THE GREAT
CONTEMPORARY
ISSUES

CHILDHOOD, YOUTH AND SOCIETY

THE GREAT CONTEMPORARY ISSUES

**THE GREAT
CONTEMPORARY
ISSUES**

CHILDHOOD, YOUTH AND SOCIETY

𝔗𝔥𝔢 𝔑𝔢𝔴 𝔜𝔬𝔯𝔨 𝔗𝔦𝔪𝔢𝔰

ARNO PRESS

NEW YORK/1980

FRED M. HECHINGER
ADVISORY EDITOR

GENE BROWN
EDITOR

Library of Congress Cataloging in Publication Data

Main entry under title:
Childhood, youth, and society.

(Great contemporary issues)
Consists of articles which appeared in the New York times.
Bibliography: p.
Includes index.
1. Children — United States — Addresses, essays, lectures. 2. Youth
— United States — Addresses, essays, lectures. 3. Socialization — Ad-
dresses, essays, lectures. 4. Social perception — Addresses, essays, lectures.
5. United States — Social conditons — Addresses, essays, lectures. I.
Hechinger, Fred M. II. Brown, Gene.
III. New York times. IV. Series.
HQ792.U5C42   305.2'3'0973   80-26288
ISBN 0-405-13398-7

Manufactured in the United States

The editors express special thanks to The Associated Press, United Press
International, and Reuters for permission to include a number of dispatches originally distributed by those news services.

Book designed by Stephanie Keylin.

Contents

Publisher's Note About the Series

It would take even an accomplished speed-reader, moving at full throttle, some three and a half solid hours a day to work his way through all the news The New York Times prints. The sad irony, of course, is that even such indefatigable devotion to life's carnival would scarcely assure a decent understanding of what it was really all about. For even the most dutiful reader might easily overlook an occasional long-range trend of importance, or perhaps some of the fragile, elusive relationships between events that sometimes turn out to be more significant than the events themselves.

This is why "The Great Contemporary Issues" was created—to help make sense out of some of the major forces and counterforces at large in today's world. The philosophical conviction behind the series is a simple one: that the past not only can illuminate the present but must. ("Continuity with the past," declared Oliver Wendell Holmes, "is a necessity, not a duty.") Each book in the series, therefore has as its subject some central issue of our time that needs to be viewed in the context of its antecedents if it is to be fully understood. By showing, through a substantial selection of contemporary accounts from The New York Times, the evolution of a subject and its significance, each book in the series offers a perspective that is available in no other way. For while most books on contemporary affairs specialize, for excellent reasons, in predigested facts and neatly drawn conclusions, the books in this series allow the reader to draw his own conclusions on the basis of the facts as they appeared at virtually the moment of their occurrence. This is not to argue that there is no place for events recollected in tranquility; it is simply to say that when fresh, raw truths are allowed to speak for themselves, some quite distinct values often emerge.

For this reason, most of the articles in "The Great Contemporary Issues" are reprinted in their entirety, even in those cases where portions are not central to a given book's theme. Editing has been done only rarely, and in all such cases it is clearly indicated. (Such an excision occasionally occurs, for example, in the case of a Presidential State of the Union Message, where only brief portions are germane to a particular volume, and in the case of some names, where for legal reasons or reasons of taste it is preferable not to republish specific identifications.) Similarly, typographical errors, where they occur, have been allowed to stand as originally printed.

"The Great Contemporary Issues" inevitably encompasses a substantial amount of history. In order to explore their subjects fully, some of the books go back a century or more. Yet their fundamental theme is not the past but the present. In this series the past is of significance insofar as it suggests how we got where we are today. These books, therefore, do not always treat a subject in a purely chronological way. Rather, their material is arranged to point up trends and interrelationships that the editors believe are more illuminating than a chronological listing would be.

"The Great Contemporary Issues" series will ultimately constitute an encyclopedic library of today's major issues. Long before editorial work on the first volume had even begun, some fifty specific titles had already been either scheduled for definite publication or listed as candidates. Since then, events have prompted the inclusion of a number of additional titles, and the editors are, moreover, alert not only for new issues as they emerge but also for issues whose development may call for the publication of sequel volumes. We will, of course, also welcome readers' suggestions for future topics.

Introduction

The myth of America as a child's paradise is, like all myths, fiction affected by some elements of fact. The early optimism of a New World could not help but influence society's view of its children and youths. In a young nation, with dreams of growth and expansion, the young personified the promise of the future. In contrast to the Old World where children were expected merely to follow in the footsteps of their parents, the American psyche drew strength from the expectation that the young would exceed the success of their elders.

Foreign visitors to the United States reacted to American parents' relationships with their children with a mixture of awe and concern. In 1837, Capatin F. Marryat, a British naval officer, recorded in his diary the following exchange between an American father and his son:

Father: Come in, Johnny.

Son: I won't.

Father: I tell you, come in directly, sir — do you hear?

Son: I won't (runs away)

Instead of being angry, the captain noted, the father said with a smile: "A sturdy republican, sir."

But such indulgence, and the generally optimistic and supportive approach by American families toward their children, should not obscure another side of the picture: the harsh, often cruel and at least uncaring attitude toward the great mass of those unfortunate children and youths who could not bank on the support of their families. Over the years, the children of poverty, immigrants, blacks and other minorities, experienced something quite different from the child-centered America that has often been admired from afar and denounced by "Spare the rod and spoil the child" advocates at home.

This volume provides a realistic insight to the realities of childhood and youth in American society. Since it consists of reports, articles and comments in the news, the emphasis is inevitably on problems and deficiencies, on the lot of those who suffered or were in trouble rather then of those who prospered and were at ease. This is as it should be; for no society can move toward the prospectus of its ideals without paying attention to the obstacles on the road, particularly to those obstacles that are of its own making. What makes this chronicle fascinating is that it nevertheless also provides an account of progress. There is a message of great encouragement in a historic journey that starts with almost total denial that children had rights and ends with the ratification of such rights by the Supreme Court itself.

There are many ways of savoring this historic slice of American history. One way is to weave together the strands of progress, the slow but ulitmately victorious march of the prochild forces. Another is to look at the zigs and zags along the way, as in the recurring signs of youth revolt followed by eras of acquiescence. Yet another way is to compare conservative adult reactions to new forces that exert their influence on the young, as in such reactions first to books, then to motion pictures and, ultimately, to television. Each time, the alarms appear virtually the same, forecasting a dire end in sight; and yet, the race survives.

Time and again, society looked with fear and despair on its street children — the truants, delinquents, gangs or whatever designation the particular period gave them. In 1887, an editorial — a remarkably advanced commentary for its time — deplored the plight of the "Large Boys" of the streets, the adolescents who were neither children nor adults. They were too old to be newsboys or bootblacks and too young for gainful employment or apprenticeship. The schools washed their hands of them. So did the churches. They ended up in prisons or workhouses which the editorial characterized as the "kindergarten of crime" where youths learned "all the foul secrets of crime and lust, and graduated to begin a new round of thievery, burglary and vagabondism." Hardly an obsolete concern, though aired almost a hundred years ago. It is worth noting that 15 years were to pass before a news report in 1902 informs us of the creation of a "New Court for Children."

There can be no responsible reading of American history without attention to two aspects of childhood: the low value placed on the lives of poor children and, related to it, child labor.

It is left to a news item of three paragraphs, dated January 22, 1899, to tell us, as did the headline, what then was the "estimate of a Child's Value." A little boy in a small town in Indiana fell into an uncovered sewer and drowned. The jury, after deliberating for 53 hours, awarded the father $599.95. The child, the jury figured, between the ages of eight to ten would be able to earn only 45 cents a week, against the 85 cents in weekly upkeep. From ten to 12 "it" would earn 75 cents, and so on until, between 15 and 18 years of age, the weekly income of $5 would actually exceed by $2.25 the father's expense for keeping the son. Thus was a child's value arrived at.

The fight against child labor remained a losing battle — until changing conditions in a newly industrialized nation made such labor unwanted. Early opponents fought valiant skirmishes. For example, the Rev. Dr. Joseph Silverman, rabbi of Temple Emanu-El in New York City in 1906 preached on "The Abolition of Child Slavery," comparing the lives of some two million child laborers with those of the affluent children in progressive new kindergartens.

The shame of child labor extended from coast to coast. The Third Annual Report of the Illinois Factory Inspectors in 1895 cited the example of the Chicago stockyards where "in several places a boy has been found working at a dangerous machine because his father had been disabled by it." Children toiled, were maimed, and often disabled for life. And yet, the courts continued to uphold the practice. In 1885, the New York Court of Appeals struck down a law forbidding cigar manufacture in tenements on the grounds that the "hallowed associations and beneficent influence" of the home could best protect the health and morals of the child. Twice the Supreme Court declared anti-child labor legislation unconstitutional. In 1918 and again in 1922, the Court held that if Congress could so restrict a local authority's power "all freedom of commerce will be at an end, and thus our system of government be practically destroyed."

At Columbia University, president Nicholas Murray Butler, a man with extraordinary influence on public opinion, supported the court by intoning: "Surely no true friend of childhood can wish to support a measure which will make possible the substitution of Congressional control of childhood and youth for the natural relationship of parent and guardian."

Fortunately, these grim reminders of the reactionary force that often stood in the way of any efforts to relieve the suffering of poor children were beginning to be answered by the humane voices of those who knew that the rights of children and youths are of piece with the rights of men and women. Justice Oliver Wendell Holmes, in a historic dissent, from the 1918 ruling in *Hammer v. Dagenhart*, wondered why it was proper to translate popular moral outrage into the prohibition of alcoholic beverages under the Volstead Act, but impermissible to

prohibit the evil of child labor. "If there is any matter," Holmes wrote, "upon which civilized countries have agreed . . . it is the evil of premature and excessive child labor."

Although American society, and the Supreme Court, eventually changed their minds and conceded the evils of child labor, the high court continues, through rulings as recently as 1975 and 1977, to approve of corporal punishment of children in school. The practice persists in the majority of states today. Those who defend it ignore such questions as the one asked in 1853 by the Indiana Supreme Court, after noting that it had become illegal for a husband to beat his wife, a master his apprentice or an officer in the Navy a sailor: "Why the person of the schoolboy should be less sacred . . . is not easily explained."

When problems arise that are difficult to explain and even harder to solve, society looks for scapegoats or at least explanations. Children have, of course, always misbehaved; and youths have tended to violence — especially whenver there is much violence in adult society.

"The boys of New York," bemoaned a new report in 1878, "are furnished every week with as vile and degrading a supply of . . . corrupting literature as unscrupulous men can buy and publish, or greedy news-vendors spread broadcast across the City." In 1911, a headline proclaimed "Comic Supplements of Source of Evil" and complained of "an invasion of vulgarity" that was undermining the morals of children, driving them to drink and other evil ways. In 1933, a study of the movies' effects on children wound up between the covers of a book, "Our Movie-Made Children," which showed that the majority of films children saw dealt with love, sex or crime. Skip four decades and arrive at a familiar theme, as in "The Plug-in Drug," a book on television's effect on children.

The fact that the experts disagree on these issues makes the debate particularly interesting, if inconclusive and this volume follows the debate in enlightening detail. Whatever the reader's views and conclusion, it is worth noting the contrast between society's rather cavalier record of concern with the welfare of children in such matters of child labor and the intensity with which it focuses on the things children hear, read or see.

Perhaps the most intriguing chapter in the history of this country's reaction to childhood and youth is the discovery of "teen-age" circa 1945. A rather remarkable item, dated December 31, 1893 provides a prescient glimpse of the mysterious realm of adolescence that would so dominate the public attention and curiosity some 50 years later. "The time from ten to 15 years of age," this item reported, ". . . is of all the periods of life the most lacking in reverence. The problem of how to live with this young person . . . is an abosrbing problem in the minds of parents." It was dubbed "the age of disrespect," and the youths of that age were called "bumptious boys and girls."

And so they are. Yet, it was not until the 1940's that the "problem" of adolescence was to move into the limelight under the new label of teen-age. The difficulties of adolescence — growing up, seeking an identity, groping for independence while deadly in fear of it — were hardly news to those who had long been dealing with that age group *en masse*, particularly the teachers in the junior high school. But it was not until the 1940's that "The Adolescent Society," as sociologist James Coleman called it, came to the fore.

The era was new and dramatically different, not because human nature had changed but rather because the environment and the values that surrounded American adolescents had undergone drastic changes. For the first time — in sharp contrast to the days of child labor — youths found themselves essentially unneeded and unwanted in economic terms; but these same young people, at least the affluent majority, had at their disposal, either personally or through their parents, substantial amounts of money. They were hitherto untapped consumers in a consumer society, and they were consumers with a great deal of money not committed to buying the necessities of life.

Inevitably, this mass of teen-agers became a target for commercial appeals. They were buyers of records, clothes, junk food, cosmetics. They dictated styles in all manner of design, including automobiles. They influenced grown-up living patterns because adults longed to be young. The "generation gap" came to be a key word in popular psychology, and few parents or other middle-aged Americans wanted to be at the wrong side of the gap. Imperceptibly, teen-age extended its tyranny, first, over families and, in time, over society as a whole.

In the 1950's and early 1960's teen-agers became the most analyzed sector in American society. Their elders often dealth with them in a love/hate manner that may, in part, have been caused by simultaneous admiration for, and envy of, their magic possession — youth. The intensity of feeling generated by the issue, aggravated by the peer pressure common to that age group and by its exposure to commercial exploitation, created what came to be known as the Youth Culture. It was in reality an adolescent culture, adolescent in values and intellect; but it was imitated so avidly by so many adults that there seemed a new

risk that it would retard youth's process of growing up, while making their elders grow down.

In the 1960's, Youth Culture gave way to Youth Revolt. It was a rebellion with many causes, some merely the extension of rebellious adolescence into the increasingly dangerous realm of revolutionary action. It frightened the academic leadership with the result that it gave in to many demands for reforms, some of them beneficial and others at best superficial and at worst harmful. Ultimately, the banner under which the young rebels could not only rally their peers but could also join with their elders in pursuit of more mature goals and values was the war in Vietnam. What started out as a battle over the length of teenage hair was to culminate in the battle over America's right to ask its youth to die in a civil war in Southeast Asia. Symbolically, the end may well have come with the death of four young Americans at Kent State University. It came a year after the Supreme Court — the same court that once had viewed children and youths as little more than property — had upheld the right of students to join in public demonstrations against the war.

Growing up in America is not a process that can be readily reduced to a formula. It could, at various times in history, be benign or harsh, depending on the child's place in society. For the affluent majority, the process has become more indulgent, if not always easier. For those born to poverty, serious hardships remain, even though some of the extreme cruelties of child labor have been eliminated. The reform movement which, in the last century, relied largely on occasional good intentions of upper-class gentility, has become broadly based, shored up by other groups fighting for their rights.

Much remains to be done. Once exploited in sweatshops, too many adolescents today suffer from being shut out of the labor force or from being exploited by those who merely count them as consumers. If economic growth continues in low gear, the American dream of greater accomplishments for each new generaton will seem harder to attain. But as new trends alternate with a repetition of yesteryear's experiences, this chronicle of Childhood, Youth and Society assumes the instructive role, not only of history but of a predictor. It offers not certainty, but shrewd hints of risks and possibilities.

—Fred M. Hechinger

CHAPTER 1

Beyond the Family: The Child and Society

Television has proven to be a source of entertainment and socialization. A good deal of controversy has arisen over the effect of T.V. on the young.

Ken Laffal/NYT Pictures

BIRTH OF THE DELINQUENT

What Shall Be Done with Pauper Children?

Our exchanges from Albany give us an interesting account of a convention of the Superintendents of the Poor from the various counties of the State, held in that city on Wednesday last. Some idea of the importance of the administration of these officials can be gained when we state that every person in 150 of the whole population is under public charge and supervision, and that over $24,000,000 of property is held by the public charities of the State. The convention was addressed by Dr. CHAS. S. HOYT, Secretary of the State Board of Charities, on the important question of disposing of able-bodied paupers. The very interesting topic of the care of pauper children was also considered by the convention, and an address was delivered by Mr. CHAS. L. BRACE, of this City. The speaker urged that the true solution of this question was to be found in the plan adopted by the Children's Aid Society during the past twenty years, of distributing poor children in country homes, rather than placing them in poor-houses or asylums. He cited the experience of the Poor Law administration in Sweden and Norway, in Prussia and in Great Britain, to show that this distribution was attended with far better results than keeping children in almshouses. The remarkable success, also, of the French authorities in disposing of foundling children by a similar plan, was cited as an instance of the superiority of this system over the one pursued in this country.

The importance to the community of the proper care of pauper children cannot be exaggerated. No greater evil can afflict a people than hereditary pauperism. When once two generations of paupers have been born, it becomes almost impossible to eradicate the dependent habits and criminal tendencies of those persons. The only cure is the terrible cure of nature, which seldom suffers "the sins of the fathers" to be trans-mitted "beyond the fourth generation." Families of paupers and criminals die out from their own vices. Hereditary paupers are the worst members of "the dangerous classes" in all modern communities. The nursery and school of hereditary pauperism is the modern almshouse. The young and tender children grow up with older vagabonds, and learn the habits of a criminal class before they reach maturity. The pauper mother begets the pauper child, and it enters life only to return to the institution after a few years a worse character than the mother. Even if the children are kept by themselves, they acquire all the low habits and tastes of the place, and are disinclined to all manly labor afterward. Within thirty miles of New-York, in Westchester County, there are sixty pauper children kept in an ordinary almshouse, and, if we are rightly informed, under the charge of a pauper woman of pauper ancestors. They will grow up there inevitably to be members again of the poor-house, or they will be found to be the pests and nuisances of the villages where they are placed. Such a mode of caring for unfortunate children is a disgrace to that wealthy and intelligent county, and should at once be reformed. It ought to be a foundation principle of the Poor Law administration of the United States that no unfortunate child should ever be put in the poor-house.

The almshouse is no place for these little creatures. They are corrupted there in mind and body. Such is the demand for children's labor, and so great the generosity of our rural families, that every unfortunate pauper child of the whole country can be placed in a good home. The only exceptions are such children as are defective in mind or body, and for these we have asylums for the deaf and dumb, the blind, the insane, the idiotic, the crippled, and for almost every kind of infirmity. There are abundant provisions, also, for the orphans, and the orphan asylums, at least in this City, are frequently not half filled. The remedy suggested by Dr. HOYT, of intermediate asylums scattered through the State, where pauper children could be sent by Superintendents of the Poor, is good so far as it goes. The Susquehanna Valley Home, at Binghamton, though not so complete as might be desired in all its arrangements, is a good example of this new method of treatment. It is certainly infinitely better than the almshouse. But it will take time and much expense to found these institutions in various parts of the State. In the meantime, the unfortunate children of the poor are becoming pauperized and degraded. A new class is growing up with inherited vagabondism and criminal tendencies. The shortest and most practical method of curing the evil is that suggested by the Secretary of the Children's Aid Society to this convention of the Superintendents of the Poor—that is, the employing the machinery of the society in distributing these children in country homes.

It is almost useless to put out an almshouse child in the immediate neighborhood of the house. The child is known as a pauper. The stigma is fastened upon him in his earliest years. His pauper relatives and criminal friends find him out. He grows up unconsciously a member of that terrible class—hereditary paupers. No; the only just and humane method is to transfer these children to homes far away from their associates; to give each unhappy child of poverty and crime the same general chance which we give the child of the fortunate. This can be done in this State—thanks to the machinery of the Children's Aid Society—with but little expense. Let our County Superintendents of the Poor try the experiment.

February 2, 1873

HOW TO PREVENT VAGRANCY AMONG CHILDREN.

It is well known to our readers interested in educational reform, that we have excellent legislation in this State for enforcing education, but that it has not been executed. This City is a good instance of the neglect of the law. Every quarter of the Metropolis swarms with children who are not technically "truants," and therefore are untouched by the Truant Agents, but who are non-attendants at school, and, so far as public schools are concerned, are unaffected by our expensive system of popular education. Our readers have only to look at the great numbers of little Italian boot-blacks, the German children engaged in rag-picking and bone-gathering, the Irish-American newsboys, and the like, to be convinced how great a multitude of youth in New-York are practically outside of our public-school system. This is the more remarkable, as we have had in Boston an excellent instance of the working of the Compulsory law. Boston has faithfully carried out for years this legislation, and the result has been all that the friends of the law could desire. The city is practically freed from homeless and vagrant children. Some benevolent individuals undertook recently to found in Boston a charity similar to those which have accomplished so much good here—the Boys' and Girls' Lodging-houses—but discovered, to their amazement, after diligent inquiry, that there were no homeless children in the city of the kind for which these institutions were designed. The whole roving population of boys and girls are either schooled or forced into houses of detention. Vagrancy is rooted out from the very bottom. We have at hand no statistics of juvenile crime in Boston, but we have no doubt that the proportion to population is far less than in this City.

In this State, one great difficulty in executing the law has been the want of proper places of detention. If truants or non-attendants were arrested in villages or small towns, there was no place to put them except the poor-house or the jail. The constables or officers executing the law have naturally felt a great reluctance to consign these roving children, who are not yet contaminated, to the society of thieves and paupers. Then, the larger towns dreaded the additional expense of founding another "institution" of charity, so that finally the children were left untouched by the law. We doubt if, on the whole, truants and non-attendants in our rural districts are forced to attend school any more than they were before the passage of the act. In this City, the former Superintendent and the majority of the Board of Education have only given the law a half-hearted support. They have contented themselves mainly with the appointment of Truant Agents, and the forcing into school of the runaway and truant children. This work, though useful, is not precisely what the law intended, and does but slightly touch the great evil in the City, of children's vagrancy. The same difficulty has been experienced here as in the rural districts. It seemed harsh and unwise to confine a merely roving and restless child with petty criminals in the House of Refuge, or with legally vagrant children in the Juvenile Asylum or the Roman Catholic Protectory. There was no proper place of detention, unless the Board of Education would open one. This they have not thought fit to do. Fortunately for the City, the same thing has occurred as does with many of our charities, private energy and ingenuity have taken the place of public and official neglect. The various night and "half-time" schools of the Boys' and Girls' Lodging-houses, and of the Children's Aid Society have reached great numbers of the vagrant class of youth. Several thousands are thus schooled and brought under some degree of training. But there is still needed the execution of the law and the final breaking up of childish vagrancy.

Brooklyn has already led New-York in the matter of "model lodging-houses" for working people. Our sister city seems to contain a few young men of capital and of brains, who care for something besides wealth, who are ready not only to work for public matters, but to "pay with their persons." That is they risk both money and reputation in philanthropic and political reforms. Some of these persons, we suppose, have created a wise series of institutions in Brooklyn for making education universal. The truants are first sought after, then the non-attendants, by appointed officers. These children are then brought to the public schools; if they still absent themselves, they are taken the next time to a

kind of truant day-school, where only truants attend. Here, if they run away two or three times, they are "warned," and then, if persistent, conducted to an asylum in the outskirts of the city—a "Truant Home"—where they are kept in arrest for several months or a year. None of these schools or places of detention are very expensive, and, though Brooklyn is as much loaded with taxes as New-York, there has been, as yet, no complaint from tax-payers as to the increased expense. Such institutions soon pay for themselves in diminished crime and pauperism.

Other cities in the State might imitate Brooklyn in this matter; and one "Truant Home" could serve for several counties, thus diminishing the expense on particular towns. New-York could easily arrange such places of detention. The intermediate school is already supplied by the

"Industrial Schools," now under the supervision of the board. Their officers could—as they often do now—send truant and vagrant children to these schools, without any additional expense to the board. Then, for the final place of detention, they could open a Truant Home on Randall's Island, for which the board could be empowered by special act to draw moneys from the Excise fund or the charity fund of the City. The next step would be, as we have often indicated, for the board (according to the present act) to "instruct" the Police to arrest all children engaged in work or play on the streets who did not have certificates with them of attendance on a night or half-time school. This would be the beginning of the reform so much needed in New-York—the breaking up of children's vagrancy.

December 25, 1879

VAGRANCY AMONG CHILDREN.

A very proper act has just been passed by the Legislature, forbidding the employment of children in such semi-vagrant occupations as picking up cigar stumps, bones, rags, or garbage in the streets. On Wednesday the first arrest occurred under this law, of an Italian child, who was subsequently committed to the Society for the Prevention of Cruelty to Children, and whose mother was fined $25. There can be no question of the necessity of such an act in this City. Thousands of children begin lives of crime and shame in these irregular occupations. A young girl spending days and evenings picking over the gutters for rags and cigar stumps will, as a matter of course, become hardened and bold and soon addicted to criminal practices. A boy falls in with all sorts of bad company in these occupations, loses school discipline, and finally takes to thieving as a more agreeable pursuit than this disgusting business. The little *chiffonniers*, the rag and bone pickers, the swill-gatherers, and young collectors of tobacco, beer, and garbage soon crowd the ranks of the youthful criminal population. It is in the interest of the public that these occupations should be broken up among the children. The older German and Italian peasants can follow these pursuits, and, except for the nuisances they create in their cellars and yards, may be no worse off than they were before; but with the children the danger is great and the usefulness of the work small.

Equally with these should another street trade be held in strict check, which, though useful and necessary, is a cover for much idleness and vagrancy. It is well known that many Italian lads never enter a school in New-York, but spend the days nominally busy with their brushes

and blacking, but really gambling and pitching pennies. They form the idle and vagrant *gamins* of the Metropolis, and, as they grow up, will naturally enter the class of gamblers, sharpers, thieves, and vagabonds. This is the more to be regretted as they are a remarkably bright and intelligent class of youth, and would make skillful and tasteful artisans. There has been formed for them, through American generosity, a very suitable and complete system of schools in the night and industrial schools for Italian children of the Children's Aid Society. Here, after their hours of work are over, they can be cleansed in the baths, refresh themselves in the gymnasium, and then learn various English branches of common school education, or be trained in industrial trades or practice themselves in music.

They have no excuse for truancy, vagrancy, or ignorance. But the parents, especially among the Neapolitans and Calabrians, are indifferent to the education of their children, and are perfectly willing they should grow up ignorant provided they can earn a few shillings each day. The lads escape the action of the Education law of 1873 by being "engaged in a lawful occupation" apparently, though their real employment is roaming the streets and petty gambling. The industrial schools, without a compulsory education act, cannot reach them all, and many of these children form a dangerous element in the growing youthful population, especially as the Italian immigration increases each year to a formidable extent.

The Board of Education can alone correct this evil. By the act of 1873 they are empowered to make such "rules and regulations" as can secure the attendance of vagrant and street-wandering children, and

they have only to pass a rule that every child between the ages of 5 and 14, engaged in street trades, must have a certificate of school attendance such as is required by that act and its amendments, and they would completely break up this incipient vagrancy. The law allows eight months' half-time attendance in place of four months' full schooling, so that the certificate of any night or industrial school for this period would be sufficient. The act also allows the board to call on the Police for assistance in carrying out their rules and regulations, so that next Autumn, when the board meets again and the schools resume their sessions, a vigorous action on the part of the Trustees would completely put an end to this growing evil.

It is also very much for the interest of New-York that the youthful population should not be consumed and wasted too early by labor in the shop or manufactory. The present law (of 1873) is defective in many of its provisions, and it was sought to amend it in this Legislature, so that too early labor might be prevented in this City and elsewhere. The indifference, however, of that body to such reforms has defeated this effort. Still, enough remains in the old law to enable the Board of Education to hold both grasping manufacturers and selfish parents in check when children of tender years are placed at constant labor. We rejoice to know that the present useful Superintendent, Mr. JASPER, is already instructing the truant officers to inspect the factories closely, and that the employers show a creditable humanity in seconding these efforts. Much can be accomplished, even under the present laws, toward correcting juvenile truancy and vagrancy and restraining overwork.

July 17, 1881

WORK FOR THE YOUNG.

CONVENTION OF SOCIETIES FROM MANY CITY CHURCHES.

The first convention of Young People's Associations attached to the Protestant evangelical churches in New-York was held yesterday for the purpose of effecting a permanent organization. There were two sessions, afternoon and evening. The first was held at the Church

of the Strangers, on Mercer-street, and 250 delegates, representing 50 church societies, were present. The convention was called by a committee which held a preliminary meeting, the Rev. Dr. Howard Crosby presiding, on Sept. 27. The Rev. Dr. C. F. Deems opened the session with an address of welcome. He said that the power of young people for effective work in the church used to be ignored, but he was glad to see this mistake was no longer made. The "old men for counsel" adage had been so universally acted on that the churches came near dying of wisdom.

It was resolved to permanently organize the association, and the committee appointed for the purpose submitted a plan. The only parts of the proposed constitution which were not accepted without debate were those relating to the title of the association and admission to membership. The committee had recommended the name "The Young People's Union Association of New-York City," but this was not deemed euphonious or expressive enough and was changed to "The Young People's Christian Association of New-York." The clause in the constitution which provided that only societies attached to Protestant evangelical churches should be admitted to membership was not acceptable to Dr. Deems, who said he did not believe in keeping out good people because of denominational differences. He did not see why young Catholics should be excluded if they wished to enter. An amendment to the effect that wherever the words "Protestant evangelical" occurred in the Constitution they should be stricken out, and the word "Christian" substituted, caused a warm debate. It was carried finally by the close vote of 83 to 74.

The following officers were elected: President —G. R. Boyd; Vice-Presidents—S. Williams, Miss M. L. Welden, and Miss Nellie West; Secretaries

—J. Halsey Terrell, Jr., and A. L. Whitelaw, Jr.; Treasurer—H. A. Hallock. W. L. Amerman read a paper on "Young People's Opportunities for Christian Work," on which the Rev. L. A. Crandall commented, and George W. Glaentzer presented his ideas on "Individual Responsibility to the Church." W. R. Collins's paper on "The Successful Conduct of a Young People's Association" was discussed by Dr. Crosby. He said that in regular church work there were generally two classes who kept in the background—young people and ladies. He was glad to see that an organization was forming by which their great power for ef-

fective Christian work could be utilized. He thought, however, that the societies constituting the organization should form integral parts of their particular churches and be under the control of the officers of the church.

In the evening a session was held in the Collegiate Church, Fifth-avenue and Twenty-ninth-street. Addresses were delivered by the Rev. Drs. Ormiston, MacArthur, Virgin, Masden, Kittredge, and Hulburd.

December 10, 1886

WASHINGTON'S DEPRAVITY

ALARMING STATISTICS OF YOUTHFUL CRIME.

THE VICIOUS CHILDREN OF THE NATIONAL CAPITAL — MR. EVARTS TO OPPOSE THE INTER-STATE COMMERCE BILL.

WASHINGTON, Jan. 8.—About a year ago Mr. Dorman B. Eaton provoked a storm of criticism by directing the attention of the people of the District to some alarming statistics of crime in Washington which he had gathered to show the necessity for affording the best of school facilities to the place. Senator Vance and Mr. Eaton are not men whom any one would expect to find working together, but Mr. Vance on Thursday introduced a petition carrying some further statistics of just the sort quoted by Mr. Eaton for his purpose. He did it in the interest of juvenile reform at the suggestion of a newly formed society called the Guardian League, of which H. B. Moulton is President. The petition was accompanied by letters of commendation from Judges McArthur and Cox, of the Supreme Court; Judge Snell, of the Police Court; Major Moore, Chief of Police, and Gen. Crocker, Warden of the jail.

It contained some statistics of crime in the District of Columbia, and some statistical comparisons of the District with the large cities of the North, which are startling to contemplate. The petitioners are very solicitous that they should not be understood as representing that the young people of the District, which is practically the same as Washington, are any more depraved than the young people of other places. On the other hand, they are inclined to think that the children of the District are more tractable and less inclined naturally to vicious habits than the children of most large cities. But the petitioners contend that in consequence of the entire absence of wholesome laws, and the absence hitherto of any benevolent society organized to shield them from corruption, these children are being led into drinking and gambling habits, and consequently are finding their way into the police court in larger numbers than almost anywhere else in the country. They say that there never has been any law punishing the sale of liquor to minors throughout the District, or prohibiting their presence in pool rooms. The nearest approach to this is an old ordinance of the city of Washington, in force nowhere else, prohibiting the keepers of tippling houses from selling liquors to minors, and this is so meagre and so easily evaded that it is a dead letter.

The first comparison instituted is between the number of general arrests for crime and the population, taking the census of 1880 as a basis, and it is said that in Springfield, Mass., these arrests were only 44 for every 1,000 of the population; in Cincinnati and Brooklyn, 48; in Providence, 58; in Columbus and Philadelphia, 60; in New-York, 61; in Buffalo, 70; in Boston, 79; in Baltimore, 80; in Chicago, 81; and in the District of Colum-

bia, 126, or more than twice as many as in New-York, Brooklyn, or Philadelphia. The second comparison made is between the number of general arrests for crime and the number of juvenile arrests in the year 1885-6, and it is said that in Columbus there were 99 juvenile arrests for every 1,600 general arrests; in New-York, 108, in Springfield, Mass. 116, in Boston, 137; in Chicago, 155; in Buffalo, 172; in Cincinnati, 178, in Brooklyn, 205, and in the District of Columbia 208, nearly twice as many as in New-York. The third comparison instituted is between the number of juvenile arrests in the years 1885-6 and the population, and it is said that in Columbus, Ohio, and Springfield, Mass., there were only 5 of these juvenile arrests for every 1,000 of population; in New-York and Newark, 6; in Cincinnati, 8; in Albany and Brooklyn, 9; in Boston, 10; in Hartford, 11; in Chicago and Buffalo, 12, and in the District of Columbia, 26, or more than four times as many as in New-York, and more than five times as many as in Columbus and Springfield. The fourth comparison instituted is between the District of Columbia now and five years ago, and it is said that, while in that time the population has increased only 15 per cent., the retail liquor sellers and wholesale liquor sellers have each increased 40 per cent., the pool tables 90 per cent., and the juvenile arrests 72 per cent. The officials of the District deny that these figures indicate a bad state of morals, and attribute them to the large number of frivolous arrests made. But the explanation is probably to be found in the colored people who constitute only one-third of the population, but furnish at least two-thirds of the criminal arrests.

January 9, 1887

THE "LARGE BOY" OF THE STREETS.

It is earnestly to be hoped that the Mayor will accede to the request of the State Board of Charities and cause a bill to be prepared for the next Legislature which shall establish a temporary reformatory for the older boys and girls of a vagrant class in this city. The "large boy" of the streets of New-York is the terror of all philanthropic societies. He can do nothing at street trades. The little newsboy or bootblack is too active for him and secures all the business, while the compassionate public always prefer to employ the younger rather than the older lad. The position of apprentice is closed to him by the selfishness of trades unions. The boys' lodging houses cannot receive him because of his age. The Western farmers do not want him because his habits are fixed and he cannot easily learn new ways. He is the outlaw of the city and naturally tends to vagrancy and crime. If he commits an offense or is arrested as a vagrant, his prospects for reform and improvement are not bettered. The Roman Catholic reformatories will not take him because he is too old. The only institution which may receive him —the Protestant House of Refuge—is already crowded by the courts with young ruffians and criminals, and does not want an older member of the same class. The large boy, accordingly, on the slightest offense—vagrancy, fighting, disturbance, drinking, petty thieving, and the like—is packed away to that kindergarten of crime on Blackwell's Island, the workhouse,

or penitentiary, to spend ten or twenty days, as the case may be, in close companionship with the most abandoned vagabonds, drunkards, "revolvers," and outcasts which any large city ever produced. As Mrs. Lowell has recently stated in her excellent report, there were in the five months ending May 31 last 351 commitments to Blackwell's Island of such lads over 16 years of age. These boys, without much supervision or any useful occupation, spent their term of sentence with the very outcasts of society, learning all the foul secrets of crime and lust, and graduated to begin a new round of thievery, burglary, or vagabondism. It is only natural that over one-half of the inmates of this school of crime on Blackwell's Island should be "revolvers," or those who have been there before, and some of them many times.

The various reformatory and preventive efforts of New-York for the outcast children have indeed produced vast effects in diminishing youthful crime. But, with the single exception of Col. Auchmuty's remarkable trade schools, there is scarcely any reform institution for the larger boy—nothing to keep him from criminal courses or to make him better if he is once entangled in them. Dr. Hoyt, the faithful Secretary of the State board, proposes that the city of New-York should found a graded reformatory for this class of boys similar to the best graded prison of the United States—that at Elmira. He would have the age of those sentenced limited, so that offenders clearly matured and sunk in crime might not be received.

The sentences should be indeterminate, and this we regard as one of the most important features of the plan. The boy's release and early freedom will depend on his conduct in the prison and the judgment of the Superintendent and managers as to his habits and character. It is this peculiarity which has made the Elmira Reformatory under its able Superintendent such a great success. The life on Blackwell's Island will then have the same motives to elevate it that are felt outside. Moreover, there will be classes and grades as at Elmira, and the young offender will not be put with the old criminal or "revolver," and the entrance to given grades will be a coveted prize and honor. The managers will have great freedom in discharging, either on probation or finally, according to the moral improvement of the inmate.

The Elmira prison has had a similar and even worse class of youth in its subjects, and has made a wonderful success in their reform and improvement. The proposed New-York Reformatory could no doubt accomplish similar results if the right kind of Superintendent were found and a similar plan adopted. Mayor Hewitt would surely like to distinguish his administration by the founding of such a useful and philanthropic institution. The expense would scarcely be greater than that of the present slipshod and useless management of our youthful criminals, and the saving in diminishing crime would be important.

August 25, 1887

A CHILDREN'S FRIEND DEAD

THE REV. CHARLES L. BRACE DIES IN SWITZERLAND.

THE CAREER OF A MAN WHO HAS DONE MORE THAN ANY OTHER FOR THE LITTLE OUTCASTS OF A BIG CITY.

Word reached this city yesterday of the death of the Rev. Charles Loring Brace, the founder and, from its organization, the Secretary of the Children's Aid Society. The information came to the office of the society in a letter sent from a Summer resort near Portland, Me., by Prof. James Crosswell, whose wife is a daughter of Mr. Brace. He had received a cable dispatch from Switzerland announcing the fact of the death, but he was unable to make out just where it occurred or when. His inference from recent advices was that probably the end had come Monday at Campfer, in the Tyrol, in Upper Switzerland, Mr. Brace having located in that neighborhood late in July.

The news did not come wholly without warning, for Mrs. Crosswell received a cable dispatch about a week ago saying that her father was then seriously ill, and, under date of July 24 and 28, letters came from Mr. Brace and his wife, dated St. Ulrich, in which mention was made of their purpose to journey to Campfer as the next stage of their trip. They were in Switzerland for the purpose of getting the advantages of what is known as the after-cure, having previously spent about two months at baths in Bohemia, where Mr. Brace was under treatment. Their trip to Europe was made in the hope that he would be able to recover from the effects of overwork, and until within a month the reports from him and his family were quite encouraging. It was their intention to return here about the last of September.

Mr. Brace's death is a most serious loss to the cause of practical charity in this city. His was the moving mind in the various projects for the relief of the poor and needy associated with the Children's Aid Society. In the prosecution of this work he was tireless. It was the kind of work that required special aptitude and energy. Mr. Brace seemed not only fitted for it himself, but he had the rare faculty of selecting as his associates and assistants men of the right quality of mind and heart to carry on the work on the lines he had mapped out. His influence and example furnished a constant inspiration, and the policy of executive management which he devised has been so firmly impressed upon the character of these various charities that they are no longer dependent for their success upon the efforts of any individual. Otherwise the loss to this city in his death would be irreparable.

It was a happy circumstance in his career that he was prepared for the ministry, and that the bent of his mind during his early years was in the direction of religious endeavor. When the demand was made upon him that he abandon his idea of preaching and give himself up to other but no less important work he committed himself to this change as if to a mission divinely endowed. He did not find it necessary to divest himself of his training and culture in order to labor among and for the wretched poor. On the contrary, he needed all of his acquirements, for with them he was enabled to reach the highest and most exclusive of society, and they were no hindrance to him when he stooped to help the most lowly. They enabled him, moreover, to interest the world in his work. He had pronounced literary ability. There was abundant occasion for him to employ it, and in his own judgment the influences which he was able to enlist in behalf of his work could have been reached in no way so well as through the efforts of his pen. In the prosecution of his labors also he was helped by a temperament that was sunny and gracious at all times and under all circumstances. He would never allow himself to become discouraged, and he had a way of imparting his hope to those for whom he desired aid, and of interesting in the various enterprises of charity which he projected every one who was at all versed in these subjects.

In the organization of the Children's Aid Society he was a pioneer. While never averse to suggestions, but on the contrary always grateful for them, he was a man of original character and strong convictions, and no combination of circumstances was ever effectual to turn him from the general plan of charity that he organized when he embarked upon the project of helping others as his life's work.

Mr. Brace entered upon this field of labor while he was a very young man. He had been graduated from the Union Theological Seminary after having taken a degree at Yale College, and in 1850, at the age of twenty-four years, he went to Europe in company with Frederick Law Olmsted for the purpose of a pedestrian journey for pleasure. Their travels through Great Britain and Ireland were not specially eventful, but in the following year, having spent a Winter in study at Berlin, Mr. Brace visited Hungary, and he was the first American to go to the interior of that country. While at Grosswardein he was arrested on suspicion of being a secret agent of the Hungarian revolutionists in America, and was imprisoned. No information of his arrest was sent to the American Minister, and he found himself in a strange land with no friends upon whom he could call and with a trial ahead of him upon twelve different charges. An opportunity, seemingly accidental, enabled him to communicate the fact of his arrest to Charles J. McCurdy, the United States Chargé d'Affaires at Vienna, who instituted vigorous efforts for his release. There was a bitter diplomatic correspondence with the Austrian Minister, and finally after having suffered imprisonment for a month, Mr. Brace was discharged with an apology. During his visit to Hungary he met Kossuth, of whom he became a great admirer, and with whom afterward he maintained the most friendly relations.

It was not until after this experience that his life was cast. Leaving Hungary, he visited Switzerland, Italy, and Ireland, and in those countries his attention was specially called to the condition of the masses. Incidentally, also, he gave some study to the management of the schools, the prisons, and the reformatory institutions. He was specially impressed with the work of the Rauh Haus in Hamburg and of the Ragged House in London. The Hamburg institution furnished the beginning of the kindergarten system which has since been developed all over the world. Its operations when Mr. Brace visited it served to impress him with the importance of industrial training for the young. The London home was impressive to him, rather because it convinced him of the things that he should avoid than of the things that he should imitate. In its function of providing support for the poor he approved of it, but in its practice of clothing all of those who benefited by it in uniform and in its offensive name it incurred his disapproval.

When he returned to America he was filled with the subjects upon which he had been lately studying. Naturally his attention was turned to the condition of the tenement districts and of the immigrant poor. Then without any special preparation other than that indicated, the work of his life was unfolded to him, and early in 1853, which was only a few months after his return, he had interested a large number of philanthropic people in the organization of the Children's Aid Society. In 1854 the work inaugurated by this society indicated the importance of providing a lodging house for newsboys. This was done, and the results have for the past thirty years been apparent to all charitably-disposed people in this country. Although the Children's Aid Society is founded only upon the broad principles of charity, the Newsboys' Lodging House is unique and is the only institution of its kind in the world.

The great idea in Mr. Brace's work was to enable the young to help themselves. The principle laid down from the first year of the organization of the Children's Aid Society was that for an outcast or homeless or orphan child not tainted with bad habits the best possible place of shelter and education, better than any prison or public institution, was the farmer's home. In this shelter the child was to be taught good habits and good morals, and, with no expense to the public, was to be brought up a self-supporting man or woman. During the thirty-five years since the organization of the society more than 70,000 children were thus placed in good homes. Many of them have since grown up as worthy citizens, and all of them have fully justified the broad principles of self help upon which Mr. Brace organized the society.

By planting, in various parts of the city, lodging houses for boys and girls, Mr. Brace sought to provide means by which the young wanderers of the street, instead of drifting into dens and haunts of vagabonds, might be brought into clean, healthy, well-warmed, and well-lighted buildings, where could be found amusement, instruction, and religious training, and where good meals, comfortable beds, and abundance of washing and bathing conveniences could be had at a low price. This plan was distinctly not intended to pauperize children, but it was intended to provide a sort of children's hotel, in which every one could pay his or her way and yet in which no one one would be inconvenienced to do so. The lessons of self-help were thus learned very early in life by those who came under this beneficent influence. The books show that more than 200,000 boys and girls have availed themselves of these lodging houses since they were started. In connection with these general projects for helping the poor and the young, Mr. Brace organised industrial schools in various parts of the city where children could also be taught the important lesson of self-reliance. It was quite in the line of his work, also, to find that children who were too young to be of any service to themselves in the way of self-support were in need of quite as much attention at the hands of the charitably disposed as were larger children, and from this discovery proceeded arrangements for the establishment of Summer homes for infants and for the collection of the fresh-air fund, which ever since then has been maintained under the Children's Aid Society.

This special movement was started about 1873, when THE TIMES united with the Children's Aid Society in inviting subscriptions to this fund. Excursions for children were given to Staten Island, and with such success that Mrs. Anson Phelps Stokes offered the society a Summer home for children on the Staten Island shore. In the course of a year or two it was found that the situation of this home was too well protected to secure the wholesome result that was desired, and provision was made for the construction of cottages and other buildings at Bath Beach and Coney Island, where they have since been maintained.

Mr. Brace's training and talents were of constant service to him in interesting the public in his labors and in directing modern thought into wise channels on the subject of the dispensation of charities. For many years he devoted a good part of his time to writing for journals and to delivering addresses designed to educate the charitable and to enlist sympathy with his policy of making charity in a measure self-supporting. His ideas and methods were eminently practical and they appealed always with force to those to whom they were addressed. The confidence of the charitable in him was unbounded, and so positive and salutary was his influence in directing thought and action that he took a commanding position among promoters of philanthropic endeavor, almost from the outset of his career, and he was able to bring ample support at all times to his undertakings.

In 1856, when only thirty years old and but two years after he organized the Children's Aid Society, he was a delegate to the International Convention for Children's Charities in London. In 1865 he carried out a special sanitary investigation in the cities of Great Britain. He was a delegate to the International Prison Congress in London in 1872, afterward visiting Hungary and Transylvania, where his reputation had preceded him and where he was received with marked attention. Meanwhile and afterward he published several works which were honored with reproduction abroad. "Hungary in 1851," "Home Life in Germany," "Norse Folk," and "Races of the Old World" were his earlier works, completed by 1863. In 1869 his book, "The New West," dealt more particularly with his specialty. "Short Sermons for Newsboys" came out in 1866 and "The Dangerous Classes of New-York" in 1872. Three editions of this book were exhausted, the publication continuing until 1880. In 1879 he published a work entitled "Free Trade as a Promoter of Peace and Good Will among Men," and in 1882 his now famous work, "Gesta Christi, a History of Humane Progress Under Christianity," was issued and commanded wide attention. His last book, published about a year ago, "To the Unknown God," tracing the history of the different forms of religion, was equally fortunate in the impression it made as a valuable compendium of sacred history.

For more than twenty years Mr. Brace was a contributor to the editorial columns and to the book reviews of THE TIMES. Theological and philanthropic subjects were intrusted to him for treatment. He brought to this work a graceful and vigorous pen and a ripened judgment. His attainments as a classical scholar also served him in his newspaper writing, especially in reviews of books dealing with the classics.

Mr. Brace's father was John Pierce Brace, a noted educator of Connecticut. Litchfield was Mr. Brace's birthplace. His mother and the mother of Henry Ward Beecher were cousins. His own home for some years was Ches-Knoll, at Dobbs Ferry, where he had a most delightful retreat. His family, consisting of his wife, two sons, and two daughters, all survive him. Mrs. Brace and a son and daughter were with him at the end.

August 14, 1890

POOR "DELINQUENT CHILDREN."

A Great Conference Discusses How They Should be Punished.

The conference on the care of dependent and delinquent children closed yesterday in the Associated Charities Building, after morning and afternoon sessions. The subject was "Delinquent Children."

At the morning session Evert J. Wendell, Secretary of the Board of Managers of the Society for the Reformation of Juvenile Delinquents on Randall's Island, declared that the whole attitude of a reformatory should be that of encouragement, and that boys should be taught what splendid fellows they might become, not what bad fellows they were.

"I believe in all manner of good employment," he said. "We have a full-rigged ship built on our lawn where the boys are taught to furl and unfurl sails and perform other nautical work."

On the question of corporal punishment Miss S. E. Minton, Associate Director of the Burnham Industrial Farm, said a large slipper without any heel was kept in that institution for spanking children. The blows were given, she said, in the presence of a witness and according to a fixed schedule.

Mr. Pierce, Superintendent of the Westchester Temporary Farm, believed in punishing children by depriving them of something they looked forward to. "For instance," he said, "a boy in washing dishes may break a bowl, and is sent to bed after a supper of bread and water."

Mr. Carpenter, Superintendent of the New-York Juvenile Asylum, said he thought whipping necessary at times, but that the one punishing the boy should be calm.

"But can you keep your temper?" a demure woman in black asked. "I know I lose mine when I whip my boys," she added.

Mr. Otterson of the New-Jersey Reform

School said: "I used to have a boy whom I had to whip three times a day. He came out all right and thanked me for whipping him."

Others did not believe in corporal punishment. An animated discussion of the subject followed.

Dr. Felix Adler commended industrial training for boys. He suggested that manual training be supplemented by instruction in the natural sciences.

"It seems hard," he said, "that a child must be a semi-criminal to get the advantages of these training schools. I think in time the schools will be accessible to all children."

In the afternoon William J. Fanning, Secretary of the New-York Catholic Protectory, described the work of that institution. Mrs. C. R. Lowell of New-York, in discussing Mr. Fanning's paper, said: "I think it unwise for the Protectory to keep so great a number of boys together. I think, too, that boys are kept there often too long. I know of instances where the removal of boys has been opposed by the authorities of the institution, when the Superintendents of the Poor of Westchester County, whence the boys came, tried to get them out. As long as the institution receives public funds I think, also, its reports should show what becomes of the children that are sent out of there."

Mr. Fanning said the Reformatory records showed this. He added: "We only offer opposition to a boy's removal when it seems for his interests to remain longer."

The Rev. W. F. Johnson, Superintendent of the Brooklyn Colored Orphan Asylum, took Mr. Fanning's part. "I thank God for the Catholic Protectory, though I am a Protestant," said he. "It is the Catholics alone who receive the white and black alike into their institutions, and who give the colored boy a chance to learn a trade. We are careful about the indenture when we place a boy in a family, for we are sensitive on the point of bondage. We were slaves for 250 years and received nothing for it, and now we are very cautious."

Francis Wayland, Dean of the Yale Law School, said: "The State has duties in these matters. You know that you can only touch the fringe of the evil. The State has full power to act and should do its duty. It must take children from the homes of vice and put them in proper places."

The closing address was made by Dr. George S. Wheelock.

November 17, 1893

NEW COURT FOR CHILDREN

The Governor Signs the Bill Providing for Its Operation.

Additional Special Sessions Justice to Preside—Offenses Below Capital Crimes to be Dealt with as Misdemeanors.

Gov. Odell on Monday signed the bill in its amended form providing for a Children's Court in this city. Although the court was to be opened in the Old Charities Building, at Third Avenue and Eleventh Street, on Jan. 1 last, amendments in the law necessary for its management and other delays have deferred the opening. In the opinion of Magistrate Joseph M. Deuel, President of the Board of City Magistrates, and who is the father of the bill, the court will probably be in operation in the building originally selected for it the middle of May.

The law provides that within twenty days after the Governor's approval an additional Special Sessions Justice shall be appointed to preside over the court. He is to have two assistants to be selected from the Board of City Magistrates, perhaps twice a week, it being at the discretion of the parents or guardians of the children whether the juvenile offenders shall be tried by one or three Judges.

The purpose of the new court, as has been heretofore stated, is to guard children against the exposure and environment of crime. In this respect, as was frequently urged by the advocates of the bill in the Legislature, New York has lagged behind, many cities having already established juvenile courts. This is so in cities in Pennsylvania, Illinois, and Wisconsin.

The law has been so amended that all offenses of children under sixteen years of age, save capital offenses, are to be regarded as misdemeanors. That permits of their being finally dealt with in the Children's Court, without the necessity of going to a higher tribunal.

Magistrate Deuel, when seen last evening in regard to the bill, had this to say.

"The new court will be a great improvement over the present system. It will be a model for other cities, and you will find that we will have delegations here to see it. It is something the Magistrates, and, I must admit, I myself, have given much consideration to. I was at Albany upon three different occasions to speak for the bill.

"It will be quite important that the new Justice who is appointed shall keep in mind that the court was established as a corrective measure—that is to say, that he punish only with a view to reform. That is one of the great reasons for which the court was established. It is quite natural in the Special Sessions to judge children on the basis of the law for adults. In the Children's Court this will be obviated, and by the same Justices, who will naturally be impressed by the environment of the Children's Court."

Within the last few days President Cantor has awarded the contracts for the work upon the new court.

There is considerable speculation regarding the selection of the additional Special Sessions Justice.

April 16, 1902

WORK OF CHILDREN'S COURT.

First Annual Tabulation Shows That Probation Should Be Exercised Only After Twelfth Year.

E. Fellows Jenkins, Chief Probation Officer of the Court of Special Sessions, yesterday afternoon submitted to Presiding Justice Holbrook the first tabulation of the work of the parole officers at the Children's Part of Special Sessions, otherwise the "Children's Court," since the opening of that court, in September last.

It shows that in the justice of the court the quality of mercy has not been strained; accused of offenses ranging from disorderly conduct to forgery, robbery, and grand larceny, children, according to the report, have been paroled and reparoled as many as six times, to give them a chance to mend their ways. Fifteen per cent. of all who had been paroled violated their parole and had to be committed to institutions.

In all, 616 boys and 23 girls were paroled between Sept. 3 last and June 27 this year. Disorderly conduct was charged against 125 boys; petit larceny, 226 boys and 7 girls; grand larceny, 59 boys; burglary, 83 boys; begging, 2 boys and 1 girl; no proper guardianship, 19 boys; assault, 21 boys; robbery, 13 boys; malicious mischief, 8 boys; ungovernable, 3 boys and 2 girls; disorderly children, 41 boys and 8 girls, and forgery, 3 boys.

"This report," says Mr. Jenkins, "indicates what satisfactory improvement may follow when erstwhile well-behaved children are given a chance to 'mend their ways.'

"I regret to have to report that of the 639 children enlarged on probation since the opening of the Children's Part of the Court of Special Sessions, about 15 per cent. have had to be committed to institutions for violating the provisions of their release. Of the number so committed it may be interesting to know that children under twelve years of age formed the larger part. And this goes to emphasize, in my opinion, that probation is productive of the most good when exercised over children over that age, children under twelve, having in most cases absolutely no conception of the position in which their misconduct places them."

July 1, 1903

WHY SOME CHILDREN ARE BAD.

Because of Parents' Neglect and Intemperance, Says Chicago Juvenile Court.

Upon the parents of Chicago has been placed the blame for conditions which have brought about the greatest year's work in the history of the Juvenile Court. The report of the court's work, prepared by Chief Probation Officer J. J. McManaman for Judge Mack, puts neglect and intemperance in the front rank of the causes of crime in children.

During eleven months past 1,460 "bad" boys and 328 wayward girls have been tried in the court. In the same time Judges Mack and Tuthill have been asked to decide the future for 786 homeless boys and 641 neglected girls. Records of the court stand as accusing drunkenness, laziness and their resultant poverty of parents as causing the children's plight.

"Whisky causes poverty. Poverty causes crime. That summarizes the situation," said Officer McManaman. "Children come to us first as dependents, but with age dependency becomes delinquency. Parental neglect lies at the foundation of work of the Juvenile Court."

During part of the time covered by the year's report statistics have been kept to learn how great an influence on the court's work is exerted by the "divorce evil." There was disappointment for those who expected much would be shown to have followed separation of parents. Only sixteen cases were discovered.

Pointing the force of the charge that intemperance and neglect, and not misfortune, has caused the work of the courts, reference is made to a table of causes of dependency in children, the first ever prepared in connection with the Chicago Juvenile Court. The table deals with cases of children taken into the court for the first time.

The causes of the little ones' poverty are shown thus:

Causes.	Girls.	Boys.	Total.
Lack of parental care.	162	148	310
Drunkenness of father..	85	75	160
Drunkenness of mother..	40	52	92
Drunkenness of both....	31	32	.63
Desertion by mother.....	15	14	29
Desertion by father.....	51	96	147
Desertion by both.....	10	15	25
Separation of parents....	9	7	16
Neglect by father.......	8	5	13
Mother immoral	8	5	13

All the foregoing are considered preventable causes for the appearance of children in court, as having no proper care and home. The following causes are held as impossible to avoid by the parents and guardians of the children figuring in the cases studied:

Causes.	Girls.	Boys.	Total.
Death of father.........	30	53	83
Death of mother....	41	32	73
Death of both parents..	24	41	65
Insanity of parents......	13	19	32
Poverty of parents......	3	22	25
Sickness of parents......	39	41	80
Incorrigibility	5	32	37
Grand totals—			
Preventable			468
Non-preventable			395

Of the causes listed officially as non-preventable, the probation officers who investigated the cases say fully 75 per cent. could be traced to their origin in the neglect and drunkenness of parents.

Of the 1,460 delinquent boys taken to the court 859 were there as their first appearance. The others had made previous trips to the court as follows: Second offenses, 305; third, 160; fourth, 91; fifth, 54. Girls never made more than two appearances, as a second offense means with them imprisonment in a State or city institution. Of the 328 girls made subject of inquiry during the year seventy-two were in court before.

There appears a striking difference in the average ages in which boys and girls are charged with wrongdoing. More than half the boys taken to court as delinquents are between twelve and fourteen years old. Girls find their period of greatest misconduct between the ages of fourteen and sixteen. Seventy per cent. of the girls' cases fall within these years. Larceny is the offense which brings the downfall of a great number of boys.—Chicago Post.

January 2, 1905

Successful Club for Boys

Millionaires and Tenement Dwellers Equally Interested in an Avenue A Experiment. ♣ ♣ ♣ ♣

MILLIONAIRES and tenement dwellers seem to have achieved a cordial friendship for one another at the Boys' Club, whose spacious building is at Avenue A and Tenth Street. The captains of industry attend the frequent entertainments, while their sons teach classes once a week, sip two-cent cups of coffee, play games, and mingle familiarly with hundreds of youngsters of every race. There is apparently no condescension on one side or deep awe on the other.

Such men as E. H. Harriman, Percy A. Rockefeller, Philip T. Dodge of the Mergenthaler Linotype Company, Otto H. Kahn of Kuhn, Loeb & Co., Mortimer L. Schiff, Herbert L. Griggs, Gordon F. Brown, nephew of J. Pierpont Morgan; Albert Kessler, and H. Kinnicutt are well known to the numerous members of the club. If these men have any other than an amiable side it has not been detected in the vicinity of Tompkins Square. They are held to be ideal patrons, joke-makers, and comrades.

Now that Christmas is coming the boys look forward to the vaudeville show by professionals on the evening of Dec. 21. This entertainment, afforded by Mr. Schiff, is held in the large hall, and there are always many uptown visitors to see the fun. The small boys receive boxes of bonbons and other presents. Bankers, railroad magnates, and heirs of oil kings will be on hand to guarantee the dividends of merriment. A later entertainment is a minstrel show, with native talent, and Spring brings the annual operetta, which is always a screaming delight.

The Boys' Club is a remarkable institution in several ways. It is really a club without rules, discipline, ostensible instruction of any sort. There is a gymnasium, reading room, library, parlor, restaurant, pool and billiard room, and many small clubrooms, all furnished in expensive and artistic style. An evening visitor hears a roar of voices and a noise of feet throughout the large building, for there are some 10,000 boys and youths who belong to the institution. The movement and noise disconcert one at first; he soon discovers they are not due to disorderliness, but to mere numbers. The boys are neatly dressed, bright looking, good mannered.

It was the discovery of Francis H. Tabor, the athletic young Superintendent, who hails from England, that boys act best without rules. He has found that on a system of honor they are never guilty of mischief, and guard the club property as if it were their own. The practice of never giving advice results in many coming to seek it, which is the only time advice is efficacious.

The object of the club being social, instruction is a side issue, and the knowledge imparted in the various weekly classes has a mask of extra entertainment. Even if anything difficult were taught, the junkets given by the leaders would atone for all pains. There are thirty-two so-called clubs which meet weekly, with a total membership of 720 youths and young men. The dues for all privileges average 10 cents a month, while every year there are issued 15,000 annual tickets at a cent apiece to the small boys of the neighborhood. Since many tickets are lost the number does not represent the exact membership.

The weekly club meetings are held in small rooms on the second floor, and the leader usually makes the boys organize with a President, Secretary, Sergeant at Arms, and so forth. He suggests parliamentary methods, corrects mistakes, and speedily devises a new game when attention flags. Oratory, debate, and study of literature and science are relieved with chatty intervals. The leader smokes a short pipe or cigar; everything is free and easy.

Gordon F. Brown, nephew of J. Pierpont Morgan and a former Yale football Captain, is the leader of the Boys' Athletic Club. He often practices with them in the gymnasium or exhibits the tricks of Old Eli on the Columbia Oval for the benefit of his admirers.

E. H. Harriman is always interested in athletics, and so is Henry S. Brooks, Jr., of the telephone company, who used to be a champion quarter-mile runner at Yale. The latter gives points on track work, and varies instruction by taking the boys to the theatre.

Morris U. Ely, former Yale quarter back, teaches the athletic class Monday nights, and besides football practice in the gymnasium goes in for expert basketball. The quality of athletic material is shown in the results of many amateur games played in this city and out of town by club representatives. John Hein, for instance, is a champion 105-pound wrestler of the National and metropolitan tournaments, and he took second prize at the St. Louis Olympia. Ben Bradshaw, at 135 pounds, and R. Wolken, at 145 pounds, are also wrestling champions.

The Camera Club is the hobby of Philip T. Dodge, who provides all the materials used. H. Kinnicutt, the banker, calls the picture makers to order every Wednesday night, and suggests new subjects for experiment.

Percy A. Rockefeller lately managed a social club, and was well liked, despite his inherited quietude and reticence, but since his marriage to Miss Stillman he has not been seen very often.

Meredith Howland, Jr., takes charge of the Brownies' Club on Tuesday nights. This is a social organization, and the leader often treats his class to supper parties, theatres, and the Hippodrome. Coney Island was visited last Summer.

The Natural History Society, which is making an especial study of birds at present, is in the efficient charge of A. C. Barrell, who belongs to an arms manufacturing company. Loyall Farragut, a son of Admiral Farragut, likewise helps the students of natural history along.

R. Bayard Cutting, son of Fulton Cutting, conducts the Out of Door Club on Tuesday evenings. The stalwart, large-jawed young man has welded the members to him by hooks of steel, and perhaps in part by the frequent entertainments of theatre parties and dances. A dance is planned for the near future by this club. Eliphalet Potter, a banker and nephew of Bishop Potter, collaborates with young Mr. Cutting in leading and amusing the Out of Door members.

J. Duane Pell has the Irving Pleasure Club on Friday nights, and Walter T. Stern, a lawyer, manages the Tompkins Athletic Band.

A hilarious organization is the Primrose Social Club, under E. Trowbridge Hall, head of the firm of Rogers, Peet & Co. The boys are studying just now for a minstrel show.

The annual operetta, when small boys are dressed as girls and beautiful ladies, pirates and soldiers, creates a furor all over the upper east side, and the repeated performances have thousands of spectators.

December 17, 1905

CHILD'S ENVIRONMENT MAKES ITS CHARACTER

Children's Court Report Says Heredity Is a Minor Matter.

After giving the subject three years of careful study the officers of the Children's Court of New York don't believe that heredity controls character. Drawing their conclusions from the thousands of cases of girls and boys arraigned for misconduct, they think heredity does influence the life of a youth, but that the character of a boy or girl is largely determined by his or her environment before reaching maturity.

Statements to this effect are made in the report for 1905 of E. Fellows Jenkins, chief probation officer of the court. After reviewing the 1,188 cases which came before the court, he says:

"Removing a boy or girl from improper environment is the first step in his or her reclamation. The theory that heredity has its influences has not yet been entirely exploded, but that heredity controls character is no longer believed to be a fact. Perhaps the best proof of the contention that environment has the strongest influence on the development of character is found in the records of the New York Society for the Prevention of Cruelty to Children, which during thirty years has investigated cases involving the social and moral welfare of over half a million children. Instances of this fact are of every day occurrence. "No less than in the permanent removal of children from improper guardians and their being placed in the control of individuals and institutions is the force for good found in their being placed by any court of competent jurisdiction on parole. In three years 3,377 children arrested for various crimes and convicted at our Children's Court have been so released in the custody of their parents and guardians. The results have been by no means discouraging, even though they show that 16.8 per cent. of such children have been arrested for recurrent misbehavior and committed to institutions.

"The more important fact is that 83.2 per cent. have profited by the privilege of parole and have not later become wards of the court or prisoners of the police for any cause whatever. Unfortunately too great stress has been laid upon the number of 'parole boys gone wrong.' These instances should

rather be used to emphasize the number who have 'gone right,' and who are today the best witnesses of that system."

The report shows that the greatest number of juvenile arrests last year were made for petit larceny, 302 boys and 8 girls being taken into custody for the offense. On the charge of disorderly conduct 190 boys and 2 girls were arrested, and for burglary 131 boys. One boy was arrested for passing a worthless check, while seven girls were designated as totally depraved morally.

Officers of the society say that the wave of immorality among girls in Chicago, as reported by a prominent sociologist there, does not extend to New York.

"The dance halls are said to be the root of the evil here," said Mr. Jenkins's deputy, E. K. Coulter. "We have seen none of it here. We had about 120 girls up on charges of immorality last year, an exceedingly small number.

"What we are discouraged about, is the constant growth of pocket picking among youths of New York growing out of the maintenance of basement pool parlors. There are many of these on the lower east side. We are trying to break them up. These poolrooms, in a majority of cases, are schools for pickpockets. The Fagins who run them are busy every day getting recruits from among the school children of New York. They select the brightest and best behaved boys of a class. In many cases basement pool parlors have been exposed, fitted with dummy figures used for instruction in the art of pocket picking. The men who do the teaching can be arrested only on a charge of impairing youthful morals. They never do the actual stealing. The boys, after being instructed, are sent out upon the work, but the Fagin gets the lion's share of the plunder. "In one case we noted that a boy got 10 cents for stealing a $50 gold watch. The worst feature of the whole thing is that in 999 out of 1,000 cases when a youth once becomes a thief of this character he remains so all his life."

January 4, 1906

The Youthful Delinquent: A New Way to Deal with Him

Judge Lindsey of Denver, Pioneer Apostle of the Juvenile Court ❧ Idea, Gives an Interesting Explanation of His Methods. ❧

THE Juvenile Courts in the United States are going to bring about a complete reorganization of our methods of dealing with criminals. We are already beginning to realize that by working against the lawbreaker we are only making of him an implacable enemy of the court that convicts him, the Government that supports the court, and the authorities that administer the Government, whereas the juvenile courts are teaching us that by working with the lawbreaker we gain his friendship for the court, his respect for the Government, and his obedience to the authorities. It doesn't make any difference that the individuals dealt with in the juvenile courts are children, while the material of the criminal courts is grown-up men and women. Men and women are pretty much like boys and girls, and they are all accessible to the same appeal—a sympathetic understanding of their difficulties."

This is what Ben B. Lindsey, the "little Judge," who has made the Denver Juvenile Court the marvel of modern legislation, has been saying in New York and Boston to audiences composed of legislators, educators, boys and girls, and members of small clubs. He was invited to come East to explain his method of dealing with delinquent children by James J. Storrow, President of the new School Board in Boston, and by Dr. A. E. Winship of The Boston School Journal. The object was to strengthen the chances of the juvenile court bills now pending in the Massachusetts Legislature. During his six days' stay in Boston he spoke twenty-one times, including once at Harvard University. In New York he addressed only four or five small meetings called together in private parlors by persons particularly interested in his work, owing to the heavy tax which his Boston talks had levied upon a vitality already greatly reduced by his regular labors in Denver.

+ + +

In talking with him the cause of the threatened nervous breakdown becomes evident. Judge Lindsey gives all of himself all the time. People who have seen his influence with apparently hopeless boys have accused him of using hypnotism. The "power" that he employs is, however, only the power of an overwhelming earnestness poured forth with passionate

energy. Judge Lindsey is to himself only the instrument of a cause, and he lets the cause use him as it will. He has no wife, no child, no home. He holds court every hour of the twenty-four in which his services are needed—not on an easy bench in a comfortable courtroom, but on the up-turned washtub in a squalid shanty under the railroad viaduct, on a soap box in a "newsies' alley," on the edge of a cot in the detention home.

"A Judge in Boston asked me when and where I hold court," said Judge Lindsey with the gentle smile out of the gentle brown eyes under the big, bulging forehead. "I couldn't tell him. Another Judge wanted to know how long I took to try each case. All I could tell him was that we don't try cases. We hear the boys' stories, and if the boys want to tell their stories at home, or at their place of business, or in the detention home, or at my house, or out on the street—why, the Judge has to go to the boy that's all. It's impossible to say when we hold court, because we make a point of listening to the boy when he wants to talk and of not forcing him to say anything until he gets ready. He always tells us the truth then. If we tried to make him talk when we wanted him to he would probably tell us a lie. You can't blame him for that. And as for saying how long it takes us to try a case—that's impossible, because it may be three hours and it may be three weeks. It all depends upon how long it takes the boy to make up his mind to tell us the truth. We don't hurry him. We let him take his time—and meanwhile we look up his home surroundings.

+ + +

"The trouble with all our work in the criminal line is that we pay more attention to the act than to the cause of the act. Our chief concern with the lawbreaker is, What did you do?' whereas it should be, 'Why did you do it?' Nobody—man or boy, woman or girl, breaks a law just for the fun of doing it. There is a reason for all the acts that we call crimes. It seems to me that the only preventive for an act of that kind is to find out the cause and remove it, instead of inflicting punishment for the crime.

"For instance: Not long ago a boy was brought into our court for stealing coal off the railroad tracks. He didn't deny his guilt, and, under the law,

I could have sent him up or put him under the probation of a perfect stranger. I did nothing of the kind. I knew that Micky wasn't stealing coal off the tracks just to be vicious. I went to see his mother.

"Exactly as I expected, his mother admitted to me that she had sent Micky to pick up coal along the tracks. She didn't know that it was against the law, and she couldn't see why the poor people shouldn't have the benefit of the waste coal from the box cars. She was perfectly right from her point of view, but I explained to her that it was against the law for people to pick up coal along the tracks—not because the State didn't want them to have the coal, but because the State is interested in those people, and it doesn't want them to lose a leg or an arm, or perhaps their lives. Then I went on to show her that in the case of boys like Micky it was only a step from the track to the box car, and from loose coals to fruit and grain and brasses, and, finally, the corner grocery and the penitentiary.

"'Now, Mrs. Brown,' I said to her, 'if you need coal we will get coal for you, but we want you to keep Micky off the tracks. We are just as much interested in Micky as you are, and we want to be your ally in bringing him up. If you're a widow, we want to act as a sort of foster-father to him. He's as valuable and important to us as he is to you, and it would be even harder upon us than upon you if he should happen to go wrong.

"Do you suppose we had any trouble with Micky after that? Why, Micky now considers himself the divinely appointed guardian of all the tracks and box cars of his neighborhood, and he believes it his solemn duty to reason seriously with all the boys who hang round them. The boys whom he finds inaccessible to reason he reports to me.

"You see, out in Denver we have progressive ideas in regard to 'snitching' or 'squealing,' or whatever you call telling on the other fellow in this part of the country. We think that the first duty of every citizen, big or little, is toward the State, and that it is as much a part of his duty to enforce the laws as to keep them. Then our boys understand that the evil is not in getting caught, but in doing the thing. Lastly they know that the fellow they 'snitch on' is not going to be betrayed into the hands of a prosecutor, but that he is going to be treated as 'square' as they were themselves. Sometimes they don't have to 'snitch' on him. They just bring him into court. He's usually willing to come, because he knows that he is only going to have things explained to him. Two years ago one gang of four who had been caught, brought in forty-four others who hadn't. None of those boys is in institutions. There has not been a single complaint lodged against one of them since we had things out the first time.

"Instead of sending to jail the four boys who were caught and making of them imbittered little enemies of the State, we got at the cause of their act—which in this instance was 'the gang'—and then we got hold of the other boys and showed them why it was against their own interests to break the laws.

"In this way we get the boys who are caught to work for us, instead of against us, and we are enabled to reach the boys who are not caught. There is no opprobrium attached to a boy for having been in the Juvenile Court in Denver. The boys speak proudly of belonging to the court.

"Now in other States the juvenile laws do not allow the court to act until the child has transgressed the law. Then he has to be arrested and tried. Even if he is only charged with delinquency or misdemeanor there is a certain stigma attached to it, and even if the Judge is kind and humane in his examination of the child there is a certain bitterness in the child's heart at being brought into court and exposed to public criticism. In a measure the court is still working against the prisoner instead of with him. Our law permits us to take control of the child if he even 'enters a condition tending to delinquency.' We have just as much jurisdiction over a boy who, we hear, is hanging about the railroad tracks as we have over a boy who has been caught stealing coal from a car. We get hold of the boy before he has committed a delinquent act and remove him from

danger. If we can't remove him from danger we remove the danger from him.

"This is where some of your conventional Easterners think we have gone too far. The Gerry Society people will tell you that our 'adult responsibility' law is unconstitutional and that some day somebody will make an attack on it and prove it so. Maybe the Gerry Society is right, but nobody has made an attack on the law yet, and in the meantime it is doing some mighty effective work.

"I sent a father to jail for three days not long ago for swearing in the presence of his boy. Parents in Denver understand that if they do not perform their proper functions toward their children they are liable to fine or imprisonment. We don't consider a child responsible for his truancy if his parents are keeping him out of school to work. We don't send a boy up for stealing brasses off the railroad cars as long as his father is encouraging him to steal as a source of income to himself and as long as a pawnbroker is paying the boy a good price for his booty. We arrest the father and the pawnbroker. We don't blame a boy for vicious habits as long as the messenger companies are sending him into improper places and the saloon and dive keepers are setting their traps for him. We go after the messenger companies and the saloon and dive keepers.

"Through our adult responsibility law and through the loyalty of our boys we have been able to close up all the wine rooms in Denver. At the time when the Juvenile Court was first started these places were running wide open, but it was generally understood that they were not. I had written the Police Commissioner and warned the wine-room men, but my boys kept telling me that the places were still running. The Police Commissioner paid no attention to my letters and the wine-room men only laughed at me, so finally I planned a coup that, I fancy, was pretty sensational.

"There was a hearing before me of a number of wine-room cases. The Commissioner and a number of other public officials were to be there. I got about two hundred boys who had been keeping me posted in regard to the wine rooms to come down and stow themselves away in one corner of the court room.

"During the hearing the Commissioner made the statement that all the wine rooms had been closed. This was the cue for little Johnny Simpson. Johnny jumped up and said right out loud:

"'Yes, they were closed one night and opened the next. Ain't it so, kids?'

"The other kids yelled in chorus that it was so, and the Commissioner had to back down. After that he got busy and cleaned up the town.

"The boys understand their duty as citizens. Whenever they hear of a boy being admitted to a saloon they come and tell me about it. Whenever they find a man who sells cigarettes to 'kids,' they let me know. There is no bitterness in their hearts toward the State because they have been in court. Through their experience with the court they have learned that the State is a citizen's best friend, and that it is to a citizen's interest to work for and with the State.

"Even when I am forced to commit a boy to the State Industrial School in Golden, I do my best to make him feel that, in committing him, I am doing it only because I feel that it is best for him. In fact I tell him that I am going to let him go up to the school absolutely alone and that he can cut and run if he wants to. I give him his papers and I say, 'Now, Johnny—or Tom, or Bill,' or whatever his name may be—you can ditch the papers if you want to. If you think it's best for you not to go out to Golden, you ditch and run. Nobody is going to follow you and nobody is going to bring you back. All I want is to do the best thing for you.'

"At first people used to think I was crazy, but when they found out that there wasn't a boy that didn't take the train and go straight to the school they began to think that there might be something in my idea, after all. Dozens of young men whom I've tried in the criminal court I've sent to the State Reformatory or to the penitentiary in the same way. Not one has ever betrayed my trust. In the Juvenile Courts of Salt Lake City, Portland, and Omaha, where they have adopted my system, they have had the same experience, with the exception of one boy in Portland. Do you know why he broke his word? As he was buying his ticket he saw the Sheriff watching him. Naturally he cut and ran. Why not? He had meant to be square with the court, but the court had not been square with him. No one can blame him for feeling that he had a right to flee from a traitor. I've sent a hundred boys to Golden since our Juvenile Court was opened and not lost one.

"Of course it will take a good many years of quiet, steady growth before the complete system of working with, instead of against, the wrongdoer can be applied to adults, but it will come in time. What if it will require trouble and money and an elaborate system to put it into operation? We have expended plenty of money and trouble and built up an elaborate enough system to create deadly enemies to the State.

✛ ✛ ✛

"You can't bring an individual—man or boy, woman or girl—into a courtroom full of people and stand them up before a perfect stranger, whom they have every reason to believe has designs upon their liberty, and expect him, or her, to tell the truth. His frightened instinct will only prompt him to say that he didn't do it. But talk to him quietly, as a friend, for an hour or two; make him see that what he did isn't half as important as why he did it; win his confidence and let him know that you are not going to betray it; make him feel that you are not going to take away his liberty and happiness, but that you want to find the best way to insure him the fullest measure of liberty and happiness; then see whether your prisoner will tell the truth.

"Under circumstances like these he will be satisfied with whatever measures you take with him. You'd be surprised to see how things come out under this process. Not long ago a little boy was brought before me charged with assault. A little girl had

accused him of having struck her. Imagine those two children up before a Judge in a crowded court for a three-minute examination! The boy's denial would, of course, be discredited, and, at the very least, he would have been sent home with a reprimand. Naturally he would hate the Judge and he would hate the little girl as long as he lived.

"I took that boy and girl aside and talked to them for three hours, and finally the little girl opened her heart to me and admitted that it was all a lie and that the boy had not struck her at all, but that she had a grudge against the boy and wanted to get even with him by getting him into trouble. Then the boy admitted that he had been 'mean' to the girl, and that he had lied as well as she had. The parents were involved in the matter and there was a whole mountain of neighborhood hatred to be cleared away before the boy and girl finally shook hands and agreed to be friends. But they did it at last. Then I got the parents to bury their differences and to admit that they, too, had been in the wrong.

✛ ✛ ✛

"Now that took a long time and a lot of energy, but I say that it was worth it. It saved endless Police Court transactions—maybe a murder trial. More than that, though, it made both that boy and girl and their parents firm friends of the State.

"Newell Dwight Hillis says that the degree of skill necessary for the handling of marble is nothing compared to the degree of skill necessary for the handling of men, and yet we treat men as if they were blocks of the roughest granite. We must learn to handle men as men, and the best time to handle a man is when he is a boy. We will never get anywhere in the problem as long as we try to overcome evil with evil. We may begin to hope when we adapt to men the Juvenile Court system of overcoming evil with good."

F. M. B.

February 25, 1906

Big Brothering Boys Who Are in Law's Grip

Judge Hoyt Tells How the Work of the Children's Court Is Aided by Great Volunteer Organization Which Gives the Boy in Trouble a Helping Hand

EFFICIENT as is the Probation System in the courts of New York City, and enormous as has been the help given by the Children's Court in solving the problem of society's dealings with the juvenile offender, these powerful agencies are glad to avail themselves of the aid freely supplied by a great volunteer association. This organization is the Big Brothers.

Although this rapidly growing organization is generally known, the methods it employs are as a rule only vaguely comprehended. It was with the purpose of giving a clearer understanding of its workings that Judge Franklin Chase Hoyt recently talked to a TIMES reporter about the value of the Big Brothers movement to the community as he had seen it exemplified in the exercise of his judicial duty.

Judge Hoyt, it may be said, is doubly interested in this particular branch of philanthropic endeavor. He is the Presiding Judge of the Children's Court of New York City, and he is also President of the Big Brothers.

"There are two classes of children with whom the Court has to deal," he said, as he sat at his great desk in his private office in the Children's Court Building. "They are the neglected child and the delinquent child, the child that has been offended against, and the child that has offended. The courses of procedure differ radically in the two cases.

"All delinquency cases, if they are of a serious nature and seem to warrant supervision by the Court, are put on probation. Such children never are handed over to the Big Brothers or to any other volunteer organization. Such is not the practice of the Court. We have our own probation officers, adequately trained and equipped for their work, and it is to their care that the delinquent children are committed.

"Although I am President of the Big Brothers, I don't turn the delinquent children directly over to the Big Brothers. I put them in the care of the probation officers. But if the case is not serious enough to warrant putting it on probation, then the Big Brothers and similar volunteer organizations are decidedly useful.

"In such cases of delinquency as I have mentioned, in which it is necessary for the Court to put the child on probation, the great value of the Big Brothers is that they stand ready to co-operate with the probation officers. The Big Brothers offer the children facilities that are, of course, beyond the reach of the

probation officers, among them being employment and change of environment. Personally, I do not see how the work of the probation officers and that of the Big Brothers could ever clash and interfere with each other.

"You see, the Court is able to keep the child under strict supervision only for a comparatively short period of time. As a rule the period of probation runs from six months to a year. There is every reason why the help and the interest of the Big Brothers should be continued indefinitely. As a matter of fact, to continue that help and interest for a longer time than is possible to the probation officers is the chief aim of the Big Brothers.

"In the case of a child that is not delinquent, but has been neglected, advantage is taken of the services of the Society for the Prevention of Cruelty to Children. But this by no means precludes a co-operation of a volunteer organization. As a matter of fact, it is sought and encouraged.

"The aim of the Big Brothers is to continue their interest in a case as long as may be necessary. This care may and often does continue for many years.

"The probation officers cannot be expected to do for the children committed to their care many of the things which are easily in the power of the Big Brothers. There is, as I have said, the employment which individual members

of the Big Brothers organization are able to procure for the boys in whom they are interested.

"And then there are the Summer Camps. Boys who otherwise would not leave the city may now go to Summer Camps of Princeton, Saint Paul, Groton, and Choats School. Boys are sent to these camps through the instrumentality of the Big Brothers.

"Also the Court in the course of its work cannot fail to observe the beneficial effects of the five clubs which the Big Brothers conduct in various centres of the city. Thirty boys have attended each of these clubs three times a week within the past year.

"The Big Brothers have provided gymnasium work and instruction for 150 boys. And most of these boys have come from the Children's Courts.

"One important phase of the Big Brother movement is illustrated by the fact that many boys have through the instrumentality of the Big Brothers been placed in private schools. If the Big Brothers had not taken care of the boys in this manner, it would have been necessary for the Court to commit them to corrective institutions.

"Then there is a matter which I have already mentioned—the matter of employment. The probation officers cannot, of course, find employment for the boys given over into their care. But through the agency of the Big Brothers many boys are placed in positions which otherwise they could not hope to secure.

"Nor do the Big Brothers neglect the important question of providing adequate instruction for the boys whom they intend to supply with employment. Through the Y. M. C. A. and the Training School for Office Boys, the Big Brothers provide special vocational training for many of the boys who have appeared before the Court.

"It is one of the principles of the Big Brothers' movement," said Judge Hoyt, "that every child should receive some religious training. The organization does not attempt to dictate what that training shall be. But the Big Brothers have been instrumental in establishing close relations between the churches and the boys. Of course, it is the probation officer who is directly responsible. But back of the probation officer stand the Big Brothers, ready to give their powerful aid.

"Recently the Big Brothers established a system of Saturday trips for the boys to points of interest, some of which might also be of value from a vocational point of view. The boys have visited the Museum of Natural History, the navy yard, the Aquarium, hotel kitchens, bakeries and various mills and factories. This has given the boys on probation a chance to spend a part of their time pleasantly and profitably, and the results have been extremely gratifying to the Big Brothers and to the Court.

"The point which I mentioned that the Big Brothers are able to continue their supervision after that of the probation officers has terminated is of special significance. Because of the vast numbers to be dealt with by the Court, the supervision of the probation officers can necessarily be exercised only for a short time. But the friendly interest of the Big Brothers often continues on until the boys have grown up and taken a responsible place in society.

"In this connection it is interesting to note that there are now among the active workers in the Big Brother movement men, who, as boys, came before the Court at the time of the establishment of the Big Brothers. Now they are befriending and taking care of boys who are brought before the Court, just as they were years ago.

"I said some time ago that the Big Brothers believe that every child should have some religious instruction. Apropos of this it may be stated that since the inception of the Big Brothers similar organizations have been started, notably movements for providing special care for Catholic, Jewish, and colored boys.

"Now, there is no doubt that the lack of the facilities which are furnished by the Big Brothers would greatly hamper the Court in its efforts to use the probation system efficiently. The fact that the probation system is backed up by the Big Brother movement is of a value that is readily apparent. At every Court session the Big Brothers' investigator is present, and he takes down the name of every boy who is brought before the Court."

Judge Hoyt smiled reminiscently. "I remember," he said, "one case I had some time ago. A boy came up before me for the third time. It is true that the charge against him was merely one of assault, and did not necessarily indicate any great moral delinquency. But the mere fact that the boy had been arrested three times, and had become an intolerable nuisance in his own neighborhood, made it difficult for me to come to a decision on the case.

"After a careful consideration of all the facts in the case the Court found itself clearly justified in giving the boy another chance instead of committing him to an institution. At the same time a need of the services of the Big Brothers was indicated.

"Both through its own officials and through the Big Brotherhood, the Court endeavored to do what it could for the boy's welfare. The first offer of the Big Brothers, of which advantage was taken at once, was to remove the boy from his environment for two or three weeks.

"He was taken to a Summer camp. Here he had life in the great outdoors instead of in the narrow and noisy city streets, he had wholesome outlets for the natural energy which had led him into mischief, and, what is especially important, he found that he had real friends who took a genuine interest in him.

"After this boy's return to the city, his friends among the Big Brothers secured for him employment in a large brokerage office. There he has since risen to a position of considerable responsibility. Since his first visit to the Summer camp he has never missed his yearly trip to it.

"Lately he has taken charge in the Big Brother movement of various groups of small boys at the very camp to which he was sent after his early appearance in Court. When he reached his majority he was eager to show his willingness to do his share of the work, and since his election to the Big Brothers he has devoted many of his evenings to work among the boys at the club centres.

"While I have spoken of the work of the Big Brothers movement alone in connection with the Court, it is because as its President I have direct interest in its organization. There are other volunteer societies carrying on a similar work, and their activities and helpful service are fully as great. As Justice of the Children's Court I cannot close without testifying to the great debt which the Court owes to such societies as the Catholic Protective Society, the Catholic Boys' Protective League, (otherwise known as the Catholic Big Brothers,) the Jewish Big Brothers, the Catholic Ladies' Committee, the Protestant Big Sisters, the Jewish Big Sisters, and the Catholic Big Brothers."

October 17, 1915

SEE IN SCOUT WORK END OF THE BAD BOY

Students of Juvenile Delinquency Blame Misdirected Energy for Most Cases.

ALL NEED CHANCE TO PLAY

Malicious Mischief Another Name for Animal Spirits Turned to Wrong Channel.

That juvenile delinquency would be largely prevented by an extension of the Boy Scout movement is the opinion of the head of the New York Children's Court, Justice Franklin Chase Hoyt. Concurring in this decision is Magistrate Joseph Fitch of Long Island City, who is the leader of a band of Scouts. Also concurring in this opinion is Judge Ben B. Lindsey of the Juvenile Court of Denver.

Justice Hoyt believes that the scout movement turns the gregarious instincts of boys to useful purposes. He says in a statement issued through the Scouts' headquarters:

"Over one-half of the cases that come before the Children's Court are due to the environment of the children, using the word environment in its largest sense. The test is whether a change of surrounding conditions would remove the motive that led to the delinquency. The activities of scouting would act as a great preventive against the formation of bad associations and give direction to energies which, when misdirected, lead the boy into trouble. A large part of delinquency is a gang phenomenon, the same natural tendency to act in groups which the scout movement utilizes for constructive purposes as well as amusement."

Justice Hoyt is President of the Manhattan-Bronx Council of the Boy Scouts of America, and chairman of the Advisory Committee for Greater New York, which is in charge of the $200,000 campaign.

Magistrate Fitch puts the matter somewhat differently. "A large majority of the offenders in any court," said he, "are youths from 16 to 25 years of age. The civil war, like the present European war, was fought by youths under 25. Youth is enterprising and moving about. That is the time of life, the age when vital impulses assert themselves most vigorously; after that age things become set and men do not take the chances they do before life settles down into a rut.

"This morning a young Italian of 18 or 19 was arraigned before me on a charge of insubordination and vagrancy preferred by his own father. The old man is a street paver, a rammer, the father of seven children, a wizened day laborer, about half the size of his delinquent son. The son had grown away from his parents. His education in the public schools had so thoroughly instilled in him the idea of keeping clean that he carried it to the point of keeping away altogether from any manual labor which might possibly soil his hands. The hard working father couldn't see why his broad-shouldered son should not take a pick and shovel and get to work as he did. He had watched him do nothing for so long that he was ready to throw him into the street, a vagrant without any means of support.

"I asked the boy what was the matter, and he said he was not strong enough to work. When I pressed him for details he complained of bad wind. Cigarettes! I made him admit it.

"The whole trouble was that his education had been such as to make him look down on manual labor to such an extent that he couldn't get the point of view of the old man. But if that boy had been brought up as a Boy Scout he never would have been haled into court on any such charge. Some one must do the commonplace work of the world, and scouts learn that no work, no matter how menial, is disgracing. On the contrary, a scout is taught that the disgraceful thing is to have anybody do anything for him that he can do for himself; to be ashamed to ask for help from others wherever he can help himself.

"The discipline of the Boy Scouts would have met this particular case in two ways. He would have been trained to be clean, to omit cigarettes or anything else that was impairing his health. In my own troop the boys have prohibited the use of all tobacco in their by-laws, and I abstain from it when I am with them as rigidly as they do. If this young Italian had been a scout he probably never would have got into the cigarette habit. Secondly, he would have been taught the dignity and decency of common labor. As a scout, while he would have been stimulated to prepare himself for a more skilled position, he would have felt that even a pick and shovel were not only permissible, but desirable.

"I put him on probation for six months on condition that he quite cigarettes entirely and find any honest work that he can lay his hand to. But it would have been much better if the idea had been instilled into him by the Boy Scout discipline at the proper age when habits were forming. If scouting is widely extended throughout this city, youthful delinquents ought to be entirely wiped out."

Judge Lindsey is much more emphatic. He declares that if the Boy Scout movement had the support that it rightfully demands the Juvenile Court would soon be needed no longer.

"The Juvenile Court is not a remedy for so-called juvenile crime," he says. "It merely insures a better handling of the delinquent child. It may, and sometimes does, reduce delinquency. But if we are to solve the problem effectively we must go deeper; we must conserve and direct the energies of boyhood.

"Courts and jails will never do away with the gangs of lawless youths that infest cities. It is absolutely futile for any community to stand the terrible expense of police departments, prisons, criminal courts, or even juvenile courts, if it does not at the same time wholeheartedly support every effort to conserve and prevent.

"The Boy Scout movement is our greatest hope, the greatest single activity in this country promising a solution, not only of the boy problem, but the girl problem, for the best protector of girls is the youth who lives up to the laws and ideals of the Boy Scouts.

"Devoted, far-seeing men have given us this remedy, and it is the duty of every parent, teacher, and citizen, to support it. The youth of the land is anxious to join the Boy Scout movement, for there is fun in it, besides every kind of instruction and opportunities to serve.

"After fifteen years of juvenile work I say without question that if you will give the Boy Scout movement the moral and financial support it rightfully demands, the Juvenile Court will soon no longer be needed."

William C. McKee, Clerk of the Kings County Children's Court, said of the Boy Scout movement as related to juvenile delinquency: "People sometimes refer to the Juvenile Court as a great preventive agency of juvenile delinquency. That is hardly correct. The Children's Court treats symptoms merely, symptoms of disease whose causes lie back in the social environment, where only such organizations as the Boy Scouts can reach. It is noticeable in Brooklyn that the interpreter is the most important person in the Children's Court. The great majority of delinquents are foreigners who frequently err through ignorance. Lack of proper amusements, lack of interest for idle hours, physical defects, and ill health—these are all causes of delinquency which the Boy Scout program attacks much further back than the juvenile courts can reach."

Another man who has had much experience with delinquent chilldren and who strongly indorses the movement, is Charles Edwin Fox of Philadelphia, who, as Assistant District Attorney in Philadelphia, is in charge of the Juvenile Court work of the office.

"Close observation of hundreds of lads who have been haled before the bar of the Juvenile Court in the last four years," says he, "had brought me to the conclusion that there was one underlying cause for about 50 per cent. of their offenses, gray or gay, as they might be. It was this: They did not have adequate opportunity for play, and so they fell into one form or another of mischief that brought them afoul the law.

"Others assign much more formidable-sounding reasons, such as heredity or environment or adenoids or high-grade feeble-mindedness. But really I cannot use words that sound more serious than these—'lack of play.' To my mind these words are quite serious enough, for they are an indictment not of the boy before the Court, but of the community which sent him there. Given an average young American citizen of the Juvenile Court age (up to 16,) and he is bound to have an outlet for all that splendid energy and enthusiasm and sheer love of living that is the very fibre of his being. All of us grow more or less sentimental over the abstract thought of youth, because of its light-heartedness, its lack of responsibility, its pleasure in simple joys, and all that sort of thing.

"But do we all make this idea a concrete one by giving youth, born and imprisoned in the city, an opportunity to breathe purer air than the city contains. In short, do we give youth a chance to play? If it stopped there and went no further, it would have its great value. The real need of affording city youth the opportunity for play for play's own sake needs no more than mere mention, now that the playground movement is firmly intrenched in all of our big cities, and in Philadelphia has given rise to a separate municipal department with constantly expanding usefulness.

"The wise men of Greece thought it well to give their best thought over many centuries to the perpetuation of the greatest system of play for their young people that the world has ever seen. Our wise and good men, who have uplifted a phase of modern administration of law by creating the Juvenile Court, have now to go a step further and consider the establishment of those preventive forces that can anticipate the efforts of this same court. I earnestly urge the extension of every facility for play as one of the most potent of these preventive forces. And let it be the play of the Boy Scouts wherever possible."

December 5, 1915

YOUNG DELINQUENTS FEWER IN 9 CITIES

Juvenile Offenses in New York Show a Marked Decline From 1915 to 1925.

NATIONAL DECREASE SEEN

Children's Bureau Holds Fears of Country-Wide Wave of Youthful Crime Are Groundless.

Special to The New York Times.

WASHINGTON, April 4.—Challenging the contention that there are any real grounds for any youthful crime-wave scare in the United States, the United States Children's Bureau, in a statement issued today, asserted that available figures indicated a reduction rather than an increase in juvenile delinquency rates during the past decade.

The bureau declared that there had been no significant increase in the actual number of children committed to jail for grave offenses—homicide, robbery and burglary—between 1910 and 1923, and recommended "sane and thoughtful consideration of this problem rather than newspaper headlines."

New York, Philadelphia, Boston, Chicago, Buffalo, Detroit, Minneapolis, New Orleans, Providence, Richmond, Rochester, St. Louis, Seattle and Washington are the fourteen cities for which the bureau was able to obtain statistics from, in most cases, 1915 through 1924 and, in some cases, through 1925.

Decreased juvenile delinquency rates at the end of the period as compared with the beginning were found in New York, Boston, Buffalo, Chicago, New Orleans, Providence, Richmond, St. Louis and Washington. The rate in Rochester was stationary for the three years for which statistics were obtained, 1922, 1923, 1924. Increased rates were found only in Detroit, Minneapolis, Philadelphia and Seattle.

With reference to decreases and increases the bureau's statement reads:

"A study indicates for most of the cities lower delinquency rates at the end of the period than at the beginning, with a tendency toward higher rates during the war years, 1918 and 1919. Slight fluctuations from year to year are to be expected and are not especially significant.

"For example, in Chicago the rate has fluctuated around a lower level since 1920 than before. The decrease in New York has been quite marked.

"Contrary to opinions which have been expressed, there seems to have been no marked decrease in the age of commitment to prisons, reformatories, jail and workhouses. On the contrary, only 9.4 per cent. of the commitments in 1923 were of persons between the ages of 18 and 20 years, as compared with 9.8 per cent. in 1904 and with percentages of 11.9 and 12.1 based on persons present in prisons in 1880 and 1890, respectively."

April 5, 1926

CHILD CRIME REDUCED BY CLINIC, SAYS JUDGE

Psychiatry Has Proved Value, Smythe Tells Westchester Women at Meeting.

The importance of psychiatry in checking juvenile delinquency was emphasized yesterday by Judge George W. Smythe of the Children's Court of Westchester County, in an address at the Winter meeting of the Westchester County Federation of Women's Clubs, held in the Wanamaker Auditorium.

Judge Smythe, who established a Child Guidance Clinic in his jurisdiction last year, said that the results have indicated the need of this adjunct to the court. "Our experience convinces us of the place of psychiatry in checking delinquency and through it we expect to reduce the number of these children who are being brought to court," he declared.

The conference was opened by Mrs. Gridley Adams of New Rochelle, president of the organization. Brief addresses were made by Mme. Alma Gluck Zimbalist, on behalf of the Musicians' Emergency Aid, and by Mrs. William Dick Sporborg, Mrs. Theodore Stolz and Mrs. Jane Deeter Rippin. Mrs. D. Theodore Kelly presided at the afternoon session.

February 27, 1932

THE CHILD AS WORKER

TOILING FOR THEIR BREAD

CHILDREN WHO ARE EMPLOYED IN WORKSHOP AND IN FACTORY.

THE LAWS REGULATING CHILD LABOR IN THIS AND OTHER STATES—EFFORTS OF THE BOARD OF EDUCATION TO SECURE ATTENDANCE AT SCHOOL.

Of the great quantity of varied products contributed to the world's wealth by the thousands of toilers daily at work in shop and factory in this City, few who have not investigated the subject could form an idea of the large share contributed to the general result by children of tender years. To the children of the wealthy, or of those in moderately comfortable circumstances, the years of childhood at least are free from care and toil. The conning of their lessons is the severest task they know, and this is relieved by hours of healthful play. Money is to them a word whose real meaning is as yet unlearned. When the time comes for them to enter the battle of life both mind and muscle have had the opportunity to become fitted for the burden that is to rest upon them, and into their days of earnest labor they carry the memory of a happy, sunny childhood to brighten the shadows that manhood or womanhood may bring. To the children of the poor, on the contrary, the stern reality of a never-ceasing struggle for existence becomes familiar with the dawn of reason. Their passage from the cradle to the work-bench is a short one, and at a time when the children of the wealthy are still the occupants of tenderly guarded nurseries they have taken their places in the ranks of the great army of labor.

What the number of little laborers of both sexes between the ages of 5 and 16 years in this City may be it is difficult to ascertain with any degree of exactitude. Mr. Charles L. Brace, of the Children's Aid Society, who has given to this subject much attention, some time since estimated the number of children thus employed at 100,000. To enumerate the employments in which they are engaged would be a difficult task. In tobacco factories they prepare the leaf for the cigar makers, pack chewing tobacco in its paper and tin-foil wrappers, and make cigarettes. They are employed in making envelopes, as gold-leaf workers, as burnishers of gold and silver and china, in paper collar factories, as makers of paper boxes of all kinds, in twine-making, in the manufacture of artificial flowers, of torpedoes, of toys, and of a hundred other articles to be found in the great bazaars of commerce. The skill displayed by many even of the youngest of them is astonishing to the uninitiated observer. Following the system of the division of labor, they thoroughly learn their own task, in almost every case a simple one, and then by unremitting practice acquire a degree of dexterity that in many instances approaches the marvelous. In the packing of chewing tobacco it is not unusual for a girl of 10 to wrap in a day of 10 hours 22 gross in paper wrappers and 10 gross in the foil. In the manufacture of artificial flowers and in dozens of other employments in which children are engaged, the little hands display the same skill. In fact many of them perform as much work and perform it as well as adults could. The work in which children are engaged in this City is in many cases injurious to their health. In no cases, of course, can it be healthy for children of very tender years to pursue one unvarying, unremitting round of labor for a long number of hours, but in addition to this there are additional causes of injury to their health to be found in the lack of proper ventilation in many of the places in which they work, and also in the nature of the work they perform. Gold-leaf workers, for instance, are compelled, from the nature of the material in which they work, to keep the windows of their shops closed even on the warmest days. It has been claimed by physicians that work on several kinds of artificial flowers is not only injurious but positively dangerous, from the fact that arsenical poisons are used in the dyes employed in coloring the flowers. Certain branches of paper-making in which children are employed are also said to be dangerous for the same reason. In tobacco factories, in which it is said that fully 5,000 children under 15 years of age are employed, many of the boys work under-ground in a damp atmosphere preparing, brining, and sweetening the weed preparatory to "stemming." In the twine factories "hackling machines" are attended by boys from 10 to 15 years of age. The attention of the boys running these machines must be closely riveted on them or there is great danger of the loss of a finger or a hand. The "twisting-machines," which are attended by girls of a similar age, are equally dangerous. Another frightful source of danger to the fingers of the youthful toilers is the stamp-dies used in manufacturing tin toys, and which are also very generally operated by children. Probably one of the most dangerous employments in which children are engaged, however, is that of manufacturing torpedoes, an employment in which there is constant danger of an explosion by which life or eyesight may be lost.

The question of childrens' labor is a subject to which philanthropists have given much attention. The abuses of the system in England were at one time much more flagrant than they have ever been in this country, but, on the other hand, much more has been done there to remedy them than has been accomplished in this State, at least. The English Factory bills, which are quite numerous, were passed after much opposition on the part of both parents and employers. By these bills the age at which children may be employed, and the limit of hours they may be permitted or compelled to work, are strictly regulated. By them, also, children are assured of a certain amount of education, and are provided with safeguards for the protection of health, limb, and life.

Connecticut was the first State in the Union to pass a law limiting the age at which children might be employed and the number of hours they should work. This law was passed in 1842. In 1869 a more stringent law was adopted, in which regulations as to the agricultural as well as the manufacturing labor of children were established, and in which the responsibility of ascertaining whether the children are too young or whether they have attended school for the specified time is placed on the employer under a penalty of $100. In the great manufacturing State of Massachusetts, where children's labor was largely employed, the necessity of providing legal safeguards was strongly felt. In 1866 the Legislature passed an act "restraining the employing of children of tender years in manufacturing establishments." This was subsequently repealed, and a more thorough and stringent law passed in 1867. By this act no child under 10 years of age could be employed in any manufacturing establishment in the State, nor any child between the ages of 10 and 15 who had not attended a day school for at least three months of the year preceding, or a half-time school for six months. The "10-hour provision" is also in force, which forbids the employment of children under 15 years of age for more than 10 hours a day, or 60 hours a week. By a violation of this law both parent and employer incur a penalty of $50. Some employers have established half-time schools for their employes, and work the children in double gangs, one gang relieving the other. Others have established night schools. In Rhode Island the law adopted is very similar to that of Massachusetts, excepting that no child under 12 years old can be employed, and that the time children over that age are permitted to work in the day is 11 hours. Similar laws have been adopted in several other States in the Union.

In this State, notwithstanding the large number of children employed in its numerous manufacturing establishments, no provision for their benefit has ever been made by the Legislature excepting that found in the Compulsory Education law. This law contains the following provisions:

SEC. 2. No child under the age of 14 years shall be employed by any person to labor in any business whatever during the school hours of any school day of the school term of the public school in the school district of the city where such child is, unless such child shall have attended some public or private day school where instruction was given by a teacher qualified to instruct in spelling, reading, writing, geography, English grammar, and arithmetic, or shall have been regularly instructed at home in said branches, by some person qualified to instruct in the same, at least 14 weeks of the 52 weeks next preceding any and every year in which such child shall be employed, and shall at the time of such employment deliver to the employer a certificate in writing, signed by the teacher or a school Trustee of the district or of a school, and countersigned by such officer as the Board of Education or Public Instruction, by whatever name it may be known in any city, incorporated village or town, shall designate, certifying to such attendance or instruction; and any person who shall employ any child contrary to the provisions of this section shall for each offense forfeit and pay a penalty of $50 to the Treasurer or chief fiscal officer of the city or Supervisor of the town in which such offense shall occur; the said sum or penalty, when so paid, to be added to the public school money of the school district in which the offense occurred.

SEC. 3. It shall be the duty of the Trustee or Trustees of every school district, or public school, or union school, or of officers appointed for that purpose by the Board of Education or Public Instruction, by whatever name it may be known, in every town or city, in the months of September and February of each year, and at such other times as may be deemed necessary, to examine into the situation of the children employed in all manufacturing and other establishments in such school districts where children are employed, and in case any town or city is not divided into school districts it shall, for the purposes of the examination provided for in this section, be divided by the school authorities thereof into districts, and the said Trustees or other officers as aforesaid, notified of their respective districts on or before the 1st day of January of each year, and the said Trustee or Trustees, or other officers as aforesaid, shall ascertain whether all of the provisions of this act are duly observed, and report all violations thereof to the Treasurer or chief fiscal officer of said city or Supervisor of said town. On such examination the proprietor, Superintendent, or manager of said establishment shall, on demand, exhibit to such examining Trustee or other officers as aforesaid, a correct list of all children between the ages of 8 and 14 years employed in said establishment, with the said certificates of attendance on school or of instruction.

As will be seen, this law does not forbid the employment or children at any age, provided they have attended school, nor does it fix any limit to the number of hours the child may be so employed. The duty of enforcing the provisions requiring attendance at school devolves on the agents of truancy employed by the Board of Education. According to the records of the board there have been issued during the present year 668 certificates to children between the ages of 8 and 14 years who are employed in stores and manufacturing establishments in this City. If the law were strictly enforced this number of certificates should, of course, represent the number of children under 14 years of age thus employed, but no one acquainted with the facts pretends that this number even approximates the actual total number. The subject of the employment of children was considered at the last annual meeting of the State Medical Board, and a committee consisting of Drs. Jacobi and Sturgis, of this City, and Dr. Lansing, of Albany, was appointed to take suitable action. In connection with the New-York Society for the Prevention of Cruelty to Children there was prepared and offered at the last session of the Legislature a bill containing the following provisions:

SECTION 1. No child actually or apparently under the age of 14 years shall be employed by any manufacturing corporation within this State; and no child shall be employed in any factory-work, unless it shall have been previously examined by two physicians duly licensed and admitted to practice residing within the county wherein such child is to be employed, and designated in writing for that purpose by a Justice or the Supreme Court, and who shall certify that such child is not suffering from any chlorotic, anaemic, scrofulous, scorbutic, bronchitic, or physical condition, and is not in anywise so disabled or crippled as to render its employment in such factory work dangerous to its life or injurious to its health or limb. No child at any time so suffering or so disabled or crippled shall be employed in factory work, and the certificate of such physicians shall be in writing, duly verified before a notary public, and shall be delivered to the person in charge of such factory, who shall exhibit the same to any person requesting to examine it.

SEC. 2. No child over the age of 14 years shall be employed by any manufacturing corporation in this State for a longer period than 10 hours a day, and no child shall be employed by any person in any mining, glass-work, rag-sorting, mercury, lead, arsenic, iron, or brick works, or in refining petroleum or other hydro carburetted oils, or in any match factory, or in the preparation or application of any aniline or other poisonous dyes, or in the manufacture of any explosive substances.

SEC. 3. No child shall be used or employed in the manufacture of cigars or cigarettes, or in the preparation of tobacco in any room or apartments which in any city are used for the purpose of living, sleeping, or for household work therein; nor in any trade, business, or occupation involving the use of any machinery dangerous to life or limb.

SEC. 4. Any person violating any provision of this act shall be guilty of a misdemeanor.

This bill passed the Senate, and it was supposed that it had also passed the Assembly, but when the Legislature adjourned the friends of the bill could learn nothing of its fate, and no information on the subject has yet been obtained. It is supposed that it was mysteriously "lost" during the confusion which marked the closing hours of the model Democratic Legislature. In the absence of any law on the subject, the Society for the Prevention of Cruelty to Children is unable to take any effective steps for the protection of the working children unless specific acts of cruelty are charged. Even in cases where it was proved that children were employed in places where machinery dangerous to them was used it has been held that the children were there of their own volition, and that by the exercise of ordinary prudence they could avoid accidents. So also, in cases where physicians have declared certain employments injurious to health, employers have always succeeded in finding other physicians to contradict their statements. The officials of the society say that if any law for the protection of children were in existence in this State they would see that its provisions were enforced, but that in the absence of such law they are practically powerless. All who have given thought to the subject and outspoken in their declaration that it is of the utmost importance that the children should receive some protection from the present existing evils of the system under which they are compelled to toil.

December 26, 1882

ESTIMATE OF A CHILD'S VALUE.

How an Indiana Jury Figured Out Damages for the Parent.

ELWOOD, Ind., Jan. 22.—Some time last Autumn the little son of Paul Addison of this city fell into a sewer and was drowned. Mr. Addison brought suit against the city for $5,000 damages at this term of court. The suit was tried last week, and the jury gave a judgment in favor of Mr. Addison for $599.95, after being out for fifty-three hours.

This is said to be the first time in the history of the county that a jury was out so long, and brought in a verdict. The most interesting feature of the jury's finding was the method of deciding upon and determining the value of the child to the parent, had the child lived. In doing this it went into detail, and decided the wages a child could likely earn at different periods of its life, and the probable cost of keeping it.

The jury figured that from eight to ten years old the child would be able to make 45 cents a week. During that period it would cost 85 cents a week to keep it. From ten to twelve it would make 75 cents a week, and it would cost $1.25 to keep it. From twelve to fourteen it could make $4 a week, and the living cost would be $2. From fifteen to eighteen it could make $5 a week, and the living cost would be $2.75. From eighteen to twenty-one it could make $6 a week, and the living cost would be $4. By the jury's calculation, the most valuable time of the child's life to the parent would be from fifteen to eighteen. The parent is not supposed in law to benefit from the child's earnings after it is twenty-one, and the figures began at eight years, as the child was drowned at that age.

January 23, 1899

INFANT LABOR IN SOUTHERN MILLS.

An appeal "To the people and press of New England" relative to the employment of children in the cotton mills of the South controlled by Northern capital has been printed in the Boston and other New England papers, and appears to have been well received. The most significant paragraph of this appeal is that which we quote below:

While the proportion of the children under twelve in our Northern and Southern mills is approximately the same, yet in the mills representing Northern investments the number of such children employed is twice as great as the number found in the mills controlled by Southern capital.

This statement would be difficult of credence on any less respectable authority than that of its signers, the Rev. EDGAR GARDNER MURPHY of Montgomery, ex-Gov. THOMAS G. JONES of Alabama, J. H. PHILIPS, State Superintendent of Schools, and two members of the Alabama Legislature, Messrs. JOHN CRAFT of Mobile and A. J. REILLY of Ensley. It is undoubtedly true, but the wonder is that foreign influence should be potent in obstructing the course of legislation in Southern States when such legislation appears to be desired by the local manufacturing interest, or at least not opposed by it.

Our suggestion is that this is a matter which every Southern State should decide for itself, on broad grounds of public policy, independent of any dictation from cotton mill owners. The difficulty of discussing it grows out of the fact that the practice as to the employment of children of tender age in mills varies in different localities and in different mills. In some of the plants the school facilities are admirable, and it is insisted by the management that no children of parents employed shall be deprived of the elementary education which such schools are able to provide. In other plants we have no doubt that the absence of any legal restraint upon the employment of children is abused, but where this is done it is probable the blame rests chiefly with the parents and in very much less degree with the mill managers. The number of children which can be profitably employed in a cotton mill is very much smaller than is commonly supposed; but throughout the cotton manufacturing district the pressure upon the mill managers to employ more children than they need, to keep them "out of mischief" while their parents are at work, is very strong. In many cases it is necessary to let the children play around the mills that the mothers may earn support, and the visitor to Southern mills is often misled by what he sees into believing that the system is generally much worse than it is.

Enforced idleness will do the children of the mountaineers of the Piedmont district very little good if it does not carry with it the opportunity for and the obligation of primary education. The desire for knowledge and the power of assimilating it do not come naturally to the children of an illiterate ancestry, and to some extent it must be enforced under strict truancy laws. The subject is one which the public interest demands shall be dealt with on broad lines, and from the intelligent activity of such representative Southern citizens as those whose names are identified with the movement for the protection of children in Alabama, we have no doubt satisfactory laws will be passed within another year or two which will effectually reform the evils of a system open to abuse by those who find profit in abusing it.

November 11, 1901

EVILS OF CHILD LABOR.

Longer Attendance of Children at School and Prohibition from Dangerous Occupations Suggested.

In the sixteenth annual report on factory inspection, which was issued yesterday by Commissioner McMackin of the State Department of Labor, are several recommendations for the amendment of the laws regulating child labor. The Commissioner suggests that children between twelve and fourteen years of age be required to attend school through the entire school year instead of eighty days every year, as provided for at present. He recommends also that a certificate of birth, instead of the parents' affidavit of age, be required before a child under the age of sixteen years can obtain employment in factories, and that children under that age be prohibited from employment in dangerous occupations, to be designated by the Governor.

The report says:

Some children when asked their age will say, "Do you mean my school age or my real age?" They have been deliberately taught by their parents to report themselves to the school teacher older than they really are, in order that later they may begin employment before they reach their fourteenth year. The greatest trouble thus comes from the misrepresentation of a child's age by his parents. The connivance of parents at this mode of violating the law was fully proved by the Reinhard investigation of female labor in 1895. As remarked by that committee, "a parent who is willing to permit his child to work in a factory at an age under fourteen is ordinarily just as willing to perjure himself as to the age of the child. The only effective remedy for this sort of thing is the requirement of a certificate of birth in place of the parent's affidavit of age.

Eighty per cent. of the children in New York State, outside of New York City, to whom certificates were issued during the ten months covered by the report, were born in New York State, and it may be assumed that most of these were duly registered by the proper local officers. Hence the age of most of the children applying for employment certificates could be accurately determined by applying to the records of the State Department of Health. Provision could be made for the recording of the birth of children born outside the State. The only objection to such an amendment to the law would be the increased expense to the Department of Health on account of additional clerical work. But the great value of such a system should more than counterbalance the small appropriation needed for two or three additional clerks.

The evils of child labor are much greater outside than inside our factories, namely, children working at home, in stores, at household service, and in offices, messenger service, &c. The failure of the New York City Government to enforce the provisions of the mercantile law led Gov. Roosevelt in 1899 to recommend that its enforcement be transferred to the State Factory Inspector, but the Legislature did not act upon the recommendation.

In greater need of regulation, however, is the employment of children in tenement work, and also as delivery and messenger boys in business outside the scope of the factory and mercantile laws. The most practicable method of regulation is doubtless to be found in strict enforcement of the compulsory school law, which requires all children between eight and twelve years of age to attend school during the full period of the session, and makes their employment within that term unlawful.

February 13, 1903

Child Labor as a Factor In The Increase of Pauperism

Children Unfitted for Larger Tasks When Manhood and Womanhood is Reached, and in Many Cases Parents Willingly Become Dependent Upon Their Offspring.

BY MISS JANE ADDAMS OF HULL HOUSE, CHICAGO.

EACH age has of course its own temptations, and above all its own peculiar industrial temptations. When we ask why it is that child labor has been given to us to discuss and to rectify rather than to the people who lived before us, we need only remember that for the first time in industrial history the labor of the little child has in many industries become as valuable as that of a man or woman. The old-fashioned weaver was obliged to possess skill and enough strength to pull his beam back and forth. With the invention of machinery the need of skill has been eliminated from many processes, and with the application of steam and electricity strength has also been largely eliminated, so that a little child may mend the thread in a textile mill almost as well and, in some respects, better than a strong and clumsy adult. This is true of many other industries, until it has come about that we are tempted as never before to use the labor of little children and that the temptation to exploit premature labor is peculiar to this industrial epoch.

What, then, are we doing about it? How deeply are we concerned that this labor shall not result to the detriment of the child, and what excuses are we making to ourselves for thus prematurely using up the strength of a child? Of course, it is always difficult to see the wrong in a familiar thing, and it is a test of moral insight to be able to see that an affair of familiar intercourse and daily living may also be wrong. I have taken a Chicago street car on a Winter's night in December at 10 o'clock when dozens of little girls who have worked in the department stores all day are also boarding the cars. I know, as many others do, that these children will not get into their beds much before midnight, and that they will have to be up again early in the morning to go to their daily work. And yet I take my car almost placidly—I am happy to say not quite placidly—because I have seen it many times. Almost every day at 6 o'clock I see certain factories pouring out a stream of men and women and boys and girls. The boys and girls have a peculiar hue, a color so distinctive that any one meeting them on the street even on Sunday in their best clothes and mixed up with other children who go to school and play out of doors can distinguish almost in an instant the children working in factories. There is also on their faces a something indescribable, a premature anxiety and sense of responsibility which we should declare pathetic if we were not used to it.

SENTIMENTAL EXCUSE.

How far are we responsible when we allow custom to blind our eyes to the things that are wrong, and what excuses do we make for ourselves? The sentimental excuse is the one we use most frequently in the North. It is said that the labor of these little children is needed for the support of widowed mothers. Some of us are sure that the widowed mother argument has been seriously overworked. In every community there can only be a certain number of widowed mothers unless some plague has carried off the men in the prime of life. Out of that number of widows only another certain number will be absolutely impecunious, for if the community is prosperous some of the workingmen by benefit societies and insurances will have made some little provision for their families. Out of that certain number of impecunious widows only a few will have children between the ages of ten and fourteen, in which short space of time the temptation to the premature use of children's labor always lies.

In a certain manufacturing town it was discovered that 3,600 children on the school census roll were not to be found in the schools. We have a much larger number than that in Chicago; according to our school census we lose 11,000 between the first and second grades. In this particular manufacturing town it was suggested that the children be looked up and the number of those who were supporting widowed mothers be verified. Out of the 3,600 children it was found that 1,100 were legitimately out of the public schools, i. e., that they had moved out of the district, that they were ill, that they were attending private institutions, or that they were legally at work. That left 2,500 to be accounted for, and out of those it was found that exactly 66 were the children of widows. Out of the 66 only 23 were in any real sense contributing to the support of their mothers. The other mothers had older children or other means of support, so that only 23 were in any way absolutely dependent on the wages of those children, which wages could be only supplementary at best. It was certainly a great deal better for the community, for the widows and the children, that grown-up, vigorous people should take care of these 23 widows for a few years, until the children were old enough to go out to work and bring in a decent wage with which to support the family, and that the children should be saved from the breakdown which premature labor so often implies.

When children are thus broken down it means that we do not stand up to the obligations which belong to our own time, but insist upon using up the energy which belongs to the future.

CAUSES OF PAUPERISM.

What connection do we find between child labor and pauperism? One of the first causes of pauperism is non-employment. Those who are first to lose their places in an industrial crisis are those who have never had sufficient training and who curiously lack strength and vigor. In our municipal lodging house in Chicago it is surprising to find how many tramps are tired to death with monotonous labor and begin to tramp in order to get away from it. This inordinate desire to get away from work seems to be connected with the fact that the men have started to work very early, before they had the physique to stand up to it, or the mental vigor with which to overcome its difficulties, or the moral stamina which makes a man stick to his work whether he likes it or not. But we cannot demand any of these things from a growing boy. A boy grows restless, his determination breaks down, and he runs away. At least this seems to be true of many of the men who come to the lodging house.

Another cause of pauperism is illness. A potent cause of disease is due to the breaking down of the organs which were subjected to abnormal uses before they were ready to bear it. I recall a tailor for whom the residents of Hull House tried to get medical assistance. He died at the age of thirty-three, and his death certificate bore the record of "premature senility" due to the fact that he had run a sewing machine since he was six years old. It is no figment of the imagination to say that the human system breaks down when it is put to monotonous work before it is ready to stand up to that work, and that general debility and many diseases may be traced to premature labor. No horse trainer would permit his colts to be so broken down.

Then we have the pauperizing effect of child labor on the parents. Many of our European immigrants resent the monotonous petty work of the factory, but their children become adapted to it, and you get the curious result of the parent of the household being more or less dependent upon the earnings of the child. This tends to break down the normal relation between parents and children.

The pauperization of society itself is another serious charge.

When an industry depends upon the labor of boys and girls it takes them at a time when they ought to be at school. The wages paid to them are wages of mere subsistence. In almost all factories the work at which the children are employed leads to no trade. By the time they are old enough to receive adult wages they are often sick of the whole business. Such an industry is parasitic on the future of the community. We recall that when the recruiting officers went into the factory regions of the North of England they found the bulk of the people below the standard in stature required in the English army. They were found specially dwarfed in that part of the country where the third generation recorded in their frames the effects of child labor.

The gravest charge I have to bring against child labor is that it pauperizes the consumers. If I wear a garment which has been made in a sweat shop or a garment for which the maker has not been paid a living wage—a wage so small that her earnings had to be supplemented by the earnings of her husband and children—then I am in debt to the woman who made my cloak. I am a pauper, and I permit myself to accept charity from the poorest people of the community. All that can be said against the parasitic character of sweating industries can be said against the parasitic character of child labor, with this difference that the latter robs the assets of the community, it uses up those resources which should have kept industry going on for many years.

We may trace a connection between child labor and pauperism, not only for the child and his own family, bringing on premature old age and laying aside able-bodied men and women in the noontide of their years, but also the grievous charge is true that it pauperizes the community itself. I should also add that it debauches our moral sentiment, it confuses our sense of values, so that we learn to think that a bale of cheap cotton is more to be prized than a child properly nourished, educated, and prepared to take his place in life. Let us stand up to the obligations of our own age. Let us watch that we do not discount the future and cripple the next generation because we were too indolent. I was going to say because we were too dull, to see all that it involves, when we use the labor of little children.

October 4, 1903

CHILD LABOR COMMITTEE.

Complete Membership Announced—Permanent Office to be Opened Soon.

The National Child Labor Committee, recently formed with a membership of prominent men from all parts of the country, has been organized with Former Commissioner of Public Charities Homer Folks as Chairman and Edward T. Devine, General Secretary of the Charity Organization Society, as Secretary. Funds are being raised, and it is understood that a permanent office will be opened soon and the committee's campaign begun. Both Mr. Folks and Mr. Devine, it is understood, are holding office temporarily, while the organization of the committee is being completed.

The Executive Committee in general charge is composed of the Chairman and Secretary and the following: Dr. Felix Adler, John S. Huyler, V. Everit Macy, Isaac N. Seligman, Paul M. Warburg, John W. Wood, Robert W. De Forest, Florence Kelley, William H. Baldwin, Jr., and Edgar Gardner Murphy. The Finance Committee is composed of Isaac N. Seligman, V. Everit Macy, William H. Baldwin, Jr., Paul N. Warburg, and John S. Huyler.

The committee, according to one of its members, will organize local committees in fields where they are needed, and will not so much work for Federal legislation, as has been suggested; as to educate public opinion in the matter of child labor and create a demand for the best industrial conditions for all minors.

The membership of the committee, now completed, is announced as follows: Dr. Felix Adler, New York; William H. Baldwin, Jr., New York; Edgar Gardner Murphy, Montgomery, Ala.; Homer Folks, New York; William E. Harmon, New York; Jane Addams, Hull House, Chicago; Florence Kelley, New York; Mrs. Emmons Blaine, Chicago; Lillian D. Wald, New York; Stanley McCormick, Chicago; Hugh F. Fox of New Jersey; Cardinal Gibbons, Baltimore; Hoke Smith, Atlanta, Ga.; V. Everit Macy, New York; John W. Wood, New York; Robert W. De Forest, Bishop David H. Greer, New York; Edward T. Devine, New York; John Graham Brooks, Cambridge, Mass.; Isaac N. Seligman, New York; Paul M. Warburg of Kuhn, Loeb & Co., New York; Dr. C. B. Wilmer, Atlanta, Ga.; Dr. J. H. Kirkland, Chancellor of Vanderbilt University; Talcott Williams, Philadelphia; Judge N. B. Feagin, Birmingham, Ala.; Senator B. R. Tillman, South Carolina; John S. Huyler, New York; Adolph S. Ochs, New York; Judge Ben B. Lindsey, Denver, Col.; A. J. Cassatt, Robert Hunter, Noroton, Conn.; Grover Cleveland, Princeton, N. J.

June 4, 1904

FIGHT ON CHILD LABOR.

Dr. Silverman Fires the First Gun—Bishop Greer Heads Campaign.

The Rev. Dr. Joseph Silverman, rabbi of the Temple Emanu-El, preached yesterday to his congregation on " The Abolition of Child Slavery." The sermon was one of many to be delivered from pulpits of all creeds in an agitation to obtain a special day of the year on which National protest shall be made from the pulpits of the country against child labor.

A committee of ministers, headed by Bishop Coadjutor David H. Greer, is at work on a plan for bringing before the executive bodies of the various religious denominations the proposition for a National Children's Day in church and synagogue.

" The antithesis of the Froebel kindergarten," said Dr. Silverman yesterday, " where the child is carefully developed physically and mentally, is the shop, the factory, and the coal mine, where the beautiful and sacred image of God is distorted by the satanic greed of man.

" The army of child laborers is constantly increasing, and it is now estimated authoritatively that it has reached the incredible figure of 2,000,000. Nearly every State in the Union is more or less culpable for permitting child labor, and in not enforcing laws already made to prevent it."

Dr. Silverman quoted from reports of those who had made personal investigations of child labor conditions in mines and factories, saying that these reports should make clear the great crime that is being committed against the Nation as well as against the children themselves.

" We might rightly say," he declared, " that while we have abolished adult slavery, we have permitted child slavery to fasten itself upon our land and cast a stigma on our claims to civilization."

Of the evil results of a citizenship infested with human beings born of parents who have been stunted by labor in childhood, Dr. Silverman said: " Of such poor stuff will thousands upon thousands of our citizens be constituted. They will grow into men and women without education, minus morals, spirituality, religion, or ideals, and yet they will have it in their power to aid in shaping the political, industrial, and social destiny of our country."

Of the obstacles in the way of enforcing the laws now existing in a number of the States for the protection of children, Dr. Silverman said that the selfishness of parents was one and the greed of manufacturers another.

February 5, 1906

President Signs Child Labor Bill.

WASHINGTON, April 9.—The act of Congress creating a Bureau of Child Labor in the Department of Commerce and Labor was signed to-day by President Taft. The pen used by the President was given to Dr. A. J. McKelway, Secretary for the Southern States of the Child Labor Committee.

April 10, 1912

EVILS OF CHILD LABOR WORSE IN WARTIME

By BABETTE DEUTSCH.

ON Forty-eighth Street, just east of Fifth Avenue, is a wide show-window made conspicuous with flaring signs and charts, and especially because of a whirling ball of metal in the very centre. This ball is just one of the interesting features of an exhibition that is of importance to every citizen of New York.

The exhibition was prepared under the auspices of the National Child Labor Committee. Their good work in trying to uphold labor standards during the war has been commended by the President, a copy of whose letter may be seen there. Not the literature, however, but the ball in the window is what first attracts the attention of passers-by. To this revolving sphere little figures are attached, which appear to be moving past the spectator. They represent the working children of the United States, and if the onlooker were to watch them all go by, at the rate at which they are moving, he would have to stand before that window for 139 days and 139 nights.

The interested beholder, however, is more apt to go in. There he finds a

15

museum complete in its kind. The walls are covered with pictures and charts, with guides to point out the significant features. The photographs show boys and girls of every kind and condition, at play as well as at work, and at all kinds of work, in the mines and the mills, in the shops and the factories, in the streets and in the tenement homes. One presents a group of sturdy, smiling youngsters, placarded: "Good material at first," a factory building, labeled "the process," and beside it thin, bent little bodies and pale, indifferent faces, "the product." The whole is a graphic presentation of "Making Human Junk."

Then there is a picture of a small boy poling logs for a sawmill, and beside it photographs of youngsters whose work is taken for granted by New Yorkers: newsies and messenger boys, whom one is accustomed to see about the streets of the city. These pictures are placed side by side to indicate that the street trades expose children to great moral dangers.

An official inquiry was made recently under the direction of the United States Commission of Labor with regard to the relation between juvenile delinquency and employment. It was found that 62 per cent. of more than 4,000 delinquents studied were engaged in work. The report shows, moreover, that 54 per cent. of these delinquent child laborers were engaged in street occupations: selling newspapers, running errands, blacking boots, and that "it seems rather difficult to escape the conclusion that being at work had something to do with their going wrong." One finds here the boy who "hain't grown none since he was 6," and the girl whose monotony of dreary labor made her "wish she was a machine, too." Three times as many industrial accidents occur to children as to adults.

There are other photographs which show that it is not in the factory or on the street alone that the child worker suffers. Thousands of boys and girls are working in stuffy tenement rooms under insanitary, unhealthful conditions. The Irish lace and artificial flowers on the side tables are the product of such child labor.

But the room is not entirely a picture gallery. There is a great mass of documentary evidence for the interested student as to the conditions and evils of child labor and the means of protecting children from both greedy parents and exploiting employers. Enormous charts show that more education pays, and that safeguarding the children of today is of vital importance for the society of tomorrow. The farsighted employer has long realized that the product made by the tired youngster is not equal to that of the strong man. The farsighted citizen knows that the child worker makes the exhausted adult. Yet there is a shock in these vivid pictures that brings the lesson home with new emphasis. These cold, clear diagrams make it self-evident that the greatest cost of child labor is not to the individual worker or to the individual employer, but to society. It is society that foots the bill. And that bill is paid in a multitude of wrecked human beings, in institutions filled with dependents whose working capacity was drained in childhood, and in prisons crowded with criminals who were taught their trade on the city streets of their youth. Society pays in its mass of uneducated boys and girls who are the ignorant adult citizens of the coming generation.

The law of the United States protects those children who are working on articles that are shipped in interstate commerce. But there are almost 2,000,000 children who are working in local industries and are not affected by the Federal law. Here in New York State the protection that has been afforded to our children in the past is in imminent danger of removal. Before the interested spectator leaves the Child Labor Exhibit, before, indeed, he has had an opportunity to examine all the well-collated and graphic material which is open to his inspection on Forty-eighth Street, he is bound to be made to realize the very personal appeal of this display. For it presents to the voters of the State, men and women, a clear picture of the dangers and evils of child labor.

The high cost of child labor never needs to be reckoned with so urgently as in time of war. The workers are going into the trenches. It seems logical that their places should be filled by the women and children. It seems essential that industry, and especially war industry, should be speeded up. It follows that those who go into the industrial field must be safeguarded even as those who enter the war zone. For in the intensity with which war industries are to be pursued it is easy to forget the necessity for maintaining good conditions in the busy factory.

Indeed, there are bills pending at Albany which aim at letting down all the protective restrictions on the labor of women and children who are engaged in the manufacture of munitions or other things pertaining to war. The Elon R. Brown bill, which was vetoed last year by Governor Whitman, removes all protection now surrounding women and children who are working for war purposes. It makes possible absolute disregard of health and safety in munition factories. It means that the working mothers and the boys and girls of New York will be permitted to toil for unlimited hours at unregulated work under unhealthful conditions.

Just what all absence of safeguards implies is graphically illustrated in charts and photographs to be seen at the Forty-eighth Street exhibit. The eager patriot who wants to speed up war industry can see there as plainly as actual pictures and hard facts can show that he is working against his own warmest interest if the bill is passed. For it means not merely exploitation of the women and children, but a menace to the health of the community, and wastage all around.

There are two further bills pending at Albany which are of supreme interest to the New York voter. These would wipe out all safeguards for children under 16 who are working in stores and in theatres and bowling alleys, or in the telegraph service and street trades during the Summer months. This means that boys and girls in the years when they need exercise in the open, plenty of food "to grow on," and healthy occupations more than at any other period, will be shut in humid rooms, in basement alleys, and stuffy theatres, or running about the burning city pavements for endless hours, even throughout the night, and for seven days a week. That children cannot suffer this kind of thing and grow up into strong, capable men and women is patent. Statistics, in this case, merely back up common sense by proving the enervating effect of long hours and unregulated work on boys and girls who need all their strength to mature properly.

The pending legislation threatens to run up a bill for New York State in accidents to children, in industrial waste, and in the depleted health and power of the coming generation, which the voter would have to pay or hand on to his own children for payment. He has a chance to foresee the future on East Forty-eighth Street. And the people who have built up this interesting and important exhibit claim that he cannot merely foresee the future, but he can vitally affect it at once. But whether or not he believes that the American Nation, or even the State of New York alone, can afford to pay the price of child labor now, it will be worth his while to pass the Forty-eighth Street show-window. He will perforce stop, and then go in. The practical business man and the newly enfranchised woman must find their common ground of interest and achievement.

March 10, 1918

CHILD LABOR LAW UPSET BY COURT

Action of Congress Declared Unconstitutional by 5 to 4 on Final Test.

HELD TO EXCEED POWERS

Holmes Reads Dissenting Opinion—Move for New Law or Constitutional Amendment.

Special to The New York Times.

WASHINGTON, June 3.—On the ground that Congress, in passing the child labor law, unwarrantably invaded the rights of the States to control their own commerce, the Supreme Court today declared the law unconstitutional.

The decision was concurred in by five of the nine members of the court, Chief Justice White, and Justices Day, Van Devanter, Pitney, and McReynolds. Justice Holmes read a dissenting opinion, concurred in by Justices Brandeis, Clarke, and McKenna.

The court's action caused the utmost surprise. It was received with much regret by those who worked for nearly fifteen years in Congress for the passage of the law, which prohibited the shipment in interstate commerce of the products of child labor.

"The controlling question for decision is," said Justice Day, who handed down the prevailing opinion, "Is it within the authority of Congress in regulating commerce among the States to prohibit the transportation in interstate commerce of manufactured goods, the product of a factory in which, within thirty days prior to their removal therefrom, children under the age of 14 have been employed or permitted to work, or children between the ages of 14 and 16 have been employed or permitted to work more than eight hours in any day, or more than six days in any week, or after the hour of 7 o'clock P. M. or before the hour of 6 o'clock A. M.?"

Called Purely Local Question.

This question the majority opinion answered as follows:

"To sustain this statute would not be in our judgment a recognition of the lawful exertion of Congressional authority over interstate commerce, but would sanction an invasion by the Federal power for the control of a matter purely local in its character, and over which no authority has been delegated to Congress in conferring the power to regulate commerce among the States."

Justice Day said:

"All will admit that there should be limitations upon the right to employ children in mines and factories. That such employment is generally deemed to require regulation is shown by the fact that every State in the Union has a law limiting the right thus to employ children.

"We have neither authority nor disposition to question the motives of Congress in enacting this legislation. The purposes intended must be attained consistently with constitutional limitations, and not by an invasion of the powers of the States. This court has no more important function than that which devolves upon it the obligation to preserve inviolate the constitutional limitations upon the exercise of authority, Federal and State, to the end that each may continue to discharge, harmoniously with the other, the duties intrusted to it by the Constitution.

Boundaries of Trade Freedom.

"In our view, the necessary effect of this act is, by means of a prohibition against the movement in interstate commerce of ordinary commercial commodities, to regulate the hours of labor of children in factories and mines within the States, a purely State authority. Thus the act in a twofold sense is repugnant to the Constitution. It not only transcends the authority delegated to Congress over commerce, but also exerts a power as to a purely local matter to which the Federal authority does not extend.

"The far-reaching result of upholding the act cannot be more plainly indicated than by pointing out that if Congress can thus regulate matters intrusted to local authority by prohibition of the movement of commodities in interstate commerce all freedom of commerce will be at an end, and the power of the States over local matters may be eliminated, and thus our system of Government be practically destroyed."

Justice Day pointed out that the making of goods or the mining of coal were not in themselves commerce, even though the goods or the coal were afterward to be shipped in interstate commerce. He cited this in support of his argument that the law in effect aims "to standardize the ages at which children may be employed in mining and manufacturing."

"If the mere manufacture or mining were part of interstate commerce," Justice Day said, "all manufacture intended for interstate shipment would be brought under Federal control to the practical exclusion of the authority of the States, a result certainly not contemplated by the framers of the Constitution when they vested in Congress the authority to regulate commerce among the States."

Dissenting Opinion by Holmes.

In the dissenting opinion, Justice Holmes stated that Congress in his judgment was clearly within its rights, as defined by the Constitution, in enacting the law, even if it constituted interference with the individual rights of States to regulate commerce.

"The national welfare," said Justice Holmes, "is higher than the rights of any State or States, and Congress was clearly justified in using all its efforts along that line."

Justice Holmes expressed surprise that this question of the right of Congress to invade State rights of commercial control should have entered into the decision. He pointed out that in the oleomargarine case, various cases under the Sherman anti-trust law, and under the Pure Food and Drug act, as well as under the Mann act, the Supreme Court had decided that in the broad general interest of the nation, Congress had a right to trample upon the individual rights of States.

The suit decided today was brought by Roland H. Dagenhart in behalf of his children, Roland, Jr., Reuben, and John, who were employed in the mill of the Fidelity Manufacturing Company at Charlotte, N. C. Mr. Dagenhart sought an injunction to prevent the concern from discharging his children.

The Federal Court for the Western District of North Carolina decided that Mr. Dagenhart's contention that the law was unconstitutional was well founded. The Government at once appealed, and today's decision is the result.

Representative Keating of Colorado and Senator Kenyon of Iowa, ardent supporters of the child labor law, stated today they would immediately begin a campaign for a new law, or for an amendment to the Constitution, which would permit Congress to enact such a law. Mr. Keating suggested that the situation might be met by taxing the products of factories employing children.

A meeting will be held in Washington soon to plan a new campaign for a child labor law that will meet the Supreme Court's objections.

June 4, 1918

CALL THE CHILDREN FROM WAR PLANTS

"Back to School" the Message of the Government and Societies Interested in Child Welfare

An important movement in the work of reconstruction after the war is the drive now being started by the Children's Bureau of the United States Department of Labor to bring back into the schools of the country the thousands of children who during the period of the war have left them for the purpose of getting into well-paying industries.

Raymond G. Fuller in an article in The American Review of Reviews entitled "Child Labor and the War," makes the following statements which give in brief the conditions of child labor as they are today:

"The United States Commissioner of Education says that this year four or five times as many children as normally are leaving school. Reported violations of compulsory education and child labor laws are numerous in all parts of the country. State boards having in charge the administration of the workmen's compensation laws are handling case after case in which children illegally employed have become victims of industrial accident. The pressure of those conditions which have caused the large and rapid augmentation of the ranks of child labor is growing stronger all the time.

"The President of the United States, the Secretary of Labor, the Secretary of War, and other officers of the executive branch of the Federal Government have repeatedly called attention to the necessity of maintaining and extending, even in these stressful times, ["this was published before peace was declared,] the application of such protective labor standards as have already been established for men and women and children: and they have urged the raising of these standards in the interest of economy of production as well as in the service of national morale. The Government is practicing its own preaching in its own sphere of opportunity. Thus the following clause has been made a condition of all war contracts:

"'The contractor shall not directly or indirectly employ in the performance of this contract any minor under the age of 14 years, or permit any minor between the ages of 14 and 16 to work more than eight hours in any one day, more than six days in any one week, or before 6 A. M. or after 7 P. M.'"

The above ruling has helped things a little. The more conscientious holder of war contracts made an effort to toe the line as far as child labor was concerned. Where, however, too great an inroad was made in the profits of an industry or the output of an industry, the heads of it were not backward about openly stating that they would either ignore the law or refuse to accept Government contracts under such conditions. The American Cotton Manufacturers' Association was one of the organizations to take the second stand. Proclaiming itself to be actuated solely by motives of patriotism, it protested the ruling of the board and wired the State associations advising that no Government contracts be taken until the disagreement had been adjusted. Special exception was taken to the provision as to the number of hours children might be employed.

Other industries in the country were less open about their objection to the clause. They just simply disobeyed it. As a result thousands of children under 14 years of age and without permit did work and are working in mills, factories, and canneries throughout the States of the Union.

In those industries not directly bearing upon the war the Government, even if it would, cannot bring the offender to justice. The revocation of the child labor law of 1916 made that impossible. As will be remembered, the law went into effect on Sept. 1, 1917, and went out of effect on June 3, 1918, on the ground that it exceeded the authority of Congress under the interstate commerce clause of the Constitution. On June 4, 1918, the day after the law was declared unconstitutional, the cotton mills and canneries of the South were using child labor on the old scale of the eleven-hour day. This condition has obtained throughout the last year. During the nine months of the operation of the law conditions were speedily being changed for the better. Investigations made by the Child Labor Division in 686 factories and 26 mines and quarries covering an area of twenty-four States and the District of Columbia showed that 158 children under 16 years of age were employed in mines and quarries, 1,363 under 14 in factories, and 1,024 between 14 and 16 were working more than eight hours a day. Since June 3, in only 9 States and 392 factories investigated, 909 children under 14 were found employed, 818 under 16 were working more than eight hours a day, and 149 were employed at night. In 13 mines investigated 62 children were found employed.

The State of North Carolina stands out foremost with its record of employing children of five who work for more than eight hours a day. In twenty-four States, where the eight-hour day is not required by State statute, investigations proved that the return to the nine, ten, and eleven hour day for children under sixteen is general. School laws are disregarded, and children from seven to sixteen years of age are found employed in vegetable canneries taking a hand in all the processes, including peeling tomatoes and husking corn. Those too small to reach tables stand on boxes placed on wet and slippery floors. In 270 canneries in Maryland and Virginia there are 1,094 children under fourteen at work.

These conditions are by no means true of the South alone. In Texas, for instance, the Superintendent of the schools of the City of Dallas recently announced that the State compulsory education law would be suspended in Dallas until Jan. 1. The Fall session of the school term began Sept. 11. The attendance, it can readily be understood, was not very large. The Dallas Despatch naively mentioned the fact in its columns, stating that beginning Jan. 1 the State school law would apply to children between the ages of eight and fourteen for the remainder of the school year, adding that the School Board had decided upon this course on account of war conditions and because more children were needed for work in the Fall months than in the Winter months.

In Massachusetts the school enrollment this year has been 14 per cent. below normal. Fifty thousand children in that State have during the last year been sucked up into the industries of that section of the country. In Philadelphia it was found necessary by the Bureau of Compulsory Education to inaugurate a city-wide raid in order to bring back to school 2,000 school delinquents who were found working illegally, that is without the necessary papers.

Here in our own city, the number of children between 14 and 16 years old who have taken out working papers this year is more than 10 per cent. above that of last year. On July 1, 1917, the records showed that 42,145 children had received permission to go into industries. On Aug. 3 of this year the figures were 46,887. These of course are entirely apart from the numbers of children who are working without legal papers.

An item in the news column of The Lexington Leader in Kentucky openly comes out with the fact that the industries in that section of the country are draining the schools with the full permission of the educational authorities. It reads as follows:

"If business men and others who want to employ boys within the provisions of the child labor law will send their needs in writing to Attendance Officer J. Sherman Porter, McClelland Building, he will recommend boys for such places. All boys who want to work this year who are under 16 years of age and over 14, and through the fifth year of the public schools, will be given certificates if they ask for them."

The opening of the schools for the Fall term gave the Children's Bureau an opportunity to find out to just what extent children were leaving school prematurely, whether those who had worked on vacation permits had returned, and in general, the conditions among working children. A series of inquiries were made in typical industrial and commercial centres to throw light on these and other questions. The cities studied included New York, Philadelphia, Chicago, Boston, Baltimore, Pittsburgh, Washington, Wilmington, St. Louis, Cincinnati, Louisville, and several smaller cities. In Washington it was found that this year 1,095 permits to work either outside of school hours or full time had been granted under the law which permits children of 12 or 13 to work, if in the opinion of the Juvenile Court the poverty of the family justifies it. In 1916-1917 only 277 such permits were issued. This is a gain of 235 per cent. In Wilmington 61 per cent. more children have taken out permits this year than last. Practically all of this 61 per cent. have definitely left school to enter industry on full time.

Reports of greatly increased shifting from job to job seem to indicate that the child is not finding in his work a steadily progressing training. The figures do not show that children are staying at their jobs because of higher wages or that they are staying long enough to gain from their industrial training experience which will make them increasingly useful.

The attitude taken by all those industrial heads of the country who have been engaged in this exploitation of child labor is that it is a war measure, or, now that the war has ended, a necessary reconstruction measure; that in order to meet the requirements made upon them they must employ children. From the very moment we entered the war President Wilson has repeatedly stated that the children of the nation are in no way necessary to carry along the increased demands made upon industry, that there was sufficient man and woman labor to meet the needs.

England at the very beginning of the war thought it wise to let down the barriers in its child labor legislation. The result was that juvenile delinquency increased 40 per cent. To meet this situation President Fisher of the English Board of Education proposed a bill providing for the compulsory education of English children as well as controlling the conditions under which children might be employed. In urging its passage, President Fisher said:

"At the beginning of the war when first the shortage of labor became apparent, a raid was made upon the schools, a great raid, a successful raid, a raid started by a large body of unreflecting public opinion. The result of that raid upon the schools has been that hundreds of thousands of children of this country have been prematurely withdrawn from school and have suffered an irreparable damage, a damage which it will be quite impossible for us hereafter adequately to repair."

Mr. Allan Lovejoy, Secretary of the National Child Labor Committee, in speaking of the situation here, declared that the first step of democratizing the world lay in the proper care and education of the children.

"Democracy has been saved from autocracy," he said, "but democracy is a process and its completion is for the future. That is the biggest meaning of reconstruction. Problems of commerce and finance must be faced and solved for America's sake, but for God's sake and America's, too, let us not neglect the human factor in reconstruction, which means, in part, getting down to some small but very important things, the children.

"France in war times stuck to her guns and children, winning not only against a foreign invader but against a domestic danger, namely, neglect of her defenses of tomorrow. As well as she could, she kept her schools going and she kept her children in the schools, which was good for the boys and the girls, and good for France. No matter what she may have failed to do in wartime for the protection and education of her children, she tried hard and with wonderful success. What more could be asked? She lived up to her reputation of being thrifty.

"But here in America, where the experience of war has not touched us in any way as it has touched France, here we plunged headlong into a policy of child exploitation. We have lived up to our own reputation of not being thrifty. We took our children out of the schools when there was no reason or necessity for it whatever, except, of course, the closing down of hundreds of schools because of the exodus of 40,000 teachers to better paid jobs. Other schools were closed because the former pupils had begun their curriculum of child labor.

"The executive officers of the State, from President Wilson down, protested repeatedly against this violence, not only of the rights of childhood, but of the best interests of the nation, and the War Labor Policies Board issued an order prohibiting the employment of children under 14 years old in Government contract work. This, however, is the only protection of the kind that the United States has been affording the children of America since the Child Labor act of 1916 was annulled by the decision of the Supreme Court last June.

"The executive branch of the Government has not been able to prevent the enormous increase in child labor, the State Legislatures have done nothing to prevent it, and the social, civic, and religious organizations of the country have been unable to stop it. There are influential people and organizations that don't want it stopped, just as in Great Britain similar interests were able to secure an amendment to the Fisher Education and Child Labor bill, postponing its going into effect until the end of the war. In this country, bearing in mind that child labor was not born and will not die with the war, the most needed and most effective action to take against the evil is that which President Wilson urges, the passage of a new child labor law.

"This law can be based on the taxing power of Congress. It is hoped to do with child labor products of mines, quarries, canneries, and factories exactly what was done by the use of the taxing power with State banknotes, artificially colored oleomargarine, and poisonous phosphorus matches—that is, tax them out of existence."

The situation is considered serious by the Children's Bureau of the Department of Labor. The back-to-school drive inaugurated by it will attempt two things: to return to the schools and keep there the children who have deserted them for industry and to keep the children now in school from leaving prematurely. The actual work of the drive will be done through the Child Conservation Section of the Council of National Defense. This is organized into State, county, and local units. In each school community, committees are being formed whose first duty will be to study child labor and school attendance laws. After that they will go to the County Superintendent, the school Principals, and teachers to get accurate lists of the children who have not returned to school. Then begins the real work of getting the children back. Parents will be called upon and the committee members will talk over with them why it is important not only to the

child but to the country that he be well prepared for work before attempting it. Where the reasons for leaving school were pecuniary, an adjustment will be attempted so that the child can return. The adjustment will doubtless take the form of a scholarship similar to those in practically all of the colleges and in certain city school systems. The average amount of school scholarship is $120 a year. It is hoped that as a result of the drive an average of at least one will be founded for each of the 281,000 school houses in the United States.

A general order has been sent to all branches of the United States Employment Service to discourage all children under 16 from leaving school. If a child of 16 is placed, Federal standards of child labor will be followed unless the standards of the particular State in which he works happen to be higher. In

that case the State standards will be observed. An effort to put the children in suitable progressive positions will be made, and, so far as possible, the conditions under which they work will be investigated.

The United States Boys' Working Reserve refuses to give recognition to boys under 16 who are employed in farms or in industry. It maintains that children under 16 should be kept in school by all the pressure that can be brought to bear, on the ground that the future welfare of the nation depends on the educational training of its youth.

Not the least important feature in the drive will be the work of the National Child Welfare League. In those sections of the country where child labor conditions are at their worst, the capacity for appreciating their dangers is much below par on the part of the members of the

community. It is difficult to make them understand the evils that follow in the wake of abnormal child life. Just at the present time it means an inflation of the family budget. That in the future it will mean an ill-afforded decrease is way above their heads. By a series of attractive charts, with simple captions and pictures, the National Child Welfare League has inaugurated a system of education that is within the scope of the intelligence of the most illiterate. A set of pictures depicting the childhood, youth, and maturity of the man who has been trained in industry and a corresponding set of the man who was not, together with the comparative wage scales of the two, is one of the features of its work.

November 24, 1918

CHILD LABOR SEVERELY CUT

Decrease of 40 Per Cent. in Cotton Mills, Canning, and Coal Mining.

WASHINGTON, Nov. 15.—Child labor in the United States has decreased more than 40 per cent since the child labor tax provision of the revenue act went into effect April 25 last. This act levied a tax of 10 per cent on the net earnings of plants employing children under 14 years old or between 14 and 16 years for more than eight hours in the production of commodities entering interstate commerce.

Reports of internal revenue bureau agents, it was announced today, indicated that the greatest decrease had taken place in the cotton mill industry of the Southern States where more than 25 per cent of the mills are now operating on a basis that exempts them from the child labor tax. A marked reduction in child labor was also reported in the coal mining and canning industries.

The action of employers in avoiding the tax liability, it was said, indicated a general expectation that the constitutionality of the provision would be upheld by the Supreme Court when it comes up Dec. 8.

November 16, 1919

IN PLACE OF CHILD LABOR.

Not Child Idleness, but Work and Play.

To the Editor of The New York Times:

Substitutes for child labor may be recommended as substitutes for child idleness. People sometimes say that child idleness is as bad as child labor, or worse, while others reverse the statement. It is a futile argument. Child idleness and child labor are both bad. But it is poor logic that assumes child idleness to be the alternative to child labor, or child labor to be the alternative to child idleness. For child labor there are several substitutes: schooling is one; play, and especially supervised play, is another, and suitable children's work under home and school supervision is a third.

There exists a rather common belief that child labor is better for children than play. Play is often regarded as practically identical with idleness. It is regarded as a waste of time. The real waste of time is in not playing and in going to work too soon. Play is pleasurable to children because of its instinctive basis, but it is not pleasure as such; it is the most serious business of life, and it is tremendously real. It is real life. Idleness in the case of children is the exact opposite of play—it is the lack of play. Habits of idleness are not developed by play; habits of idleness are encouraged by its absence. It does not develop love of ease, it often involves and welcomes hardship. Play gives the pleasure of doing

the unpleasant and the moral training of overcoming difficulties and "playing the game." It makes the most exacting demands upon patience, perseverance, concentration and skill. It develops, not the qualities of the loafer, the shirker or the quitter, but the qualities needed by the efficient, effective, successful worker, not least of which is good bodily development and health.

Children's work, as distinguished from child labor, does not interfere with childhood as playtime—that is one of its chief distinctions. Children's work and children's play are both substitutes for child labor. In many communities parents actually treat child labor, on the contrary, as a substitute for children's work and children's play. Are they unaware that substitutes for child labor are available in such definite and specific forms as home chores and household tasks, boys' and girls' agricultural clubs, manual training and vocational courses, continuation schools, boy and girl scouts and similar organizations, public playgrounds, evening social centres and so on? These are available to parents as substitutes for child labor; that is, parents can make them available to children. They are not yet, however, universally available to children as substitutes for child labor. To establish them as substitutes is the task of home, church, school, community and State.

Child labor may be defined as the absence of its substitutes in the lives of children. Establishment of its substitutes in the lives of children, in city and in country, is both a method and a goal of child-labor reform. Not an unoccupied but a well-occupied childhood is the aim. The method was prescribed of old; it is that of overcoming evil with good—of putting in the place of child labor its substitutes.

RAYMOND G. FULLER.
Brooklyn, April 11, 1921.

April 19, 1921

COMPULSORY ATTENDANCE.

EVERY State now has a compulsory school attendance law, according to information recently furnished by the United States Department of Labor through the Children's Bureau. The bureau recently completed an analysis of education laws affecting child labor, the results of which are published in a chart entitled "State Compulsory School Standards Affecting the Employment of Minors."

In five States attendance is required until 18 years of age, in two of these in certain districts only; in three until 17, and in thirty-two until 16. One State requires attendance until 15, six others and the District of Columbia until 14, and one State requires attendance until the age of 12 years, but applies this to illiterates only.

Unfortunately, the exemptions in the majority of States are so numerous that they greatly limit the application of the law. The most common exemptions are for employment, or upon completion of a specified school grade. Four States specifically exempt for work in agricultural pursuits, three with no age provision. The laws of fourteen other States contain loosely worded provisions exempting a child at any age, which might be used to cover absence for farm work as well as for many other purposes. Several States exempt a child whose services are necessary for the support of himself or others, without any age or educational provision.

July 31, 1921

THE OVERWORKED FARM CHILD

Two Million Children Now Injuriously Employed, According to Department of Labor

By FLORENCE C. SMITH.

NOW that we are all devising ways and means to keep the farmer, why not at the same time give some attention to the farmer's children? Evidently they need our help fully as much as any ever employed in the canneries or mines or any other injurious labor, for "life down on the farm" is one round of hurtful drudgery to many a farm child. According to a conservative estimate of the National Child Labor Committee, nearly 1,500,000 children, 10 to 15 years

of age, inclusive, are employed in farm work, either upon the home farm or "working out." This committee does not claim that all of these million and a half suffer from this employment. But the Children's Bureau of the United States Department of Labor takes the decided stand that they are laboring on the farms to their own injury, and the number estimated in its report is 2,-000,000.

When we realize that the total population living on the farms in the United States is somewhere near 38,000,000 and

that the total number of adult men employed in farming is 8,000,000 we can begin to appreciate the vital importance to the solution of the agricultural problem is the fair play accorded these million and a half youthful farm workers. "Keep the Farmer Through His Children" is the slogan proposed by Owen R. Lovejoy, General Secretary of the National Child Labor Committee. "There is $100,000,000 worth of children on the farm," says Mr. Lovejoy. "Why not increase their value by giving them a chance to develop by means

of work and play and education? Give these children a chance, and the interest in the investment will be repaid manyfold over any investment in gold dollars. I firmly believe that no plan for keeping the farmer will be adequate or insure permanent assistance that does not involve, first of all, practical help for that farmer's children."

"But," some one objects, "we already have in every State adequate child labor laws. Surely the children who work out of doors have had plenty of State and Federal care!"

But have they, when such things as these are happening?

As recently as this Fall the Massachusetts Society for the Prevention of Cruelty to Children reported that boys and girls from 10 years of age upward were working in the tobacco fields of the Connecticut Valley. Out in the fields, working under canvas, the boys pick the tobacco leaves from the stems and lay them on the ground, working nine and one-half to ten hours a day.

All the girls and women work standing for the full nine and a half hours.

$1.50 to $3 a Day.

Illegal? Scarcely. For the work on which these little Connecticut Valley toilers exchange their youth for $1.50 to $3 a day is on a farm or in sheds in connection with a farm, and as such is not a violation of the existing statutes governing child labor.

An investigator of the National Child Labor Committee went through the farming section of Ohio in the Summer of 1917. Truck gardening and general farming were found to employ comparatively few children, yet their employment was possible. Those who were working labored about ten hours a day, and the average earnings were $1 a day. In the big onion fields of this State, however, many children toiled, the average age of the workers being 11 years. Picture acres of muck land with rows on rows of tiny onion sprouts, and every row carefully weeded by children who have to crawl on hands and knees from one row's end to the other until the "weeding season" ends.

The Michigan sugar beet fields offer an excellent illustration of the bad effects of migratory labor. Investigation proves that, "extensive child labor prevails, there is lack of educational provision, a shocking degree if insanitation in living quarters and an exploitation of adult and for the most part foreign labor." Whole families have been imported from New York City, Buffalo, Erie, Philadelphia, Akron, Cleveland, Cincinnati, Chicago, Milwaukee, Toledo and cities in Iowa and Minnesota. In the last two or three years workers have come even from San Antonio, Texas. Much is promised—"easy work, good pay, free rent, free fuel, a large garden, and above all an opportunity for every child to work and help the family save money."

Disillusionment comes soon to the poor foreigners, aglow with the hope of bettering their condition. "Going to Beets" doesn't turn out to be what was dreamed. Living conditions are very bad. "Fourteen families of four and five persons, and four families with from six to nine persons were found living in one-room shanties. One family of eleven, the youngest child 2 years, the oldest 16 years, lived in an old country store which had but one window; the wind and rain came through the holes in the walls, the ceiling was very low, and the smoke from the stove filled the room. Here the family ate, slept, cooked and washed.

In Tuscola County a family of six was found living in a one-room shack with no windows. Light and ventilation were through the open door. Little Charles, 8 years of age, was left at home to take care of Dan, Annie and Pete, whose ages were 5 years, 4 years and 3 months, respectively. In addition he cooked the noonday meal and brought it to his parents in the field. The filth and choking odors of the shack made it almost unbearable, yet the baby was sleeping on a heap of rags, piled up in a corner.

Little Beets Weeders.

It can be readily seen that one of the most serious effects of beet work on children is its interference with their education. According to the Children's Bureau of the United States Department of Labor, the proportion of beet-working children who are retarded in school was commonly 25 to 35 per cent. higher than that of non-beet workers. Physical defects are bound to be the consequence of overworking youthful, undeveloped bodies. Postural deformities were shown by 70 per cent. of more than 1,000 of these beet-working children examined by a physician of the Children's Bureau.

But Michigan is not the only sinner in the beet industry. In the State of Colorado alone, where great quantities of beets are raised, 5,000 children, between 6 and 15, were found regularly engaged in raising beets. One family boasted that they made $10,000 a year in beets. They worked their 7 and 11 years old children even during school hours. One Colorado man frankly stated that his boy was worth $1,000 to him in the beet season, but was nothing but an expense in school.

Exploitation of children is not an Eastern vice alone, however. When we enjoy the delectable California asparagus tips on toast how many of us realize that children, not yet in their teens, work in California asparagus fields? Their working day is ten or twelve hours. Often the bosses are Chinese or Hindus. Would it whet our appetites if we could glimpse these child-laborers who live in wretched overcrowded shanties?

Violation of the existing child labor laws is flagrantly committed in the Imperial Valley. A State commission estimates that between 2,500 and 3,000 children under 16 years of age are out of school picking cotton. The cotton fields of the valley are crowded with pickers—children are everywhere; even those as young as 3 years pick—for cotton picking in itself is not hard work.

Special Cases.

Here are a few wage accounts that might be taken as typical:

Father and two children aged 12 and 8, $97.67 in two weeks, or an average of $16.27 per person per week.

Father, mother and four children, $121.68 in two weeks, or an average of $10.14 per person per week.

Father, mother and two children, $126.91 in two weeks, or an average of $15.86 per person per week.

In order that such wages could be earned work was continued daily until dark. Usually the mother hurried away a little earlier than the rest in order to cook a hastily prepared hodge-podge meal. After this was gulped down everybody turned in for the night.

California has laws governing child labor, yet in agricultural sections it is especially true that some employers are not interfered with, not fined, not imprisoned, when they disobey the laws. Oklahoma, another cotton-growing State, is open to the same criticism as is California, for children as young as 5 pick cotton regularly.

The absolute lack of educational opportunities that should be the right of all children to enjoy was shown when the National Child Labor Committee made a study of 300 Baltimore families who were seasonal migratory workers. From May to July they had picked peas and strawberries in the country regions near Baltimore; from August to October they had worked in the tomato and corn factories of Maryland and Delaware, and 100 families had worked in the Southern oyster and shrimp canneries from October to April. If the children of these families ever should rise above the dregs of the social stream would it not be miraculous?

If farm workers could once be made to see the actual money value of an education there is no doubt that the agricultural industry would be revolutionized. Various agencies are attempting to do this. The Missouri College of Agriculture proved recently that it pays a farmer to get an education. A study was made of 656 farms in one county. Of these 554 were operated by men who had received a district school education only; the remaining 102 by men who had gone beyond the district school. The better educated farmers operated 33 per cent. more land; they owned four-fifths of the land they operated as compared with three-fifths owned by those with only a district school education; they kept one-sixth more live stock; worked 14 per cent. more land per workman, and earned 77 per cent. more labor income per year.

A new attitude of mind must be created in the farmer himself. When he realizes that he is crippling himself either by losing his children from the farm altogether or if they stay by getting only a small fraction of returns possible from their work, he will enter upon a new era of permanent prosperity. It is only here and there that one finds a new attitude of mind toward education and play and work developed in farming sections, for first, last and all the time the farmer is an individualist. The very fact that he is a farmer makes him an individualist. His home is isolated from other men. He works alone in the fields. Work is the alpha and omega of his existence, as it was of his grandfather and his father before him. To rank as "a great worker" is to achieve the highest measure of praise. So every child is expected to work. And the highly individualistic parents sees no tyranny in choosing and directing the work, determining the hours of labor and coolly pocketing all the returns.

To Solve Problem.

It has long been thought that employment in agricultural work was not injurious to children, and probably in thousands of cases it is not harmful because the children labor under intelligent parental supervision. However, recent studies by the Children's Bureau of the National Child Labor Committee and other organizations show that rural child labor is injurious to health and education, and it is not confined to any particular locality or crop. It is widespread as agriculture itself.

There are no provisions in State or national laws giving protection or supervision to agricultural child laborers. Moreover, in every State in the Union farm work does not come within the purview of the law or else is made a legal excuse for children to stay out of school.

It is interesting to note that fourteen States specifically exempt agriculture from any restrictions as to hours; twenty-three others do not mention it in the occupations for which hours are regulated, and only eleven limit the hours. "Because of the old conception that country life is idyllic it is difficult to make the average citizen appreciate the fact that rural child labor is fully as flagrant an evil as was ever factory child labor," is the statement of one well-known investigator, and this opinion is backed up by the Children's Bureau of the Department of Labor. It estimates that 2,000,000 country children are engaged in farm labor to their injury, and sees that the only remedy for this condition is compulsory school attendance.

Without waiting for laws to be passed, the Farm Bureau and the County and Home Demonstration Agents, through the Boys and Girls' Club, are doing most of any agency to eliminate the evils of rural child labor. Approached in this way, many parents have been won over to entirely new methods of child management. And they never go back to the old ways, for the new are productive of interest and contentment, two things that keep children at home.

January 22, 1922

CHILD LABOR LAW DECLARED INVALID

Supreme Court Holds 1919 Act Unconstitutional in That It Usurps State Function.

TAFT DISCUSSES TAXATION

WASHINGTON, May 15.—The Child Labor Law was declared unconstitutional today by the Supreme Court.

The law, enacted in 1919, was intended to regulate the employment of children in any mill, cannery, workshop, factory or manufacturing establishment, under the age of 14, or in any mine or quarry under 16 years, by imposing an excise tax of 10 per cent. upon the net annual profits of those employing such labor. It was attacked on the ground that it attempted to regulate an exclusively State function in violation of the Federal Constitution and the Tenth Amendment and was defended as a mere excise tax, levied by Congress under its broad power of taxation conferred by the Federal Constitution.

The opinion was delivered by Chief Justice Taft with no dissent announced. The case was discussed at length in view of previous decisions involving questions bearing upon the taxing power of Congress, and the law was held invalid as an attempt by Congress to regulate through its taxing power something entirely within the jurisdiction of the various States in the exercise of their police power.

"Does this law impose a tax with only that incidental restraint and regulation which a tax must inevitably involve," the Chief Justice asked, "or does it regulate by the use of the so-called tax as a penalty? If a tax, it is clearly an excise. If it were an excise on a commodity or other thing of value, we might not be permitted under previous decisions of this court to infer solely from its heavy burden that the act intends a prohibition instead of a tax. But this act is more."

After analyzing the principal features of the law and its operation, the Chief Justice said, "in the light of these features of the act, a court must be blind not to see that the so-called tax is imposed to stop the employment of children within the age limits prescribed."

"Its prohibitory and regulatory effect and purpose are palpable," he added. "All others can see and understand this. How can we properly shut our minds to it?"

Declaring it the duty of the Court to decline to recognize or enforce laws of Congress dealing with subjects not entrusted to Congress but left by the supreme law of the land to the control of the States, the Chief Justice said the Court must perform that duty "even though it require us to refuse to give effect to legislation designed to promote the highest good."

"The good sought in unconstitutional legislation," he added, "is an insidious feature because it leads citizens and legislators of good purpose to promote it without thought of the serious breach it will make in the ark of our covenant or the harm which will come from breaking down recognized standards.

"Grant the validity of this law and all that Congress would need to do hereafter, in seeking to take over to its control any one of the great number of subjects of public interest, jurisdiction of which the States have never parted with and which are reserved to them by the Tenth Amendment, would be to enact a detailed measure of complete regulation of the subject and enforce it by a so-called tax upon departures from it. To give such magic to the word 'tax' would be to break down all constitutional limitations of the powers of Congress and completely wipe out the sovereignty of the States."

May 16, 1922

PASSES AMENDMENT FOR CHILD LABOR LAW

Senate Votes, 61 to 23, in Favor of Proposal Which Now Goes to the States.

WASHINGTON, June 2.—Approval was given by the Senate tonight to a Constitutional amendment which would empower the Federal Government to limit, regulate or prohibit the labor of children under 18 years of age. It previously had been approved by the House and now goes to the States for ratification.

The vote was 61 to 23 or five more than the necessary two-thirds.

Under the amendment Congress would have the power of regulation, but the enforcing power would be vested in the Federal and State Governments.

The vote of three-fourths of the States is necessary for ratification.

The Senate refused to provide for ratification by special convention or to require completed ratification in five years.

June 3, 1924

DENIES CHILD LABOR IS A FEDERAL AFFAIR

National Association of Manufacturers Opposes Proposed Amendment.

BRANDS IT AS SOCIALISTIC

The National Association of Manufacturers made public yesterday a summary of the arguments against the proposed Child Labor (Twentieth) Amendment, which has been prepared by its counsel, James A. Emery. In the course of his argument Mr. Emery attacks the proposed Child Labor Amendment at both socialistic and communistic and holds it to be unjustified and unnecessary.

"Wherefore," says the statement, "an American association of manufacturers free from child labor in the mechanical departments of its members urges that this politically revolutionary amendment be rejected."

Mr. Emery's report discloses that "on the day Calvin Coolidge became President of the United States his 14-year-old son received $3.50 a week for his labor in a neighbor's tobacco field." The announcement of the manufacturers concerning Mr. Emery's analysis and criticism of the proposed Twentieth Amendment in part reads:

"His study of the problem leads him to the conclusions that the proposed amendment is unnecessary and is also subversive of the principles of American life, as well as an unjustifiable invasion of State's rights.

"To prove that there is no such necessity, he quotes figures from the census of 1920 showing that of the 12,502,582 children in the United States from ten to fifteen years old, 1,060,868 were reported as gainfully employed; 647,309 in agricultural pursuits and 413,549 in others. Of those employed in agriculture, 569,324 worked on their parents' farms, leaving 77,485 working for others.

"Of the 413,549 other children at work, he argues that they must have been employed legally, as they were 14 or 15 years old, and the Child Labor Tax act of 1919 was then in effect. This left only 49,105 children whose employment might be questionable. He cites, too, the fact that these figures include all kinds of intermittent work done by children outside of school hours. He asks:

"'Can it be contended that the employment of 126,590 children (those employed on farms other than those of their parents and those engaged in pursuits other than agricultural) out of 12,502,582 demands the grant of power to Congress which is sought?'

"One of Mr. Emery's chief arguments against the proposed amendment is that it raises the prescribed age limit to eighteen years and that up to that age the Congress will have the power to 'limit, regulate and prohibit the labor' of such persons.

"Mr. Emery contends that regulation of child labor is the function of the State and he declares that the States have not been neglectful of their obligations. Mr. Emery quotes as applicable to the proposal the complaint against the King in the Declaration of Independence:

"'He has erected a multitude of new offices and sent hither swarms of officers to harass our people and eat out their substance.'"

August 18, 1924

FOR REPLACING CHILD LABOR

Miss Abbott Says Ban Would Give Jobs of 1,000,000 to Adults.

Special to The New York Times.

WASHINGTON, Jan. 24.—Two suggestions for relief of the unemployment problem were offered today by Miss Grace Abbott, chief of the Children's Bureau of the Department of Labor, on the eve of Child Labor Day, nation-wide observance of which was organized in 1907 by the national child labor committee of New York.

"Ratification of the Twentieth or Child Labor Amendment to the Constitution," Miss Abbott said, "would take out of industry more than 1,000,000 children. At this moment 250,000 jobs could be released to adult workers by raising the age limit for compulsory school attendance from 14 to 15 years."

According to statistics of the bureau, 33,399 children of 14 and 15 years of age received first employment certificates in New York last year, 10,455 in Philadelphia, 3,486 in Chicago, 2,847 in Boston and 1,033 in Detroit.

A total of 1,060,000 children between 10 and 16 are reported to be gainfully employed in the United States, it was stated. Between the ages of 16 and 17 the young workers number 1,712,648.

January 25, 1931

YOUNG WORKERS.

Child labor is called an aggravating factor in industrial depression by the American Federation of Labor. Yet child labor in the United States is not predominantly an industrial problem if one uses industry in the sense of manufacturing or other urban occupation. The great body of child labor is on the farm and not in the factories, and it is the agricultural States that have been sternest in their opposition to the proposed constitutional amendment. Perhaps it is necessary to define the precise meaning of "child" as well as of "industry." The amendment would make the age limit under 18, and that is the usual objective in such legislation. But the argument against child labor undoubtedly profits by the emotional response to the case of child workers who are in a very real sense children, workers under 15 and workers of 13 years down to 10. But it is not generally made plain that these very young child workers are so rare in industry as to be virtually non-existent.

Occupational figures from the 1930 census are now being published for localities and States. Enough material is in hand for instructive comparisons. Manchester, N. H., has about 34,500 persons gainfully employed. The workers between 10 and 13 years number 7; those of 14-15 number 139; those of 16-17 number 1,222, or 3.5 per cent of all workers. Wilmington, Del., in 47,770 workers has 5 wage earners in the 10-13 year class, 143 workers of 14-15 years, and 1,428 of 16-17 years, the last being 3 per cent of all the workers. Winston-Salem, N. C., out of 36,100 workers has 28 workers in the 10-13 class, 368 of 14-15 years, and 1,343 of 16-17 years, the last being 3.7 per cent of all workers. But Arkansas, an overwhelmingly agricultural and non-industrial State, has gainfully employed more than 14,000 children between 10 and 13, or 2.2 per cent of the entire working population, 16,000 children of 14-15 years, or another 2.4 per cent, and 26,000 workers of 16-17 years, or 4 per cent. The Arkansas workers under the age of 18 constitute nearly 9 per cent of the workers of the State, as against something between 3 and 4 per cent in the industrial communities cited. And if we are speaking of real children, those of 15 and under, Arkansas would have more than 30,000, against an average of less than 250 in those sizeable industrial communities.

Even in the rural districts there has been a sharp reduction in the number of very young workers since 1920. In Arkansas the 14,000 workers between 10 and 13 compare with 26,339 workers in the year 1920, and in view of the increase in population the proportional decline is still larger. For the 14-15 year class the reduction is from something less than 22,000 to 16,000. Idaho had very nearly 500 child workers under 14 in 1920, and only 237 last year. The 14-15 year olds were down from 1,111 to 800. Manchester, N. H., had 50 workers under 14 in 1920, and 7 last year; Wilmington, 64 and 5; Winston-Salem, 61 and 28. For the 14-15 year olds the decline in these three cities has been respectively from 318 to 139; from 743 to 143; from 543 to 368. Finally, it should be noted that these very young workers in the cities are in all probability not industrial workers, but gainfully employed as newsboys, messenger boys, and the like.

August 16, 1931

The Physical Risks in Child Labor

Reasons for Children's Charter Pledge of Protection Against Tasks That Stunt Growth Are Summed Up by Harvard Expert.

Why do we pledge, as the White House Conference on Child Health and Protection did for the nation in Point XVI of the Children's Charter, "For every child protection against labor that stunts growth, either physical or mental,

that limits education, that deprives children of the right of comradeship, of play and of joy"? The facts behind this determination are summed up in the following article by a member of the Harvard School of Public Health faculty. It

is the last of a series of six articles on points in the Charter.

By ALICE HAMILTON.

In considering the possible evils of child labor it is important to remember that the children who leave school for the factory at 14 or 15 years, if the law allows, are in the great majority the children of poor families, and that means that they have more than their share of physical handicaps.

They come from homes where

there has never been enough to go round, not enough milk, butter, eggs, meat; not enough rooms; not enough beds; not enough parental attention; not enough medical care. The home is crowded, and there is no quiet spot, no privacy. It is hard, if not impossible, to get to sleep early. It is often impossible to have a bed to oneself. For amusement or for refuge from the jarring of family life, there is only the noisy street. Often the atmosphere of the home is one of anxiety and insecurity. If the child develops a nervous disorder, how can it be wisely handled by an overburdened mother in an overcrowded house.

It is the product of life like this who, just at the age of puberty with its special strains, asks to be admitted to the factory. Compared with the children of the well-to-do, this child is likely to have several handicaps. Tuberculosis is pre-eminently the disease of the poor, and the children of poor families are more likely to be suffering from a latent infection. Such an infection is very common in all classes, but if the resistance of the body is normal, the infection is held in check. But among the poor this resistance is likely to be lower because of lack of proper food and of sunshine. Industrial work indoors through all the sunny hours of the day may be the last straw for such a child.

The heart disease of childhood which has assumed so much importance of late years is, according to St. Lawrence of New York, a disease of the poorer class as clearly as diabetes is a disease of the well to do, coming as it does from neglected infections, from the failure to secure proper medical care in time. Even if it is arrested, there must be a long period of anxious watching and care to bring the heart back to its normal strength. Think how difficult this is for a mother in a crowded tenement.

Every one will admit that the boy or girl of 14 years is still immature. Skeleton and muscles are not yet developed. The work he is required to do will almost inevitably make uneven demands on his body, devel-

oping part of it at the expense of others; he will have to stand or sit most of the time, with a possible resulting curvature of the spine or cramping of the chest from faulty posture.

The normal life for a boy or girl of that age is one of periods of quiet work alternating with periods of intense muscular activity in the open air. A steady, unvarying monotonous job for eight hours is for a growing boy or girl unnatural in the extreme.

Where Tuberculosis Strikes.

The nervous system is immature and is passing through an especially trying period with the development and functioning of the ductless glands. As every parent knows, the boy or girl of 14 years is likely to be more unstable nervously than a younger child and to need in a special sense the steadying influence of home and school and protection against premature sex stimulation.

The resistance to tuberculosis is weaker than it will be later on, for each year diminishes the danger. Under the strain of industrial work the latent tuberculous infection, which is almost surely present in the body somewhere, may find a chance to break out and spread and the young worker may succumb to it, while if he had had only a few more years of life before the strain came on he might have resisted successfully.

Drolet's statistics of deaths from

tuberculosis in New York City show that there is an increase when boys and girls pass from the 10 to 14 year old group to the 15 to 19, the increase being almost three times for the girls and almost four times for the boys.

The young people cannot resist poisons as well as older people. Lead, wood alcohol, benzol, naphtha, carbon monoxid, these are all industrial poisons which are fairly widely encountered and which cause much more damage to young things under 20 years of age than they do to the mature.

And, finally, the 14 or 15 year old who enters industry is immature in judgment, self-control, capacity for concentration; he is naturally heedless and impulsive, easily distracted, and therefore much more liable to accidents of all kinds.

We must remember that modern industry is quite different from the kind of industry that prevailed fifty years ago. It has become increasingly a machine industry, monotonous and requiring less and less intelligence as the machine is perfected year by year.

A Machine-Made Dilemma.

The saying is now that in most industries all that is needed is a stupid little girl to feed the machine and a skilled machinist to keep all the machines in order. There is no educational value in such work; there is no possibility for the worker to gain a sense of achievement and pride in increasing skill.

We know that this machine-made industry has come to stay, that there will be no return to the old hand work. What, then, can we do to provide for the workers a share in the fullness of life which we, more fortunate, are determined to give to our own children? The factory for work, the movie for pleasure: what kind of men and women does that program promise us?

If we cannot give the children of the workers what the child of the farmer and the craftsman used to get inevitably, we can postpone as long as possible the entry of such a child into industry so that the strain of machine work shall not begin until bodies and minds are more nearly prepared for it.

We can shorten the hours of work, recognizing that eight hours a day is far too long even for 16-year-olds; and by intelligent training in school we can give the child some way of using his leisure that will let him share in the beauty and richness of modern life.

If we do not do this we may find that we are building up in our country a separation of classes which is quite contrary to our ideal of democracy; on the one side, the well to do, whose lives are fuller and richer than ever before; on the other, the poor, who are shut off from the great gains of our modern life because they are incapable of appreciating them.

May 22, 1932

CHILD LABOR'S END FORESEEN AS OUTCOME OF TEXTILE CODE

The Recovery Act Supplies a Weapon Against the Exploiting Of Childhood, But State Safeguards Are Still Needed

By GRACE ABBOTT,
Chief of Children's Bureau.

WASHINGTON.

IN signing the cotton textile code, the first to be agreed to under the National Industrial Recovery Act, President Roosevelt listed the prohibition of the employment of children under 16 years of age first among the "many significant circumstances" attending this result. "Child labor in this industry is here abolished," he declared. "After years of fruitless effort and discussion, this ancient atrocity went out in a day, because this law permits employers to do by agreement that which none of them could do separately and live in competition."

Commenting again on this subject in his recent radio talk, President Roosevelt declared that the abolition of child labor in the cotton textile code and other agreements already signed had made him personally happier than anything with which he has been connected since he came to Washington. "As a British editorial put it," he said, "we did more under a code in one day than they in England had been able to do * * * in eighty-five years of effort."

After a Century.

It is of interest in this connection that it is exactly a hundred years ago that the first factory act was passed in England and in the world. That early act prohibited the employment of children under 9 years of age in textile mills and limited

the hours of those under 13 years of age to nine a day and forty-eight a week. The leader in the long Parliamentary struggle which resulted in this legislation was later to be the Earl of Shaftesbury. It was, perhaps, because of his own unhappy childhood that this great aristocrat devoted his life to promoting the welfare of children and especially the welfare of working children.

Some twenty years before this first law was passed, Robert Owen, who was not only a manufacturer but also a cotton mill operator, believed that child labor was unfair to children and demonstrated it was not necessary for business success if the cotton mills were well managed. Owen had thought that he had only to lay before his fellow manufacturers the results of his experiment to secure their cooperation. He was bitterly discouraged by their indifference to what happened to the children of the poor. Certainly the spirit of Owen was in the code which the textile operators submitted to the President. One wonders why it should have been so long in coming—why, indeed, child labor ever developed in democratic America.

Favored by Hamilton.

At about the same time that Robert Owen was writing his tracts against the employment of young children in factories the Secretary of the Treasury of the United States, who is so frequently used as a measuring rod of the greatness

of those who have followed him in that high office, was advocating the employment of little children in the mills which he hoped a protective tariff would bring to America. The great capitalists of that day were the landlords, who hesitated to support a policy which, by creating a new demand for labor, would jeopardize the labor supply for agriculture in our then sparsely settled country.

Hamilton had a ready answer. Adult men, he said, in his famous "Report on the Subject of Manufactures," were not needed in a machine-equipped factory; women, and children of 8 and 10, "who would otherwise be idle," could be used as operators in the textile mills. He was right. The machinery which came from England for what was then truly an infant industry was especially built to accommodate little children.

Old Cruelties of Child Labor.

The regulation of child labor in this country was delayed not because the leaders in social reform were converted to a ruthless industrial nationalism, but because the absorbing struggle over the abolition of slavery and the problems of reconstruction which followed the Civil War delayed the development of the whole social reform movement in America. Before 1860 labor unions secured a few laws, which generally went unenforced, in some of the New England States and in Pennsylvania, but the real child-labor movement did not get under way until the last decade of the

nineteenth century.

The periods of greatest progress in State legislation were between 1890 and 1909, and again between 1917 and 1922, when one of the most important effects of the first and second Federal child-labor laws was the raising of State standards to the level established by the Federal law—14 for children employed in mills and factories and 16 for children in mines and quarries. The hours of work in the Federal statute for employed children between 14 and 16 years of age were eight per day and forty-eight per week.

A century ago the hours in a textile mill were from 5 in the morning until 7 at night during ordinary times and in rush periods often ran from 3 in the morning until 10 at night, and the children who worked these long hours were often as young as 7 and 8. Royal commissions in England and legislative committees in the United States found that many of them had literally to be driven to go to work or to keep it up after they were there.

As I read the official reports of little children of 6 and 7 working in the dark mines, harnessed to coal cars to drag them through small openings; of the chimney sweeps or "climbing boys" compelled to go up the chimneys by beatings, and under whom fires were sometimes lighted when they became frightened and refused to climb, I have the same feeling of unreality that I had about the cruelties with which the fairy tales of my childhood were filled. Yet these cruelties were condoned and even justified as necessary in an industrial society, and long after official reports had been made and after laws were passed prohibiting them these practices continued.

New Code Benefits Thousands.

But it is not by a hundred-year period that we measure the importance of the child-labor provisions of the cotton textile code.

21

THE 'PATCHWORK' OF STATE MINIMUM AGE LAWS

CHILD LABOR LAWS OF THE STATES

☐ 16 YEARS　　⬚ 15 YEARS　　▨ 14 YEARS　　▧ NO AGE MINIMUM

Courtesy of the Children's Bureau.

The Map Shows the Minimum Ages Established by the States for Employes of Factories and Stores. Nearly All States Permit Some Exceptions to Their Laws, Such as Allowing Children of Less Than the Established Minimum Age to Work After School Hours. Under the National Industrial Recovery Act Many Industries Voluntarily Agreed to Higher Minimum Ages Than Required by State Laws.

One asks, how much have the children of today gained? The latest national figure we have for the number of children employed is for 1930. Then the census enumerators reported 20,625 under 16 employed in textiles, about half this number being in cotton mills alone, more than in any other manufacturing industry. But the cotton textile code in establishing a standard which is being followed by other branches of the textile industry will do more than liberate these 20,000 children.

As child labor was more strongly entrenched in textiles than any other industry, we can expect that the codes adopted by other industries will provide at least a 16-year minimum for children. Many of the codes already submitted have done so. For some of the more hazardous occupations, the entering age should be higher. It is, therefore, important to review briefly where we stand with reference to this whole subject of the employment of minors.

Legislation varies greatly from State to State, as does the effectiveness of the administration of all labor laws. It is not possible to give these variations in detail, but a summary, which omits the many exceptions and exemptions, may be said to give the general picture.

In spite of revolutionary changes in industry, bringing more and more machinery and greater and

greater speed. 14 has been the general age minimum established by law and frequently indifferently enforced. Seven States have for some years had a higher minimum. Ohio led the way with the enactment of a 16-year age law some twenty years ago. Montana also has had a 16-year minimum for many years and California, Maine, Michigan, Texas and Rhode Island a 15-year minimum. This year the State Legislatures of Wisconsin and Utah adopted a 16-year minimum. There are textile mills in Maine. Rhode Island and Texas where the 15-year standard has received legislative approval, but the great textile States of Massachusetts, New York, Pennsylvania, North Carolina and South Carolina have only a 14-year legal minimum. For the children of these States, the textile code raises the age for employment two years. Their working hours will also be shortened.

Shorter Working Days.

Before the depression, eight hours had become the working day for so many men and women workers that the theory that the young and immature workers should begin with a shorter working day than adults was no longer met by the usual eight-hour legal day for children between 14 and 16 years of age. But even this provision was not universal. In some parts of the South boys and girls of 14 and 15 are still permitted by law to work ten or eleven hours a day and

even longer; in Georgia "from sunrise to sunset" is the legal limitation. The cotton textile code specifies a forty-hour week for all workers. No State has specified so short a work week for children; in only five widely separated States— New York, Virginia, Mississippi, New Mexico and Utah, where it is forty-four—is the legal working week for children between 14 and 16 less than forty-eight hours.

The fact that the code will affect textile mills in all States is of special interest. The maps which we make in the Children's Bureau to show the labor laws of the different States resemble a crazy patchwork quilt. The movement for a national minimum reached the halls of Congress as long ago as 1906, when the first bills proposing a Federal child-labor minimum were introduced in Congress. Among the authors of these bills introduced before 1916 were Senators Beveridge of Indiana and Lodge of Massachusetts, and Representative Parsons of New York.

The one that passed Congress in 1916 and was signed by President Wilson was sponsored by Edward Keating of Colorado in the House and by Senator Owen of Oklahoma. It had been actively supported by the National Child Labor Committee, the National Consumers League, the American Federation of Labor and the General Federation of Women's Clubs. This law, which sought to take advantage of the interstate

commerce clause of the Constitution, and the one passed in 1919 as a tax measure were each in turn held unconstitutional by the United States Supreme Court.

After the second decision, on May 15, 1922, some twenty-eight proposals for a child-labor amendment were introduced in the Senate and the House. In the latter, Mr. Foster of Ohio was the author of the resolution finally submitted to the States. In the Senate, Mr. Jones of Washington, Mr. Lodge of Massachusetts, Mr. McCormick of Illinois and Mr. Wheeler of Montana introduced resolutions. Senator Walsh of Montana and Senator Shortridge of California were active supporters of the amendment in the Judiciary Committee and on the floor of the Senate. It was submitted in June, 1924; in the Presidential campaign which followed, the three leading candidates, President Coolidge, John W. Davis and Senator La Follette, all declared for the amendment.

The Depression as a Teacher.

That year and in 1925 the amendment was ratified by four States only—Arkansas, Arizona, California and Wisconsin—and rejected by twenty. In the years between 1925 and 1933, two other States, Montana and Colorado, ratified. But the depression seems to have brought a new appreciation of the importance of a national minimum standard. The textile code and other codes to follow will establish a national minimum.

Moreover, the Legislatures of nine States — Illinois, Michigan, New Hampshire, New Jersey, North Dakota, Ohio, Oklahoma, Oregon and Washington—have ratified the child-labor amendment this year, and in all of these, except Illinois and New Jersey, the amendment had previously been rejected by one or both houses of the State Legislatures. All of this is evidence of the fact that the depression has profoundly influenced the thinking of many of us on this and many other questions.

The number of children gainfully employed had, to be sure, greatly decreased before as well as after the debacle of 1929. The census enumerators reported that in April of 1930 there were 235,328 children from 10 to 13 years of age gainfully employed and 431,790 who were 14 and 15 years of age, giving a total between 10 and 15 inclusive of 667,118.

The largest number, 70.4 per cent, were in agriculture and the next largest, 10.2 per cent, were employed in manufacturing and mechanical industries. Except in a very few States, notably Ohio and Wisconsin, almost no attempt has been made to regulate the employment of children in agriculture. While evidence has been presented of real exploitation of children in what we might call industrialized agriculture, where large numbers of children are employed, generally speaking, the children employed in agriculture, particularly when they work on the home farm, are in a very different category from the children who work in factories, in textile mills, or the clothing industry.

Child Labor in Hard Times.

Omitting the children employed in farm work, we find that in 1930, 1.4 per cent of all the children between 10 and 15 years of age inclusive were at work or, to use the more accurate language of the census, were "gainfully employed." This is very much less than the Census Bureau reported for 1920. The decline in the number of children employed in non-agricultural occupations from 1920 to 1930 was 53 per cent. This striking decrease was not spread evenly over all States or all occupations.

The bulk of the decline in the number of 14 and 15 year old children in occupations outside of agriculture occurred in the Northern and Eastern States, which had been hardest hit by the depression and where unemployment was, in consequence, widespread in 1930. In

the South, where unemployment had been less severe up to 1930, a few States showed an increase in the number of such children at work; for example, South Carolina showed an increase of 29 per cent; Florida, an increase of 7 per cent, and Georgia, an increase of 2.5 per cent.

The number of employed boys and girls of 16 and 17 years had declined less; nearly a million and a half were employed in 1930. In many cities there had been a very large increase in the number of boys and girls of this age employed as waiters and servants; for instance, in New York the number had increased 60 per cent; in Philadelphia, 70 per cent; in Atlanta, 92 per cent; in Pittsburgh, 99 per cent; in Chicago, 153 per cent, and in Detroit and Cleveland, more than 175 per cent.

Although there was a general decline in the number employed in manufacturing and mechanical industries from 1920 to 1930, there were a few significant increases for the younger age groups. In several Southern States textile workers of 16 and 17 years showed an increase, and in the clothing industries in certain of the New England and Middle Atlantic States there has occurred a shift from older to younger employes. Thus, in the clothing industry of Connecticut the number of workers of 16 and 17 increased by 123 per cent, in New Jersey the increase was 81 per cent, in Pennsylvania 62 per cent and in Massachusetts 52 per cent. For all the younger age groups the census indicated that the better-grade jobs were disappearing faster than less desirable types of employment.

Exploitation Goes On.

In general, child employment follows the industrial trend. The number moves up and down, corresponding roughly with the peaks and valleys of adult employment, although the general trend has been downward. It is to be expected therefore that when adult employment increases child labor will increase, except as preventive legislation or temporary agreement under the National Industrial Recovery Act prevents young boys and girls from getting a share of the jobs that become available.

In the last year there has been striking evidence of a tendency greatly to increase the proportion of young children in certain industries, particularly in the needle trades. Indeed, we have a development of new sweated industries reported for Pennsylvania, Massachusetts and Connecticut. Under such

conditions exploitation is always greatest among the younger workers. A study of the clothing industry in Pennsylvania made last April by the Department of Labor and Industry of that State showed that half the children of 14 and 15 at work were earning less than $2.76 a week each.

Recently a general survey of the shirt industry was made jointly by several bureaus of the United States Department of Labor, including the Children's Bureau. In one Pennsylvania plant visited, 20 per cent of the female workers were under 16, and in several factories practically the whole working force, according to the management, was under 20 years of age. Continuation schools have been opened up in communities which hitherto have not had enough child workers to make the establishment of such schools mandatory.

The Connecticut Commissioner of Labor reported last Winter that child labor and fearfully low wages characterized the sweatshops in the clothing industry operated in that State. In spite of the large number of adult women unemployed, children of 14 and 15 are going to work in these and other industries in Connecticut at wages rarely exceeding $3 a week and often less.

In the study of the Federal Labor Department it was found that proceedings for violation of the Connecticut law had been filed against a number of the firms visited; because of flagrant abuse of child labor one firm had been refused permits for child workers by the State Department of Education; one contractor said that 75 per cent of his employes were learners fresh from school, whom he was training.

Children in Sweatshops.

Attention has been focused on child-labor conditions in Pennsylvania because of the recent strikes of children for higher wages, and in Connecticut because of the publicity campaign carried on last Winter by the Labor Commissioner, but reports of departments of labor in other States indicate that there has been this mushroom growth of sweated industries throughout the industrial East.

There will be some opposition on the part of unemployed and discouraged parents if a minimum wage and a 16-year age minimum are adopted for this or other industries, for it will mean that in many cases a child who has been the only employed member of a family will be out of work. The parents often see only their immediate necessities and not the vicious circle which poverty and child labor make. These jobs will be

taken by adults who will be paid some five or more times what most of these girls—and most of the workers in the needle trades to which reference has just been made are girls—have received.

The wages of children follow the general trend of wages for adults. Always low, wages for children last Spring reached a level which would be ridiculous if it were not tragic. It is for this reason that the establishment of a minimum wage in the textile and other codes is important, and even more important is the enactment this year by New York, New Jersey, New Hampshire, Connecticut, Ohio, Illinois and Utah of minimum or fair wage laws.

Increased buying power means industrial recovery in its larger aspects. In the individual family it means milk and fruit and vegetables, attractive clothing, and a happy home for children. Women as well as children have been unwilling underbidders in the labor market. A legal minimum for them will protect the wages of other workers.

Vigilance Still Needed.

The question which every one interested in the welfare of children is asking is, Will the National Industrial Recovery Act and the codes adopted under its terms make further legislation unnecessary? One must remember that, important as these codes are, the Recovery Act runs for a two-year period, or for less if the President decides that the emergency has passed. It is therefore essential to keep up the struggle for legislative standards.

Many manufacturers who dismiss their child employes in accordance with the industrial code which has been agreed to for their industry will not want to re-employ them when the emergency no longer exists. But this will not be true of all. A small minority greedy for profits or seeking to make labor pay the costs of poor management will want a cheap labor supply and will re-employ the children if the law permits it; some of them in spite of the law, if enforcement is poor.

Most laws are made necessary by the anti-social practices of the few. Industry is no exception. Should we let the few destroy the standards of the many by unfair competition? In this event, the children will be the first to suffer, but their losses will eventually affect all workers and society as a whole.

August 13, 1933

MORE CHILD LABOR SEEN OVER NATION

By SAMUEL MINES

The march of child labor into the mills and factories of the nation—halted for a time by the provisions of NRA codes—has been resumed. Reference is made to it, it was learned last week, in a report to President Roosevelt that compared

NRA and post-NRA conditions in various industries.

Despite the voluntary agreements of many industries to abide by the spirit of the now extinct Blue Eagle, the Children's Bureau of the United States Department of Labor reveals a 58 per cent increase in the number of employment certificates issued to children 14 and 15 years of age in 129 cities of twenty-nine States reporting for the seven-month period following the decision of the United States Supreme Court invalidating the NRA.

New York City presents an even

more striking picture. Figures assembled for the last four months of 1935 by the National Child Labor Committee show a rise of almost 400 per cent in employment certificates as compared with the like period of 1934. Certificates issued to children of 14 rose from 266 to 570 and those issued to 15-year-olds from 1,139 to 4,659—a total increase from 1,405 to 5,229.

Count of Permits

In the same period certificates issued to 16-year-olds declined from 8,730 to 8,424—a certain indication, according to members of the committee, that older children (and

adults) are being displaced by younger and cheaper laborers.

Other sections of the country, according to reports received by the committee, reveal similar conditions. In Maryland work certificates issued to children of 14 and 15 for the last half of 1935 totaled 190, as compared with eleven in the like period of 1934. In North Carolina, despite the efforts of the textile industry to prevent a breakdown of standards, eighty-two permits for full-time work in cotton mills and twenty-four for other types of factory work were issued to children of 14 and 15. Permits issued for work in the "service trades," including laundries and restaurants, increased more than 100 per cent.

"Fly-by-Night" Firms

With the return of child labor come stories of hardships and indignities inflicted upon the young workers. New England and Pennsylvania both report the return of the old-time "fly-by-night" textile sweatshop, which sets up in an abandoned barn or factory, works its employes mercilessly for a few weeks, and then moves secretly at night without paying even the meager wages promised.

Sweatshop conditions also are claimed in the New Jersey silk industry. It is said that small mill operators set up in rickety, old buildings, which sway and vibrate to the motion of the looms. The National Child Labor Committee declares that many children are working in such factories, often partitioned off with chicken wire in units of four to fourteen looms. Since doors are locked during working hours, the only exit is by means of fire-escapes—when there are fire-escapes.

The New Jersey Department of Labor and the Paterson Chamber of Commerce emphatically deny these charges, but investigators of the Child Labor Committee insist they saw children apparently 10 to 15 years old working in such places.

Even under NRA regulation child labor was far from stamped out in many lines of work. This was particularly true in agriculture and in domestic service, which were covered by no codes. The nation's farms employed some 100,000 children in 1930, according to the census of that year, and this figure is believed to have increased sharply during the depression. In 1930 some 40,000 children, mostly girls, were employed at low wages as domestic servants.

Similarly, in the anthracite coal mines, in the field of telegraphic communications and in some branches of the publishing industry children under 16 were exploited even during the rule of the Blue Eagle because satisfactory codes were never worked out.

Ranks Cut by NRA

However, the NRA went a long way toward reducing child labor during its life. The census of 1930 showed more than 68,000 children under 16 employed in manufacturing and mechanical occupations and about 50,000 in other industries later covered by codes. The depression cut into these figures somewhat, but the National Child Labor Committee estimates that 100,000 were still so employed in 1933, when the NRA came into being.

Under NRA codes the textile industry alone quickly released some 20,000 children, the clothing industry about 9,000, other branches of manufacturing about 40,000 more. Hotels, restaurants, beauty parlors and laundries yielded 8,000, from stores came 28,000, and from various clerical occupations, chiefly errand and messenger boys and girls, 17,-000 were released.

These figures do not include boys and girls just above the minimum age who were barred from dangerous occupations by the NRA codes. An 18-year minimum was established for specially hazardous occupations such as work with explosives and quicksilver and in the wrecking and salvage industries. The minimum for underground work in coal mines was fixed at 17 and that for work above ground at 16.

Control Is Shown

Estimates of the Children's Bureau place the reduction of child labor at 90 per cent in industries affected by the NRA. Eighteen per cent of the decline is attributed to the forces of depression, leaving a 72 per cent reduction to be credited directly to the NRA. These figures, it is asserted, show how easily the exploitation of children can be controlled with proper legislation.

With the passing of the Blue Eagle agencies interested in child welfare are renewing their efforts to bring about final ratification of the child labor amendment to the Constitution.

To date twenty-four States have ratified the proposed amendment. Ratification by twelve more is necessary to make the amendment a part of the Constitution. Eight States which have not ratified, including New York, have legislative sessions during the current year, at which ratification could be voted. But even if all eight ratified, the amendment could not be made effective before 1937, when the Legislatures of other non-ratifying States hold sessions.

In the meantime seven States have adopted their own laws establishing a 16-year minimum age for working children. New York is one of the latest of these, but her legislation does not become effective until next September.

March 22, 1936

Old Evils of Child Labor Curbed by Wage-Hour Law

With Cooperation of the States and Backing of the Public, a Long Crusade Is Believed to Be Approaching a Successful Ending

By BEATRICE McCONNELL
Director, Industrial Division, Children's Bureau, U. S. Labor Dept.

The child labor provisions of the Fair Labor Standards Act of 1938 offer a challenge and a hope to all those concerned with the protection of working children throughout the United States—a challenge to develop standards whereby boys and girls who go to work anywhere in the United States will be protected from the harmful effects of oppressive child labor in so far as they come under the Federal act; a hope that in setting these standards through Federal legislation and administering them in cooperation with the forty-eight States which make up our Federal Government, oppressive child labor will vanish entirely from these United States.

There is no place in a successful democracy for oppressive child labor, and the Fair Labor Standards Act is designed to stop that evil in industries engaged in the production of goods for interstate or foreign commerce.

The act, which went into effect Oct. 24, 1938, defines oppressive child labor as the employment of children under the age of 16 years in any occupation, although it makes exceptions in the case of a parent, or person standing in place of a parent, employing his own child or a child in his custody under the age of 16 in an occupation other than manufacturing or mining. Children employed as actors in motion pictures or theatrical productions are not covered by the act, nor are children employed in agriculture except when legally required to attend school. The employment of minors between the ages of 16 and 18 in any occupation which is found and declared by the chief of the Children's Bureau to be particularly hazardous for children of that age or detrimental to their health or well-being is also defined as oppressive child labor.

Recognizing the fact that some employment may not be "oppressive" for children between the ages of 14 and 16 if it does not interfere with their schooling and if the work is carried on under conditions which will not interfere with their health and well-being, Congress gave to the chief of the Children's Bureau the duty of determining under what conditions and in what occupations such child labor would not be "oppressive." But in no case may children under 16 be permitted to work at any time in manufacturing and mining occupations.

The chief of the Children's Bureau is charged with the administration of all provisions of the act relating to oppressive child labor.

This provision in the act has made it possible for the Children's Bureau to start where it left off when the first Federal Child Labor Law went into effect Sept. 1, 1917, and was administered by the bureau until it was declared unconstitutional by the Supreme Court June 3, 1918. The regulations drawn up at that time, the forms worked out, the methods of cooperation with the various States which were tried, have been invaluable background for the industrial division of the Children's Bureau in its task of putting into effect the child labor provisions of the new act.

States Progressed

But even more important as a background for successful administration today is the progress that has been made in legislation in the States since those early days. Standards that were incorporated in the first Federal act and recommended to the States by the Children's Bureau in the intervening years have since been made a part of the child labor and education laws of many States.

Some States that permitted children as young as 14 years or even less to leave school for work in factories and mines have since raised the age requirement to 16 for such occupations. Some States that twenty years ago had no State-wide system for the issuance of employment certificates have amended their laws to provide for such systems. Other States have strengthened their school attendance laws, and in many States labor departments have been established and special inspectors appointed for the enforcement of child labor laws.

A Wise Provision

Congress wisely provided in the act that the chief of the Children's Bureau, with their consent and cooperation, might utilize the services of State and local agencies charged with the administration of State labor laws. Such cooperation has come readily from nearly all of the forty-eight States and plans are being worked out to avoid overlapping of functions, duplication of work and conflict of authority in the carrying out of the program.

Basic to effective administration is the provision in the act for proof of age for children entering employment, as a safeguard against employment of such children below the legal age. The act provides that "oppressive child labor shall not be deemed to exist by virtue of the employment in any occupation of any person with respect to whom the employer shall have on file an unexpired certificate issued and held pursuant to regulations of the chief of the Children's Bureau certifying that such person is above

24

the oppressive child labor age." Therefore, the first basis for co-operation with States has been the development of systems of issuance of certificates of age for all children going to work

Cooperation in Effect

By Nov. 22, 1938, less than a month after the law went into effect, forty-one States and the District of Columbia had been designated for a period of six months as States in which State employment and age certificates will have the same force and effect as Federal certificates. In Idaho, where the State law does not provide for the issuance of work permits, Federal

certificates will be issued through the Department of Public Instruction under an agreement which has been worked out with that State.

Plans for cooperation have been worked out with two other States and will be put into operation shortly. At the beginning of January only four States remain in which no cooperative plan has been agreed upon, but a temporary regulation has been issued to take care of the situation in those States.

Hazardous Occupations

Another phase of this program to outlaw oppressive child labor is the determination of occupations hazardous for the employment of

minors between 16 and 18 years of age or detrimental to their health or well-being. Basic procedures governing the determination of occupations as hazardous under the act were set forth by the chief of the Children's Bureau in regulation No. 5, issued Nov. 4, 1938. This regulation guarantees to interested parties opportunity for a hearing on any proposed order before a final order is issued.

The provisions determining maximum hours and minimum wages for all workers covered by the act apply regardless of age. Since child labor has always been a problem of low wages, the wage and hour provisions, applying as they do to

minors the same as to adults, will undoubtedly be a most effective deterrent to child labor.

There are, of course, many limitations in the administration of the Federal act. There are many related problems which must be solved along with the attempt to wipe out oppressive child labor through legislation. But all of us together, legislative bodies, administrative officials, organized groups of people everywhere, can help meet the challenge and keep alive the hope that oppressive child labor is on the way out in the United States of America.

January 8, 1939

WAGE LAW UPHELD BY SUPREME COURT; OLD DECISION UPSET

Justice Stone Writes Opinion Overruling a 22-Year-Old Child Labor Case

TEXTILE WAGE IS BACKED

Industry Committee's Finding Is Supported Despite Plea of South for Differential

By LEWIS WOOD
Special to The New York Times.

WASHINGTON, Feb. 3—The constitutionality of the Federal Wage and Hour Law, last of the major New Deal statutes to face a legal challenge, was unanimously sustained by the Supreme Court today in an opinion affecting minimum wages for millions of workers.

Justice Stone ruled that Congress was empowered to prevent shipment in interstate commerce of materials produced by employes receiving less or working longer than the standards set in the act. Remarking that Congress intended the Wage and Hour Law to bar interstate traffic in goods produced under substandard labor conditions, the court specifically overruled the twenty-two-year-old decision holding the Federal child labor law invalid.

Dealing with another phase of the Wage and Hour Law, the court, again through Justice Stone, upheld the validity of the determination of a special industry committee setting a 32½-cent minimum hourly wage for cotton textile workers. Southern cotton mills at-

tacked the determination, which was made as part of an order fixing this minimum wage for all the 650,000 workers of the textile industry.

The Wage and Hour decision, together with another holding Federal anti-trust laws inapplicable to jurisdictional disputes of labor unions, stood out in a list of nearly twenty decisions handed down from a bench reduced to eight justices by the retirement of Justice McReynolds, who was 79 years old today.

Lumber Company Is Involved

Justice Stone handed down his principal opinion in the case of the F. W. Darby Lumber Company of Statesboro, Ga., indicted for failure to pay the required 25-cent minimum hourly wage and time and one-half for hours longer than a forty-four week, failing to keep proper records and shipping into interstate commerce lumber produced by workers paid less than the provisions of the act.

The indictment was based on actions of the concern shortly after the law became effective in 1938. Since then the wage level has been raised to 30 cents hourly and the work week set at forty hours.

The challenge to the special industry committee finding came from the Opp Cotton Mills of Opp, Ala., and ten other Southern cotton mills.

In this case Justice Stone upheld the Fifth Circuit Court of Appeals. In the Darby case he upset the Southern Georgia Federal District Court. In the latter Judge William H. Barrett quashed the indictment on the ground that the Wage and Hour Law, which he interpreted as a regulation of manufacture within the States, was unconstitutional.

Almost at the outset of his ruling Justice Stone commented that while manufacture was not of itself interstate commerce, the shipment of manufactured goods in interstate commerce "is such commerce." He added that the prohibition of such commerce by Congress was "indubitably" a regulation of commerce.

Commerce Power Is Defined

"The power to regulate commerce," he continued, citing authorities, "is the power 'to pre-

scribe the rule by which commerce is governed.' It extends not only to those regulations which aid, foster and protect the commerce, but embraces those which prohibit it.

"It is conceded that the power of Congress to prohibit transportation in interstate commerce includes noxious articles, stolen articles, kidnapped persons and articles such as intoxicating liquors or convict-made goods, traffic in which is forbidden or restricted by the laws of the State of destination.

"The power of Congress over interstate commerce 'is complete in itself, may be exercised to its utmost extent, and acknowledges no limitations other than are prescribed by the Constitution.'

"That power can neither be enlarged nor diminished by the exercise of State power. Congress, following its own conception of public policy concerning the restrictions which may appropriately be imposed on interstate commerce, is free to exclude from the commerce articles whose use in the States for which they are destined it may conceive to be injurious to the public health, morals or welfare, even though the Senate has not sought to regulate their use.

"Such regulation is not a forbidden invasion of State power merely because either its motive or its consequence is to restrict the use of articles of commerce within the States of destination and is not prohibited unless by other constitutional provisions.

"It is no objection to the assertion of the power to regulate interstate commerce that its exercise is attended by the same incidents which attend the exercise of the police power of the States."

The motive and purpose of the Wage and Hour Law, Justice Stone said, is plainly to make effective "the Congressional conception of public policy that interstate commerce should not be made the instrument of competition in the distribution of goods produced under substandard labor conditions, which competition is injurious to the commerce and to the States from and to which the commerce flows."

"The motive and purpose of a regulation of interstate commerce are matters for the legislative judgment upon the exercise of which the Constitution places no restriction and over which the courts are given no control," he added.

At this point Justice Stone took up the 1918 decision in Hammer v.

Dagenhart, in which the Supreme Court in a five-to-four decision ruled that Congress was powerless to exclude the products of child labor from interstate commerce. In this case the late Justice Oliver Wendell Holmes delivered what Justice Stone called "a powerful and now classic dissent." Justice Brandeis joined Justice Holmes in saying that Congress had the right to bar any interstate commerce it saw fit.

"The reasoning and conclusion of the court's opinion there," Mr. Stone said of the child labor case, "cannot be reconciled with the conclusion which we have reached, that the power of Congress under the commerce clause is plenary to exclude any article from interstate commerce, subject only to the specific prohibitions of the Constitution.

"Hammer v. Dagenhart has not been followed. The distinction on which the decision was rested, that Congressional power to prohibit interstate commerce is limited to articles which in themselves have some harmful or deleterious property, a distinction which was novel when made and unsupported by any provision of the Constitution, has long since been abandoned.

"The conclusion is inescapable that Hammer v. Dagenhart was a departure from the principles which have prevailed in the interpretation of the commerce clause both before and since the decision and that such vitality, as a precedent, as it then had has long since been exhausted. It should be and now is overruled."

Later Justice Stone discussed the interpretation of "production for commerce" and said that Congress evidently intended that these words meant woods which, at the time of production, the employer intended to move in interstate commerce.

"There remains," he remarked, "the question whether such restriction on the production of goods for commerce is a permissible exercise of the commerce power. The power of Congress over interstate commerce is not confined to the regulation of commerce among the States.

"It extends to those activities intrastate which so affect interstate commerce or the exercise of the power of Congress over it as to make regulation of them appropriate means to the attainment of a legitimate end, the exercise of the granted power of Congress to regulate interstate commerce."

Congress may, said Justice Stone, regulate "intrastate activities where they have a substantial effect on interstate commerce."

"A recent example," he stated, "is the National Labor Relations

Act for the regulation of employer and employe relations in industries in which strikes, induced by unfair labor practices named in the act, tend to disturb or obstruct interstate commerce.

"But long before the adoption of the National Labor Relations Act this court had many times held that the power of Congress to regulate interstate commerce extends to the regulation through legislative action of activities intrastate which have a substantial effect on the commerce or the exercise of the Congressional power over it.

"The Sherman act and the National Labor Relations Act are familiar examples of the exertion of the commerce power to prohibit or control activities wholly intrastate because of their effect on interstate commerce."

In the ruling sustaining the textile industry wage, Justice Stone denied that here was an invalid delegation of legislative power to the Wage and Hour Administrator.

"The mandate of the Constitution that all legislative powers granted 'shall be vested' in Congress has never been thought to preclude

Congress from resorting to the aid of administrative officers or boards as fact-finding agencies whose findings, made in conformity to previously adopted legislative standards or definitions of Congressional policy have been made prerequisitive to the operation of its statutory command," the Justice stated.

"The adoption of the declared policy by Congress and its definition of the circumstances in which its command is to be effective constitute the performance, in the constitutional sense, of the legislative function."

In the same opinion the court sustained the validity of the procedure set up for establishing wage minima above those prescribed in the act and ruled that the cotton textile industry committee and the administrator had complied with that procedure.

The cotton mills challenged the wage-hour administrator's findings, which were based on the committee's study, on the ground that a wage differential should have been granted to the South because of the difference between conditions existing there and in other textile centers.

"We conclude that the administrator's findings are supported by substantial evidence," Justice Stone stated. "Any different conclusion would require us to substitute our judgment of the weight of the evidence and the inference to be drawn from it for that of the administrator, which the statute forbids."

Notwithstanding the pronouncement of Justice Stone on the Child Labor Law as it affects interstate commerce, Gerard D. Reilly, Labor Department solicitor, said that neither the opinion nor any Congressional enlargement of the Wage and Hour Law would remove the necessity of State ratification of the Child Labor Amendment if the labor of minors in intrastate commerce was to be protected.

According to experts, an interesting sidelight on the wage and hour decision and the setting aside of the child labor ruling was that by its action the court automatically resurrected the child labor law fostered by former Representative Edward Keating which had been declared illegal in 1918.

In the same way, the court, it was said, held valid a minimum-wage law which also had been adopted for the District of Columbia, a Federal territory, at Mr. Keating's motion, which was also declared unconstitutional in 1918.

To Press for Amendment
By The Associated Press.

WASHINGTON, Feb. 3 — Miss Katharine F. Lenroot, chief of the Children's Bureau, said that efforts to get the long-pending Child Labor Amendment ratified would continue because the Wage-Hour Law, upheld today by the Supreme Court, covers only children in interstate commerce industries.

To protect all children it is necessary to have legislation regulating their employment in intrastate industries as well as interstate, Miss Lenroot said.

In 1924 Congress approved the Child Labor Amendment and it was submitted to the States. Since then twenty-eight States have ratified it. Eight more States are needed.

Miss Beatrice McConnell, head of the industrial division of the Children's Bureau, estimated that only one-fourth of the children gainfully employed were in interstate industries.

February 4, 1941

CHILD LABOR DROP NOTED IN REPORT

Plight of the Migratory Farm Youth Deplored by Group —Accidents Cited

Legislation has virtually eliminated the employment of children in canneries, factories and mines in the United States, but agriculture continues to be the last stronghold of child labor.

This situation is pointed out in the fifty-second annual report of the National Child Labor Committee, which cites the plight of the children of migratory farm workers. These children also follow the crops and help their parents to plant and to harvest. Frequently these children "labor in the fields at arduous toil unprotected by state labor regulations and inadequately safeguarded by Federal laws," according to Sol Markoff, executive secretary of the committee, who prepared the report. He quotes from a study of the United States Children's Bureau, which notes that few of the migratory children "ever see a doctor, a teacher, a child welfare worker or a nurse."

Children injured or killed while operating tractors are singled out for attention in the committee's report.

"Fragmentary reports culled from the nation's press last year," Mr. Markoff said, "show that 235 boys and girls were involved in serious accidents last year. Among this group, seventy-seven were killed and the rest badly crippled. The majority of these youngsters are under 14 years of age."

Part-time employment of children is also mentioned in the report. It states that last year nearly four million young people, or about 42 per cent of the 14-to-17-year-old population, were employed some time during the year. This employment was largely in part-time jobs outside of school hours and during school vacations.

Noting that many youths who drop out of high school before graduation have a difficult time in obtaining employment, Mr. Markoff said that "it is socially undesirable for youths to be out of school and out of work."

The National Child Labor Committee is a voluntary organization with offices at 419 Fourth Avenue. It was organized in 1904 and was incorporated by Congress in 1907. Dr. F. Ernest Johnson is the chairman of the board of trustees.

The organization seeks to promote the welfare of society with respect to the employment of children in gainful occupations; to investigate and report the facts concerning child labor; to raise the standards of parental responsibility with respect to the employment of children, and to assist in protecting children by suitable legislation against premature or otherwise injurious employment.

December 2, 1956

Yes, Child Labor Is Still a Problem

By CASSANDRA STOCKBURGER

Lewis Hine wrote in 1911: "I am sometimes inclined to think that we must mutilate these infants in industry before the shame of it can be driven home. The horror of placing an industrial mortgage upon the back of a perfectly good child does not seem to be obvious."

Many Americans find it difficult to believe that child labor remains a legal and moral problem in this country. The fact, however, is that children employed in agriculture are not adequately protected under the child-labor provisions of the Fair Labor Standards Act. While no child under sixteen can work during the hours school is in session, outside those hours and during vacation periods there is no Federal regulation governing work by children of any age in agriculture. In addition, only a few states have child labor laws applicable to agricultural work.

This is not a problem that affects only a small group of children. In 1971 the Department of Labor reported that more than one-fourth of the country's seasonal farm work force—roughly 800,000 out of 3.1 million—were children under age sixteen. Of these almost half were between ten and thirteen. The proportion has reached as high as 75 per cent in some states, such as Oregon, Washington and Louisiana. In Maine 35 per cent of the potato harvest is gathered by more than 15,000 children aged five and older.

Defenders of the present situation say that work in the fields is good for children: they get fresh air, exercise, lessons in good work habits and the value of money. They ignore the fact that agriculture, along with construction and mining, is one of the three most hazardous industries. Dangerous machinery and lethal pesticides are constant threats to many children in the fields. Fatal and crippling accidents are frequent.

When the pseudohumane myths are uncovered, supporters of child labor contend that without the children's work the crop would go unharvested, small farmers would be bankrupt, agricultural laboring families could not support themselves. Yet, in spring 1972 the present child-labor law was enforced in the Louisiana strawberry harvest where 75 per cent of the workers were children illegally employed during regular school hours. No crop went unharvested. No farmer went bankrupt. Local unemployed adults were recruited at higher wages than those paid the migrant children.

Work contributes to widespread educational retardation, especially among migrant farm children. The Department of Labor reports that 84 per cent of the fifteen-year-olds found illegally working were enrolled below the normal grade level for their age. Only 22 per cent of migrant children remain in school beyond the sixth grade.

The inhuman conditions of child labor in other industries were banned in 1938. Yet children still work in the fields for as long as ten hours a day— there are no regulations governing working hours—in 100-degree heat, at poverty wages, all over America. A study of child labor in agriculture in summer 1970 gives a typical case: "One family the Maine team observed included seven children, of whom six worked in the fields. Their average day began at 5:15 A.M. with breakfast. In the field by 6 A.M., they worked to 5 P.M., with a one-hour break for lunch. On one day, these children brought in 200 barrels of potatoes— everyone gets the piece rate of thirty cents per barrel. This means you have to pick 45 barrels a day to gross at least $70 for a five-day week."

In midsummer the Senate passed a bill to amend the Fair Labor Standards Act. This bill, which is now under consideration by a joint Senate-House conference committee, would improve, if not completely remedy, the situation. It would extend the protection to children in agriculture outside of school hours that the law now applies to children working in other industries. It would also prohibit agricultural work by children under twelve;

those between twelve and sixteen would be permitted to work under certain conditions.

The Senate bill, while it would not provide the maximum protection necessary for children in agriculture, would mark an important step forward. Its provisions are the absolute minimum protection that we can offer a truly victimized group of American children. On the basis of my experience working with migrant children, I am convinced that employment in agriculture must be governed on the same basis as in all other industries. If that were the case, no child under sixteen could be employed except on his parents' farm.

Public support and favorable action by the conference committee on the Senate bill amending the Fair Labor Standards Act is essential. Thousands of children with no legal protection against exploitation, with no real hope of educational and economic advancement and social mobility, are calling on the conscience of the country.

Cassandra Stockburger is director of the National Committee on the Education of Migrant Children.

September 4, 1972

THE CHILD AS VICTIM

PROTECTION FOR CHILDREN.

ORGANIZATION OF A SOCIETY FOR THE PREVENTION OF CRUELTY TO CHILDREN— ITS SCOPE OF ACTION AND ITS OBJECTS.

The apprehension and subsequent conviction of the persecutors of little Mary Ellen, some time since, suggested to Mr. Elbridge T. Gerry, the counsel engaged in the prosecution of the case, the necessity for the existence of an organized society for the prevention of similar acts of atrocity. Upon expressing his views among his friends, he found plenty of sympathizers with the movement, but no one sufficiently interested to attempt the formation of such a society. About this time he met Mr. John D. Wright, to whom he stated his plan. The latter at once became warmly interested, and undertook the necessary steps toward effecting an organization. Invitations were extended to a large number of prominent citizens interested in the welfare of children to meet at Association Hall on Tuesday afternoon, and many promptly responded. Mr. Gerry defined the object of the meeting, which, he said, was to organize a society for the prevention of cruelty to children. There were in existence in this City and State, he said, many

excellent institutions, some as charitable corporations, and others as State reformatories and asylums, for receiving and caring for little children. Among these might be cited the Children's Aid Society, Society for the Protection of Destitute Children, &c., and in addition each religious denomination had one or more hospitals and similar institutions devoted to the moral and physical culture of helpless children. These societies, however, only assumed the care of their inmates after they had been legally placed in their custody. It was not in the province of these excellent institutions to seek out and rescue from the dens and slums of the City the little unfortunates whose lives were rendered miserable by the system of cruelty and abuse which was constantly practiced upon them by the human brutes who happened to possess the custody or control of them; and this was the defect which it was proposed to remedy by the formation of this society. There were plenty of laws existing on the statute books of the State, which provided for all such cases as had been cited, but unfortunately no one had heretofore been held responsible for their enforcement. The Police and prosecuting officers were engaged in the prosecution and conviction of offenses of a graver legal character; and, although they were always ready to aid in enforcing the laws when duly called upon to do so, they could not be expected to discover and prosecute those who claimed the right to ill-treat the children over whom they had an apparent legal control. This society proposed to enforce legally, but energetically, the existing laws and to secure the conviction and punishment of

every violator of any of those laws. The society would not interfere with the numerous institutions already existing, but would aid them in their work. It did not propose to aid any single religious denomination, and would be kept entirely free from any political influences. Its duty toward the children would be discharged when their future custody should be decided by the courts. The counsel for the society volunteers his gratuitous services in the prosecution of cases reported by its officers during the first year. The Secretary will be entitled to a moderate compensation, but no salary will be paid to the remaining officers.

The following board of officers was elected:
President, John D. Wright; Vice Presidents, James Brown, Peter Cooper, William E. Dodge, Cornelius Vanderbilt, John J. Cisco, Robert L. Stuart, August Belmont, Theodore Roosevelt, Henry Bergh, Elbridge T. Gerry; Secretary, John L. Griffen; Treasurer, William L. Jenkins; Counsel, Elbridge T. Gerry; Executive Committee, Wilson G. Hunt, Louis J. Jennings, Joseph Seligman, D. Willis James, Robert Colgate, Evan T. Walker, Jonathan Thorne, Benjamin H. Field, Burden B. Sherman, Israel Corse, William M. Vermilyea, Henry Bergh, John Howard Wright, J. G. Bennett, Thomas C. Acton.

The Secretary will be provided with a book in which all parties who desire to enroll themselves as members may do so at the office of the society, which will be located temporarily in the office of the Society for the Prevention of Cruelty to Animals, No. 100 East Twenty-second street. The first annual meeting of the society will be held on Dec. 23, 1875.

December 17, 1874

HOW CHILDREN ARE ABUSED.

MEETING OF THE SOCIETY FOR PREVENTING CRUELTY TO CHILDREN—THE WORK DONE DURING SIX MONTHS—TYPICAL CASES SHOWING MALTREATMENT AND NEGLECT.

An important meeting of the Board of Managers of the New-York Society for the Prevention of Cruelty to Children was held yesterday afternoon at the rooms of the society, No. 50 Union-square. Hon. Thomas C. Acton presided. Among those present were John D. Wright, Frederick De Peyster, Charles Haight, Wilson M. Powell, Lewis L. Delafield, William H. Gibson, William L. Jenkins, Benjamin H. Field, B. B. Sherman, Jacob W. Mack, Sinclair Tousey, and others. Forty-three members of the society

were elected. The following report of the society's work for the past six months was made by the Secretary:
Complaints received...........................380
Complaints investigated........................361
Advice given in cases of complaints.............19
Prosecutions for cruelty.......................154
Children sent to homes for adoption or to institutions..199

Among the cases reported were many showing most outrageous brutality and cruel treatment toward children of tender years. Many cases were also reported where young girls had been taken from the streets and from vile dens, and placed in homes or institutions. Among some of the typical cases presented in the report, and the result of the society's interference, are the following:

Herman Meyer, for assaulting a little girl 6 years

old, was sent to the Penitentiary for 18 months. Sabina Quigley, for drunkenness and beating her 6-year old daughter and badly cutting her head with a pitcher, was sent to the Penitentiary for one month. Norah Campbell got drunk and neglected her children, who were found in a frightfully filthy condition, with hardly any clothing on their persons. The room in which they were was absolutely devoid of all furniture. The mother was sent to the Penitentiary for one month, and the children were provided with clothing and homes. The mother has reformed and is in respectable employment. She has returned and has thanked the society for its work. She says she will soon be able to provide a home for her children.

Timothy Collopy assaulted a girl 10 years of age and knocked her down. He was imprisoned for four months. James Kearney, for striking a 6-year old

27

boy across the face with a whip, was fined $20. Luigi Tenasa, who brutally assaulted his 8-year old daughter and bruised her back and side terribly, was sent to the Penitentiary for one month. Antonio Lagruta, for letting his children out to beg, was given the option to pay $50 or be imprisoned for 50 days.

Catherine McGuckin went about the street in an intoxicated condition to beg. With her was a child 9 years old, and a baby. She was sent to the Work-house for six months, and homes were found for the children. Patrick Tenety, a widower, for drunkenness and neglecting his four children, was sent to the Penitentiary for one month. Rosanna Cusick, for neglecting her 3-months old child, was sent to the City Prison for 10 days. Kate McLaughlin beat and scratched her step-daughter, who is 10 years old, so that the child's face is badly marked. The woman was sent to the City Prison for 10 days, and a home was found for the girl. Catherine Welsh, who neglected her 2-year old child, was sent to the Penitentiary for three months. Catherine Farley, for neglecting her 16-months old child, was imprisoned for two months. The child was suffering from disease, and was removed to a hospital for treatment.

James and Catharine Noonan were arrested for neglecting their two children. The family were in a terrible condition when found. They had hardly a stick of furniture. The children were without clothing, and one of them was nearly dead from neglect and disease. The father was found lying intoxicated in a hallway, and the mother, also intoxicated, was roaming about the streets. One of the children was removed to St. Mary's Hospital, and the other to the Roman Catholic Protectory. The father was imprisoned for 10 days, and the mother for three months. The case of Patrick and Catharine McCahill was much the same as the above. These persons with their six children were found almost wallowing in filth. One of the children was dead in the arms of its mother, who lay on the floor stupefied with liquor. The children were cared for and the parents were sent to the Penitentiary for four months.

Mary Pfeiffer was found with her five small children in a very filthy condition. Her husband is said to have deserted her, and she was partially demented. The members of Engine Company No. 22, and some neighbors, rendered aid to the woman, but she was in such a state that she refused to cook or care for the children. She was removed to Bellevue Hospital for treatment, and the children were cared for by the Society of St. Vincent De Paul and by the woman's relatives. The latter had refused to do anything for the children until the Society for the Prevention of Cruelty took action in the matter. Bridget Connolly, who, while intoxicated went begging in the street, accompanied by a child, was sent to the Island for 30 days. A home was found for the child. Theodore Stock, for assaulting a 6-year-old girl, was sent to the Penitentiary for a year. Peter Epson was sent to the Penitentiary for one month for cruelly beating a 9-year-old girl in his employ. A good home was found for the girl by the Women's Aid Society.

Frank and Mary Mason were found in an attic with two children, one of whom was 15 months and the other 4 weeks old. Both parents were grossly intoxicated. The room was frightfully filthy and the children were very dirty. The parents were sent to the Penitentiary for six months. Terence and Mary Boyle, for neglecting and beating their two children, were sent to the Penitentiary for two months each. Homes were found for the children. Annie Love, for drunkenness and begging with her two children, was sent to the Work-house for three months. The children were provided with homes. Mary Bohan was sent to the Penitentiary for three months for neglecting her children. One of the latter was in such a condition that it was necessary to remove it to St. Mary's Hospital for care and treatment. Thomas Ward, for cutting the face of an 11-year-old girl with the lash of a whip, was sent to the City Prison for 15 days. William McClusky, for neglecting and abusing his children and putting one out of doors late at night, was sent to the Penitentiary for three months. William Porcher, for neglecting and abandoning his three children, was sent to the Penitentiary for one year. The children, who had been aided by Police Capt. Petty, were provided with good homes.

In cases where families were found in extreme destitution the children were clothed, and, where desired, homes were found for the little ones. The society makes an appeal for cast-off clothing, to be used for destitute children.

October 12, 1877

WORK OF CHILDREN'S BUREAU

WITH the appointment of Miss Julia C. Lathrop of the Illinois State Board of Charities as Chief of the Children's Bureau the first National agency for child welfare has entered upon its active work.

The Children's Bureau, in its work, will cover the entire field of childhood in America. Everything that has to do with child life will come under the headings of the Bureau's activities. Its function is to "investigate and report," to quote the bill as the President signed it—"upon all matters pertaining to the welfare of children and child life."

It will have, of course, no power to act, no authority to direct the passage or the enforcement of laws, yet it needs but a cursory examination of the bureau's field, child workers explain, to see that the bureau's results in action will be more far-reaching than anything that has ever been accomplished for the children of America.

Infant mortality, the birth rate, blindness in children, disease in children—all that pertains to children's health—forms one of these special features. Physical, mental, and moral degeneracy is another. Children's playgrounds and recreation centres will be reported upon. The problem of the child orphan, to which we pay now little systematic attention, will fall within the province of the Children's Bureau. The entire field of child delinquency, child reform, and the juvenile court, will be investigated by the Bureau. Deserted children will be objects of the Bureau's attention. And the whole wide question of child labor, in all its details and with all its ramifications, will be open to the light that the Bureau's investigations will throw. The Bureau in all these matters, will report conditions, trace causes, advise relief.

The work of the Children's Bureau, generally speaking, will be to provide a common channel into which all the streams of child interests flow. It plans to do this in two ways—first by considering the welfare of children as a whole, with the interrelations of various child-problems; and second by considering the United States of America as a whole, with the interaction of various State laws and customs. No such study of interrelations has ever been made: no such central and disinterested consideration of the differing rulings of different communities has ever been possible. The problem of the American child has been split up into bits, and has been therefore, insoluble. The Children's Bureau, to the minds of all child workers, offers the first possibility of a solution.

Summed up as briefly as possible, and in its barest outlines, the work of the Children's Bureau will be to collect and disseminate information regarding children. In so doing the Bureau will inevitably establish precedents, as when the measures taken for the care of a deserted child in New York, made public by the Bureau, serve as a model for the treatment of a similar case in Birmingham, Alabama. It will, as inevitably, work for the higher efficiency of the various State and city departments touching upon child problems, and it will sooner or later tend toward the establishment, if not definitely of uniform laws, certainly of uniform customs, in regard to child labor, truancy, juvenile courts, infant mortality, defective children, and the other problems, for the solution of which the different States adopt such different methods.

Among the early undertakings of the Children's Bureau will probably be the sending out of a series of questions to truant officers and compulsory education boards in the large cities of the country, applying for definite information as to truancy and its causes and effects.

"This particular work gives a good example of how the Children's Bureau, unempowered for action as, of course, it must be, will still be a means to raise the standard of department efficiency," said Owen R. Lovejoy, Secretary of the National Child Labor Committee. "The bureau, in sending out these questions, uniform for all cities, will take no 'action' on them. But the mere fact that the questions are there to be asked, that the truant laws and their enforcement in each city will be made public, will spur the officials to greater care and greater efficiency.

"At the same time, the information as to living and working conditions, the knowledge of how problems are solved in various communities will, when made public by a Federal, disinterested bureau, act toward the establishment of uniformity, toward the adoption of the best methods known. No State Legislature likes to be told that it ought to do things a certain way in its State because another State does it thus and so. But when it is pointed out by a Federal bureau that, for instance, the Factory Inspection Bureau of one State is a better thing than the management of the factory problems of another, the comparison is more likely to result in action.

"The National Child Labor Committee has worked very hard for the establishment of the bureau, and we feel that if we have never accomplished another thing this alone would have justified our existence. The creation of the Children's Bureau is undoubtedly the greatest thing that has been done for the children of this country. Many people consider it, and I agree with them, the greatest piece of legislation in years. The interest of the Child Labor Committee in the establishment of the Children's Bureau is due to two causes.

"First, we know that the reports of a Government authority, known to be a public bureau, known to be disinterested, will of necessity be received with greater attention and will be productive of greater results than the investigations, however careful, of a private organization such as our own. We are very particular about our investigation, very conservative in our reports. But we can always be attacked as 'hysterical' just because we are a private body with no Government authority behind us. That, of course, will not be the case with the Children's Bureau or its findings.

"In the second place the Children's Bureau, being National, will be able to get over State boundaries. And it will be able also to work with problems of child labor not only as child labor problems, but as they are bound up with the other problems of education, health and citizenship.

"Here is a case in point: In certain oyster canning plants in Florida, little children are employed all Winter, under conditions, by the way, of absolute filth, as 'helpers.' Some of them are negro children; most of them are Poles and Hungarians. And these Poles and Hungarians are not Florida children, they are imported from Baltimore.

"Every Fall these children are sent down from Maryland to Florida, and every Spring they are shipped back again. All Winter they work in the oyster canneries on the Florida coast, and our agents are told that it is all right for them to work in the Winter because in the Spring the oyster season is over and the children go to school. But as soon as their work in Florida is ended and they are sent back to Maryland, they are put to work immediately on the fruit canning—and our agents are told that of course they work in the Summer, but then they go to school all the rest of the year. Now it is not possible to do anything with that inter-State commerce in children; we found it out only by accident. The Children's Bureau, being a Federal body, will be empowered to investigate just such cases as that.

"And what is more, the case of little

Maria in Baltimore, investigated by the bureau, will serve as a precedent in caring for some other little Maria in New York or Boston or Los Angeles."

The idea of a Federal Children's Bureau originated five years ago with Miss Lillian Wald, headworker of the Henry Street settlement in New York and a member of the Board of Trustees of the National Child Labor Committee. Other workers before had felt vaguely the need for a concentration of child interests, but Miss Wald was the first to give articulate form to the conception of a need.

In formulating the plan for a possible Federal organization she was immediately aided by Mrs. Florence Kelley, National Secretary of the Consumers' League, who made the first definite outline of the matters to be investigated by such a Bureau were it formed. Miss Jane Addams, Dr. Samuel McCune Lindsay of the New York School of Philanthropy, and Owen R. Lovejoy, General Secretary of the National Child Labor Committee, entered at once upon the campaign for the creation of the Children's Bureau, and these five have been the leaders in the movement that has led to the Bureau's establishment.

For the last four years, Dr. A. J. McKelway, Secretary of the National Child Labor Committee in the Southern States, has been in Washington directing the campaign there. From the first formulation of the plan, the Child Labor Committee has been in the forefront of the movement to bring about a Federal department for children; but as soon as the movement was under way other associations took up the fight; the Bureau's establishment is the victory, not of any one organization, or of any small group of workers, but of the various activities for the welfare of the American child.

Miss Wald, in reviewing the history of the campaign for a Children's Bureau, said that in 1906 she brought the matter to the attention of President Roosevelt.

"When it was our pleasure to bring this suggestion before the President," she explained, "his first expression of approval was, if I remember rightly, 'That is bully.' It was a coincidence that the Secretary of Agriculture was departing that same morning for the South to find out what danger to the community lurked in the appearance of the boll weevil. That brought home, with a very strong emphasis to the appeal, the fact that nothing that could have happened to the children would have called forth, at that time, such official action on the part of the Government."

In 1909, the Conference on the Care of Dependent Children unanimously adopted a resolution calling for the creation of a Children's Bureau.

Practically every State Board of Charities and every juvenile court was represented.

The bill, as it finally passed the Senate on Jan. 31, and the House on April 2 of this year, to be signed by the President soon after, says:

That the said bureau shall be under the direction of a chief, to be appointed by the President, by and with the advice and consent of the Senate, and who shall receive an annual compensation of $5,000. The said bureau shall investigate and report upon all matters pertaining to the welfare of children and child life, and shall especially investigate the questions of infant mortality, the birth rate, physical degeneracy, orphanage, juvenile courts, desertion, dangerous occupations, accidents and diseases of children, employment, legislation affecting children in the several States and Territories. No official or agent or representative of said bureau shall, over the objection of the head of the family, enter any house used exclusively as a family residence. The chief of said bureau may from time to time publish the results of these investigations.

Miss Lathrop was chosen by President Taft. She is the first woman to be made head of a Federal commission in this country, and she will be paid the highest salary of any woman in the Government employ. Hers will be unquestionably the most important position held by any woman in this country.

Miss Lathrop has been for twenty years a member of the Illinois State Board of Charities, and has long been associated with Miss Addams at Hull House. She is a member of the Board of Trustees of Vassar College, and is a Vassar graduate. She has recently returned from a trip around the world to study the penal systems of various countries, and she is known as an authority on criminology.

There was no question of the appropriateness of choosing a woman as head of the Children's Bureau. As President Taft said in a letter to Owen Lovejoy, the position was one in which there could be no consideration of sex. Miss Lathrop was chosen because she was considered both by the President and by the various associations interested to be eminently fitted for the leadership of a work which should unite the interests of childhood.

In his letter to Mr. Lovejoy, President Taft pointed out that the creation of the Children's Bureau and the choice of its head was a matter that had nothing to do with sex or with politics. That it has not been a political question has already been proved by a canvas, before the bill went through, of the Presidential candidates. President Taft signed the bill and has long been known to favor it. Col. Roosevelt, during his term in the White House, urged the bureau's establishment in a special message to Congress. At the present Congress Speaker Clark insisted that his name be called in the roll when the bill was brought up, in order that he might vote for it. Mr. Underwood used his influence to bring about its passage, and Woodrow Wilson, Senator La Follette, and Eugene Debs have all spoken in its favor.

September 29, 1912

CHILD-ABUSE LAW URGED ON STATES

Government Steps Up Effort as Cases Increase

By MARJORIE HUNTER
Special to The New York Times

WASHINGTON, Dec. 19 — The Government plans to increase pressure on the states next year to enact legislation aimed at reducing the abuse of children.

Child abuse is not new. But in recent years there has been a marked increase in the violence of attacks on infants and small children by parents or caretakers, according to officials of the Department of Health, Education and Welfare.

Reports of abuse come to the department's Children's Bureau from all over.

In this city, for instance, a father held his infant son under a scalding hot-water faucet.

In Cincinnati, an infant boy was chained to the bed when his unwed mother went out on dates.

In Chicago, a 27-month girl was sexually abused by her drunken stepfather.

Called a Disease

Hospitals report admitting infants and small children with strap marks, multiple fractures, ruptured livers, crippled limbs and even brain hemorrhages.

Doctors and social worker refer to such abuse as a syndrome. But it is not a reportable disease. The Government believes it should be as reportable as gunshot wounds or typhoid fever.

The Children's Bureau recently sent suggested legislation to the states. It would require that all cases of child abuse be reported by doctors and hospitals to the appropriate police authorities.

Legislation is needed, bureau officials say, because many doctors and hospitals do not report such cases, fearing civil or criminal liability in the event their reports cannot be proven.

The suggested legislation would grant them immunity from civil and criminal liability.

Recent surveys have underscored the seriousness of the problem. A Denver study showed that of 302 such cases, 33 children suffered a fatal injury and 85 permanent brain damage.

The Cook County Family Court in Chicago has reported it receives 100 cases a month.

Files of the Children's Protective Service in Cincinnati are heavy with case histories of physically abused babies and youngsters. In some, parents were found to be retarded.

Children's Bureau officials say the cases occur in all levels of society, but most are among low-income families and involve children under 2.

December 20, 1963

Child Beating Attributed To Parents at Wit's End

MIAMI BEACH, March 11 (AP) — A team of pediatricians said today that child beating stems from stresses in the home because parenthood is not always what it is ideally supposed to be.

"If one is honest, one must admit that children are a mixed blessing to the average parent," the team said in a paper presented to an American Medical Association symposium.

Dr. John B. Reinhart and Elizabeth Elmer of the University of Pittsburgh Medical School said: "Children do limit the activities of parents. They are not always easy to deal with and, indeed, some are most difficult. There is nothing so exasperating as a crying, colicky infant, whom one cannot comfort no matter what one does. Perhaps we should be amazed that more children do not suffer assault by parents who have reached their wit's end."

March 12, 1967

Abuse of Children Remains a Puzzle

By JOHN LEO

Psychiatrists are beginning to put together a rough portrait of parents who beat their children, sometimes fatally.

They are finding that race, sex, religion, intelligence quotient and even marital stability are not significant factors in identifying the potential or typical child-beater.

But they are finding that child-beaters, whether slum-dwellers or well-to-do suburbanites, come from authoritarian homes, tend to feel victimized by life and are prone to criticize their children for not meeting impossibly high standards.

There have been a number of child-beating incidents in this area recently, and the Mayor's Task Force on Child Abuse is studying the problem. Yesterday, two more cases were brought to light.

In State Supreme Court in Brooklyn, a 45-year-old ex-convict pleaded guilty to beating his 6-year-old son.

And in Hicksville, L. I., a 41-year-old security analyst, father of three girls, who is under arrest on charges of beating a 9-year-old boy, was accused by parents of eight other boys and girls in alleged assaults.

Last night the chairman of the legislature's judiciary committee on court organization, Peter J. Costigan, Republican of Suffolk County, said that he and a subcommittee member, Alfred Lerner, Republican of Queens, would introduce legislation to improve the handling of child-abuse cases.

He said one bill would provide legal representation for a child by a Police Department lawyer or District Attorney in Family Court. Another proposal would put priority on serving of warants in child mistreatment cases.

In a study of 60 families involved in child-abuse cases, Dr. Brandt F. Steele and Dr. Carl B. Pollock of Denver found that offending parents tend to isolate themselves unnecessarily, and find practical affairs — such as repairs of household appliances — impossibly difficult.

"We have jokingly remarked," the two psychiatrists wrote recently, "that if one goes down the street and sees a house with the blinds drawn in broad daylight, with two unrepaired cars in the driveway, and finds the people have an unlisted phone number, the chances are high that the ihabitants abuse their children."

A more central finding in the Steele-Pollock study, conducted at the University of Colorado School of Medicine, is that in beating their children, a great many parents are re-enacting the treatment handed out to them by their own parents.

"It is axiomatic to the child-beater," Dr. Steele said, "that infants and children exist primarily to satisfy parental needs, that children's and infants' needs are unimportant and should be disregarded and that children who do not fulfill these requirements deserve punishment."

Parents reared this way go on to raise their own children along the same lines, he said.

"It is transmitted from parent to child, generation after generation," he added. To a large extent, it has been socially acceptable, although sub rosa, and to some extent it has been culture-bound."

Dr. Steele's conclusions have been "generally accepted," according to Dr. William Barton of Children's Hospital in Washington, co-author of one of the early articles calling attention to "the battered-child syndrome" in The Journal of the American Medical Association.

However, Dr. Barton, like some other critics, believes the Steele study underestimated the connection between child-beating and poverty.

"Physical punishment, impulsive behavior and the inability of parents to get away from their children for a period of time are all more common to the working class than to the middle class," he said.

Many analysts believe the child-beater is likely to do the most damage while their children are still infants.

"Anxieties are likely to be provoked when the child begins to move, sit and stand," said Dr. Emanuel Schwartz, a psychologist at the Postgraduate Center of Psychotherapy in New York.

"The mother wants to pacify the child, keep it immobile," he explained.

Most analysts offer their opinions tentatively, arguing that research was still in a primitive stage.

"We don't know anywhere near enough," Dr. Schwartz said. "My guess would be that the problems of lower-class living are a major factor. Frustrations are higher among the poor, they live in more cramped quarters and they have less access to outside help."

However, Dr. Steele doubts that the incidence of child-beating follows the poverty line, and points out that he was unable to find a single case of child abuse among poor Spanish-American agricultural workers in the Denver area.

April 10, 1969

2-Year Study Links Child Abuse To the Role of Force in Rearing

By ROBERT REINHOLD
Special to The New York Times

WALTHAM, Mass., Dec. 12— A major nationwide study has traced the high level of child beating in this country to a widespread acceptance among Americans of the use of physical force as a legitimate procedure in child rearing.

This conclusion was reached by Dr. David G. Gil of Brandeis University after an analysis of 13,000 child beating reports in all 50 states. It conflicts with past interpretations, which have generally attributed the abuse to the mental illness of the beater.

"The context of child rearing does not exclude the use of physical force toward children by parents and others responsible for their socialization," Dr. Gil said. "American culture encourages in subtle, and at times not so subtle, ways the use of 'a certain measure' of physical force in rearing children in order to modify their inherently nonsocial inclinations."

But, however bad child beating may be, Dr. Gil said that it constituted only a minor social problem in comparison with what he calls the "collective societal abuse" of the offspring of the poor.

Sees 'Violence Syndrome'

"Millions of children are living and growing up under circumstances of severe social and economic deprivation which tend to inhibit the fullest possible development of their innate capacities," he said, citing poor nutrition, poor medical and dental care and poor education.

He concludes, "Society's violence against its young generation in the form of poverty and discrimination may constitute an important aspect of the violence syndrome, or the 'cycle of violence.'"

These findings are outlined in a new book, "Violence Against Children," just published by the Harvard University Press. They are based on what the Children's Bureau of the Department of Health, Education and Welfare, which sponsored the work, calls the most extensive research on child abuse ever undertaken.

The subject is likely to figure in the White House Conference on Children, that opens tomorrow in Washington.

The "battered child syndrome," as the more severe forms of abuse are known, is one of the most perplexing problems facing health officials. Dr. Gil, who is a professor of social policy, estimated in an interview that as many as 2.5 million children are abused every year. However, reliable statistics are hard to obtain.

Dr. Gil's study encompasses a survey of every incident of child abuse reported nationally through legal channels in 1967 and 1968, as well as detailed analyses of incidents in selected cities. In addition, samples of public attitude were taken by the National Opinion Research Center at the University of Chicago.

Dr. Gil's belief that child abuse stems from society's sanctioning of corporal punishment is based upon the very low incidence of abuse in cultures that have strong taboos against striking children, such as the American Indians. The Indians disciplined their young mainly through example and shame.

The public opinion poll found a "culturally determined permissive attitude" toward corporal punishment among Americans in general.

The study found that abuse tended to occur most often in large families of low socio-economic status and educational achievement. In a sampling of 1,380 reported beatings in 1967, more than half involved Negroes and other non-whites. However, statistics are not entirely reliable because children beaten in more prosperous homes are more likely to be treated by private physicians and to go unreported.

Statistics on Religion

By religion, the breakdown conformed roughly to the proportions found in the general population. Of the 1967 sample, 62 per cent were Protestant, 25.5 Roman Catholic, 0.7 Jewish, 1.8 other religions and 10.1 per cent unknown.

Bruises and welts were the most common type of injuries,

followed by scratches and cuts. Other common injuries were burns and bone fractures.

A majority of the 13,000 incidents reported in 1967 and 1968 were found to have resulted from "more or less acceptable disciplinary measures taken by caretakers in angry response to actual or perceived misconduct."

As a remedy, Dr. Gil called for a "revolutionary change" in the underlying value system that permits striking of children, backed up by laws against corporal punishment in homes, schools, juvenile courts and child care facilities. He also urged a reduction in poverty and said that improved family assistance and counseling were needed.

"Rarely, if ever, is corporal punishment administered for the benefit of the attacked child," Dr. Gill wrote, "For usually it serves the immediate needs of the attacking adult who is seeking relief from his uncontrollable anger and stress."

December 13, 1970

Cathy Hull

A Satisfying Job: Helping End the Abuse of Children

By LINDA CHARLTON

WASHINGTON — About a year and a half ago, Congress established the National Center on Child Abuse and Neglect. This month the center finally got its first director, a New York City lawyer who is a specialist in the problems of children.

Not that the center has been inactive: Under an acting director, it has funded millions of dollars worth of projects around the country, all aimed at defining child abuse, discovering the many reasons that it happens, and above all, doing something about it.

As part of its funding so far, the center has granted $198,000 to Parents Anonymous, to expand its chapters; this group works on the Alcoholics Anonymous principle among parents who abused, or fear they may abuse, their children. Other projects are trying to determine the effects of drugs and alcohol on child abuse, what kinds of treatment are most effective, and what makes a parent relapse into abuse after having stopped it.

To carry out its program, the center currently has an annual budget of $10-million. It has 28 staff members, 15 at headquarters here and 13 others in 10 regional offices being set up around the country.

The new director, Douglas J. Besharov, is a man with many ideas about the tasks his agency faces. He has served as counsel to the New York State Assembly's subcommittee on the family courts, as executive director of the Assembly's select committee on child abuse and neglect, as assistant corporation counsel in New York City working in the family court there.

"There are a lot of ways to abuse a child," Mr. Besharov said in a recent interview. The one that comes to most minds, because it is the most visible and the simplest, is the physical abuse of children, the "battered child" horror. Even here, however, there are many sorts of abuse, Mr. Besharov stressed.

Kinds of Abuse

There are the "sick psychotics" who burn and kill children, torture and maim them for reasons clouded by their own distemper; there is abuse that is corporal punishment, the kind that "gets out of hand," when a parent becomes enraged and loses control; there is abuse by alcoholic parents; there is the abuse of neo-natal drug addiction, which submits newborn infants to days of withdrawal; above all, there is the abuse that is the product of stress, of parents striking at children because of unbearable pressures.

"A lot [of these parents] are normal people, like you and me," Mr. Besharov said.

It is a class-linked phenomenon, Mr. Besharov said, only "to the extent that less verbal people resort to violence to express anger." But he added that while physical abuse does tend to be more prevalent among the disadvantaged, "emotional abuse and neglect—that's more middle-class."

"We know more how to hurt a kid in the head than that poor ghetto mama can with a belt

buckle," he said. "It's just a different version."

Mr. Besharov sees contemporary mores as contributing: "Society doesn't make it easy for parents to raise kids." He would favor a proposal that has been floating around for a "family policy impact statement" to be required on every new piece of legislation, similar to the "environmental impact" statement required now of relevant legislation.

"We don't strengthen family life," he said, citing housing, taxation and transportation as areas in which the Government leans toward policy that does not generally enhance the family structure.

Mr. Besharov estimated that there are about 450,000 cases of abused children reported in the United States annually and that the true, unreported figure could be "two, three or four times as many." A better reporting system is one thing he would like to work out.

He also would like to change the systems society has devised supposedly to "protect" children. "The existing child-protection system too often abuses children and parents," he said.

Mr. Besharov cited "incredible delays and snafus" in the family-court systems, and "no commitment to help natural parents while their kids are in foster care," as some of the areas in which present programs are faulty.

He would like fathers to be more involved with their children. He would like to develop "public understanding of what child-rearing practices ought to be about," just as there is at least a vague, general understanding of sound public-health practices, such as washing one's hands before eating. He is a bit annoyed at the women's liberation movement, which he said had "unnecessarily made a lot of women guilty about being mothers."

Ideas for Action

The new director would like to

coordinate existing neighborhood resources, such as family service and mental health agencies, church and school guidance counseling, to provide counseling for abusive or neglectful parents.

He would like to mobilize the parents, largely in city slums or rural poverty, whom he calls the "walking dead" — men and women, the mothers especially, who "can't mobilize themselves" to cope with life, much less with their children.

These are the children, he said, who "suffer silently. They're going to grow up the same way." He added, "We can really help 'em, we really can."

Some of his ideas include providing trained homemakers to teach these women how to function; to make some kind of day-care available to "give parents a break," to relieve the stress that is the dominant factor in the neglect and abuse of children.

"I'd really like to encourage baby-sitting co-ops," he said, adding, "We really have to provide an early way of helping families at risk, or vulnerable families. When a mother or a father realizes they're having problems meeting child-rearing responsibilities, they ought to have somewhere to go . . ."

Mr. Besharov and his wife, a social worker, have a four-year-old son, whom he refers to as he talks to illustrate points: How he himself snapped at the little boy because he was annoyed at himself and "he did the really minorest thing," how easy it is for any child to become a target. But later he said: "I take care of my son a lot. It's one of the nicest things you can do."

Linda Charlton is a reporter in the Washington bureau of The New York Times.

August 24, 1975

HIGH COURT RULES PUPIL SPANKINGS ARE PERMISSIBLE

By LESLEY OELSNER
Special to The New York Times

WASHINGTON, Oct. 20—The Supreme Court ruled today that states may permit school teachers to spank misbehaving stu-

dents, even over the objections of parents, as long as the teachers use lesser punishment when appropriate and also give the children some procedural safeguards—such as warning them ahead of time what misbehavior warrants a spanking.

The ruling does not invalidate statutes that prohibit corporal punishment, for the Supreme Court only sets minimum standards and the states may give students more rights. But the ruling does make corporal punishment legal, provided

that the procedural safeguards are followed.

Corporal punishment is prohibited in New York City and New Jersey schools. There is no statute specifically banning it in Connecticut or New York State.

The Court issued its decision in the case of a sixth-grade student from Gibsonville, N.C., Russell Carl Baker, who was paddled along with two classmates for playing with a ball when they were not supposed to.

'Familial Privacy' Cited

The Court issued no opinion. Instead, it simply affirmed without comment the decision of a three-judge Federal court that had considered the matter at the behest of Russell and his mother, who had previously asked school officials not to spank the child because he was frail.

On another issue, the Court accepted for review the question of just what a city can do to prevent development of a concentration of shops and theaters that specialize in pornography. The case arose in Detroit, whose zoning limitations on such places were struck down by an appellate court.

In the spanking case, the Bakers had argued that the state law permitting corporal punishment in the schools was, as applied in this case, unconstitutional on several grounds —that it violated the mother's right to "familial privacy," that it was applied to Russell without procedural safeguards and that it was arbitrary and applied with excessive force.

The three-judge court, though —whose judgment now becomes the judgment of the Supreme Court, and the law of the land—agreed only that some procedural safeguards must be followed.

It held that while the 14th Amendment includes the right of a parent generally to control the means of disciplining his or her child, the "state has a countervailing interest in the maintenance of order in the schools." In this case sufficient to sustain the right of teachers "to administer reasonable corporal punishment for disciplinary purposes."

The three-judge court noted that the Supreme Court several times before had given great force to various rights of parents—their rights to send their children to parochial school rather than public school, for instance, and their right to assure that children get an adequate education.

Tradition for the Rod

The court said, though, that the right to keep one's child safe from spanking was not of the same stature. It is not so widely regarded, the court said. "Quite the contrary, it bucks a settled tradition of countenancing such punishment when reasonable," according to the three-judge court.

"Opinion on the merits of the rod is far from unanimous," the court said at another point.

The court specified, however, that due process must be guaranteed the children. It said that except in cases of conduct so extreme as to be shocking, corporal punishment should not be used unless the student has first been warned that that specific form of misbehavior might lead to corporal punishment.

The court said, too, that subject to the same exception, corporal punishment should not be the "first line" of punishment. That means in effect that corporal punishment would not be considered reasonable if the offense was slight enough to be adequately punished by keeping the child after school, for instance.

In addition, the court said that a second teacher should observe the punishment and that if a parent wanted a written explanation, he or she should get one.

Complainant Loses Plea

The court did not specify precisely what types of corporal punishment would be "reasonable" and thus permissible. It did rule that the punishment in Russell's case was not cruel and unusual punishment.

Russell was in the sixth grade at the time, in December, 1973. His teacher paddled him either twice, as he remembered it, or three times, as the school said, with a wooden drawer divider that was about two inches wide, 13 inches long and three-eighths of an inch thick.

How much more of a spanking the courts will allow is unclear. Since the ruling spoke of "reasonable" corporal punishment, however, it seems unlikely that a severe beating could be justified.

Conceivably, the ruling could have two contradictory effects —it could force schools that now allow spanking but have no procedural safeguards to adopt a fairer procedure; it could also prompt areas that have banned corporal punishment to reconsider the matter.

Dr. Edward Keller, deputy director of the National Association of Elementary School Principals, suggested in an interview that most schools who now have corporal punishment already follow safeguards similar to those ordered by the court.

Corporal punishment is generally considered by experts such as Dr. Keller to be declining in the United States. However, it is still hardly uncommon. A study conducted by the Norfolk, Va., school district and published in the June, 1974, issue of Phi Delta Kappa, the magazine of Phi Delta Kappa, an organization of academics, says that 70 of the country's largest school districts were queried on the subject, and of the 50 that responded, 80 per cent, or 40 districts, permitted corporal punishment.

Eleven of those 40 districts permitted only the principal to administer the punishment, however, rather than the teacher.

The North Carolina statute at issue in the Baker case says not only that corporal punishment is allowed but also that local school boards may not ban it.

October 21, 1975

U.S. Finds 'Epidemic' Child Abuse Rate

WASHINGTON, Nov. 24, (UPI)—More than a million American children suffer physical abuse or neglect each year, and at least one in five of the young victims die from their mistreatment, the Government announced today.

Disclosing tentative results of the first nationwide child abuse study, an official of the Department of Health, Education and Welfare said the figures represented a "social problem" of "epidemic" proportions.

The statistics were gathered for the agency by the American Humane Association. They were made available in an interview with Douglas Besharov, director of the agency's National Center on Child Abuse and Neglect.

With no previous data against which to compare the new findings, Mr. Besharov said he did not know whether abuse and neglect were increasing.

Mr. Besharov cited the findings in a single city, New York, to describe the scope of the child abuse problem. In 1973, he said, about 110,000 children were born in New York and the next year there were reports of abuse and neglect of 2,300 infants in the city under the age of one.

"If you had a communicable disease that struck as great a rate of children, you'd say you had an epidemic on your hands," he said.

Until he took charge of the abuse center, Mr. Besharov was a New York City lawyer and expert on child abuse law. The H.E.W. Child Abuse Center was created last year to study the national incidence of abuse and neglect and to conduct research on its causes, treatment and prevention.

Based on reports from 30 states involving more than 311,000 children, the agency estimated that with complete reporting about one million cases would be reported annually.

The statistics indicate that 1.6 million cases of child abuse or neglect are reported each year but that 20 to 40 percent of these reports cannot be substantiated, Mr. Besharov said.

By the narrowest definitions of the terms, he said, 200,000 children a year die from circumstances associated with abuse or neglect. He said that under such definitions the 500 to 1,000 children killed annually by such accidents as falling out of windows were not included as 'victims of neglect.

Mr. Besharov said most reports involved neglect, and he denied that such reports reflected cultural biases, such as middle class social workers reporting abuse in low income families.

About three-fourths of the neglect reports come from friends, relatives and neighbors sharing the same cultural life as the young victims, Mr. Besharov said.

November 30, 1975

Children's Rights Drive Centered in Courtroom

By BARBARA CAMPBELL

The struggle for human rights has found a new frontier—America's children. A movement has arisen, not one of marches, petitions and boycotts, but one of constitutional arguments and legal theories.

It is a movement of the courtroom and the legislative chamber, aimed at reaching beyond patchwork protections against child abuse to establish clearcut constitutional rights for America's children.

But this movement is no less vigorous for its low profile. A spot check of 24 states by The New York Times disclosed that every one of their major cities had some legal group fighting for children's rights.

"Children's rights is a frontier area of legal thought," said J. Harvie Wilkinson, a professor of law at the University of Virginia, "and it will be a major concern of the United States Supreme Court in the next decade."

There are some state laws and regulations governing the mistreatment of children, some going back for decades. But until the early 1970's, there was no organized movement to gain individual rights for children.

That children should be protected by the Bill of Rights is a new area of social, philosophical and legal thought. "We had always assumed that parents looked after children," said Robert E. Shepherd, professor of law at the University of Baltimore.

The leaders of the children's rights movement, which encompasses thousands of persons, in religious, fraternal, social and labor organizations, make a distinction between their goals and those of the advocates of racial or sexual equality. Their aim, they say, is not to let children determine their own destiny. Adults, they say, must ultimately be responsible for children.

What they hope to do is establish that a child has a right to a safe, stable home, to a reasonable education, to due process of law and to freedom from abuse and neglect. They hope, in other words, to prove that adults and institutions have obligations to the young as well as powers over them.

John M. Rector, chief counsel of the Senate Juvenile Delinquency subcommittee in Washington, summarized the movement by saying, "We want to stop adults from being able to do anything to children and get away with it."

In the view of the movement's leaders, adults have historically been able to get away with an awesome list of injustices against the young. Among those they cite are the following:

¶Committing children to mental institutions at a parent's whim, without the same medical evidence required to commit an adult.

¶Placing children in reformatories although they have committed no crimes, other than so called "children's crimes" —truancy, incorrigibility and running away from home.

¶Forcing children to take powerful drugs to subdue them in schools, mental and penal institutions and foster homes.

¶Committing children to one foster home after another, or consigning them to foster care virtually until adulthood.

¶Sending children to institutions far from the states in which they live, in effect banished by their states and cut off from their families.

"We have kidded ourselves that we love children in this country," says Peter Sandman, who heads the Youth Law Center in San Francisco, a federally funded children's-rights law firm. "In fact, we treat kids as chattels and have done so for as long as there has been an America. Children are the last oppressed minority."

The drive to end that oppression has had some successes.

For example, to encourage states to stop locking up juveniles for "children's crimes," the Federal Juvenile Justice and Delinquency Prevention Act was passed in 1974. Sponsored by Senator Birch Bayh, the act provides money for states that can find alternatives to locking up children in detention centers and reformatories.

Double Jeopardy Barred

The children's rights movement has also come to the attention of the courts. The United States Supreme Court ruled last year that states cannot, without due process, deprive children of education for disciplinary reasons and that a student can recover damages from school officials whose actions breached his right to attend school.

Last year the Supreme Court held that the double jeopardy clause of the Fifth Amendment also applied to juveniles in a case brought by the Youth Law Center in San Francisco. A minor cannot now be retried in an adult court for the same offense for which he was tried and sentenced in juvenile court.

All of the children's rights activity in the last few years has resulted in unusual activity in the area before the Supreme Court. The Court has agreed to review at least five cases this term that deal with the constitutional rights of children.

State legislatures are beginning to move, also. In South Carolina, for example, the General Assembly is considering a bill to prohibit the placement in adult jails of those under 17 who are awaiting trial. The bill was introduced after the filing of a Federal suit in behalf of six boys aged 12 to 15 who alleged that they had been sexually abused, burned and beaten in adult jails.

In 1972 Massachusetts instituted a controversial and innovative plan. State officials began closing down all reformatories and children's prisons and substituting group homes, foster homes and other residential settings for juveniles.

Now 92 percent of 2,400 children, who would otherwise be in reformatories, live in their community. However, three secure facilities with a total capacity for 49 juveniles were reopened for youths who could not be treated in community-based residences.

Every state now has a child-abuse registry where people witnessing child abuse, or strongly suspecting it, can call a central number and report it.

Some states have just begun to set up these registries, but others like New York, have had them for several years. There has been in recent years an increased awareness by the public that children are abused and neglected, prompted in part by widely publicized cases of child abuse and a paper called the "Battered Child Syndrome" written in 1962 by Dr. C. Henry Kempe of the University of Colorado.

Despite the successes, though, much remains to be done. All states except Hawaii, Massachusetts, New Hampshire and Vermont still incarcerate children in adult jails.

Senator Bayh has had difficulty in acquiring the authorized funding for the 1974 act, which gives money to states that find alternatives to locking up juveniles. "For fiscal years 1976," said John M. Rector, counsel for the Senate Juvenile Delinquency subcommittee headed by Mr. Bayh, "President Ford allocated zero dollars." Congress, he said, had allocated $40 million of the $125 million requested by the Senator, a Democrat of Indiana.

Mr. Rector said that President Ford had requested $10 million for the program for the fiscal year 1977 although the act authorizes $150 million.

Another problem facing children's rights advocates is that in cases involving juveniles Federal judges tend to rely heavily on precedents that favor the adult and the state rather than the young.

Nonetheless, the advocates continue to pepper the courts with suits—often class actions—that challenge the constitutionality of the treatment thousands of children receive in mental and penal institutions, schools, foster homes and even in their families' homes.

One such case, to be argued before the Supreme Court this fall, challenges the practice of committing children to mental hospitals without due process of law.

The case, known as Bartley v. Kremens, is a class action brought in behalf of all mentally ill or retarded children 18 or younger who have been confined to Pennsylvania mental institutions.

"It is the first case to reach the Supreme Court involving the rights of children independent of their parents," said Robert Walker of the Youth Law Center in San Francisco. "It goes directly to the ancient concept . . . that parents make decisions for their children."

The suit accuses the State of Pennsylvania of violating the 14th Amendment rights of due process of four children who were confined to mental institutions "against their will" but with the consent of their parents and a physician. David Ferleger, the attorney representing the children, is asking that an independent review be required before a child is placed in a mental institution.

State officials are arguing that parents have a right and an obligation to decide what is best for their children.

According to Mr. Ferleger, there will be "tantalizing" implications if the Supreme Court decides that parents have no right to sign their children into mental hospitals.

"Potentially every area in which parents make decisions for a child can be challenged by the child," he said. However, "a child will receive the protection of law where he can be potentially harmed and the law will not interfere where there is no threat to the child.

"The whole effort here in children's rights is forcing the recognition of children as equal in our society with adults."

Several similar cases involve the right to treatment—the question of whether children who are institutionalized have a constitutional right to education and medical and psychological treatment. One of them is a case filed by the New York Civil Liberties Union in behalf of a 10-year-old boy who allegedly did not receive the necessary treatment to correct degenerative mental retardation while he was confined to a foundling hospital.

Obligation of State

The suit contends that the boy had a constitutional right to treatment while he was in the care of the state, but child-welfare officials argue that no such right exists.

Most children's rights cases tend to turn on such technical points, for the public officials who usually find themselves defendants are reluctant to base their arguments on the quality of the treatment children receive from the state.

While the right to treatment is a fundamental issue, it is not the foundation for all legal activity in behalf of children.

Alaska Legal Services, for example, has filed a suit challenging a practice that is widespread in that sparsely settled state—boarding children far from their homes while they attend school. The suit maintains that children should have ready access to schools.

In Detroit, the American Civil Liberties Union is suing the state Department of Mental Health in an effort to stop what it says is the use of mentally retarded children to test experimental vaccines. The children "are being used as ready-made guinea pigs," said David Wineman of the Detroit A.C.L.U. The suit challenges a parent's right to give permission for such testing.

"Banishment," the widespread practice of sending children out of state for institutionalization when local facilities are not available, is of particular interest to children's advocates. The Children's Defense Fund, based in Washington, has sued Louisiana and Texas for placing Louisiana children in child-care institutions in Texas.

Although there are some reputable institutions that accept out-of-state children, critics say there is a growing number of substandard facilities that operate for profit only.

Critics charge that banishment is cruel to children because it separates them from their families and homes and because it is costly. Virginia for instance, sent 596 children out of state at a cost of $2,999,770.38 in 1975.

While agreement is virtually unanimous that children should be given proper treatment and a decent education, some observes are wary of the kind of broad rulings the movement is seeking. They argue, for instance, that a favorable decision in the Bartley case, which challenges the commitment of children to Pennsylvania mental institutions, could establish a precedent for challenging almost any parental decision.

Such rulings could "destructively tamper with the relationship between parents and children as we know it," said Seth P. Stein, a Long Island custody lawyer. "I don't think we are ready for that kind of change."

Helen Buttenweiser, a New York lawyer, who is acting as law guardian for children involved in a foster care case that the Supreme Court agreed to hear recently, said she was opposed to court cases that pitted children against adults.

"The rights of all contending adults are taken care of in these court fights," she said, "and no one is paying too much attention to the children although the cases are brought in the guise of helping the children."

In the case now before the Supreme Court, for example, she said, the New York Civil Liberties Union wants the Court to decide whether foster children

have a right to an impartial hearing before they are removed from a foster home. This, Mrs. Buttenweiser said, is essentially a fight between the foster parents and the biological parents."

"A lot of people," said Seth Stein, "are now arguing for children's rights and arguing against the concept of the presumption in favor of natural parents. But they should realize the family is the most effective unit we have in this society. Before these sociological issues are decided by the courts, we should make sure the alternatives are not worse."

October 31, 1976

Toward a U.S. Secretary for Children

To the Editor:

At this time when President-elect Carter is organizing his new Cabinet and other advisory positions, it is my sincere hope that he will consider establishing a Cabinet position that represents children. Since children lack voting power, a Cabinet position established on their behalf would offer some direct representation in the executive branch of government.

The focus of this office would be to consider the rights and needs of children, and the effects of all national developments and programs on children and their future. Recognition of their needs through H.E.W. is not sufficient. The establishment of such a position would indeed be innovative and consistent with the image President-elect Carter and Mr. Mondale created in the campaign. Because children have no voting power, politicians have tended to ignore their needs. (I have always been concerned with how politicians have used children in their campaigns, and then neglected their needs afterward.)

In my years as an advocate for children I have come to realize that

S. Harmon

children are indeed a neglected segment of our society when it comes to providing for their optimum physical and emotional growth.

I am specifically concerned with

meeting the emotional needs of infants, children and parents to prevent the development of serious emotional problems. I believe the family is of the utmost importance for the development of human strengths.

Unfortunately, in our society the family has been given little or no support, in spite of our knowing that crime, violence and mental retardation are related to weakened ties between children and families. The deterioration of human values and family ties in this country demands that we consider this an important responsibility of our government. Direct recognition of children and the family by government would lead Americans to see the importance of meeting the needs of our children to prevent the kind of social and emotional problems that have been plaguing us.

I have written a letter to President-elect Carter urging him to give serious consideration to this suggestion.

LEE SALK
New York, Nov. 18, 1976

The writer is clinical professor of psychology in pediatrics and psychiatry, Cornell University Medical College.

November 27, 1976

CONSTITUTION NO BAR TO SCHOOL SPANKING, HIGH COURT RULES

Beatings, No Matter How Severe, Not Covered, 5-4 Decision Says —Other Curbs Noted

By LESLEY OELSNER
Special to The New York Times

WASHINGTON, April 19—The Supreme Court ruled 5 to 4 today that the spanking of schoolchildren, no matter how severe, by teachers or other school officials does not violate the Constitution's

Eighth Amendment ban against cruel and unusual punishment.

But, according to the court, teachers and school officials almost everywhere in the nation are subject under other laws to criminal or civil penalties for using "unreasonable" or "excessive" force to discipline pupils. It said that the prevalent rule in the nation was derived from common law that the force used should be "reasonable but not excessive."

The Court also ruled that a student has no constitutional right to have even an informal hearing before the spanking on whether the punishment is justified.

Ban in Some Areas

The Court's decision, written by Lewis F. Powell Jr. in a case involving allegedly excessive punishment in a junior high school in Dade County, Fla., does not mean that all types of corporal punishment are now legal in all localities.

Some areas, such as both New York City and the State of New Jersey, bar

physical punishment in their public schools. Since the Supreme Court sets only minimum standards as to what protections must be provided and since states can thus create extra protections, these bans are unaffected by today's rulings.

The Court relied heavily on this prevailing law to justify its decision. It said in effect that as long as the common law rules were standing, children would be protected and teachers would be hesitant to be unreasonable in administering corporal punishment.

Justice Byron R. White wrote a dissenting opinion and was joined by William J. Brennan Jr., Thurgood Marshall and John Paul Stevens. Joining Justice Powell in the majority were Chief Justice Warren E. Burger and Justices Harry A. Blackmun, William H. Rehnquist and Potter Stewart.

The majority seemed confident that the current law provided enough civil and criminal sanctions to deal with cases of abuse by teachers and other officials of their disciplinary power.

The dissenters contended that the current remedies might be inadequate. It may be impossible to sue officials successfully in some areas, they said; for example, if the official can be shown to have acted in good faith.

Also, they noted, "the infliction of physical pain is final and irreparable; it cannot be undone in a subsequent proceeding."

Somewhat as it did in its opinion last summer ruling that capital punishment is not inherently unconstitutional as a cruel and unusual punishment, the Court stressed the broad public acceptance of the practice it was considering.

"The use of corporal punishment in this country as a means of disciplining school children dates back to the colonial period," the majority said. "It has survived the transformation of primary and secondary education from the colonials' reliance on optional private arrangements to our present system of compulsory education and dependence on public schools.

"Despite the general abandonment of corporal punishment as a means of punishing criminal offenders, the practice continues to play a role in the public education of school children in most parts of the country. Professional and public opinion is sharply divided on the practice and has been for more than a century. Yet we can discern no trend toward its elimination'," the Court said.

The majority contended that the Eighth Amendment was designed to protect persons convicted of crimes.

"The prisoner and the schoolchild stand in wholly different circumstances, separated by the harsh facts of criminal conviction and incarceration," it said. "The schoolchild has little need for the protection of the Eighth Amendment," it argued, in part because of the protections of the common law regarding corporal punishment, in part because the school is an "open institution" subject to community supervision.

The dissent contended that the Eighth Amendment should be viewed as applying to "punishments," not just to criminals.

"If there are some punishments that are so barbaric that they may not be imposed for the commission of crimes, designated by our social system as the most thoroughly reprehensible acts an individual can commit, then a fortiori, similar punishments may not be imposed on persons for less culpable acts, such as breaches of school discipline," Justice White's dissent said.

"Thus, if it is constitutionally impermissible to cut off someone's ear for the commission of murder, it must be unconstitutional to cut off a child's ear for being late to class."

Today's case was started in January 1971 by James Ingraham and Roosevelt Andrews, who at the time were enrolled in the Charles R. Drew Junior High School in Miami. They complained of paddling incidents that each had suffered the previous fall and they sought to have the case considered a class action on behalf of all students in the county schools.

The youths' case at trial included testimony regarding allegedly severe punishment. The Ingraham boy allegedly was struck more than 20 times with a paddle "because he was slow to respond to his teacher's instructions," with the result that he suffered a hematoma (a blood mass) that kept him out of school for 11 days. The Andrews youth was paddled several times, for supposedly minor infractions, and at one point was deprised, as a result of the paddling, of the full use of his arm for a week.

The trial court ruled against the youths. A panel of the United States Court of Appeals for the Fifth Circuit reversed, finding violations of the Eighth and Fourteenth Amendments; subsequently, the full appeals court reversed the findings of the panel.

It is presumed that an effect of today's ruling was to tell the plaintiffs in this case (Ingraham v. Wright, No. 75-6527) that they could seek remedy for any allegedly excessive punishment by school officils in the Florida state courts.

Today's decision also expanded considerably upon a 1975 decision by the Court in which the Justices, without having heard argument on the matter and without issuing an opinion, summarily affirmed a lower court decision permitting corporal punishment in certain cases.

The lower court had found that it was not unconstitutional for teachers to spank misbehaving students, even over the objections of parents, as long as the teachers used lesser punishment where appropriate and also gave the children some procedural safeguards—such as warning them ahead of time what behavior warranted a spanking.

When the Supreme Court summarily affirms a lower court decision in that manner, it adopts the judgment of the lower court, though not necessarily its reasoning. Thus, the full meaning of the Court's action in the 1975 case was not clear.

In today's decision, the court merely referred to the 1975 action in a footnote. It said, "This Court has held in a summary affirmance that parental approval of corporal punishment is not constitutionally required," and cited the 1975 case.

April 20, 1977

POOR AND MINORITY-GROUP CHILDREN

NEGRO CURB CITED BY PSYCHIATRISTS

By EMMA HARRISON

Special to The New York Times.

CHICAGO, Feb. 27—Dramatic evidence of the impartment of intellectual functioning in the Negro child by socio-cultural factors was presented here today.

Negro and white children who scored nearly the same in early intellectual and developmental potentials show greater variance at the age of 3, when environmental factors enter into the picture, two psychiatrists said.

The differences occur largely in adaptive and language behavior, areas most susceptible to socio-cultural influences, while motor behavior, which is largely the result of basic neurological endowment, remains the same.

Drs. Hilda Knobloch and Benjamin Pasamanick, a husband-wife team conducting a study on causes and effects of prematurity, made the report to the annual meeting of the American Orthopsychiatric Association here.

The researchers, whose studies of 1,000 Baltimore children have turned up much vital statistical material on results of both organic and environmental defects on the infant, reported on a study of 300 of these youngsters, measured for capacities as infants and later as 3-year-olds. The group comprised about half white and half Negro youngsters.

The youngsters were used as "controls" on normal births in the larger study of prematurity being conducted by the Pasamanicks, who are now in Columbus, Ohio. The measurements were made by means of the Gesell Developmental Test, which operates very like intelligence-quotient tests, relating achievement and ability of infants to their chronological age.

Behavior Change Noted

A comparison of the full-term, controlled youngsters at the age of 3 showed a "marked racial divergence in adaptive and language behavior, while the motor and personal-social behavior are essentially unchanged."

The general developmental quotient rose for the white children, while it fell for the Negro youngsters; language ability rose in the whites and fell in the non-whites.

Failure in these areas is quite understandable among the non-white groups, usually of the lower socio-economic background, Dr. Pasamanick said. There is less motivation to learning in most of these non-white homes in the study, because there is more of a deterrent to it.

There is more sickness, more working mothers, lower nutrition and less, if any, stimulus to intellectual achievement. The Negro children in the study just did not have the motivation to achievement in all phases of their development, intellectual and physical, he observed.

They observed that in infancy, the factors producing differences in intellectual potential were largely organic. Other of their studies have maintained that even organic differences are the result of certain environmental factors, such as malnutrition, time of conception, etc.

Social Differences Stressed

Thus, the study is putting statistical measurements to the environmental factors in intelligence that social scientists have long discussed.

"It is perhaps fitting," they say, "to comment here that evolution in man no longer appears to be on an organic structural level. The major changes are social and cultural and small differences in intellectual potential due to organic factors cannot be detected within this larger framework."

They noted that while the studies of the intelligence indicated need for a hard look at educational and social welfare activities, the emphasis was still on genetic factors. They asked for a reversal of emphasis, with increased socio-cultural research into problems related to intelligence, and organic research into such mental disturbances as schizophrenia.

It is true, they observed, that there are organic factors determining mental behavior, but intellectual functioning can also be controlled by environmental conditions.

February 28, 1960

36

INTEGRATION HELD A HELPFUL STRESS

Psychiatrist Finds Children Profiting by Experience

By JOHN D. POMFRET
Special to The New York Times

WASHINGTON, May 16 — The reaction of Negro children who have desegregated Southern schools has raised questions about some of the fundamental presumptions of child-raising, according to a child psychiatrist who has been studying the children.

Dr. Robert Coles of Concord, Mass., the psychiatrist, thinks that the experience of the Negro children shows that stress can be creative and positive.

Dr. Coles, with the aid of foundation grants, has been studying the impact of school desegregation on Negro and white children and their families in New Orleans and Atlanta since 1961.

Despite the threats and the isolation to which the Negro children were initially subjected, Dr. Coles said in an interview, they show surprisingly few symptoms of mental disorder.

"The Negro children were not hand-picked," Dr. Coles said. "They came from all sorts of backgrounds. Of course, they had moments of pain and anguish, but they have survived successfully with astonishingly few psychological symptoms.

"I went to New Orleans expecting to find them developing reactions to constant threats and isolation and the struggle of meeting the social and academic challenge of the switch from Negro to white schools.

"What I discovered was that they had already developed ways to deal with these hurts. What I considered a stress was exactly the opposite and a challenge to them.

"We tend to put a cellophane bag around kids—to be protective. What the experience with desegregation shows is that stress can be a positive thing—a creative thing."

The experience of white children in desegregated schools, Dr. Coles found, has created a subtle split between them and their parents.

"Even if there are only one or two Negroes in a school," Dr. Coles said, "the white children learn things about them that they otherwise never would have.

"For a Negro to answer a question in a math class conflicts with the white stereotype of the Negro. And when a Negro child is called on in class and does not know the answer, and a white child does not know the answer either, it creates a bond between them whether the white child realizes it at the time or not."

In the majority of white families Dr. Coles studied, the children were telling their parents that they believed what the parents had taught them about the inferiority of the Negroes and the evil of school desegregation. But, in fact, they were questioning these concepts by telling their parents that they liked a particular Negro child and asking what was wrong with him.

Dr. Coles found the same reexamination of stereotypes going on within Negro families.

"Many Negro parents teach the laws of segregation to their children," he said. "They teach their children to be fearful and distrustful of whites. It is very hard for these parents to go against their own advice. The do not easily relinquish these attitudes."

Dr. Coles continued:

"But we are dealing with the influence of reality on a child's life and mind. Although a parent can fight reality, he cannot deny its nature.

"The desegregation experience shows how hard it is for adults to keep up with what history does for and to their children. The continuity between parents and children is not total. It sometimes is a matter of children leaving their parents behind and becoming the future."

Dr. Coles found that it was much easier for the elementary-school children in New Orleans to adjust to desegregation than for the older high-school children in Atlanta. Desegregation works better if it is started in the lower grades rather than the higher, he has concluded.

Over-all, Dr. Coles has found that social policies and laws are much more important in regulating conduct than what heretofore has been presumed to be deeply rooted attitudes.

"It turns out that they are not deeply rooted after all," he said.

Dr. Coles, a research psychiatrist with the Harvard University Health Services, undertook the Southern school-desegregation study with the financial support of the New World Foundation and the General Education Board. His findings have been published by the Southern Regional Council and the Anti-Defamation League of B'nai B'rith.

The school study is one of a group of investigations Dr. Coles intends to carry out on how the life of the child is affected by certain social situations that might be considered stressful. He currently is studying the children of migrant farm workers.

May 17, 1964

Inferiority Feelings Hold Negro Back, Spock Says

By JOAN COOK

ONE OF the serious problems faced by Negro children is their belief that they are inferior because of the color of their skin, according to Dr. Benjamin Spock. Psychological studies show that the Negro child, by accepting the white man's prejudice against him, becomes prejudiced against himself by the time he is 4 or 5 years old, the noted pediatrician declared.

"At a later age," Dr. Spock said in an article in the September issue of Redbook magazine, "experiments involving Negro and white students who take tests in one another's presence show that a Negro who actually scores the same as a white student will characteristically rate his own performance as inferior. This unrealistic sense of inadequacy gets expressed, of course, in low expectations for himself in school and career. It also follows that the Negro comes to think less well of his family, his friends and his race than they deserve. And they, in turn, have less esteem for him."

Dr. Spock's remarks parallel those of Dr. Joseph S. Himes, head of the sociology department at North Carolina College, Durham, N. C. Dr. Himes advanced the theory of what he calls "learned apathy" among Negro children at a recent conference held by the Washington School of Psychiatry and the National Child Research Center.

Young Children Active

"Very young children of whatever class or race are, if healthy, spontaneous and active," Dr. Himes said. "Middle-class parents, with the time, economic resources and understanding, recognize, conserve, guide and cherish this quality. Deprived parents, however, tend to find spontaneity troublesome and even sometimes dangerous or threatening. They tend to repress it, unintentionally to be sure. They want the child to stay out of mischief, danger, the way and so on and not to ask trouble-some and embarrassing questions."

Dr. Himes goes on to say:

"His [the Negro child's] extra-family world also contributes. The social institutions—police, economy, church, mass media, all of them — limit his field of options and show him the stereotype he is or is supposed to be like. For example, if he goes to work it is hard, heavy, dirty, low-paid low-prestige work and everybody and everything tells him this kind of work is not good. So he doesn't like work and sees no evidence to prove that 'hard work' will help him get anything but tired. He learns, rationally and realistically, the habits, attitudes and skills of work avoidance."

Like Dr. Spock, Dr. Himes argues that the apathetic person is not an activity vacuum but at person acting in terms of a pattern or value that is divergent from that of the middle class.

Dr. Spock takes note of experimental projects carried out by the Bank Street College of Education here, which show that some of the most withdrawn and indifferent Negro pupils—those classified as "unteachable" in the existing school system—respond dramatically to teachers who like them, believe in them and are able to go halfway to find their interests.

Dr. Frank Riessman, a psychologist currently engaged in Mobilization for Youth Inc., has taken this a step further by suggesting that "apathetic" and "non-verbal" youngsters in the classroom are lively, vocal youngsters at play and that the teacher's problem today is to divest himself of middle-class teaching patterns and meet these children on their own ground in terms they can understand.

Harmful to White Child

Dr. Spock also deals with the harm that discrimination does to white children. In addition to teaching fear and hate, Dr. Spock points out, white parents communicate to their children a less easily seen anxiety when they find them playing with an unknown Negro child or discuss the possibility of a Negro family moving into the neighborhood in apprehensive tones.

"...the mere fact that a white child's parents don't meet Negroes socially will give him a slight sense of strangeness and uneasiness, which most of us realize is still in us in adulthood when we try to overcome this barrier," he says.

Taking note that other groups in America's past have started from poverty and slums but were able to escape as soon as they learned American ways, Dr. Spock says:

"The Negro, because of his

skin, is chained to a slippery incline. He must struggle more intensively than a white person to climb upward, but if he or his children are not able to persevere, they'll slide more easily to the bottom again."

Shows Less Aptitude

Dr. Spock scored the opposition to school integration that is based on the theory that Negro children on the average have lower scores on intelligence tests and show less aptitude than average white children.

"In actuality, there are very bright Negro children as well as average and dull ones — the same range as for white children," he says. "But there is a larger proportion of Negroes in the lower-score brackets, and this is what brings the average down. There is no proof, however, that Negroes are innately less endowed with gray matter.

Most psychologists believe that the intellectual and academic differences are explained by the cultural deprivation of the Negro."

Studies of the effects of school integration in Louisville, Ky., and in Washington show academic improvement for the Negro children and no academic disadvantage for the white children, he states. In advocating that people of goodwill take part in opening schools,

jobs and residential areas to Negroes, Dr. Spock further notes that news reports show clearly that "those who are aroused to fear and antagonism at the prospect of integration are quick and vigorous in expressing their feelings. It is the people of goodwill who most often fail to speak up."

August 20, 1964

New Criteria Show 15 Million Children In Poverty Families

Special to The New York Times
WASHINGTON, Jan. 28 — Fifteen million American children, one-fourth of all those in the nation, live in poverty, the President's Council of Economic Advisers estimated today.

This new estimate of the number of children who are

members of poor families was 4 million higher than the one used by the Council last year. It results from an attempt by the Government to refine the manner in which it identifies poor families.

The new estimates of the extent of poverty take into account the size of families as well as their income. Last year, poor families were defined simply as those whose total income was less than $3,000.

Now, however, the Government has attempted to work out more sophisticated standards for identifying the poor. These criteria take into account the fact that smaller families can live with less money than larger ones and rural families with less than urban ones.

The result of the new criteria has been to reduce the number of adults defined as poor, especially the number of elderly couples, and to increase the number of children. Under these standards, families with many children can be classified as poor even if their income is somewhat above $3,000.

The total number of families in the poverty classifica-

tion, by the old test of income of less than $3,000, actually fell by about 300,000 to a total of 9 million in 1963, the Council said. It said that a similar drop probably occurred last year.

Even with the changes brought by a rising economy, however, most families classified as poor remain poor year in and year out, the report said. Studies of the last available figures on family income showed that about 70 per cent of those with incomes below $3,000 in 1962 remained below this level in 1963.

January 29, 1965

'Hidden Language'

Ghetto Children Know What They're Talking About

By JOHN M. BREWER

BROKEN homes are "trees without roots."

Meat markets are "great flesh parlors."

Outsiders looking for thrills are "toys on a fairy lake."

This is the colorful, private speech of the children of America's ghettos, a "hidden language" of haunted phrases and striking subtlety. It is a language little known in the world outside, but for many it is more meaningful, more facile and more developed than the language of standard English.

During the period I was the principal of a large elementary school in the heart of a Negro slum, I became fascinated by this secret language developed by a rough-and-ready group of ghetto children. I found this idiom to be as

---

JOHN M. BREWER, slum-born himself, heads a "compensatory education" project for slum children in the Pittsburgh school system.

dazzling as a diamond, invested with the bitter-sweet soulfulness bred by the struggle against poverty's dehumanizing forces.

I discovered that it was developed by the children even before they came to school, passed on from mother to child, and that a quarter of the students came from homes where it is the usual household speech. It is equipment for survival in the black ghetto. Normally it is used only in easy social settings like the home and after-school gatherings, and not in front of outsiders — which helps to explain why the children are often inarticulate when they try to use conventional English in talking to teachers, doctors, the school staff, etc.

As they advance in their schooling these children also advance their hidden language vocabulary, become infatuated with this kind of verbal play and help it to flower with additions from the standard

English they meet in class. They, and their parents, are fully aware of the aliveness of their words and make a serious effort to master the idiom. But, of course, this development conflicts with the formal school pattern and teachers who demand that only conventional English be used, and it often happens that verbally bright children suddenly clam up or become inarticulate in the classroom.

AN illustration of the wonderful possibilities of the language of the ghetto helps one to judge how rich and interesting it is.

About 9:45 A.M. one day, Junebug—a small, wiry, shabbily dressed boy with large brown eyes — came into my office. As I looked up, it was obvious that he was hosed down and deep in the mud [embarrassed and had a problem]. Very quickly I got up and asked, "Why are you

stretched so thin by joy? Are you flying backwards?" ["Why are you so sad? Are you in trouble?"]

Junebug took a cool view [looked up], cracked up [smiled] and answered, "My special pinetop [favorite teacher] is smoking [angry] and wants to eyeball [see] you fast." I said to him, "I'm stalled [puzzled]. What is this all about?"

He answered, "I wasted [punched] one of the studs [boys] for capping [insulting] me. Teach blasted [yelled] at me and told me to fade away [go] to the hub [office] and fetch you."

I stood up and told Junebug to cool it. "Don't put your head in the bowl and pull the chain" ["Don't do anything rash"]. Hurriedly he grabbed my arm and said: "I hope I don't get a big slap on the rump."

As I headed up the stairs toward his classroom I was deeply concerned. What did he mean by that "slap-on-the-rump" remark? A paddling never fazed him before. Suddenly the message came through loud and clear: He had played the part of an unlikely wrongdoer to tell me something was wrong in his classroom. He was tough and cruel, cunning and ruthless, a master of all the skills needed to survive in his jungle; he was too shrewd to be trapped this way, with so many witnesses, without a motive. He

was very fond of his teacher.

I knew his twisted code of honor, which did not allow him to be an informer. He had got in trouble himself so that I would see and uncover something about his class.

Very reluctantly I eased open the classroom door and entered the room. I could sense that the hum of industry was missing. The children—chronologically aged 11-13 but actually precocious young adults —were impenetrable, as though encased in glass, sitting stiffly at their desks. The teacher walked over to me and said, "Whatever has come over this class this morning defies interpretation by anyone—most of all myself."

In a booming voice I said to the class, "Operation Jappin' [teacher harassment] has shot its load [is all over]." Operation Jappin' goes like this:

The tomcat [the sly and ruthless student leading the operation] begins with a stinging hit [first attack] and the sandbaggin' starts—things are thrown, strange noises come out of nowhere, children are unresponsive. The tomcat tells all his tadpoles [classmates] that it is now time for the chicken to become an eagle [for more aggressive action] and they had better trilly along [join his group] because the sun has fallen on its belly [it's too late to back out].

The first step is to unzip the teacher [make her back down], so the tomcat takes the long dive [openly defies her], hoping she puts him in cold storage [punishes him] so he can then dress her in red tresses [insult her]. He and his friends get bolder, and outflap [out wit] and scramble [gang up on] her daily. All morning they shoot her down with

grease [play dirty tricks on her] until finally she is ready for the big sleep [gives in]. They continue the heart-deep kicks [fun] until they are sure she is frozen on the needle [does not know what to do].

The tomcat then decides to wring [exploit] the scene. Now his glasses are on [he's in control], his ashes have been hauled away [his problems are gone]. He sends hotcakes [notes] to some of the children demanding money; the rabbits [timid children] know they will be erased [beat up] unless they pay him. He tells them he is a liberty looter [good crook] who will protect them because he carries a twig [big club]. Five-finger discount [stealing] pays off. The cockroaches crow [gang members are happy].

Poor Tiny Tim [the teach-

er], her nerve ends are humming [she is overwhelmed], her fleas [nice children] and bust-heads [smart children] have twisted the knob [lost respect for her]. The tomcat doesn't have to waste any more hip bullets on her [continue the harassment] — after all, a cat can't tell a dog what to do [he is the new leader]. He will keep his shoe laces tied [control everything]. Hail the Stinking King.

QUICKLY I singled out the group I thought was capable of organizing Operation Jappin', and together we went to my office. I told Junebug to go to the outer office and sit down. In spite of the imperturbable look on his face, I knew he was aware that I had captured the scene [found out what was going on]: these cub scouts [amateurs] were bleedin' [exposed].

The climate was a sticky one. I had to converse with them in their hidden language. But since I was a ghetto linguist, they could not victimize me by their idiomatic ambushes so neatly booby-trapped with sudden jolts and dead-end phrases.

I also had to ready them to pay their dues [accept disciplinary action]. I could not offer them two tricks for one until they were ready to turn a somersault [promise them anything until they confessed]. And I had to burn some time [give them time] to talk it over.

Finally, of course, I had to discipline the ringleaders. Operation Jappin' was sandbagged. In the end, I couldn't help but feel sorry for Junebug, and yet how could I tell

his teacher how he had sacrificed himself in her behalf? Conceivably all of this might terrify her.

Yet I had to try to provide a bridge between her world and his. It is imperative that teachers see the ways in which the hidden and formal languages cut across, support or collide with each other. In fact, the term "hidden language" is really a misleading

one, because in the out-of-school setting it becomes the primary language while the formal language used in the schools is secondary.

I suspect that many teachers are unaware of this inversion. And they are baffled as well by the odd structure of the primary language of the street-corner society. The logic is nonlogic, for instance: "I am full of the joy of being up front" means "I am disgusted with my circumstances. The appeal is illusion and fantasy: "It goes to the back of your head and pulls out beautiful things."

If one looks for substance instead of smut, meaning instead of obfuscation, it is possible to harness some of the positive features that lie behind the crust of degradation and depravation explicit in the hidden language. The schools in our urban ghettos are full of children who communicate this way.

IT was to make clear the hidden dynamics of the hidden language — realistic, tough, practical, with a broad sweep of understanding—and to explore the inversion process that I began "Operation Capping."

Operation Capping can best be described as a "tug of war" between formal and restrictive language. The long-range goal was systematically to strip away the students' addiction to a hidden language that thwarted their progress with

Color It Vivid

Adapting the hidden language to their own experience, slum children turn standard English into phrases like these:

A nice teacher . . . My golden butterfly, my luscious lollipop, my special pine-top, Little Eva, star apple-smooth.

A mean teacher . . . Headshrinker, killer ape, Bloody Mary, Swinging Tillies, The Vulture, The Beast.

A strict teacher . . . Clyde Beatty, Smokey the Bear, caged quiet, my ball and chain, rifle-hard, double-edged.

Patronizing teacher . . . Untouchable, tack-head, huckster, hard and odd, foggy, my caddy.

A well-taught lesson . . . Easy eats, heart-deep kicks.

Poor lesson . . . Same tired paths, cracked my skull, tucked me in tight.

Textbooks . . . Passport, license, retreads, sheets.

To cheat in class . . . Fix the meter, boosted goods.

A reading class . . . Living it twice, the line up, here comes the birds.

An arithmetic lesson . . . Tops and bottoms, halving, splitting.

the language of the school and textbook.

I developed a two - pronged approach. One was not to deny the validity of the child's world, his pragmatism, his unwillingness to be deluded, his suspicious nature and his perceptions, his quickness, toughness, and agile imagination. The other was to manipulate and redirect what was already a favorite pastime of the children, called "Capping," which in my youth was called "Playing the Dozens." In it, children try to outdo each other in trading insults and deprecating each other's family. For example: "Your Mama wasn't born, she was trapped"; "Your sisters are side-show bait"; "You ain't got no pappy, you're a S.O.B."; or "So's your Mama."

I decided to borrow this practice and give it a classy academic personality. The technique was simple, because the kids were already highly motivated to surpass each other in verbal intercourse. So I would meet a group for a "buzz session" [dictionary skills and English grammar] and introduce one of their well - known idioms, such as "pad," "crib" or "bread," and the children had to "cap" each other in formal English by providing a synonym.

As time passed we introduced antonyms and moved from simple sentences to complex ones. The kids were so highly competitive that they took up practices to which they previously were indifferent: They used the dictionary, read books, brought samples of word lists and resorted to all the conventional practices of the classroom. They had to win the capping game at any cost.

The spin-off from Operation Capping touched many sensitive and intriguing areas. The students discovered for themselves the built - in disadvantages of their idiomatic phrases; it didn't take them long to determine that these phrases didn't convey the meanings to others that their hidden language did: For example, they were stumped as they tried to find a standard English idiom for such hidden language phrases as: "rising on the wings of power" [a pocketful of money]; "gold is my color" [pay me in advance]; "trailing dark lines" [a hopeless search for something]; "I'm on ice" [in trouble].

The students openly expressed a real concern about their verbal deficit in formal language. But at the end of Operation Capping, they had become less dependent on their hidden language to express themselves, and began to stockpile new standard words and phrases and to wrestle successfully with grammar for the first time.

They also had a purpose for reading, and their ability improved significantly. Learning became fun and exciting because they no longer labored under unfair handicaps. There was a change in their value system, and they had a new sense of identity.

I believe that the operation helped to provide richer opportunities for these children to experience the forces in the tug of war between their two languages and to come to know the language necessary for effective communication in the mainstream of contemporary American society.

December 25, 1966

Study Finds Welfare the Last Step in a Series of Insults Brought On by Living Conditions

By NANCY HICKS

A Columbia University research team has concluded that welfare by itself does not cause psychological impairment, but is, rather, the last step in a series of environmental insults that poor people face throughout life.

This finding was documented last week in a continuing five-year study of the causes of emotional illness in welfare and nonwelfare children in New York City. The study is being conducted by a six-member team at Columbia's School of Public Health and Administrative Medicine.

It is being sponsored by grants from the National Institute of Mental Health, the Health Research Council of the City of New York and the Social and Rehabilitation Service of the Department of Health, Education and Welfare.

Dr. Thomas S. Langner, a sociologist and professor of psychiatry, who is the principal investigator for the project, said that welfare as a separate cause of psychological illness almost "cancels out" when the full range of problems accompanying poverty are considered independently.

2,000 Children Involved

The study involved 1,000 children who live between Houston Street and 125th Street in Manhattan, and another 1,000 children whose families are welfare recipients. One third of the welfare sample is white; one-third is black, and one-third is Spanish-speaking. All the children were between the ages of five and 18 when the research began five and a half years ago.

Each child's mother was interviewed for two and a half hours and answered a 90-page questionnaire designed to determine the child's behavior in school and at home, and his relationships with his brothers, sisters, parents and peers.

After the questionnaire was completed, psychiatrists evaluated the answers, looking for keys to psychological impairment.

In each case, the child's background was not known to the psychiatrist but was stored in a computer. After the psychiatrists evaluated the behavioral information, they rated the child in areas such as family relationships, school adjustment and relationships with peers and then gave him a total "impairment rating."

In addition, the mother of every fourth child was interviewed by a psychiatrist to check the effectiveness of the questionnaire. All the findings were put into the computer with the ethnic and socioeconomic data. Similar patterns emerged.

These were the research team's findings:

¶Psychological development is most risky for young boys of lower socio-economic families who live in broken homes where families tend to move a great deal.

¶School adjustment is most difficult for Negro boys who come from welfare homes.

¶Children of working welfare mothers are less impaired than children of nonworking welfare mothers for unknown reasons that are to be studied.

¶There is more sibling rivalry in middle-class homes than in lower-income homes.

¶White children with severe psychological problems tend to become depressed, while Negro children with such problems tend to express themselves in outgoing physical acts.

¶Although the phrase "he'll grow out of it" is commonly used to dismiss many forms of childhood behavior, it is not always true. Children tend to make more demands, become more involved, become less anxious, less sexually curious, and fight less as they get older. However, the problems of delusions and isolation (no friends) show no variance with age.

The first phase of the study, completed last year, reported that at least 12 per cent of all Manhattan children and 23 per cent of welfare children in Manhattan suffer from mental illness serious enough to require immediate treatment.

It also reported that Negro children, age 6 to 9, tend to be as normal as all other children but that their impairment rate rises from 4 per cent to 28 per cent by the time they reach adolescence, regardless of the income level. This phenomenon was attributed to the effects of racial discrimination.

The next phase of the project, scheduled for completion within several weeks, will evaluate the role of parental behavior in children's psychological development.

"We've been following this group for five years," Dr. Langner, the principal investigator, said, "and some of the 'children' are now 23 years old and are parents themselves.

"One question we will be exploring," he continued, "is can people really behave in a way that is different from the way their parents treated them? Some bend over backwards to do so, but I really don't know."

The other members of the team are Dr. Edward L. Greene, Dr. Joseph H. Herson, Dr. Jean D. Jameson, Jeanne A. Goff and Elizabeth D. McCarthy.

March 2, 1970

Reverse Effect Feared in Pushing Black Pride

By THOMAS A. JOHNSON

According to two black psychiatrists, though most effects of black consciousness have been beneficial, "it is possible that drilling black pride into a child's head in a stereotyped and isolated manner may actually have the reverse effect."

These are the contentions of Dr. Alvin Poussaint of Harvard and Dr. James P. Comer of Yale.

In an article in the January issue of Redbook magazine, the two psychiatrists write: "Those who teach by rote the slogans of black dignity — 'I am Afro-American,' 'Black is beautiful' — may be too extreme in their approach."

Now, they said, parents must "provide the proper love and guidance for their children or

2 Black Psychiatrists Urge Parents Not to Overdo Racial Dignity Talk

the rhetoric of racial dignity will be self-defeating."

Cite Responsibility

Black parents, the psychiatrists maintained, face a greater responsibility than ever before to "try to raise men and women who are emotionally healthy in a society that is basically racist."

"We believe the first crucial step must be to emphasize a spirit of community with all black people, making clear to our children that they are not alone in the struggle," they declared. "We must encourage them to know our history, to appreciate our heritage and to fight for our rights."

They noted that during slavery, black mothers established "excessive control over their children, particularly the males, because any show of aggression toward whites might cost them their lives."

They said that fearful blacks of past generations were partly victims of "parental teachings that sought to fit the child into a repressive society."

"Our job is to help our children develop that delicate balance between appropriate control and appropriate display of anger and aggression, love and hate."

Need for Article

Dr. Poussaint, former director of the Medical Committee for Civil Rights, said during an interview yesterday that the article was prepared "because there is no place black parents can go and get information unique to the psychiatric needs of the black community."

He said: "Dr. Comer and I felt we should take what we knew on the subject and impart it to black families since there is so much racism continually bombarding their community."

While there is much material published on child care in books, newspapers and magazine columns, Dr. Poussaint said, it is, for the most part, intended for white, middle-class families.

"There is practically nothing published for the white poor either," he said.

Dr. Poussaint is an associate professor of psychiatry and associate dean of student affairs at Harvard Medical School and Dr. Comer is an associate professor of psychiatry at the Yale Child Study Center and associate dean of the Yale Medical School.

December 22, 1970

For Him, There Is No Exit From the Cellar

By Kenneth Keniston

Current trends that are depopulating families and narrowing judgments of children to measures of their intellects directly touch *all* American children. But a particular group is afflicted by all these pressures and one more besides—exclusion. These are children born in the cellar of our society and systematically brought up to remain there.

Our sentiments in their behalf are always touching. Our treatment of them is heartbreaking. Our excluded include one-quarter of all American children, and the tragic truth is that today *one-quarter of all American children are being brought up to fail.*

Why? The reasons include race, poverty, handicap and being born of parents too overwhelmed by life to be able to care responsively and lovingly for their children.

◼

The one out of every five children in America who is nonwhite must somehow cope with institutional and psychological racism that the rest of us are seldom aware of because we do not experience it. The one out of every three children who lives below the minimum adequate budget established by the Labor Department must face the multiple scars of poverty. One out of every twelve children is born with a major or minor handicap, and all of these children face the stigmas and social burdens that accompany any disability.

Approximately one-quarter of all American children do not receive anything approaching adequate health care, nor did their mothers before they were born—whence our disgraceful in-

Maurice Sendak

41

fant mortality rates. Millions of children live in substandard housing. Millions attend deplorable schools. And how many parents are themselves so overwhelmed by the stresses of their lives that they are unable to provide responsive care to their children? We don't know, but there are millions, rich and poor.

What makes these facts even more disturbing is the frequency with which they occur together. Poverty is irrevocably linked to inadequate medical care. Children who most desperately need good schools most often wind up in bad ones. To speak of the poor and the hungry is almost redundant—and a hungry child can rarely do well in school.

But the most powerful results of exclusion are social and psychological. The children of the poor live in a world more dangerous by far than that of the prosperous. The poor child's is a world of broken window glass, lead paint and stairs without railings. Or it may be a rural world, where families cannot maintain the minimal levels of public health considered necessary a century ago.

Urban or rural, it is a world of aching teeth without dentists to fill them, of untreated ear infections that result in permanent deafness. It is a world wherein a child easily learns to be ashamed of the way he or she lives. Such a world teaches many children to suppress any natural impulse to explore, to reach out. And it teaches many others that the best defense against a hostile world is constant offense — belligerent aggressiveness, sullen (and justified) anger, deep mistrust, and readiness for violence. Harsh as it is to say it, such children are systematically trained for failure.

Our social and political history sings with our commitment to equality and fair play. Nothing in our constellation of basic value even hints that our

society should impose special burdens upon special children. How, then, can we understand the perpetuation of exclusion?

One answer, put forward for almost two centuries in America and repeated again today, is that those at the bottom deserve to be there. They are said to lack virtue, merit, industriousness or talent. Or they are thought immoral —lazy, dependent, unreliable, spendthrift or licentious. Or they are said to inherit from their unfortunate parents a genetic propensity toward "low I.Q." or "concrete thinking."

But far more persuasive, I believe, is the suggestion that the excluded are among us not because of their individual inadequacy or immorality but rather because of the way our society works, the way it has worked for more than a century.

Let me point to one cold and significant fact: The distribution of wealth and income in this nation has not changed materially in 150 years. While many people have moved ahead of their parents economically, groups ahead of them have moved up also, leaving little net change. The distribution has not been changed by our promises of equal opportunity, or by our efforts at schooling, or by all of the general increases in our national prosperity, or by all of our efforts to reform, change, uplift or "help" those at the bottom of our society.

Exclusion persists not because of the evil motives of robber barons or the wicked intentions of capitalists. It persists because we all live in a system driven by the relentless quest for innovation, growth and profit. That system has worked well given its goals. It has made us the most prosperous and technologically advanced nation in world history.

But the prosperity of our comforta-

ble groups at least partly depends on having a pool of cheap labor—individuals and families driven by economic need to accept menial, dead-end, low-paying work. There are menial jobs to be done in any society, of course—but the question is whether they are to be filled by paying decent wages, or by impelling desperate souls to do them out of chronic need.

America's economic success has been reaped at a price that does not appear on corporate ledger sheets or the gross national product. For children this neglected price includes the pressures that are emptying families and cudgeling children to be narrow thinking machines. And it includes the misery and despair and neglect and hunger and want of that vast fraction of us whom I have called the excluded.

Some prices we should not be willing to pay. In the long run, the price of exclusion is enormous—not only in dollars laid out for remedial services, for prisons, and for mental hospitals, but in the anguish and pain exacted by social tension and discontent.

And this nation pays a continuing price far more serious, and beyond quantifying. This is the moral and human price we pay simply by tolerating a system that wastes a significant portion of the potential of the next generation, lets the advantage of some rest upon the systematic deprivation of others and subtly subverts in all of us our best instincts for loving our children.

Kenneth Keniston, Mellon Professor of Human Development at the Massachusetts Institute of Technology, is chairman and executive director of the Carnegie Council on Children. This article is adapted from a speech to the American Orthopsychiatric Association.

February 20, 1976

CHILDREN AND SOCIAL VALUES

WAR INCREASES TOY SOLDIER SALES

Shotguns Also Best Sellers Now, and New War Games Being Devised for Children.

By Elsie Clews Parsons.

WE thought there were soldiers enough being killed off, so we put dogs in here," said the toy agent, pointing to the little target figures at the end of the toy rifle range he was showing me. His exhibit was the first I visited; the other toy manufacturers, I soon found, had not made such pacifist compromises with the prevailing war spirit.

To take the place of the lead soldier made in Germany, one firm had made a steel soldier very durable and quite

neutral, his breeches Magyar, his coat English, his helmet German. He is cheap, too, the little set of fifteen infantrymen and three cavalrymen costing 25 cents, as against the price of the imported pewter set of soldiers, $1. As for the sale of the paper and wooden soldier of a neighboring exhibit, it has gone up from the rate of three million a year before the war to five million since. The sales of the toy shotguns have also increased. In one firm the employees have been increased from sixty to one hundred and eighty, and they work in day

and night shifts. This firm made not only guns but war games. Their history is interesting because it is so recent. They are an adaptation of the peaceful map game made by the firm before the war, a game of the shortest routes for parcel posts or a game to be won by locating the capitals of the States or by naming rivers and harbors. Today a boy will learn geography, not in puzzling out the quickest means of transport or communication, but in planning how to outwit the enemy and capture his forts and his men. Similar map war games, let me add, are sold

by several firms, and by the thousand.

Although war games were in the market before the European war, since the war their sale has greatly increased. This increase impresses me as one of the most important effects in this country of the European war. Disputations about this impression I cannot be, for my evidence will not be available for another decade or two, not until our little boys have grown up; but I can argue that it is by the most militaristic of the European countries that the toy soldier has been produced, and I can reflect upon the con-

"Soldiering Is Indorsed and Made Familiar in the Nursery."

attributes, then, of a soldier, mixed together in the mind of the child, and to please mother and get the rewards she holds out one must be like a soldier.

This complex of feelings, impulses, and ideas about soldiering or fighting, given as it is at the early, impressionable age, is not easily analyzed at a later period. No such early association is. Early associations are hard to break up; they resist the analysis of reason. They are resentful of the processes of criticism. To force them to relinquish their hold is so painful to most of us that we search for excuses and means of escape. Often we take refuge in the plea that what is asked of us is against human nature. When I allege that a given course of conduct is against human nature, what I usually mean is that it is destructive of the associations made in my mind when I was a very young child.

"But why not make these early associations?" asks the earnest mother. "I want to impress my boy with a standard for bravery," she urges, "and, though I do not believe in war, I can do it best through the war standards. What a boy believes in he must be ready to die for. Tell me, if you can, what gives him as great a spirit of self-devotion as playing soldier, not to speak of the glamour in it, the sense of adventure?"

In pioneering, in exploration, in surveying, in bridgemaking and railroading there is adventure; in discovering the secrets of nature or fitting them to man's service, in making beautiful things, in all

such effort or accomplishment there is glamour. Discovery and adaptation may be equivalents to the imagination for destruction. Outside of military circles how many men there are after all in whose lives the heroic may be a commonplace. The engineer who saves the bridge he has built from flood, his railroad from landslide, the bacteriologist who saves unnumbered thousands from yellow fever or typhoid, the forest conservationist or fire fighter, the irrigationist, the miner, the steeplejack, is not each quite as potential a hero as a soldier?

Records of life-saving may be quite as thrilling as records of war, and toy life-savers might be just as alluring, I fancy, as toy life-takers. Indeed, were I a manufacturer and a bit of a pacifist, the experiment of making toy life-savers would appeal to me—firemen, coastguards, lighthouse keepers, deep-sea divers, forest rangers, railroad signalmen, the monks of St. Bernard and their dogs, Red Cross workers. For all these and their outfits or paraphernalia, would not there be a market—a market for the rescue toy against the war toy with "to mothers who do not believe in war" the text of its advertising? From the pacifist point of view the experiment is undoubtedly worth while. Commercially it may also be warranted.

April 4, 1915

sequences in general of war toys and games.

Taking war for granted, must they not habituate to it the mind of the child? To the little boy who shoots down with his popgun his row of pewter (or steel) soldiers, does not the idea of killing people become a familiarity of a kind, freed at any rate from the dismay caused by novelty? It is not as thorough a familiarization, I grant you, as that thrusting of spears into a worn-out old crone the lads of Borneo are sometimes forced into by their militaristic elders, still it

serves as an introduction to the idea of killing people, an idea, I venture to say, that does not come easily to either the savage or the child. To inculcate it, the instincts of fear or of play are necessary.

Soldiering is indorsed and made familiar in the nursery by other associations. "Stand up straight, like a soldier," says a mother to her ambitious toddler. "Be brave, like a little soldier," she urges, as she pricks a splinter out of a finger. "If you're good, mother will make you a soldier's cap." Poise and self-respect, bravery and virtue, are the

MORAL TESTS REVEAL CHILDREN'S STANDARDS

Investigators of Teachers College Discover a Readiness to Cheat in School—Moral Codes of Parents and Children Compared and Value of Home Training Shown

By EUNICE FULLER BARNARD.

MOST students in elementary school and college will cheat when conditions are favorable; a minority even when the risks are great. Public school children cheat, on an average, four times as much as do pupils in private schools. Girls cheat more often in the classroom and boys more often in games—though girls' standards of right and wrong are, on the whole, higher than those of boys.

Even among four and five year old children, those with the highest moral standards are likely to be the most popular; children with the lowest standards have the fewest friends. The moral teachings of school and Sunday school teachers seem to have little influence. In spite of the prevalent idea that the younger generation is in moral revolt, children's ethical codes are derived mainly from their parents, especially from their mothers, though the standards of mother and father generally coincide to a remarkable extent.

These are not mere opinions. They are statistical results of the new moral tests. For today, almost twenty years after the invention of the intelligence tests, psychologists are beginning to devise workable measuring scales for character.

An Honesty Index.

For a decade, ever since its use in the draft suggested that the average citizen had a mental age of about 14 years, the "I. Q." has been almost as familiar a term of intellectual rating as is Bradstreet's of financial. Ten or twenty years hence, political orators may not dare vaunt their candidate's sterling honesty, for their opponents can look up his honesty index and see what his percentage of alloy really is. A scale is already being devised to show not only whether a man is honest but also to determine his degree of resistance to dishonesty. The "still, small voice" is rapidly becoming a loud-speaker.

Between 1920 and 1925 some 200 books and articles were written on scientific tests for various character traits—deception, conscientiousness, perseverance, fair-mindedness, ability to "mix" and some seventy others. Since that time the whole investigation has been focused by the establishment of the character education inquiry at Teachers College, Columbia University. In the last two years Dr. Mark May, Dr. Hugh Hartshorne and

their associates have classified and in some cases evaluated existing tests, and have tried out new ones in all types of schools—Sunday schools, boys' and girls' clubs—even in the children's homes. Already the results give a new insight into children's conduct and moral standards and their relation to age, intelligence, sex and training.

Honesty is one of the most investigated traits of the long laboratory list. The scale the Teachers College inquiry is evolving consists of a graduated series of tests to show attitudes toward cheating in school. Dishonesty, for the purposes of scientific inquiry, is not to be thought of as either good or bad. It is simply a form of energy, like heat, and as such is to be measured by the work done. This work can assumably be measured by the resistance overcome in doing it. The measuring-scale tests must therefore have a series of obstacles to cheating ranging from the difficult to the negligible.

The technique adopted by the investigators is simply to give children a series of ordinary written tests in information, language, spelling and arithmetic. These papers are then taken to the office and duplicated. A

43

day or two later the original papers are returned to the children with answer sheets, and each child is allowed to grade his own paper. These are then compared with the duplicates in the office.

In grading the first test it is made hard to cheat without detection, as it involves erasing a circle drawn in ink and adding another. Besides, there is no special motive for cheating, the child having been urged to guess at each answer he did not know. On the last tests it is easy to cheat, involving only the erasure of a pencil check mark or figure or adding another. Moreover, in marking the final test there is an incentive to cheat, the child being told that it will count in his monthly grade.

Results of the Tests.

These tests were tried out on 263 children from 8 to 16 years old in grades IV to VII. Eighty-four per cent. made at least one change in their papers. Two per cent. cheated even on the first test, where cheating was hardest and the risk greatest; 17 per cent. on the second, 43 per cent. on the third, and so on up to 80 per cent. on the last, where cheating was easiest.

Roughly, it did scale the children's classroom honesty. Some apparently cheated habitually, even under the most adverse circumstances, and the great majority cheated when conditions were favorable. Interestingly enough, while, as in all honesty tests, the duller children on the average did most of the cheating, the 2 per cent. who took the risk of erasing the ink circle were among the more intelligent.

By such methods the investigators hope to build complete scales for honesty and other traits. "Suppose," they say, "this scale for classroom situations be perfected. Suppose that another be constructed for games; then another for situations involving money or business transactions. These could be placed alongside each other, so that at each level there would be two or more situations. Such a scale would give a measure of the whole complex of behavior tendencies called dishonesty." Already there are individual tests for both games and money dealings. One of the latter determines whether the child will return overchange. Another shows whether he will keep money sent him through the mail "by mistake."

Apparently the amount of cheating is affected by the classroom atmosphere; the teacher's relation with the taught. Comparing 1,200 public school children with children in six private schools, it was found that four times as many public school children deceived. "This may be due," says the report, "to either a highly selected population in the private schools or to fundamental differences in school procedure. If method is what does it, then children from equivalent homes in public school and private school and with equivalent intelligence should still show a difference in favor of the private school. We equalized two sets of children and the differences were still maintained."

Next they compared an ordinary public school with a school connected with a normal school using freer, more progressive methods. Again the amount of cheating was much less in the more progressive school. "The case is not proved," says the report, yet it seems to indicate that "changes in school procedure which change the traditional hostile attitude between pupil and teacher to one of friendly confidence may tend to eliminate dishonest practices in school work."

Again, the examiners tested 3,600 children in schools using two popular moral education schemes involving membership in a league or order. Here they found that members cheated as much as did non-members—in some cases more. Children's own moral codes seem to determine their conduct. For instance, 91 per cent. of those who, on a moral knowledge test, said they thought it all right to let another pupil copy one's work and hand it in as his own actually cheated themselves, as did 93 per cent. of those who answered that it was right for a boy to cheat in order to help his class win.

A Search for Moral Codes.

But what are children's moral codes? Are they individual or more or less alike? Do they come from the home, school, Sunday school or club? To determine this, identical tests were given to 1,159 children and their teachers in Grades V to IX in seven schools located in different towns. More than half of these children took another form of the same test in their homes, in most cases one or both parents taking it with them. In the same way it was given in Sunday schools and clubs, teachers and club leaders participating.

Five tests were used, two asking more or less abstract ethical judgments, the other three more personal. For instance, in one of the latter a list of "duties" was given which the person taking the test was to mark "Yes," "No," or "Sometimes," according as he believed each to be a genuine duty. Some of them were:

To take a temperance pledge.
To sell tickets to your school entertainments.

To keep every secret that you promise to keep.
To keep quiet when older persons are talking.

On many of these subjects the judgments of adults are very much divided. For the purpose of the test, however, the answers must be scored right or wrong. The investigators, therefore, took as their main criterion a 75 per cent. majority opinion of a class of graduate students, reversing them only on a few items. The graduate class by a majority of 4 to 1 answered "Yes" on the temperance pledge. The investigators thought the right answer was "No." Similarly on the other three items the class majority voted "Yes." The investigators considered the better answer to be "Sometimes."

Even more controversial was a test called "Provocations," with such questions as:

The neighbors had been kept awake at night by two cats fighting. So Fred set his bulldog on them.
Was this right, wrong but excusable, or entirely wrong?

The majority of the graduate class voted it excusable. The examiners thought "Wrong" a better answer.

On the five tests, each demanding ten to thirty-six judgments of this type, the scores of public school teachers averaged highest—ten points above those of club leaders, parents and Sunday school teachers, who were almost tied for second place.

More significant, however, was the correspondence of the answers of the different groups. According to the figures, children's moral codes are based first on those of their parents, and secondarily on those of their friends, with little relation to the codes of school or Sunday school teachers or of club leaders. Again, the moral codes of the children resemble those of their mothers more than those of their fathers.

The relation between the child's moral notions and those of his friends was obtained by asking the child to write down the names of three or four chums at school. Their average moral scores and his own code were com-

A MORAL TEST FOR YOUNG CHILDREN

The Question Asked Is: "What Would You Do if Somebody Hit You Without Meaning to Do It? This One (1) Says 'I'd Tell His Mother,' This One (2) Says 'I'd Hit Him Back,' This One (3) Says 'I'd Cry,' This One (4) Says 'I'd Not Do Anything.' What Would You Do if Somebody Hit You Without Meaning to Do It? Mark It." A Test Devised by Dr. Bess V. Cunningham of Teachers College.

pared. Mainly the children named classmates, but, contrary to the usual assumption, boys named girls and girls named boys as friends almost as freely as they designated members of their own sex. Seventy-nine children, or nearly 7 per cent., named no friends at all, while 145, or 12 per cent., were not named as friends by any other child. Within the groups of friends, figures indicated that moral ideas tended to be more alike among the older children, showing friendship to be more and more influential with increasing years.

Moreover, as the children grow older their moral knowledge scores improve. The scales show a steady rise, with a total of thirteen points of difference between the fifth grade and the ninth.

In the Columbia graduate class 45 per cent. marked it right, 42 per cent. wrong but excusable, and only 13 per cent. unqualifiedly wrong. In a sixth grade 85 per cent. marked it right, 6 per cent. wrong but excusable, and 9 per cent entirely wrong. The examiners, on the other hand, in scoring gave a credit of one to "excusable" and of two to "entirely wrong."

Consistently through every grade the girls' scores are from three to four points higher than are those of the boys. Possibly this is due, the investigators think, to the fact that as a rule girls spend more time at home with the mother.

March 20, 1927

Child Frustration Breeds Race Hatred

Columbia Scientist Asserts Punishment of Baby May Be Seed of War

North American Newspaper Alliance
WASHINGTON, Dec. 21—Spanking the baby may be the psychological seed of war.

Out of this and similar punishments are formed the repressed hatreds which find their outlet later in the race prejudice which is making a shambles of Europe in the hands of a clever manipulator, declares Dr. Montague Francis Ashley-Montagu, Columbia University anthropologist, in a report on the basis for race differences just made public by the William A. White Psychiatric Foundation here.

The aggressiveness which adults exhibit, Dr. Montagu says, "is originally produced during childhood by parents, teachers, nurses, or whoever else participates in the process of socializing the child. By depriving the infant of all those means of satisfaction which it seeks—the freedom to cry at will, to scream and shout, to stay up as late as one wishes, to be the thousand and one things that are forbidden—frustration upon frustration is piled up within the child. Such frustrations lead to resentment, fear, hatred and aggression.

"In childhood this aggressiveness is displayed in bad temper and in general naughtiness. Such conduct almost invariably results in further frustration—in punishment. At this stage the child finds itself in a state of severe conflict. Either he must control the expression of his aggressiveness or else suffer the punishment and loss of love which it provokes.

Conflicts Seek Expression

"Such conflicts are usually resolved by excluding the painful situation from consciousness and from direct motor expression—in short by the repression of one's aggressive energies. But the evidence renders it overwhelmingly certain that these energies are never to any extent destroyed. Being a part of the total organism they must, in one way or another, find expression. The ways are innumerable. Race hatred is merely one of them."

The original feeling of aggression is against the frustrators, Dr. Montagu says. But against them any expression of it must be repressed. The child depends on them for everything and can go only a short way in risking their displeasure. Besides, the moral background of the race dictates that they must be respected and obeyed.

"This aggressiveness which is more or less common to all human beings," Dr. Montagu says, "is not itself the cause of race prejudice, but merely represents an effective energy which can be attached, among other things, to the notion that other groups are hateful, and may thus serve to keep such ideas supplied with the emotional force necessary to keep them going.

"Since the infliction of mental and even physical pain, as well as the frustration and depreciation of others, is involved in the process of race prejudice, and since much of the aggressiveness of the individual owes its existence to early experiences of the same sort, it is perhaps not difficult to understand why most people are so ready to participate in the exercise of race prejudice. By so doing they are able to find an object for their aggressiveness."

Says Few Avoid Race Prejudice

There are few individuals anywhere, he says, who have not shown race prejudice at some time, and most individuals are capable of being brought to a state of mind in which they are really glad of the opportunity of freely releasing their feelings against some group. When society lends its sanction to the attachment of such feelings to any group the free exercise of racial intolerance is enjoyed as a happy release for feelings.

Those tensions which must find an outlet, he comments, continue to be built up through life on the base of those laid down in early childhood.

It will do little good, Dr. Montagu says, to teach tolerance between peoples. Education, he says, "must be in the processes which lead to a completely integrated human being—humanity first and facts afterward. For of what use are facts unless they are intelligently understood and humanely used?"

Actually, he insists, all the data available show that the differences between races are very insignificant, especially in the mental and emotional fields.

December 22, 1940

War Need Not Mar Our Children

By MARGARET MEAD,
Assistant Curator of Ethnology,
American Museum of Natural History

CAN we protect our children in wartime? In the bottom of their hearts most Americans believe that we cannot, that we are condemned to seeing a whole generation of little children marred by war. This basic belief shows through the barrage of nervous, excitable questions, of rumors and cross-rumors, about evacuation and air raid shelters, about nutrition plans, identification tags, and discussion of what to tell the children about the war.

From the mother of young children to the welfare worker, the nurse, the teacher, come the anxious, recurrent, worried questions, sometimes cast in personal terms, sometimes including all the children of America within their scope. What is going to happen to education? Won't all the school routines be interrupted? Isn't there going to be a dreadful increase in juvenile delinquency? Have we the available child psychologists to deal with the children who are war-shocked?

On the surface, these all appear merely reasonable questions, which should be answered quietly, informatively, with facts about how evacuation is finally working out in England, with authoritative statements from the best child psychiatrists about how slightly children have actually suffered from the Blitz itself, and how much more they suffered from evacuation away from parents, friends and teachers. Child-guidance experts can be brought in to state clearly, definitely, that if the adults are calm, unhysterical, serene, the children will not show any serious signs of shock. The best experience in England, backed up by two years of careful work, shows these signs to be true. If we tell inquiring and anxious mothers these things, will they not be reassured?

SIMILARLY, with the welfare workers. They recognize the immense unfilled needs in this country for better health and welfare work. Isn't their anxiety merely a reasonable and responsible insistence on the things to be done? And the teachers, worrying about the interruptions of education, the problems of possible school evacuation? Well, they were problems in England. Education was terribly interrupted. In 1941 the Minister of Education, broadcasting, announced that, of 5,000,000 elementary school children, 700,000 were receiving only part-time instruction and 800,000 were "unaccounted for." If this happened in England, isn't it reasonable for teachers to be worried about what is to happen here?

But when we analyze all these fears and worries into those which appear reasonable and those which appear to be due to ignorance, and carefully remove the ignorance, explain that evacuation is working very well in England, advance programs for welfare action in this country, do we find that the persistent fear disappears? No, instead we find that it continues, and those who have tried to explain it have been driven to various sorts of indictment of Americans, mothers and teachers and welfare workers, as hysterical and unable to take it. They say that this recurrent fear of "what the war is going to do to our children" is just a projection of our own instability. And then those people who

45

enjoy spreading accounts of how low morale is tell about a welfare council meeting entirely devoted to identification tags and sand boxes for putting out bombs.

But an anthropologist who has watched attitudes of adults toward children in many different societies will give a different answer. Admitting that wartime brings dislocation and confusion, admitting that people are badly misinformed about conditions in England and know only of the failures and very little of the successes, and do not realize that evacuation of children through careful stages of day nurseries and then to country school camps is now a very going concern, the anthropologist recognizes that there is more behind this fear than lack of information or individual hysteria.

AMERICANS have been reared in the belief that any contact with the facts of life and death is dangerous to children. Birth, sex, dying and death are occasions for which children have been hustled away. The ears of mothers and teachers and social workers have been filled with accounts of the terrible effects which such scenes, accidentally witnessed, have had on children's tender minds.

We know, of course, that in the slums children often see such things, but that is vaguely felt to be responsible for the amount of crime which comes out of the slums. Children must be protected, at all costs, from any close contact with the realities. Even the modern educational methods which have mocked at the flowers-and-bees stories and insisted upon telling children "the facts of life" have halted before the suggestions of telling children very much about the facts of death.

On every hand we find traces of this attitude—movies which are regarded as unfit for children, plans to take the older child away when the new baby is born, disapproval of those of European or simple country background who would take a child to a funeral or allow it to see a laid-out body. Our comfortable urban classes have been protected from birth and taught that they must protect all children from these scarring contacts.

Then suddenly, and for the first time in our lifetime, there is the possibility that mothers and teachers and welfare workers will not be able to protect children from such things, that bombs may fall and people die before their eyes, that no will in the world can give them the safety from the harsh realities which we have believed are lethal to children's psychological welfare. Therefore, people are worried, worried as they would be if they were told that their children's diet for the next two or three years was to contain a daily dose of poison.

It is not merely the chance of death from bombs—for most people know that only one-quarter of 1 per cent of the civilian population of London were casualties in the midst of a Blitz far more terrible than American cities are likely to encounter—but it is the chance of psychological maiming from the knowledge and experience of death to others, by bombs, which seems so dangerous.

BELATEDLY, those who have lectured on child care and warned of the extreme sensitivity of the growing human organism are now trying to reassure mothers and

teachers by telling them how tough, how superficial, how "don't carish" children naturally are. They also reiterate the point made by psychiatrists who have watched English children, that if the adults are calm the children will be calm.

But none of this gets at the root of the trouble. Persistently, at the back of their minds, people continue to believe, as they have been taught, that contact with death will maim their children's minds for life. Unless this basic issue is faced all the job of reassurance and information and exhortation to calmness will fail and the fear of what will happen to the children of America will remain a terrible vulnerable point in American morale.

And so the anthropologist is asked: "It is true? Will scenes of dying mar a child's mind for life?" And to this the anthropologist can answer: "No, not unless the adults expect them to." I have seen a group of Samoan children clustered with their elders around an open grave in which a post-mortem Caesarian operation was being performed, interested, curious, but unhurt, going away afterward to play, discussing the scene lightly afterward.

Neither the adults nor the children were upset. It was sad that the mother had died, sad that the baby—yes, it was a girl and a pretty one too—had died, but people did die, every month or so in the village and those immediately bereft wept. No one shooed the children away, no one suggested that they weren't able to watch quietly, as their elders. And the shared experience brought no nightmares. Yet this was a scene which would send a certain thrill of fearful repulsion down the spine of the average American adult.

ON the other hand, I have seen children fall into paralyzed fear-sleeps, fear from which they could not be awakened except by five minutes of severe shaking, in Bali, during an ordinary birth, when no one had died and no one was going to die. Folklore, in Bali, surrounds a birth scene with witches, dreadful long-nailed harpies, ready to snatch the new-born child away, and children have been so terrorized by such tales that they go into these terror sleeps in the midst of all the excitement of a birth scene.

In other parts of the South Seas I have seen children take part in mourning scenes of great violence, where the mourners, arriving in canoes, ran the length of the rocking pile house and flung themselves on the corpse with such force that sometimes the whole house floor broke and the mourning crowd, adults and children, fell into the sea. But the night after scenes like this no nightmare cries rang through the village.

Children are not maimed by contact with death or with life. They are maimed if they have to face such contact alone or if all

those around them expect them to be maimed, or if, as too often happens, their only contact with the facts of life and death comes to them in the death of a member of their own family. Unprepared to face any reality, and suddenly confronted with its full impact in their own families, they have, of course, been traumatized, and child-guidance experts have told us of their cases. In England, also, children who have seen members of their own family injured or killed have suffered psychologically, though not to such a degree that psychiatry cannot restore them to full functioning.

BUT the simple facts of life and death, as they occur in war or peace, in the community, do not hurt children. We have been overprotecting children for fifty years, and now, faced with the circumstance that we can overprotect them no longer, Americans are worried. Unless they can learn to believe that their worry is needless, that they can protect their children simply by including them, serenely, within the community circle as the community faces whatever disasters may come—the children will be hurt, not by bombs, but by the isolation thrust upon them as their parents tensely put them off with feeble fibs and tales that the blackout is to keep the naughty Japs from stealing their toys. The children can stand up to reality, however grim, if the adults can, and if the adults believe in the children's strength.

When those responsible for planning—citizens, welfare workers, civilian defense officials have crossed this cultural hurdle, have shaken off the fear that no child can stand contact with death, then we can get on with the business of considering just what methods are best to give children the health and educational protection which they will need during this emergency period.

WHAT those practical plans should be is now fairly well known. Bombed cities, sabotaged cities without adequate heat or light or sanitation, are no places for children. Many defense areas in which the majority of women are working and where living conditions are incredibly bad, are very doubtful places for children.

On the other hand, foster home placement on any large scale is equally not recommended. In England far more psychological casualties have been found in children placed in foster homes away from the Blitz than among children left with their parents, schoolmates and teachers, right in the Blitz. But from this very well-documented fact many American planners here have drawn the hasty conclusion that therefore children should not be moved anywhere, even if by moving they would be given better health and educational opportunities.

Actually the English experience has shown that school groups, nursery school, kindergarten and elementary school groups, first grown accustomed over a few months to being away from their mothers and with their class and their teachers, can be moved to the country together, without the penalties which accompanied placing children in strange foster homes. Adjust-ment to school as one step away from home is something that all of us expect, that parents and children alike are prepared for. The teacher does not replace the mother in the child's affections; there is no conflict between the own mother left behind and a foster mother on whom the child is dependent.

The United States may never have to face any sort of evacuation. But the people of the coastal cities will have to live as if air raids were a possibility for the duration. This means preparing to protect our children. Such preparation involves cultivating the belief that greater contact with the facts of life and death will not, in itself, hurt them, and developing more nursery schools, more day nurseries, more kindergartens, closer ties between parents and teachers, all as insurance against possible evacuation.

If evacuation should come, the child who has never been away from his mother's side for half a day is the child whom it will be most difficult to protect. Left in the city, his health, his sleep, his education will be endangered. If he is taken suddenly from his mother his whole psychological adjustment will be equally endangered. Provisional weaning, a few hours every day in some sort of nursery or kindergarten for every child, will guarantee, as no other measure can, protection for our children in wartime.

February 15, 1942

URGE PARENTS ACCEPT JUVENILE WAR GAMES

Psychology Experts Call 'Kill Jap' Play Harmless Outlet

CHICAGO, Aug. 8 (AP)—Parents whose youngsters play such blood-thirsty games as "kill the Japs" or "mow down the Nazis" need not be afraid the children will grow up with anti-social over-aggressive complexes, according to three experts in child psychology. They said the war games were harmless provided they were held within reasonable limits.

Charlotte Towle, associate professor of psychiatric social work at the University of Chicago, and Dr. Robert N. McMurry, assistant professor of psychology at the Central Y. M. C. A. College, asserted that the war games might have a definite therapeutic value, while the third expert, Dr. John J. P. Morgan, Professor of Psychology at Northwestern University, said it was only natural for the youngsters to play militaristically in wartime.

"The danger," said Dr. Morgan, "lies not so much in the games children play as what they see and hear concerning the viciousness of our enemies. This develops hatred much quicker than playing war games. These tactics were used by the Nazis to develop hatred among children for everything non-German.

"But even this particular brand of hatred is apt to prove superficial, since it's born during the stress of war. Such feelings will be inclined to disappear when peace returns."

Professors Towle and McMurry said that playing at "killing the Japs and Germans" provided a good emotional relief to the "rage" which accumulated in children because of frustrations imposed by parents, teachers and others. Such a harmless outlet, they felt, was preferable to the children damming up.

August 9, 1943

'Prejudice Can Be Unlearned'

By CATHERINE MACKENZIE

PHILADELPHIA.

BARRIERS of dislike and distrust exist everywhere in America. Unspoken or openly declared, prejudice is our number one problem in getting together and working together. Where does prejudice come from? What can we do about it? Obviously no one is born with prejudice. Many persons contend that young children are friendly, get along together, do not see differences, or ignore them if they do. Still children, as well as adults, have prejudices.

What prejudices do children have? What can be done about them? Since 1945 the Philadelphia Early Childhood Project has been trying to find the answer to the questions the first research of its kind ever attempted. The experiment was the joint project of the Philadelphia public schools, the Bureau for Intercultural Education, the Research Center for Group Dynamics of the Massachusetts Institute of Technology and the Philadelphia Fellowship Commission. Work was carried on in the kindergartens and the first and second grades of five schools. The major aim was to find ways for the school to deal with prejudice, to combat and prevent it. The project has ended in the schools, but analysis of the data is far from complete.

In launching the project it was necessary first to know more about children; what prejudices they have, if any; "what children feel about their world," as the sponsors put it.

CATHERINE MACKENZIE received last year's $1,000 Lasker Award, and a special citation this year from the New York State Council for Early Childhood Education, for her contributions to education. She is parent-child editor of The Times.

MRS. HELEN G. TRAGER, project director of the Bureau for Intercultural Education, says it is a common assumption that "children catch prejudice in the middle years, 9 to 11; that they come to school at age 5 and 6 with minds like clean slates, accepting of and friendly toward all people." It is also widely assumed that young children are aware only of persons, unaware of "groups" or group differences, "and have no particular feelings about group membership." In other words, that little children are as vague about their own or other children's race, religion and national origin as they are about such conceptions of time and space as "a year" or "ten miles."

Because of these assumptions, and not by accident, the project holds, school intercultural programs have been directed toward older children. Mrs. Trager reports that school people are especially tenacious of the clean-slate view of children's minds. "Nonsense, little children don't feel prejudice," protested one principal at the outset of the study.

The Philadelphia research disputes this theory. Preliminary findings of the study show that five-year-olds bring to kindergarten definite feelings about race, awareness of religious differences and of the significance of "we're rich" or "they're poor." These feelings are strengthened in the first grade; still more strongly held by grade two.

Moreover, the inquiry shows that the source of prejudice is not exclusively "the home" or "the school," that prejudice is all around us. It is a basic part of our thinking, and feeling, and of the way we live. As the project staff puts it, "Preju-dice is part of our culture."

It is not a new idea that prejudice takes early root. As Sister Mary de Lourdes once stated, "Our prejudices begin to tell on our children from the seventh month on; the tone of our voice rather than the word itself carries meaning to them." Previous studies made by means of question and answer, or by classmate choices, had charted the prejudices of school children. Still other studies supported the common observation that prejudice has its source in the precepts and attitudes handed down by, and reinforced, in homes and surroundings.

THE Philadelphia project was the first effort to test the validity of these views. In many ways it was pioneer research. It went back to early childhood. Its observations were not made in a laboratory or a clinic, but in everyday life and at first hand. The study went on as the children learned, played, fought, called names, made friends, in classrooms, on playgrounds.

There were no guideposts for such a study. New test materials, new methods of approach had to be devised. A notable development was the active cooperation of classroom teachers. Mary V. Thompson, a classroom teacher, gave full-time leadership. Whatever was learned had to be understood, accepted and applied by teachers, Mrs. Trager explains; it seemed a sound idea to enlist their help from the start.

Besides, no one was better situated than the teacher to observe and record the rich, revealing stuff of children's lives, the things they did and said, showing likes and dislikes. *(Continued)* their feelings about themselves and their companions. It was not a strange observer, but a child's own teacher, in the ordinary run of the day's work, who noted their answers to formboard and picture tests, their choices of partners in games. Teachers collected the children's drawings, talked with their mothers, learned how they lived at home, and jotted it all down for the record. Trained psychologists assisted in collecting much of the material, under the direction of Dr. Marian Radke of M.I.T., who was responsible for all scientific aspects of the study.

SOME four hundred children have been observed—Negro, white and Oriental; Catholic, Jewish and Protestant; Italian, Central European, English and Scotch-Irish in family origin. The project considered them a fair cross-section of the children who go to school in an American city.

Moreover, 230 children were interviewed and retested, individually, to gain an all-around picture of a number of "whole" children. Particulars of their home life, their feelings about themselves, their families, form part of this amplified record. It is hoped that from this data something may be learned about the personality make-up, and the emotions tied up with prejudice, and about ways in which ideas and attitudes develop.

There is no question of what the ideas and attitudes are. On the basis of values absorbed in their first five years the children came to school avoiding or accepting other children; knowing what it was to be avoided.

"They won't let him play because he's colored," white children said to explain why a Negro child was left out of a game. Forty-three per cent of the children knew this by kindergarten age. By the second grade seventy-three per cent of the children knew it. Negro children also understood their exclusion. " 'Cause he ain't white" was their comment on why one of their number was not asked to play.

ACCORDING to Mrs. Trager, the facts so far analyzed indicate that the children's awareness of differences parallel the "anti-" feelings reflected in adult opinion polls, and in the same order of intensity—Negro, Jewish, Catholic.

Early awareness of differences, of "group belongings," is a finding stressed by Mrs. Trager. Identifying themselves with religious groups, children said:

"Only Protestant schools have dentists, don't they?"

"I go to Hebrew School . . . we got to learn how to be with Jewish people."

"Catholics are better'n everybody."

Such off-hand remarks are only a fraction of the research material. Few of the emotional overtones are conveyed in print, yet they offer little surface signs of strong undercurrents running deep and dividing us.

THE preliminary findings show that of all prejudices that of color is most marked, the feeling expressed most hostile. Analysis of fifty-seven interviews by M.I.T.'s Research Center revealed these descriptions of Negroes:

"They kill people. Sometimes when people are coming out of the movies they slug them. They go in beer saloons and get drunk."

"There was a colored maniac at my sister's school, brown skin."

"Germans are real light and niggers are real black."

"Colored people — there are some in this school, just people like us."

The report shows that even when describing the Negro in terms of skin color—as more than half the children did—the implications are "not good." For example:

"You'd be afraid of them 'cause some are real dark. Some have guns in their pockets. If I see one I walk away."

"They do things bad and all, they're brown and don't have no hair. They'se bad. White people don't allow colored people in their church. They have all kinds of diseases all over them."

The report adds: "A stereotype which occurs very frequently includes references to weapons and killing, such as: 'Nigger man with a knife, wanted to cut white man's head off.' "

Descriptions of their own group by Negro children are "noticeably" similar to those of white children (carrying knives, killing people, and so on) and at the same time they say, "I like colored the best." This may be due to the fact that Negro children are badly mixed up in their feelings. At least there were indications of "severe conflict" in their responses toward their own group and the white group.

In contrast the investigators found a sharp difference in responses on conflict between groups: "Well over half of the white children describe Negroes in terms of conflict, whereas only one Negro child out of thirteen mentions it. This seems to be an over-avoidance of it by the Negro children."

IN describing "white" the

Project finds the Negro child's feelings often "masked" in such responses as, "They are nice. They smiles at you." Some Negro children dwell on physical appearance. Such responses as "Their face is white, arms—all over white" represent a preoccupation in which the investigators find "wistful yearning," and one more example of the confusion which adds up to "I like what I am, but I'd like to be what you are."

Most descriptions of "Jewish" by 6 and 7-year-olds were in terms of customs:

"They talk funny."

"They sell all kinds of stuff."

"They's home on Jewish holidays."

"Sunday's can't eat nothing. Not a sip of water. It would be a sin."

"They sell Jewish crackers, bread. They cheat you."

"Stereotypes on 'Jewish' appear most frequently in specific unfriendly terms," the report states, "a reference to language occurs frequently. 'They talk like they're coughing'. 'They talk just like a Jewish person, they make the words sound funny so you can't understand.' . . . 'They're stingy, that means Jews. When Sisters go around for money they don't give it.' . . . 'They pray to idols, make pictures and pray to them.' . . . 'Jewish people are mean. They are selfish and mean and never good. They tell lies.' 'They say bad words, sloppy words. They hit.' "

Descriptions of "Catholic" are most often given in terms of the institution:

"You have to go to church on Sunday." . . .

"It's a Catholic School."

"You don't eat meat on Friday." . . . "Have candles."

"They wear pins, they go and make first communion."

ACCORDING to the analysis: "There are few responses on Catholic which characterize the whole group as good or bad; such as 'I think Catholics are better than Protestants' or 'I think Catholics ain't so good.' Specific stereotypes refer mostly to Catholic school: such as 'Catholic School is where Sisters hit them around.' Another child sees Catholic mainly in terms of nuns and says 'Catholics is ladies. Black cape over head, white around their head—just ladies.' "

"Don't know" is the most frequent answer to "What is Protestant?" Some children said:

"You go to Protestant school and don't go to Catholic."

"Not like Catholic, they vote different, against each other."

"You sing hymns and say

prayers. That's American."

In the interviews analyzed there were few "stereotypes" about Protestants—these are positive and given by Protestant children. "Protestant, that's American." . . . "Protestants are white." "Protestants are best."

The data comes from a small sampling which shows "no differences evident between Catholic, Protestant and Jewish children in frequency of rejection of Negro children" . . . and no evidence of difference between Catholic and Protestant children in their reaction to Jewish groups. There is a small number of rejections of Catholic (four Protestant children)."

WHAT can be done about prejudice?

The Project's sponsors believe that the school can help. It is held that no matter what she teaches, the teacher communicates her own attitudes to the children. Regardless of subject matter, or phrases on the blackboard, the teacher's feelings toward people, and her values, become part of the lessons learned.

To test this hypothesis, three groups of first and second grade children, ten to a group, were picked from four schools and matched by age, intelligence and background. Boys and girls were equally paired.

Each group met twice a week, led by a teacher (not from their own classrooms) who had special training. Opinions held by the children before, during, and after the experiment, were carefully tested. Trained personnel made the observations.

To the children these were "club" periods, similar to other classroom clubs formed for pupils not in the experiment.

The groups were led on the assumption that the teacher could help children in understanding, accepting and respecting their neighbors, or she could strengthen prejudices already held. Group A was deliberately led on the theme of "cultural democracy," Group B on that of the "status quo." In the third group, serving as a control group, nothing was done either way. Omitting intercultural content from the children's classroom work offered a further control.

The setting was the neighborhood because everything so far learned about the children reflected the neighborhood.

In leading Group B, the teacher followed the line of things as they are, minimizing or ignoring differences in people and beliefs, stressing conformity to the majority group. This represents the status quo.

IN leading Group A the teacher made conscious efforts

to show that the neighborhood has many groups, that many are discriminated against, that groups are made up of many kinds of people, that people should be accepted as individuals. These themes were carried into games, stories, acting-out and neighborhood trips.

The program took its cue from the children. Since "storekeeper" was a common sterotype for "Jewish" and "Jewgyp" was noted to be one word, the club visited reputable storekeepers. The children discovered that "storekeepers" might be Jewish, or non-Jewish, that there were honest storekeepers. They found that Jews had other occupations.

When a dentist cooperated in one club excursion, showed the children his office and equipment, they found that he too was Jewish. "The children were flabbergasted," according to an informal report.

Because hostility to Negroes had been expressed as "they're dirty," "they kill people," the children met kindly, well-educated Negroes; their club outings included visits to clean, attractive homes of Negro families.

When a Catholic nun came to play games with the children, she showed her rosary, let the youngsters examine her habit and explained its significance. She was the first "Cath-

olic" some of these children had ever known as a person, the first of whom they could ask questions including, "Don't you beat kids?" Natural and charming, she won the children completely.

IN visits to homes, to churches, the children discovered that "Protestant," "Catholic," "Jewish" apply to differences in beliefs and forms of worship of one God, that all are "religion." It was a new idea to youngsters to whom "religion" had meant their own faith and excluded all others.

In this direct approach the Project sponsors seem to feel,

with Cardinal Newman, that man is not a reasoning animal, he is a feeling, seeing, hearing, acting animal.

The findings show how intensely children live in the world immediately around them, that the thing they see and hear and feel is the thing they become, that prejudices are not "taught"; they are "learned." The classroom experiment suggests that prejudices can be unlearned; that the understanding, acceptance and respect of democratic living can be taught; and that by seeing, hearing, doing together, the schools can teach it.

July 25, 1948

Codes of Youthful Behavior

By DOROTHY BARCLAY

WE passed a group of up-and-coming boys on the Lower West Side the other weekend—youngsters ranging in age from 11 to 14—and, as we listened to their chaff, we thought for a moment the Kefauver committee was back in town. With tones and gestures that neatly parodied those of Senators and witnesses alike, they carried on their own little version of the investigation, to the delight of a cluster of girls looking on.

As Dr. Elias Lieberman, associate superintendent of schools in charge of the junior high school division, pointed out to us shortly thereafter, the audience of millions that sat for hours on end before television or radio sets during the recent hearings in Foley Square wasn't made up of adults alone. Youngsters educated to understand the intricacies of United Nations procedure are more than capable of following the activities of a Senate committee. Hardened as so many of them are today in the school of "B" pictures and crime comic books, children, so far as we could observe, weren't particularly shocked or shaken to see how different life in high places can be from the orderly picture presented in civics books. And, right there, danger lies. At least one group of parents we know is pretty concerned about it.

IN 1948, during the annual meeting of the representative assembly of the National Education Association, a study

group was assigned to consider the role of the public schools in the development of moral and spiritual values. Their report ("Moral and Spiritual Values in the Public Schools," $1, from N. E. A., 1201 Sixteenth Street, N. W., Washington 6, D. C.) was made available in February. At that time, it was discussed widely in the education press and, with parents' concern in mind, we've been watching for examples of

how the American values it enumerates and analyzes tie in with the thoughts and activities of school-age boys and girls.

Two good examples have just reached our desk. One is "The Junior High School Code of Behavior and Manual," just re-issued by the New York City Board of Education. The other is a list of "group goals" compiled by 10 and 11 year olds in Denver

public schools and included in a new technical publication of Teachers College, Columbia University. It is called "Understanding Group Behavior of Boys and Girls," and was written by Ruth Cunningham and associates.

Both these codes are written in the language of childhood and give, as examples of moral problems, situations so simple that an unthinking adult might pass them off with a smile. As a matter of fact, that was our first inclination—until the Kefauver investigation set us thinking. Looked at more sharply, however, the elementary behavior rules and moral values worked out by youngsters here and in Denver, and doubtless in hundreds of other communities as well, cover pretty much the same points outlined in finer language by the Educational Policies Commission of the N. E. A.

WE asked some of the teachers we know whether or not they thought the material revealed in the Kefauver hearings would have any directly adverse effect on youngsters and the answer, naturally enough, was: "It's hard to tell—but it certainly won't help any." The Educational Policies Commission underlines that fact in one passage that might have been written yesterday, it is so apt: "If observant young people see that the realities of political and community life differ sharply from the ideals which are presented to them by their teachers, they are bound to conclude that their teachers are either ignorant or untruthful."

WHAT then are the "commonly accepted American values" the commission believes schools—and mothers and fathers, of course—should try to encourage? They are ten: the basic value of human personality; the individual's moral responsibility for the consequences of his own conduct; the belief that institutions are the servants of man, not the other way 'round; the principle of common consent; devotion to truth; respect for excellence; moral equality; brotherhood; the pursuit of happiness; the right of all to spiritual enrichment.

The New York youngsters' code includes many of those points in five rules of behavior: I will never knowingly by word or deed injure anyone's person, feelings or property in any manner; I will al-

ways respect the religious beliefs of others, as I will respect my own; I will show courtesy to other people at all times, particularly to my elders; I will abide by the laws and regulations of my school and community; I will be honest with myself and others and I will practice cleanliness of mind and body. As a summing up they have written the Golden Rule: "Do unto others as you would they should do unto you."

THE boys and girls in Denver set thirty goals for themselves which boiled down to such basic desires as these: to learn to play and work well together; to learn to like each other; not to argue or fight; to be unselfish; to listen to others; to learn to obey; to be polite, truthful, honest, brave, respectful of property; to learn to think

and decide for themselves; to know when to be serious and when to be silly; to know where authority lies.

Offhand, some of the Denverites' "goals" might seem unrelated to morals, but the children's explanations fit right in with the N. E. A.'s listing of American values: the inherent worth of every human being ("If someone is fat or skinny, we should play with them." "Learn not to call people names."); moral responsibility ("If you did something and you know you did it yourself tell the truth about it."); common consent ("Play what other people want to sometimes and not what you want to play all the time."); devotion to truth ("Always tell the truth, even if it isn't the easiest way out."); respect for excellence ("If you didn't listen to other people's good ideas you'd be

dumb."); moral equality ("To like each other no matter what they look like or what color they are."); brotherhood ("Help people when they need it."); the pursuit of happiness ("Don't be silly all the time and don't be serious all the time.").

LAST week Senator J. William Fulbright, directing yet another Governmental investigation of ethical matters, cited the country's general "callousness to scandals" and urged a moral revival. Thinking through by parents of their own standards and values and discussions with the youngsters of behavior they deem right and fair is important at any time. Right now it is especially apropos.

April 8, 1951

Outside the Group—and Happy to Be So

By DOROTHY BARCLAY

EARLY this month, Dr. William S. Carlson, new president of the State University of New York, called for development of an educational philosophy that would "give everyone an opportunity to seek out the contribution that he and he alone can make," one that would "encourage the thinker, the creative artist, the research scientist and the leader in political affairs."

Although Dr. Carlson was not discussing parent-child relationships nor education at the nursery and elementary school level, his remarks have easily as much pertinence for those concerned with youngsters' early development as for those working with university students. They sent us looking for a folder of notes we've been gathering for several years under the general heading "children different from the group—and happy to be."

We'd been prompted to start this collection because of an uneasiness we felt about what seemed to us a contradiction between two main themes stressed time and again at meetings we attended. One was an emphasis on "respect for individual differences." The other was constant stress on "integration with the group."

Time after time we had

listened in at meetings where all speakers agreed that children were unique personalities.

WITH scarcely a break for breath, however, these speakers often went on from there to describe "the well-adjust-

ed child," and here was a mid-twentieth century paragon—no longer the Good Child who sat quietly on a sofa while his mother's friends drank tea but a new ideal — "outgoing," inquisitive, talkative, popular and "well rounded." Apparently

the feeling was that so long as youngsters were all these nice things there was plenty of room for difference. If a boy didn't like baseball, basketball was just as good. But what about the fellow who didn't like either? Ah, here was a problem.

There was the incident of the young entomologist at day camp. At a special "carnival" celebration other youngsters ran about throwing darts at pictures of counselors painted on paper plates, drenching one of their fellows—who had volunteered as victim—by knocking over a pail of water with a towel. But this little boy hovered on the outskirts of the picnic grove and watched ants. "Our social workers," the camp director said, "have failed to make him feel a part of the group."

We don't know the personal details of this actual incident. Perhaps the little boy, as the director implied, was indeed miserable and attempting to forget his sorrows in a preoccupation with crawling things. But supposing he wasn't. Suppose he or other boys and girls like him are honestly and deeply interested in the ant's life and ways, the piano or a chemical set, ancient history or short-story writing? Must their parents and teachers worry? Must their interests be broadened? Must they be rounded-out?

These are questions, we know, which in varying degrees plague a number of parents. We wish we had a clear-cut answer. Those who feel that such youngsters need skillful treatment aimed at making them more like their contemporaries believe, apparently, that intense interest in more or less solitary pursuits during childhood is either a compensation for the lack of group acceptance or a reflection of parents' pushing, conscious or otherwise. Specialists of this mind feel also that social skills are by far the most important ones a child must master and these should be the main concern of his formative years. The very future of the world depends on it, many of them insist.

Although we have heard various specialists question the current emphasis on the importance to the child of being "part of the group," we have never heard the case of the happy - outside - the - group child discussed in detail by anyone but David

Riesman, Professor of the Social Sciences at the University of Chicago. Emphasis on individuality plus group acceptance or popularity, he holds, demands that a child be "different but not too different" — the proper degree of difference in this case proving that he is "conventional and up-to-date." The only easy measure of acceptance by the group is popularity and therefore the child whose interests differ too radically from those of the other youngsters about him is likely to be judged wanting. (Is this the juvenile counterpart of what Dr. Carlson has called "smoking-car standards of popularity"?)

Mr. Riesman feels that in some cases at least it certainly is. As parents more and more are taught "the gospel of adjustment to the group," he feels, they will have more and more difficulty helping youngsters to develop freely according to their own innate and acquired differences. In an article published in a past issue of the Child Study

Association's quarterly, Mr. Riesman presented the hypothetical case of a teen-age girl whose passionate interest in music was setting her apart from her contemporaries.

*I*S their acceptance more important than music, he asks? And his answer is No. "Thousands of parents," he holds, "throw away their children's special gifts—which can best be cultivated during youth—in return for gifts of social adjustment to a particular group at a particular time and place. They ignore the fact that as the children grow older they could make their own place among another group who shared their interests and pleasures."

We made a point of talking to Mr. Riesman about this and he held that such efforts to change a child are in line with the "short-run point of view prevalent in this country today, a selling short of the child's future for the present under the label of security." Loneliness, he

holds, need not be looked upon as the worst evil that could befall a child. Failure to develop real potentialities, he feels, may well be far worse. With support and protection from parents, the child who is different-from-the - group - and - happy - that-way, can learn to defend himself against the demands of his peers for more conformity, develop in his own way his genuine differences and in adulthood know the joy of real congeniality with others like himself.

*T*HE question, clearly, has no easy answer. Parents who are troubled by it must consider carefully two basic points. First, do the child's solitary interests bring him real satisfaction now and are they likely to continue to in the future? And, second, are they a genuine expression of his own desires, or a reflection—however well masked —of his parents' wishes?

May 18, 1952

Too Much Popularity

By DOROTHY BARCLAY

*F*IVE or six months ago we took up on this page the matter of the child who is "different from the group"—and happy to be. The article occasioned considerable comment from our readers. Several wrote us their thanks for a "fresh point of view" in terms that made it clear the question had concerned

them for quite a while. One put it sharply thus: " 'Well-adjusted' has been griping me for a long time, because the emphasis is upon conformity and not upon further progress. A glance at any newspaper shows wars, famines, crime, prison riots, disease, ignorance, bigotry and human misery upon a vast scale. Anyone who can be

'well-adjusted' to this sort of thing must be either extremely selfish or extremely stupid."

On the other side were comments, some from the best known leaders in early childhood education, stressing that many of the very horrors of present civilization referred to by the correspondent quoted above exist largely because so many people today are not "adjusted to their group." Therefore, they held, group adjustment—and with it the development of social mindedness and a co-operative spirit—must be made one of the principal aims, if not perhaps The Aim, of childhood education both at home and in school.

The idea that children should be helped to understand and respect the rights and needs of others is not likely to cause argument. Neither is the effort to help boys and girls get along well together and enjoy one another's companionship at work and at play. As in the case of so many other Big Ideas in education and child development, however, the emphasis on "social adjustment" has been mistaken by many—parents and teachers alike—to mean "social success" in the sense of general popularity. From the ideal of the "good" child, widely held

in the past, many adults have swung to a new model of perfection—the "all-American boy" or girl who is bright, well-rounded, talkative, outgoing and "liked by all."

*I*NCREASED knowledge of child psychology—as well as a quick look at the world around us—unquestionably indicates the importance of good social development. Misinterpreting the meaning of this "adjustment," however, has led to endless arguments and discussions on the relative merits of individuality versus conformity. Those we have listened to have been for the most part based on personal opinion, developed by the "armchair philosophy" method. Therefore we found of extreme interest and significance, reports of research on children's social relationships included in an article titled "So You Want Your Child to Be Popular? A Second Glance at Social Relations." This piece, written by Dr. Mary L. Northway, in charge of research at the Institute of Child Study, University of Toronto, appears in the institute's latest bulletin. (Reprints may be had for 10 cents from The Bulletin of The Institute of Child Study, 98 St. George Street, Toronto. A longer and more technical discussion of the material is included in Dr. Northway's "A Primer of Sociometry," published last month by the University of Toronto Press, $2.25.)

Seeing the clear eye of scientific investigation turned on a topic that has prompted so many futile discussions is a thoroughly satisfying sight and we made a point of checking with Dr. Northway on the institute's activities along these lines. Continuing studies of children's social relationships have been going on there for over ten years, she told us, in an effort to see what kinds are best for children in terms of their psychological security and mental health.

We had been under the impression that our cousins to the north were not so concerned with the ideal of popularity as were many Americans. Dr. Northway felt this to be generally true. However, she told us, the specialists at the institute had seen enough instances of parents trying to force their youngsters into the "Campus Favorite" mold to be concerned about the unfortunate results. The findings of some of their researches will come as a shock to certain parents who have held up to their children the ideal of "being liked by all" or to others who have been basking in the golden haze surrounding a youngster

who is universally applauded and sought after.

FOR the extremely popular child, as determined by sociometric techniques which ascertain how thoroughly a child is accepted by others in his group, is, the researchers have found by using still more psychological tests, often beset by inner anxieties, tensions and conflicts which are not found to the same degree in less popular children. It would seem, Dr. Northway told us, that with some of these overly popular children the desire to retain their high social rating becomes an "over-powering self-impelling motive." Such youngsters are usually children who further the interests of other people, and help them to do what they want to. They are usu-

ally considerate and in sympathy with their companions, giving considerable attention to their desires, wants and needs. They frequently carry the burdens of others as well as their own. They can become too responsible for their commitments and obligations and may develop a gnawing fear of what may happen if they ever let down.

Not all popular youngsters are under such strain, of course, Dr. Northway emphasized, but the "ordinary child" —neither left out of his group nor continually extolled by it —is in the most generally comfortable spot. Sociometric tests indicate the average youngster will be liked by some, ignored by others and disliked perhaps by a few. The pattern of social rela-

tionships that he develops will be uniquely his own and not that of either the child down the street or the child his parents ideally imagine he should be.

To us, however, the most interesting material the Toronto researches have brought out is that which distinguishes between the child who likes, or is liked by a great many others—but without much depth, and the youngster who has "learned to be friends." Studies of children who have personal friends as opposed to those who have not, regardless of their general acceptance by the group, seem to indicate that from the point of view of psychological security and mental health, to have a friend is worth infinitely more than any amount of general popularity. To be accepted by the group the child must be what the group wants and expects him to be; with his friend he can be himself. In the group he must subordinate his own wants and desires, hopes, fears and pleasures, to the conventions and expectations of the group; with his friend he can increase his spontaneity and reduce his energy. He is more relaxed, less inhibited and more creative.

October 19, 1952

Television and A Child's Values

By DOROTHY BARCLAY

SEVERAL years ago a young University of Pennsylvania psychologist set a parents' meeting aflame with indignation by declaring that values could—and perhaps should — be taught by machine. The values to be taught, he said, adding fuel to the parental ires, could be decided by "industry."

What was the thinking behind his bizarre recommendation? So many homes and schools have abdicated their responsibility for the teaching of values, he explained, that industry—through advertising and public relations techniques—already is a major influence in shaping the standards we live by.

Experimental machines of the electronic-brain type have proven their effectiveness in

teaching basic educational skills, the psychologist said, and "within a generation" the teaching of values could be handled automatically as well.

The general parental reaction to this prophecy, as we've indicated, was one of outraged denial and disbelief. However, revelations concerning the television industry during the past months indicate just how far one machine—and those who set its standards—can go in shaking values, if not in shaping them.

One aspect of television has been discussed repeatedly— the effect on children of continual exposure to programs saturated with violence and bloodshed, programs in which life is cheap and the lesson repeatedly told is that "might makes right." Less often considered but equally vital are

questions of a somewhat subtler nature. What cumulative effect does television have on such values as respect for truth and beauty; for responsibility and the worth of work; for independence, initiative and original thought; for loyalty, cooperativeness, kindness and human understanding?

EDUCATORS have been stressing for some years that moral and ethical values such as these cannot be imposed from the outside but must develop from within as a result of the child's own experiences and his evaluations of them. Is the power of television such, however, that the vicarious experiences it provides a child can produce the same kind of inner reactions that actual experience does? In at least some cases, we believe,

the answer is an emphatic yes.

Those who disagree with this point of view hold that only children who are "sick" or "warped" to begin with will be adversely affected by crime programs and the like. Yet among the latest theories on delinquency is one that emphasizes that much of it is "a culture pattern."

As Albert K. Cohen, University of Indiana sociologist, described it recently, delinquency is a "pattern" in which destruction is valued over constructive activity, disruptive behavior over cooperation, meanness over kindness and consideration, fighting over attempts to understand. Foolhardy daring and defiance of the world are valued over sane courage and respect for the rights of others.

"A child learns delinquency

much as he learns any other culture pattern," Dr. Cohen declared.

If this is so, continual exposure through television to dramatizations of the mores of delinquent society would seem certain to have some effects. So would continual exposure to evidences of the crimes, weaknesses, lies and crooked dealings of real-life men. Although comparatively few children have direct experience with these, they are brought daily into the home on television newscasts.

It is a question whether the great mass of men today are any weaker or more evil than they were in earlier times. A wider knowledge of the world's wrongdoing is, however, unquestionable.

Pertinent to the present situation, we think, is a comment made by James Dumpson, now New York City's Welfare Commissioner, at the time of the Army-McCarthy hearings on television. This scandal, he said, was certain to have its effect on the moral values of young people because, "no matter how much or how little they understand of the details, they cannot help realizing that there are men in high places who are mishandling the truth."

The current television scandal, then, is only one in a continuing series of unwholesome events brought forcefully to children's attention in one form or another just about every day. The fact that television itself created the idols whose destruction it now details simply adds a bit of irony to the situation.

*W*HAT does all this mean

to parents? Throw television out? Keep newspapers and magazines out of the reach of children? Obviously not. Insulating a child from all evidences of the world's evil will not insure the development of sound values any more than a realization of wrongs and inequities need destroy them. The powerful appeal of television, however, and the immediacy of its impact make its power as a possible molder of values incalculable. This is frighteningly true in situations where, as the young psychologist held, parents and teachers have abdicated their re-

sponsibility in guiding children's development of values through a searching for truth and right.

*I*T is true that parents cannot "impose" their values on children. Values cannot be tattooed into the hide or indelibly stamped on the brain. Many factors influencing the development and maintenance of moral standards are still to be discovered. There may even be genetic differences, research suggests, between those who are easily swayed by others and those who hold fast to their values even under duress.

In regard to television, however, parents can be alert to the potential dangers of total permissiveness in program choices and the hazards of uncritical acceptance of life as it is presented even in worthwhile shows. Because they deal with aspects of human behavior, both dramatizations and news reports often provide the raw material for discussions in which parents can present their point of view and make their values known.

The spontaneous comments children make on the actions they observe can also provide insight for parents on some of the points their young may be struggling with. In the child's world these might involve a conflict between principle (telling the truth about an episode of vandalism, perhaps) and loyalty to friends; a struggle to decide between gratifying some immediate personal desire and doing the work required for a future event involving others; a decision between helping out an unpopular newcomer or going off with the crowd.

*I*N households where the television set is permitted to take the parents' place as educator and guide, the values children develop are likely to be confused and conflicting at best. Knowing what children are watching as well as what they are doing in real life, parents will be better prepared to straighten out misconceptions and help settle conflicts in terms of their own honest beliefs.

November 29, 1959

Status Seekers, Junior Grade

By MARY ANNE GUITAR

*T*HE most fascinating aspect of our status-conscious society may well be the cool way the younger generation accepts the inevitability of status distinctions.

The status symbol is, above all, a means of communication. One guitar player meeting another guitar player needs no verbal contact. The sight of

that peerless symbol serves the same purpose today as the aborigine's peace pipe did in times past. It suggests instantly that these two understand one another and can safely become friends. Or, as one boy put it: "Without your blanket, you are nothing. You have to carry your status symbol with you or fade."

The "blanket," however, has become so richly ornamented that it can be described only by those who wear one—the under-20's. Any adult who grew up with such simplistic symbols as dirty saddle shoes and beat-up jalopies is understandably mystified by the complex status system presently in force among the young.

*W*ITH a total lack of self-consciousness, a high-school junior explained what is obligatory in his circles:

"You have to have long hair, but not Beatle length. The crew cut is out. Your hair should be thick, smoothed down, parted on the side and swept across the forehead.

"It's a good thing to own

a car. A sports car. Healey Sprites are the best. And if you don't own a car, you should be able to talk about them as if you really knew.

"Vespa motor bikes are good and Hondas are even better. They only cost $400. Nobody has one. It's like the sports car. You have to know enough to talk about them.

"It's a good thing to have a summer house on Cape Cod, Fisher's Island, Fire Island. If your parents don't own one, then you should get an in-

Mary Anne Guitar, who reports on the manners and mores of the young, still yearns for the status symbol of her youth—a Ford phaeton, preferably robin's-egg-blue.

teresting job in one of these places.

"It's important to travel," he concluded, "particularly without your parents."

STATUS mobility, be it upward or crabwise, starts early. A 10-year-old began an English composition with this awesome—if somewhat misleading—sentence: "I rarely travel abroad without my parents, but. . . ."

Happily for the great majority of the status-seeking young, most of the prevailing status symbols are based on an awareness of what's in. They do not involve a high price tag or a heavy investment in resort real estate or European travel. The Upper East Side boy who urges his father to join the exclusive River Club with, "It's really quite reasonable, I hear" is sure he would be in if they made it. But he also knows that he can make it in other ways more in scale with the average father's income. A youngster can, for example, dress in an approved fashion without breaking the family bank.

ALTHOUGH the young are acutely aware of high-priced haberdashery ("Brooks' blue shirts are almost purple!"), they favor a uniform notable for its low price tag. It consists principally of blue jeans that are cropped just below or just above the knee—and the stringier the fringe the better. These are used as swimming trunks on occasion and are said to improve with each bath of salt water. The idea is to season them until they are a weak-eyed blue and virtually threadbare.

"Store-bought jeans are out," says one young oracle.

MOTOR-MINDED—Sports cars and motor bikes are the teen-age male's ultimate status symbol, but luckily you don't have to own one; it's enough to be able to talk about them.

Presumably they must be faded into heirlooms handed down by siblings or found on the beach at Cape Cod, Fisher's Island, Fire Island. White Levis are making some inroads on the popularity of blue jeans, but to qualify as a status symbol they must be darkened and dirty.

Striped shirts are—at the moment—in. So is the madras jacket. Neither is particularly cheap, but the boys who wear them are not out to demonstrate their affluence. For dress, the knowledgeable boy will wear his ragged jeans topped by a madras jacket. The good thing here is the contrast, the implied value system neatly balanced between not caring and yet possessing impeccable taste.

The status-conscious boy is usually shod in loafers. The more advanced wear them without socks. Some, however, regard this as sloblike. Sneakers are okay. The unmatched pair has gained some favor, but this borders on the fad and is not a symbol.

THE true status symbol must convey more than mere group addiction to what is currently in fashion. It must

suggest an image. One high-school boy said, for example, that it is good to go to big-name colleges on weekends and boast an older friend. You must, in short, appear to be worldly beyond your years and dress the part.

A Rockland County mother

apprehended her 15-year-old boy just as he was about to take off for a Princeton weekend wearing "his usual grubby rags." She ordered him to change into a proper dark suit and tie. Upon his return, she said smugly: "Well, I suppose you're glad you were properly

IN, OUT—Hair should be long today; crewcuts have had it.

HARMONY—The status symbol is a means of communication. One guitar player meeting another guitarist can establish instant rapport.

dressed." Not at all. The Princeton "guys" were wearing torn blue jeans, loafers, madras jackets and the sublime confidence that comes with status.

IT may be assumed from this ritualistic emphasis on dress that boys, not girls, are clothes crazy. Indeed boys today do seem to defy the male stereotype, as more than one observer has noted. In his book, "The Vanishing Adolescent," Edgar Z. Friedenberg comments: "Boys seem to me usually more concerned with their appearance than girls and also to have more idea what they actually look like and how other people will respond to the way they look . . . Boys are often very vain. . . . They bask in physical regard like alligators on a log."

Some girls cannily achieve status by adopting male clothes habits, a fact well-known to Seventh Avenue The buttoned-down shirt, blue jeans and loafers have long been female status symbols. A new and rather alarming identification with boys is reported from some feminine quarters. A girl will often wear the talcum powder, shaving lotion and cologne of the beloved. "It makes me feel close to him when he's not around," one 15-year-old explained.

STATUS symbols for the young fall chiefly into the display area. Food and drink labels, family tree, proper address — all so important to their parents — carry little

UNIFORM—"In" attire for boys pairs a madras jacket with faded blue jeans that are cropped above or below the knee.

weight with the younger generation. What counts is what you wear, drive or play. The more visible the better. This must be why the guitar is the all-purpose symbol from coast to coast. If you own one, you are immediately identified as a person of parts, one who is conversant with Bob Dylan and Joan Baez. You are obliged to teach yourself or learn from a friend—ideally, a Radcliffe girl. Nobody dreams of taking lessons, except "the High Ape or Low Human group and they would play an electric guitar anyway." This do-it-yourself cult severely restricts the number of players who can achieve status. "If I could play it bet-

ter, it would be a symbol," said one boy who has since switched to a banjo.

BEING good at sports is as status-making as facility with music. The football hero is fading in favor of the skier and tennis star. Skiing, as a matter of fact, offers even the beginner plenty of status scope. The type of skis, the mountain itself, the way the skier gets to the slope (bus, train, family car) all influence the amount of prestige gleaned from a down-hill run.

Although "the brain" does not want for respect from his peers, he reaps little status from cerebral achievement. In describing a brain ("He built

his own computer"), a classmate admitted that the brain got some recognition when he exhibited the computer, but "none when he ran it."

This last observation makes one wonder if the critics of status seeking don't have a point. They maintain that the wrong values are emphasized by those youngsters who set the status goals. Why, the critics ask, don't parents have more influence? This question implies that adults are uncorrupted by the search for status. Some are, of course, but their children will not necessarily adopt their values. The offspring of a couple who had deliberately turned their backs on consumermanship (thus achieving the status of the pure nonmaterialist) asked Santa Claus: "Please bring us real toothpaste instead of salt and soda. And bring us cereal that crackles."

HAPPILY, status symbols change. If a youngster doesn't like what's in, he can simply bide his time. Or he can make a virtue of his dislike. If you believe what you read, you "know" that everyone is dancing the Frug and the Mashed Potato. But a recent high-school graduate says confidently: "I don't dance anymore." She is superbly gifted as a dancer, but she also has the true instinct of a status setter. She may well be in the vanguard. Sitting out the Frug could be this fall's choicest status symbol.

August 16, 1964

Bridging The Prejudice Gap

By KATHARINE DAVIS FISHMAN

"MISS JONES, do I have to hold hands with that black boy?"

"Mommy, how come all the kids in the dumb class are Negro and Puerto Rican?"

"No one can escape all contamination of racism in an essentially racist society," says Dr. Kenneth Clark, professor of psychology at City College and the first Negro member of New York State's Board of Regents. "So-called liberals must face up to their own ambivalence and learn to fight it."

A public school on Manhattan's West Side enrolls many white students from comfortable families who could well afford the price of a private education; the parents, presumably, have opted for public schooling out of the best liberal sentiments. Recently, a well-dressed white mother voiced this complaint to the school's guidance counselor: "It seems as if all my child's friends are Negro and Puerto Rican. Why does he have such a low opinion of himself?"

In sophisticated Northern so-

ciety, condemning racial prejudice is like coming out against sin. Many Northern parents, told when they were 5 years old that "we're all the same inside," quote Rodgers and Hammerstein's old slogan, "you've got to be taught to hate and fear," to show that their children will grow up untainted by bigotry. But when a Negro talks frankly about the subtler brand of Northern prejudice, it cuts deeply into white complacency. Mrs. Anna Arnold Hedgeman of the Commission on Religion and Race, National Council of Churches, says the old humanitarian clichés are not only inadequate but often further racial misunderstanding. " 'We're all the same inside,' " she observes, "implies that there is something wrong with Negroes outside. 'I'm color-blind' is condescending and dishonest."

PREPARING one's children to live in a progressively more inte-

grated world requires soul-searching. In "How to Bring Up Your Child Without Prejudice," a pamphlet published by Public Affairs Pamphlets, Mrs. Margaret Young writes: "The first step for any parent who would bring up his child without prejudice is to examine his own feelings about people who are differt. Sometimes this self-appraisal is the most difficult step if the readjustment threatens an old comfortable pattern of living." Dr. Robert Coles, a psychiatrist on the staff of the Harvard University Health Services who spent five years studying the effects of school desegregation on Southern children, notes that "there is a definite relation between prejudice and the rigidity of parents' general attitudes toward strangers and toward differences in race, income, habits and customs."

The preferred answer to a small child's first questions about race begins, "All kinds of pretty flow-

55

ers grow," and goes on to explain that Negroes, like white people, come in a variety of shades. But just knowing the proper responses to 10 common questions is not a foolproof method for raising children without prejudice.

PSYCHOLOGISTS seem to agree that children first notice racial differences at about age 4, while 5- and 6-year-olds understand that these differences affect status. "I don't believe in indoctrination of 2- and 3-year-olds," Dr. Clark says. "With race, as with sex, premature discussion tends to block communication. The average child will make it clear to sensitive parents—by his questions, his statements and his actions — that he is ready to learn. When this time comes, you must respect the child's curiosity by being perfectly forthright. Tell him that discrimination exists and is wrong, and that we must all work to change it. If a Negro child has abused your child, you get angry just as if he were white. On the other hand, you direct your anger at the individual, not his race. When a dispute does have ugly racial implications, it's time again to be honest about the problems of discrimination."

News of civil-rights marches, trials and even of racial violence should be included in this frank discussion, Mrs. Young advises. Parents should point out that demonstration is an honorable means of protest. They might then tell their children that the policemen who mistreat demonstrators are prejudiced, but many other policemen are helpful to all races; and that "the people who riot, breaking the windows and looting, are wrong. . . . Grown-ups, like children, don't think clearly when they are hot, tired or hungry. . . ."

While most white parents accept the truism that bigotry stems from ignorance, few are well-informed about Negroes. When a child asks why the sky is blue or what makes rain, dutiful mothers pull down the encyclopedia, but a question about Negro life usually elicits a simple "I don't know." Both Mrs. Young and Mrs. Hedgeman feel that this hesitancy nourishes prejudice and urge that white parents read more books by and about Negroes.

Often, the first Negro a white child gets to know is the family's maid, and the way she is treated has a strong effect on the child's attitude. "This is the age of the working mother," says Mrs. Alaine Krim, a psychiatric social worker at the Child Study Association. "She might explain that household help makes an important contribution to the family, freeing the mother to go on with her job and spend time with her children." Dr. Clark, however, warns against go-

Katharine Davis Fishman is a freelance writer.

66Prejudice is visceral, not intellectual, and no expert can propose a magic formula to do away with it.99

ing overboard: "I certainly wouldn't invite the maid to join the family at dinner, just to show how democratic I was."

The maid or cleaning woman is frequently not just the first but the only Negro a child gets to know. One parent reports riding with her son in their apartment house elevator, in company with a well-dressed Negro woman. After the woman had left, the boy observed, "Someone on the seventh floor has a new maid." Dr. Clark puts it squarely: "White parents have got to work very hard to show their children that difference in race doesn't mean difference in ability. Of course, when a child asks why most maids are Negro, you should explain about job discrimination. But it's even more important to widen your social sphere to include Negroes in the professions, the arts, or business. Inevitably, I suppose, your first attempts to find Negro friends may be slightly forced. But you should genuinely like the Negro families you befriend. No Negro wants to be anybody's test case and besides, children can always spot a phony situation."

DESIRABLE as a mixed circle of friends may be, the question, "How do you meet Negroes?" seems to stump the experts. Even when children attend integrated schools, the chances of encountering Negroes from a variety of backgrounds are slim. "There are the rich white kids from the co-ops on Central Park West," observes one parent whose child goes to public school, "and the poor Negro and Puerto Rican kids from the brownstones on the side streets. Upper - middle - class Negroes seem to send their children to private school or move out of town."

The racial situation is certainly considered, either directly or obliquely, by parents choosing a school for their children. The common complaint, "I'm not going to sacrifice my child's education for noble principles" conjures up pictures of jaded teachers manning old buildings with peeling plaster and rank smells for hordes of ineducable pupils. Certainly in the districts where white parents who can afford to choose are

likely to live, however, this picture is unrealistic. P.S. 87, for example, an elementary school housed in a cheerful 11-year-old building on 78th Street and Amsterdam Avenue has a yearly magazine which has won many Columbia Scholastic Press Awards, an annual art show, and several choral groups. The ethnic composition of its 989-student population is listed as "31 per cent Puerto Rican and other bilingual children, 14 per cent Negro children, and 55 per cent other children." A Human Relations Committee, composed of faculty volunteers, concerns itself with intergroup problems. A story told at a recent meeting shows that 87's children know the racial facts of life. Two Negro and two Puerto Rican children were picked for some innocuous reasons, to lead an assembly. When a teacher asked the student body why they had been chosen, a little girl swiftly answered, "Because they're underprivileged."

"We reorganized the lower grades to avoid clustering of groups," says Arthur Block, the principal. "We want the classes to reflect our actual ethnic composition, but we must also balance this somewhat with achievement levels. We've found the mixing doesn't interfere with the education of either bright or slow students —it simply requires more individual attention. We do have grouping by ability in the fourth and fifth grades, and the intellectually gifted classes are predominantly white English-speaking. But I think we need to re-evaluate the standards by which we judge students' performance. Many children who don't read quickly have lively, imaginative minds. Our mixed classes are more spirited than the old homogeneous groups. Recently, I was asked if our problem children were mostly from minorities, and we studied our records. The problem group came out 55 per cent white English-speaking, 31 per cent bilingual, and 14 per cent Negro, just like the school."

THE private-school attitude toward Negroes ranges from vague benevolence to serious efforts to provide a realistically mixed student body; formal segregation has certainly gone out of fashion. Trinity School, founded as a charitable enterprise, has had Negro

students since 1956. "Before that," says Richard Garten, the headmaster, "none applied." The present nonwhite population of Trinity is 16, 10 Negroes and six Orientals, out of a total of 485 boys; some are on scholarship and others pay full tuition. "We took one Negro student last year," said Mr. Garten, "on a 'challenge' basis, admitting him without the usual testing requirement. We are anxious to have more Negroes, and hope they will apply."

MR. GARTEN reports no racial problems at Trinity. The president of the school's social fraternity last year was Negro. It is, we assume, relatively easy to absorb 10 Negroes and six Orientals into a student body of 485. Downtown Community School, on the other hand, is 25 per cent Negro and its awareness of the subtleties of prejudice parallels that of P.S. 87. Norman Studer, the director, explains: "We were founded 20 years ago as an intercultural school, but we've had large Negro representation only in the past 10 years. The Negro revolution made our Negro parents more active and articulate about school problems. When integration is just tokenism, these problems are purely theoretical. We try to find Negro and white children from all classes and backgrounds. Integration involves the daily life of children in the classroom, their parents' attitudes and efforts to break across race lines, and of course, curriculum study. When feasible, there has been social mixing. Many of our Negro students live far away, which makes it difficult for the younger children." Mr. Studer, like Mr. Block of P.S. 87, questions ability grouping: "I'm dead opposed to competitive intellectualism. Some kinds of intelligence don't show up on tests."

Elementary school children seem to adjust rather well to differences in background. Adolescence, however, and dating give rise to new problems. In her pamphlet, Mrs. Young quotes a Negro teen-ager: "Donna and I were real good friends all through elementary school, but when we got to high school, something happened. I don't get invited to her parties now that she has boy-girl parties. And we don't call each other any more." Parents are likely to get emotional when boys and girls start liking each other even when they are of the same race, and many mothers and fathers are terrified by the thought of interracial dating.

Mrs. Krim, Dr. Coles and Dr. Clark suggest discussing your fears frankly with your child. Dr. Coles says, "It's not horribly racist to admit you're troubled, as long as you respect the child's ideas as those of a different generation. We must come to terms with our children, who see a different world than we did."

DR. COLES is optimistic that these difficulties will one day be resolved. "More and more interracial dating will occur as time passes, and will progressively bother parents less and less. They will feel that it is a logical part of white America's getting involved not only with the Negro but with the whole world. The barrier will be lowered as children go out with people their parents know and like. It may take a hundred years, but it will happen."

In this hundred years there are no easy answers to any of the problems that arise as our society becomes more interracial. Prejudice is visceral, not intellectual, and no expert in child care or civil rights or both can propose a magic formula to do away with it. But the suggestions of the experts do point to a need for self-examination, honesty and information which must make the road to understanding between white and Negro somewhat smoother.

October 23, 1966

'Look, This System Is Not Working'

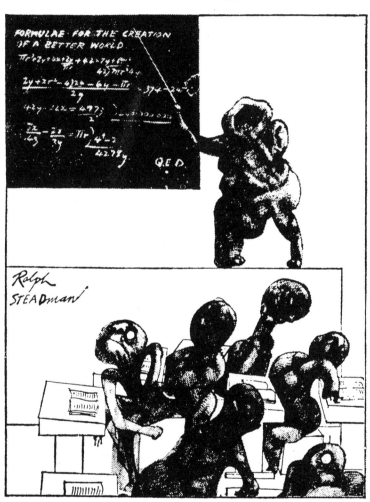

Ralph Steadman

By JONATHAN KOZOL

Five years ago, when many of us began to write and speak about the problems of the public schools in cities such as Boston and New York, it seems to me that we were more than innocent in one regard. We would point out that schools in the United States were not encouraging children to think freely and to question bravely, to fight for justice and to cry for those in pain. We would point out that schools contained and silenced, muted and anesthetized our children. We would point out that this was not the way to turn out honest souls like Thoreau or good men like Gandhi or brave men like Malcolm X or Martin Luther King. We would complain like children standing by a huge and slightly obsolete machine. "Look," we would say, "this system is not working."

The innocence of this approach now seems quite overwhelming. Public school was never in business to produce Thoreau. It is in business to produce a man like Richard Nixon and, even more, a population like the one which could elect him. It does not require the attribution of sinister motives, but only of the bare survival-instincts, to know that an interlocking network of industrial, political and academic interests does not exist to subsidize the demolition of its methods.

Businessmen are not in business to lose customers, and schools do not exist to free their clients from the agencies of mass persuasion. School and media possess a productive monopoly upon the imagination of a child.

It is not bizarre, it is not unexpected, it is entirely logical, that public schools should serve the public interest in this fashion. That we can continually lose sight of the indoctrinational function of the public school is only perhaps the more persuasive evidence that we ourselves are well indoctrinated.

We are a rich nation living well at the expense of others. It is of the essence that schools should teach us how to live at peace with an uneasy sense of conscience. Just children are a terrible danger to an unjust nation unless they can be etherized successfully. It is the major function of the public schools to offer us that ether.

Often we hear each other speaking in frustrated or in disappointed tones about a particular school or a particular school system that seemed to us for a little while to be moving industriously outward in the direction of some kind of new and promising "wide-open" freedom, where the kids might probe into the activities of their own school board, examine the motives of big business and the Department of Defense, scrutinize chauvinism, condemn false offerings in press and television, take sides with the powerless against the dominant and strong. When it does not turn out to be like this at all, we grow enraged and bitter, and protest the great deception that we were so willingly led into.

There is, I now believe, a terrible innocence about the character of our reiterated disappointment. Schools are not intended to lead children into avenues of ethics, candor or dissent. Children are not expected to come anywhere close to speculations of this order. They are intended to think *about* not *into*. They are intended to acquire information *regarding*, not leverage *upon*.

They are intended to conceive themselves to be free people by the exercise of unimportant liberties and semblances of ineffective options.

The walls that stand around the flag and chalkboard of the U.S. public school will not be leveled by the sound of trumpets or by another research-project sponsored by the Ford Foundation. We should not fool ourselves about the nature of the task before us. There is a terrible yearning in us all, as I believe, for almost any variety of warm, placating and believable deception: anything, it seems, no matter of what shape or origin, so long as we shall not be forced to put our bodies on the line or stake our lives for something we believe in. We turn in desperation to complex technologies (called systems), new phantasies of "open schools" within closed buildings, new phrases ("Discovery," "The Integrated Day") for old deceptions. What is the realistic meaning of alternatives "within the system," if the system is the primary vehicle of state control?

A school that flies the flag and conscientiously serves the interest of that flag it flies, cannot serve those of justice. School cannot at once both socialize to the values of an oppressor and toil for the liberation and the potency of the oppressed. If innovation is profound, it is subversive. If it is subversive, it is incompatible with the prime responsibility of public school. The public schools may be inept, archaic, old and unattractive, but they are not suicidal.

Indoctrinational schooling and the mandatory practice of a twelve-year house arrest are the keystone of a mighty archway in this nation. It will not be taken out without grave consequences for the structure it supports; nor will it be taken away without the kind of struggle and the kind of sacrifice for which young people in this nation are now only beginning to prepare themselves.

———

Jonathan Kozol, author of "Death At An Early Age," is involved in the creation of a network of student-operated free schools.

April 1, 1971

Taking a Child's Shame Away

By VIRGINIA LEE WARREN

There is too much concern in this country with a disadvantaged child's slum environment and not enough concern with the child himself, says Dr. Martin Wolins, a specialist in child care who was here recently from Jerusalem's Hebrew University where he is director of the University of California's Education Abroad program.

"We're too concerned here with slum clearance and housing," said Dr. Wolins, who is an associate professor in the School of Social Welfare at Berkeley on leave for a two-year appointment in Israel.

"But it is not possible to eradicate a slum," he went on, "because the slum dweller will go somewhere else and create a new slum. What we must do is to take the slum out of the person and the way to do this is to give that person an opportunity to be a creative human being. And this means starting with the person when a child and placing that child in a moral environment in which he has a chance to see himself as a potential member of the community."

An example of a moral environment, Dr. Wolins said, could be a hospital and he suggested that sometime in the future a plan be worked out whereby children from the age of 10 or 11 be placed in "a hospital situation."

After describing a hospital as "a moral place, where people do not take advantage of each other," he pointed out that it also comprises such a wide range of occupations that a child could see himself growing up to become "anything from a janitor to a surgeon."

'He Must Learn'

Also, in such a place, according to Dr. Wolins, "a child who has locked himself out of education, suddenly finds himself in a situation where he realizes that he must learn. And things take on more meaning than in a classroom. For instance: To a child there is no reason to learn arithmetic, but if he had to count sheets and figure out how many could go into a washing machine and how many loads the machine could handle in a day, he would be learning arithmetic and it would take on meaning."

The child welfare specialist said he would not be reluctant to pick certain business enterprises as places for putting children, "if those enterprises had a wide range of occupational opportunities and if those opportunities were exciting."

"And it's fine," he went on, "when the children can be taken to work with their parents and do something there. The world we have built separates adults from children so that what is often lacking in the life of a deprived American child is an intelligent and compassionate adult, or adult-like figure."

Dr. Wolins, who came to this country to consult with United Nations officials and other authorities involved in child welfare, was sitting in Hadassah's headquarters as he spoke. It was during a brief interval between appointments, and the talk got around to his studies among the kibbutzim and Youth Aliyah villages in Israel.

With Meir Gottesman, educational supervisor of Youth Aliyah in Israel, Dr. Wolins co-edited the recently published "Group Care: An Israeli Approach" (Gordon and Breach, $12.50)

While Dr. Wolins says that kibbutzim are not feasible in the United States—"there would have to be individual living habits even if there were cooperative production and cooperative consumption" —he does think that some aspects and attitudes of the Youth Aliyah movement might be transplanted advantageously. (The movement got under way in 1934 to rescue and rehabilitate the child refugees of the Nazi holocaust, but it is now caring for boys and girls whose families are unable or unwilling to do so.)

The fact that Israel is a country in the process of being built and has a sense of purpose, Dr. Wolins said, makes it easier to bring up children there—"Every person counts and knows he is needed."

"In Israel," said Dr. Wolins, "we have a large number of disturbed children from parents who have not yet become integrated, but instead of dealing with their problems as a serious deviance or illness, we look at them as problems of development; these children are treated as if they had a normal capacity for growing up.

A description in a Youth Aliyah pamphlet of boys and girls in a Youth Aliyah village might well be applied here, Dr. Wolins said. The pamphlet says: "It is as if the children were aliens in their own homeland. At least one parent is illiterate; there are no books or magazines at home to stimulate interest in the world of wonder opened by reading. Many children in the family battle for corners of overcrowded apartments. Homes may be broken by divorce."

Then, when the children are brought to a Youth Aliyah village: "The first step is to free the child from shame. At home he may have been ashamed of his parents or himself; the whole neighborhood knew about his problems. In the relaxed atmosphere and peace of the Youth Aliyah village he is liberated from his past.

"For the same reasons, the child is not graded. Instead, classes are given the names of flowers. He is moved from class to class according to his development. Never does he have to feel shy about his own backwardness. At the same time, there are no fantasies; he has to cope with reality, to deal honestly and truthfully with himself. He must know where he stands before he can walk onwards."

What Dr. Wolins says he finds so striking is that the problem child in Israel usually does walk onwards.

November 30, 1971

Girls' Liberation

By *LETTY C. POGREBIN*

Where sexism is concerned, certain children's books can be said to offend with fair warning.

I'm prepared for the male eye of perception in the magical, marvelous worlds of Roald Dahl, Maurice Sendak or E. B. White. With the fairy tales, Babar, Christopher Robin and Pooh, The Little Prince or Paddington I know in advance that there will be precious few female characters with whom my daughters can make positive identification.

While I regret this deeply, as a feminist and a parent I try to overlook male bias in books that are overwhelmingly literate and durable.

Instead of banishing "Peter Pan" from the shelves because Wendy flies back to Neverland every year to do Peter's spring cleaning, it seems more constructive to engage my daughters in some bedtime consciousness-raising. That way, a literary

———

Letty C. Pogrebin, editor of children's features for Ms. Magazine, is writing a book on non-sexist child-rearing.

classic survives while the stereotype of the domestic female doesn't filter into their dreams unchallenged.

On the other side of the spectrum from the "good" books are all those bland, undistinguished volumes one can live without on several grounds —including, but not limited to their sexist content. Here again, we have fair warning. It's no surprise to find sex-typed occupations (male doctors and police; female nurses and teachers) or sex-role rigidity (ferocious daddy tigers; gentle mommy pussycats) in books that are altogether ordinary and conformist to begin with.

In this vast category the Peter Pan principle doesn't hold. There's no cause for compromise unless one gets quality. What's to be gained from a visit to Richard Scarry's unimaginative animal community, where aproned mother bears are forever dishing up breakfast treats and pushing shopping carts? In the vapid career guidance series, such as the "I Want to Be Books" (Children's Press), it's only "natural" for a little girl to have to chart her future from such limited offerings as waitress, airplane hostess, beauty operator, homemaker or secretary. We're not shocked to discover that virtually every book about cars, trucks or trains shows only men at the wheel. Conventional concepts reflect conventional myopia.

And, with few exceptions — like Joe Lasker's attractive "Mothers Can Do Anything" (Whitman) and Eve Merriam's lovely perennial "Mommies at Work" (Knopf) — it is only predictable that books about mothers are set in the kitchen, oblivious to the truth of everyday life for 6 million preschool children whose mommies work outside the home.

Most of these instances of sexism in children's books no longer surprise me.

What I do find both amazing and appalling are the scores of books that at first description seem to be responsive to the sex-role revolution but, once read, reveal themselves as standard fare. Lately I have been deceived by too many books that sound promising or safe, enlightened or at least innocuous—but turn out to harbor a hidden punch.

Take simple science. Only a paranoid could anticipate sexism in the Random House Step-Up Book, "Animals Do the Strangest Things" by Leonora and Arthur Hornblow. The blurb guarantees "little known facts about some well known animals." As my 4-year-old son and I begin reading we learn that camels' eyelashes keep out the desert sand; that lions fear a campfire; and that otters sleep in the sea. Then suddenly, on page 20, in the chapter on little

brown bats, we read: "Sometimes women are afraid of bats. They are afraid that bats will fly into their hair."

Aside from the "little known fact" that few *men* are relaxed about the prospect of bats in *their* hair, the authors' comment does not contribute to my son's body of knowledge about little brown bats. But it does have something invidious to say about women. It reinforces stock myths about the "fearful female." Because such gratuitous statements are so typical, we cannot excuse them as trivial. For when we allow trivia to accumulate in layer after layer of literary and cultural reference we end up with girls who believe fearfulness is "feminine" and boys who disdain "hysterical" women.

Beware of trivia in datebooks too. I gave up on Macmillan's "Calendar for Children" after living with author Ruthven Tremain's version of a recent year. Marginalia accompanying her January calendar page included a time capsule sequence in which a boy was shown flying an airplane in the 1930's and walking on the moon in the future. The girl, on the other hand, was pictured wearing a cloth dress in the old days and a paper dress in the future. What progress!

With the more than 50 famous and obscure men honored in the datebook there were three women, all portrayed in reference to men: Queen Elizabeth I (shown knighting Sir Frances Drake), ballerina Maria Tallchief (identified as a descendant of Chief Peter Big Heart) and Katie Weeks, whose brother is said to have "invented" the potato chip when *Katie* dropped a sliver of potato into hot fat.

Frequently we seek books to help a child with a new situation or a special problem. More often than not, however, in the process of solving one problem the book creates others. "Jane's Blanket" by Arthur Miller (Viking) treats the Linus syndrome with heavy doses of sexist brainwashing. Jane's security blanket (pink, of course) represents her desire to cling to babyhood. Jane's mother, who cooks, bakes and cleans, represents maturity. No wonder Jane needs her blanket.

An even more disturbing example is Behavioral Publications' "Illustrated Books for Small Children on Psychologically Relevant Themes." Two titles by Joan Fassler concern temporary parental absence.

In "All Alone With Daddy" Ellen's mother goes to Grandma's for an overnight visit. Ellen's way of amusing Mama's place in the house involves putting on make-up, jewelry and high heels. She sets the table and pours Daddy's juice. Then she and Daddy walk in the park; and on the very next page it's night. (What

did they do all day? Who made the beds, dusted, cooked? Where are the tears, tantrums and conversations?) Ellen gets into her parents' bed on Mommy's side. Clearly, taking a mother's place means becoming a beauty symbol, domestic servant and sex object. When the mother returns, Ellen dreams about "little girls who grew up and really did marry their daddys. And had little boy babies for them too." Direct quote, I kid thee not.

As if this spoonfed Freud weren't pernicious enough, the companion volume, "The Man of the House," adds injury to insult. Here Daddy is the one who leaves—and he's gone for several days, not just overnight. David takes his Dad's place by announcing that he'll "slash" off the heads of dragons that scare Mommy; he'll "stamp down" on whatever wolves invade the house, or he'll "shoot" a crocodile and "burn" a monster to bits. David's violent phallic image of manliness gives one pause —if not hives.

In contrast to these "problem-solving" disasters, "Danny and His Thumb" (Prentice-Hall) is a bright example of a book in need that delivers indeed. Kathryn F. Ernst's spare text and Tomie de Paola's straightforward illustrations reassure the thumbsucker that this too shall pass. And while absorbing the message, one does not plow through sexist background detail. Danny's mother is shown painting the ceiling and emptying the garbage (distinctly male chores in bookland); his father is pictured carrying a sack of groceries and caring for a seedling. Given such relaxed realism, who cares that it's still Dad who drives the car? What feminist would quibble when Danny, detached from his thumb, takes up football? No one is asking for complete role reversal between the sexes. Balanced variety, that's all.

Ranking high in the category of unfulfilled promises are books about fathers. Each time one is announced I vainly hope that the shadowy "other parent" in a child's life will be given some kind of solid participatory presence. It seems a futile wish.

"The Daddy Book" by Robert Stewart (American Heritage) boasts several progressive assets: Don Madden's pictures are refreshingly interracial, fathers' clothes run from hat to hippy, a few daddies' jobs are not your average Golden Books he-man occupations (there's a poet and hairdresser here), and the fathers are shown warmly involved with their kids. However, the underlying structure assumes that, no matter how diverse the daddies' lifestyles, all mommies stay home all day.

When Daddy comes home from work it's a special event. He sits in his big chair, eats dinner, uses his tools. Still, the hackles don't rise until I reach the disclaimer: "Daddy often does what Mommy does." That's how Stewart introduces the idea of a man who changes diapers, cooks dinner, washes dishes, bathes children, dresses them and tucks them in. As soon as Daddy becomes involved in the domestic (not the fun-and-games part of parenting), his activities are characterized as someone else's job.

"The Day Daddy Stayed Home" by Ethel and Leonard Kessler (Doubleday) sounded all right. Would Daddy take over the house, kids and all the chores? Did Daddy stay home that day because Mommy went out on job interviews? Or because his child was sick and Mommy couldn't take a day off from harnassing the

atom in her lab? Perish the thought. Pop's only stuck at home because of a major snowstorm, and he starts his day down in the kitchen, where Mom serves him breakfast. Later, father and adoring son spend the time shoveling snow and watching the snowplow while Mom observes the happy scene from a window in the house, where she is undoubtedly ironing socks or peeling Daddy's camembert.

Often in the struggle against stereotypes, one looks for non-sexist stories about bravery and heroism. The problem here is that courage is usually tested within the context of violence or amorality. "Molly and the Giant" by Kurt Werth and Mabel Watts (Parents') proves that little girls-can be daring against great odds, but in the process of outwitting the giant, Molly must be a sneak thief. And, not incidentally, the rewards are still measured in husbands.

"The Practical Princess" by Jay Williams (Parents') is a charmingly told tale about a sensible, well-educated princess with a mind of her own. One

can object that she decimates a dragon with gunpowder and deceit, thereby emulating macho tests of valor. However, lacking a time-tested formula for "proving one's womanhood" outside of the nursery, it would seem that girls are damned if they're active and dulled if they're not.

A few more not-so-rhetorical questions for this Sunday morning:

Why do so many assertive, independent female protagonists have to be given neuter or "boyish" names—as though a girl with such qualities must have a little maleness in her?

Why are so many of the gracefully written books not feminist and why are most of the books with a feminist consciousness not particularly well written? There must be a way of enlightening good writers to the virtues of open options and non-sexist characters. And there must come a time when feminist writers will express to young readers the rage, vision and frustration of the female experience without proselytism weighing down their prose.

And, finally, can we inspire

our children through books that come out of good intentions but not out of realty? While "Firegirl" by Gibson Rich (The Feminist Press) is an admirable effort, not every little girl can stowaway on a fire truck; and there aren't any real-life women in boots and slickers to serve as models for a little girl's aspirations. It's not enough to have Norma Klein's "Girls Can Be Anything" (Dutton) or "What To Be?" by Meredith Powell and Gail Yokubinas (Children's Press) as long as women cannot really be space pilots and Presidents in our society.

I don't think it's that easy to soothe our consciences or fool our children. We shouldn't be replacing old myths with new fairy tales about everyday life. Make-believe space pilots and Presidents can wait. What we need now are airtight truths and well-supported challenges to the status quo; stories about strong, endearing females and tender, companionable males; and maybe even a picture book about a terrific woman driver. ■

May 6, 1973

Between Parent and Child, What Does Watergate Mean?

By NADINE BROZAN

To 10-year-old Sarah Hilsman, morality has become a simple equation.

The other day, she had a lengthy discussion on the consequences of Presidential impeachment with her father, Roger Hilsman, a professor of government at Columbia University who served as Assistant Secretary of State for Far Eastern Affairs in the Kennedy Administration.

Then she pronounced her verdict: "Well, you have to do it. In the fifth grade, we have to be extra good to be an example to the younger kids, and he's the President."

Sarah touched a nerve that is apparently pinching many a parent.

They are convinced, on the one hand, that the moral image they beam to their children shines a more potent light than that of a distant bureacracy, a remote President. But, on the other hand, they remember that they once equated the Presidency with a man who could not tell a lie, so they worry about the ethical example being set by Nixon Administration figures caught in the Watergate labyrinth.

"When we try to teach children respect for people and institutions, and then they see that those very people for whom we instill respect are above

the law, it creates tremendous confusion," said Mrs. Beatrice S. Frank, the mother of two and associate director of the New York University Law School/ Channel 13 Consumer Help Center.

"Even parents are losing a certain amount of credibility," she lamented.

Mrs. Claire Flom of Manhattan, mother of three, concurred.

"The chief problem in raising children is our desire as parents to teach them the ethical approach to people in life situations," she said. "That's a difficult enough lesson without Watergate, and now they're seeing a total lack of conscience at the highest level. Our message doesn't relate to what they're seeing now."

What they do relate to, at least at

younger levels, is their own experience.

"Young children perceive the morality of Watergate in very simple terms," said Dr. Bernice Berk, psychologist at the Bank Street College of Education School for Children.

"The President appears to have been bad in terms they understand," she said. "When they lose their gloves, they may lie to their mothers, and they think the President did the same thing with the tapes." The difference, she pointed out, "is that they judge the President by much harsher standards."

And so it was in the Bernard Goldstein household in Brooklyn. When Nicholas Goldstein, 8, asked why the President had refused to relinquish the tapes, Mr. Goldstein, who, like many

---

"When we try to teach children respect for people and institutions, and then they see that those very people for whom we instill respect are above the law, it creates tremendous confusion.... Even parents are losing a certain amount of credibility."

---

parents, turns his son's questions into provocative dialogues, asked, "What do you think? Should the President be punished if it turned out he were involved?"

"That's not right," Nicholas retorted. "He's the President and is supposed to be protecting the people against crime, not making crime. He should be punished *more*."

Indeed, the question of guilt doesn't often arise among the young. "They haven't asked me if the President has been bad: they've decided he has," said Mrs. Andy Pettee of Westport, Conn., the mother of five children ranging in age from 6 to 20.

"The older ones are disappointed that there seems to be no moral fiber left after all the years they've been imbued with it," she said, adding that David, one of her 10-year-old twin sons, had declared the other day, "Nixon has a bad look now, and so does the Government."

If children have no trouble comprehending the ethics of the Watergate morass, they do have difficulty absorbing the facts.

Those 10 years old or less have asked: "Mommy, what is Watergate?" "Why is the President making mistakes?" "If Nixon resigned or got impeached, would he still be buried in the President's cemetery?" "Why doesn't Agnew have more money than Daddy?" "Who are the good guys, and who are the bad?"

Adolescents, more knowledgeable and sophisticated, have raised the issues of constitutional crises, Presidential succession, special prosecutors, separation of power, executive privilege.

With the younger children, responses tend to focus on elementary facts, with the older ones, they are more theoretical.

Mr. Goldstein, for example, told his son: "Watergate is the place where the Democrats had an office because they were trying to get elected. That office had a lot of papers and some people broke in to find out what they [the Democrats] were going to say and where they were going to say it so that they could think up answers and win the election."

Implicit in the most rudimentary queries is the curiosity about who the President is and what he does.

Shari Hyman, 7, of Great Neck, L. I., asked her mother, Mrs. Mimi Hyman, "Is he the boss of Daddy's office? Does he tell you what to do?"

Mrs. Hyman, executive director of the Nassau County Chapter of the New York Civil Liberties Union, remembers replying: "Basically, he's the most powerful person in the country, but he's not interested in everything that happens everywhere every day. He's in charge of every place in the United States, but each little place has its own officials."

Anne Siegel, 8, of Weston, Conn., was also troubled by the powers of the Chief Executive.

"It dawned on her recently that Nixon stood for the whole country and for all Presidents of all time," her mother, Mrs. Sue Siegel, said. "It bothered her that one human being served as symbol of an entire nation. I told her, 'This is just one man in the office at the moment. Whether you agree or disagree with him, he is not the whole country.'"

Anne, who wonders "What Senator Dean's wife's name is?" also asked her mother, "Why is the President bugging himself?"

"Why don't you write and ask him," Mrs. Siegel suggested.

And so she did, along with a query, "What does the inside of the White House look like?"

The answer: a photograph of the White House enclosed in a note that read: "The President appreciated your thoughtfulness in writing."

Despite the efforts of the parents, no matter what their personal convictions, to maintain some objectivity in answering questions — for instance, many stressed presumption of innocence until proof of guilt—their approaches tended to differ according to party allegiance.

"Michael knows we've never liked Nixon, he knows we voted for McGovern, but we have always tried to say, 'It's still a decent country, and there are still enough good people around so that if Nixon did do wrong, he will be punished,'" said Mrs. Carol Rinzler, editor-in-chief of Charterhouse Books.

(When Michael, 8, suggested that a book for children on Watergate would clarify his confusion, Charterhouse Books began planning such a volume.)

"Yes, it's probably more difficult emotionally [for Republicans]," said a lifelong Republican whose husband worked as an advance man in President Nixon's 1952 and 1960 campaigns.

The woman, who didn't want to be identified, said her 13-year-old son had asked her if she were sorry she had voted for Mr. Nixon.

"I said no, that maybe he has let people around him get out of hand in this [Watergate] area, but that in many areas, such as foreign affairs, he's done brilliantly.

"I also told him," the mother continued, "I think people change when they get into office, just as they change when they get a lot of money, when they get old, when they get sick."

When the same question arose in the Pettee family, "I told them yes, we had voted for Nixon; we thought we were doing the right thing at the time," Mrs. Pettee said. "We made it clear that we back the man rather than the party [in fact, Mrs. Pettee voted for President Kennedy], but that, in general, we stand more for what the Republican party represents.

"But," she emphasized, "what is happening now is simply wrong."

November 23, 1973

Poor Little Rich Children? Study Shows They Often Are

By DEE WEDEMEYER
Special to The New York Times

CONCORD, Mass.—Robert Coles, the child psychiatrist who has written extensively about the children of the poor and working class, has completed a study on the children of the rich and upper middle class in which he records their developing a class and money consciousness, a sense of entitlement he calls "mind-boggling" and their struggles with the moral ambiguities of their wealth.

He said he observed enormous opportunities and at the same time disadvantages associated with the opportunities and their class.

Too many choices, he said, can cause confusion in some children. Indulgence can lead to finickiness. Traveling from home to home, country to country can lead to a sense of rootlessness akin to that of migrant workers. Some children with enormous homes actually become afraid of some rooms. As these children are taught manners, they are also isolated and aloof from other people.

Some became skeptical of their own abilities and felt teachers might show them deference because of their parents' position.

A 10-year-old told Dr. Coles: "The principal has to be more careful than anyone else. When Daddy sends a check, he gets a nice letter back. He's shown it to me—because the principal says nice things about me. I only half believe him. He has to say nice things, when he's getting hundreds of dollars— thousands, I think. . ."

In an interview in his home here, Dr. Coles said, however, that he believed that his new work, entitled "The Privileged Ones: The Children of the Well Off and the Rich," would be a disappointment to "some some who for understandable reasons might want a book that will portray upper class life into a wasteland."

"One can be against injustices without turning people on top into King Farouks," he said. "Remember these are not Farouks. Some of them are lean, spartan, hard-working and, yes, decent and idealistic parents, whose psychological dilemma is that of having a lot, wanting to hold on to it and yet feeling in many cases troubled, even in some cases tormented by what they have, which is in turn passed on to their children."

Dr. Coles, who is also a pediatrician, is a child psychiatrist on the staff of the Harvard University Health Services. He has published three volumes in a series known as the "Children of Crisis," and won a Pulitzer Prize for nonfiction in 1973 for volumes two and three, subtitled, respectively, "Migrants, Sharecroppers, Mountaineers" and "The South Goes North." Volume four, "Chicanos, Eskimos, Indians," will be published simultaneously with the volume on the privileged next year by Atlantic - Little, Brown, he said, bringing the series to a conclusion after more than a million words. He is now beginning to study children of other countries.

61

Since he began studying poor and working-class children in 1959, he said he has been quietly studying the privileged also, beginning at the suggestion of Vivian Bridges, the then 9-year-old sister of one of the first black children to integrate the New Orleans schools.

"She said, 'Why are you studying us?'" Coles recalled. "Over here we are only the poor. Not only us but even those white people who are hurting us, they are poor too. If you want to know what's happening, you better go to the Garden District."

Others reinforced her suggestion so Dr. Coles began in the Garden District, a section of New Orleans with many wealthy residents, and continued to seek out the wealthy in Atlanta, Boston, Princeton, N.J., Connecticut, Westchester County, N.Y., New York City, Winnetka, Ill., New Mexico, Texas, Florida and Alaska.

As he interviewed children of maids, he sought out children of the employer; slum dwellers and tenement owners, migrant workers and farm owners, mineworkers and mine owners. He interviewed segregationists and integrationists and, in the case of one prominent New York family, a family in which philanthropic work in Harlem was a tradition. He said he saw 85 children, some over a period of four years, none less than a year, several hundred others on a group basis and also interviewed parents and teachers.

None in the new study were from families earning less than $40,000 a year in 1960 and many came from families worth several million dollars. Names and places are disguised in the study to provide anonymity, he said, and in some cases, children with similar situations are made into a composite figure.

Dr. Coles said that one of the most obvious differences in the children of the privileged and poor and working-class children was in their drawings. Typically, he said, a poor child might draw pictures of himself, minus some physical features or without detailed landscaping.

The privileged child drew elaborate houses, exotic landscapes, well-dressed people and objects Dr. Coles found unusual until he realized the objects were toys "in proportion to the grandeur of their lives."

"Believe it or not, one child drew for me an enormous hippopotamus," recalled Dr. Coles. "I had never seen a child draw a hippopotamus. It turned out to be the biggest toy I've ever seen in my entire life, and I think the ugliest. I think the hippopotamus was about as large as a real baby hippopotamus. It would go into

Dr. Robert Coles, a child psychiatrist, said he was startled when a privileged child drew a picture of a hippopotamus for him. "I had never seen a child draw a hippopotamus," he said.

United Press International

the pool and the child could control it. It could either go up or go down."

Sometimes they asked for more paper to elaborate.

"I never had a ghetto child fill up paper the way they did," said Dr. Coles in a moment of levity. "They have the wherewithal to fill up paper."

He said the "common denominator" of the privileged children was a sense of "entitlement" which he defined as "a sense of one's position in the world and a sense of real self-assurance about the future, at least the social and economic part of that future."

As the privileged child grows up, Dr. Coles said, he becomes increasingly aware that he is special, that people respect his parents and are sometimes awed by them. They see that they have money and possess status symbols.

In contrast, he said, even if the poor or working class child starts out feeling secure, as he grows older he observes the contempt society has for him.

"These children get stronger," said Dr. Coles, patting the unedited manuscript of the volume on privileged children. "These children get weaker," he said, tapping the manuscript on "Chicanos, Eskimos and Indians."

When he first heard the privileged children talking about trips they would take, places they had been, ambitions they had, he said he

found it "mind-boggling."

Dr. Coles said that social scientists had substantially documented the rituals of the poor, working class and middle class but the resources of the rich had enabled them to keep many of their rituals unobserved.

He compared the poor child's visiting the welfare office with the privileged child being taken to meet his trust officer or having lunch at the bank.

"I think that is an event in the lives of these children," he said. "They are being educated, told what their lives are about. One child is learning the family dependency and how rude and condescending the treatment often is. One child learns entitlement and the other child learns vulnerability."

The advantages and disadvantages of Little League baseball have been written about, he said, but riding or sailing, for example, could also be excruciatingly competitive. "Among certain quite well-off children the performance at a show or on a hunt can be an occasion

for fear, self-doubt and fierce rivalry," he said.

He also compared the staff —maids, instructors, gardeners —to the extended family of the ethnic working class. Some servants, he said, could be cruel; others provided some of the most meaningful childhood moments and their presence often precipitated the introduction of moral

questions about the child's wealth and position in society.

Contrary to myth—that the rich are less conscious of money than the poor—he said he found money consciousness a big factor in the children's life and some children, who had heard their parents talking about taxes, unions, shiftless welfare recipients, feared for their future. Even a 6-year-old New Orleans girl was aware that she would inherit $500,000 some day and a 12-year-old boy who lived on an estate north of Boston worried about living up to family standards.

"He [the father] says that if we don't demand a lot of ourselves, then we'll become fat and stupid—and we'll live off our capital, and we'll amount to nothing and we'll become rich bums, and our children will become comfortable bums, and our grandchildren will become poor bums of good families or of families that once were good," the child told Dr. Coles.

Dr. Coles said the children had moments of what he called "exquisite sensitivity" in which they ask "Christ-like questions" about the problems of the poor. Inevitably, he said, parents become "uncomfortable and fidgety" and handle the situation in such a way as to inhibit future questions. The child is often made to feel that he is weak, subversive, or that something is wrong with him.

"What they end up doing is drawing the line," he said, "because there is no answer."

Poor and working-class children ask the same kinds of questions, he said, citing a migrant worker who as a child hated the landowners and wondered why the workers did not rise up against them. When her own children tormented her with the same questions, she urged them not to ask those questions because they would become known as troublemakers.

Similarly, he said the child of a Boston banker began watching a television show about Robin Hood and concluded that when he grew up he might like to be Robin Hood, taking from the rich to give to the poor. The child's parents consulted their pediatrician. A teacher asked the boy whether Robin Hood was acting on impulse and lacked the ability to implement change. The boy's father said the television show was for "younger children" and suggested a science program instead that was for "older children."

The father offered to watch the show with the boy. Before long, Dr. Coles said, the boy was watching "Gilligan's Island."

August 3, 1976

Dinner-Table Talk Can Be a Family Alternative to Preaching

By RICHARD FLASTE

Your child has just been caught cheating. It comes as a real shock. It's so unlike him, you say—when, manifestly, it was exactly like him.

A method of communication that could avoid such shocks—either because you would know that the child was prone to cheat, and why, or because the child who had been a cheater had been helped to stop—is called "values clarification."

It's a method used and ballyhooed in thousands of schools, and one of its main spokesmen, Dr. Sidney Simon, an educator, is attempting to make it at least as big a success in families.

In a new book called "Helping Your Child Learn Right From Wrong" (Simon and Schuster, $7.95), Dr. Simon and Sally Wendkos Olds, a veteran author of child-rearing books and articles, adapt the values clarification approach to families.

The title is somewhat misleading, however. It seems to imply that there is some absolute notion of right and wrong and this approach will help your child learn it.

No such luck. Dr. Simon, describing his thinking in an interview the other day, said he saw right and wrong as concepts each individual decides for himself; Dr. Simon simply wants to help make that a reasonably rational choice, based on a clear understanding of one's own values.

Dr. Simon's definition of a value—a principle of life—is that it is something you choose freely, are proud of once it's chosen, and act upon it aware of the consequences.

That leaves a lot of latitude: there are people who greatly value punching others in the face and do so fully aware of the consequences. And the values clarification approach has been attacked as a potential buttress for amorality.

But Dr. Simon, who teaches at the University of Massachusetts Center for Humanistic Education, appears to believe that most people have within them the power to be responsible, wholesome and happy, given the chance.

Values clarification gives them the

chance—around the dining room table. Dr. Simon described dinner-table conversation as revolving around such requests as "pass the ketchup." But dinner is a time, he said, when the whole family is together for a change and to waste it on trivial conversation is a tragic "missed opportunity."

Instead, he said, parents can pause before dessert to help children, and themselves, confront a chaotic world in which "Watergate is only the most obvious example."

"Do you realize," he said, "that in the supermarket there are whole aisles of cookies? Whole aisles of dog food? There are more choices and more confusion about everything today than at any other time in history."

What he has done to clarify matters is draw up games to be played by families whenever the spirit moves them. One game is called Priorities. A sample question: What is the most important thing for parents to give their children —independence, compassion, motivation to succeed?

Opposite Views

Such a question can lead to emotional discussion. The parent who values compassion over independence and the child who holds the opposite view would find themselves, in no time at all, exploring what they mean to each other and why they choose to behave the way they do. They might even choose to change as a result of the discussion. The talk could certainly lead to personal vulnerability. "It's a beautiful thing," Dr. Simon said, "for a child to realize his parent is frail."

Another game is called My Last Lie, in which everybody tells about the lie, why they told it, how they felt and what alternatives there were to lying at the time. The book—like Dr. Simon's previous works, which aimed primarily at teachers instead of parents—provides a great many of these "strategies." There are 84 games in the book for families.

Such discussions can readily lead to abuses, in which parents attempt to guide a child to the right answers. Or use the talks mainly to pry into secrets.

The rules of the game prohibit manipulation, outlaw judgment of right or wrong on the part of the listener and demand that there be no moralizing.

Dr. Simon said he thinks that when parents try to teach values they fail. What they have to do, he said, is help children arrive at values the children feel comfortable with.

The Drug Issue at Home

Children often feel quite comfortable using drugs, of course. Should parents who disdain drugs quietly accept their children's use of them? No you're allowed, in Dr. Simon's world, to express your own opinion with "quiet dignity, and not necessarily without passion."

When Dr. Simon's teen-agers were smoking marijuana, he told them, "I would be humiliated if there were a drug bust at my home." They stopped smoking around the house, and eventually stopped altogether.

Dr. Simon leads his life in what some will see as an eccentric fashion. When his family goes to a supermarket, they only buy what they listed beforehand. When they make New Year's resolutions, they don't mess around—they draw up contracts and check on each other. When, in earlier years, Dr. Simon took his four children to a county fair they were given a set amount of money, worn in cans around their necks. They were forced to walk through the entire fair once without buying anything and then set free to buy what they wanted. When the money was gone, there was no more forthcoming.

Dr. Simon's approach and life may sound awfully rigid. But he asserts that by clarifying what you are and what you like there's less anxiety about choices and more time to enjoy life.

His co-author, Mrs. Olds, got involved with this book because, she said, she found Dr. Simon's approach helpful in her own family and far from rigid.

"I found it particularly useful," she said, "for raising issues that wouldn't have been easy to raise without it. It's a lot better than preaching to the kids."

October 8, 1976

CHILDREN AND THE MEDIA

WHAT SMALL BOYS READ.

RANK LITERATURE FOR THE YOUNG.

NEWSPAPERS, MAGAZINES, AND NOVELS TEEMING WITH CORRUPT AND SENSATIONAL STORIES FOR JUVENILE READERS.

The boys of New-York are furnished every week with as vile and degrading a supply of "flash" and corrupting literature as unscrupulous men can buy and publish, or greedy news-vendors spread broadcast throughout the City. There are published in the City of New-York every week not less than 10 newspapers whose titles denote that they are intended exclusively for boys and young men, and as many monthly magazines, all filled with such matter as no boy, nor no young man, can read without filling his mind with preposterous bosh; trash fatal to the storing up of

anything useful or true; stories in which the outcast, the desperado, and the criminal always figure in glowing colors, and the decent person is overthrown and thoroughly vanquished.

Until a short time ago, these newspapers confined themselves to the telling of improbable stories of successful burglaries, millionaire highwaymen, and tales well calculated to turn the respectable working boy into a midnight prowler and Bowery rough. But recently they have gone a step further, and lecherous and impure stories, in which fallen women figure prominently, ornament their columns.

It is a safe proposition, that not one of these newspapers is fit to go into the hands of any boy or young man in this city. And it is not to be supposed that they would make the enormous sales by which they now grow fat were the parents of these budding boys aware of the character of the reading that employs

their sons' leisure hours. These papers circulate largely among schoolboys and boys employed in workshops and factories. Where three boys are seen riding in a street-car, two of them are poring over this abominable trash. At the times of day when working-people are going to or returning from their work the sidewalks are full of them. All through the down-town streets, in Park Row, Broadway, Chatham-street, Third-avenue, the streets of the East Side, Sixth and Eighth avenues, and even in some of the principal hotels, the news-stands are plastered over with this pernicious literature—a sure sign that it sells quickly and profitably.

A TIMES reporter bought three of these newspapers at a down-town news-stand yesterday. They were three of the principal ones, and they can be bought of almost any small news-dealer in New-York. Every one of them has the word "boy" in staring letters in its heading, to attract the attention of its young customers. A brief description of the contents of these three papers will give the public some idea of what "the boys of New York" feed upon.

Almost the whole front page of the first is covered with a rough wood-cut. It represents a man shackled to the stone wall of a prison. A flashily-dressed woman has her arms thrown about his neck, and his expression denotes the greatest terror. At his feet kneels a boy with a file in his right hand, evidently preparing to cut the shackles. Through a small hole in the cell door a revolver and a hand are seen, the revolver smoking and flashing. Underneath this picture is the explanatory line, "A sudden flash and report of a pistol, held by a hand thrust through a hole in the bars, illuminated the room, and Earle Dudley sank down with a groan at the feet of Leonora Cressleigh." This picture is supposed to illustrate the leading story in the paper, "Shot in the Dark," by the author of "Jack Dauntless, the Boy Privateer," "The Burglars of New York," &c. Another picture in the same paper is of a dwarf perched upon the back of a chair, with a revolver in each hand, pointing them both at a man who cowers in a corner. Underneath this is printed, "Wheeling around, he was paralyzed with horror on seeing the dwarf, a grinning imp of hideous deformity, perched on the back of a chair." The two other illustrations are of very much the same character. The titles of the other impossible stories in this paper are: "Escaped from Justice;" "Kickapoo Joe: or, the Struggle for a Mine;" "Thirteen: or, the Brotherhood of Death;" "The Burglars of New York; or, the Crimes of Jerry O'Keefe;" "Tricks; or, Traveling with a Variety Show;" "Stump; or, Little but Oh, My!" "Bad Murice, the Looney Detective," and "Under the Gallows," by a United States Detective. Among the advertisements is, "Hell, by ——, the most wonderful book ever published; price 25 cents." Among the answers to correspondents is this: "Charley Masher.—You want to mash, hey? Buy 'How to Do It,' just out, and you will be able to get all of your girl friends on a string; price, 10 cents."

The second of these papers also fills the greater part of its first page with a wood-cut. This one is a triumph of the blood-curdler's art. It represents a half-sunken ship, with the body of a man lying in the hold, half floating in the water. A young man is looking through a sky-light and two boys are in the hold, one with a lighted candle in his hand. A score or more of enormous water-rats have just been frightened from the body. They are coming out from under the dead man's vest, eating his hands, and swimming away in the water. Underneath this picture is the line, "A scene lay before them, and at their very feet, which was enough to freeze the blood in the veins of the most hardened sinner the world had ever seen." Another illustration is of a man tossed against a monkey's cage, on the horns of a "sacred cow," with the line below, "The cow made a dive at the Professor, and, catching her horns just under his coat tails, sent him flying through the air." Another represents a man thrown overboard from a steam-ship by a party of young roughs. The titles of some of the stories in this paper are unique: "The Wharf Boys of New-York; or, Together as One," by the author of "Bang Up," "The Mysterious Messenger," &c., "Three Yankee Chums; or, Dr. Dodd's Exploring Expedition," by the author of "Sassy Sam," "Barnum's Boy Ben," &c., &c. Then comes the announcement, "The Bowery, Night and Day! Ready in two weeks. A rattling boy's story, descriptive of life in that most fascinating of all Metropolitan thoroughfares, the Bowery, entitled

THE FOUR JACKS;
OR
THE DOG DETECTIVE.

"This thrilling romance will introduce to the readers a series of characters that can be found in no other part of the world than the place in which the story is located, and the scenes are written in a graphic style, and by one who has been 'A Bowery Boy' all his life. No one who wishes to obtain a glimpse of the stirring scenes daily and nightly enacted in the great East Side portion of the Empire City should fail to read 'The Four Jacks; or, The Dog Detective.'" The other stories are, "Shorty, Jr., on His Ear; or, Always on a Racket," by the author of "Shorty," "Shorty in Luck," "Shorty, Jr." &c., &c. "The Boy Clown; or, The Star of the Pantomime," by the author of "Teddy O'Lynn," "Billy the Boot-black," &c., &c., "The Scarred Hand," "Hale and Hearty: or, the Boys of Columbia College," "The Tell-tale Paper," by a New-York detective, and "Red Leary, the Bill-poster; or, The Murder on the Pier."

The third of these interesting publications also leads off with a large picture. It represents four masked men in a sleigh, the horses dashing madly in front of an approaching locomotive, and a boy, writhing and twisting in the air. Underneath is the line. "'Now or never for a bold jump for life,' cried Maurice. Then, with a sudden bound and a wild yell, he sprang from the sleigh into a snow bank." This picture illustrates a story entitled "Mad Maurice; or, The Crazy Detective." Titles of other stories in the same paper are: "Jim Jams; or, Jack of all Trades;" "Out with Stanley; or, Young America in Africa;" "Laying a Ghost;" "Lured to His Ruin;" "The Boy Bohemian; or, The Adventures of a Young Reporter:" "Tim of the Mail Train; or, Steel to the Last." There is also announced for early publication, "Nip and Flip; or, Two of a Kind," by the author of "Skinny the Tin Peddler," "Corkey," "Jim Jams," &c.

All the stories in all of these papers are full of impossible adventures, or something worse, and the situations are such as, if reached in real life, would send the heroes to the Tombs and Blackwell's Island.

Two or three brief extracts, selected at random, will show the literary character of these productions. Here are a few lines out of "The Boy Bohemian; or, the Adventures of a Young Reporter":

"To say that the Duke De Aches and Jack Ralston were thunderstruck when the French detective climbed through the trap-door in the floor, would but poorly express their feelings.

* * * * * * *

"Here was the man whom but an hour or two before they tied in a loaded bag and threw into the bay, standing before them.

"When Ned Looney bore the French detective to the surface, he made for the Long Island shore, and landed between Bay Ridge and Fort Hamilton."

Here is some news from Stanley, from the story "Out with Stanley":

"Again all was hushed in breathless silence, but no tiger appeared.

"'Confound the brute!' roared Stanley, hitching about the top of his bush in an agony of impatience.

"'Blaze away, men; give him more fire; blow the cowardly rascal to the devil.'"

This is from "The Burglars of New-York"

"'I've hacked these two in true butcher style,' said Jerry, as he threw his dripping knife under the bed. 'There's lots more up stairs, but they won't trouble us.'

"They then went down stairs, and immediately proceeded to open a safe, which Wolf kept in a small room at the rear of his store.

"It was full of valuable property.

"Diamonds, watches, jewelry of all kinds, and money.

"'There's a fortin',' cried Jerry, cramming the valuables into his pockets.

Two of these newspapers are published at the same number, in the same street, and, presumably, by the same firm. In these two is an advertisement of "The New-York Boys' Library. Well-known, Valuable, Juvenile Works, almost given away." These works are published in the same style as the "Seaside Library," and many other cheap novels, and are sold for 10 cents each. The list starts off with such well-known works as Thomas Hughes' *Tom Brown's School Days,* De Foe's *Robinson Crusoe,* and Marryat's *Peter Simple,* but it soon degenerates into flashy and impossible stories. In the list, which includes 120 numbers, are *The Devil's Diamond, The Pirate Doctor, The Pirate Chief, The Smugglers, The Masked Highwaymen, The Hangman of Newgate, The Demon of the Deep, Tom, Dick, and the ——, The Pirate Schooner, The Pirates of America, The Pirate Cutter, the Black Pirates, Three-fingered Jack, The Devil on Two Sticks, The Highwayman's Fate, The Light-house Murder, The Assassin's Doom, The Pirate of the Shoals, The Robbers of the Rhine, Duval and His Pals, On the Scaffold, The Highwayman's Ride, Duval in the Cloister,* and a score of others of the same kind.

Any philanthropic person who is interested in knowing the result of such reading may find it, unwashed and ragged, in the boys' prison in the Tombs.

March 31, 1878

WHAT SMALL BOYS READ

CHOICE TALES OF INDIANS AND PIRATES.

A GLANCE AT THE CONTENTS OF SEVERAL PUBLICATIONS, SELECTED AT RANDOM FROM A NEWS-STAND.

It is two years since THE TIMES directed the attention of its readers to the abominable trash that is daily set before the boys and young men of this and neighboring cities, under the misnomer of literature; and in that short time the number of pernicious newspapers and cheap books for the young has greatly increased. Two years ago there were three or four weekly publications in this City, filled with the trashiest of stories of Indian hunting and impossible adventure. This number has now increased to fully a dozen, and there are published, in addition to the newspapers, cheap pamphlets, after the style of the "Franklin-Square Library" and the "Seaside Library," but sold at half the price, full of the same abominable stuff. The boys of the streets and factories have nearly all had a taste of the public schools, and they must have something to read. That they do read, and that they read principally the unwholesome trash printed in the publications mentioned, may be seen in any street car, or on any ferry-boat. The boy of the time is no sooner seated in any conveyance than he whips out his paper or his pamphlet, and falls to reading—and, nine times out of ten, he reads these trashy papers that fill his head with notions of Indians, and pirates, and successful thieves. There is plenty of antidote to these unhealthy tales in the shape of several wholesome juvenile publications; but the working boys, with nobody to care what they read, take heavy doses of the poison, and let the antidote severely alone. Hardly a day passes in this City but the Police capture runaway boys, many of them the children of respectable parents, who, having filled their heads with these wonderful adventures, run away to this City to see the great sights. The sight they usually do see is the inside of a Police station, and a penitent return to their homes; but this side of the picture is not shown in the story papers. Two humorous cases of this kind have lately come to the notice of the writer, one in the dispatches of the Associated Press, the other by personal observation. Two boys in St. Louis, who had been reading tales of imaginary frontier life, concluded to start out to see something of the world. One was 13 years old, the other 14. Instead of going West, they went southward. But they desired to travel by rail, and they had only money enough to buy one ticket. So they procured a large trunk, bored some airholes in it, and tossed a penny to see who should travel in the trunk and who should go as passenger.

The boy who lost the toss coiled himself up in the trunk; a loaf of bread and a bottle of water were put in with him, and the trunk was locked. All went well till the trunk was hustled into an express car and stood on end. It happened to be stood on the end where the boy's head was, and the express passenger soon began to scream. The runaways were thus discovered and sent home. The other was a New-York case. One of the bootblacks always on duty in the vicinity of the City Hall, a boy from Troy, was telling one of his companions of a recent visit from two of his old friends in Troy. "They was the biggest fools you ever see," said he. "They'd been readin' about 'Muddy Jack; or, the Thief of the Docks,' and they come down here a-purpose to see him. Nothin' would do but I must show 'em the robber's cave under the docks, an' then they wanted me to show 'em Muddy Jack. I picked out another bootblack and showed him to 'em, an' he did just as well. If I'd told 'em there wasn't no such person as Muddy Jack they'd thought I lied."

Not only have these pernicious newspapers for boys increased greatly in number, but they have grown in recklessness, publishing now with impunity shameless advertisements that two years ago they would not have dared to publish. They are for sale at every news-stand, at every depot, everywhere. The writer of this article went to a news-stand in Park-row on Saturday afternoon, and for 31 cents bought a rare assortment of them. Three or four of them, taken as samples, will give an idea of them all.

Here is the first one with a title indicating that it is published for the boys of New-York. It is about the size of the story papers for older folks, and sells for 5 cents. The first page is almost filled with a rough wood-cut of a bare-headed hunter kneeling in the bulrushes, with his cocked rifle at his shoulder. Underneath the picture are these two lines in explanation of it: "'You've trapped the trackless at last. I'm durned sorry now that I didn't put that bullet in Hard-Heart's noddle-box. Wonder if I couldn't fetch him now—I'd feel then as if I'd sorter squared accounts,' and he raised his rifle and took a careful aim." This picture is to illustrate the leading story, "'The Arkansas Scout,' by —— ——, author of 'The Mark of Mystery,' 'The Red Circle,' 'Tracked,' 'The Blue League,' 'Red River Pilot,' 'At 12 o'Clock,' 'The Detectives' League,'" &c. Then, after several short stories, comes 'Among the Fire-Worshipers; or, Two New-York Boys in Mexico,' by —— ——, author of 'Castaway,' 'Boy Whaleman,' 'Sea-Dog Charlie,' 'Midshipman Ned,' 'Burt, the Detective,' 'Dick Halliday,' 'The Orphan Boy,' 'That Boy of Tony Pastor's,'" &c. The next story is the "'Shorty's Trip Around the World,' by —— ——, author of 'Ebenezer Crow,' 'Stump; or, Little, but Oh, My!' 'Chips and Chin Chin,' 'Stuttering Sam,' 'Tommy Bounce,' 'Tom, Dick, and the Devil,' 'Shorty; or, Kicked into Good Luck,' 'Tommy Dodd,' 'Shorty in Search of His Dad,' 'Tumbling Tim,'" &c. This is also an illustrated story, and the picture is supposed to be explained by the line, "'Whew! who would think there was so much dance in it?' cried the King, and, being unable longer to contain himself, he seized the horrified missionary woman, and began to dance with her." The next illustrated story is "'Ned Kelly and His Bushman,' a story of robber life in Australia, by a United States Detective." Then follow "'Young Capt. Prery, the Hero of 1812,' an exciting privateer yarn," and "'Billy Button, the Young Clown and Bare-back Rider,' a story of the circus," and "'A Balked Murderer,' by a New-York Detective." Here is a choice variety to feed the mind of that dear young creature who is said to be father of the man—fire worshipers, robber life in Australia, a privateer yarn, a story of the circus, and a detective's story of a murderer! A single verse of the "poetry" of this exciting newspaper will no doubt be quite sufficient. It is the chorus of a song called "The Widdy McCarty's Boarding-house," and comes under the general caption of "'The Singer's Corner,' containing the latest songs of the day:"

"Then here's success to the Widdy McCarty,
An' her boarding-house on Mulberry-street;
So if ye wish to get fat an' hearty,
Don't forget to go there an' eat."

This is what your boy is reading in his leisure hours, Mr. Parent. Is it quite to your liking? But if you are dissatisfied with the stories, what will you think of the advertisements? Here are a few of the things advertised: "Night Scenes, rich and very rare, three for 10 cents, twelve for 25 cents. ——, Boston, Mass." "How to Dance." This is a book, price 10 cents. "On the Stage, or How to Become an Actor," another book, for 15 cents. "'How to Flirt;' just out," another book, 10 cents. "The Boys of New-York. Minstrel Guide and Joke Book," 10 cents. "How to Do It," another book, "that tells you all about it; there's happiness in it," 10 cents. These are some of the advertisements that, by a little stretch of the proprieties, may be mentioned. There are others of such a character that they will not bear mention at all in the columns of any respectable newspaper.

The second one of these papers professes to be published by a pair of New-York minstrels, and the leading story is entitled "'Dan Bryant; or, the Romance of a Minstrel,' by —— and ——, authors of 'Edwin Forrest's Ward.'" Another story is "Bryan O'Lynn, the Irish Detective; or, There Never was a Coward Where the Shamrock Grows." The other stories, with big heads, are "Paddy Miles's Boy," "The Middy Spy; or, Commodore Decatur's Protégé," "Hancock's Pet; or, the Drummer Boy of Gettysburg," and "Harry Howard; or, Life in Public School and College." This paper is very much on the plan of the one first named, but more "stagey," and contains no objectionable advertisements. The third paper is intended for "young men." It is pretty much the same as the others, only the pictures are of young men instead of boys. It is a paper that some of the young men of the East Side might delight in—full of gore and Indians and murders.

On the top of these three valuable additions to American literature comes a pamphlet in the shape of the cheap novels of the day, but printed in large type, and sold for 5 cents. This is only one of many, all modeled in contents after the dime novels of the past, full of Indians and pirates and thieves. It is dangerous reading for a boy, nauseating for a man, and it is multiplying and spreading much faster than all the good books of all the good publishers.

November 25, 1880

HEALTH AND GROWTH IN CHILDREN.

A recent sketch in our news columns calls attention anew to the pestiferous stream of printed trash which enfeebles the minds and depraves the morals of children. For every periodical of a healthful sort offered—and the juvenile field has received so much attention from publishers of late years that the number of these is not behind the demand—there are some half-dozen of the pernicious sort. They are a source of mental intoxication, and their stimulus is so fascinating that delicately nurtured children, whose parents keep the stuff out of their homes, have been known to stand on the sidewalk and greedily devour the "continued story" through the news-dealer's windows. The number of these publications has greatly increased, and their success seems to justify the opinion that the most profitable printed matter is that which appeals to the lowest grade of intelligence. How to meet the evil is a problem, and yet society cannot afford to be inattentive to an instrumentality so profoundly affecting its health and morals. That strong manhood and healthy girlhood can follow this mental debauchery is as impossible as that the body can be nourished on sawdust; yet society has never gone so far as to interfere with education beyond a fixed compulsory course. But the "flash" story leads by a natural gradation to the seductive correspondence and the immoral advertisement. There is a publication in Boston, misusing one of the most honored names in literature, which is not only made up of the most abominable dish-water imaginable, but is positively unfit to enter any family of children, its immorality being made the worse by being disguised under polite phrases. Shall we establish a public censor? Nothing more opposed to the spirit of republican institutions could be suggested, the theory being that the press must have liberty up to license. The latter has been held to cover only two abuses, libel and obscenity. It has long been a maxim in law that any trade obviously and necessarily corrupting to morality has no title to use the facilities of protection and exchange ordinarily furnished. Thus, no device of such sort can be patented; no obscene publication or thing can be passed through the Customs; lotteries, obvious frauds, and obscene publications are denied the use of the mails, and the exclusion of publications which admit lottery advertisements has even been urged. The press is not and can not be free without limit, because debauchery of public morals is often a profitable business, and society is bound to act in self-defense. To make laws, build jails, and maintain courts is foolish if the corruption of youth is to be unrestricted. How far society may rightfully and wisely go in deciding that this or that publication is too injurious to be permissible it is not easy to define, because the standard of tolerable literary merit is hard to establish; but to define what degree of immorality in print the law will permit should not be difficult. The just line is considerably overstepped already, and it is time the poisonous trash exposed on news-stands was critically examined. Some of it may be subject to correction under existing law, and the law itself may require amending.

November 27, 1880

Books for Children.

A healthful sign is the increasing attention which has been given within the past two or three years to books for children. This subject has risen to such importance that it now occupies a distinct place of its own in library methods, and more care is being taken each year in the department of literature for young people and children.

In the library world Miss Caroline M. Hewins of the Hartford Public Library stands as the recognized authority on the subject of children's books. Its present importance is largely due to her efforts, and some of the results of her study of this subject were given to the recent assembly of librarians in Philadelphia in a brief but decidedly interesting and instructive paper. Not only to librarians in general, but to teachers and others having the care of children, will its suggestions upon juvenile literature be found valuable. Miss Hewins's paper is as follows:

"Before giving an opinion on individual books it is well to keep in mind that the children who take books from public libraries are of all grades of intelligence, a few from homes full of books where fathers and mothers read the best from English literature, and many from houses where there are no books, and the father cannot read enough to vote. The first have a large vocabulary and are familiar with historical allusions and the names of poets and artists before they go to school. The second have a meagre choice of words, but pick up with surprising quickness crumbs of information about historical characters or the poets whose verses they read in class.

"Between these two extremes is a large number of boys and girls, whose fathers and mothers read newspapers and poor novels. What books should a library buy to meet the wants of these three classes of children? First, books should be written in good English, which they all could understand. A recent reviewer defines a good style for children as that which Andrew Lang has adapted in his fairy books, a little old-fashioned and abounding in such expressions as 'Vastly well, madam!' The abridgments of his fairy books are models for the children to whom English is an unfamiliar tongue, and who find Hawthorne's Wonder Book and Tanglewood Tales full of long words and involved sentences. It is, however, a fatal mistake to simplify Hawthorne, as the writer of a little book called 'In Mythland' has done, into such chopped sentences as 'This made Pandora cross. She would not play. The dear boy felt sad. He went out to play alone. Pandora looked at the box. How pretty, is it not? Flowers men carved upon it; leaves, too, and children.'

"If the book is in an easy, flowing style, the child reader becomes interested in it and goes on just as you and I read a French story, occasionally meeting an unfamiliar word, but guessing it by the context.

"Second, children's books should be imaginative in the best sense, or give information to be understood of the people. Children like history in story form, but once in a while there is a boy or girl who prefers it undiluted. One class in history that I know of children, from twelve to fifteen years old, reads and enjoys Parkman's histories.

"Third, books should appeal to the best instincts of children. There are two which always touch the chord that vibrates to tales of suffering bravely endured. These two are 'Uncle Tom's Cabin' and 'Black Beauty.' Stories of children who are cruelly treated should not, I think, be placed in children's libraries, and, with the exception of these two books, there should be little on the shelves to excite their tears.

"Stories of happy, sunny childhood in sheltered homes, of simple country pleasures or home life in cities where the father and mother rule the household gently but firmly and the children do not decide important question for themselves, are still to be found. So are wholesome tales of school life, stories of animals, lives of great men, books teaching handicrafts or resources for vacation and rainy days and selections of poetry.

"On reading several hundred letters from children about their favorite books, I find that none of them cares for books about music or art, and few for out-of-door writers, books of games and sports. Most of them like fairy tales, if they speak of them at all. One thinks 'Gulliver's Travels' silly, but another writes: 'A year or two ago I found in reading fairy stories that what seemed to me to be rather silly corresponded to what was real facts, and might have happened.'"

Some of the books of the year which were recommended for children are: Brooks's "True Story of Abraham Lincoln," Brooks and Alden's "Long Walls," Crockett's "Sweetheart Travelers," Joel Chandler Harris's "Story of Aaron," Henty's works, Andrew Lang's "Animal Story Book," Nora Perry's "Three Little Daughters of the Revolution," White's "Little Girl of Long Ago," and Paul Leicester Ford's "True Story of George Washington."

August 7, 1897

Children's Rooms in Libraries and Their Popularity.

In the library world one of the most encouraging features is the progress of the work for children. Special rooms for children have been set apart in many libraries, and under competent management have generally been productive of more beneficial results than in many cases was first imagined. Our New York libraries, however, are at present lacking in this children's department, but the Pratt Institute Free Library of Brooklyn has a children's room, started a little more than a year ago. Provision has been made for this necessary feature of library work in the coming building for the New York Public Library, but it will be some time before this can be realized.

In connection with the growing popularity of library effort for children it may be interesting to call attention to the remarkable success of a plan organized in Cleveland last Spring, which has since been adopted by one library in this State, the Prendergast Library of Jamestown, while news now comes that the library enthusiasts in Utica are preparing to put the scheme into practical working order there.

This plan originated with the Cleveland Public Library, and was an experiment toward providing broader and better facilities for children in the use of the library, these facilities not only meaning better conveniences in using books, but the education of children so that they themselves may become judges of good books. Briefly, it may be said that this is the underlying principle in all of this children's library movement, and a very laudable one it is, too.

During the Summer conference of the American Library Association, in Philadelphia, a report of this Cleveland system was given for the first time, the league, known as the Cleveland Library League, then having a membership of 3,500. Now the membership is close to 13,000, and in the November number of The Library Journal Miss Linda A. Eastman of the Cleveland Public Library furnishes an instructive account of the first league mass meeting, held early this month, which was attended by over 5,000 children.

One of the distinctive and not least popular features of the movement is a neat white-metal badge, supplied to each of the members at 3 cents apiece. No one can secure a badge unless a bona fide user of the library, and, while it is obvious that many children will probably commence using the library solely for the purpose of wearing one of the badges, it is the very beginning of literary interest in children that the league seeks to develop, no matter whether book interest is first engendered through the pride of wearing a badge or not. Upon the badge is an open book, bearing the words Cleveland Library League. The utility of the league has been greatly enhanced by the method of sending parcels of books to the schools, so that the children can draw their books from the library through the schools. The teachers, also, have shown great interest in the movement and have contributed largely to its success.

The large membership of the Cleveland League has recently led to the formation on a small scale of several reading clubs, in which the interest of the children can be more carefully directed by older persons. Miss Eastman, in speaking of the possibilities which have been revealed by the league, says:

"The one great point which our league seems to be proving conclusively is that our city—and ours is not an exception in this respect—contains thousands of children who are not being reached by the ordinary methods of library work. The league in itself is sufficient to reach but a small fraction of these children. We were told by a teacher of an instance of several members of the league to whom the coming down town to that league meeting was the event almost of their little lives—so narrowed have their lives been within the limits of the poor suburb where they live, that they actually did not remember having seen our public square before that day."

And with very much the same idea in mind Miss Mary Wright Plummer, director of the Pratt Institute Free Library, in Brooklyn, writes regarding her experience with children's libraries in the same number of The Literary Journal: "It will not be long after the opening of the children's library before an insight will be gained into domestic interiors and private lives that will make the librarian wish she could follow many a child to his home, in order to secure for him and his something better than the few hours' respite from practical life which they may get from the reading of books. When the boy who steals and the girl who is vicious before they are in their teens have to be sent away lest other children suffer, it is borne in upon the librarian that a staff of home missionaries connected with the library, to follow up and minister in such cases, would not be a bad thing—and she has to remind herself again and again that it is not incumbent on any one person to attempt everything, and that Providence has other instrumentalities at work besides herself."

The Prendergast Library has already secured over 1,000 members to its league, and a special room for little ones was opened in October. The statement that the children's room was formerly the Trustees' room brings up the query of how many libraries may have Trustees' or other rooms used as little as Trustees' rooms usually are which might be employed in giving delightful and helpful instruction to hundreds of children.

November 27, 1897

FIGHTS PICTURE SHOWS.

Father Gardiner of Bath Beach Warns Mothers to Keep Children Out of Them

The Rev. William A. Gardiner, rector of St. Finbar's Roman Catholic Church, in Bath Beach, Brooklyn, made an attack in his sermon yesterday morning on the moving picture shows within the limits of his parish. There are now three such shows running in almost as many blocks.

Father Gardiner warned the mothers that they must keep their young children away from these resorts, declaring that many of the pictures shown, particularly those depicting crimes, had a demoralizing effect on the young mind. He admitted that many of the pictures were pleasing, but said the objectionable ones did creep in, and do a great amount of damage among the young.

Father Gardiner also warned the parents against allowing children to spend whole days along the swimming beaches during the Summer. He suggested teaching the youngsters how to enjoy the privileges of the water front with moderation. Father Gardiner made a vigorous fight some years ago in favor of allowing the boys of his parish to play ball on Sunday, believing it better for them, as he said, "than hanging around the corners."

May 2, 1910

COMIC SUPPLEMENTS A SOURCE OF EVIL

Principal Chubb Says Lurid Sunday Pages Distort the Views of Children.

AN INVASION OF VULGARITY

The Child Is Following His Elders, He Says, in the Use of Beautifiers, Beverages and the Like.

The comic supplements of some Sunday newspapers were censured yesterday by Percival Chubb, Principal of the High School department of the Eethical Culture Society, in a speech at the Child Welfare Exhibit in the Seventy-first Regiment Armory.

These comic supplements, because of their "glorification of the cheeky, disrespectful, irreverent child," he said, tended to make children "too smart."

"They give the children a distorted view of what is commendable and desirable," said Mr. Chubb, "and one or two newspapers, on the other hand, stand apart from the rest as exhibiting an endeavor to provide wholesome material.

"Education in this city is largely to protect the child from the unfavorable adult environment with which the child is necessarily surrounded. This city is not a child's world. It is an adult world, which recks little of the effect of its adult ways on the sensitiveness and innocence of the young. The nervous rush and crush, the selfish push and greedy haste which reach a barbarous climax in the subway, the immodest assertiveness, are all unwholesome and ruinous to children. The interest of the child is everywhere nudged with things that concern his elders—beautifiers, beverages, and the like.

"Against these influences the teachers of the city have to wage a grim and uncertain war. The teachers have to counteract the influence of the adult theatre and vaudeville with its ragtime ditties, which heedless parents allow their children to patronize. The moral task of the school is to protect the boys against the smoking, drinking, and gambling which they see around them. The girls, in the same way, have to be protected by the schools from folly and immodesty in dress and from all the vagaries of flaunting fashion.

"These things will continue to happen until every school board is primarily a board of moral health which jealously guards the child against all forms of moral disease—posters, shows, sensational newspapers and songs. The newspaper should not be free to the child under sixteen, at least. Its chronicle of scandal, sin, and crime gives a distorted view to the child.

"The child should have its own periodical literature. The popular monthlies and bi-monthlies are not objectionable. But this very tameness of the monthlies may account for the Sunday debauch in flamboyant color and violent drawings. It is when we come to that American monster of misrule, the Sunday newspaper, with its lurid comic supplement for the child's particular benefit, that our trouble begins. It is, in almost every case, the product of the newspaper vaudeville artist, who has lost his sense of humor, his ethical values and his taste.

"It glorifies the smart child, proficient in monkey tricks; the cheeky, disrespectful, and irreverent child, who 'guys' his elders and betters; the libertine child of silly, humoring parents. Its so-called humor is the humor of distortion, akin to that provided for the parents in those inane cartoons which serve up daily and nightly in our yellow journals the misshapen, apelike creatures of a diseased imagination.

"It is strange that the churches and Sunday schools have not been active to suppress this Sunday invasion of vulgarity. Is any child who has feasted on this coarse food in any state of mind to attend Sunday school or church? Is indulgence in this comic supplement habit calculated to induce the right kind of reaction after the services of the Sunday School or church? If the parents, as their chief Sunday relaxation, give themselves up to the enjoyment of the average type of swollen Sunday newspaper, with its ugly mosaic of scandal, gossip, and crime, and its frequent indecent piquancy—what is to be expected of the children?"

January 27; 1911

A Study of the Movies' Effects on Children

OUR MOVIE-MADE CHILDREN. By Henry James Forman. Introduction by W. W. Charters. 288 pp. New York: The Macmillan Company. $2.50.

IN this book parents who are wondering whether or not attendance at the movies has any deleterious influence on their children, and all others who feel doubtful as to the entirely wholesome nature of the silver screen, will find answers to many of the questions they have been asking themselves and one another. The importance of these answers lies in the fact that they are authentic, the results of extensive, scientific investigation. For the first time investigations have been made of such scope and covering so many phases that conclusions can be deduced applicable to the question anywhere. The investigations of which the book tells the story continued from 1929 to 1933, and were carried on chiefly in large Eastern cities and cities and towns in the mid-West region. They were financed by the Payne Fund at the request of the Motion-Picture Research Council. Almost a score of men and women, psychologists, sociologists and members of the faculties of Yale, Chicago, New York, Iowa and other universities, and all expert investigators, did the actual work of carrying on the research. The chairman of the group, who wrote the introduction, was Dr. W. W. Charters of the faculty of Ohio State University. All the material was turned over to Henry James Forman for the study, comparison and interpretation out of which he has made this book. The sixteen chapters in which

Mr. Forman presents the most important of the figures and findings of the studies made by this group of investigators include such aspects of the motion-picture problem as the scope and character of the pictures; the age and characteristics of movie audiences; how much children remember of what they see; whether or not their sleep is affected by movie attendance; whether or not there are other physical effects; to what extent the conduct and the character of children is influenced by the movies; whether or not young people are moved by the pictures they see toward and into juvenile delinquency, criminality and sex delinquency; to what extent pictures, if ever, have a deterrent or correctional influence; the place taken and the influence exerted by the movies in a crowded city section. Thousands of children and youth, from 5 to 20 were examined in the course of the research. In one of the investigations, that into what children remember of what they see in the movies and how long they retain it, it was found that the children remembered from 60 to 90 per cent of what adults remembered of the same pictures and that the passage of weeks, even months, seemed to enhance both the amount and the vividness of their memories.

In one of the chapters are presented the results of an analysis by Dr. Edgar Dale, whose aim was to sort out and classify "the contents of the vast and ceaseless output of Hollywood." He took 1,500 moving pictures, 500 from each of the years 1920, 1925 and 1930, including all of the feature pictures produced in

those years by the leading companies, and classified their contents into a dozen categories. He found that from 75 to 80 per cent of all these films dealt with love, sex or crime.

Occasionally, it was determined, certain pictures produce socially desirable effects; there were cases in which the investigators found the desire for education or travel aroused, or even the emotion of religious aspiration. But they found also a great many more instances in which children were moved to imitate low and even criminal levels of conduct; a number of juvenile delinquents told of learning their criminal technique from the movies; large percentages of the girl inmates in an institution for sex delinquents attributed to the movies their cravings for an easy life and for wild parties, and testified to the high degree of stimulation produced in them by scenes of passionate love-making. On the other hand, a small number of pictures were found to have in some cases a deterrent effect as regards misconduct and crime.

It is reckoned by these investigators that of our vast national movie audience of 77,000,000 per week over 28,000,000 are children and adolescents. Whether or not their sleep is affected by the pictures they see is of cardinal importance, since not only their school work but their health and growth would thereby be injuriously influenced. The inquiry into this phase of the picture problem was intensive. It involved the devising of an electrical hypnograph, or sleep recorder, and its application to a

group of 170 boys and girls, who were kept under observation two and a half years, a total of almost 7,000 child-nights of sleep. The investigators found an added increase of restlessness during sleep after movie attendance, varying in the average from 14 to 26 per cent and running in individual cases as high as 50, 75 and even 90 per cent.

Mr. Forman has very capably and successfully accomplished his difficult task of sorting, selecting, organizing and presenting in interesting style the most important outlines and highlights of the comprehensive research. He does not try to make a case against the movies. He merely sets forth the facts, and does not let the reader forget that the findings he presents show the movie to be in its molding influence upon the character of children more powerful than either the school or the church, and, when attendance is frequent, more important than even the home. But he constantly insists upon the possibilities for good inherent in the film industry. He offers no constructive suggestions other than to put the situation up to parents and hopes that they will heed the obvious conclusions to be drawn from his chapters as to the evil influence of three-fourths of the films. But if the book has the wide reading and attention it richly deserves, out of it may grow some definite, determined and constructive endeavor to control and better the present situation.

FLORENCE FINCH KELLY.

June 18, 1933

Children at the Movies. What is the one big interest outside of the home that children of pre-high school age share as full partners with their elders? It is the motion picture. Figures presented and analyzed by HENRY JAMES FORMAN in the concluding chapter of "Our Movie-Made Children" leaves no doubt on this point. The nation's movie theatres have been estimated to draw from 80,000,000 to 100,000,000 spectators weekly. The audience under the age of 21 numbers very nearly 30,000,000, which is virtually equal to the entire school and college population. But most significant of all is it that there are no less than 11,000,000 weekly movie spectators of 13 years and under.

Children of that age do not read the newspapers which their elders do. They are in school, but their elders are not. They read books, but not as a rule the books which their elders read. Over the radio children and elders do not always listen to the same things. But the movies supply the same fare for the boys and girls of 13 or less, for their parents and for their grandparents.

June 27, 1933

CHILD'S LIKES AND DISLIKES OF RADIO TURN CORNER AT 10 YEARS OF AGE

THERE is probably no radio program that is good for all children or bad for all children, according to a recent report Mrs. S. M. Gruenberg of the Child Study Association made to the Radio Institute of Audible Arts. The problems of child training arising out of radio are, in the opinion of Mrs. Gruenberg, of an individual nature, varying with the type of child. Observations reveal that an exciting thriller which plunges one lad to the verge of hysterics sends another youngster to happy dreams of success and victory.

It is pointed out that parents must accept without prejudice the fact that the children's interests differ from those of grown-ups. The child, it is explained, is a developing organism, and it must not be expected that he will possess the understandings and appreciations of maturity. It is believed, however, that if the child is afforded the opportunity to exercise his judgment he will become more exacting and selective in his radio listening as he grows older.

Parents Must Be on Guard.

"Parents do have to guard against having imposed upon their children programs determined by a single group," said Mrs. Gruenberg. "It is obvious that no single group, not even an association of parents, can be allowed to impose upon the rest of the community its notions of what is suitable and proper for children.

"The greatest need in the development of radio is to have the creative efforts of talented men and women turned toward this field as worthy of serious application. Parents must come to see that the direct action of censorship and negations will not take us to our goals as quickly as this seemingly longer road."

In making the survey of children's programs, the radio committee of the Child Study Association reviewed not only those programs designed expressly for children, but also certain adult programs of possible interest to children given at hours when they might be listening.

"Between 4 and 5 years, children begin to take an interest in special programs and this interest becomes rather general at about 6 years," continued Mrs. Gruenberg. "This fact has raised the question whether children are not influenced by the group, when they come to school and discover that 'everybody'—that is, everybody in their social sphere—is talking about certain programs and characters.

"Like older people, children appear to stimulate one another in common interests that represent the fashion of the day rather than an inherent requirement. At any rate, while the interest does appear to become general at the time of entering school, it is not very intense. The peak seems to be reached at about 10 years of age. It is significant, however, that this peak of interest corresponds to the child's eager reaching out in all directions—the most avid and varied reading, the experimenting with 'stunts' of all kinds, and with companionship.

"From the point of view of the home, these facts should be helpful, since they suggest the desirability of considering not alone the child's need for the specific content of a particular program, but also his need for keeping en rapport with his fellows. The need to be 'in it' is vital, even where the program itself may be a matter of relative indifference."

June 9, 1935

MOVIES AND THE CHILD: *The Debate Rages On*

Good and bad effects of popular films presented.

By CATHERINE MACKENZIE

AT almost any neighborhood theatre on a Saturday afternoon there is occasion for parental soul-searching.

The place is well filled with children. Uproarious shouts greet the showing of a night-club brawl—glassware smashing, tables overturning, fists fetching up on jaws. Girls of 12 and 13 bounce, shrieking, in their seats as the mystery unfolds. Gratified yells drown out the dialogue as the hero of the Western gallops through the old familiar perils.

The children sit through the double-feature, a comedy short, an animated cartoon and newsreel shots of death in Belgium, and they see the "trailer" flash its gaudy promise for next week—"It's eerie, but elegant! It's sinister, but swell!"

Maybe when families go to the movies together, we shall know more about the effect of movies on children. The experience can be full of surprises for the parents. "The clinic was a medically quite incorrect place," remarked the 12-year-old daughter of a physician after seeing a movie version of a hospital scene. "But, mother," an 8-year-old protested, trudging away from Maeterlinck's classic. "I don't *see*. The bird was brown at first and then in the end it was blue."

Some parents have protested the screen fare purveyed to the youngsters and psychologists have joined them. Other parents, psychologists and movie men themselves see little cause for alarm. But the argument goes on almost constantly.

THE debate affects literally millions of young moviegoers. Around 12 per cent of all motion-picture fans are between the ages of 7 and 13, according to one attendance survey, and 22 per cent are between 14 and 21. Most children begin to go to the movies about the time they start to school, and they go, on the average, once a week.

Their own preference on the screen is action, not talk. In one representative poll, taken among children averaging 13½, the first six choices of the boys were adventure, comedy, mystery, sport, Western and war pictures, in that order. The girls went along on the first three of these, though placing mystery at the head of the list; but thereafter the sexes parted company. "Musical" was the girls' fourth choice, with drama fifth and romance sixth.

Romance, various surveys have established, makes an earlier appeal to girls—at an age when boys grudgingly concede that a picture like "Ninotchka" would be all right "if it wasn't for that love stuff." In the poll just cited girls voted overwhelmingly for "love interest" in the films they liked to see; boys were against it, 74 per cent.

However, there is a point at which the children's preferences and the parents' idea of what those preferences should be go off at tangents. If a 12-year-old boy remarks of a movie that "it should be avoided by some people because it has several bloody scenes," the chance is that he has been hearing the grown-ups talk. When a group of mothers went to see

"The Hunchback of Notre Dame" recently one of them took her 9-year-old son along. The mothers agreed unanimously that it was no picture for children to see. The 9-year-old loved it.

WHAT the average parent would like to know is whether the present screen fare contains definite harm for the young. Those who believe the answer is affirmative get support from Dr. Frank J. O'Brien, director of the Bureau of Child Guidance of New York's Board of Education.

"It is one thing to expose children to the unpleasant as well as the pleasant things of life," said Dr. O'Brien; "it is another to subject them to unnecessarily disagreeable experiences. The immature child is highly susceptible to strong emotional experiences, and he can handle only so many of them without damage."

Nightmares deriving from such horror pictures as "Dracula" and "Frankenstein" have turned up among the bureau's young patients as long as two or three years after the picture was seen. Dr. O'Brien's advice to parents of high-strung youngsters is to keep them away from terrifying movies. "After all," he said, "if a child is predisposed to tuberculosis we guard him against aggravating conditions. If he is susceptible to fears, why not guard him against a threat to emotional good health?"

"To be sure," he continued, "death and disaster may not have the implications to a child that they have to adults. 'Snow White' was more unnerving to some parents than it was to their children. When all is said and done we don't know enough about children to be sure of how much emotional shock they can take without harm, or whether in limiting a child's experiences we are only projecting our own fears. But if we are going to err, it is better to err on the side of conservatism."

Dr. O'Brien added the view that the movies—some movies—can be a waste of time. "Cheap entertainment," he said, "whether on the screen, or in print, or on the air, absorbs the leisure and interest

"The child who has nightmares from horror films can be matched by the child scared by the Planetarium."

which might better go to intelligent pursuits enriching children's lives for the future. The craving for constant excitement, the need to be always 'on the go,' is another result of keying emotional interest so high that nothing else can be enjoyed."

DR. A. A. BRILL, recently elected chairman of the National Board of Review of Motion Pictures, takes a different approach. He is one of those psychiatrists who think that thrills, slapstick, and even gangster pictures, may do the children a world of good.

"You remember," he said, "that the Greeks spoke of the play as effecting a 'catharsis' of the emotions. The movies serve this purpose. So do hockey and football games. People get rid of pent-up aggression when they go to a prizefight, and society approves of this release. Children, too, have plenty of bottled-up protest against life's little tyrannies—keeping clean, learning lessons, behaving themselves—and the screen is the greatest medium for giving the child an outlet for this revolt. Didn't an earlier generation have Nick Carter, and hang on the installments?"

Absurdities of animated cartoons also have their uses, said Dr. Brill. "Children identify themselves with the characters. They like to see that little mouse doing things they'd like to do—and getting away with it. Children like the grotesque. They like to see grown-ups getting the worst of it on the screen." Those joyous catcalls one hears as

adults come in a fumbling second-best in the juvenile serial are, in his opinion, just what the brats need to get resentment out of their systems.

"Love scenes?" Dr. Brill went on. "Of course people talk about 'children,' and we find they are referring to young people of 17 or 20. And to say that young people wouldn't have ideas about love if they didn't get them from the movies is just as sensible as to say that they wouldn't be hungry if they didn't know about food.

"Besides," said Dr. Brill, "we are apt to forget that the movies are a normal part of the modern child's environment, accepted by him far more casually than airplanes or radios are accepted by middle-aged adults; that the screen fare we view as a new and disturbing influence has always existed for him."

We have always been going on like this about the Old Adam, Dr. Brill told us. "'The imagination of man's heart is evil from his youth,'" he quoted. "You'll find that in Genesis."

FATHERS and mothers can take their choice of these opposing opinions; and they do.

On the one hand are those who contend that while some children can take the movies in their stride, others cannot, and that it is up to fathers and mothers to pick the films for them to see. This is the view of the New York Schools Motion Picture Committee, a voluntary group of parents and teachers representing some twenty-five public and private schools. The committee previews shorts, trailers and newsreels, as well as features, and in 300 co-operating theatres around town only films so approved are shown from Friday through Sunday—the time when children go.

Children like and can take plenty of excitement and action, the committee agrees, but by its standards a picture "is not considered suitable" for ages 8 to 14 if it has too much killing, terrorizing, drinking, cruelty, meanness or brutality either to human beings or to animals. Sympathetic portrayal of a criminal and overemphasis of passionate love scenes are taboo.

These standards appear to leave the children plenty of choice in entertainment, since the committee approves currently of such pictures as "Abe Lincoln in Illinois," "Grapes of Wrath" and "Dr. Ehrlich's Magic Bullet," as well as "Gulliver's Travels," "The Bluebird" and "Pinocchio."

ON the other hand are parents who say that children can and should be taught to discriminate, to take screen fare for what it is worth, and to like it or laugh at it as their elders do. They re-

"Family pictures are enjoyed by all ages."

main unconvinced of the need for censorship. They hold that children get no more ideas from pictures than they take to them: that the child who woke up screaming after seeing "Snow White" can be matched by the child scared out of his wits by a trip to the Planetarium. They assert that youngsters outgrow their taste for thrillers there are statistics to prove it—and point to the success of motion-picture appreciation courses in the schools.

Another argument for youthful discrimination is provided by the young reviewers of the National Board of Review of Motion Pictures, now organized in 4-Star Clubs throughout the country. When these young reviewers— aged 8 to 16 were first picked among New York school children and encouraged to speak their minds, they proved unexpectedly critical. Parents then learned that instead of a threat love scenes were to many minors a bore. "There are some love pic-

"Children like to see that little mouse doing things they'd like to do."

tures that I think are absolutely terrible." fumed one reviewer. He was 10. And he didn't mean what you mean by terrible.

THE increase of motion-picture appreciation courses in public schools, and the industry's co-operation in the use of film shorts in classroom teaching, are noted in a recent report of Will H. Hays, president of Motion Picture Producers and Distributors of America. Incidentally, Mr. Hays leads off with a list of seventeen films, representing Hollywood's best for 1939, and one notes that ten of these have been approved in New York City for children from 8 to 14.

In yet other ways Hollywood's commercial output has taken into account the children's quarters and dimes. Juvenile players have topped the list of box-office favorites for three years running. Mickey Rooney now replaces Shirley Temple in first place. Of 463 pictures cleared last year through the Hays office roughly 25 per cent were adventure, Westerns and other action pictures,

packed with the thrills young folk crave, and the good moral lessons elders approve.

In addition, the year's film fare provided sixteen juvenile comedies, featuring such favorites as Shirley Temple, Mickey Rooney and Deanna Durbin, and twenty-seven other pictures considered suitable for young audiences because they "contribute to human understanding by illuminating some area of history, science, biography, geography, music, literature or current reality." The children were also treated to "Gulliver's Travels" and "The Wizard of Oz."

Both family pictures which have multiplied in recent years the serial life and times of the Hardys and the Joneses and such pictures as "Mr. Deeds Goes to Town" and "Good-bye Mr. Chips" are enjoyed by all ages

June 23, 1940

Books

Pocket Books, Inc., is sponsoring a new book club to "induce teen agers to read, love and accumulate good books." Under the direction of Martha Huddleston, the Teen Age Book Club will offer its first list to members in September.

June 11, 1946

Many Doubt Comics Spur Crime, Senate Survey of Experts Shows

Special to THE NEW YORK TIMES.

WASHINGTON, Nov. 11—Widespread doubt that crime comics cause juvenile delinquency is shown among officials and others dealing with the problem in a survey by the Senate Crime Investigating Committee made public today.

The committee gave no opinion of its own nor did it summarize the views of those questioned. It quoted sixty-five public officials and eight child guidance experts, as well as ten publishers of comic books. The opinion of the majority was that comics and juvenile delinquency had no direct connection.

"Any over-all study of crime in present-day America would be incomplete if it did not include adequate consideration of the problem of juvenile delinquency," the five members of the committee said in a foreword to the report. They are Senators Estes Kefauver, Democrat of Tennessee, chairman;

Lester C. Hunt, Democrat of Wyoming; Herbert R. O'Conor, Democrat of Maryland; Charles W. Tobey, Republican of New Hampshire, and Alexander Wiley, Republican of Wisconsin.

Their interest in the subject was aroused they said, by "frequently heard charges that juvenile delinquency has increased considerably during the past five years and that this increase has been stimulated by the publication of the so-called crime comic books."

Heading the list of public officials whose views were sought was J. Edgar Hoover, Director of the Federal Bureau of Investigation He said that arrests of youths had generally leveled off during the post-war period, "although the incidence of crime among young people is still abnormally high."

"It is doubtful, however, that an appreciable decrease in juvenile delinquency would result if crime

comic books of all types were not readily available to children," he said.

He added that "the answer may lie not in wiping out objectionable crime comics but in substituting restrained presentations which will allow the child under guidance to logically set up standards as to what types of crime comics are good or bad."

Miss Katharine F. Lenroot, chief of the Children's Bureau of the Federal Security Agency, called the committee's attention to the code of ethics to which fourteen of the thirty-four publishers of comic books now voluntarily subscribe. She held that juvenile delinquency was the product of manifold factors, of which comic books glamorizing crime might be only one.

Explicit Instruction Noted

A. H. Conner, acting director of the Federal Bureau of Prisons, said that "no one can state with certainty that juvenile delinquency would decrease if crime comics were not available to juveniles."

"Nevertheless," he added, "it is clear that many such publications serve as sources of contamination of impressionable minds, provide explicit instruction in the methods by which criminals operate, and contribute to a weakening of the

ethical values of the community."

The committee submitted seven questions to the public officials. It asked whether juvenile delinquency had increased since the end of World War II, to what causes any increase might be attributed, whether there was an increase after World War I, whether delinquency lately tended to more violent crimes, such as assault, rape, murder and gang activities, whether there was any relationship between juvenile crime and reading crime comics, whether there were known examples of crimes caused by such reading, and whether delinquency would decrease if there were no crime comics.

The authorities could not reply to the question about the period following World War I, as no reliable statistics were kept at that time.

Most of them agreed that juvenile delinquency reached a peak during World War II and had somewhat subsided since. Few attempted to cite crimes directly attributable to reading comics.

Louis Goldstein, chairman of the Board of County Judges of Kings County, replied that "my own experience with comic books has been favorable."

"In the many years of close and intimate contact which I have had with thousands of defendants," he said, "both in the capacity c' prosecuting assistant district attorney and judge of the County Court, I never came across a single case where the delinquent or criminal act would be attributed to the reading of comic books."

One of the most outspoken champions of the comics was Milt Caniff, the cartoonist.

"Practitioners of the inexact science of psychiatry have long served as apologists for the present parental generation," he replied to the committee's questionnaire, "by attributing every childhood ill from measles to shyness to the reading of comic books.

Right Triumphs, Caniff Notes

"It follows that parents might find it difficult to counter the skill of the professional story tellers in catering to their children's escapist instincts, but fathers and mothers of other generations guided their youngsters during out-of-school hours because there were no radio, television, or comic-book outlets to which the sometimes irksome task could be surrendered.

"In my childhood, it was Tom Mix and William S. Hart movies which were leading us kids to damnation. No doubt Hopalong Cassidy will be blamed for many youthful escapades in the present era.

"However, any critic of these media must not forget that all the popular figures are heroes—that right triumphs. It is the good guy they seek to emulate. This is also true in the most vivid of the comic books.

"Children are natural critics, no lobby can reach them. They will follow only the line of behavior which is their natural tendency. The portrayal of the blackness of evil which makes virtue white by contrast, and, as in all folk tales, the desire to emulate the St. George of the moment slaying the current dragon, is a healthy and desirable instinct to arouse."

November 12, 1950

EDUCATORS FIND TV BENEFITS CHILDREN

Some Early Adverse Effects Wear Off, They Say, Noting Widening of Horizons

PARENTAL CONTROL URGED

Minority of Experts Consider Video a Menace That Gives False Values and Views

By JACK GOULD

Children from toddlers to teenagers are among television's most avid fans, but the overwhelming majority of school officials from coast to coast believe that the new medium is benefiting youngsters in many different ways and is not having significantly adverse effects.

In a remarkable unanimity of opinion, which undoubtedly will come as a pleasant surprise to the television industry, state superintendents of school systems, principals and teachers agree that at first children may look at the video screen excessively or neglect other activities, but that they soon return to their old habits and maintain their scholastic standing.

Parental supervision, which temporarily may weaken when a new video receiver is purchased, is quickly reasserted in the average home if a son or daughter remains unduly attentive to the screen in the parlor.

Use of television to introduce children to many personalities, events and topics to which they otherwise might not be exposed, a large number of school officials said, actually was contributing to the education of the younger generation, according to correspondents of THE NEW YORK TIMES.

Vocabulary Improvement Seen

Improved vocabularies for children in the primary grades apparently was one benefit of TV, several school officials also observed.

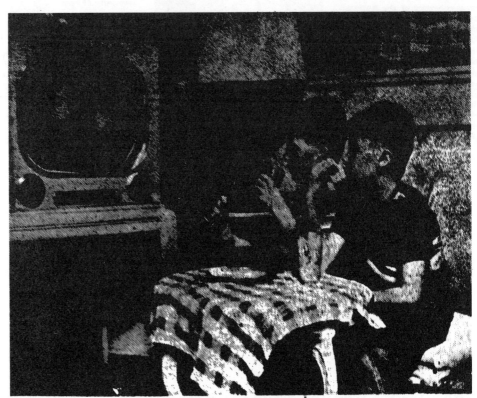

Children watching the screen while eating their meals.

The New York Times

Psychiatrists and experts in child study generally are of two minds on television's effect on children. The majority group holds that if TV is controlled and supervised properly by parents it is in no way harmful to children. The other sees video as a menace to the psychological life of the child.

Dr. Phillip Polatin, Assistant Clinical Professor of Psychiatry at the College of Physicians and Surgeons at Columbia University, observed that parents who complain bitterly about TV disrupting children's normal habits are "unconsciously confessing their own abdication of reasonable parental authority."

He held that cowboy films, despite general parental disapproval, are "an excellent outlet" for children's hostility and aggression. Critics who object to television's "passive entertainment," he said, should watch a group of boys popping cap pistols, yelling at villains and encouraging heroes as they sit before the screen.

Dr. Frederic Wertham, psychiatrist and author, on the other hand, asserted that many people glibly discount the influence of mass media on children.

He insisted that because of television children were acquiring the point of view which makes them "confuse violence with strength, low necklines with feminine ideal, sadism with sex and criminals with police."

Excess Held Temporary

In the New York area, representative high school officials believed television viewing was assuming a reasonable place in the children's life.

Elias Lieberman, Associate Superintendent of the Board of Education for the division of junior high schools, said excessive looking was only a temporary phenomenon.

"Unwritten law dictates a sensible family schedule for Dad and Mom as well as for the chastened younger set," he said.

Woolf Colvin, principal of the Seward Park High School, on the lower East Side, said television was widening the experience of youngsters, but questioned whether the screen might not be taking too much time away from home work and open-air play, a view also advanced by Jacob M. Ross, principal of the Midwood High

School in Brooklyn.

Fred Schoenberg, principal of Stuyvesant High School in Manhattan, said television's effect on children had not been significant from a constructive point of view and that its future depended on how wisely it was advanced by broadcasters, parents and teachers.

"I am sure that good citizens of several centuries past felt that youth was wasting its time in reading, time that might better have been devoted to chores," he said.

Round-Up of Opinion

The national round-up of opinion on television's effect on children follows:

Garden City, L. I.: A parent-teachers group here has made a study and survey of TV's effects with the following results:

Interests	Beneficial	Unchngd.	Harmful
Intellectual	56.6%	35%	1.7%
Creative	45.4	46.4	4
Recreational	19.5	64.2	9.6

Chicago: Harold C. Hunt, General Superintendent of Schools, says that "particularly in the lower grades, students with television sets seem to be more aware, have a somewhat larger vocabulary and seem to have a greater sense of the world at large." However, he added, there are often cases of "over-identification" with Howdy Doody or Hopalong Cassidy and some youngsters show up at school with "TV hangovers," he said.

Philadelphia: Louis P. Hoyer, Superintendent of Schools, says television has not diverted children who ordinarily read, but has proved popular among children who would not read much anyway. "When the novelty wears off, children as well as adults return to regular routines," he said.

Topeka, Kan.: TV may have reduced some reading, particularly among children who do not read much anyway, but the Kansas State Department of Public Instruction reports "boys and girls are more discriminating in their use of TV than at first."

Advantages Follow Adverse Effect

Concord, N. H.: Harold E. Hyde, chief of the division of research of the New Hampshire State Department of Education, says TV's first effects are adverse—loss of sleep and neglect of homework—but then come positive advantages in greater interest in "current events, discussions, science classes, drama and music." Schools actively encourage pupils to watch better programs, he says.

Des Moines, Iowa: Jesse M. Parker, Iowa State Superintendent

of Public Instruction, doubts if TV "in long run will detract too much from other worthy activities."

Richmond, Va.: According to William E. Lloyd, director of school-community relations for the Richmond public school system, TV interferes "at first with everything, then there is selective viewing."

Nashville, Tenn.: W. A. Bass, Superintendent of Schools for the City of Nashville, says there "seem to be some evidence of the children settling down and taking television, like they have other inventions, in stride."

San Francisco: Sue J. Convery, principal of the Lafayette School, said her institution had been conducting an experimental class in teaching children how to be selective about their entertainment, including television. She said some children were looking for five or six hours a day.

Dr. Herbert C. Clish, Superintendent of Schools, remarked: "If a youngster sees something on TV which is unfamiliar, he is likely to read up on it."

Syracuse, N. Y.: While drowsiness, inattention and loss of interest have been noted among some children, thirty teachers at one of the largest schools in Onondaga County reported that bad consequences were offset in part by beneficial effects.

School Attendance Affected

Yonkers, N. Y.: Dr. Stanley

S. Wynstra, Superintendent of Yonkers Public Schools, says TV has affected attendance at school by younger children to a "limited degree."

Long Beach, L. I.: A survey among parents of children, between the ages of six and eleven, at the East School brought these conclusions, among others, according to Dr. David G. Salten, Superintendent of Schools:

Boys and girls look at TV an average of 20 hours a week; 75 per cent of the parents set aside a definite time for their children to watch; 88 per cent said that TV was not interfering with completion of homework; 75 per cent said that TV was keeping children and parents closer together, and 21 per cent of children acquired nervous habits—"squinting, nail biting and hair curling"—from watching video.

Cleveland: School officials declare that "grades of hundreds of elementary and high school pupils dropped during the last two semesters and declare that television is primarily responsible." Number of honor students also has declined over previous year.

Dallas: Dallas school system has studied TV's effects and found that problem boils down to "whether or not a child does as he pleases at home." In Fort Worth no noticeable effect was found.

Columbus, Ohio: Ohio Depart-

ment of Education recently criticized wrestling on television on the grounds that unsportsmanlike behavior in the ring sets a bad example for children.

Bridgeport, Conn.: Some social workers say TV will keep teen-agers at home and the pool rooms may lose out.

A village doctor in the Syracuse, N. Y., area reports many instances in which parents send their children to bed at 8 P. M. and awaken them at 10 so they can see a favorite program.

In the Domestic Relations Court in New Brunswick, N. J., a husband who had left his wife and children said he might be interested in returning home if he had something to amuse him—"such as television," he said.

In Detroit, John J. Considine, Superintendent of the Parks and Recreation Department, told of two examples of influence of TV on the younger generation.

On a city rink a girl skater was taken to task for sending another child spinning with a body block.

"I learned that from the roller derby," she explained.

In a park, one tyke, wrestling with a pal, clipped his opponent in the chin with his knee.

"Chief Fractured Fox does it that way on TV," he said.

June 29, 1951

CHILD OUTLET SEEN IN ENTERTAINMENT

Experts Call Mass Media Aid in Fantasy Expression but Offer Caution on TV

Special to The New York Times.

LOS ANGELES, July 29—Entertainment media, from the legitimate theatre to comic books, are essential in child development, experts told the seventh annual Children's Theatre Convention, which ended here yesterday.

Their role, they said, is an outlet for the "fantasy life" normal in both children and adults and is dangerous if not given expression.

By the same token, the speakers said, this fantasy-expression could become harmful—as in unlimited absorption in television entertainment—if its relationship with reality were not constantly maintained.

The four-day convention, held under the auspices of the Children's Theatre Conference of the American Educational Theatre Association, and sponsored by the University of California at Los Angeles, was attended by 300 persons from the educational and entertainment fields. "Workshop" round-table sessions were held on the theatre, motion pictures, radio and television.

Mental and emotional maladjustments, Dr. Herbert Kupper of Los Angeles, a fellow of the American

Psychiatric Association, said in the keynote address, "are often due to the suppression of childish daydreams and fantasies."

Cites "Hansel and Gretel"

"Children are too frail to contain their emotions and too dependent to risk expressing them," he said. "The fact of unexpressed emotions makes the use of mass media, especially the child theatre, a key instrument to help children live these early emotions. In effect, seeing a play on a stage is primarily group therapy."

The perennial popularity of "Hansel and Gretel" with children, he suggested, is due to the fact that "the witch represents the feared, bad image of their own mother."

"They love mother," he explained, "but still resent her for her frustrations. They finally outwit the bad mother and return to the good. The fear of being eaten is a typical fear of children who want to bite and eat others."

The test of the wholesomeness of any entertainment medium for children, Dr. Kupper said, is: "Does it stimulate and arouse fantasy to a certain extent only, so that reality is also permitted to play a part?"

"Television concerns me," he continued, "because the senses often are too completely satiated. Visual, auditory, speaking, thinking are all done for the child.

"Usually a boy will see a play or read a book or see a film and then try to reconcile these with reality by asking questions or reading more books. But children gaze at television for hours on end until all fantasies become reality in itself. Usually parents are pleased

because the child doesn't bother them. So instead of pulling the child out of fantasy with realistic criticism, the child is lost."

Says Comics Fill a Need

The idea that comic-strip fiction promotes juvenile delinquency was decried by Dr. David Cole, Professor of Psychology at Occidental College, Los Angeles.

"The widespread popularity of the comics is sufficient to suggest that they meet a real need in their audience, both children and adults," he said. "This is probably accomplished through a process of identification, wherein the reader finds in the comic strip hero someone who somehow is either meeting the same problems as the reader and handling them more effectively, or is able to do the things the reader himself would like to do."

Dr. Cole said a study indicated that "in children's preferences for comics we find the same factor of vicarious experience that we see in adult reading."

"While the reader's behavior may be changed by the comics," he added, "it is equally true that the reader's personality causes the comics, in the sense of making them a salable commodity. To attribute casual significance to comics in such a thing as juvenile delinquency may be merely putting the cart before the horse.

"Rather, the regularity with which the hero emerges triumphant in comic strip literature may provide the child with an area of security which he does not find elsewhere in his daily life."

July 30, 1951

CHILDREN CHANGE VIDEO FAVORITES

Survey Shows Shift From '50 Cowboys and Puppets to Situation Comedies

If the enthusiasms of 10,000 boys and girls in Chicago are like those of other children in the nation, television tastes in the younger set have changed considerably in the last three years. Whether they have changed for the better is a moot point.

At a recent conference of the American Association for the Advancement of Science in Boston, Dr. Paul Witty of Northwestern University discussed television preferences and attitudes of pupils, teachers and parents. Whereas in 1950 cowboy programs, puppet performances and variety shows were favorites, a survey in 1953 showed that situation comedies and at least one crime show were preferred.

The 1950 top choices included Hopalong Cassidy, Howdy Doody, Milton Berle and Arthur Godfrey. Since then shows such as "I Love Lucy" and "My Friend Irma" have grown in popularity; Roy Rogers, the cowboy, and "Red" Buttons, the comedian, have become personal favorites and "Dragnet" marks the entrance of a crime detection program to the winners' circle.

The kinds of new programs that youngsters said they would like are probably closer to what would be chosen for them by their parents and teachers. Older pupils wanted more "good" comedy, more plays, more musical programs and more new movies.

The younger children asked for more comedies, cartoons and science. They also requested a wide variety of educational offerings, including dramatizations of favorite books, more children's plays and a larger number of programs about hobbies and crafts.

The over-all findings of the continuing studies indicate, Dr. Witty said, that the "distrust and antipathy" toward television shared by parents and teachers in 1950 have eased. The adults are increasingly recognizing the potentialities of video for education and enjoyment. They are guarded in their enthusiasm, however. A teacher commented that "TV is good for some pupils, bad for others."

Last May 92 per cent of the children had access to television and 50 per cent of the teachers had sets.

"Meet the press," Omnibus, "What's My Line?" and Mr. Peepers are favorites with the teachers.

January 11, 1954

Magistrate Is Made Comics 'Czar'

By EMMA HARRISON

City Magistrate Charles F. Murphy has been named official "censor" of the comics industry of America. He will administer a code of ethics whereby publishers hope to purge the business of objectionable comics. Appointment of the 44-year-old magistrate, who had been a vigorous campaigner against juvenile delinquency, was announced yesterday by the newly formed Comics Magazine Association of America at the Waldorf-Astoria Hotel. Magistrate Murphy, who will resign from the bench on Oct. 1, will have a $100,000 annual budget for the job.

Horror and terror books will go off member publishers' lists at once, Magistrate Murphy pledged. He said that had been a contingency in his accepting the position.

"I have promised the members of the industry and I am now promising the general public that the new program of self-regulation will be based on a strong and effective code of ethics and a competent staff of reviewers," said the new comics "czar."

Experience for the Post

He said he would call on his nine years of experience on the bench and more than a dozen years as the father of three children to "make the kind of careful judgment which will bear the scrutiny of millions of mothers and fathers, educators, religious leaders and government officials." He promised the "strongest code of ethics ever adopted by a mass media industry" and urged groups critical of comics to offer suggestions.

Soon after the announcement, the new administrator received a telegram of encouragement from officials of the Senate subcommittee investigating juvenile delinquency that had called some association members to testify last spring. Richard Clendenen, executive director of the subcommittee, and Herbert W. Beaser, chief counsel, expressed hope that establishment of the organization meant the enforcement of a code to "protect the children of the nation."

Similarly, the chairman of the joint committee of the State Legislature that is studying comic books said the publishers' action was "welcome news."

"We will offer every cooperation to the industry and hope that it will now begin to effectively police itself," Assemblyman James A. Fitzpatrick said. But he added that his committee would continue working on new legislation to curb the distribution of horror books in this state.

Magistrate Murphy said he had taken the job, for which he has a two-year contract, because of his desire to help the children of the country on "a preventive scale." But he added that in his time on the bench he had never had a case of juvenile delinquency which he or any official of his court could attribute to the reading of comic books.

Although the code will not be completed until Nov. 15, queries on the association's failure to include a ban on crime comics along with that on horror books, prompted Elliott Caplin, publisher of Tobey Press and chairman of the code committee, to consider some proposed regulations aimed at crime comics.

September 17, 1954

WHIP, KNIFE SHOWN AS 'COMICS' LURES

Books No Better Under Code, Psychiatrist Tells State Investigating Committee

INDUSTRY 'CZAR' REPLIES

'Can't Build Rome in a Day,' Says Murphy, and Promises Improvement Shortly

By EMMA HARRISON

A well-known psychiatrist brandished a bull whip before a comic books hearing yesterday. He said he had obtained it through an advertisement published in a magazine bearing the seal of approval of the new industry Code Authority.

The testimony was given by Dr. Fredric Wertham before the Joint State Legislative Committee, which is studying comic books. His assertion was challenged by Charles Murphy, code administrator. Mr. Murphy, a former city magistrate, had previously told the committee that advertisements for whips and knives had been banned from the books he approved.

Dr. Wertham repeated his statement under oath administered by Assemblyman James A. FitzPatrick, chairman of the one-day hearing held at the Bar Association Building, 42 West Forty-fourth Street. This followed Mr. Murphy's challenge of the psychiatrist's statement that he had clipped an advertising coupon from an approved book dated March, 1955. Dr. Wertham did not produce the book but said he would send it to the committee.

Says Books Incited Killers

Dr. Wertham cited the whip to bolster his contention that the comic books had not improved under the code. He used it also to support his belief that Brooklyn's recently convicted teen-age killers had been directly influenced by comic books.

The psychiatrist, who examined Jack Koslow, one of the killers, said there was not one crime they committed that was not described in detail in comic books. He cited the whipping, burning, drowning, and beating tortures used by the boys. He also produced a knife that he said he had obtained through a coupon in a comic book.

Mr. Murphy said he would like to know where the advertisement appeared. He assured the committee that he "didn't recall of any such ad going through" and that had it been submitted to him he would not have approved it. Mr. Murphy then produced a pocket book that he said should be "included in the 'how to do it' books" describing violence in detail.

He produced a reprint of Dr. Wertham's book, "The Show of Violence," and asked that it be put on the record.

"It's outrageous," he shouted, before Mr. FitzPatrick cut off the argument.

Adams Asks More Powers

Police Commissioner Francis W. H. Adams testified that his department saw a "direct relationship between [published] obscenity and lewdness and juvenile crime."

He asked the committee to consider more laws to enable the police to fight effectively against obscene books and pictures.

In the morning session, Mr. FitzPatrick presented a display of approved books. He pointed out where the committee considered "excessive violence" still existed.

Closely questioned by Mr. FitzPatrick, Mr. Murphy said he "couldn't destroy a business overnight." He said it was a "process of education" of the comic book industry.

"We won't have this by April or May," Mr. Murphy promised. "You can't build Rome in a day. Give me a little understanding and realize we are in the growing-up process."

Summing up the hearing, Mr. FitzPatrick, Plattsburg Republican, said his committee sought only to cooperate with any agency attempting regulation and that he welcomed the "initial steps" being taken by the industry. He said that the hearings had "manifested a real need to eliminate the sale to children of obscenity, vulgarity and violence."

February 5, 1955

COMIC BOOK COST CITED

Study Finds More Spent for Them Than for School Texts

Special to The New York Times.

BERKELEY, Calif., Feb. 28—American comic book readers spend more on their purchases every year than is laid out for the entire book supply for elementary and secondary schools. Their outlay for comic books is four times the amount spent for the purchases of all types of books by the nation's public libraries.

These findings were reported today in a survey by the Bureau of Public Administration of the University of California. The study found that 25 per cent of the nation's adults who were high school graduates were readers of comic books. Sixteen per cent of the college graduates and 12 per cent of the schoolteachers were put in the same category. Comic book sales were reported to average 1,000,-000,000 copies a year, representing an expenditure of about $100,000,000.

The study found no scientifically acceptable evidence to substantiate or refute the contention that a relationship exists between juvenile delinquency and comic book reading. Nor did there seem to exist any correlation between such reading and intelligence.

March 1, 1955

SENATE UNIT ASKS CURB ON TV CRIME

Industry Takes a 'Calculated Risk' in Such Programs, Delinquency Study Finds

NO PROOF OF HARM SEEN

But Stricter Federal Control and Voluntary Restraint Are Urged by Panel

By C. P. TRUSSELL
Special to The New York Times.

WASHINGTON, Aug. 25—A Senate subcommittee said today that the television industry was taking "a calculated risk" with crime and violence on programs during children's viewing hours.

The group recommended that the industry watch itself and that the Federal Communications Commission restrain and punish, if necessary.

The panel, investigating causes of juvenile delinquency, drew its conclusions from hearings, the monitoring of programs in many cities, opinions submitted by thirty-four psychiatrists and staff studies that lasted for months. The investigators also said that:

¶Proof that TV crime and violence programs were harmful to children was lacking.

¶There existed enough professional opinion that such programs contributed to juvenile delinquency to warrant study.

¶The television industry should adjust its programing to the fact that a substantial body of opinion disapproved of such programs.

Industry Is Thanked

Senator Estes Kefauver, the Tennessee Democrat heading the group, thanked the industry for the cooperation it had given the inquiry. This was not a report excoriating the television industry.

He and his panel, however, emphasized that many children spent more hours before television screens than they did in school. During those hours, the report stated, programs well may have brought to the juvenile mind things such as these:

"Life is cheap; death, suffering, sadism and brutality are subjects of callous indifference, and judges, lawyers and law enforcement officers are too often dishonest, incompetent and stupid.

"The manner and frequency with which crime through this medium is brought before the eyes and ears of American children," the report added, "indicates inadequate regard for psychological and social consequences."

The subcommittee recommended:

¶The formation by citizen groups of local "listening councils" to ensure good TV programming.

¶Stricter control of programming by the Federal Communications Commission, with authority from Congress to punish those who violated the present code of practices to which most producing companies have subscribed.

¶A collective responsibility among telecasting stations to present programs that would not contribute to juvenile delinquency.

¶The inclusion of motion pictures in the code on television. This would deal not only with old motion pictures that were being reproduced but also with newer ones appearing on television.

¶Further research by private and public foundations into the effects of television on children's behavior.

¶The prompt establishment, when Congress reconvenes in January, of a Presidential commission to study mass communications and report on practices and materials that might be detrimental to children and youths.

This report was Part Two of a three-part inquiry into the effects of crime and violence dramatized as the programs ran through the so-called children's hours. Previously the panel had dealt with the movies, the radio and the comic books.

The subcommittee found that there was "reason to believe" that TV crime programs were potentially much more injurious to children and young people than movies, radio or the comic books.

Other members of the subcommittee are Senators Thomas C. Hennings Jr. of Missouri and Price Daniel of Texas, Democrats, and Senators William Langer of North Dakota and Alexander Wiley of Wisconsin, Republicans. The panel is a unit of the Senate Judiciary Committee.

August 26, 1955

Expert Repeats TV Is Harmful on Young

Although most parents and specialists who work with children have gotten over their original concern about the deleterious effects of television on the young, not all have been won over. Psychoanalyst Joost A. M. Meerloo, quoted in the current issue of "Child-Family Digest," holds that with some children—and adults, too—television-watching can be habit-forming to the point of real addiction, requiring professional help to cure.

Besides being a time-stealer, he holds, television "arouses precociously sexual and emotional turmoil." Gunplay and crime scenes provide an outlet for aggressive feelings, a point that many specialists count in television's favor. Dr. Meerloo feels, however, that such satisfaction of aggressive fantasies simply adds to the child's guilt feelings. Finally, he complains, preoccupation with television prevents "active inner creativity" and interferes with personal growth. It prepares the mind more easily for cliché-thinking and persuades onlookers to "think in mass values." It intrudes into family life and cuts off "the more subtle interfamilial communication."

February 29, 1956

TV Is Found To Broaden Child's Vista

By MARTIN TOLCHIN

TELEVISION today engrosses the average child to the tune of twenty to thirty hours of viewing a week. Time that was formerly spent in a variety of children's activities is now spent quietly in front of the set.

What has been learned of television's impact on the physical and emotional growth of youngsters in the years since the medium came into its own?

Several findings are offered by the Foundation for Character Education, Boston University, in a fifty-six-page pamphlet entitled "Television for Children." It is the work of thirty-four authors, including social scientists, educators, spokesmen for child care organizations, school systems, and, of course, representatives of commercial and educational television.

Eyesight Not Impaired

According to the report, several early concerns of parents already have been proved groundless. For one thing, television has not damaged the eyesight of youthful viewers, nor has it affected school performance.

The fear that television would produce a nation of illiterates is likewise far from the truth. For example, the circulation of library books to children has increased since the advent of television. And there is some indication that the medium has whetted the literary appetite of youngsters seeking more information on subjects they first encountered as "entertainment." Certainly, television has broadened the child's world and enhanced his experiences.

But there is another side to the ledger, one that indicates that paradoxes become the rule. On the one hand, television broadens the child's base of knowledge and gives him new experiences easily and quickly. On the other hand, the report found, prolonged exposure to television makes children more stereotyped in their moral judgments and more inclined to see people as "all good" or "all bad."

Similarly, a child watching television learns, for good or bad, how people behave in certain circumstances. The report found that "much of the television fare offered to children is of excellent quality by moral, intellectual and aesthetic standards." On the other hand, a child may conclude from television westerns that, in cases of conflict, the hero is justified in imposing his will on others by force.

Unexplored Possibilities

The report declared:

"In real life, there is an enormous range of possible solutions to problems involving conflict between people. Most of these possibilities remain unexplored in the stereotyped children's dramas."

Why do most children spend more time in front of their television set than in their schoolrooms? What do they see in it?

The report found that a child became interested in a television program primarily when his emotions were aroused.

"The child, in real life small and powerless, experiences virtuous power, success and the excitement of new surroundings when he puts himself in the place of the hero of a western," it said.

Violence for its own sake is not likely to attract a young audience, according to the report. Much more important than mere violence are "action, movement, suspense and excitement." The expectation of fear also captivates many children, the report said, adding:

"The child, to the extent that the danger is controlled, enjoys fearing for the safety of his hero, whether he be a cowboy or Mickey Mouse, just as the excitement in viewing many a circus act comes from vicarious fear for the safety of the performer. But the exploitation of fear in its more gruesome aspects is less often found in children's programs (except in certain fairy tales) than in the suspense and horror stories intended for adult consumption."

Family Dramas Appealing

Family-life dramas also appeal to children, the report noted. The child's need for affection, acceptance and support is reached by those programs that depict satisfying relationships between adults and youngsters.

"Even where the relationships are exaggerated and lampooned, the appeal can be as great, because it makes ridiculous situations which are too often painfully real," the report said. "This is especially true during the transition period from viewing children's to viewing adults' television fare."

There are still other motivations. Youthful curiosity and the desire of children to explore the physical world account for the popularity of science, animal and travel programs. In addition, talent programs, both amateur and professional, stimulate the youngster's desire for achievement.

The report is available for $1.50 from the foundation at Boston University, 322 Bay State Road, Boston 15.

January 6, 1959

VIOLENCE IN FILMS SEEN ON DECREASE

Juvenile Delinquency Scripts Drop as Result of Drive

By MURRAY SCHUMACH
Special to The New York Times.

HOLLYWOOD, Calif., July 16 —Whatever the explanation for juvenile delinquency this summer, it cannot be blamed on movies. For the films about juvenile delinquency have almost vanished.

The disappearance of the inexpensively made pictures filled with youthful crime and sex has been the result of a campaign by the movie industry that began in 1958.

The fight against these movies was carried on by the Production Code Administration, the self-censoring organization of the movie industry; Eric Johnston, official spokesman for the industry, and the heads of major movie companies.

Mainly the weapon against those who wanted to make these movies was persuasion. Industrial economics also played a part and finally there were times when the Production Code Administration took an irrevocable position.

Campaign Begun in 1958

In April, 1958, Geoffrey M. Shurlock, head of the Production Code Administration, became alarmed about the flood of scripts about juvenile delinquency that was pouring into his office. He notified Mr. Johnston and pointed out that one independent producer alone had begun a schedule to turn out twenty-eight pictures during the year that would deal with this and similar subjects.

Mr. Johnston then conferred with studio executives. They agreed to avoid making movies on the subject of juvenile delinquency except in a serious and mature vein.

With this backing, the administration began applying pressure. One of the most successful methods was to point out to would-be producers that the market for juvenile delinquency films, on the basis of scripts already submitted, would soon be glutted and the producers of such films might find it difficult to make a profit.

Script Changes Made

Another effective step by the administration was to insist that changes in the scripts on juvenile delinquency be made so as to raise the ages of the characters in the films.

Finally, movie censors, when everything else failed, said flatly, after studying an objectionable script, that such a movie would never get a seal of approval.

By last year there were only two pictures distributed in this country that dealt with juvenile delinquency mainly as an excuse to display violence and sex. One of these movies was British.

However, one recent development concerns the administration. An independent producer recently purchased from a major studio a few movies made several years ago, including some of the obnoxious juvenile delinquency variety. There is nothing the administration can do to prevent such re-issues.

July 17, 1961

KENNEDY STIRRED TEEN-AGERS' GRIEF

Emotion Is Found Greater Than Would Be Expected for Adolescents' Parents

By JOSEPH LELYVELD

Adolescents displayed more grief over the assassination of President Kennedy than they might be expected to show over the death of a parent.

This observation was offered as a "paradox" yesterday by Dr. Martha Wolfenstein, an associate professor of psychiatry at the Albert Einstein College of Medicine. Her paper was presented to a conference on reactions of children to the assassination.

The "major life task" of adolescence, Dr. Wolfenstein said, is the loosening of the child's bonds to his parents. Nevertheless, the acknowledgement of loss involved in a free expression of grief often proves too difficult. By staying dry-eyed adolescents reject the fact of death, she asserted.

It was different Nov. 22. She and her colleagues, Dr. Wolfenstein said, were struck by the frank outpouring of emotion for the dead President from ordinarily inhibited teen-agers.

The assassination, she reasoned, suddenly focused their diffuse everyday feelings of loss and estrangement. As a remote figure, the President was easy to mourn, but as a kind of idealized parent, Dr. Wolfenstein observed, he summoned up some of the most painful emotions of adolescence.

Although adolescents appeared to be overwhelmed by the death of President Kennedy, speakers at the conference found that younger children were preoccupied by the violent way in which he died. For young children, death is not necessarily an irreversible phenomenon, Dr. Sybelle Escalona, a psychiatry professor at Einstein, remarked.

Their confusion on this point, other speakers noted, may have been intensified by the detailed television coverage of the assassination. President Kennedy, whom they had mostly known as a television figure, was still before their eyes.

At the same time, the notion that something catastrophic had happened was graphically shown by the reactions of their parents and, also, by the cancellation of all their favorite television programs, the speakers asserted.

Two Boys Regressed

Dr. Augusta Alpert, associate director of the Child Development Center, presented a paper on the reactions of four disturbed boys between the ages of 4 and 6. In response to the slaying of the President, each of the boys adopted defensive postures that represented regressions to more infantile states.

Analysis showed that the boys had fused fragments of what they had heard of the assassination to fantasies of violence against their fathers. The murder of Lee Oswald, the accused assassin, seemed to impress them as a sign of the retribution they might suffer.

The two-day meeting at the Abraham Jacobi Hospital, which continues today, is being attended by 27 psychiatrists, psychologists and social scientists. Some of them said they had conducted the studies to relieve their own feelings of grief and shock over the President's death.

April 4, 1964

SCHOOL FOR VIOLENCE

By FREDRIC WERTHAM, M.D.

Dr. Wertham is a psychiatrist in the criminal field and author of "The Show of Violence."

THE British Government has recently set up a committee to study the effects of television on young people. The secretary of this Television Research Committee, sociologist J. D. Halloran of Leicester University, conferred with me last month about my material, methods and conclusions. He wanted to know particularly to what extent television, in relation to other influences, plays a part in shaping young peoples' attitudes and concepts. Inevitably the question of violence was in the center of interest.

The influence of television is part of a much larger problem. Has the technological development of mass media, especially television, progressed so far that it transcends man and has outstripped its human controllers? I don't believe that we are pawns to advanced machines. Technology is everybody's servant. As spectators and viewers of TV, we are involved in the results and responsibilities, so we must inform ourselves what the real effects are.

Two sets of facts are indisputable. First, in real life certain kinds of violence have increased, and our attitudes about violence have changed. Secondly, there is an inordinate amount of violence on television. More than 15 years have passed since I pointed out that younger and younger children are committing more and more serious violent crimes. Today that is common knowledge. Murders by children under 14 used to be a rarity. They are not any longer. In addition, many of them show more brutality and cruelty now. As for young adults, it has become so prevalent for young parents to beat up and seriously injure their infants or very young children that the condition has been given a name, the "battered baby syndrome," and laws are being considered to cope with it. A new attitude on the public's part has been highlighted by recent cases where men and women were attacked, beaten or killed on the street, in open buildings, on the subway or on ferryboats in front of bystanders who did not either help the victims or call the police.

Mass Murder

The amount and matter-of-factness of violence on TV is easily documented. An innumerably repeated promotional blurb for "Cheyenne" (a Western series no worse and no better than others) illustrates its monotonous insistence. Within a few seconds two men are slugging it 'out and two men shooting it out, with one of them apparently killed.

One television station showed in one week, mostly in children's viewing time, 334 completed or attempted killings. Promotion spots showed over and over again 8 murders within 60-second periods (sometimes it was 30 seconds and 4 murders).

I have studied adolescents who in comic books, movies and TV have seen more than 10,000 homicides. Crime and violence are just that, whether shown in the setting of ordinary life, in pseudo-patriotic Westerns or pseudo-scientific settings in outer space. For the overall picture, quality is as important as quantity. A man brandishes a knife in a pretty girl's face on TV and threatens to cut her tongue out. A group of giggling attractive girls are shot down cold-bloodedly. A man is suspended by his feet with his head over a fire. Afternoon programs promise "hideous torture and terrifying horror"—and keep their promise. Typical are scenes of what I have called "sneering sadism," where the torturer or murderer expresses cynical contempt for his victim while hurting him. Children have learned to love that. For example, while one man lies on the ground with an arrow in his chest, a second man comments: "Don't worry, it won't hurt much longer" and pushes the arrow deeper into his chest and kills him.

Questionnaire

The question is: Are there relationships between acts and attitudes in life and representations on TV?

This is not a matter for speculation and facile generalization. It needs sober and concrete scientific investigation. The much-used questionnaire method is not enough; even if they want to, children cannot tell you whether or how much they have been influenced. Artificially set-up experiments (similar to animal experiments) to measure aggression are not adequate either, because children are not rats. Moreover, the immediate effects after seeing a show are relatively insignificant compared with the important long-range consequences.

We must study the whole child and not just one facet. The only method that can give valid results is the clinical method. That is to say, the child has to be examined and all the psychobiological and psychosocial factors with a bearing on his life have to be considered. The influence of TV has to be taken up and analyzed unobtrusively and incidentally. Follow-up study of development is necessary and what young adults say later about their childhood is most relevant.

I have been studying the effects of mass media (first comic books, then television) for many years. My definite opinion is that continuous exposure of children's minds to scenes of crime and brutality has had a deeper effect on them than is generally realized—just as the constructive effects of good shows (quite apart from strictly educational programs are more far-reaching than is generally assumed. Television in the life of the young is either educational or mis-educational—but never—in the long-run—neutral. For children, the television screen has become a second reality.

When Lee Harvey Oswald was actually murdered on the screen, some adults for a moment did not believe their eyes. They did not understand what had happened. Children blended their realities and knew right off: "He shot him in the stomach." That is what always happens in the serials; they had seen it a thousand times. In one of my group therapy sessions, a boy brought up the point that Oswald was completely defenseless since he was handcuffed to two sheriffs when Ruby shot him point-blank. "Why not?" asked another boy.

Robert Stack as Eliot Ness on "The Untouchables."
TV, says Dr. Wertham, is a second reality for children.

Eliot Ness (the crime-fighter hero of "The Untouchables") is a good guy and he gives a prisoner a terrific sock while two cops hold him. Many modern children fail to see the evil in horror and the wrong in violence and have lost their natural sympathy for the suffering of others. The trouble it not that they get frightened, but that they do *not* get frightened.

TV Factor

Of course the TV factor never works alone. The cult of violence lurks in many areas of our own social life.

We speak glibly of the casualties of the next war in terms of minutes and millions. We kill each other recklessly on the highways. Human life has become more devaluated than the dollar. The fact that there are so many other influences working in the same direction does not make the television factor less potent, but more so. The witnesses who did not come to the aid of the girl who was being stabbed, the young people who shouted "Jump!" and "Chicken!" and "What's the matter—ya yellow?" to would-be suicides on the top of the building in Albany and

the bridge in Brooklyn were conditioned in many ways. The mass media, and especially television, make up one part of this conditioning.

Whether crime and violence programs arouse a lust for violence, reinforce it when it is present, show a way to carry it out, teach the best method to get away with it or merely blunt the child's (and adult's) awareness of its wrongness, television has become a school for violence.

In this school young people are never, literally never, taught that violence is in itself reprehensible. The lesson they do get is that violence

is the great adventure and the sure solution, and he who is best at it wins. We are training not only a peace corps but also a violence corps. I do not advocate that violence should be entirely eliminated from TV. But it should be presented as a fact of life, not as life itself. We want to show younger people how the other half lives; but that does not mean we have to overload their imagination with images of how the other half dies.

July 5, 1964

SENATORS STIRRED BY VIOLENCE ON TV

View Films at Inquiry Into Juvenile Delinquency

WASHINGTON, July 30 (AP) — Senators investigating juvenile delinquency showed samples of what one of them called "brutal violence" in television programs today. Then broadcasters were told:

"The people won't take it forever. You better mend your ways."

The statement came from Senator Thomas J. Dodd, Democrat of Connecticut, who with other members of the Senate Subcommittee on Juvenile Delinquency watched monsters and murderers perform on a screen in a darkened hearing room as they renewed an inquiry into television programming.

After the showing, Senator Dodd lectured industry witnesses about the content of programs being watched by children and teen-agers and said the mail was heavy from parents who object.

Trouble Is Foreseen

"I don't think you care," Senator Dodd said. "But unless you do care the American people

are going to make you care."

Senator Dodd and Senator Kenneth B. Keating, Republican of New York, said they were opposed to Federal regulation of programming and that they hoped the industry would "clean up" its practices and avert what could become a great public clamor for Government action.

Senator Keating said that "as a politician I have as much of an elephant hide as anyone else" but he still found some of the violence depicted on television "hard to take."

By better self-policing, Senator Keating said, the industry could head off what might develop into an "overwhelming outcry in favor of the Government doing something."

Senator Dodd said he agreed, and added "that's the purpose of these hearings."

Thomas W. Moore, vice president of the American Broadcasting Company, protested that scenes shown at the hearing from such A.B.C. shows as "Outer Limits," "Breaking Point," and "Combat" were taken out of context and were not necessarily representative.

Mr. Moore insisted that the industry "can and does police itself." He said it strives constantly for better programs, periodically alerts its producers to the problems involved, and has developed codes for the guidance of its personnel.

July 31, 1964

Senators Declare TV Violence Spurs Juvenile Crimes

WASHINGTON, Oct. 25 (UPI)—A still-secret report charges there is a conclusive link between crime and violence in television shows and juvenile delinquency.

The report has been signed by a majority of the Senate

Subcommittee on Juvenile Delinquency headed by Senator Thomas J. Dodd, Democrat of Connecticut. It will be released shortly.

In its summary, based on years of study and public hearings, the subcommittee reported it found "on the basis of expert testimony and impressive research evidence, that a relationship has been conclusively established between televised crime and violence and anti-social attitudes and behavior among juvenile viewers."

In another section of the re-

port, the subcommittee said that in its view "the excess amount of televised crime, violence and brutality can and does contribute to the development of attitudes and actions in many young people which pave the way for delinquent behavior."

Little Improvement Seen

At the opening of the latest hearings in July, Mr. Dodd said that despite the reduction of TV violence predicted by network officials in 1961 and 1962, he found very little improvement except with the Columbia Broadcasting System.

In addition, Mr. Dodd said he

found that most of the violent shows from the 1961-62 season had been syndicated and reshown on independent networks.

"No serious student of juvenile delinquency contends that television is the sole cause of delinquent behavior," the report said. "Nor does the subcommittee hold this view."

At the same time, the report said, "it is clear that television is a factor in molding the character, attitudes and behavior patterns of America's young people."

October 26, 1964

DOCTORS FIND TV MAKES CHILD ILL

New Syndrome Symptoms Include Fatigue, Loss of Appetite and Vomiting

By WALTER SULLIVAN

Excessive television viewing can make a child ill, it was reported yesterday. The illness

was named the "tired-child syndrome."

Its symptoms are those typical of anxiety conditions: chronic fatigue, loss of appetite, headache and vomiting.

The ailment was discussed in a report to the American Academy of Pediatrics based on a study at two Air Force hospitals. Those suffering from the syndrome, all from 3 to 12 years of age, were spending an average of three to six hours in front of television screens on weekdays and six to 10 hours on Saturdays and Sundays.

This was well above the aver-

age, established in a separate survey of 160 children of Air Force personnel. There the average weekday television time was found to be two and a half hours, with six hours on weekend days. In some of the younger children this amounts to roughly a quarter of their waking hours.

Children Become Addicts

A syndrome is a combination of symptoms often characteristic of a given disease. The study concerned 30 children brought to the hospitals at Lackland Air Force Base in Texas and Fairchild Air Force Base near Spokane, Wash.

In none of the cases did the

parents mention excessive time spent in front of television. This came to light only through questioning of the family and in most cases only after several examinations.

It was then found that in some sensitive, introspective children television could become a form of addiction. They fall into a cycle in which long hours of viewing produce such fatigue that the children have only enough energy for television watching.

In each of the 30 cases the parents were told to terminate the child's television viewing completely. The effects were dramatic. In the 12 cases where the instructions were followed fully, the symptoms vanished within two to three weeks. The 18 other children, allowed as much as two hours of viewing a day, were free of symptoms in three to six weeks.

Parents Break the Rules

Later follow-ups showed, however, that the parental habits were as much of a problem as those of the children. Several families, and particularly the fathers, were unwilling to forgo evenings in front of television and soon the children had drifted back into their old practices.

Thus, of the 26 patients whose cases were followed for several months, only nine remained free of symptoms, all of them having restricted their viewing. Of the rest, 13 had been released of all restrictions and 11 of these were again suffering severe symptoms. The four others were allowed limited viewing and had limited disorders.

Chlorpromazine, a sedative, had been prescribed in some of these cases to aid in sleeping during the early days of treatment. Some of the parents who

were reluctant to curb their own viewing asked for further sedation of the children, but it appeared that medication by itself did not remove the symptoms.

The report was presented by Capt. Richard M. Narkewicz and was co-authored by Capt. Stanley N. Graven. Both are pediatricians with the Air Force Medical Corps. The meeting was at the New York Hilton Hotel.

At a news conference Captain Narkewicz told how, in his

view, susceptible children become emotionally involved in shows that they were watching, even including animated cartoons aimed at the very young.

"They are living right inside that little box," he said. He also told how nightmares and other manifestations disclosed a direct link between the childrens' anxiety and the shows they had been watching.

October 27, 1964

Violence in TV Cartoons Being Toned Down

Saturday Programs for Children Turn Toward Comedy

By ROBERT WINDELER
Special to The New York Times

HOLLYWOOD, July 19 — Cartoons, which transformed Saturday morning from "television's garbage heap" to prime time and in the process became some of the most violent fare on the tube, are turning toward comedy and science-fiction adventure.

Protests by parents and educators have caused the networks to re-evaluate programming and substitute less violent half-hours for the "zap-pow" superheroes.

Although the networks have not announced their final schedules for the fall season, it is known that the superheroes will be all that extinct.

"They were just about exhausted anyway, everybody was doing the same thing," said Norman Prescott, a partner in Filmation, one of the leading producers of cartoons for television. "But it was the recent wave of antiviolence which really killed them off. The parents had every right to holler: I'm with them all the way."

No Choice for Children

One parent who complained is Mrs. Irvin Hendryson, national president of the Parent-Teachers Association.

"Television cartoons are worse than immoral," she said. "They are full of horror and violence and negative values."

The P.T.A. at its last three conventions has sponsored strong resolutions condemning the kind of violent cartoon fare offered by the networks. These actions and those of other civic groups and hundreds of thousands of letters from parents and teachers, particularly after the assassination of Senator Robert F. Ken-

Archie and his comic strip friends will be on TV this fall

Mightor, one of television's many Saturday superheroes

nedy, have apparently begun to have their effect.

In much of the Saturday morning programing period, children do not have a choice:

they can watch one of three superhero programs, or what the networks and animators call "adventure shows."

Fred Silverman, daytime pro-

graming vice president of the Columbia Broadcasting System, said his network's shift from virtually all-adventure to half comedy in its six hours of cartoons was "an effort to achieve a balance and because comedy has always been a staple of children's programing—most children like to laugh."

Edwin Vane, the American Broadcasting Company's vice president for daytime programing, said in New York that "as a result of the protest we have re-examined two of our adventure shows which will be on again this fall, and made a very strong effort to stay away from anything that could be construed as violence."

The two shows are "Fantastic Four" and "Spiderman," both based on the superhero theme. A.B.C. executives in New York viewed all 17 segments of each show and eliminated two episodes of each on the grounds of excessive violence.

An executive of the National Broadcasting Company, who declined to be identified, indicated that his network was the least settled about what to do with holdover cartoon action shows.

"I don't think we can say with any certainty that any of those shows will be back," he said.

When the three networks began to program animated shows on Saturday mornings several years ago, millions of American children were content to watch whatever leftover theater cartoons were available. But as the audience grew, so did its thirst for something new.

Animators turned from cute little humanized animals to what one animator, Friz Freleng, calls "hard-hitting superstuff," in which superheroes "pow," "zap" and "rat-tat-tat" their enemies out of existence. The sound tracks for such cartoons sound like real-life battle scenes.

All three networks carry cartoons from 8 A.M. until noon each Saturday, but the Columbia Broadcasting System starts the moving-line drawings a half hour earlier and continues them until 1:30 in the afternoon, when an animated and updated Lone Ranger rides off into the sunset. (And Sunday morning, once reserved for religious and public service programing, is opening up as a secondary cartoon time slot.)

The present lineup of television cartoons features four other faintly recognizable old favorites: "Casper, the Friendly Ghost," "The Flintstones," "King Kong," and "Superman," the original superhero, but one who doesn't annihilate his victims, merely sends them back where they came from.

"Superman" and an animated "Beatles" half-hour limp along on name value. "You could animate Superman on toilet tissue and it would sell," says David DePatie, Mr. Freleng's

partner in two network cartoon shows, "Super-6" and "Super President," which reflect the preponderant theme.

There are also "Atom Ant," "Secret Squirrel," "Birdman," "Aquaman," "Mightor," "Shazzan" and "Herculoids."

'Action and More Action'

"You fall in line," says Joe Barberra, vice president of Hanna-Barberra, the animation facility that accounts for 11 of the 25 cartoon half hours now on television.

"You go through with a trend decided by whoever is in charge at the networks, and they want action, action and more action. Saturday mornings are so competitive now that we have script meetings and we talk about character analysis and motivation—for cartoon shows!"

But the indications this summer were that the superhero theme had begun to pall and that parents particularly were upset by the violent implications of it. They agreed with the judgment of Murray Korengold, a Beverly Hills, Calif., psychiatrist, who said:

"The superhero of today's quickie cartoon has the effect of desensitizing people—not simply children—to social and personal violence, to pain and compassion for other people's suffering. The superhero very nearly represents the American ethic of hegemony and supremacy; he uses violence without explicit application and arrogates himself very radically into everybody else's life."

Parents protested to the networks and were able to effect a major change in a whole bloc of television programing, instead of just saving a single show, like "The Dick Van Dyke Show" or "Star Trek."

Filmation, Hanna-Barbara's chief competitor, is producing cartoon segments of "Journey to the Center of the Earth," based on the Jules Verne novel, "Fantastic Voyage," based on the movie about scientists who miniaturized themselves and entered the human blood stream and "Archie," a popular comic book for 35 years.

Sold to Networks

All have been sold to networks for the fall, an indica-

tion of what animators agree are the next two trends in cartoons: nonviolent science fiction adventure and comedy ("Archie" will also feature original music by a live group called "The Archies").

Hanna-Barberra has sold an animated "The New Adventures of Gulliver" and "The Banana Splits," a live-animated musical-comedy hour.

Mr. Freleng is delighted at the success of the antiviolence protest: "I don't like to make that kind of thing; animation has better applications."

Mr. Barberra feels the effects of the protest won't last: "Television is like a snake; every two years it sheds its skin. We'll have to go back to violence, there aren't too many other ways we can go."

But Mr. Prescott of Filmation, says "I think we've seen the last of violence in TV cartoons. Anybody can pull out a gun and kill people. When you say 'No more violence,' you're saying 'Be creative again—do other things that will entertain people.'"

July 20, 1968

YOUTH ALIENATION ATTRIBUTED TO TV

Semanticist Says Children Don't Learn to Interact

SAN FRANCISCO, Sept. 3 (UPI)—A leading semanticist suggested today that youthful rioting, drug-taking, alienation and radical politics may all be unforeseen consequences of television's radical reshaping of the environment.

The semanticist, S. I. Hayakawa, gave his conclusions to the 76th annual convention of the American Psychological Association.

He compared TV to a powerful sorcerer who snatches a child away from his parents for three or four hours a day, something like 22,000 hours by the time they reach 18.

"Is it any wonder that these children, as they grew to adolescence, often turned out to be complete strangers to their dismayed parents?" the semanticist asked.

The important fact about television, Mr. Hayakawa continued, is "you have no inter-

action with it."

"A child sitting in front of a TV set gets no experience in influencing behavior and being influenced in return," he said.

"Is there any connection," he asked, "between this fact and the sudden appearance in the past few years of an enormous number of young people from educated and middle class families who find it difficult or impossible to relate to anybody—and therefore drop out?"

The antimaterialism of youth, Mr. Hayakawa said, may be an overdue negative reaction to television's message that "material possessions are everything, that this headache

remedy, this luxurious carpeting, this new model Camaro" will bring all kinds of happiness.

Looting by both whites and blacks in riots, he suggested, may be an explosive response to TV's materialistic world and its depiction of violence "as a way of life."

Mr. Hayakawa gave his impression that young militants had not lost faith in democratic processes, but rather were "totally unacquainted with them since they were rarely shown on television" except for national conventions.

September 4, 1968

Ratings to Bar Some Films to Children

By VINCENT CANBY

The representatives of the majority of American movie producers, distributors and exhibitors announced yesterday that they had agreed to set up a classification system for motion pictures. Under it, children under 16 will be prohibited from seeing certain films thought to be unsuitable.

The United States is believed to be the last major country in the Western world to adopt a movie classifica-

tion plan. Unlike the system in most other countries, however, the American system is to be set up by members of the movie industry and administered by it without government participation or authority.

The classification system is designed to answer critics of the motion picture industry, who have voiced alarm in recent years over the increasing number of films in which sex, nudity or violence is depicted or obscene language

is used.

Largely as a result of such films as "Who's Afraid of Virginia Woolf?," "Alfie" and "Blow-Up," the industry's Production Code, the body of rules by which it attempts to control film content, was rewritten two years ago to permit the production of movies with adult themes. Such films earlier were denied code approval or were given approval only by special dispensation.

The industry continued to

be attacked, however, because there were no regulations to restrict young audiences from seeing these films. Accompanying the attacks have been numerous attempts by communities to enact local classification ordinances, which the industry has continually fought.

One of the industry's severest critics, the National Catholic Office for Motion Pictures, which classifies movies for Roman Catholic patrons, warned several years ago that although it was basically against statutory censorship, it would seek some sort of Government-sponsored movie classification unless the industry acted.

Representatives of the National Catholic Office and of the Broadcasting and Film Commission of the National Council of Churches will hold a news conference at 2:30 P.M. today to discuss the classification plan. The meeting will be held at the Catholic group's headquarters at 453 Madison Avenue. Neither group had any comment yesterday.

The rating system, which goes into effect on films released after Nov. 1, will classify movies in four categories:

G—acceptable for general audiences.

M—for mature audiences.

R—restricted to those 16 or older, although younger patrons will be admitted if accompanied by a parent or guardian.

X—for those 16 or older without qualification.

The announcement of the plan was made jointly at a news conference yesterday by Jack J. Valenti, the president of the Motion Picture Association of America; Louis Nizer, the association's general counsel; Julian S. Rifkin, the president of the National Association of Theater Owners, and Munio Podhorzer, a member of the governing board of the International Film Importers and Distributors of America. The conference was held at Mr. Valenti's office, 522 Fifth Avenue.

His association, whose members are the major American movie producer-distributors, and Mr. Podhorzer's, whose members are primarily concerned with the distribution of foreign films, handle all but a small percentage of the films that go into general theatrical release in this country.

Mr. Rifkin estimates that his group represents 10,000 of the nation's 13,000 movie theaters. The burden of enforcing the movie ratings will fall on the theater owners and managers.

The rating will be done by the Production Code Administration, a branch of the Motion Picture Association, headed by Geoffrey Shurlock, whose office is in Hollywood.

The present five-man code staff will be augmented by two people, one of whom will be in New York. Mr. Valenti said he expected that one of the new staff members will be a woman with a background in child psychology.

In addition to Mr. Shurlock, the staff members, each of whom has been with the code for 3 to 20 years, are

The New York Times (by Barton Silverman)

Youngster gazes at photos outside midtown theater showing film made for adult audience. Motion Picture Association of America is issuing a system classifying content of movies.

Eugene G. Dougherty, Morris V. Murphy, Albert E. Van Schmus and Richard Mathison.

The adoption of the classification system represents a major change in policy. Under the late Eric Johnston, the association fought off all suggestions that the industry rate its pictures with classifications that would be enforced at the theater box office.

The adoption comes two and one-half years after Mr. Valenti succeeded Mr. Johnston as the group's president, and two years after the code was rewritten and updated at Mr. Valenti's request.

The revised code of September, 1966, eliminated many of the specific taboos that had been in the original code, written in 1930 and slightly modified several times over the years.

According to Mr. Valenti,

two United States Supreme Court decisions paved the way for the adoption of the rating plan. In one the Court struck down a Dallas classification law because of vague wording, but it acknowledged that some sort of movie classification to protect children would be legal.

In another, the Court upheld a New York statute under which a newsstand owner had been convicted for having sold an obscene publication to a boy under 16.

Mr. Valenti said each picture would be judged independently. If a producer objects to a rating, he can submit his case to an appeals board composed of Mr. Valenti, four of his association's directors, eight exhibitors, two independent distributors and two independent producers.

A movie that has not been rated by the code, but whose distributor wants it to play

a theater that is cooperating in the classification system, will get an "X" rating automatically.

In an effort to get as many producers and distributors as possible to submit their films to the code, the fees charged will be lowered—in Mr. Valenti's words—for "poverty stricken producers."

The fees will thus vary from $25 to $3,000, depending on the film's cost and the gross annual income of the distributing company.

According to Mr. Valenti, all but one of the major theater circuits—he declined to identify it—have agreed to participate in the plan. This covers 4,000 to 6,000 theaters. If most theaters of the National Association of Theater Owners cooperate, he said this would represent 90 to 95 per cent of the movie business done in this country.

October 8, 1968

TV FOR CHILDREN TIED TO VIOLENCE

Psychoanalyst Finds Harm in Too Much Viewing

By JOHN LEO

Soupy Sales and Captain Kangaroo can produce as much violence in children as blood-and-gore television shows according to a new book, "Psychoanalysis, Uses and Abuses," by a Los Angeles psychoanalyst.

The book's thesis is that regular television viewing renders children passive, denying them the normal outlets for aggressive energy until that energy accumulates to the point where it explodes in some form of violence or destructive action.

"The programming is irrele-

vant," says the author, Dr. Lawrence J. Friedman, a senior faculty member of the Los Angeles Psychoanalytic Institute. "All television, except in small doses feeds children ready-made fantasies at a time when fantasy-making and intellectual activity is crucial for their development.

"If a child watches enough television, he will automatically become violent because he has nowhere else to go with his normal aggressive energy that he should be working off in creative activity."

Case Studies Cited

Dr. Friedman, a native of Hungary, was interviewed about his book during the Pan-American Congress for Psychoanalysis held last week at the Waldorf-Astoria Hotel. He said his theory tested out in his psychoanalytic practice.

"I had three children, aged 11, 9 and 7, who had regressed into bed-soiling," he recalled. "It took me a year to convince the parents that long hours

before the TV was making the children regress, but when they finally agreed to take the television away, the passivity disappeared and the bed-soiling stopped."

He said a study in Pasadena, Calif., of 750 middle-class children, aged 8 to 12, showed a correlation between long hours of television viewing and poor scholastic performance.

"We're just beginning to see the results of long exposure to television in adolescents today," he said. This is the first TV generation and much of its violence can be traced directly to their television habits."

Dr. Friedman also believes that there may be a connection between television and "dropping out and turning on" with LSD.

Push-Button Society

"Many adolescents today take for granted that everything comes from the outside, that satisfactions come easily and can be enjoyed passively without taking others into consideration. These are attitudes

that television encourages," he said.

"A generation that grew up just pushing a button to be entertained is finding it extremely difficult to establish an object relationship with others. In general, the consequences of TV are much more far-reaching than ever described."

Although the effects of television have not yet been accurately measured, he said, he believes an hour of television a day for children of 8 to 10 is probably not harmful. "But I'd prefer that small children, 2, 3 and 4, not watch any at all," he added.

He believes that most children who watch more than 28 hours of television a week are encouraged to do so by parents who want them quiet and out of the way. Eighty-two per cent of the students in the Pasadena study, he said, indicated that they would rather do things with their parents than watch television.

March 2, 1969

Panel Links Violence to That on TV

By JACK ROSENTHAL
Special to The New York Times

WASHINGTON, Sept. 17— The National Commission on the Causes and Prevention of Violence is expected to ratify tomorrow a final draft report that concludes that violence on television encourages real violence, especially among the children of poor, disorganized families.

The draft report also includes sweeping recommendations intended to reduce sharply the volume and type of violence portrayed on television.

The findings and recommendations are contained in a 31-page "Proposed Final Draft, Violence and Television Entertainment Programming," which has already been circulated to the 13-member commission.

The commission, headed by Milton S. Eisenhower, president-emeritus of Johns Hopkins University, was established June 10, 1968, by President Johnson after the assassination of Senator Robert F. Kennedy. It is a study and advisory body without enforcement powers.

Associated Press
Milton S. Eisenhower

The draft report does not propose Federal enforcement of its television recommendations, but rather voluntary action by the three national networks and an enlarged role for the Congressionally established Public Broadcast Corporation.

Since the commission has already reviewed the television section of its report once, the final draft is expected to be approved readily at the com-

mission's meeting in Washington tomorrow and Friday.

The recommendations call for:

¶An over-all reduction in programs that require or contain violence.

¶Elimination of violence from children's cartoon programs — probably excepting the fanciful, exaggerated violence of films like "Popeye" and "Tom and Jerry."

¶Adoption of the British practice of scheduling crime, Western and adventure stories containing significant violence only after 9 P.M.

¶Permanent Federal financing for the Public Broadcast Corporation, to enable it to offer high-quality alternatives to violent programs for children.

¶Intensified research by the networks into the impact of television violence.

"Violence on television," the final draft asserts, "encourages violent forms of behavior and fosters moral and social values about violence in daily life which are unacceptable in a civilized society."

Many children and teen-agers can emulate the patterns displayed by parents, schools and other social institutions. But for many poor children,

"in the absence of family, peer and school relationships, television becomes the most compatible substitute for real life experiences," the draft report says, adding that: world which most children get from television drama is by and large an unwholesome one."

The television report, which is to be part of the commission's final report, may be issued separately. It will be based on, but will not necessarily endorse, a much longer and more detailed report to the commission by a study group.

That study began a year ago, and the report is now awaiting publication by the Government Printing Office. The television work was directed by Dr. Sandra Ball of the University of Michigan.

Another report of the same study group, as yet unpublished, deals with the news, rather than the entertainment, functions of television and the press. Two other study group reports also remain to be issued—one dealing with assassinations and the other with law enforcement.

The commission has already issued three study group reports dealing with group violence, firearms and the history of violence, and four special reports, including the controversial Walker Report on the 1968 Democratic National Convention in Chicago.

September 18, 1969

The violent Bugs Bunny et al.

By JOHN F. McDERMOTT

TODAY'S parents who are worried about the violence on children's television programs might rest a little easier if they would look back for a moment. Our parents went through the same bit a generation ago when we seemed to be completely beguiled by comic books. And most of us turned out to be solid citizens. Our parents were also subjected to the same conflicting advice and theories. Fortunately, in the span of a generation we have learned a number of things about ourselves and our reactions to violence that may clarify some of the conflicts in our thinking about the subject.

TV violence is said to corrupt morals and encourage violent behavior in children. It is also said to provide a vicarious outlet for aggressive feelings, something fervently to be desired. No wonder parents are confused.

The fact is that it can do either or both depending on the circumstances. Aggressive and violent thoughts *do* exist in the mind of the child. Television *does* influence these thoughts and the way they are expressed. It also provides an experience that is the basis for much of children's play, especially group play. Youngsters often turn the TV experience into action. Emotionally healthy children keep the actual violence at an imaginary level, however, when they are playing out the story.

We have seen instances where a youngster who is not allowed to watch a certain program that all his schoolmates follow is turned into a "social isolate" because he is unable to talk about or engage in play based on the program. Many parents who dislike certain programs still let their youngsters watch them for just this reason.

Many of us tend to let our adult prejudices and perceptions cloud our thinking on TV violence. It is more important to examine the

John F. McDermott, M.D., is chairman of the department of psychiatry at the University of Hawaii School of Medicine.

differing perceptions that young children and adults have of the same experience than it is to argue whether certain television programs are good or bad for children. Too frequently, we make judgments concerning our children and television because a program has upset *us.* Adults have become much more sensitive about children and television because of the tragic events of the recent past—assassinations, riots, war. They puzzle us and deeply trouble us. What many parents do not realize is that these events are just as upsetting for young children as they are for us, possibly more so, because they are on live television showing real adults losing control of themselves.

Most parents do not actually watch their children's programs.

They overhear or glimpse fragments. TV thus offers a convenient scapegoat when we need to find a reason why our little angels are fighting or acting up. We may also need to fight against our own secret enjoyment of violence and our guilty conscience over it. After all, the deluge of Western shoot-'em-ups in the fifties was mostly watched by adults. Batman and Superman are old friends of ours from childhood and their revivals were initially enjoyed immensely by adult audiences. They, of course, did not make us killers. But we have no difficulty in deciding that the new television mythology and folklore—for example, the outer-space programs —should be condemned. Yet these third-rate modern-day fairy tales are only technologically advanced versions of the old-fashioned tales of giants and witches who devoured and destroyed people themselves—without benefit of scientific gadgets.

THE problem has been that we tend to judge TV from our own standpoint, rather than the child's. Sit down sometime and watch television with your pre-school child. Observe him,

Scenes like this one—of A.B.C.'s Spiderman being given a hard time by Vultureman — could be harmful or they could be "vicarious outlets for aggressive feelings, much to be desired."

after he has gotten over the shock of your interest, and ask him to explain the television program to you. You may notice that the dialogue on many of the programs is way over his head, more oriented toward adult minds. He may ignore the actual story, and instead focus on the pictorial action upon which he superimposes his own experience and interpretations. When several children watch the same program, they often see parts of the story differently and argue about who is right about what is going on. Often a youngster sees mainly what appeals to him at his particular developmental stage. Thus some may act withdrawn and hypnotized while others are restless or perhaps even acting up during the same episode.

IF you have been pleased because of the newspaper reports that parental pressure has forced changes in the Saturday morning viewing for young children, then I suggest that you watch the "improvements." The Saturday morning programs are indeed slowly changing from programs developed around the semi-human space monsters repugnant to adults. But these bizarre animals and people, atomic guns and radioactive destructive devices usually appealed more to older children anyway. Pre-schoolers preferred the simpler themes of cartoons. Now the familiar animal cartoons are back. They are considered healthy, perhaps because the figures don't look so much like us, so that we adults can relax and enjoy them. The form of aggression has changed, perhaps, but hardly the amount. Bugs Bunny is still the model of a lazy, irresponsible, selfish individual who outwits and frustrates the serious purposes of the adult world. The action enters on a repetitive chase. Bugs and his adversaries, alternately destroy and are destroyed by each other, but bounce back quickly. They are inevitably flattened and squashed into paper-thin images, burned, shot, stabbed, blown up, drowned, and have their bodies distorted and changed in a variety of ways. A favorite is falling from or being exploded to great heights. We laugh and tolerate this because it is all in fun, impulsive and not carefully planned, and, of course, it's "only animals. Yet animals are much closer to people in the minds of children. They often secretly represent their own inner experiences. Children's stories have utilized animals for genera-

"Batman and Superman are two old friends of ours from childhood, and their revivals were initially enjoyed immensely by adult audiences. They did not make us killers. But we have no difficulty in deciding that the new television mythology is to be condemned."

tions because of this.

So Bugs Bunny has fooled the adults once again. Violence has not disappeared or even been reduced; it has simply become more acceptable to us. Adults object less to "unrealistic" forms of violence like the kind of body changes that the Bugs Bunny characters go through (always quickly restored to their oroginal shape) as these seem to us to have no possibility of fulfillment. We can laugh at them. It is only when characters and their forms of violence begin to resemble human form and behavior that we are bothered. The behavior and motives of cartoon animals, however, are much closer to the inner life of the child. In fact, when small children see animals facing experiences that resemble too closely their own experiences it can be extremely upsetting even though there may be less actual violence displayed. In fact, such programs are usually considered "good, wholesome" shows. Lassie, a program generally approved of by parents of small children, is on just before bedtime. Animals and human family members are very much involved with each other, in this program and routinely experience

series of injuries or near-injuries. If a particular episode is divided into two parts, part one may end with Lassie about to be killed. Parents may then wonder why their youngster can't sleep that that night. They may not realize that he has been left at bedtime like Lassie, alone and in terrible danger with no solution for another week.

On one psychiatric ward the hardened delinquent abolescent boys would not watch Lassie. We members of the staff assumed that it was because it was a "baby" program until the boys corrected us and told us that it was too "scary" for them. On the same ward, the girls became intrigued with an afternoon soap opera called "Dark Shadows." Each afternoon they were spellbound by this program with its plots and counterplots, threats of intrigue, death by poisoning or at the fangs of vampires. After an active debate among the staff of the effect of this program on the girls, it was decided to study their reacations during and after watching it before deciding whether or not to forbid the program. However, before any direct evidence of adverse effect on the children or their behavior was found, the staff turned off the program and terminated the study, because the program was so repellent to them.

WHILE some programs may prevent resolution of very young children's fears of injury and death by making them too real, others, with all their violence which is done, redone, and then undone, not only may be less disturbing but also may help them outgrow their fears. For instance, the themes of cartoon violence fit more with the pre-school child's understanding, both intellectual and emotional, of death, which is quite different from our understanding. At that age the youngster has a heightened fear of being hurt, hence his enjoyment of the repetitive themes in cartoons which help him laugh at this fear. He sees death as reversible and this, too, fits in with the cartoon theme. When he is 7 or 8 years old he will lose some interest in these programs because his concepts change and approach ours more closely. He begins to view death as final—and something from which he is not immune. We see small youngsters playing and toying with death every day in their games. The angry small child who says, "I wish you were dead," really means, "I wish you would go away because you bother me and I can't cope with you in actuality." This sharp difference in the conception of death between adults and children is very much evident these days when children play with toy guns. They are surprised when adults say, "Don't ever point your gun at me or anyone else." The youngster knows that the gun play was not real, only pretend, and is startled when adults take seriously his magical power as if he and his gun have real potential for killing.

Superman and Batman, with their daily diet of violence, always occurring at the same point in the program and in the same way, illustrated with fireworks and labels, "Zap, Pow," etc., can become so predictable and routine to children that after a while they become boring. Television westerns with the barroom brawl and showdown on the main street are also so easily anticipated as to be routine. On the other hand, a television "special" or "good" children's movie, classics such as Snow White or Hansel and Gretel, can be terrifying to the same child because he is not used to that form

and expression of the violence. Perhaps we should be more concerned that the daily diet of violence may produce children who are immune, callous and indifferent rather than children who want to emulate it.

THERE are other themes within these programs that may appeal to some children more than we suspect. The fact that Bugs Bunny outwits adult-like figures may provide his real appeal for children. Superman, Batman, and their newer version, Spiderman, all have two identities: one that is very harmless, almost foolish, and "childlike," in the real world. The other, unknown to the outside world, is one of limitless power, strength, scientific intelligence and tricks. Children like to imagine what it would be like to have the ability to unleash this secret power whenever necessary. It helps them deny the helpless position they often find themselves in. Other themes commonly encountered are children rescuing adults in trouble, little people versus big people, protection of one's own group from unknown outside dangers of "other worlds," etc. The violence may be incidental to these themes in importance, although we are likely to react to the violence as it is more obvious to the casual viewer—i.e., the adult, as opposed to the child who is absorbed in other aspects of the story.

If you take the time to watch your children's programs for a few days, you may find yourself becoming more annoyed at the commercials than at the programs. The seductive commercials about food just before a youngster's dinner time are inevitably more attractive than the dinner awaiting him. Commercials are supposed to be "true," and to be believed. The TV programs they surround are "pretend." Yet the commercials advertise shoes that will "run faster and jump farther" than their competitors and cereals that will bestow "superpower." A TV child who refuses to drink his milk at mealtime finds it magically transformed into a candy bar which is supposed to be its exact equivalent nutritionally. His mother marvels at this and suggests that this candy bar substitute for his milk thereafter.

Children remember, repeat and sing these commercials for days and weeks. They are much more firmly imprinted on their minds than the content of the program.

Compare the amount of excitement and activity children show during the commercials to that during the actual program itself. They are likely to be much more active during the commercials, shouting insistently that their parents get them something that is advertised.

NATURALLY the child's own life experience will shape the way in which he is influenced by a television show. If violent or bizarre programs are interwoven into a good mixture of life events and experience, and thus do not become a "life" in themselves, they will be less influential than for the child in whom they assume special significance. The most important people in children's lives are their parents, not television actors. Children who see or experience aggressively violent behavior in their own parents are most likely to be aggressive in their own relationships.

Children will also identify with TV characters to the extent that their parents are unavailable. When a mother uses TV as a babysitter and leaves her 2 year old in front of the set for most of the day, the child may very likely find television actors to be the only models to imitate in his vacuum-life.

Youngsters from families in which violence is commonly experienced will see television violence as representing the world as it really is rather than as a fantasy world that is detached from their own experience. The youngster who has been deprived of and isolated from a variety of stimulating and satisfying experiences may view the violent world of television as representing the way things really are on the "outside." All this accords with the report this month of the National Commission on the Causes and Prevention of Violence, which found that TV violence encourages violence, particularly among children of poor, disorganized families.

Furthermore, a certain type of show may produce very different reactions in children from different socio-economic levels. The child from a disadvantaged lower class family may have much greater violent feelings aroused in him by a pleasant 'family type" show with warm, close relationships in a spacious happy home in a middle class neighborhood than he would from a program involving outer space monsters killing each other. And for him, Bruce

Wayne, alias Batman, is no amusing pedantic fop; he is "whitey," with too much of everything in life.

Parents have the responsibility to know what their children are watching and to balance their day, to keep the children interested in other things. Parents' interest in the television programs their children watch and their "censorship" of these reflect the level of their own interest in their children. For most children, individual judgments must be made as to whether a particular program allows aggressive feelings to remain in and perhaps be drained off in fantasy, or whether it only builds up excitement without providing discharge and thus it spills over into his behavior.

But certain youngsters must be even more carefully considered. TV may indeed suggest patterns of behavior as outlets for anger in youngsters who are already angry with others. A few children seem to fuse with characters on television and actually "become" those characters, unable to pull themselves out of the shoes of the character when the program is over. Thus, for some children with their own problems of behavior, certain programs must be limited: just as a diabetic child may not eat sweets while others may, some children have a deficient mechanism for handling television's violent ingredients which other youngsters can manage without difficulty.

IT is wise for the parents to re-examine their children's TV diet but to examine it with *them* and observe their reactions Television specials which can be anticipated for several days and for which interest, curiosity and excitement can be built up, are often good vehicles for this interaction between parents and child. A parent who talks to his youngster about such a special will see that his interest, curiosity, and excitement action over this "special event" is responsible for most of the emotion he shows, regardless of how exciting or disappointing the show might turn out to be. ∎

September 28, 1969

Survey Faults Children's TV in U.S.

By GEORGE GENT

A survey of children's programs in 16 countries shows that the United States is the only major country that does not have network programs for children on weekday afternoons.

The survey also shows that American network programs for children are marked by a high degree of commercialization and a low level of informational content compared with other countries.

The survey was sponsored by the National Citizens Committee for Broadcasting, a non-profit group that seeks to upgrade broadcasting. It was released yesterday at a news conference at the Biltmore Hotel.

At the same time, Thomas P. F. Hoving, the group's chairman, announced that a petition urging the upgrading of children's programing had been submitted to the Federal Communications Commission. The petition, which bore 8,300 signatures as well as those of organizations representing 32 million members, was the committee's response to an F.C.C. notice of inquiry of last January.

Age Division Asked

The petition urged a minimum of 14 hours of children's programing a week on all television stations, divided into at least two hours a day, and particularly in the after school and early evening hours. It asked that programs be provided for children in the 6 to 9 and 10 to 12 age groups, as well as for those in the preschool years.

The petition said that at least 50 per cent of such programing should be more than pure entertainment, that there should be no commercial interruptions and, in no case more than two commercial breaks an hour.

The survey, which was written and researched by David Fleiss, a political scientist, and Lillian Ambrosino, a writer and founding member of Action for Children's Television, is believed to be the first comparative study of American programing and foreign countries with similar network structures and highly developed broadcast technologies.

The countries studied were Austria, Australia, Canada, Denmark, Finland, France, Britain, Ireland, Italy, Japan, the Netherlands, Norway, Sweden, Switzerland, the United States and West Germany.

Among the key findings were:

¶American network television is alone in allowing more commercials on children's programs than on adult evening television programs.

¶Twice as much advertising is allowed on children's programs on American networks as on any other country surveyed. In this country, 16 minutes an hour are permitted (12 network and four local minutes) on children's show, while the maximum in other countries surveyed is 8 minutes.

¶The United States is only one of five countries out of the 16 surveyed that permits advertising on children's programs. The others are Japan, Canada, Australia and Britain. Eleven of the 16 do not permit advertising on children's shows, while seven of those do permit advertising on adult shows.

¶The American television programs tend to be for the entire range from 2 to 12 years, while other nations aim at more specified age groups.

Mr. Hoving said that the publicity being given to the networks' plans for more informational shows for children next season was "overblowing" the significance of the actual changes in prospect.

"We will still be only catching up with the rest of the world," he said, "and there will be no real change as long as there are no weekday afternoon network programs and as long as 16 minutes per hour of advertising are permitted."

July 2, 1971

Federal Study Says TV Can Make Youths More Violent

By BOYCE RENSBERGER
Special to The New York Times

WASHINGTON, Sept. 3 — Violence in television programs can lead children who watch the programs to become more violent in their behavior, a team of psychologists sponsored by the office of the Surgeon General of the Public Health Service has found.

The findings will become part of evidence on which an official report by the Surgeon General's Advisory Committee on Television and Social Behavior will be made later this year. The psychologists' report, one of four prepared for presentation tomorrow at the annual meeting of the American Psychological Association, concludes:

"At least under some circumstances, repeated exposure to televised aggression can lead children to accept what they have seen as a partial guide for their own actions. As a result, the present entertainment offerings of the television medium may be contributing, in some measure, to the aggressive behavior of many normal children. Such an effect has now been shown in a wide variety of situations."

Contention Discounted

The study was conducted by Dr. Robert M. Liebert of the State University of New York at Stony Brook, L. I., and Dr. Robert A. Baron of Purdue University. Both men are research psychologists.

The contention that televised violence may stimulate children to aggressive behavior has been repeatedly discounted by the television industry. It has been suggested by industry spokesmen that, instead of stimulating violence, television programs may reduce it by providing a cathartic experience. The new study appears to weaken that contention.

Dr. Liebert and Dr. Baron say that there can be little remaining doubt of the effects of televised violence. Of 18 situations studied, they said, 16 support the belief that "viewing aggression can instigate subsequent aggression among observers."

In one test, which the researchers themselves conducted, groups of school children were shown episodes from "The Untouchables," an old television series with a substantial amount of cops-and-robbers-style violence, and then exposed to opportunities to help or hurt a child playing in another room. Children shown the television program were found more likely to hurt their peers and hurt them more intensely than were children of the same age who were shown a highly active but nonaggressive sports event.

Public Debate Sought

"The findings," the psychologists report, "appear to warrant formally advancing some tentative conclusions into the arena of public debate."

Dr. Eli A. Rubinstein, an assistant director of the National Institute of Mental Health, who is coordinating the research being done for the Surgeon General's advisory committee, said today that the psychologists' study would be included with 22 others to be submitted to the 12-member committee. The studies are expected to be published later this year in a five-volume technical report.

The advisory committee, which includes several representatives of the television industry, will weigh the reports before making its official conclusions. Dr. Rubinstein said, however, that he did not expect the final conclusions to disagree with those of the psychologists.

Network Comment

A spokesman for the Columbia Broadcasting System declined to comment on the study. "We certainly don't want to comment on just one paper," he said. "We'll wait for the final report."

A spokesman for the American Broadcasting Company refused to respond, saying: "There have been many studies and we don't want to talk about this one until we've had a chance to see it."

Officials of the National Broadcasting Company were unavailable for comment.

Other studies sponsored by the Surgeon General's office are also scheduled to be reported tomorrow.

In one, a team of journalism researchers from the University of California, Los Angeles, reported that, compared with children of 10 years ago, today's youngsters are watching substantially more television each day, although the amount of viewing time declines markedly as the child grows into adolescence.

Weak Parental Control

The researchers, Dr. Jack Lyle and Heidi R. Hoffman, also found that most of the programs watched by children were not specifically produced as children's programs but, rather, were shows aimed at adults or a family audience. They also report that, of most families studied, parental control over a child's television fare is weak, particularly for children over 6 years of age.

Another study, from Bradley S. Greenberg and Thomas F. Gordon of the department of communication of Michigan State University, concluded that the way in which a child regards the violence he sees on television is influenced by his socio-economic level.

According to this study, children from poor homes, when shown violent television scenes and later questioned, rated the violence level much lower than did middle-class children shown the same scenes. Boys from lower-class neighborhoods found violent scenes to be more "real-istic" than similar scenes without violence.

Still another study examines various forms of parental control on television viewing.

Two researchers found that children who view the most violent programs tend to come from homes where the parents are highly protective of the child, frequently insulating the child from ideas different from the family norm.

By contrast, the findings showed, children who are least violent in their personal behavior and who view the least amount of televised violence tend to come from homes where the children are relatively free of social constraints and are encouraged to explore new things on their own.

The researchers, Stephen H. Chaffee and Jack M. McLeod of the Mass Communications Research Center at the University of Wisconsin, suggest that improved methods of controlling actual violent behavior might be developed. They support the idea of attempting to interpret televised violence and to explain its psychological and social sources so that children may come to understand violent behavior without emulating it.

September 4, 1971

Violence in Children's Literature Eyed

Special to The New York Times

NEW HAVEN, Oct. 31—The fantasies of princes, fairies and beanstalks in children's literature often hide the harsh realities of broken heads and mutilated bodies. In a colloquium on children's literature at Yale University today, a distinguished panel of writers, illustrators and critics found that the fairy tale confronts real problems, such as violence, but at the same time avoids the shock of adult literature or television.

The panelists included the noted children's author and illustrator Maurice Sendak: Lore Segal, author and creative writing teacher at Columbia University; John Stone, producer of "Sesame Street," and Michael DiCapua, children's editor.

Mr. DiCapua noted that children's literature as an art form did not work on the same scale as adult literature. "Children are not miniature adults," he said. "They are to be given as much of the world as they can absorb."

Mrs. Segal opened today's session on "Violence and Death in Children's Literature" by reading "The Juniper Tree," a Grimms fairy tale in which a mother chops off her stepson's head, cuts him up, and feeds him to his real father. Unlike adult literary violence, the panelists pointed out, the fantasy of "The Juniper Tree" realizes the harshness of death but allows a loophole for children to escape.

"Children's literature often makes the assumption that children have violent feelings," said Mr. Sendak, who has illustrated and written dozens of children's books. "One has to be honest to a child and tell him what he already knows."

Mr. Stone, who labeled himself a descendant of the "Captain Kangaroo school" ("We deny that violence is there at all"), said he had tried to work out a compromise in "Sesame Street."

"I think the compromise is to admit that violence exists and to try to make some message out of it, either positive or negative," he said.

November 1, 1971

TV Violence Held Unharmful to Youth

By JACK GOULD

The office of the United States Surgeon General has found that violence in television programing does not have an adverse effect on the majority of the nation's youth but may influence small groups of youngsters predisposed by many factors to aggressive behavior.

This finding was contained in a study conducted by the Surgeon General's Scientific Advisory Committee on Television and Social Behavior. The study became available yesterday in Washington, but full details were not officially disclosed.

The formal release of the study, which includes 43 separate papers, is expected in two weeks to a month but the overall conclusions of the long and controversial examination have been approved by the committee. No significant last-minute revisions are anticipated.

The complete study will be submitted to Senator John O. Pastore, Democrat of Rhode Island and chairman of the Senate Subcommittee on Communications, who had requested the study more than two years ago.

In relying on 43 studies to make up the summary, the Surgeon General's committee used a variety of methods, including the testing, in different parts of the country, of children who watched television avidly and those kept away from TV receivers. Interviews with parents, friends of the children and academicians were also part of the research process, estimated to cost $1-million or more.

Each of the studies, not all of which agreed in every detail, were written as separate reports. These, in turn, were distilled into a final summary, which was reviewed by the advisory committee.

The Surgeon General's Scientific Advisory Committee reported that the general prevalence of violence on TV as a whole remained constant between 1967 and 1969, but that the nature of the violence altered.

"Fatalities declined and the proportion of leading characters engaged in violence or killing declined," the summary, which studied daytime and nighttime network fare, said.

"The former dropped from 73 to 64 per cent; the latter from 19 to 5 per cent. The consequence is that as many violent incidents occurred in 1969 as in 1967 but a smaller proportion of characters were involved and the violence was far less lethal."

Violence in Cartoons

In the case of cartoons and comedies, however, the Surgeon General's committee will bolster complaints made against the Saturday morning fare on the networks.

"Violence increased from 1967 to 1969 in cartoons and in comedies, a category that included cartoons," the summary said. "Cartoons were the most violent type of program in these years."

A study early in 1971, embracing both cartoons and adult material, said that 3 out of 10 dramatic segments were "saturated" with violence and that 71 per cent involved at least one instance of human violence

with or without the use of weapons.

The committee noted, however, that the real question was quantitative. The summary said it had obtained limited data of a frequent if short-run tendency to respond to aggressive TV stmuli.

On the other hand, the summary continued, the effect of TV may be small compared with many other causes, such as parental attitudes or knowledge of and experience with the real violence of today's society.

The summary continued:

"First, violence depicted on television can immediately or shortly thereafter induce mimicking or copying by children. Second, under certain circumstances television can instigate an increase in aggressive acts.

"The accumulated evidence, however, does not warrant the conclusion that televised violence has a uniformly adverse effect nor the conclusion that it has an adverse effect on the majority of children."

"It cannot even be said that the majority of children in the various studies we have reviewed showed an increase in aggressive behavior in response to the violent fare to which they have been exposed."

Viewer Is Profiled

The committee drew up this profile of the viewing habits of a human being: Pre-schoolers pay full attention to the tube. By first grade, children begin to exhibit individual tastes. Sixth graders prefer situation comedies and adventures. Tenth graders prefer adventures and music and variety. At 13 years interest in TV starts to decline, not to be revived until young people marry and have their own families. After middle age, when grown children leave home, TV viewing rises again.

Dr. Jesse L. Steinfeld is the Surgeon General of the United States Public Health Service in whose name the summary and accompanying papers will be released.

Members of the advisory committee were:

Ira H. Cisin, professor of sociology, George Washington University.

Thomas E. Coffin, vice president, National Broadcasting Company.

Irving L. Janis, professor of psychology, Yale University.

Joseph T. Klapper, research director, Columbia Broadcasting System.

Harold Mendelsohn, professor of communications, University of Denver.

Eveline Omwake, professor of child development, University of Connecticut.

Charles A. Pinderhughes, associate professor of psychiatry, Tufts University.

Ithiel de Sola Pool, professor of political science, Massachusetts Institute of Technology.

Alberta E. Siegel, associate professor of psychology, Stanford University Medical School.

Anthony F. C. Wallace, professor of anthropology, University of Pennsylvania.

Andrew S. Watson, professor of psychiatry and law, University of Michigan.

Gerhart D. Wiebed, dean of communications, Boston University.

January 11, 1972

Findings on TV Violence

To the Editor:

Before the publication of the Surgeon General's Advisory Committee Report on the impact of televised violence, The Times ran a reasonable story about it with a misleading headline, "TV Violence Held Unharmful to Youth." Since then, Congressmen, editorialists, letter writers, mothers and others, whether they have read the report or not, have interpreted the report in the light of The Times' headline.

The report reaches no such conclusion. The lead finding in the topic sentence in the one paragraph summary in the report itself is that of an "indication of a causal relation between viewing violence on television and aggressive behavior."

As the text of [Jack] Gould's article explained well, the committee was at pains to distinguish between the lack of evidence of "an adverse effect on the majority of the nation's youth" and some mounting evidence of a possible effect on a minority. The

committee on which we served was fully conscious of the profound social significance of an effect on a minority amounting to possibly millions of young people. We hope that public discussion of the report can focus equally on both halves of our complex findings. ITHIEL DE SOLA POOL
IRVING L. JANIS, ALBERTA E. SIEGEL
Massachusetts Institute of Technology
Cambridge, Mass., Jan. 21, 1972

January 27, 1972

Study Aides Voice Misgivings About Report on TV Violence

By LINDA CHARLTON

In the month since the public release of the Surgeon General's report on the impact of television violence on children, a growing number of those involved have begun to air their misgivings about the report's accuracy in reflecting the research on which it was largely based.

The 279-page report, which conceded the existence of a modest link between televised violence and aggression in some "predisposed" children is being described by these critics in terms ranging from "purposeful fraud" to "misieading" and "a compromise." Senate hearings on it are scheduled for March.

It was written by an appointed 12-member group, the Surgeon - General's Scientific

Advisory Committee on Television and Social Behavior, which reviewed the research data and added its own expertise and conviction in reaching conclusions.

The data, the product of 23 studies by social scientists inquiring into whether televised violence is related to children's 'aggressive behavior," will be published in five volumes next month.

The harshest general assessments have come from such researchers as Dr. Monroe M. Lefkowitz, of the State Department of Mental Hygiene; Representative John M. Murphy, Dr. John Murray, a research coordinator for the project, and Dr. Robert Liebert of the State University at Stony

Brook, a researcher who also reviewed all the other research.

It is the report itself, "Television and Growing Up: The Impact of Televised Violence," a 19-page summary of findings and conclusions followed by nine chapters and appendices, that is being questioned and attacked. In style and substance, its critics maintain, the report tends to support the television industry's position that children are not significantly affected. This, they say, is clearly contradicted by evidence demonstrating a stronger link.

The committee "tentatively" concluded "that there is a modest relationship between exposure to television violence and aggressive behavior or tendencies." It cautioned: "It must be emphasized that the causal sequence is very likely applicable only to some children who are predisposed in this direction" and the indications of cause-and-effect were "preliminary and tentative."

In an effort to uncover the

roots of the controversy, The New York Times interviewed more than a dozen people involved with the project.

Many of the ritics see it as no coincidence that the television industry was given veto power over proposed members of the advisory committee.

This right led to the vetoing of seven of the 40 names proposed—including several of the best-known specialists in the field of children and television who had previously done work that they said tended to illustrate the harmful potential of televised violence. The committee itself, in the report, was critical of the selection method.

Of the twelve committee members five had links with the television industry. Two are full-time executives of networks; two others serve as consultants, and another has done so.

Some particularly embittered critics make much of the fact that Richard A. Moore, who has had a long career in television, served as liaison with the committee for Robert H. Finch, then the Secretary of Health, Education and Welfare.

Mr. Moore, a close associate of President Nixon and now on the White House staff, said yesterday that he was "only lightly involved for a fairly short time" early in the project.

Dr. Jesse Steinfeld, the Surgeon General of the United States Public Health Service, was out of the country this week and could not be reached for comment on the criticism. He has already implicitly acknowledged that it exists by saying at a news conference that he did not feel the report was a "whitewash."

Aside from those involved with the $1-million project—the researchers, staff members of the National Institutes of Mental Health, which was responsible for implementing and administering the project, and members of the committee — perhaps the most outspoken criticism has come from Representative Murphy.

Mr. Murphy, a Staten Island Democrat, has railed in the House against "the shabby machinations of the TV moguls on the latest study," has recalled the findings of previous studies, including the National Commission on the Causes and Prevention of Violence, and reintroduced legislation asking that a new study be made by the Federal Communications Commission.

Carl Perian, Mr. Murphy's legislation assistant, and the staff director of the 1964 Senate subcommittee that did an abortive study of the same subject, said that the Congressman had reached his judgment after going over the research data himself and talking with many of those involved.

Mr. Perian said:

"It isn't a question of opinion or even judgment, it's a matter of looking at the documents, and concluding that, yes, indeed, the Surgeon General's report is misleading."

Considering "the involvement of the TV industry," he declared neither he nor Mr. Murphy has any doubt "that the report is a fraud—purposeful fraud."

Senator John O. Pastore, chairman of the Senate Communications Subcommittee and the man, at whose request, in 1969, the study was undertaken, plans to hold public hearings starting March 21 to explore what he called the report's "tentative and limited conclusion."

The 19-page summary was the best-read part of the report, and the best-reported. This has led to criticism by such persons as Dr. Steven Chaffee of the press's handling of the report—including what they say was an inaccurate headline in The New York Times, "TV Violence Held Unharmful to Youth."

Dr. Chaffee, a psychologist at the University of Wisconsin, was one of the research scientists and also wrote one of the "overviews"—that is, reviews of data supplied by the other studies—submitted to the committee.

Dr. Ira Rubinstein, vice chairman of the Surgeon General's committee and the over-all administrator of the project, said in an interview that he, too, felt the report had been misinterpreted in part because,although intended for the public, it was written in "social-science language." He called it a "reasonably good report . . . albeit conservatively stated."

He also contended that a stronger statement about a causal link between aggression and TV violence might have done harm rather than good, might be "dysfunctional." He pointed to data showing that previous criticism of violence in children's television programs had resulted in less lethal violence but more "sanitized violence"—that is, fewer people are killed, but there are more violent acts. And violence shorn of its ultimate effect, he suggested, might be even more harmful.

Dr. Rubinstein and many others stressed that the document was a compromise, a committee paper.

"There was a big move to get a consensus report," said Dr. Murray of the National Institutes of Mental Health, a research coordinator. "There was a lot of anger, the meetings were extremely tense," he went on, with the warring factions "sitting at either end of the table, glaring at each other,

particularly toward the end."

The report as finally released, Dr. Murray said, gives "the over-all impression . . . that the findings are trivial." Dr. Murray, who has also read all the data, said this impression was "absolutely wrong."

The first draft of the report was written by staff members, and then rewritten by the committee. "The report as initially drafted," Dr. Murray said, "was, I think, much clearer," before "everyone began tacking on their own caveats to the sentences."

There was, he said, some sentiment in favor of having at least two reports issued, but the sentiment for consensus was stronger. "Looking back, I personally am sorry," he said.

"A mass of equivocations" was the way Douglas Fuchs described the report in an interview. Mr. Fuchs served as senior research coordinator on the project until June, 1970, when, learning that his contract would not be renewed, he resigned. He had said publicly that the study's "scientific independence" had been "subverted to some kind of political consideration."

Among the most outspoken critics of the report have been three researchers based at the State University of New York at Stony Brook, L.I.: Dr. Liebert, Dr. John Neale and Emily Davidson. Dr. Liebert also wrote one of the overview papers.

The recent studies, as well as research done in the past, Dr. Liebert said, "quite clearly" demonstrate "that watching violence in a television context can instigate aggressive behavior in children."

None of the studies, he conceded, suggest that it is the only cause, or even the prime cause; but it is, he said, "changeable"—that is, it is one cause of such behavior that can be altered far more easily than a family's emotional climate or economic status or a child's genes.

"We don't want to take the baby-sitter away," he said, "we just want to stop her from committing murder in the living room." As for the report's as-

sertion that only a "modest" relationship has been established, Dr. Liebert contended that research showed only a small number of cigarette smokers — "some" cigarette smokers with a predisposition to malignancy—develop lung cancer. "A modest relationship is clearly enough to take action," he declared.

However, according to several persons close to those who wrote the report, the possibility that a strong indictment of televised violence might prompt some remedial action by the Government was one element in the decision to hammer out the "compromise" report.

One of the committee members, Dr. Alberta E. Siegel of Stanford University, agreed that this fear of Government moves toward control or censorship of the media was present, adding: "And the statements that Vice President Agnew has made make that into a real threat."

Dr. Siegel said that while the report was "very cautious and conservative," it was significant that there was unanimous agreement on a report that stated watching TV violence caused aggressive behavior.

Criticizes the Press

She said she was "very disappointed" with the way in which the press and public had failed to discern that "hidden in all that obfuscation are some positive statements," although she said, "A stronger statement could have been made in light of the evidence."

Several other members of the committee have also said that they felt that the committee's report was really stronger than it seems. A careful reading with a trained social scientist, one of those involved with the research, turned up a number of statements that support this view.

One example might be the repetition of the statement "there is evidence that a modest relationship does exist between the viewing of violence and aggressive behavior"—in which according to social science parlance, modest does not mean insignificant or trivial.

February 19, 1972

Ban on Sugary-Cereal TV Ads Urged

By RICHARD D. LYONS
Special to The New York Times

WASHINGTON, March 5—Warning that sugary breakfast cereals harm children's diets and teeth, nutrition and dental experts urged Congress today to ban children-oriented television ads for the products, and food makers reacted by boycotting the Senate hearings.

During the opening of five days of hearings before the Senate Select Committee on Nutrition and Human Needs investigating the television advertising of food for children, four witnesses testified that many children's breakfast cereals were nutritionally "hollow," containing over 50 per cent sugar; children were exercising "unconscious blackmail," forcing parents to buy the foods; both old and young Americans were on a sugar binge, eating more of it annually than flour and that increased sugar con-

sumption from breakfast cereals, soft drinks, chewing gum, candy and other snack goods had caused an epidemic of tooth decay and fostered other diseases.

Prominently displayed at the hearing room was a table with boxes of 30 breakfast cereals having such names as Cap'n Crunch, Crispy Critters, Frosted Rice Krinkles, Apple Jacks, Kaboom, Sweet Wheats, Great Honey Crunches and Super Sugar Crisps.

Many of the boxes, whose labels identified sugar as the principal single ingredient, contained ads for toys such as dolls, balloons, helicopter models, magic kits, circus patches, robots, monster cutouts and something called a "kanga-zoom."

The witnesses noted that the average child, who sees several thousand food commercials on television yearly, was not the best judge of what is good for his health, and that ads aimed at children who are 6 years old or under should be prohibited.

"I don't think it's asking too much of the mothers of the nation to get up 10 minutes earlier to make hot cereal rather than feed these sugar-coated nothings to their children," said Dr. Jean Mayer, a professor of nutrition at Harvard.

During the hearing the committee chairman, Senator George McGovern, Democrat of South Dakota, announced that eight leading executives of food producers and their advertising agencies, who had been scheduled to testify at Wednesday's hearing, had declined to appear as witnesses.

Both Senator McGovern and Senator Charles H. Percy, Republican of Illinois, denied reports that the hearings had been "rigged" against the cereal makers and advertisers and in favor of their critics.

Senator Percy, noting that the

hearing opened at the start of "American Nutrition Week," insisted that the committee members "are not prejudging any industry" and that the investigation was held to find out what is going on in the food industry.

Dr. Mayer, who was chairman of the White House Conference on Food, Nutrition and Health, said "many children's food advertisements are nothing short of national disaster."

"Small children would be better off if they did not see TV ads," he said, because commercials have equated "goodness with sweetness," a notion that is reinforced through advertising and is difficult to change past the age of 6.

Dr. Mayer said each year the average American eats slightly over 100 pounds of flour, but also consumes about 115 pounds of sugar and corn syrup.

The statistics prompted Senator Percy to comment that "the sugar lobby is almost as good as the highway lobby in Washington."

But Mr. Meyer said there was evidence that the switch in sugar-rich and snack foods may be causing nutritional deficiencies of such necessary trace elements as chromium and zinc.

The remaining witnesses, three dental researchers, seconded Dr. Mayer's call for a halt to cereal ads aimed at children and called tooth decay the country's most widespread health problem.

"If all the 100,000 dentists in the United States restored decayed teeth day and night, 365 days a year, as many new cavities would have formed at the end of the year as were just restored during the previous year," said Mr. Abraham E. Nizel of the Tufts University

School of Dental Medicine in Boston.

Dr. Nizel said the frequency of eating sugary foods, such as chewing gum and candy, contributed as much to tooth decay as the amount of sugar consumed. He also said that during the nineteen-sixties food producers had increased the use of sugar in their products by 50 per cent.

The other witnesses were Dr. Juan Navia of the Institute of Dental Research at the University of Alabama and Dr. James H. Shaw, a professor of Nutrition at Harvard. Dr. Shaw said that new studies at Harvard found that the feeding of sugar-coated cereals to animals had increased their tooth decay.

March 6, 1973

Survey Finds 82% of Mothers Endorse TV Fare for Children

By LES BROWN

A survey of attitudes toward children's television, commissioned by the Association of National Advertisers, a service organization and sometime lobby for major users of advertising, has concluded that mothers with children between the ages of 2 and 20 overwhelmingly approve of television and consider its programs beneficial to their children.

Of the 442 respondents in the survey, which was conducted nationally by telephone by the consumer research division of the A.C. Nielsen Company, 82 per cent called television's effect on children positive while only 9 per cent rated it negative. The remainder offered no opinion.

According to a spokesman for the association, the results will be submitted to the Federal Trade Commission and the Federal Communications Commission in rebuttal to arguments put forth by various consumer and parent groups that have been pressing for reforms in television programs and advertising directed at children.

Guidelines Considered

Both agencies are considering issuing policies and guidelines in the children's area. The F.T.C. has already proposed a specific guideline that would ban the advertising of premiums to children and has set a Monday deadline for replies from the industry. The F.C.C., meanwhile, has indicated it would act this fall on the question of whether it was necessary to adopt a policy for children's broadcasting.

Such consumer organizations as Action for Children's Television and the Council on Children, Media and Merchandising have urged the agencies to ban all advertising in children's programs.

In the survey, the mothers interviewed were considerably less sanguine about television commercials than they were about the effects of TV in general. On the question of whether it was of benefit to children to acquaint them with products through commercials, 41 per cent of the respondents felt it was beneficial while 43 per cent answered that it was not.

A similar Nielsen survey had been commissioned by the advertising association in 1971 and was introduced, at that time, into the public record of the F.T.C.'s hearing on advertising practices. The data for the latest survey had been gathered from March 30 to April 1.

"The surprising revelation of the two surveys is that the over-all attitude hasn't changed," said Sam Thurm, the association's Washington executive vice president. "There has been virtually no change in three years, in spite of all the publicity given to the views of the consumer critics of children's television."

Doubts Raised

In the 1971 survey, 80 per cent of the mothers interviewed rated television's effect on children good and 6 per cent called it bad. Mr. Thurm said there was an equally close comparison in the two surveys in the responses to questions relating to commercials.

Mr. Thurm contended that the surveys raise doubts about whether the critics are correct in their assumption that they are speaking for all housewives and mothers. He said it was clear that they represented "a public" and not "the public."

Representatives of the consumer groups expressed skepticism about the validity of the

surveys and challenged Mr. Thurm's conclusions.

Peggy Charren, president of Action for Children's Television, called the survey "meaningless" if it defined children as between the ages of 2 to 20 when the broadcast industry's own definition has always been "under 12 years old." The programs and commercials the consumer-action groups were concerned with are those on Saturday mornings, which are usually not watched by persons over 12.

"It's to be expected that parents would say television is good. If they really felt television was bad for their children, over-all, they wouldn't have a set in their homes. You can assume that, without talking a survey," Mrs. Charren said.

She added that much of the favorable response in the surveys may well have been for children's programs on public television, which do not carry advertising.

Robert B. Choate, a leading consumer advocate in the field of television advertising, stated that not to have popular support does not invalidate the consumers' concerns. "Wrong is wrong, whether or not the majority of people is aware of it," he said.

September 5, 1974

F.C.C. Approves Policy on Children's TV

By DAVID BURNHAM
Special to The New York Times

WASHINGTON, Oct. 24—The Federal Communications Commission gave final approval today to a policy statement that all television stations must provide a reasonable amount of

programing for children and that a significant part of it should be educational.

The 37-page policy statement also said that broadcasters should provide for the viewing needs of the preschool child, that children's programing

should not be shown only on weekends and that television hosts should not serve as salesmen.

While approving the general policy statement, the commission rejected the request of Action for Children's Televi-

sion, a consumer group, that it adopt specific rules banning advertisements on children's programs and requiring specific amounts of programing at specific times.

Concerning advertising, the commission accepted the code recently worked out by the National Association of Broadcasters under which advertising on weekend children's programs would drop from 12 minutes an hour to 9 minutes and 30 seconds an hour on Jan. 1, 1976. This is the same level of advertising now permitted by the code on prime-time television.

The policy statement results from an inquiry into children's television and advertising begun by the commission in January, 1971, at the request of Action for Children's Television, which is based in Boston.

According to the commission, the proceedings prompted an "overwhelming" response, with more than 100,000 citizens expressing their opinions about children's television.

The commission defended its decision not to impose specific rules as consistent with its historic and court-sanctioned role of imposing only general affirmative duties on broadcasters in return for their right to use the public airwaves.

"We believe this traditional approach is, in most cases, an appropriate response to our obligation to assure programing service in the public interest and, at the same time, avoid excessive governmental interference with specific program decisions," the commission said.

Critics of the commission have expressed disappointment with its decision not to issue specific rules. Some lawyers familiar with F.C.C. procedures, however, believe the policy statement will strengthen the hand of citizens' groups in influencing the broadcast patterns of individual stations which must renew their licenses every three years.

"One of the questions to be resolved here is whether broadcasters have a special obligation to serve children," the commision statement said. "We believe they clearly do have such a responsibility."

The commission said it therefore expected television broadcasters, as trustees of a valuable resource, to develop and present programs to serve the needs of children.

The statement said it was "not enough, however, to state that children have a right to programing particularly designed for them. Children, like adults, have a variety of needs and interests that cannot be fully served by programing which provides entertainment and nothing more."

"While we are convinced that television must provide programing for children, and that a reasonable part of this programing should be educational in nature, we do not believe that it is necessary for the commission to prescribe by rule the number of hours per week to be carried in each category," the F.C.C. said.

Here, as in several other parts of the policy statement, the copy available for newsmen in the commission's press office appeared to show a slight last-minute softening of the F.C.C.'s position. In the phrase concerning how much programming should be devoted to education, the word "must" had been scratched out and replaced by the word "should."

A similar deletion appeared in the statement where the commission said it had found a few stations that presented no children's programs. "We trust that this report will make it clear that such performance (or other low levels) will not be acceptable for commercial television stations which are expected to provide general program service to their communities," the original statement said.

In the policy statement in the press office the words within the parentheses had been ruled out.

The commission said that to help determine if the television stations were adhering to the advertising limits imposed by the broadcasters' code, the license renewal form would be amended to require information on how many minutes of commercials were broadcast in each hour of children's programing.

October 25, 1974

TV Designates 7-9 P.M. as 'Family Time'

By LES BROWN

The board of directors of the National Association of Broadcasters has voted overwhelmingly to adopt an amendment to the Television Code designating the period between 7 and 9 P.M. as "family viewing time."

The provision, which becomes effective next September, generally prohibits subscribing stations and networks from broadcasting "entertainment programs inappropriate for viewing by general family audiences" during the indicated hours. If occasionally a single program in a continuing series is deemed unsuitable for children, the program is to open with an advisory to that effect, which would be repeated later.

The advisory, or warning, would also accompany all promotional materials and would be suggested to newspapers and magazines carrying program listings.

The period for "family viewing time" consists of the first hour of network service in prime time and the local hour preceding it. Approximately two-thirds of the television stations in the United States subscribe to the television code, the industry's instrument for self-regulation.

Prime time begins in the East and the West at 7 P.M., and 6 P.M. in the central and mountain time zones. Therefore, the family viewing time in the last two areas will be from 6 to 8 P.M.

Stations violating the provision would be cited by the Television Code Review Board. The penalty for excessive citations would be revocation of code membership, which could affect a station's community relations and even its license renewal, an official of the broadcast association said. The vote on the amendment was taken Tuesday night in Las Vegas, where the association is holding its annual convention.

While the new amendment does not attempt to define what is suitable for family viewing, the history of the proposals leading to it has given the industry to understand what the prohibition embraces: programs involving sexual candor, gratuitous violence and subject matter considered too sophisticated or risqué for juveniles.

During the last year, several Congressional committees voiced concern over the increasing adult orientation of prime-time television and directed the Federal Communications Commission to present a plan that would protect children from the mature themes and dialogue of such programs.

Because the F.C.C. is prohibited by the Communications Act of 1934 from interfering in program content or taking action that would constitute censorship, its chairman, Richard E. Wiley, proceeded to "jawbone" the television industry for a voluntary mechanism that would assure greater discretion in programing.

Arthur R. Taylor, president of CBS Inc., last December took the first step in proposing to the broadcasting association's review board that the networks be required to present family-oriented programing before 9 P.M., when great numbers of young children might be watching television.

When the other networks made similar proposals, Mr. Wiley urged the National Association of Broadcasters, representing local stations, to include the local hour of prime time (7 to 8 P.M.) in the "family viewing" period.

Mr. Wiley called the network and station proposals "a landmark in the development of industry self-regulation."

He described the plan as creating a "reasonable balance" between the objectives of shielding children from objectionable programs and permitting television to continue to present sensitive and controversial themes for adult audiences after 9 o'clock.

Networks and stations have been left to determine in their own ways what is suitable for family viewing.

Last week, Elton H. Rule, president of the American Broadcasting Companies, Inc., gave some indication of how ABC-TV would respond when he announced that the police series "The Rookies" and the ABC "Movies of the Week" would be scheduled after 9 o'clock next season.

"The Rookies," which frequently has episodes of violence, is now on at 8 P.M. on Mondays. The "Movies of the Week," films made for television that sometimes deal with mature subjects, are carried at 8:30 on Tuesdays and Wednesdays.

In adopting the code amendment, the association's board agreed to a "grandfathering" provision designed to provide some relief for stations not affiliated with a network, although it is applicable to all stations.

The provision gives stations two years to play off "unsuitable" syndicated programs in the family viewing hours if they were purchased before April 8. In those instances, however, the stations would have to post advisories that the programs are not family fare.

April 10, 1975

Children's Fare Taking a Giant Step on Local TV

By LES BROWN

Since there is no mandatory school attendance in Mississippi and no kindergarten level in the public schools, a television station in Jackson is developing a daily half-hour program designed to prepare preschoolers for the classroom experience.

In Waterloo, Iowa, a station is planning a daily after-school show that would be entirely the work of school-aged children of the area.

A Tampa, Fla., station is working on a monthly program by and for children between the ages of 9 and 13. A broadcaster in Jacksonville, Fla., wants to incorporate cultural and informational elements in an existing daily children's show that has been moderately successful for more than five years.

Comeback Locally

Around the country, the local television show for children is making a comeback, but on wholly different terms from the early models of the nineteen-fifties and sixties, which mainly featured old animated cartoons with local personalities as hosts—Fireman Fred, Officer Dan, Jerry the Clown.

Supported by a recent Federal Communications Commission policy statement on children's television and the unrelenting cricism of consumer groups, the new activity by local stations centers on programing that promotes positive or "pro-social" values and contributes in some way to the education of children.

A conference on children's programing in Washington this week, arranged by the National Association of Broadcasters, was attended by about 170 broadcasters in quest of ideas for wholesome and culturally uplifting children's programs that will be produced on stringent local budgets.

Many showed interest, too, in the more pretentiously produced syndicated programs for children that were being promoted by distributors in the corridors of the Washington Hilton. Along with such widely praised new series in the syndication market as "Call it Macaroni" and "The Big Blue Marble" are a return of "Kukla, Fran and Ollie" and a reissue of "The Mickey Mouse Cub," Which has been sold to 130 stations.

"The F.C.C. has created a children's market for us," one syndicator said.

The agency's 1974 guidelines on children's television calls for broadcasters to devote a "reasonable" amount of time to educational programing for the child audience and to diversify the scheduling of such fare so that it is not concentrated on Saturday and Sunday mornings.

Significantly, the policy statement added the category of children's television to the areas of broadcast service it normally considers for license renewals.

Stating that the F.C.C. can neither mandate quality nor call for specific programs at specific times, Richard E. Wiley, chairman of the agency, said at the conference:

"I am challenging each of you to examine the depth and degree of your commitment to children's television. You know how well you are serving the child audience."

Mr. Wiley, saying that children make up about 20 per cent of the television audience, accused broadcasters of treating them as a "sideline" while programing primarily for older viewers.

"What this means," a broadcaster from the Middle West said, "is that we have to do something in the children's area or answer for it."

Another told of being "hounded" into producing an informational children's show by local consumer organizations.

But a few broadcasters indicated that they were responding also to their own pangs of conscience about commercial television's service to the young.

"Having children of my own," I'm as concerned about their well-being before the TV set as any other parent," said William H. Dilday, general manager of WLBT, Jackson, Miss.

Broadcasters have little expectation that the new "purposiv" children's fare will be profitable and most have resigned themselves to supporting the programs from the profits of other shows.

"We were wrong in applying the same profit standards to children's programs that we have for other shows. That's why they've disappeared from the stations," remarked James Bradley, executive vice president of Blackhawk Broadcasting in Waterloo, Iowa. "We've got to think about it differently now."

With the notable exception of General Foods, which has made good on a commitment two years ago to buy commercial spots in well-executed local programs for children, most national advertisers avoid local productions. Largely this is because local programs, as a general rule, receive lower ratings than the network or syndicated shows they may compete with, and because rating information on them is usually scarce. Ratings are taken in most markets three times a year, so that a show may be on for months before the size of its audience can be estimated.

Bob Keeshan, who for 19 years has been the CBS-TV children's star Captain Kangaroo, appealed to broadcasters at the conference to give up their competitive ways where worthwhile children's shows are concerned.

Answering to their business instincts, most stations will attempt to demolish a rival station's quality show by scheduling an exploitative program at the same time, to overwhelm it in the ratings.

"Broadcasters have to stop this practice in the interest of the young people of this country," Mr. Keeshan stated.

Peggy Charren, president of Action for Children's Television, the organization that prompted the F.C.C. inquiry that led to its policy statement, expressed her approval of the local programs screened at the conference.

"Some interesting things are happening. Local stations with small production budgets are doing better shows than the networks are on Saturday mornings," she said.

June 5, 1975

Commercials' Impact on Children

By PHILIP H. DOUGHERTY

Some supporters of advertising contend that exposure to sometimes misleading commercials helps develop consumer skills in the young. However, a recently completed research project indicates that such evidence of allowable "institutional hypocrisy" actually causes conflict in children that is possibly harmful and may permanently distort "their views of morality, society and business."

This problem with children is not among the 5 and 6 year olds who were thought to be the most threatened, but in the 7-to-10 year-old group, which "is most vulnerable to the manipulation of TV advertisers."

Interestingly enough this project was principally conducted by an adman and a psychologist—Martin L. Smith, a co-founder of the Smith/Greenland agency, and Dr. Thomas G. Bever, professor of psychology and linguistics at Columbia University.

•

Their study, done through interviews with 48 New Jersey youngsters, did not deal with any particular advertising or its effectiveness, but rather attempted to learn, in the words of Mr. Smith, "how children develop and utilize their cognitive skills to process the information they receive from TV advertising."

The children were divided into three groups, the 5 and 6 year olds, the 7-to-10 age group and the 11 and 12 year olds.

The youngest group is not badly affected because it's "insulated" and members tend to believe everything on television, including the commercials, is entertainment.

The oldest group is partially out of the woods because its members appear to have already made "certain accommodations to the adult world and its values.'

It's the middle group that is "angry because they feel forced to accept practices that they believe are immoral."

In an article due in the November-December Harvard Business Review the principals and their co-authors, Barbara Bengen of Columbia and Thomas G. Johnson of the agency, write, "The 10-year-old's anger appears to reflect the first realization that advertising is an accepted part of society. This shows him that society allows for institutional hypocrisy, a fact that violates moral precepts he has been taught as "a young child."

•

This anger of the 10 year olds as well as the tolerance of the older children, they write, "raises serious questions about the role of TV advertising in the socialization of children."

"In most cultures," they note, "adolescents have to deal with social hyprocrisy and even with institutionalized lying. But today, TV advertising is stimulating pre-adolescent children to think about socially accepted hypocrisy. They may be too young to cope with such thoughts without permanently distorting their views of morality, society and business."

Announcement of this research project was made yesterday at a news conference in the Harvard Club.

•

In his remarks Dr. Bever noted that contrary to popular thinking "our findings suggest that children are not misled by specific advertisements more often than adults."

Children, he said, "are not passively manipulated by advertisments; rather they actively attempt to figure out a place for advertising in their mental life."

But, as the Harvard Review piece asks in its conclusion, the conclusion, "How can current practice be modified to reduce the conflicts that TV advertising appears to impose on children?"

Mr. Smith, who is 50, explained that he began doing graduate work in psychology because "I was bothered by the imprecise nature of what we do on Madison Avenue. It's tough being in a business that sometimes doesn't make any sense."

October 29, 1975

The Plug-in Drug

By Marie Winn.
231 pp. New York: The Viking Press. $8.95.

By STEPHANIE HARRINGTON

In our terminal stage of stupefaction, unable even to marshal our forces to rise up against Donny and Marie, having someone tell us one more time that television is the opiate of the people is about as startling as confirmation from the White House Press Office that Jimmy Carter brushes three times a day. But would we allow ourselves to be so lulled by the comfortable familiarity of our contempt for television if we were convinced that the national addiction is responsible for not only a decline in reading and writing skills, diminished socializing experiences, hyperactivity and the fragmenting of the nuclear family, but the rise of the drug culture, the emergence of a new breed of remorseless young criminals and generations of children suffering from no less than an imbalance of the brain?

These are the components of the multiple warhead launched against the great American pacifier by Marie Winn, a writer and translator of "10 books for parents and children." Her primary focus is the effects of television on children and family life. And she argues that children's development is distorted not by the content of television shows but by "the very nature of the television experience." It doesn't matter, she contends, whether they are watching "Sesame Street" or "Popeye" or "Mod Squad."

What matters is that just at the age when they can begin to take an active role in the world, television drugs children into their previous state of infantile passivity. What matters is that before they have developed language skills, they are immersed in a world in which they are talked at, but in which they play no responsive verbal role. Before they have learned to read they are given a substitute that eliminates both the need and the time to read and discourages the kind of sus-

tained concentration necessary for reading comprehension. Before they have worked out the rituals of social behavior, they are lost in an isolate experience, one that interferes with the sort of family interaction that helps children learn to relate to other people. Before they have learned to separate reality from fantasy they are assaulted by a medium that deliberately blurs the boundaries.

These are familiar indictments. But Winn ventures further: "Just as the lungs of a chain smoker are demonstrably different from a nonsmoker's lungs, is it not possible that the brain of a 12-year-old who has spent 10,000 hours in a darkened room watching moving images on a small screen is in specific ways different from the brain of a child who has watched little or no television? Might not the television child emerge from childhood with certain left-hemisphere skills — those verbal and logical ones—less developed than the visual and spatial capabilities governed by the right hemisphere?"

To someone as equipped to refute Winn's physiological theory as to analyze the rinse cycle, the suggestion that thousands of hours of exposure to television might affect the development of the brain is not implausible. But readers might feel better about sticking with Winn through 214 pages of indirect evidence, inference and appeals to common sense if she cited just one expert or one piece of research that directly supported her hypotheses.

Not all her assumptions are as unquestionable as she seems to think. There is evidence that violence on television desensitizes children to actual violence. But not even the study referred to by Winn substantiates her claims that "six hours daily of 'The Waltons' seem just as likely to affect a child's ability to respond normally to human realities as an equal amount of 'Mod Squad' or 'Adam-12' . . ." If a child lives in a home or a neighborhood where violence is routine, isn't it possible that watching characters on television

relate to each other respectfully, gently, lovingly might help to balance that child's idea of human reality? And if program content is irrelevant, how would Winn explain the intense reaction to "Roots"?

She points to the "frightening new breed of juvenile offender" capable of committing "unspeakable crimes with a complete absence of . . . guilt or remorse." And she reasons that since poverty, family pathology, neglect and inadequate schools pre-dated this "new breed," its appearance can be accounted for only by "the great new element that has been introduced into children's lives . . . television." Television, she argues, conditions them to deal with people as if they were images on a screen that can be turned off "quite simply, with a knife or a gun or a chain . . ."

There is, however, another new element in the lives of those children who are likely candidates for criminality— the children of the poor today have less stake in American society than they did 20 years ago, while, at the same time, the *content* of television shows holds before them visions of the "good life" and violent scenarios for getting a piece of it.

The generation that came of age in the 60's, she says, was an electronically mutated right-lobe generation that, in its non-linear, disconnected thought, its nearly non-verbal speech, its flight from reason and reality into loud music and drugs, was engaged not in evolving a new spiritual realm called Consciousness III, but merely in reproducing the television-induced trance in which it passed through its childhood.

The connections she keeps finding between television and social phenomena are intriguing but her methodology is too reminiscent of the panelist who announced that since he had such a short time to speak, he would present only the conclusions on which his evidence was based. Still, until research into the effects of television prove or disprove Winn's assumptions, her book may provide just the kind of hell fire we need to rouse us from our lethargy long enough to switch off the set and force on our children the opportunity to nourish that neglected hemisphere of the brain that gave us Sid Caesar.

March 20, 1977

Stephanie Harrington has written frequently on television.

Study Finds Children's TV More Violent

Young people who watch much television are more apprehensive about their own safety and more likely to think that people are mean and selfish, according to researchers at the University of Pennsylvania's Annenberg School of Communications. They noted that violence in weekend children's television programming rose to nearly record levels on the three major networks in the fall of 1978.

The study shows strong associations between patterns of network dramatic content and conceptions of social reality among children and adolescents. It found that television cultivated an exaggerated sense of danger and mistrust in steady viewers compared with similar groups of those who watch television less frequently.

School children who watch a great deal of television are also more likely to believe that the police frequently use force and the average officer will shoot fleeing suspects.

It was noted that there were 15.6 violent incidents an hour in 1977 in children's programs, but that figure rose to 25 an hour in 1978. Dr. George Gerbner, co-principal investigator for the project, said the definition of violence used in the research project was "that of unambiguous physical violence — hurting or killing a person or the credible threat of hurting or killing."

April 23, 1979

Children's TV Is Short Of Its Goals, F.C.C. Says

By ERNEST HOLSENDOLPH

Special to The New York Times

WASHINGTON, Oct. 30 — The staff of the Federal Communications Commission reported today that television broadcasters had fallen short of commission goals for children's programming, but the commissioners hesitated to order the industry to increase the programs immediately. Instead, the commission plans to issue sometime in the next two months a variety of new proposed rules, including the most far-reaching programming requirements yet contemplated for television.

One version of the requirements

TV RATINGS

Following are the top 15 national television shows of the past week (Monday, Oct. 22, to Sunday, Oct. 28), listed according to their rank in the ratings compiled by the A.C. Nielsen Company. A rating is a percentage of the total number of United States households with television sets.

Rating	Program	Network
1 30.9	Sixty Minutes	CBS
2 30.6	One Day At A Time	CBS
3 30.2	Alice	CBS
4 29.3	Three's Company	ABC
5 27.5	The Jeffersons	CBS
6 26.3	Dallas	CBS
7 26.2	Taxi	ABC
8 25.4	M*A*S*H	CBS
9 25.2	Mork And Mindy	ABC
10 25.0	Archie Bunker's Place	CBS
11 23.5	Dukes Of Hazzard	CBS
12 23.5	"And Baby Makes Six" [S]	NBC
13 23.1	Eight Is Enough	ABC
14 22.8	Hart To Hart	ABC
15 22.8	Quincy, M. E.	NBC

[P]remiere   [R]epeat   [S]pecial

would compel television broadcasters to carry seven and one-half hours of educational programs a week for children, including five hours for preschool youngsters and two and one-half hours for school-age children.

The staff study, which was set up last year to examine the television industry's response to a commission policy statement issued in 1974 to encourage more children's programs, found that in the long run a number of developments may enhance the prospects for a wider variety and higher quality list of productions.

Some of the Developments

These include an increase in the number of stations in the communities, Government funding for program production, subscription broadcasts, the expanded reach of cable-television systems, and improvements in UHF technology that could expand the number of television stations available.

In a five-volume study, to be issued this week, the staff found that the economics of commercial television today do not support an extensive offering of children's shows, especially during the weekdays when most children are watching. (The staff found that only eight percent of the television watched by children includes the so-called Saturday morning children's shows.)

"The economics of the marketplace simply have not worked for children's programs," said Nina Cornell, chief economist of the commission, during a meeting today.

Children simply do not command the attention of television broadcasters or advertisers, Dr. Cornell said, because of the children's willingness to watch television voraciously regardless of what fare is offered — as well as their lack of influence in the commercial marketplace.

In a finding that clashes somewhat with testimony in the children's advertising proceedings before the Federal Trade Commission, the F.C.C. staff found that children had little influence over their parents' choice of what to buy — and consequently it is not so important that advertisers cater to them. In the F.T.C. proceedings, some consumer groups called for regulation of children's ads on the grounds that they can influence parental choice of purchases even though they are highly gullible to the pitch of advertising.

Even on the public-television side, the staff concluded, money for children's programs has been drying up and even such popular shows as the highly acclaimed "Sesame Street" and "Misterogers Neighborhood" are mostly broadcast in reruns now.

"The Public Broadcasting Service, which built its reputation through its offerings of outstanding children's programs, is now offering mostly old things," Dr. Cornell said.

Even in public broadcasting, she said, corporate sponsors would prefer to have their names associated with adult shows such as "Masterpiece Theater," and producers of programs are inclined to be more attentive to the adults who make the monthly contributions rather than to the children.

Regarded as 'Free' Audience

"Most broadcasters consider children to be free, and consequently are due little in return," she said.

Only cable television has been offering freshness in daily children's shows, the staff said, and parents have been so willing to pay premiums for them that it appears a lot of dollars are waiting for the producers who can get their material into the homes.

Cable material that has been popular, the commission staff found, includes the children's offerings of Home Box Office, UA Columbia and Warner's Nickelodion — which is on 13 or 14 hours a day seven days a week and has more than one million paying subscribers.

October 31, 1979

The Research on TV: A Disturbing Picture

By KATE MOODY

THEIR biggest enemy, many teachers say, is never present in the classroom, has no control over budgets or labor policies and is the parent of no child. It is the television set in the pupil's home.

Like concerned teachers, many physicians say children who are heavy television viewers are the worst stu-

dents — aggressive, easily distracted and lacking in imagination and reading ability. These observations are often backed up by research.

"I can spot the heavy TV viewers right away," said Alison Stopford, a kindergarten teacher for 20 years, first in Britain and now at the Central School in Mamaroneck, N. Y. "They are usually the children whose play is copied from TV superheroes — the ones you see standing on top of the tables with towels or aprons tied around their necks as capes like Batman has. They do a lot of aimless running around, punching and shouting. The heavy viewers are often the ones who can't sit still and listen to a story without

squirming and interrupting incessantly. But if I put on a film they will sit motionless and stare at it."

How many of these heavy viewers are there? Studies at the Annenberg School of Communications at the University of Pennsylvania compared behavior and attitudes of heavy viewers, those who generally watch six or more hours a day, with light viewers, who watch less than two hours a day. While these studies offer insights into the effects on extreme viewers, the vast majority of American children approach the "heavy" level in their "normal" habitual viewing patterns. According to the A. C. Nielsen Company, the typical child spends three to four hours a day watching television.

The most comprehensive study to date is the Surgeon General committee's report on television and social behavior, commissioned by the Federal Government at a cost of $8 million and published in 1972. The report presented data on many social effects of television, including whether viewing

© Marvel Comics Group

Average Hours of TV Viewing by Children Per Week

		Age Group 2-5	Age Group 6-11
Mon.-Fri.	7 00 A M -10 00 A M	2 85	1 25
	10 00 A M -1 00 P M	2 21	60
	1 00 P M -4 30 P M	2 84	1 72
	4 30 P M -7 30 P M	5 36	5 07
Sat.	7 00 A M -1 00 P M	2 53	2 23
	1 00 P M -4 30 P M	48	72
	4 30 P M -7 30 P M	69	73
Sun.	7 00 A M -1 00 P M	1 41	88
	1 00 P M -4 30 P M	34	58
	4 30 P M -7 30 P M	74	92
	4 30 P M -7 00 P M	52	67
Mon.-Sun.	7 30 P M -8 00 P M	1 41	1 56
	8 00 P M -11 00 P M	5 44	8 13
	11 00 P M -11 30 P M	14	33
	11 30 P M -1 00 A M	14	42
	1 00 A M -7 00 A M	21	34
Mon.-Sun. 24-Hour Total		**26.79**	**25.48**

© Warner Brothers Television

television and film violence encouraged the use of violence as a means of solving problems in real life.

Each of the experts on the committee, after reviewing hundreds of published papers, testified that viewing television violence made children more willing to hurt people and more aggressive in their play and in their methods of resolving conflict situations.

One of those experts, Dr. Joseph T. Klapper, director of the Office of Social Research for CBS, argues that "the jury is still out" on the issue. Noting in an interview that there had been a considerable number of studies since the Surgeon General's report, he said: "With all the research and discussion, there is one statement on which all would agree: that some kinds of TV violence has some kinds of adverse effects on some children and adults under some circumstances."

Anecdotal evidence from parents and teachers tends to confirm that all the bumping, zapping, zonking, chasing, squashing, shooting and punching has some effect. Teachers observed that students bring the images of television aggressiveness to school and that the video values and tough language get recycled in the playground: "Oh yeah? So? Who cares? Dummy! Dingbat!"

Philip A. Harding, a member of Dr. Klapper's staff at CBS, expressed about anecdotal reports. "I don't think the effects of television can be validly defined purely on the basis of anecdotal reports," he said. "I would feel as a researcher that this simply underlines the need for empirical research findings to document either alleged socially desirable or socially undesirable effects of television."

On the matter of heavy and light television viewers, he said: "It is not sufficient simply to compare persons who watch relatively more TV with persons who watch relatively less and then to infer that any differences in behavior or attitude are therefore attributable to television. One has to know a good deal more about the ways in which the so-called heavy-viewing children differ from the light viewers."

In one of the Annenberg studies, when schoolchildren were asked, "How often is it all right to hit someone you are mad at?" the heavy viewers were more likely than the light viewers to respond that it was almost always all right. In another survey, by the Foundation for Child Development, in New York, heavy-viewing children tended to be more fearful of the world and more apt to have bad dreams.

Statistical evidence is also beginning to show how the use of various media affect the imagination and thinking process.

Researchers in Harvard's "Project Zero" concluded that how a person received information made a difference in how the brain could use it. In one study, they aimed at discovering the differences in learning when children watched a story on television or had that story's content read aloud to them from a children's book. Laurene Mer-

ingoff, in her substudy, used a book called "The Three Robbers" by Tomi Ungerer and a television version of the same story that had been specially produced to be "identical" to the print story. Equivalent groups of youngsters experienced the story, either via print or video.

The children who heard the book read aloud remembered the story language more precisely and tended to integrate their own experience to make inferences. While all the children reached approximately the same conclusions, the television-viewing group rarely went beyond the "picture language," either to pay attention to the audio portion or to integrate their own real-life experiences with the vicarious television experience. Those who heard the book version paid attention to the words and conjured imaginative inner pictures by drawing on their own experiences. The project director, Howard Gardner, concluded: "Clear differences are attributable to the medium of transmission; and the younger the child, the greater the difference."

For some generations the daily use of print and radio required the person to conjure inner pictures because these media leave the pictorial part of the image incomplete. This process involves making one's own pictures.

By contrast, television delivers the pictures to the viewers who don't have to participate in the inner picture-making activity.

Michael Morgan and Larry Gross, at the Annenberg School of Communications, found that heavy viewing and low reading ability usually go hand in hand. but did not claim that heavy viewing causes poor readers.

Eye movements necessary for reading are inhibited by television viewing. To read, the eyes must first scan the line of print with a left-to-right sweep while the brain connects and de-codes symbols across the line; then the process must be repeated, again and again, line after line, until the paragraph is completed.

However, Dr. Edgar Gording, director of the Gording Institute of Developmental Vision, said that "While it is often recognized that eye movements are necessary in order to read, what is not generally realized is that habitual television viewing trains eyes *not* to move.

"When we see a child who can't read, we first check out how his eyes are moving. Older kids who aren't reading often have faulty eye movements. The first objective is to get those eyes moving, and part of the therapy is to reduce the amount of television viewing."

A study by Prof. Adele Fasick at the University of Toronto showed that the language of children's books consistently offers wider vocabulary as well as more varied and complicated sentence patterns than television does. She found that the predominant sentence form on television is the incomplete sentence.

"Hearing the complicated language of story books, which utilizes most of the syntactic possibilities of English," she said, "may help children to under-

stand and to use the more complicated language they will have to employ in school."

While there is no solid statistical evidence on TV's effect on the attention span of viewers , many educators believe that habitual viewing breaks perception into bits and reduces the ability to remain engaged in one subject or sustain attention to one topic for any length of time.

Indeed, television's most successful techniques — quick cuts, short segments, fast action — condition the brain to change, but not to continuity of thought. If there is not enough flash-and-dash on one station, the viewer flips to another and further interrupts any continuity of thinking.

Psychologists and educators report anecdotally that the "television environment" and habitual viewing interfere with many children's ability to pay attention or persist in classroom activities.

Drs. Dorothy and Jerome Singer , co-directors of the Yale Family Television Research and Consultation Center in New Haven, said: "No sane parent would present a child with a fire engine, snatch it away in 30 seconds, replace it with a set of blocks, snatch that away 30 seconds later, replace the blocks with clay, and then replace the clay with a toy car. Yet in effect, a young child receives that kind of experience when he or she watches American television."

According to the late Dr. Dorothy H. Cohen, professor of early childhood development at the Bank Street College of Education, "Children whose lives are a kaleidoscope of changing figures and inconsistent responses — for whom things and people disappear and fail to reappear with frequency, or children whose environment is heavily dominated by the frantic pace and speed of television — are children likely to be easily distracted. For them, focusing and paying attention are a strain."

However, Dr. Edward Palmer, vice president for Research at the Children's Television Workshop, doesn't concur in this thinking. "There are no measures of attention span. I wish we had a good definition of attention span, and some measures and data indicating that there had been changes due to TV, because then we'd know what to do."

Television has been found to expand children's world view by showing them the moon, the floor of the sea — or "Sesame Street," where they will see people of many racial and ethnic backgrounds playing together and cooperating.

Yet, schools are destined to deal with the effects of heavy and habitual television viewing by young children whose preschool level of vicarious experience is higher than ever before and whose skills and perceptions may be shifting as a result.

Kate Moody is a consultant on television and education and author of "Growing Up on Television," to be published in June.

April 20, 1980

CHILDREN IDEALIZED

THE EDUCATION OF GIRLS.

Whatever we may think of what our girls ought to be, and however severely we may criticise some of their tendencies and characteristics, we must in all our discussions start with the facts of the case, and see our daughters as they are, before we try to make them what they should be. Thus, there can be no doubt that the American girl, as such, differs much from her European sisters, because she is born in this new country and in this long-established Republic, and that she is thus placed in conditions that alike stir her ambition and task her strength. Her brothers are born with the right of suffrage, and she in her way has virtually the same right, although she cares to use it, not by her vote, but by her social freedom, or by having her say in the choice of a husband, and in all other matters within her sphere. What is quite memorable, and not in all respects advantageous, this democratic freedom, which gives the brothers a certain dashing independence, adds in a measure to her dependence by going with a certain homage to women as such, and making them a kind of aristocratic caste who have high expectations, and to whom all men are to pay deference. So the American girl is at once tempted to queen it over men as her vassals, and claim tribute from them, and also obliged to a great and often painful extent to stand upon her own feet and make her own way in the world. The proudest of queens, and often the hardest of workers, she has a peculiar lot, in view of which the topic of the education of our daughters has now a great and growing interest.

The present discussion of the higher education of young women, as also the question as to opening our colleges and universities to them, is important, but not most important. But few girls can at best be thus educated, and we are concerned more for the general drift of our school and home instruction, which is to give character to the daughters, wives, and mothers of the nation. It is evident that in view of the new strain that is now put upon our girls, alike by their privileges and their burdens, a suitable education must be secured to them. The old routine of household discipline that trained girls mainly to be cooks and seamstresses will not do now, nor can we be for a moment content with the new-fashioned rage for accomplishments, that aims to fit them for the marriage market by dress, the dance, and the piano. Our girls have too much refinement in their make and their manners to be drudges, and they have too much mind and opportunity for using it to be dolls or parrots or music-boxes. Life is becoming for them somewhat serious, and they are looking for teachers and helpers to guide them in the new calls upon their powers and their patience.

What is more obvious than that our girls need to be educated to be reasonable? It is,

perhaps, asking too much to insist that they shall be great reasoners, for reasoning is a gift that apparently does not fall to the majority of men, and does not abound even among bright women. But to reason with logic and to be reasonable in conversation and conduct are quite different things, and a girl with little show of logic may be trained to see the bearing of words and actions, and to secure herself against her own flighty fancies and the reigning follies and fashions of the hour. In one form of severe reasoning, in that purest of logic which goes by the name of mathematics, a girl may be an adept, and in this way she may save herself and her family from ruin. Because our women are so seldom used to keeping accounts, and so little in the habit of counting the cost of things, vast mischief comes to our people, and many a man who is a close calculator is sadly perplexed by a wife who, without meaning wrong, forgets that two and two make four, and that we cannot spend twice what we have and have anything left but debt. Woman's will is a constant power, and should go with prudence as constant, or the evil day comes when wants clash with ability. A careful training in arithmetic and geometry, with perspective and drawing, goes well with the study of physiology, psychology, history, and literature, in teaching girls to see the nature of things, the bearings of actions, and the conditions and the play of character. Language, which is so often thought to be the breath of folly or caprice, is really the word of reason, and, when well taught, the gift of speech itself is seen to be at once the life of history and the soul of humanity, if not the revelation of heaven. Woman, as such, has a certain eloquence of her own, and the American girl ought to know the worth and the meaning of the sparkling gems that so often drop from her ruby lips, well aware that her words do not lose charm in losing folly, and that the finest diamond has beauty most when its light is purest.

We have, of course, no objection to our girls being as pretty as they can be or GOD has made, or as charming as the choicest schooling in social arts can make them; but they gain nothing in the long run by being fools or seeming such. A lovely girl with genuine good sense holds her charm long after the shallow prattler has played out her little game. Our girls should have, for their own sake as well as for ours, a more rational education, and so, also, a more practical one. This may be repeating the same thing in other words, yet fairly considered it is but carrying the idea out, since what is reasonable needs to be carried out in order to be practical. Here comes the pinch of the whole matter—the practical education of girls, **and any man who dares to be honest and tell the whole truth must expect a storm of indignation in certain quarters, and would have his ears pulled by gentle hands if little feminine tempers could be put into action.** There can be

no doubt that, according to a certain standard of gentility, all useful industry is under a ban, and that the young lady, as such, is supposed never to see the kitchen or to know anything about the dull utilities of the household. Yet a better day is coming, and many of the most honored teachers and the most prominent leaders of society, are ready to go with us in maintaining that well-educated girls ought to know how to do all the work of the house, even if they expect only to see that it is properly done by their servants. How to wash, cook, cut garments and make them, to nurse the sick, care for the garden, provide for the table, and look after the whole economy of the home belongs to a well-trained woman, however gentle her blood and breeding, quite as much as to know the etiquette of society and the arts of dress and the methods of amusement. Of course, those useful branches do not exhaust the range of practical education, but they belong to it; and few women go through life without suffering much, and making others suffer, from their ignorance of plain household uses. These do not by any means sacrifice the elegances and accomplishments, and may sometimes serve them in a dark day, or a perplexing emergency. As health secures to beauty its wholesome and lasting bloom, so economy secures home comfort, and, prosaic as it seems, it rises into poetry like pure water and good bread, which give light to the eye, bloom to the cheek, and music to the step.

It is hardly necessary to add that the true education for our girls should give them their just social power by securing that genial play of natural spirits which is their great, and sometimes their almost mystical, prerogative, and also by fixing them upon solid ground of purity and principle which prevail so with the best men. Our girls have the future of American society in their hands, and they need all that belongs to them to keep and to exalt their power. They are in league with the occult forces of nature and life that give them a faculty of being possessed, not always, indeed, from on high, and of possessing others not always for good. Let no hard bookishness, no rough masculine mannerism, no pushing rudeness, no coarse competition, rob them of their delicacy and shut the gates of heaven that are ready to open into their affections and their homes and social sphere. The true girl may not paint pictures, or write poetry, but she ought to be herself a picture whom God's own light and love have painted with expression, color, and warmth, and a poem too, which heaven has filled with thrilling meaning and set to charming music. The census that is soon forthcoming may not note these facts, but our American history and life depend upon them for thrift as well as joy.

March 23, 1879

BOYS IN AMERICA.

There is good reason for believing that there have always been boys in the world, because there have always been men; but in these latter days, and in this new country, the boys do not allow us to wait until they report themselves as men, for they insist upon being seen, and heard, too, before they have cut their wisdom teeth, and they often make more noise in the world by their precocious mischief than by their mature experience and ability. The worst of it may be over, but it is bad enough; and there have been some grounds for fearing that we are not to have any more boys and girls, but only little men and women, with the knowing ways and forward manners of age, and the ignorance and feebleness of childhood.

It is said that boys will be boys, and that we must expect and excuse a certain amount of rush and rudeness in them. It is easier, however, to excuse them for being boys than for trying to be men, and it is one of the crying evils of American society that we are not content to leave this young life to stay awhile in the bud, but we insist upon pushing it forward into flower and fruit before its time. This tendency belongs in part to our age, and this nineteenth century of liberty and progress has made its mark upon the nursery and school as well as upon the college and the workshop; and comic art in every country amuses us with caricatures of little misses and masters who bluster and swell in a marvelous way. But the Old World still keeps childhood and youth very closely to their own place; and while free-

thinking Germany still allows teachers to bully and beat stout school-boys, Mother England is not yet quite motherly to her children, and she has not yet decided that even young men shall not be flogged with rods that draw blood. It is well that we Americans have outgrown that brutality, but it is not so well that we have set aside the due subordination of childhood to authority under influences more humane and commanding than blows. We make a sad mistake in our forcing processes that are crowding our children forward into the cares and also into the indulgences that are suited to mature years, and sometimes our very thrift, that sets a boy to making money before his time, goes with a laxity that tempts him to a dissipation quite as untimely.

Let boys be boys in the best sense of the

word. Let them have the education and the enjoyment that are proper for them, alike from regard to what they are now that they are boys and from what they are to carry forward in their preparation for manhoood. It is not fair to treat them as if they had no duties and rights of their own, and as if they were good for nothing except in the prospect of being men. The boy as such is a precious creature of GOD and an important member of the family and of society, as well as of the nation and the Church. He can enjoy and make others enjoy a great deal, and without him the house is not home, and life is without its true geniality. He should be encouraged to have his own proper expression, manner, and activity, so that while his boyhood continues he is a recognized power, and when sober years come, those early days are still a pleasant remembrance and a motive energy which cheer him and the whole world with that light from the past.

If we would have our boys to be truly boys, and not prematurely old, we must allow them to have the education that belongs to them, or what is called the first education, with its full awakening of the perceptive senses and the wide range of observation of nature and life, and large round of healthful exercise, instead of the perpetual drill over books and definitions and all manner of abstruse notions that so task the brain and dry up the vital juices. The great thing is to give the boy a healthy body and to build up a vigorous brain, instead of making his limbs and chest puny with long sitting at the desk and cramming his head with words and sentences that do not come in through the eager senses, and are not digested by earnest thinking. All honor to JULIUS FROEBEL for the emancipation of children from the tyranny of books before their time, and for his exchanging the dull school for the pleasant garden and its stirring round of plays and objects which aims to set life and its work to cheering music and marches. Our boys are

having the benefit of this movement, and our American sagacity and pluck are bound to carry out that ideal German's theory to more practical uses by adding wide observation to careful study, and by making the fields and woods and waters and mountains, as well as the workshops, laboratories, and museums, interpret books and instruction into light and life.

Of course, boys are to do their part of serious study and work, alike for the sake of knowing what they ought to know and doing what they have to do, and also for the sake of impressing them with the fact that they have duties as well as rights, and that not pleasure only, but principle, is the rule of conduct and the key to true living. Yet in our estimate of the serious part of a boy's life we are not to overlook that higher kind of exercise in which play and work meet together, and the just pursuit of pleasure at once strengthens the muscles and stirs the spirits and tends to make him something of a hero in action as well as something of a poet in his ideals. Perhaps the old round of games may be made to serve a new turn by being carefully studied, refined, and completed into a kind of life-drama, and it may be seen that in such sports a more thorough culture of body and mind may be found than in such specialties as rowing and racing, that do not stir the whole constitution and bring every sense, nerve, and muscle to the true bearing. Somewhere in the future our boys are to have a "Year of Play" that, in its way, shall help out the year of study, and not shame the "Christian Year" which so many of them are learning to love in their hymns and lessons. Such genial and uplifting sports do much to form character as well as to secure health; for character depends much for its life and force upon a certain fullness of animal spirits that is greatly favored by judicious play.

Our boys need very much a genial temper and original force to carry them forward to manhood and to fit them for the best joy, and

also for the best work. Their lot is to depend not merely upon how much they are to possess, but upon how much they can enjoy—not merely upon what new thoughts or fancies they can start, but upon what plans and purposes they can originate. They often come sadly short of these resources, whether by plodding care or precocious dissipation, and we are abounding in wretched specimens in both directions. There, on one side, are puny little book-worms, with as little vital juice as the pages over which they pore, and here are pale and tremulous little reprobates, who have lost digestion and strength and comeliness under their diet of sweet-meats, perhaps drugged with tobacco and wine and whisky, and depraved by vices which cannot be named without offense. These extreme cases do but prove the extent of the mischief that comes from the improper education, or no-education, of our boys, and they urge the need of an honest and thorough treatment of the whole subject by the physician and preacher, as well as the teacher.

There are signs of a better day for them alike from the progress of physiological knowledge, the improvement in methods of instruction, and from the admirable example of teachers who have added the charm and the power of personal character to the influence of their learning and persevearance. Such men as Dr. ARNOLD, of Rugby, live and speak in their words and system after they have gone, and their names are held in honor in our American homes and schools. They are teaching us what we ought to know, that character is more to be considered than knowledge in the training of our boys, and that we should associate with the routine of learning the charm of a kindly disposition, the dignity of a noble purpose, and the elevation of high principle. Boys are willing to look up to their superiors, and to remember in after life the traits and lessons that may be too deep for present understanding.

March 30, 1879

ROOSEVELT TALKS ON AMERICAN BOYS

Tells Archie's Schoolmates to be Brave, Strong, Gentle, and Kind.

Special to The New York Times.
WASHINGTON, May 24. — President Roosevelt delivered an address to-night at the annual presentation exercises of the Friends Select School in this city, where Archie Roosevelt is a student. His subject was "The American Boy." The President said:

"I want to see the boy enjoy himself. The boy at play sometimes exhibits these qualities which determine the kind of man he will make. If he dislikes his work, if he shirks his studies, he will develop into a great failure in everything else. If he hasn't character to study, he won't have character to play. Play hard when you play, and work hard when you work. Right here there is as great a lesson for the grown-ups as for the younger ones.

"I want to see the boy work hard, but at the same time I want to see him remember the other side of life. I want to see you brave and strong, and I want to see you gentle and kind. These are the qualities that make up the good citizen. I want to see you so conduct yourselves that among your fathers and mothers there will be a feeling of re-

gret, and not relief when you are away from home."

The element of courage in the young boy, as essential and imperative along with any other trait, was the basis for some references by the President.

"When you are out among your playmates," he said, "don't be afraid of the little boy who happens to be rude to you. The boy who is too nice to hold his own is not the boy who will grow to be the best citizen. When you boys grow to manhood I want to see you put the wrongdoer out of the way, and to make the man who does wrong feel that you are his superior both in strength and character. If you can't hold your own you will be a curse in any environment and remain the dread of those around you.

"The bully, the boy who would maltreat a weaker boy or an animal, is one of the meanest boys in the world. I want to see you protecting those who are weak against those who would oppress the weak. It's a boy who becomes a citizen that will be strong enough to abhor and despise the betrayal of a trust and strong enough to stand for the right."

At this juncture the President made some amusing allusions to the "eleven," and told the boys some of his observations as to what constituted the good player and the qualities which helped to win. In passing, he remarked that some of the youngsters who could make a plunge into the line, could tackle in the roughest places, and could stand the greatest endurance would sometimes exhibit pronounced feebleness if his mother should ask him to go upstairs and get something.

The President looked squarely into the beaming faces of the youngsters on the eleven at this moment, and muffled snickerings emanated from the little coterie

of the football heroes on the front seats. The President admonished the boys not to misuse their strength.

"You will find," said he, "a certain number of boys who have strength and who have misused it by oppressing the boy or the girl who is weak. That kind of a boy has a weak streak in him and hasn't in him real strength or the real courage that makes for character. I abhor the boy who uses his strength against those who cannot help themselves."

The President concluded his address by what he termed "just a word to the grown-ups, the fathers, and especially the mothers." He said he desired particularly to talk to the mothers, upon whom the greatest responsibilities and burdens in directing the course of the boy's impressionable life rested, and who were charged with the duty of developing in the boy the sturdy traits of bravery, courage, gentility, kindness, morality, and respect for others among his fellows.

"Hardness of heart and softness of head" was the term applied by the President to many parents whose boys were utter failures, and who lacked the fundamental principles for good citizenship. He declared that the mother who permitted her boy to have his own way without restraint and whose selfish wishes were always granted without a single curb, would see that boy develop into an undesirable citizen and a "selfish and brutal husband or father."

"Now, I have finished, and just a closing word to you boys," said the President. "I am going to give you some of the rules of which I am fond and which are as applicable in life as on the football field: 'Don't flinch, don't foul, and hit the line hard.'"

May 25, 1907

CHILDREN OF HOLLYWOOD'S GOLD RUSH

A New Get-Rich-Quick Scheme Dazzles Their Parents, but Prizes Are Won by the Few

By EUNICE FULLER BARNARD
HOLLYWOOD.

OUT in Hollywood a 7-year-old child with blond curls is drawing a salary reputedly three times as large as that of the President of the United States. For looking after her health and welfare her mother is paid a sum which in itself would mean to most families luxury beyond their dreams.

And suddenly a new American get-rich-quick vision dazzles thousands from coast to coast. In miners' shacks in Montana, in breathless Philadelphia flats, in farmhouse kitchens in Kansas, parents are looking appraisingly at smart little Susie or Sam. If only a movie director could see him now, they are thinking, it might be the end of all our worries about meeting the rent or the mortgage payments. Masses of able-bodied Americans are plotting to make the youngest and weakest member of the family the chief breadwinner.

Already, like the Forty-niners, scores of sober citizens have left hearth and home to seek their fortunes in California—with their hopes centered on a child rather than on pick and pan. Mothers who would shrink from risking $10 in the sweepstakes are putting all their savings into two bus tickets to Hollywood, a $20-a-month apartment and singing and dancing lessons for the young hopeful, purchased sometimes in lieu of food.

Ten thousand parents last year besieged the Central Casting Bureau, which serves the larger film studios in Hollywood, in an attempt to register their children as screen extras. Thousands of others are trying to reach the movies through other channels—radio and stage appearances; beauty contests; special child-placing directories, agents and dancing schools of alleged influence with the Hollywood powers. One such dancing school alone, with twenty-seven branches in near-by California towns, has 10,000 pupils, mostly between the ages of 3 and 5.

"And suddenly a new American get-rich-quick dream dazzles thousands from coast to coast."

• • •

ACCESSIBLE to the Hollywood scene, then, are a host of active, not to say passionate, aspirants to juvenile movie fame. Constantly through the casting offices moves the procession of youngsters, submissive but weary in their pink and tinsel costumes, shoved by doggedly hopeful mothers. "Can't you give us something soon?" the mothers beg. "We've got to meet the gas bill, and the grocer is threatening." But—despite the vogue of the baby star, despite the fact that Shirley Temple tops Garbo and Gable as the premier box-office attraction of the country—the eight big studios all together probably do not employ on the average fifty children a day, and the majority of these are $5 extras. Thus it is only the exceptionally lucky or talented child who can support his parents in the luxury of estates, swimming pools and chauffeurs.

Still, the parents feel they are right. They are rushing to be among the first to knock at the door of the most glittering of professions ever opened to children. It may be narrow, but nevertheless, as they correctly insist, it is a real door. And it has already opened to some of the youngest and poorest in the land.

Cinderella today has her big chance at 6 perhaps more often than at 16. Not one child alone but a dozen in recent years have achieved a millionaire's income and world-wide acclaim beyond that of the princelings of Europe. Few youngsters in history have been so fantastically publicized and fêted.

In luxurious bungalows in the Hollywood hills child stars, yesterday sunk in complete obscurity, live a life and wield an influence on style, manners and business that occasionally is more than regal. Guarded from kidnappers, besought by interviewers, surrounded by publicity men, taught by special tutors, petted by studio attachés, protected in their health, work and morals by emissaries of the State, they live necessarily in the center of a world of more or less hushed adulation.

From the outside, too, it rushes in, in the shape of "fan" presents — dolls, books and toys sent from Buenos Aires, Bangor and Berlin— and fan mail, which in the case of the three or four most popular children reaches a total of 2,000 to 4,000 letters a week. "Fans" are parts of their lives as familiar as cousins or aunts, and they refer to them in the same casual way. A veteran prima donna is scarcely more accomplished in dealing with her admirers. "Which photograph of me would you like?" the movie child will casually ask the interviewer as she prepares to append her autograph with a practiced hand.

When the young stars venture out, they have practically royal ovations. Though Shirley's parents say they try to shield her from publicity, they take her shopping in downtown Los Angeles, and a mob follows them about the stores. The noted film children, at previews of their pictures, enter the theatre in a blaze of lights and a rush of autograph-seekers. And unlike certain bashful princes, they have no inhibitions about addressing their populace in person. Both Freddie Bartholomew and Jane Withers have spoken impromptu to large theater audiences with entire nonchalance.

Children have set styles before, but they have been royal children or more frequently dream children, evolved, like Little Lord Fauntleroy, from an artist's or author's imagination. Never before the advent of the movies had any one conceived the scheme of ingratiating into the affections of the public the personality and mannerisms of an everyday child without rank or fortune. And only in the past few years have the film magnates themselves fully realized how profitable such exploitation might be.

But already certain movie children, all from average homes and backgrounds, are setting the patterns of juvenile dress and conduct around the world. Mothers in Austria and Australia, as in Tampa and Tacoma, are twisting their babies' hair into curls like Shirley's, teaching their children Shirley's little songs, dressing them in copies of her frocks.

Shirley's face may

not have launched a thousand ships but it has probably sped a thousands freight cars of merchandise on their way. And on a thousand counters Shirley Temple and Jane Withers dolls are a bulwark of the toy industry. In lofts and factories and shops uncounted adults owe their jobs to the vogue for imitating Shirley's clothes, underwear and furniture, on which, it is said, her own royalties alone amount to $100,000 a year.

Everything conspires to gild the modern fairy tale in the eyes of aspiring families. Moreover, the end is not yet. All over the country "talent scouts" are still avid in the pursuit of possible new starlets. At the moment every major studio feels it almost as important to have a Freddie Bartholomew as a Wallace Beery. And movie directors are zealously thumbing through the pages of the "Elsie" books and the collected works of Frances Hodgson Burnett as well as goading on their own scenario writers to achieve new child vehicles.

• • •

WITHIN obvious limits there has been this year a bull market for children in Hollywood. Film companies are gambling on child personalities like automobile manufacturers on a new model, putting their money on this or that unknown in the hope that he will catch the public fancy.

"Children!" exclaimed a motion-picture executive recently. "Why, they're carrying the industry. Even up in Alaska and down along the Ganges the child picture is catching on."

Whether this year has perhaps seen the zenith of the child star's orbit is a moot question. At any rate, while the former screen deities, the siren and the G-man, have languished relatively neglected in the playhouse around the corner, millions of Main Streeters have flocked to see innocent childhood winning the heart of a crusty millionaire or even hurling a tomato at his head. Older stars are more or less ruefully aware of the trend. "The only way I can get my picture in the paper is to pose with Shirley," said Warner Baxter.

In an era of violence and hardship there is apparently a kind of flow of the popular preferences back to the dear, safe Victorian shores. Sentiment at the moment pays better than thrills. Such children as Shirley Temple and Freddie Bartholomew give the same sort of psychological satisfaction as did the chromos of babies, sleeping or saying their prayers, which used to adorn the old-fashioned guest room. Their candid charm, understandable to all, provides an obvious spiritual resting place in a complex age. It is no wonder that producers are reverting to Laura E. Richards, Alice Hegan Rice and other "heart-string" writers of the turn of the century, in their search for scripts to the public taste.

No sign of the movie times, however, seems to inflame the average ambitious parent more than the fact that the child stars almost invariably have come from his own more or less obscure station in life. The old folk-tale, in which the goose girl or the shepherd boy won the kingdom, was no more cunningly calculated as a wish-fulfillment for the bulk of its auditors than is the true story of the young movie favorite of today.

Filmdom has become the happy gambling ground of the child of the middle class because from that class to date most of the prize-winners have been drawn. No special qualifications of coin or culture have been necessary. A few children, like Jackie Cooper and Mickey Rooney, have come from film or stage families. But in general the lightning of film fortune has struck indiscriminately among the progeny of butcher and baker around the world.

In the movie companies' search for a "natural," neither possessions nor parentage necessarily has any bearing. Among 200 children who tried out last Summer for a leading part in the new film, "Valiant Is the Word for Carrie," Paramount chose the 7-year-old daughter of the delivery man for a bread company who had recently come to Los Angeles from Tulsa, Okla. Sybil Jason, the 7-year-old star whom Warner Brothers brought across the ocean, is the daughter of a traveling salesman in South Africa. Jane Withers came from Atlanta, Ga., where her father was employed by a tire company. Shirley Temple's father has a job in a branch bank in California. Look at random down the list of young newcomers who recently got contracts in Hollywood. Here is a child of a farmer in Indiana, of a Ford em-

ploye in Detroit, of a shipbuilder in New Zealand.

* * *

TO the parent outside looking eagerly in, this miscellany of origin is heartening. Right in his own household he has a child who, he is sure, is just as beautiful, just as talented as any of the young stars. Potentially he feels like a man who has struck oil in his front yard or who suddenly discovers that the old kitchen table is a genuine Sheraton. In days of unemployment, when he has been casting about desperately for a new means of livelihood, he has been peculiarly ready to stake the family savings on "selling" his child in Hollywood.

Others have done it and won; why not he? It needs, he decides, only complete determination and persistence and some training of the young hopeful to dance, recite or sing. Before him glitters the career of Freddie Bartholomew, who crossed the ocean and the continent with his aunt on the 1-in-10,000 chance that he might land the part of David Copperfield. He thinks of Jane Withers, whose mother took her from Georgia to California at the age of 5 and in the best success-story tradition stuck it out for two and a half years before she got a chance for her in a real film part.

So at crowded dancing schools throughout California "kiddies" in abbreviated uniforms are going through their routines of tap and ballet dancing and acrobatics. Babies are lisping over the microphone; learning how to arouse stage tears over a hypothetical "broken dolly," and raising their tenuous and uncertain sopranos in jazz melodies. Some day, somehow, every child's mother believes, a movie scout will "discover" her youngster, much as one picked out 3-year-old Shirley Temple in a California dancing school.

* * *

MEANWHILE telegraphing, telephoning, driving, sometimes even flying to Hollywood, mothers and children apply at the Central Casting Bureau at the rate of forty or fifty a day. The bureau is usually the first line of assault upon filmdom. In its files are listed the juvenile movie "extras"—some 1,600 children of all sizes, shapes, colors, nationalities and talents—from whom every day are chosen children for mob scenes and "bits."

Hopefully, sometimes hysterically, the mothers plead their case: Mary is the very image of Shirley Temple—the same curls, the same cute ways, the same smile; the family has even gone to the ex-

pense of providing her with false teeth in the gaps where the baby ones have fallen out. Won't the lady take the time to see her dance? Father has been out of work a long time now.

Patiently the bureau officials go over the disillusioning explanations: What the studios most often want is not the curly headed darling of the Shirley Temple type, nor yet necessarily the child who can dance. Day in and day out, it is the homely, freckled-faced youngster, the everyday boy or girl, who is most in demand to fill in the average scene—on the street, in the schoolroom, orphan asylum or children's party. Moreover, no child can support his family by his calls as an extra. The most fortunate do not average a day's work a week or make more than $200 a year.

Into the studios the mothers of the extras carry their desperate warfare, contriving for position, watching for the openings which, quickly seized, may mean a fortune for the family. "Try to stand next to Shirley, dearie," they whisper to their youngsters. "Move up beside the nice director man. Show him how cute you can imitate Charlie Chaplin. Just push right in."

October 4, 1936

Children's Photos Lead Demand
Children continue to be the most popular advertising and editorial subjects in America, according to the Free Lance Photographers Guild, Inc., 219 East Forty-fourth Street. Pictures of children accounted for 16 per cent of sales of color photographs by the organization to advertising agencies and magazines during the year ended July 30. Pretty girl pictures were in second place, 14 per cent, and animals third, 9 per cent.

August 29, 1950

Junior Rules the Roost

THE CHILD WORSHIPERS. By Martha Weinman Lear. 251 pp. New York: Crown Publishers. $3.95.

By BEVERLY GRUNWALD

THERE was a time when everyone said it was a man's world—though sociologists viewing the matriarchal position said it was a woman's

Mrs. Grunwald is a first-hand observer of the problems of the younger generation, vis-à-vis their parents.

world. Lately, it is being called a children's world, a child-centered society. Never before have so many parents spent so much time, effort and money on trying to understand their children. Never before have so many children been so misunderstood. And perhaps never before have children so influenced and controlled our daily lives. Among others, Leslie Fiedler noted this phenomenon in his essay on the Cult of the Child, "The Eye of Innocence." Now a diligent re-

porter, Martha Weinman Lear, has recorded the most recent evidence in all fields of child worship.

Mrs. Lear spoke to mothers and pediatricians, psychologists and advertisers, builders and educators. She spoke to the children themselves. The result is an often funny and always provocative book which should produce soul-searching among all parents, whether they belong to the Cult or not. Undoubtedly, we all have a tendency to live for our children, to give them the "best." Do we do this for them or ourselves?

Mrs. Lear believes that many people are not as altruistic in this respect as they believe, that countless parents are wearing their children like a string of pearls or a Balenciaga gown. For those that have them—and use them—children are a built-in status symbol.

THE "Good Mother" makes motherhood a career. Since this is the way she "fulfills" herself, she expects her child to succeed for her sake in the competition with other parents. He must oblige her by being best-be-

99

haved, dressed, adjusted. He must get the best grades, make the best schools. He should have a high I.Q.—and what joy if he is an I.G. (Intellectually Gifted)! He must be popular in the right circles, for such a child can help his parents make the social grade. As one new-rich father put it, "My son associates with people of a higher level than I would have dared seek out. . ... He pulls me up by my own bootstraps."

People of moderate means overextend themselves to buy a $100 christening dress or a $360 four-poster bed for the nursery. The child may even determine where the family is to live—the right house in the right neighborhood. Many parents don't have the home they want or decorate it as they'd like; it is antiseptic and formicaed, tiled and generally childproof. Edward Stone, the architect, declares: "Parents today do a home that can be hosed

down like a latrine." A frustrated decorator wonders whatever happened to parents: "Can't they say, keep your grubby paws off it?" The answer is, of course, "No." Today's parents don't want to create feelings of "rejection." They are so Freud-ful that they have forgotten how to relax and enjoy their children—or even how to relish a good family fight.

In the battle to keep up with the Junior Joneses, the birthday party has become a production. It frequently has to have a theme, professional entertainment or "party coordinator." Sometimes it is elaborately catered—with special favors and fancy food one expert feels are wasted on children, who would prefer hot dogs. But mothers like to boast about how expensive the party was, including that "little nothing" designer-dress their toddlers wore. They also vie for the most expensive camps, which are becoming

more like country clubs with social and cultural benefits. It is a special triumph to show neighbors a returning son who can now say, "Bonjour, Mama."

THE private-school "interview" is one of the most talked-about and worried-over situations wherever mothers meet. For weeks children are coached, and parents try to act casual as they nervously await the day and the results. One whose child was rejected said, "No reasons. They never give you any reasons. You can't imagine how it feels. Here you've gone through medical school and your wife was a philosophy major, and you both got honors—and your three-year old kid is turned down by a nursery school."

These are some of the parental problems explored by Mrs. Lear. She also delves into the harried life of pediatricians and the way TV turns children into salesmen pressuring the whole

family. She presents a hilarious depth survey of the emotional and psychological factors surrounding the $50 million-a-year diaper-service industry, designed to expand coverage beyond the usual six months and to spare mother any guilt feelings about not washing the diapers herself. One happy trend can be noted. Togetherness is now being combined with apartheid. It's all right to take the children on a vacation — provided there are separate recreational facilities and baby-sitters.

"The Child Worshipers" is a book to be read and discussed, if only while waiting for that recorder session to end or for that last twirl in ballet class. Though occasionally exaggerated, it hits home. And that's where the child is—sometimes.

November 17, 1963

To the Children, 'Cute' Is an Offensive Word

By RICHARD FLASTE

In no time at all, Julia Hendricks, a fast-thinking, fast-talking 10-year-old at P.S. 41, can rattle off a whole list of complaints about adult attitudes toward children—how they belittle them in everyday dealings and how they portray young people as if they were "so dumb."

She most especially resents the "cute" way adults depict children in comic strips. Grabbing a pad and pencil from a visitor's hand, she said, "They always make us look like this:"

The complaints Julia expressed, as did many other fifth and sixth graders around the city, reflected a ground swell of resentment against being stereotyped—whether in the minds of adults generally or in the entertainments such as comics and television shows they create.

There is at least one grownup who sympathizes with the youthful anger. "Adults who think they like chil-

dren," John Holt, the author of "Why Children Fail," said the other day, "often treat them like puppy dogs, like pets."

Mr. Holt, who deals with these adult attitudes in "Escape From Childhood," which will be published this spring, said he believes that children know intuitively that this kind of sentimentality "quickly turns to cruelty when a child doesn't live up to the idealized view."

The concept of "cute," he said, "is also disrespectful, and children have quite a strong sense of dignity."

Traveling from school to school in the city, one finds that observation continually borne out.

The words the children typically use to describe blatant portrayals of them—"stupid," "corny," "dumb" —indicate their feeling of being insulted, and show they can be insulting in turn.

¶On Mason Reese, the television-commercial child star and, to the children, a kind of Cousin Tom: "He's such a big show-off," and "he's so corny."

¶On the comic strip, Dondi: "He's just a goody-two-shoes."

¶On the Partridge Family television show: "One of the boys, Danny, says all the yukkie jokes. At least they could give him a decent line, but, no, everybody thinks he's s-o-o-o cute."

¶On cartoons generally: "Grownups in cartoons can be beautiful, like Brenda Starr, but did you ever

The New York/Times/Gene Maggio
Adults may find Mason Reese adorable. But children don't.

see a beautiful child?"

¶On stereotypes: "There are always these bullies and teacher's pets and smart-aleck kids—but that's not the way most kids are."

At the crux of the matter are grownup attitudes ("Adults," one child said, "lie like crazy"). And, invariably, the talk turns from comics and television shows to the subtle and demeaning moments that are part of every child's experience with the adult world.

At St. Ann's Episcopal School in Brooklyn, for instance, there was this bit of dialogue:

Anne Wiese, 9: "Grownups think

© The Chicago Tribune

Goody-goody Dondi vs. loudmouthed Virgil, an example of stereotypes children find offensive

they are superior in everything, but they're not. You can see through it when they say, 'Oh dear, the picture you did is beautiful,' and you know it's not."

Karen Petras, 10: "It's not fair if they tell you something is nice but it's obvious they don't like it — you know they're hiding something."

Anne: "They think you'll be so hurt."

Cyril Jermin, 11: "But it hurts you more if they turn around and, when they think you're not looking, go snicker-snicker-snicker."

Elise Burton, 11, conceded that "these are hard times for adults." (So much for sympathy.) But she also thinks children can demand a bit more respect.

"When our parents were in grade school, they didn't know half as much as we know," she said. "But they think we're only as smart now as they were then."

The children's view is not as bleak as it may seem. Some adults, rather than being villainous, are actually considered "neat-o," as are some entertainments, notably the "Fat Albert" television show. And the children are even optimistic enough to offer some remedies.

One favors the a-little-child-shall-lead-them proposition. At Hunter College elementary school, Christopher Stoecker, 11, said there should be "a kid President." But as soon as he put forward that idea, his peers argued loudly that a child wouldn't know how to handle important things, money, for instance.

No, David Hyman, 11, had a better idea, "How about," he said, "lowering the President's age to 18 so he could be close enough to children to remember how it felt."

Margaret Harris, 11, advised: "We know how we want to be treated and we know what's fair—parents should listen to our point of view."

Whether or not adults decide to take children more seriously, Charles Zorn, 10, has found his own, secret remedy. At 6:30 in the evening he watches "Beat the Clock," a television game show that gets adults to do slapstick tasks.

"That show," he said gleefully, "makes *parents* look stupid."

February 8, 1974

FILM VIEW

VINCENT CANBY

Thoughts About the Fear of Kids In Current American Movies

America's domination by its youth culture will not have properly peaked until we have as the nation's number-one television entertainer a stand-up comic no older than 8. At that point everything will have come together—our fear of the young, our desire to appear hip, our inclination to give children more material rewards than they could possibly think of on their own, and our worst nightmare, the expecta-

tion that one day we'll wake up to find ourselves rendered obsolete by toddlers, who then may well decide at what hour we should be put to sleep.

This is the only way I can explain the extraordinary fear and loathing of children, including babies, being expressed in current American movies. These films seem as determined to alert us to the potential dangers of totdom as the Warner Brothers films of the late 30's and early 40's were devoted to exposing the Nazis. Look closely at your kid, says "Demon Seed," because its father may have been a computer. "There's only one thing wrong with the Davis baby," says the ad for another film. "It's alive!" (which is also the title of the movie).

This peculiar American obsession with children-as-monsters is made even more apparent by the availability here of a number of European films that persist in treating children seriously and childhood as a normal part of the maturation process, not as a sentence to Hell.

In the space of one week there opened in New York "Cousin Angelica" and "Cria!," two unusually sensitive and sensible films about childhood, both directed by the Spanish filmmaker, Carlos Saura, and one ("Cria!") starring Ana Torrent, the tiny, dark-eyed 9-year-old whose responsive face made last year's "The Spirit of the Beehive" so memorable.

They regard children unsentimentally in European films, and with admiration and affection, as in Truffaut's "Small Change." Here we've reached the stage where it's a laugh to watch a short-tempered mom, fed up with non-stop squalling, toss her baby out the window of her high-rise. ("Andy Warhol's Bad").

About the only normal—or normally neurotic—children to be seen in a recent American film are the three boys in Franklin Schaffner's screen version of Hemingway's "Islands in the Stream," and the film isn't really about the boys. It's about their Hemingway-like dad and what *he* feels about *them*. More in the fashion of the day is "Audrey Rose," the Robert Wise-Frank De Felitta spin-off from "The Exorcist" about an 11-year-old New York girl named Audrey Rose, who was killed two minutes before Ivy was born.

• • •

The movie is supposed to be about reincarnation (and its pitfalls) but it's essentially an exercise in the good old pastime of Kick the Kid (Before He Kicks You). The little girl in "Audrey Rose" is a tortured nonentity, a spectacle to be observed much as we might watch Old Faithful in Yellowstone National Park. We don't feel any special sympathy for the child, and I don't think we are meant to, only a terrific relief that she's theirs, not ours.

The little boy in "The Omen," we are given to believe, is the natural son of the Prince of Darkness, come to earth to claim his legacy. "It's Alive" is about a murderous new-born infant who, after dispatching the doctors and nurses in the delivery room, crawls around Los Angeles at will, killing milkmen, senior citizens and other innocent adults. Near the end of "Demon Seed" we witness the birth of the child that's been "given" to Julie Christie by an amorous, ambitious "artificial intelligence system" that wishes to rule the earth. The baby, which we see briefly, is a superbeing who looks like a brass-dipped Mickey Rooney.

Ray Bradbury has wittily exploited adult fears of and guilts about children in a number of short stories, but the movies we're getting today have less to do with wit than with paranoia. That paranoia, though, in being a delusion, is not too different from the unreal way in which American movies have always depicted children, particularly as represented by such child stars as Mary Pickford, Shirley Temple, Jackie Cooper, Margaret O'Brien and Hayley Mills. These idealized representations of children—wise beyond their years, stanch, loyal, self-sufficient—have little need of the state of grace that Truffaut says, in "Small Change," envelops childhood. They are plaster saints, and quite as kid-freaky as the malignant monsters American movies are now presenting to us.

It's no wonder that the best child actor to appear in American movies lately, Jodie Foster, has made her mark playing essentially adult roles (the teen-age prostitute in "Taxi Driver," the speakeasy singer in "Bugsy Malone" and the daughter in the daughter-mother role-switching Disney comedy, "Freaky Friday"). Actresses complain about the dearth of good roles for women, but there are none at all for children as children.

• • •

That European filmmakers are able to explore childhood so successfully while Americans deal largely in distortions has, I suspect, more to do with the difference between the way films are made here and abroad than with any innate difference in sensibility. The best European films, which are the ones we see here, are the product of a cottage industry, of director-writers who pursue their personal visions away from the kind of pressures that have historically shaped American films since they became a global business. Though American movies are not exactly mass-produced, children in American movies tend to be as doll-like as toys produced for sale both at home and abroad. Would anyone want to buy a Barbie Doll with a crooked nose or thin hair? Perhaps a few eccentric little girls, but most want dolls that look exactly like the dolls their friends have.

European filmmakers recognize that movies that contain child actors needn't be designed for children. This is something that has perpetually confused Hollywood filmmakers and, I think, has been responsible for the odd distortions we've come to accept by saying with a shrug, "That's Hollywood." In American movies children tend to be miniature adults, and thus without any real stature or individuality. Not so in a film like Saura's haunted "Cria!", which is about the desperate attempts of a 9-year-old child to make some sense out of the chaos she sees in the adult world around her. It's not a film for children (though I don't believe it would disturb a child). It's a film for adults who haven't forgotten that they too were once at a terrible disadvantage for being small and, in the ways of the world, ignorant.

Saura, Truffaut, Hans Geissendorfer (director of the excellent German adaptation of "The Wild Duck"), Pascal Thomas (director of "Les Zozos") recognize that children are different from you and me by taking them on their own terms. The reaction of American moviemakers is to turn kids into either saints or beasts, a process that not only facilitates the product merchandizing but also relieves us of any responsibility towards them.

May 29, 1977

Hollywood's Kids Are Becoming Cherubs Again

By MILES BELLER

Cute, lovable movie kids are back. In a dramatic break from their portrayal in recent years as little and sometimes fiendish monsters, Hollywood's children are again behaving "admirably," as they did in the films of the 1930's. In "The Black Stallion," which was screened at the New York Film Festival last night and enters commercial release on Thursday, the young hero who befriends the horse of the title is shown as resourceful and determined against forces that might defeat grown-ups. In the current "Rich Kids," about children suffering through their parents' marital miseries, and "A Little Romance," an updated Romeo and Juliet, the protagonists react to love with a fervor that adults have presumably outgrown. And in last summer's tearjerker, "The Champ," the emotional focus is on the heart-tugging little boy who was first played by Jackie Cooper in the original, more than four decades ago.

That film makers should return to the 30's image of model children in our uncertain time is not surprising. For as Alfred Appel Jr. notes in "Nabokov's Dark Cinema," few moviegoers under age 40 are aware of the pervasiveness of child performers during the 30's, a decade hit by the Great Depression, progressive education and Freud's insight into infant sexuality.

Yet as the 30's lapsed into the 40's and 50's, baby's face took on an increasingly evil sneer. In "The Bad Seed," blond and blue-eyed Patty McCormack cheerily played a piano after torching a man to death. With "Village of the Damned" (1962), kids changed from figurative monsters into literal monsters — no longer of our flesh, but aliens from space now on earth to take control of a world run by adults.

The birth of "Rosemary's Baby" in 1968 began a long-term preoccupation with devil children; the fetus became evil incarnate. "Rosemary's Baby" begot "The Exorcist" (1974), an explicit film about a possessed child who takes to killing priests and masturbating with a bloody crucifix. In turn, "The Exorcist" spawned "The Other," "The Omen," "Audrey Rose," as well as legions of low-budget productions populated by pint-size ghouls and hideously deformed beasts sprung from the womb. By the mid-1970's, Satan and the child were one.

And yet now, at the end of the decade, Hollywood has rediscovered the innocence of childhood. In "The Black Stallion," Kelly Reno, a newcomer to the screen, portrays Alex Ramsey, an angelic-looking lad who survives a shipwreck and is washed ashore on a deserted island with a fellow passenger — the black stallion. Set in the 1930's, the film uses the boy/horse relationship to develop an image of an idyllic childhood in which a young survivor ably takes care of himself in a world without adults. Even when rescuers "save" boy and horse, and return them to civilization, their union is a magical bond that can't be broken. (As if in homage to yesterday's child stars, Mickey Rooney, the ever-smiling Andy Hardy of the 30's, is cast as Alex's friend and trainer of his horse.)

Another current film imbued with the 30's notion that children are naturally nobler and brighter than adults is "Rich Kids." Here two schoolmates, Franny and Jamie (Trini Alvarado and Jeremy Levy), develop a special relationship because of divorces in their families. Jamie, having gone through his parents' break-up, counsels Franny on how to handle her parents' impending split. In the movie, parents are dimwits locked into sad routines. The film also advances an if-adults-would-only-act-more-like-children philosophy, for adults are pictured as acceptable only when they drop grown-up concerns and pretentions, and again see the world through a child's eyes. When Franny sadly asks Jamie, "Why can't they [adults] be like us?," the boy bitterly replies, "Someday we'll grow up just like them."

The recent "A Little Romance" depicts children as keenly sensitive souls who instinctively feel life more deeply than their parents. As most of the adults bumble and fumble, the two youngsters (Diane Lane and Thelo Bernard), with the aid of an old man (Laurence Olivier), flee Paris for Venice to kiss beneath the Bridge of Sighs; while the adults merely play-act at flirting and coquetry, the children experience and understand the "romance" of the film's title, which describes their liaison as well as that quality the children see as essential in life.

In the coming months, Columbia Pictures will begin production on a film of the Broadway musical "Annie." M-G-M, responsible for the original and remake of "The Champ," has started "Why Would I Lie?", about a welfare worker (Treat Williams) who unofficially adopts a little boy (newcomer Gabriel Swann) from a child care home and then discovers the woman he loves (Lisa Eichhorn) is the lad's mother; the studio also wants Franco Zeffirelli, who made "The Champ," to direct a comedy starring Ricky Schroder of that film. And at Universal, a remake of the 1934 Shirley Temple film "Little Miss Marker," starring Walter Matthau, Julie Andrews and 6-year-old Sara Stinson as the tot who finds herself used as a "marker," or gambling I.O.U., is set for spring release.

Nor is this fond view limited to prepubescent kiddies. The current "Breaking Away" is about teenagers who, though known to curse, are essentially innocents. In the forthcoming "French Postcards," college students spending their junior year abroad in Paris show a naïvete that is touching in this jet age. And next year, Paramount will present two erstwhile "child stars" — Tatum O'Neal and Kristy McNichol — in "Little Darlings," about two girls (Miss O'Neal rich and shy, Miss McNichol poor and streetwise) who meet at summer camp and become close friends.

The youngsters now gracing movie screens embody our 'wishful projections,' says Dr. Bruno Bettelheim.

Some of these films will no doubt remind audiences of the days when freckled Mickey Rooney romped with winsome Judy Garland in Andy Hardy movies; when that bunch of little rascals called "Our Gang" performed their endearing escapades; when roles were tailored to the talents of such as Jackie Cooper, Dickie Moore and Freddie Bartholomew. But of course the No. 1 child star of the age was Shirley Temple. Through deeply dimpled cheeks and 47 years of movie history, the tiny actress now smiles beatifically down from revival house screens: she is the patron saint of child stars, destined to dance forever in America's collective consciousness.

Why has Hollywood today become so eager to present children as cherubs and saints when just a few years ago moviegoers thronged to films that portrayed them as killers and sinners? What does this recycled film image of the child reveal about larger cultural attitudes toward children and society?

The child psychologist Bruno Bettelheim believes that today's film view of children and childhood represents "a general tendency to glorify the past, denying feelings we really experience." According to Dr. Bettelheim, who finds Hollywood's cute innocents offensive, the depiction of youngsters as simple sweet souls, in an age when studies and newspaper headlines underscore quite the contrary, provides adults with readily acceptable sons and daughters. "Adults today don't want to be bothered understanding children. When a child comes to us with a nightmare, we tell him there are no snakes under his bed. But dismissing the nightmare doesn't dispel the child's real anxiety." The youngsters now gracing movie screens embody our "wishful projections," notes Dr. Bettelheim, and not any God-given attributes in the child's nature.

Americans are not known for being benevolent toward their children, says Dr. Lee Salk, president of the child/youth division of the American Psychological Association. "In the past, making kids into demons and monsters reflected this anti-child attitude, a thinking that we had to beat the 'little devils' into submission to get them to behave." Yet Dr. Salk finds nothing to applaud in Hollywood's current depiction of children. For the re-emergence of innocent kids on film is just a change in image, not essence. According to Dr. Salk, the cute squeezable kids now before us are as "emotionally alien from real children" as were their depraved predecessors. One poorly fashioned caricature has been replaced by another. Since neither depiction takes children seriously, concludes Dr. Salk, the ersatz youngsters in films are safe and non-threatening to adults, providing synthetic reactions in place of the joys and terrors of real children.

Amitai Etzioni, professor of sociology at Columbia, characterizes Hollywood's current portrayal of children as "flat and one-dimensional. We all either have or know children; yet as revealed in these films, we know as much about them as if they were Martians." For Hollywood either bedevils or romanticizes childhood, he observes, never presenting this stage of development as it truly is. "When films like 'The Exorcist' were out, we were at the height of the anti-child feeling in this country. When we later sold Third World countries the idea of 'zero population growth,' we wound up buying the idea ourselves. Now we've come to see a society without children as sick and infirm." As a result, Dr. Etzioni believes, Hollywood and the public now see children as gentle spirits pure of soul instead of as evil. Like Dr. Bettelheim, Dr. Etzioni finds Hollywood's current depiction of kids symptomatic of our need to "strip children of their complexity" and see them as virtuous innocents.

M.I.T. professor Kenneth Keniston is wary of the oversimplifications often found in films: "People harbor mixed feelings about children, which is not the case in films that show children either as 'good' or 'bad.'" Dr. Keniston traces this tendency in part to America's early attitudes toward kids. Childrearing practices back in the Puritan days were harsh, he says; compared to the past, today is a relatively good time to be a child.

"I'm suspicious of adults sentimentalizing children," says the pediatrician Dr. Benjamin Spock, commenting on today's film image of youngsters. For such movies often refuse to see the "dignity of the child," instead satisfying adults' needs at youngsters' expense. Like a grownup cooing baby talk to a 6-year-old, Dr. Spock says, these films underestimate their subjects, ad-

Adults who indulge a sentimental view of childhood are 'mourning their own lost innocence,' notes François Truffaut.

dressing them in a patronizing voice. "I think the image of children in films swings so dramatically in this country," he concludes, "because of a deep-seated ambivalence we feel toward our children. We'll spend hundreds of dollars straightening a child's teeth or giving him or her piano lessons, yet at the same time scream our lungs out at that same child and be positively abusive."

The French film director François Truffaut, who since the 1959 "400 Blows" has made many films about children, views the current affinity for "cute" kids with some alarm. In a story he wrote for the UNESCO Courier several months ago, Mr. Truffaut states that "The adult cinema-goer sees childhood as linked to the idea of innocence and above all to the idea of purity." Yet the adult who becomes "emotional when he sees a child on the screen" is, in Mr. Truffaut's words, "actually indulging in self-pity and mourning his own lost 'innocence.'" The French director sees the public expecting children to play on its heart strings, but cautions that giving in to this sentiment is the worst thing film makers can do. For such movies ring false, reveal nothing about the nature of children, and only perpetuate a cliched view of childhood — a view, that, however comforting to adults, cheats children "out of their due."

Yet perhaps in an age when, according to Dr. Spock, "We've come to expect too little from people, . . . taking pride in our cynicism," it's only natural that the child become the fountainhead of innocence and purity. For, as in the 30's, a period faced with economic woes and an uncertain future, we've lost faith in traditional solutions and grown-up logic. Thwarted and frustrated by our inability to get what we want, low on fuel, options and morale, we cherish our illusions. And the illusion of an idealized childhood tempers remembrances of our own youth and brings us back to an age when everything, to quote Dickens, "was happy and there was no distance and no time." So we reinvent children and childhood, Geppettos carving Pinocchios, whittling "what was" into "what should have been."

Miles Beller, a Los Angeles freelance writer, has a special interest in films.

October 14, 1979

CHAPTER 2

The American Teenager

Part of the audience at one of disk jockey Alan Freed's rock 'n' roll stage shows of the 1950's.

Larry Morris/NYT Pictures

THE AGE OF DISRESPECT.

Bumptious Boys and Girls and How They Should Be Accepted.

The time from ten to fifteen years of age, writes Kate Upson Clark in a paper on the above subject, is of all the periods of life the most lacking in reverence. The problem of how to live with this young person, often three or four strong in a single family, is an absorbing problem in the minds of parents.

Even in a well-managed household, it must have been remarked by every observer that the boy or girl of from ten to fifteen, especially if he or she be bright and ambitious, is likely to be bumptious. A boy may have comported himself up to the age of ten or twelve with modesty and propriety; but he often takes a turn about that time, and becomes impertinent, heedless of advice and even of command, scornful of father and mother, and generally unendurable. It is a time for the exercise of the choicest wisdom within our reach. These children are full of life and hope; they are successful in school, leaders among their mates, and so far instinct with confidence in themselves that it is not strange that they find themselves cribbed, cabined, and confined by the restrictions of home. They do not realize that their parents have been through just such a series of triumphs and successes as they themselves are enjoying, (and, if the truth were known, were probably as disagreeably conscious of it as their children now are of their own small cleverness!) and they regard the heads of the family with something which savors not remotely of contempt. It is easier for a mother to bear this than for a father, and yet the mother usually comes in for the greater share of the disdain. Some one has written that if we could realize how our mothers love us, there would be a new force in the world. These children are very far from realizing it. They cannot realize it until they are fathers and mothers themselves.

"No chance, no fame,
No wealth of love can ever compensate
For a dead mother."

But these unseeing ones, wrapped in the dense, opaque brightness of youth, have little perception of these deepest truths.

"But how shall we manage them?" asks a perplexed mother. "How can we make them listen to us, take our advice, treat us with proper respect in the presence of others, do the drudgery which falls to their share in the household work thoroughly and well, believe that when we forbid a pleasure it is for their best good—from 'that sharp and waspish word "No"'

pluck the sting?"

In the first place, do not find fault too much. Pass some things over. Do as much as you can of the neglected work. If the child has, as is likely, real nobility at bottom, this course will touch his heart. We all hated drudgery at his age. Talk with him alone as much as you can. It is hard to make any impression on a child when he is surrounded by others. Show an interest in his pursuits, even if you feel none.

Don't be cross to him when he litters up the reception room, and when he persistently, day after day, keeps his own room looking as much like a kennel as he can. Good Jan Ridd calls "scolding and crossness" "the curse of clean women and ten times worse than the dustiest dust." Many a boy and girl, at this critical age, have been turned permanently against their homes by the faultfinding and captiousness of overclean mothers.

But the great general rule (to adapt the directions in the "Faerie Quene") is "Be patient, and again be patient—but be not too patient." A little wholesome spirit in parents is a good thing now and then for these "bumptious" children. One must, in short, apply to the dominion of the home what Tennyson has written of a greater kingdom, or republic, in which "the common sense of most shall hold a fretful realm in awe." The great gift of common sense is never more needed than during the age of disrespect.

December 31, 1893

Teen-Age Decalogue

By Catherine Mackenzie

JUDGING by the opinions they express in questionnaires and polls, teen-age boys and girls hold decided views on how they should be brought up. One more expression of their views is contained in a "Decalogue for Parents," reported to the National Recreation Association by Dr. Philip L. Seman as the outcome of a Chicago Youth Congress "held to discuss the problem of juvenile delinquency and to suggest cures."

Parents who aren't too worn out to cope with this subject on Sunday morning may care to see how they measure up.

The ten items of the "decalogue" are too detailed for this space (Recreation publishes them in full). In essence they go like this:

(1) Make a friend of your child,

take him into your confidence. . . . Show your child the right way by example.

(2) Make it your business to know the whereabouts of your child at all times, but don't allow him to feel "haunted."

(3) If a child errs, it is chiefly because he has never been shown the right way . . . don't punish him to excess . . . show him the right way with kindness.

ITEM 4 deals with the wabbly discipline implied in such threats as, "Just wait till your father comes home," leading, the young people say, to "loss of affection for the 'discipline-parent' and a realization of the weakness of character in the other parent."

Item 5 lays down and expands the injunction, "Don't give your child the impression that he is a nuisance when adults are present."

The sixth and seventh of these commandments go into detail on the "duty" of every father and every mother, respectively, to explain to sons and daughters "the facts of life." Mothers are charged, in addition, with "impressing" upon a daughter "the righteous trends of young ladies of high character."

There is something touching in the solemnity of all this, and something sobering too; the young expect so much of adults, make so few allowances—just as we did at their age. (Is it necessary to add that these "Ten Commandments," accepted by 250 delegates representing 176,000 high school students, were drafted by a boy of 16?)

IN the foregoing, and in items 8 to 10, the young people said in so many words that they want to be "proud" of their parents; to be sure that parents "count" on them; to feel that their friends are welcome at home; to be encouraged to go to church, to love their country, and to enlist their energies in "patriotic movements of high caliber."

In short, by their own account, the boys and girls seem to want just what the experts have been saying they need.

January 21, 1945

Teen-Age Social Life

By CATHERINE MACKENZIE

LEARNING from some recent research that a fair proportion of little girls—aged 12—were trying the effect of lipstick for social occasions, we made a mental note to look into the phenomenon of early stepping-out.

So we asked Dr. Esther Lloyd-Jones what she could tell us about it. Director of the Guidance Laboratory at Teachers College of Columbia University, Dr. Lloyd-Jones had not seen the study we quoted, but said that it was not news to her that the wartime acceleration of growing up had reached as far down as the sixth and seventh grades.

As we went into the war, specialists in guidance told us that as older teen-agers suddenly took on mature roles, the younger group would also step ahead. And they did. Dr. Lloyd-Jones has been hearing about this from teachers and parents for several years.

Parents tell her that one sign of sud-

den precocity is the tendency of 12 and 13 year old boys and girls to pair off, to go to the movies in couples, to have "dates." Parents ask her about this, suggesting that maybe, since the urge is sweeping this age group, it is just as well to let them go ahead. But Dr. Lloyd-Jones doesn't agree. She thinks that to permit this early "dating" is to deprive the youngsters of something else they need, and shouldn't skip—the wholesome fun of normal 12 and 13

year old group gatherings. This is part of the normal experience of growing up and shouldn't be missed. She realizes that parents—and teachers—have to get together to plan for it. For example, she says, grown-ups have to know which house can take care of the "gang" on which night.

LITTLE did we think that we'd soon find out about this trend at first hand. In the course of recent weeks, in an-

swering the telephone for the busy mother of four, our role consisted largely of relaying messages from young friends, intermittently for the twin boys, aged 9, and regularly for their sister, aged 11.

Back from their first season at camp, the children had suddenly become intensely social. Gone were the leisurely days when we read aloud, played jacks or provided an audience for the "Watch me!" stage of growing up. Now we jotted down the invitations, most steadily those from a contemporary whom we'll call Billy, whose open admiration for the lass of 11 years was discussed by the children frankly and with utter calm.

Some parental astonishment was privately expressed. ("I didn't know this started so young"), but no special family problem was posed. The accelerated social life of ages 9 to 12 seemed to have pervaded the neighborhood. (Perhaps the return of gasoline and tires helped.) Parents had it well in hand. We observed that mothers took turns piling the youngsters into station wagons, convoying them on trips to beaches and on picnics; that on weekends fathers supervised swimming and fishing trips.

Children swapped overnight visits, came to play and stayed to lunch. Family permission was sought, reports on whereabouts duly given. We saw no evidence of "pairing off," even at ages 12 or 13, but we discovered what Dr. Lloyd-Jones meant by parental planning for social occasions. Judging by our interlude with the telephone, the planning is intensive and starts sooner than we thought.

September 8, 1946

Unchanging Teen-agers

By CATHERINE MACKENZIE

TOM is "always on the go," Grace "comes home just long enough to change her clothes and go out again." Jane must see every moving picture. . . .

Teen-age boys and girls behaved this way in 1933 when the United States Children's Bureau first published "Guiding the Adolescent." A revised edition has just appeared, and Tom, Grace and Jane are still in its pages, behaving the same way.

Three-quarters of a million copies of this booklet have been used by parents,

according to the new foreword. The lack of major revision is one of the most interesting things about it.

Changes of phrase, a few new sentences, a paragraph added here and there represent alteration in the American scene since pocket flasks were part of it (noted as a factor leading to "petting" and not mentioned now).

But basically there is little difference —in the behavior which is normal to the years between 12 and 20, in the way parents feel about it and in the counsel written in 1933 by Dr. Douglas A. Thom, director of the Habit Clinic for Child Guidance of Boston.

Here are the boys and girls, acutely aware of bodily changes, sensitive to criticism, afraid of being "different," at once wanting the security of home life and wanting to escape from it.

And here are their parents, expecting the young to account for their comings and goings, expecting to continue the companionship built up over the years, and finding doors to intimacy shut—if not banged—in their faces.

THE advice, keyed to everyday problems common to normal growing-up, deals with attitudes toward sex, with education, work and earning. Family headaches are here too—stealing, cheating, truancy, drinking.

One statement on physical growth seems to us outdated by newer findings, but the behavior involved is not. And it is noteworthy that Dr. Thom long ago spoke up in behalf of the "great masses of boys and girls of this country." He asked for "more respect and less criticism from adults," a view with which some of us have only just caught up. He also cautioned about the assumption that "every adolescent boy or girl is drifting about in an emotional whirlpool." No such thing, he said, in 1933, and he sticks to it now.

In a section on "Education in the Use of Leisure" parents are told that by giving thought to it early, a backlog of family enjoyment can be established. This applies to the years in which fathers and mothers plan picnics, trips to the zoo, to see boats load and unload, to watch airplanes land and depart, to explore historic spots, visit pet shows.

MANY parents have done all this, and still find Tom and Grace—at adolescence—"always on the go." Since we haven't space to quote a great deal, we pick this as bearing on one of the harder facts to face in middle age:

"No matter how pleasant the family life and how much the children enjoy their leisure-time activities with their parents, the normal adolescent, as he grows older, will want to spend more time doing things with the boys and girls of his own age and less with his family. This is something which parents should be prepared to welcome as a sign that their growing son and daughter are developing in an entirely normal way and making a good adjustment to life."

That's what the booklet said thirteen years ago, and says now. But the new edition adds this:

"Parents should make sure that their children are not obliged to have all their social contacts away from home through lack of any privacy from an interested family. A boy who has a room of his own to which to bring his friends will spend a lot of time there; the girl who knows that her parents may be depended on not to attach themselves like limpets to the living room chairs when she brings the 'gang' home with her will spend less time joy-riding."

THIS is not to imply that parents abdicate control when they go early to bed, vacate the living room, or wave the children off to the debating club: "There may be a rule—or perhaps a tactful understanding—about the hour for coming home, and parents should certainly know where and with whom their adolescents are spending their time."

Thirteen years ago the text read, "Adolescence is the time when companionship and confidence may be sought by the child or invited by the parent, but it is too late for the parent to force it." Today this comment continues, "Nor should he risk making a boy or girl feel guilty because he is growing out of his earlier intimacy with and dependency upon his parents."

Many more families have moved around the country since the year in which Hitler became German Chancellor, and the new edition notes that—depending on the "essential security" of the family relationship—these removals are not necessarily a handicap. The contemporary tendency to pair off, and to "date" with only one person, is noted now as "a fad of the moment" requiring "real ingenuity" of handling.

And in the section "Needs of the Parent" appears that timeless character, Isabel's mother—young, gay, anxious to share her daughter's life, hurt when rebuffed. This is the mother who calls from her bedroom, "Hello, dear, did you have a good time? Come and tell Mummy all about it." This is the daughter who stamps off to her room with a poker-faced "Good night." It is such an old story. The locked diary. The plaint, "You seem to forget I'm your mother."

If Isabel was 17 in 1933 she must be 30 now. And if she marries as young as her mother did, any day now it may be her turn.

December 8, 1946

'Calling All Teens'

By CATHERINE MACKENZIE

PARENTS should have something to say about how teen-age allowances are spent. Boys should meet the girls' parents when calling for a date. Parents should set the hour for coming home from a party and expect an accounting for being late.

These are the majority views of some three hundred boys and girls between the ages of 13 and 16. Other opinions, on friends, school, manners, dress and dating appear in the latest round-up of youthful opinions to reach our desk. Of course, the young people have their own ideas on "reasonable" hours of getting home at night, on just how much—and no more—parents should govern outlay of spending money. They want parents to meet them half way. They are firm about the proprieties of dating, but they also wish mother would be out of her apron and ready with some "friendly conversation" when the escort calls.

"This is how we act, how we feel, how we think," declare the young compilers

of a brisk little document "Calling All Teens."

Clarence G. Moser of the field staff of the Y. M. C. A. Central Atlantic Area tells us that this material originated last year with the teen-age crowd of Evanston, Ill., first as a protest against an adult mass meeting on "juvenile delinquency," then as a means to set standards among their own crowd.

SEEMS the boys and girls were unrepresented at the mass meeting, thought the approach should have been more positive. Discussions ensued. Then came the opinion poll. Graduate students from Northwestern University helped. At this time Mr. Moser was City Boys' Work Secretary of the Evanston Y. M. C. A. and he cooperated in interpreting the findings. He assured us that the point of view and the language are strictly teen age. We said we were sure of this.

The scene is new. Terminology changes with the generations. But emotions do not change, and only the young of this age group would be as conventional and as touchingly in earnest as these youngsters are.

The young people refer to a girl who smokes as a "fag-nag." Ninety-nine per cent of the boys—sorry, "guys"—

consider her "strictly off the beam." Sloppily dressed boys are termed "mothballs." When they mention paper money they call it "folding lettuce," in case you didn't know—we didn't.

But this is superficial. In matters of dating, conduct in public places, in appraisal of their peers, these young people are as conservative, we almost said "strait-laced," as we were at their age.

IN their disapproval of noisy or unseemly conduct in public they say to girls, "Making a general fool of yourself is strictly 'off the cob.' " To the boys, "Can't you have fun without being so childish?" And on destroying public property: "You don't impress your crowd by the way you can break up a park bench or smack a street light. * * * Get hep, folks, get hep."

Particular as they are about a scrubbed, trim exterior, they have this to say about girls' personal appearance: "It's not the cost that matters as much as the clean, neat touch."

Under the general heading of "Junior Mess" the young people are unsparing in criticism of personal grooming, and say severely, " 'You'll Walk Alone' if you fix your make-up and hair in a place that is more public than the ladies' lounge."

Some of the teen-age counsel to girls

on "dating" is freer than it used to be. For example: "Maybe he wants to hold hands in the movies—O. K. If you can't stand this, better not date him. Eventually he may try a kiss. If you can't accept graciously, then don't give him the 'come-on.' But get too chummy and you cease being out of this world."

But they continue—so little have times changed since grandma was a girl: "You may not think it fair, but the boys expect you to be finer and gentler than they are. * * * If the party looks like it is getting out of hand, find a good reason to go home."

THEY point out to girls that in saying good night, "lingering on the doorknob hoping for another invitation is very poor strategy." They remind boys of their social responsibilities this way: "If you're a date-breaker for anything less than illness, you're on the skids."

Mr. Moser tells us that a small edition of this pamphlet has been issued at 35 cents a copy by The Progress Press. (19 South Wells Street, Chicago 6, Ill.) He finds that it has "clicked with teen-agers." And since coming to the East he has found the material helpful in parent counseling.

Most unusual feature, in his opinion, is the comment for parents, derived by the young people from the poll and its

interpretation, and all their own idea. Here are a few excerpts.

"Most of us don't want to date girls you pick for us. We want to please you, but we'll get around to her in time if she has all the glamour you think she has."

"You will find it a poor investment to select clothes for your son without consulting him. Trying to change his style may end up in a family fight if you go against the crowd."

"You have a right to crack down on us when we are too late, but it is hard to operate when the hour is not flexible. * * * Just remember that late hours do not mean low morals with most of us."

"You will not only find it cheaper to give your boy or girl an allowance, but you will find it a good chance to counsel with your children about handling money."

"Egg beaters" is their term for the elders who pursue "the steady lashing that beats us into froth." A parent is a "Good Egg" when "you realize that the hatching season is over and you don't try to sit on us all the time."

"Lubricated Lugs and Lugesses" is the heading for teen-age comment on drinking. This is what they say to parents:

"MOST of your children do not approve of smoking or drinking and they feel you do not approve, yet they are being pulled into it by advertising, radio, the crowd, or drinking within their home, often with their parents. You ought to see that your children have the facts on both of these subjects. Those who are smoking or drinking to convince themselves they are big stuff are to be pitied. Some of your children will be hurt. You can't dodge this issue."

This isn't all. A summary of the poll includes this finding:

"Do you expect to give your children more, less or the same discipline you have had?" Of the girls 47 per cent said "same," 33 per cent "more"; 29 per cent of the boys said "same," 42 per cent "more."

January 26, 1947

Parents of Adolescents Are Urged to Span Rapidly Widening Gap Between Generations

Normal differences between teen-age children and their parents have been accentuated by the rapidity of change in this generation, according to Dr. Evelyn M. Duvall, executive secretary of the National Council on Family Relations.

Dr. Duvall's examination of this subject and her conclusions are contained in a pamphlet made public yesterday by the Public Affairs Committee, Inc., a non-profit educational organization at 22 East Thirty-eighth Street.

"Times are changing so fast," Dr. Duvall wrote, "that each generation lives in a world that is only partially known to the one that precedes it or the one that follows. Understanding these shifts, what they are, what they mean, and how they affect the thinking and behavior of the people who live

through them, is one span in bridging the generations today."

Dr. Duvall attributed to "ruralization" some of the problems in parent-child relations. She asserted that when city children grow up and make friends outside the family circle, they may reject or minimize patterns of behavior encouraged by their parents.

"Each youth," she said, "is brought up in the way of life of his parents. As soon as he is old enough to make friends outside the family circle, he finds that many of the ways he has always considered 'right' are not taken seriously by some others. Behavior that is forbidden in one group is condoned or even encouraged in a second. The 'right' is not absolute but relative to the time and the place and the people."

March 31, 1947

Topics of The Times

Parents and Children

When people speak about the gulf between the generations, as Dr. Evelyn M. Duvall does in a pamphlet released by the Public Affairs Committee, there is a first temptation to say something bright and flip. Of course there is a gulf between parents and children because the youngsters know so much more than their elders.

Only it would be a pity to yield to a show-off impulse and so miss Dr. Duvall's wise and moving words on the subject. She is executive secretary of the National Council on Family Relations. She makes the point that it is not a question of one generation knowing truer and more important things than the other generation, but of knowing different things. "Times are changing so fast that each generation lives in a world that is only partially known to the one that precedes it or the one that follows."

Highly Perishable Slang

Times change fast, indeed; not only in tastes, morals, manners, but in language. The old generation, in a fine endeavor to keep up with the young, will quote at the dinner table a picturesque new bit of slang encountered that very day. There will be a general teen-age laugh around the table, not unkindly, and it turns out that this new bit of slang is three years old and very much old hat. The old generation mentions a new bit of crooning over the radio and is informed that it is eighteen months old. The world does change fast.

Confusion of Tongues

The language gulf between the generations will grow wider and wider as time moves on and the older generation finds its stock of standard quotations fall on deafer and deafer ears. The familiar things from the Bible, from Shakespeare, from Kipling, from Longfellow, grow paler and paler with the years, not to speak of our occasional lingering remnants from the classic tongues. One wonders how safe it is now to speak to a teen-age audience about shibboleth and sibboleth, the coat of many colors, the walls of Jericho, the Good Samaritan, the Gadarene swine, the road to Damascus. How much longer will it be safe to allude to all the pomp of yesterday which is now like Nineveh and Tyre; or the youth who bore midst snow and ice a banner with the strange device; or *Sic semper tyrannis* or *Labor omnia vincit?*

One might argue that ultimately the problem will be solved by the elder generation passing from the scene. There will be nobody left to quote outworn things which the young do not understand and so the gulf will be bridged. But how about the former younger generation, now grown elderly, being misunderstood by a new younger generation?

April 4, 1947

Party Code of Conduct for Teen-Agers And Parents Is Issued in Hartford Area

Special to THE NEW YORK TIMES.

HARTFORD, Conn., Dec. 8—A code of conduct for teen-agers and their parents while both are out on parties was issued this week by the parent councils of five schools in this area.

The code sets up a standard of conduct for the schoolboys and girls and gives general advice to parents. The code was drafted by the parent council of one of the schools. It was received so well that copies were distributed to parent councils in the other schools, and they, too, approved it.

The code follows:

1. "Insist that your boy or girl go to no party to which he or she is not invited and insist that no one be allowed at your party who is not invited.

2. "Have no parties at your house unless you are there. The parent council feels strongly that every party of teen-agers should be adequately chaperoned.

3. "Impress upon your son or daughter that when he or she is driving someone in a car, he or she is responsible for that person's safety.

4. "Think of this: Do you, as a parent, have the right to serve any intoxicating drinks to someone else's children? If you do serve them or have alcholic beverages available, then you, as an adult, are responsible.

5. The parent council disapproves of parties running into the small hours of the morning. Please insist that your boy or girl telephone you if he or she is to be out later than agreed.

6. "We feel that our boys should ask the parents of their girls what time the girls are expected home and comply with the parents' wishes. They should also advise the parents where they are going."

The codes, described as "a sensible basis of good conduct and good manners," has been approved by the parent councils of Kingswood School in West Hartford, Oxford School in Hartford, and Loomis and Chaffee Schools in Windsor, all private schools. The parent council of William H. Hall High School in West Hartford, a public school, also approved the document.

December 9, 1951

Allowing for Teen-Age Tensions

By DOROTHY BARCLAY

PARENTS of teen-agers don't have to be told that these youngsters can be pretty baffling. Their perception, their understanding and their knowledge at times surprise adults. At other times their perverseness (or what looks like it to adults) is enough to tempt parents to disclaim ownership. Mothers and dads whose relationship with their adolescent young is alternately a puzzle and a delight have company in their perplexity. "The experts" are puzzling about teen-agers too.

A week or so ago there reached our desk a 316-page report on "Personality Development in Adolescent Girls," a monograph of the Society for Research in Child Development. This is a technical study intended for use by professional workers in education, counseling and organized youth services. It presents,  however, so clear a picture of what goes on under the often-smooth surface of many teen-age girls that we felt some discussion of its assumptions and findings would be both interesting and helpful to parents.

Five specialists share authorship of this report—Ross

Harrison, Elisabeth Hellersberg, Karen Machover, Meta Steiner and—a name well known to our regular readers —Lawrence K. Frank. Mr. Frank was director of the over-all study as well.

*I*T was a tremendous undertaking. Three hundred girls, ranging in age from 10½ to almost 20 and coming from a wide variety of backgrounds, were included in the research, based on a series of specialized psychological tests. Fifteen hundred separate analyses had to be made. These were individually studied and interpreted, girl by girl, and then by groups according to evidence of physical maturity.

The tests given were the kind in which persons are asked to tell what they see in a series of ink blots or to make up a story about a provocative picture that could mean any number of things. This method was used in an attempt to discover some of the things girls in these age groups are not likely to say about themselves — either because they are not aware of, or do not understand, what they think and feel or because they prefer not to talk about these things with grown-ups.

A good many adults don't like this sort of approach to youth. Teen-age girls are, to them, delightful creatures in pastel dresses and little flat shoes sipping a soda with an equally delightful young man —or perhaps, instead, the girls are harum-scarum creatures in blue jeans and boys' shirts. Either way, they are Happiness, they are Youth, and these adults would rather not hear about psychologists "stirring up trouble" in Paradise.

*T*HESE individuals very likely will not accept the re-

searchers' conclusion: That the teen-agers studied, as a group, were more seriously disturbed emotionally than even the researchers had anticipated.

The girls, especially those of about junior and senior high school age, appear "in some of the tests and with few exceptions to be unhappy and tense." They show in some of their responses "a pervasive fear of life." The girls in the middle and upper social-economic groups "show the effects of the continual pressures they are under from ambitious or intellectual parents, often reinforced by idealistic teachers." Some of the girls were rated as highly intelligent and capable with a wide range of knowledge, "but they are anxious and tense and show little desire to mature as feminine personalities." This talk of "confusion about the feminine role" abounds throughout the report.

*W*E talked with Mr. Frank about this and some of the other implications of the study for parents. Considering the number of books and articles currently appearing

on the confusion of grown women about their place in life, he said, it's not surprising that the situation exists among young girls. In part, it helps to explain the prevalence of the "glamour girl," described by the researchers as "a socially approved stereotype" dictating manners, grooming, dress, speech, gestures and attitudes.

Hiding behind this social front, the girl can act as popular thinking seems to indicate a woman should. This new idea of her role might be most helpful indeed were the pattern not completely superficial, leaving the girl still adrift so far as all basic considerations are concerned.

In the midst of this confusion, how can parents help? Mr. Frank's answer may surprise many. During adolescence, he told us, that period of emancipation, young people almost from necessity must look for their principal counseling outside (that's right, "outside") the family. Just as the 2½-year-old had to assert himself, to stop being a baby and become an individual in the family, the teenager must complete this

"journey" and stand at last as an individual in the world outside his home.

*T*HE long periods of solitary day-dreaming, the seemingly endless sessions of talk with others the same age are vitally necessary to adolescents in this process. Counseling services at schools and in youth agencies would not relieve parents of their responsibility for guidance but would help them carry it more effectively.

Adolescence may be a time of explosive emotional outbursts or of emotional withdrawal from parents. If parents react in kind the situation can grow acutely worse. As in the case of younger children, Mr. Frank said, parents would do well to try to accept negative feelings without taking them as personal affronts. Battered and sore though they may sometimes feel, parents will help all concerned if they can serve as a buffer between the conflicting interests of the older and younger children, trying to explain the needs of each to the other.

*F*OR parents, just being willing to recognize the strain their daughters may be under can be a first step toward helping. Once they have accepted this idea they will find it easier to loosen up on demands for perfection and achievement. They will in every way they can help their daughters build their strength and develop healthy confidence. They will allow time and provide opportunities for healthy relaxation and fun, alone and in groups, and encourage such activities as painting, dance and creative dramatics, with their opportunities for emotional release and self-discovery.

June 7, 1953

Coexisting With Teen-Agers

By EDA J. LESHAN

*I*N any discussion among parents of adolescents, sooner or later one question is almost certain to arise: What shall we do when we know our children are doing things we don't approve of? Shall we voice our objections? Or shall we accept the behavior on the theory that in this

way at least we avoid secrecy and deceit?

Do we, because a 16-year-old insists that "it's done," serve cocktails to youngsters at a birthday dance? ("Otherwise," the adolescent may insist, "somebody's liable to spike the punch!") Do we buy cigarettes for a 12-year-old and

sit by while he smokes them? ("I can get them for 2 cents apiece from a guy at school. You wouldn't want me smoking in the street, would you?") Do we, to prove our broadmindedness, laugh at—and thus encourage—the 14-year-old's off-color stories or ignore his locker-room language just

because we know it is commonplace among other youngsters his age?

For many parents the course is never in doubt. No child of theirs will do thus and so! Others, however, may have been confused by warnings against "indoctrinating" their children with their own thinking, or attempting to "mold them in their own image." These are the ones who suffer doubts when questions like the above arise.

*M*ETHODS of control that worked in earlier years are

useless now. (The 12-year-old who wants to try smoking will not be "distracted" for long by a lollipop!) By this time, too, youngsters have learned to hide what they are doing. Or they may not even resort to subterfuge but will announce, "If I can't do this in front of you, I'll just do it behind your back!"

Parents who want urgently to keep their youngsters' confidence by acting as "pals" might consider the experience reported recently by a young social worker. On his first job as recreation leader in a community center, wanting very much to be accepted by the neighborhood adolescents, he decided to gain their confidence by "meeting them at their level."

He began spending a good deal of time at their local hang-outs. Then after several months, thinking he had been accepted almost as a member of the gang, he joined a crap game one night and rolled the dice like a veteran. He noticed a stiffening in the group around him, an uneasiness later as they all walked home. Finally, one boy said: "You know, Doc, you get more and more like *us* instead of us getting more like you!"

In their attempts to be "modern" some mothers and fathers may run the risk of a reaction similar to the social worker's experience. Yet parents want to keep up-to-date. They've been cautioned against making their youngsters "different" from their friends. The adult wish to get a clear picture of the youngster's social scene today has prompted an increasing number of surveys among parents and students of various schools on such matters as clothing considered appropriate for school and parties, use of make-up, smoking, dating behavior. (One recent survey included a question on whether or not lights should be left on during parties.)

Interestingly enough, the results of a recent questionnaire given to 2,000 parents and students in a big city junior high school indicated that the students were just as uncertain about standards and limits as their parents. While the youngsters demonstrated a wish for many signs of increasing freedom (such as being permitted to earn money and have full responsibility for handling allowances), they also showed a strong desire for parental controls in matters where they seemed aware that their own impulses might get the best of them.

These youngsters said they thought parties should be planned, should have adult supervision; felt their parents should know where they were and with whom. Two-thirds of the students thought they ought to be home by midnight on week-ends and holidays, and seemed to want help in scheduling homework and keeping to a reasonable bedtime during the week.

The results of such a questionnaire suggest that, useful as such surveys may be in giving parents a picture of the social scene today, youngsters in the complicated business of growing up need more than the statistical analysis of a questionnaire to guide them. It is important for children of all ages to have direct guidance and a clear understanding of what their parents expect of them, even though they cannot live up to parental standards all the time.

OFTEN mothers and fathers can help youngsters understand what behavior is appropriate and acceptable merely by their own steady example of maturity and good judgment. At other times they may have to point out in no uncertain terms the hazards of certain conduct, and suggest more acceptable ways of doing.

But growing up is slow. Even with the best of adult guidance, youngsters will experiment with new forms of behavior in ways that parents may not like. There will be times when their self-control will fail, when they will feel they must challenge parental authority, when they must satisfy special needs whether their conduct has parental approval or not. Adult sanction for inappropriate behavior, however, may just add to adolescent confusion.

IT is certainly true that young people must learn to think for themselves. In a time of rapid social change they will inevitably face situations requiring new judgments that we cannot make for them. But it is quite possible to encourage individual thinking, while still keeping in mind the inexperience and immaturity of youngsters which make them need a strong foundation from which to move forward. We must give them both "roots and wings."

Young people gain strength in controlling their impulses when we hold to our point of view with firmness, accepting the fact that behind-the-back experimentation may be the price we will pay occasionally for sticking to the validity and worth of our standards.

Dorothy Barclay, Parent and Child editor, is on vacation. Mrs. LeShan, today's guest columnist, is a staff member of the Great Neck School's Adult Education Department and a member of the United Parents Associations' professional leaders' panel.

July 17, 1955

Teen-Agers Talk of Sex

THE battle of the sexes usually is a flourishing one—even where teen-agers are concerned. The ammuntiion used in such youthful skirmishes is the lively subject of a new booklet whose aim, it is explained, is to ease the situation.

The authors base their illustrations on the actual but anonymous views of a group of 3,000 teen-agers who were asked to discuss the problem, "What I Can't Understand About the Other Sex." Typical of some of the complaints aired are:

¶"Talk about girls being fickle—a boy can be completely over a crush in two weeks."

¶"Girls will go with one boy just long enough to hook somebody better."

¶"The fellow who had the most to say about girls wearing too much make-up had his hair so full of oil it looked terrible."

¶"Girls want you to spend a lot of money * * * but after one or two dates a week, I'm broke."

¶"Boys talk about necking, petting as though they were accomplishments similar to winning a fight. I wish they could consider a girl's side of it."

¶"Why does a girl want to get serious? They talk about marriage after the first date."

Called "Understanding the Other Sex," the booklet is available for 50 cents from Science Research Associates, 57 West Grand Avenue, Chicago 10, Ill.

March 2, 1956

This Is the Way They Are as They Grow Older

YOUTH: The Years From Ten to Sixteen. By Arnold Gesell, M. D., Frances L. Ilg, M. D., and Louise Bates Ames. 542 pp. New York: Harper & Bros. $5.95.

By ELIZABETH JANEWAY

IN 1943 Dr. Gesell and Dr. Ilg, in collaboration with Miss Ames and Janet Learned, published a book called "Infant and Child in the Culture of Today." This was followed, in 1946, by "The Child From Five to Ten," Miss Ames and Glenna E. Bullis being listed as collaborators with the two doctors. In the years since, tens of thousands of mothers and numerous teachers have not only read these two volumes but used them as handbooks; and the question "What do you think of Gesell?" has provoked discussion throughout the length and breadth of the land.

Great as has been the influence of the first two books, "Youth: The Years from Ten to Sixteen" will undoubtedly be read with even more intensity. "O Adolescence, O Adolescence," wrote Ogden Nash, "I wince before thine incandescence", a cri de coeur that has echoed down the ages and rings louder today than ever when the word "teen-ager" has, as the authors say, become "a cliché * * * too closely associated with * * * delinquencies and glamours." It is a word they use sparingly; but the contemporary emphasis on, and anxiety about, the problem gives this third volume an interest even greater than that of its predecessors.

In view of this interest it would be well to see if Dr. Gesell's theory and practice can be disentangled from what might be called the "Gesell effect," for a certain amount of misinterpretation seems to be present in the latter. Briefly, Dr. Gesell believes that neither authoritarianism, with its rigid rules and schedules, nor over-permissive laissez-faire is a proper approach to the understanding and rearing of children. The child, he says in the first volume, "needs discerning guidance rather than rigid regimentation."

ON the other hand, "the developmental point of view does not mean indulgence * * * (but) a constructive deference to the limitations of immaturity." The core of Gesell's work, and its great value, has been a careful clinical (yet imaginative) search for these limitations and for their corollary, the laws of growth. "It is clear," says the second volume, "that the significance of a child's behavior depends upon the position of that behavior in a developmental sequence." It is clear, but without the work of Dr. Gesell and his colleagues, most people would know little about how the developmental sequence of growth actually develops.

The authors, then, offer their readers a systematic, sensible harvest of observations upon children's behavior and attitudes. Unfortunately, both the earlier books have been taken as something rather different from this by many readers. "Of course," said one mother to me recently, "it was awfully reassuring to look up Gesell and find that all 6-year-olds call their mothers names. But I got so tired checking the children against their age-groups to see if they were keeping up with them, that I finally gave the books away."

Now Dr. Gesell, Dr. Ilg and their collaborators would hold up their hands in horror at this use of their books. They disclaim, ever more emphatically, that they intend their compilations of frequent behavior at any age to be taken as "rigid norms" of activity. They point out with great care in the new volume that the young people they observed and interviewed differ both in intelligence ratings and in family background from the statistical averages of the urban population of the United States. Their opposition to authoritarianism certainly includes their own appearance in this role.

Yet it is easy to see how it has come about. Where is a puzzled young mother to turn? The traditions upheld by grandmothers and nurses have been largely discredited; the grandmothers and nurses are themselves absent from the almost universal two-generation family unit; nor does the mother, herself usually the child of a small family, have experience of numerous little brothers and sisters to fall back on. No wonder that, in our transitional and competitive culture, she tends to take Dr. Gesell's "behavior patterns" as more absolute than he intends.

PERHAPS this will be less true for the present volume than for the earlier ones, just because each child, as he grows to maturity, becomes more individual and differentiates himself more, and more articulately, from the pattern. This is as true of the young people with whom the authors worked as it is of those whose parents will seize upon this book for understanding. It is a longer, fuller book than the others not only because the subjects are closer to maturity, but also because they are more varied.

Though a pattern of growth emerges, it is one that must often be qualified by the words "some, a majority, a few": Some 13-year-old boys get mad at their friends, though on the whole they get on well. A few 13-year-old girls date. There are 14-year-olds on the outside of groups as well as successful insiders. Fourteens for whom a full academic program is too demanding and too unsatisfying must be considered. Some 12-year-olds read nothing but comic books, some use libraries effectively.

Yet within the variations a sequence of growth is clear. How pleasant it is to read about it! "This is a book," I found myself thinking, "about successful children." It must be, of course, if it is to be about growth at all, about the achievement of maturity. But in an atmosphere of rather condemnatory scrutiny of "teen-agers," it is good for us to be reminded that growing up is not only possible, but usual. What one carries away from this book is a sense of the capabilities of youth, of its wide-ranging interests and of its ability to meet the challenge of a difficult, multifarious world.

Fiction has made us perhaps over-familiar with the agonies and absurdities of adolescence. They are not ignored here. Thirteen-year olds tend to withdraw into themselves. Fourteen is given at times to yelling and shouting. The parent of one 15-year-old remarked, "It's like pulling teeth to get anything out of him"; and Ogden Nash springs to mind again—"When anxious elders swarm about/ Crying 'Where are you going?' thou answerest 'Out'."

So they do, indeed. But these difficulties are seen in proportion and set in a framework of increasing mastery of the world and of self. No parent of an adolescent is likely to have time to become complacent. But the bulk of the material recorded here suggests convincingly that overanxious parents would do well to relax and cultivate a sense of humor instead of permitting the specter of juvenile delinquency to distort what can be a rewarding and delightful relationship.

HAVING said this, it is important to note that—as the authors point out—their work is limited in scope. The young people they interviewed and observed are of high average to superior intelligence. They come from stable middle-class and professional homes in a prosperous community. One of the most pertinent questions that the "Gesell effect" has raised in thoughtful minds is, How far are these theories of growth true for children from other classes and in other countries? Obviously, there can be no sensible answer until comparable work has been done among—say—Negro children in Montgomery, Ala., or French adolescents working for their bachots.

The very limitations of the present work, however, suggest some conclusions. Eleven-year olds, for instance, seem to have a passion for forming and joining clubs, often absorbed for the children under study into membership in the Scouts or something similar. In underprivileged urban children this certainly offers a clue as to how and when gangs begin. Again, the 12-year-old is so active that space is a prerequisite for his fulfillment — space, organized athletics and, above all, a bicycle and a place to ride it. How many children in Harlem have bicycles and a place to ride?

Pilfering occurs in early adolescence, though—it's amusing to note—never indulged in by the particular child being interviewed but occasionally reported about someone else. These children grow out of it. Their parents can give them enough to make the game not worth the candle, and also they are able quite easily to find ways to make money themselves. But how many Puerto Rican girls can become camp counselors? Held up to the light, Dr. Gesell's positive picture indicates the existence of a negative.

I would guess, however, that this limitation is more significant philosophically than pragmatically. Who, after all, will buy and read "Youth: The Years from Ten to Sixteen"? Will it not have an audience very like the families of the young people who contributed to it—stable, middle-class, professional, concerned about their children? Dr. Gesell's earlier book could not have produced the "Gesell effect" if they had not gone straight to the anxious hearts of their readers and provoked those cries of "My goodness, yes! Mine behaves just like that!" which connote the shock of recognition.

Years ago I worked for a large book club. My job was to deal with such correspondence as could not be answered by printed form. One day I opened an unforgettable letter from a woman who wrote only this: "Please send me a book. I think it would help." If you have lately locked horns with a sulky young man, if your 11-year-old daughter is planning to become a veterinary, if your 13-year-old son reminds you hauntingly of Walter Mitty, if his twin sister won't read anything that isn't about horses and his older brother wants nothing for his birthday but a driver's license, if the television set is yours now only because the telephone isn't —then please read this book. I think it will help.

Mrs. Janeway is a novelist and mother of two teen-aged boys. Her most recent novel, "Leaving Home," deals with family relationships.

May 13, 1956

The Telephoning Teens

By DOROTHY BARCLAY

IF the ancient art of heraldry were flourishing today, many a family with telephone-happy teen-agers in residence might well be in the market for a new coat of arms. Instead of being held aloft by a lion or unicorn, the center shield would in this modern adaptation be somewhat shakily supported on each side by an adolescent couchant. The field between, a tangled maze of cable and wire, would be liberally covered with telephones rampant. The new family motto: Yak, yak, yak.

It's no news to anybody with teen-age relatives that adolescent love for Mr. Alexander Graham Bell's brain-child has been growing in recent years until, in some cases, it has become a consuming passion. Telephoning is actually rivaling televiewing as a recreation in some sets; and, what's more, so great is the adaptive power of the young that a few hardy pioneers are already developing the skills necessary to view a show and simultaneously discuss it by phone with a friend two blocks—or two miles—away.

Newspaper and magazine stories have already carried word of the great telephone craze to those outside the adolescents' realm. This word is likely to be carried even farther as telephone companies press their campaigns extolling the virtues and convenience of a second telephone—not an extension, but a separate line with its own number and listing "just for the children."

THE Illinois Bell Telephone Company is already reaping the results of one such campaign, with an estimated total of 500 special installations in and around Chicago at last count. In one prosperous Chicago suburb the number of these "younger generation" listings has about doubled in the past year. The New York area has its share of special telephones for young people, too, even though the local company has made no special effort to encourage the trend to date.

This matter of private lines for teen-agers has touched off considerable discussion among parents in groups where the topic has been brought up. Some think the extra telephone idea is great.

Others are horrified by the very thought of it, vow no such "useless time-consumer" will find a place in their households. Basic to the whole discussion are adult attitudes about unlimited teen-age phoning, whether the family has one or a dozen lines at its disposal.

At least one member of the "pro" party has labelled the "anti" group basically "anti-children," reactionary and spoilsport to boot. A representative of the "anti" contingent feels the "unlimited calls" supporters are "over-permissive to the point of destructive indulgence." The truth probably lies somewhere in between.

"Look," a father told us. "The kids love to talk. At their age ideas are the fire of life to them. If they're talking on the phone, I know where they are. They're not doing their gabbing on the streetcorner, where I did twenty years ago, or in bars, where plenty of them end up today. I don't listen in on their talk but I hear enough to have some idea what's on their minds. They get confidential and whispery sometimes but most of the while it's out where anybody who wants to can hear. I think it's a good thing."

Other advocates of the unlimited approach held, "It's just the way the kids live today. You can't lay down the law on these things. It makes your child the 'queer' one. What's wrong with it? They're happy."

OPPONENTS of "too much" telephoning by teen-agers had usually reached their state of mind the hard way. Father's inability to get through to headquarters when necessary, a stimulus for installing a second phone in some families, had determined other parents to limit their children's calls to specific periods of the day. This approach was reinforced in still other households by the desire for a relaxed meal hour. ("When it reached the point where each of the three children was averaging twenty minutes on the phone in the course of one meal, we had our choice of serving cafeteria style or spending two hours over dinner.") Soaring bills in other families made some parents decide to tighten up. ("When bills that have run nine to ten dollars start hitting twenty-five and thirty, it's time to start encouraging face-to-face visiting!")

Of the specialists who have considered this problem there are a number who have suggested the family council method as a step toward confining talk-fests within reasonable bounds. Others have held that families who can afford it would do well to install a second telephone and stop worrying.

Dr. Goldie Ruth Kaback, psychologist in charge of counselor training at the City College of New York, pointed out that in the crowded life adolescents lead today the friendly after-school

talk is not always possible. Distances teen-agers travel are greater. Youngsters have to rush for buses and trains. They have special classes to get to. The leisurely homeward walk of boon companions is pretty much a thing of the past, in this city at least. As for talk between boys and girls, at these early stages it is frequently eased by the invisibility and possibility of immediate retreat a phone affords.

THE telephone is quick; it's efficient. News or a fresh thought can't wait when you're in your teens. Impulsiveness and spontaneity are the essence of youth. Unlimited telephoning is a new form of conspicuous, though intangible, consumption. Then, too, the telephone has become a symbol of adulthood—and a "prestige symbol" at that. Picture the stereotype of the important executive with six phones on his desk, all busy. And the café society celebrities who must be within plug-in reach of a phone even during an intimate supper for two.

Some opponents of too much telephone talk feel their teen-agers use it as a defense against ever thinking quietly for themselves. "Let them hold onto an idea for a while, mull it over in their own heads instead of constantly batting the conversational ball." Adherents, on the other hand, hold that rubbing ideas together is, for some youngsters, the only way to refine them.

But telephoning itself—or the pros and cons of private lines for kids—is not the important issue. The point to be considered is how and why the telephone is being used and how its constant demands affect family life in general.

Parents who emphatically resent the over-use of the phone by adolescents would do well to work the problem out with their youngsters and determine some fair method for limiting the number and length of conversations. Allowing it to become the source of constant bickering and contention will create a situation that can do more harm to family life and individual dispositions than the effects of the conversations can overcome.

May 20, 1956

'It's Love—It's Really Love'

By DOROTHY BARCLAY

IN a cottage down the lake road angry words are flying fast. For the third time this week, Katie, 16, has come in after midnight.

"If this is the way you and Lee are going to behave, you'll just stop seeing him. If necessary, we'll all pack up and go home."

"I won't go home and you can't make me. I love him and I'm going to see him. Every night."

Three houses away 14-year-old Jean lies on the porch hammock, swinging listlessly and humming bits and pieces of songs. All of them, her parents have noticed, center on romance. After six months of trying, as valiantly and blindly as an 8-year-old boy trying to learn to wiggle his ears, she is in love at last. All her girl friends have been in love "at least once already." Now she, too, has a chance of achieving that Seal of Merit, that Stamp of Acceptability— a boy's ring on a locket chain to wear around her neck. The badge is so obvious (or conspicuous by its absence) in the season of sun-dresses and bathing suits.

Across the lake, Jack, 17, is wearing out his voice and his parents' patience. They had planned a final "family summer" before his entry into college in the fall. Now he wants to go to work in town every day.

"Janet isn't the kind of a girl you can just buy a Coke for once in a while. There's competition for a girl like that. She wants to go out *right*—and I want to take her." The boy "has it bad," his parents agree. He has spoken briefly of marriage. What if he decides to drop his college plans!

YES, summer, as the song writers let none of us—least of all teen-agers—forget, is the time for romance. In countless families around the country right now the joys and pangs of first loves are affecting the lives of adults and adolescents alike.

Vacation time with its ultimatum to have fun, the new faces and places summer travel provides, help stimulate a tendency toward emotional attachments which needs little encouragement among teenagers at any season.

Parents react in a variety of ways to these youthful romances — sometimes with fear, sometimes with pity, sometimes with indulgent humor or unkindly wit. Some give young love every encouragement. Others may see it as a threat to the future and use a heavy hand in attempts to discourage it.

As various as the reactions of the parents themselves are the reasons for and the meaning of love to the youngsters involved. Specialists who work with teen-agers have identified a number. To some, they have observed, being loved and loving in return is proof of one's attractiveness and grown-upness, a vital business to fledglings who, in reality or in their own minds, are awkward, undistinguished and frailly young.

OTHER adolescents who may have hugged dreams of glory to their hearts find in love an "inspiration," someone and something "to work for." The world which had begun to seem dull is again brave and new with deeds to be done and problems conquered in the name of the beloved.

To some, being in love means catching up with friends who have achieved that blissful state before them; to others it may signify superiority to their friends or their "hopelessly dull" and singularly unromantic parents. Just as Mom and Dad's love and support sustained them in their grade school days, being loved and "believed in" by a contemporary gives the adolescent new confidence and courage at a time when life ahead may seem especially complex and difficult.

This sort of crisis in a youngster's life is often very difficult for parents to handle. At best the young may be only moony or erratic. ("Deedee! For the fourth time!· Get that wet bathing suit off the bed!") At worst they may be demanding, sullen, now elated, now depressed. ("You never *have* liked any of my friends. You want me to be miserable!") Whatever the quality of the youngsters' emotional state, there's likely to be lots of unusual behavior—and just about none of it amenable to reason.

A first step in handling the problems young love may create for the family is an effort to understand its meaning to those involved as well as to the parents themselves. Anger, fear and frustration frequently characterize adult reactions when youngsters are rebellious and unwilling even to try to think "sensibly." It's wise for parents to let off this steam—but not in the direction of the youngsters themselves. True enough, the youngsters may be irrational. Angry dramatics on the adults' part will only compound the confusion.

PARENTS who have maintained an attitude of easy give-and-take in discussion over the years will find it not too great a strain to continue it at this time. Ideally, they will try to be friendly but tactfully frank in giving an opinion of the beloved; reasonable but firm in setting and enforcing limits as to where the young couple may go, with whom and for how long; sympathetic and understanding of the youngsters' feelings but still aware of their own adult responsibility to protect them from unfortunate consequences.

Lawrence K. and Mary Frank have some important things to say about youngsters in love in their forthcoming book, "Your Adolescent at Home and in School," to be published by the Viking Press on Aug. 24. ($3.95.)

Early love, they warn, can be a form of retreat or withdrawal for young people—unless we provide them with opportunities for wholesome activities together. If we haven't done so in the past, we can help adolescents find interests and pursuits which will not leave them wholly dependent on parties and dating for personal satisfaction and prestige.

This is a time for parents to help youngsters realize the responsibilities which love for other people involves and to recognize the occasional hurts which any kind of love will bring. The youngster must be helped to realize that although in the fullness of his heart he would gladly give "all" to his beloved one, he has both the right and responsibility to consider himself and his own goals and wishes, and should expect others to consider them as well.

*I*T takes a long time to develop the capacity for mature love. In their first loves, youngsters discover their ability to communicate with others, to trust others, to learn what is harmful and what is good for them (and for everyone) in love relationships. They develop the ability to give as well as to get.

Parents of youngsters "in love" may also find helpful Rudolph Wittenberg's excellent "On Call for Youth," Association Press, $3.50, and Lester Kirkendall's pamphlet "Too Young to Marry?", 25 cents a copy from Public Affairs Committee, 22 East Thirty-eighth Street, New York 16.

July 22, 1956

Early Teens A Likely Age For Idolizing

By DOROTHY BARCLAY

The early teen-age years are a time for great enthusiasms. The boy who never "cracked a book" may suddenly begin devouring volume after volume. The once cool-headed girl may get dreamy-eyed at the sound of a voice on radio or the sight of a special face on the television screen. In recent weeks several different aspects of this phenomena have come to our attention.

Random House, for instance, reports that it has sent out more than 50,000 "Walter Farley" buttons. These are badges of membership in an unorganized but highly vocal group, the Black Stallion Club. Mr. Farley is the author of a series of exciting books about a black stallion and his assorted equine friends and relatives.

Youngsters who wear the pin —as well as countless others who read but do not write letters—have pushed sales of the twelve volumes in this group over the million mark. The communicative ones keep a steady stream of mail flowing into the publisher's office. Many pour out the young writers' love and longing for horses. ("I have always wanted a horse, but I cannot have one in an apartment.") telling about 'the story I like best" and offering suggestions for more books for Mr. Farley to write. Although boys and girls are believed to read the books in equal numbers, most of the letter writers are girls.

Baseball Fan Club

Another theoretically masculine interest for which girls have organized is reflected in the Chicago fan club set up to do honor to Nellie Fox, second baseman for the White Sox. Decorum is its keynote—Mrs. Fox has been elected an honorary vice president—and worthy activity its goal. The group distributes gifts and refreshments to hospital patients in honor of its ideal.

Similarly high in tone but nearer to the sort of thing that makes many adults shake their heads is the network of fan clubs for The Four Lads, a vocal group whose recordings are consistently high on popularity listings. Michael Stewart, manager of the quartet, has a quite understandable interest in the psychology of "fandom." As he sees it, fan clubs are "a healthy outlet for youthful energy, a challenge to initiative and a means of building confidence."

Obviously such organizations fill a need for certain youngsters who, at about 12 or 13, have become aware of the world outside their own circle and seek some contact with fame and prestige.

When such youngsters choose to organize, it is usually on behalf of relative newcomers in the performing arts, and often club members work diligently to build their success. As members of a fan club, they are more likely to have an opportunity to meet their favorites and in such situations they are, for the most part, quiet, shy and reserved..

Many have raised the promotion of their idols to a science—making and distributing posters, bombarding radio stations with requests for their favorites' current recordings and touring record shops after school to make sure these hits are in stock and well displayed. Members of many of The Four Lads fan clubs have gone beyond these celebrity-building activities, however, to attempts at civic service as well.

As parents who have survived their daughters' adolescence have usually found, the fever pitch of such enthusiasm usually begins to cool by the time the girls are 15 or 16. A gentle interest in the idol may continue into adulthood, however, as one mother found to her surprise when a Leslie Howard film showed up unexpectedly on television.

September 4, 1956

Further Notes on Teen-Agers

By DOROTHY BARCLAY

*O*NE good way to liven up a dying conversation is to make a provocative remark about "teen-agers." We heard one recently—at a conference of the New York State Congress of Parents and Teachers — that has already touched off plenty of heated talk. The fighting words? "Although only a small minority of teen-agers are delinquent, a much higher percentage of them are obnoxious."

Just who the jaundiced author of this statement may be we have not been able to determine. Although quarreling with this anonymous critic's choice of words, a good many parents, teachers and innocent bystanders have ruefully agreed there's a kernel of truth in what he said.

A case in point is the recent opinion poll conducted by the National Education Association's research division. While stressing that their answers should by no means be construed as a blanket indictment of youth, the reporting teachers indicated that, in their eyes at least, various acts of misbehavior—including such items as impertinence and discourtesy to teachers, failure to do homework and other assignments—"are definitely occurring more frequently now" than they did ten to twenty years ago.

*W*ITHIN a week we had heard three stories from reasonable and intelligent parents who felt that no matter how they tried to prevent trouble, their early teen-agers—agreeable youngsters as a general rule—were out to cross them, thwart them and precipitate family battles. One mother, after half a day of provocation, told her 15-year-old to stop looking for trouble. "I refuse to argue with you about trivialities," the mother declared. "Well," asked the girl, all matter-of-fact, "what *would* you be willing to fight about?"

Disturbing though it may be, the thoughtful parent must consider such behavior in its proper perspective, says Dr. Elizabeth Lee Vincent. Formerly Dean of Cornell's College of Home Economics, she is now Professor of Human Development and Behavior at Chatham College, Pittsburgh. In a panel discussion on adolescence during the recent Academy of Pediatrics conference, Dr. Vincent emphasized, as do other specialists on the adolescent, the considerable stresses and strains these youngsters are going through. They must wean themselves away from childish dependence on their parents. They must choose and prepare for a life's work. They must work out new relationships with the opposite sex. They must clarify for themselves what they are really like as persons and what their role in adult society may be. All this is further complicated by physical changes and spurts of growth. Small wonder that the adolescent at times behaves in ways that some might term "obnoxious."

In groups, on buses, trains and street corners, these youngsters may behave raucously to attract one another's attention or just to see what adult reaction they will get. "Usually they get a strong one from somebody. This adds to the 'fun.'" As for picking fights with their parents, that's understandable, too. When pressures and frustrations build up, something's got to give. Some adolescents find it safer to strike out at their parents than at their peers. Then, too, the cutting comment, the lively argument, the heated spat are frequently without special significance to the young.

*U*NDERSTANDING the reasons for such behavior, shall adults just ignore it, take whatever punishment is handed out and let the adolescent go his way? Dr. Vincent says a firm "No" to this. Often, she agrees, it's easier and best to overlook minor points—the slang, the untidiness, the feet-in-air sitting posture. Attempts at provoking fights can be side-stepped, though any real issues the youngsters may be raising should be seriously considered.

Dr. Vincent most emphatically stressed, however, that she is opposed to a do-nothing policy when the youngster's own health and welfare or the rights, comfort and privileges of others are involved.

Although adolescence must be a time of expanding freedoms, certain definite "limits" are as essential for the teenager as for the toddler, Dr. Vincent believes. "I am not for letting the adolescent go through this period without improving in self-control and appreciation of the rights of others. There are few sadder sights than the child who is victim of his own whims."

November 4, 1956

...And the Sex Problem

*B*OY-GIRL matters being one of the principal problems of adolescence, the pediatricians also heard, proper sex education might almost be considered a "medicine." On the premise that if a little is good a lot is better, some youngsters today are being overdosed, one speaker implied.

Adolescents mature at different rates. The degree of their sex interests vary in intensity. They differ widely as to ideals and activities. Slow maturers who don't seem especially concerned may be irritated or embarrassed by much talk. Those with normal sex interests but plenty of wholesome activities to absorb their energies can have the matter magnified beyond its actual importance to them by too many lectures or "little chats." As for the minority to whom the problem is of intense and consuming interest, "frank talks" and "strong inspirational guidance" from

their physician can be definitely helpful.

Parents who bring 10 or 12 year-olds to the doctor to be told the facts of life are themselves in need of a friendly talk, another pediatrician declared. Although the doctor on good terms with a young patient may certainly discuss the matter with him when it seems pertinent, sex education is a job best done by parents, at home. The doctors were advised to give the parents a good book on the subject and suggest that, after reading it, they come back and discuss the next steps to be taken with the child.

Gunnar Dybwad, executive director of the Child Study Association of America, also made a point on this score last week. Too many of the books written for small children today, he held, go into minute biological details that few parents — unprompted by diagrams and the written word—would ever think of getting involved with.

Children need to have their questions clearly and simply answered, Dr. Dybwad stressed, but they do not need to be crammed with facts. Far more important to the very young child is a parent's warm and accepting attitude toward questions, backed by a readiness to talk further whenever new questions—or even the same old ones—are raised.

November 4, 1956

YOUTH PANELISTS VIEW TEEN-AGERS

Pupils Decide Elvis Presley Craze Is Largely a Case of Following Others

The New York Times Youth Forum addressed itself yesterday to a topic close to home: "What Makes Teen-agers Tick?" The adult guest, Dr. David Abrahamsen, a psychiatrist who directs the Institute of School Consultation Services, said that in this period of biological development there were likely to be "rebellious attitudes which parents can't do much about."

Jerry Brand, 16 years old, of the McBurney School in Manhattan, was quick to point out that his parents helped him a great deal. Sigburga Quintus, 15, of Public School 60 in the Bronx, said that, in spite of differences, "deep down, teen-agers understand that their parents are trying to help them."

The discussion was televised over Station WABD of the DuMont network at 1 P.M. Miss Dorothy Gordon, who presided, raised the question at what age boys and girls should be treated as older persons.

The youngest panelist, Edwin Pate, 14, of P.S. 120 in Manhattan, suggested 16 to 18 years. Susan Wolfe, also 14, of the South Orange (N.J.) Junior High School, thought it should be a gradual process.

Dr. Abrahamsen said that each child was an individual and that one could not lay down rules in such matters. He also said that there was a difference between boys and girls in this respect, with girls usually needing more affection.

When Miss Gordon asked about conformity among teen-agers, Sigburga Quintus cited "this Elvis Presley business." She said a girl started screaming because other girls did "when he starts his singing and motion." It takes a lot of strength not to follow the others, she said.

Dorothea Ewald, 15, of St. Barbara's Diocesan High School in Brooklyn, chimed in to say, "It means a lot to be like the rest of the bunch."

Jerry Brand disagreed with those who saw obscenity in the Elvis Presley performances. He said, "Just because teen-agers seem to cling to Elvis Presley is why parents dislike him."

Dr. Abrahamsen described Mr. Presley as "a very interesting personality." These crushes, involving mostly girls, are "more or less a phase", he said. He saw no harm in this and said that if there were no Elvis Presley "they would find something else to be concerned about."

Yesterday's forum will be rebroadcast over the WQXR network on Saturday at 10:30 A.M. It will also be televised at 11 A.M. on Dec. 15 over Channel 5, Station WTTG, in Washington, D.C.

The topic for next week's forum will be, "Are Trust Territories Becoming Independent?" The adult guest will be Dr. Benjamin A. Cohen, under-secretary of the United Nations for trusteeship and information from non-self-governing territories.

November 26, 1956

STUDY FINDS GIRLS ECHOING THE PAST

Scout Survey Reports Little Change in Teen-Agers From Mother's Day

By DOROTHY BARCLAY

Those who have been worrying about the nation's teen-age girls now can relax. By and large, today's youngsters have been found to be as idealistic and practical, as romantic and down-to-earth, as rebellious and as conservative as their mothers before them.

Actually, there are no statistics available to indicate just what today's mothers were like during adolescence. A clear picture of the attitudes, interests and aspirations of their daughters, however, was made avail-able yesterday by the Girl Scouts of the U. S. A. It was a reassuring picture.

The details were supplied by the University of Michigan's Institute for Social Research, which conducted a survey for the Scouts. Under the "microscope" was a scientifically selected sample of 2,000 girls, 11 through 18 years old, representing American girls in the sixth through twelfth grades.

The research explored the girls' hopes, worries, relations with parents and friends, dating, and plans for education, work and marriage.

At a conference yesterday in the Carnegie Building, 345 East Forty-sixth Street, Girl Scout executives joined with Dr. Elizabeth Douvan, director of the study, to interpret the findings to reporters.

Representing the Girl Scouts were Mrs. Roy F. Layton, national president; Miss Dorothy Stratton, executive director, and Miss Edith W. Conant, director of the program department.

That adolescent girls have changed somewhat from the general pattern their mothers followed as teen-agers in the Nineteen Thirties is to be expected. Dr. Douvan said the researchers found this change to be primarily a matter of increased independence and advanced education ambitions.

More girls today, they found, have ample allowances, part-time jobs, freedom to participate as they choose in games and sports and more voice in helping to set the family rules that they must follow.

Today's girl is ambitious. One in three says she wants a college education; fewer than one in fifteen dreams of a factory worker or farmer as a husband. Most look forward to both a job and marriage. But the girls are practical as well. Only two in a hundred aspire to the super-glamour **of a movie or television star's position.**

Talk of the American female's tendency toward domination of the male would not seem to be supported by the study's findings. Only 2 per cent of the girls want to run their own businesses. For the most part, the youngsters look forward to jobs that require the feminine characteristics of helpfulness and service to others — secretary, nurse, teacher and social worker. As for husbands, they want men who are intelligent, independent, responsible and self-directing.

With regard to their present activities, the girls as a group are consistently conservative. Less than one-fifth said they liked the idea of "going steady." Sixty per cent of those over sixteen thought there were more disadvantages than advantages to the practice.

The Girl Scouts undertook their study to find out what actually is typical of schoolgirls in this age group so that the Scout organization might keep its program up to date with the youngsters' interests and needs.

January 16, 1957

The Between-Agers: 11 to 14

By DOROTHY BARCLAY

ONCE upon a time, when the world was young and life was much simpler than it is today, there were two age groups: children and adults. By and large, so long as a human being was dependent on his parents for financial support, he was considered a child. When he went out on his own he was a grown-up, with all the responsibilities and privileges pertaining to the rank.

In the minds of many, this distinction may still hold true. But the more researchers study in the field of human growth and behavior, the more classifications they come up with.

Modern parents are aware of many distinctions. We have the infant, the toddler, the nursery school child; the young school child, the pre-adolescent, the early adolescent and so on up the scale. (We've even heard the designation "older youth," to cover that in-between period from twenty-eight to thirty-five!)

REPEATEDLY in recent months our attention has been drawn to considerations of the early adolescent, a grouping not too easy to classify by calendar years alone but generally considered to include youngsters ranging in age, roughly, from eleven to fourteen. Early adolescence in-cludes that period of rapid growth which suddenly follows upon the slow, steady growth period of late childhood. The trousers which only yesterday draped over the instep now reveal three or four inches of ankle to the startled adult eye. What's more, the youngster's sense of his own self-importance is likely to have shot up just as rapidly —and with it his willingness— nay, his mission—to set adults right whenever they err and to reveal to them their obvious inadequacies.

As we indicated earlier, we've been increasingly aware of growing interest in this age group among parents. It is paralleled — as a matter of fact, it was preceded—by a similar, even more searching, interest among educators. We talked this over with two of them at Teachers College, Columbia. They were Dr. David B. Austin, in the Department of Educational Administration, and Dr. Arno A. Bellack, in the Department of Curriculum and Teaching.

AS evidence, Dr. Austin pointed to the steady decline in the once all but standard division—eight years of elementary school, four years of high. At the present time, he reported, over three-fifths of the country's school systems have abandoned the eight-four arrangement for some combination of years which makes special provision in set-up and curriculum for these seventh, eighth and ninth graders with their special needs, special interests and, at times, very special problems.

As Dr. Bellack put it, the junior high school student is neither a young child nor an adolescent. He is still quite dependent on the adults in his life for supplying his basic needs but in mind and spirit he is developing great independence.

Such a youngster must be given plenty of opportunity to explore new problems, to grow in freedom, to develop his own interests, abilities and understandings. At the same time, Dr. Bellack held, he must be guarded from the consequences of his excesses and helped to adjust to reasonable restrictions.

Parental concern over youngsters in the pre-and early adolescent age groups—as evidenced in the desire for more discussion about them — may be increasing for a variety of reasons. Dr. Bellack pointed out that the current crop of junior high school pupils is actually quite different in many ways from those preceding them. Most were born during or just at the close of World War II. The great majority in one way or another were influenced by the unsettled and abnormal home conditions of that time. Many moved about the country a great deal, making friends and then having to leave them behind, attending different schools with different teaching methods, sometimes studying the same materials twice and others not at all. Many have been in overcrowded classrooms or on split-shifts part or all of their school lives.

THESE youngsters today represent as well the first group of early adolescents to have had television as an important influence in their lives. Their scope and accurate knowledge in some spheres often exceeds that of adults but—it's our observation—their fund of misinformation, picked up the same way, must not be overlooked.

We think there may be significance in the fact that the parents of today's early adolescents, some at least, were also among the first to try out the "total permissiveness" approach during their children's early childhood. Now they find little tricks and distractions are no longer enough for controlling and guiding high-spirited youngsters with minds of their own.

The world expects more of young people today, Dr. Austin held, when it comes to directing their own conduct. "Kids now have to solve problems for themselves that years ago no one would have trusted them with—if the problems had even existed."

Dr. Austin offered as an example the freedom given young people today to decide for themselves on a question such as smoking. We've heard many parents express concern over such matters as children's time-budgeting, their handling of allowances, homework, clothing, social behavior and similar matters which, in an earlier day, would have been settled by parental edict. Now, these require a fine balancing of freedom with guidance and control.

AN outstanding example of how one parents' group went about helping its members find that "balance" for themselves is summed up in "Our Teen-Agers," publication of the Parents Association, Andries Hudde Junior High School 240, Brooklyn. Two years of surveys of parent and pupil opinion, as well as discussions with professionally trained leaders, preceded publication of the thirty-two page booklet, written by Ruth L. Simon of the Board of Education's Bureau of Guidance. The booklet covers questions raised by parents and children themselves on such matters as appropriate dress, household chores, allowances, smoking, "curfew," dating and conduct at parties.

"Absolute freedom, even to adults," the booklet concludes, "is a somewhat frightening prospect. At this time of rebellion against authority, therefore, it is vital that parents maintain their own balance and judgment. Discuss matters instead of giving lectures or 'laying down the law.' At this age, your youngster is trying to master self-control at the same time that his family is trying to maintain control of him. The most effective way of developing self-discipline is exchanging views and ideas rather than issuing parental sermons."

February 24, 1957

CATHOLIC WARNS ON 'GOING STEADY'

Head of Family Life Bureau Calls Practice Threat to Christian Marriage

By RICHARD J. H. JOHNSTON
Special to The New York Times.
MILWAUKEE, March 19 — Protracted "steady dating" among the nation's youth threatens the Christian concept of marriage, the twenty-fifth National Catholic Family Life Convention was heard today.

The Right Rev. Irving A. De Blanc, director of the Family Life Bureau of the National Catholic Welfare Conference, spoke at the opening general session of the convention.

It brought together more than 300 Catholic laymen and clergy for a three-day discussion of the responsibility of the family in preparing children for adult life. Msgr. De Blanc declared:

"Going steady is pagan unless there is a reasonable chance of marriage within two years. The habit of going steady must be stopped if the Christian concept of marriage is to be saved."

Warns on Steady Dating

While steady dating is often construed as "marriage in miniature," the speaker said, "it is not preparation for marriage" when the practice is devoted to individual pleasure.

Too many families, he said, do not provide children with the love for which a substitute is sought through steady dating.

In a speech later in the day, the Rev. John R. Cavanagh, a Georgetown University psychiatrist, also attacked steady dating among teen-agers.

He urged parents to "do everything in their power" to prevent the going steady of teen-agers and pre-teen-agers. He declared:

"It limits their friendships and if continued is likely to promote at best a brother-sister relationship in marriage. In addition, it may lead to a consummated sin even in their early teens."

Steady Dating Denounced

By Religious News Service.
CINCINNATI, March 19—The Roman Catholic Archdiocese of Cincinnati has denounced teenage "going steady" as an evil. A bulletin directed the clergy to preach sermons and use "all prudent means at your disposal to effect a cure of this evil."

March 20, 1957

GIRL SCOUTS ISSUE REPORT ON DATING

Most Youngsters Start at 14, Survey Finds—Conflicts With Parents Noted

Adolescent American girls undergo the most stress between 14 and 16 years of age—when they are beginning to establish new relationships outside the family—the Girl Scouts reported yesterday.

The report also disclosed that most girls begin dating at 14. It noted that 70 per cent of those up to 16 dated almost every week-end. Ninety per cent of girls 16 through 18 said they dated every week-end.

Some of the findings of the survey, conducted for the Scouts by the University of Michigan's Institute for Social Research, were made known in the Scouts' 1956 report to Congress. It was submitted in accordance with the group's Congressional Charter.

The survey, which included the opinions of 2,000 girls aged 11 through 18, also found that only 10 per cent of the girls "go steady."

As a group the girls overwhelmingly expected to marry "some day." At the same time, only 3 per cent said they wanted to become housewives. Sixty per cent of the sample now hold jobs outside the home, with baby-sitting the most common occupation. The girls listed their choice of occupations as secretary, nurse, teacher and social worker.

In their relations with parents, the group reported that the area of disagreement ranged from clothes to matters of intellect. The younger girls took issue with their parents primarily over dress and the "use of make-up." Those over 14 cited conflicts over "driving and dating" or over "ideas."

The report to Congress put the growth in Girl Scout membership at 250,000 between September, 1955 and September, 1956. The total enrollment was calculated at 2,860,050.

More than half of this number were Brownie Scouts aged 7 through 9. In New York, New Jersey and Connecticut, the densest area of Girl Scout population in the nation, one of every eight girls was said to be a member of the Scout movement in 1956.

The Scout organization also expanded abroad in 1956. More than 20,000 Girl Scouts were in troops established in forty-three countries. The Girl Scouts were founded in 1912 with 12 members.

June 10, 1957

Inside the World of the Teenager

By DOROTHY BARCLAY

ANY parent who has engaged in extensive discussion with a group of articulate high school students knows that the opinions poured forth in these lively sessions are often, in the full sense of the term, "fearful and wonderful."

Some youngsters, to be sure, express themselves in the measured terms and tones of their elders. But more often than not these youngsters, or so their voluble statements indicate, have opinions definitely their own. They know what's wrong with the world and they know the cures. Their opinions are often fresh, sometimes startling, occasionally disheartening.

The parent, on the other hand, who has only observed his adolescent, pensively engaged in silent meditation would be something less than normally curious if he did not wonder what thoughts were passing through that youthful brain.

Researchers, who are at least as curious as parents and in a far better position to allow their inquisitiveness full rein, have been looking into adolescent attitudes and opinions for some time. Their findings can be helpful to parents in several ways. Those parents who think their youngsters' opinions bewildering or disturbing may find—for whatever comfort this may be—that these opinions are by no means unique. In cases where little communication of any kind goes on between parents and teenagers, the findings of research can give parents a better insight into the problems and concerns which upset their youngsters and, even more important, pinpoint the barriers and stumbling-blocks to free give and take in discussion.

TAKE, for instance the matter of disheartening opinions. Much has been made recently of the findings of the Purdue Opinion Panel in the matter of teenagers' beliefs in the political sphere, and their attitudes toward the freedoms guaranteed in our Bill of Rights. Over half the teenagers in America, this long-term study has indicated, feel that politics is "over their heads, a dirty game run by unscrupulous insiders," that we should help Federal and

local police maintain order by legalizing wiretapping and the third degree; that we should put censorship of books, movies, radio and television into government hands "to protect ourselves against improper thinking." What's more, nearly half are ready to dispense with freedom of the press; one-quarter think police should be free to search homes and persons without warrants; a third that free speech should be denied certain people if it seems convenient.

THE interpretations put on these findings vary, but they have been generally, and understandably, viewed with alarm. What the holding of such opinions may mean in the case of individual adolescents only individual study could reveal. One thing we are convinced of, however. Not every young person ex-

pressing these opinions is an authoritarian zealot. Immaturity, inexperience, typical youthful impatience with slow procedures—these are as likely to be at the root of such opinions as base motives.

This does not mean that parents should shrug off the implications of such findings, or of whatever out-of-line or out-of-bounds opinions their own youngsters may express in free debate. Such findings or opinions serve to underscore the responsibility of parents to make their own beliefs and values clear to their children—not by preaching but by rational explanation and living example. The panel's findings represent but one sample of the material reported in "The American Teenager," by H. H. Remmers and D. H. Radler (Bobbs-Merrill, $3.75). Other studies conducted by the Purdue panel within a scientifically selected sample of the nation's high school students reveal, for parents of more silent children, the prevalent worries and concerns of growing youth—concerns that center on themselves, their minds and bodies, their relationships with their parents, their school work, their dates, their money problems, their hopes and fears for the future.

FIFTY-TWO per cent want to gain weight or lose it; 37 per cent are seeking to improve their posture or, in the case of boys, their "body build." Fifty-four per cent wish they knew how to study better and a like number admit to difficulties in concentration. Forty-one per cent suffer severely when they try to express themselves in words; 38 per

cent have trouble expressing themselves in writing. Fifty-six per cent wonder what kind of work they're best suited for. Forty-two per cent aren't sure what their real interests are and 40 per cent wonder seriously how much ability they actually have. Nervousness, excitability, guilt feelings about things they've done, unsuccessful attempts to shake an undesirable habit or just plain unsureness of themselves—these are all complaints of about a third of the nation's adolescents.

COMPLAINTS about parents, although not overwhelming in number, center largely on "strictness." Parents, the youngsters feel, are too strict about their going out at night, dating, using the family car. Parents nag about studying, interfere in their selection of friends and in their use of money they earn. Parents "hate to admit I'm sometimes right," they play favorites, they don't treat the adolescent as "sufficiently grown up." Complaints like these came from 10 to 18 per cent of the sample. Nineteen per cent said they were afraid to tell their parents when they had done wrong.

This final statistic bears out a similar finding in another study, this time of college students, carried out by Marvin C. Dubbe at Oregon State College and reported in the bulletin of the Oregon Coordinating Council on Social Hygiene. It was found that fear and a belief in their parents' conservatism combined to keep college young people, especially boys, from discussing some of their problems at home. Nagging was another deterrent, as was lack of time together—especially for fathers and daughters. Mothers' tendency to violate confidences also discouraged a number of young people.

THE opinions of a 17-year-old girl, offered in a letter written as part of the Purdue research, may revive the wilting spirits of parents at this point: "Most parents do try, I think, to understand us, but it's not an easy thing to do. Teenagers seem to live in a world of their own. They want to be boss in everything. It takes an awful lot of patience and understanding to know how to cope with us."

August 25, 1957

LIPSTICK CHARTS YOUTH MATURITY

Its Acceptance Among Pupils Is Said to Reflect a Rise in Sophistication

---

STUDY COVERS 20 YEARS

9th Graders of '50's Found on a Level With 11th and 12th Graders of '35

By BESS FURMAN
Special to The New York Times.

WASHINGTON, March 20—Ninth grade youths of today are as mature as eleventh and twelfth graders of twenty years ago, as measured by lipstick.

This facet of modern life was disclosed at the twenty-fifth anniversary meeting of the Society for Research in Child Development by Dr. Mary Cover Jones, Professor of Education, University of California at Berkeley.

Dr. Jones was comparing the interests, activities and opinions of seventy-two boys and seventy girls in the ninth grade in 1935 and ninety-five boys and seventy-eight girls twenty years later in the same Oakland, Calif., junior high school. They were questioned on the same 250 items.

"By the Nineteen Fifties for both boys and girls the per cent approving of the use of lipstick was higher than for the eleventh grade sample in the Nineteen Thirties," she said.

"Lipstick symbolizes as well as any one specific item could the sensitization in early adolescence toward a new sex role and toward being grown up," Dr. Jones explained.

"While its use is confined to girls, opinions about it are not."

She also noted in the study a greater concern of 14-year-old boys in dating and grooming than was true two decades ago. Both boys and girls expressed greater interest in church and religion, she said. Both were more responsible in doing home work, more interested in the contemporary scene including politics, and more tolerant in social attitudes.

A greater proportion of today's ninth graders earned money, took care of their rooms and their clothes, and "thought it appropriate to worry about the future," she said.

Girls More Active

The girls of today were found to be more active in sports, less interested in careers though expecting to hold down jobs to supplement the family income, and more tolerant of gambling, betting, and women smoking.

The members of the 1935 group are still interviewed from time to time as part of the continuing study, she said, adding:

"There may be some relationship between their frequent complaint in interviews: 'Why didn't someone make me study more when we were in school?' and our findings that ninth graders say they do study more now."

Dr. Leland H. Stott, leader of the longitudinal studies program of the Merrill-Palmer School, Detroit, described daily observations of sixty-six preschool children analyzed as to natural leadership, bossiness, individualistic tendency, and social irresponsibility.

He said that natural leadership was a matter of inner resourcefulness, whereas bossiness was closely correlated with high activity, high gross muscular skill, and low fine muscular skill.

Dr. D. Bruce Gardner, of the Child Development Research Laboratories, Iowa State College, said that the response of two-year-old children to stress situations showed no group differences as between adopted children; children who lived in Iowa University home management houses and had as many as eighteen "mother figures" and children always cared for by real mothers.

March 21, 1959

Teen Profile

Seventeen magazine has completed a survey of 4,532 teen-age girls to determine the characteristics of the 9,750,000 American girls in their teens. Some of the results:

She weighs an average of 114.7 pounds and is 5 feet 3.2 inches tall. She arises at 7:34 A. M. and goes to bed at 10:49. She listens to the radio two hours a day, can cook a wide range of things varying from spaghetti to chocolate cake, goes to church on Sunday, confides in friends (not father) and worries about not having a date on Saturday night.

More to the point, as far as Seventeen magazine is concerned, the young woman spends an average of $300 on her wardrobe; she has a good deal of leisure time and the $4,500,000,-000 earned each year (those babysitting fees do add up) is hers for the spending; she goes to the movies three times a month and 2,700,000 of the girls bowl and another 1,800,000 are going to travel this summer.

For mother's information, on Saturday morning three-quarters of the girls help with household chores. Clip and show this to the teen-ager who does not.

July 21, 1960

Adolescence: Time of the Rebel

By EDA J. LeSHAN

WHENEVER parents of 12- to 14-year-olds get together, there is bound to be a certain amount of mutual commiseration about the difficulties of living with those disturbing, irritating, delightful and perplexing creatures-in-revolt of early adolescence.

Yet, despite parental agitation, there is in most families a deep, underlying current of love that carries parents and children through these difficult days. Moments of youthful arrogance and anger, balkiness and seemingly unending arguments are balanced by others of sensitivity and

Mrs. LeShan, a psychologist, holds the title of Director of Education of the Manhattan Society for Mental Health.

thoughtfulness, charm and gaiety to sustain adults through this necessary period of rebellion.

Today's parents, as distinct from those of twenty-five years ago, are schooled, for the most part, in the art of expecting and accepting periods of revolt in their youngsters.

But many parents, while willing to accept expert advice intellectually, are still subject to emotional misgivings. Coming from backgrounds that differed materially in fact and concept from their children's, they are fearful that some of their own difficulties may be reflected in their young.

In addition, having been placed in the limelight in recent years as the source of all good and evil in their children, parents are unusually sensitive to feeling unloved by their offspring. In the face of the 12-year-old's "I hate you" or the 14-year-old's obvious disdain for their appearance, intelligence and judgment, the strongest parents can be shaken in their resolve to remain self-confident and understanding throughout the "trying" years.

THE strength to endure the more difficult days with humor, patience and self-confidence needs to be reinforced, from time to time, by taking a fresh look at the facts that help us to sustain a sense of perspective.

We have ample evidence that severe, militant authority —the kind that borders on dictatorship—carries a high price tag. Behind us, there is a long history of this approach to child care, and there is no dearth of literature to indicate the pitfalls of "breaking a child's spirit."

Yet, some parents who would find it unacceptable to browbeat a rebel today are, in fact, bringing about the same end result by a far more subtle technique. They use their own visible misery and hurt as a disciplinary weapon.

These are the parents who, because they cannot bear to feel unloved, are likely to make their youngsters feel so guilty about defiance that the children give it up entirely. A child surrenders not out of fear of severe punishment or tight control, but because he cannot endure his parents discomfort and unhappiness. Thus, the parents encourage obedi-

121

ence, not through authoritarian discipline, but by their disappointment that their own child could be so defiant and critical of the very people who love him most.

As this kind of control becomes more widespread, it is possible to see what happens to the child who abandons revolt, the nice youngster who cannot bear to make his parents unhappy. We find, increasingly, that the results of the make-him-feel-guilty approach, in its way, can be just as damaging as those of the iron fist.

WHAT happened to one youngster I know, now an 18-year-old college student, may help to illustrate. Her parents were decent, kind people, perfectionists when it came to their own family. Having had unhappy childhoods themselves, they were desperately eager to give their children something more.

Always a happy, loving youngster, the girl gave her parents a deep sense of gratification. They were doing a good job. It was not until the age of 12, when she began to flutter her wings experimentally in her first attempts to-

ward independence, that the difficulties began.

Never having been allowed to express angry, rebellious feeling toward their own parents, and having made impossible demands on themselves to be patient and understanding at all times, this girl's mother and father expected the same from her. With her first attempts at defiance, her father found himself trembling with rage, and her mother began to have violent migraine headaches. Without resorting to severe punishments or rigid limits, they soon let her know what her change in attitude did to them.

As a result, the child gave up. Once more, she became their beloved baby girl. At the same time, she became increasingly shy and withdrawn with her playmates, clung to her parents and gave up all evidences of being "fresh" or "talking back." Helpful at home, she obeyed her parents' rules, studied hard at school, but, unfortunately, she also stopped really growing up.

For all of the attention currently focused on the rebelliousness of adolescence, the truth of the matter is that college teachers, guidance coun-

selors and employers are seeing an increasing number of young adults who, like this girl, never really grew up. Those of us concerned with the problem find ourselves faced with a novel challenge: How to spark some courageous rebellion in the lives of these young people to help them move on to a genuine maturity and a life with their own generation.

UNLIKE some, my young friend's story has a happy ending. With professional guidance, her parents were able to face the unrealistic standards they had set for themselves. Gradually, they understood that in a loving, devoted family, rebellion is neither dangerous nor undesirable.

Parents must grasp the difference between the normal, momentary flare-ups that are part and parcel of the adolescent years, and the constant, secretive, smoldering resentment that in both quantity and quality indicates a more serious disturbance.

The rebellious adolescent knows intuitively that his parents are strong and competent, that they are equal to the fray. Secure in this knowledge, he

has the courage to test himself and move forward in his growth toward independence. When defiance can be seen as an act of integrity—the wish to grow—parents can stop feeling threatened and begin to develop the skills needed to meet the daily challenges to their authority. They can learn to roll with the punches, with humor and an abiding sense that the family members' devotion to one another will come through intact.

AS a result, parents become clearer in their own minds about the essential controls that must be maintained, despite the youngsters' objections to the contrary. They can and should make reasonable demands to preserve their own rights, unafraid of any storms that may ensue. In this way, parents become free to enjoy the good times and learn, gradually, to let go as their offspring's challenges bear fruit in greater responsibility and wisdom. Seen in this light, adolescent rebellion is no longer a threat but one of the many essential ingredients for the fullest flowering of the human spirit.

October 9, 1960

Anxieties Over College Heighten Youths' Woes

TEEN-AGE anxiety over college admission is becoming a mental health problem in this country, a pediatric psychiatrist warned yesterday.

Dr. George E. Gardner, Professor of Psychiatry at Harvard Medical School, said that this anxiety aggravates a period of life that is fraught with conflicts and tensions. He noted that many parents also become

unstrung in their efforts to help their children gain admission to college.

Among the adolescent's most difficult tasks, Dr. Gardner said, was his need to modify his unconscious concepts of his parents. While the security of the infant and young child depended on a concept of all-knowing, all-powerful parents, the elder child learns that this concept does not square with

the facts. He is beset by anxiety and insecurity, and usually reacts by investing other adults with the role of supreme counselor, much to the chagrin of his parents.

This accounts for the extreme vulnerability of all adolescents —and adults who remain adolescent—to leaders who appear omniscient and omnipotent; and are willing to do his thinking for him. In time, however, the adolescent learns that he must look to himself.

Another task of adolescence, Dr. Gardner said, was the modification of the view that genuine, lasting love relationships mean either slavery for oneself or subjugation of the beloved. This is based on the relation-

ship between the infant and his mother, whom he virtually enslaves.

The adolescent reacts to these conflicts by becoming indecisive, by assuming shifting, fleeting roles, and by dedication to varying ideals and values, according to Dr. Gardner. He said that 95 per cent of the adolescents come through this period with flying colors, while the remainder needed professional help that was sometimes unavailable. The psychiatrist addressed a meeting of the thirty-eighth annual convention of the Woman's Auxiliary to the American Medical Association, at the Roosevelt Hotel.

June 28, 1961

Whatever Happened to 'Please'?

By EVELYN S. RINGOLD

"THE manners of the children who come into our house are terrible. They wolf their food. Use their fingers. Treat my wife and me like over-aged zombies—or ignore us completely. They're totally concerned with consensual validation—that's a sociological term

meaning they care only about their peers. But—" wound up a suburban father, "ask my wife. She may think they're O.K. She's child-oriented."

The reaction of this father of three epitomizes the attitude of many parents on the matter of teen-age manners. Adults know what they see as

they drive car pools, travel in public and answer their own doorbells—but they are hesitant to deplore it lest they be charged with lack of understanding and sympathy for youth.

Many adults modestly assume that their own observations are personal and limited.

They hesitate to judge the intrinsic worth of a youngster by his manners and appearance. They know that the older generation has been decrying the customs of the young since society began — viz. Plautus, who wrote around 200 B.C.: "Manners are always declining." Others, not cowed by a sense of history—"we have to live with them *now*"—respond with a yelp of disapproval to party-crashing, total disregard for elders, the uncombed hair of the boys and the overcombed hair of the girls. The more child-centered, knowledgeable about "the turbulent feelings of adolescence," "the need for rebellion" and "peer approval" force themselves into an attitude of understanding to forestall an immediate reaction of revulsion—even resentment.

*N*o matter how adults react, however, they do have the distinct impression that manners among the young have

TEEN-AGERS *seem to be too wrapped up in themselves to be able to bother about others.*

suffered an undeniable decline. Even the simple formalities compulsory in earlier childhoods—the "please's," "thank you's" and "excuse-me's"—are often missing today. Parents observe a casualness in table manners that sometimes borders on the appalling. The more formal courtesies such as rising when introduced to an adult, addressing him by name and holding the door for a woman are rarely extended by contemporary teen-agers.

Parents note casual manners and mannerisms that match the omnipresent skinny pants and chewing gum. They see the extreme casualness of hair-clips and sausage - sized rollers worn in the subways, in the elevators of Fifth Avenue department stores and in college lecture halls. They see short shorts and bare feet on a young girl walking her poodle on Park Avenue. They see boys with crumpled chinos, an unfresh shirt and little evidence of a recent shave,

haircut or shower arriving for dates with pretty teen-age daughters in their "best."

Teen-age manners are probably the most disturbing where "peer culture" reigns supreme—at the local movies, where there is often more dialogue and action in the audience than on the screen, and at the hamburger hangout, where adolescents have been known to upset toothpicks, mustard jars, sugar bowls and the nerves of all adults within earshot.

A CHILD analyst in Philadelphia told me, "I do not go where teen-agers go. No sensible adult would!" An official in the Winnetka school system said, "I wouldn't be caught dead in a suburban movie on a Friday night." Amy Vanderbilt, an authority on good manners, disagrees with this resignation. "It is the responsibility of the theater," says Miss Vanderbilt, "to see that everyone who buys a ticket can enjoy the performance."

Boys and girls defend their

"hangout" manners. "It's hard to bother with 'please' and 'thank you' when you're ordering 'four shakes' into a little box," points out the editor of the newspaper in a large, urban high school. The assistant editor added: "Sometimes waitresses and drugstore clerks have no manners with *us*. They throw down the silver and growl 'What do you want?' They make all of us feel like juvenile delinquents."

Both children and parents agree, however, that mass behavior brings out mischief, latent hostilities and trouble. A psychiatrist says: "Kids wander around in packs, charged with unused energies, anxious to show how daring they are . . ." A high-school senior sees it from the inside: "One kid starts clowning. He's show-

WORST MANNERS prevail at hangouts where adolescents congregate.

ing off. Without his crowd—he wouldn't act that way."

*P*ARENTS are familiar with group behavior and group approval as the trademarks of adolescence—itself a challenging condition that overhangs and obscures the issue of teenage manners. But more and more parents are coming face to face with the question: how much must be excused in the name of adolescence and its classical accompaniment, rebellion? When current teenage standards conflict with adult standards what gives way?

Of course it is a matter of degree. Outright misbehavior and destructive manners—such as destroying property at a party—are obviously close to vandalism or delinquency, and call for clear-cut action. But a strong, outspoken minority of adults sees an equally portentous and insidious lowering of standards in the prevailing

thoughtlessness and sloppiness currently classified as "casual." This somewhat bitter minority feels we have crossed the borderline of good taste and sense.

Criticism of manners is almost indistinguishable from a deeper criticism of the current crop of children. "While they may eventually learn to say 'Thank you,' will they ever learn to *feel* it?" asks one disenchanted adult. "These children have been the center of *our* attention so long, they have naturally become the center of their *own* attention. No one has trained them in the theory and practice of thinking of the next fellow—especially if that fellow happens to be a parent!"

*O*BVIOUSLY, something has gone wrong. But what? While it is generally accepted that manners begin in the home, all the evidence points to considerable backing and filling on the part of parents. Even those parents who believe deeply in good manners hesitate to drill their children in the forms.

A mother of two girls and one boy says: "I was insistent on teaching manners when my children were young, because I did not want to be embarrassed by their behavior. But I had the guilty feeling that I was *too* insistent, that it was no longer considered important to teach young children their manners."

This view that "it's not important to teach manners" is undoubtedly still held by many parents in the deluge of con-

THE PENDULUM may be swinging back to an era of good manners.

temporary insights into childhood. It is felt that the age-old insistences: "Don't slouch over your food;" "Don't forget to thank Mary's mother when you leave the party;" "say 'Please pass the bread' not 'Pass the bread!' " will not produce manners but only a resentful set in the child *against* manners. There is also the feeling that real manners are not rooted in the outward formalities, such as shaking hands and saying the proper "how-do-you-do's," but rather in an ingrained sensitivity to and consideration for other people. "Such a child," a mother tells me, confidently, "will have an attractive manner, if not rule-book manners."

STILL another viewpoint, expressed with some heat, brushes aside the question of manners. "Kids should be thinking of more important things—how to work out racial tensions, their love lives, their views on existentialism. Our kids are too blasé. They don't need more manners. They need more involvement."

This attitude, however, brings forth fierce contradictions from other parents. "Consideration!" echoed one father. "Children are little animals that have to be civilized. We have to lead them—not follow their instincts."

"Involved!" retorted a mother who has seen her children through high school, college and into early marriage. "The only thing these kids are involved with is themselves—*their* racial tensions, *their* love lives. Where are they going to practice the art of living with and adjusting to *some one else's* needs—if we forgive so much, so quickly, in the name of puberty?"

PLENTY of parents are holdouts who refuse to be "modern"—who insist on the forms without too much self-conscious thought, who do not find clean finger nails a threat to mental health. But even among these there are bewildered parents who ruefully confess they are simply unsuccessful in their efforts.

"When the asparagus is served, I don't have to teach my children how to eat it," says one mother. "They take one look and say 'Ugh! Not for me!' " And a father who is a child analyst in the Westchester area says he *does* insist upon the proprieties with his children, but "I might as well be talking up a wall." In

a reflective mood, he adds "perhaps we are not teaching the absolutes with the same absolute convictions as our parents."

SOME educators feel that while the home is the source of a child's original manners, there is a definite need to implement the work of the home with additional instruction and incentive from the school.

Miss Ruth E. Bishop, an educational consultant in New York City, familiar with both public and private schools in a wide area, observes that in the more traditional private schools, they do go after table manners and behavior, that faultless manners are implicit and that the boys and girls know when they enter that this code of behavior is expected of them. (She tells of one boarding school for girls in Pennsylvania where a failing mark in deportment means dismissal—no matter how impressive the academic grades.)

In Scarsdale, the parents sponsor an after-school dancing program in the junior high, where, reportedly, children are "as interested in learning the social graces as in learning to dance." Some schools set up situations to practice manners. At Cheltenham High School in suburban Philadelphia, an annual junior-senior reception is designed to give students an experience with introductions on a formal receiving line. In one Ohio high school, the parents turned the senior prom into a dinner dance—against the protests of their children—

so that boys and girls would have an opportunity to show off their company manners at the table.

However, not all parents agree that public schools should take a role here. One Great Neck mother, when asked if her school or PTA did "anything about manners," replied flatly: "I hope not. We all have more important things to do. If my daughter wants to know a point of etiquette, she can look it up in a book."

IS the pendulum possibly swinging back to manners? There are many scattered indications of dissatisfaction and a renewed appreciation of what manners mean. Adults, teachers and counselors are beginning to wonder why children in other eras and other places seem able to go through adolescence without such a disturbing show.

MANNERS do not come naturally, but have to be learned.

They are weary of hearing comments such as that of a Pakistani member of the United Nations staff: "American children have no respect for adults, for nature or for life."

Child therapists report that youngsters tell them: "I certainly wouldn't let *my* children get away with the things my folks let me do."

A high school adviser says "Parents have been confusing development with training. A child grows from within, but needs pruning and firm stakes in the process."

Everything points toward a fresh view of manners in the near future. Not a revival

of the elaborate superstructure that was torn down with the great old town houses, but a return to simple, workable courtesies based on a recognition of the existence and rights of others. This must be reinforced with knowledge.

Amy Vanderbilt, who considers herself a proponent of "relaxed" good manners, feels that these must be *consciously* taught and practiced at home from a very young age, in a clear, good-humored way. She says that "whenever I speak before a group, some one in the audience will ask: 'If a child is innately kind and considerate, won't he automatically have good manners?' I reply 'No.' The greatest kindness in the world will not help a child to eat an artichoke in public—or save him the embarrassment if he doesn't know how."

No one seems to be making a brief for the reinstatement of the fingerbowl, nor for what social - critic Paul Goodman calls "the icy-grin of the upper middle-class." New manners will be a simple blueprint for behavior—a set of expectations and habits designed to make life pleasanter in spite of pressures and tensions; to protect feelings — one's own as well as the other person's. Children will have to be taught to say "thank you" and yield the center of the stage. Such good manners will not be regarded as a mark of pathology in a child, or a bid for status on the part of the parent—but simply as one way in which a child can find acceptance in the eyes of others.

WHEN the parents' job becomes boringly repetitive and seemingly unsuccessful—as it undoubtedly will—some might find refreshing insight into the matter in the views of two children.

A 14-year-old girl says "My manners are best when I'm shy or afraid." A 9-year-old boy writes definitively on the subject: "I have good manners. I say good night and good morning. I say hello and good-by, and when I see dead things lying around the house I bury them."

Evelyn S. Ringold, a frequent contributor to this page, has had considerable exposure to adolescent manners — good and bad. She confesses that she is the "asparagus mother" mentioned in the article.

Of Youth and Health

By ROBERT and PHYLLIS GOLDMAN

"**I** LOOKED in the mirror and what I saw made me sick. I was fat. Unfashionably fat. As I stood there, I realized that I was disappointed and angry with myself. I decided to lose weight. I said to myself, "It's now, today—not tomorrow.""

The speaker is an attractive if plump 16-year-old girl. Her self-assessment is indicative of the self-doubt and anxiety which many adolescents feel about their health, their "body image," their face to the world.

"Ordinarily, during childhood preadolescence, the body image changes slowly," declares Dr. William A. Schon-

"IMAGE"—A teen-ager can be troubled by the face he thinks he presents to the world.

feld, a child psychiatrist at Columbia Presbyterian Medical Center, who recently published a report on more than 200 teen-agers with "body image disturbances."

"Later, during the upheaval of adolescence, the tempo of change is greatly accelerated. It is a time when youth is in the midst of emotional conflict and turmoil. Often the adolescent feels that his body is unfamiliar to him, alien, not really part of him."

All this comes at a stage—

Robert and Phyllis Goldman are husband and wife and often collaborate on articles concerning child-rearing.

the adolescent years—when there is almost inevitable insecurity, feelings of inadequacy and an overwhelming desire to conform. Taken together, these forces can produce all sorts of symptoms.

To cope with the situation —and to help their teen-agers cope — parents must understand the extent of adolescent concern with health, says Dr. Joan Morgenthau, director of the Adolescent Clinic, New York Hospital-Cornell Medical Center.

"Some teen-agers will talk about their problems," says Dr. Morgenthau, "but some won't. This is a period of life when it is normal to withdraw."

Actually, recent studies show that teen-agers have innumerable unanswered questions about health; frequently, they do not seek answers from parents. At times, they develop psychosomatic complaints because of real or imagined inadequacies.

A University of Washington study of 700 teen-agers shows, for example, that 80 per cent of them had pressing questions about "personal hygiene, body functions or sex matters." Yet, the medical scientists who carried out the study, Drs. Robert W. Deisher and C. A. Mills, found that only about one in three adolescents take these questions to their parents. About one in two reported that they asked "a friend, a brother or sister, or no one at all."

WHAT are the deepest health problems in the adolescent's spectrum? Headaches, stomach aches, insomnia, muscular pains and menstrual disorders. All these are fairly common emotionally induced problems of adolescence, according to Dr. Morgenthau.

Probably the three most common complaints of teenagers are skin blemishes, growth and development deviations (the youngster is or thinks he is too short, too tall, too thin or too fat) and what might be called "deviations from the average."

This comes from Dr. J. Roswell Gallagher, director of the Adolescent Unit, The Children's Hospital, Boston. The irony of the teen-agers' concern, says Dr. Gallagher, lies in the fact that adolescence

is the healthiest period of life —at least from a physical standpoint.

DR. SCHONFELD points out, however, that this feeling of difference can be agonizing for a teen-ager. What parents must realize, he says, is that "today, we have a teen-age culture. Records, clothing, books, hair styles all are aimed at capturing the burgeoning teen-age market."

Many adolescents are overly concerned about their physical growth and development because they are afraid they will not fit into the "ideal image" created of them by television and the movies, says Dr. Schonfeld.

"They are constantly comparing themselves to these imagined ideals," he explains. "And this is the source of many of their health worries."

THIS is borne out by the University of Washington study, which found that among adolescents who complained of physical symptoms, a great number really had problems, adjusting and "integrating" into an effective role in life. In other words, their physical complaints actually paled in significance to their worries about being accepted as one of the group.

What can parents do to help

their teen-agers over the difficult moments of physical insecurity?

"Obviously, every teen-ager should be seen by a doctor regularly," says Dr. Gallagher, "a doctor with whom the youngster has rapport. If the teen-ager has a skin problem, for example, the task of parent and doctor is to convince him that the condition is temporary—that it will go away, that it is common to the age group."

"What the adolescent requires is repeated reassurance, continuing interest and help," says Dr. Schonfeld, "so that he may understand the vast difference between being abnormal and not being average."

"The girl who is secure and loved need not even *be* attractive in order to feel attractive," Dr. Morgenthau points out.

Dr. Schonfeld goes a step further. "The capacity to adapt socially depends more on the family and cultural attitudes toward body structure than on any actual defects." Thus, if the family accepts the teen-ager "as he is," the youngster's path will be comparatively smooth — no matter what his physical makeup.

PARENTS must understand that if they themselves are preoccupied with illness, their

MONKEY SEE, MONKEY DO—A young person exposed to his parents' ills may decide that he is suffering from the same complaint.

teen-agers will begin to worry about their own well-being. A mother or father who complains constantly about abdominal pains can actually "spread" these pains to everyone in the household.

In one New York clinic, a 16-year-old boy told the doctor that he suffered from tension headaches. When questioned closely, he told the doctor: "Well, I don't exactly have headaches with real pain. But my father and mother have them and I just sort of expect to have them, too."

Parents can help their teenagers greatly by pointing out to them the broad range of "normal or average." This, so the youngster will not suddenly begin to feel that he "is a strange one."

For example, says Dr. Schonfeld, the onset of menstruation can come at age 10. Or it may come as late as age 16. At either age, it is considered normal, although most girls experience it at ages 12 to 14.

"For boys, the onset of pu-

REASSURANCE—Although the "patient" may find it hard to believe, doctors say that adolescence is really the healthiest period of life

berty can come all the way from age 12 to 17," he explains, "and still be considered normal. Most boys reach puberty between ages 13 and 14."

One source of psychosomatic complaints, and even overweight, lies in the adolescent's need to loosen the bonds that hold him to his parents. Parents who "can't let go" are inviting their teen-agers to

develop physical and emotional problems.

"Emancipation from parental control is especially important," says Dr. Schonfeld. "The teen-ager wants to shift some of his dependence from parents to his peers because he feels he can conform to the latter group more readily."

FINALLY, parents should remember that pressure can intensify the youngsters' doubts about themselves.

"Parents should ask themselves," says Dr. Schonfeld, " 'Am I exerting too much pressure on my teen-age child to get good grades, apply to the right schools, join the right clubs, cultivate the right people?' 'Am I pushing him beyond his tolerance?' "

To this, Dr. Morgenthau adds: "Teen-agers are individuals. Each should be given the support he needs before adolescence if he is to thrive during adolescence."

September 6, 1964

The Best Of Teens, The Worst Of Teens

By MARTHA WEINMAN LEAR

IT was only a statistic. But poised upon its frail angularities, like the Koran inscribed upon the head of a pin, were volumes of significance. Before the year is out there will be 3.7 million 17-year-olds among us, according to figures released by the Population Reference Bureau, a Washington research organization. That means a million more than we had last year—a mas-

sive jump. And what with their tribe increasing each successive year for the next decade, the country is due for an inundation of 17-year-olds. They have flowered, all those buds of the 1947 baby boom. Who are they? What are they like?

There they stand, on a big threshold and awesomely hip. They cut their baby teeth on television, sharpened their bite on space, grew up to marry sooner, pay later, become dropouts and juvenile delinquents, crowd the colleges and the Peace Corps, act distressingly complacent and painfully idealistic, head straight for hell and be the bright new hope of tomorrow. In short, to mess briefly with Dickens, they are the best of teens, they are the worst of teens, and they are surrounded by adults who know one view or the other to be absolutely true.

Some facts, then. The 17's are 51 per cent male, half from middle-income families, two-thirds living in urban and suburban areas, 80 per cent in high school—seniors, mostly—almost three out of 10 destined not to graduate and almost half of those who do graduate (45 per cent of them girls) college-bound. One out of eight (female) and one out of 50 (male) are married. And the rest is mostly conjecture. Despite the cherished national myth that 17's,

and all teen-agers, are a distinct and mildly schizophrenic species, and despite the heady "teen-age world" summoned up by popular pollsters, the 17-year-old dropout in Harlem is unimpressed by all he has in common with the 17-year-old basketball star in Kansas City or the 17-year-old cocktail-party veteran in Connecticut, all of whom whoop it up on Saturday nights in vastly different ways.

THE Great Divide, at 17, is tomorrow. Asked what they worried about most, in studies conducted by the Boy Scouts, the Girl Scouts and Seventeen magazine, boys who were not college-bound overwhelmingly cited future employment as their single biggest worry. Boys and girls who intended to continue their education had the predictable obsession with competition for college. Apparently only girls bound for the labor market can afford to worry in the present tense; their chief concern, as revealed by the studies, is popularity with boys.

The lines were clearly drawn at a discussion, recently, among 10 seniors in a (Continued)

MARTHA WEINMAN LEAR often writes on sociological topics. She is the author of "The Child Worshipers," published in 1963.

middle-class suburban high school that will send 60 per cent of its graduates to college. The college-bound reported an average of two-and-a-half to three hours of homework nightly ("just to keep our grades up") and were further bogged down by extracurricular activities — student government, sport, church, community. The reason? College.

"I would do more but there just isn't *time,*" said one girl. "The second day of school there were nominations for student elections, and our English teacher told us, 'Go! Run for office! It will look *great* on your college records.'"

Mere participation is not enough. "You can't just take part in the Student Council, you have to be a leader," a boy explained. "That's what the colleges like."

Youngsters not headed for college are generally less involved with extracurricular activities. The activities they *do* pursue in school are, quite simply, those they enjoy. As one girl, a member of the Dramatics Club and a rabid football enthusiast, pointed out, "We lead completely different lives. I think one of the big differences between you [the college group] and us is that right now we have more fun." And not a soul called her wrong.

STILL, there are common points of reference: the instant joke, the instant fad, the instant dance, the instant celebrity, instantly communicated by television and relays of disk jockeys from coast to coast. (The communication may be faster, but the herd instinct is no greater than it used to be; Beatlemania has nothing on the raccoon coat, the Big Apple, or those "Three Little Fishes in an Itty-Bitty Pool"). And there is a common problem, severing the umbilical cord, which is crucial at 17.

"In this sense they're all in the same boat," says Lillian Opatoshu of the Child Study Association of America. "This is the final struggle to loosen the parental grip. You need support in any struggle, and they get it from each other. That is why they seem to look alike and talk alike and think alike. In a few years the struggle will be over, and then they won't look alike at all."

Currently, the look-alikes are wearing remarkably restrained protective coloration. The Beatnik Look may still prevail in some dim corners of the land, but the mainstream of 17-year-olds never went for all that grime. "What they *did* do," says Ruth Whit-

Teen-agers at a suburban high school —"Today's 17-year-olds stand on a big threshold and are awesomely hip."

ney, executive editor of Seventeen, "was to take the Beat Look, slick it up and make it come out clean and tasteful."

WHEN the boys discuss style the operative word is "conservative." "Nowadays everybody's got to be a good dresser, and the good dresser looks conservative," one said recently, adding with commendable frankness, "We all try to look like college students." Loafers and pin-stripe shirts are considered very Ivy League, and the hair style of the moment is the Peter Gunn look, patterned after the tonsorial effects of a television star. It is of moderate length, combed to the side and slightly forward, and exceedingly neat.

For the girls, the magic word is "casual." The teased hair of recent seasons has given way to longer, straighter locks. Loafers, sweaters and dark, patterned stockings are favored. On both coasts (typically, the fads appear there first and move inland) there is a strong trend to pierced ears. The result is they all look at least as much alike as the women in any theater on any opening night.

For what 17's like, their current glossary includes fabulous," as well as "gear" and "tuff," both of which also mean fabulous. For what (or whom they do not like, the words are "animal," "gross" and "skag," the last of which means what "jerk" used to mean to their parents.

They dance the monkey, the frug and the swim, all loosely derived from the twist and all characterized by almost as

much explicit sexuality as the shimmy.

Following a period of intense devotion to elephant jokes last year ("How can you tell if there's an elephant in the room?" "You smell the peanuts on his breath"), the 17's—and all teen-agers —had a brief fling with grape jokes ("What's purple and swings through trees?" "Tarzan the Grape"), and moved on to assorted food-and-color jokes ("What's red, hangs from a tree and goes *d-pah, d-pah?*" "A retarded apple") from which they are only now recovering. Adults who find none of this funny are referred to the knock-knock jokes of the thirties.

Such traditional idiosyncrasies aside, it is all but gospel that 17-year-olds are smarter, more ambitious, more precocious and less respectful than they used to be. But how much change has there been?

Well, they are taller: The 17-year-old boys have picked up an inch and a half since the turn of the century, the girls half an inch (the girls have also shed three pounds). They are better educated: Only half of their parents and a quarter of their grandparents finished high school, as compared with the current seven out of 10.

THEY have more money and drive more cars, according to Gilbert Youth Research, Inc., a leading Boswell of the teen-age market. Eighty-five per cent of the boys and almost as many girls work at some time during the year. Their earnings and allowances add up to $2.8 billion annually which gives Madison Avenue long and

thoughtful pause. Most of them have drivers' licenses, and while estimates on ownership range wildly, it is nothing if not conservative to say that used-car dealers would be in trouble without them.

Their aspirations are almost solidly middle-class—particularly the girls'. In college, half the boys will pursue a profession (the favorite: engineering) and a third of the girls will go into education. Most of the boys who are not going to college want "interesting work," whatever it may be. The noncollege girl wants to work for several years in a white-collar job and then marry—if not one of those engineers—a white-collar man. Nothing too new there.

ARE their tastes more sophisticated than their parents' were? Are they more aware of politics, the world, the arts? The Gilbert people report that their polls show greater political awareness "since Kennedy. The kids worshiped him, and he made them more conscious of politics."

They may *know* more; after all, they are better-educated, and almost all of them have access to television, which has made everyone more aware of politics, the world, the arts. But there is no real evidence that the proportion of Bach-to-Beatle fans is any greater than was the proportion of Bach-to-Sinatra fans. In three widely disparate high schools the favorite extracurricular reading for senior boys was Playboy magazine; the girls said they didn't have time for extracurricular reading. And Republican and Democratic leaders in several districts say—unofficially—that the 17's who volunteer for duty are proportionately the same small corps of exceptional youngsters ("the cream of the college - preparatory crop," one calls them) who have gotten involved in every election in memory.

Socially, at least, they are surely more sophisticated than 17's-gone-by. The mass media have made them glib. Permissive parents have made many of them feel more poised with adults and freer to criticize them (one principal vividly recalls a student referring to one of his staff as "an old stereotype teacher." An expanding pattern of apprenticeship for dating that begins in the elementary grades with parties and dances has given a whole community of them a veneer of precocity.

BUT the possibility exists that change is more apparent

than real as regards sex standards — which everyone knows have changed most drastically of all. *Doesn't* everyone? Despite the accessibility of cars, more going steady and rising out - of - wedlock birth rates, Yale's August de B. Hollingshead says, "I do not think that premarital sex behavior has changed significantly in 40 years." This sociologist and long-time observer of American youth notes:

"We tend to overemphasize change. You find more of it in large communities where there are new masses of people who have been uprooted and transplanted. In the relatively small group or community, where everyone knows the social system, very little

has changed.

"In each generation the gatekeepers and curators of morals have to defend them from violation—because they are being violated. Kids always misbehave. Generations of them have been going to the dogs since there were dogs. The difference today is that they are more willing to talk about it."

Discussions with groups of 17-year-olds in three communities do suggest a more clear cut change in attitude than in behavior. "Some of us do it, some of us don't," one girl said simply; "most of us don't." Another: "I think if you've been going steady for a long time, and you're really serious, you might go all the way. But just

to play around—no." "I hear about kids jumping in and out of bed," a boy said. "What I'd like to know is, where?" Some probably *knew* where, but then some 17-year-olds have always known.

S URELY they are not precisely the same old breed, these 17's; they are not in the same old culture. But the differences may be exaggerated by (1) adults with short memories and (2) a clear-eyed fleet of entrepreneurs creating a new image of new youngsters with new needs for new products.

The fact is, 17-year-olds still fight with their parents over the same old things: In those

Scout surveys, both boys and girls reported that the chief bone of contention was control of hours. They still think they are unique. "Do you kids think you are the only ones who ever rebelled?" one mother reports asking her son recently. "Your father once disowned his family's religion— that's how strongly *he* felt the need to rebel." The youngster grabbed hold of his near-Beatle hair, yanked it in frustration and said: "And I have to express myself through *this* kind of nonsense because in the *big* things I *agree* with you—dammit!"

And they still, of course, are going to the dogs.

November 1, 1964

TEEN-AGE SUICIDE REPORTED ON RISE

Panel at Parley Here Warns Parents and Schools

By NATALIE JAFFE

For every one of the 600 American teen-agers whose deaths are recorded as suicide each year, there are at least 100 who fail in the attempt or who take their own lives under the guise of accident, a group of social scientists and teachers was told yesterday.

Although suicide is ranked as the 10th leading cause of death for all Americans, for teen-agers it ranks fourth—after

accident, cancer and rheumatic heart disease—and the rate is rising.

The annual figures themselves are not dramatic—about 4 teenagers in 100,000 take their lives —but the rate has doubled in the last decade while the figures for all suicides have increased by about 50 per cent, according to Dr. Harry Bakwin, professor of clinical pediatrics at New York University.

A panel of psychiatrists at a convention of the American Orthopsychiatric Association at the New York Hilton Hotel urged parents and school officials to watch for early signs of depression.

Children show their depression very differently from adults, according to James Toolan, former head of adolescent psychiatric services at Bellevue Hospital. Constant

complaints of fatigue, poor work in school, disruptive behavior or running away from home should not be automatically labeled "mere deinquency," he said.

Although many attempts at suicide are more a cry for help than a bent for self-destruction, and many bouts with depression do not end in suicide, the symptoms must be respected, Dr. Toolan said. He is now head of the student mental health service at Bennington College.

Dr. Toolan's successor at Bellevue, Dr. Robert E. Gould, said that at least one-third of the 350 girls admitted to his service each year were referred to him after unsuccessful attempts to take their own lives. For the boys, it is one in five. Statistically, more boys commit suicide than girls, but more girls try.

Discussing those deaths that are not identified as suicides,

Dr. Gould said, "From what I've seen at Bellevue and in private practice, many of the accidents --hot rod crack-ups and the like—have to be suicide."

The reasons for a suicide attempt, he said, "cut across class lines." At the core, in his opinion, is depression, arising from feelings of being rejected, abandoned, unloved.

Although national figures show a higher suicide rate for city-dwellers, a recent study of New Jersey school children disclosed a higher rate in rural areas.

James Jan-Tausch of the New Jersey State Department of Education said his study of two groups of emotionally disturbed children, had shown that those who attempted suicide were "uniformly" the isolated, withdrawn youngsters with no close friends.

March 20, 1965

THE TEENAGE SUB-CULTURE

Teen-Age Slang

By Catherine Mackenzie

A PPLE-POLISHING, as a term for currying favor, has passed into our vernacular; so has "corny," as applied to the obvious and the sentimental, and where we once said "okay," the expressions "on the beam" or "in the groove" are slang terms in good standing, accepted, or at least understood, even by the middle-aged.

All these currently punctuate the speech of the young. But did

you know that the latest of everything is now designated by teenagers as "burnt to a crisp"? That A. W. O. L. means to them not only the traditional "absent without leave" but "a wolf on the loose"? And that in conversational exchanges with their peers the conventional salutation (meaning "How have you been?" or "What have you been doing?") is "What gives?"

This week's researches have included study of a breezy little

booklet, published by Scholastic Magazine, written for the teenagers on their own manners and mores, in their own idiom, by a staff member calling herself Gay Head, and entitled "Hi There, High School." From this valuable little document we have dredged up some information for parents, who may be unaware, as was this reporter, that the lads and lasses nowadays retort "Harvest it" upon hearing a tiresome joke (sorry, boys and girls, a corny

joke); that to raid the refrigerator is to "blitz the cold-storage plant," and that as a favorite expression meaning "wonderful" they exclaim, "Mur-der!" "Collapse," they say, meaning sit down.

Here are a few more of the fifty-odd expressions with their teen-age definitions from the dictionary of high school slang listed in the Scholastic booklet (20 cents a copy, 220 East Forty-second Street, New York 17, N. Y.):

Cooking With Gas or Cooking on the Front Burner — "Doin' all right; on the beam; okay."

Drip — "A wet smack of the human species; 'way off the beam."

Gruesome Twosome — "A couple who 'go steady.'"

Hep — "In the know or groove; very o-kay."

Ice Up — "Give 'em the cold shoulder. Usual, and often effective, treatment for wolves."

Jackson — "Anyone. Most often used in addressing a smooth-looking boy."

Jam Session — "The result when a swing band gets 'hep'; ditto when the jitterbugs gather around the juke box."

On Fire — "Super-colossal."

Off the Cob — "Corny."

Step Up Closer to the Mike — "I didn't get what you said. Come again!"

Shove in Your Clutch — "Get going!"

Tizzy — "A dither; a 'mad.'"

You Ain't Woofin'? — "You aren't kidding?"

You Shred It, Wheat — "You Figure it out."

Taking a little time to figure them out, all of the terms but one seemed clear to this reporter. This one was "Military Objective," defined as "A good number, but not one found in the multiplication table." This particular point was made clear by a telephone call to Miss Gay Head, who compiled the list.

"That means," she said, "a very nice number; a smooth cookie; or, in plain English, a very dateable girl."

Parents may care to note that the current "exclamation denoting approval, astonishment or dismay" is *ZOWIE!*

December 5, 1943

Sinatra Fans Pose Two Police Problems And Not the Less Serious Involves Truancy

Some 25,000 crooner fans, most of them early teen-age girls clad in bobby socks and sweaters, created intricate traffic problems outside the Paramount Theatre in Times Square yesterday waiting their turn to see Frank Sinatra. But one police squad watching their antics was concerned with more serious problems than traffic snarls.

Twenty policewomen and a group of patrolmen in plainclothes from the Juvenile Aid Bureau investigated the bobby socks phenomenon, one of a series staged by swing maestros and crooners that has lured teen-age children into Times Square at 4 A. M. in spite of Mayor La Guardia's 9 P. M. curfew for them and that caused mass truancy from the schools on Wednesday.

The police investigation, which began at 7 A. M., one hour after a goodly crowd had lined up outside the box office on Broadway, ninety minutes before the doors were opened, came as George H. Chatfield, member of the Board of Education and former director of the board's bureau of attendance, called for a concerted program by the board, the police and the courts to deal with the problem.

"We don't want this thing to go on," Commissioner Chatfield said. "We can't tolerate young people making a public display of losing control of their emotions."

The first few times the crooners and swing band leaders staged fan displays on Times Square that appealed to children of school age the Board of Education was inclined to overlook it, hoping it would not recur, because only single-day absence from school was involved and the absentees were back before case studies could begin, Commissioner Chatfield explained.

But since it was getting to be a regular part of these players' promotion, a plan would have to be worked out to deal with it, he said. The number of truancies is too large for the bureau of attendance to handle with its present staff and there are not enough judges in the Juvenile Courts at present to handle the cases if a drive were made, he explained.

The police investigators from the Juvenile Aid Bureau worked from 7 A. M. until last midnight, when the investigation was taken over by plainclothes patrolmen from the Third Division. In a previous case, the police learned that a press agent had started the fan demonstration by engaging young people to appear at the theatre and idolize the star. The police were seeking to learn yesterday if any grown-ups were in back of the present demonstration.

"If we find anybody encouraging truancy," Mr. Chatfield explained, "we can prosecute them directly. If there is evidence of that, we will do so."

When the theatre's doors opened at 8:30 A. M. yesterday, the queue, mostly of girls released by the Columbus Day holiday from grammar and high school classes, extended west along Forty-third Street and then north to Forty-fourth. From then on, the lines grew, and nearly 200 policemen had to be called to keep pedestrian and vehicular traffic moving.

Up in his dressing room, the windows of which were covered with heavy draperies so he would not absent-mindedly show his face and throw the girls in the street below into an impromptu swoon on the wrong side of the box office, Sinatra decided he would have to have his meals indoors. The crowds had become so big he could no longer go out.

"The crowd is swell, but I'm always afraid of somebody getting hurt," he said.

October 13, 1944

Kaleidoscope of Teen-Age Fads

From yesterday's yellow slickers to today's letter-writing craze, signs of 'epidemic lunacy' confirm that adolescents will be adolescents.

By LESTER RAND

IF in the next few months the teen-age males of this country start wearing silk hats with their dungarees and the young females start wearing rubber boots to school proms, no one will be surprised.

There is no sign of either trend right now. But who can say what bizarre and generally inexplicable mode of dress, style of speech or mass mannerism youthful faddists will adopt next? It has been going on for years, of course, but nowadays it goes on faster than ever before. To some parents and educators these fads are signs of epidemic lunacy in the younger generation; to others (myself included) they are simply reflections of the uneasy mixture that is adolescence—part childhood and part maturity, part conformity and part individualism.

In any case, the sudden manifestations are fascinating to observe. In my own travels around the country, and in reports from some 1,800 correspondents in schools and colleges, many strange and often amusing things turn up. For instance, right now in the Middle West (there are indications that the same thing is occurring in other sections) teen-age girls are engaged in a frenzy of letter writing. They are not letters to editors or to Congress or to movie and TV stars. They are letters to their dearest chums, whom they have seen all day and will see again tomorrow. And they are no hurried notes, either. They are five and six pages long.

How did this come about? Parents cracked down on those endless telephone calls every evening. The girls, however, simply couldn't keep their thoughts and their gossip bottled up overnight. So they began writing these long screeds—and handing them to their friends in the morning. An incidental discovery in all this is that there is more privacy in a letter than there is over the family's living-room telephone. Yet no one expects this fad to last long—it involves too much work.

FROM Texas to Oregon, from Omaha to Nashville, the reports come in. They describe what fads the youngsters are going in for at the moment, what fads are waning. Our correspondents are also field interviewers, but more often than not they can get no satisfactory answers to such questions as: How did you catch on to this? Why did you take it up? Do you think it will last? To this and similar questions the all-embracing answer seems to be: "Well,

LESTER RAND is president of the Youth Research Institute, a marketing and opinion research firm specializing in the youth field.

129

all the other kids are doing it."

In the case of the letter writing, it is possible to pin down the origin of the craze. But no one seems to know why, for a few examples:

Teen-age couples walk along the street "handcuffed" by means of paper clips attached to their wrist-watch bands.

High-school youths go around with small placards pinned to their neckties, viz.: "Who's Louise's new boy friend?" and "Don't forget the dance Friday night."

Girls are wearing as many as three "Slim Jim" or "Texas" ties on their blouses at the same time.

Some Midwestern boys simultaneously go into full "mourning" when flunking an exam.

Girls in various parts of the country are known for a few days at a time by the names of ranking movie stars (they announce the names themselves).

Similarly, a few seasons ago, no one seemed to know why girls wore dog-collars around their ankles (or different-colored ribbons to denote their dat-

"Couples who are going steady' carve each other's initials in the soles of their shoes."

ing status), and boys put "hashmarks" on their sleeves to indicate their years in high school, and a couple "going steady" would draw up an elaborate nonaggression pact after a quarrel.

Whatever starts them off, the fads tend to spread rapidly and bite deeply. They may begin in Texas or New York, in a Chicago suburb or in Southern California. They may last six months or a year (seldom longer). Very few of them become nation-wide in scope, and when they do they are likely to be in the field of dress—the ubiquitous blue jeans, for example. Certain catchwords from movie and TV comics occasionally have a sudden vogue—"I like it, I *like* it" or "I'm with *you!*"—but they will be short-lived.

Some fads go on for years: charm bracelets with everything imaginable clipped on have been popular for the better part of a decade. Some die away and then are reborn: the business of pinning buttons and gadgets of various kinds onto a beanie or pork-pie hat seems continually resurgent; the yellow slicker painted with emblems and

mottoes appears to be coming back right now, after a lapse of some thirty years.

The way that a fad spreads is easier to trace than its motivation. A boy visiting Tulsa or Detroit or any town hears some new slang or sees a new trick of dress and he takes it home. A girl writes a friend some distance away and raves about the latest fun with necklace or hair-do, and the thing spreads faster than the merchants can keep up with it. Clothing manufacturers in particular do their best to outguess the newest rage and they follow it up with promotion in the teen-age magazines and general publications, spreading the word on a massive scale.

THE "why" of it all is pretty elusive. Broadly speaking, the teen-agers want acceptance by their contemporaries; "conformity" within the social group is a form of self-reassurance at an age when things can be pretty confusing. It is a period of natural resistance to —if not alienation from—the control of parents and teachers, so the youngsters find comfort in being like others of their own age. In doing this they nevertheless seek to express their individuality by wearing more and crazier charms or being the first to use a new bit of slang.

Beyond this, they would appear to be responsive to larger social forces around them. The extreme "Sloppy Joe" styles among the girls that marked the end of World War II may well have reflected the facts that: (1) many of the older girls were going off to factory jobs in slacks and sweaters; (2) there was a general austerity that made fancier dressing seem out of order; (3) there were fewer young men around for whom to look attractive. Now there is a definite trend toward trimmer dress, even in casual clothes; the girls continue to wear "man-tailored" shirts, but they are in fact very feminine—and the shirt-tails are tucked in. They are using more cosmetics, but using them better. Why? Probably because there is more social life, more dating, than the war years afforded.

DURING and just after the war the boys who were too young for military service admired those in uniform. Maybe that explains why they all dressed and walked, as nearly as they could, like bomber crews heading out for a mission—the bulky jackets and long scarves, the shambling stride as though they were loaded down with parachutes and oxygen masks. Now the young man in his teens wears a much more conventional demeanor, while preserving the right to a few zany manifestations.

So the going-together couples carve each other's initials in the soles of their shoes; they use locks of each other's hair as bookmarks; they wear the names of their opposites in their lapels. They are, all in all, pseudo-sophisticates teetering on the edge of growing up. And, while teetering, they are having a wonderful time.

October 17, 1954

Drawings by Leonard Shortall
"The only explanation for any of this seems to be: 'All the other kids are doing it.' "

Bridgeport Ban Stops the Music: Halts 'Rock 'n Roll' Teen Dances

Special to The New York Times.

BRIDGEPORT, Conn., March 25—Police Superintendent John A. Lyddy has forbidden, until further notice, the issuance of permits for "Rock 'n Roll" teen-age dance parties.

Explaining that he was doing so because the situation was getting out of hand, he said today that he had acted upon the recommendation of Lieut. Joseph Couglin.

"We did this on our own, without a specific request from any church or community group," Mr. Lyddy said.

"Recently there was real trouble in New Haven, where half a dozen Bridgeport youngsters were arrested, and the authorities outlawed this 'Rock 'n Roll' business. I think the musicians start it with their capers. The kids take it up and pretty soon the whole thing is out of hand."

Drinking Is Cited

According to William E. Kelsey Jr., a business man who has organized such parties, "Rock 'n Roll" is less to blame for the situation than are the alcoholic beverages taken straight by boys and girls from 16 to 19 years old.

"A couple of nights ago, a group of teen-agers met at my house to talk it out," Mr. Kelsey said. "I asked them to expose the liquor dealers selling to minors, but they refused. These are their friends now, I was told."

Mr. Kelsey, a 32-year-old furniture manufacturer, has four children, the oldest a boy of 14. A director of the Bridgeport Teen Club, his objective has been to create an outlet for young people in town.

"Clear through from here to Stamford the problem exists," he continued. "The kids will go to New York, and you know what that means. I've always tried to let them all in, good and bad. The police tell me the bad ones must be kept out, so we are going to issue identification cards hereafter to let the good ones in."

A month ago Mr. Kelsey organized a "Rock 'n Roll" party for 2,000 at an armory here. After the New Haven fracas, he withdrew a request for permission to hold three more such parties in April.

March 26, 1955

Rock-and-Roll Called 'Communicable Disease'

HARTFORD, Conn., March 27 (UP)—A noted psychiatrist described "rock-and-roll" music today as a "communicable disease" and another sign of adolescent rebellion."

Dr. Francis J. Braceland, psychiatrist in chief of the Institute of Living, called rock-and-roll a "cannibalistic and tribalistic" form of music. He was commenting on the disturbances that led to eleven arrests during the week-end at a local theatre.

It is insecurity and "rebellion," Dr. Braceland said, that impels teenagers to affect "ducktail" haircuts, wear zootsuits and carry on boisterously at rock-and-roll affairs.

Six of those arrested were fined from $15 to $25 yesterday in Police Court. One hundred more were ejected from the theatre.

March 28, 1956

Segregationist Wants Ban on 'Rock and Roll'

BIRMINGHAM, Ala., March 29 (UP)—A segregation leader charged today that the National Association for the Advancement of Colored People had "infiltrated" Southern white teen-agers with "rock and roll music."

Asa Carter, executive secretary of the North Alabama White Citizens Council, said the group was starting a survey in the Birmingham and Anniston areas and would ask juke box operators to throw out "immoral" records in the new rhythm.

Coin music distributors said this would mean eliminating most of their hits. Mr. Carter said other records featuring Negro performers also should be "purged."

Roy Wilkins, executive secretary of the N. A. A. C. P., commented in New York: "Some people in the South are blaming us for everything from measles to atomic fallouts."

March 30, 1956

ELVIS PRESLEY

Lack of Responsibility Is Shown by TV In Exploiting Teen-Agers

By JACK GOULD

TELEVISION broadcasters cannot be asked to solve life's problems. But they can be expected to display adult leadership and responsibility in areas where they do have some significant influence. This they have hardly done in the case of Elvis Presley, entertainer and phenomenon.

Last Sunday on the Ed Sullivan show Mr. Presley made another of his appearances and attracted a record audience. In some ways it was perhaps the most unpleasant of his recent three performances.

Mr. Presley initially disturbed adult viewers—and instantly became a martyr in the eyes of his teen-age following—for his strip-tease behavior on last spring's Milton Berle program. Then with Steve Allen he was much more sedate. On the Sullivan program he injected movements of the tongue and indulged in wordless singing that were singularly distasteful.

At least some parents are puzzled or confused by Presley's almost hypnotic power; others are concerned; perhaps most are a shade disgusted and content to permit the Presley fad to play itself out.

Neither criticism of Presley nor of the teen-agers who admire him is particularly to the point. Presley has fallen into a fortune with a routine that in one form or another has always existed on the fringe of show business; in his gyrating figure and suggestive gestures the teen-agers have found something that for the moment seems exciting or important.

Quite possibly Presley just happened to move in where society has failed the teen-ager.

Certainly, modern youngsters have been subjected to a great deal of censure and perhaps too little understanding. Greater in their numbers than ever before, they may have found in Presley a rallying point, a nationally prominent figure who seems to be on their side. And, just as surely, there are limitless teen-agers who cannot put up with the boy, either vocally or calisthenically.

Family counselors have wisely noted that ours is still a culture in a stage of frantic and tense transition. With even 16-year-olds capable of commanding $20 or $30 a week in their spare time, with access to automobiles at an early age, with communications media of all kinds exposing them to new thoughts very early in life, theirs indeed is a high degree of independence. Inevitably it has been accompanied by a lessening of parental control.

Small wonder, therefore, that the teen-ager is susceptible to overstimulation from the outside. He is at the age when an awareness of sex is both thoroughly natural and normal, when latent rebellion is to be expected. But what is new and a little discouraging is the willingness and indeed eagerness of reputable business men to exploit those critical factors beyond all reasonable grounds.

Television surely is not the only culprit. Exposé magazines, which once were more or less bootleg items, are now carried openly on the best newsstands. The music-publishing business— as Variety most courageously has pointed out—has all but disgraced itself with some of the "rock 'n' roll" songs it has issued. Some of the finest recording companies have been willing to go right along with the trend, too.

Distinctive

Of all these businesses, however, television is in a unique position. First and foremost, it has access directly to the home and its wares are free. Second, the broadcasters are not only addressing themselves to the teen-agers but, much more importantly, also to the lower age groups. When Presley executes his bumps and grinds, it must be remembered by the Columbia Broadcasting System that even the 12-year-old's curiosity may be overstimulated. It is on this score that the adult viewer has every right to expect sympathetic understanding and cooperation from a broadcaster.

A perennial weakness in the executive echelons of the networks is their opportunistic rationalization of television's function. The industry lives fundamentally by the code of giving the public what it wants. This is not the place to argue the artistic foolishness of such a standard; in the case of situation comedies and other escapist diversions it is relatively unimportant.

But when this code is applied to teen-agers just becoming conscious of life's processes, not only is it manifestly without validity but it also is perilous. Catering to the interests of the younger generation is one of television's main jobs; because those interests do not always coincide with parental tastes should not deter the broadcasters. But selfish exploitation and commercialized overstimulation of youth's physical impulses is certainly a gross national disservice.

Sensible

The issue is not one of censorship, which solves nothing; it is one of common sense. It is no impingement on the medium's artistic freedom to ask the broadcaster merely to exercise good sense and display responsibility. It is no blue-nosed suppression of the proper way of depicting life in the theatre to expect stage manners somewhat above the level of the carnival sideshow.

In the long run, perhaps Presley will do everyone a favor by pointing up the need for earlier sex education so that neither his successors nor TV can capitalize on the idea that his type of routine is somehow highly tempting yet forbidden fruit. But that takes time, and meanwhile the broadcasters at least can employ a measure of mature and helpful thoughtfulness in not contributing further to the exploitation of the teenager.

With congested schools, early dating, the appeals of the car, military service, acceptance by the right crowd, sex and the normal parental pressures, the teen-ager has all the problems he needs.

Mercenary

To resort to the world's oldest theatrical come-on just to make a fast buck from such a sensitive individual is cheap and tawdry stuff. At least Presley is honest in what he is doing. That the teen-ager sometimes finds it difficult to feel respect for the moralizing older generation may of itself be an encouraging sign of his intelligence. If the profiteering hypocrite is above reproach and Presley isn't, today's youngsters might well ask what God do adults worship.

September 16, 1956

TELEVISION MAILBAG: MR. PRESLEY

To the Radio-Television Editor:

JACK Gould's column last Sunday on Elvis Presley was excellent. As a teacher facing youth of today, I cannot help but feel alarmed at the reaction I have noted to this alleged entertainer. And to know that he is aided and abetted by powerful networks is most disturbing.

My quarrel is not with Mr. Presley but with those who push him on further and further. * * *

G. SCOTT CREE.
Syracuse, N. Y.

RESPONSIBILITY

To the Radio-Television Editor:

I am 18 years old and have wide contacts in teen-age circles. My experience would seem to indicate that if it were not for the dubiously sincere moralizing of such men as Mr. Gould, the whole question of Mr. Presley's sexuality might never have arisen and he might not be the national craze that he is today. * * *

FRED BARREIRO Jr.
New York.

COLLABORATIONISTS

To the Radio-Television Editor:

In aiming his criticism at the recording industry, the music publishers and the television producers, Mr. Gould placed most of the responsibility where it belongs. Let us not, however, overlook the aiders and abettors, like Ed Sullivan and Steve Allen, who introduce such performers as Elvis Presley with elephantine fanfare. * * *

In order to be accepted by our present-day TV and entertainment entrepreneurs, the performer must be more primitive, more elementary, more mediocre than ever before. * * * One shudders to contemplate the cultural level of the next generation.

HARRY A. FELDMAN,
Chairman, Music Department,
William C. Bryant High School.
New York.

MISUNDERSTANDING

To the Radio-Television Editor:

The teen-age minds reacted toward Elvis Presley as they have toward other American favorites. In no way did they feel a sense of stimulation with a sex-defined attitude. It was puppy love and no more than any admiration that exists between the idol and his fan.

Adults who forever misunderstand the desires of these teen-agers immediately took up the cries of "suggestive performance," "degrading routines" and "sexual gyrations." * * * Believe me, the teen-agers were not aware of this interpretation until it was presented to them by the unhealthy few. * * *

Mrs. RHODA FRANK.
New York.

COMMENDATION

To the Radio-Television Editor:

I want to commend Mr. Gould for his excellent column regarding Elvis Presley. * * * If the adverse public reaction that follows an unfortunate performance such as this were directed at the sponsor as well as the broadcasting industry, would it not cause advertisers to consider more carefully what they wished to present to the public?

HOWARD SPALDING,
Principal, A. B. Davis High School.
Mount Vernon, N. Y.

APPRECIATIVE

To the Radio-Television Editor:

I am one of Elvis' frantic fans. * * * I really appreciated the way Mr. Gould outlined the position of teen-agers in this controversy to our parents. Also, I hope and believe that with proper handling Elvis Presley can become a good actor as well as a truly popular singer. * * *

FRANCES McCARTHY.
New York.

MASTERLY

To the Radio-Television Editor:

Thank you for presenting Jack Gould's masterly arraignment of the Elvis Presley entertainment routine. ERNEST BRISTOL.
New York.

SENSIBLE

To the Radio-Television Editor:

A line of appreciation for Mr. Gould's fine column. Its common sense should be irresistible to all well-intentioned and thinking people.

CATHERINE C. FENZEL.
Tuckahoe, N. Y.

September 23, 1956

Gas Ends Rock 'n' Roll Riot

FAYETTEVILLE, N. C., Nov. 3 (UP)—Several persons were injured when the police fired tear gas to break up a rock 'n' roll riot here last night. They fired gas grenades into ventilation ducts at the dance hall where the Fats Domino band was playing. Mr. Domino said the fight was caused by "the beat and the booze." He and three band members received minor cuts. George L. Ahumade and Roy E. Williams, both of Fort Bragg, were stabbed.

November 4, 1956

Rock 'n' Roll Teen-Agers Tie Up the Times Square Area

Line Up at Theatre 18½ Hours—175 Police Called

By EDITH EVANS ASBURY

Teen-age rock 'n' roll enthusiasts stormed into the Times Square area before dawn yesterday and all day long they filled sidewalks, tied up traffic and eventually required the attention of 175 policemen.

They began lining up at 4 A. M. to see the show at the Paramount Theatre. It wasn't until eighteen and a half hours later—at 10:30 P. M.—that the last of the line entered the theatre. Late arrivals continued buying tickets, however, until the box office closed shortly after 1 A. M. The show featured Alan Freed, a disk jockey who takes credit for coining the phrase rock 'n' roll.

The rock 'n' rollers stamped their feet so vigorously in the theatre that firemen became alarmed and sent for inspectors from the Fire and Buildings Departments at 5 P. M. The management cleared three-fourths of the 1,600 youngsters from the second balcony as a precautionary measure.

All but the first four rows, seating 206, were refilled at 7:30 after a preliminary report by a building inspector, and at 8 o'clock occupancy of the entire second balcony was approved by Nicholas Lanese, chief construction inspector of the Building Department.

A theatre spokesmen said that 15,220 patrons had attended the six stage and seven movie shows between 8 A. M. and 1 A. M. The attendance figure and receipts of $29,000 set opening day records for the thirty-one-year-old theatre, the spokesmen said.

When the last stage show ended most of the crowd left, leaving only a handful of persons watching the final showing of the movie.

"Rock 'n' roll is really swing with a modern name," Mr. Freed said in his backstage dressing room between performances. "It began on the levees and plantations, took in folk songs, and features blues and rhythm. It's the rhythm that gets the kids. They are starved for music they can dance to, after all those years of crooners."

Other experts described rock 'n' roll as essentially a rolling two-beat rhythm with the accent coming on every second beat.

In the streets and in the theatre the youngsters gave a lot of evidence of fierce enthusiasm for the rhythm.

They shouted, tried to crowd past policemen and burst screaming through wooden barriers set up to hold them in line. Policemen on horseback were jeered as they galloped along Forty-third Street trying to thwart break-throughs during the morning.

Two girls suffered leg injuries and were taken to St. Clare's Hospital. Other youngsters hobbled around, with bruised shins, bemoaning lost shoes and rubbing bumped arms. The street was littered with sandwiches, apples and other lunch-box contents tossed at the police.

A glass restaurant door was shattered, and so was the ticket seller's box in the Paramount entrance.

The noise of the crashing glass, at 10:10 A. M., had a sobering effect on the teen-agers, who fell back from the barriers they had been trying to overturn and stopped shoving the police trying to hold them back.

Shortly thereafter, two dozen more policemen marched down Forty-third Street from Broadway, hailed and applauded by the exuberant but now somewhat calmed youngsters. Traffic, which had been barred from the street, was cautiously resumed at 10:30.

More policemen continued to arrive, and they held the upper hand over the crowd. By midafternoon 175 policemen were engaged in coping with the youngsters in and outside the theatre. Throughout most of the day the crowd stretched along Forty-third and Forty-fourth Streets nearly to Eighth Avenue, and along Broadway between the two streets.

Theatre Expected 'Crowd'

"We expected a crowd, but not such a large one," said Robert Shapiro, managing director of the theatre. "Thats why there were not more police earlier.

"This is the largest opening crowd we have ever had," he added. Previous records established for a week at the Paramount by Frank Sinatra, Nat King Cole, Dean Martin and Jerry Lewis, and others may totter before this show ends next week, he believed.

Five thousand boys and girls were in line—or breaking out

The New York Times

In West Forty-third Street, mounted police worked to keep crowds awaiting admission to the theatre behind barriers.

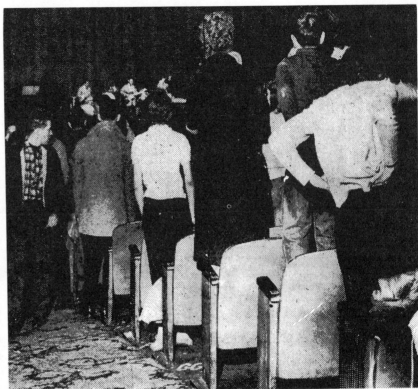

At earlier shows, there was dancing in the aisles, and many enthusiasts stood on seats to see better. Later, things quieted — somewhat.

of it—when the theatre doors opened at 8:15 and admitted 3,650. Those left outside were quickly joined by new arrivals, who swelled the figure to 5,000 again. The line thinned out during the afternoon. But many who arrived in the morning had to stand in line for hours because most of the first-show audience stayed for the second show.

Inside the theatre, boys and girls danced in the aisles, the foyer and the lobby, stood in their seats and jumped up and down, screamed with delight as performers were announced, stamped their feet in time with the music, and sang with the singers.

They knew all the songs, especially those played nightly over Radio Station WINS by Mr. Freed.

"He's the greatest, the mostest, I love him," declared 16-year-old Carol Verzielo, a student at Manual Training High School.

Seven other girls who had spent the night in her home in Brooklyn in order to be at the theatre at 8 o'clock, vied to surpass her praise of the disk jockey and rock 'n' roll.

"It's not true what they say about rock 'n' roll," declared 13-year-old Rosemary Samaritano, also of Brooklyn. "Rock 'n' roll keeps kids off the street. They stay home and listen to it on the radio and phonograph."

Although the police preparations had obviously not contemplated so exuberant and large a reception for Mr. Freed's Times Square debut, Mr. Shapiro had "had a feeling" that the show would be a success, he said.

Mr. Freed's only previous appearance in Manhattan was a week's engagement at the Academy of Music on East Fourteenth

Alan Freed, star of show

Street during Christmas week, 1955.

He had already demonstrated his popularity with teen-agers in Brooklyn, however. He appeared at the Brooklyn Paramount Theatre during Easter week of 1955. That theater, which has 700 more seats than the Paramount in Manhattan, was packed all week, and he returned three times.

According to Mr. Shapiro, the crowd that turned out yesterday had had ten days' notice. The show consisted of a motion picture. "Don't Knock the Rock," music by a twenty-piece orchestra directed by Mr. Freed, and twelve groups of performers, usually five in number, singing and playing rock 'n' roll.

The motion picture, which features Mr. Freed playing himself, tells the story of a famous rock 'n' roll singer who is rebuffed when he returns to his hometown. The rebuff is delivered at the railroad station by the mayor, who denounces rock 'n' roll as a menace to the morals of youth.

Screams of derision and boos from yesterday's audience drowned out the mayor's speech.

"They are not bad kids, they are just enthusiastic," Mr. Freed said in his dressing room. "I look out the window and see them standing there, and say to myself, how can they stand there so long, in the cold?

"But I used to do it myself. When I was a boy in Ohio, I drove twenty-five miles to Youngstown and stood in line three hours to see Benny Goodman.

"I see those scrubbed faces looking up at me from the orchestra, and I know they are like my own kids. If they want to jump and clap hands, that's all right. If the theatre gets a few broken seats, that's their problem."

Mr. Freed is 35 years old, dark and personable. He grew up in Salem, Ohio, and was graduated from Ohio State University, where he majored in mechanical engineering.

He has four children, ranging in age from 1½ to 11 years old. The older ones are rock-'n'-roll addicts, "and the baby is beginning to jump up and down in his play pen," said Mrs. Freed, known to her husband's audience as Jackie. She travels with him and does his secretarial work.

Show Considered a Gamble

Mr. Freed said he had regard-

ed his engagement at the Paramount as "somewhat of a gamble." Previously he had appeared during holiday weeks when schools were closed. "This is my first New York engagement with four school days," he said. Schools were closed yesterday in observance of Washington's Birthday.

The terms of engagement provide that the Paramount Theatre receives the first $50,000, with 90 per cent of subsequent receipts going to him, Mr. Freed said.

Out of his "take," Mr. Freed will have to pay $32,000 to the performers he engaged for the show. He rounded them up in a hurry, having received only two weeks' advance notice of the engagement, and had to buy off bookings to which some of the performers were committed.

When the doors of the theatre opened, admission was $1.50. It went up to $2.00 at 10 A. M., and rose to $2.50 at 2 P. M.

Some of the youngsters who reached the box office after hours of waiting had only $1.50, and howled. "We took care of them," Mr. Shapiro said.

Some of the boys and girls seemed to be well provided with funds. They exhausted the popcorn and candy dispensers in the lobby as fast as they were stocked and put away hundreds of hot dogs.

"We didn't used to sell hot dogs," Mr. Shapiro said.

"But lately we do—for this type of show," he added, gazing at the blue-jeaned girls and lumber-jacketed boys racing around the ornate, marble lobby, up and down the stairs as if they were in a high school building at recess time.

February 23, 1957

Frenzy 'n' Furor Featured at Paramount

DON'T KNOCK THE ROCK, written by Robert E. Kent and James B. Gordon; directed by Fred Sears; produced by Sam Katzman for Columbia Pictures. At the Paramount.
Featuring Alan Dale. Alan Freed; Bill Haley and his Comets; The Treniers; Little Richard; Dave Appell, and Patricia Hardy, Fay Baker, Gail Ganley and others.

A SO - CALLED "rock 'n' roll" musical program opened yesterday on the Paramount's screen and stage. And somehow, as reported elsewhere in this newspaper, the roof stayed on. The occasion (and the theatre experience of this reviewer's career) was a terrible little Columbia film called "Don't Knock the Rock," stringing together some musical sequences, and a stage bill that takes up exactly where the other leaves off.

•

The extremely young audi- ence, and apparently Columbia, wanted no part of the picture's plot—something about how such "cats" as Bill Haley and his Comets (band), Alan Dale, Alan Freed and more, or worse, manage to overcome small-town, adult hostility toward their art. Most of the dialogue couldn't even be heard above the restless din.

What is "rock 'n' roll"? Well, to one comparatively middle-aged man who made the awful mistake of grabbing a seat down front, it goes thump, *thump,* thump, *thump.* The audience roared it right back, number for number, as it continued the scouting parties up and down the aisles, the open warfare over seats and, of course, the aisle-dancing.

At 12:47 P. M., as Little Richard, who must be seen to be believed, cut loose with "Long, Tall Sally," this viewer, nudged by two young ladies tussling over a souvenir program, made a perfect three-point landing at the feet of two aisle-rocking belles. "Ya mashin' my foot, ya square ya," bellowed one.

•

About then, as seen in flight, the picture ended with the view of a slogan, "Dig It Soon." Your own grave, no doubt, and fair enough.

Legging it up to the mezzanine for a crouching aisle position (on a giant wad of gum) this spectator watched the stage platform rise from the pit, as the entire, chanting audience mounted seats.

"Come on up here," offered a pig-tailed girl in dungarees. She extended a hand. "I didn't know you old folks went in for this stuff."

The stage portion, dominated by Alan Freed, again, and his orchestra, was obviously what the spectators had come for, and they thumped it on down with the whole performing gang. There were the Platters, Ruth Brown, Jimmy Bowen, Nappy Brown, Frankie Lymon and the Teenagers, the Cadillacs (human) and even more.

And O-Daddy-O, those cats had it! Anybody above 30 who elects to brave the Paramount's new program may find himself amid a composite of a teen-age revival meeting and the Battle of the Bulge. And O-Daddy-O, with a slight case of St. Vitus Dance, compliments of the house—if it's still standing. H. T. T.

February 23, 1957

Rock 'n' Roll Exported To 4 Corners of Globe

The rock 'n' roll mania that gripped Times Square yesterday has manifested itself in just about every corner of the world.

Youngsters have torn up theatre seats in London. They have danced in the streets in Sydney, Australia. As at the Paramount in New York, the balcony of a local theatre in Jakarta, Indonesia, once swayed precariously to the stamping feet of youths in the grip of the rocking rhythm.

In Leningrad, recordings by Elvis Presley cut on discarded X-ray plates sell for $12.50 a copy. In Vancouver, B. C., a singer had to be rescued by the police when a crowd of 2,000 juveniles he was entertaining went wild.

The Navy at Newport, R. I., banned rock 'n' roll at the enlisted men's club after ten sailors were injured and nine arrested in a riot touched off by rock 'n' roll rhythms.

In Japan a showing of a rock 'n' roll movie touched off what the police called riots and the movie "Rock Round the Clock" touched off similar disturbances in just about every continent.

February 23, 1957

FAD ALSO ROCKS CASH REGISTERS

Sales Jump in Many Fields —Records, Clothing, Films and TV Feel Impact

By ALEXANDER R. HAMMER

The rock 'n' roll fad is increasing sales for many segments of American business.

Such diverse fields as phonograph records, clothing, motion pictures, emblem-making, television commercials and dance studios are increasing their volume as a result of the craze.

Rock 'n' roll has made its biggest impact on the music industry. Many record companies are operating on a three-shift basis to fill orders for this type of record. R. C. A.-Victor last year sold 13,500,000 records and 2,750,000 albums of rock 'n' roll's No. 1 singer, Elvis Presley.

Retailers of soft goods last year sold more than $20,000,000 worth of Presley products. Such items as pre-teen and teen-sized jackets, skirts, T-shirts, jeans, hats, nylon scarves, charm bracelets, sneakers and nylon stretch bobby sox, all bearing the Presley insignia, are big sellers in the nation's stores.

Chain, drug and novelty stores now feature lipsticks in autographed cases bearing color names for such Presley hit tunes as Hound Dog orange, Love You fuchsia, and Heartbreak pink.

70,000 Dungarees

One large manufacturer of dungarees has sold more than 70,000-odd pairs of black twill jeans with emerald green stitching for the nation's youths.

Rock 'n' roll motion pictures also have been doing well at the cashier's booth. Columbia Pictures Corporation rang up profits of $3,000,000 on the film, "Rock Around the Clock," which cost only $350,000 to make.

Alan Freed, whose rock 'n' roll stage show opened at the Paramount Theatre in Times Square yesterday, broke the house record set by the Brooklyn Paramount Theatre with the show he put on there last Easter week. The gross for ten days was $204,000. Mr. Freed has appeared at the Brooklyn Paramount five times, including an eight-day stretch last Christmas, when the theatre grossed about $180,000.

Like most devotees of fads, the rock 'n' roll cult is emblem conscious. John Atkinson, director of sales of Lion Bros. Company, Inc., of Baltimore, a large maker of emblems, said that his company was turning out 47,000 emblems a month for teen-age rock 'n' roll clubs.

The premium and box-top people, who ordinarily capitalize on every craze from Davy Crockett to space men, have been slow to take up the fad. Gordon C. Bowen, president of the Premium Advertising Association of America, explains that "since parents by and large disapprove of rock 'n' roll, many advertisers are reluctant to appeal to young people with premiums which may antagonize the parents."

On the other hand, major advertisers like Coca-Cola and Schaefer beer have used rock 'n' roll music for singing commercials with good results, and a growing number of radio and television commercials are rocking now.

One advertiser that has it both ways is the Ralston Purina Company of St. Louis, maker of cereals and mixed animal and poultry feeds. A recent commercial on its television program had the announcer satirize rock 'n' roll, singing:

Who-ho-ho-ho
Rock that rock
And roll that roll
Get that Ralston in the bowl.

The popularity of rock 'n' roll also has affected the earnings of dance studios. Arthur Murray, president of the Arthur Murray Schools of Dancing, said yesterday that the craze had led to an influx of teen-age pupils that had raised total registrations 10 per cent. He said the trend had started last summer but had hit its stride in the late fall.

Some rug manufacturers have benefited from the fad. Edward Fields, president of E. Fields, Inc., rug maker, observed that rock 'n' roll had brought about a good increase in area (small) rug sales. He attributed this increase to the fact that parents of the gyrating youngsters preferred to buy this type of rug because it was easy to remove for dancing.

February 23, 1957

EXPERTS PROPOSE STUDY OF 'CRAZE'

Liken It to Medieval Lunacy, 'Contagious Dance Furies' and Bite of Tarantula

By MILTON BRACKER

Psychologists suggested yesterday that while the rock 'n' roll craze seemed to be related to "rhythmic behavior patterns" as old as the Middle Ages, it required full study as a current phenomenon.

One educational psychologist asserted that what happened in and around the Paramount Theatre yesterday struck him as "very much like the medieval type of spontaneous lunacy where one person goes off and lots of other persons go off with him."

A psychopathologist, attending a meeting of the American Psychopathological Association at the Park Sheraton Hotel, feared that this was just a guess.

Others present noted that a study by Dr. Reginald Lourie of Children's Hospital, Washington, indicated in 1949 that 10 to 20 per cent of all children did "some act like rocking or rolling." The study went into detail on the stimulating effects of an intensified musical beat.

Meanwhile, a parallel between rock 'n' roll and St. Vitus Dance has been drawn by Dr. Joost A. M. Meerlo, associate in psychiatry at Columbia University, in a study just completed for publication.

Echo of Fourteenth Century

Dr. Meerlo described the "contagious epidemic of dance fury" that "swept Germany and spread to all of Europe" toward the end of the fourteenth century. It was called both St. Vitus Dance (or Chorea Major), he continued, with its victims breaking into dancing and being unable to stop. The same activity in Italy, he noted, was referred to as Tarantism and popularly related to a toxic bite by the hairy spider called tarantula.

"The Children's Crusades and the tale of the Pied Piper of Hamelin," Dr. Meerlo went on, "remind us of these seductive, contagious dance furies."

Dr. Meerlo described his first view of rock 'n' roll this way: Young people were moved by a juke box to dance themselves "more and more into a prehistoric rhythmic trance until it had gone far beyond all the accepted versions of human dancing."

Sweeping the country and even the world, the craze "demonstrated the violent mayhem long repressed everywhere on earth," he asserted.

He also saw possible effects in political terms:

"Why are rhythmical sounds and motions so especially contagious? A rhythmical call to the crowd easily foments mass ecstasy: 'Duce! Duce! Duce!' The call repeats itself into the infinite, and liberates the mind of all reasonable inhibitions * * * as in drug addiction, a thousand years of civilization fall away in a moment."

Dr. Meerlo predicted that the craze would pass "as have all paroxysms of exciting music." But he said that the psychic phenomenon was important and dangerous. He concluded in this way:

"Rock 'n' roll is a sign of depersonalization of the individual, of ecstatic veneration of mental decline and passivity.

"If we cannot stem the tide with its waves of rhythmic narcosis and of future waves of vicarious craze, we are preparing our own downfall in the midst of pandemic funeral dances.

"The dance craze is the infantile rage and outlet of our actual world. In this craze the suggestion of deprivation and dissatisfaction is stimulated and advertised day by day. In their automatic need for more and more, people are getting less and less."

"The awareness of this tragic contradiction in our epoch," Dr. Meerlo said, "must bring us back to a new assessment of what value and responsibility are."

February 23, 1957

Principals Toss a Rock At Presley-Mimic Role

WASHINGTON, Feb. 24 (*P*) —Several high school principals put their backs up today against blue jeans, the ducktail haircut and Elvis Presley.

They were interviewed at the convention of the National Association of Secondary-School Principals. Here are some of the things they said:

R. B. Norman of Amarillo (Tex.) High School—"You can't put a kid into a monkey suit like one of these blue jeans outfits and expect him to make any kind of good record for himself."

Howard F. Horner of David Douglas High School near Portland, Ore.—"It's a rare, rare day that anybody comes into school in that kind of outfit and (his) record does not show a long list of difficulties in and out of school."

Orren T. Freeman, of the Senior High School, Wichita Falls, Tex.—"We do not tolerate Elvis Presley records at our dances, or blue jeans or ducktail haircuts."

February 25, 1957

Why They Rock 'n' Roll—And Should They?

The Big Beat is more insistent than ever and the younger generation is all shook up. A reporter attempts to explain What It All Means.

By GERTRUDE SAMUELS

Come on over, baby,
Whole lotta shakin' goin' on.
Come on over, baby,
An' baby you can't go wrong.
Ain't nobody fakin'.
*Whole lotta shakin' goin' on.**

"ROCKING" the song as though in a life and death struggle with an invisible antagonist was a tall, thin, flaccid youth who pulled his stringy, blond hair over his eyes and down to his chin. He shook his torso about as the beat of the band seemingly goaded him on. Screams from thousands of young throats billowed toward him. In the pande-

*1955 by Marlyn-Copar, New York

monium, youngsters flailed the air with their arms, jumped from their seats, beckoned madly, lovingly, to the tortured figure onstage.

The song could scarcely be heard over the footlights. No matter. The kids knew the words. They shrilled them with the singer—and kept up their approving, uninhibited screams. The singer finished off at the piano. The applause and yells all but raised the roof. Then a Negro quartet raced onstage, adjusted the microphones, and a new tune brought on a new cascade of screams and energetic handwaves.

This was the teen-age bedlam at the Paramount Theatre in New York where in recent days Alan Freed emceed a rock 'n' roll show. Now the spectacle is moving on to the national scene, to

Philadelphia, Washington, Cleveland, Chicago, Detroit, Los Angeles.

What is this thing called rock 'n' roll? What is it that makes teen-agers mostly children between the ages of 12 and 16—throw off their inhibitions as though at a revivalist meeting? What—who—is responsible for these sorties? And is this generation of teen-agers going to hell?

For some understanding of the rock 'n' roll behavior which has aroused a great deal of controversy, at least in adult circles, one must go to the sources.

GERTRUDE SAMUELS, a staff writer for The Times Magazine and a parent, has long studied trends in music and adolescent behavior. She took the pictures with this article.

AN important source, of course, is the music itself. Technically, rock 'n' roll derives from the blues. But rock 'n' roll is an extension of what was known as Rhythm and Blues, a music of the Thirties and Forties that aimed primarily at the Negro market; that music emphasized the second and fourth beats of each measure. Rock 'n' roll exploits this same heavy beat—by making it heavier, lustier and transforming it into what has become known as The Big Beat. It is a tense, monotonous beat that often gives rock 'n' roll music a jungle-like persistence.

In his Encyclopedia Yearbook of Jazz, Leonard Feather comments that "rock 'n' roll bears the same relationship to jazz as wrestling bears to boxing." Freed claims to have invented the term "rock 'n' roll" back in 1951 for a radio show in Cleveland because "of the rocking beat of the music."

Of the top sixty best-selling records in 1957, forty were rock 'n' roll tunes, the biggest seller being Elvis Presley's "All Shook Up" which sold 2,450,000 across the country.

Another rich field for research is found among the children themselves. They come from all economic classes and neighborhoods, sometimes lone-wolfing it, but mostly with their pals, dates, clubs and gangs. Outside the theatre they seem to become one class rocking the neighborhood with wild and emotional behavior as they break through the wooden police barriers to improve their positions in line or fight toward the box office and their heroes inside.

Like young teen-agers generally, they tend to keep the sexes segregated; girls are mostly with girls; boys with boys. Their clothes and manners bespeak a kind of conformism: so many of the girls wear a sort of uniform— tight, revealing sweaters with colorful kerchiefs, skin-tight toreador pants, white woolen socks and loafers; so many of the boys conform to a pattern —leather or sports jackets, blue jeans, loafers and cigarettes.

Physically, it would seem as though

the children feared to look different from one another, or lacked confidence in individuality. Indeed, many admit to this cheerfully: "All the kids have this jacket," said one boy, "and I don't want to be different."

Inside the theatre, the emotional conformism is even more obvious. A scream of approval or delight starts— mostly a girl's scream—and everyone starts screaming. An arm shoots up fifth row center, and instantly all arms appear to be flung up and bodies leap up or start swaying crazily. Anyone can touch off the stampede of screaming youngsters who always rush the stage after a show is over. Sometimes, they fling themselves onstage, as did one member of a Brownsville gang who jumped on, zip gun and all, "as though he was Superman," and was firmly ejected.

How do the teen-agers feel about rock 'n' roll?

A black-haired, starry-eyed beauty of 15, emerging from the theatre looks as though she had returned from outer space.

"It's just instinct, that's all," murmured Roseann Chasen of Norfolk, Va., visiting in New York. "I come to hear it because I can sing and scream here.

Because it's not like at home where your parents are watching TV and you can't. Here you can scream all you like. And the stars wave to you, and don't act like they don't care whether you're there or not."

Roseann had about fifteen favorite tunes, "but the best are 'Teardrops,' 'At The Hop, and ''Great Balls of Fire.' "

"He was rocking the house with that 'Great Balls of Fire,' " she said, "did you hear it, when the kids went crazy? It was just instinct with him, that's all," she added dreamily as she went off to join her girl friends. She didn't sound as though she could raise her voice to a scream.

KENNY PUNCERELLI, 16-year-old from Englewood, and his two pals, Bob Brennan of Tenafly and Wayne Whalen of Hillsdale, N. J., tried to find words to describe their favorite, Jo-Ann Campbell, the diminutive singer in a shimmering green dress whom no one could have heard over the footlights because of the screams.

"Just say she's the greatest. It's the beat. It's different from any other beat," Kenny said, talking almost with a beat. "It's the rhythm. It's easy to listen to."

"It's the beat," the others confirmed knowingly.

Three 15-year-old girls from Queens, one with braces on her teeth, another in pin curls, the third smoking ("gee, I wouldn't want my mother to know I was smoking,") had saved their money for the show. Every day they listen to the rock 'n' roll show over Channel 7 "because it's music we can understand."

"And here we can look at the actors and wave to them," one caroled. "They're cute, they're young, and we don't have to do the housework."

The Lords, who called themselves a "sports gang" from Flower Park and Melrose in the Bronx, had been waiting for hours in the queue, lost their place when they went to buy lunches, and failed to persuade a policeman that they deserved their old position in line when they returned. The red-jacketed 15- and 16-year-olds moved to the back to start waiting anew. Why?

"Because it's great music." * * * "It makes you feel good." * * * "We like to go crazy." * * * "It hops us up. It's different from the records when you can see them and be with them." Some of the boys play instruments. Two were planning college careers (one to be an engineer, another a veterinarian).

VIVIAN STOKER, 16, and Jerilyn O'Neill, 16, juniors at the Villa Maria Academy in the Bronx, had sat through three shows with Vivian's mother. Both girls "like classical music, too" and have Beethoven, Mozart and Chopin records as well as rock 'n' roll.

"The main thing about this music," said brown-haired Vivian, "is that it's lively—it's not dead. It makes you want to dance. With a waltz you have to be in a good (Continued)

GOAL ATTAINED—After a long wait, these boys and girls have found seats to hear rock 'n' roll. "They say, 'It's music we can understand. It makes us feel good.' "

mood to dance to it. But with rock 'n' roll, no matter what your mood is, it gets you."

Did they think the effect of the music, the lyrics, the physical contortions of the actors, was making delinquents?

"SOME of the kids say that Presley affects them," Jerilyn put in. "My girl friend says he sends chills up her spine. But I think the majority of the girls just like the beat. It's new."

And Mrs. Stoker added: "I like it. The girls have their record collections and keep their minds occupied. They just enjoy it all."

Eddie Cook, 14, and Frankie Mielke, 13, of Queens, attend the same parochial school. Eddie wore a religious medal on a chain around his neck. Said Eddie: "I don't like this symphony stuff that my father puts on the radio. My mother doesn't mind rock 'n' roll though."

Frankie said: "In my house, they don't mind it as long as they're not around." And Eddie adds reflectively: "If there wasn't this music, we might be getting into trouble you know, there'd be nothing to do at night."

* * *

IN show business circles there has been bitter controversy about the worth and effects of rock 'n' roll.

Frank Sinatra, a veteran showman, was quoted in a Paris magazine recently as follows: "Rock 'n' roll smells phony and false. It is sung, played and written for the most part by cretinous goons and by means of its almost imbecilic reiteration, and sly, lewd, in plain fact, dirty lyrics * * * it manages to be the martial music of every sideburned delinquent on the face of the earth."

Between shows at the Paramount the other day, Alan Freed replied to Sinatra and other critics.

"I was shocked when I read what Frank said. He has no business knocking show busi-

ness. It's been good to him. As for charging that this music is 'dirty' and making delinquents of children, I think I'm helping to combat juvenile delinquency. If my kids are home at night listening to my radio program, and get interested enough to go out and buy records and have a collection to listen to and dance to, I think I'm fighting delinquency.

"This music," he went on, "comes from the levees and the plantations. It's simple to dance to, and to clap your hands to, and the kids know the words to every song. That's why they come. This is an audience-participation kind of music. They come in and pay to sing louder than the performers.

"And it's natural that kids should look for excitement and thrills. Well, I'd rather that they find it in the theatre than in street gangs. I say that if kids have any interest in any kind of music, thank God for it. Because if they have the interest, they can find themselves in it. And as they grow up, they broaden out and come to enjoy all kinds of music."

* * *

WHAT does it all prove? One on-the-scene observer, Robert Shapiro, manager of the Paramount Theatre, pointed out that back in the Thirties Bing Crosby,

Benny Goodman and Glen Miller were idolized by the young jazz fans. With the advent of Frank Sinatra, Shapiro recalled, teen-agers "swooned, moved and screamed with his every gesture—and now the daughters of those teen-agers are here."

"The young people of all generations," Shapiro said, "are only looking for a chance to express their enthusiasm."

A. D. Buchmueller, a psychiatric social worker and the executive director of the Child Study Association, a national organization working in the field of child development and parent education, said:

"Kids, just like adults, get caught up in a mass kind of hysteria, which is contagious. Some get hurt by it, physically and emotionally.

"But it is not helpful, and may even be harmful, for adults to take a strong and condemning attitude and action toward adolescents in their rock 'n' roll behavior. This behavior is part of their individual as well as collective or group rebellion against the strictness of adult society.

"This doesn't mean that I approve of rock 'n' roll. I don't. I think there are many other kinds of music, more beautiful and culturally more valuable, that they might be hearing. And also the suggestiveness of a sexual nature in crude and open exhibitionism, used by some singers, is to be deplored.

"THE charge that rock 'n' roll may be an outlet for impulsive behavior or sexual aggression by the youngsters may be true. But this has not been proven by any thorough studies. The charges are mostly hunches that people have been having. The rock 'n' roll behavior seems faddish, as was the behavior for other generations that liked the Charleston, the black bottom, jitterbugging. I don't think it does a bit of good to outlaw it. It will pass, just as the other vogues did."

Finally, Judge Hilda Schwartz, who regularly pre-

sides in Adolescents' Court and has made many studies of youth problems, had this to say:

"Rock 'n' roll does not produce juvenile delinquents. The causes of delinquency and youth crime are far more complex and varied. But for the disturbed, hostile and insecure youth, the stimulation of the frenzied, abandoned music certainly can't be considered a therapy.

"However, only a tiny proportion of youngsters lining up around the theatre are hostile and insecure. The vast majority are wholesome boys and girls following an adolescent fad as only adolescents can.

"But what a pity that this tremendous hero worship, this yearning for something and someone to look up to, this outpouring of energy and love should have been concentrated on a fad that can only be a passing interest. It is our fault. We haven't stirred the children with something to live by, to worship, to put their hopes in. They haven't the inspiration because we ourselves haven't put a high value on courage and liberty and working for others. Perhaps we have taken the glamour out of the good life — and, because they're young, they're looking for excitement and outlets."

* * *

ENTHUSIASM, hysteria, misguided hero worship? On one thing all experts agree: rock 'n' roll will surely be with us for a while longer. For apprehensive adults who think nothing as alarming as The Big Beat has ever existed, there may be comfort in a college joke of some years back. An Englishman, watching some contorting American dancers in fascination and disbelief, turned to his friend, murmuring, "I say, old boy, they get married afterwards, don't they?"

And that was in the foxtrot and shimmy days, long before rock 'n' roll appeared, amid commotion, on the scene.

January 12, 1958

BOSTON, NEW HAVEN BAN 'ROCK' SHOWS

BOSTON, May 5 (P)—Rock 'n' roll musical shows in public auditoriums were banned in Boston and New Haven today.

Other New England cities braced for the same show that preceded violence in Boston late Saturday night.

Fifteen persons were stabbed, beaten or robbed by gangs of roving teen-agers and adults after an Alan Freed show ended at the Boston Arena.

Albert Raggiani, 18-year-old sailor from Stoughton, was stabbed repeatedly in the chest. He was taken to Chelsea Naval Hospital. His condition was reported satisfactory.

Mayor John B. Hynes of Boston said promoters for such shows in the future will not be granted licenses.

"I am not against rock 'n' roll as such," Mr. Hynes said, "and not when it is conducted under the auspices of an established organization. However, I am against rock 'n' roll dances when they are put on by a promoter. This sort of performance attracts the troublemakers and the irresponsible.

"They will not be permitted in Boston."

Mayor Hynes can ban such shows by directing the City Censor not to issue a license to a promoter.

May 6, 1958

Blue-Jeans Are Getting Bad Name

By JOAN COOK

BLUE-JEANS, the most durable and once the most wholesome kind of American clothes, are getting a bad name. Through no fault of their own, these sturdy adjuncts to the family wardrobe have fallen into disrepute. After years of constancy as a best-seller, which they still are, blue-jeans, by being adopted as the favorite garb of young hoodlums, have innocently gained an unsavory reputation.

Ever since the "motorcycle boys" started wearing blue jeans in anything but a neat manner, many schools over the country have banned this attire from the classroom, save in the elementary grades. The controversy over jeans as school garb has had repercussions in principals' offices and at parents' meetings.

A 13-year-old boy recently told his mother that, off the baseball diamond, otherwise friendly adults regarded him with suspicion if he was wearing jeans. Store keepers, he said, kept him under close surveillance and an apartment-house acquaintance cut him cold when he appeared attired in what she apparently regarded as an irrefutable badge of gangdom.

The Picture Has Changed

Sears-Roebuck reports that denim blue-jeans were the whole story six years ago. Today, chinos, twills, Bedford cord and the like have eaten into more than 50 per cent of the business. However, although these other fabrics and styles — notably the buckled-in-back Ivy League sort—are cutting into the total blue-jean trade, Sears is picking up customers as a result.

"As other stores diminish their blue-jean stocks, some even dropping them altogether, customers come to us knowing that we, if anyone, will have them on hand," a spokesman for the store said.

Blue-jeans have held their own for more than a century. In "American Ways of Life," published some years ago, George R. Stewart wrote:

"Blue overalls and jeans, for working clothes, have become as typical of the American working man as the blue shirt is of a French laborer. They have become standard wear for the American small boy and even for many American small girls. * * * *"

Became College Craze

During the Thirties, when the country's economy was at a low ebb, women began wearing blue-jeans and students at the University of California at Berkeley reportedly touched off the college craze.

Since then, blue-jeans have spread from their starting point on the West Coast to all parts of the country. If jeans are losing face at home, it is some consolation to know that they amount to a real craze in Europe. Some smart French women even have theirs tailor-made.

It is a matter of record that the jeans worn by Constance Bennett for her singing engagement in a New York hotel a few years ago cost $100.

Perhaps this counter-trend will help to re-establish blue-jeans to their former state of respectability.

August 19, 1959

PRODUCERS RUSH MOVIES ON TWIST

Low-Budget Pictures Show Quick Box-Office Return

By HOWARD THOMPSON

Having twisted its way out of Manhattan's Peppermint Lounge and across the country, the current dance rage is appropriately returning home to roost, at least temporarily, on the screens of metropolitan movie houses. Leading the parade are Columbia's "Twist Around the Clock," due on Jan. 22 at R. K. O. ciruit theatres, and Paramount's "Hey, Let's Twist," another low-budget entry also slated for a double-bill unveiling at neighborhood theatres later this month.

More films are expected in the near future, with the two "leaders" reportedly holding their own in out-of-town engagements and doing even better financially in current overseas bookings. An independent production titled "Doin' the Twist," with Louis Prima and June Wilkinson co-starred, is expected here after successful holiday bookings by National Theatres and Television, Inc., a West Coast exhibitor organization. Already rushed before the cameras in London is "It's Trad, Dad" (translation: "It's Traditional, Father"), a Columbia-Vanguard Productions project using such British and American entertainers as Chubby Checker, the Dukes of Dixieland, Chris Barber and a "gentleman singer" (according to Columbia) named U. S. Bonds.

Film to be Made in Paris

Furthermore, Harry Romm, who produced "Hey, Let's Twist' for Paramount, disclosed yesterday that he now has a tentative starting date (March 2) for a second twister called "Viva La Twist!" It will face the cameras in Paris with Joey Dee, the Starliters and Jo-Ann Campbell featured.

Finally, United Artists plans an updated opening for a year-old musical called "Teen-Age Millionaire." First intended as a rock 'n' roll vehicle for Jimmy Clanton, the popular young singer, the film will now be advertised as a twist movie with Chubby Checker, the idol of the newer craze, who appears in the footage briefly. It opens on the local Loew's circuit and other outlets on Wednesday, billed with "Paris Blues."

Yesterday, without labeling either the Twist or the movies as art, both Paramount and Columbia home office executives conveyed the impression that money still talks. A Paramount spokesman, declining to give figures, said simply that "Hey, Let's Twist" was "holding its own very nicely" in pre-Manhattan engagements at a few Long Island theatres. He noted that the company had bought some 600 prints of the picture for national and foreign circulation.

The picture has already opened in London, Paris, Rome, Trinidad, Puerto Rico, Australia and Greece.

Grosses Are Called 'Good'

Columbia, reporting "unusually good" grosses in foreign engagements, has shipped "hundreds" of prints of "Twist Around the Clock" to forty-one countries overseas. The film received ten pre-Christmas bookings and 500 during the Christmas-New Year span. Some 4,000 additional engagements are scheduled before the end of the month. The picture drew $20,000 in a five-day run at Boston's Pilgrim Theatre, and $15,000 for the same period at the St. Francis in San Francisco. The 400-seat Granby Theatre, in Norfolk, Va., took in $6,773 during five days. The take for the frist three days at the R. K. O. Regent in Grand Rapids, Mich., was $4,426, and the small Weis Theatre in Savannah, Ga., reported a six-day gross of $5,577.

January 6, 1962

Serious Epidemic of 'Automania'

With alarm mounting at the rate of accidents among young drivers, how do teen-agers feel about their passion for driving?

By GRACE and FRED M. HECHINGER

A NASSAU COUNTY judge recently charged that suburban teen-agers suffer from a "serious malady —automania." He defined the term as "an overobsession with the automobile as a status symbol, as a means of getting someplace in a hurry, as a vehicle for a flight from tensions, or to indulge in a craving to show off."

The judge, Douglas F. Young, said he was disturbed by the number of teen-agers in suburbia who feel they just cannot live without a car, by the resulting increase in the number of youngsters from good homes who steal cars or go for joy rides without permission, and by their tendency to go "showboating" in cars to such an extent that the vehicles become deadly weapons.

How much cause is there for Judge Young's alarm? How widespread and serious is teen-age automania? And if the disease is truly epidemic, what are its causes?

At the outset, it ought to be clearly understood that whatever the excuses and rationalization, the stark facts of

GRACE and FRED M. HECHINGER are co-authors of the book "Teen-Age Tyranny." He is The New York Times education editor.

139

accident statistics leave no doubt that teen-age driving presents a serious problem in public safety and law enforcement. Surveys show that over half the nation's male youths have been involved in auto accidents, either as passengers or as drivers. Their understandable fascination with speed, reinforced by the sense of power that comes from being behind the wheel of a modern machine, is sure to take its toll. More than one-fourth of the high-school seniors in a Gallup poll admitted they had driven faster than 90 miles an hour.

The problem is aggravated by the teen-age tendency to move about in large groups. When a car is crowded with teen-agers, they are likely to put pressure on the driver to ignore the caution he might have observed if he had been on his own. For the same reasons, an accident involving a teen-age driver is apt to endanger more lives because of the greater number of car occupants.

TODAY'S teen-agers are the first generation to have grown up with cars as an indispensable part of life. The car, like the television set, is no longer considered a luxury but a necessity. The two-car suburban home came about through the wife's desire for mobility while her commuter husband's car remained in readiness at the railroad station. Today, the mushrooming of the latest architectural design — the three-car-garage house—is a monument to the growing acceptance of the teen-ager's right to an automobile, too.

Suburban houses that give more floor space to cars than to the living room are sure to influence adolescent thinking. Moreover, teen-agers deposit money in drive-in banks, shop in centers built around parking areas, go to drive-in movies and eat in drive-in eateries. As small children, they are chauffeured everywhere, including to Scout meetings. Many suburban communities seem no longer to permit walking, having long abandoned the sidewalk as an unnecessary expense.

FOR many teen-agers, reared in the no-privacy layout of the modern home's "family living area," the car is almost the only enclosed means of escape from togetherness. It has replaced the screened back-porch and the parlor— the traditional, semiprivate courting spaces. This role has been underlined by the heavy play on sex appeal in automobile advertising.

Against this background, how many teen-agers actually own their cars? And what do the young people themselves — not the judges, the social critics or police — say about the importance of the automobile?

The statistics are full of discrepancies, and the picture differs from community to community. But one insurance company reports that, nationally, 75 per cent of all high-school juniors and seniors have drivers' licenses, and nearly 60 per cent have access to the family car for "social purposes." In two comfortable but not excessively wealthy suburban communities used for a sampling of views—one on Long Island, the other in Westchester—the estimate of actual teen-age owners of cars was put at below 25 per cent, but the majority had access to their parents' cars. (In very wealthy suburbs, teen-age car ownership is probably more than twice as high and in cities, such as New York, where keeping cars is difficult and expensive, it is much lower.)

WHAT did the youngsters themselves say about the reasons why they want to drive? Their answers prove the car to be a prestige symbol, a conclusion underlined by frequent references to the type of cars they or their parents own and by the pleasure car owners get from driving their less fortunate contemporaries around Main Street. A 14-year-old freshman aspirant to car ownership said: "I don't know how to explain it, but when you have your own car, you've got it made. You can get where you want when you want. It's a lot better than having to take the bus...."

Another boy confirmed this: "It has something to do with reaching the age of freedom. Having a car gives a person more liberty, without having to ask permission."

A thoughtful teen-age boy added: "As soon as you first get your license, you like to show off. But after a while, it's just transportation. When a father buys a kid an expensive new sports car for his birthday, most of us are morally disgusted."

These differ- *(Continued)* ences and distinctions, incidentally, are confirmed by sociologist James S. Coleman in his study of adolescent culture. He points out that there are subtle subdivisions in teen-agers' attitudes toward cars, with the "élite" group using cars for dating but not to show off, while the "lower" ranks *use* cars with the kind of show-off immaturity with which

teen-age girls moon over rock 'n' roll singers.

AMONG the teen-agers questioned for this report, there was general agreement that it is more important for a boy to have a car than for a girl. By the same token, a boy's prestige among girls is directly related to the kind of car he drives, whether it is his own or his family's. Without a doubt, girls prefer to date boys with cars. A Long Island girl, who has a steady boy friend, felt that transportation is very definitely his responsibility. If he cannot get his father's car, they will double-date with another couple who do have a car—or take a taxi—rather than have the girl drive her own or her family's car. Most of the boys appeared to share this view—an indication that there is a link between cars and masculine dignity. Probably for the same reason (in addition to the advantage of privacy), once a boy is past his predriving teen-age, usually after his 16th birthday, parents are dismissed as chauffeurs. "It is degrading," said one boy.

A RECENT reflection of this trend came when doubts were raised about new legislation concerning learners' permits for 16-year-olds. The Roslyn motor vehicles registrar received hundreds of phone calls from confused parents.

Driving, said one teen-ager, makes you feel "old and competent." Another added: "Without a car, social life is dead." Perhaps in keeping with the current vogue for psychological explanations for every action, one boy told of a friend for whom driving brought about "the big change in his life." It seems the youngster was short and had always been self-conscious — never daring to ask girls to go out with him. But now, with a driver's license in his pocket, "it's like the car gives him the extra height." While popular youngsters and those who have always ranked high in their school work can apparently take cars or leave them, those who have been socially "out" were reported to find a car a big boost.

Most teen-agers agreed that driving their parents' car is a fully acceptable compromise. It doesn't matter, "as long as it's available," one boy put it. But there are subtle nuances. "Of course," said a Long Island youngster, "it de-

pends on the kind of car your parents drive. Now, if I was to take off in my father's [small foreign car], why, that's a bomb. It has no power. Driving wouldn't mean a thing. But, if my father had a '61 [powerful American make], driving that would be no disgrace." He pointed to a powerful $7,000 sports model as the "top prestige car," but said wistfully that no teen-agers in his community owned one, although a few youngsters in a nearby high-income suburb did. He added that, while it was felt that only "the sharpies" drove such show-off cars, everybody gathered around to have a look. "They like the car, but not what the driver represents," he said. In his neighborhood a $5,000 domestic sports model is "top car" and several high-school students own them.

Although denials of the importance of owning an expensive car come fast in the course of any interview, all the youngsters, including student leaders, are conversant with models and prices and the up-to-date details of who owns them. One boy, who condemned ostentation, said that Cadillacs are now looked down upon while powerful sports cars are all the rage — "not because they are expensive, but because they are classy. Teen-agers like to associate themselves with things that are classy."

If teen-agers hedge over the prestige aspects of car ownership, they are even more reluctant to discuss the importance of the car for "social" purposes. Among teenagers, "parking" is pretty much a synonym for necking or petting. One teen-age girl, quoted in a recent Darien, Conn., survey, said that ac-

cepting a date to a drive-in movie was the equivalent to agreeing to sexual intercourse, but most young people, understandably, just won't talk about this to adults.

A Long Island mother of two teen-agers, with no illusions about the tempting nature of a car for "social privacy," feels the automobile may now be losing out, however, as a place for "making out" (as the current jargon puts it). "Teen-agers today have enough freedom at unsupervised parties to make the car less important," she said.

WHAT about the economics of the teen-age car? Some parents make a car their 16th-birthday or graduation gift. One girl said her parents paid all the expenses for her car, while another was required to cover the cost of keeping the car clean. Several boys had to pay for the gas they used in the family car.

Usually, when a teen-ager has to save up to buy his own car, he is also expected to pay for its upkeep and maintenance. Many youngsters take part-time jobs largely to support their cars. Often they cut down on expenses by learning to do a good deal of the repair work themselves. "You want to put in a new transmission, or a four-barrel carburetor," said one boy, "so you shop around for the part in a junk yard, then you invest $30 for it and get a bunch of kids to come over and help install it." But the cost of buying and running a car is an important reason why many youngsters appear to be satisfied merely with access to one.

Uninformed adults often assume that teen-age driving and hot-rodding are one and the same problem, but they are wrong. Hot-rodders are a highly specialized minority group—single-minded to the point of fanaticism. A middle-class Long Island boy described them as members of a clique who work on their cars a lot, have old, souped-up vehicles, talk a language that barely resembles English and often become school dropouts.

But the snobbism works both ways. Members of the hot-rod élite look down on some of the automania-infected high-school youngsters, whom they call "squirrels." These are "the crazy kids with loud dual exhausts and a foxtail on their cars," said a serious teen-age hot-rodder. "The squirrel doesn't race his car; he's just an exhibitionist. He spins his tires when leaving a drive-in. The real hotrodder spends all kinds of money to prevent his tires from spinning, because spinning reduces speed."

AMONG the "squirrels" is that dangerous minority which goes in for dare-devil drag-racing, or "dragging," on highways, usually to impress girls. "We don't drag much when the girls are not around to watch," one teenager said. But none of the suburban youngsters interviewed in Westchester and Long Island showed much interest in these excesses, or in the teen-age game of "chicken" in which two cars race toward each other on a collision course and where the shameful tag goes to the one who first loses his nerve and swerves to avoid a crash. The popularity of this motorized

form of Russian roulette seems to be on the wane, leaving teen-age speed demons as the major danger.

WHAT about the youngsters' views on the influence of cars on academic work? They dispute the findings of a national survey which shows that car owners get lower grades. "If a person is intelligent, the fact that he owns a car is not going to make any difference in the grades he gets," said a 16-year-old blonde. An assistant high-school principal agreed: "As far as our experience goes, many kids who have free access to a family car, or even a car of their own, actually save a lot of time when they can drive, and this may help them with their school work."

Teachers generally seemed to feel that the issue is whether or not an adolescent has a sense of responsibility—with or without a car. (There is, however, some indication that car ownership tends to be more of a threat to school work among lower economic groups where the upkeep of a car becomes a major drain on a student's time and energy —and frequently even a cause of school drop-outs.)

In recent years, more and more communities have begun to make rules about the use of cars. Roslyn High School has a "law" that once a car is brought to school, it may not be removed from the parking lot until the end of the day. Only a few youngsters were found to be dodging this rule by parking on nearby streets so that they could drive their friends around town during the lunch hour. Most students said they approved of the rule, and one boy even expressed the opin-

ion that students should not drive to school at all. "It's a waste to leave the car in the lot all day," he said. "And it isn't nice for the teachers. A teacher may drive a '55 Chevy, and the kid parking next to him gets out of a '63 sports car. It revolts me to see this."

In Pleasantville, school authorities have restricted the use of cars to those students who live some distance away and who have parental permission. The rule was laid down after complaints from local residents about loud engines, traffic problems and other hazards.

IN Petaluma, Calif., after a series of fatal accidents among students who went joyriding during the lunch period, the schools issued a series of detailed traffic-control regulations. Driving out of the school parking lot during the day was prohibited, for example—although, as an interesting commentary on the "social" functions of the automobile, students were still permitted to eat lunch in their parked cars.

Initial reactions showed some of the symptoms of an advanced stage of automania. Great numbers of bicycles appeared — not as substitute transportation but as a protest against "confinement." (In fact, many of the bicycles had been driven to school in pickup trucks.) Several days later, dissident students (estimated at about 10 per cent of the total enrollment) staged a sit-down strike. But by now the rule is accepted and, with the community's support, continues to be enforced.

In spite of the apparently sensible and sometimes slightly self-righteous attitudes of most of the teen-agers interviewed, serious problems of teen-age driving do exist. While they may be right in saying that only "a minority" are extreme automaniacs and reckless drivers, the minority is getting bigger and the widespread use of cars by the majority is not without its dangers.

A number of adults, when told about the teen-agers' calm and sensible attitudes in their communities, smiled knowingly and said the report might not be so reassuring if the youngsters were less hep to what grown-up questioners wanted to hear.

As for repeated protestations that the automobile is really nothing more than a means of getting places, one Long Island assistant principal described the day when 20 high-school seniors, all members of the Key Club, an honor society for those of outstanding scholarship and service, were to go with him to entertain the children of an orphanage. At the appointed time, the 20 teen-agers arrived at the school in 19 cars. When the principal suggested that they could make the trip —a considerable distance—in four cars, they objected. Even among this outstanding group, everybody wanted to be in the driver's seat.

August 11, 1963

Why the Girls Scream, Weep, Flip

The path to understanding is psychological, anthropological and a whole lot besides.

By DAVID DEMPSEY

WITH the predictability of a plague of locusts, teen-age America is swept to its feet every few years by the newest craze in popular music. Although symptomatic relief of this seizure is not difficult for most young people—they can dance all night—the side effects are disturbing to say the least. In the presence of their latest folk hero, many admirers often stand in one place and jump up and down. Usually this is accompanied by incessant screaming and, on the part of girls, by protestations of undying love.

Sometimes this hero worship takes a violent form and the singer is mobbed by his fans. At other times, the kids go into a Zen-like trance. The pupils of their eyes dilate, a rapt expression comes over their faces, and they achieve a state of teen-age Nirvana. (In this condition, they are given those posthypnotic suggestions that send them all out to buy crazy-looking wigs, photos of their heroes on lam-

DAVID DEMPSEY is a novelist and critic (and father of three) who often comments on the phenomena—beat and offbeat—of our time.

inated buttons, toss pillows and tight, very tight, pants.)

The newest outbreak of this madness, as everyone knows, was occasioned by the Beatles, four young singers from England who have, indeed, brought a new kind of love to millions of females between the ages of 10 and 30. The chant of "Yeah! Yeah! Yeah!" follows them everywhere and their travels have inspired the largest mass following since the Children's Crusade.

What is happening here is significant. Although idolatry in popular music is nothing new, the method of expressing this idolatry seems to be changing. A generation of youth that shrieks at the sight of a Fabian, or packs the Cotton Bowl to cheer Elvis Presley, seems 100 years removed in spirit from the generation that tuned in on the Ipana Troubadours or settled back to the nasal tones of Rudy Vallee. As our singers get progressively more frantic, their followers become increasingly frenzied, and an audience that once swooned in the presence of its favorite singer, or at best squealed, has given way to a mob that flips.

THE cause of this malady is obscure

—so obscure, in fact, that modern scholarship, in its quest for an etiology, has expanded its investigations into four major fields: the anthropological, the psychological, the socio-economic and the moral. All appear to play a part, at one time or another, in influencing the mass behavior patterns that sweep the country from time to time when a new type of music—or musician—appears on the scene. If you are of the opinion that youth today is simply out for fun and excitement, skip it. This is much too simple an explanation. (In fact, let us pretend that this possibility was not even mentioned.)

To begin, first, with the anthropology of rock 'n' roll. It is generally admitted that jungle rhythms influence the "beat" of much contemporary dance activity. Every man, according to this theory, is instinctively aboriginal in his feet, if not in his heart; much of today's jazz-dancing—as anyone knows who has seen it—is strongly reminiscent of those tribal dances performed to the tune of a nose flute and the beat of a tom-tom. Aboriginal society being collective, however, the group catharsis that takes place is not only highly ritualized, but is frequently carried out as a supplication to certain mythic beings —the god of the hunt, or of fertility— that are lacking today. The idolatry in this case is totemic.

By comparison, contemporary rock 'n' rollers lack a social focus for their energy, which is thereby visited on the godlike individual. According to this notion, modern society, with its emphasis on decorum, suppresses a need in man for uninhibited kinetic self-expression. Today's music is a throwback, or tribal atavism, made endemic through mass communication. It is probably no coincidence that the Beatles, who provoke the most violent response among teen-agers, resemble in manner the witch doctors who put their spell on hundreds of shuffling and stamping natives. Far- *(Continued)*

142

fetched? Not for some anthropologists. At any rate, it is a theory worth thinking about.

The aborigines, of course, have no monopoly on fancy footwork. Nor are they the only ones who dig the music. An example closer in spirit to our own times is Orpheus, who except for the fact that his lyre was not an electric one, might easily pass for the Elvis Presley of Greek mythology.

You may remember that Orpheus could charm the stones right out of the field. What is sometimes forgotten is that he, too, was set upon by screaming females who were determined to devour him. His music alone held them at bay until, finally, ". . . . the wild shouts which they . . . raised deadened the sound of the notes and so left Orpheus helpless. So great was the rage of the Bacchantes that they actually tore him limb from limb," reports Prof. Frances E. Sabin in her aptly titled book, "Classical Myths That Live Today."

It is clear from this that the problem of modern teen-age behavior was not altogether different, with respect to popular musicians, from that of the classical world, although the Greeks had the good sense to keep the whole matter decently in the lap of the gods.

A MORE fashionable line of inquiry into the mob response so prevalent in popular music today is psychological. At its simplest, this view holds that the young are undergoing a hysterical reaction to a craze. Whether dancing, or merely listening and jumping, those taking part are working off the inner tensions that bedevil a mixed up psyche. For these young people, the singer performs a healing role.

Nor is there anything uniquely modern in this behavior. Parents concerned about such dances as the Twist or the Slop can draw some consolation by thinking back to the wildest and strangest dance of all, the tarantella. A product of rural Italy, where it achieved its peak popularity in the 16th and 17th centuries, the tarantella comes even closer to simulating insanity than that now-famous drug, LSD.

It has been described by the Sicilian scholar Ernesto de Martino, in "The Land of the Bad Past," as "an instinctive experiment in madness." The dancer goes into a frenzy in order to kill frenzy; she is finally "cured"—or at least exhausted, for the tarantella is said to "reintegrate the people after the collapse of psychical balance."

WOULD this not indicate that a fairly recent counterpart, jitterbugging, was possibly a deliberately induced outer frenzy aimed at staving off the inner frenzy that threatens young people during a difficult period of adjustment? Such an idea is suggested by a lengthy study of the jitterbug addict in an article by Dr. T. W. Adorno, with the assistance of George Simpson—it takes two to write on jitterbugging—that appeared in the scholarly journal Studies in Philosophy and Social Science at the height of the jitterbug movement in 1941.

Adorno and Simpson distinguish between two major types of mass behavior toward popular music, the "rhythmically obedient" type, and the "emotional" type. The latter are likely to get a crush on a movie star and let it go at that; in general, they remain passive, and give little trouble. The "rhythmic obedients," on the other hand, make up the vast, noisy and clamorous mob of adolescents whose star has been in the ascendant ever since the onset of Frank Sinatra. They like to keep time to the music, and the crazier the music, the better they like it.

But they are not just letting off steam; in fact, although they may not know it, they are expressing their desire to obey. They are products of a conformist, and sometimes authoritarian, society, and their obedience to the beat "leads them to conceive of themselves as agglutinized with untold millions of the meek who must be similarly overcome."

Here again, such activity, no matter how eagerly participated in, should not imply joy. The jitterbug can't help himself. He is not really having a good time; he only thinks he is, since the craze for a particular fashion, in the Adorno-Simpson view, contains within itself the latent possibility of fury.

"Likes that have been enforced upon listeners [by press agentry, mass media and an age of conformity] provoke re-venge the moment the pressure is relaxed." The Bacchante syndrome? Possibly. The authors add that "the whole realm of jitterbug fanaticism and mass hysteria about popular music is under the spell of a spiteful will decision." It is based on such superficial enthusiasm that it must be continually reinforced by repetition and the safety of numbers if it is to survive. Hence its mass character.

THE conclusions reached by Adorno and Simpson are, at first glance, discouraging. These "rhythmic obedients," they believe, will inherit the earth. Yet this prospect is not as deplorable as it may seem. "To become transformed into an insect [i.e., a jitterbug] man needs that energy which might possibly achieve his transformation into a man."

Here again, the parallel with Beatlemania is apparent. Beatles, too, are a type of bug; and to "beatle," as to jitter, is to lose one's identity in an automatized, insectlike activity—in other words, to obey. Do not underrate this hypothesis in trying to understand your teen-age daughter.

Let us turn now to the socio-economic interpretation of the present craze over pop singers. This can be summarized as follows: hero worship, such as that conferred on Fabian, Johnny Mathis and the Beatles, is ultimately the product of an affluent society which, for the first time in history, has made possible a leisure class of professional teenagers.

OUT of this new class has come a culture which, in turn, constitutes an enormous market of consumers. One of the products sold to this market is the hero, along with all the ikons of worship (records, rings, pin-ups, Beatle clothes, etc.).

"The religion of teen-age culture, as such, may be said to be the cult of popular personalities, singers, actors and performers of all kinds," writes Prof. Jessie Bernard, of the Pennsylvania State University, in The Annals of the American Academy of Political and Social Science.

A unique feature of this religion is the insistence by those who practice it that the gods be approximately the same age as the worshipers. The day when young people "looked up" to their heroes is gone; instead, for the first time they now have a self-identifying culture which they need not transcend in order to find the values that reflect their own aspirations. The hero is not only an idol but an image.

MOST contemporary pop singers get their start at 16 or 17. As they grow older, their popularity with the bandstand set wanes and their places are taken by new idols. Presley, for example, at 29, is a comparative oldster, as is the once fan-ridden Pat Boone, who is also 29 and has a family. The 19-year-old Paul Anka, and the 21-year-old Bobby Rydell typify those who now hold down the tabernacle.

All of this makes it easier for the female members of the cult to go berserk. This is especially true of those who, for one reason or another, are alienated from their peer group. Fabian has observed that many of the young girls who besiege him are lacking in physical attractiveness, and it has been noted that membership in the screaming and jumping societies includes a high proportion of the homely, and of those who are lonesome, or ill at ease in social situations. They can act out their feelings most easily in a group.

Moreover, by "mobbing" a singer, they are thus able to reverse the boy-girl roles, in fantasy at least, for in a sense they are saying, "I wish the boy would go after me, but because he won't, I'll go after him; and since there's no danger that I'll get him, the whole charade is safe." For these teen-agers, such a troupe as the Beatles is made to order —four young men instead of the customary one.

AS long as teen-age culture remains an entity in itself, a large percentage of its members will continue to jump with joy—or what they think is joy. Such a prospect raises the fourth, or moral, line of inquiry, namely, that youth today has found a new, and perhaps a last remaining, excuse for being young. In this sense, young people are rebelling against an adult world that pretends to higher standards of entertainment. Much exhibitionism among teenagers is carried out in a spirit of defiance. This is the "last fling" theory, and it proves again that rock'n'rollers are rather desperate even in fun.

Paradoxically, however, this rebellion is taking place against a society that has shown no real indication that it really cares about the standards of teen-age entertainment. Upholders of this view point out that young people today are exploited by popularity "ratings," payola-taking disc jockeys, press-agent ballyhoo, sponsored fan clubs and a communications industry that panders plainly to the "kookie" interests of the teenage group. The violent and spectacular diversions of the young are taking place in a moral vacuum caused by the abdication of their elders. If this vacuum is filled with tin gods, it is largely because the adult world has not offered them a valid religion.

Such criticism, to many psychologists and others who work with teen-agers, is unduly harsh in that it ignores the fact that the tin gods are highly temporary, to be worshiped only until the real thing comes along.

"THE teen-ager, after all, is entitled to be young," states Dr. Jane Vorhaus Gang, a psychiatrist in the New York area who works with this age group. "You can't expect girls of 15 or 16 to have a mature set of values. They are trying their wings at this age, and hero worship is a fairly normal and harmless way to go about it. The bobbysoxer, with all her silly behavior, often turns out to be the responsible P.-T.A. chairman of tomorrow."

Even assuming that parents have abdicated in the face of the insect invasion, there is evidence that youth is taking the problem into its own hands. The increasing popularity of folk music and the hootenany, which appeals to the same rhythmic instincts as pop music, yet requires a more creative participation, and in a somewhat higher cause, is an encouraging trend. Although a craze in its own right, the movement can be said to represent a step upward by drawing on certain indigenous American values; in any case, the vapid banalities of much of pop music are discarded.

MOREOVER, an influential segment of teen-age America is now throwing its rhythmic energies behind the Freedom Rider Movement. Possibly most of these young people were never serious candidates for rock 'n' roll, but in any case they have shown that the generation to which they belong is not the monolithic stereotype that has been pictured. Seized by an equally strong desire for the beat, they are keeping step to a different breed of guitar, while singing another kind of song, "We Shall Overcome."

As for those who remain obedient—who are waiting to be overcome—it is well to remember that they exhibit a form of madness that has baffled mankind for centuries. The compulsive shuffle of the aborigine, the rage of the Bacchante, the frenzy of the tarantella dancer and the hysteria of the Beatlebug are all expressions of a common, and complex, demon. No wonder the jumpers can seldom explain what makes them jump. And no wonder that they have such a miserably happy time doing it (Yeah! Yeah! Yeah!).

February 23, 1964

THE TEENAGE CONSUMER

1,500 TEEN-AGERS CAN'T BE WRONG

That's the Theory Behind Market Service Using the Panel of Adolescents

The American teen-ager, whose spending for consumer products is put at $9,000,000,000 a year, with the added hope of building brand loyalty early, is to be asked in detail what he wants to buy.

A panel of 1,500 high school boys and girls will make up the Teen National Consumer Board, and the views of this group, supplied monthly on tastes, fads, needs, preferences, brands, colors and packaging, along with their reactions to names, slogans and advertising copy and their likes and dislikes generally will be quickly obtainable.

Ward J. Jenssen, Inc., market research concern of Los Angeles, has been retained by Petersen Publishing Company, publisher of Teen and various other magazines and books, to direct operations of the teen group. The reports will include statistical findings, interpretation of the data and analyses of its implications.

Dr. Ward J. Jenssen, head of the concern, and his associate, Dr. Shoi Balaban Dickinson, will send questionnaires to the 1,500-teen-agers each month, with one-third of the number questioned being changed monthly. The questionnaires and products to be tested are to be mailed on the 15th of each month, with final reports available about four weeks later.

The purpose of the board, Dr. Dickinson explained, is to "relieve the advertiser from basing sales messages on what he thinks will appeal to teen-agers."

"It makes advertising results more predictable," she said, "by informing advertisers of what teen-agers themselves find appealing or what they reject.

"There is probably no other single population group which is so aware of what other members of their group are doing, thinking, wearing, buying. Conformity to the group is more important for a teen-ager, who lacks personal security about individual taste in products, than is true of any other group.

"This fact also tends to make the teen market more of a mass market, in spite of income differences, than is true of any other population segment.

"However, for the advertiser to be successful with this market he must keep up to date on the latest conformities of the teen group, because this age group is characterized by shifting tastes and the quick and ready adoption of new products or ideas."

Results of the first survey by the board currently are being compiled. The initial survey dealt with Teen magazine readership, phonograph records, hobbies and favorite colors. Merchandising and sales promotion programs to assist concerns making use of the board are being developed by Teen magazine; a national advertising campaign also is being scheduled by the magazine through its agency, Compton Advertising.

Dr. Jenssen, who holds a Ph.D. in psychology from the University of Southern California, has been a special consultant to advertising agencies, directing consumer and motivation research studies.

Dr. Dickinson, who holds Ph.D. degrees in sociology and social institutions from the University of California at Berkeley, has directed consumer research studies on various types of products and services.

June 28, 1959

Advertising: Why Youths Spend

By CARL SPIELVOGEL

Parents concerned about their teen-agers' seemingly insatiable desire to spend are advised to relax. The youngsters are suffering from "planned obsolescence," according to a marketing expert.

"The fact that they want the very latest in almost everything makes for a somewhat paradoxical situation," said Lester Rand, president of the Youth Research Institute. The organization has worked in the youth field for clients such as the Ford Motor Company, the Parker Pen Company and Smith-Corona, Inc.

"On the one hand teens stick doggedly to a highly vintaged pair of jeans or shoes, which should have been discarded long ago. But then again they want the latest model" in most other things, he said.

"A teen with a wrist watch or two expects a better one for graduation or a birthday gift and if he has a portable radio, he's yearning for a smaller, transistor type," Mr. Rand asserted.

He listed a telephone as the "hottest" item on teen-agers' shopping lists, noting that within the last five years the number of youngsters having their own phones had doubled.

If all of this comes as good news to American manufacturers, Mr. Rand does not see as bright a picture for savings institutions.

"Teen-agers are extravagant and carefully avoid the lines in savings banks," he asserted. "Only one out of three is committed to savings on a long-term basis. The rest are living right up to and even beyond their incomes."

Based on his studies, Mr. Rand has concluded that "there is no such thing as the 'teen who has everything.'"

July 15, 1959

Teen-Type Credit

More and more department stores are offering credit or charge accounts to teen-agers and the results reportedly are pleasing to the merchants. Such accounts are opened only with the consent of parents. But parents are not asked to guarantee payment.

The accounts are teaching future full-scale customers how to budget expenses, the importance of good credit and the value of merchandise, it was reported by Amos Parrish & Co., Inc., retailing and marketing consultant organization. Most stores are highly selective of their applicants in the teen group and watch performance carefully. The accounts usually are handled as regular revolving credit with a maximum limit and a specified weekly payment.

December 3, 1959

Advertising: Hints on Selling to Teen-Agers

By ROBERT ALDEN

With the teen-ager market now estimated at something close to $10,000,000,000 a year and its present population of 17,000,000 expected to increase sharply by 1970, it becomes important for advertisers to know something about adolescents.

Oddly enough, the gum-chewing, hot-rodding stereotype of a teen-ager that has emerged from all the fuss and publicity that has been given to the group, apparently is a false one.

Dr. Shoi Balaban Dickinson, who, as research consultant for 'Teen Magazine, polls a rotating group of 1,500 teen-agers each month, finds that advertisers have what she calls a "Salvador Dali image" of this group—an image in which the central subject-matter may be distorted.

For example, Dr. Dickinson has found that while most adults, including advertisers, believe that teen-agers are nonconformists, the fact is that this age group may well be the most conformist group in society today.

Follow the Leader

A teen-ager wants to do just what every other teen-ager is doing whether it is wearing a beanie hat or dancing the pachanga. Dr. Dickinson has found, therefore, that it is a mistake for advertisers to emphasize the exclusiveness of a product when selling the teenager market.

The research has turned up the fact also that adolescents are not sophisticated or tolerantly liberal in their views. On the contrary, they are conservative and their efforts at rebellion are kept within rigidly defined areas.

For example, while a group of boys may all wear duck-tail haircuts that look distinctly rebellious to adults, the group is conforming to its own standards. It would be a rare boy who would be willing to break away from the pattern and adopt another hair style.

The bad publicity given to advertising has not helped the advertisers' case with the teen-agers. Dr. Dickinson finds that the group tends to view advertising "as an occult and evil force, not unlike smog—an integral part of the atmosphere that is unhealthy but cannot be escaped."

The teen-agers, Dr. Dickinson says, "resent and resist" advertising that overstates the value of the product or makes false claims about it. "Although," Dr. Dickinson says, "we also find this reaction to some degree in studies with adults, it is far more pronounced among teen-agers. Teen-agers may love music played triple forte. But they hate advertising at that volume."

The research consultant warns advertisers of an important pitfall in dealing with teen-agers. She says that it is dangerous for them to think back to their own youths in building an approach to the teen-age market.

Dr. Dickinson says that there has been a drastic change in society and in the economy. What was valid even a relatively few years ago, she finds, is not valid today.

Another mistake commonly made by advertisers is in the matter of age. Age, Dr. Dickinson warns, is extremely important to a teen-ager. A model who looks young to an advertiser may seem ancient to a teen-ager.

As an example of the conservatism of the group, the research consultant cites a survey of opinions of the bikini bathing suit. Most adults would assume that teen-agers approve of bikinis.

However, of the 1,500 teen-agers polled, three-quarters denounced the suits as "absolutely repulsive," "disgusting," "vulgar," "cheap" or 'horrid."

Even the one-quarter of the group that approved, hedged and said that their use should be confined to film stars or for wear in a private pool.

Just to show the limits, which even the sophisticated teen-ager places upon her acceptance of the bikini, one girl said that bikinis were "all right" unless worn "by girls who are too fat or too thin, by my mother or any other female relative or by any of my girl friends."

Thus, the teen-ager in the mid-twentieth century. The problems of travel to the moon are complex, but no more complex than the problems of trying to understand the problems of adolescence: what youth wants, how it goes about getting it and the unwritten laws it sets for its own behavior.

June 16, 1961

Teen-Ager Courted As a Big Consumer

By MYRON KANDEL

The American teen-ager, in his increasingly important role as a consumer, is being courted as never before by the nation's retailers and manufacturers.

These business men have discovered that the youth market, fed by a spiraling birth rate, has more and more money at its command, and is ready—and even eager—to spend it.

The complaints of harried fathers to the contrary, most of this sum, which has been put at more than $10,000,000,000 a year for the 13-to-19-year-old group, does not come out of Dad's pocket in the form of allowances.

Eugene Gilbert, a research and merchandising specialist in the youth field, estimates that more than one-third of the nation's teen-agers work either full time or part time the year around, while about 59 per cent hold jobs during the summer.

Having no hungry mouths to feed—other than his own—and not being limited by the fixed financial obligations that his elders must meet, the youthful consumer can expend almost all his purchasing power on himself.

In addition, teen-agers have achieved in recent years an important role in purchases by their parents, particularly of items for the home.

While in the past even their own clothes were bought for them, today's teen-agers are helping pick out living-room furniture, major appliances and even the family automobile.

Ninety-five per cent of teenage boys now choose their own clothes, says Jesse S. Siegel, president of Henry I. Siegel Company, Inc., a leading manufacturer of sportswear for boys and young men.

He also reports that young men are becoming increasingly clothes conscious and interested in style.

"The rate of fashion change is greater than it's ever been before in the youth field," he notes. "We must continue to come out with new styles each year, or even twice a year, to satisfy the young man's appetite for buying new things."

In an effort to stimulate this appetite rather than merely satisfy it, manufacturers in the youth field are constantly seeking new styles that will capture the teen-age taste.

Mr. Siegel's company, which sells about 8,500,000 pairs of slacks a year, as well as sport coats, suits and outerwear, mostly under the H.T.S. label, has spearheaded the recent changes in young men's slacks that emphasize the narrow, tapered look.

In the teen-age girls' field, which is even more mercurial in its stress on new fads and fashions, the present rage is the interne coat, popularized particularly by the "Ben Casey" television series.

The fad, which started catching on about four months ago, mushroomed so fast that manufacturers were unable to keep up with the demand.

A Detroit high school recently reported that almost half its girl students were wearing the high-necked white coats or similarly styled blouses and dresses.

Sigfried Alper, chairman of Devonbrook, Ltd., a leading New York producer of junior coats and suits, believes that today's teen-age girl "is less conservative than her older sister and more willing to wear something exciting and off-beat."

"And she wants to change her fashions regularly," he adds, "so that she can be the belle of her speciale set. Gone are the days when young people were content to walk around with sloppy shoes and pigtails."

Spending by teen-agers ranges across the entire merchandising spectrum. In the variety chain field, the F. W. Woolworth Company notes that costume jewelry with a "Twist" theme is selling briskly now.

The company also reports strong interest by teen-agers in exotic pets. According to Hyman L. Hammond, Woolworth's director of pet operatons, these include alligators, iguanas, horned toads, guinea pigs, hamsters and whtie mice.

Even the prosaic rubber band appears to be on the verge of a new teen-age fad. Last fall the B. F. Goodrich Company introduced inch-wide rubber bands in nine school colors to be used instead of the old-fashioned bookstrap.

However, reports William A. Drisler Jr., the company's vice president for marketing of consumer products, "school girls from coast to coast are wearing them as colorful headbands and cinches for their waists."

Desptie the growing importance of the youth market, however, some merchants still appear to be neglecting it. In speaking to a boys' wear group recently, William Hellman, president of the Kennedy chain of men's and boys' stores in the Boston area, observed that in many stores, "the huge student market is almost ignored."

"In the great number of department stores," he said, "we find youngsters from 14 to 18 floating between the boys' and men's departments. Fashion conscious for the first time in their lives, they react quickly to new style concepts and are looking for sound guidance.

"Furthermore, their influence is tremendous on their friends and schoolmates, and often their purchase of a particular wardrobe item provides a chain reaction of repeat business.

"Yet, in store after store, we find no department for these young men who are a huge market now, and one that is growing by leaps and bounds."

May 20, 1962

Advertising: Teen-Age Markets Are Wooed

Specialized Media Aim Particularly at Young Girls

By PETER BART

The teen-ager, whose formidable purchasing power was once all but ignored by advertisers, has become perhaps the most pampered of purchasers. Advertisers lavish their attention — and advertising dollars—on the teen-age trade, and meticulously study teen-age habits and foibles to uncover emerging trends.

The nation's 11,065,000 teenage girls, the researchers say, directly spend some $6,300,000,000 a year and indirectly influence the spending of billions more. The average high school girl spends about $177 on new clothes each year, buys a new lipstick every other month, owns her own hair dryer and uses abundant eye make-up. She listens to the radio about two hours a day, devotes nearly all of her Sunday evenings to television and spends an astonishing amount of time thinking about marriage.

Indeed, about 1,000,000 teenage girls each year not only think about "that day" but actually get engaged, and about 600,000 of these end at the altar.

Having scrutinized these and similar statistics, advertisers have long since decided that the teen-age girl is someone worth paying attention to, and specialized media appealing to teenagers have amply reflected this determination.

20th Anniversary Near

Seventeen Magazine, which is approaching its 20th anniversary, is a case in point. When it was first started toward the end of World War II it was thought a rather chancy venture. Today, Seventeen has a monthly circulation of 1,110,712 and says it has carried more advertising linage over the last decade than any other magazine appealing to a female audience. Indeed, the magazine is widely regarded as a handsome moneymaker, though its publisher, Triangle Publications, Inc., declines to give any details.

The typical teen-age girl has acquired an aura of sophistication in recent years, and Seventeen has adapted itself to this change. The once girlish, almost giggly format has been brought up to date, and today's Seventeen is awash with smart-looking young ladies in bouffant hair styles and ma-

ture attitre. Indeed, a chance reader thumbing through the magazine might easily think he had picked up McCall's or the Ladies Home Journal.

Despite this adult aura, Seventeen still knows what the typical adolescent girl wants, and dishes it out in generous portions. Says the banner on the April issue: "How to bring romance into your fashion life.... How to have prettier skin . . . How to make a boy say wow!"

Advertising in Seventeen runs heavily to fashions and cosmetics, but also includes many other categories of ads. Significantly, it carries more advertising for diamond rings than any other periodical.

Seventeen's pages are decorated with such a plethora of ads that it can well afford to pursue a fairly strict set of advertising standards. The magazine accepts no liquor, beer or cigarette advertising, no hotel ads featuring honeymoon facilities, no ads containing the word "pimples" in the headline and no ads for bridal gowns. Though it accepts ads displaying some of the most elaborately made-up girls imaginable, Seventeen steadfastly declines to take any ads for hair dyes.

These advertising policies, and, in fact, the magazine's entire editorial slant, are largely the product of a slim, flawlessly groomed woman, Mrs. Enid Annenberg Haupt. Mrs. Haupt directs her magazine from a pink, thronelike swivel chair in a large office dominated by pink curtains and pink flowers. She addresses visitors and employes in a manner that is quiet but commanding.

Mrs. Haupt was brought up in Milwaukee, the daughter of the late publisher, Moses L. Annenberg. She was married young and brought up a daughter. During World War II she went to work as a newspaper reporter and later became special assistant to her brother, Walter Annenberg, president of Triangle Publications (TV Guide, The Philadelphia Inquirer). She was named publisher of Seventeen in 1954, editor a year later and editor in chief in 1962.

The recently widowed Mrs. Haupt enjoys the company of teen-agers, but candidly refers to herself as "an awful square."

"A square," Mrs. Haupt said, "is someone who follows old-fashioned standards. That's what it used to mean, anyway —you know teen-agers, they may have another definition by now."

September 8, 1963

Teen-Agers Said to Take Mother's Job as Buyer

Macy's New York President Assays 'New Influentials'

By ISADORE BARMASH

Mother is no longer the chief family purchasing agent, according to David L. Yunich, president of Macy's New York.

Her job has been taken over by the nation's teen-agers, who not only have $11 billion of spending power of their own but also influence an additional $30 billion of family purchasing, Mr. Yunich said yesterday in a speech before the American Marketing Association.

"In our generation," he told an audience of 300 at the Waldorf - Astoria Hotel, "you had to keep up with the Joneses. Today, it's more important to keep up with the Joneses' kids.

"In short, in the child-oriented society where we now find ourselves, the teen-ager is the new influential."

Profiling the teen-ager as the "new consumer," Mr. Yunich described the affluent young shopper as "a revolutionary force at work in the marketplace."

If manufacturers, marketers, sales promoters and merchants are to be successful in the years ahead, "we had better start paying real attention to this market," he urged.

Noting by implication that the teen-age market is widely misrepresented, he added:

"The teen-ager is not one market but several. Subclassification can be worked out, however, to the point of absurdity, but there is one subdivision that is important.

"Since over 40 per cent of the brides today are teen-agers and since more wives have their first child in their 19th year than in any other, we obviously have two markets—the teen-

David L. Yunich

ager, per se, and the young marries—both with money in their overstuffed wallets—both at peak periods of spending, when they want more, need more and buy more."

The challenge is to take these two distinct groups and make customers out of them for the present and the future, he told the audience of marketing and media men and competing retailers.

The president of the R. H. Macy & Co. division assailed the prevailing philosophy that dictates that the industry should ignore the teen-ager while waiting for him to fall into adult buying patterns. There were "four very good reasons why

Marketing Men Urged to Pay Attention to Youth Market

they should now be accepted for what they are," he asserted.

One is that the teen-age years are the time when loyalties are formed. The second is that teen-agers have money to spend as they wish.

By 1970, he noted, teen-age disposable income is expected to climb from the present $11 billion a year to $21 billion. Teen-age girls make up only 13 per cent of the female population, but they buy 27 per cent of the cosmetics, 50 per cent of all phonograph records and 25 per cent of all greeting cards. And teen-agers today own a million television sets, 10 million record players and 20 million radios.

A third reason for meeting the challenge of this consumer group is the teen-ager's influence on family purchasing, he said.

"One myth some of us still hang on to, because giving up a Claus, is that mama is the family purchasing agent," he said. Today's teen-ager, however, influences every area of consumer-goods purchasing.

The fourth reason, Mr. Yunich said, centers on the married teen-agers, who today have better taste than their parents did at the same age and accumulate goods with "a discrimination far beyond their years."

When they marry, they don't want the bed from mother's spare room, he said. "They want to start in the style they're accustomed to at home."

To capture this new market, he added, Macy's has set up separate shopping areas for teen-

age apparel, since "teen-agers hate being catered to as children." In Macy's new stores, junior merchandise is being put in main-floor prime selling space.

This plan has a double-barreled effect by attracting teen-agers and making a store's merchandise seem youthfully appealing to older customers, he noted.

"A corollary of the youth kick in this country is that mature women prefer to shop in a store that looks young and thinks young," he said.

Macy's also has a teen-age board, a special teen-age coordinator and a monthly newsletter called "The Pacesetter's Notebook," which acknowledges the trend-setting role of teen-agers and gives them fashion news and information on such things as how to bake a cake or how to use eye-shadow.

However, he emphasized, much more remains to be done by Macy's, other stores and suppliers, particularly on developing more effective means of reaching the teen-ager for a direct influence.

Cosmetic clinics and beauty workshops could be increased tenfold and the pattern imitated in other services, he said.

Direct mailings, direct phone solicitation and perhaps even the use of teen-agers for this purpose would be advisable, he said, and he suggested that covers of records might be used for advertising merchandise.

Forty per cent of the country's population is now under 20 years of age and most birthrate projections indicate that this ratio will remain fairly constant. "That means," he added, "that the teen-ager is here to stay, and probably in increasing numbers, since children seem to become teen-agers earlier every year."

February 19, 1965

AFFLUENCE HELPS TEEN-AGE TRAVEL

More Youths Visit Europe as Summer Tourists

"Good-by, baby.

"Don't forget to take your salt pills. Watch out for foreign men."

"You're so young to go so far away alone."

"Cable Daddy if you need money."

With these or similar words, hundreds of anxious parents said good-by to their teen-aged children one recent afternoon at Kennedy International Airport.

Each day in early summer the scene in the jet-line terminals is likely to be the same

as thousands of youths 15, 16 and 17 years old depart for travel or study abroad.

A few years ago, most of the teen-agers would have spent July and August at camp, the family's summer home or selling hot dogs at Jones Beach. Today they visit such spots as Crete, the Soviet Union, Turkey and Argentina.

Travel Becomes Common

"In this affluent society, a summer abroad is becoming common for middle-class kids," said Laurie Simmons, a 17-year-old from Dallas who was waiting at Kennedy for her flight to Rome.

"All my girl friends' parents gave them either a nose bob or a trip to Europe for a high school graduation present," Miss Simmons said, wrinkling her small, upturned nose. "I got a trip."

Many teen-agers spend the summer in study-travel programs run by American

secondary schools.

Phillips Exeter Academy, Exeter, N. H., for example, offers four weeks of intensive Russian language study followed by a three-week tour of the Soviet Union. The total cost is $1,600.

On Tuesday, 31 students will leave for a five-week program of study in Greece at Athens College. Sponsored by the Horace Mann School, a boys' school in the Bronx, the session is co-educational, includes a five-day cruise to Crete and costs $1,150.

"European summer study programs are going to mushroom in the next 10 years," said Robert A. Tomasson, headmaster of Horace Mann. "It's part of the general parental attitude of turning kids loose and placing more confidence in them.

"But the real reason for the boom in foreign travel for kids is affluence. Their parents

have the money to send them anywhere in the world."

Many go to summer language institutes run for English-speaking students by foreign universities, such as the University of Oslo in Norway and the Goethe Institute near Munich, Germany.

Today 192 recent high school graduates are to leave for Israel to take a two-month intensive course in Hebrew before entering Tel Aviv University in October.

Other teen-agers spend a month or two living with a foreign family and learning the language. The 36-year-old Experiment in International Living has paced 800 teen-agers with families in 40 countries this summer.

Some 850 teen-agers, half of them less than 17 years old, sailed from New York last week to spend two months with foreign families under the American Field Service program.

Still others spend their vacations on organized sight-seeing tours. For example, 300 high school students will leave on Wednesday for seven weeks in Israel on a tour sponsored by Histadrut, Israel's labor foundation.

"Our tour has become amazingly popular in the past year," said Max Mermelstein, executive vice president of the Histadrut Foundation for Educational Travel. "Kids today are very sophisticated. They think it's square to go to camp."

However, a spokesman for the American Camping Association said the camping business was still excellent, despite competition of foreign travel. "There are more teenagers today—enough to fill both Europe and the camps,"

he explained.

And, according to the American Youth Hostel Association, more and more youngsters—especially boys—are traveling to Europe on their own, often living on a budget of $1 a day.

June 30, 1968

Advertising:

The Secret of Reaching Youth Market

By PHILIP H. DOUGHERTY

Any parent sharing his pad with a teen-ager doesn't have to be told that the record companies know the secret of reaching the youth market. The parent has already had the vibrations; the pulsations; the loud, loud sound of rock.

Companies like Capitol, London, Columbia, RCA, Motown, Stax, A. & M. and Warners are not reaching the teen-agers through TV or slick national magazines like advertisers of other products. No, they're going after this highly volatile market (where many another manufacturer has failed) through radio, college papers and radio and the underground press.

And they advertise with complete honesty, so they say, because they have to.

"You kind of lay the truth out for them. You can't even give them a hype any more," said David Herscher, who is in charge of ad production at Warner Brothers.

"They're a very sophisticated audience and you can't talk down to them for a second," said Hastings Baker, ad director of Elektra. "You got to be honest and informative. Most advertising talks down. We can't."

●

That might explain the headline in the Oct. 4 issue of Rolling Stone from Mercury that read, "Four albums guaranteed to prevent the feeling you've been cr------ on again." It didn't use the dashes.

But you really can't equate any other product aimed at the youth market with records.

"They're not just to listen to, they're a way of life," said William H. Lucas, advertising and sales promotion manager at RCA.

"Acne cream has no emotion involved," said Mr. Baker Elektra.

The nation's annual retail sales are put at over $1-billion by the people involved and some estimate that teenagers make up 75 per cent or more of that spending.

And because of the changing nature of youth ("Hot today, cold tomorrow," according to Phil Jones of Motown), the recording com-

The New York Times (by Neal Boenzi)

Customers looking over rock offerings at Sam Goody's on West 49th St. Annual record sales are put at $1-billion. Some estimate teen-agers spend 75% of that.

panies have to remain flexible, which they can do far more easily, say, than a cosmetics company.

"They make you or break you," said Dene Parker of Stax. "They fool you. When you think you've got a hit or when you think you've got a flop."

Mr. Lucas of RCA breaks the rock record buyers into three age groups—the 9 to 13 set, which goes for what he called "bubblegum rock;" the 13 to 18, and the 18 to 25.

His advertising is primarily in radio in what his trade calls the "Top 40" stations, the stations that play the top 40 songs.

●

"Radio and records go together. One is the lifeblood of the other," he said. Other record companies must feel the same way, since, according to the Radio Advertising Bureau, record companies spent almost as much in the first half of this year as the $1.1-million they spent in all of 1968.

College radio stations are getting a play and so are college papers. The National Education Advertising Services, the Reader's Digest subsidiary that is the national advertising representative

for 900 college papers reports that while six record companies placed $59,694 worth of ads during the 1966-67 academic year, 18 companies placed $119,388 during the 1968-69 year.

But the media you use on the audience you're trying to reach and the audience you try to reach depends on the artists you have under contract.

"We got lousy response from the college press. We advertised in four college papers and not too successfully," said Mr. Herscher of Warner Brothers, which also puts out the Reprise label.

"But we got great response from Ramparts and Evergreen," he added later.

His artists he described as "underground groups — a kind of folk rock—like the Grateful Dead—that are not accepted by 'top 40' stations."

So their Burbank Advertising Agency, a house agency (many of the record companies have them), places its ads in what he calls underground FM radio and underground press.

To reach the trade Burbank, like the others, probably places its ads in Billboard Cashbox, Record World and perhaps Variety,

to reach the buyers it has been advertising in the underground press even more than in radio. He includes The Village Voice in the group but calls it "the grandfather."

The others, which stand out in his mind, covering music exclusively or extensively, are papers like The Rolling Stone, The Boston Fusion, New York Changes, The Los Angeles Free Press, or magazines like Rock Magazine, The Seed in Chicago, or Creem Magazine in Detroit.

Rolling Stone, which Mr. Jones of Motown describes as "the biggie," is published in San Francisco, is two years old and has a national circulation of 74,000, of which 20,000 is subscription.

It started out with almost all of its advertising record advertising but is now carrying about 85 per cent records with the rest of the paid space taken by book ads and hi-fi equipment.

Its readership, according to its ad director, is 49 per cent under 21, 40 per cent in school and 90 per cent male.

And 0 per cent digs "23 skidoo."

December 21, 1969

TEENAGERS AND SOCIETY

Drawing by Susan Perl.

Menace—Some grownups view today's teen-agers as a threat to adult sanity, likely to sweep away civilization as we know it.

Teen-Agers Mirror Their Parents

If we want to know what the growing population of juveniles will do to our world, a father suggests we look at ourselves.

By RUSSELL LYNES

THE number of 13-year-olds is increasing at a rate twenty times faster than the rest of the population. "Between 1958 and 1960," a recent report of the David L. Babson Company of Boston says, "the number of children crossing the 13-year-old threshold will rise by nearly 40 per cent. By 1965 there will be a 35 per cent increase in the 14-17 age group." The total population grows by a com-

paratively sluggish 2 per cent a year. We are obviously reaping the whirlwind of post-World War II romance.

One of the specters that haunt our time is the sprawling expansion of the population, and it is more and more difficult not to picture the future as though it were going to be life in a sardine can. If the figures on the teenage population are correct (and they must be), it's going to be a boisterous,

noisy, squirming can indeed.

There are those who view this prospect with alarm for they fear that civilization, as we know it, will be swept away by juveniles—if not entirely delinquent, then at least objectionable. Others, who have a hand in the teen-ager's pocket, consider the explosion the best sort of news. It seems to me unlikely that civilization is doomed, at least not by teen-agers, and

I would like to suggest that if we want to know what the teen-agers will do to us, we should look at ourselves.

In all the brouhaha about teen-agers we are inclined to forget, it seems to me, that they are primarily reflections of us, of our foibles and fumblings and aspirations, our fears and frustrations, our hopes and our beliefs. They are, in effect, a magnifying mirror of their elders—like a shaving mirror in which our eyes seem to bulge, our pores to be extinct volcanoes, and our eyebrows thickets of thistles.

Consider their rebellious natures. Of a New York Times Youth Forum last year it was reported: "A group of high school students said * * * that teen-agers were increasingly rebellious toward authority—especially parental authority. And the tension behind teen-agers' attitudes comes from a lack of close understanding with their parents." The students also blamed this rebelliousness on "the terrible age we live in" and the "looseness of family ties."

This is where we come in. These are not things the teen-agers thought up for themselves; they are ideas that have been impressed on them by the rest of us. We have drummed into their heads their "need to be understood," and they would be less than human not to use this ready-made excuse as an escape hatch for their natural high spirits.

A FEW years ago two revealing studies of teen-agers appeared, one of them something of a shocker, the other reassuring. They both throw some light on ourselves. The first was a book called "The American Teen-ager," a summary for the general reader of the findings of a fifteen-year investigation of teen-agers made at Purdue University under the direction of Dr. H. H. Remmers. The second was called "Adolescent Girls" and was a study made for the Girl Scouts by the Survey Research Center at the University of Michigan.

From "The American Teen-ager" one gets the superficial impression that our youngsters are monsters. (One also gets this impression from the newspapers, of course.) Teen-agers believe, the book says, in wire-tapping, in search without warrant, in "censorship of books, newspapers, magazines and other media as protection of the public against improper ideas." Furthermore, they believe that "most people aren't capable of deciding what's best for themselves," and they "see no harm in the third degree." Not all of them, to be sure, but a good many more than half of them.

I FIND this rather chilling, less because of what it says about the teen-agers than what it says about their parents. But the Girl Scouts' report takes a somewhat more optimistic view.

Their study found that by and large the youngsters of this era are "conservative." Far from being rebellious, the study exposed them as idealistic

RUSSELL LYNES, a parent-emeritus of teen-agers, is managing editor of Harper's Magazine and the author of such books as "Snobs," "Guests," and "A Surfeit of Honey."

and practical, more eager than their mothers had been for advanced education, but not, in general, wanting to be high-powered executives or movie stars. Fewer than a fifth of them had a good thing to say for "going steady." In many respects they are more independent than their mothers were at the same age. They have weekly allowances that give them more freedom to choose their fun; they have part-time jobs, and they play a larger role in making family plans. The attitude of the family has come a long way since the "children should be seen and not heard" era.

CHATTER—The more teen-agers there are, the more telephones will be endlessly tied up.

No one would now say, as my wife's grandmother used to, that there was nothing to do with children but "put them in a barrel and feed them through the bunghole until they're 21."

Somewhere along the line we stopped thinking of teen-agers as just young people in transition between childhood and the state of being "grown up," and we began to regard them as a minority pressure group in our society. We now look on them not as just "kids," as we used to, but as a sub-culture with a powerful effect on the culture as a whole.

You will look in vain (or at least I have looked in vain) for references to "teen-agers" in the literature of my parents' day. You will find "youngsters" and "schoolboys" and "schoolgirls," but you will not find teen-agers as a group, treated as though they were something between menaces and the hope of the world, a class by themselves, a threat to adult sanity.

THE change came during and after the second World War, the result of the dislocation of families both physically and spiritually. Children were asked to adjust to change rather than to continuity, to pulling up stakes rather than to putting down roots. They began to look more than ever

to their contemporaries for security, and they began to look for their own set of rules to live by. The practice of "going steady," for example, was an attempt to establish formal relationships that promised some sort of continuity and sense of belonging to some one person.

The songs popular with youth, you may have noticed, belie the old Tin Pan Alley cliché that a hit can't be made on the theme of married love. As Arnold Shaw has pointed out, "Honeycomb" and "Kisses Sweeter than Wine," both songs of marriage, have been taken to the hearts of teen-agers whose popular hits are "a growing literature of * * * protest." "Born Too Late," they sing, and "Why Won't They Understand?"

At the same time they want to be a self-sufficient and rebellious group, they reach out for a hand to guide them. Their accusation that adults "fail to understand" them is a reflection of our "wanting to

SUCCESS—Only one out of many makes the college of his choice.

understand," and their "rebelliousness" is, in part at least, a reflection of our fairly new belief in "permissiveness" and in our encouraging them to make up their own minds. They seem to be in a terrible hurry to be grown-up, to have grown-up respect paid to them, at the same time that they resent the group they most want to be part of—a not uncommon human condition.

They have reason to resent us, and if the reflection of ourselves that we see in them is not a pretty one, we should not be surprised. Let's look a little deeper into the mirror of our society and see theirs.

THERE was a time not long ago when parents not only preached the virtues of work but practiced them. The work week was ten or fifteen hours longer than it is now for father, and his day off each week was a restorative to enable him to do a better job on the other six days. Now leisure has become a kind of job in its own right, and it is going to become still more of a job. When the work week shrinks, as economists say it will, to twenty hours, it is going to be difficult indeed for father to preach to his children the old gospel that "the devil finds work for idle hands." There is plenty of evidence around us now of what happens to young people deprived of the opportunity to work and without the resources, either cultural or social, to put their time to good use.

But time on parental hands has still further effects. At its worst it is corrosive and it is stultifying. It passively accepts what is put before it. It wallows in ways to make time pass—hours of sitting before the television or in aimless puttering. Or it can be dangerously aggressive against society, or against self, as in dope addiction or alcoholism.

Less spectacular, but also corrosive, undirected leisure takes itself out in consumption for consumption's sake, in buying gadgets that save time, when time is the thing that least needs saving for the already time-ladened. It shows itself in ostentation and in competition with one's neighbors. Everyone wants to be the biggest Jones in the block. These are the lessons that the young learn when leisure is not constructive and does not enrich the spirit. It can, of course, be otherwise, but it is the parents who show the direction.

There is another direction they show. A good deal of journalistic space is occupied these days by articles about the number of young people who cheat on exams. Is this, after all, very different from padding an expense account or, more important, shading the truth on an income-tax return? If colleges and universities promote gifts in such a way that it is sometimes possible for a donor to make money by giving gifts to them, doesn't the line of academic honesty become a little blurred?

OR take another matter that is related to schools. It is not uncommon today to find youngsters who, when they have graduated from high school, wish they had been made to work harder. Why? Suddenly adults have been spurred into believing that only education will save us from lagging behind the Russians; suddenly bright students have a new status which a few years ago they sadly lacked—often to the point of being ostracized by their contemporaries. The "grind" and the "brightie" were looked down upon, a reflection of intellectual distrust on the part of parents. Now the winds blow in a different direction.

Or take the shibboleth of "conformity" with which the critics of our society plague us. (In my opinion this is a convenient tag that has been greatly overused to describe one aspect of a highly industrialized nation.) How is the teen-age custom of "going steady" a reflection of our own insecurity? To what extent is it, as I have suggested, an attempt to inject a kind of formality into relationships among young people that they miss in this age of informality?

The Girl Scouts may say that they are against it, but it has become a tribal custom of the young that they observe with almost universal respect all the same.

We are inclined to be indulgent about the hero-worship of the teen-ager for the movie glamour boys, for the Presleys and the James Deans and Eddie Fishers and Ricky Nelsons. We should be. We are hero-worshipers ourselves. It is evident in our political attitudes, in the numbers of us who don't even bother to vote, presumably because we are willing to "leave it to the boss." It is evident in our reverence toward leaders of business and industry, toward scientists, toward anybody who we think can lead us by the hand through the maze of complications that beset us.

To what extent is our fear of the Russians, for example, responsible for the teen-ager's belief in censorship, in wire-tapping, in search without warrant? If we are worried, as we should be, about their attitudes toward personal liberties, hadn't we better look to our own?

It is easy to take this subculture, this minority group, the teen-agers, and read our characters and future in them as though they were tea leaves. We can see adumbrated in them our attitudes toward religion, toward the arts and toward education more clearly than we can by looking at ourselves. We are likely to be more indulgent in looking at ourselves than at them; we smooth over our own exaggerations while we view theirs with alarm.

But I can see no reason why the simple statistical fact that there are going to be a great many more teen-agers in the next few years should be cause for anything more than the usual alarm. Unquestionably they will cause problems, just as we caused problems when we were teen-agers. But they will also give delight. There will be more noisy households than we are accustomed to, more telephones endlessly tied up, more records strewn around the living-room floor, more starry-eyed young lovers, more hard questions to answer, more nonsensical fads to throw up the hands about.

THERE will be something that will take the place of rock 'n' roll, bobby socks, and hot rods, something that will seem ludicrous to those who will have recently grown out of their teens into adulthood, and alarming to the parents who have to put up with it.

Possibly I am lucky. I have just lived through the teen-ages of a son and a daughter. There were moments when I thought murder was too good for them; there were moments when they thought murder was much too good for me. Sometimes their anguish was my anguish; sometimes their cussedness was my fury; occasionally their pleasure was my despair. But I saw myself sometimes distorted, sometimes all too clearly, in them as a mirror. I suspect I learned from them as much as I taught them, and I wouldn't have missed it for anything.

June 28, 1959

Teen-Age Tyranny Extends Its Empire

Young people, able to obtain charge accounts, automobiles and almost anything else they desire, are becoming rulers of the roost.

By GRACE and FRED M. HECHINGER

A RECENT newspaper advertisement, offering "teen-age charge accounts," emphatically made the point that no adult signatures were required. "Pick it out. Take it with you," the ad told its young readers.

This is only one of many manifestations of a growing and unreasonable domination by teen-agers over American adults, American life and American standards.

The teen-age tyranny is partly the result of adult abdication of responsibility. It is also the natural consequence of widespread misinterpretation by parents and teachers of the meaning of freedom in the growing-up process. And it is, to no small degree, the effect of the great and increasing economic power enjoyed by youth.

The young slowly are capturing an ever-growing snare of the nation's market, both through their own purchasing power and, more important, through effective dictation to parents. Financial columnist Sylvia Porter, calling the teen-age market "a most enticing prospect" for retailers, estimates it at a "fabulous ten billion dollars a year, of which three billion goes for girls' clothing alone."

This teen-age tyranny is not, of course, the outcome of a conscious play for power; it is, rather, in an affluent society, a mutiny of the bountiful.

151

BUT the economic factor is only one symptom of a serious condition. False, or distorted, permissiveness has moved from the home to the schools where, in some instances, pupils are asked whether or not they approve of such rules as the honor system. In extreme cases, they even are asked whether the curriculum meets with their favor.

Teen-age tyranny is reinforced by the pseudo-psychological jargon that did so much harm to American education by equating adult guidance with authoritarian despotism. To prevent youngsters from aping anything that "is done" by "the peer group" is considered reactionary and repressive. Those parents who have not been indoctrinated by academic theorists are being "reached" by television's many psychological teen-operas in which youngsters play their tyrannical role to the hilt.

On a recent Tom Ewell show, the hard-pressed and, as always, slightly imbecile father is hit for $5 by the bright-eyed, pony-tailed, teen-age daughter who "must" have a man's shirt because this has been proclaimed the required uniform for the class dance. Daddy cheerfully offers one of his shirts but is told that only a new one will do. When he protests, a teen-understanding mother comes to the defense of teen-law. "Do you want her to be different from all the others?" she asks. Dad, by now properly ashamed, shells out the cash.

IN such an atmosphere, it is hardly surprising that teen-agers have come to dominate American cultural tastes, at least in much of the mass market. The teen-age tribal beat of popular music haunts the radio. One top network executive had a long-playing tape system built into his car to escape from the adolescent fare that saturates his and his competitors' stations.

Of course, much of the teen-age influence on the radio and record industry is to be attributed to the efforts of good salesmen, who know a potential

Drawings by Susan Perl.

ADOLESCENT RAMPANT—Parents now find it hard to say "no" to their children.

market when they see one. Since they correctly estimate that the most doubtful tastes of the least sophisticated of the group will prevail, they appeal to that element.

But, whatever the explanation, there is little excuse for some of the wailing distortions that contaminate the air. Nor is it easy to find an alibi for those television "productions" that show hordes of awkward, self-conscious youngsters milling around a dance floor

and making a spectacle of adolescent romance.

Even the most respectable adult, mass-circulation magazines have blossomed forth with lengthy columns about teen "problems," running the gamut from dating to going steady. They are generally written by, or ghosted for, those depressingly look-alike idols of teen-agers, the disk jockeys and "actors." The language, though unimaginatively wholesome, is always on the verge of the ungrammatical and in that teen-jargon which has been creeping into much "adult" advertising copy, as well.

TEEN influence on the culture may be a slow subversion; the economic domination is quite overt. The makers of leotards, ballet slippers and Bermuda shorts know and cherish the story. The boom in snack foods and hero sandwiches is merely another chapter of the same tale. Few parents of today's teen-agers suspected, when their babies were in diapers, how expensive the teen years would be and how persuasive salesmen of the teen products would become.

There is nothing basically wrong with the desire to provide teen-agers with attractive things—until it gets out of hand. The teen charge accounts are an example. They assume that few par-

KEY FIGURE IN THE ECONOMY—The teen-ager's patronage is the quarry increasingly sought by business. This market is now put at "a fabulous ten billion dollars a year."

GRACE and FRED M. HECHINGER often work together on stories about young people. He is education editor of The New York Times.

ents are reactionary (or courageous) enough to prevent their children's extravagance.

A RECENT survey by Seventeen magazine showed that teen-age charge accounts have doubled since 1959 and that some of them start at the 13-year-old shopping level.

Going along with the trend, some observers now praise the charge-account gimmick as an "educational" device for teaching thrift. One enterprising jeweler, following through with the "educational" theme, recently advertised "Going-Steady Rings" at $12.95—"Nothing down, 50 cents a week to pay."

A better educational case could be made *against* the teen-age carte blanche as a blatant symptom of ridiculous permissiveness. At any rate, the "educational" potential is seriously diminished by the proven fact that few stores ever try to sue or collect bad debts from the minors themselves. A letter or discreet telephone call to the parents usually results in quick settlement. And so ends a lesson.

Deeply involved in all this is the confusion over the outward symbols of success and status. Parents often find it hard to say "no" to their children—not because

they don't realize that it may not be unwise to make certain concessions, but rather because they fear loss of social status among parents of other teen-agers.

This is especially true among parents who had few outward "advantages" in their own youth; they may want to buy precarious prestige and status by permitting their children to have the status symbols of the gang.

N ATURALLY, adolescents are quick to exploit this parental attitude. How contagious this national weakness tends to be was shown when the small son of a foreign diplomat, stationed in New York, made the rounds of his American neighbors and told them that his father was "un-American" because he refused to buy a television set.

Status-seeking is not the whole story, however. Also to blame are the uncritical philosophy of permissiveness, introduced in the Twenties, and a misinterpretation of the meaning of democracy, both in the home and in the school. Today, adults who ought to establish standards of adolescent behavior frequently resort to that convenient substitute for policy-making: the opinion poll.

A group of educators recently asked tots in the second grade whether they thought they were learning what they needed most to know. School "administrators" have tried to determine, by way of majority opinion, whether today's high-

CHOICE—Should kids smoke? Often today it's up to them.

school students should be allowed to smoke in school and, if so, what kind of special smoking rooms ought to be provided. (Lest this kind of action be erroneously ascribed only to mass education, it must be added that the same debate raged in the alumni magazine of one of the country's most venerable private academies.)

In many communities, high school almost invariably means car ownership. Last fall, the opening of a new public high school in Norwalk, Conn., led to so vast a traffic jam that many commuters missed their trains.

When Norwalk's police chief asked that the school authorities limit student use of cars, a Board of Education spokesman said he could do nothing about it since anybody over 16 is legally entitled to drive. Norwalk's adults "compromised" by taking earlier trains.

The news from Norwalk brought testimony of similar dilemmas from other parts of the country, including complaints about the "need" for expensive parking lots for new schools. When one community urged that this noneducational expense be covered by charging parking fees, the school superintendent said plaintively that this might lead to student parking in residential neighborhoods. Nobody considered it possibly to lay down rules and enforce them.

T HIS spectacle of adult helplessness goes on in the face of a recent study showing a direct relationship between students' use of cars and failure in their school work. Moreover, the National Safety Council reports that in 1959 teen-agers were involved in about twice as many accidents as their numbers would warrant. (Perhaps it was these statistics that inspired one major automobile manufacturer to advertise his product as road-tested by teen-agers!)

In its total effect, teen-age

tyranny is not merely an inconvenience; it can be desperately harmful to the adolescents themselves. In extreme cases, it leads to heartbreak and ruined lives. Members of a parents' committee in an upper-middle-class commuter town recently complained "in confidence" that their small high school had seen more than ten "forced marriages" in one term. But those who wanted to counteract the dangerous trend by taking open measures of education and discipline were met with violent protest.

T HE hectic search for "popularity," says school psychologist John J. Morgenstern in the Journal of the National Education Association, leads to such as this: approved dating for 9-year-olds, so that they will be "ready for junior high school" and won't feel "left out." An elementary-school principal comments, "I don't like it, but my P.-T. A. wants me to have fifth- and sixth-grade dances, and sometimes the fourth grade is invited to even out the number of boys and girls." But too many school authorities who "don't like it" lack the guts to be right rather than unpopular.

Educators almost unanimously deplore the trend toward teen-age marriages, but they rush nevertheless to provide "married-student housing." To suggest that they swim against the stream is not a plea for the impossible, as shown by the continued courage of a few of the best colleges. Swarthmore, for example, still rules that if an undergraduate couple gets married, one of the two must leave the college.

Instead of protecting the teen-ager from the pressure of

WRATH—"I've given you everything! Where have I failed?"

his peers, adults permit the pressure to become the accepted norm. They do so even though, as anthropologist Margaret Mead warns, many a marriage becomes "a prema-

ture imprisonment of young people, before they have had a chance to explore their own minds and the minds of others."

H OW far adults still are from heeding such warnings may be gauged from a course offered in an upstate New York high school. Entitled "Family Living," it provides for "units" in which "each girl plans, either alone or with her boy friend, a home that would be possible to build and furnish on a limited budget." Other "units" are concerned with "learning to be livable, lovable and datable."

A further danger signal is the increase of delinquency—not in the slums, where economic conditions make it explicable, but in the well-to-do suburbs. Last year, summer residents in one fashionable New York commuter town were shocked to find that teen-agers had been stealing cars from the railroad parking lot; it was their favorite relief from boredom.

In Englewood, N. J., seventeen youths were arrested after a long period of housebreaking, in which they had totaled $10,000 worth of loot. Most of the young burglars admitted having liberal allowances from home but went on their lawless sprees "just for kicks and because it was thrilling."

Westchester County's District Attorney last year issued a report on 251 persons, most of them in their teens and some as young as 13, who had used an extensive assortment of narcotics regularly at dances, club meetings and parties. Some of these gatherings had been held in homes while parents were absent.

The youngsters came from well-to-do communities, from Port Chester to Pelham, and were joined regularly by "guests" from Fairfield County and New York City. According to a New York Times report, most of them were "high-school and college students from prosperous families."

When one of the boys confessed, his father shouted: "I should take you by the throat and kill you. I have given you everything. Where have I failed?"

O NE experienced educator replies that this father and other parents like him have failed exactly because they have given their children everything. Miss Sophie Jaffe, a teacher in New Britain, Conn., told an education congress last year: "Children must learn as children that one cannot have everything

LIGHT FANTASTIC — Now even fifth-graders attend dances.

one wants." She told of 4-year-olds in kindergarten who boast of the price of their dresses and of the fact that they "know how to get what they want."

It is not easy for parents, in a prosperous society, to limit their generosity toward their children. Much of their desire to give is rooted in genuine love. But, at least in part, the excess of giving springs from feelings of guilt: It is a material substitute for lack of personal attention.

What can be done to halt a pernicious trend? Psychologist Morgenstern says: "Our child-rearing methods emphasize development of the individual so much that many parents find it difficult to apply sensible limits to children under 12, and even more difficult as the youngsters reach adolescence and make their strongest bids for independence and feel the strongest need for conformity to their peer groups."

Increasingly, the experts are therefore abandoning the old extremes of permissiveness. They warn that, in the absence of adult "laws," the only law tends to become that of the lowest common adolescent denominator. The challenge of the "peers" is to explore the limits to which one dares go. The "dare" then becomes the tribal substitute for law, and the only punishment is to be considered "chicken" or to be hurt. Undoubtedly, the majority of teen-agers would prefer to have an "out" rather than to be dragged along by the dictatorial tribe.

IRONICALLY, many articulate teen-agers try to tell their elders that they really don't enjoy their own regime. When recent years brought about a tightening of academic requirements in the schools, many students responded with enthusiasm and gratitude to hard work, intellectual chal-

lenge and the sensible new government by adult law. At a teen-age convocation of the Wayne County (Mich.) Camp Association last fall, the youngsters agreed that "teenagers are punished by being pampered," and that they are "led to become accustomed to too much too soon."

One danger is that some panicky adults will try to cope with the teen-age tyranny by attacking the symptoms rather than the source of the disease. Others, attuned to the current faith in the magic of public relations, think that the "problems" can be made to appear insignificant by simply playing up "good news" about teen-agers.

The latter course is clearly no solution at all. As for the former, experts are convinced that no remedy can be found in a primitive "get tough" policy, such as is advocated in legislative proposals to introduce corporal punishment in the schools.

WHAT the experts do want is a re-establishment of sensible adult authority, coupled with admirable adult values.

"An adolescent has the right to know the best judgment of those whom he respects as to what his strengths and weaknesses are," says Eric W. Johnson, head of the Germantown (Pa.) Friends Junior High School.

Turning to the specific problem of establishing rules, Mr. Johnson adds: "Teen-agers appreciate a clear understanding about the time of return (from a party) and a definite word (from the parents) so that they do not have to make the self-belittling decision that it's now time to go home."

In exercising their authority, parents must, of course, make it clear that they are doing so not just because they are bigger and stronger, but because they have the benefit of greater experience and the burden of greater responsibility.

By taking this view, they inevitably will encounter "crises" and opposition. They will find it especially difficult to remain firm when the majority of parents in the neighborhood continues to be excessively permissive. On this problem — not of keeping up with the Joneses, but of keeping the Joneses in line—specific advice comes from Dr. Benjamin Spock:

"The parents' best defense is to keep in touch with the parents of their children's friends, and to devote P.-T. A. meetings to discussion of such matters," he wrote recently. "* * * It's often a surprise and a pleasure to find that most of them share your point of view (contrary to reports from

your children), and that everyone is ready to come to a neighborhood agreement. Such a code is a comfort to the children, too, because it assures them that they will not be ridiculously out of line."

Naturally, the courage to establish laws and regulations is needed as much in the school as in the home. If cars are harmful to high-school learning and mores, for instance, there is practical precedent for law enforcement: Some of the best colleges, including Princeton, have had the courage to outlaw cars, simply by basing their decision on the fact that it is better for education.

HAZARD—"In many communities, high school almost invariably means cars." The accident rate is high.

THERE is steadily growing agreement among today's experts that the extreme permissiveness of a generation ago has done great harm to teenagers. In his new book, "The Education of Nations," Robert Ulich, James Bryant Conant Professor Emeritus at Harvard University, asks:

"Would it not be more conducive to a person's development if he were more free when he could profit from his freedom, namely, as a young man, or woman, and more controlled when control might be at the right place, namely, as an adolescent?"

Prof. Ulich urges today's parents and teachers to understand that the difficult business of growing up demands "not only freedom from false authority, but also respect for rightful authority."

If adult authority is one part of the fight against teen-age tyranny, the establishment

of challenging goals is equally important. Dr. Edward D. Eddy Jr., president of Chatham College, recently conducted a study of college students on many campuses. He observed that teen-agers, perhaps misinterpreting the psychologists' stress on individualism and "child-centered" schools, have developed a dangerous streak of "privatism." Their key question is: "What's in it for me?"

BUT the antidote, as Dr. Eddy points out and as recent events have underlined, is in kindling in young people a joyful sense of their talents and

the expectation of excitement as the reward for effort and service. That this is not a Utopian idea has been demonstrated by the electric response of young people across the country to such challenges as the Peace Corps, and by the less spectacular but equally important involvement of teen-agers in science projects.

It is no accident that so much of the "good news" about teen-agers has come from the science laboratories, where laws and regulations are adult-established and clearly defined, and where adult knowledge is expected and respected. It is a ready hint as to how parents and teachers, willing to risk the loss of "palship" by acting like responsible adults, can make adolescence a step toward growing up, not a privilege to be exploited.

March 19, 1961

Teen-Agers Are An American Invention

By BENNETT M. BERGER

"Youth culture functions to keep the young happy while being kept out of an adult society." Above, the springtime student frolics in Florida.

THERE is a notion abroad in the land—one can hardly call it an idea—that ours is an adolescent-dominated society. The notion should not be taken seriously, and rarely is—least of all by those who voice it most frequently and audibly. It is, rather, typically expressed with that peculiar combination of coy bewilderment and mock helplessness which men affect when pleading their domination by women or by servants or by any group which actually has little power but which for one reason or another occupies a highly visible, perhaps strategic, and yet somewhat protected position in the society.

But the notion that we are a society dominated by adolescents is especially perverse because it is not only not true but is close to being the direct opposite of the truth. Indeed, it was not very long ago that the leaders of the world's major countries (Eisenhower, de Gaulle, Khrushchev, Mao, Macmillan and Adenauer) were men who, were they not rich and powerful, would have qualified for the old folks' home. Far from being adolescent-dominated, modern societies tend to be gerontocracies.

It is true, however, that most modern societies do seem to have a problem with their adolescents, teen-agers—call them what you will. The very fact that we do not have a straightforward, unselfconscious, unmincing word in our language to describe the group is in itself evidence, as Edgar Friedenberg, the sociologist, has pointed out, of the problem that youth presents, and our apparent reluctance to face it squarely. I think that it is precisely because our kind of society has as yet found no honorable, serious and productive place in it for young persons that we have no word to describe them with respect, and that our discussions of them have a tendency to be patronizing or cloying or clinical.

BENNETT M. BERGER is chairman of the department of sociology at the University of California in Davis.

CHILDREN everywhere, of course, pass through the sudden crisis of puberty, and the gradual maturation of their physical and sexual powers. But whereas in many societies the onset of puberty and the strength to do a man's or woman's work qualify a young person for membership in adult society (at a low status, perhaps, but at a low *adult* status), industrial societies like our own introduce into the culture a special *age grade* we call "adolescence"—a social category that *defines* that part of the population which fits it as not children, exactly, but not quite adults either. Adolescence is one of the ways in which culture violates nature by insisting that, for an increasing number of years, young persons postpone pressing their claims for the privileges and responsibilities of common citizenship, and by persuading young and old alike of the justice of that postponement.

Since the early 19th century in England, and probably the middle of the century in the United States, that postponement has been both institutionalized and prolonged, as more and more occupations required higher levels of skill. The most usual defense of postponed adulthood is the alleged "complexity" of our society, and hence the longer period of preparation needed for adequate functioning in it. But although there is little question that many modern occupations require extended training, the evidence is far from convincing (far, even, from being adequately gathered) that an American adolescent, for example, has more to learn about adult functioning *in general* than a young member of a "primitive" society, who may have to master the intricacies of a very complex kinship system or a system of highly elaborate religious ritual.

In any case, it is clear enough that adolescence is a relatively recent social invention which prolongs the exclusion of young persons from adult society until they are deemed "ready" to assume adult roles. There have al-

ways been people between the ages of 12 and 20, but "teen-agers" are an American invention (not discovery)—invented within living memory.

The well publicized conflicts and tensions of the teen-age "transitional stage" stem from the combination of an acceleration in the individual's physical and cultural growth with the continued refusal by society to grant to adolescents many of the rights and opportunities of adults: when sexual desires are more powerful than they will ever again be, sexual opportunities are fewest; obedience and submission are asked of adolescents at precisely the time when their strength, energy, and desire for autonomy are ascendent; responsible participation in the major social institutions is denied or discouraged at the moment when their interest in the world has been poignantly awakened. These tensions, generated partly by our age-grading system itself and exacerbated by a decline in parental control and a world in a state of permanent crisis, are a major source of general adolescent problems.

But given the severe tensions of adolescence, the surprising thing is that there isn't more trouble and turmoil among (Continued) teen-agers than there actually is. I say this not to defend adolescents against the bad press they have had in recent years nor to minimize the magnitude of the "adolescent problem" but simply to point out that despite the general problems of adolescent psychology and by now legendary storminess of the teen-age years, the overwhelming majority of adolescents seem to make their way through to full adult status without getting involved in riots, orgies, or other serious delinquencies, without a dominating hedonism and without generalized attitudes of rebellion toward parents and the world.

We don't have nearly as much adolescent rebelliousness as the tensions of adolescence suggest we might have because society has at its disposal a great armory of means to control the implicit threat of adolescent disorder posed by the anomalies of their status. I mean not the police and the courts or the more informal weapons wielded by parents, school principals, and other authorities; I mean the community youth center, the chaperoned dance, organized sports, extracurricular clubs, and the junior auxiliaries of business, religious, fraternal and veterans' organizations—to say nothing of the comprehensive high school itself. Potential adolescent rebelliousness is controlled by a complex network of adult-sponsored youth organizations and by their promise of a bright future to those adolescents who can learn to live with and tolerate the temporary frustrations and deprivations of adolescence.

Of course, the effectiveness of these organizational weapons in coping with youth varies with the location of particular youths in the social structure. Where adult leadership is poor and community facilities limited (as frequently occurs in urban slums and certain new suburbs) or where sudden discontinuities in style of life create intergenerational tensions (as frequently occurs in immigrant or highly mobile families), or where failure or anticipated failure in academic competition leaves the failed with the perception of a bleak future and with no approved, alternative sources of self-respect (as frequently occurs among Negro and lower-class boys in predominantly middle-class schools) — where these conditions exist we can expect to find high rates of adolescent disorder.

Most of the kids who get into trouble, in short, are those who are denied *both* the rights of adults *and* the com-

pensations for this deprivation which the society tries to provide.

NOW, for a society to subject so substantial a part of its population to such severe pressures, and then to devote so much of its energies to avoiding explosions, seems like a particularly wasteful way for it to handle its youth. But we really don't know what else to do with them, for the "problem" of adolescence is inherent in something we are unwilling to change — the very structure of industrial societies.

The imposition of adolescence on young persons is not a simple accident of history nor the ethical result of revulsion with the facts of child labor, nor even an attempt by gerontocracies to postpone the succession of generations. It is by now quite common knowledge that, as societies industrialize, their need for the relatively unskilled labor of the young declines, and this tends to render a large part of youth economically superfluous.

Such societies have the problem of coping with economically useless persons while encouraging them to develop the skills which the economy needs. "Adolescence"—that is, the definition of young persons as not fully competent citizens—justifies the control that society exerts over them. It helps keep youth juvenile until society has readied an adult place for the young.

One of the functions of adolescence, then, is to keep young people off the labor market. But not only must they be kept off the labor market but off the streets and out of trouble as well; hence the whole range of adult-sponsored organizations designed to keep the young wholesomely occupied and distracted while they are readied for participation in the world of grownups.

The comprehensive high school, of course, is the most important means of controlling adolescents, and although the current campaign to reduce the number of "dropouts" is without doubt correct in warning those who are contemplating dropping out that their future

occupational chances will be severely reduced, staying in high school is less important for the jobs it will qualify one for than for the reduced pressure it provides on a labor market unable to absorb the unskilled. I severely doubt that a high-school diploma equips one to perform very many jobs that a person with a 10th or 11th-grade education could not perform.

Another thing that adolescence helps industrial societies to accomplish is the detachment of young persons from their families and locales, which helps fit them for social mobility. One of the features of traditional societies that industrialism destroys is the capacity of families, particularly fathers, to train their children for economic roles. As families are rendered inadequate to the task of training children for making a living as adults, this task falls increasingly to public agencies, which segregate the young for a large part of the day in places called schools.

But schools do more than simply take over the education-

What, besides age, identifies the teen-ager? Exuberance (as shown by Beatle fans, opposite), concentrated study, telephonitis. Not to mention jukeboxes, movie stars, romantic love, hot rods, panty raids, hamburgers and basketball games.

al function from families; by bringing large numbers of young people together for a common purpose, the schools help shift the orientations and loyalties of teen-agers from their families to their peer groups, and in a way this makes excellent sense for the future. Getting ahead in the adult world increasingly means the necessity for physical removal from the persons and place of one's youth, and strong family and kinship feelings as well as sentimental ties to "soil" and locale discourage social mobility.

On the other hand, strong peer-group ties (so long as they are not ties to specific persons) equip one for mobility by promoting experience and poise in "getting along" with friends and acquaintances who are one's age-mates. Blood may indeed be thicker than water, but for the sustenance of the kind of society we are making, it had better not be.

The price of social advancement is frequently separation from kin and community. The telephone company knows this, and can undertake a national advertising campaign for long-distance calls under the safe assumption that one's kin live at such distances that one can see them only infrequently. Where this is true, friends must be able to serve as a kind of substitute for unavailable relatives. But friends not obligated by blood must be found, and once found, kept, and are kept best by the sort of skill in casual cordiality developed in an adolescence crowded with one's age-mates.

ADOLESCENCE, then, by creating teen-agers and defining them as less than fully competent citizens, helps keep young unskilled persons off a labor market which has little need for them; and the pseudo-society of adolescents, created by their segregation for a large part of the day in schools, helps detach them from the more traditional kinship influences which might impede their mobility. But perhaps the most important function credited to adolescence is the achievement of personal "identity."

One of the most civilizing features of adolescence is what certain psychologists and psychoanalysts call the "psychosocial moratorium" it provides, that is, a period of years free from adult pressures, commitments and responsibilities, in which young persons may engage in "the search for identity," that stormy process in which adolescents may play and experiment with social roles in an attempt to find out who and what they are.

In this view, adolescence terminates with the development of a firm and stable "identity" capable of adult choices and commitments, and this development, promoted by a long adolescence, is frequently praised as one of the triumphs of modern civilization because of the individuality it engenders. I find two serious difficulties with this view.

First, I see little evidence that the institutions designed to care for adolescents during the "psycho-social moratorium" are contributing much to "identity play" or experiments with social roles. Rather, it seems that the high schools and other youth organizations are more devoted to the rapid, assembly-line fabrication of junior grownups than they are to the cultivation of individuality. Moreover, the feared shortage of college openings creates great pressures among middle-class children for premature commitment, especially occupational commitment, which tends to restrict rather than expand the horizons of personal identity.

Second, even if the conditions were optimal, there would still be a serious question about the value of a "firm identity." I see no good psychological reason for the stormy search for identity to end with adolescence (though I see how socially convenient this would be); nor do I see any good reason to believe that a "firm" and "stable" identity is under all circumstances preferable to a flexible and unstable one.

These days, a firm identity often seems to manifest itself as pig-headedness, and a stable one as stubborn rigidity. Moreover, in a rapidly changing society where social and geographic mobility puts enormous pressures on larger and larger numbers of people to anticipate the new demands that unfamiliar life situations may make on them tomorrow, a flexible, unstable identity seems like a very useful thing

to command however offensive such plasticity of personality may seem to those who have been intellectually bred on psychiatric euphemisms for "strength" of character.

IF the very concept of adolescence is an idea which has functioned historically to keep the young out of adult society, the complex phenomenon we have come to call "youth culture" has functioned to keep them distracted and happy while kept out. Whatever sense there is to the notion that adolescents dominate our culture rests on the fact that they constitute a major market, perhaps *the* major market, for several of the important industries of mass entertainment and popular culture. Young persons "consume" TV, movies and popular music, for example, so far out of proportion to their numbers in the population that in this country "popular culture" is very nearly identical with "youth culture."

But there are several varieties of youth culture in America, varieties as wide as the different cultural contexts and opportunity systems offered by a pluralistic society. At its broadest and most innocuous, youth culture touches the fringes of what is called "teen-age culture": popular songs, rock and roll, disk jockeys, jukeboxes, portable phonographs, movie stars, dating and romantic love; hot rods, motorcycles, drag racing and sports cars; panty raids and water fights, drive-in hamburgers and clandestine drinking, football games, basketball games, dances and parties, and clubs and cliques, and lovers' lanes.

At its delinquent extreme, youth culture is black-leather jackets, gang rumbles and switchblades, malicious mischief and joyriding in stolen cars. Politically, it is expressed in sit-ins, freedom rides, peace marches and folk songs; it is jazz at Newport, vacations at Fort Lauderdale — and their attendant riots. And it is also bohemians and beatniks and beards and hipsters, and coffee-shop desperadoes plotting everything from literary magazines to assaults on the House Committee on Un-American Activities.

To the extent that the sound and images of popular culture invade the eye and ear at every turn, they create much of the surface texture of perceived everyday life in America, and hence reflect the influential role played by youth in the creation and the marketing of mass culture.

Now this is rather puzzling because there is no immediate

"The proverbial idealism of youth may be channeled into politics . . . topical folk songs, freedom rides, sit-ins." Here, young pickets outside a Federal office in New York.

self-evident reason why popular culture should be dominated by youth except, perhaps, the very existence of adolescence and consequences attributable to it. By defining young persons as "teen-agers," that is, as "not ready" for the serious matters of adulthood, adolescence invites their absorption in the frivolous matters of "teen-age culture," and the leisure and the unprecedented affluence of teenagers predispose them to accept that invitation.

It may well be that the very fact of their *exclusion* from responsible participation in the major adult social institutions increases the sensitivity of adolescents to the more purely *symbolic* aspects of the culture. The proverbial "idealism" of youth is without question partly a matter of this absorption with the symbolic, and the "irresponsibility" which adolescence imposes on them.

The dominant tendency among teen-agers is to channel this idealism into a sentimental preoccupation with romantic love, as this is expressed in the music, lyrics and rhythm of popular culture; less often, the idealism is channeled into politics. For some it is the purity of the Beatles and the pure erotic frenzy of their appearances; for others it is topical folk songs, freedom rides and sit-ins.

I do not mean morally to equate these two modes, but only to emphasize their common source in the adolescent condition: alienation from practical adult affairs and a compensatory absorption with the symbolic, the ideal, the ideological. But regardless of whether their major preoccupations are the Beatles and

basketball or peace and civil rights, adolescents tend to throw themselves into these preoccupations with great purity and idealism.

AT the same time, adolescence as we know it in this country ill prepares young persons for the futures that actually await most of them. The qualities of the young that our culture celebrates the most — the purity and the idealism, the passion, candor, bluntness, spontaneity and so on — are precisely the qualities that the conditions of adult life make most difficult to sustain.

This is probably why most of the culture heroes of youth (not the men and women they say they want to be like, but the figures who actually affect their style, demeanor and orientation) are not the political or economic or religious or other leaders of major institutional sectors of the adult world but figures from the various worlds of show business, whose milieux are closest in feeling and style to the adolescent world itself.

The "adolescent problem" is at root a problem of age grading, to which our society has found no systematic solution—except to keep pushing up the chronological age at which people may still be legitimately referred to as "kids." It is altogether likely that the problem of adolescence, like the problem of slums and poverty and urban traffic, is a problem we will simply have to learn to live with and work at piecemeal since we are unwilling to change the basic conditions which generate it.

June 13, 1965

JUVENILE DELNQUENTS

BOY GANGS ON RISE, GIRLS A PROBLEM

Young 'Runaways' Increase, Says OWI, Since 'Father Has Gone to War, Mother to Work'

WASHINGTON, Oct. 9 (U.P.)— The war has brought a tremendous increase in the number of boys' "gangs" and young "runaways," unprecedented growth in truancy and theft cases, and an alarming spread of venereal disease, particularly among young girls, the Office of War Information stated tonight.

In a comprehensive report on juvenile delinquency in the United States, based on information from a source of public and private agencies, OWI said that the number of juvenile delinquency cases involving boys increased 11.3 per cent from 1940 through 1942, while delinqeuncy among young girls jumped an alarming 38 per cent.

Discussing the various "patterns" of juvenile delinquency, the report put "pick-up girls" high on the list. It said a survey of 878 cities showed such girls were increasing in number and decreasing in age.

Pick-up Girl "Menace"

Describing the pick-up girl as "a public menace, particularly in communities near military camps and war plants," the OWI said she "frequently has uniform hysteria." Often these girls are infected with general disease, the report said, and in many of the 162 areas investigated "girls as young as 12 and 13 are infected."

Juvenile delinquency throughout the country increased 16.6 per cent during the three years, and in one community it jumped 77 per cent, the report said.

The number of cases coming before eighty-three courts increased from 65,000 in 1940 to 75,500 last year, it added. All age groups showed increases, with the greatest being noted in the group 14 years of age and over. The percentage of increase was two and a half times as great among white children as among Negroes, the OWI said. In past years juvenile delinquency cases involving boys outnumbered girl cases six to one, the report went on, but the ratio now is five to one.

"There is a definite connection between war and delinquency," OWI said. "Father has gone to war; mother has gone to work. Homes are crowded. There is no place for the youngster to play; no place for the older girls to entertain. The living room is a bedroom. The youngsters are pushed into the street; may end up in the cheap hotel."

Boys always have belonged to "gangs," OWI said, but in recent years the average number of gangs has grown from two or three to 15 or 20, and in one instance 32 boys were listed in one "gang." Also, they involve more boys from the "privileged" classes, the report said.

"Commando gangs, often the result of misdirected war enthusiasm, try to imitate the older brothers in service, and sometimes begin by stealing real guns to replace their wooden one," the report continued. "Stealing is often a requisite, and in some instances, an illicit sex experience is a requirement for membership."

Concerning remedies, the report said, Federal, State and community governments must coordinate public and private efforts to solve the problem. Some of the most effective remedies are the "Dry Night Club," YWCA-USO dances and entertainments, and curfew laws. Recreation is not a magic cure-all but is an important preventive measure, the report asserted.

October 10, 1943

Boy Gangs of New York: 500 Fighting Units

Boys' conflict gangs demand strong loyalties. Can these qualities be turned to good account?

By BRADFORD CHAMBERS

THERE are more than 500 conflict gangs of boys in New York City, boys banded together to fight other gangs. Every day somewhere in the city there are street battles between them. Often boys are stabbed, occasionally shot, sometimes killed.

Gangs are an old story in New York. But today the activities of the boys and girls—for there are many girls' auxiliaries to these gangs—are inspired to some degree by racial and religious hatred, a manifestation of two of our most pressing social problems—juvenile delinquency and racial antagonism.

During the last year I have been trying to find out what is behind this racial gang warfare and what, if anything, can be done to combat it. For some time I had been working with the Friends of Democracy in New York, where reports kept coming in that the gang wars were being aggravated by fascist and Nazi sympathizers. I went to the gangs themselves for information. I hung around boys on street corners and in back alleys, offered them cigarettes, asked them what they had to gripe about, and invited them to my home. Gradually I was lucky enough to gain their confidence and friendship. I could find little evidence of subversive activities, but I did learn a lot of other interesting things.

The evolution of the gang out of the young people's natural play group is almost inevitable in certain communities. The conflict gang must not be confused with the loosely knit social or athletic club, or the street club, of which there are thousands, all comparatively harmless. The conflict gang aims to excel in battle with gangs of a different race or religion. Its greatest sport is a good fight. Such gangs exist because they provide security and excitement to their members in insecure surroundings. They satisfy the urge for adventure, a natural desire of all youth, and give opportunity for the exercise of loyalty to the group that is also strong among boys, even the bad ones. And a good many members of these fighting gangs have been in reformatories.

The ganglands I have come to know are in the borderline districts—neighborhoods situated between segregated communities of different race, creed or nationality. The dominant attitude here is one of fear, suspicion and antagonism. The young people, above all else, lack security and constructive direction. The gangs in these communities have primarily one purpose—protective security.

IN the case of the white communities, protection is sought from the Negroes who are being crowded out of their segregated areas. The Negro gangs in turn fight them. In some sections Catholic gangs fight Jews, and the Jews fight Catholic and Protestant gangs. There are Italian, Spanish and Puerto Rican gangs, which fight one another for various reasons.

Though the size of the gangs varies considerably, their organization is fairly uniform. Members range in age from 11 to 17 years. Many of the boys left school before finishing or are confirmed truants. Each gang has its name (often printed on the shirt), its leader and its hang-out—a street corner, alleyway or cellar. Cellar hang-outs are much scarcer than they were before the war, as the police have hedged them with many restrictions.

Gang leaders are generally called "captains" and are almost invariably chosen on the basis of personality and physical prowess. A captain must be bold and successful in combat, a "big shot." He must also be a "right guy." In most gangs major questions are submitted to a vote, and the captain may be overruled, but not if he has the personality to be a real

159

leader. And this mere fact of the gang as a group yielding to majority rule is one of the little things that indicates how fundamental this need of group association is in boys, and how it might be turned to good account.

In conflict and out of conflict the gang acts as one. Solidarity is one of the gang's strongest features. Fear of being ridiculed or kicked out of the gang, and a keen desire to be looked up to by fellow-members, compel uniformity to the wishes of the gang, no matter what outsiders may say. Unlucky is the boy who does not show up for a designated battle.

Some gangs are highly organized. The "Chancellors" in Harlem, for example, are divided into definite sections—Tiny Tims, Midgets or Cubs, Juniors and Seniors-ranging from 7 through the 'teens. One gang also divides its members into "fighters," who beat up members of opposing gangs on sight; "maybe-fighters," who give battle only in arranged forays, and "peacefuls," who fight only when the gang is attacked. The purpose is to gain such a fighting name that no other group will ever dare start anything. It is like an army with so many reserves that it is irresistible.

The girl auxiliaries of gangs are called the "debutante" or "sub-deb" divisions. Occasionally these divisions serve as the harems of the senior boy members, for there is considerable sexual promiscuity. The girls frequently carry the boys' weapons, walking slightly behind them or across the street so that if a policeman should search the boys, no concealed weapons will be found.

THESE weapons are nothing to joke about. Clubs and knives, usually fish knives, are the most common. To use a knife on another boy is to "mess him up," "topsy" or "shank" him. Brass knuckles (ash or garbage can handles), crude blackjacks (sometimes made in school workshops), pieces of broken bottles and ice picks are also handy weapons.

But the boys show remarkable ingenuity in making their guns. They use a four-inch piece of pipe with an opening large enough to take a .22-caliber bullet, and fasten the pipe to a block of wood with wire or tape. Then a firing pin is made from another piece of metal, and the metal of which the pin is a part is pulled back against the pressure of a heavy rubber band, the other end of which goes around the forward end of the block to which the tube is fastened. When the band is released the firing pin strikes the cartridge with sufficient force to explode it and send a bullet two or three blocks. The guns are usually used at short range, where they are reasonably accurate and deadly. Boys have been killed with these things.

The sources of the metal tube and the rubber band are interesting. The tube that receives the collapsing radio antenna on an automobile makes a pistol barrel when cut down to size. There is also a piece of metal tubing in street-light lamp posts, behind the little door where the light can be turned off, that can be used. (One reason lights sometimes go off in certain sections of the city.) A source of rubber is the inner tube of an automobile tire that can be reached by carefully cutting through the shoe of the tire. A short section of tubing will make a lot of tough rubber bands.

I have seen several battles, one that might truly be called a planned blitz. I happened to be on the corner of Amsterdam Avenue and 122d Street with six Negro boys, members of the Buccaneers, an athletic gang who had been playing baseball earlier.

I HAD been talking with the Buccaneers for about an hour and was just leaving when four white boys, no more than 12 years old, rushed by and grabbed the baseball bat. The Buccaneers, seeing that they were older and that they outnumbered their attackers, gave chase, yelling, "Let's beat the hell out of those white skunks." In the middle of the next block the fleeing boys (from the Midget division of the Robbins, a white gang) were caught.

At once from two corners of the intersection streamed ten or more Robbin Seniors. Simultaneously cans filled with pebbles and ashes toppled from the roof tops on both sides of the street. The six Negroes turned to flee, but escape had been cut off. From the opposite side of the street came more Robbins, and what appeared to be a massacre was on. Soon, however, hearing the racket, a brother gang of the trapped Buccaneers came to the rescue. The fight that resulted was definitely not play. By the time military police, who happened to be in the district, broke up the fight more than thirty boys had participated.

"We'll get them yet," screamed one of the Robbins, as I dragged him against his will to a drug store for treatment of a badly slashed face. I asked the only policeman in the neighborhood if he had made any arrests.

"Look," he said, "I'm on night duty and this is a pretty common occurrence. If I arrest these kids I have to appear in court tomorrow to bring charges. That's extra time for me and I don't get paid for it."

GANG warfare is not a summer pastime. Nor is it confined to boys. The girl auxiliaries are trained by the boy members of some gangs. They make vicious fighters and have the boys' respect. One of their weapons is a more than adequate vocabulary. They also serve as decoys to waylay the gang's enemies.

To the gang, to fight is to be tough; to be tough brings respect and power. But gangs can be utilized for worth-while ends. In fact, because of their influence, gangs can become real preventive forces against delinquency and crime. For, with all their anti-social points, gang philoso-phy has hidden in it the worthwhile elements of leadership, discipline, initiative, spirit and loyalty. If we were to make use of these characteristics and redirect the gang into constructive activities, then their influence on their satellites would be as great as before but it would be a constructive pattern the gang would set in its community.

WHAT can be done for them? Some of these boys are undoubtedly hopeless. They will always be toughs, and many of them will be criminals. They have gone too far to conform to a new pattern. But the majority of them can be helped. They all come from poor homes; poverty is one thing they have in common. But whereas some of their homes are repulsive, others are neat and clean, and the parents in these better homes do their best to guide their sons and daughters, but without much influence against the gang spirit.

It has been suggested that a start might be made by forming athletic and civic leagues in a few small communities in the city, leagues which would be associations of the existing gangs. We must keep their group organization, and let the boys themselves govern it, without imposing too much authority on them from the top, something they resent. And what they do must be made exciting to attract them.

Each community would have a store or other suitable meeting place as headquarters for its local league. Members of the league would meet here with older district leaders to decide on their activities. Tournaments within the league, block parties, civic and other activities could be developed. And of great value would be a larger meeting place where these leagues could meet together to discuss their affairs, and listen to persons they respect, star athletes, baseball and football players and boxers. Motion pictures of college and professional games could be shown.

THE local organization, or league, would express itself through a weekly newspaper, written largely by the boys themselves, for they dearly love publicity. The paper would criticize and make constructive suggestions. If they had their own paper, published by their own organization, it would be anticipated reading material each week. And the possibilities of reaching and arousing the parents and the general public through such a dramatic enterprise are also many.

It can be done. In one or two test communities ways can be worked out to reach most of the tough boys, and, if successful, these leagues would spread all over the city.

December 10, 1944

NEGRO CRIME RISE LAID TO SLUMS, BIAS

Delinquency Among Children Called Social Problem by Citizens Committee

While noting a comparative rise in delinquency among Negro children, the City-Wide Citizens Committee on Harlem in a report issued yesterday branded as "lurid fiction" and a "myth" the generalization that Negroes were "criminalistic" and declared that the roots of crime were the same among all ethnic groups.

Responsibility for the increase was ascribed to conditioning factors, slums and discrimination, and

not to the physical characteristics of a "generally law-abiding people." The report was prepared by Edwin J. Lukas, chairman of the sub-committee on crime and delinquency.

"Until the economic and social and political welfare of the Negro are improved," it said, "there will be no substantial diminution of crime and delinquency among Negroes. There is no delinquency and crime problem ascribable to the Negro as such; it is a problem chiefly involving the attitude of officialdom in particular and of society in general toward the Negro."

The most "shocking" of the statistics, according to the report, was that while the number of "neglected" white children was 24 per cent less for the first four months of this year than for the corresponding period in 1944, the number of "neglected" Negro children was 16 per cent greater.

In the more serious category of

delinquency, Negro children reflected an increase of 9 per cent over 1943 in the same period that cases of white children dropped below 1943, the report said. The total of delinquent Negro children in the first four months of 1945 was 6 per cent greater than in the same portion of 1944.

The report declared that the race discrimination amendment adopted in 1942 had not fully solved the problem of placement of Negro children in institutions to aid them. Some institutions were said to be accepting Negro children only in "token quantity," while others were alleged to have "refused to alter their policy of discrimination." Still others, it was said, had reversed their former attitude of non-acceptance and had "discovered that these children live with white children in complete harmony in an intramural atmosphere."

The committee said it planned to meet with Welfare Commissioner

Harry W. Marsh this week to "discuss ways to insure full compliance" with the amendment.

Other phases of the committee's activities in prevention and treatment were cited as extension of Big Brother work to Negro children, adequate probationary and psychiatric care for Negro children in the courts and schools and provision for playgrounds and community centers and play space in parks, to be extended in equal portion to Negro children.

A city-wide Harlem Week sponsored by the committee will begin today. Tomorrow at a meeting in Town Hall the principal speaker will be Irving Ives, majority leader of the Assembly and sponsor of the State anti-discrimination bill bearing his name. A report will be submitted on the city's gains and goals in race relations.

May 27, 1945

THE YOUTHFUL CRIMINAL

Although it has many other problems on its mind, this nation is not too busy to look forward with deep interest to the program for action that will develop from the National Conference for the Prevention and Control of Juvenile Delinquency, which is closing its three-day session in Washington this evening. Representatives of more than a dozen Federal agencies have been taking part in this conference, attended by about a thousand delegates from all over the country.

President Truman told the meeting that the roots of their problem lay in the homes, the schools, the neighborhoods and churches of our nation. This makes it the task of every one of us, and it is a task whose aspect grows

increasingly alarming. Only ten days ago J. Edgar Hoover gave us the figures: all crime in the United States up 8 per cent between 1945 and 1946; arrests of persons under 21 accounting for 51 per cent of all auto thefts, 42 per cent of burglaries, 25 per cent of rapes and 28 per cent of robberies.

This conference was in the making for nearly a year, with Attorney General Tom Clark its moving spirit. He counts "helping youngsters who are in trouble" one of the important functions of his department. This nation, which knows how fully the future rests upon the moral integrity of its boys and girls, awaits leadership and a program that attacks that problem with vigor and intelligence.

November 22, 1946

NOTES

WAYNE—Delinquency Study

Over 80 per cent of the boys who get into trouble with the police come from average homes with adequate incomes, according to a study by Dr. William W. Wattenburg of Wayne University. Based on statistics compiled and collected by the Crime Prevention Bureau of the Detroit Police Department, the study found that only 15 per cent of the delinquents came from substandard slum neighborhoods. The majority of the youngsters suffered neglect from their parents.

January 11, 1948

DELINQUENCY LAID TO HOME FACTORS

10-Year Study of 500 'Bad,' 500 'Good' Boys Is Pointed Up in Five Groupings

Special to The New York Times.

CAMBRIDGE, Mass., Oct. 21—The quality of home life determines whether a child will become a juvenile delinquent, it was reported here in one of the most comprehensive studies of the causes of juvenile delinquency ever made.

This was the major finding of a ten-year study conducted by Prof. Sheldon Glueck and Dr. Eleanor Touroff Glueck of the Harvard Law School, under auspices of the school and financed by a number of leading foundations.

A husband and wife team noted

for their research in the field of criminology and delinquency, the Gluecks based their findings on a study of 500 delinquent boys living in the slum areas of Boston, and a control group of 500 boys from the same area who did not get into trouble with the police.

They found that if the child's family life was adequate, the chances were only three in 100 that he would turn out to be a delinquent, whereas if his family situation was poor, the chances were ninety-eight out of 100 that he would become a delinquent.

Most Common Factors

The factors that showed up most among delinquent boys were: A father whose discipline was lax, or overstrict or erratic (not firm and kindly); a mother who left the boy to his own devices without provision for a healthy use of his leisure time; a father or mother who rejected the boy emotionally, and a family whose home was "just a place to hang your hat."

The Gluecks found differences between the delinquents and the

non-delinquents on two major points—character traits and personality traits. If a boy was markedly willful, assertive, defiant of everyone, suspicious and hostile without reason, wanted to destroy or hurt others and himself and "exploded" emotionally regardless of consequences, there was "every chance in the world that he would turn out to be a delinquent," they predicted.

If his personality was such that he was usually looking for excitement, change or risk, if he ordinarily did what he pleased, if he usually resisted because he felt thwarted, and if his feelings were in conflict and he had "unharmonious or inappropriate" feelings, the chances were ninety-three in 100 that he would become a delinquent, they estimated. If he scored low on all these points, the chances were only five in 100 that he would develop into a delinquent.

Family Relationships Stressed

They concluded that the kind of relationships that existed in a home between the boy and his par-

ents had far more to do with delinquency than whether he lived in a slum area, or grew up among conflicting cultures, or came from a large family or from a family where there was much ill health, or had a high or low I. Q.

"It is clear that in the home and in the parent-child relations are to be found the crucial roots of character which make for acceptable or unacceptable adjustment to the realities of life in society," they said.

They warned that "little progress can be expected in the prevention of delinquency until family life is strengthened by a large-scale, continuous, pervasive program designed to bring to bear all the resources of mental hygiene, social work, education, and religious and ethical instruction upon the central issue."

The Gluecks developed "prediction tables" from their findings that would separate, at an early age, the "probable" future delinquents from those likely to stay out of trouble. This can be used only by skilled specialists, they asserted.

Minor Offenses Written Off

Minor childhood offenses, such as smoking, staying out late and petty stealing are no indication that a boy will become a persistent violator of the law, they found. One-fourth of the non-delinquent boys "had been guilty of the usual boyish pranks and peccadilloes which might have caused a passing policeman to arrest them."

Among the delinquent boys more than half were older than eight years at the first "clear" signs of a persistent tendency to misbehavior. The I. Q. scores of the two groups ranged from 60 to 120, with the average for delinquents 92, and for the non-delinquents 94.

Summarizing their findings into what they called "a dynamic causal pattern," the Gluecks held that the delinquents, as a group, were distinguishable from the non-delinquents in the following way:

1. Physically — In being solid, closely knit, muscular in consti-

tution.

2. Temperamentally — In being restlessly energetic, impulsive, extroverted, aggressive, destructive, often sadistic.

3. In attitude—By being hostile, defiant, resentful, suspicious, stubborn, socially assertive, adventurous, unconventional, nonsubmissive to authority.

4. Intellectually—In tending to direct and concrete, rather than symbolic, intellectual expression, and in being less methodical in their approach to problems.

5. Socio-culturally—In having been reared to a far greater extent than the non-delinquent boys in homes in which the "under-the-roof culture" was "bad," that is, homes of little understanding, affection, stability or moral fiber.

"In general, the high probability of delinquency is dependent upon the interplay of the conditions and forces from all these areas," they concluded.

October 22, 1950

Youth Narcotic Use Growing

LEXINGTON, Ky., Nov. 4 (UP) —The addiction of teen-agers to narcotics is increasing rapidly, an official of the United States Public Health Hospital here said today. Dr. Victor Vogel said the hospital roll showed the number of patients under 20 years of age rose from thirteen in 1948 to 203 this year. "It looks like a definite effort on the part of peddlers to contact teen-agers," he said. The hospital, which is the only one of its kind in the United States, has one 14-year-old under treatment.

November 5, 1950

CHILD CRIMES RISE AND GROW WORSE

Survey Links Trends to Wars and Shows Sharp Increase Since Korean Outbreak

WASHINGTON, Jan. 3 (AP) — Children in scores of cities are committing more crimes and worse crimes than at any time since World War II.

The Associated Press, in a survey of juvenile court records in nearly all major cities, has found that juvenile delinquency started to increase in many cities in 1948, that the rate jumped in more cities after the Korean outbreak and that it was now rising fast in many areas.

If the rise continues it will soon reach the rate of the World War II peak.

Juvenile crime always increases in wartime. Experts at the United States Children's Bureau are deeply concerned about the heights it may reach if the Korean conflict and the cold war mobilization program continues for many years.

Associated Press bureaus throughout the country endeavored to obtain statistics on delinquency from juvenile courts in all cities of more than 100,000 population. It received the figures from sixty of the 106 cities of that size in twenty-six states and from this city.

Survey Factors Variable

Juvenile crime has decreased in only four of the sixty-one cities. In nine there was no trend up or down. In forty-eight cities the number of juvenile delinquency cases has increased.

The figures in most instances represent cases referred to the courts, although in some cities only figures on total police cases among children were obtainable.

The situation is not quite so bad as at first it appears to be. In a considerable number of the cities showing an increase the population rise accounts for all or part of it. And in some cities the systems of keeping records or the age limits for juveniles subject to the court have been changed. Some city boundaries have been extended. All these factors could affect the count.

After World War II the juvenile crime rate began to decline. In thirteen of the forty-eight cities now showing an increase the low point was reached in 1948. In twenty-two cities the decline continued until 1950.

The population was growing during the years that the juvenile delinquency rate was falling. The number of children between 10 and 17 — juvenile court age in most jurisdictions — increased between 1948 and 1951 at almost exactly the rate of the total population: 5 per cent.

The number of children from 10 to 17 is expected to increase 42 per cent between 1951 and 1960 while the total population will be increasing only 16 per cent. The Census Bureau bases this estimate on the high birth rate during the war and post-war years.

Rate a Million a Year

About a million children get into trouble with the police each year. If the total increases only in proportion to the child population the courts and police will have to handle 1,420,000 child cases in 1960. If the increasing rate of juvenile delinquency continues the total of cases in 1960 will be much greater.

The survey revealed a rise in serious crimes committed by juveniles. It is difficult to think of children as burglars, gangsters, drug addicts or murderers. Such has become the reality, however.

A San Diego official said that the use of narcotics — marijuana mostly at first, with later switching to heroin—was "not on the decrease." New Orleans authorities reported that the use of narcotics by children was increasing.

Juveniles who get into trouble are younger than they used to be in many of the cities. H. J. Palmieri, in charge of social work for the Washington Juvenile Court, said that the average age of offenders had dropped three years. Juvenile housebreakers used to be 16 or 17, he added, but now they were often 13 to 15. Some housebreaking has been committed by children from 10 to 12.

Sex offenses among children have increased so much in Tulsa, Okla., that they exceeded the number of burglaries in 1951. Usually there are not many offenses of this type among boys, but many courts find sex figuring in most crime by girls.

Nearly all juvenile court judges and social workers declare home influences to be a major factor in juvenile delinquency. Nearly all agreed also that the two wars started much of the trouble for children. Wars tend to break up homes and create other factors adverse to the welfare of children.

"Delinquent parents" were blamed by many of the officials. An official in Tampa, Fla., went back to "delinquent grandparents," saying that the parents probably would have been better mothers and fathers if they had had proper home environment.

Indianapolis authorities ascribed much of the increase in juvenile delinquency to the increase in divorce.

January 4, 1953

CHILD DELINQUENCY SHOWS NEW TREND

Rise in Middle Class Homes Is Cited—30% of Youngsters Held Emotionally Disturbed

'PUBLIC APATHY' NOTED

Dr. Bloch, Sociologist, Tells Crime Institute 'Distrust' of Psychiatrists Harms Work

By MURRAY ILLSON
Special to THE NEW YORK TIMES.

CANTON, N. Y., Aug. 17—Recent investigations show that 30 per cent of the country's juvenile delinquents suffer from serious emotional disturbances and that increasing numbers of these youths are coming from middle-class homes, a nationally known sociolo-

gist said here today.

Speaking at the fourth annual Frederick A. Moran Memorial Institute on Delinquency and Crime held at St. Lawrence University, Dr. Herbert A. Bloch, chairman of the university's Department of Sociology and Anthropology, declared that "public apathy and distrust of social scientists and psychiatrists" were handicapping efforts to cope with the problem.

Dr. Bloch said that specific types of homes, dependent on social and cultural circumstances, apparently were providing characteristic behavior traits in children. He asserted that youngsters with "fundamental neurotic disturbances seemed to emerge with considerable regularity in areas of relative stability, where parents presumably are intent upon giving the child normal and effective guidance, but where marital tensions tend to make the child overdependent upon one parent, usually the mother."

Poorer Areas Surveyed

"Characteristic of depressed economic areas," he said, "we find children who, in identifying themselves with gangs and anti-social teen-age groups, engage in delinquent activity, but do not necessarily reveal the emotional disturb-

ances of the economically favored children."

Dr. Bloch completed nine years of research in preparation for writing a volume on social disorganization, which was published recently. He declared that the increasing emergence of delinquent youth from homes of average or better than average economic status was a relatively new trend. As an indication of this he cited studies of Negro children and said that those from poorer economic surroundings were "emotionally sound but socially maladjusted" while "middle-class Negro children tend to reveal basic anxiety patterns characteristic of other groups of middle-class children." He went on to say:

"The trends in delinquency, as minority groups rise in economic status and are assimilated into the community, appear to be in their direction of contributing toward an increase in this rising neurotically orientated delinquency."

Dr. Bloch held that there was a general failure to "implement adequately the results of research so that it could indicate how we should attack the causes of delinquency." He urged that social scientists and psychiatrists "take an organized position" in the recommendation of policy for communities' guidance on delinquency problems. As a step in this direction he advocated popularizing the findings of the social sciences.

"Prediction For the Future"

Dr. Walter C. Reckless, Professor of Sociology at Ohio State University, told a session of the institute that "the prediction for the future" was an increasing disinclination to report so-called minor violations of legal codes. Among such violations he listed alcoholism, prostitution and statutory rape.

Msgr. Joseph E. Vogt, Roman Catholic chaplain at the State Agricultural and Industrial School for Boys at Industry, N. Y., said that most delinquent boys came from homes that did not have religious training and that there was a direct relationship between a lack of such training and delinquency. He added that 72 per cent of the boys who were discharged from the school would not get into further trouble.

The institute, which was named for the late chairman of the New York State Board of Parole, will continue through Friday. It is being attended by 450 police officers, teachers and workers in the field of social welfare, mental hygiene and correction. The meetings are supported by a $50,000 grant authorized by the state as a result of a request by Governor Dewey in his January message to the Legislature.

August 18, 1953

PSYCHIATRIST SEES CHILD-ADULT WAR

Delinquency is an Outgrowth of That Conflict, Chicagoan Tells Toronto Parley

By MURRAY ILLSON
Special to The New York Times.

TORONTO, Aug. 12—A generation of children is at war with a generation of adults and juvenile delinquency is an expression of this conflict, an international meeting of psychiatrists was told today.

Dr. Ruolf Dreikurs, Professor of Psychiatry at Chicago Medical School, termed delinquency a social problem "intensified by democratic development." He said "our children are becoming our equals and can no longer be pushed down by adults."

He spoke at the first International Congress on Group Psychotherapy, which is being held

in connection with the fifth International Congress on Mental Health that will open here Saturday and continue for a week.

The social values of juvenile delinquents are merely a distorted image of the values of the community, Dr. Dreikurs held. These values are centered on "personal prestige and glory, the seeking of gratification and making easy money," he continued.

Community Held Involved

Dr. Dreikurs, who is also director of Chicago community child-guidance centers, maintained that treatment of the problem must involve the community as a whole because delinquents generally did not respond to individual treatment.

He asserted: "We have to make peace between adults and children. We have to give juveniles a place in society. We must change adult attitudes toward children."

Dr. Joshua Bierer, medical director of the Institute of Social Psychiatry in London, said that 70 to 90 per cent of the effectiveness of child guidance depended on how effectively parents were

guided. He held that in most cases of disturbed children, the parents rather than the child needed intensive psychiatric treatment.

Too frequently, he added, the child gets the intensive treatment while the parents, who most likely are responsible for his mental or emotional disturbance, receive only the attention of a social worker.

Dr. Bierer declared that in the past the practice of psychiatry had involved "too much of an attempt to adapt the patients to the treatment, rather than the treatment to the patients." He said that in the London psychotherapy center all schools of psychiatric thought and methods were represented, and that staff members "get along very well, which is rare among psychiatrists."

Traditional time-consuming treatment methods will have to give way to shorter methods that are less costly for the average patient, he stressed.

Group psychotherapy, which is the treatment of patients in a group setting, was originally believed to be the answer to this problem, Dr. Bierer said, but he indicated that such treatment

was not satisfactory for some types of patient.

St. Louis Program Cited

A. D. Buchmueller, director of mental health service of the St. Louis County Health Department, described a program in the St. Louis area for developing comprehensive community care for emotionally disturbed children. He said the program was the only one of its kind in the country, having received a $38,000 research grant from the National Mental Health Institute of the United States Department of Health, Education and Welfare.

The program, which has been conducted in three school districts with 300 families taking part, seeks to train parents and teachers to detect early signs of emotional disturbance in children.

After three years of experiment, Mr. Buchmueller said, some tentative conclusions have been reached. One is that the program operated most smoothly with parents "in a lower-middle to upper-lower class area where there is a degree of social uniformity and no unusual minority or discriminatory sentiments."

August 13, 1954

CHILD DETENTION CALLED DISGRACE

By MURRAY ILLSON
Special to The New York Times.

ST. PAUL, Minn., June 21—Most of the country's detention facilities for delinquent children today were called "a disgrace to

the nation."

They were described by Sherwood Norman, director of detention services of the National Probation and Parole Association, which has its headquarters in New York. At a session of the association's annual conference being held here this week, he said:

"For all our professed concern about children, we show our contempt for those who are delinquent by locking them up by

the thousands to await hearings in a court which was intended to offer protection and treatment. I know of no other country in the world which engages in this practice so extensively.

"Not only do we detain far too many children, but the type of detention care we offer is primitive. It is estimated that nearly 100,000 children from 7 to 17 are detained annually in jails and jail-like places of detention throughout the country. Most of these county jails have

been classified as unfit for Federal adult prisoners."

Our Western Cultures

Mrs. De Etta Taylor, assistant director of the Essex County Detention Home in Newark, N.J., declared that "in our western cultures people have been beating and abusing children for centuries and are still doing so." She went on to say:

"I believe that those of us in child protective work have found no great reduction during the past ten years in the frequency of physical assaults upon children by parents or parental figures, acting in the name of character building or similar subterfuge.

"There still are bruised, welted and bleeding children as periodic exposés of institutions and prosecutions of parents for felonious assault reveal. I would expect

'back to the woodshed' advocates to deny any identification with sadism, but it is important to know what you are sponsoring when you encourage an increase in the frequency and severity of corporal punishment."

Dr. Adelaide Johnson, psychiatrist at the Mayo Clinic, Rochester, Minn., told the conference

that one or both parents often unconsciously permit or even foster delinquent behavior in their children. These parents, she said, unconsciously enjoy satisfaction from the child's anti-social actions.

June 22, 1955

DELINQUENCY RISE OF 9% IS REPORTED

500,000 Children in Nation Brought Into Court Last Year, U. S. Estimates

Special to The New York Times.

WASHINGTON, May 19—A 9 per cent increase in juvenile delinquency in 1955 was reported today by Dr. Martha M. Eliot, chief of the Children's Bureau of the Department of Labor. Dur-

ing that year the child population in the age group involved, 10 to 17, went up only about 3 per cent, she said.

Preliminary estimates based on reports from 977 juvenile courts to the bureau showed the 9 per cent increase over 1954. These reports would indicate that about 500,000 children had been brought into juvenile court between Jan. 1 and Dec. 31, 1955.

Preliminary estimates based on reports of a trend group of 383 courts, which have been reporting to the bureau for many years, likewise showed a 9 per cent increase for the year.

Dr. Eliot said that figures gathered by the Federal Bureau of Investigation bore out these preliminary findings.

The latest F. B. I. uniform crime report, she explained, shows an 11.4 per cent increase in police arrests of young persons under the age of 19 in 1955 as compared with 1954. Their report was based on data from 1,162 cities.

Dr. Eliot said that the bureau's juvenile delinquency consultants, a comparatively recent service, were working with the states in both prevention and treatment programs.

May 20, 1956

FEW GANG BATTLES LAID TO RACE BIAS

Experts Report Most Involve Neighborhood Factions— Housing Problem Cited

By IRA HENRY FREEMAN

Social workers agreed yesterday that racial antagonism had been the cause of only a small minority of the many battles among juvenile gangs in New York.

The gangs are organized, for the most part, along ethnic lines. But they rarely fight over those differences, experts on the problem insisted.

James E. McCarthy, deputy executive director of the New York City Youth Board, an official agency combating juvenile delinquency, estimated that of perhaps fifty serious "rumbles" fought or threatened in the city in a year, not more than 10 per cent had been caused by racial hatred.

"The boy gang is a neighborhood club, organized among the kids who live on a certain block," Mr. McCarthy explained. "If the street is tenanted by Negroes, the boy gang is Negro; if Puerto Rican, the gang is Puerto Rican, and so on.

"We must face the fact that the slums of New York, in which the juvenile gangs flourish, are mostly segregated—black ghettos, Puerto Rican, Irish, Italian ghettos. In the few mixed areas, like the Lower East Side, where the most recent gang war was

threatened, the boy gangs are mixed."

Two of the gangs involved in the threatened East Side "rumble," the Enchanters and Sportsmen, are composed in that neighborhood of Negroes, Puerto Ricans and Irish boys. On the other hand, the divisions of the Enchanters in West Harlem are virtually all Negro, because the community also is.

"Ninety per cent of the gang fights are between like ethnic groups," Mr. McCarthy said. "For example, the Dragons and Viceroys have been fighting each other in East Harlem almost exclusively for a long time, yet both are solidly Puerto Rican."

One "shocking" result of prejudice against Negroes and Puerto Ricans, Mr. McCarthy said, was to turn the resentment of the minorities against their own kind.

"To that extent," he commented, "you could say gang warfare is race warfare. It is not far-fetched to say that injustice by whites against Negro boys helps stimulate Negro boys to fight against other Negroes. Often race prejudice increases the hostility of the victims toward one another instead of toward the oppressor."

Racial gang fights are found mostly on the boundary line between segregated neighborhoods. For example, the Youth Board has noted that Puerto Rican boys who live between Third and Fifth Avenues in the vicinity of 110th Street do not dare swim in a public pool in Jefferson Park, at 110th Street and First Avenue. The streets east of Third Avenue are the "turf," or territory, of Italian gangs, who forbid Puerto Ricans to enter. The Puerto Rican youths from East Harlem travel to the pool at St. Mary's Recreation

Center in the Bronx, which is Puerto Rican "turf."

Housing Problem Cited

Other Youth Board executives noted that new public housing projects had increased juvenile delinquency in their first years, as different ethnic groups were mingled in previously homogeneous communities.

A spokesman for the City Housing Authority conceded that all its seventy-nine projects in the city were more or less interracial, but denied that that policy had contributed toward delinquency or gang fights. She did admit that one white-versus-Negro gang war had occurred in the neighborhood of Red Hook Houses in Brooklyn last November and December. Twenty-one families whose children had been involved were evicted from the project.

The Authority is so sure that desegregation is a good thing that it is still trying, after two years of indifferent success, to induce families other than Negroes and Puerto Ricans to move into Forest Houses in Morrisania, the Bronx. Up to now, the ratio of 657 families is: 59.4 per cent Negro, 34.8 per cent Puerto Rican, 5.8 per cent others.

Miss Betty Murrell, executive director of Forest Neighborhood House, leading settlement of the district, said her policy was to avoid grouping Puerto Ricans and Negroes in separate clubs. In three years of mixed activities, she has found no friction because of ethnic, religious, or language differences.

The Board of Education also does not believe that interracial mingling creates conflict in schools. Proposals by its com-

mittee on integration for rezoning school districts to bring Negroes, Puerto Ricans and other groups into the same classrooms are now being studied by the Board of Superintendents. The proposals may be effected, in part, this year.

The Police Department policy is not to discuss race as a juvenile delinquency problem at all. A spokesman would say only: "We do not regard race, religion or nationality as a major factor in juvenile delinquency or gang fights; it is a matter of individual personality."

Nevertheless, social workers grant there are some ethnic groups in New York who, because of tight family and community organization, produce remarkably few juvenile delinquents regardless of poverty, slum homes, or minority status.

Youth Board executives could recall only one Chinese delinquent in all their years of experience and only one family of Moslem children, all psychopathic. Few Jewish children are adjudged to be delinquent, but comparatively many are emotionally disturbed, these social workers said.

"Instead of knocking someone's head off," one of them said, "a disturbed Jewish child takes his tensions out inwardly, on himself."

Jacob Trobe, assistant executive director of the Jewish Board of Guardians, said that only 2.2 per cent of all children brought into Children's Court for misbehavior in 1952 were Jewish, while about 31.5 per cent of the total city population was Jewish. He vigorously denied, however, that Jewish children were more neurotic than others.

August 19, 1956

Gang Delinquency Defined

It Is Called the Rebellion Against Society of the Underprivileged

TO THE EDITOR OF THE NEW YORK TIMES:

A news story in The Times of Aug. 19, reports that James E. Mc-Carthy, deputy director of the New York City Youth Board, minimized ethnic-racial antagonisms as a cause of juvenile gang fighting and estimated that only about 10 per cent of gang fights were due to "racial hatred."

It should be noted, however, that gang warfare and delinquency are largely characteristic of adolescents of lower socio-economic groups. The fact that the great majority of Negroes and Puerto Ricans are in this category is definitely part of the pattern.

The precise role of ethnic discrimination is complex and not obvious on the surface, as Mr. McCarthy indicated when he said: "Injustice by whites against Negro boys helps stimulate Negro boys to fight against other Negro boys." A study of delinquency in Baltimore by Professor Landers shows lower delinquency rates for those districts which are completely Negro in composition than for those in which Negroes are a minority.

The gang type of delinquency—and most, though of course not all, delinquency is of this type—would appear to be a specific pattern in which many underprivileged adolescents express their rebellion and resentment against a society which promises much but actually gives them few rewards.

We need to reduce the isolation and ecological segregation of our lower socio-economic areas and open up opportunities in every aspect of living. Housing and education are vital fields for improvement.

The recent study sponsored by the Public Education Association showed that elementary and junior high schools which are largely Negro or Puerto Rican offer inferior opportunities to the very youngsters who are most in need of assistance. Our junior high schools, originally designed for the guidance of the young adolescent, still have to meet that challenge.   HENRY MILLER.
Assistant Professor, School of Education, The City College.
New York, Aug. 20, 1956.

August 27, 1956

The Teen-Age Gang— Who and Why

A reporter visits 'the Devils' for clues to the growing problem of delinquency.

By MURRAY SCHUMACH

THAT murky nursery and training ground of American crime—the juvenile gang—has become one of the nation's most important areas of first-hand investigation by the police, social workers, clergy and psychiatrists. In the weird social patterns and violent outbursts of these asphalt gangs, the experts are trying to find the answers to what produces the juvenile delinquent and how to cope with him.

The problem is growing more acute. A survey of 1,477 American cities by the Federal Bureau of Investigation shows that 42.3 per cent of those arrested in 1955 for major crimes—such as murder, rape, grand larceny and extortion—were under 18 years of age. This was an increase of 11 per cent over 1954. In New York City, a particularly favorable climate for youth gangs, the statistics are even more disturbing. Arrests of juveniles for major crime in the world's richest metropolis rose 41.3 per cent during the first six months of this year over the same period last year. The city's Youth Board says sixty-five anti-social gangs, with 3,000 members, endanger orderly life in the city. The police say the figure is higher, but refuse to say how much. Statistics of organized gangs, at any rate, tell only part of the story. For individual gang members, operating independently of their street-roaming parent groups, are responsible for much of the city's crime. They learned the way in the gangs.

Although no one of the New York City gangs can be considered "typical," most of them have a great deal in common. Membership is almost entirely from the neighborhood. This, more than prejudice, explains the racial character of so many gangs. Dictatorship and strict discipline mark the organization. Force is its guiding social principle. It recruits members by offering "rep"—prestige—and by intimidation. Almost always, each gang is part of a loose federation for warfare that may range from sneak raids with fists to massed attacks—"rumbles"—with guns. Headquarters may be a street corner, lot, park, playground, candy store, cafeteria, hallway or cellar. Most members do not attend school or hold regular jobs. Generally, these youths do not use dope.

IN most other respects, however, the gangs vary widely. Some gangs are recruited from slums, others from middle-class environments. Some have members largely from broken homes, others from apparently stable families. Some are children of immigrants, or are themselves immigrants. Others were born to native Americans. Some adorn themselves in flashy blazers, sneakers and Levis and let their hair grow long. Others dress without affectation. Some have auxiliary girl gangs, others repudiate such an idea.

Recently I spent a few days with a gang of juvenile delinquents—they call themselves a "crew" or "clique"—to try to learn its organization and composition; how it lives in peace and war; the forces that bring and hold the gang together; the values and mores that comprise its rather primitive code; the gang members' attitudes toward one another, the community, the police, social workers and adults in general.

The members of this gang—we shall call them the Devils—are almost entirely of Irish and Italian stock, with just a few of Jewish and German origins. Their parents were born in this country, mostly in the same Park Circle section of Brooklyn where they now live. Their environment is middle class, with a family income ranging from $3,000 to $6,000. They live mainly in one- or two-family homes along clean, tree-lined streets. For the most part they are nice-looking boys, who dress like most adolescents, in sport shirts, slacks and shoes. In rainy or cool weather they wear unmarked zipper jackets.

"If you're man enough," explained a Devil, "you don't need a name on your jacket."

THE Devils claim a membership of 175. This is probably greatly exaggerated. I met about twenty-five, and their hard-core membership probably does not exceed fifty. They are supreme over a territory—they call it "turf"—of nearly a square mile. Most of them have left school, though their average age is about fifteen and a half, ranging from 13 to 18. (Boys can leave school at 16. Those who are younger usually have truancy records so long they indicate chronic absenteeism.) Very few have regular jobs. Their organization is topped by a Leader, a War Counsellor and two Main Guys.

Tension hangs over the gang members, even now when they are virtually unchallenged and at peace with all except one of eight bordering gangs. When they gather at night at their headquarters outside a playground they are wary of every car that rolls by the bench around which they cluster. The car could contain invaders or detectives. With careful military sagacity they maintain outpost groups in other parts of their realm. Important members of the   *Continued*

MURRAY SCHUMACH, of The New York Times staff, has been reporting on New York City and its people for more than twenty years.

gang carry a list of telephone numbers for emergency mobilization.

"A clique could get in," conceded a Devil, "but they'd never get out. We'd cut them off before they knew what happened."

The police take no chances. One night a radio car passed slowly by the group at least once an hour for three hours. The last time—it was nearly midnight—the car stopped. One of the Devils whispered:

"Watch this. They're gonna bust us (disperse us). They're gonna pad us down (search us)."

The police studied them slowly and drove off without interfering.

THE next night, however, when some twenty of them were being noisy about 9 o'clock along a brightly lighted street, the police ordered their dispersal, then fragmentized the smaller groups. This was done without force. The youths obeyed, reluctantly. One of them muttered, "Some cops need a beating." But another youth had said, the preceding day, "Most cliques are breaking up. The cops are too hot."

The threatening atmosphere that envelops the Devils is accentuated by the incessant tendency to "rank" or "sound" one another. This is a combination of threat and insult in loud, foul language, whereby the members are constantly measuring one another. Their sudden bursts of sparring sometimes seem close to violence. Their derisive laughter, their swaggering, boisterous manner and eternal suspicion are reminders that the Devils are more than just hearty adolescents. So, too, is their warfare.

Their favorite tactic in gang fights, they say, is "pulling a Jap," or sneak raid. A group of Devils will drive at night into enemy territory and park a few blocks from the hangout of the enemy. When the rival gang breaks up, the Devils will follow by car one or two who have broken away from the main body. When these "strays" are beyond help, the group of Devils will beat them and drive off. Such an attack lasts only a few minutes. The raids continue until the enemy surrenders—"turns it off."

THEN there is the military maneuver known as "a fair one." On the surface it seems honorable. Each of the hostile gangs sends forth its champion, accompanied by five cohorts. The figure of six has become accepted because that many fit comfortably in a car. In a "fair one," the champions fight without weapons,

but everything goes—kicking, stomping, kneeing. In theory, there is no interference. Actually, the Devils admit their five "seconds" always attack the rival quintet.

The Devils say they have access to guns, but prefer to fight without weapons. They contend they were forced to acquire guns when they learned a rival gang had them. But they avoid the "rumble," or massed gang fight. They say only stupid gangs fight this way; it is the surest way to get picked up by the police.

THE fights stem from numerous causes. But these can be boiled down to two—invasion or insult. The Devils assert they always check rumors of boundary violation or of their crew being demeaned by others. They seek out witnesses, question them and then send out emissaries to the other crew for confirmation.

"We talk before we hit," says a Devil. "If we find out it's true, we hit."

I never saw the Devils violate the law. But sixteen of their members or alumni are in jail on charges that include extortion, grand larceny, and violation of the Sullivan Law. Most of those I met said they had been arrested—mostly, they declared, for unlawful assembly. They hinted at serious crimes but, for obvious reasons, refused to discuss them. They admitted they had committed wanton destruction of property in public or private buildings. Some of them, for instance, talked of having destroyed toilet fixtures at a recreation hall. They "used to" extort money from youngsters at school, some admitted, and "when we were kids" used to attack youngsters without gang affiliation "just for the kicks." They admit having carried guns in fights.

LIKE most organizations created for military operations, the Devils seem to spend a great deal of their time idly hanging around. Usually, they wake up about noon and reach the playground benches between 1 and 2 o'clock. Three or four afternoons a week they go to a nearby movie.

"You go to pick up girls," explained a Devil. "If there's no girls you watch the movie. If there's girls you make out with them—and watch the movie." The term "make out," in this case, usually means vigorous necking.

Occasionally, they will go swimming. Almost invariably they choose an area near Mill Basin not frequented by the public. They say they avoid

such places as Coney Island.

"We don't like to go where there's a lot of people," a Devil said. "Anytime we go to a place like Coney Island we get into trouble. A guy gives you a funny look. You say: 'What the —— you lookin' at?' You can't let guys get away with that stuff. Next thing you know there's trouble."

NOT long ago, the Devils agreed to accompany social workers on an outing to a Long Island beach. Soon after they arrived, there were objections from another bather about their loud, foul language. They told him to move. When he tried to silence the Devil who had made this suggestion, a few other Devils jumped him. A state trooper ended the picnic a short time later by ordering the Devils back on the bus and home.

Most evenings they loiter at the playground or wander in groups through the neighborhood. Sometimes, on hot nights, they dive from trees in Prospect Park into the lake. Thursday nights they meet at the playground to learn if any enemies have besmirched their rep or violated their turf. At this meeting they also consider whether any of their own members have to be "straightened out," punished. The transgression could be failure to attend meetings without good reason or consorting with an enemy group. Punishment could range from warning to beating. On this night they also plan their campaign for the dance the following night in Prospect Park. There they go in strength because it is alien territory and because they think it might be fruitful for girl-hunting.

Saturday nights they may go to parties, to a Coney Island rock-and-roll session or just drape themselves around the bench and sip a few cans of beer while they argue loudly.

They rise much earlier than usual on Sundays, for the 10 A. M. mass. Afterward, they watch a softball game in the playground, played by alumni of the Devils. They lunch at home—almost all their meals are at home—and return to the bench. In the evening, except for those with dates, they gather at the benches or patrol the turf.

BENEATH all their apparently reckless hostility and confusion, the Devils have a strict code — one that seems not too far advanced from the cave. They do not, they insist, attack neutrals, either adolescent or adult. They grant the right of passage to all gangs

except the one with which they are currently at war. They believe they have the right to beat up any member of this warring gang found in their territory. They respect, they say, pacts with rivals. They are respectful of their parents and particularly of their mothers — known as "moo" in their jargon. A slighting remark about one's mother must be avenged. The mother-insult is a reliable device for provoking an enemy or making him admit he is a "punk."

One reason they try to avoid trouble near home stems from the wish to keep their gang activities a secret from their mothers. When arrested for unlawful assembly—gathering for a fight—they may tell their mothers they were preparing to defend themselves or that they were arrested unjustly. One boy hangs out with a faction of the gang that meets a few blocks away from the playground because he lives near the playground and doesn't want his mother to see him there. Generally the parents admit their sons are "wild," but hope they will outgrow this phase.

The gang code applies to girls as well as mothers. The Devils brag that "our girls are clean." They literally shout it through the streets, while the girls giggle on near-by benches. By this boast they mean they desist from immoral acts with girls in their neighborhood. These are girls, they say, they will marry some day. However, they crow just as loudly about their lack of restraint with girls outside the neighborhood.

Most important, the code calls for loyalty of gang members to one another. "We stick together," says a Devil. "Everything we do we stick together. We got it made right. The clique is good. When we're men, the guys will still be friends and our wives, too."

AT times, carried away by the fervor of their code, they see themselves as protectors of a homeland that, without their resistance and courage, would be overrun by enemy gangs.

That the community does not judge them by this code is irksome to the Devils. They think it unfair that several candy stores and cafeterias will not admit them because they sometimes endanger property by their "fooling around." For the legal arm of the community, the police, they express hatred. To them a policeman is a bully, for sale to "anybody with scratch." Nor do they think much more flatteringly of social workers. The social worker, they say, "makes himself a hero." They make an exception of the Youth Board worker now assigned to them.

AT times, in self-appraisal they are capable of withering honesty. In bragging that none of their members takes dope, one of the Devils said sadly, not boastfully, "We're bad enough without dope." The others nodded silently.

The primordial pattern of the Devils emerges clearly in the ritual for admission. The aspirant, having been questioned carefully at earlier interviews, presents himself before the group in the playground on a prearranged night. There he is beaten by any Devils present. He has the right to fight back. If he makes no complaint he is admitted. But if he cries or begs mercy, he is called "punk" and barred from membership. Members are proud of having "caught my beating."

The Devils were not always this sort of organization. The group was formed fifteen years ago as a football team. The game was often marked by fist fights. During World War II, athletics became less important to the Devils and gang fighting increased in importance. Clashes with other gangs led to brushes with the police, and an anti-social group developed.

MANY Devils say they joined the gang because they grew up in this neighborhood and wanted to be with their friends — for excitement; for protection against other gangs; for "rep." To them the gang seems a normal transition process before they grow up, leave the gang, get jobs, marry and settle down in the neighborhood, honorably retired from "gang busting."

Adult workers, surveying the whole field of juvenile delinquency, come up with somewhat different explanations of the gang. In the gang, they say, boys find the recognition and status they do not receive elsewhere. They are not good at school, they rarely distinguish themselves in athletics. Only in the gang can they gain "rep." This sense of comparative adequacy in the gang makes them increasingly dependent upon it, increasingly fearful of being deserted by the gang or thrown out of the group. This leads to the irony that these boys who rebel so strongly against the normal discipline of society impose upon themselves the sterner disciplines of the gang.

Researchers in the field also discern other factors in the formation of gangs. First, they point out, it is normal for teen-agers to join groups in the difficult period when they are making the transition from adolescent dependence on the family into adult independence of the family. The vast majority of teen-age groups fit the community pattern and usually contribute a great deal.

IN the case of anti-social groups, the members feel cultural deprivation as well as strong personal difficulties. They are convinced they have no future and that society will not give them what they deserve. If, in support of this conclusion, they can find considerable evidence of discrimination—as in the case of Negroes and Puerto Ricans—their leanings toward delinquency are that much stronger. Such youths may think they have no choice but to live for the pleasures of the moment. Delinquents, with little sense of obligation toward society, have little compunction about violating the rules of society.

Some researchers say that the main reason underlying this overpowering sense of deprivation is a broken or inadequate family life. Dr. Alfred J. Kahn, professor at the New York School of Social Work, says a recent large—and random—sampling of court cases of juvenile delinquency showed this to be an almost unvaried pattern. Where family life has been adequate, he believes, it has been a bulwark against corrosive factors in youth. The values offered by healthy family life explain why, amid poverty, the vast majority of youngsters do not become delinquent.

WHAT is to be done about the gangs? One of the most unusual techniques is that adopted by the New York City Youth Board. This public agency, set up to work with juvenile delinquents, assigns workers to some of the most difficult gangs. These young men try to win the confidence of the youths by the force of their personalities and then to deter them from anti-social activities. Theirs, they concede, is an enormously difficult kind of missionary work. In overcoming the strong distrust of the gangs to which they are assigned they must put up with criticism and insult.

How many delinquents this method has saved from crime in its five years of experiment it is impossible to estimate. The Youth Board is not very optimistic on that score. However, Youth Board workers can easily cite cases in which they have played important roles in averting gang warfare. Clergymen, such as the Rev. C. Kilmer Myers, who works among Puerto Ricans on the lower East Side, have also had some success in this work.

The position of the police is different. Though the Police Department is apprised of mediation efforts among the gangs by social workers, it has not always approved. Recently, when a pact to avert territorial gang warfare was negotiated by social workers, Police Commissioner Stephen P. Kennedy warned his officers:

"You shall meet violence with sufficient force, legally applied, to bring violators to justice swiftly * * * You shall not enter into treaties, concordats, compacts or agreements of appeasement — because of such are storm troopers made."

IN explanation of this position, Capt. Frederick J. Ludwig, head of the Juvenile Aid Bureau, points out that very often social workers gain a gang's confidence but lose their own prestige, because to win the gang's friendship the social workers must, at first, "say and do things the gang likes." Too often, he believes, the social worker must make more concessions to the gang than the gang makes to the social worker.

"Our method," says Captain Ludwig, "is to know the gangs and their members and to get their respect. They must know that policemen have a shield, a gun and a billy. We must not stand for unlawful assembly or illicit behavior. We want respect for all who walk the streets. If any adjustment is to be made, they have to adjust to law and order—if they can. We can't compromise law and order to their subculture."

Yet it would be a mistake to say the police are using only force to combat juvenile delinquency. The Police Athletic League has long been a beneficent influence in poor neighborhoods, organizing athletic and social events for underprivileged youngsters. The Juvenile Aid Bureau, which has hand-picked men with college degrees, has been making careful studies of the problem and is currently compiling a report based on information gathered from all parts of the country. In one precinct in the Bronx the police "beefed up" their juvenile delinquency work and in little more than a year virtually eliminated gang warfare in one of the toughest sections of the city. In this experiment the police worked with social agencies and parents of gang members.

THE over-all picture in the nation shows that, despite occasional friction, all groups engaged in fighting juvenile delinquency are learning from one another. It has become obvious that, in curbing youthful crimes, the work must certainly be as much preventive as punitive. For, as Commissioner Kennedy said recently:

"It must always be remembered that when a youth comes to the attention of the police the damage has already been done."

September 2, 1956

NEW TRENDS SEEN IN JUVENILE CRIME

By EMMA HARRISON

Juvenile delinquency is not increasing as rapidly as is the public furor over it, a group of psychologists said yesterday.

Serious youth crimes, which are not typical of deviant juvenile behavior, receive all the headlines, one of the members of a symposium on juvenile delinquency at the American Psychological Association reported.

Dr. Isidor Chein of the Research Center for Human Relations at New York University noted that the total youth crime figures for another high anxiety period, 1949-52, showed a rise in misdemeanors, but no increase in felonies. He recalled that the furor was even greater then than now.

Dr. Chein said that there was no reason to believe that the rise in serious youth crime now was any greater than it was in that earlier period. Increased misdemeanors and more arrests spurred by public furor have inflated the youth "crime" figures, he said.

The psychologist also observed that most youngsters "outgrow" juvenile delinquency. This is shown, he said, by a study of prison populations that show that juvenile delinquents do not generally become professional criminals later.

In any event, the patient is not the delinquent, but the community, the group of psychologists agreed.

Also, efforts to bring about changes in the community are often blocked, said Dr. Walter B. Miller, director of a special youth project in Roxbury, Mass. He said this was due to the fact that many of the social institutions interested in preventing delinquency have a "stake in the maintenance of conditions that cause it."

Thus, the police department,

which the public expects to be the keeper of the peace, must continue to arrest; settlement houses that are equipped to handle those lower-class youngsters who are ambitious to move into upper-class brackets, must continue to provide services for the "good" youngsters and ignore the tough element. Society itself, applauding the "tough and manly" virtues, often encourages delinquent behavior, Dr. Miller noted.

It is Dr. Miller's thesis that the present public furor is due not so much to the increase in delinquency, as to the increase of it among middle-class youth. There has been, he says, a diffusion of lower and middle-class characteristics that causes middle-class youth to commit acts formerly done by lower-class youngsters.

This has aroused the middle class, which is startled to find its children committing acts once believed to be only in the province of the less privileged, he said.

Dr. Miller used the popular rock 'n' roll fad to illustrate how lower class culture speech and dance patterns were pervading the whole of youth in this country.

He characterized this as the fourth and most effective of such movements occurring in this country. He listed the others as the ragtime period of the Twenties and the swingtime and jitterbug periods of the Thirties.

September 1, 1957

Helping the Youngster in Trouble

By DOROTHY BARCLAY

FIVE teen-agers in a comfortable suburban community in Maryland are currently at work two nights a week, the papers tell us, polishing up brass and chrome and doing whatever other chores may be necessary in the town's firehouse. These boys, reportedly from "well-to-do" families, have also been put on probation, required to pay damages and restricted in leaving their homes. Their offense? Setting off fires and explosions in homes because they were "looking for something to do."

News items like this one, which rated four paragraphs in a recent newspaper, seem to be on the increase. Indeed, according to one psychologist, Dr. Walter B. Miller, the current public furor over juvenile crime is due not so much to the increase in delinquency itself as to the increase of it among middle-class youth. Middle-class parents, startled to find their children committing acts once believed to be "only in the province of the less privileged," have become frightened and aroused, he believes.

Statistics on this point are unclear, but whether or not delinquency has increased among middle-class youngsters, it is our opinion that concern about it among parents definitely has. Obviously the best way to prevent delinquency is to have had a close and friendly relationship with the youngsters of the family from their earliest days. Even so, however, there can be misunderstandings when preadolescence arrives and what "the other kids" do means more than mom and dad's old-fashioned opinions.

A PARENT'S best insurance against a sudden call from the police is probably to be found in knowing a youngster's

friends, encouraging them to come to the house, sharing enough of their spontaneous chatter to see how their thinking goes, checking informally now and then on the places where the youngster plays and "hangs around," sharing interests with him and providing constructive outlets for youthful energies, fun and the spirit of adventure.

At the other extreme are possible danger signals to be aware of. As outlined by Dr. John Briggs, a psychiatrist, these include "clamming up," a really cold refusal to share ideas and experiences; sudden difficulty in school — either with subject-matter or discipline; a "superior" attitude toward organized activities; demands to be allowed to go out without letting parents know

where; habitual reckless driving and overemphasis on speed. The strained relations that symptoms like these indicate should suggest that major reconciliation efforts are in order.

But even in the most well-meaning families things can go wrong. In the latest issue of Child Study, journal of the Child Study Association of America, there is a rather unexpected article by William A. Wattenberg, titled "Normal Rebellion—Or Real Delinquency?" It is no theoretical discussion, but a practical piece addressed directly to parents —solid middle-class parents— whose children have been in, or may get into, minor difficulties with the police.

Professor Wattenberg, who teaches educational psychology

at Wayne State University, serves as research consultant to the Youth Department of the Detroit police. He is quick to admit that there is such a thing as a real delinquent. The "genuine tough boy or girl," he says, is easy to recognize but hard to treat.

IT is important to realize, he points out, that only a small minority of preadolescent and teen-age youngsters are delinquent in the true sense of the word. The majority never get into trouble or, if they do, their difficulties are a product of poor judgment, group loyalty and a flare-up of antagonism to adults.

But supposing a youngster does hit trouble? How can parents and other adults recognize the difference between the boy or girl who will learn a valuable lesson from his first encounter with the law and the true delinquent whose police record will grow? According to Professor Wattenberg, the immediate reaction to getting caught tells part of the story. Many relatively normal boys and girls are very contrite. They are worried, feel very uncomfortable and clearly do not want to repeat the experience. Others hide their anxiety by acting silly. By contrast, the seriously delinquent child is more apt to go in for "slick lies or angry outbursts of blaming other people."

Whatever the circumstances surrounding the offense and its detection, Professor Wattenberg believes that parents have three tasks to perform— seeing the behavior in perspective, standing by their children, and indicating clearly and forcefully that there are limits on behavior.

As for point one, and with no desire to minimize or shrug off the offense, Professor Wattenberg holds that it is important for parents to try to understand the motivation of the act. "If girls pick up a few knickknacks from store counters, it is more accurate to regard them as testing their courage than to act as though they were members of a professional shoplifting ring. If a group smears paint on a building, they are probably engaging in a thoughtless and impulsive expression of anger rather than in cold-blooded vandalism * * *. Adults have to be alert to recognize the why of actions, to see them in the perspective of pre-adolescents' need for group approval and for displays of independence from adult domination."

*W*HEN misconduct is the result of serious disturbance or of disordered character, professional help is called for. In either case, parents have a direct part to play in helping the youngster in trouble. "The boy or girl in the police station," Professor Wattenberg tells us, "needs mother and father as seldom before. However chagrined or ashamed they may feel, parents should recognize that now is the time to give son or daughter the realization that family bonds have great significance."

Unless, of course, there are well-founded reasons to question the charges, in Professor Wattenberg's experience nothing is as reassuring to the police or as calming to the adult victim of a juvenile offense as the recognition by parents of guilt and responsibility and their ready assumption of responsibility for the child and for restitution for damages. On the other hand, overprotection—in the form of trying to "fix" the case by bribery—may be interpreted as approval of the delinquency.

*W*HATEVER official disposition may be made of the case, parents have a job to do in indicating that in their eyes certain behavior is bad, that there are limits which must be observed. "Appropriate punishment," says Professor Wattenberg, "is in order. Typical penalties may involve limitation of social activities, reducing allowances to help pay for restitution, extra work to obtain money for the same purpose."

After two or three weeks, he suggests, it would be well to hold a conference to make sure the youngster has recognized the necessity of keeping himself out of similar situations. "The promises most children will make under these circumstances are usually kept. If they cannot be trusted, something is very wrong and outside help may wisely be used."

(The theme of the fall issue of Child Study is "Aggressiveness in Children." Single copies are 65 cents from Child Study Association, 132 East Seventy-fourth Street, New York 21, N. Y.)

September 29, 1957

Teen-Age Gangs Speak Strange Tongue; Here's Glossary of Common Expressions

Here is a glossary of terms and expressions commonly used by New York's teen-age gangs:
A fair one—A fair fight between gangs or gang members, fought in some accordance with rules.
Bop—To fight.

Bopping Club—A fighting gang.
Cheesy—Traitorous.
Cool—An uneasy armistice.
Coolie—Non-gang boy.
Cool it!—Take it easy!
Debs—Girl affiliates of gang boys.
Diddley bop — First - class gang fighter.

Drop a dime—Give me a dime.
Duke—To fight (with fists).
Gig—A party.
Go down—To attack another gang, to declare war.
Heart—Courage.
Jap—To ambush or attack an individual.
Jitterbug—To fight.
Meet—A meeting, usually of gang chiefs.
Pot—Narcotics.
Punk out—Display cowardice.
Rank—To insult (usually profanity concerning a boy's mother).
Rep—Reputation, usually fighting reputation.

Rumble—Gang fight.
Shin battle — Intra-gang practice or test-of-mettle fight among gang members.
Shuffle—To engage in a fist fight.
Snag—To attack an individual.
Sneaky Pete—Cheap wine.
Sound—Talk.
Stenjer—Alpine - style hat with narrow brim.
Swing with a gang—To be a gang member.
Tight — Friendly, as between gangs.
To sound—To joke or needle.

March 24, 1958

LEIBOWITZ URGES CUT IN MIGRATION TO COMBAT CRIME

Judge Offers Statistics to Hearing on Delinquency Among Puerto Ricans

VIEWS HOTLY DISPUTED

Javits, Celler and Civic Body Defend the Newcomers— Senate Inquiry Adjourns

By PETER KIHSS

Kings County Judge Samuel Leibowitz called on Mayor Wagner and other officials yesterday to discourage migrants "from all parts of the country and the Caribbean" from coming here until the city had overcome crime-breeding slums.

The often outspoken judge stirred up new controversy when he made public figures that

Puerto Ricans, with only 7 per cent of the city's population, were involved in 22.3 per cent of the city's juvenile delinquency cases. Puerto Ricans, the figures also indicated, were involved in 20.8 per cent of the cases of older individuals awaiting trial in one institution.

The figures were contained in a document the judge submitted while appearing before a Senate subcommittee on juvenile delinquency, which is holding hearings here.

Price of Discrimination

The figures also indicated a similar pattern among Negroes, who are estimated to total 11 per cent of the city's population. Negroes were reported to total 46.3 per cent of the city-wide cases awaiting trial in the Brooklyn House of Detention.

At the hearing in the United States Court House in Foley Square, Council President Abe Stark declared that "the price we pay for discrimination against minority groups is reflected in the fact that their resentment and frustration cause them to commit almost half of the crimes of violence in the nation, even though they represent little more than 10 per cent of the total population."

Mr. Stark's statement, his as-

sistant, Leonard P. Stavisky, said later, referred to Negroes and Puerto Ricans, and was based on studies by his office of reports by the Bureau of Census, Federal Bureau of Investigation and other sources.

A quick reaction against the figures submitted by Judge Leibowitz came from Joseph Monserrat, chairman of the Puerto Rican Community Self-Help Program. Mr. Monserrat said he was sure they were accurate on what they covered, but "the danger lies in the possibility of misinterpreting them."

Referring to the youthfulness of the Puerto Rican population here, Mr. Monserrat said Puerto Ricans comprised 33 per cent of Manhattan's school children — but less than 30 per cent of Manhattan's juvenile delinquency cases.

He said "The Puerto Rican Study, 1953-57" by the Board of Education—the only one of its kind—"showed that the Puerto Rican children had a lower delinquency rate than the other children in the same neighborhoods."

The study was by Dr. J. Caye Morrison and was made public last April 6. It covered School District 10 in East Harlem and District 11, stretching from West Harlem to the Hudson River. In these districts, the report said, "the Puerto Rican children were offenders at the rate of 12 per 1,000; the non-Puerto Ricans at the rate of

14 per 1,000."

Yesterday's hearings, conducted by Senator Thomas C. Hennings Jr., Democrat of Missouri, chairman of the subcommittee, closed two days' sessions. The subcommittee plans to move on to other cities to study increasing teen-age gang violence around the nation.

Javits Disagrees

At yesterday's sessions, Senator Jacob K. Javits, Republican of New York, as a witness, disputed Judge Leibowitz's plea against migration. "I believe that ultimately, as was true of other waves of migration, we will integrate the migrants," Senator Javits said. He said every citizen was "entitled to freedom to travel and the best we've got."

Representative Emanuel Celler, Democrat of Brooklyn, had testified before Judge Leibowitz spoke. Mr. Celler noted outside the hearing, as had Judge Leibowitz in testifying, that Puerto Ricans had a constitutional right to come here.

"We should not discourage them from coming," Mr. Celler said. "We need them for the hard chores and rough work. If they do not come, most of our hotels, restaurants and laundries would close. We need new-seed immigration."

Answering some of the criticism, Judge Leibowitz later said:

"The Puerto Rican Government itself has been trying to divert these people from coming to New York City. All I wanted to do is to get the man in City

Hall to open his mouth, to do a little talking not only to Puerto Ricans but others who are going to be jammed into these terrible slums which cause juvenile delinquency."

With this comment he reported he had received a letter from the Puerto Rican Department of Labor, Migration Division, dated Tuesday, that said in part:

"The Puerto Rican Government has done extensive work to make conditions in New York City known to persons thinking about migration. They have been informed of the extremely poor housing, the cold weather, the high cost of living, the probabilities of exploitation, the existence of prejudice and discrimination. Such information has not notably affected the size of the migration."

Judge Leibowitz, who has presided over county grand jury inquiries into relief and housing problems, told the hearing that he had first made his plea on migration to Mayor Wagner after their joint tour of Brooklyn slums last February.

Links Crime to Slums

He said he had noted that migrants from other parts of the mainland and the Caribbean were coming here, "looking for a better life," but crowding "into rat-infested places where they can't have a chance in the world." He said he had asked the Mayor "to get on the radio and tell them to give us a chance to catch up."

Asserting that he wanted to avert delinquency caused by slum - dwelling, the judge charged the city was "pampering and protecting slumlords." The Welfare Department, he said, was paying slum rents in "thousands of cases" for relief recipients.

Although the State Rent Commission may reduce rents to $1 a month when city departments certify buildings as dangerous to life and health, Judge Leibowitz said city agencies had certified only seventeen such cases in Brooklyn last year.

Recalling how the late Mayor Fiorello H. La Guardia had occasionally sat as a magistrate, Judge Leibowitz urged that Mayor Wagner act as a judge some time and personally 'sentence "slumlords" to jail.

Judge Leibowitz also called for a state law to require one year's residence in the state before eligibility for relief here. Only Rhode Island and New York, among all states, he said, have no such residence law.

Mr. Monserrat insisted in his comment later that Puerto Ricans came here for work, not relief, as evidenced by the fact that migration has dropped during mainland recessions.

The Puerto Rican Labor Department's letter to Judge Leibowitz had reported that states with high residence require-

ments for relief got more migrants than New York. Among these were listed California, Florida, Michigan, Ohio, Arizona and Maryland.

Judge Leibowitz's submission of figures on Puerto Rican delinquency came as a rebuttal to an advertisement in Wednesday's newspapers by Mr. Monserrat's group of 162 organizations representing Puerto Ricans here. The advertisement had said "Puerto Ricans are involved in only some 8 per cent of the city's crime, which is roughly equivalent to our proportion of the population."

Judge Leibowitz said he was offering "the true figures" from Presiding Justice John Warren Hill of the Domestic Relations Court and from other official quarters.

September 25, 1959

KENNEDY OFFERS PLAN TO COMBAT JUVENILE CRIMES

Urges a 5-Year Program to Curb Delinquency — Cost Is 10 Million First Year

CABINET GROUP SET UP

Attorney General Will Head Agency—A 'Total Attack' Proposed to Congress

By ALVIN SHUSTER
Special to The New York Times.

WASHINGTON, May 11 — President Kennedy urged Congress today to initiate a "total attack" on the growing menace of juvenile delinquency.

Expressing "serious concern," the President proposed a five-year program to prevent and control youth crime, treat offenders and train youth workers. The cost was put at $10,000,000 for the first year, beginning July 1.

At the same time, the President issued an Executive Order creating a Committee on Juvenile Delinquency and Youth Crime to coordinate Federal efforts in a program to aid states and local communities in their fight on delinquency.

Committee Membership

The committee members will be Attorney General Robert F. Kennedy, the President's brother, who will serve as chairman, Abraham A. Ribicoff, the Secretary of Health, Education and Welfare, and Arthur J. Gold-

berg, the Secretary of Labor.

David L. Hackett, a 34-year-old special assistant to the Attorney General, will serve as the committee's executive director.

The Department of Health, Education and Welfare appointed Dr. Lloyd E. Ohlin, a 43-year-old Professor of Sociology at the New York School of Social Work, to be its special consultant on delinquency. The school is a graduate division of Columbia University.

A Citizens Advisory Council, composed of authorities on youth crime, will be selected by the Attorney General later to advise his Cabinet group.

Serious Problems Cited

In his letter to Speaker of the House Sam Rayburn asking Congressional action, the President said that expanding juvenile delinquency was evident in both urban and rural communities.

He said it affected particularly youths who dropped out of school, unemployed juveniles faced with limited opportunities and children from broken homes.

"I view the present trend with serious concern," he said. "Juvenile delinquency and youth offenses diminish the strength and vitality of our nation; they present serious problems to all the communities affected; and they leave indelible impressions upon the people involved, which often cause continuing problems."

To point up the need for the legislation, the President sent along figures compiled by Mr. Ribicoff showing the steady rise in youth crimes. Since 1948, the Secretary said in a letter to the President, court delinquency cases and juvenile arrests have more than doubled. If the present trend continues, he said, up to 4,000,000 children will come before the courts in the next decade.

The President, accordingly,

asked for funds to work in three major areas.

The first would be in demonstration and evaluation projects. This would involve grants for developing special techniques and practices that hold promise of preventing or controlling youth offenses.

Such projects might include rehabilitation facilities such as outdoor work camps, or short-term training centers where emotionally disturbed youths would be given intensive group therapy. They might also involve so-called "half-way" centers where delinquents would be permitted to go to work or school during the day but be kept under surveillance at night.

Would Train Personnel

Secondly, funds would be used for training personnel such as probation officers, policemen, social workers, youth gang workers and others. Moreover, funds might be used, for example, to give psychological training to public school teachers so they could detect potential delinquents before they had the opportunity to begin their careers in crime.

Thirdly, the funds would be used to increase the technical assistance services the Government is now providing in a limited way to public and private agencies dealing with juvenile crime. These services include advice on the control of delinquency as well as on the treatment of offenders.

The proposals generally are in line with those made by the Senate Juvenile Delinquency subcommittee, which for several years has conducted youth crime studies. As an outgrowth of its latest hearings, the Senate last month passed legislation authorizing $5,000,000 a year for four years to fight delinquency along the lines suggested today by the President.

It is now expected that the House will approve the Administration's bill and that it will then be reconciled with Senate-passed legislation. Somewhat similar legislation was blocked by the House Rules Committee last year.

May 12, 1961

YOUTH CRIME RATE CALLED ALARMING

Senators Note Rise Among White-Collar Families— Ask More Funds

WASHINGTON, Aug. 27 (AP)—A Senate investigation group reported today a continued rise in juvenile delinquency, "largely among the children of the so-called white collar classes."

The Juvenile Delinquency subcommittee said its figures covered a detailed study from 1940 through 1959, plus a significant preliminary study covering much of 1960. It asked for more Federal aid to combat the problem.

In an accompanying statement, Senator Thomas J. Dodd, subcommittee chairman, said the group's inquiries had shown that illegal traffic in narcotics and narcotics addiction among children were "at an all-time high" in the United States.

The Connecticut Democrat said a poll of Federal judges and other officials showed 75 per cent believed the narcotics laws needed changing.

The report told of "an alarming change in patterns" of juvenile delinquency since 1940. It said the number of cases was 177 per cent greater in 1959 than in 1958, reaching a high of 773,000 juvenile court cases involving 666,000 children 10 to 17 years old.

Rise in Rural Areas

The report said "big cities are still by far the greatest producers of delinquents." But it told of a 7 per cent rise in youth delinquency in suburban areas and a 15 per cent rise in rural areas in 1959.

"This 'trend to the suburbs' in juvenile crime is a clear indication that the increase is largely among the children of the so-called white-collar classes," the report said.

"National and state police officials report that there are increasing occurrences of vandalism, muggings, burglaries, larcenies and crowd disturbances emanating from the ranks of those who have no reason for committing these crimes except for so-called thrills," the subcommittee said.

The report contended that the need was urgent for more Federal aid for training social workers to deal with delinquency.

August 28, 1961

U.S. AND CITY OPEN 12.6-MILLION WAR ON DELINQUENCY

3-Year Plan Aims to Reform Entire Lower East Side as Example to Nation

By MARJORIE HUNTER
Special to The New York Times.

WASHINGTON, May 31—President Kennedy announced today a $12,600,000 mass social experiment on the Lower East Side of New York. It is part of a program designed to strike eventually at the roots of the national juvenile delinquency problem.

The three-year project, called Mobilization for Youth, will be financed jointly by Federal, city and private funds. It was called "the most advanced program yet devised to combat delinquency on a broad scale."

The announcement was made in the White House garden, just outside the President's office. Attending the ceremony were Attorney General Robert F. Kennedy, chairman of the President's Committee on Juvenile Delinquency; Abraham A. Ribicoff, Secretary of Health, Education and Welfare; Secretary of Labor Arthur Goldberg, Mayor Wagner and members of the New York Congressional delegation.

'Action by All' Urged

The President said juvenile delinquency was a "matter which requires action by us all in this decade."

Using the Lower East Side area as a giant laboratory, project officials will seek to reform the social patterns of an entire community as a way of guiding youth into conforming with the accepted patterns of American life.

They will cover a broad range of social activities, from organizing the play of 7-year-olds to examining the political structure and community attitudes of adults.

There will be an Urban Youth Service Corps to provide jobs for 16-to-21-year-olds, an Adventure Corps on paramilitary lines for boys 9 to 16, "cool and jazzy" coffee shops featuring art and folk music, and improved welfare services to "troubled" families.

Special Programs Set

And there will be special school programs for both youths and adults, community development programs, a narcotics demonstration project, and a program to rehabilitate juvenile offenders.

The project is based on a theory, developed by Mobilization for Youth, Inc., of 214 East Second Street, New York City, that there must be a systematic approach to the problems of juvenile delinquency.

The administrative director of the project will be James E. McCarthy, a 45-year-old graduate of the University of Notre Dame who has specialized in youth and social work.

Officials here said that the Federal and state funds for the project would be available July 1 and that the program would get under way this summer. They said they hoped to begin the educational phases of the program with the opening of school in September and to have the entire project under way by late fall.

In a 617-page outline of the project, Mobilization for Youth called it an effort to "bring together the actionist and the researcher in a joint program of social engineering."

The theory is that the central factor controlling whether young people follow accepted behavior standards is the opportunity presented to them. The program is organized to improve opportunities for youth

The New York Times   June 1, 1962
Area of youth project is shown by diagonal shading.

and guide young people into pursuing them.

Summing that up, Attorney General Kennedy said underprivileged youth must be given "a stake in conformity if they are to accept the normal values of society."

Mayor Wagner said the project was intended to enlist new forces to attack "the continuing rise in delinquency, through preventive action that offers young people expanded social, educational and job opportunities."

One of Worst Areas

He noted that within the last thirty years public and publicly aided housing had provided new homes for 60,000 residents of the lower East Side and that in the last eight years space for 10,000 students had been added in the schools.

"Despite all that we have done and in spite of all the good that has come from all that we have done, there are still some gnawing problems in the area which require accelerated and increased effort," he said.

The project area, with a population of about 107,000, has one of the worse juvenile delinquency records in New York City.

The New York City Youth Board reported recently that delinquency offenses for each 1,000 youths between 7 and 20 years old in the area rose from 28.7 in 1951 to 62.8 in 1960, an increase of 118 per cent. During the same period the over-all increase in the city was 110.9 per cent. The delinquency rate in the city is 41 for each 1,000.

The project area is bounded by East Fourteenth Street, the East River, Brooklyn Bridge, St. James Place, Pearl Street, Park Row, Chatham Square, Division Street, Canal Street, Rutgers Street, East Broadway, Grand Street, Rivington Street, Clinton Street and Avenue B.

A survey indicated the following population groups: Jewish, 27 per cent; Puerto Rican, 26 per cent; Italian, 11 per cent; other white, 25 per cent; Negro, 8 per cent, and other non-white, 3 per cent.

The survey also showed that 35.6 per cent of the housing in the area was substandard and 28.5 per cent more overcrowded; that the average family income was $68.92 a week, and that only 14.9 per cent of the adults had completed high school.

2 Years of Planning

The project follows two years of planning by Mobilization for Youth, Inc., a nonprofit corporation headed by Winslow Carlton of the Henry Street Settlement.

Mayor Wagner announced that New York City would contribute $1,400,000 to the project for the first year and an estimated total of $4,500,000 for the entire three-year period.

Federal contributions are a three-year grant of $1,900,000 from the President's Committee on Juvenile Delinquency and a one-year grant of $1,500,000 from the National Institute of Mental Health, Public Health Service.

The remaining funds will come from foundations and private sources.

Much of the work will be carried out by existing groups, such as settlement houses, welfare agencies, religious organizations, civic clubs and the New York School of Social Work of Columbia University.

Job Help Slated

One phase of the project will seek to create new jobs and find existing work through these programs:

¶Urban Youth Service Corps, to hire about 1,000 unemployed, out-of-school youths and pay them $1 an hour for up to thirty-five hours a week. They will repair tenements, construct-

Playgrounds, manufacture toys, repair furniture, beautify the neighborhood and serve as aides in public and nonprofit private institutions.

¶Youth Jobs Center, an employment agency for counseling and job placement.

¶Exploratory work course, to be offered in junior high schools to inform students of job possibilities and requirements.

Another project phase will be to meet the problems of "slum children in slum schools" through these programs:

¶Home visits by teachers.

¶A planning committee to develop a curriculum for slum schools.

¶Reading centers in all elementary schools and reading clinics in two elementary schools.

¶Experimental classes for retarded children.

¶A homework helper program, with 300 good high school students being paid to tutor failing elementary school pupils.

Recreation and community development programs will include the following:

¶Three coffeeshops, furnished and staffed by young people, to serve refreshments and feature folk music, art, sculpture and other cultural activitites.

¶An Adventure Corps for boys 9 to 16, to provide marching bands, educational programs, camping, athletics and vocational training. The boys will be organized in jacket-uniformed squads of twenty to twenty-five, six or seven squads to a division. Two divisions of 150 boys each are contemplated.

¶Neighborhood service centers, or helping stations, to offer casework service for families with special problems.

¶Neighborhood councils, to develop community development programs.

In addition a pilot narcotics demonstration program will work with fifty or so teen-aged and young adult addicts. It will offer psychiatric medical and social services and provide job training and placement services.

The project will study the strength of the city political machines over the last thirty years. Project planners expect to find that political machine strength has increased in middle-class areas and decreased in lower-class districts.

"The machine is no longer dealing with persons whose only barter goods are their individual votes," the Mobilization for Youth outline says. "Persons with higher status tend to organize the resources in their community, which gives them a position from which they can bargain.

"Instead of the previous parent relationship between machine and voter, a contract is negotiated in whic representatives of middle-class communities offer to deliver a body of votes in return for a larger slice of the political pie."

The entire project also will include a large-scale training program in the behavioral sciences, including social work, sociology, education, psychology and research. This training program will be coordinated by Columbia University.

The Pesident's Committee on Juvenile Delinquency, authorized last year by Congress, has authority to spend $30,000,000 over a three-year period.

New York City is the first to get a demonstration project grant. However, the committee has made grants for planning of projects in New Haven, Cleveland, Houston, Philadelphia, Los Angeles and Minneapolis.

June 1, 1962

Affluent Delinquency

Outburst After Debut on L.I. Follows Pattern of Rowdyism in the Suburbs

By FRED M. HECHINGER

A riotous Long Island coming-out party last weekend, at which a chandelier, furniture and more than a thousand window panes were broken, underlines a trend of growing delinquency among upper-class and middle-class youth. The outbreak after the debut of Miss Fernanda Wanamaker Wetherill in Southampton, in which 125 teen-age and post-teen socialite youths ripped up the house set aside for them by their hosts, following a pattern of destructiveness among affluent youth.

News Analysis

With damages now estimated at between $3,000 and $10,000, this instance differs from less prominent suburban affairs only in the size of the bill.

The incident occurred only a day after a rash of teen-age rioting in vacation spots, such as Hampton Beach, N.H.; Ocean City, Md.; Lake George, N.Y., and a racetrack near Indianapolis.

The headlined outbreaks, however, are only the visible peak of an iceberg. In recent weeks, the police of a well-to-do Connecticut community have had to intensify patrols of the local country club, after a rash of attempted burglaries of the golf shop by teen-agers.

Even more routine, the habit of party-crashing has increasingly terrified suburban parents to the point of making requests for police protection almost standard procedure in some areas.

Constructive Activities

This increase in affluent delinquency stands in contrast to constructive activities of many other adolescents who spend their free time serving the community, representing their country in the Peace Corps abroad or contributing their talents to the tutoring of underprivileged children.

The contrast becomes devastating in view of the disciplined actions of teen-agers and even younger children in the civil rights movement. The rise in this type of delinquency threatens to turn into hostility the resentment of underprivileged youths in slums who face arrest and reform school for transgressions far less destructive to property.

With the debutante season almost at its end—it will run roughly through Monday—there is little significance to the Southampton story on that particular level. In fact, observers of the society scene predict that the remaining affairs will probably be especially sedate, in reaction to the Southampton fiasco.

But the impact of society vandalism on adolescent mores is far-reaching. Teen-agers and even pre-teeners, from 11 to 17, shape their behavior largely in the image of models or idols. For serious-minded youngsters, the image to live up to may be the adult scientist or artist or astronaut; but in the adolescent mass-culture it is more likely to be the rock 'n' roll singer, with his immature dating and mating habits or the glamour of the social set.

The activities of society—ranging from the established élite to the pseudo-social jet set—unofficially substitute an outside view of high life in America for that provided by nobility and royalty in older societies.

This is reflected in the current teen-age obsession with large parties, preferably the "open house," which is a thinly disguised invitation for party-crashing. In imitation of huge society parties and adult conventions, the teen-age "blast" is a status symbol, with popularity measured by the turnout.

What are the causes of the destructiveness such as in Southampton's free-for-all?

Drinking is a factor. Last month, Dr. Frederick Hudson, director of a clinic at the Presbyterian Medical Center in San Francisco, confirmed what observers of the teen-age scene had increasingly found: that alcohol had become a trap for the very young, beginning at the age of 11.

Responsibility Abdicated

More basic is the abdication of adult responsibility. Suburban parties often are — as was after-the-ball blast in Southampton — conducted in the absence of adults. As a result of earlier permissiveness, leading to a lack of discipline, young adults continue the pattern of adolescent immaturity.

A common complaint of the participants in an outbreak is that "there is nothing for us to do." This excuse might be more convincing in a slum than in an affluent suburb.

Psychologists assign part of the reason for the vandalism to the fact that in modern society teen-agers are given fewer useful outlets than their predecessors in rural society. Probably at least as important a factor is parents' tendency to give too much to children and adolescents too soon. Many parents tend to buy their way out of giving their children more of their time and adult guidance.

Children who have had professional entertainment at parties when they were 5 years old are likely to be bored with ordinary social functions as teen-agers. They turn to the thrill of destruction.

Southampton offered another clue. The youths involved shrugged off the damage, saying they would pay for it. Generally, parents are ready to pay for teen-agers' destruction. Teen-agers know that, in an air of easy affluence, money will take care of all consequences.

September 5, 1963

GANG STUDY FINDS 'RUMBLE' IS PASSE

9-City Survey by Professor Credits Special Police

By JOHN H. FENTON
Special to The New York Times

BOSTON, Sept. 14—A Boston University professor of social work finds that juvenile gangs are showing signs of more sophistication.

After a seven-month study in nine cities, Prof. Saul Bernstein said that changing styles indicated the end of "rumbles" of juveniles gangs that marched into other neighborhoods to wage pitched battles on pre-arranged fights.

Professor Bernstein said today that much of the change for the better could be credited to policemen who had been detached from regular patrol duties to work with young people. Boys on street corners, said Professor Bernstien, "come to know and trust the youth police worker to a much larger degree than they do the regular cop on the beat."

The Boston educator conducted his study here and in New York City, Chicago, Los Angeles, San Francisco, Cleveland, Detroit, Washington, and Philadelphis. He said he had found gangs to be less obvious than they once were. Gangs' names no longer were splashed on walls and members no longer flaunted dark colored jackets advertising who they were, he said.

In place of the rumble, Professor Bernstein said, he found many gangs indulging in "snagging." Under this system, he said, a lookout discovered where a rival gang or an individual member passed daily.

Then, five or six from the lookout's gang, all probably dressed quietly, would wait for the victims and methodically beat them up. Just as unconcernedly, the gang would return home, change clothes and go about its business.

"No show of power, no advertising, all 'cool,'" said Professor Bernstein.

But all of the problem of revenge was not solved, he went on. A technical change included a technique known as the "fair one." This involved choosing a member from each of two gangs to settle differences openly in front of other gang members with their fists.

But pressures on the representatives in openly upholding the "honor" of the gang and the difficulty other gang members had of restraining themselves from joining the battle militated against the success of this technique, said Professor Bernstein.

But the technique of selecting leaders from each gang to discuss differences on neutral territory, in the presence of youth workers, was a promising one, he said.

The youth workers, the professor said, functioned at many levels. In addition to trying to induce the gangs to talk out their differences, the workers try to find recreational space for gangs. And if a boy is picked up by the police, the worker may appear in court with him.

A considerable number of antisocial gangs, Professor Bernstein found, were made up of boys who had dropped out of school and had no skills. Although social work had helped these youths, he said, they needed a chance "to get on the opportunity escalator, an opportunity to obtain an education and skills so that they can eventually get decent jobs."

Professor Bernstein's studies will be published in a book entitled "Youth on the Streets," by Association Press of New York later this year. The study was made possible through funds from the Duncan Russell Memorial Committee on Juvenile Delinquency of the Boston United Community Services of Metropolitan Boston.

Professor Bernstein is chairman of the committee that will meet to draw up plans for a national conference of social workers on youth groups in conflict. He has been a member of the faculty at Boston University since 1946.

Professor Bernstein is associated with the establishment of New England's first training center to combat juvenile delinquency and youth crime at Boston University's Law-Medicine Research Institute.

September 15, 1963

U.S. WILL ASSIST YOUTH OF HARLEM

$110 Million Plan Approved by Johnson Panel—3-Year Program to Open July 1

By SAMUEL KAPLAN

A "last hope" program to salvage the youth of central Harlem has been approved by a Presidential committee headed by Attorney General Robert F. Kennedy.

The three-year, $110 million program is scheduled to begin July 1. Its architects describe it as an attempt to defuse the social dynamite of Harlem—its 71,000 youths.

The President's Committee on Juvenile Delinquency and Youth Crime has not announced the program because an intricate system of financing has yet to be worked out. Also, it is understood that President Johnson wants to announce the program personally "at an appropriate time."

Extra Pay Is Planned

Among other things, the program will seek to upgrade Harlem's schools by establishing pre-school and after-school centers and by providing extra pay for teachers and administrators.

The program also involves vocational training, job centers and the creation of jobs.

Harlem Youth Opportunities Unlimited, Inc., a group of professional social workers and leading citizens formed by the city two years ago, developed the program. About 150 Harlem teen-agers assisted HAR-YOU in the research and development under a $330,000 city-Federal grant.

Most of the $110 million will come from Federal agencies, including the Department of Labor, the Department of Health, Education and Welfare, the National Institute for Mental Health and the President's committee.

May 7, 1964

SHAME FOUND KEY TO DELINQUENCY

Expert Says Youths Strive to Avoid Humiliation

By NATALIE JAFFE

Special to The New York Times

SAN FRANCISCO, April 16—The paradox of dealing with delinquency is that "the more we publicize it, the more we fear it, the more we associate it with evil, the more dramatic and heroic a model it becomes for certain of our youth," a New York psychologist said here today.

The glamor of wickedness and danger is cultivated by teen-agers, according to Dr. Murray Bilmes, to avoid feelings of shame.

"The major problems of the adolescent include achievement, pride, identity, sexual success, independence and attaining respect," he declared. "A failing in any of these is a loss of face and humiliation—the experience of shame."

One of the reasons for the great success of the Peace Corps, for example, is that it provides a moral equivalent of delinquency, Dr. Bilmes said.

"The same elements—adventure, thrills, courage, prestige—that so often promote delinquency were here utilized constructively," he declared.

An associate professor at the New York School of Psychiatry, Dr. Bilmes, has worked extensively with troubled teen-agers.

Parley Attracts 7,000

He addressed one of the closing sessions of the American Orthopsychiatric Association's 43d annual meeting, which concluded here today. More than 7,000 psychologists, psychiatrists and social workers attended the four-day meeting — the annual gathering of all professions in the mental health field.

Dr. Bilmes noted that his studies and treatment of teen-agers disclosed that shame was a more powerful force than guilt.

"Guilt is the sense of having done something wrong, shame the sense of having failed to live up to one's desired image," he explained.

In trying to change teen-age behavior, he said, appealing to a sense of guilt—telling a teen-ager not to do something because it is wrong — has little effect. But calling up feelings of shame—telling him that he is "chicken, yellow, a sissy or soft"—usually works, he said.

Dr. Bilmes stressed, however, that this distinction should be used as evidence of the power of shame, not as a recommendation for treatment.

In addition to the biological changes that make the teen years a time of turmoil, Dr. Bilmes said, there are new social factors today that make the adolescent particularly vulnerable to shame.

He pointed to the sense of futility among the uneducated at a time when education and achievement were so closely linked, the sense of failure in a "have-not" when the world was so full of "haves," the sense of ignominy among minority group members who saw themselves through the eyes of those who were prejudiced.

In addition, he said, adolescence is a time when "closeness to parents has become associated with a humiliating infantilism." A "tenderness taboo" is created because compassion, warmth and love are associated with dependency on parents.

As a result of all these pressures, Dr. Bilmes declared, "the problem of becoming a decent, law-abiding citizen is not that the teen-ager would feel guilty not doing this, but rather that he would feel déclassé, reduced to a mediocrity and a nonentity, doing it."

He urged therapists, and social planners to devise antidelinquency programs that would not force a teen-ager to repudiate his desire to be special, but would give him the opportunity.

April 17, 1966

Experts Here Doubt Vandalism Is Rising At Significant Rate

By PAUL HOFMANN

A rash of arson on Powell Street in Brooklyn's depressed Brownsville-East New York section has been drawing firemen to the scene week after week. "It seems they want to burn down the entire block," a Fire Department official remarked recently.

Elsewhere in Brooklyn, unidentified raiders have made havoc of a 100-year-old Baptist church in a series of incursions, inducing the small Spanish-speaking congregation to move a few blocks to storefront quarters that it considers safer.

Throughout the city, and in many parts of suburbia, new schools look like prisons, with electric alarm systems and wire-mesh screens to protect windows.

Vandals Stone Trains

Suburban newspapers set aside space to record cherry bombs in mail boxes, toppled headstones in cemeteries and air-rifle salvos at autos almost as regularly as they report on women's club meetings and church rummage sales. The Long Island Rail Road has been plagued for years by rocks hurled into train windows, and a maintenance man said in resignation recently: "They're still stoning us."

Arsonists have just driven a half-blind Mount Vernon newsvender out of business, burning what had remained of a shed adjoining the New York, New Haven and Hartford Railroad station that had been half destroyed in an earlier fire last winter.

This is the kind of needless destruction of public and private property that costs New Yorkers tens of millions of dollars every year. Yet many authorities are not particularly concerned. An official in a responsible position says: "Vandalism? I have myself engaged in that sort of thing as a kid and fortunately was never caught—but don't mention my name."

In this fairly widespread boys-will-be-boys approach, willful damage to property is considered an inevitable result of youthful exuberance and love for action and daring in an increasingly urban civilization. Consequently, many acts of vandalism go unreported, and few vandals are ever apprehended. According to the scanty official statistics there are only four arrests to every hundred complaints.

There is a popular impression that vandalism is on the increase in the metropolitan area, but this was dispelled by a round of interviews with officials, community leaders, psychologists and sociologists. This study by The New York Times also exposed as misconceptions the widely held views that most vandals are Negroes and that vandalism is "senseless" behavior.

Instead, a consensus of experts who were consulted showed that:

¶The over-all cost of destructive acts has not risen significantly and may even have decreased slightly in some areas.

¶The typical vandal is not Negro or Puerto Rican but a white teen-age boy from a middle-income family, often living in a stable neighborhood.

¶Vandals often vent frustration, anger, protest or need for excitement, and the community should explore the motives behind what looks like acts of deliberate wantonness.

Little could be elicited from some juvenile offenders who were interviewed. A Long Island youth tried to explain why he and his friends had tossed stones into store windows: "We had a couple of drinks at a party, then got hopped up on pot (marijuana), and went out in a car to have some fun."

Did It for Kicks

Other youngsters who had committed acts of vandalism were even more elusive or outright hostile. Law enforcement officers said teen-agers caught smashing school windows, setting fire to shrubbery in a park or daubing housewalls obscenely usually clam up or mutter sullenly: "I did it for kicks."

If the offender is under 16 years of age, he is usually charged with juvenile delinquency in Family Court. A bill passed by the New York State Legislature in 1964 that would have required parents or guardians of children to pay up to $250 in damage from vandalism was rejected.

Persons older than 16 years involved in destruction of property normally face charges of malicious mischief, because vandalism is not a legal charge in itself.

For the police and the courts, false fire alarms also fall under malicious mischief, and they account for much of the substantial increase in complaints on such charges that is being observed lately—from 56,236 in New York City in 1963 to 66,507 in 1965. The Fire Department in collaboration with other city agencies has just started a drive to curb false alarms.

To most experts, however, false alarms represent a problem quite distinct from destructive vandalism. The latter costs nearly $500,000 annually to the Park Department and about $5-million to the Board of Education with another $5-million hidden in its budget for repairs of damage to school buildings and equipment beyond normal wear and tear.

City Transit Problems

The Transit Authority said its vandalism bill last year amounted to $411,600, but was unable to make a comparison with earlier years because of a recent change in its statistical system concerning property damage. It is still unclear as to whether the authority's Operation Shield—policemen riding on subway trains—has reduced vandalism.

"There are just possibly fewer cases" of destruction in buses, a spokesman for the authority stated. The substitution of plastic materials for upholstery in subways and buses has eliminated one target of vandals.

Counter measures have also reduced vandalism at installations of the New York Telephone Company. A company official attributed the decrease to stronger locks on coin boxes and other changes. However, the company's annual losses from vandalism total around $4-million.

Estimates as to the aggregate cost of wanton destruction to the community vary widely. Some writers have asserted that it runs up to $100-million in New York City every year.

"A nice, round figure," Deputy Mayor Timothy J. Costello commented. "Nobody can disprove it." However, he wouldn't endorse it either. As the city administrator and an expert in business psychology, Dr. Costello appears particularly qualified to evaluate vandalism.

"It has been around for a long, long time," he remarked. But he stressed that he saw no evidence of any upswing.

Social Symptoms Discussed

For Dr. Costello, vandalism belongs "to the same syndrome that makes kids truant," a set of symptoms denoting "a feeling of being excluded, of reaction to unnecessary restriction, of alienation" that should not be overdramatized. The deputy mayor suggested that teen-age groups be given governing responsibilities in their community as an antidote to destructive tendencies.

Discussing the incidence of acts of vandalism in the case load of city courts, Administrative Judge Florence M. Kelly of Family Court said she had "no knowledge of any rise," while Administrative Judge John M. Murtagh of Criminal Court pointed to the deepening narcotics problem, rather than to vandalism, as his overriding worry.

While there were acts of looting and destruction of property in the Harlem riots of summer 1964, several authorities consider the Negro involvement in vandalism minor. One sociologist observed: "As a rule of thumb, policemen do not normally consider Negro youngsters the most likely suspects whenever something is vandalized. Acting empirically, the police first look for white teen-agers."

The Police Department has no way of telling how many whites and how many Negroes were among the 2,330 persons who were arrested in 1965 on charges of having committed the misdemeanor of malicious mischief or the 256 arrests for felonious malicious mischief (respectively 16 and 13 fewer than in the preceding year).

However, there are "shreds of evidence" in what little ethnical crime statistics is available, that Negroes are far less apt to be vandals than whites, according to John M. Martin of Fordham University. Certainly, Dr. Martin affirmed in an interview, Negro involvement in vandalism was much smaller than in other types of delinquent behavior.

Although ethnic arrest statistics are not available here, it appears from the data for commitments to correctional institutions that most criminal offenses in New York City are laid to the Negro minority.

In 1963 Negroes accounted for 51.9 per cent of new commitments, whites for 26.8 per cent, and Puerto Ricans for 21.0 per cent.

Seeking an explanation of why the average vandal is white, sociologists suggested that the destruction of property was the delinquent behavior most easily accessible to the "nice kid" in a "nice" neighborhood. In the material and moral decay of racial ghettos, this theory holds, the police neither notice nor mind what additional damage is being done to slum property.

The comparatively small role of Negroes in vandalism was first suggested by Dr. Martin in 1961 in an observation on Negro vandals that was based on 1955 crime figures for the Bronx.

In his study, Dr. Martin also introduced the categories of "vindictive" vandalism, motivated by prejudice and resentment, "predatory" vandalism, such as wrecking a vending machine to get at the coins, and "wanton" or seemingly senseless vandalism. In 1962 Dr. Martin and Herman D. Stein of Columbia University published a study on a particular form of "vindictive" vandalism, swastika daubing. They pointed to the fact that almost no Negroes or Puerto Ricans had been rounded up for painting anti-semitic symbols.

The civil rights movement may have a byproduct in more Negro vandalism, Dr. Martin asserted in the interview: "When the strains of inequality are becoming acute, something is bound to happen and some of the strains may find expression in more vandalistic acts, especially by Negro youths."

April 24, 1966

AGENCIES UNABLE TO AID CHILDREN

Facilities for Youths in Need of Supervision Inadequate

By KATHLEEN TELTSCH

In a Bronx courtroom, a black-robed judge recently faced a teen-ager who alternately sat sullenly silent and wept.

The girl alone on the bench was 14 years old and seven months pregnant. She also had a record as a chronic truant and runaway. Her mother had told the police that she could not control the girl and had asked the Family Court to take charge of her.

The girl was a "person in need of supervision"—or, in the jargon of the courts, a "PINS." The number of boys and girls in this classification, who are not lawbreakers, brought to the city courts last year was 4,382.

Because the judge knew exhaustive efforts already had been made without success to place the teen-ager in a private maternity shelter, she chose instead to invoke a previously unused legal provision giving the City's Commissioner of Social Services responsibility for placing the girl.

Agencies Object to Action

The action precipitated an interdepartmental problem—still unresolved—because the Social Services Department and other agencies say they have no facilities for caring for such children.

The predicament of the 14-year-old prompted the calling of a meeting between Jack R. Goldberg, the Commissioner of Social Services, and the other high-level administrators most directly involved.

Besides the Commissioner, the meeting was attended by Judge Florence M. Kelley, Administrative Judge of the Family Court, John A. Wallace, director of probation, his deputy C. Boyd McDivitt, and Wallace Nottage, deputy director of probation for institutional services.

The consensus developed at the meeting, Mr. McDivitt said, was that the state department of social services would have to provide for such difficult cases as those presented by the PINS girl. There also was agreement that more money would be needed to care for all PINS cases.

In 1967, the city's Family Court handled 3,000 to 4,000 child-neglect cases, along with the 4,382 PINS cases and 7,679 delinquency cases.

The city's Department of Social Services objects that it already is beset by difficulties in finding institutions or private homes for a backlog of neglect cases and currently is caring for 24,000 of these nondelinquent cases. Until now, it has not been asked to take on the added burden of PINS or delinquent children and it has facilities for neither, according to Miss Elizabeth C. Beine, director of child welfare. There is no facility operated by the department for pregnant girls.

Mr. McDivitt said the probation office has developed a central placement unit that will work with public and private agencies in seeking placement for children.

However, he maintains that the department is not equipped to take on the placement responsibilities and says this function belongs logically to the state and city social-service offices since these agencies inspect, license, supervise and reimburse the institutions caring for boys and girls.

There are 80 to 90 institutions accepting neglected children but fewer than 20 will take PINS or delinquency cases and this total includes the state training schools operated outside the city.

The training schools have been refusing in recent years to accept pregnant girls. The state school for mentally retarded PINS children has a two-year waiting list.

Children like the 14-year-old girl whose case started the current review are sent to the city's Juvenile Center until a permanent place can be found for them. Often children stay there for weeks or months.

August 25, 1968

PANEL SAYS CRIME BY YOUTHS IS KEY TO U.S. VIOLENCE

Report to Johnson Hopeful on Early Identification of Most Likely Offenders

By JOSEPH A. LOFTUS
Special to The New York Times

WASHINGTON, Jan. 30 — A Government report made public today said that the key to violence in American society seemed to lie with the young, possibly with a relatively small number of them, whose identity science may be able to establish early for purposes of preventive action.

The point was made in a report of the National Commission on the Causes and Prevention of Violence.

The 13-member commission, headed by Milton S. Eisenhower, submitted the report to President Johnson on Jan. 9 in fulfillment of a request made by Mr. Johnson when he established the commission last June after the assassination of Senator Robert F. Kennedy.

The report contains no recommendations. These will be made in a final report to President Nixon in the spring.

Separate Study Projects

All 13 members signed a brief statement that included 10 "themes of challenge for the leaders and the people of America." The bulk of the volume consists of reports by seven study groups describing their missions. These include the titles of research projects assigned largely to outside research teams and individuals.

Lloyd N. Cutler, executive director of the commission, said the full reports of the study groups were being made available for study by the commission this month and next month.

One of the themes of challenge dealt with youth, who, the report said, "account for an ever-increasing percentage of crime, greater than their increasing percentage of the population."

Many Chronic Offenders

The commission said that it may be here, "with tomorrow's generation, that much of the emphasis of our studies and the national response should lie."

One study group reported that "recent research suggests the possibility of identifying the youths most prone to violent or antisocial behavior, especially those prone to commit the more serious crimes."

A continuing study of boys born in 1945 who grew up in Philadelphia has developed such a technique, which may make it feasible to establish priority targets in programs for crime prevention and rehabilitation of offenders.

Of nearly 10,000 boys in the study, 3,475 became juvenile delinquents, committing a total of 10,214 delinquent acts ranging from petty offenses to homicides.

Half of these boys were only one-time offenders. More significantly, 627 were chronic offenders (five or more delinquent acts) who accounted for 5,305 crimes, or 52 per cent of all offenses committed by the entire group.

Moreover, their offenses tended to be the more serious ones, including a majority of the homicides.

Although they represented only a small minority (18 per cent of the juvenile and 6 per cent of the total group), these 627 youths accounted for the major cost to society from juvenile crimes.

"Clearly these chronic offenders merit special attention and study," said the study group, "especially as a means for judging when and how society might best take preventive and therapeutic action."

The group said that the statistics on violent crimes reported in 1967 compared unfavorably, "both absolutely and on a per capita basis, with other industrial nations." It continued:

"A dramatic contrast may be made between Manhattan Island, with a population of 1.7 million, which has more homicides per year than all of England and Wales, with a population of 49 million. And New York's homicide rates are by no means the highest among American cities."

These figures, the study group said, can be read in another perspective, namely, the number of Americans who do not commit violent crimes. "We might note that despite the recent trends 99 per cent of the population do not engage in crimes of violence," the report said.

The heavy concentration of crime, according to the report, is among the poor, the ethnic minorities in the city slums, areas of lowest per capita income, of highest unemployment, of lowest level of average educational attainment, of poorest housing, and of highest infant mortality.

A recent Chicago study indicated that the annual risk of physical assault for the Negro slum dweller was one in 77; for the white middle-class citizen, the odds were one in 2,000, and for the upper-middle-class suburbanite, the odds were one in 10,000.

A study group on mass media and violence said that examples of violent acts by persons who had just watched violence on years of exposure to television suggested a cause and effect that was not supportable by the evidence so far in hand.

"Most persons will not kill after seeing a single violent television program," the study group said, adding: "However, it is possible that many persons learn some of their attitudes and values about violence from vision, and that they might be more likely to engage in violence as an indirect result of that learning."

The group said that studies indicated that 40 per cent of the poor black children and 30 per cent of the poor white children (compared with 15 per cent of the middle class white children) believed that what they saw on television represented an accurate portrayal of life in America.

January 31, 1969

Schools Hire Own Guards As Violence Rises Sharply

By WAYNE KING

Crime and violence appear to have increased sharply in public schools in urban areas.

This trend is documented in interviews with school officials in 20 major cities and in the preliminary results of a Senate subcommittee study to be released later this year.

The school officials also reported that some school systems were moving to meet the growing problem, in part, by bringing private guards and other nonteaching personnel into the schools to maintain order.

The Senate subcommittee study links what it calls a dramatic rise in school violence over the last few years with adverse socio-economic conditions, particularly in the inner cities. The study also says that the most dramatic rise in violence involves nonstudents who congregate in and around the schools. Examples of school violence abound:

¶In Washington last week, policemen were stationed at each of the city's 46 junior and senior high schools following several incidents on Jan. 5. On that day, a 15-year-old student was shot to death by a classmate; another, 14, was wounded in the leg when a derringer brought to school by a friend accidentally fired; a third was arrested for carrying a pistol, and a fourth reported being shot at on a school playground. The incidents occurred at four different junior high schools.

¶In Nashville, two students involved last year in a dispute with the band director at East Nashville High attacked him with their fists, knocking out several teeth and breaking his nose.

¶In Detroit, a 25-year-old substitute science teacher suffered a punctured lung last year when he was stabbed by a gang of youths who burst into his classroom during one of a series of disruptions at an East Side high school. Later in the year, a 26-year-old elementary school teacher was wounded when a youth, not a student, asked for a match outside the school, then pulled a pistol and shot her when she said that she had none.

In the face of such incidents, coupled with student disruptions and evidence of racial polarization in some schools, a number of large urban school systems are relying on private guards, hall monitors and other nonteaching personnel to maintain order.

While the problem of violence in urban schools has been cited for several years by teachers' unions and others, no reliable system of reporting incidents on a nationwide basis has been developed.

However, the Senate Subcommittee to Investigate Juvenile Delinquency, headed by Senator Thomas J. Dodd, Democrat of Connecticut, is now compiling data from questionnaires sent to 153 school systems in all parts of the country.

The Dodd report, while it stresses that its figures do not reflect a definitive picture, concludes that "it is possible to say that homicide, forcible rape, robbery and other crimes on which statistics were developed have dramatically risen."

Statistics compiled so far, contained in a draft of a statement Senator Dodd plans to make in opening hearings on school violence in the early spring, show sharp increases in specific categories of crime and violence.

The statistics, based on responses from the 110 districts that replied to the questionnaire, showed that between 1964 and 1968 the number of homicides in the schools responding rose from 15 to 26, forcible rape from 51 to 81 and robbery from 396 to 1,508.

In other categories, the reports show that the number of aggravated assaults in the 110 districts increased from 475 to 680; burglary and larceny from 7,604 to 14,102; instances of vandalism from 186,184 to 250,544; weapons offenses from 419 to 1,089; narcotics violations from 73 to 854; drunkenness from 370 to 1,035; assaults on teachers by students from 1,601 to 4,267; other offenses from 4,796 to 8,824, and expulsions for incorrigibility from 4,884 to 8,190.

In another category, the report cited what it called "perhaps the most dramatic increase," a rise in crime by nonstudents from 142 instances in 1964 to 3,894 in 1968.

The report continues: "There is every indication that despite his triumphant bravado, the dropout is deeply affected by his failure in school. In almost every case of vandalism, destruction of school property and attacks on students, former students who were dropouts are involved."

Cost of Vandalism

The report also notes that the nation's 36 largest cities reported that school vandalism, including arson, caused damage totaling more than $6.5-million in 1968.

The report tentatively suggests that the causes of school violence are the same as those listed as causes of general violence by the National Commission on the Causes and Prevention of Violence. These are:

Low income, physical deterioration of housing and surroundings; dependency; racial and ethnic concentration; broken homes; working mothers; low levels of education and vocational skills; high unemployment; high proportion of single males; overcrowded and substandard housing; low rates of home ownership or single-family dwellings; mixed land use and high population density.

The report said that these conditions were particularly prevalent in the inner city.

At the same time the statement suggests that laxity on the part of school officials may be a cause:

"It is in the interest of the school system that whatever untoward violence occurs be hushed up," the report said. "It reflects on the school system itself. . . . . The fact that these events are treated so gingerly is not lost on the student body, which feels considerable encouragement from this failure to report violent incidents."

While teachers in some cities reported a reluctance to discipline unruly youngsters, sometimes out of fear of making a bad situation worse, there were also indications that more schools were turning to nonteaching personnel for discipline.

After the incidents in Washington last week, for example, school officials held an emergency meeting and authorized the hiring of 80 "community aides," mostly young men, for duty in the schools. Uniformed city policemen, meanwhile, have been assigned to schools on a temporary basis, a step school officials had been trying to avoid as possibly inflammatory.

In New York, a $500,000 pilot program that puts 170 unarmed security guards in 29 high schools and 19 junior highs has been in operation less than a year. The Board of Education is requesting $2,656,901 to "provide additional security for pupils and teachers" and to make it unnecessary to call the city police to schools "except in rare instances."

Program Called Successful

Irving Anchor, assistant superintendent of schools, said

that the guard program had been generally successful, although "some of the militants feel that these are pigs in the schools." About 60 per cent of the guards are Negro, 20 per cent Puerto Rican.

In Chicago, the public schools have recently increased the number of part-time security guards in the schools from 390 to 420. The guard program cost $912,000 last year and Edward D. Brady, director of security, said that he hoped for more money in the new budget.

As part of security arrangements, he has a direct-dial police phone on his desk that enables him to reach all police district stations and major police officials quickly. Other schools reported similar direct ties to police precincts.

With the increase in school security personnel, Mr. Brady reported that he was handling organization of a new school security directors association to be formed in Fort Lauderdale, Fla., in April.

In Philadelphia, the school system spends about $3-million a year to employ 532 nonteaching assistants, 48 fulltime security guards and varying numbers of "per diem security offi-cers" hired as needed and numbering up to 170 at any one time.

The nonteaching assistants are not hired specifically to control violence, "but they come in pretty damn handy for unruliness," a school board spokesman said.

Public school officials in the last two years have also had to cope with student demonstrations and disruptions. Although disruptions in secondary schools have received far less public attention than incidents like those at Berkeley, San Francisco State and Columbia, the nation's public schools have been far from immune.

In a recent study titled "High School Student Unrest," published by the National School Public Relations Association, it was reported that 59 per cent of the high schools and 56 per cent of the junior highs had experienced some form of protest by January of last year. By May 25, according to Alan F. Westin, director of the Center of Research and Education in American Liberties at Columbia University, the number of protests had reached about 2,000.

January 12, 1970

Senators Told of Brutality to Young Offenders

By NAN ROBERTSON
Special to The New York Times

WASHINGTON, May 3 — Stories of brutality, corruption and flouting of the law by juvenile judges, parole officers and those who run detention homes for children unfolded here today before a Senate subcommittee headed by Birch Bayh of Indiana.

Witnesses told of children being sent for months to jails and reformatories without a court hearing or an attorney, having committed no "crime" other than being runaways or being described as "uncontrollable" by a parent.

Bill Payne, an investigative newspaper reporter, described "juvenile justice" in El Paso and throughout Texas as a disgrace and an abomination. He said this "justice" was "conceived and executed in bad faith and designed solely for the profit of the keepers even as they speak nobly of solicitude for the children they catch and cage."

Judge Is Criticized

Steven Bercu, a public assistance lawyer in El Paso, contended that "the greatest single cause of juvenile crime" in his county was Juvenile Judge Edwin F. Berliner. Mr. Bercu said

Juvenile Justice in Texas Described as a 'Disgrace' by El Paso Reporter

the judge, "for the past five years," had sent about "75 children each year" to detention homes hundreds of miles away without a hearing or legal counsel.

Mr. Bercu, who works for the El Paso Legal Assistance Society, said he believed that no more than four or five of these children could have been committed if they had had an attorney.

"And what kind of judge would commit a child without a hearing?" he asked. "I know of now way this can be justified under the laws of the United States."

Mr. Bercu and Mr. Payne, a reporter for The El Paso Times who has investigated the Texas system dealing with delinquent children for the last nine months, criticized Judge Berliner and Morris W. Raley, the El Paso County chief probation officer, in the strongest terms.

Senator Bayh said he had invited Mr. Raley to testify, but that he had been hospitalized in El Paso. "Judge Berliner will be invited in view of the comments made today," the Indiana Democrat added. Judge Berliner, reached later by telephone and asked if he would say anything about the accusations made against him, replied that he would not.

Mr. Payne testified that the Texas schools were "characterized more by homosexuality than anything else."

He also contended that the legal treatment of children in Texas seemed designed "to pander to the very worst type of parents—the boozers and the perverts and the brutes—because the probation officers themselves" were the same.

Mr. Payne noted that a former chief guard at the El Paso detention home had been hired by Mr. Raley "while the man's own children were in protective custody in the home during a Child Welfare investigation of the children's allegations that their father 'handcuffs us to the bed and beats us.'"

The reporter also spoke of alcoholic caseworkers, of children being fed "slop" while the employes ate sirloin tips with mushroom sauce, of inmates' suicide attempts and of inmates sitting on the floors of their cells every day because their mattresses were taken from them until nightfall.

Another witness, John A. Cocoros, Texas director of the 65-year-old National Council on Crime and Delinquency, said that only 12 Texas counties had a juvenile detention home. In the remaining 242 counties, delinquent children are sent to jail.

"Although the quality of services in these detention homes vary greatly, all, in my opinion, are much superior to any Texas jail for detaining children," Mr. Cocoros added.

Senator Bayh asked if the problems in Texas were unique to that state. "No, sir," Mr. Cocoros replied.

The Senator said the Judiciary Subcommittee on Juvenile Delinquency had also found that the abuses were nationwide. Many institutionalized children are "beaten, brutalized and subject to vicious sexual attacks," he said.

Senator Bayh introduced legislation last Friday to protect juveniles in courts and detention homes. The hearings will continue tomorrow and Wednesday.

May 4, 1971

YOUTH PENALTIES HELD TOO SEVERE

Reformatories Blight Lives, Senate Hearing Is Told

By NAN ROBERTSON
Special to The New York Times

WASHINGTON, May 4—A 16-year-old boy told a Senate subcommittee today that he had been committed to an Indiana state reformatory for stealing 75 cents, and a 17-year-old girl said she had been "sent up" for carrying a can of beer down a small-town main street on a Saturday night.

The boy, Sherril Ness, and the girl, Sharon Rushin, appeared with the superintendents of their institutions as examples of the kind of teenager those officials felt should not be incarcerated for such minor offenses.

Under questioning by Senator Birch Bayh, Democrat of Indiana, the subcommittee chairman, witnesses described overcrowded, antiquated, understaffed "dumping grounds" and "baby-sitting" warehouses that doomed delinquent children to uncertain or blighted futures.

Witnesses who had so-called "criminal" records because of such acts as drinking, breaking parole by changing seats on a school bus or running away from home spoke of hostile home towns and schools after release and of the difficulty of getting jobs.

Dorothy A. Vanbrunt, superintendent of the Indiana Girls' School in Indianapolis, said a study of the 208 inmates there showed that 125 had been committed solely because they were runaways and 19 because they were school truants.

"These offenses are not criminal nor a threat to public safety," she said. "There ought to be resources short of expensive, closed, institutional care."

About the most serious misdemeanor was petty shoplifting, she added.

She also said the housing in her institution had been condemned as "unsafe and unfit to live in" by state fire and health authorities and that the plumbing in most cottages date back to 1907, when the school was built.

She and Alfred R. Bennett, superintendent of the Indiana Boys' School in Plainfield, testified that retarded children were passed in bucket-brigade fashion from families to welfare agencies to state mental hospitals to foster homes and finally to state reformatories, where they received minimal education, mental and physical health care and job training.

One 11-year-old retarded girl was finally admitted to the Indianapolis school, where the ages of inmates are supposed to range from 12 to 18, because the "only alternative for this tiny thing" was the county jail, Miss Vanbrunt said. The child had already spent one month in jail.

Mr. Bennett told of a boy named Robert, 16, who was committed for disorderly conduct and violation of curfew. He was given the Stanford-Binet intelligence test and showed an I.Q. of 43 with a mental age of 6 years.

"But almost a year was lost" before a court sent the boy where he should have been in the first place, "an appropriate mental health facility," Mr. Bennett said.

Carried Beer After Curfew

Sharon Rushin said she had been committed twice to the girls' school. She said she had been strolling with a can of beer in Attica, Ind., after the town curfew for minors and had been stopped and questioned, then "sent up." When she was released, she returned to a hostile atmosphere, she said. Her fellow-students and adults "thought I was a criminal," she said after testifying.

She ran away from home. When she was found, she was committed the second time. No lawyer represented her, she said. She and young Ness, who comes from Rochester, Ind., will be released on probation later this month, and both will be going to schools in nearby towns where they hope for a new life.

Miss Vanbrunt also told of the difficulty of finding and keeping jobs for reform school "graduates."

In filling out forms asking if the applicant has a "criminal record," many write "Yes" although this is not literally true. They are usually not hired. Those who write "No" live in fear that the employer will find out their backgrounds and dismiss them, Miss Vanbrunt added.

Another witness, Luther C. Hicks, director of a newly organized Dignity House in Indianapolis, said his institution merged with the neighborhood along with "all other family structures." The small group of boys live in cheery surroundings, go to public schools, are fed and clothed well, do chores and are made to feel like part of a family, Mr. Hicks said.

This is "one possible alternative," he said, to juvenile detention centers and reform schools.

The hearings before Senator Bayh's Judiciary Subcommittee on Juvenile delinquency resume tomorrow.

May 5, 1971

CHILDREN'S CRIME RISING ACROSS U.S.

Serious Offenses Committed by Youngsters Under 13— Violence Not Uncommon

By WAYNE KING

Crime by children, some of it serious and committed by youngsters not yet in their teens, is arousing growing concern among parents, the police and school authorities across the country.

While it is not new, juvenile authorities generally agree that the problem has grown substantially worse in the last few years, both in the number of offenses and their seriousness. And while there is a lack of national statistics that might back it up, there is a feeling that both the victims and the perpetrators are getting younger.

For the most part, the crimes are "petty" in terms of the money or property involved—shakedowns for lunch money, bicycle thefts, pilfering from school lockers—but some are serious and violence is not uncommon.

Reports from school and law enforcement officials in 13 cities indicate that the trend noted in 1969 by the National Commission on the Causes and Prevention of Violence is con-tinuing. The commission found that in the 10-year period 1958 through 1967, there was a 300 per cent increase in assaults by 10 to 14-year-olds and a 200 per cent increase in robberies by this age group.

"We've had just about everything in schools short of murder," says Harry S. Hodgins Jr., chief security supervisor for the Baltimore city schools, "everything from ordinary shakedowns for lunch money right through armed robbery in the halls at pistol point."

Off the school grounds, the problem is worse. The Baltimore police report that last year there were 12,835 arrests of suspects under 18, up from 10,594 in 1969.

526 Under 10 Arrested

Moreover, in the age group 10 years and under, there were 526 arrests, including one for murder, 22 for robbery, 169 for burglary, six for auto theft, 12 for arson, nine for aggravated assault, 104 for larceny and four for narcotics violations.

In Los Angeles, as in most other cities, bicycle theft has become commonplace, and the police department there is considering creating a 25-man "bike section" to handle the problem.

In the Roslindale section of Boston, a woman complained that "in our neighborhood, I hear you can go up to a kid in front of the local ice cream shop and say you want a 10-speed Peugeot racing bike and he'll ask you what color."

The Best Indicator

Although not considered the most serious child crime problem — shakedowns and "muggings" are regarded as more dangerous—bicycle thefts are probably the best indicator of the growth of crime committed by children against other children.

The police and other juvenile authorities generally agree that the other categories, particularly shakedowns, are not reported as often because of the threat of reprisal and the generally lower dollar value of the stolen property.

Robert Ehrman, a disciplinary officer in the Sacramento school system, says instances of extortion, backed up by threats, are increasing more noticably than other problems.

"It's usually a two-or-three kids-on-one thing," he said, "extortion or just the sheer delight of scaring the hell out of some small kid."

A Common Pattern

The greatest increase and highest incidence is from the fifth or sixth grade through the ninth grade, Mr. Erhman observed, a pattern reported by most other school officials.

Although the problem of petty extortion is not a new one—a Pittsburgh school principal recalls a situation 12 years ago in which one student demanded and got 50 cents from another student each school day for two years — juvenile officials say it has grown serious within the last three to five years in most areas.

The reasons given by police and school officials vary, but those most often cited are "a general breakdown" in family discipline, racial animosities and changing school patterns that place poor children in contact with the more affluent. The general increase in crime by all groups is also cited.

For whatever reasons, juvenile crime rates have been rising far faster than the adult rate. From 1960 through 1970, according to the Federal Bureau of Investigation police arrests for all criminal acts except traffic violations rose 31 per cent, while arrests of those under 18 more than doubled—a pace more than four times the population increase in the 10 to 18 age group.

Lesser Rate for Adults

Adult arrests for violent crime in the same period went up 67 per cent, while for juveniles they increased 167 per cent.

Generally, the police and other officials who deal with juvenile offenders keep no related statistics on the victims of juvenile crime, and there is, thus, no accurate gauge of an increase in children's crime against their peers, although there is general agreement that the problem is getting worse.

Reaction to increased youthful crime has largely taken the form of more policing of schools and surrounding areas, usually with private guards. Dade County schools had a security force of five men in 1968: today it has 98. Most other school systems have bolstered their patrols similarly, but parental concern remains.

"Mothers are frightened these days of what might happen to their daughters at school," said a Miami teacher whose three children attend public schools. She reported that at a Coral Gables Junior High, many girls were afraid to enter lavatories because of shakedowns by other girls, some of whom have brandished razors.

And a Boston father said: "My 14-year-old son got punched in the mouth at a park the other night because he wouldn't yield up a radio when ordered to by a peer who was drunk.

"It was not a traumatic experience," he said. "My kid was a little bit small and thinks that most things can be settled nonviolently."

October 4, 1971

Rise in Youth Gang Killing Alarms Police in 3 Cities

By ROBERT A. WRIGHT
Special to The New York Times

LOS ANGELES, Nov. 26—Youthful assassins in three major American cities have committed more than 100 murders this year in what some police officials fear may be a resurgence of the street gang warfare that swept urban America in the nineteen-fifties.

The cities are Los Angeles, where there have been 31 deaths caused by gangs; Philadelphia, where the total is 37, and New York, where there have been 30 gang killings in the Bronx alone, the borough with by far the highest gang toll.

Last Monday, 18-year-old Sergio Trujillo of Avila was beaten and shot to death behind a church where he had sought to hide from a gang of youths in south central Los Angeles. That was the 31st death here.

"It would have been many more except for bad shots," says Lieut. R. L. Appier, head of the Los Angeles police department's gang activities section. "We've had more than 300 attempted gang murders this year."

Ten days earlier, youthful assassins abruptly ended a football team homecoming celebration at Jefferson High School in the same primarily black section of town with a volley of gunshots that left five teen-agers wounded. The police said it had been a gang retaliation.

Another Jefferson High School, 3,000 miles across the nation in the East New York section of Brooklyn, was closed re-

cently when teachers canceled classes to protest "rampages" by youth gangs and violence in the school.

Sgt. Craig Collins of the New York police, who is in charge of youth gang intelligence for the Bronx, says: "To my knowledge the largest number of gang homicides in any one year was 12 for the whole city. Already this year we have had 30 in the Bronx alone."

The police and social workers cannot explain why gangs and violence are proliferating in Los Angeles and New York, or why it is a continuing problem in Philadelphia. In Chicago there has been a sharp decline in gangs and associated crimes. There is little violence from Cleveland's gangs and no evidence of any gangs in Pittsburgh.

In San Francisco, the Chinese community has been terrorized by gangs of youthful extortionists. Recently, the police arrested six members of a reputed teen-age gang, composed mostly of Filipino-Americans, and charged them with four armed robberies, including one in which a policeman was shot at.

In Philadelphia, William Jones, school district spokesman, said 15 to 20 gangs in the north, west and central sections of the city caused the most trouble. "Hardly a day goes by that we don't have a clash between a couple of gangs outside one of our schools," Mr. Jones said. Gang fights and assaults on pupils increased 150 per cent during the first four months of this year from the 1971 level, he reported.

Ron Bloomberg, an adver-

tising executive, recently placed an advertisement in The Philadelphia Bulletin with the headline, "Say a prayer for the children of Philadelphia." It appeared over a photograph of a black boy sprawled on a street clutching his stomach, which had been blown open by a shotgun blast.

The text asserted that the city had done nothing to alleviate gang violence, although city officials say they are spending $4-million a year in programs aimed at ending gang violence. Mr. Bloomberg said in an interview that he found that "gang killings don't make the papers any more, especially if you're a black kid. Maybe they'll get a couple of lines on the back pages."

Gang activity, the authorities say, is as cyclical as adolescence. But there was an apparent eclipse of youth gangs during the sixties when a broader section of the population was affected by violent confrontations associated with civil rights and student protest. In the last two years, the police here say, dormant gangs have revived and recruited new members. When one gang "gets hot," others are formed as a challenge or as a defense.

Where they have revived, today's gangs differ from those of the fifties in armaments and tactics.

The occasional, crudely home-fashioned zip guns of the fifties have been replaced by sophisticated automatic pistols and shotguns. The spontaneous fight, and the organized confrontations of rival gangs in rumbles, has been replaced by the planned assassination of one or two of the enemy in killings more like those of the adult underworld.

"They have an inexhaustible supply of guns and a penchant to use them," says Capt. Jack L. Eberhardt of the Los Angeles police, who is in charge of the Newton division, which encompasses Jefferson High. "These kids are willing to take revenge

That's a thing you used to see just on television. They will retaliate against the report of a crime. So people don't want to talk to us when we go to the scene. Not even the victims."

Los Angeles now has some 150 gangs, compared with about 75 in the fifties, according to Police Lieutenant Appier, with memberships as small as eight or 10 and as high as in the thousands. They range from 11 years of age to, usually, 18. Most are males, although increasing numbers of girls are admitted or formed into auxiliaries. Most gangs are black or Mexican-American. White gangs tend to be motorcycle or car gangs, the police say.

In New York, the police say, gangs have more than doubled in the last nine months. A proliferation that started in the Bronx has spread to Manhattan, Brooklyn and Queens, with a total of 285 distinct gangs identified by the police. Police Sergeant Collins says gangs vary in size from 35 to 100 members. "We're dealing with 9,000 kids running around," he says. Most are black or Hispanic, but the police say that white gangs have been formed in defense.

Other People Victimized

In the fifties, gangs fought mostly for territory, or turf, and among themselves. Their names, once more reflective of pride in race or neighborhood, now more often describe their violent intentions. And today, while gang activities are concentrated in the slum areas, more persons who are not gang members are victims of gang crimes ranging from petty extortion, muggings and thefts to misdirected "hits."

On the third day of school this semester at Jefferson High School in Los Angeles, one gang member shot a rival. That night, the gang, seeking revenge, went to the wrong address and fired a shotgun from a passing car in the dark into a family gathering of about 20 persons in front of a home.

Two teen-age girls, a woman and a 3-year-old boy were wounded.

A code of silence among gangs and the fear of retaliation in the black community present the biggest problem to the Los Angeles police in dealing with the gangs.

"The answer is parental guidance and community involvement," Lieutenant Appier says. "Many gang crimes go unreported. We need people to report crimes and then to come forward as witnesses if we are going to be effective."

Just this kind of community involvement is credited in Chicago with a sharp decline in youth gang crimes. Louis Burke, community organizer for the Chicago Urban League, and Lieut. John J. Hart of the police department's gang intelligence unit agree that the decline in delinquency in that city stems from the arousal of the black community, programs to redirect youth and the jailing of many gang leaders and the indictment of others.

Since the Jefferson High incident, the California school authorities and some parents have expressed concern and have begun to explore ways that school security might be improved and gang activity dissipated.

Street workers continue to try to redirect youths, some by working through the structure of established gangs to reorient them. But the police are convinced there will be little success until the communities themselves become involved and cooperate with the police.

Dr. Malcolm W. Klein, a faculty member at the University of Southern California and for six years a street gang worker, says: "I don't see how you can expect the gangs to disappear. Gangs are just a by-product of other social ills and they have been established for 40 years in these communities as a viable alternative."

Dr Klein said his experience had indicated that programs to work within gang structures reinforced the organizations and led to increased delinquency.

In his 1970 book, "Street Gangs and Street Workers," he declared, "Getting older is still the gang member's best hope and will be until social theorists and practitioners are able to translate their observations into theory and their theory into action more powerful than the natural variables of urban society."

November 27, 1972

Skyrocketing Juvenile Crime: Are Stiffer Penalties the Answer?

By ENID NEMY

The staggering increase in the number of violent crimes committed by the young is prompting both a re-examination of the efficacy of present juvenile laws, and a hardening of attitude on juvenile rights. There is a growing belief that youths of 14, 15, and 16 years of age, particularly recidivists who commit such crimes as murder, rape and armed robbery, should be tried as adults.

Legislators who, in the past, have attempted unsuccessfully to stiffen juvenile laws in their states, believe that increasing public pressure and indignation will accomplish their purpose this year. But despite mounting criticism of the frequent minimal sentences given violent young criminals, there is also a body of opinion that believes that most young offenders are salvageable, and that they should not be treated as harshly as adults.

The number of juveniles arrested for serious and violent crimes increased 1600 per cent in the 20 years between 1952 and 1972, according to Federal Bureau of Investigation figures gathered from 6,000 law agencies covering 155 million people. Almost 4 per cent of arrests for homicide, and more than 9 per cent of rape arrests, were youngsters under the age of 16.

'Not Hubcap Stealing'

"Juvenile crime has risen because youthful offenders know they will not be punished," said Joseph Busch, District Attorney of Los Angeles County. "They'll be back on the streets bragging about how nothing is happening to them. We're talking about murder and rape, not hubcap stealing."

The mounting dissatisfaction at the built-in restrictions of Family Court prosecution and sentencing, and the resulting "turnstile" or "revolving door" effect — where youngsters are back in court two, three and four times in one month, and back on the streets four to eight months after being convicted of murder—have led to various proposals for a "more realistic" treatment of juvenile criminals.

Among them are:

¶A bill just introduced in the New York State Legislature that would allow juveniles 15 years of age or over, who have been charged with such crimes as homicide, kidnapping, rape and armed robbery, to be tried as adults. The present law prohibits this procedure until a youngster reaches his 16th birthday.

¶A bill to be introduced in the California State Legislature that would allow 16- and 17-year-olds arrested for serious crimes to be treated as adults. (California law now treats anyone under 18 as a juvenile). The move for such a bill was led by Mr. Busch, and strongly backed by Los Angeles Police Chief Edward M. Davis.

¶A bill to be introduced in the Illinois General Assembly within the next few weeks that would lower the minimum age for a criminal trial as an adult from 17 to 14 years.

¶A bill prepared for submission to the Washington State Legislature that would make trial in an adult, rather than a juvenile court, mandatory in some cases of violent and serious crime.

¶A Police Department lobby at the Texas State Legislature that is seeking amendment of the state's 1973 Family Code, which police spokesmen claim restricts their handling of juvenile crime.

"I'm more optimistic because there's been a great deal of public sentiment toward a more realistic juvenile stance," said Mr. Busch in Los Angeles, adding that Assemblyman Julian Dixon, a Democrat, had agreed to sponsor the California bill.

"Community pressure for stiffer measures against serious crimes by juveniles is causing this," said Geoffrey Revelle, a deputy prosecuting attorney in Seattle. "There should be some changes in the law, mostly to provide more protection for society."

Lieut. John Rumsey of the Dallas Police Youth Division noted that "public attitude is changing . . . there's a hardening . . . they want us to deal severely with these kids who commit violent crimes . . . but the law is becoming more relaxed about the culprit. I personally feel someone ought to look at the victims' rights."

Illinois State Representative Raymond W. Ewell, a Democrat, who plans to introduce the bill in his state's Legislature, said he was doing so "because if we believe in some obligation to society, there must be a certain deterrent factor, and the only one is some punishment . . . these kids understand what they are doing."

He said communities throughout the nation were disintegrating because they were "unsafe" and warned that if some action wasn't taken, "our cities will become holding centers for the unfortunate."

"I don't think you're doing a kid a favor by letting him off easy the first or second time he comes in," observed William K. Hanger, chief of police in Pontiac, Mich. "Something should happen to that kid that creates a healthy respect and/or fear."

Police Chief Davis in Los Angeles said he believed that juvenile justice in California worked "pretty well for a while . . . but the machinery must be changed with the protection of society in mind, and not the protection of a particular juvenile."

(California law allows a youngster under 18, who commits a serious crime, to be detained in a youth authority facility for a maximum of two years. When the youngster reaches 18, the record can be erased. Police officials contend that juveniles are rarely detained for more than six months, no matter what the crime.)

Decries Philosophy

"There are too many people with a Father Flanagan philosophy that there is no such thing as a bad boy," Chief Davis added. "There are plenty of bad boys."

There are also, apparently, plenty of bad girls. F.B.I. figures indicate that, between 1960 and 1973, there was a 296 per cent increase in the number of girls under 18 arrested for murder. This compared with an increase of 102 per cent in the number of women of all ages arrested for murder.

"The percentage change among the young has really gone sky-high," an F.B.I. spokesman said.

According to Douglas J. Besharov, author of "Juvenile Justice Advocacy," a law text, there are now 42 states that give their family courts authority, in certain situations, to transfer cases of serious juvenile crime to the criminal court.

In some states, any youngster over the age of 14, charged with murder or rape, is charged as an adult, unless the case is waived back to juvenile court. Advocates of stronger legislation and stricter measures are usually in states where such transfers are not allowed, or in communities where authorities are inclined to release youngsters after minimal confinement.

In New York State where, between 1970 and 1974, the number of juveniles charged with homicide more than tripled (from 32 to 98), and the number of rape charges doubled (from 83 to 165), Assemblyman Alfred A. Delli Bovi, Republican - Conservative of Queens stated that "we have to start coming to grips with the problem."

"It's all right to think of kids and rehabilitation," he said, "but kids aren't being rehabilitated and society is being terrorized. More and more public officials are realizing that you've got to start thinking about society and the victims."

Mr. Delli Bovi, who with co-sponsor Joseph R. Lentol, Democrat of Brooklyn, introduced the juvenile bill, said the juvenile justice system wasn't created with a view to handling "the type of kid we get now."

Few who believe in harsher punishment for juveniles question the desirability of rehabilitation but many, like Mr. Delli Bovi, believe that the price being paid, for efforts that are seemingly not working, is too high.

Protection of Public

Judge Simeon Golar of New York's Family Court commented that a rational case could be made for both punishment and rehabilitation but that he found it difficult to condone the fact that neither one nor the other was being done.

"Youngsters who are violent and a threat to the community must be removed from the community for the protection of the public,"

he added. "Hopefully, they can be rehabilitated but even if they can't, one of the objects of the courts is public safety."

"American society has given up punishment for rehabilitation but rehabilitation hasn't succeeded, so society stands naked and helpless before the assault," said Assistant Police Chief Anthony Bouza, commanding officer of the Bronx.

To Assistant Police Chief Jules Sachson, commanding officer of Brooklyn South, "rehabilitation is a phrase used by social workers and psychologists . . . there's a shoveling of money into it but that doesn't mean it works."

Of particular concern in New York State, (where, in the year ending June 30, 1974, 62 per cent of juvenile homicide arrests and 69 per cent of juvenile rape cases, were dismissed, withdrawn, discharged, adjourned or suspended) is the fact that a great majority of youths sentenced up to the maximum three years, are released within four to eight months. The Family Court sentences the youngster but the New York State Division for Youth can effect his release whenever it deems appropriate, without going back or consulting the court.

"It is their policy to release dangerous and violent teen-agers into society in six to eight months," said Judge Shirley Kram of Family Court. "They have stated to me that after six to eight months, a child 'is not motivated to stay.'"

Although there is some consensus of opinion that stricter measures should be taken about juveniles committing violent crimes, there is little unanimity as to the method that might prove most effective.

Rena K. Uviller, who heads the Juvenile Rights Project of the American Civil Liberties Union in New York, suggested that juvenile courts be reserved for law violators only.

"There should be a voluntary community effort for kids running away from home and school . . . these cases should be eliminated from court, she said. "The

courts should deal only with law violators and there should be greater specifics in sentencing depending on the crime . . . a scaled-down version of the adult situation, but more realistic than it presently is."

Favors Special Center

Concern was also voiced about the facilities available for punishment. Judge Frank Montemuro, chief of Philadelphia's Juvenile Court, acknowledged a trend toward "stiffer punishment for youthful offenders." He said he would agree to setting up juvenile maximum security centers, but would not agree to putting juveniles into adult institutions.

Richard Buckland, acting director of a juvenile court in Seattle, expressed the view of many when he suggested that "children who come in for reasons of care should be separated from alleged delinquents."

The importance of separating first-time offenders and recidivists was emphasized by State Senator Roy M. Goodman, a Republican-Liberal of New York. Senator Goodman also advocated spending a little less money on educating normal children and devoting the difference to "those in deep trouble."

In Michigan, where youths of 16 and under are considered juveniles, L. Brooks Patterson, the prosecutor of Oakland County, would like to see a "limbo" category between the ages of 15 and 17. The category would leave to the prosecuting attorney the decision as to whether the charge should be adult or juvenile.

Statistics notwithstanding, moves to stiffen juvenile laws are opposed by many throughout the country.

"I think the move to change the law is predicated on fear and overreaction," said Ramona Ripston, executive director of the A.C.L.U. in southern California. She agreed that liberals and conservatives now seem to be more in agreement on dealing more severely with serious youthful offenders but, "what bothers me is that they want to put them in prison . . . that's not what deters crime."

"Institutionalizing is a thing of the past," said Henry J. Albach, president of the Dallas A.C.L.U., who added that he was not aware of any upward trend in juvenile crime. He said proposals would be made to establish diversion programs for juveniles.

"We definitely don't take a get-tough attitude," said Jan Payton of the Urban League of Philadelphia. "We support alternative programs such as group homes."

Darrel L. Longest, deputy state attorney of Montgomery County, Md., said "there is a substantial public interest in treating people under 18 different from those over 18."

More Services Urged

A greater emphasis on helping people and more services for juvenile offenders were suggested by people as diverse as Assemblyman Alan Sieroty of California, Charles Schinitsky of New York's Legal Aid Society and Capt. Francis J. Daly, commanding officer of the Youth Aid division of the New York City police.

Although agreeing that solutions must be found outside the court, as well as within it, Judge Golar of New York refuted the claim that rehabilitation and treatment are answers to the problem.

"Most youngsters who are charged with juvenile delinquency are not psychotic and are not more neurotic than the rest of us," he said.

"But we continue a commitment to the idea of diagnosis and treatment of the problems of children in trouble, on the medical model. Twenty-five per cent of the entire New York City Family Court budget, I am told, is spent on psychiatric services—diagnostic services. All of this totally excludes the idea of individual accountability or any reference to right or wrong."

"We have taught young people that crime does pay," Governor Carey of New York recently said. "One of the most indefensible practices today is the release of juvenile offenders who have committed unquestionably heinous acts." avo

February 21, 1975

Violent Crime by Young People:
No Easy Answer

By ENID NEMY

Why is it happening?

Why are an increasing number of youths committing brutal, violent and often senseless crimes?

Why is the curve of violence rising, even as the

percentage of juveniles in the general population is decreasing?

There is general unanimity, among people associated with criminology, that there is neither an easy nor a single answer. The seeming

inability of many youngsters to differentiate between right and wrong, and to feel any sense of personal responsibility for their actions, is the result of a combination of factors. And, it is noted, once the causes are accepted and

understood, solutions, while difficult, are more readily planned and adopted.

The experts, whose studies are outgrowths of their areas of concern—sociology, law, psychoanalysis—list among major reasons for the upsurge in juvenile violence:

¶The American dream and the country's emphasis on brawn, rather than brains.

¶The easy availability of guns and lack of a national gun law.

¶The disintegration of the family and the deterioration of discipline in schools.

¶The prevalence of violence in the media, particularly on television and in films.

¶The lack of deterrents in the form of positive punishment.

¶Racial attitudes that neutralize guilt feelings.

"The American dream is, in part, responsible for a great deal of crime and violence," said Dr. David Abrahamsen, a psychoanalyst specializing in behavorial disorders. "People feel that America owes them not only a living but a good living, and they take short cuts to get what they feel is owing to them . . . frustration is the wet nurse to violence."

Dr. Abrahamsen, author of "The Murdering Mind," (Harper & Row) added: "Unfortunately, we in the United States are not very easily given to contemplation . . . we have a masculine self-image. I think it's time it was a little more feminized, a little more passive and peaceful. If you have a brain, you are thought to be a sissy. If you have muscles on the football field, you are an American. It's almost un-American to have a brain."

Violence as an accepted technique of getting something, with no sense of personal responsibility for actions, was noted by Wayne Mucci, the former director of the Bureau of Institutions and Facilities for New York City.

Most kids tend to be highly impulsive and seek immediate gratification," said Mr. Mucci, who is now director of the American Bar Association Institute of Judicial Administration, Juvenile Justice Standards Project.

"They didn't plan to murder the person they were robbing, but it seemed to happen if someone got in their way . . . it seemed incidental."

Mr. Mucci said that one characteristic common to many juveniles in serious trouble was "a highly disorganized environment . . . no controls or highly inconsistent controls."

"Juveniles tend to become disengaged earlier, not only from families but from society," he said.

Dropout Parents

"An increasing number of parents have resigned their responsibility for the character of their child," said Dr. Amitai Etzioni, professor of sociology at Columbia University.

"It's as elementary as that —where is a child supposed to get the distinction between right and wrong— from the home and school. The schools focus ever more on cognitive skills and less on character building.

Dr. Etzioni also attributed the increasing number of children "who don't know right from wrong" to broken homes, rotating "partners" and the lack of a permanent philosophy.

"There's a continuing disintegration of the social context . . . of links . . . and the family and community are central in this," said Richard (Rick) Carlson of Santa Barbara, a lawyer involved in the criminal justice field.

To Dr. Marvin Wolfgang, professor of sociology and law at the University of Pennsylvania, the reduction in discipline, supervision and monitoring of adolescents is "an important variable."

"Important studies have confirmed empirically a lot of laymen's ideas about discipline," he commented.

Dr. Wolfgang, director of the Center for Studies in Criminology and Criminal Law, questioned, too, the race relation between victim and perpetrator. He believed that a high proportion of violent and sometime senseless crime was committed "by a minority group against a majority group."

"I believe a lot of kids have a neutralization of guilt about attacking [a majority racial group] . . . they feel justified . . . and the easiest targets are the disabled and the old."

Dr. Wolfgang, who is also the research director of the National Commission on the Causes and Prevention of Violence and the commissioner of the National Commission on Obscenity and Pornography, observed that a display of sex in the media and television wasn't hurting anyone "but a display of violence has more of a response . . . people imitate violence."

Although violence had, he believed, become "the norm" in society, Dr. Abrahamsen suggested the necessity of television controlling its content better than it does now.

"There are no doubts about it, it serves as a stimulus," he said. "It can trigger hostile actions."

Mr. Mucci said he had seen research figures that indicated that children who watched television had seen about 11,000 murders by the time they were 14 years old, "and that's really shocking when you come to think of it."

"We don't need to have violence liberated," said Dr. James Short, visiting professor of law and sociology at Stanford University. "I'm not suggesting a direct connection [with television] but it's inconceivable that there is no effect. I don't view it with equanimity."

Dr. Short was one of many who were inclined to attribute the increase in lethality to the greater presence of weapons on the streets.

Urges a National Law

"What we need is a national law," he said. "We can't prevent people from killing when hand guns are so easily available."

Dr. Etzioni concurred, as did Mr. Carlson, a former visiting fellow at the Center for the Study of Democratic Institutions in Santa Barbara.

"Guns make a physically disadvantaged person—someone smaller, less strong than an adult—into an accomplished person," Dr. Etzioni said.

Although there is some belief that the rising juvenile crime figures reflect both better reporting and an increase of the percentage of juveniles in the general population, police officials question the general validity of the first premise, and census figures refute the second.

The Census Bureau reports that although the juvenile (16 years of age and under) percentage of the general population increased from 35 to 49 per cent between 1965 and 1971, it has fallen steadily since then. Juveniles accounted for 31 per cent of the population in 1972, 30 per cent in 1973 and slightly under 30 per cent last year. There were 67,151,000 juveniles in the country in 1965 and an estimated 63,055,000 last year.

The figures reinforce the beliefs of some criminologists that lack of deterrents in the judicial system encourages young first offenders.

"I used to see kids who had been through the juvenile court system laugh at what the court could do," said Mr. Mucci, whose former work brought him in contact with hundreds of delinquents in New York City. "They told me it was an 'easy' time. I believe there should be definite sentences and the length should be related to the seriousness of the crime."

"We probably imprison too many for too long but there is an incorrigible minority of those who engage in violent crime that you can't do anything with," Mr. Carlson said.

Although deterrent research is still in its infancy, Dr. Robert Martinson, who is involved in the field, noted that initial results indicated that "people can be deterred by threat of punishment."

"Until recently, deterrence was set aside as an archaic notion," he said. "I'm not interested in pushing any position. I try to base my arguments on the facts of the matter. I think the police have a prima-facie case that couldn't be made 10 years ago. There is no fear among kids . . . they know if they are caught, they'll get away with it.

Sees Little Effectiveness

Dr. Martinson, who, with two colleagues, spent eight years looking into thousands of studies on correctional treatment, said his research had indicated that "rehabilitation doesn't have much effect, if any."

"There is an American tendency to think that there is a cure for every disease . . . we have rather strong evidence that, on the whole, if you look at all rehabilitation programs they don't seem to have much effect, or any effect, on recidivism."

Dr. Martinson, co-author with Douglas S. Lipton and Judith Wilks of "Effectiveness of Correctional Treatment," a book scheduled for publication within the next few months, added that treatment—"almost an axiom of American penal policy for 50 to 75 years" — had begun to be questioned very seriously.

"The present system is clearly out of line somewhere . . . . it is certain that money poured into rehabilitation is not the answer."

"The certainty of punishment, rather than the severity, would have the effect," he said.

> 'There is a continuing disintegration of the social context . . . of links . . . and the family and community are central in this.'

March 17, 1975

RADICAL CHANGES URGED IN DEALING WITH YOUTH CRIME

Panel Led by Judge Kaufman Would Limit the Discretion of Court in Sentencing

A PHILOSOPHICAL SHIFT

End to Indeterminate Terms Is Asked — Proceedings Would Be More Visible

By MARCIA CHAMBERS

A national commission set up to establish the country's first comprehensive guidelines for juvenile offenders has recommended radical philosophical changes that would base sentences on the seriousness of the crime rather than on a judge's view of the "needs" of the youth.

At the heart of the recommendation is the belief that disparity in juvenile sentencing must end. To accomplish this, the commission would limit a juvenile judge's discretion and make the judge accountable to the public by putting down written reasons for his sentencing decision. The decisions would be subject to judicial review and public scrutiny.

Moreover, the report recommends that juvenile proceedings be made more visible to achieve greater judicial accountability.

Shift Is Major

Thus, certain court procedures would be open to the public. Either the youth or the judge could request the admission of certain persons, including reporters, to certain hearings.

This would be a major shift from the present system in New York, and most other states, where secrecy pervades the juvenile process. Under the recommended guidelines, however, the names of juveniles would still remain confidential.

Irving R. Kaufman, chief judge of the Court of Appeals for the Second Circuit here and chairman of the Juvenile Justice Standards Project, said the commission's major principles would "significantly alter the concepts now prevailing in juvenile courts and agencies throughout the country."

He said the juvenile courts had traditionally based dispositions on the "best interests" of the youngster. The commission, however, would supplement this criterion for sentencing with other factors, including the gravity of the crime, the degree of the juvenile's guilt, his age and his prior criminal record.

To make a juvenile's sentence commensurate with his crime, the panel would abolish indeterminate sentences, which are now used in 25 states, in favor of required maximum terms prescribed by state legislature.

The proposed guidelines are an attempt to standardize the handling of juvenile offenders that now varies considerably in the 50 states. The recommendations come, Judge Kaufman said, at a time of "community outrage" over violent crimes committed by youths.

They also come at a time of public indignation over sentencing disparities that may permit an incorrigible juvenile who has committed no crime to spend more time in a state facility than a youth convicted of murder.

Discussion Sought

The commission hopes to stimulate public discussion of its recommendations before next summer's convention of the American Bar Association, which sponsored the project along with the Institute of Judicial Administration.

At the convention, the commission will ask that the guidelines be adopted. Subsequently it hopes that the 50 state legislatures will enact these new legal principles into law.

The panel's recommendations, the first to be disclosed during its four-year effort to draft uniform laws affecting juvenile offenders, are set forth in more than a score of reports, several of which were made available to The New York Times last week. Commission spokesmen were interviewed about other reports.

In a six-page press release outlining the commission's principles, Judge Kaufman did not disclose the suggested duration of the required maximum terms, but the report on juvenile delinquency adopted by the commission recommends two-year sentences for serious juvenile felons and the transfer, under rigid restrictions, to adult court for violent juveniles 16 and 17 years old.

According to the Federal Bureau of Investigation's uniform crime reports for 1974, children between the age of 10 and 17, who make up 16 percent of the population, account for almost half of all arrests for violent cries and theft.

Rise Noted in 1975

A recent study by The Times shows that arrests in New York City of juveniles under 16 for the violent crimes of murder, rape, assault and robbery increased by nearly 20 percent in the first six months of 1975, compared with the similar period in 1974.

The following are the major recommendations described in the reports and in Judge Kaufman's statement:

¶Juvenile offenses would be divided into five classes, three for felonies, two for misdemeanors. A required sentence of two years would be imposed on juveniles who committed crimes for which adults normally would be sentenced to death, life in prison or 20 years in prison. Juveniles could be sent to a secure or nonsecure facility. The minimum sentence for a misdemeanor or crime would be two months. In some instances, conditional freedom could be granted instead of confinement.

¶The criminal code for juvenile offenders would cover the ages from 10 until a youngster's 18th birthday, an age limit imposed by nearly two-thirds of the states and the District of Columbia. New York, along with Alabama, Connecticut, North Carolina and Vermont, limit delinquency jurisdiction to youngsters under 16.

¶Certain victimless crimes would be decriminalized—possesion for personal use of marijuana and alcohol, gambling and possession of pornographic material.

¶"Persons in need of supervision," children defined as habitual truants, incorrigibles or ungovernable or beyond the control of parents or other law authority, would be removed from the juvenile court's jurisdiction. The commission points out that these children have committed no crime. They would be cared for by community agencies, including crisis-intervention groups and peer-counseling programs.

¶Juveniles would be given the right to counsel at every stage of the proceeding.

¶The most violent 16- and 17-year-old offenders could be transferred or "waived" to an adult court following a hearing in juvenile court. Adult courts could impose a life term in prison for convicted murderers, for example.

Provision Opposed

The so-called "waiver" provision appears to be the most stringent recommendation to emerge from the reports. It was adopted over strong opposition by some commission members who believe that juveniles should never be sent to mix with adult prisoners.

Some of the panel's members were said to have contended that a two-year mandatory sentence for youngsters, even for murder, was too harsh. To incarcerate a juvenile longer, said Barbara Flicker, the project's director, breeds recidivism and "endangers the public more."

"The two-year term for a juvenile is a long period of time," Mrs. Flicker said, adding that studies showed that after 18 months in custody, a juvenile reaches "the point of diminishing returns" and could no longer be salvaged.

As New York law now stands, the waiver provision would not apply to the state's violent 16- and 17-year olds because they are now prosecuted in adult court. A waiver statute transferring 15-year-old New Yorkers to adult court on murder charges was repealed in 1967 by the Legislature.

Full Term Rare

Data obtained by The Times show that in 1973 and 1974, a total of 64 juveniles 15 years old were arrested for murder in the city. If adjudicated juvenile delinquent in a murder case, the juvenile, if 15, could be sent to a reformatory for up to three years or to a non secure state facility for up to 18 months. Youngsters under 15 face an 18-month sentence.

In practice, juveniles sent to either place rarely serve the full term, and parole boards or state administrators decide when, and without the permission of the judge, to return a youngster to his community. Thus, regardless of the crime, a youngster usually servies about one year.

Under the commission's proposals, however, no one could tamper with the disposition except if a petition was brought to the judge to review the sentence. The only other sentence reduction possible would come by way of 5 percent time off for good behavior.

When administrators have the power to release juveniles, thereby aborting a sentence, the result is disparate treatment of juveniles serving time for similar conduct, the report says.

The intent of the indeterminate sentence—to treat each juvenile individually, according to his needs and release him when ready—has been carried out rarely. Often youngsters have been forced to stay in juvenile centers for the sake of rehabilitation that is never provided.

"The rehabilitative ideal," Judge Kaufman said, "has proved a failure frequently causing needless suffering in the name of treatment. Sentencing geared to the gravity of the offense on the other hand reduces arbitrary sentencing disparities and prevents harsh, vindictive sanctions from being imposed in the guise of benevolence."

Judge Kaufman noted the recent case of Rodney L., a 15-year-old youth sentenced to up to 18 months in an unlocked rehabilitation center for killing Michele Godbout, 18, with a golf club after he took the bicycle she had been riding through Central Park last spring. In all likelihood Rodney will serve only six to eight months of his sentence.

Factors Called Unfair

The Family Court judge, whose name has not been disclosed, had been told by the Probation Department and lawyers in the case that Rodney had no prior record and showed great remorse for his act. The judge was also told Rodney came from a good home and had parents who cared for him.

These were some of the factors weighed in sentencing Rodney, factors that Judge

183

Kaufman says are unfair.

"Flagrant injustice is seen in the likelihood that a poor minority child from a 'bad' home who committed the same crime would be confined in a correction institution until he or she reached majority," he said.

Under the commission's guidelines, the judge would not be able to consider the nature of Rodney's home life or his remorse, but could note that he had no prior record. The judge would also have to weigh the gravity of the crime and the degree of Rodney's guilt.

Under those rules, Mrs. Flicker predicted that Rodney would most likely have been sent to a secure state facility for two years. With good behavior he would be free in 19 months. But Mrs. Flicker's prediction may not be that precise.

According to one of the commission's reports, judges must employ "the least drastic" punishment and duration of sentence commensurate with the crime. Incarceration behind locked doors, the commission says, is a step to be taken only "as a last resort."

November 30, 1975

Issue and Debate

Juvenile Criminals an Increasing Problem

By JOSEPH B. TREASTER

They are smooth-faced, not more than 14 or 15 years old. Yet nothing they see on television is more violent than their daily lives.

They are members of a small army of muggers, stick-up men and purse-snatchers who have beset New York and other cities in the country in the last few years, confounding the police and the courts, terrorizing neighborhoods and creating an intense debate on how to cope with them.

For decades, authorities have dealt with juvenile delinquents as troubled individuals, rather than as criminals. The delinquents have been offered help, but have seldom been punished.

But now, with a tougher, more dangerous delinquent emerging, committing more violent crime than ever before, it is clear that the old approach is not working.

That fundamental changes are essential seems to be universally accepted. What is at issue, however, is the degree of the change. And these days, a handful of concerned legislators are searching for answers.

On the one hand, there is a group of so-called "hard-liners" urging that 14- and 15-year-olds accused of violent crimes be dealt with in the criminal courts and be sent to adult-style prisons for terms of up to life.

Others, at this end of the spectrum, say that all youths under 16—the demarcation line for juveniles in New York State — should remain within the jurisdiction of the Family Court but that sentences of up to six years should be levied for the most heinous crimes, compared to the present maximum term of 18 months, which is usually shortened to a year or less.

Still others, maintain that youths should be tried in the Criminal Court, then returned to Family Court for sentencing of up to five years.

Another group is rallying around a number of more moderate revisions, including one providing for a minimum of one year of detention in secure confinement for a youth found guilty of such violent crimes as murder and rape with at least two more years of supervision either in or out of an institution.

None of the reformers wants to eliminate the basic goal of trying to rehabilitate errant youths, they say. But the steep rise in violence has convinced them that the system must shift away from its original focus on just helping the troubled youths so that some measure of protection can be provided for the community. Generally speaking, the reformers want to impose a standard of accountibility on young lawbreakers—to make clear to them that they "can't get away with murder," — and this appears to mean, for the first time, establishing punishment as a part of the juvenile justice system.

The Background

The first juvenile court was established in Cook County, Ill. in 1899, rooted in the concept that youngsters who got into trouble ought to be accorded special care and treatment because of their immaturity. Within the next decade or so there were similar courts in all the states.

From the beginning, however, the juvenile justice system was treated as a stepchild within city and state governments. It was never adequately financed and, while children were institutionalized separately from adults and interned for periods thought to be relevant to their needs rather than their offenses, efforts at rehabilitation were generally limited.

In the late 1950's and 1960's, there was great concern that the system, however benevolently conceived, was more harmful than helpful to its charges. This set in motion a number of reforms for the protection of the child.

But in the last few years something, still unexplained, has been happening: Increasing numbers of youngsters have been turning to violent crime, and the crimes are not just an isolated murder or robbery, but scores of them.

For example, the New York City police say 54 youths under 16 years of age were arrested for murder in the city in 1975; there were 5,276 arrests for robbery and 1,230 were charged with felonious assault. There were also 173 arrests for rape and 125 for sodomy. These youths are often thought to be more dangerous than adults because many of them are unpredictable, easily upset and remorseless.

As a result, the pendulum has began to swing away from protecting the child and toward protecting society. The two sides in the debate disagree to some extent on this point, however, with those in the moderate camp arguing that harsh treatment of juveniles in adult facilities will not serve the community well but will create a more disturbed person to deal with in later years.

Severe View

Assemblyman Burton G. Hecht, liberal Democrat from the Bronx, who introduced one of the bills that would sent 14- and 15-year-olds charged with violent crimes to the Criminal Court, argues that Family Court is simply not equipped to deal with these cases.

He recalls a recent study by a state agency that showed that of more than 4,800 youths taken to Family Courts on felony charges only a little more than 4 percent of them were sent to institutions.

According to Senator Donald M. Halperin, Democrat of Brooklyn and chairman of the Democrats' Senate task force on juvenile delinquency, longer incarceration and sentences directly related to the magnitude of the crime would provide a deterrent that does not currently exist.

Both Mr. Hecht and Mr. Halperin see their measures as offering protection to society by removing youths from the community.

Senator Ralph J. Marino, Republican of Oyster Bay, says he favors trying youths accused of violent crimes in the Criminal Court and then having them sentenced by the Family Court and sent to youth facilities for up to five years because of a great "log jam" in the "adjudication process" in the Family Court.

He and the others in this camp feel the proposals for a minimum of one year in secure detention, which have been advanced both by Governor Carey and Assemblyman Richard N. Gottfried, liberal Democrat from Manhattan and chairman of the Assembly's standing committee on child care, are far too lenient.

"One year is not enough time to turn around a kid who's done a major crime," Senator Marino says.

Furthermore, he says, "it's ridiculous to focus on the age of 16. Kids are maturing much earlier now. The determination of maturity should be based on the seriousness of the crime and not an artificial chronological age. A kid who commits rape is not a child."

Moderate View

Mr. Gottfried's more moderate proposal provides a flexibility that he suggests is invaluable in trying to cope with young people. Beyond the initial three years of supervision, his proposal also makes it possible for the state to extend control over the youth for one year at a time until his 21st birthday.

"I don't think you can mandate a specific sentence," he says. "Fourteen and 15-year-old youngsters are going through very rapid changes. No two are at the same point in change. No two of them are moving at the same pace."

He feels strongly that the Family Court and the other elements of the present juvenile justice system can be made to work effectively and has advanced several other proposals, which, as well as tightening up current procedures, would shift the mandate of the court so that it is clearly obligated to consider the safety of the community in its dealing with youths.

Mr. Hecht, on the other hand, says he feels it is "a

lot worse," to put a 15-year-old murderer into an institution with 13- and 14-year-olds who have not committed major crimes and "who still may be saved," than to put the older boy into the adult system.

The Outlook

According to a number of legislative sources, the harshest of the proposals—partic-.

ularly those that would send juveniles into the adult system—appear to be losing ground, partly because it is strongly felt that they would be rejected by the Governor.

At the same time, the proposals put forward by Mr. Gottfried are becoming the focal point of the Legislature. For the last several days, Mr. Gottfried and Mr. Hecht have been negotiating a compro-

mise that is expected to result in the death of Mr. Hecht's plan to send youngsters to the adult system and a toughening of Mr. Gottfried's sentencing proposal.

Just how tough Mr. Gottfried's proposal might become is something he says he would prefer not to discuss.

May 25, 1976

Study Finds Drinking—Often to Excess—Now Starts at Earlier Age

Eric, who is 14 years old, gets drunk several times a week, but does not think he has a drinking problem. He drinks only beer or fruity wines, considered innocuous in his circle of friends, and his idea of an alcoholic is a bottle-clutching bum lying in the gutter.

Eric is among the 1.3 million preteens and teen-agers in this country with serious drinking problems, according to the National Institute on Alcohol Abuse and Alcoholism. Young people today are starting to drink earlier than ever before, according to a report by the Advisory Council on Youthful Alcohol and Drug Abuse Problems, which was set up by Mayor Beame two years ago to combat alcoholism among the young.

About 70 percent of high school students have tried alcoholic beverages, and the number who have become intoxicated doubled in the last 20 years. These statistics were related by Dr. Ernest Noble, director of the National Institute on Alcohol Abuse and Alcoholism, to a Senate subcommittee in Washington last week.

Started on Beer at 12

"My friends were all drinking beer when I was 12," said Kari, now 17, in an interview. She and several other teen-age alcoholics consented to be interviewed, provided their names were not used. "They used to get it from older brothers and sisters, and they were always getting drunk. At first I couldn't get drunk. I just kept getting sick and throwing up. I wanted to get drunk, I wanted to feel like a part of the good times."

By the next summer, Kari had learned how to get drunk, but she was 15 before she learned that her father was an alcoholic. Children of alcoholics, according to the study by the advisory council, have a 50 percent chance of becoming alcoholics.

"I used to drink out of my father's Scotch bottle and then fill the space with water," Kari recalled. "The summertime was always the biggest party time. I felt liked and accepted when I was drunk.

I was always the one to get people's drinks, too, because then I could drink a little more when I was out there in the kitchen."

Kari began going to Alcoholics Anonymous last November and has not had a drink since, but acknowledging her dependence upon liquor was "really hard."

"There was this whole insane denial thing," she recalled. "I was really defensive, it was getting out of control. I think teen-agers always tend not to believe they can actually be alcoholics. You say you're too young, it's something that happens to old people."

According to a study conducted by two Hunter College professors, Dr. Essie Lee and Dr. Gilbert Shimmel, in 93 high schools in New York City of those surveyed, 80 percent of the boys and 75 percent of the high school girls drink, most of them irregularly. However, 12 percent drink enough to be considered abusers.

Katie, now 15, was 9 the first time she and her sister got drunk on beer they found in the refrigerator at home.

"In my school you weren't normal if you didn't drink," she said. "Vodka—that was my specialty. When I was drunk, after a couple of years, I began going through this whole personality change. I used to be really friendly but I got paranoid, didn't want to be bothered while I was drinking."

Last summer, after she took a trip to Florida with a man who had a wife and four children, Katie became frightened of what was happening to her, and went to Alcoholics Anonymous. She is back in public school in the Bronx, where she lives, and has not had a drink in nearly eight months.

"I drink to forget, mainly," said Nancy, 16. "I started in the seventh grade, on scotch and Coke, because my friends all drank and I was unhappy at home and school. I've been doing really badly in school and my parents yell at me to stop drinking. But they drink their martinis every night. What's the difference?"

Getting alcohol is easy, even for those under 18, according to one 13-year-old boy who attends a suburban New Jersey high school.

"You go to a bar, they might ask you for proof, but you can give them a phony ID with no hassle," he said.

Of the pupils surveyed by Dr. Lee and Dr. Shimmel, 25 percent of those who reported they did not drink said it was because they disliked the taste and smell liquor. But today, Dr. Lee points out, adolescents may choose from a wide range of alcoholic beverages that taste like chocolate milkshakes, fruit drinks and soda pop.

Drinking in High School

Last fall Kickers, a 30-proof, milk-shake flavored beverage whose advertising depicted young people enjoying the drink, was withdrawn from the market by its producer, Heublein, after a suggestion by the National Council on Alcoholism. But car cards advertising the drink may still be seen on the subway in New York, and Heublein's similar sweet alcoholic drink, Hereford's Cows, is still being advertised and sold and the company has no plans to take it off the market.

This month has been labelled Alcohol Education Month by the New York State Education Department and the State Division of Alcoholism, which are previewing their new alcohol education curriculum around the state.

"Every study shows that kids today are drinking younger," said Dr. Patricia O'Gorman, director of the Department of Prevention and Education of the National Council on Alcoholism. "We know, too, that today's adult alcoholics started drinking earlier than their adult counterparts who are not alcoholics. What everyone is wondering is, since youth as a whole is drinking younger, this means we are going to have more alcoholics in 20 years. We just don't know."

March 27, 1977

The Curfew: It's at Center of a National Controversy

By NADINE BROZAN

"It is 10 P.M. Parents, do you know where your children are?"

That question is asked every evening on radio and television stations in Salt

Lake City, and it is by no means meant lightly. According to the law there, a minor who is under 14 years of age is prohibited from being "on a sidewalk, street, alley or public place after 10 P.M." Those under 18 are given until

midnight to be off the streets and, presumably, go home.

Quaint though the curfew may seem today—New York City has none—it is still imposed not only in Salt Lake City but with varying degrees of vigi-

185

lance statewide in Indiana. Illinois and Oregon, the cities of Milwaukee, San Francisco, Chicago, Columbus and Portland, Ore., and countless villages such as Middletown, Pa., Del Rio, Tex., and Modesto, Calif.

The curfew has fueled ongoing controversy in the courts, the legislatures and at the kitchen table. Some officials, parents and even children find it an appealing way to maintain discipline; others abhor it. Although some advocates of the curfew contend that it reduces crime, there does not appear to be any conclusive data to support that argument.

In recent weeks the curfew has been introduced in at least two communities Nassau, in Rensselaer County, N.Y., and Uvalde, Tex.—and is about to be challeneged in a Wisconsin court.

Why One Village Acted

On Dec. 12, children under 18 in Nassau, a tiny resort village 12 miles from Albany, were ordered by the village trustees to be off the streets from 10 P.M. to sunrise.

"We're an average village for anywhere in the United States," said Mayor Gerrold Van Deusen of Nassau, "and we were beginning to get physical resistance from the young, vandalism and property damage."

The Mayor said he had personally canvassed parents and proprietors of businesses before the trustees voted the move, and that he had heard no objections. "Some said we should have done it 10 years ago—it might have prevented problems with those who are now in their 20's," he said.

Other residents, like Angela Somers, 17, contend that the ordinance was provoked by acts of vandalism on Halloween attributed to an out-of-town youth of 21.

"I think it's strange," Miss Somers said, "that as a result kids under 18 have to be home by 10." She said she would continue to stay out later than 10 and so, she predicted would her friends.

"My parents," she went on, "realize that I'm responsible. When I'm out that late, it's because I'm coming home from baby-sitting or from somebody's house."

But it is not just equity that bothers some critics of the curfew: it is the fundamental question of constitutionality of ordinances that restrict individuals solely on the basis of youth.

Martin Guggenheim, a staff lawyer with the American Civil Liberties Juvenile Rights Project, said "The curfew infringes too greatly on fundamental rights. The goals—to reduce crime, by juveniles and to protect juveniles—are in and of themselves laudable and within the state's appropriate concern, but the means are totally inappropriate."

It is as if the state, in trying to educate children," he went on, "were to confine them to institutions for 10 years. The curfew legislation prohibits the thing a nontotalitarian society should cherish: the right to walk around freely.

"With curfew laws, the police can look with concern at anyone on the street and make them justify where they are going, who they are and how old they are. That's totalitarian."

The ordinances also diminish parental rights, Mr. Guggenheim said, adding, "Parents have the right to decide for themselves the limits of their trust in their children."

Divided Opinions From the Bench

So far the judiciary has taken no definitive stand on the matter. Some courts have declared curfews unconstitutional, usually because of vagueness. Other courts have upheld them, generally on the ground that the state has greater authority to regulate the activities of children than it has to regulate the activities of adults.

The question is to be tested again Monday in Wauwatosa, Wis., when the County Court of Milwaukee County will decided if the curfew in the suburb is constitutional. If the court rules against the legality of the curfew, the case of Dennis Buckett, a father of six, will be dropped. If not, he will stand trial for infractions of which two of his sons are accused.

In some locales, only the children are held culpable for curfew violations; in others only the parents are considered responsible. In still others, such as Wauwatosa, the blame is divided.

On Feb. 14, 1976, Mr. Buckett's son John, at the time 16, was arrested at

Curfews can be as strict as 10 P.M. or as liberal as 1 A.M.

2:15 A.M., reportedly because his car had run out of gasoline a block from home. Shortly afterward, on April 17, Robert Buckett, 15, was apprehended for being a passenger in a car that overran a stop sign at 11:45 P.M.

An earlier curfew case, involving John Buckett in a restaurant incident, had been dismissed on appeal but Mr. Buckett, John's father, used that occasion as the basis of a Federal Court challenge to the constitutionality of the ordinance.

Mr. Buckett is determined to see the curfew abolished. "Every man," he said, "has the right to raise his family as he sees fit. We do things together as a family. We like to go to midnight bowling because that's the only time I can go. But if I can't go and the boys want to go alone, they should be able to."

He said that both John and Robert have nighttime jobs as dishwashers that require them to work until 2 A.M., and so Robert, not yet 17, must be picked up and taken home by his father.

James Walrath, the family's lawyer and a volunteer with the Wisconsin Civil Liberties Union, said of the case: "This would be the first time an ordi-

nance would be declared unconstitutional on the grounds that it interferes with parental rights to control children. It could also be ruled unconstitutional on other grounds."

It would not be the first time a court had ruled on parental rights. In 1975, Jo-Ann Bykofsky and her son, Shaw, then 13, of Middletown, Pa., filed suit in Federal District Court contending that the curfew violated Mrs. Bykofsky's right to rear her children as she saw fit and that it interfered with the guarantee of family autonomy.

Last year the circuit court of Mrs. Bykofsky's area affirmed the district court's ruling and a petition to the Supreme Court for appeal was denied. So, today, the Bykofsky family lives by the law, "unhappily and with great inconvenience," according to Mrs. Bykofsky, who serves in a legislative liaison capacity for the Pennsylvania Human Rights Commission.

"If I sent my child to the drugstore after a certain hour, he could be arrested," she said. "The Middletown curfew does permit exceptions but prior notice of the after-hours activity must be submitted in writing to the police.

"How can I get a note to the police when my children want to do something that violates the curfew and I'm not here? I'm a single parent who works," she said.

Curfew regulations vary widely. They can be as strict as Nassau's, which takes effect at 10 P.M., or as liberal as those of the state of Indiana, commencing at 1 A.M. Some places, such as Middletown, Columbus and Salt Lake City, proscribe different hours for different ages, and most curfews start later on weekends than on school nights. Minors are allowed out at any hour if accompanied by a parent, guardian or adult who is considered to have custody.

Nearly all the ordinances provide for exceptions, such as a nighttime jobs emergency errands and standard organized teen-age activities such as proms, Scout meetings and sports events.

"The police know when there's a basketball game and when the buses arrive home, so the youngsters are given 15 or 20 minutes extra to walk home," said Mayor Van Deusen of Nassau. "On Friday night; the Catholic Church has a coffee hour, so the police give them 15 minutes' leniency."

No matter what the hour specified by the law, it is generally enforced with the gentlest of controls—or even ignored. In many small towns where the police officers know all the young people, they simply drive them home, perhaps with a warning to the parents. In larger cities, the young people are taken to a police station or detention center, and the parents are notified.

Although they rarely do so, judges have the right to put offenders on probation or send them to reform schools. Sometimes they levy fines on parents.

Only if a youngster is a habitual offender or is suspected of having committed a more serious offense is a punishment for curfew infraction imposed. In Portland, Ore., last year for example, of the 2,993 children apprehended for all causes, only 63 juveniles were taken into custody over curfew violations.

But the police of Portland found the law a useful mechanism for curbing "cruising," a teen-age fad for driving in a circuit around Broadway, the main thoroughfare, catcalling at each other and pedestrians.

In August 1975, at the peak of the craze, 276 "cruising" children were taken into custody on curfew charges.

In San Francisco, the police use the law to clear out the notorious Tenderloin District, where youths of both sexes solicit for prostitution, and a stretch of seaside highway where drivers congregate for drag-races.

But the San Francisco law lost most of its muscle last year when California decriminalized all so-called status offenses—those acts, such as truancy, which would not be violations if committed by adults.

Now, according to Sgt. Walter Garry of the San Francisco Police Youth Services' patrol division, "We can't jail a kid. If a curfew violator is taken into custody, he's put into a nonsecure facility. So he can come in the front door, have a shower and a meal and slip out the back. It's a standing joke among the runaways. We can't hold them."

Indeed curfews seem a joke to many of the youngsters whose lives are ostensibly circumscribed by them.

As Robert Hill, 17, of Portland, said: "I don't think anyone even pays attention to the law. I stay out after curfew.

We go out with friends and eat or just go riding around.'I don't even pay any attention to the police."

On its face, the existence of the curfew seems an anachronism in an age when children are emancipated in unprecedented ways.

F. Raymond Marks, counsel for the childhood and government project of the School of Law at the University of California, Berkeley, theorizes that the curfew represents the problem adults face with the young today.

"The puzzle is, 'What are we going to do with our children?' " said Mr. Marks, whose own 16-year-old son was once picked up in Chicago as he was returning to his mother's home from a job in a pizzeria. "There is a climate of fear that we can't control them," he said.

"And, to some extent the curfew is felt to be more necessary as children show more readiness to be independent. Parents are unable to control children. The curfew is not a control, but it makes the administration of controls easier."

While many parents were adamantly opposed to the concept of the curfew, including even those whose own rults were more strict, a great number said they were grateful for it. As Lorin Wiggins, a Mormon bishop in Salt Lake City, put it: "It's an ace in the hole for control purposes. It gives me a lever."

Mary Ellen Kilpack, also of Salt Lake City said, "We've been having trouble with our teen-age daughter lately. This last time she stayed out till 2 A.M. We called the sheriff, and he had a deputy sitting there in the driveway when she came home. He told her she was violating the curfew and that there was a reason for the law: to help parents keep their youngsters out of trouble and away from harm."

The chastised daugher, Cori, 17, said:

"Well, if my parents are that serious, if they're that concerned, I guess the midnight curfew is reasonable enough, although I don't like being hassled by a deputy sheriff. Having the police car there sure surprised my boyfriend."

January 6, 1978

JUVENILE JUSTICE: A PLEA FOR REFORM

The nation's juvenile courts, says the author, should focus their attention on the gravest problems that are confronting them: the twin evils of violence by and against the young.

By Irving R. Kaufman

n July 27, 14-year-old Luis Bonilla sat impassively in the starkly modern courtroom of the Bronx Supreme Court, waiting for the jury to return. He was accused of shooting and killing a teen-ager who had resisted Luis's attempt to steal his portable radio; at the time of his crime Luis was 13 years old. If the jury convicted him on charges of second-degree murder, his sentence would be mandatory life imprisonment, with no chance of parole for at least five years.

That Luis had been tried in an adult criminal court at all was extraordinary, for criminal suspects below the age of 16 had long been under the exclusive jurisdiction of the family court. Even for the most serious offenses, that court could impose at most five years of "restrictive placement," only the first 18 months of which would be spent behind bars. But two months before the fatal Bonilla shooting last October, New York's new juvenile-offender law

took effect. It requires that 13-year-olds accused of second-degree murder (as well as 14- and 15-year-olds indicted for a variety of offenses, including burglary and assault) be treated as adults in the eyes of the law and tried in the adult court system. (To protect young convicts from premature contact with adult offenders, however, the new law still requires that a convicted youth be confined in juvenile facilities until he or she is old enough for transfer to an adult prison.)

Spurred by a series of brutal and highly publicized killings in the New York City subways, the State Legislature, in an extraordinary session in July 1978, enacted this far-reaching transformation of New York's criminal law within a few hours after the bill's submission. Luis Bonilla was the first 13-year-old tried under the new law, but though convicted, he was not sentenced as an adult. When the jury finally did return, after 15 hours of deliberations, it found him guilty of manslaughter — an offense not within the ambit of the new law for 13-year-olds. Accordingly, he was returned to family court for sentencing. The process had come full circle. The New York Family Court does not place manslaughter in the highest

severity category, so the maximum sentence available — which Luis received — was three years, of which only the first will be in secure detention.

The case of Luis Bonilla illustrates only one of the problems facing those who have attempted to reform laws dealing with juveniles. Eighty percent of the 328 youths arrested under the new law during its first seven months were charged with theft, rather than with the more vicious crimes that were the principal target of the lawmakers. Over 60 percent of the youths initially charged as adults were returned to the family court — but not before some had undergone such experiences as pretrial detention in the filthy, windowless holding pens used by the Kings County Criminal Court in Brooklyn to house adult defendants.

All this, critics assert, demonstrates that the new law was drafted too broadly, sweeping within its purview many youths who *(Continued)*

Irving R. Kaufman, chief judge of the U.S. Court of Appeals for the Second Circuit, is chairman of the Joint Commission on Juvenile Justice of the American Bar Association and the Institute of Judicial Administration.

should not be exposed to the adult criminal-justice system. Most states have long provided for the transfer to adult courts of juveniles who have committed particularly serious crimes. But in virtually all these states the family court determines whether transfer is necessary, thus minimizing potentially harmful pretrial contact with adult criminals.

The new law's defenders, however, point out that cases of neglected, abused, runaway or disobedient children, as well as child-support controversies, make up the bulk of the family court's docket. This court, they contend, was established to deal with youthful criminal mischief and petty thefts, not the brutal, heinous crimes that the public fears today. They also emphasize that many dangerous offenders are treated too leniently, simply because the few available secure juvenile detention facilities are already overcrowded by runaways and other nondangerous offenders. Removing youths accused of serious crimes from the family-court system, these policy makers concluded, would result in stiffer penalties, and thus serve as a more powerful deterrent of juvenile crime. But perhaps because juries are unwilling, except in compelling cases, to condemn youthful criminals to adult prisons, the "tough" new law has produced fewer and shorter detentions than the juvenile-offender law that preceded it.

New York's unsatisfactory experience with its new juvenile-offender law is illustrative of the age-old dilemma in this field. It is a fact of life that juveniles, no less than adults, are capable of killing and destruction, and must be punished for such deeds. Yet society is unwilling to abandon young delinquents to the often hopeless fate that awaits adult criminals.

On one issue, however, both sides in this often bitter debate are in agreement: the present system of juvenile justice is plagued by serious problems, problems that run too deep to be rectified by last-minute legislative fiat. Recognizing this fact, the American Bar Association, in cooperation with the Institute of Judicial Administration, a research organization, has sponsored a comprehensive nine-year study, now nearing completion, of our entire juvenile-justice system. This project's goal has been to re-evaluate and produce a detailed set of guidelines, or "standards," that may serve as the basis for reform of every aspect of the child's manifold interactions with the law.

For each of 22 distinct topics, an expert, termed "reporter," was appointed to draft proposed standards and commentary. The work of the reporters was then reviewed by drafting committees drawn from the full spectrum of professionals in the field. Many were lawyers; the roster included three past presidents of the American Bar Association. The project also consulted judges, scholars, psychiatrists, psychologists, social workers, educators and experts in corrections and police work. This process insured that the standards would be well-integrated and internally consistent. In addition, they would reflect the varying perceptions of those involved in different aspects of the juvenile-justice system.

The standards, now being considered by those concerned with juvenile-justice reform, are not an exercise in theoretical armchair sociology. Rather, they draw on the best of existing, tested statutory reforms. Covering such areas as police handling of juvenile problems, youth service agencies, pretrial proceedings, juvenile records and information systems, and rights of minors, the first 17 volumes of the standards were approved by the American Bar Association this February. Five more volumes will be submitted to the A.B.A. at a later date.

The standards represent the latest chapter in the history of troubled children in America, a history that reflects some of the meanest and the most noble aspects of the American character.

□

Seventeenth-century London was beset by every type of problem child now encountered by our family courts. Young criminals terrorized the middle classes, and were tried and punished in the same manner as adults. "Rogues and vagabonds," as well as "idle and needy" children who had run away from their parents and masters, were brought to the courts for punishment; orphans and neglected or abandoned children were bound out or cared for at public expense. But the Londoners had a "dispositional alternative" (in the jargon of the day's juvenile justice) that is unavailable now: they shipped many of these children to the Virginia colonies as indentured servants. The Dutch, for their part, pursued a similar policy in New Amsterdam.

The colonial policy toward children and their families was marked by a stern Puritanical view of the responsibilities of the child to his parents and of the parents to the state. The dead hand of this view continues to mold today's policy. The colonial government lent its force to the absolute rule of the parents, permitting up to 10 stripes at the public whipping post for incorrigible children who displayed a "rebellious carriage" toward their elders.

The colonies also expected much of parents. Virginia provided in 1748 that unfit parents who were either too poor to raise children properly, or who failed to bring them up "in honest courses," could lose custody of them forever.

The New England colonies (and later New York as well) provided for dependent persons, including young abandoned children, by a reverse auction known as vendue. The state offered subsidies of ever-decreasing amounts to prospective caretakers, with the lowest bidder winning. Apart from a cursory check to ascertain whether the child was being grossly abused, the child's best interests were not even considered.

By the 1820's, this reality gained broad recognition as the nation's increasing prosperity alleviated the financial pressures that had made the vendue acceptable. The search for a more humanitarian approach was galvanized by a dilemma in governmental policy toward juvenile delinquency, which was already beginning to emerge as a heated issue with the massive influx of European immigrants. In the eyes of the criminal law, youths reached maturity at age 14, and suspects as young as 6 were legally considered as adults if the state could show that they knew right from wrong. Thus, several cases are recorded of 12- and 13-year-olds tried for murder, and of 7- and 8-year-olds locked up in adult prisons. The sympathy of judges and jurors toward the young mitigated the harshness of this common-law rule; even in 1820 all were aware that brutality and instruction in "the most artful methods of perpetrating crime" awaited the youth incarcerated with adults. But if acquitted, as the New York Society for the Reform of Juvenile Delinquents noted in an 1826 report, "they were returned destitute, to the same haunts of vice from which they had been taken, more emboldened to the commission of crime, by their escape from present punishment."

The New York reform society therefore recommended the establishment of specialized institutions for children. These homes would provide a refuge not only for young criminals but also for those who had been dealt with by the vendue — the homeless, the neglected and the vagrant — and children beyond their parents' control or whose parents were considered "unfit."

The institutional movement spread rapidly, at first under private auspices and later supported by public funds. These early "child savers" deemed several years of stern, regimented discipline essential to reform. They therefore thought it necessary that institutions and the state be given extensive authority over these children, even over parental protests. In 1838, the seminal case of In re Crouse established this power.

Mary Ann Crouse was consigned to the Philadelphia House of Refuge on her mother's assertion that she was "incorrigible." The Pennsylvania Supreme Court rejected her father's petition to recover custody, defending its usurpation of the rights of "unworthy" parents by stating, "She in fact has been snatched from a course which must have ended in confirmed depravity, and, not only is the restraint of her person not unlawful, but it would be an act of extreme cruelty to release her from it."

With these noble-sounding words, the court planted in American jurisprudence a dangerous and alien seed that flourished most fully in the juvenile-court system founded 60 years later. A central principle in Anglo-American law is that crimes must be charged and proved precisely. One is convicted not of "being a robber" but of robbing John Jones at 2 P.M. on the corner of Fifth and Main. A law that confines a child in an institution because a parent is "unworthy" or because the child is destined for "depravity" presupposes that a court can divine

the most salutary remedy for an individual by peering through some magic window into the soul. A homogenous community like Puritan New England may tolerate such official moral judgments, but in the diverse society dedicated to free thought that the United States has become, such institutional presumptuousness appears pernicious.

These considerations did not impress those active in the institutional movement, nor reformers who attempted other means of grappling with the problems of youth. The Children's Benevolent Society, for example, like its predecessors in London 150 years before, sought to "drain the city" of its delinquent children and ship them westward to "the best of all asylums, the farmer's home." And as the frontier began to close after the

Civil War, yet another new phenomenon — the reform-school movement — swept the North and the West.

Two principles were central to the reform school ideal. First, youths could be properly treated as criminals for offenses peculiar to their status as minors: for example, truancy, running away, incorrigibility. Second, because the mission of the reform school was a benign, rehabilitative one, the normal procedural protections of the adversary criminal trial — the rights of confronting witnesses, of prior disclosure of specific charges, of counsel and of trial by jury — could be abrogated with no constitutional qualms.

Initially, these principles suffered a major setback. In *People v. Turner*, the Illinois Supreme Court rejected a statute that mandated the confine-

ment of children under 16 "growing up in mendicancy, ignorance, idleness or vice." "Vice is a very comprehensive term," wrote the court. "Acts, wholly innocent in the estimation of many good men, would, according to the code of ethics of others, show fearful depravity. What is the standard to be? What extent of enlightenment, what amount of industry, what degree of virtue, will save from the threatened imprisonment? The principle of the absorption of the child in, and its complete subjection to the despotism of the State, is wholly inadmissible in the modern civilized world."

The *Turner* decision represented a subtle wisdom that would not become widely evident for nearly a century. The Illinois child savers ignored its warning and lobbied to create a new institution that would

A Randalls Island (New York) reformatory workshop, c. 1900. Inset: An 1882 drawing of a 3-year-old arraigned in a New York court for "inaugurating a reign of terror."

further their interventionist, paternalistic goals within constitutional limitations. Finally, in 1899, at the prompting of the Chicago Women's Club, Illinois founded the nation's first juvenile court. Its jurisdiction encompassed all children in trouble, including those found living "with any vicious or disreputable person." This idea of a separate court for juveniles, able to address and cure the problems of youth with a special fatherly concern, quickly spread to every major city in the Union.

The juvenile court was the culmination of a growing belief that children were institutionalized far too frequently, both in degrading, unhealthy almshouses and in reform schools, which were already perceived as dehumanizing in their regimentation and brutal in their operation. Foster care and adoption were the practices preferred by the juvenile court for children with unsatisfactory homes, and for the first time home relief was offered on a broad basis to "worthy" mothers of dependent children. Juvenile probation officers were another innovation. These men and women — at first, unpaid volunteers — were to supply the court with investigations of the young offender's background. More importantly, they would supervise the child living at home, thus providing an alternative to punishment in an institution.

"Juvenile courts," noted Thomas D. Eliot, a critic of the system, in 1914, "were to fill every gap in the child-caring system. However, if this be granted, no line can be drawn short of a court administering all the children's chari-

ties. . . . Some courts actually state this as their ideal; they are all things to all men." The juvenile courts had, indeed, set themselves an ambitious, perhaps impossible, task. As a leading juvenile-court judge, Paul Alexander, noted in 1944, the judge must apply "not only man-made law, but the moral law and the laws of social science, psychology, psychiatry and the general laws of human nature." But the states never gave the juvenile courts the resources to carry out their mission. As late as 1967, one-third of the juvenile courts in the country did not have social workers or probation officers available to them, and 83 percent lacked psychologists or psychiatrists.

Confronted with massive waves of runaways in the 30's and the 40's, as well as a steady increase in youth crime, the system steadily broke down. Insufficiently staffed to follow its proclaimed purposes, the juvenile court -- despite its origins as an alternative to institutionalization — with increasing frequency referred delinquents to an ever-growing network of misleadingly and euphemistically named "reform" and "training" schools. By 1966, 51,000 children were living in 292 institutions for delinquents.

Discipline, rather than rehabilitation or education, preoccupied these prison-like facilities. As late as 1949, the punishment for possession of tobacco at the Indiana State School for delinquent boys was 10 strokes on the bare back with a leather paddle; for impudence and vulgarity, 15 strokes. At the Hudson School in New York State in the 1950's, rebellious girls could be locked in solitary confinement for up to 81 days and fed only milk and bread for two of their daily meals. And reports emerged in the 1960's from one Massachusetts training school of children who were punished by "staff dunking youngsters' heads in toilets, dousing them with pails of water, forcing them to march around with a pail over their heads, and using one 12-year-old boy as a mop and dragging him through urine in the boys' washroom."

With the heightened social consciousness of the 1960's, many of these aspects of the juvenile-justice system began to appear archaic, if not cruel. Recognizing at last the essentially punitive nature of reform schools, Justice Abe Fortas, writing for the Supreme Court in 1967, noted that "however euphemistic the title, a 'receiving home' or an 'industrial school' for juveniles is an institution of confinement." Before making a finding of delinquency, therefore, juvenile courts were required to observe the "essentials of due process and fair treatment."

The 1960's also witnessed a second, more massive deinstitutionalization movement. It took its most striking form in Massachusetts, where the entire training-school system was closed and replaced with a network of small-scale, community-based residences.

There was, therefore, little disagreement in 1967 when the President's Commission on Law Enforcement and the Administration of Justice wrote: "The great hopes originally held for the juvenile court have not been fulfilled. It has not succeeded significantly in rehabilitating delinquent youth, in reducing or even stemming the tide of juvenile criminality, or in bringing justice and compassion to the child offender."

☐

The Juvenile Justice Standards Project of the American Bar Association and the Institute of Judicial Administration thus convened in a day of growing disenchantment with the institutions used to deal with problems of youth. At that time, it was clear that a substantial number of adult criminals had started as juvenile offenders and invariably returned to lives of crime. The depth of dissatisfaction, however, provided the project with an ideal opportunity to achieve its ambitious goal: to structure a new juvenile-justice system that by heeding the lessons of the past would better serve us in the future.

After nearly a decade of research and discussion, the project members concluded that the juvenile court must abandon the "moralistic" model that had guided it since the turn of the century. Some members supported this view because they believed courts could not meaningfully pass upon the "worthiness" or "depravity" of those who came before them. Others argued that such judgments have no place at all in modern society. All agreed that the juvenile courts — like all other courts — should be tightly bound by the rule of law. Acts that would be crimes if committed by adults should be charged, proved and punished in a similar manner. Senator Edward Kennedy, chairman of the Senate Judiciary Committee, has forcefully decried the cruel ironies of the present system: "If juveniles want to get locked up, they

Critics of the present family court emphasize that many dangerous juvenile offenders are treated too leniently because the few available secure juvenile detention facilities are already overcrowded by runaways and other nondangerous offenders.

should skip school, run away from home or be deemed 'a problem.' If they want to avoid jail, they are better off committing a robbery or burglary." Children whose actions do not amount to adult crimes — the runaways, truants and incorrigibles — should be dealt with outside the judicial system. The term "delinquency," therefore, with its attendant stigmatization and possibility of incarceration, should be reserved exclusively for juveniles who have committed crimes.

A few examples will illustrate the basic philosophy that undergirds the Juvenile Justice Standards Project:

Parental Abuse and Neglect. Under the standards, children may not be removed from their homes because of alleged parental misconduct without a finding that specific physical harm, clinically recognized psychiatric disturbance, or sexual abuse has occurred or is imminently threatened. This standard is intended to reduce sharply the widely deplored extent of state intrusion into family life that the child savers thought proper. Although state intervention is clearly called for when a child is, for example, battered by a parent, physical abuse was reported in only 10 percent of the 300,000 neglect petitions filed annually. More often, the petition for juvenile-court intervention to remove the child from the home is based on such complaints as the tendency of a single mother to bring home overnight male visitors. Separation of child from mother in such cases, which once may have appeared imperative, has become distasteful in a society that has learned respect for the dignity of all and has come to recognize the necessity of keeping hands off the parent-child relationship except in particularly dangerous situations.

Experts agree that unnecessary intervention often harms rather than helps the child, shattering parental bonds. The wiser course, the standards conclude, is for the state to leave the child with the family and supply voluntary social services to assist the family unit in the home.

Youth Crime. In cases of juvenile delinquency, the standards frankly recognize that although reform schools may have rehabilitative goals, they are dominated by their punitive aspect. Clichés about saving a child from a life of crime do not alter the stark reality — and necessity — of punishment. For the protection of society, it is necessary that legislatures increase many of the maximum prison sentences for juveniles who have committed serious crimes. And, under carefully defined circumstances, juvenile courts must be permitted to transfer the most hardened young criminals to the adult system for the severest punishments allowed by law. But in either court, juveniles accused of crime should have the right to the same adult procedural protections that guard against conviction of the innocent. Consequently, the standards accord accused juveniles, beyond the minimal due process that the Supreme Court has held is constitutionally required, the rights to counsel and to a six-person jury. The juvenile-court judge must remain free to act leniently in an appropriate case. The standards require no minimum sentences, but where the judge deems a heavier determinate sentence necessary, no parole commission should be permitted to release the offender prematurely. Under the existing system, as Senator Kennedy recently said, "certainty of punishment is a joke."

Noncriminal Misbehavior. The standards permit incarceration only for conduct forbidden by the adult criminal law. Large segments of juvenile court jurisdiction would therefore be removed, for adults cannot be convicted for disobeying their parents, truancy or running away. In recent years, some states have begun to treat youngsters who have committed such acts, but no crimes, as "Persons [or Children] in Need of Supervision" (PINS or CHINS), rather than as delinquents. The change, however, is one in name only. PINS children continue to be confined alongside young criminals, an experience destined to do more harm than good. In fact, through PINS petitions, juvenile courts have intervened in family disputes over household chores, abusive language and undesirable boyfriends. The juvenile courts, in these cases, have allowed themselves to be used as birch rods by angry parents disgusted with, but unable to control, their adolescent children's behavior.

The project concluded that all services rendered to PINS children should be provided on a strictly voluntary basis, and preferably outside the judicial system. For example, in recent years, concerned adults — many of them former runaways — have established "crash pads" and runaway houses where young people who have left home can live for a time, safe from the dangers of the street. At first, these shelters were often hostile both to parents and authorities, but today, with the help of government funding and state certification, they have evolved into an important adjunct to the social-services system. Experience has shown that after a runaway child spends a few days in such a shelter, an amicable reunion with parents usually ensues. The standards endorse this system of licensed shelters and recommend that it be augmented substantially.

For other troubled children who have not broken the law, the standards prescribe voluntary psychiatric or other medical care, and educational, vocational and legal counseling appropriate to the needs of the particular child. Where a child chooses to avail himself of such services, the chances of success will be enhanced by the fact that he has chosen this course voluntarily. The key, then, is to make these services adequate, well-known and easily accessible.

□

The long history of justice and injustice to our nation's children counsels that the juvenile court focus its power, its wisdom and its compassion on the gravest problems that confront it: the twin evils of violence by and against the young. Courts must mete out fair and even-handed justice to young criminals. No longer should they try to serve as surrogate parents in attempting to control youthful mischief. As the legislatures of our states join in this effort and draw upon the standards' recommendations, the age-old promise of justice for our nation's youth may at last be fulfilled.

October 14, 1979

CHAPTER **3**

Youth Cultures

Long hair on young men became a symbol of rebellion and
liberation in the 1960's.

Jack Manning/NYT Pictures

Pocket Flask and Younger Set

*Governor Edwards
and Mr. Anderson Enter the
Mrs. Grundy Contest*

By HELEN BULLITT LOWRY

SOMETHING has really happened to cleave the Young Generation of today from the generations that have gone before it. Something specific has happened in the history of sociology to mark the two sides of 1920-21 as the Before and After Taking. Even though this contest between the Young Generation and the Old Generation we have had with us always, even as we have had playful kittens and dignified cats!

Usually the contest between the two runs on uneventfully—the bone of contention is some change in the mere machinery of courting. Church sociables and holding hands in church chairs merge gently into holding hands at the movies. The ripple of disapproval purls on, muttering that religion is disappearing in the Young Generation. The romantic two-by-two buggy flows into the romantic twosome roadster, and the buggy-reared elders cry " Pie! " In the fourteenth century ladies began to wear dresses that laced down the front, revealing a muslin blouse, and the clergy railed against the new mode, calling it " Hell Gates," even as the clergy before them had railed at the mode that preceded.

But once in a half century something does really happen that cleanly cleaves the past from the present—something that ushers in a new social era. It was so about a half century ago when the waltz came in. To the strains of " The Blue Danube " Man took Maid in his arms upon the public ballroom floor, and the manners and thoughts of the Old Generation dropped from the gay young blade's back.

It is so today, when the hip-pocket flask has got into mixed society.

Prohibitionists and anti-prohibitionists alike will tell you what the result is on the young things who are the " victims " of the new hip-pocket habit.

" Take away Liberty and you get Libertine," is the way Governor Edward I. Edwards of New Jersey, champion of " personal liberty," expressed his idea.

With equal assurance, William H. Anderson, member of the Executive Board of the Anti-Saloon League of America, said:

" It is the working out of the law of compensation that has given dissipated children and robberies to the man who has fostered lawlessness by breaking the law of the Eighteenth Amendment."

Each has taken the theme of the pocket-flask-munitioned Young Generation, has pointed a moral and adorned his opinion. The report that many 18-year-old girls of formal American society are for the first time indulging in intoxication and in some of intoxication's by-products causes the theme to be laid by each side—" wet " and " dry "—at the other side's door. One difference is that Mr. Anderson, having predicted the betterment of the nation through prohibition, naturally has to picture the rumored condition of youthful laxity as a mere " temporary manifestation." As for Governor Edwards, his hope is that " Mothers will realize that their daughters are bound to meet new temptations, and will arm them more intelligently with knowledge of the pitfalls than has been the custom of the mothers of the past."

Each of these advocates, one " dry " and the other " wet," was asked to discuss the cause and the corrective of the hip-pocket flask.

" The source of the infection was the rich man's private stock," said Mr. Anderson. " The man who laid up whisky didn't play the good sport and abide by the conditions that the law had placed on the great middle class. Instead, he bought liquor and stored it away. After July 1, 1919, he began to carry it with him against the law, and this brought about a new standard for the ostentatious display of wealth. This encouraged those who wanted to look as if they had wealth to patronize the bootlegger.

" Not only that—but soon the rich man discovered that his stock was not holding out as he had expected. He decided to buy more—and for this more he pays such profiteering prices that it pays the bootlegger to take the most awful risks of discovery. The rich man, with every reason to protect the laws of the existing order, became as deliberate an anarchist and lawbreaker as is the radical from Russia.

" And now he is getting his reward in the lawlessness that is abroad in the land. Because he, a mature and influential man, has broken the law with a certain amount of discretion, he has made it safe for these young girls and boys to break it with utter indiscretion. Because the older society men and women have connived at the hip-pocket flask, even welcomed it because it saved their own stock when they entertained, these children have taken to the excesses to which indiscriminate drinking inevitably leads."

So it would seem that, according to the Anti-Saloon League theory, Nemesis is striking the older generation when a youngster takes an illegal flask drink. Colloquially speaking, the older generation is getting what's coming to it.

" These same silk-hatted anarchists, these rich men who purchase illicit whisky, are responsible for the demoralized New York police force," continued the speaker. " The police force has been subsidized to protect the illicit whisky traffic, in which these rich men and the speakeasy are engaged together.

" But some day—and that not so very far off, either—the rich man is going to wake up to the startling fact that he's been silly. Because he has the most to lose, he will realize that he has most cause to foster law abidingness. And the same day he will realize that it is the children of the rich, instead of the children of the middle classes, that are carrying about flasks of whisky. Why, the very fact that we hear so much about these conditions shows that the rich drinking man already is horrified when he sees the vices of liquor drinking intensified and made silly in young faces. He is as a man who may swear himself, but unexpectedly hears curses on the lips of a baby."

A year and a half ago, Mr. Anderson recalled, the law against carrying the hip-pocket flask could not have been enforced. " Public sentiment would have been in tumult at arrests for this violation of the law. Instead of trying to enforce it, the prohibition officers have allowed abuse to bring about its own condemnation. Very shortly there will be such a general demand that carrying liquor be abolished, and that this demoralization of youth cease, that every citizen will become a prohibition enforcement officer."

And who is to prove that Mr. Anderson is not correct in his prophecies of a community shocked into enforcing, however unpleasant, a law " to save the morale of the young generation that is the future of the nation." For, wherever you turn, New York, Middle West or South, the formal societies of the cities give forth the same tale.

" We were accustomed to seeing older people drink, and college boys, but not young girls in their teens," is the frequent comment.

" And it is because the Government has placed the fascination of the forbidden on drinking," commented Governor Edwards of New Jersey. A sad minor key crept into the voice of this enemy of prohibition, who adds certain dramatic quality to his opposition by being himself a teetotaler.

" It has added that fascination," he continued, " and then has proceeded to pour the temptation into the young hands—not to mention their hip-pocket and muff. The Government is responsible, remember, through its agents, since it is inconceivable that the Government would have passed a law which is unenforceable. I am informed that more whisky has been taken out of bond during this last year than in any previous year of the business. And it is the Government that has done it. If people want this law, why don't they see that it is enforced?

" I hear that drinking has increased. I hear that drinking among young people has increased. Why did the worldly wise old churches, the Catholic and the Episcopalian, not throw their strength as a body toward prohibition? Individual members may have backed it—but the churches that did so as a body were the emotional churches that think you can convert a sinner in ten seconds.

" And, instead of converting,'

"Instead of letting some young man take his daughter to the Broadway restaurants, * * * let the father take her himself."

they've merely succeeded in making a crime and a mystery of drinking. Instead of a responsible hostess serving young girls a glass of wine at her table, young girls are getting off to secret places to be served a surreptitious drink from some young man's pocket. They break the law, and they know that they break the law. A loosening of the moral code in other ways is bound to result.

"Those of us who opposed prohibition through no self-interested motives foresaw just this wild abandon that comes of bottling up the human inclinations. The openness of drinking was what protected it. With their elders and contemporaries sure to be looking on at any results of drinking, moderation was the natural, self-interested thing for the young.

"It is the law of human nature that breaking one law leads to breaking a more serious law. The moral retrogression is sure and steady. This particular manifestation is at present showing itself most unpleasantly in the stratum of society that we erroneously call the 'top.' But will the new social code which this secret drinking will bring to us spread to the other strata? We can only hope that this will not happen generally. But certainly those young women who are weak will adopt the customs of the richer class. And those girls who have not received the intelligent home training in knowledge from their mothers will be in the gravest danger.

"The only hope in sight is that the mothers and the fathers realize the seriousness of the country's condition and strip the veil of mystery from all of the vices, so that the young eyes can see them without the fascination of the occult. Instead of letting some young man take his daughter to the Broadway restaurants, with perhaps a flask under the tablecloth, let the father take her himself. I have taken my daughter.

"Conditions will have to get a great deal worse than they are today before the turn of the tide will come, and the country either rise up against prohibition or else see that prohibition is enforced. Meantime the problem of the young people we have with us."

February 6, 1921

Ban All Forms of Jazz Dance In Syracuse Public Places

Special to The New York Times.

SYRACUSE, N. Y., Feb. 11. — No more will the toddle, the camel walk, the Chicago flop, the face-to-face or any other of the shivering, shaking, sinuous, distorting convulsions that have passed as terpsichorean interpretation be seen in this city.

For the Common Council today unanimously passed an ordinance prohibiting all forms of the jazz dance in the hotels and public dance halls, ordering that all such places close their doors at midnight and forbidding any person under 16 years of age to attend these places, which hereafter must be brilliantly lighted.

Some parents had complained that dance halls were not being conducted as they should be and there was too little of the foot and too much of the rest of the body in the dances that have been popular.

February 22, 1921

CENSOR FOR NUTLEY DANCES

Members of Board Condemn Steps Seen at High School Reception.

Dancing in Nutley, N. J., is to be regulated hereafter, so far as the high school pupils are concerned, by a censor, a professional dancing teacher, whose word will be the law which the School Board will enforce.

The School Board held an indignation meeting yesterday afternoon at which the dancing at the high school freshman reception last week was condemned as highly improper. Mrs. Arthur B. Proal, President of the Federated New Jersey Women's Clubs and a member of the board, who attended the dance with Mrs. Perley A. Prior, another board member, said that they had ordered the music stopped and had asked a student to request that those dancing improperly cease.

"Our request had little effect on the dancers, however," said Mrs. Proal.

Mrs. Prior described one of the dances, which she said she was told was the "Camel Walk." "The girl rested her chin on her partner's shoulder," she said, "and then apparently went to sleep. At least she seemed to doze off, for they scarcely moved and her eyes were closed."

November 30, 1921

Condemns Dress Extremes of Chicago School Girls

CHICAGO, Jan. 25. — Chicago's Board of Education condemned the shimmy dance, jazz music, short skirts, low necks, joy riding and cigarettes today, following an investigation by Peter A. Mortensen, Superintendent of Schools. Suggested alternatives are keeping early hours and studying five nights a week.

"No effort on our part can counteract these evils unless the parents realize the danger and help us maintain the standards," Superintendent Mortensen said. "Extremes in dress are deplorable. Mothers should know that modesty and simplicity in high school girls' costumes are the most healthful and uplifting to school ideals."

January 26, 1922

WANTS SCHOOL GIRLS TO HIDE THEIR KNEES

Member of Newark Board Opens Five-Day Crusade on 'Immodest Dressing.'

When Joseph M. Hauber, a member of the Newark Board of Education, visited a high school in Newark recently he saw some bare knees. He went back a few days later and saw some more bare knees, and Wednesday night, with only five days more of his term to serve and no possibility of reappointment, he said he would devote the whole five days to covering the knees of high school girls who "wear 'em rolled."

Mr. Hauber's disapproval of bare knees was made known at a meeting of the Committee on Instruction, when Mrs. Mary Poland, dean of the high schools, applied for permission to attend the meeting of the National Association of Deans, to be held in Chicago on Feb. 24. Hauber objected.

"You have enough to do at home," he said to Mrs. Poland. "Recently when I visited the high school, I saw girls showing their bare knees. I complained about it, and on other visits saw more bare knees. I think you ought to stay here and give some attention to the immodest dressing of high school girls."

Mr. Hauber's objection was voted down, and Mrs. Poland, who defends her girls, received permission to go West.

And there isn't a high school girl in Newark who isn't critical of Mr. Hauber. There may be a few bare knees about, particularly when the wind is blowing and a girl has to climb aboard a trolley car, but if one didn't look for bare knees one wouldn't see them, is the girl's argument.

Mr. Hauber was appointed by Charles P. Gillen, the former Mayor. He was not named for reappointment by Mayor Archibald and will leave office on Feb. 1, but in the meantime he is going to do something about those knees.

January 27, 1922

Mothers Complain that Modern Girls "Vamp" Their Sons at Petting Parties

The boys of today must be protected from the girl "vamp" and if standards of young people are to be raised the boys must do it, said Janet Richards of Washington, at a meeting in the home of Mrs. Otto H. Kahn at 1,100 Fifth Avenue yesterday. Miss Richards discussed the girl of today and she said that although she had not seen much of the petting parties which are talked of so much, she had heard enough to realize that some girls were deliberate vamps.

"I have recently been told by the mothers of five sons of some of their problems," said Miss Richards, "and they told me that the most serious thing I had to face was the saving of their sons from the girl 'vamp.'

These boys have gone to their mothers, said Miss Richards, and said: "Mother, it is so hard for me to be decent and live up to the standards you have set me, and to always keep in mind the loveliness and purity of girls. How can I do it with this cheek dancing, and if I pull away they call me a prude. And when I take a girl home in the way that you have told me is the proper fashion she is not satisfied and thinks I am slow."

Miss Richards said that she was trying to get some of the boys to band together to raise the standards of the set in which they move, in which the girl "petter" holds sway.

"These girls are a small percentage of the whole, and there are not enough of them to condemn them all," she said, "but it is sad to think that the girls are setting such standards for the boys." Middle-aged people, who remember the old-fashioned girl, must interfere in the young people's affairs, she said, and help to restore them to wholesome standards.

Others who spoke were Mrs. Francis Rogers on the work of the Girls' Protective League, and the Girls' Service Club, and Mrs. Charles Cary Rumsey.

February 17, 1922

TOPICS OF THE TIMES.

A Competent Judge Speaks Out. Mrs. ASQUITH, asked what she thought of the much-discussed and much-denounced younger generation of these days, is quoted as replying that all such talk was "very silly," and then she added: "From my own observation, they are no worse than they were twenty years ago, or since time immemorial."

Mrs. ASQUITH has not been an observer of young men and women "since time immemorial," but she is right, of course, in what she meant by that phrase—if a speaker as cautious as she really used it so carelessly. The older generations always have been nearly, or quite, in despair over the manners and morals of the young, and the reason always has been the same—the younger generation has insisted on having ideas of its own as to propriety, and invariably has made changes in the established standards, regardless of the pain thus given to predecessors who insisted on being also contemporaries.

It is on this insistence that the irrepressible conflict ever has been based and presumably ever will be. The too quick despairers of today well might learn what history tells them—that all is not lost merely because the young folk are doing and saying things which their fathers, mothers and maiden aunts hold unseemly or even wicked, and either didn't do or did only when spectators were absent. Indeed, it is more than possible that the chief difference between the present and the highly vaunted past lies in a new or increased frankness in action and discussion, not in any essential alteration of conduct.

The moralists of the Victorian era were not less unhappy than our own, though their eyes perhaps were less often shocked by the sight of what was going on. They knew, though they didn't see, and that was enough to set them scolding. It may be that the new courage is merely a new audacity, but, on the other hand, it may be a new honesty and decency, a revised estimate of relative values.

February 24, 1922

SAYS FLAPPER HAS A SOUL.

Dr. Reisner Tells Parents Their Duty Toward Wonderful Youth of Today.

The Rev. Dr. Christian F. Reisner, pastor of the Chelsea Methodist Episcopal Church, 178th Street, preached last evening on "A Religion for Today." He said, in part:

"It is too common to abuse the youth of today. They are wonderful in their possibilities. Underneath the flapper and the flipper is a royal soul that will die for a great cause or grow up to fill a large place if inspired and nourished. Instead of adults abusing them they ought to review their own lives to see how much they are helping to give youth a chance to grow up clean and strong. It is a wonder they are so sane and clean and ambitious along right lines when it is remembered that father boasts of law-breaking in getting his hootch, mother smokes and easily and flippantly says 'My God,' much like the husband swears, and beats the girl in jazz dress and looks, and both laugh carelessly as they relate youthful escapades.

"How many children today get religious training in the home? What would have happened to most of the big men today if they had received no more religion in their youth than their own children get. Tomorrow's citizenship cannot be built big enough to meet the issues sure to face them without parents and teachers and leading citizens adopt a real religious program and follow it openly and honestly."

March 19, 1923

WOMEN'S COLLEGE HEADS DEFEND THE MODERN GIRL

Dissent From Critics' Charges of Unconventional Habits and Attire—Agree She is More Intelligent Than Her Mother and More Self-Reliant.

THE question as to whether the college girl of today is better or worse than the college girl of yesterday has again been raised by recent statements that the modern young woman lacks the seriousness of past generations and is given over to cigarette smoking, drinking and unconventional attire and habits. The Presidents of several of our largest women's colleges, asked by THE TIMES to express their opinion, dissented vigorously from the critics.

The discussion was started by remarks attributed to Dr. Charles J. Smith, President of Roanoke College, Virginia, who recently spoke before the eleventh annual meeting of the National Lutheran Educational Conference in New York on the social life of our college students. Subsequently Dr. Smith denied the statements alleged to have been made by him, and said that he referred to "a new type of American woman which has been produced by the present social order," and not to the college girl.

"Distrust of Youth Ridiculous."

According to President Henry Noble MacCracken of Vassar College the present profound distrust of youth is ridiculous.

"What we all need is to be infected with youth," said this guardian of eleven hundred and some odd undergraduates. "Then we will understand better what youth is driving at and youth will have more tolerance for what we think and say."

Through the four big windows of the President's office in Vassar's old main building one caught glimpses of that much discussed "youth" swinging along with uncovered head and book-laden arms. It walked alone and it walked in groups. Sometimes it stopped to exchange greetings and sometimes those greetings were tossed in passing with a wave of the arm and a backward smile. Small chance apparently not to be infected with youth if one stayed long at that old farm of Matthew Vassar's at Poughkeepsie on the Hudson River.

"Youth hasn't been living in a vacuum," ruminated the boyish-looking President. "The modern girl sees all of life that she can see. She knows a great deal about her father and mother. More, perhaps, than they know about her. She thinks a great deal about life. The girls who come here are serious about their work. All of them are doing what they want to do most. They make study a major sport. It is the business of the instructors to see that students like this sport best. We can learn a great deal from the modern girl. We do learn a great deal from her, and incidentally we learn something about her.

What Vassar Has Learned.

"We've learned that she has a fine mind, that she has originality, that she can apply herself to scholastic work with brilliant results. The debates between Vassar and the men's colleges have proved our girls can compete creditably with undergraduates of Harvard, Yale and Princeton. In the last State medical examination a Vassar graduate stood third, with two Harvard men first and second. Our graduates have many of them taken important positions, some as instructors in colleges, others in equally responsible posts. But I'm boasting," smiled the man who refuses to distrust youth and advises those who do to become "infected with it."

"Faculties take themselves too seriously. The members are apt to be pompous, aloof, inaccessible. I am only an older brother to these students. I am not here to criticize. I'm here to help. And the only way to help is to listen to what they have to say. This office is always open to them. They may come here at any time to talk over matters which bother them. Just now there has been a request from the student body for a change in the curriculum. A conference has been arranged between a Faculty committee and a student committee. The change will be made if it is found desirable.

"During the four years a girl is with us we try to give her the necessary equipment for her later life outside of college. If there is a protest against the college environment, she is given an opportunity to voice that protest. But we do not let her burn down a chemical laboratory. We do not give her an uncontrolled environment. We tell the students what control is needed in a laboratory; that if certain precautions are not observed definite disaster follows. Then we say, 'Go ahead and learn chemistry.' It is our duty to point out the dangers of the environment in which the girl works and lives. Fire laws must be obeyed or there is a conflagration. Other laws must be obeyed or there is apt to be a catastrophe.

Stop Criticizing, Says MacCracken.

"Psychology has been showing us the way to solve many difficulties. Within the last ten years, it has given us a much better understanding of things we formerly knew little about. Not only are we learning more about the study capacity of the student, but more about her physical and mental state. There is no use blaming any one when he is sick. And certainly some people are sick. Take the young girl who committed suicide the other day in New York because she was taller than the rest of the class. That girl was sick. She should not be blamed for what she did. Those are things to be guarded against. In most cases they can be prevented. That is the responsibility of the modern school. Statistics show, I think, that 80 per cent of the human race are honest the other 20 per cent. are victims of social heredity and bad environment.

"The purpose of a college is to catch up with one's own past, including one's self. By this I mean the history of the human race from the beginning and its relation to the present. The process of education is the process of taking advantage of a controlled environment. During the time students are here they are catching up with their environment. They discover this environment for themselves, and they develop a power of selection.

"Let's get down to our jobs. Let's stop criticizing the modern girl. I think one of our teachers hit the nail on the head the other day when she said that the conduct of the observed was apt to be reflected by the mind of the observer."

Dr. MacCracken's only comment on the recent discussion of specific habits of a harmful nature attributed to college girls was that Vassar had declined last year to join a committee of college representatives investigating this matter, as there was no evidence to warrant such action.

More Self-Reliant Than of Old.

Dean Virginia Gildersleeve of Barnard College remarks that: "It is true that a good many of the younger generation do foolish things at times, but so have they always done in the past. For the young women of the present I have great respect. They seem to me on the whole an admirable lot. Harmful and offensive habits are, I believe, much less prevalent in colleges than among girls of the same age outside college walls. They are not causing us particular anxiety at Barnard."

Miss Mary E. Woolley, President of Mount Holyoke College, does not concede that as a group undergraduates are either superficial or conspicuous.

"I am not at all sure that the college girl of today is to be criticized more than the college girl of yesterday," she says. "Notwithstanding the fact that her sport clothes would have seemed remarkable ten years ago and her manners somewhat frank and outspoken, I find her just as responsive and earnest, perhaps more self-reliant and independent. The colleges naturally are affected by the tone of society outside, and in the large college groups throughout the country there are doubtless small elements of the superficial and conspicuous. I doubt whether in any group of young women it is possible to find so much real earnestness of purpose and high idealism as in the undergraduates in our colleges."

Another Dean of a woman's college, Miss Ada L. Comstock, President of Radcliffe, mentions restlessness alone as a possible danger to the steady development of the modern college girl. She is on the whole, according to Dean Comstock, more intelligent than her mother.

"There is, I believe, only one safe generalization to make about the college girl of today. This is, that she is more numerous than ever before and she represents a greater variety of homes. Consequently, she probably reflects American life more truly than in earlier days when she came from the exceptional home."

As Seen at Hunter College.

The statement of President George S. Davis of Hunter College is of particular interest, coming as it does from the head of a school whose students are not under his jurisdiction after a day's classes are over. Hunter College is not a boarding school.

"In view of the fact that Dr. Smith of Roanoke College did not say the things attributed to him concerning college girls of today, it seems to me improper and impertinent to discuss the matter in relation to him. He has been very unfortunate in having been the unintentional occasion of statements in the press derogative of college girls, when his strictures on feminine conduct were intended to call public attention to certain social improprieties among young women in general: improprieties which are alleged to be committed by some of them irrespective of their connection with educational institutions. From this point of view I believe that the warning given by Dr. Smith is not without some justification.

"Personally, I do not consider that there is any such person as 'the modern college girl.' The expression implies a type, whereas the girls who go to college are infinite in their variety. They cannot be standardized and labeled in that way and then be subjected to adverse criticisms as a whole because of alleged vagaries in conduct on the part of a very limited number of individuals.

"At Hunter we have never seen any indications of the particular offenses properly condemned by Dr. Smith, and I can assure the public that they have not been committed by our students while under our jurisdiction. After our students leave for the day they are absorbed into the life of the city and behave, as far as I know, after the manner of other girls, but with such self-restraint as their ideals as college girls and their own breeding may impose.

"Hunter girls, as classes and societies, have had many social functions, such as dances, dramatics, &c., in the various hotels and theatres of the city, and we have never had an instance of such offenses as pointed out. I do not wish to imply that Hunter girls are entirely without imperfections, but only that while under the college jurisdiction or patronage they naturally respect the ideals which they themselves have set up. I also believe they respect them at other times, but what they do elsewhere and at other times is a matter for their parents, none of whom have ever complained that their daughters gave them trouble in the ways criticized.

"I have found, in these later days, that when girls enter college a great change takes place in their attitude toward things. In the first place, there is an increase in dignity from the very fact that they are in college. They are thrown more upon their own resources than formerly, and in consequence they develop a greater sense of responsibility. Their interests become much wider and they obtain a more intelligent understanding of social, political and, to some extent, economic conditions. They form opinions and are able to defend them.

"Comparing, as you suggest, college girls of today with college girls of yesterday, I should say that some of them are better and some of them are worse; but taking them for better or worse, I have found the young college women of the present day quite efficient, very reasonable and altogether delightful persons to work with and for."

February 17, 1924

'Drug Store Cowboy' Target Of Salvation Army Campaign

"The drug store cowboy," known in small cities as a corner loafer, is to be the object of an especially vigorous attack during the coming year by the Salvation Army. This was announced yesterday when Army representatives from the Eastern and Southern States met in the First Presbyterian Church.

This type of youth wears spectacular clothing, subjects women and girls to flippant remarks and talks familiarly on the subject of liquor, where it can be bought and at what prices, according to the Salvation Army. Commissioner Thomas Estill, head of the Army in the Eastern territory, said his number is growing fast, and although such youths are not vicious, they often drift into careers of crime.

September 24, 1924

SAYS AUTO HARMS STUDENT

Illinois University Dean Also Lays Loose Morals to Machines.

Special to The New York Times.

URBANA, Ill., Nov. 8.—The morals, scholarship and physical safety of students at the University of Illinois are endangered by those whose parents permit them to bring automobiles to the university, according to a letter sent today by Professor Thomas A. Clark, Dean of Men, to the parents of the 400 students who use automobiles.

"The university has made no regulations about the automobile and does not wish to do so, hoping that the co-operation of parents may be able to solve the problem," the letter reads.

"The automobile is a waster of time and money. It encourages loafing and the taking of frequent and unnecessary trips out of town to the neglect of the students' regular work.

"The possession of a car involves more than ordinary physical danger. A half dozen students crowd into a machine intended for two or three. There is excitement and fast driving and frequent serious accidents.

"There is moral danger in the car. Whatever of drinking and stealing and immorality exists among the college students is largely in connection with the automobile. The passion for driving seems often to stimulate other passions and unconventionalities and actual immorality often results.

"Youth is perhaps no more irresponsible now than it has always been, but the automobile is an added temptation to moral irresponsibility."

November 9, 1924

CO-EDS GET AN ULTIMATUM.

Nebraska College Gives Them Four Days to Appear in Modest Styles.

LINCOLN, Neb., Feb. 12.—Co-eds of Union College, at College View, a Lincoln suburb, are allowed four days in which to abandon short skirts, low-necked dresses, rouge and lipstick, and adopt attire specified by the President, W. W. Prescott, in an ultimatum issued at a meeting "for girls only" at the college yesterday.

The girls were ordered by President Prescott to garb themselves in clothing in no way conspicuous. He prescribed the following: Skirts not more than nine inches from the ground, elbow-length sleeves, closely-fitting collars and rougeless faces.

After the meeting, Mr. Prescott said:

"The model girl should be so inconspicuous in her mode of dress that people might not remember her for clothes but for her personality."

Girls who fail to comply with the ruling will not be permitted to attend classes, he said.

February 13, 1925

DEFENDS NEW GENERATION.

To the Editor of The New York Times:

The best in social life is not undermined; if it were, it would not be the best. The social life of our younger generation is becoming fuller, richer and more intelligent than that of the older generation now passing on. Any "resulting excesses" that may appear are due primarily to the influence of restraints, prohibitions and moral values imposed on us and our ancestors in the past. The younger generation is slowly progressing toward firmer and nobler ideals, and is taking a more practical and hence a healthier view of sex matters.

Puritanism, which is responsible for much of the uglier aspects of modern life, is gradually dying under the potent influence of higher education. Calamities, tragedies, moral lapses, social troubles, &c., are no longer regarded as a sign from God, but rather as the direct or indirect result of hereditary and environmental influences. Truth reposes relatively in the highest and noblest conceptions of life, that can be logically supported by verifiable facts and ample evidence.

HOWARD THOMAS LAKEY,
Jersey City, N. J., Aug. 2, 1925.

August 9, 1925

MASS TRAINING OF YOUTH.

"The flapper of today," said Professor SNEDDEN of Teachers College, "is a perfect example of 'the herd mind.'" She pays small heed to her parents, to her minister, even to the high-school teachers whom Professor SNEDDEN was addressing. "Ninety "per cent. of her vital personal reac- "tions come from other persons of "her own type." Civilization trembles on the brink—until one turns to what Dr. SHERWOOD EDDY said to the League of Youth. Returning from a tour of Europe, he declared that everywhere a deeply moral and far-sighted "revolt of youth" is "in the air." We elders are sunk in "sordid materialism," prostrate beneath an "absolutism" that is at once "political, economic, racial and intellectual." But it "lies in the power of youth" to stop all this "just as slavery was stopped sixty-three years ago." The famous prophecy of ELLEN KEY missed it by only a negligible fifteen years. Though not precisely "the century of the child," this is indeed the century of boy-sheik and flapper.

Miss KEY did not tell us whether her "child" was to salvage civilization or to sink it. Ministerial outgivings last Sunday were burdened with woe. According to the Rev. C. A. Ross, who addressed the Forum of the Y. M. C. A., that vital and salutary institution of all our forefathers, the home, is no more. Once a industrial plant of the first order, producing its toys and its music, its teaching and nursing, its cooking and its very spanking first-hand, it now imports them all. The delicacies of home life have become mere delicatessen. As to who is to blame for all this Mr. BASIL HENRIQUES had no doubt. It rests, he said, addressing the Free Synagogue in Carnegie Hall, not so much with the young people as with their parents—whose interests are in night clubs, "shows" and parties rather than in bringing up their children.

The description is familiar. But have not moralist and divine put the cart before the horse? Disintegration of the home comes not from within but from without. In transforming our industries, mass production has transformed our very lives. It began with the public school and the popularization of the university. Then came canned and package food. Hospital and trained nurse wiped out the old family doctor and the maternal nurse, so loving and so blundering. Theatre and moving picture, restaurant and cabaret, did for crude parlor games

and parlor dancing. The latest invasion is that of visiting teachers and visiting nurses, of Boy Scouts and Girl Scouts. Can any one undo it all, or would he if he could? These are the real source of Professor SNEDDEN's herd psychology, as of Dr. EDDY's revolt of youth.

Will insurgent sheiks and flappers create a valid substitute for the home of yesterday? That is the real question for moralists and divines. It will not be answered by one generation. Meantime parents deserve some little sympathy. To have children at all is a triumph. When they grow up and,

under the promptings of the mass mind, desert their shrunken simulacrum of a home, what is left their parents but to put on the mask of a decent cheerfulness and join the giddy rout at theatre and cabaret?

March 2, 1926

A MISDIRECTED "REVOLT."

Professor THORNDIKE of Columbia is not so much wrought up as are some by the current "revolt of youth." Perhaps he has seen it too often to be afraid of it. Possibly he was in it himself at a time when it was bliss to be alive and very heaven to be young. Anyhow, he thinks rather better of young men and women because they rebel at a good deal of what they see in the world. He is confident that their red fire of protest will in time pass into the steady light in which constructive work can be done.

It is naturally in the colleges that most of this youthful revolt is detected. But at what things is it mainly aimed? College boys want to get rid of compulsory chapel, and small blame to them. They would like better courses of instruction, with more inspiring teachers, and still less blame to them. They are repelled by current standards in literature and art and morals.

Every kind of censorship outrages them. They crave entire freedom to utter the thoughts that arise in them. At social conventions and customary proprieties of human intercourse which they believe to be without reasonable justification they snap their fingers in scorn. In brief, their instinct of revolt directs itself, as is natural enough, against traditions and, practices and rules with which they are most immediately in contact, and which they would radically change or abolish outright.

Ought they not, however, to lift up their eyes so as to be able to see reforms which should be striven for outside the social and academic walls behind which they live? What we mean is indicated in the remark of an English lecturer who has been spending some time in an American university. Writing of the impressions he derived from the youth he was trying to teach, he speaks enthusiastically of

their energy, their keenness to learn, their hopeful outlook, their organizing ability, their group activities, their happy confidence that the world of thought and art lies plastic under their hands. But one lack he noted. It was that all this stir and enlargement of life in our colleges had almost no influence upon American "political conditions." It almost seems as if he thought of the revolt of youth in our universities as, after all, a cloistered virtue. It did not impinge upon the great community about it.

Doubtless the contrast with England and the Continent was in the back of this lecturer's mind. It is not simply that English and French and German and Near-Eastern universities send a great many men into public life; their students, before graduating, take a livelier interest in political affairs, and class themselves as radicals not only on the intellectual and theoretic side, but on public questions. We do not

have so much of that in this country, though it would be well if we had more. We should like to see our youth in revolt against corruption in politics, against ignorance and want of character in public men, against laws that have outlived their time and their usefulness, against stupid and oppressive methods of administration, against every lurking form of injustice in the social order. By all means let our youth revolt. There is no means of stopping them, if we wished to. But one cannot help thinking what a fine thing it would be if their rebellious and reforming spirit could be directed less to private grievances and restricted evils and more to the public mischiefs and wrongs which cry out for correction and redress.

April 14, 1926

JANE ADDAMS SEES SOBERING OF YOUTH

Believes Young Americans Are Settling Down From Hectic Post-War Self-Determination.

IN PARIS FOR CONFERENCE

Copyright, 1926, by The New York Times Company.
By Wireless to THE NEW YORK TIMES.

PARIS, June 29.—Miss Jane Addams of Hull House, Chicago, who will be the outstanding figure at the International Settlements Congress, arrived in Paris today with some interesting things to say about the rising generation. The subject is one of the problems uppermost in the minds of the delegates, who are gathering here from all parts of the world.

Although the present situation appears rather bad on the surface, Miss Addams believes there are signs of a settling down process on the part of the younger people of America.

"In the language of the moment, I believe that thousands of young men and women who since the war have been possessed of independence of movement are beginning to snap out of it," explained Miss Addams smilingly. "I am extremely anxious to know how the problem is working itself out in other countries, especially England, where the young people have been causing as much worry as they have at home. I intend to arrange a symposium of all nations so that each group can tell about its respective young folks and how they are behaving. I think in this fashion we shall get some excellent ideas and at the same time learn if young America is really as bad as the youth of other countries or worse, as some would have us believe."

Blames Automobile and War.

Miss Addams blames two things for this so-called wildness of American youth—the automobile and the late war.

"The motor car, now within the reach of any workingman, has made

it possible for a young man to take his girl into the country, away from the social restrictions of home and city life, and that has been bad," she continued. "The parents are just as much to blame, because, if the children don't take the car, they do, leaving the children alone for the evening or the week-end, as the case may be.

"Then there was the war. What an unfortunate psychological effect that had upon young people! A distinct change has taken place in the United States since the war days. One notices it even when living there all the time, but it is especially apparent to those who have been away from America since then. A peculiar idea of independence and freedom has taken hold of the younger generation. For example, certain heads of colleges have told me how they discovered with horror that many young girls were freely discussing the theory that every woman was entitled to sexual experience, aside from marriage, which they placed in the companionship or later period of life. One woman President, when she discovered that this idea was apparently being accepted, contemplated resigning, feeling that she could not possibly cope with the consequences of this theory. Fortunately most girls have not put the idea into practice, but it is a dangerous one

even to discuss and can easily lead to disaster.

Wildness of Sons Also.

"Parents are really having a terrible time of it. They complain that they are irritated beyond measure with the wildness of their sons. There are definite indications, however, that the settling down process I have already mentioned is beginning. There are thousands of normal-living young people of both sexes throughout our country, and I think their number is increasing all the time. Of course you hear more about those who are not living normally, and that leads to the opinion that the young Americans are all going the pace."

Miss Addams speaks with peculiar authority. Besides being the oldest settlement worker in point of service in America, she has spent a great part of her live studying American social problems, viewing them always with wide vision and kindliness. After thirty-seven years of strenuous work in the social field she looks upon the young people of America as a sound investment for the future, despite the censure leveled at them from many directions.

June 30, 1926

YOUTH REVOLT FAILING, SAYS NORMAN THOMAS

American Students Educated Too Much in Creed of Success and "Get Ahead," He Asserts.

Norman Thomas, former Socialist candidate for Mayor and Governor, told an audience of students yesterday

that the widely heralded American "revolt of youth" had failed to live up to its press notices.

The reason, he explained, was that American boys and girls had been so thoroughly educated in the philosophy of success and "get ahead" that they were not interested in revolting at all. Dr. Thomas spoke at a meeting of the Students' Forum of Temple Emanu-el, Fifth Avenue and Forty-third Street.

"A great many of our young people are drunk with our apparent prosperity," he said. "They have taken one

smell of the bottle of materialism, and they like it. For the most part, American youth has been badly exploited in the way it has been taught. From the earliest grades in grammar school it has been told to get ahead—to get there honestly, if possible, but at any rate to succeed.

"We in America are educating our youth in the success religion. We are teaching our young people not to learn, not to emancipate their spirits, but to 'get ahead.' And there are just enough Cinderellas who marry fairy-story princes, just enough poor boys who be-

come millionaires, to give color to the success religion."

Dr. Thomas warned against the dangers of the "herd mind," especially as reflected in war-time hysteria, and said that although human nature could not be changed, human beings should not allow themselves to be exposed to "herd" influences.

"A great deal of skepticism is wholesome," said Dr. Thomas. "But we cannot afford the luxury of cynical pessimism while we cling to life."

April 4, 1927

FINDS YOUTH FACING GREAT REVOLUTION

H. J. Golding Tells Ethical Society New Generation Inherits Burden of Change.

A CALL FOR SOCIAL VISION

"We are in the midst of the greatest revolution the world has ever experienced," Henry J. Golding declared in an address yesterday morning in the meeting house of the Society for Ethical Culture, Central Park West and Sixty-fourth Street. His topic was "The Plight of Youth."

"Religion, the family, education, government and industry are undergoing profound modification," he said. "Science is more revolutionary than the revolutionists. It opens vistas that outrange our vision; it thrusts upon us vital problems, for the solution of which the past yields little guidance. Never before has the contrast between the fatherland and the children's land been more acute.

"The new generation inherit this burden of bewildering change. They must control the forces that now control and drive us. They must master the industrial machine and make it the servant, not the tyrant, of life. The new civilization that will grow out of the old calls for statesmanship, social vision, fresh moral insight. It demands a new birth of beauty and a greater and stronger conviction than ours of the meaning and value of life.

"Without these, life, however encumbered with material riches, is cheap and dreary.

"Youth enters on a heritage of spiritual chaos. The austere values of a harder life—values never really accepted by the mass of men—go down before the gospel of enjoyment."

The result, he held, would eventually be the evolution of "an ethic that will exalt—as supreme, lofty intellectual standards, long range vision, self-discipline, the cooperative spirit, the joy of creativeness, and reverence for the deepening marvel of human personality."

April 15, 1929

TOPICS OF THE TIMES.

Sophistication in Iowa. So little has been heard recently of the sad young men and emancipated young women of Greenwich Village that they were in danger of being forgotten until a recent play restored them to public attention. High rents or business depression or something unaccountable appeared to have driven most of them from their old haunts, and they do not seem to have collected again in a single community. Perhaps many of them have gone back to their families to hibernate.

Some of them must have been Iowans, for a description of a group observed by Mr. BRUCE BLIVEN and reported in The New Republic indicates the importation to that State of some genuine Greenwich Village color. He attributes the ostentatious boredom of these condescending young people to Mr. SINCLAIR LEWIS. When "Main Street" was published they discovered the pangs of bucolicism and at once set about to get a remedy.

Outward signs of proud decadence are not lacking, though they are not the most depressing. The gaudy roadsters, the incessant smoking, the ghastly make-up used by the young ladies are only surface indications. These young Iowans read "the little expatriate magazines of Paris," and when they go to the movies or listen to the radio, as they are bound to do sometimes, they wear a satirical smile. It is nothing new for youngsters to pity their parents, but Mr. BLIVEN doubts "whether there has ever been so much concentrated pity as is going on in the Mississippi Valley in 1930." If these boys and girls are not returns from Greenwich Village, they are ripe to come and rehabilitate it.

October 2, 1930

WHERE IS THE REVOLT OF YOUTH HEADING?

Its Attack on Old Traditions, Says Zona Gale, May Be Only the Prelude to Useful, Constructive Energy

The beginning of a new decade finds a younger generation still puzzling to an older generation whose ways are not the ways of modern youth. What is the status of this ever new and ever continuing revolt of youth? The following analysis is by one of America's best-known novelists and a recognized student of changing society.

By ZONA GALE

"FIRST," says the average American man, "I had to get used to the new woman. Now I have to get used to the new daughter and the new son."

The average American man, it would seem, is about the only one in his family who is not new. He goes right on, earning the living and a good deal more—if he can keep the pace—and saying that everything is different.

Two decades ago he was trying to understand his wife. That gentle soul, who had kept "his" house and looked after his needs, abruptly developed new needs of her own, outside "his" house; and she proceeded to fill them. His daughter found that the interests which he and his kind had projected for her were not enough, and she took an apartment, went into business, lived her own life. Much earlier, his sons had declared their right to turn from his business, no matter how carefully he had built it up for them, and to choose their own occupations.

To all this he adjusted himself.

He first endured, then tolerated, then cooperated in his wife's new interests. He bought stock in her club buildings and non-professional theatres, subscribed to her lectures, even attended those that she herself gave. His own daughter he hired to do his interior decorating, he patronized her gift shops; and he lent her money to go into business, even as he had been doing for his sons.

All was quiet, and adjusted. Then came Another Dawn.

This time it was not only that the younger generation came knocking at the door. This time they did not trouble to knock, and if they entered at all, it was merely to say: "Mother, don't expect me for dinner," and "O dad, I'll have to have a check." No, it was not that they knocked and demanded their share, their place in the sun; and it was that they said, "This place is nothing, and what is the sun anyway?" They made for themselves new orbits and new poles. And today there is the average man, standing on his heaped hearth, by his well-provided dining-room table, with a copy of unregarded family rules and regulations in his hand; and there is the average woman, wife and mother, in the same position, her own revolt long ago accepted and out-moded; and now together these two face not the younger generation but a new race of individuals who say that they know precisely what they want and are taking it.

THE average American woman, not less than the average American man, seems to think that Rome before the fall is repeating itself in the life of their children; and they argue or they weep or they pray, according to their natures. They do everything save to try to understand what is happening.

What is happening?

It is childish to say: "But I remember that my parents said the same thing—thought I was going to the dogs. Every generation thinks the same. These young people will come out all right—just as we did."

It is true that every generation has felt that its children were in danger, were likely to come to no good end. But in America one has only to look back, generation by generation, to the beginning of this century, to our Civil War times, to our Revolution, to discern that no period has offered to us any general younger generation whose choice of actions was similar to that of this period. There have been aberrations of conduct, vagaries, daring, independence, defiance, but never has there been anything like this. If in the past, convention was defied or flaunted, if there was sharp divergence from tradition, this divergence was recognized as such and a part of the fun was in diverging; but always the old standards were still there, a mighty background. For us in America the standards themselves never have crashed, until now. That is why the adult comfort of "every generation thinks the same" is specious. We in America have never before observed this that we are observing now. The average man, the average woman, is aghast.

Even as man was bewildered by the new woman (and how moderate she was!) so now man and woman together are bewildered by their offspring.

What has come upon them? There is a stock set of replies: Loss of inhibitions consequent upon both the great war and the Eighteenth Amendment. A new psychology. "The" single standard. Break-down of the family, break-down of religion, break-down of respect for and belief in age. Loss of illusion. Desire for self-expression. Hunger for reality. The new freedom.

These offerings, some generic and some specific, are not explanations. These are all results, not causes, of whatever it is that is happening to American youth. Such replies do not explain. They merely partially enumerate.

However, this enumeration does disclose one truth: It is that alarm for the new generation must be based not so much on what they actually do (though Heaven knows that, too, occupies the field) as on what they say they believe.

"We have been talking for twenty minutes," I said to a newspaper woman, "and we have spoken of nothing that matters."

She answered: "But what is there that matters? Living doesn't matter, dying doesn't matter. * * *"

"To whom?" I interrupted.

"To me," she said, "to anybody."

Was there then, I asked her, anything that did matter?

She replied positively: "Having a good time."

"Why that?" I asked, puzzled.

On which she merely looked suspicious.

She was a college woman, an honor student, a Phi Beta Kappa. She was 22 years old. It was thus that she was meeting life, and death, which did not matter.

199

However, I respected her reply, which is also the reply of a host no man can number. It was not vague, it was not hypercritical, it was not based on the accustomed. The one possible flaw in its sincerity was that it may have been caught by contagion from the jargon of others—may have become as much a convention as any convention which her age was deriding. But this kind of contagious jargon, accounting as it does for the loose talk of the unthinking, by no means explains the psychology of those who do think. And most of the younger generation do think. It is as shallow to say that the majority do not want any other solution of life as it is to say that the majority of the unemployed do not want to work. It takes more to account for a general social condition than contagion. One might as well say that diphtheria is caused by "catching" diphtheria.

The young people of today in America are thinking alike and are thinking as they do think because of some stimulus beyond their control. They did no more originate their present psychology than they originated the measles and mumps of their childhood. Just as the unemployed are unemployed because of vast economic crevasses in our loose social formation, so the younger generation "got this way" because of some wash of energy that caught them up as, in the past, youth has been caught up again and again.

At least twice in America has youth reacted to some vast appreciable intellectual and emotional stimulus. And both times this was a stimulus by which adults also were moved. Once by the cause of American independence. The majority of the "boys" of '76 were literally boys; they were boys at Lexington and Concord, boys at the Boston tea party, boys who joined with their own elders and defied the royalists. That time the young people expressed themselves, and their elders approved. And again in the cause against or for slavery in America, and—for or against—the preservation of the Union. That time, too, the young people expressed themselves burningly, and their elders approved and encouraged and—when the enthusiasm wavered—even conscripted.

There is, perhaps, a third cry for self-expression, that of the boy and girl who wants to go to college; but that goes on so quietly and with such cooperation and sacrifice on the part of the elders that we hardly think of it as a youth movement at all—even though in reality it is such. These social and political and educational upheavals have risen and swept young America, with the approval and cooperation and even the instigation of the older generation. But this present upheaval has its rise and its support from the younger generation alone, without the smallest by-your-leave to the elders.

* * *

NOW this that we are undergoing may not be an upheaval for the better. Just as in Europe the Crusades and the Reformation—youth movements both—are not now by some considered blessings; so in America, in the future, this present uprising of youth against tradition, against convention, may not be regarded as a source of good—may prove to be regarded as an evil and a mockery. Its effects may be either to upset our whole social convention or to cause but a slight shift in our values. The Crusades shook Europe and died away to an echo. The Reformation shook Europe and left a chasm which four centuries have not bridged. But whatever are the results of this present subversion, at this moment it should be taken as seriously as any other youth movement that the world has ever known.

In America, as elsewhere, youth always has been secretly in revolt One has only to remember one's own youth to be convinced of that. Youth has always questioned the omniscience of the elder generation in its rules, its solemnities, its politics, its religion, its sense of reality, and the brands of freedom which satisfied it. But before youth could get up its courage effectively to object, middle life usually overtook it, and it settled down to expediency, and it conformed. It remembered—

"The Young People of Today in America Are Thinking Alike and Are Thinking as They Do Think Because of Some Stimulus Beyond Their Control."

for a while—but it conformed. And then it began teaching the next generation to conform, too.

But this time—for reasons which we need not agree upon—youth somehow made a concerted movement, formed an abrupt invisible union, and generated the energy to sound a single note:

"I protest. I accuse. I express myself."

This time, in America, right or wrong, they have made themselves heard.

And now, whether we like it or not, the older generation faces two pitfalls. The first is the pitfall of berating and suspecting and still seeking to dominate youth. The second is the pitfall of pretending to agree with youth and pretending to sympathize with it in all its new points of view, simply because the older generation is in terror of being cut off, shut out, regarded as Victorian. In both these ways the elders fail the younger generation—as they have failed so many times before.

What then shall be the way of the average American father, the average American mother, in dealing with this amazing manifestation of a youth movement surpassing in possible effect any revolt that America has yet known?

Certainly the first need is to try to understand the great change which is taking place in youth. To understand that it is not a matter of individual "insubordination," or self-will or defiance; but that a vast wave of challenge to old social standards has swept the land, and that, conceivably, it may have something to contribute to social progress. In America the last stronghold of open autocracy has been in the family—and among certain employers of labor. Perhaps it is only that now in the family, too, autocracy is giving place to some degree of democracy. Or perhaps what is happening is very much more. But whatever it is, it must be regarded as a social problem and not a problem of the individual young person in his or her family relationships.

But how shall we define such a social problem?

ANY reply to such a question can be only tentative, can be only one's own guess, hazarded from one's own scant observation or perhaps faulty theory. But at any rate we can argue from known facts:

First, that there seem to be, at certain periods and in certain areas, unprecedented outpourings of an unknown energy. The Europe of the Crusades and the Reformation; the Greece and Rome of their great day; the Italy of the Renaissance; the England of Elizabeth; Asia as the cradle of all great religions; the Europe and America of twentieth century science; and such little outpourings of energy as that which motivated the Lake poets in England or, in America, the Concord of Emerson and his friends. In these times and places something tremendous occurred—some enormous silence and conformity was shattered by strange happenings. In most cases the older generation must have believed that their world was headed for the rocks.

Here and now, in America, is as great an outpouring of power, of a kind of fresh creative energy as ever motivated any group of young people in the world. Fresh thinking, fresh convictions, fresh determinations of fact. Something as different as research is different from memory. A sweep of new power flowing mysteriously through the young people of every remote town as definitely as ever it flowed through any youth in the world, in any movement which possessed them.

• • •

ALL the ways in which we see the younger generation expressing itself may be but the first awkward handling of new powers which they shall transform into uses of which as yet we, and they, have no conception. Heaven knows, they deal with these energies awkwardly enough. Drunkenness seems a silly way to express a new and god-like desire to be linked up closer to life. Shattering old ideas of order and procedure seems not enough to do, without offering some form of new order and new procedures. And still, when they do offer suggestions, nobody listens—yet.

"It is," I heard a poet say, "exactly as if a vessel with a cargo of musical instruments had been wrecked on a far-away island. And all the islanders came down and seized on the strange instruments and began to blow and pound and pluck. That is the confusion of the younger generation now. Wait until they develop a theory of music and a technique. Wait until they form their orchestra. Then—"

It lies with the younger generation itself. It can keep on playing wildly, expending the new energy in obvious ways. Or it can make a new music. Even if now it does not wish a new music, and says, "The world doesn't matter. Life doesn't matter. Death doesn't matter. Nothing matters but having a good time • • •" Even that need not be too disconcerting. Any new form of expression modifies behavior and, consequently, beliefs. There must have been drunken Crusaders, and, even among these, many who never knew what it was all about; who indeed died without seeing themselves as figures in a spectacle connected with anything but having a good time. Perhaps they weren't otherwise connected—not, however, in the sense which they intended. It is not to be expected that those in any new stream of tendency should be self-conscious from the first. A Spengler period is as predictable after war as is a financial panic after a time of expansion.

The avowed disillusion of the younger generation in America does not interfere with its own generosity, its kindliness, its urge to do a good turn. No more than secondary symptoms are its mental confusions, its despairs, its refuges here and there. The main symptomatic revelation which it makes is that of an energy unprecedented in the general life of American youth, an energy expressing itself in new forms of behavior, in new attitudes of belief, in a striking-out toward new areas in every form of reaction. This is the one aspect that matters.

• • •

WHATEVER we may call the rebellion of youth, it is never ultimate. Already among the sophisticates, among that small group of those who rebound most sensitively from any standardized behavior, there is to be noted a certain return. Perhaps it is because of the fundamental sanity of the American, even of the human, temper and spirit; or, perhaps, it is because of the old-new shadow of humanism; or it may be only because of Victorian clothes; but for some reason this return, a flair for decorum, is observable now among certain young people. There is here and there even a slight spiritual renaissance. Before the war in France there was a society of young intellectuals formed for and dedicated to the worship of The One, The Being. In the American colleges there is a frank seeking for new values, for a standard more reasonable than that of despair.

All these are symptomatic of factors on the long, long road, the eternal road, of the quest of the young human spirit. In less than another hundred years there may be a younger generation that is serious and spiritual and inordinately bored by the vagaries and intoxications of the generation older.

The need of any generation is obviously to come to understand itself and its own peculiar powers—to be aware. This new generation is likely to make—not that it wishes it now, but that is unimportant—a contribution to America and to the world such as no other group has ever made, not excepting those earlier youth movements of 1864 or 1776. For the defiances at the Boston tea party did not include a perception of a nation of forty-eight States. The excesses of the French Revolution did not contemplate an eventual United States of Europe. And the concerted effort of the youth of America to break down traditions and to find a new freedom may be but the immediate expression of an energy which shall yet apply itself to undivined constructive ends.

Meanwhile, America awaits the directing of this new creative energy, whose primitive splashings it is enduring—and enduring, if it is wise, with a great sympathy.

March 8, 1931

Books of The Times
By Christopher Lehmann-Haupt

THE DAMNED AND THE BEAUTIFUL. American Youth in the 1920's. By Paula S. Fass. 497 pages. Oxford. $15.95.

WE THINK of the American 1920's in clichéd images of jazz, gin, Charlestons and flappers, which, in case you've forgotten, or, like me, never knew before, took their name from the fact that the young women so called took to wearing their galoshes open. We also think of the 20's as the time when traditional institutions and values lost respect among the middle-class young, and, depending on your point of view, youth was either free to be damned or liberated to progress into a better future.

But Prof. Paula S. Fass, author of "The Damned and the Beautiful: American Youth in the 1920's," says all this is nonsense. Our images of the 20's may have a certain validity, although they do so for reasons a lot more complex than we are accustomed to thinking. But the notion that young people were either damned or beautiful is simply wrong, Professor Fass insists. It was the figment of traditionalist and progressive commentators who correctly perceived that the behavior of youth had become a mainstream problem of the decade, but who solipsistically projected their own hopes and anxieties onto youth's true concern. As for F. Scott Fitzgerald: For all the luminousness of his art, what he did "with uncanny insight" was "to play on the public sensibility and its alarm" and "expose the way in which the culture had betrayed its past, all the while feeding the public's hungry curiosity about the present."

Peers Filled the Gap

Meanwhile, back on the college campus, youth was simply adjusting to certain profound changes in American culture, and doing so with considerable success, Professor Fass insists. Owing to a complex variety of causes having to do with the industrialization of the country and a declining birthrate among the urban middle-class, the previous several decades had seen a redefinition of the American family. Where it had once been a Victorian institution whose function was to prepare the child for society, it was now a more democratic unit whose end was to provide the child affection. That change left a gap in the socializing process, which was filled by the child's adolescent peers, who happened, for reasons related to the increased democratization of the family, to be flocking to university campuses in greater numbers than ever before.

In Professor Fass's scheme, everything about youth in the 20's follows from this peer phenomenon. The predominance of fraternities and sororities in campus life; the high level of conformity they demanded; the greater respect paid to extracurricular activities — especially athletics — than to academic pursuits; the liberalization of sexual mores; the smoking and drinking, and the passion for fads involving dances, games, pop philosophies, clothing styles and slang — all were young people's way of preparing on their own terms for the adult society that they understood to be awaiting them.

The result was America's first youth culture, whose passions, not for the last time, became "one effective way in which the needs of the young were channeled into the historical conditions of a changing society." In short, and to bring to a close this vast oversimplification of Professor Fass's complex and attenuated thesis, young people of the 20's were neither damned nor beautiful. They were simply working new things out in new ways.

May 4, 1977

A SKEPTICAL MOOD FOUND IN COLLEGES

The Majority of Students Are Serious but Disillusioned, an Observer Asserts.

NOISE BY THE MINORITY

Flaming Youth and the Heroes of Yesterday Are Reported Missing, but Social Ideas Are Few.

By ANITA BRENNER.

What has become of the "wild young generation" which not long since furrowed so many elderly brows? Where now is the flapper, and where is Flaming Youth, with its hip-flasks, its speedy cars and flamboyant clothes and many tacit declarations of freedom? Not, indeed, on the campus. The traditions they created there are now regarded with indifference; "the collegiate business and all that" are definitely old-fogeyish and as dated as balloon trousers.

To be sure, many of the things once looked at askance have become normal and familiarly accepted—smoking by co-eds, for example. But also fashion has turned, outlawing excesses and social flashiness from their once high places and substituting new habits, new interests and a changed idea of what is and what is not admirable and smart.

The new era on the campus began, it is now apparent, about 1930. It was manifest first in a marked drop in attendance at football games, a drop in the number of students trying out for teams, an increased registration in economics, history and social-science courses, and a flare of interest in politics.

The nonchalant and well-dressed man chiefly notable for his social successes is still, to be sure, prominent on the campus, but he is now recognized as a "smoothie." On the other hand, the greasy grind is no longer so funny as he once seemed, though he is not a model

either. The brawny athlete is no longer a campus hero, and is apt to be looked upon as a "dumb egg" by the rank and file of his fellow-students. Instead, the limelight is often on the editor of the college daily, who, for the first time in history, perhaps, may be a non-fraternity man.

The Signs of Change.

These are the signs that the American college is turning somewhat from football and its equivalents—to what? Can it be veering toward politics and social problems? A growing undergraduate minority is. Student strikes are by now familiar items in the daily news. Agitation against war and, to the same end, against military training in school has appeared in one form or another in most of the large colleges in the country, both co-educational and otherwise. Liberal clubs, social problems clubs, Socialist clubs, chapters of student federations of a liberal or radical character have been formed in most universities.

One bulletin board, noted at random on the Columbia campus recently, announced the following: An anti-war meeting; a lecture on the Negro problem; a debate, "Should Palestine Be Rebuilt Along Socialist Lines?"; a meeting to protest the discharge of a faculty member active in student politics; another meeting to discuss art from a Marxist angle; and one to protest against German fascism.

Do these signs mean that the United States is slowly producing a "youth movement" and that in the future American students may take as important a part in shaping the destiny of their country as do their European and Latin-American fellows?

At first glance it might seem so. But more probably the frequent items of news about campus political struggles in our country mean that the minority which in other days devoted itself to things radical in literary, dramatic and artistic fields is reflecting the intellectual temper outside of the campus by going politically leftward. The great majority of the students are indifferent so far to the burning issues thrust before them.

Seriousness Is the Mood.

What has happened, apparently, is, first and most strikingly, that the student body as a whole has acquired a deeper respect for the practice of reading and research, which authorities and educators call "the new seriousness." But

it is not a respect for study as such, nor are high marks and other signs of academic distinction the motive. Rather it is simply a need to know, an interest in techniques and information, which has established in many students the habit of carefully reading a daily paper and which in some colleges, one student observes, "has driven so many people to the library that the faculty is alarmed."

There is a sharp difference between the pre-war student, ambitious and hopeful, with phrases such as "the public good," "service" and "patriotism" in his vocabulary, and the present generation, which is neither very ambitious nor very hopeful, and looks upon such words as decidedly quaint.

More than anything the most characteristic student of this generation is a skeptic. The self-assured young man with the flask on his hip has been replaced by a young man no less self-assured, but sure especially of his right to doubt. Frequent exposures of graft in politics and shadiness on a grand scale in finance have impressed upon him the idea that this is a cut-throat world, in which the clever and not too scrupulous man is rewarded.

Youth Accuses.

Such disclosures have convinced him that most of what he has been taught about the goodness of the great and the mundane rewards of virtue is "bunk." As a result he takes plenty of salt with his academic fare. His mood is often acid; his pose, a tough flippancy; his tone, a cross between Ernest Hemingway and The New Yorker.

That the world is in a mess and his own future dubious, at best full of ifs and buts, is the fault, he feels, of the muddling middle-aged and elderly, of precisely those generations who once cried that youth was going to the dogs and taking the world with it. Now it is youth's turn to criticize, and youth concludes privately that they, the oldsters, have been blind and selfish hypocrites, and are now either unwilling or incompetent to mend their ways. So the younger generation feels it must straighten things out, not because it wants to save the world, but because in self-interest it must. Meanwhile, who wants to make his way must do it by the common method of each man for himself and no holds barred.

Underneath this hard philosophy is a deep sense of loss, and a determination to avoid trite illusions

that constitute a far more significant revolt than the naughtiness of the Twenties. Many students are saying to themselves that "All the idols are broken. There is nothing left to believe in."

One with the face and expression of that "radiant American girlhood" to be seen on the covers of magazines says that she "and many young people" feel "a certain emptiness. * * * Religion hasn't the appeal and the prestige any more, nor the comfort. * * * And is chasing after money worth anything? Playing around is just too empty * * * one can forget things in working. Maybe intellectual and cultural values might be worth something. * * * Music, I guess.

"We've got to break away from the old traditions. We need a new idea to believe in. It's up to America, and what America does is up to us. Still, we don't want to throw everything away. * * * Maybe we could find a new way of stating old principles so they would have a meaning. * * * Sort of combination of individual freedom and social responsibility."

And another, more brusquely, finishes with "Well, anyhow, we can at least try our hand. We couldn't possibly make things worse."

The Campus Groups.

Many students, of course, feel that they will fare well somehow and are not much interested or perturbed by anything outside of their private concerns. They devote their leisure to being amused.

The more socially aroused have programs ranging from communism to vague approval of the six-hour day, cooperative housing, State insurance, voluntary control of profits. They have hope, and a little faith, in the New Deal. Most of them agree that a greater measure of socialization in almost everything would be a good thing and advocate more responsibility for the welfare of the working class.

In the extreme group are the picketers and the glum romantics, who dare the world to do its worst. And the embryo anarchists, such as the law students at Michigan who left school because "What is the use of studying for a profession in which we will have to defend property, when we don't believe in it?"

Certainly youth now trusts youth alone; it must, it feels, make for itself if it can, what age has lost—the security of a dignified, satisfactory and useful way to live.

June 11, 1933

Topics of The Times

Young Are Impressionable. Youth looms large in the rehabilitation plans of the Republican party. The chairman of the membership committee of the National Republican Club has addressed a pamphlet to the young men urging them to come forward and avail themselves of the opportunities for leadership. Colonel THEODORE ROOSEVELT writes: "Where there is no vision the people perish. Those who have vision and idealism are generally young."

One way in which the Republican party can make heavy inroads among the young is by going ahead and electing a Republican Congress this year and a Republican President in 1936. Youth will thereupon rally to the Republican standard in great numbers. Youth always rallies to the party in

power or the party that seems to be heading for power. This lies in the nature of youth. The young are impressionable. They take color from the dominant note of the moment.

Many Young Ideals. The young have vision and idealism, but can be easily manipulated. No one knows this better than the "authoritarian" political engineers. MUSSOLINI, STALIN, HITLER are always heaping laurels on the brow of youth, but in practice they are convinced that when you have secured control of the State, including the newspapers and the schools, you can make the young toe the mark and think they love to.

German youth after the Armistice was the Wandervögel type, youth seeking the poetic values of life in comradeship, music, the open air, universal brotherhood. German youth today is in Storm Troops and hand-grenade practice.

June 8, 1934

AMERICAN YOUTH SEEKS SECURITY

For the First Time It Sweeps Across the Country in a General Movement to Demand a Fair Chance and a Wholly New Place in the National Scheme

By EUNICE FULLER BARNARD

TWO million boys and girls are filing out of school and college this month to join the waiting throngs in the employment offices. Like thousands of their ten million predecessors since 1929, many will wait in vain. Yet beyond the office windows already gleams a prospect newly brightening for youth.

This year has seen America's first real youth movement. To be sure, no general juvenile crusade with banners has swept across the country. Yet awkwardly gathering here and there in small, heterogeneous groups, youth without any single concerted effort has gained a wholly new position in the national scheme. Slowly it is coming into recognition as a separate class or bloc, with needs and grievances of its own almost as distinct as those of labor or capital or the American Legion.

Unlike youth movements in other countries, ours has been impelled by no revolutionary or nationalistic enthusiasms. It is a straightforward drive toward the protection of youth's own interests. After centuries of apathy American young people are being aroused to effective defense of their own collective future.

Despite the fact that for thousands of individual boys and girls the past year has been hard and despondent, for youth in the mass it has marked an immense advance toward adult, and even government, support of its pleas for special security, education and employment. In Washington for the past two months high officials have been discussing two independent proposals made by the Department of Labor and the Federal Office of Education, which would earmark from $96,000,000 to $288,000,000 of relief funds for a new guidance system for jobless, out-of-school youth.

But the matter goes deeper than any temporary expedient. More or less consciously youth and its counselors are looking toward some permanent youth provision in our social scheme. It is no accident but merely an adroit answer to this largely unspoken demand that Huey Long, for instance, is emphasizing a college education for every boy and girl as part of his promised political program. It is a recognition on his part of the new mass psychology of, and toward, youth.

AS the depression has continued, many observers have begun to say that if we are in for technological unemployment, it will be largely an unemployment of youth. Only ten years ago on the railroads, it has been pointed out, 16 per cent of the employes were under 25 years of age, whereas today less than 3 per cent are in that age group. "The applications of science have enabled adults to produce all that we need in the way of food, clothing and shelter with far less effort than a few years ago," remarks Dr. George F. Zook in his recent report as director of the American Council on Education. "Except on the farms there is little work for young people to do."

What we are up against, youth and its educators have both protested, is prolongation of dependency—of infancy, if you will—not alone for the privileged, college-going few but for all youth into the early twenties. If in this period of work deferred, youth's heart is not to be made sick, if there is not to be a breakdown of morale, loss of skill and a strong urge toward crime, some new sort of school or occupational service must fill the gap, it is argued.

All youth, to be sure, is not agreed upon the cure, but of the sickness already there is no doubt. A kind of resentment against an unequal fate widely pervades youth thinking.

IN earlier days there was perforce no more rugged individual than the youngster starting out in life. The rule here in America was every boy for himself, with the odds in his winning through to a modest livelihood. Today, with the odds frequently against him, he almost instinctively is turning to a mass approach to the problem.

Haltingly thousands of youngsters, in the upholstered ease of the college fraternity as well as in the bleak barracks of the transient camp, have come to the conclusion that their generation lacks the traditional heritage of American youth—confidence and opportunity. The old counsel to the young man to go West, or even to go Wall Street, no longer holds much promise. Neither place, they suspect, has nowadays much pay dirt for the youngster.

Moreover, there is no one to tell him in what other direction he may hopefully turn. Employment bureaus, many a boy has realistically decided, are apt to regard his problem from the viewpoint of their own pocketbooks rather than his vocational future. And school and college, despite their protestations, have in youth's uncompromising view done little to help. Too often schools have been apathetic or confused as to what kind of guidance to offer.

Behind much of youth's protest is also the thwarted biological urge toward marriage and family-rearing. The traditional American hope of love in a cottage, with the roses peeping in, the babies peeping out, seems like a mirage to thousands at the very age when their fathers were experiencing the reality. Today, as speakers at a recent youth conference put it, a young couple often seems to have but three choices: either to postpone marriage till youth is gone; to marry and live with their parents; or, if they are lucky, to marry and both pick up what jobs they can get. Almost for the first time in American life John and Jane are beginning to look not alone for personal escape but for some adjustment of jobs and job-training that will provide a way out for the majority of young people.

HITCH-HIKING, crawling over hundreds of miles of road in superannuated buses, sitting up all night in railway coaches, youngsters have stopped at little this year to get together and talk over their common plight. College students, young workers and members of various religious and reform groups have held congresses and formed new youth organizations. Radical campus groups—still probably comprising less than 1 per cent of college undergraduates—have reported notable gains. At the other end of the scale several hundred transient boys and girls this Winter organized as the Unattached Youth of America to alleviate "the sufferings of the hundreds of thousands" like themselves.

Dozens of young people, too, a number of them college graduates, are sitting in cramped, precariously financed offices editing papers, answering letters, as their contribution to some youth cause. Often without permanent headquarters, some of these groups seem to grow merely by the faith that is in them. Take the American Youth Congress, for instance, one of two continuing organizations resulting from the stormy meeting of that name held in New York last August. Today, almost wholly without the aid of funds, it has built up, it claims, a membership of nearly two million in its affiliated groups and has held a series of seventeen regional conventions from coast to coast.

As never before, too, youth is being heard. From college students to Boy Scouts, all sorts of young people have conferred with Cabinet members and Senators on youth problems. Youth is being given the rostrum at community meetings and welfare conferences. With all the eager curiosity with which our grandfathers might have viewed Fiji Islanders or runaway slaves, solemn citizens have gathered in lecture halls to hear the home youth tell of its problems. They have listened with a new sense of responsibility. In the Oranges and Maplewood, N. J., for instance, a community jury, sitting in the case of Youth vs. Society, found Society guilty of lack of proper provision for Youth. Fortnightly, during the Winter and Spring, following similar youth meetings in New York, Mrs. Franklin D. Roosevelt invited representatives of various youth organizations to meet with her at her Manhattan house to talk things over.

Thus, bit by bit through the year, upon the screen of the national consciousness has been projected the figure of American youth in the rôle of a feller needing a friend.

What has been the least common denominator of the pleas and the platforms of these curiously varied youth meetings? Mainly, of course, a demand in some form for more social, economic and educational security for youth in its 'teens and its twenties—the same things for which idle youth in Europe asked when a delegation, 200 strong, appeared the other day before the International Labor Organization in Geneva. As in the Geneva instance, youth also has made frequent protests against war and war preparation.

BRIEFLY, what youth is newly demanding is some assurance of a fair chance. In that chance different youth conventions have included a wide variety of elements—from unemployment insurance and subsidies for young married couples to birth-control information. And these specific demands, incidentally, have been made quite as emphatically by youths drawn from character-building agencies as by the more radical groups.

But even more generally youth includes in its chance a security of future, without war. These vocal youngsters of the new confederations seldom pass the academic resolutions about peace that their fathers sometimes did. Their attitude is more apt to be personal and realistic: They do not want to be "cannon-fodder" in an aggressive war, and for the first time some of them don't mind saying so. Moreover, the glory that was war has been dimmed in many of their eyes by recent revelations of Congressional investigating committees. It is a phenomenon of our times that the anti-war crusade of the past year or two has been largely a youth cause.

Three years ago the resolution in no circumstances to fight for king and country, passed by students at the Oxford Union in England, was the occasion for shocked outcries and a box of white feathers sent to the voters. Since that time similar votes have become more or less commonplace in America. The nation-wide college poll taken last Winter by The Literary Digest showed the undergraduate anti-war sentiment spread beyond the confines of any one group. Four to one, the 90,000 students replying registered as willing to defend our shores, but unwilling to fight in any war of invasion. Moreover, the majority apparently are convinced that the United States Government should control munition manufacturing and that it could, if it would, stay out of another conflict. In a national policy of acquiring the largest navy and air force they see no insurance of peace.

Increasingly organized youth has gone actively, even defiantly, into the anti-war drive. A year ago 25,000 students, mainly in the Eastern colleges, took part in a spectacular anti-war strike. When it was repeated this Spring the young strikers' numbers multiplied to 184,950, according to figures gathered by the National Strike Committee. Behind the movement was a motley assortment of youth organizations—from the National Council of Methodist Youth to the Student League for Industrial Democracy. Such groups do not represent all youth, of course, or probably even a majority, but their existence is a new factor in American life.

* * *

THE more immediate issue on which youth has been clamoring for help is, of course, unemployment. How many million youths are at present out of school and out of jobs no one accurately knows. The conservative estimates of the Department of Labor and the Office of Education coincide in putting the wholly unoccupied youth at about 3,000,000. Others have reckoned twice that number. Shortly in some sixty typical cities the

Office of Education will start a census of all young persons between the ages of 16 and 24 to determine the question. Scattering surveys already made show that in certain communities almost half of the young people are idle.

Already, however, youth and government experts agree that to meet the problem something more than the present relief provisions of CCC camps and work subsidies for college students is needed. Even if these facilities were doubled, as is now proposed, they would care for only 800,000 young people. What we now need, it is argued, is a nation-wide service combining guidance, education, recreation and part-time work for the idle millions in a more permanent way in their home communities.

Autumn, Winter, Spring, without rest the National Student Federation, the organization of college student government officers, has urged such a plan. And its president, a graduate who serves without pay, has traveled over the country in its behalf.

* * *

A DETAILED program to care for 2,000,000 youths on these lines has been drawn up by the Federal Commissioner of Education, John W. Studebaker, and presented through Secretary Ickes to the President's Emergency Fund Allotment Committee. A somewhat similar plan has been transmitted to the Senate by the Department of Labor. Some compromise between

the two is being favorably considered.

In the Office of Education plan (which is also to some extent youth's own) the nation's school-houses would become, so to speak, mental, moral and, temporarily, financial first-aid stations for jobless youth. There young people would resort to counselors for help in planning their immediate lives. Each would be aided in working out an approved program covering at least forty-two hours a week of supervised education, recreation and part-time employment on community projects.

Schools, libraries, museums, hospitals, recreation centres and all sorts of government offices would supply the jobs, which would be paid at the rate of about $12 a month by FERA funds. Youngsters, for example, would reclaim vacant lots for playgrounds, build trails, clear camp sites, help in nursery schools. Essentially, this phase of the project would be an extension to all youth of the work-relief given during the past two years to needy college students.

But beyond the individual encouragement of real work and real wages lies the implicit promise of a mammoth extension of our school system. It points to a time when every boy and girl, and not just the college student, up into his twenties, would have in a new sense a guardian alma mater.

"To the extent to which this proposal emphasizes youth guidance, it

is the beginning of a permanent program," says Commissioner Studebaker. "From this point on in our national development the educational system must accept the definite responsibility of guiding the youth of the country to successful integration into the life and work of the nation."

Already educational designers are at work on the blueprints of this new system. The American Council on Education has decided to devote five years to the task, as well as a fund of $800,000, which it has just obtained from the General Education Board for the purpose.

Whether or not the need for work-relief continues, one permanent feature of the new school, all authorities agree, must be real jobs, paid or unpaid. According to the American Council's Director, Dr. Zook, the school must "cooperate with industry, agriculture and the home in setting up work experiences that are real and educative" and it must provide practical contact with the institutions of local, State and national government. Somehow too, school must "build up more intimate relationships" with wholesome recreation activities.

Whatever may happen to any or all of these particular projects, it seems indubitable that this year has set forces in motion toward a new philosophy of education; toward serving youth in a way never before contemplated by a national government.

June 23, 1935

SURVEY SEES YOUTH LOSING INFLUENCE

Resources Group Finds We Shall Have Twice as Many Persons Over 60 by 1960.

MORE 'STABILITY' AHEAD

Trends Indicate Fall in School Needs, Changes in Occupations and Other Shifts.

Special to The New York Times.
WASHINGTON, Oct. 15.—Under present population trends the United States will be converted within twenty-five years into a country populated and ruled largely by elderly people, and youth will be on the wane as to both numbers

and influence, the National Resources Committee has concluded on the basis of a preliminary analysis of findings of planning boards of several States.

The committee was set up by President Roosevelt in June, 1934, to devise and recommend a plan for the general social and economic advancement of the people through wider use of the nation's resources.

The population expectations indicate that by 1960 there will be twice as many citizens above 60 years of age. This will make for a more stable population, with a considerable slowing down of the average American's present pace in daily life, the committee believes.

This change in our national character would be accompanied, in the committee's opinion, by a decreased demand for primary educational facilities in some sections, by marked changes to quieter forms of recreation, and shifts in general types of occupations.

The resources committee assumed in its predictions that present trends as to birth and death rates and immigration restrictions would continue.

October 16, 1935

YOUTH STATES ITS CASE

Preceding Generation Apparently Has Much to Answer For.

To the Editor of The New York Times:

I am a member of the so-called "lost generation," born during the World War and come to maturity during the great depression. I am a member of that generation which indulges in peace strikes, which has produced such organizations as the Veterans of Future Wars, which is able to pronounce the word "communism" without hissing the last syllable.

I am of the generation which has heard its activities described as "radical," "subversive," "un-American"; which has seen a boorish clown maintain a dictatorial rule over one of our forty-eight States and represent it in our chief law-making body; which has seen a priest, through persuasive oratory and by means of the radio, convince a large following that he alone has the remedies for our economic ills, in terms of economic reasoning which would make any student of the subject hurt his sides with laughter; a generation which has seen a medical practitioner obtain a large number of converts for his idea of paying $200 a month to every one over 60 and in this way curing the depression; a generation which has seen the veterans of the World War, a militant minority, force their will on a weak-spined Congress and filch on one hand a billion or so dollars from the citizens of the country, while on the other hand they were forcing equally weak-spined State Legislatures to pass bills compelling students to salute the flag and teachers to take oaths of allegiance to the Constitution, thus entering the wedge of fascism and dictatorship.

We have seen one from San Simeon control a large portion of the public press and by means of his newspapers convince a large public that he is brimming over with love of country, while any one who dares to suggest that it may not be quite perfect is a "Red," a "dangerous radical," and probably an anarchist.

No Apology Necessary

I make no apology for our generation, for none is necessary, but I ask you in all sincerity, what is the matter with yours?

You have a great deal more to answer for than the relatively trivial offenses cited and their like. It is your generation at whose door may be laid the blame for the most costly and destructive war ever waged during the history of mankind. And before you draw the line and total up the sum, set down the cost of the greatest depression in economic history and make it a roundish sum, for the price of human suffering is rather difficult to count in dollars and cents.

I read the other day that the Daughters of the American Revolution were going to start a campaign to instill the spirit of patriotism into the youth of America which had lately shown "radical tendencies." They were instructed that to do this they must see that youth is first clothed, housed and fed, or it would not be receptive. Do they suppose that the youth of America think with their bellies? If so, America is degenerate indeed. Do they think because we don't rush around waving flags and shouting "America is the best damn country on earth"; because we have anti-war strikes and form future veteran organizations to mock our elders who have made such a mess of things, that we are any less patriotic than

those who trace their ancestry back to the Revolution?

Past the Ukulele Age

Or does it mean that patriotism and thinking do not mix? Our college generation is not that which is typified by the ukulele, the coonskin coat, the Ford covered with slang expressions, though the American Legion, from its recent utterances, seems to think so.

Most of us do not consider ourselves "radicals" unless our sensitivity to the problems of the day, our search and anxiety to find answers to those problems, and our willingness to change, if necessary, the most traditional and moss-covered institutions put us within the boundary of that term.

Most of us, at least of the student bodies, are not driven to thought by economic necessity. I, myself, have never known a day of hardship, but that does not make my mind less acute nor prevent my seeing the incongruity of your generation's admonishing our generation as though you were saying to a naughty child, "Go away and don't bother papa."

I think I speak for my generation when I say that we are sick to death of platitudes and clichés, of flag-waving and heroic attitudes, of "Red" scares and patriotism that is talked rather than felt, of Father Coughlins and William Randolph Hearsts, of Huey Longs and Dr. Townsends, of soothing talks and accusations, of political parties and political corruption, and all the other paraphernalia which are our unsavory heritage.

No, Mr. Editor, it is not ours which is the lost generation. It is yours. We only ask that you don't take us down with you.   H. R. BYERS.

Cambridge, Mass., April 23, 1936.

April 27, 1936

Letters to the Editor

THE HERITAGE OF YOUTH

Younger Generation, It Is Held, Has Much to Be Thankful For.

To the Editor of The New York Times:

H. R. Byers, in your issue of April 27, has joined the army of recrimination in the endless conflict between the generations. After pronouncing himself sick to death of platitudes and clichés and other political and economic odds and ends of hypocrisy and ambition, he adds: "And all the other paraphernalia which are our unsavory heritage. * * * We only ask that you don't take us down with you."

In a world richer than ever in its heritage, richer than ever in opportunities, Mr. Byers is sorry for himself. He has begun by blaming some one else for the tasks he has to meet, and if he does not toughen quickly he will end by demanding that the government feed and clothe him for not meeting them.

From generations past Mr. Byers inherits citizenship in a society where freedom of thought, expression and enterprise have been traditionally preserved and honored. Let him look to it that these traditions, young in history though old in America, are preserved by

him at whatever cost. Anglo-Saxon civilization struggled to secure them for over a thousand years. They and the scheme of government by w..ich they are insured and protected, are probably the richest political heritage that any people have to offer their children.

From your generation and mine, Mr. Editor, Mr. Byers inherits the internal combustion engine with its great by-products, the automobile and the airplane, the motion pictures, the electrification of toil, with the accompanying achievement of a more generous day's work in eight hours than preceding generations accomplished in twelve. He inherits the wireless and the radio and a splendid advance in the technique of surgery and sanitation.

If these and the achievements which have accompanied them in the field of science and engineering have created new and troublesome relationships, such as that of employer and employe; have more than doubled the population and preserved millions of lives in comfort which could not have endured a more exposed or rigorous existence, and thereby created difficult political and economic problems which our generation has not had time to solve, the only question for Mr. Byers is whether he

is one of those of the next generation who are competent to carry this great heritage further.

MURRAY T. QUIGG.
New York, April 27, 1936.

Self-Reformation Needed

To the Editor of The New York Times:

I am a young man of 25 years who has been reading with interest, but not approbation, the condemnations from the pens of other young people launched at our present older generation. I have found, to my disappointment, little of serious value for curing society's evils.

It is a great temptation to be eloquent and pick out all the errors and mistakes of our past generation, but do we merely criticize and condemn, or have we the desire to understand, because if we do not understand these errors and how they came about, how can we adequately correct them?

What are the mistakes of the past generation? Was it lack of good judgment? Are they merely violations of "good economics"? Can youth, by means of its education and enlightenment, eradicate these mistakes?

It is evident, if we regard Mr. Byers's examples of our public men, such as Long, Coughlin, Townsend and Hearst, that there is something radically wrong with society. We must go into the philosophy of our civilization and see that materialism, dialectical or otherwise, is at the root of this whole problem. The great god Gold is our only god. With such a root is it any wonder that society grows such ugly flowers and weeds?

Mammon has become a part of our natures; therefore, criticizing is only self-criticism.

It is all very well for one to say that he is willing to change "the most traditional and moss-covered institutions"— but what if he finds out that these institutions, in spite of appearances to the contrary, are tied up fundamentally with his own needs and desires in a very real way? I refer to our individual luxuries, pleasures, prides, hatreds, prejudices, neuroses, of which all our public institutions are a shadow, while our passions are all too real. Such a change, then, to be a real change, would involve the tearing down of our own inadequacies.

The only solution, tragic as it may seem, is that those heroic youths who can see clearly that they must practice radicalism with their own character, who will examine their own desires and thoughts in the light of the highest and best ideals, and undertake to practice self-reformation, shall come together to create this new kind of society.   BURTON STONE.

New York, April 27, 1936.

Age and Youth Indispensable
To the Editor of The New York Times:

Your correspondent who states the case for youth has acquired a clear style and a knack at exposition. That is a good beginning for any young man. It is creditable to his intelligence that he dislikes war, depressions, unemployment, jingoism, Hearsts, Coughlins, Longs and Townsends.

It is natural, though less commendable, that, finding the world not to his liking, he catches up the nearest stick to beat the cat, in rather arrogantly accusing us elderly men of producing or, at least, of not preventing, all these ills.

The right to an opinion is not conferred by being alive, but has to be earned. To concentrate on passing the buck is profitless. The fact that errors now visible have been made all through the past is no evidence that they will not be made in the future and by those now young or even unborn; quite the reverse. The only coupling that draws envisaged fine results straight in the wake of high purposes is a knowledge which comes out of painfully verified and reverified experience, not out of wishful thinking.

For one, I have not the slightest apology to offer for my generation, any

more than Mr. Byers has for his, or than a doctor in these days has for not being able forthwith to rid a victim of cancer. Age and youth, like male and female, are indispensable constituents of any society. The one is not superior to the other, for indispensability makes both superlatives. Their job is to co-operate and carry on. Censoriousness between "generations," and mutual sneers, get nowhere. In a relay race you cannot stop to scold the running-mate who passes you the stick.

A. G. KELLER.
New Haven, Conn., April 28, 1936.

Stripping the Nude
To the Editor of The New York Times:

In reply to H. R. Byers's letter I would like to ask him if he has been sleeping so soundly that he has not heard of "platitudes and clichés—flag-waving and heroic attitudes—'Red' scares and patriotism" being broadcast before? Mr. Byers seems to be stripping illusions that have been nude a long time.

Despite the fact that I belong to the generation that was born during the World War, I fail to see the necessity for tearing out foundations on which we have, as yet, built nothing.

Mr. Byers's fears for the stability of this country, which, he says, is being easily swayed by clowns, priests, elixir-bearing medicos and sensationalists. Such fears have already been expressed in this and every other country, publicly or privately, quite frequently. I do not know the comparative percentage of the "rights" and "wrongs" in the government of the United States in the last century and a half, but I do know that the "rights" must have exceeded "wrongs" by a great deal. After all, it is the "wrongs" who get the publicity. The mistakes in this government are the same, in numbers and character, as occur in any government of its type.

The only experience that we of the younger generation need is the experience of creating and standing by our creation as destructive criticism tears it down. Then we may gain a little tolerance, understanding and patience.

Do the youth of America think with their bellies? I suggest that Mr. Byers try thinking when his has been empty for several weeks. When he has kept it full, by his own efforts, then the time will have come to look higher.

JAMES E. BURR.
Englewood, N. J., April 26, 1936.

Open Mind Essential
To the Editor of The New York Times:

It seems to me that youth could have

had no better exponent of its grievances against the older generation than H. R. Byers in his letter to THE TIMES. His charges are not easy to answer or to contradict. We surely did make a mess for those of the present generation to unscramble.

As one of the older generation, I might say in extenuation of our sins that we also inherited the bad seeds sown by our preceding generations, and are not entirely responsible for what we turned over to our succeeding generation. By all means, let youth study and search unafraid for changes in our economic system; let them state clearly their remedies. They need not be deterred by opprobrious names.

My only hope is that youth will also curb its emotions and keep an open mind when listening to the advocates and promisers of plausible "sure cures" of the evils of our present system. Youth might study history and find that nothing of permanent value was ever achieved in a hurry.

GREGORY WEINSTEIN.
Brooklyn, April 28, 1936.

Approval of Views
To the Editor of The New York Times:

I read the illuminating letter from H. R. Byers in THE TIMES today. I believe it is the epitome of the thought of every normal and intelligent individual not enslaved by allegiance to the self-seeking, handout-grabbing organizations mentioned in the letter.

ARTHUR L. VAN VEEN.
New York, April 27, 1936.

Clear-Sighted Youth
To the Editor of The New York Times:

Three cheers for H. R. Byers and for the frank way he has stated youth's case! I too am fed up on this flag-waving form of "patriotism" which covers a multitude of sins of powerful groups—sins that seem to be more clearly comprehended by the younger generation than by the older.   J. W.
Woodmere, N. Y., April 28, 1936.

Complete Confidence
To the Editor of The New York Times:

I am hastening to confirm the splendid sentiment expressed by H. R. Byers in his letter to THE NEW YORK TIMES. It is with confidence and assurance that we of the "lost generation" accept our chaotic heritage, for we feel that we are equal to the task of molding the better society that should have been molded fifty years ago.   EUGENE TURNER.
New York, April 27, 1936.

April 30, 1936

A Youth "Champion"

A new militant youth magazine, with a first issue optimistically set at 300,000 copies, comes off the press this week. Entitled The Champion, it will deal with "the insecurity of youth," "the efforts toward the militarization of youth, the danger of war, the abrogation of civil rights, the struggles of labor"; it will contain also fiction, sports and scientific features. Its editorial board, composed entirely of young people, includes Roger Chase, former editor of The Columbia Spectator; James Wechsler, director of the publications of the American Student Union, and Beryl Gilman of the American Youth Congress. Governor Floyd Olson of Minnesota contributes to the first issue a discussion of America's youth problem.

May 17, 1936

POLITICAL INTEREST OF STUDENTS RISES

Balloting on Military Drill in Oregon an Example of Their Pressing of Issues.

WIDE RANGE OF ACTIVITIES

Some Run for Offices, While a Utah Group Helped Elect Prof. Thomas to Senate.

By RICHARD L. NEUBERGER

The recent vote in Oregon on a bill proposing the abolition of compulsory military drill in schools, which was placed on the ballot through the efforts of college students, calls attention to their growing political activity on campuses throughout the country.

The Oregon measure was put before the voters by a group of students who through months of work financed, circulated and sponsored initiative petitions. Another formidable student group opposed the bill, which was defeated by the voters, and the State was treated to a campaign virtually headlined by students.

In the Presidential campaign in all parts of the country party leaders addressed numerous appeals to the citizen who had just reached his majority. Governor Landon and President Roosevelt issued specific messages to the young people of the nation. The third-party advocates circulated "An Appeal to Youth," written by the late Governor Floyd B. Olson of Minnesota. Even Dr. Townsend's old-age revolving pension movement, for persons over 60 years of age, added a youth division.

Young Republicans were as tireless as young Democrats, and vice versa. Straw polls attempted to canvass voters according to age groups, a survey of the Institute of Public Opinion indicating that young citizens tended to favor President Roosevelt over Governor Landon.

Student branches of the American Liberty League were formed at such institutions as Northwestern, Yale, Princeton and the University of Nebraska, with other members attending several hundred other leading colleges.

At the opposite pole was the radical American Student Union, the leaders of which come largely from the Student League for Industrial Democracy. The union has subordinate groups in numerous schools; it publishes The Student Advocate and has a regular legislative program adopted at its national convention. The main points include support of the Nye-Kvale bill to abolish compulsory military training and of the Benson-Amlie Youth Act to provide for relief and assistance to needy young people.

The Epworth League of the Methodist Church has also won a large number of student members, and has aroused considerable agitation because of the alleged left-wing beliefs of the league's spokesmen.

Of an antithetical trend has been the formation of student vigilante groups, composed largely of athletes, to combat the spread of "subversive" doctrines.

In the last four years local political undertakings have attracted thousands of students, especially in the West and South. Among the few outspoken adversaries confronted by the late Senator Huey Long in Louisiana were several undergraduate editors at Louisiana State University, who rebelled against alleged censorship.

In 1932 the support of students at the University of Utah was instrumental in electing Professor Elbert Thomas to the United States Senate over the veteran Republican leader Reed Smoot.

In the State of Washington college students have been prominent in the Washington Commonwealth Federation, several of them running for the Legislature under the egis of that organization.

A year ago students at the University of Oregon referred to the voters a compulsory athletic fee measure passed by the Legislature. The people upheld them at the polls by a margin of more than 3 to 1.

In California students have been active in the struggle for and against mandatory military drill.

November 15, 1936

YOUTHS 'SIT-DOWN' AT WHITE HOUSE

700 of 2,500 Marchers Drop to Street in Demonstration for $500,000,000 Lundeen Bill

---

TWO LEADERS ARRESTED

'Want Scholarships, Not Battleships,' Paraders Chant— Roosevelt Sees a Group

---

Special to THE NEW YORK TIMES.

WASHINGTON, Feb. 20.—Representatives of youth organizations from all over the country held a "sit-down" practically at the door of the White House today as part of their demonstration in favor of the Lundeen bill, providing $500,-000,000 for jobs, scholarship assistance, and vocational training for all persons between 16 and 25 years of age. Two of the leaders of the movement were arrested on charges of violating their parade permit and obstructing traffic.

The members of the "pilgrimage," as it was termed, gathered for a session over the week-end, under the auspices of the American Youth Congress. The high point of the gathering was to have been a parade from the Capitol to the White House, after which petitions in favor of the bill, with "hundreds of thousands" of signatures, were to have been presented to the President.

However, when the parade arrived at its dispersal place on the

Times Wide World Photo.

YOUTHFUL MARCHERS SIT DOWN IN STREET AT WHITE HOUSE

Some of the demonstrators who arrived in Washington yesterday to present a petition in support of the Lundeen Youth Bill as they staged a sudden "sit-down" near the Executive Mansion, shouting their demands that Congress pass the bill.

---

broad drive which bounds the south side of the White House grounds, the leader gave the signal to sit down, and hundreds of the paraders dropped to the ground, much in the manner of a falling house of cards.

Two minutes later, William Hinkley, 25, of New York, chairman of the Congress, and Abbott Hinkley, 21, also of New York, its "legislative representative," were under arrest, both of them being described by Captain P. J. Carroll of the National Park Police as being "the ringleaders." Each was held in $25 collateral for a hearing on Monday.

New Problem for the Police

Mr. Simon was the holder of the parade permit and Mr. Hinkley was arrested as his colleague, the captain said.

The officer changed his mind on the question of arresting the rest of "the ringleaders." He told the prisoner that they had no permit for a down parade, although he admitted that a sit-down parade was a new problem for police.

Whatever it was, the paraders could not hold it in Washington and block the streets, Captain Carroll said, and promptly set a force of fifty patrolmen to clearing the thoroughfares. This was finally accomplished with no disturbance, mainly by the expedient of turning traffic through the sit-down group.

Mr. Simon and Mr. Hinkley said that the sit-down was caused by the postponement of an appointment for a delegation of seven to present the marchers' demands to the President—an appointment originally set for the end of the parade this morning at 11 o'clock but later put off until 4:30 o'clock this afternoon.

The youths said that the sit-down was called merely to rest the marchers, some of whom had hitch-hiked from New York, while they were waiting for a covered wagon, which had been towed from California by an old automobile, to be brought up with the petitions.

The petitions were to have been presented to Marvin McIntyre, one of the President's secretaries, the prisoners said, explaining that the seven youths who were to see Mr. Roosevelt did not want to carry "thirty or forty pounds of petition."

However, Mr. McIntyre, who, the youth leaders said, caused the failure of an arrangement made through Mrs. Roosevelt for the President to address the entire "pilgrimage" on the lawn of the White House, was not on hand when the marchers arrived, and thus the contretemps developed, according to the leaders.

Late in the day, after the sit-down, a seven-man delegation went to the White House, headed by Mr. Hinkley and Joseph L. Lash, of the American Student Union. Also present was Aubrey Williams, National Youth Administrator, who, according to Mr. Hinkley, received instructions from the President to "take care of" Mr. Hinkley's arrest.

Mr. Hinkley quoted the President as saying that the youth's demands were too advanced for him

to accept, but that he was in favor of their activity as enabling him to get greater aid for needy youths. He also quoted the President as saying that he planned to make the present National Youth Administration a permanent agency and would ask Congress for more money for its work in the coming fiscal years.

Members of the group said that they told Mr. Roosevelt their impatience over any delay in the passage of the Lundeen bill was similar to his own feeling in regard to his measure for reorganization of the judiciary.

There were 2,500 marchers in the parade, of whom at least 700 took part in the sit-down. The principal feature of the parade was the covered wagon which bore signs saying: "Go East, Young Man, Go East."

The marchers, many of them well dressed, and including several pretty girls, bore signs indicating their school, college or other affiliation, and reciting their demands. They chanted "Pass the National Youth Act—We want jobs." "Scholarships, not battleships." "Homes, not barracks," and sang songs to the same effect.

The marchers held a mass meeting in the afternoon. Tomorrow they will hold an open-air religious ceremony at the Washington Monument, with clergy of all faiths officiating. Police Captain Carroll at first threatened to stop this ceremony as a result of the sit-down, but later relented.

February 21, 1937

STUDENTS DIVIDED ON WAY TO PEACE

At Campus Rallies Throughout Nation They Unite in Opposing War, but Split on Methods

MAJORITY CHANGES STAND

Renounce Oxford Pledge and Declare for Security—Rival Group for Pacifism

Divided into two camps, students in colleges and universities in various sections of the country demonstrated their desire for world peace yesterday at campus rallies, convocations and chapel exercises.

The United Student Peace Committee issued the national call for the annual April peace movement. It was estimated that 10,000 undergraduates met on the local cam-

puses, and in the neighborhood of 100,000 elsewhere.

Student leaders said yesterday's demonstrations were among the mildest on record. They were quiet and orderly throughout, with no serious disturbances reported. Even where the rival groups met on the same campus, no untoward incidents occurred. Both sides stressed the need for peace; the only question raised was the best way to assure it.

The issues of neutrality and collective security, however, split the students. Unable to follow the security "line" laid down by the peace committee, the Youth Committee Against War, held rival "strike" meetings, proclaiming the virtues of neutrality and taking the Oxford Pledge.

Renouncing the Oxford Pledge that would bind the students not to participate in any war, the American Student Union avoided the word "strike" in its call to the students. Rather, the union stressed the need for supporting President Roosevelt's policies and of stopping the aggressor nations.

The Youth Committee Against War called upon its adherents to resist any war, and to force this country to maintain a neutral stand. By a queer turn in the political cycle, it had now become the "radical" group, and accused the

American Student Union of "selling out" to the administration and the reactionary groups.

At all the local colleges the Committee Against War had the smallest attendance. In some cases they were heckled by "collective security" adherents.

At the end of the day the American Student Union, through its secretary, Joseph P. Lash, issued a statement saying it was "highly pleased" with the various peace meetings. Over and above all differences of opinion that might exist on the campuses, he said, one factor stood out sharp and clear: "American youth does not want war with anybody."

Large crowds gathered on the local campuses to hear the peace messages, as the meetings got under way at 11 A. M. Many professors and deans permitted students to "cut" to attend the rallies.

Columbia University's demonstration on South Field gave a hearing to both sides in the controversy, but a viva voce vote indicated that most of the 1,500 present were for collective security. The youth committee distributed leaflets announcing that a "genuine anti-war strike" would be held today at noon on the campus.

Dean Herbert E. Hawkes, principal speaker, told the students it was well to discuss all approaches to the

peace problem, but reminded them that any program must be based on "mutual understanding, scrupulous rectitude, tolerance and goodwill." McAllister Coleman, Socialist, appealed for the Ludlow amendment, saying: "Let's count noses before we crack heads."

While 750 students met at the City College School of Business at Twenty-third Street and Lexington Avenue, 400 Hunter College girls and "neutrality" adherents of City College joined in a rival outdoor meeting in Madison Square Park. Student orators exhorted their "classmates not to be misled by the "collective security" slogans.

At City College, participating students divided into two groups and conducted separate meetings in the Great Hall of the Main Building and Lewisohn Stadium. About 300 students took the Oxford pledge.

Thirteen hundred Hunter College students attended simultaneous peace rallies at the Bronx division of the college and at the Adams Memorial Church.

At Brooklyn College, 3,000 undergraduates held rival meetings on the college athletic field.

Fifteen hundred students participated in the demonstration at the New York University downtown center.

April 21, 1939

AMERICAN YOUTH GROUPS SCRUTINIZED

By FRANK S. ADAMS

The sixth annual American Youth Congress held at College Camp, Wis., a week ago, focused attention anew on the youth of this country and on the problems they face. Is there a youth movement in this country comparable to those in some foreign lands? Is the A. Y. C. truly representative of the young people of t   nation? What sections of the organized youth groups are aloof?

Any effort to answer such questions immediately meets with serious difficulties. It is true that there is no organized, national youth movement in this country similar to the movements in Germany and Italy, where the young men and women are regimented under the

Many Organizations In Country Have Diverse Aims

ict rule of the dominant parties. There are, however, very large numbers of youth organizations in this country with an almost endless variety of aims and purposes. A Directory of Youth Organizations issued last Spring by the National Youth Administration lists 281 national and local youth groups, with a total claimed membership of about 32,000,000. In this total there must be, of course, a large amount of duplication.

Some of those familiar with the situation contend that American

youth organizations are so divergent in nature and in aims that it is impossible to unite them behind any aggressive program that seeks to deal with political, social and economic questions. They add that some youth groups are debarred by their charters or constitutions from such activities.

Supporters of the Youth Congress reply that it has already succeeded in exercising a unifying influence on the youth movement, and that its influence in this respect is steadily growing. They point to the number and the virulence of the attacks made on it as the best proof of the effectiveness of the congress. They often refer to the congress as the "spearhead" or the "van" of the country's youth "movement." The whole question is complicated

by the fact that there is no general agreement as to what constitutes youth. The N. Y. A. endeavored to confine its compilation to organizations whose members ranged in age from 12 to 30 years, although in a few cases it included groups where the upper age limit ran as high as 35 or even 40. A more common age grouping for youth, frequently used by some government sources, is from 16 to 24. It is estimated that about one-sixth of the population, or between 21,000,000 and 22,000,000 persons, fall in this age group.

A. Y. C. Age Standard

The American Youth Congress, made up as it is of member organizations and not of individuals, does not attempt to set very precise age standards. It merely requires that member organizations must have memberships at least 60 per cent of which are under the age of 30. This provision enables many organizations which are not ordinarily thought of as primarily youth organizations, for instance such trade unions as the United Electrical, Radio, and Machine Workers and the International Longshoremen's and Warehousemen's Union, to qualify for membership.

There is a major division in the youth movement between the organizations directly controlled and run by young people themselves and the so-called youth-serving agencies which, though existing for the benefit of young people, have their policies determined by governing bodies of adults. Many of the best-known youth organizations, including "character-building" groups like the Boy Scouts and the Girl Scouts, are in the latter category.

Attacked by some of its more vehement foes, notably Gene Tunney, as an assemblage of "paper" organizations, the sixth Youth Congress claimed, through the report of its credentials committee, to consist of 533 delegates, representing 5,159,495 young persons, and ninety-five observers, representing 2,190,966 others. It held that thirty-four national organizations were represented by national delegates; that twenty-four other national organizations were represented by local delegates, and that sixty-seven local councils and 116 local and State affiliated bodies were also represented.

Outside the Congress

Many well-known youth groups do not participate in the Youth Congress. Thus the 4-H Clubs and such governmental agencies as the Civilian Conservation Corps and the National Youth Administration are not in its ranks. The Boy Scouts and the Girl Scouts do not participate, in accordance with their long-held policies of not affiliating with other organizations. The Catholic Youth Organizations not only have refused to participate but their spokesmen have been strongly critical. The Y. M. C. A. and the Y. W. C. A. do not participate as national organizations in the congress, although some of their member groups take part.

The American Youth Commission, a non-partisan group of leading citizens under the chairmanship of Owen D. Young, discussed the problem of youth organizations not long ago. It argued that while their activities "may be irritating to many adults, they should not be suppressed on that account" and that they "can have major values"

in contributing to the educational processes of youth.

A Warning Given

Expressing its conviction that, notwithstanding present difficulties, youth-led organizations are here to stay, the group warned that "the violent and hysterical persecution of young intellectual radicals is in itself a childish procedure." On the other hand, it urged upon youth groups "special care to avoid outraging the adult community through conspicuous bad manners and through gross failure to give a hearing to adult points of view."

It concluded that "rejection of the curative though irritating processes of public discussion is un-American and might be suicidal."

July 14, 1940

Youth Seeks No Sympathy

Present Generation Held Aware of Its Duties and Responsibilities

To THE EDITOR OF THE NEW YORK TIMES:

On June 17 I graduated from Brown University. As we left the chapel after the commencement exercises newsboys were selling papers with headlines screeching "France Gives Up." The fury that is in me now started at that moment, for a member of the faculty approached me and said, "Well, Bradford, it is a terrible world that you are getting into." Since then many people have expressed pity and sympathy for my generation.

This letter, then, is an answer to all the people who are feeling sorry for my generation. This letter is for all the mothers who lament that their boys were born in such dreadful times. This letter is for all the synthetic cynics who tell us "to live for today and forget tomorrow."

"Outlook" is the one word all these sympathizers grasp. "What a terrible outlook you have," they say. The way I feel about the outlook is as follows: Certainly it looks black. I don't suppose the outlook of the world ever looked blacker; but that is no reason to feel sorry for my generation, for there is much to be gained from this blackness.

There is no room in our generation for sham. Ours is not the day of hidden smut, of synthetic morals that filled the Victorian era. We face an unconditioned reality. Fakes are recognized. The false members of our generation

cannot stand the glare of this realism. I am thankful, therefore, that I can be sure of my generation.

Preceding Generation Fooled

The generation immediately preceding mine was fooled. They lived for wealth. Came 1929 and they realized the weak bridge they had been crossing. Now they are trying to stay above the water, but the current is strong. The generation caught in the last war let itself be swept away by banners we now know were false. My generation has gained from their loss, for we will never fight for a slogan.

This Wednesday I will register for the draft. This draft has caused more pity from my elders than any other incident. Let them forget their pity, for I welcome the draft. I have said that our generation will not fight for a false banner, and certainly the reasons for which we are asked to prepare do not make up a false banner. We have seen the collapse of Poland, Holland, Belgium, Denmark and France; there is nothing false about that. We are now watching the valiant defense of Britain; there is nothing false about that.

We see all around us the unpreparedness of this country; there is nothing false about that. Come Wednesday, I will fill out the registration blanks, and if called I will go; but as I go I will not be filled with sham heroics nor with gilded patriotism. The necessity of this action has no room for blaring bands and hysterical flag-wavers. Because of a job that has to be done with deep sincerity and sacrifice, I will be glad to go. The reasons for the draft are smeared over the map of Europe.

We cannot ignore this smear; we can try to stop its spreading and finally to clean it up completely. Our generation has a cause for living, a purpose to follow. We need no pity.

Religion Seen as Need

The need for religion has never been more vital than to our generation. We are rather bewildered by religion, for the preceding generation seems to have turned away from the church. They have not turned against it, but rather have ignored it. Their sophistication, their materialism, have fooled them into thinking they had no need for religion.

This problem is one that my generation must face and attempt to understand. We need religion, but we do not need the conscience comforter that the older people have made out of the present-day church. I feel sure that the "black outlook" which my elders think has me completely damned will bring religion closer to my generation than it has been in many a generation. I don't suppose that faith was ever harder to have than now. Hope was never more keenly felt. But it is not a false faith nor a false hope. Man cannot have faith and hope without some kind of religion. Ours will not be a false religion.

To all the insipid well-wishers, to all the sympathizers, to all those who pity my generation, I say that I do not want pity nor do I want condolences. From the "black outlook" that you condemn will come deeper hope, deeper faith and truer religion. For these reasons I am glad I was born a member of this generation. BEN BRADFORD.

Niagara Falls, N. Y., Oct. 13, 1940.

October 16, 1940

Thoughts of an 18-Year-Old

A minor by law, a man by national necessity, he says it has taken a war to give him a real objective in life.

By Jay Topkis

I AM 18. A minor in the eyes of the law, a man by national necessity. Very soon now I shall be making the jump from drowsy lecture rooms to the crashing grimness of war. I am excited, like the rest of the fellows I know, and these days whatever else I'm thinking about, that lies pretty close underneath.

My whole life has shifted focus, as if I were in a plane making a landing and the world tilted to meet me. It's ironic, but it's taken a war to give me an objective, and I think that is true of most of the fellows around my age. I, frankly, have been floundering; I haven't known how to aim my life. Sometimes I have thought I am a writer and I am registered in college as pre-law. My thoughts, hopes and judgment of my capacities move about like pieces in a kaleidoscope. But there is one hard, solid central piece that does not change, and this is the fact that I am enlisted in the Army Reserve.

Growing up as we did in depression years, the question has been not what would you like to do but what can you learn that will give you some sort of future? There didn't seem to be room in anything, no matter how pared our ideas of what a living is. Few of us dreamed of luxuries. To get an education and to attain just security — a foothold — has seemed quite a chancy question in itself.

NOW, suddenly, there is room. Suddenly we are desirable, important citizens; we rate high as manpower in jobs and as manpower in the armed services. It sets you up. But if we had all been asked:

Do you consider yourself a grown man, able to take on an adult's responsibilities? we would probably have said promptly, yes, of course; and then have begun to wonder. For instance, if we were now asked: Do you think you should have the vote? we would probably say yes. Yet most of us distrust ourselves somewhat, and I think especially we distrust our educations. We are not sure that what we have learned is any real base upon which to make judgment.

This sudden change in status has hit us in different ways. We are all, I think, keyed high with excitement, and nervousness too, but we take it out according to our temperaments. There's Mike, for instance. Mike used to be a playboy. Private schools. Comic jaloppy. Girls. Smooth man on the dance floor. Mike is a likable chap, and intelligent, though his grades were seldom above C, and often less than passing. He was in college mainly because his old man kept arguing. It was a jumble to him. He'd rather be in a plant, he said, or go to work in a shipyard and make good money, too. But for a family in their position——

After Pearl Harbor Mike got edgier and edgier. He tried to get in the Navy but there was some sort of test he didn't pass, I don't know exactly what. Made him sore. He boned up and made Air Corps training, aiming at bombardier. He's out in Texas now, and the way he writes you would think he had been a Phi Beta Kappa prospect. Making 100 straight in math and physics, and being proud of it. Thinking about getting married. All set—I figure—to be, after the war, an upstanding householder somewhere in Westchester. In the story books they would say at this point that Mike has found himself. But real life has put a surprising twist in the plot, making his character fall into pattern from behind a bombsight.

In contrast to the rakish Mike I knew, there's Jim, who quit school halfway through his freshman first term and got a job in a war plant. Jim is a slight, quiet fellow, with not much to say and quick with his hands. He used to squeeze every nickel and dole the pennies—he had to; and he was a dogged, literal sort of student in college because "you have to have a degree to get ahead." Now he's making more a week than his father does in a month and there's swagger in the way he walks. He has bought himself the best collection of jazz records of any one I know. He's become quite a wolf, too, and drinks and tears around. But he's fresh on the job in the morning. Good, too; for they seem to be pushing him right along. It so happens there is considerable danger

in the particular job he is doing. Jim kids around about that, as about everything. But with a couple of drinks in him he's ready to fight over anything. He says we college boys blabber too much. Says his feeling is: live now, nothing comes after.

THE most serious-minded boy I know is Bob, a pre-med. Most of these budding doctors are serious. He doesn't pay much attention to anything outside of his studies, and I suppose he couldn't even if he were interested, because those boys have to grind. Bob had his plans made for public health work; they're postponed, of course. Right now Bob wonders whether he'll be called to service at once or whether he will get through his studies. And, though the one thing in the world he wants is that M. D., he is restless at the idea of staying in school while the rest go off to fight.

"It won't be a cinch going through med school in three years or less," he says, "but nothing about this war is a cinch. I'll be getting away with a lot, going to school while you are fighting. And when I do get in my part won't be so much. I won't be sacrificing anything. I'll be practicing medicine, helping heal you fellows so you'll be able to get back in there and fight again. Besides that, I'll be learning a lot—much more than I would have picked up in years of interning. But I'd rather have to interne for the rest of my life—and have no war."

Nothing Bob says suggests the fact that he will be in as much danger as the soldiers or sailors he may be tending. Danger is the one topic none of us talk about. We just don't. We know pretty well what to expect. And heroics don't go with it. But when I think of courage Johnny comes into my mind. He graduated from high school a year ago and went right to work, turning out munitions. When he starts out from home every morning his jaw sets; same thing coming home from the plant. He is in perfect physical condition and keeps seeing himself in khaki, but—they badly need what he earns at home, and the plant is short of manpower.

JOHNNY wrote to me recently: "People stare at me on the trolleys. They look me over, visualizing me in uniform like their sons are; sometimes they say things I don't get much of a kick out of. Maybe now that's going to be finished, and it won't be my choice to make any more. And let me tell you, there's pressure up. When and if I ever do climb into uniform, those monkeys on the other team are going to get plenty from me in exchange

for the delightful times their war has been giving me."

On the train back to school after the holidays I ran into Sam. He's from near my home town in Delaware. To me he was just a hunched-up boy asleep in his Navy uniform, but when I sat down next to him he woke up and in the dim night coach there he was, sure enough: Sam. He had just finished his training course at Great Lakes and was going to New York for his first leave, in his newly issued uniform. He started talking, and what was uppermost in his mind was this—he wanted to go to a specialists' school. Before being in service he had just worked on the farm, but the Navy had given him a taste of being a machinist and he was hungry for more.

"You see what happened was this," he said. "Everybody in the neighborhood was clearing out. All the kids were joining up, and, heck, I didn't want to be left behind. I guess if I'd stayed I might have been able to get deferred, but it didn't seem right. Great Lakes was tough as hell; but gee, this is a war, not a hay-ride. We've got to get it over with, and fast. I think sometimes: What'll I do afterward. Maybe I'll stick, serve a couple of hitches and then come (Continued on Page 29) home and get a job in a garage. Maybe I'll even be able to save enough to buy my own garage."

Dick, a fellow from Colorado that I see quite a lot of, is a sophomore and a philosopher. He is supposed to be the most brilliant boy in his class, a sure Phi Bete. One of those wizzards with a phenomenal I. Q. and a dazzling future, because he has personality as well as brains. Dick's favorite topic is something he thinks about a lot—a decent, hopeful, post-war world. But there's one calculation that keeps cutting across all the other things building up in his mind. It's a split-hair calculation. Dick is trying to figure by just how much the war might be shortened, counting him in. He figures something like thirty seconds.

"AND they count," he says. "For all I know, I might prolong the end by that much time, pulling some boner in the Navy. But the point is that if I do shorten it by a very little, somebody won't be killed who would have been. And a little bit more damage that

might have been done, won't be. Which will mean just a little bit of a difference in the kind of peace we get. And that's the whole point—the peace we get. Planning now isn't visionary to me. It's architecture.

I suppose I have picked this particular batch of boys, 18 and able-bodied, because each of them represents something of how I feel. I'm a junior in college, and fortunate, I think, to have been able to get that far with an education. By peacetime calendars I would graduate in June, 1944. But last August I got to the blow-off point and enlisted in the Army Reserve. I was permitted to come back to school and continue my studies while awaiting call. Graduating, I would probably have gone on into law school, and right now I firmly intend, when I come back, to pick up my work where I left off.

Yet I know that, like many others in this war period, I shall have had far greater opportunities of education, among people from all parts of the globe, than I would ever have obtained in cloistered halls.

SO to me, going into military service doesn't mean all loss. We're embarking on an unusual phase of life, because we must; there can be no future for any of us unless this war is won. This has to be our life for some time to come, and I doubt whether my generation sees any special glory in it. But on the other hand we don't regard ourselves as sacrificed, as a lost generation.

The point—the big point—and I suppose for our elders as well, is what comes out of this war. The big point! We expect to have some say in that. We expect to come back having learned a great deal and therefore being more able to contribute our share toward thrashing out common problems and taking on common responsibilities. We are boys now, teen-agers, but we will come back with something more than just years added. We will come back sure that we are men.

January 10, 1943

INTERREGNUM

RAID TESTS SHOW CHILD ANXIETIES

Increase in Nail Biting and Thumb Sucking Reported During School Drills

By DOROTHY BARCLAY

The statement that most children take "sneak attack" atom bomb drills in school "matter of

facly or as welcome interruption of classroom routine," is not so in the opinion of Dr. Wilfred C. Hulse, psychiatrist at the Children's Center and Mt. Sinai Hospital.

Dr. Hulse said yesterday that close observation of youngsters during such a drill would show a marked increase in thumb sucking, nail biting or other repetitive compulsive movements that represent defenses against anxiety. He spoke at a meeting of the Conference Group on Child Care of the Welfare Council of New York at the Academy of Medicine, 2 East 103rd Street.

To lessen the tension during such drills, Dr. Hulse recommended, the prohibition against children's speaking should be removed. "Talking is one of the best means for relieving accumulated tension," he said. "It is nonsensical to increase the anxiety and pressure in the child by putting him under a restriction not to speak. The children should be encouraged to speak in a low voice during the drills. The supervising adults always find plenty to say!"

To increase the children's security further, he added, the teacher should "take cover" herself.

"No leader should ever segregate himself from his group," Dr.

Hulse said. "If taking part in the practice drill makes observation difficult, two classes could be combined, one teacher taking part and one observing."

Discipline Is Scored

Instances of abuse of the drill idea for disciplinary purposes have come to his attention, he said. He told of one teacher who used the command "take cover" whenever her class became unruly. Such actions will confuse air-raid precautions with punishment in the children's minds.

"Freedom from fear does not depend on environmental circumstances, not on reality, but on a close relationship to a secure and protecting adult," Dr. Hulse asserted.

Dr. Leona Baumgartner, Assistant Commissioner, Department of Health, pointed out that latest population figures showed 50 per cent more children under 5 now than there were in 1940. Many of the difficulties in the child care field, she said, exist because facilities and budgets have not been expanded to keep up with the increase in population."

"If it weren't for the tremendous strides forward in medicine," she added, "we would probably be in as bad a spot in child health work as we are in child welfare. Luckily, progress has kept ahead of us there."

The annual group report was made by A. Bernice Quimby, retiring chairman. New officers named were Mrs. Edna Baer, New York Jewish Child Care Council, chairman; Joseph M. Linda, Catholic Charities, Archdiocese of New York, vice chairman; Ruth Weisenbarger, Sheltering Arms Children's Service, secretary, and Dorothea P. Cee, chairman of the nominating committee.

June 13, 1951

'This Is the Beat Generation'

Despite its excesses, a contemporary insists, it is moved by a desperate craving for affirmative beliefs.

By CLELLON HOLMES

SEVERAL months ago, a national magazine ran a story under the heading "Youth" and the subhead "Mother Is Bugged at Me." It concerned an 18-year-old California girl who had been picked up for smoking marijuana and wanted to talk about it. While a reporter took down her ideas in the uptempo language of "tea," someone snapped a picture. In view of her contention that she was part of a whole new culture where one out of every five people you meet is a user, it was an arresting photograph. In the pale, attentive face, with its soft eyes and intelligent mouth, there was no hint of corruption. It was a face which could only be deemed criminal through an enormous effort of righteousness. Its only complaint seemed to be "Why don't people leave us alone?" It was the face of a Beat Generation.

That clean young face has been making the newspapers steadily since the war. Standing before a judge in a Bronx court house, being arraigned for stealing a car, it looked up into the camera with curious laughter and no guilt. The same face, with a more serious bent, stared from the pages of Life magazine, representing a graduating class of ex-G. I.'s, and said that as it believed small business to be dead, it intended to become a comfortable cog in the largest corporation it could find. A little younger, a little more bewildered, it was this same face that the photographers caught in Illinois when the first non-virgin club was uncovered. The young copywriter, leaning down the bar on Third Avenue, quietly drinking himself into relaxation, and the energetic hot-rod driver of Los Angeles, who plays Russian roulette with a jalopy, are separated only by a continent and a few years. They are the extremes. In between them fall the secretaries wondering whether to sleep with their boy friends now or wait; the mechanics, beering up with the guys and driving off to Detroit on a whim; the models studiously name-dropping at a cocktail party. But the face is the same. Bright, level, realistic, challenging

ANY attempt to label an entire generation is unrewarding, and yet the generation which went through the last war, or at least could get a drink easily once it was over, seems to possess a uniform, general quality which demands an adjective. It was John Kerouac, the author of a fine, neglected novel "The Town and the City," who finally came up with it. It was several years ago, when the face was harder to recognize, but he has a sharp, sympathetic eye, and one day he said, "You know, this is really a *beat* generation." The origins of the word "beat" are obscure, but the meaning is only too clear to most Americans. More than mere weariness, it implies the feeling of having been used, of being raw. It involves a sort of nakedness of mind, and, ultimately, of soul; a feeling of being reduced to the bedrock of consciousness. In short, it means being undramatically pushed up against the wall of oneself. A man is beat whenever he goes for broke and wagers the sum of his resources on a single number; and the young generation has done that continually from early youth.

ITS members have an instinctive individuality, needing no bohemianism or imposed eccentricity to express it. Brought up during the collective bad circumstances of a dreary depression, weaned during the collective uprooting of a global war, they distrust collectivity. But they have never been able to keep the world out of their dreams. The fancies of their childhood inhabited the half-light of Munich, the Nazi-Soviet pact and the eventual blackout. Their adolescence was spent in a topsy-turvy world of war bonds, swing shifts and troop movements. They grew to independent mind on beachheads, in ginmills and U. S. O.'s, in past-midnight arrivals and pre-dawn departures. Their brothers, husbands, fathers or boy friends turned up dead one day at the other end of a telegram. At the four trembling corners of the world, or in the home town invaded by factories and lonely servicemen, they had intimate experience with the nadir and the zenith of human conduct, and little time for much that came between. The peace they inherited was only as secure as the next headline. It was a cold peace. Their own lust for freedom, and their ability to live at a pace that kills, to which war had adjusted them, led to black markets, bebop, narcotics, sexual promiscuity, hucksterism and Jean-Paul Sartre. The beatness set in later.

IT is a post-war generation, and, in a world which seems to mark its cycles by its wars, it is already being compared to that other post-war generation, which dubbed itself "lost." The Roaring Twenties, and the generation that made them roar, are going through a sentimental revival, and the comparison is valuable. The Lost Generation was discovered in a roadster, laughing hysterically because nothing meant anything any more. It migrated to Europe, unsure whether it was looking for the "orgiastic future" or escaping from the "puritanical past." Its symbols were the flapper, the flask of bootleg whisky, and an attitude of desperate frivolity best expressed by Noel Coward's line: "Tennis, anyone?" It was caught up in the romance of disillusionment, until even that became an illusion. Every act in its drama of lostness was a tragic or an ironic third act, and T. S. Eliot's "The Wasteland" was more than the dead-end statement of a perceptive *(Continued)*

CLELLON HOLMES is the 26-year-old author of the novel "Go," and therefore one of the generation which he describes in this article.

211

poet. The pervading atmosphere was an almost objectless sense of loss, through which the reader felt immediately that the cohesion of things had disappeared. It was, for an entire generation, an image which expressed, with dreadful accuracy, its own spiritual condition.

BUT the wild boys of today are not lost. Their flushed, often scoffing, always intent faces elude the word, and it would sound phony to them. For this generation conspicuously lacks that eloquent air of bereavement which made so many of the exploits of the Lost Generation symbolic actions. Furthermore, the repeated inventory of shattered ideals, and the laments about the mud in moral currents, which so obsessed the Lost Generation, does not concern young people today. They take it frighteningly for granted. They were brought up in these ruins and no longer notice them. They drink to "come down" or to "get high," not to illustrate anything. Their excursions into drugs or promiscuity come out of curiosity, not disillusionment.

Only the most bitter among them would call their reality a nightmare and protest that they have indeed lost something, the future. But ever since they were old enough to imagine one, that has been in jeopardy anyway. The absence of personal and social values is to them, not a revelation shaking the ground beneath them, but a problem demanding a day-to-day solution. *How* to live seems to them much more crucial than *why*. And it is precisely at this point that the copywriter and the hot-rod driver meet, and their identical beatness becomes significant, for, unlike the Lost Generation, which was occupied with the loss of faith, the Beat Generation is becoming more and more occupied with the need for it. As such, it is a disturbing illustration of Voltaire's reliable old joke: "If there were no God, it would be necessary to invent Him." Not content to bemoan His absence, they are busily and haphazardly inventing totems for Him on all sides.

FOR the giggling nihilist, eating up the highway at ninety miles an hour, and steering with his feet, is no Harry Crosby, the poet of the Lost Generation who flew his plane into the sun one day because he could no longer accept the modern world. On the contrary, the hot-rod driver invites death only to outwit it. He is affirming the life within him in the only way he knows how, at the extreme. The eager-faced girl, picked up on a dope charge, is not one of those "women and girls carried screaming with drink or drugs from public places," of whom Fitzgerald wrote. Instead, with

Painting by Reilly Nail

" 'Beat' means being undramatically pushed up against the wall of oneself."

persuasive seriousness, she describes the sense of community she has found in marijuana, which society never gave her. The copywriter, just as drunk by midnight as his Lost Generation counterpart, probably reads "God and Man at Yale" during his Sunday afternoon hangover. The difference is this almost exaggerated will to believe in something, if only in themselves. It is a *will* to believe, even in the face of an inability to do so in conventional terms. And that is bound to lead to excesses in one direction or another.

THE shock that older people feel at the sight of this Beat Generation is, at its deepest level, not so much repugnance at the facts, as it is distress at the attitudes which move it. Though worried by this distress, they most often argue or legislate in terms of the facts rather than the attitudes. The newspaper reader, studying the eyes of young dope addicts, can only find an outlet for his horror and bewilderment in demands that passers be given the electric chair. Sociologists, with a more academic concern, are just as troubled by the legions of young men whose topmost ambition seems to be to find a secure berth in a monolithic corporation. Contemporary historians express mild surprise at the lack of organized movements, political, religious or otherwise, among the young. The articles they write remind us that being one's own boss and being a natural joiner are two of our most cherished national traits. Everywhere, people with tidy moralities shake their heads and wonder what is happening to the younger generation.

PERHAPS they have not noticed that, behind the excess on the one hand, and the conformity on the other, lies that wait-and-see detachment that results from having to fall back for support more on one's human endurance than on one's philosophy of life. Not that the Beat Generation is immune to ideas; they fascinate it. Its wars, both past and future, were and will be wars of ideas. It knows, however, that in the final, private moment of conflict a man is really fighting another man, and not an idea. And that the same goes for love. So it is a generation with a greater facility for entertaining ideas than for believing in them. But it is also the first generation in several centuries for which the act of faith has been an obsessive problem, quite aside from the reasons for having a particular faith or not having it. It exhibits on every side, and in a bewildering number of facets, a perfect craving to believe.

Though it is certainly a generation of extremes, including both the hipster and the "radical" young Republican in its ranks, it renders unto Caesar (i. e., society) what is Caesar's, and unto God what is God's. For in the wildest hipster, making a mystique of bop, drugs and the night life, there is no desire to shatter the "square" society in which he lives, only to elude it. To get on a soapbox or write a manifesto would seem to him absurd. Looking out at the normal world, where most everything is a "drag" for him, he nevertheless says: "Well, that's the Forest of Arden after all. And even it jumps if you look at it right." Equally, the young Republican, though often seeming to hold up Babbitt as his culture hero, is neither vulgar nor materialistic, as Babbitt was. He conforms because he believes it is socially practical, not necessarily virtuous. Both positions, however, are the result of more or less the same conviction—namely that the valueless abyss of modern life is unbearable.

A GENERATION can sometimes be better understood by the books it reads, than by those it writes. The literary hero of the Lost Generation should have been Bazarov, the nihilist in Turgenev's "Fathers and Sons." Bazarov sat around, usually in the homes of the people he professed to loathe, smashing every icon within his reach. He was a man stunned into irony and rage by the collapse of the moral and intellectual structure of his world.

But he did nothing. The literary hero of the Beat Generation, on the other hand, might be Stavrogin, that most enigmatic character in "The Possessed" by Dostoevski. He is also a nihilist, or at least intimately associated with them.

But there is a difference, for Stavrogin, behind a facade very much like Bazarov's, is possessed by a passion for faith, almost any faith. His very atheism, at its extreme, is metaphysical. But he knows that disbelief is fatal, and

when he has failed in every way to overcome it, he commits suicide because he does not have what he calls "greatness of soul." The ground yawned beneath Bazarov, revealing a pit into which he fell; while Stavrogin struggled at the bottom of that pit, trying feverishly to get out. In so far as it resembles Stavrogin, there have been few generations with as natural and profound a craving for convictions as this one, nor have there been many generations as ill-equipped to find them.

F OR beneath the excess and the conformity, there is something other than detachment. There are the stirrings of a quest. What the hipster is looking for in his "coolness" (withdrawal) or "flipness" (ecstasy) is, after all, a feeling of somewhereness, not just another diversion. The young Republican feels that there is a point beyond which change becomes chaos, and what he wants is not simply privilege or wealth, but a stable position from which to operate. Both have had enough of homelessness, valuelessness, faithlessness.

The variety and the extremity of their solutions is only a final indication that for today's young people there is not as yet a single external pivot around which they can, as a generation, group their observations and their aspirations. There is no single phi-

losophy, no single party, no single attitude. The failure of most orthodox moral and social concepts to reflect fully the life they have known is probably the reason, but because of it each person becomes a walking, self-contained unit, compelled to meet the problem of being young in a seemingly helpless world in his own way, or at least to endure.

More than anything else, this is what is responsible for this generation's reluctance to name itself, its reluctance to discuss itself as a group, sometimes its reluctance to be itself. For invented gods invariably disappoint those who worship them. Only the need for them goes on, and it is this need, exhausting one object after another, which projects the Beat Generation forward into the future and will one day deprive it of its beatness.

D OSTOEVSKI wrote in the early Eighteen Eighties that, "Young Russia is talking of nothing but the eternal questions now." With appropriate changes, something very like this is beginning to happen in America, in an American way; a re-evaluation of which the exploits and attitudes of this generation are only symptoms. No simple comparison of one generation against another can accurately measure effects, but it seems obvious that a Lost Generation, occupied with disillusionment and trying to

keep busy among the broken stones, is poetically moving, not very dangerous. But a Beat Generation, driven by a desperate craving for belief and as yet unable to accept the moderations which are offered it, is quite another matter. Thirty years later, after all, the generation of which Dostoevski wrote, was meeting in cellars and making bombs.

T HIS generation may make no bombs; it will probably be asked to drop some, and have some dropped on it, however, and this fact is never far from its mind. It is one of the pressures which created it and will play a large part in what will happen to it. There are those who believe that in generations such as this there is always the constant possibility of a great new moral idea, conceived in desperation, coming to life. Others note the self-indulgence, the waste, the apparent social irresponsibility, and disagree.

But its ability to keep its eyes open, and yet avoid cynicism; its ever-increasing conviction that the problem of modern life is essentially a spiritual problem; and that capacity for sudden wisdom which people who live hard and go far, possess, are assets and bear watching. And, anyway, the clear, challenging faces are worth it.

November 16, 1952

STUDENTS ASSAIL CONFORMITY HERE

Parley at Sarah Lawrence Says Many Lose the Urge to Become Individuals

By MILDRED MURPHY
Special to The New York Times.

BRONXVILLE, N. Y., March 2—Students, discussing the values of the present generation, said here today that they were not fully using their college years to prepare them for life in a progressively more conformist society.

While preparing, for the most part, to meet the challenges and pressures of employment in large corporations, the students asked whether they were giving sufficient thought on how to meet the pressures against individualism.

These questions were raised at a conference at Sarah Lawrence College here to discuss the character of the present generation. Attending were several hundred student government members

and writers on newspapers in forty Eastern colleges.

Karl Haffenreffer of Princeton University said in one panel discussion that many students were wearing "psychological sneakers" and were concerned more with being "mild, the good guy and the well-rounded person" than with becoming a whole individual.

A life of ease without friction and conflict in society prevents an individual from becoming whole, he said. He can achieve this by understanding himself and by using solitude to probe his relationships to others.

John Aldridge, a member of the faculty of Sarah Lawrence College, told the group that Americans had lost the feeling for "thrift, hard work and of being true to one's ideals in the face of a hostile society."

Individualism Stressed

W. H. Whyte Jr., another panelist and author of "The Organization Man," spoke of the growing urge in society to accommodate to its needs rather than to those of the individual. Asserting that there is a great danger in not realizing the pressures against individualism, he said students could be warned of the

subtler forms of conflicts that will face them.

Earlier Dr. Robert Hutchins of the Fund for the Republic said that the crisis in education, if not confronted soon by the public, would eventually lead to the disappearance of the esteem in which intellectual activity was held.

Progress in education, he continued, is at an impasse because of a prevailing spirit of "cant." Aside from a few publicized changes, there has been proposed no real re-examination of education, he said.

"The present task of educators is to figure out the purpose of education and interpret it unceasingly to the public," he declared. To seek reform through education, however, is foolish unless society, wishing reform, looks for education to play a prominent role.

The purpose of a university should be to teach its students to live lives that have significance, he said. It should be a place for independent thought and include emphasis on how to make the democratic system work, he added.

March 3, 1957

LIFE OF 'BEATNIK' LINKED TO STRESS

Psychiatrist Views Behavior as Symptom of Conflict, Not of Rebellion

Special to The New York Times.

SAN FRANCISCO, April 1—The "beat generation" of San Francisco's North Beach and the religious healing cults of the Sudanese bush shared the psychiatrist's couch today at the annual meeting of the American Orthopsychiatric Association.

Dr. Francis Rigney, staff psychiatrist for the Veterans Administration Hospital here, declared the "beatniks" had walked out on society, and like any group of sick people they want to be left alone."

He reported that "except for their jargon, which is really protective coloring," their lives were little different from those of the artists and writers in the "Roaring Twenties" who settled in New York's Greenwich Village.

Dr. Tigani el Mahi, the first psychiatrist in the Sudan, attributed valid psychological insights to his country's religious healers and medicine men. Often, he said, he referred patients to the religious healers and they, in turn, were beginning to refer patients to him.

The convention sessions, held in the Civic Auditorium and the Sheraton-Palace Hotel, closed tonight.

Dr. Rigney reported on the "beat generation" after spending more than 100 nights in party rooms and beer parlors of North Beach and giving personality tests to about 150 persons. These, he estimated, represented about one-fourth of the hard core of the "beatniks."

About two-thirds, he said, classified themselves as creative people. His study had showed a "wide spectrum of behavior—happy, sick, tragic, creative and just plain no-good."

Half From The East

In the generation's hard core, he related, the men's average age was 30, the women's 23. Fifty per cent came from the East Coast, 10 per cent of them from New York City. Men outnumbered women about three to one. The "week-end bohemians," he said, were "primarily high school and college students who have been attracted to the area by recent publicity."

Dr. Rigney put the average educational level of the "beatniks" at two years of completed college work.

Social events, the investigator reported, were largely in the partly furnished apartments known as pads and ranged from the tender to the barbaric, from the meaningful to the absurd."

Dr. Rigney said about one-third of the hard core classified itself as writers, one-fourth as painters and one-sixth as musicians. They represented, he declared at a press conference, "the externalized acting-out of internal conflicts and needs rather than a conscious and deliberate response or rebellion toward alleged states of affairs in contemporary society."

Dr. Tigani said at a news conference that on his return to the Sudan after training in Lon-don he was surprised by the insights of religious healers.

He described as being of "much more value than Freud" for his people a dream book written by a Moslem healer named Ibn Sireen more than 1,000 years ago.

Dr. Otto Klineberg, Columbia University psychologist, called on Western workers in the mental health field to study their results carefully to determine whether their ideas were "exportable" to other cultures.

"We are influencing mental health practices in many parts of the world, just as our mechanization and industrialization are influencing the economies of other areas," Dr. Klineberg said.

"One criterion for mental health we sometimes cite," Dr. Klineberg said, "is the person's adaptability to reality. But what about the culture where the highest value is withdrawal from the world? Who would be sick in such a culture?"

April 2, 1959

Educator Holds U. S. Adolescent Lacks Rebellion

LIKE the whooping crane, the koala bear and the duckbilled platypus, the American adolescent has become all but extinct.

In his natural habitat—the ice cream parlor, the football field and the drive-in theatre—may be found specimens that bear a striking superficial resemblance. But, although their voices crack, their glands rebel and their skins erupt, this species lacks the fundamental quality of the Real McCoy—a passion for rebellion.

This is the lament of a long-time student of the American adolescent. Dr. Edgar Z. Friedenberg, Assistant Professor of Education at Brooklyn College. He has placed his findings in a book, "The Vanishing Adolescent," soon to be published by Beacon Press ($2.95).

Dr. Friedenberg elaborated on his thesis in a recent interview. Adolescence, he said, does not merely define a biological process, but a social process as well. The social process, he said, is rebellion. This is the method by which a youngster tests concepts, principles and persons.

In Dr. Friedenberg's view, the American adolescent has been "conned" out of his rebelliousness. He has succumbed to intense pressures to "adjust," "adapt" and "conform."

Worse yet, the American parent and the adults with whom the adolescent comes in contact also have been conned, according to Dr. Friedenberg. In their efforts to act "tolerant," "reasonable" and "democratic," he said, they have relinquished their standards and now stand for nothing. They thereby deprive the adolescent of a bona fide authority against whom to rebel.

The troublesome youngsters, in Dr. Friedenberg's view, are hostile but not rebellious. He observed:

"In the careers of these kids, they often have never met an authority worthy of respect, an authority that they could recognize as such and rebel against. The delinquent adolescent is enraged, not at the tyranny of adults but at their blandness, their weakness, their emptiness."

October 10, 1959

It's Purpose That Counts

GROWING UP ABSURD. Problems of Youth in the Organized System. By Paul Goodman. 296 pp. New York: Random House. $4.50.

By JOHN K. GALBRAITH

I HAVE a feeling that a considerable part of the current spate of criticism of American life is coming to display the qualities being criticized. It is slick and superficial—designed for, and merchandised to, the mass market in criticism. If you are feeling a little at odds with your world, then there is nothing like a good, readable book on the sterility of suburbia, the sex mania of exurbia, the banality of Detroit design or the wastes of advertising to attest to your wholesome anger and

Mr. Galbraith of Harvard wrote the best-selling economics book, "The Affluent Society."

show that you are right and the society wrong.

Criticism could not be put to a worse (or lesser) purpose. It imposes no responsibility upon the individual except the reading. Little is said of underlying causes and less of remedies. To put any blame on the President would be partisan. The networks must remain sovereign in their sadism; one doesn't want to raise the issue of government regulation. The automobile may have got out of hand but do its critics come up with studious proposals for solution? Much too controversial. I for one can see little merit in the man who finds much wrong but seeks neither an explanation nor a remedy.

All of this is by way of saying that Paul Goodman, a man deeply dissatisfied with things as they are, deserves more attention than other less conscientious objectors. His book is anything but slick. From the awkward title to the last appendix, reading is something of a struggle. And it is not strong on prescription, but it is a highly serious effort to understand the relation between society and the disaffected youngster.

IN a common view, the disaffection which produces the delinquent—and also the angry and the beat—is the result of a failure in communication. Bring these young people into a proper relation to society, develop an understanding of social goals, and they will be all right. Mr. Goodman strongly disagrees. The youngsters understand society all too well. They see it as it is—excessively organized for unimportant purposes. Once an apprentice mechanic could tackle a recalcitrant Model T with the interesting and useful object of making it run. Now the same automobile will have banged up some functionless protuberance or it will have lost the use of some organ which was developed as a sales point in the first place. The job no longer seems very important. If the youngster chivies the repair bill . . . well, wasn't the manufacturer also engaged in bamboozling the buyer a bit?

Everywhere the diminishing marginal urgency of goods—the lessening importance of economic function—is robbing work of its purpose. "Thwarted or starved in the important objects proper to young capacities, the boys and young men naturally find or invent deviant objects for themselves * * *. Their choice and inventions are rarely charming * * * we cannot expect average kids to deviate with genius."

This is an interesting and disturbing argument from which, incidentally, I have here extracted the merest core. It shifts attention, when one turns to remedies for (say) delinquency, from what society does or fails to do for the individual to the quality of the society itself. Accepted solutions such as firm and just law enforcement, intelligent elimination of the slums, recreation and educa-

214

tional opportunity do not become less important. They become, however, part of a commitment to much more comprehensive cultural goals. Mere economic achievement, being no longer sufficiently urgent, is no longer sufficient.

I THINK there is much to that. The point is one, as the reader discovers, that stimulates thought along a great many different lines. Possibly the author underestimates the facility with which, given opportunity, other and more engrossing goals are adopted by the individual. In the community with which I am most familiar, economic goals are certainly in decline. If Harvard undergraduates could look forward only to a life in a commercial money-making enterprise their reaction might also be rather unpleasant. Aided by what (unhappily) is a privileged education, they are able to adopt and pursue a variety of other goals from politics and public service to the fine arts and the theatre.

Mr. Goodman of the Columbia faculty tells of the great improvement in performance in a New York high school when it was made clear to students that college was not beyond their horizon—that if they were sufficiently determined, the means of attending could be found. The point is, I think, that society only enforces a narrow economic purpose on people who are qualified for nothing else. The great purpose of education in a moderately well-to-do society is to make this goal less inevitable and to allow others to be not only attractive but possible.

October 30, 1960

DRUGS, SEX AND ROCK 'N' ROLL

Surf Music, a New Rock'n' Roll, Rides Wave That Rose on Coast

Teen-Age Albums' Sales Are High in California Craze Started by a Sport

By PAUL GARDNER

If the gushing sale of surfing records continues to engulf the country the ho-daddies and their beach dollies may inherit the earth.

America's newest musical craze, which drowned traditional rock 'n' roll, has set up Dick Dale, 23 years old, as the king of surfing music. It began last winter in California, where surf boards have replaced cars as the teen-age status symbol, and this summer it has surged to the East Coast.

Surfing music can be defined as wet rock 'n' roll. The instruments used are one saxophone, three guitars and one drum. The music, often composed spontaneously at recording sessions, has the monotony of rock 'n' roll, but the lyrics are more humorous and require linguistic gyrations.

Surfers and their disciples, all bronzed beach lovers, spend their days on or near salt water, speaking and singing with a special surf beat and argot.

A beach dolly, for example, is an older woman—about 17—whose ho-daddie is a hot-rodder with sideburns and long hair. He may even be a hot-dogger which means, in surfese, a showy performer on the board.

Dick Dale's surfing albums have sold more than 200,000 copies. The Surfaris, a musical group of five teen-agers between the ages of 14 and 18, recorded "Wipe Out," a single disk, which has sold almost 1,000,000 copies. Other successful surfing groups are known as the Beach Boys, the Chantays, the Dartells and the Astronauts.

Record officials noted yesterday that surfing was the first sport to emerge with its own music. Murray Wilson, a composer and music publisher, said:

"Surfing music has to sound untrained with a certain rough flavor to appeal to teen-agers. When the music gets too good, it isn't considered the real thing."

"My Son, the Surf Nut," a comedy album, includes such numbers as "Some Gremmie Stole My Hair Bleach" and "The Teen-Age Surfing Vampire." A ditty about a battle of the surf bands suggests that the combatants dive for shelter beneath seaweed.

Mr. Dale formed a band three years ago and played for two years at the Rendezvous Ballroom in Balboa, Calif. Unlike some of his competitors, who could not balance a surf board in a bath tub, Mr. Dale has a custom-made board and a secret surfing beach in California called "Mile Zero."

Terry Melcher, a producer at Columbia Records, said:

"Surfing bands are beginning to entertain at private parties and in night clubs. The market is booming. Even Chubby Checker is making surf records."

August 10, 1963

MORAL QUESTIONS STIR CAMPUSES

Sex, Drugs and Psychoses Posing New Problems

By Dr. GRAHAM B. BLAINE Jr.

The college psychiatrist sees only a small proportion of the student population (usually from 5 to 10 per cent) in his work. But these disturbed students represent in dramatic form more widespread sicknesses, which afflict many other members of the college community at large in more subtle but nonetheless destructive ways. Encounters with the tragic consequences of the changing sexual mores, the deep depressions that may follow upon a prolonged period of apathy and the bizarre psychoses that can be triggered by a single drug experience have impelled deans and doctors to search out causes and cures for the current ills on campus.

The principal difference in sexual mores today as compared with 20 years ago has been a change in the type of sexual companion preferred by college men. By means of statistical studies and, more recently, because of the clearly expressed admission of the students themselves, it has been determined that more male undergraduates are finding sexual partners on their own and neighboring campuses.

Some students are beginning to expect the colleges to cooperate with them in making these liaisons easy and comfortable. Perhaps this trend away from finding sexual satisfaction with prostitutes or pickups should not be thoroughly deplored. The logic of combining sex with love rather than isolating it in an otherwise casual and meaningless relationship seems valid and appealing at first blush; but looked at in the light of the increasing number of unwanted pregnancies and hasty, ill-advised marriages, it seems far less attractive.

One hesitates to advocate a return to the era when the brothel and the taxi dance hall were a favorite source of female companionship for the younger generation, but surely society should be able to effect a compromise solution to the complex problem of how desire may be safely and morally satisfied in a young man strongly driven sexually by nature and yet unready emotionally or economically for fatherhood and marriage.

Our culture in theory seems to demand continence and chastity but in practice our behavior has demonstrably strayed far from the rules since the very earliest times. Witness "The Scarlet Letter." We need to be more honest with ourselves and to try to narrow the gap between our ideals and our way of living without sacrificing too much of our idealism. The means of doing this are still far from being worked out.

Reasons For Trend

The trend towards greater sexual freedom among college women seems to have been initiated by a number of factors. More widely disseminated information about contraception and its increased efficiency has reduced fear of unwanted pregnancy and the decrease of the incidence of veneral disease as well as the ease with which it is now cured has almost entirely removed this threat from the minds of those contemplating a sexual relationship.

Moral injunctions against premarital sexual activity are less clearly spoken in today's world. Many of the religious leaders who deal directly with college students are reluctant to make an emotional or spiritual appeal for adherence to the old standards for fear of being ridiculed by the more science-oriented, materialistic students who take nothing on faith but instead demand a logical reason for every rule. Actually, these students are a vocal minority that does not deserve the attention given it by those who should be more concerned with the substantial portion of the student population that is looking to religion for support for its own high standards.

However, the strongest factor influencing this change in mores is the increasing demand on the part of women for equality with men in all areas. This has led to resentment about the double standard that allows men to be relatively free in their sexual behavior while demanding that women remain chaste. Instead of attempting to impose their continent standard upon men, women have chosen to adopt the more permissive ways of the male for

215

themselves. However, the differences between men and women are more than anatomical. From an emotional, physiological and psychological viewpoint there are many reasons why the double standard makes sense, and in time we may well see a natural swing back towards it.

In light of the fact that this present trend is hard to evaluate, the colleges must be cautious in their attitudes in regard to dormitory visiting privileges. The rules they set up will be regarded by the students as reflections of the administration's own moral standards in this area. Universities that allow unrestricted use of bedrooms by men and women even for only a few hours each week cannot help but be understood by students to be condoning or encouraging sexual intercourse.

While greater liberality in regard to sexual behavior is evident throughout the country, the average American family does not allow its son or daughter to entertain the opposite sex in a bedroom.

Maintaining The Line

Until the meaning of the present shift in mores has become well understood, the colleges should not put themselves ahead of the times by promulgating a moral code that is out of line with present family and cultural standards. Instead they should provide facilities that allow for a reasonable amount of privacy where entertainment, chatter and various other appropriate intimacies can take place. They should also make available to freshmen and sophomores opportunities for small group discussions —dialogues between generations—where issues concerning morality can be openly discussed.

Thus many of the facts regarding sex can be learned and at the same time many of the myths dispelled and, most important, the confusion about standards and values and the discrepancy between theory and practice can be thoroughly aired.

Such discussions will help students realize the significance of what they are doing and keep them from simply falling into intimacies with each other just because it is the thing to do or to prove something that is quite irrelevant to the relationships.

While one segment of our college youth is enthusiastically jumping over barriers in the field of sexual behavior, others are plagued by apathy and disillusionment. They feel that life has no meaning and that they therefore have no obligation or responsibility, much less any desire, to take action. Many of this group interrupt or discontinue their education, and unfortunately among them are brilliant students.

No Memory of Suffering

It is hard to believe that this apathy is wholly caused by existialist philosophers who have brought to the surface much of man's inner uncertainty about his place in the world. Nor can we put all the blame on the threat of atomic annihilation. More important is the fact that these young men and women have no memory of witnessed suffering or deprivation. War and depression are items of history for them, not experiences involving genuine hunger or fear. Few, if any, college students of today have ever had to worry about where their next meal would come from.

Having been part of an affluent society since the day he was born, the college man understandably yearns for a challenge. Unable to find any, except those which he terms artificial or meaningless such as making the dean's list or being another graduate student, businessman or salesman, he loses ambition and slumps back into the arms of the system.

To counteract the womb-like environment it has unwittingly provided in the form of scholarships, loans and multimillion-dollar dormitories and classrooms, the university must provide challenges that reach the heart and soul of the students and engage them in an encounter that grips them in a truly emotional sense. Speakers from foreign lands, controversial national leaders, encouragement to study and work abroad, faculty participation in action groups, independent study projects that carry students far from the regular curriculum are ways in which the college can help potentially apathetic students from losing their feeling of participation.

One increasingly common resort taken by the apathetic student is the drug. As a way to find a new and more exciting environment or as a means of stimulating themselves to feel more enthusiastic about their present surroundings, some college men and women have recently begun to smoke marijuana, swallow mescaline, LSD and psilocybin, or inject opium and heroin. Students feel that these drugs increase their perceptiveness and sensitivity, bring out latent talents and inspire a feeling of extraordinary togetherness among the group which is enjoying the "drug experience." Of course, the drug generally provides only the briefest of delusional respites. But some of it leads to hopeless addiction or months of insanity.

While marijuana has not as yet been proved medically harmful, it is classified as a narcotic by the Treasury Department and possession of the drug can lead to severe penalties. Its use should also be discouraged because smokers of marijuana are easily led to taking other drugs by those from whom they obtain the drug. Opium and heroin can quickly lead to addiction, while a single draught of LSD or psilocybin may cause psychotic illnesses necessitating prolonged hospitalization, even in persons with no previous history of emotional instability.

University administrators are duty bound to prohibit the use of drugs on their campuses and to enforce their rules as stringently as possible. Without knowing it, some colleges are themselves the source of supply for drugs used irresponsibly by their students. Laboratories and pharmacies must be carefully supervised to prevent potentially dangerous materials from falling into unauthorized hands.

The number of college students who come to grief each year is small. The vast majority are conscientious, forward looking, and virtuous. They have achieved renown in the Peace Corps, various teaching projects in our slums and abroad and in many other ventures. Colleges and universities, however, must recognize the trouble spots on campus and take the steps necessary to keep the sickness of a few from spreading to contaminate the many.

Dr. Graham B. Blaine Jr. is a psychiatrist to the Harvard and Radcliffe Health Service and author of "Patience and Fortitude: The Parents' Guide to Adolescence."

January 16, 1964

MACABRE SONGS COME FROM COAST

'California Sound' Dwells on Crack-Ups and Danger

By PETER BART
Special to The New York Times

HOLLYWOOD, Jan. 21 — The other day, Jan Berry, a young medical student, was sitting in a lecture hall when he had an idea for a song.

"The song is about a motorcycle cop on the Hollywood Freeway who likes to catch teen-age kids for speeding," Mr. Berry said. "So one day the cop chases a kid who doesn't feel like stopping. They all crack up."

This may not seem like the makings of a song, but Mr. Berry knows better. He and his partner, Dean Torrence, have written and sung rock 'n' roll tunes that have sold about 10 million records. They are leading exponents of what is known as the California sound.

This week, the partners planned to inject the California sound into their first movie, for Paramount Pictures, "Myron, the Musican Ape, Meets Jan and Dean."

The California sound, though rhythmic, is less influenced by wailing rhythm and blues than most rock 'n' roll, with its strong Negro ethnic strains.

While rhythm and blues, which dominate rock 'n' roll, dwell on unrequited love, most of the California lyrics deal with surfing, skate-boarding, drag-racing and sky-diving.

"The California sound is like folk music in that it reflects the way of life of a region," observes Lou Adler, president of Dunhill Music Company, a small company that handles California rock 'n' roll singers.

The sound first attracted attention when surfing music became a fad. Out of the surfing craze evolved such groups as The Beach Boys and The Fantastic Baggys. (Baggys are loose-fitting swimming trunks worn by dedicated surfers).

When surfing music started to subside, the Californians switched to skate-boarding, referred to as sidewalk surfing, and more recently to what is called carburetor love songs. In these songs teen-agers express affection for their automobiles.

"The first thing a kid really loves is his car," said Steve Barri, a chunky 22-year-old Californian who has written 75 rock 'n' roll songs. "So the lyrics express this love. Personally, I think it's a bit nauseating."

The carburetor love songs recently gave way to humorous or macabre songs about automobiles. Mr. Berry and his partner have a record called "The Little Old Lady from Pasadena," about a spinster who likes to drag race. And there is another record, "Dead Man's Curve," about teen-age lovers who crack up their new car.

California's young rock 'n' roll singers are hunting for new fads. One young songwriter, Guy Hemric, believes that parachute-jumping will be the next teen-age craze, and he has been writing sky-diving songs. Mr. Berry, the medical student, believes that a coming fad will be for love songs for girls and boys younger than 10 years old.

January 22, 1965

The Beatles Will Make the Scene Here Again, but the Scene Has Changed

By ROBERT SHELTON

John, Paul, George and Ringo are bringing it all back home.

That means the Beatles are returning to the United States. They will arrive Friday to begin a third concert tour of the country from which they have gleaned much of their musical inspiration and probably half their earnings.

John Lennon, Paul McCartney George Harrison and Ringo Starr will perform Sunday night for their largest live audience, about 55,600 persons, at Shea Stadium in Flushing, Queens.

They will then whirl through 11 concerts by the end of the month in the San Francisco Cow Palace, the Hollywood Bowl, the Astrodome in Houston, the Maple Leaf Gardens in Toronto and at ballfields in Chicago and Minneapolis and stadiums in Atlanta, Portland, Ore., and San Diego, Calif.

In less than two years, the Beatles have inspired an upheaval in pop music, mores, fashion, hair styles and manners. They have helped conquer a growing number of adults with their charm, irreverent wit and musical skill. They have, in this country, provided marching songs for the teen-age revolution.

New Culture Heroes

They have helped raise to the level of culture heroes such figures as Murray (the K) Kaufman, a disk jockey, and Phil Spector, a young record producer. The Beatles have brought rock 'n' roll, which many have tried to dismiss as ephemeral since its start in 1954, to its third and greatest fever pitch of popularity.

It is estimated that more than 100 million single recordings and more than 25 million LP disks of the Beatles have been sold throughout the world. There have also been Beatle fan magazines, wigs and bubble gum.

However, some reports from Europe indicate that all is not box-office triumph for them. There were 150 policemen on call at the Rome Airport last spring, but only four docile Beatle fans turned out. Concerts in Vienna were canceled this week for lack of advance sale. Britain's record-popularity lists have been yielding increasingly since spring to the American invasion, with hits by Elvis Presley, the Byrds, Bob Dylan, Joan Baez and the Everly Brothers.

Certainly, the promoter of the Shea Stadium concert, Sid Bernstein, has had no cause for concern, despite his guarantee to the Beatles of $100,000 for part of one evening's work. Mr. Bernstein reported that 50 per cent of the tickets had been sold before they were printed.

The slight popularity decline for the Beatles has been caused by the strong competition of such groups as the Rolling Stones, the Dave Clark Five, Herman's Hermits, the Animals and Wayne Fontana and the Mindbenders. They and others have done well with recordings and in concerts.

The music of the Beatles is a form of American music that ricocheted to Europe, became infused with the group's personality and has since bounced back here. Mostly, the "Liverpool sound" is a buoyant, urgent, infectiouly rhythmic series of cadences, with some unsettlingly exciting harmonies (in open fourths and fifths), a bedrock blues beat and an aura of youth, channeled sexuality and exuberance. Often there is a wistful, plaintive quality to their slower ballads.

The Beatles were influenced, while working in the Cavern in Liverpool, by contact, directly or through recordings brought by American seamen from the Gulf Coast, with American rhythm and blues, rock 'n' roll or rockabilly interpreters, such as Mr. Presley, Little Richard, the Everlys or Buddy Holly and the Crickets. From this, with a dash of the British folk-jazz called "skiffle," the Beatles style emerged. Mr. Lennon and Mr. McCartney have written about 100 songs for their group.

More is happening in rock 'n' roll than those who do not appreciate it might suspect. Perhaps most encouraging is the emergence of more meaningful lyrics, long a point of attack for hostile critics.

Although not-yet reflected in Beatles records, there are more and more "message songs" in rock 'n' roll. A new recording by the British group the Animals is a cameo describing social entrapment and hope for release from the tedium of meaningless work:

In this dirty old part of the city
Where the sun refuse to shine
People tell me it ain't no use in tryin'.
My little girl, you're so young and pretty and one thing I know is true
You're gonna die before your time is due.
See my daddy in bed a-dyin', see his hair turnin' gray,
He's been workin' and slavin' his life away,
I know, he's been workin'—yeah, Everyday
Slavin' his life away. He's been workin', workin', work—work.
We gotta get out of this place
If it's the last thing we ever do.
We gotta get out of this place, girl; there's a better life for me and you . . .
© 1965. Screen Gems Columbia Music, Inc. Used with permission.

The song is by Barry Mann and Cynthia Weil, a New York husband-and-wife team. They have also composed "Uptown," which finds solace in a tenement life, and "It's Gonna Be Fine," which stresses patience and hope in a problematic situation.

Also part of the trend of meaningful rock 'n' roll lyrics is "The Eve of Destruction" by P.F. Sloan, a 19-year-old West Coast writer. The song was recorded two weeks ago by Barry McGuire, formerly of the New Christy Minstrels:

The Eastern world
It is explodin' ,
Violence flarin'
And bullets loadin'.
You're old enough to kill
But not for votin'.

Don't you understand
What I'm tryin' to say,
Can't you see the fear
That I'm feelin' today?

Marches alone
Can't bring integration
When human respect is disintegratin'.
This whole crazy world is just too frustratin'
© 1965. Trousdale Music Publishers, Inc. Used with permission.

Other songs recorded in recent weeks by Bob Dylan, the Byrds, Sonny and Cher, Jackie De Shannon, the Rolling Stones and Jody Miller examine conformity, the nature of freedom, teen-age clothes, brotherhood, recording executives and the right to wear long hair.

There is no clear-cut name for this trend, although "folk rock" or "folk pop" are frequent. Essentially, the trend is toward a marriage of the vitality and popularity of rock 'n' roll with the folk movement's general concern for saying something about reality and injustice.

Recording the Sound

The British invasion has helped re-invigorate American musical thinking and activity. There are now many categories of rock 'n' roll, from the "Spector sound," to the "Chicago sound" and the "Rebelation sound" of the Lake Charles area in Lousiana. But knowledgeable persons in pop music think the strongest element of American rock 'n' roll now, musically and financially, is the "Detroit sound."

The leading recordings of Detroit pop music are issued by the Motown Record Corporation on Motown, Tamla, Gordy, V.I.P. and Soul labels. Motown is operated by Barry Gordy Jr., whose six-year rise to musical success antedates the Beatles. At the age of 35, Mr. Gordy, a former assembly-line worker, has a roster of nearly 200 Negro performers and is considered by one authority to

217

be the greatest producer of single pop disks in the world. Essentially, the "English sound" is a white derivation of Negro music, while the "Detroit sound" is Negro pop music and rhythm and blues. It is refined out of the church choirs and ghetto bars where many of its stars, such as the Supremes, Marvin Gaye, the Miracles, Smokey Robinson, the Temptations and Martha and the Vandellas learned their music.

One technical definition of the "Detroit sound" is that it uses a muffled double drumbeat with tambourine and a large brass section. A less technical definition was offered by the Supremes, who are appearing at the Copacabana. The three girls defined the sound as "rats, roaches, guts, struggle and love."

Whatever the school of rock 'n' roll, the groups continue to proliferate, often with outlandish names to attract attention. There are the Guilloteens, Georgie-Porgie and the Cry Babies, the Rotten Kids, the Detergents; Little Caesar and the Consuls, the Turtles, the Leaves and the Bees. Sam the Sham and the Pharaohs wear Bedouin costumes, and the Great Scots wear kilts.

Few spokesmen for pop music would predict what the outlook for rock 'n' roll is. Tastes are fickle, and trends change mercurially. But the British popularity of American rock 'n' roll and folk music has not reached its peak. Although folk purists regard "folk rock" as opportunism now, it can be only to the good that rock 'n' roll lyrics are moving away from banality. In whatever form, rock 'n' roll appears to be with us for a long time.

And promoters here are still scrambling about for a group that could become the American Beatles.

But, as their coming tour will undoubtedly prove, and as Queen Elizabeth II indicated when she named them members of the Most Excellent Order of the British Empire, there are only four Beatles.

August 11, 1965

Police Called In to Control Young Rolling-Stone Fans

ROCHESTER, Nov. 1 (AP)— The appearance here tonight of the Rolling Stones, a long-haired rock-'n' roll quintet popular with teen-agers, touched off a demonstration that required police control.

A policeman and a teen-ager were injured slightly.

More than 3,500 teen-agers screamed and hurled objects as the singers performer in Community War Memorial auditorium.

Police Chief William Lombard, who halted the performance once in an effort to quiet the crowd, finally stopped the show after the group had completed seven of their 11 numbers.

"This is a hick town," yelled the Group's vocalist-guitarist, Keith Richards, as the police stepped in to quiet the crowd. "They were twice as wild in Montreal. They [the audience] won't get hurt. You're too hard with them."

The police escorted the British singers from the auditorium. Within an hour, they were on their way to New York.

November 2, 1965

Public Writer No. 1?

By THOMAS MEEHAN

FOR the past three and a half years, since the death of William Faulkner, on July 6, 1962, American literary critics have been nervously scanning the horizon in search of a novelist or poet who can be definitely called the nation's Public Writer No. 1, in the way that Faulkner and, before him, Hemingway, answered to this title. Not surprisingly, the critics, gazing out the windows of The Partisan Review, etc., have been keeping a close eye on who is being read by the country's college undergraduates, who are, after all, today's more selective readers as well as tomorrow's writers, professors of English and even critics for The Partisan Review. Thus, in intellectual circles from Berkeley to Philip Rahv's apartment, where all the talk has been of writers like Robert Lowell, Saul Bellow and Norman Mailer, a number of jaws dropped noticeably a couple of weeks ago when an informal survey of students majoring in English at three prominent Ivy League colleges revealed that their favorite contemporary American writer is a

THOMAS MEEHAN is a writer who in the course of his assignments has learned to swing with, if not wholly to subscribe to, the opinions of the young.

24-year-old folk-song writer, composer and singer named Bob Dylan.

Unlike Lowell, Bellow, Mailer or any of the dozen or so other writers esteemed by the quarterlies, explained the students, Dylan, whose songs are mainly of social and personal protest, is writing about things they care about.

"We don't give a damn about Moses Herzog's angst or Norman Mailer's private fantasies," one earnest Brown University senior noted. "We're concerned with things like the threat of nuclear war, the civil-rights movement and the spreading blight of dishonesty, conformism and hypocrisy in the United States, especially in Washington, and Bob Dylan is the only American writer dealing with these subjects in a way that makes any sense to us. And, at the same time, as modern poetry, we feel that his songs have a high literary quality. As far as we're concerned, in fact, any one of his songs, like 'A Hard Rain's Gonna Fall,' is more interesting to us, both in a literary and a social sense, than an entire volume of Pulitzer Prize verse by someone like Robert Lowell."

(The undergraduate vote was not, of course, unanimous. One Harvard unbeliever, for example, asserted that it was "absurd" to take Dylan's writing seriously.)

If Bob Dylan is, indeed, an emerging major literary figure, he will then have things going for him three ways, for he is already a leading figure in the American folk-singing world and, at the same time, a teen-age popular-music idol whose recordings of so-called folk-rock songs, a hybrid form of his own recent invention, like "Positively 4th Street" and "Like a Rolling Stone," have in the past few months frequently been nestled next to Beatles numbers near the top of WABC's All-American Super-Hit survey. Folk rock, by the way, is nothing more than a folk song sung to a rock 'n' roll big-beat background, but when Dylan introduced this new form at the Newport Folk Festival and at an outdoor concert at Forest Hills last summer, singing for the first time to the electronic accompaniment of a blaring rock 'n' roll combo, he was roundly booed by folk-song purists, who considered this innovation the worst sort of heresy. "It's all music," drawled Dylan in reply, "no more, no less."

For those who are not familiar with him, Dylan is, in appearance, the Ultimate Beatnik; cowboy boots, jeans, wrinkled work shirts and dark glasses, plus frizzy, unkempt hair and a lean, pale and haggard face. He somehow curiously resembles a combination of Harpo Marx, Carol Burnett and the young Beethoven. Most often accompany- *(Continued)*

Who needs Saul Bellow? There are those who say that the literary voice of our time—and a poet of high degree—is a guitar-playing, harmonica-blowing songwriter-singer named Bob Dylan.

POET WITH GUITAR—He took the name Dylan out of admiration for the late Dylan Thomas.

Photographs by DAVID GAHR

ing himself on a guitar—between verses he plays a harmonica attached to a contraption slung around his neck—Dylan tends to snarl his songs rather than sing them, spitting out the iconoclastic lyrics in a whiny, high-pitched hillbilly wail.

IF and when Dylan makes it into the pages of "Twentieth Century Authors," the entry will show that he was born in Duluth, Minn., on May 24, 1941, the son of a pharmacist, and was raised in Hibbing, Minn., a small mining town near the Canadian border, where he lived off and on until he was 18. "Hibbing's a good ol' town," wrote Dylan not long ago. "I ran away from it when I was 10, 12, 13, 15, 15½, 17 an' 18. I been caught and brought back all but once." Dylan's real name was Bob Zimmerman. He changed it because of admiration for poet Dylan Thomas.

His first excursion from Hibbing was to Chicago, where, at the age of 10, he bought his first guitar and taught himself to play it. By the age of 15 he had further taught himself to play the piano, the autoharp and the harmonica, had become hooked on singing folk songs—and, indeed, had written his first folk song, a love ballad he dedicated to Brigitte Bardot.

After graduating from Hibbing high school and spending six desultory months at the University of Minnesota, Dylan struck out on a hitchhiking career as an itinerant folk singer, roaming about from places like Gallup, N. M., to Cheyenne, Wyo., to Sioux Falls, S. D., for more than three years before finally heading East in the late fall of 1960 to pay a call on Woody Guthrie, the famed folk singer of the thirties who had a profound influence on Dylan as a writer, a performer and a thinker, and who was then lying seriously ill in a New Jersey hospital.

In early 1961, Dylan made his New York performing de-

but at Gerde's Folk City on West Fourth Street in Greenwich Village, the La Scala of the American folk-singing scene, and at once he took the place by storm, bowling over everyone from Pete Seeger to Joan Baez with verses like this one from his "Talkin' New York," a comic, Guthrie-like talking blues:

Winter time in New York town,
The wind blowin', snow around
Walk around with nowhere to go
Somebody could freeze right to the bone.
*I froze right to the bone.**

From talking blues, Dylan quickly progressed to more serious work, including a series of anti-war songs ("Masters of War," "God Is On Our Side," etc.) and a series of songs protesting social injustices ("The Lonesome Death of Hattie Carroll," "The Ballad of Hollis Brown," "Who Killed Davey Moore?", etc.). In 1962, Dylan wrote "Blowin' in the Wind," which became the rallying song of the civil-rights movement and which made Dylan nationally famous.

Earlier, in the fall of 1961, he had made his first record album, for Columbia Records, called simply enough, "Bob Dylan," and the album had been at once an enormous success. And he has made five subsequent albums, all of which have been equally successful. Meanwhile, he has sung to overflow audiences at colleges and in concert halls over the country and, in New York, has given several standing-room-only one-man concerts at Town Hall, Carnegie Hall and Lincoln Center.

His songs, sung either by himself or by such other folk and folk-rock interpreters as Joan Baez, Odetta, Judy Collins, Pete Seeger, Peter, Paul and Mary, Sonny and Cher, the Byrds and the Turtles,. have in the past couple of years virtually revolutionized

*Copyright 1962 by Duchess Music Corporation. Used by permission.

American popular music. "Until Bob Dylan came along, all of the hit songs were lachrymose teen-age laments about unhappy high school love affairs," a New York recording executive commented the other day. "But now, to an amazing degree, the hits are about things like war, foreign policy and poverty. Dylan started it all with 'Masters of War' and 'Blowin' in the Wind,' and his imitators are now making it big with folk-rock songs like 'Eve of Destruction,' 'Home of the Brave' and 'We Gotta Get Out of This Place.'

"All in all, Dylan has had a great deal of responsibility for the surprising interest the younger generation has today in serious questions like civil rights and Vietnam. In fact, he's probably had more direct influence on what's going on with young people in America today—protest marches, picketing, and so forth—than almost any other one person in the country."

MOST of Dylan's reputation rests on his talents as a performer and a writer of lyrics rather than as a composer, for his melodies are fairly ordinary and decidedly derivative — although perhaps unique in that they mix for the first time the sounds of Negro blues with the twang of Nashville country music. "Dylan breaks all the rules of song writing," folk music critic Robert Shelton has writ-

ten, "except that of having something to say and saying it stunningly."

As a literary stylist, he seems something of an anachronism, for many of his songs are written in a manner reminiscent of the protest, "Waiting for Lefty" pseudo-poetry of the thirties. For example, in 1937, Odets — or Maxwell Anderson — might well have written these lines from "Masters of War":

You fasten the triggers
For the others to fire
Then you set back and watch
When the death count gets higher
You hide in your mansion
As young people's blood
Flows out of their bodies
*And is buried in the mud**

On the other hand, future Ph.D. candidates in English, writing their theses on Dylan, will not find him that easy to pigeonhole, for he tends to write in a number of styles, among them an extraordinarily lyrical and traditional folk-song style. "Blowin' in the Wind," for example, is very much a traditional folk song:

How many years can a mountain exist
Before it's washed to the sea?
Yes, 'n' how many times can some people exist
Before they're allowed to be free?
Yes, 'n' how many times can a man turn his head

*Copyright 1963 by M. Witmark & Sons. Used by permission.

Pretending he just doesn't see!

The answer, my friend, is blowin' in the wind,
The answer is blowin' in the wind. **

And then there are Dylan songs like "Girl of the North Country," which could have been composed in the back hills of Kentucky in 1824. with verses like this one:

So if you're travelin' in the north country fair,
Where the winds hit heavy on the borderline,
Remember me to one who lives there,
She once was a true love of mine. *

At the same time, oddly enough, mixing a traditional folk-song style with the techniques of modern poetry, Dylan can at times be extremely obscure. His "A Hard Rain's 'a Gonna Fall," for instance, is scarcely any "On Top of Old Smoky," as this verse may suggest:

Oh, what'll you do now, my blue-eyed son?
Oh, what'll you do now, my darling young one?

I'm a goin' back out 'fore the rain starts a fallin',
I'll walk to the depth of the deepest black forest,
Where the people are many and their hands are all empty,
Where the pellets of poison are flooding their waters,
Where the home in the valley meets the damp dirty prison,
Whe re the executioner's face is always well hidden,
Where hunger is ugly, where souls are forgotten,
Where black is the color, where none is the number,
And I'll tell it and think it and speak it and breathe it,
And reflect it from the mountain so all souls can see it,
Then I'll stand on the ocean until I start sinkin' *

Those conditioned by the likes of "Red River Valley" to think of folk songs as simple and uncomplicated are inevitably confused by Dylan's songs. Dylan, however, claims that folk songs have always been difficult to comprehend. "Folk music is the only music where it isn't simple," Dylan told an interviewer recently. "It's never been simple. It's weird, man, full of legend. myth, Bible and ghosts. And, yeah, chaos — watermelons, clocks, everything."

THE use of slang like "man" is typical of Dylan, for he is very much the motorcycle-riding hipster, but this surface pose masks an extraordinarily intelligent, sensitive, concerned and surprisingly well-read young man. For

example, he is familiar with most of the classic and modern poets and at times his verses sound like those of a hillbilly W. H. Auden—specifically the earlier Auden of such poems as "September 1. 1939," as these lines from Dylan's "It's Alright Ma (I'm Only Bleeding)" might suggest:

Disillusioned words like bullets bark
As human Gods aim for their mark
Made everything from toy guns that spark
To flesh colored Christs that glow in the dark *

Perhaps Dylan's principal appeal to the young (and to an increasing number of the not-so-young) is his rude defiance of all authority and scorn for the Establishment, which he puts down with unrelenting and unforgiving bitterness, as in "Masters of War," which begins with this verse:

Come you masters of war
You that build all the guns
You that build the death planes
You that build the big bombs
You that hide behind walls
You that hide behind desks
I just want you to know
I can see through your masks
And ends with this one:
And I hope that you die
And your death'll come soon
I will follow your casket
On a pale afternoon
And I'll watch while you're lowered
Down to your death bed
And I'll stand o'er your grave
Till I'm sure that you're dead **

But Dylan doesn't viciously put away only the death-plane builders; he also goes after those guilty of the most ordinary day-to-day hypocrasies, as in "Positively 4th Street," a savage little number that was near the top of the WABC survey just a few weeks ago:

You got a lotta nerve
To say you are my friend

When I was down
You just stood there grinning

You got a lotta nerve
To say you gotta helping hand to lend
You just want to be on
The side that's winning . . .

You see me on the street
You always act surprised
You say "how are you?",
"good luck"
But you don't mean it

When you know as well as me
You'd rather see me paralyzed
Why don't you just come out once
And scream it . . .

I wish that for just one time
You could stand inside my shoes

And just for that one moment
I could be you

Yes I wish that for just one time
You could stand inside my shoes
You'd know what a drag it is
To see you *

Dylan himself refers to his compositions as "stories" rather than as songs, and most have a kind of narrative line to them, a straight narrative, as in "The Lonesome Death of Hattie Carroll," which concerns itself with the killing of a Negro maid by a wealthy young white man (based on an actual incident) or a nightmare-fantasy narrative, as in "Bob Dylan's 115th Dream which is a satiric retelling of the story of the discovery of America:

I think I'll call it America
I said as we hit land
I took a deep breath
I fell down, I could not stand
Captain Arab he started
Writing up some deeds
He said, let's set up a fort
And start buying the place with beads
Just then this cop comes down the street
Crazy as a loon
He throws us all in jail
For carryin' harpoons.

Ah me I busted out
Don't even ask me how
I went to get some help
I walked by a guernsey cow
Who directed me down
To the Bowery slums
Where people carried signs around
Sayin', ban the bums
I jumped right into line
Sayin', I hope that I'm not late·.
When I realized I hadn't eaten
For five days straight. . . .

Well I rapped upon a house
With the U.S. flag upon display
I said, could you help me out
I got some friends down the way
The man says, get out of here
I'll tear you limb from limb
I said, you know they refused Jesus too
He said, you're not him
Get out of here before I break your bones
I ain't your pop
I decided to have him arrested
And I went lookin' for a cop. . . .

Well, the last I heard of Arab
He was stuck on a whale
That was married to the deputy
Sheriff of the jail
But the funniest thing was
When I was leavin' the bay
I saw three ships a sailin'
They were all heading my way
I asked the captain what his name was
And how come he didn't drive a truck

He said his name was Columbus
I just said, good luck *

THOSE students who claim that Dylan is the best writer in America today point not only to his lyrics but also, curiously enough, to the copy Dylan writes for his record liners. This is usually a hundred lines or so of free verse, like these characteristic, somewhat Brechtian (with punctuation by Cummings) excerpts from the liner of the recent album "Bringing It All Back Home":

i'm standing there watching the parade
feeling combination of sleepy john estes. jayne mansfield. humphrey bogart
mortimer snurd. murph the surf and so forth
erotic hitchhiker wearing japanese blanket.
gets my attention by asking didn't
he see me at this hootenanny down in puerto vallarta, mexico
i say no you must be mistaken.
i happen to be one of the Supremes
then he rips off his blanket an suddenly becomes a middle-aged druggist.
up for district attorney.
he starts screaming at me you're the one.
you're the one that's been causing all them riots over in vietnam.
immediately turn to a bunch of people and says if elected, he'll have me electrocuted publicly on the next fourth of july **

Surprisingly, a number of leading American literary critics profess never even to have heard of Bob Dylan, while, among those who are acquainted with his work, the critical opinion is sharply divided between those who don't take him in the least seriously and those who agree with the students that Dylan may well be an important new figure in American letters.

"I don't see Dylan as a writer of any consequence — he's simply a pop-culture figure." says one of the anti-Dylan critics. "Granted, he has an interesting imagination, but his ideas and his techniques are dated and banal —we've been through all this before in the thirties. Like most pop-culture heroes, Dylan will soon be forgotten—he'll quickly become last year's vogue writer."

On the other hand, a pro-Dylan critic argued this way recently: "Dylan is taking poetry away from the academicians. Poetry. and the Y.M. H.A., and giving it back to the masses, which seems to me an extremely healthy development. Moreover, he is an interesting poet, even if he is a teen-age idol. After all, poetry began with Homer, wandering about reciting his verses to anyone who'd listen to them and, in a sense, stretching matters a bit, Dylan is a kind of 20th-century Homer, if, however, 'Motorpsycho Nightmare' and the rest are scarcely 'The Iliad.' "

DYLAN'S fellow poets tend also to be somewhat divided in their assessment of him, as in the opinions of:

Stanley Kunitz—"I listen with pleasure to Bob Dylan, but I would term him a popular artist, a writer of verse rather than of poetry. All in all, though, I think the interest taken in him is a healthy sign, for there is no reason why popular art and a more selective, esoteric art can't cheerfully coexist. And popular art is the foundation on which fine art rests. Thus, the higher the level of taste there is in the popular arts, the more promising is the hope for the evolution of great fine art."

Louis Simpson—"I don't think Bob Dylan is a poet at all; he is an entertainer—the word poet is used these days to describe practically anybody. I am not surprised, though, that American college students consider him

A FOLK "FIRST"—Dylan introducing his own invention, "folk-rock" (folk songs sung to a rock 'n' roll beat), with the Paul Butterfield band at Newport this year.

their favorite poet—they don't know anything about poetry."

W. H. Auden—"I am afraid I don't know his work at all. But that doesn't mean much—one has so frightfully much to read anyway."

AMONG those who tend to agree with the pro-Dylan critics is Dylan himself, who has nothing but scorn for the American literary Establishment and who not long ago

had this to say to an interviewer: "The only thing where it's happening is on the radio and records. That's where people hang out. It's not in book form, it's not on the stage. All this art they been talking about, it just remains on the shelf."

And, finally, those writers and critics who refuse to take Dylan seriously might give some thought to the second verse of Dylan's "The Times They Are A-Changin'," a song that enjoys immense popularity with the current college generation and has, in fact, become the somewhat subversive secret theme song of that generation:

Come writers and critics
Who prophecies with your pen
And keep your eyes wide
And don't speak too soon
For the wheel's still in spin
And there's no tellin' who
That it's namin'
For the loser now
Will be later to win
FOR THE TIMES THEY
*ARE A-CHANGIN'**

December 12, 1965

Offerings At the Psychedelicatessen

By RICHARD R. LINGEMAN

The generation of Americans under the age of 30 is a mutant species, sharing territory with a dangerous, deviant species (i.e., those over the age of 30 who are addicted to power, control and violence).
—TIMOTHY LEARY, in an article titled "Turn On/Tune In/Drop Out"

RUMBLINGS are audible which suggest that the arrest of Dr. Timothy Leary, a former Harvard professor, on two separate occasions for violations of the Marijuana Tax Act of 1937 and the New York

RICHARD R. LINGEMAN is executive editor of the satirical magazine Monocle. He is now working on a social history of the domestic front during World War II.

Narcotics Act (and his conviction, which he is appealing, on the first of these) has provided the small but growing group of potheads, psychedelics and other mutants in this country with a leader who has the charisma, though not nearly the following, that the Rev. Dr. Martin Luther King Jr. has among Negroes. The focal points of their first foray into social action are the state and Federal laws making possession, transportation or sale of marijuana illegal. Dr. Leary's appeal represents the first major attack on these laws that has a medicum of a chance of succeeding. Whether or not it does succeed, the climate of opinion in the nation seems to be undergoing a glacial change in the direction of the

liberalization of these laws. With the passage by the House of Representatives in early June of a bill modifying to a small extent the present Federal law, the first crack in heretofore solid stone has appeared.

There are other signs that Lady Hemp, *Cannabis sativa L.,* alias boo, pot, tea, grass, Mary Jane, grefa, muta, reefers, sticks, joints, may be changing her image. Though she is a long way from acquiring respectability, a lot more people in America today are looking at her with a lot more tolerance than they used to.

To the psychedelics, marijuana is a benign consciousness-expanding drug on the lowest level of a continuum of ecstasy culminating in LSD. To a growing number of medical men and scientists, Lady Hemp is a mild hallucinogen with a few virtues and some possible faults, who is nevertheless not the lurid temptress the moralists have painted her. To a small percentage of college and high-school students,* whether they have sampled her favors or not, and to anti-Establishment rebels, marijuana is a club of rebellion with which to belabor what Dr. Leary has called "the middle-class, middle-brow, whisky-drinking people who make the laws in this country," otherwise known as parents or, simply, the Establishment.

To Federal and state narcotics officers, however, marijuana is the same old problem. And to the large majority of adults, whisky-drinking or otherwise, marijuana summons up vague memories of movies called "Assassins of Youth" about dope-addict, bop-talking jazz musicians seducing young girls, zoot-suited Mexicans and sex orgies in the Village.

What follows is an attempt to tune into the current talk about marijuana, LSD and the like. No systematic survey is involved, but I think you will find it fairly representative.

The Groove Corps! Sights, Sounds, Cotton Candy, Cold Drinks, Electric Kool Aid—yes, & Psychedelic Treats and Trips—Midnight til 2 A.M. Wed. thru Sat., Warner Playhouse, 755 No. La Cienga, L.A., Calif.
—AD FOR A PSYCHEDELIC DISCOTHEQUE

In the ballroom of the Open Stage at 23 St.

Mark's Place, where once New Yorkers of Polish descent ate kielbasa sausages, bare tables and folding chairs are at one end of the room, a dance floor and bandstand at the other. Above the dance floor hangs one of those large, multifaceted glass globes which in earlier days revolved slowly, showering thousands of dots of light on the dancers. It does not turn now, for a newer generation responds to newer illusions. The Open Stage is a psychedelic discothèque, sometimes called intermedia or multimedia, in which slides, movies and kinetic sounds light the trips fantastic.

Vinyl screens hang at both ends of the room and on both sides. Movies are projected onto the narrow screen beside the bandstand and the full-sized one at the opposite end. The movies keep changing: old Hollywood camp items like "The Bride of Frankenstein,"

*Estimates of the extent of the use of hallucinogenic drugs in the New York metropolitan area vary widely. Dr. Louria (see box on facing page), who has suggested a "moratorium" on talk about LSD because he feels publicity has expanded the problem, says that his information shows that most published figures emphasizing its use by college students are exaggerated. He concedes that perhaps 15 per cent of local college students may have experimented with marijuana, but a report just issued by his committee declares: "We doubt that chronic abuse of marijuana [or] hallucinogens . . . in our colleges will be found . . . to exceed 5 per cent to 7 per cent except in isolated incidents, and in the overwhelming majority of our high schools this figure is undoubtedly less than 5 per cent."

with the sound turned off; on the narrow screen beside the bandstand, an underground movie slipping back and forth among several separate scenes. One recurring theme is a group of people at what may be an LSD picnic, or may not. They laugh and roll on the ground. A bearded man rides a child's tricycle. In another sequence, men and women in bathing suits are writhing about on the floor, smearing one another with mud. There are shots of trees and woods and blurred images melting into new forms. After that one ends, the reel is changed and a color documentary on India's population problem, no sound, is projected.

While this is going on, the rock 'n' roll group on stage, average age appearing to be 13, sing unintelligibly; a Negro boy in an undershirt gyrates beside them. Flanking the dancers are two slide projectionists, rapidly throwing slides of bright colored circles and dots and lines on the screen across the room, sometimes swinging the projector up and down, or pointing it at the bandstand.

The crowd is gay, very young, casually dressed, and very unorgiastic. They drink wine or liquor with setups. There is no bar. When "Bride of Frankenstein" comes on, they leave off their frugging and cluster in front of the screen to watch. Nobody's blowing his mind, but it's fun.

IN the past year or so—ever since novelist Ken Kesey* organized a big San Francisco "Trips Festival," which drew 10,000 people over its three-day run—trips, or acid (LSD) festivals or acid tests, have become very much a part of the bubbling up of underground psychedelic culture. Using slides and movies, stroboscopic lights, Indian raga music, "acid rock" and conventional rock 'n' roll, the trips festival mimics the psychedelic experience. At hard-core trips festivals in the Bay Area (at least before LSD was brought under law by the Federal Government and the State of California) Electric Kool Aid was served — punch with LSD in it.

The trips idea — and its offshoot, the intermedia discothèque — has spread to New York City, but it has lost the spontaneous mind-blowing quality it had in the beginning and is certainly unlike this acid test described by a San Francisco witness:

"Hundreds of people filling a huge dance floor, dressed in 'ecstatic clothes' — striped

*He was subsequently arrested on a marijuana charge. At last word, he had fled to Mexico after leaving a phony suicide note, although no one seems sure.

stockings, sequined and iridescent-painted bodies, flapper costumes, Victorian dress, top hats, sailor suits, Indian costumes and undefinable 'psychedelic' outfits. . . . Loud pulsating electronic music. . . . The music slows, the dancers slow, the dance takes on an Indian feeling, the music gets weirdly Oriental, then the music speeds up again and the whole place swings in a frenzied profusion of writhing bodies atune to the current dance evolution. . . .

"Then the police. In honor of a local ordinance, they have come to stop the party. What can a group of police do to several hundred Bohemians, artists, beatniks, students and freaks with a common denominator of being on 'acid,' and possessing anti-Establishment ideas? Most treated the police like poor little boys with authority hangups. . . . An hour later, the cops got down to stopping hand cymbals and finger-snapping. . . . The thing the police couldn't perceive was that each human being was entertaining himself."

Or, in the less perfervid accents of two U.C.L.A. doctors: "At various community dances which we attended, the young girls were in their 'psychedelic slacks' and the teenage boys wore long hair and sunglasses. They moved beneath undulating lights in bright 'psychedelic' color. At such gatherings [LSD] seemed to replace personal contact and to substitute for the drives of sex and aggression. We watched seven or eight sailors dancing with one girl on the floor. There was little male-female awareness or physical contact; each was in his own fantasy world."

Everyone entertaining himself . . . everyone loving everybody else. What are the mutants up to?

PSYCHEDELIC culture has now made interpenetrations into public society. What it used to be is symbolized by the KISS BIG thing at Harvard a few years ago, when Leary and his associate, Richard Alpert, were first experimenting with LSD. You dialed a phone number whose digits spelled out the words KISS BIG, waited a moment, and then a voice answered, "IFIF." That's all. IFIF—which stood for Leary's International Foundation for Internal Freedom.

Psychedelic culture started like that, a congeries of public signals with private, magical

Volkswagen ads are considered very psychedelic by some

meanings that Cambridge tripsters, potheads, acid heads, New Jersey sadhus and other mindblowers flashed to one another. This underground, loosely knit fraternity feeling still obtains, but the psychedelic scene is surfacing more frequently. It is getting like the young boy I heard of, whose father caught him with some marijuana cigarettes. Instead of being ashamed, the boy was hurt. He begged his father to try one: "How can you know, Dad, unless you've turned on, too?"

Psychedelics are like that, smiling secret Mona Lisa smiles about what they know, and what no one who has not experienced it can know: mutants walking around with the knowledge that they need only say, "Shazam," and inside their brains they will become Captain Marvel; turned on. "Turn off the drugs for a year," Dr. Leary told his young audience in a recent speech at Town Hall. "Turn on your parents." "Turn on, tune in, drop out."

In the Psychedelic Age we are now in the Year of Turning On Without Drugs, as proclaimed by the prophet, Dr. Leary. While some kids are still trying LSD, illegal or not, Dr. Leary or not, the veteran psychedelics are consolidating their experiences into public art forms. The intermedia show, with slides and movies and dancers and electronic music, is one manifestation. Recently, such a spectacle was performed at the Bridge Theater with the title "DMT" (for dimethyltrypamine, a hallucinogenic drug). "At one point," a reviewer ecstatically observed, "the screen was rolled into an exquisitely beautiful tower of light. The whole thing is very organic."

Psychedelic visions, trips and religious flip-outs (but never freak-outs, or bad trips) have given birth to a psychedelic art. Some is unintentional. Salvador Dali is an LSD artist, for example, according to Leary, "although he doesn't take LSD." By the same token, Fellini's "Juliet of the Spirits" is an unintentional LSD movie. (An intentional movie about LSD, called "Hallucination," will be released shortly.)

ONE may buy intentional LSD art at the city's first psychedelic bazaar, The Head Shop, in the East Village, where brightly colored mandala prints cover two walls. (The mandala is a circular pattern, a central artifact of Oriental mysticism.

As Dr. Leary has explained it to an inquiring television reporter: "The energy pattern of the mandala hooks up with your eye. . . .") There are also prints of candles with curving spirals of smoke rising from them, symbolizing the light of truth in the smoke of marijuana. The Head Shop also sells postcard-size visionary photo-collages.* A typical one shows faces, a crucifix, a fetus, a human brain and other symbols arranged like a cathedral tower, capped by a cross, and radiating out into a starry sky. At the base of the "tower" is an airplane instrument panel, flanked by two pilots, with the pasted-up headline: "GUIDANCE COUNSELING, NAVIGATION AND CONTROL IS OUR BUSINESS"—cult language related to the "guide" of the psychedelic voyage.

If the mandala is a key subject in much of psychedelic art, other traditional symbols come from literature: Aladdin's magic lamp and "Alice in Wonderland." Aladdin turned on with cannabis; the lamp and the jinni suggest the magical, grandiose feelings that hemp provides the smoker. The key picture in "Alice" is the illustration of the caterpillar sitting on the mushroom smoking a hookah. The magic mushroom which made Alice grow or shrink is transformed into the hallucinogenic mushroom from which the drug psilocybin is extracted and which performs, the true believers believe, a similar operation on the consciousness, while the hookah conjures up the smoking of cannabis in a water pipe.

Often psychedelic art appears in poster form. A poster issued by some Berkeley psychedelics features vertical red and white stripes and in the upper half a blue and white starred swastika—a pothead's paranoid version of the American flag. The legend reads: "BE AWARE." Another poster, used in connection with a benefit for Dr. Leary at The Open Stage, shows green marijuana leaves in the lower left with a single word, "sense," its letters breaking off and rising toward the upper right-hand corner.

One of the designers, Ralph Metzner, an editor of The Psychedelic Review and a frequent collaborator with Dr. Leary, explained to me that the poster shows marijuana lifting you to the third of Dr. Leary's five levels of consciousness. These are: (1) sleep—the most contracted stage, the stage that alcohol puts you in; (2) symbolic — the normal awakened state of language and

game patterns at which most of us operate; (3) sensory awareness — when the senses are tuned; (4) cellular consciousness — the stage when one senses his cells, and (5) "precellular flash"—the deepest awareness of all, often called "soul." Normally, our senses are out of tune, Metzner explained. Marijuana turns the senses on and increases sensual pleasures, he said, but the higher levels of consciousness can be reached only via LSD or meditation.

Psychedelics often see a psychedelic message where ordinary people see nothing: a cover of Newsweek for a story on Pop Art, for example, showing an explosion with the word "POP!" in the center. "Pop your mind—see?" a psychedelic explained. Volkswagen ads are considered very psychedelic by some of the cognoscenti, as was an ad for a dress that was all in black and white, except for a small rectangle of color in the center, the caption telling you to "see it in color."

FOR the pothead who prefers to take his in a pipe, whether conventional or water, as is the custom in India and the Middle East, there is even a small, indigenous Pipe Art movement. The Head Shop has tiny, double-stemmed pipes of Danish manufacture for the effete smoker. And for the water-pipe fan, there are modernistic versions of the hookah, shaped like tall test tubes. They are designed by an anonymous artist who signs himself the Psychedelicatessen, and are sold on consignment. For the paranoids, there is a minature water pipe disguised as a cigarette lighter. Tradition-minded smokers can find water pipes and Indian clay chillum pipes at the nearby Sindoori shop. (Of course, these pipes, like cigarette papers, can be used for tobacco as well as pot.)

Also available at The Head Shop is defraction jewelry—silvery disks that radiate colors of the spectrum from the center when turned slightly in the hand. They are worn as cuff links, as earrings, or stuck on the forehead.

A Psychedelic Shop, by that name, in San Francisco was the first of this kind. It advertises "psychedelic literature, Oriental jazz, Marvel comics, inner-journey sounds in atonal music and rock 'n' roll," which just about exhausts the list of psychedelic culture.

IN the higher stream of psychedelic culture, atonal and electronic music is much admired. Like the mandala, atonal music or "drone music," is considered helpful in consciousness expansion without

Warning!

Dr. Donald B. Louria, chairman of the New York County Medical Society's narcotics subcommittee, has urged that the Federal marijuana laws be "mitigated." Ideally, what he and his committee would like to see, he told me in his Bellevue office, is a complete recodification of the narcotics laws so that marijuana would be classified as a hallucinogen, rather than a narcotic carrying the same mandatory minimum sentences as narcotics in the opiate category.

Yet, Dr. Louria is "implacably opposed" to the complete legalization of marijuana. For one thing, he said, a person high on marijuana is a dangerous driver. Since there is at present no test for marijuana such as there is for alcohol, there would be "no legal way to get at such drivers—no way to prove they were under the influence so we can punish the guilty ones. We would be opening ourselves up to fantastic dangers without any legal recourse. A person driving under the influence of marijuana is more dangerous than a person under the influence of alcohol. The latter tends to be more aware of his incapacity and less likely to drive at all."

Second, in countries where charas and ganja (particularly potent forms of hemp) are legal, there is a connection between heavy usage of these drugs and mental illness. Dr. Louria emphasized that this is not a serious problem in the U.S., because a milder form of the drug is used. He had observed no cases of marijuana psychoses at Bellevue, such as has been the case with LSD users. But, he said, if marijuana were legalized, then it would be difficult to stop at that point. "You would have to legalize ganja and charas, too. Charas is a small LSD."

He summed up his view of the marijuana laws: "To chastise someone overly severely is wrong unless he's done something really bad, such as having an auto accident while high. Why ruin a college student's life for a minor experimentation with marijuana? The key to this whole problem of drugs is the development of character and ego strength in the kids before they try them. This can only come from a supportive home life and a return to some semblance of belief in the community and religious values as supports for the individual. Making this drug or that drug illegal doesn't solve anything. All you're doing is playing Ping-Pong with drugs; make one illegal and the kids go to another one. Sure, we should tell kids not to use marijuana because it's against the law. Sure, there is always the possibility of excessive use and abuse of marijuana. But we shouldn't get hysterical when kids experiment with it — or let this hysteria obscure the need for balanced, vigorous action to eradicate the really dangerous, addictive drugs."

As for LSD, Dr. Louria said: "In terms of potency, it is the most dangerous drug being used illicitly today. I don't mean to write off the dangers of heroin, but in terms of weight, of the tiny amount taken in a single ingestion, LSD is more dangerous. At Bellevue, we have seen the rate of admissions of persons who have had a reaction to LSD double in the past six months. Increased promiscuous use of LSD means an automatic increase in adverse reactions, which include suicidal tendencies, violence and psychoses, both acute and long-term. Anyone who advocates the administration of LSD, except under the aegis of a psychiatrist trained in its use, is being absolutely irresponsible.

"The spread of illicit use of LSD is largely attributable to the injudicious publicity surrounding the drug, which emphasizes its good aspects but totally ignores its dangers. We are not in a crisis situation now and the reports of widespread use of LSD by college and high-school students have been egregiously exaggerated. But if the increase continues at the present rate, in a year we may have a crisis.

"Let me say that I believe that research with mind-expanding drugs such as mescaline and LSD should be encouraged. The danger of unsupervised use is that it could cause restrictive legislation to be passed that would hinder such research. Those persons who advocate 'licensing' of LSD are doing a tremendous disservice. And by improperly publicizing the drug, they are creating a coterie of psychotic reactions that we otherwise would not have had."—R. R. L.

drugs. Leary has said: "Indian and Arabic music are based on a drone sound—like the voice of a hypnotist. Your consciousness focuses on a band of vibration. The needle of your consciousness follows the band of sound and you go into another phase of reality."

(Unfortunately, he neglected to specify the r.p.m.'s. Would a 33 1/3-r.p.m. record played at 45 r.p.m. set off a bad trip?)

The "low stream" of psychedelic music is found in rock 'n' roll. Just as the association of jazz musicians and marijuana produced a whole literature of pot songs, such as "Muggles," "Sweet Marijuana Brown," "If You're a Viper," "Reefer Song," "Sendin' the Vipers" and "That Funny Reefer Man," so has rock 'n' roll embraced the psychedelic vocabulary and viewpoint. It may take the form of a moralistic song like "Kicks," expressing a reproving view of the girl who took "that magic carpet ride last night" but who wakes up the morning after with the same old world around to get her "up tight" (tense). Others employ the state of being "high" as a poetic metaphor — e.g., "Eight Miles High" by The Byrds and "Rainy Day Women" by Bob Dylan.

A local government official in England called for the banning of both these songs, contending that they "have a subtle message encouraging drug-taking and I feel that it is wrong that they should be sold or broadcast in Britain." Some American stations have indeed banned them, but B.B.C. radio and Rediffusion TV in Britain have given them a big play. It is difficult to see how the following (from "Eight Miles High") encourages drug-taking, or anything else:

*Eight miles high and when you
   touch down
You'll find that it's stranger
   than known
Signs in the streets that say
   where you're going
Are somewhere just being their
   own.*

Other pot hits include "Mr. Tambourine Man," "The Gates of Eden," "Puff the Magic Dragon," "Rubber Soul," "Comin' Down" and, perhaps (who knows?), "Green Grass." Acid rock, a particularly monotonous sound produced by groups bearing such names as The Grateful Dead, Stark Naked and the Car Thieves, The Jefferson Air Planes, Dow Jones and the Industrials, and Big Brother and the Holding Company, is big on the West Coast.

The more conventional rock groups — if that adjective is possible—are beginning to experiment with Indian raga music. "Eight Miles High" shows this influence, as does "Paint It Black," by the Rolling Stones.

The basic instrument in raga music is the sitar, which was used by George Harrison in the Beatles' "Rubber Soul." Other groups, such as the Paul Butterfield Blues Band and The Byrds, employ a specially tuned 12-string guitar. An electric sitar is already in the works for American groups, many of whom think that raga rock is the coming sound.

By Jean Clark, David Crosby and Jim McGuinn ©1966 by Tickson Music Company.

One young musician explained his fascination with raga as rising from "the drone quality of the music. Like the sound a bee makes; a steady hum. It is the simplest pattern in music and it is a challenge to improvise a free melody around the one basic drone." Whether this excursion into Indian music by rock groups will make Ravi Shankar, the Indian singer, another Elvis Presley, or give rise to groups with names like Siva and the Seven Upanishads, remains, to say the least, to be seen.

IN view of the mystical and religious overtones of high psychedelic culture, it is perhaps inevitable that there should be a psychedelic church. It is called the Neo-American Church, a name that, for legal reasons, perhaps, seems an imitation of the Native American Church, an American Indian religious body whose rituals center around the ingestion of peyote, a practice now permitted by the U.S. Government. The Neo-American Church is more eclectic; it considers any hallucinogenic drug as the "True Host."

Recently, Arthur Kleps, a young man with an Apache-brave haircut who is head of the Neo-American Church with the title Chief Boohoo, testified before a Senate subcommittee investigating LSD. While Senator Quentin Burdick (D., N.D.), the lone Senator present, attended to him in baffled silence, Chief Boohoo Kleps explained that his church considers Timothy Leary its spiritual leader—on a par, say, with Christ among the Christians or Gautama among the Buddhists—and regards all his writings as its only formal doctrine.

Kleps accused the Government of "attempting to destroy a genuine religious movement" by regulating hallucinogenic drugs. He predicted that if Leary and other psychedelics went to jail "this country will have a religious war." The Neo-Americans have access to plenty of LSD, Kleps said (although he refused to discuss "the economics of its acquisition"), and "we can render most of the prisons in this country inoperative." How seriously Kleps's threat should be taken is questionable, but it conjures up a vision of the Mutants Militant, fighting a science-fiction war with the whisky-drinking Establishment, sneaking around with eye-droppers full of LSD and squeezing a few drops into the limestone springs of the Jack Daniels distillery, thus incapacitating an unspecifiable portion of the Senate.

In appealing his conviction, Dr. Leary will raise the question of freedom of religion,

Ralph Metzner told me over a drink near the Timothy Leary Defense Fund's publicity offices at 866 U.N. Plaza. Metzner, a thin, studious-looking psychopharmacologist, explained that Leary had converted to Hinduism a year ago while in India. Under the tantric form of Hinduism, each worshiper has a guru or religious instructor whom he must obey in all spiritual matters (it often works out that the guru is the guide on LSD trips). In India the smoking of ganja (the specially cultivated flowering tops and leaves of the female hemp plant, much more potent than the marijuana smoked in this country) and the drinking of bhang (a less potent concoction, similar to marijuana here, made from an infusion of chopped hemp leaves in water or milk) are intimate parts of the Hindu religion, especially in connection with the worship of Siva, the god of destruction. (Bhang and ganja are legal in India, but the most potent product of *Cannabis*, charas, the pure resin of the hemp, known also as hashish, is illegal.)

Although not all Hindus approve of the use of bhang,

66Many think 'raga rock' is the coming sound. Will we have groups with names like Siva and the Seven Upanishads?99

Metzner said, it is sufficiently a part of the various rituals and meditation that the guru might naturally invite his pupil to use it in the course of religious observances. Thus Leary will argue that, by making the possession of marijuana a crime, the Government is interfering with his right to practice his religion.

WITH the demise of The Marijuana Newsletter last year (at the behest of the police, some say), New York's pot culture lacks a full-time voice. Highbrow psychedelics, of course, have The Psychedelic Review, a sober, scholarly, if frequently arcane, quarterly, with a circulation of about 3,000, who presumably turn on with such articles as "Psychedelic Poems from the Tao Te Ching," "Transcendental Experience in Relation to Religion and Psychoses" and "Ayahuasca Drinkers Among the Chama Indians."

If Leary's Psychedelic Review is the Commentary of the movement, a small, neighborhood—but not neighborly—newspaper on the Lower East Side called The East Village Other is its National Enquirer. The Other specializes in reporting police atrocities against the avant-garde. It comes out fortnightly and has a circulation of about 10,000. Its make-up is a cross between The Enquirer and The Old Farmer's Almanac, and it is a freak-up from first page to last.

Freaking it up means to act out your social protest in a bizarre way composed of equal parts of hype (or put-on), seriousness and social paranoia. Occasionally you see a classified ad like this in The Other:

"Grass, hash and acid dealers take notice: Al Woodard is a finger man. Blond, 5 feet 7 inches, boasts of contacts, drinks, street cat. I'm serious. A Service Announcement."

"These ads are taken out by individuals," Walter Bowart, publisher of The Other, told me. "They want to warn others about informers moving among the community."

We were sitting in the back room of The Other's storefront office. Up front, the small staff was arranged at close quarters around a couple of desks and a table. The back was furnished with a bed, a desk and the staff facility. Bowart is an artist who saw an opening for an avant-garde newspaper to serve the Lower East Side's burgeoning artist population. He wears his dark hair Sonja Henie length in back in the East Village manner and speaks with halting intensity in an Oklahoma accent. Fittingly enough, for a boy from Oklahoma, he considers The Other a "frontier newspaper," the city its frontier. He promptly located the marijuana question in the bigger paranoia scene.

"Society is in a headlong plunge into totalitarianism through technology," he told me. "The marijuana cult among youth is only part of a larger revolution. The younger generation is experiencing a spiritual crisis. They are on a quest for benevolent drugs— that is what marijuana is, a benevolent herb—that will enable them to transcend the myth that every young person knows is a lie—the myth of a materialistically oriented society. Pot smokers are a tight criminal element in our society—in the sense that artists are criminal, saints are criminal, holy men and mystics are criminal. Actually, the young marijuana smokers are moral as a child is moral. The heat is on now. The middle-aged, middle-class whisky drinkers who make the laws are panicking. The President is using the marijuana laws to crack down on the anti-Vietnam protesters."

Among its other diversions, The Other features what may be the first pothead comic-strip hero, Captain High, who is described as "a hero among heroes, keeps his head tuned to police broadcasts, ready to intervene in a flash when evil Inspector Noddingact threatens to bust America's mild pot smokers. SUBSEQUENTLY he never comes down!" Whenever Inspector Noddingact is planning a raid on a mild pot smoker, Captain High immediately learns of it by means of his built-in radar, which sends out waves labeled "tense . . . tense . . . tense."

Other enemies of the Captain are the Dope Collector, who is always seeking to steal someone's stash (or cache of marijuana), and Mr. Ballast, whose aim is to bring down the Captain, or get higher than him. (The "bring-down" in the pothead lexicon is the operation of a hostile society which thwarts the pothead's desire to get high.)

OTHER staff members and visitors gathered around to talk of pot and paranoia. Here are some random samples of the conversation:

"You can buy pot in any of the bars on the Lower East Side. It's safe to sell it in bars because all the bars pay off the local cops."

"In California the pot scene is more open. New York, man, that's a deprivation scene. Out in California, well, there's that good, open highway to T.J. [Tijuana]."

"There's hardly anyone under 30 who hasn't tried pot or doesn't know someone who has. If all the kids under 20 in this country put out a newspaper they would give more information than adults could in two years."

"Practically everybody in advertising and fashions and publishing turns on."

"But the fancy rich people who smoke don't want to be caught so they won't do anything about testing the constitutionality of the laws."

"Once I had a job painting some gold leaf on the ceiling of Mrs. ——'s apartment up on Park Avenue. I saw a jar on the table; it was labeled 'marijuana.' I looked in it—and it *was* marijuana. So I just sat down, rolled me a joint and had the maid bring me a cup of coffee."

"You know the reason they don't like people to smoke pot? It's because when you smoke you see through everything, and you say, man, I'm never going to work for them again."

"The pot battle is won. All those young kids under 30 turning on now will become the D.A.'s and the legislators and they'll change the laws."

July 10, 1966

Dr. Leary Starts New 'Religion' With 'Sacramental' Use of LSD

By ROBERT E. DALLOS

Dr. Timothy Leary, the leading exponent of the controversal drug LSD, said yesterday that he had founded a new religion based on the sacramental use of that drug and of peyote and marijuana.

Dr. Leary said the name of the new religion was the League of Spiritual Discovery. He asserted that he would test in the courts the constitutional rights of the members of the sect to use the drugs in their "shrines," at home.

"Like every great religion of the past," he said "we seek to find the divinity within and to express this revelation in a life of glorification and worship of God. These ancient goals we define in the metaphor of the present — turn-on, tune-in and drop-out."

He made his announcement at a press conference in the New York Advertising Club, 23 Park Avenue. Dressed in a collarless white shirt, white pants and brown loafers, Dr. Leary wore a small pink button on the middle of his chest. It read "Legalize Spiritual Discovery," the letters L., S. and

The New York Times

Dr. Timothy Leary at his news conference yesterday, with button saying "Legalize Spiritual Discovery."

D. outsized. His long graying hair drooped over his ears and he explained that his hair was "in the state it was in when I woke up this morning."

Dr. Leary, who is free on bail in two narcotics cases, said the new religion had a 15-member board of guides, all of whom had "resigned from their jobs and were dedicating their lives to the religion." All live with Dr. Leary at his home in Millbrook, N. Y.

The sect also has 411 members, he said, who had been "initiated" by the governors. In the next two to three years, he added, he expects more than a million persons to join.

Dr. Leary, who had been dismissed from the Harvard University faculty as a result of his experiments with drugs causing hallucinations, said the new religion's first "public worship service, a psychedelic celebration," would be held tonight at the Village Theater, Second Avenue and Sixth Street. Subsequent "services," he said, will be held at the theater each Tuesday evening with seats costing $3 each.

He said no drugs would be provided at the public services.

In 1964 the California Supreme Court ruled that the use of peyote in religious ceremonies did not violate state narcotics laws and set aside the convictions of three Navajo Indians who had been arrested in 1962 for sipping peyote tea.

Dr. Leary explained the six-word motto of the religion.

"Turn-on means to go beyond your secular tribal mind to contact the many levels of divine energy which lie within your consciousness; tune in means to express and to communicate your new revelations in visible acts of glorification, gratitude and beauty; drop out means to detach yourself harmoniously, tenderly and gracefully from worldly commitments until your entire life is dedicated to worship and search."

Tax-Free Status Sought

Dr. Leary said the new religion would seek tax-free status, to "play the American social game of other religions."

"Our material life is completely dependent upon the use of chemicals," he said. "It is inevitable that chemicals will be used to develop man's neurological and spiritual potentials."

Dr. Leary said members of the religion would "turn on" with LSD every seven days because it is not effective more often but would have marijuana sessions for an hour a day.

Dr. Leary is currently appealing a Federal sentence of 30-years and $30,000 fine for possession of untaxed marijuana in Texas, and is under indictment in Westchester County on charges of possessing LSD and marijuana at his headquarters, the Castalia Foundation in Millbrook. He was released on bail of $2,500 on each case.

September 20, 1966

Hoover Scores Trend In Hairdos and Clothes

WASHINGTON, Sept. 21 (UPI) — J. Edgar Hoover today deplored hairdos and clothing styles that he said sometimes made it difficult to tell the boys from the girls.

Mr. Hoover, deploring this and other current trends, in House testimony published today, said corrective steps should start in the family but that unfortunately they were not being taken.

The F.B.I. chief said most youths were sound, and the troublemakers were in the minority. He said he saw many cleancut youngsters on tours of the F.B.I. headquarters and encouraged them to apply for employment there after they graduated.

September 22, 1966

High Court Bars Review Of Ruling on Long Hair

WASHINGTON, Nov. 14 (AP)—The Supreme Court refused today to get into the argument over the propriety of extra-long hair and beards on students.

Three men students of the Richmond Professional Institute asked the highest tribunal to strike down an institute order that they get shaves and haircuts before being registered for a new term.

The appeal to the Supreme Court was filed by Norman Thomas Marshall of Richmond, Robert D. Shofner of Charlottesville, and Salvatore Federico of Arlington, Va.

In New York, a spokesman for the High School Principals Association said: "The Court's statement to the effect that the question is one to be determined by common sense rather than by courts and that schools obviously have the authority to make rules on the matter expressed the views which we hope will now be adopted by our own superintendent of schools."

November 15, 1966

DRESS OF TEEN-AGERS UPSETS ADULTS MOST

Special to The New York Times
MEDFORD, Mass. — Miniskirts, tight pants and tight sweaters, excessive make-up and boys' long hair are the main cause of disagreement between youngsters and adults, Tufts University found in a survey of five New England communities.

The study of youth-adult interaction was sponsored by the New England School Development Council, in cooperation with the Lincoln Filene Center for Citizenship and Public Affairs at Tufts.

The young people and their parents and teachers had few significant disagreements on such matters as draft-card burning, civil rights demonstrations, classroom behavior, and school regulations.

However, 60 per cent of the students, teachers and parents polled cited dress and hairdos as the major cause of disagreements.

The study was directed by Dr. William C. Kvaraceus, professor of education at Tufts and director of youth studies at the Lincoln Filene Center.

The communities were Wilton, Conn.; Plymouth, N. H.; and Quincy, Wellesley and Westboro, Mass.

January 11, 1967

The 'Hashbury' Is the Capital Of the Hippies

By HUNTER S. THOMPSON

SAN FRANCISCO.

IN 1965 Berkeley was the axis of what was just beginning to be called the "New Left." Its leaders were radical, but they were also deeply committed to the society they wanted to change. A prestigious faculty committee said the Berkeley activists were the vanguard of "a moral revolution among the young," and many professors approved.

Now, in 1967, there is not much doubt that Berkeley has gone through a revolution of some kind, but the end result is not exactly what the original leaders had in mind. Many one-time activists have forsaken politics entirely and turned to drugs. Others have even forsaken Berkeley. During 1966, the hot center of revolutionary action on the Coast began moving across the bay to San Francisco's Haight-Ashbury district, a run down Victorian neighborhood of about 40 square blocks between the Negro/Fillmore district and Golden Gate Park.

The "Hashbury" is the new capital of what is rapidly becoming a drug culture. Its denizens are not called radicals or beatniks, but "hippies"—and perhaps as many as half are refugees from Berkeley and the old North Beach scene, the cradle and the casket of the so-called Beat Generation.

The other half of the hippy population is too young to identify with Jack Kerouac, or even with Mario Savio. Their average age is about 20, and most are native Californians. The North Beach types of the late nineteen-fifties were not nearly as provincial as the Haight-Ashbury types are today. The majority of beatniks who flocked into San Francisco 10 years ago were transients from the East and Midwest. The literary-artistic nucleus — Kerouac, Ginsberg, et al—was a package deal from New York. San Francisco was only a stop on the big circuit: Tangier, Paris, Greenwich Village, Tokyo and India. The senior beats had a pretty good idea what was going on in the world; they read newspapers, traveled constantly and had friends all over the globe.

THE word "hip" translates roughly as "wise" or "tuned-in." A hippy is somebody who "knows" what's really happening, and who adjusts or grooves with it. Hippies despise phoniness; they want to be open, honest, loving and free. They reject the plastic pretense of 20th-century America, preferring to go back to the "natural life," like Adam and Eve. They reject any kinship with the Beat Generation on the ground that "those cats were negative, but our thing is positive." They also reject politics, which is "just another game." They

don't like money, either, or any kind of aggressiveness.

A serious problem in writing about the Haight-Ashbury is that most of the people you have to talk to are involved, one way or another, in the drug traffic. They have good reason to be leery of strangers who ask questions. A 22-year-old student was recently sentenced to two years in prison for telling an undercover narcotics agent where to buy some marijuana. "Love" is the password in the Haight-Ashbury, but paranoia is the style. Nobody wants to go to jail.

At the same time, marijuana is everywhere. People smoke it on the sidewalks, in doughnut shops, sitting in parked cars or lounging on the grass in Golden Gate Park. Nearly everyone on the streets between 20 and 30 is a "head," a user, either of marijuana, LSD, or both. To refuse a proffered "joint" is to risk being labeled a "nark"—narcotics agent—a threat and a menace to almost everybody.

With a few loud exceptions, it is only the younger hippies who see themselves as a new breed. "A com-

---

HUNTER S. THOMPSON is the author of "Hell's Angels," about the California motorcycle gang. Until last fall a resident of the Haight-Ashbury, he now lives in Aspen, Colo., and is working on a first novel.

pletely new thing in this world, man." The ex-beatniks among them, many of whom are now making money off the new scene, incline to the view that hippies are, in fact, second-generation beatniks and that everything genuine in the Haight-Ashbury is about to be swallowed—like North Beach and the Village—in a wave of publicity and commercialism.

Haight Street, the Great White Way of what the local papers call "Hippieland," is already dotted with stores catering mainly to the tourist trade. Few hippies can afford a pair of $20 sandals or a "mod outfit" for $67.50. Nor can they afford the $3.50 door charge at the Fillmore Auditorium and the Avalon Ballroom, the twin wombs of the "psychedelic, San Francisco, acid-rock sound." Both the Fillmore and the Avalon are jammed every weekend with borderline hippies who don't mind paying for the music and the light shows. There is always a sprinkling of genuine, barefoot, freaked-out types on the dance floor, but few of them pay to get in. They arrive with the musicians or have other good connections.

Neither of the dance palaces is within walking distance of the Hashbury, especially if you're stoned, and since only a few of the hippies have contacts in the psychedelic power structure, most of them spend their weekend nights either drifting around on Haight Street or loading up on acid—LSD—in somebody's pad. Some of the rock bands play free concerts in Golden Gate Park for the benefit of those brethren who can't afford the dances. But beyond an occasional Happening in the park, the Haight-Ashbury scene is almost devoid of anything "to do"—at least by conventional standards. An at-home entertainment is nude parties at which celebrants paint designs on each other.

There are no hippy bars, for instance, and only one restaurant above the level of a diner or a lunch counter. This is a reflection of the drug culture, which has no use for booze and regards food as a necessity to be acquired at the least possible expense. A "family" of hippies will work for hours over an exotic stew or curry in a communal kitchen, but the idea of paying $3 for a meal in a restaurant is out of the question.

Some hippies work, others live on money from home and many are full-time beggars. The Post Office is a major source of hippy income. Jobs like sorting mail don't require much thought or effort. A hippy named Admiral Love of the Psychedelic Rangers delivers special - delivery letters at night. The admiral is in his mid-20's and makes enough money to support an apartmentful of younger hippies who depend on him for their daily bread.

There is also a hippy-run employment agency on Haight Street and anyone needing part - time labor or some kind of specialized work can

call and order as many freaks as he needs; they might look a bit weird, but many are far more capable than most "temporary help," and vastly more interesting to have around.

Those hippies who don't work can easily pick up a few dollars a day panhandling along Haight Street. The fresh influx of curiosity-seekers has proved a great boon to the legion of psychedelic beggars. During several days of roaming around the area, I was touched so often that I began to keep a supply of quarters in my pocket so I wouldn't have to haggle over change. The panhandlers are usually barefoot, always young and never apologetic. They'll share what they collect anyway, so it seems entirely reasonable that strangers should share with them.

The best show on Haight Street is usually on the sidewalk in front of the Drog Store, a new coffee bar at the corner of Masonic Street. The Drog Store features an all-hippy revue that runs day and night. The acts change sporadically, but nobody cares. There will always be at least one man with long hair and sunglasses playing a wooden pipe of some kind. He will be wearing either a Dracula cape, a long Buddhist robe,

or a Sioux Indian costume. There will also be a hairy blond fellow wearing a Black Bart cowboy hat and a spangled jacket that originally belonged to a drum major in the 1949 Rose Bowl parade. He will be playing the bongo drums. Next to the drummer will be a dazed-looking girl wearing a blouse (but no bra) and a plastic mini-skirt, slapping her thighs to the rhythm of it all.

These three will be the nucleus of the show. Backing them up will be an all-star cast of freaks, every one of them stoned. They will be stretched out on the sidewalk, twitching and babbling in time to the music. Now and then somebody will fall out of the audience and join the revue; perhaps a Hell's Angel or some grubby, chain-draped impostor who never owned a motorcycle in his life. Or maybe a girl wrapped in gauze or a thin man with wild eyes who took an overdose of acid nine days ago and changed himself into a raven. For those on a quick tour of the Hashbury, the Drog Store revue is a must.

MOST of the local action is beyond the reach of anyone without access to drugs. There are four or five bars a nervous square might relax in, but one is a Lesbian place, another is a hangout for brutal-looking leather fetishists and the others are old neighborhood taverns full of brooding middle-aged drunks. Prior to the hippy era there were three good Negro-run jazz bars on Haight Street, but they soon went out of style. Who needs jazz or even beer, when you can sit down on a public curbstone, drop a pill in your mouth, and hear fantastic music for hours at a time in your own head? A cap of good acid costs $5, and for that you can hear the Universal Symphony, with God singing solo and the Holy Ghost on drums.

Drugs have made formal entertainment obsolete in the Hashbury, but only until somebody comes up with something appropriate to the new style of the neighborhood. This summer will see the opening of the new Straight Theater, formerly the Haight Theater, featuring homosexual movies for the trade, meetings, concerts, dances. "It's going to be a kind of hippy community center," said Brent Dangerfield, a young radio engineer from Salt Lake City who stopped off in San Francisco on his way to a job in Hawaii and now is a partner in the Straight. When I asked Dangerfield how old he was he had to think for a minute. "I'm 22," he said finally, "but I used to be much older."

Another new divertissement, maybe, will be a hippy bus line running up and down Haight Street, housed in a 1930 Fagol bus—a huge, lumbering vehicle that might have been the world's first house trailer. I rode in it one afternoon with the driver, a young hippy named Tim Thibeau who proudly displayed a bathtub under one of the rear seats. The bus was a spectacle even on Haight Street: people stopped, stared and cheered as we rumbled by, going nowhere at all. Thibeau honked the horn and waved. He was from Chicago, he said, but when he got out of the Army he stopped in San Francisco and decided to stay. He was living, for the moment, on unemployment insurance, and his plans for the future were hazy. "I'm in no hurry," he said. "Right now I'm just taking it easy, just floating along." He smiled and reached for a beer can in the Fagol's icebox.

Dangerfield and Thibeau reflect the blind optimism of the younger hippy element. They see themselves as the vanguard of a new way of life in America — the psychedelic way — where love abounds and work is fun and people help each other. The young hippies are confident that things are going their way.

The older hippies are not so sure. They've been waiting a long time for the world to go their way, and those most involved in the hip scene are hedging their bets this time. "That back to nature scene is okay when you're 20," said one. "But when you're looking at 35 you want to know something's happening to you."

Ed Denson, at 27, is an ex-beatnik, ex-Goldwaterite, ex-Berkeley radical and currently the manager of a successful rock band called Country Joe and the Fish. His home and headquarters is a complex of rooms above a liquor store in Berkeley. One room is an art studio, another is an office; there is also a kitchen, a bedroom and several sparsely furnished areas without definition.

Denson is deeply involved in the hippy music scene, but insists he's not a hippy. "I'm very pessimistic about where this thing is going," he said. "Right now it's good for a lot of people. It's still very open. But I have to look back at the Berkeley scene. There was a tremendous optimism there, too, but look where all that went. The Beat Generation? Where are they now? What about hula-hoops? Maybe this hippy thing is more than a fad; maybe the whole world is turning on but I'm not optimistic. Most of the hippies I know don't really understand what kind of a world they're living in. I get tired of hearing about what beautiful people we all are. If the hippies were more realistic they'd stand a better chance of surviving."

MOST hippies take the question of survival for granted, but it's becoming increasingly obvious as the neighborhood fills with penniless heads, that there is simply not enough food and lodging to go around. A partial solution may come from a group called the "Diggers," who have been called the "worker-priests" of the hippy movement and the "invisible government" of the Hashbury. The Diggers are young and aggressively pragmatic; they have set up free lodging centers, free soup kitchens and free clothing distribution centers. They comb the neighborhood soliciting donations of everything from money to stale bread to camping equipment. Diggers' signs are posted in local stores, asking for donations of hammers, saws, shovels, shoes and anything else that vagrant hippies might use to make themselves at least partially self-supporting.

The name and spirit derive from small groups of 17th-century English rural revolutionaries, called both Diggers and True Levelers, who had a number of Socialist ideas. Money should be abolished, communal farms could support all those willing to work them, and individual ownership of land would be outlawed. The Diggers were severely harassed and the movement eventually caved in under the weight of public opprobrium.

The Hashbury Diggers have fared a bit better, but the demand for food and lodging is beginning to exceed the supply. For a while, the Diggers were able to serve three meals, however meager, each afternoon in Golden Gate Park. But as the word got around, more and more hippies showed up to eat, and the Diggers were forced to roam far afield to get food. Occasionally there were problems, as when Digger chieftain Emmett Grogan, 23, called a local butcher a "Fascist pig and a coward" when he refused to donate meat scraps. The butcher whacked Grogan with the flat side of his meat cleaver.

The Digger ethic of mass sharing goes along with the American Indian motif that is basic to the Hashbury scene. The cult of "tribalism" is regarded by many of the older hippies as the key to survival. Poet Gary Snyder, a hippy guru, sees a "back to the land" movement as the answer to the food and lodging problem. He urges hippies to move out of the cities, form tribes, purchase land and live communally in remote areas. He cites a hippy "clan" calling itself the Maha-Lila as a model (though the clan still dwells in the Hashbury):

"Well, now," Snyder says, "like, you are asking how it's going to work. Well, the Maha-Lila is a group of about three different families who have sort of pooled their resources, which are not very great. But they have decided to play together and to work together and to take care of each other and that means all of them have ways of getting a small amount of bread, which they share. And other people contribute a little money when it comes in. And then they work together on creative projects, like they're working together on a lightshow right now for a poetry reading that we're going to give. And they consider themselves a kind of extended family or clan.

"That's the model. They relate it to a larger sense of the tribe, which is loose, but for the time being everybody has to be able—from time to time—to do some little job. The thing that makes it different is that you don't have a very tight monogamous family unit, but a slightly larger unit where the sharing is greater."

The tribal concept makes a lot better sense than simply depending on the Diggers. There are indications, however, that the youthful provincialism of the Haight-Ashbury is due for a forced consciousness-expansion. For the past few months, the scene has been filling up with would-be hippies from other parts of the country, primarily Los Angeles and New York. The real influx is expected this summer. The city is rife with rumors, reliable and otherwise, that anywhere from 50,000 to 200,000 "indigent young people" will descend on San Francisco as soon as the school year ends.

The Diggers are appalled at the prospect. "Where are they going to stay?" says one. "What are they going to do?" A girl who works in one of the Digger kitchens shrugs and says: "The Diggers will continue to receive the casualties of the love generation." Local officials, from the Mayor down, are beginning to panic. Civic leaders in the Haight-Ashbury have suggested that sleeping facilities be provided in Golden Gate Park or

in nearby Kezar Stadium but Police Chief Tom Cahill said no.

"Law and order will prevail," he insisted. "There will be no sleeping in the park. There are no sanitation facilities and if we let them camp there we would have a tremendous health problem. Hippies are no asset to the community. These people do not have the courage to face the reality of life. They are trying to escape. Nobody should let their young children take part in this hippy thing."

In March, the city's Health Director, Dr. Ellis Sox, sent a task force of inspectors on a door-to-door sweep of the Haight-Ashbury. Reports of as many as 200 people living in one house or 50 in one apartment had stirred rumors of impending epidemics in the neighborhood. In a two-day blitz, eight teams of inspec-

tors checked roughly 1,400 buildings and issued a total of 65 deadline notices to repair sanitation faults. But only 16 of the 65 notices, according to The San Francisco Chronicle, were issued to occupants "whose bizarre dress and communal living habits could class them as hippies."

Dr. Sox had no choice but to back off. "The situation is not as bad as we thought," he said. "There has been a deterioration [of sanitation] in the Haight-Ashbury, but the hippies did not contribute much more to it than other members of the neighborhood." Dr. Sox went on to deny that his mass inspection was part of a general campaign against weirdos, but nobody seemed to believe him.

The Haight-Ashbury Neighborhood Council, a nonhippy group of permanent residents, denounced Dr. Sox for his "gratuitous criticism of our community." The council accused city officials of "creating an artificial problem" and harassing the hippies out of "personal and official" prejudice.

As recently as 1962, the Haight-Ashbury was a drab, working-class district, slowly filling with Negroes and so plagued by crime and violence that residents formed vigilante patrols. Housewives were mugged on the way to the grocery store, teenagers were slashed and stomped in gang rumbles, and every drunk on Haight Street was fair game for local jack-rollers.

Now, with the coming of the drug culture, even the squarest of the neighborhood old-timers say the streets are safer than they have been for years. Burglaries are still a problems but violence is increasingly rare. It is hard to find anyone outside the hippy community who will say that psychedelic drugs have made the neighborhood a better place to live. But it's even harder to find a person who wouldn't rather step over a giggling freak on the sidewalk than worry about hoodlums with switch-blades. The fact that the hippies and the squares have worked out such a peaceful coexistence seems to baffle the powers at City Hall.

A LOT of cheap labels describe what is happening in the Hashbury, but none of them make much sense: the Love Generation, the Happening Generation, the Combine. Generation and even the LSD Generation. The last is the best of the lot, but in the interest of accuracy it should probably be amended to the Head Generation.

A "head," in the language of hip, is a user of psychedelic drugs: LSD, marijuana ("grass"), mescaline, peyote, methedrine, benzedrine, and a half-dozen others that are classified in the trade as mind-stimulating, consciousness-expanding, or "head" drugs. At the other end of the spectrum are "body" drugs: opium, heroin, barbiturates and even alcohol.

WUXTRY—Across the street from the Drog Store (sic), a hippy sells a local journal of opinion. The Hashbury residents have almost no interest in politics, radical or otherwise.

66The Hashbury is full of people whose minds
have have been jerked around savagely
by drugs that were supposed to induce euphoria. Another
hazard is the widespread tendency to mix
two or three drugs at one time.99

These are basically depressants, while head drugs are stimulants. But neither type comes with a manufacturer's guarantee, and the Hashbury is full of people whose minds have been jerked around savagely by drugs that were supposed to induce peaceful euphoria.

Another hazard is the widespread tendency to mix two or three drugs at one time. Acid and alcohol can be a lethal combination, causing fits of violence, suicidal depression and a general freak-out that ends in jail or a hospital.

There is widespread concern, at least in San Francisco, about the dangers of so many people using so much LSD. A doctor at San Francisco General Hospital says there are at least 10,000 hippies in the Haight-Ashbury, and that about four of them a day wind up in a psychiatric ward on bad trips. He estimates that acid-heads make up only 1½ per cent of the city's population, but that the figure for the Haight-Ashbury is more like 100 per cent.

The estimate is absurd; if every hippy in the Hashbury took acid every day, the percentage of users in the neighborhood would still be less than 50 per cent. Many of the local squares try grass from time to time, but few have worked up an appetite for LSD; the difference in potency is roughly the same as the difference between beer and grain alcohol. Even among hippies, anything more than one dose of acid a week is considered excessive.

Most heads are relatively careful about their drug diets, but in recent months the area has attracted so many young, inexperienced hippies that public freak-outs are a fairly routine thing. Neighborhood cops complain that acidheads throw themselves in front of moving cars, strip naked in grocery stores and run through plate-glass windows. On weekdays, the action is about on a par with Macdougal Street in Greenwich Village, but weekend hippies and nervous *voyeurs* from the suburbs make Saturdays and Sundays a nightmarish traffic jam. The sidewalks are so crowded that even a mild freak-out is likely to cause a riot.

Municipal buses no longer use Haight Street on weekends; they were rerouted after mobs of hippies staged sit-down strikes in the street, called mill-ins, which brought all traffic to a standstill. The only buses still running regularly along Haight Street are those from the Gray Line, which recently added "Hippieland" to its daytime sightseeing tour of San Francisco. It was billed as "the only foreign tour within the continental limits of the United States" and was an immediate hit with tourists who thought the Haight-Ashbury was a human zoo. The only sour note on the tour was struck by the occasional hippy who would run alongside the bus, holding up a mirror.

LAST year in Berkeley, hard-core political radicals who had always viewed hippies as spiritual allies began to worry about the long-range implications of the Haight-Ashbury scene. Students who once were angry activists were content to lie back in their pads and smile at the world through a fog of marijuana smoke—or, worse, to dress like clowns or American Indians and stay zonked for days at a time on LSD.

Even in Berkeley, political rallies during 1966 had overtones of music, madness and absurdity. Instead of picket signs and revolutionary slogans, more and more demonstrators carried flowers, balloons and colorful posters featuring slogans from Dr. Timothy Leary, the high priest of acid. The drug culture was spreading faster than political activists realized. Unlike the dedicated radicals who emerged from the Free Speech Movement, the hippies were more interested in dropping out of society than they were in changing it. They were generally younger than the political types, and the press dismissed them as the "pot left," a frivolous gang of druggies and sex kooks who were only along for the ride.

Then Ronald Reagan was elected Governor by almost a million-vote plurality. Shortly afterward, Clark Kerr was fired as president of the University of California—a direct result of Reagan's victory. In that same November, the G.O.P. gained 50 seats in Congress and served a clear warning on the Johnson Administration that despite all the headlines about Berkeley and the New Left, most of the electorate was a lot more hawkish, hard-nosed and conservative than the White House antennae had indicated.

The lesson was not lost on the hippies, many of whom still considered themselves at least part-time political activists. One of the most obvious casualties of the 1966 elections was the New Left's illusion of its own leverage. The radical-hippy alliance had been counting on the voters to repudiate the "right-wing, warmonger" elements in Congress, but instead it was the "liberal" Democrats who got stomped.

So it is no coincidence that the Haight-Ashbury scene developed very suddenly in the winter of 1966-1967 from the quiet, neo-Bohemian enclave that it had been for four or five years to the crowded, defiant dope fortress that it is today. The hippies, who had never really believed they were the wave of the future anyway, saw the election returns as brutal confirmation of the futility of fighting the establishment on its own terms.

There had to be a whole new scene, they said, and the only way to do it was to make the big move—either figuratively or literally—from Berkeley to the Haight-Ashbury, from pragmatism to mysticism, from politics to dope, from the hang-ups of protest to the peaceful disengagement of love, nature and spontaneity.

The credo of the Haight-Ashbury was expressed, about as well as it can be, by Joyce Francisco, 23-year-old advertising manager of the new hippy newspaper, The San Francisco Oracle. She was talking a few months ago to a columnist from the establishment press, trying to explain what the hippy phenomenon meant: "I love the whole world," she said. "I am the divine mother, part of Buddha, part of God, part of everything."

"How do you live?" the columnist asked.

"From meal to meal. I have no money, no possessions. Money is beautiful only when it's flowing; when it piles up it's a hang-up. We take care of each other. There's always something to buy beans and rice for the group, and someone always sees that I get grass or acid. I was in a mental hospital once because I tried to conform and play the game. But now I'm free and happy."

Next question: "Do you use drugs often?"

"Fairly. When I find myself becoming confused I drop out and take a dose of acid. It's a short cut to reality; it throws you right into it. Everyone should take it, even children. Why shouldn't they be enlightened early, instead of waiting till they're old? Human beings need total freedom. That's where God is at. We need to shed hypocrisy, dishonesty, phoniness and go back to the purity of our childhood values."

The columnist then asked if Miss Francisco ever prayed.

"Oh, yes," she said. "I pray in the morning sun. It nourishes me with its energy so I can spread my love and beauty and nourish others. I never pray *for* anything; I don't need anything. Whatever turns me on is a sacrament: LSD, sex, my bells, my colors . . . that is the holy communion, you dig?"

The columnist wasn't sure if she did or not, but she passed on the interview for the benefit of those readers who might. Many did. Anyone who thinks all the hippies in the Bay Area are living in the Hashbury might just as well leave his head in the sand.

IN normal circumstances, the mushrooming popularity of psychedelics would be a main factor in any article on hippies. But the vicious excesses of our drug laws make it impossible, or at least inhuman, to document the larger story. A journalist dealing with heads is caught in a strange dilemma. The only way to write honestly about the scene is to be part of it. If there is one quick truism about psychedelic drugs, it is that anyone who tries to write about them without firsthand experience is a fool and a fraud.

Yet to write from experience is an admission of felonious guilt; it is also a potential betrayal of people whose only "crime" is the smoking of a weed that grows wild all over the world but the possession of which, in California, carries a minimum sentence of two years in prison for a second offense and a minimum of five years for a third. So, despite the fact that the whole journalism industry is full of unregenerate heads —just as many journalists were hard drinkers during Prohibition—it is not very likely that the frank, documented truth about the psychedelic underworld, for good or ill, will be illuminated at any time soon in the public prints.

If I were to write, for instance, that I recently spent 10 days in San Francisco and was stoned almost constantly . . . that in fact I was stoned for nine nights out of 10 and that nearly everyone I dealt with smoked marijuana as casually as they drank beer . . . and if I said many of the people I talked to were not freaks and dropouts, but competent professionals with bank accounts and spotless reputations . . . and that I was amazed to find psychedelic drugs in homes where I would never have mentioned them two years ago —if all this were true, I could write an ominous screed to the effect that

"Rumor is rife that anywhere from 50,000 to 200,000 'indigent young people' will descend on San Francisco as soon as the school year ends."

the hippy phenomenon in the Haight-Ashbury is little more than a freak show and a soft-sell advertisement for what is happening all around them . . . that drugs, orgies and freak-outs are almost as common to a much larger and more discreet cross section of the Bay Area's respectable, upward-mobile society as they are to the colorful drop-outs of San Francisco's new Bohemia.

There is no shortage of documentation for the thesis that the current Haight-Ashbury scene is only the orgiastic tip of a great psychedelic iceberg that is already drifting in the sea lanes of the Great Society. Submerged and uncountable is the mass of intelligent, capable heads who want nothing so much as peaceful anonymity. In a nervous society where a man's image is frequently more important than his reality, the only people who can afford to advertise their drug menus are those with nothing to lose.

And these — for the moment, at least—are the young lotus-eaters, the barefoot mystics and hairy freaks of the Haight-Ashbury—all those primitive Christians, peaceful nay-sayers and half-deluded "flower children" who refuse to participate in a society which looks to them like a mean, calculated and soul-destroying hoax.

As recently as two years ago, many of the best and brightest of them were passionately involved in the realities of political, social and economic life in America. But the scene has changed since then and political activism is going out of style. The thrust is no longer for "change" or "progress" or "revolution," but merely to escape, to live on the far perimeter of a world that might have

been — perhaps should have been — and strike a bargain for survival on purely personal terms.

The flourishing hippy scene is a matter of desperate concern to the political activists. They see a whole generation of rebels drifting off to a drugged limbo, ready to accept almost anything as long as it comes with enough "soma."

STEVE DECANIO, an ex-Berkeley activist now doing graduate work at M.I.T., is a good example of a legion of young radicals who know they have lost their influence but have no clear idea how to get it back again. "This alliance between hippies and political radicals is bound to break up," he said in a recent letter. "There's just too big a jump from the slogan of 'Flower Power' to the deadly realm of politics. Something has to give, and drugs are too ready-made as opiates of the people for the bastards (the police) to fail to take advantage of it."

Decanio spent three months in various Bay Area jails as a result of his civil rights activities and now he is lying low for a while, waiting for an opening. "I'm spending an amazing amount of time studying," he wrote. "It's mainly because I'm scared; three months on the bottom of humanity's trash heap got to me worse than it's healthy to admit. The country is going to hell, the left is going to pot, but not me. I still want to figure out a way to win."

Meanwhile, like most other disappointed radicals, he is grimly amused at the impact the hippies are having on the establishment. The panic among San Francisco officialdom at the prospect of 200,000 hippies flocking into the Hashbury this summer is one of the few things that ex-Berkeley radicals can still laugh at. Decanio's vision of the crisis was not written as prophecy, but considering the hidden reality of the situation, it may turn out that way: "I can see Mayor Shelley standing on the steps of the Civic Center and shouting into TV microphones, 'The people cry bread! Bread! Let them turn on!'"

May 14, 1967

---

30 Seized in Philadelphia As 2,500 Stage a 'Be-In'

PHILADELPHIA, May 14 (AP)—About 2,500 "hippies" and "teeny-boppers" gathered in front of Independence Hall this afternoon for what was billed as a "Happy Un-Birthday Be-In."

Some 30 members of the crowd were hauled off by the police after an incident that ended in the blocking of a police car.

James Kennedy of the Police Juvenile Aid Division said the brief sit-in around his unmarked police car began when he attempted to take a youth to the police station for questioning in connection with suspected possession of marijuana.

A crowd gathered around the car and a girl yelled, "Down, everybody, down," and they sat down, a newsman on the scene said.

The "be-in" was described as a gathering organized for unorganized activity.

May 15, 1967

Suit Over Haircut Settled

SAN DIEGO, Calif., May 30 (AP) — Sixteen-year-old Donald Demoulin, who said a teacher had cut his hair with sheep shears, won an out-of-court settlement yesterday, while jurors deliberated the suit he had brought against Karl Bakken, Fallbrook High School teacher. The amount of the settlement was not disclosed. Donald and his mother had sued Mr. Bakken on the ground that the haircut allegedly administered in January, 1966, was an assault and battery. They asked $30,000 damages. Mr. Bakken said he had permission from the school administration to cut the youth's hair.

May 31, 1967

Pravda Considers Hippies Promising Revolutionaries

MOSCOW, June 5 (UPI) The communist party newspaper Pravda has udged hippies to be good revolutionaries.

The hippies are out to change "the base and foul world in which Americans now live," Yuri Zhukov, a Pravda commentator, wrote in an article from New York.

Unlike the beatniks, the hippies "do not have the feeling that atomic death is inevitable." "They do not simply reject modern American society—they want to change it," Mr. Zhukov said.

June 6, 1967

The Runaway: 'It Can't Happen to Me,' Parents Say, but It Does

By JOAN COOK

GEORGIA PRIETO, please contact your mother. It's important. If anyone knows Georgia, please tell her to contact her mother."

This ad, which appeared recently in the personal column of "The East Village Other," is similar to hundreds that have been published around the country this summer and is indicative of the growing problem of runaway children.

So many forlorn parents are trying to get in touch with missing children that a new underground paper, "The Middle-Class Standard," has joined the ranks of publications in San Francisco's Haight-Ashbury district, the number one mecca for migrating hippies. Most of the paper is devoted to ads placed by parents who are trying to find their missing children.

In New York, at any given moment, there are an estimated 4,000 runaways under the age of 18. This year there has been an 8 per cent increase in the number of missing persons reported in the city, and, according to Capt. Joseph Lynch, head of the Police Department's Missing Persons Unit, the under-18 population accounts for most of the increase.

Leaving Home Is Easy

Nationally, the runaway problem is even more acute. Attracted by easy travel, advertisements that emphasize go now, pay later, and the aura of glamour invested by mass media in Greenwich Village, the East Village, Haight-Ashbury (Hashbury), Hollywood and Miami Beach,

youngsters hop from one city to another, using thumb and credit cards as passports to teen-age "freedom."

"Statistics are hard to come by, but there is reason to believe that as many as half-a-million kids left home last year," Rabbi Samuel Schrage, the short, voluble assistant executive director of the New York City Youth Board, said recently. "And there are thousands of parents all over the country who haven't heard from their kids for months. This creates terrific problems."

Raising his voice to be heard above the din of traffic outside his crowded Lower East Side office, Rabbi Schrage explained that while the ghetto runaway had always been with us, today's runaway was increasingly a middle-class concern.

"Too many middle-class parents are too cocksure of themselves," he said. "They say 'It can't happen to me,' but it does. And once gone, it's easier to find a pedigreed dog in this country than a runaway kid."

"The mobility of this country makes it virtually impossible to find a youngster who is moving from place to place," Rabbi Schrage said. "Besides, this is a social, not a criminal problem. There is no central means of communication for parents or kids who would like to get together but maybe need a little shove, a little follow-up."

"Some of these kids are running for their lives," said Chessor Bowles, who has 26 years of experience in counseling youths on the run. Mr. Bowles recently retired

as head counselor at William Sloane House, a residence hotel at 365 West 34th Street operated by the Young Men's Christian Association. Every night from 5 to 8 of its 1,500 beds are set aside for runaways.

"I've talked to all kinds, including plenty from Ivy League colleges and the Social Register," Mr. Bowles recalled in a telephone interview from his Vermont home. "Their problems are different from the rest. Some of them are being slowly smothered to death. They're trying to cut the apron strings, to accomplish something, anything on their own. It's hard [for parents] to understand because frequently they don't understand it themselves and express their anger and despair in very subtle ways."

Sociology of Hippies

(A recent sampling of 50 hippies by a San Francisco State College graduate student in sociology found that 90 per cent came from middle- and upper-class families and that 68 per cent had had some college education.)

"These are very strung-out kids with individual hang-ups," said Jim Fouratt, a 23-year-old hippie leader and former Harvard student, describing the modern runaway. An actor, Mr. Fouratt heads the Communication Company, which mimeographs daily bulletins for the East Village hippie community.

"We're particularly concerned about the 15, 16 and 17-year-old middle-class kids who find more sophisticated ways of running away but

are actually very naive about living," he said.

A recent case in point, he said, was that of a 16-year-old who was taken in off the street by an older girl who offered her a place to stay for the night.

"The kid was sexually abused by both men and women, shot full of amphetamine [an addictive stimulant taken in pill form] and God knows what else and kept there for nearly two weeks," Jim Fouratt said. "This is exactly the sort of thing we don't want to have happen, but this is a rough, tough neighborhood."

Frequently, it is something trivial in the battle of wills between youngsters and parents that triggers the actual runaway.

"My mother kept bugging me about school and staying out late," said Martie, a 16-year-old who ran away from Brooklyn because her mother slapped her face in front of her boy friend for being 20 minutes late one night.

"At first, I'd just stay away for the night, but then she began to threaten to lock me up or put me in a home, and I knew I'd have to split," Martie said.

For the last year Martie has been living in the East Village with her boy friend, who is six years her senior. She does not keep in touch with her family and sees no point in going back to school "until there's something I really need to learn." When she can, Martie gets "high" on "pot" or "acid" (LSD). Her hippie friends provide a substitute family.

At 17, Norman dropped out of the Ivy League college he attended and came to New York, he said, to "get a job and make it on my own." Initially, he had no desire to contact his parents, but on the advice of his residence counselor, who helped him find work, he let them know where he was.

"My father pulled every string he could, argued with me, threatened me, but I stayed, I had to stay," Norman recalled. After a year on his own, Norman plans to go back to school.

"I'm going back now because I want to, not to please my father. I had to find out first if I could make it on my own."

Girls Outnumber Boys

The draft—described by one boy as "the best locator of missing persons there is"—has made it increasingly difficult for boys to disappear, which may, in part, account for the increased percentage of girl runaways. Five years ago, boy runaways outnumbered girls by 25 per cent. Today, girls outnumber the boys.

"My mother sent me to boarding school at 13," Lenore, a short, plump girl with heavy eye make-up, said. "She thought there was something going on between my father and me, but there wasn't. Not like she meant. We just kidded around a lot and were real close and had a good time."

Later, Lenore said, she went to live with a social worker and his family and then ran away at 17, when she was given a minor punishment for having a boy in the house alone without permission.

"First I went home and asked my mother to let me stay but she wouldn't," Lenore explained. "She said it would never work out. Now my 15-year-old sister is threatening to run away because my mother's pulling the same thing on her."

At 22, Lenore said she wished she had never left home and said of her little sister: "I'd kill her before I'd let her live here [the East Village]."

To teen-agers, parents seem domineering, lacking in understanding and intent on having their way; to parents, teen-agers seem thoughtless, self-centered and immature, a threat to their own control of the situation. What may start as a minor difference can become charged with anger, hate and violence, a pattern too often doomed to repeat itself over and over again.

In an effort to try to cope with this situation, the Youth Board is readying its residence at 503 West 27th Street for homeless boys. It hopes to have it in operation by the middle of September. It will house only between 35 and 40 boys, but it will mobilize the city's resources to enable them to complete their education and to find and hold jobs.

In late September, Rabbi Schrage, backed by a nucleus of 200 volunteers, will open an office for runaways in Brooklyn.

"We are going to call our-

selves Y-O-U-T-H," he spelled out. It stands for Youth Organization for the Understanding of the Homeless. One of our hippies thought up the name."

Drawing on advice from professionals in various fields, YOUTH will serve a dual function, according to Rabbi Schrage.

"We hope to provide homes willing to take in these boys and girls until they can be returned home or other arrangements can be made—a sort of temporary foster care for teen-agers, you might say," he explained. (The city's Department of Social Services will pick up the travel tab for the trip home, if the parents can't.)

"We will also agitate to put ourselves out of business," he added. "To have national legislation passed to create a National Youth Bureau as part of the Department of Health, Education and Welfare."

August 18, 1967

Hippies Shower $1 Bills on Stock Exchange Floor

By JOHN KIFNER

Dollar bills thrown by a band of hippies fluttered down on the floor of the New York Stock Exchange yesterday, disrupting the normal hectic trading pace.

Stockbrokers, clerks and runners turned and stared at the visitors' gallery. A few smiled and blew kisses, but most jeered, shouted, pointed fingers and shook their fists. Some clerks ran to pick up the bills. After a few minutes, security guards hustled the hippies out, to cheers and applause from the floor.

"We just want to make a loving gesture to these people," one hippie, who would not give his name, said afterward. "They don't know what money is. They deal in stock certificates."

James Fourrat, who led the demonstration along with Abbie

'It's Death of Money,' Says One Leader — Guards Hustle Group Out

Hoffman, explained in a hushed voice:

"It's the death of money."

A blond girl accompanying him briefly hummed a dirge and then said, "This is a paradise earth. There's enough for all."

Newsmen Waiting

The hippies, who totaled about a dozen, entered the exchange through the visitors' entrance at 20 Broad Street at 11 A.M. and waited in a line of tourists at the third-floor gallery. An equal number of reporters and cameramen, who had been told of the planned demonstration, waited to record the event.

As they waited, several hippies casually shredded dollar

bills. Some were dressed in their normal studied shabbiness, but others had disguised themselves with haircuts, jackets and ties.

Mr. Fourrat posed for pictures with a wad of bills stuck in his mouth.

"I think they're nuts," said a woman tourist from Warren, Ohio.

Exchange officials held the line up until the gallery had cleared, and John Whighton, the captain of the security force, approached the group and warned that "no demonstrations of any form are allowed."

"Hey, did you ever work for the University of California?" a hippie shouted.

Mr. Fourrat identified himself as "George Metesky," the "mad bomber" of several years ago whose behavior has made him a hippie idol.

Mr. Whighton wrote "George

Mentsky & friends" on a pad and escorted the group to the gallery.

The hippies immediately began throwing handfuls of bills —some of them torn—over the railing and laughing delightedly.

They were escorted out almost immediately.

On Broad Street outside the exchange, the hippies joined hands and skipped in a circle on the crowded sidewalk chanting: "Free, free."

Mr. Hoffman got into the middle of the circle and set fire to the edge of a $5 bill.

But an outraged exchange runner charged into the middle of the circle shouting, "you're disgusting," and grabbed the flaming bill and stamped on it.

One hippie said the group had thrown away $1,000, but observers estimated that about 30 or 40 $1 bills had been thrown.

August 25, 1967

HIPPIES FIND WAYS TO AVOID WORKING

Some Panhandle and Some Get By With No Money

By STEPHEN A. O. GOLDEN
Special to The New York Times

SAN FRANCISCO, Aug. 28— Middle-class parents who give handouts to bums would be shocked to find their own children panhandling when they became hippies.

For many hippies in the Haight-Ashbury area here, the most popular means of support are selling one of the 26 West Coast "underground" papers or asking people if they "have any spare change."

Contrary to popular opinion in the "straight world," few hippies receive allowances from home; they don't need them.

Aside from the free hot food served in Golden Gate Park each day, a sizeable portion of greasy fish and chips costs only 65 cents.

Many hippies live in crash pads and pay no rent. A crash

pad is an apartment open to all who wish to stay a night or even for a length of time.

A few hippies hold steady jobs—the post office is a favorite place—and many get occasional part-time jobs.

The Hip Job Co-op on Cole Street helps find part-time occupations for hippies.

"We could use 200 more jobs a week," said a Hip Job Co-op employe yesterday. "Most of our jobs are baby-sitting and day labor. A lot of kids haul garbage."

Many hippie shops along Haight Street are not owned by hippies or stocked with items made by them, but some do offer a source of revenue

to hippies.

In these stores, hand-made items are brought in and off-handedly exchanged for whatever the maker feels they are worth.

One hippie used to be paid to conduct religious cymbal services in the calm center of the Psychedelic Shop. Three weeks ago he told the owners that he did not want any more money for this. His girl friend now works in a night club, he said, and this is enough money.

The hippie, Richard Webster, said he wanted to help the store, which was deep in debt, and did not need to take

233

money from it.

An indication of the hippies' lack of concern with things monetary is the sign on the door of the Pacific Ocean Trading Company on Haight Street. The sign says: "Open 12-10 Sometimes." On three consecutive days it was not open at 3 P.M.

Besides the crafts and bizarre costumes, the hippies are perhaps best known for their rock 'n' roll bands. This also is a source of revenue.

One group, The Grateful Dead, is the free band of the Haight-Ashbury. One of its managers talked recently of how the group "traveled all across this country twice this year and we played free wherever we went."

But the band does charge occasionally for an appearance, and it makes enough to support the five band members, two managers and The Grateful Dead family of six more persons.

The Light Shows

And often when a band performs there is a light show: a series of color slides, movies, colored lights and flashing images projected onto the walls.

The Family Dog, a group that does light shows, works at the Avalon Ballroom.

Bruce Conner, an underground filmmaker, also works a light show. He and many others like him have dual sources of income, some of which goes to hippy charities to support those who do not have jobs.

The hippies take drugs—lots of drugs. The law of supply and demand does not hold true in the Haight-Ashbury so some hippies are dealers.

Some deal only in one drug, but some sell marijuana, LSD, Methadrine and Dexamyl and an assortment of other pil's.

But the aim of most hippies is to create a free society in which no one pays for anything.

"It is," one hippy said recently, "the only way to fly."

August 27, 1967

Jersey Upsets a School Ruling Barring Long-Haired Students

State Orders New Milford to Admit 15-Year-Old Boy Expelled Last Fall

TRENTON, Sept. 6 (AP)—The State Board of Education ruled unanimously today that local school boards cannot tell students how long they can wear their hair.

The five-member board ordered the New Milford High School to admit Francis J. Pelletreau, who was expelled the the school last November for refusing to cut his Beatle hair style.

The action reversed a decision of former acting education Commissioner Joseph Clayton, who on March 8 had upheld the expulsion of the 15-year-old freshman.

"A school regulation forbidding long hair, in effect, regulates outside of school conduct," the board's six-page decision said. "It is not possible to have short hair in school and revert to longer hair at home."

The board emphasized the limits of its decision and cautioned "any ingenious and provocative New Jersey public school students that our concern for freedom of expression is tempered by our determination that the proper course of the educational process not be impeded and that the high standards of our schools be maintained ."

Pelletreau has not attended school since the New Milford School Board ordered the expulsion by a 6-3 vote.

The decision represents the first time the state board has decided a case involving school "dress codes." The board's decision noted: "Of course, the reasonable rules and regulations of local boards of education shall be enforced."

It said the board was not convinced that the rule governing length of hair for male students had a substantial relationship to a legitimate purpose.

The board heard arguments in the Pelletreau case last June 7. At that time it also decided that Micah Bertin, an Edison High School honor student suspended from school because he refused to trim sideburns, which local school authorities considered "extreme," should be permitted to participate in

The New York Times
Francis J. Pelletreau

graduation ceremonies the following week.

R. M. Gross, a Hackensack lawyer who represented Pelletreau, notified the boy and his mother, Mrs. Mariam Pelletreau, of the favorable decision.

"They were delighted and Frank will be ready to go to school tomorrow, Thursday, morning," Mr. Gross reported.

The lawyer is a cooperating attorney with the New Jersey Chapter of the American Civil Liberties Union, which also represented Bertin.

Boy Still Has Long Hair
Special to The New York Times

NEW MILFORD, N. J., Sept. 6—Francis Pelletreau the high school freshman who was expelled from New Milford High school last November for refusing to cut his hair, will return to school tomorrow with shoulder length locks.

In hearing the state decision ordering the boy admitted to the school tomorrow, his lawyer, R. Michael Gross, said: "This decision has confirmed my faith in our school system the need to educate everyone including nonconformists has never been greater. The free expression of the minority viewpoint is the touchstone of American democracy. I am confident that New Milford will welcome Frank in the true spirit of liberal education.

Young Pelletreau was not as optimistic as his lawyer about his welcome back into the New Milford school system. "I don't plan to cut my hair. I expect I'll have problems with some of the students as well as teachers. I'm the kid who beat the adults and some people don't like that."

September 7, 1967

NEGROES ANGERED BY COAST HIPPIES

White Youths Said to Ruin Haight-Ashbury Section

Special to The New York Times

SAN FRANCISCO, Sept. 23—Despite hippie beliefs in "love power," not everyone in San Francisco's Haight-Ashbury section loves the hippies. There is hostility and resentment against the "new community" by many Negro residents of Haight-Ashbury.

"These hippies have come in and turned a once nice neighborhood into a slum," said a Negro three-year, resident of Haight-Ashbury.

Although Haight-Asbury, traditionally a tolerant and multi-racial neighborhood, has been integrated for 20 years, most of the Negroes moved there in the last four years. They came from the nearby Fillmore District, a Negro ghetto. For many it was a step up.

Negroes point to the deteriorating conditions of the 20 blocks on or near Haight Street where most of the hippies live.

Rats and roaches are abundant in apartment houses where as many as 50 hippies cram in with an apparent indifference to cleanliness.

"Haight-Ashbury is a wonderful example to point to when Negroes are accused of running down neighborhoods," said the State Assemblyman for the district, Willie L. Brown, 32-year-old Negro.

"These middle-and upper-class kids are conducting themselves as Negroes are stereotyped by bigots," said Mr. Brown.

Negro residents complain that their children are exposed to drug-taking and to lovemaking by hippies in neighborhood parks. They also say that last summer thousands of hippies disfigured neighborhood park, which they used as temporary homes, with tons of garbage.

Whites make up 60 per cent of the population in Haight-Ashbury, Negroes 30 per cent and the remaining 10 per cent are other minority groups.

Before the large number of hippies moved in this past year, the 100-square-block neighborhood was desired by artists and intellectuals who liked the proximity to Golden Gate Park.

An eight-block extension of the park, called the Panhandle, stretches into the middle of Haight-Ashbury and is flanked by wide streets and neat rows of Tudor and Victorian townhouses.

Although Negroes are most annoyed by the hippies, whites are selling their property faster, according to Assemblyman Brown.

"It's more difficult for Negroes to move out," said Mr. Brown. "Their investment is too great and they can't afford a loss."

"Before the hippies came, it was tough to find a place in Haight-Ashbury," said a Negro, six years resident. "Now everybody is trying to get out."

Financial Problems

Mr. Brown, who owns a home in Haight-Ashbury, said that since the hippies moved in it had become difficult to get fire insurance, borrow money from local banks to buy homes in the area and to get tenants other than hippies to move into vacant apartments.

Many Negroes have ambivalent feelings toward the hippies.

One Haight-Ashbury housewife, Mrs. Faye Woods, who has a view of the Panhandle from her apartment, said: "I don't go along with their ideas, but I won't knock them because they don't bother anybody.

"But, if a hippie moved next door to me, I would move out; not because they are hippies, but because I couldn't tolerate the filth."

Apartments in the Haight-Ashbury have lower rents than comparable apartments in other areas of San Francisco.

A five-room apartment can be rented for $120 a month; a nine-room flat for $135 a month.

A big reason for Negro hostility toward the hippie is what the Negroes call a double standard set by local law inforcers and city officials because most hippies are white.

"Poor people have to get on buses and travel to clinics and then sit half the day," said one resident. "But when the hippies moved in the Haight, they got their own clinic right here in the neighborhood," he added.

"Negroes never would have been allowed to do what these white kids are doing," said Mrs. Doris Bullard, who rents a nine-room apartment a half block from Haight Street.

"They couldn't go into a neighborhood and be a vagrant without getting picked up."

Mrs. Bullard, like many Negro parents in the area, said she would move before allowing her three-year-old son to come under the influence of hippies.

"I have to give up a neighborhood with beautiful parks and playgrounds, just to let a group of people going through a fad destroy it," she said.

The most potentially dangerous situation in the Haight-Ashbury is the friction between young Negro men and hippies, according to Mr. Brown.

There have been street "beat-ins" since last September. Mr. Brown said the Negroes were hostile to the hippies because "they have odd wearing apparel and odd attitdes."

September 24, 1967

HIPPIE SCENE LAID TO 'EMPTY' LIVES

Analyst Says Well-to-Do Parents Offer Nothing

By JOHN LEO

"The evil is in Greenwich and Great Neck, not Greenwich Village," a psychoanalyst said here yesterday in discussing the flight of young people from suburban communities to the hippie section of the East Village.

"The new generation is rebelling against the nothingness breeding in the suburbs," said Dr. Benjamin B. Wolman, dean of the Institute of Applied Psychoanalysis and professor of psychology at Long Island University.

He said: "I'm tired of wealthy people who give their children cars, but no moral values, coming to me and saying they don't know what's wrong with their youngsters."

"What's wrong is that the parents are leading hollow, empty, shallow lives and not giving their children anything to hold onto."

Dr. Wolman spoke on "Psychology and the Moral Values of Religion" in a talk at Christ Church (Methodist) here, and amplified his comments in an interview.

No Parental Standards

His lecture, sponsored by the Association for Applied Psychoanalysis, was the first in a series intended to further a rapprochement between psychoanalysts and spiritual leaders.

He said parental permissiveness masked the fact that parents had no particular moral norms they cared to pass along.

"If the parents were conservative," Dr. Wolman said, "their children could rebel by becoming radical. If they were radical, their children could become conservative. But their rebellion has to be against the kind of nihilism they see around them."

Hippies are attractive to the new generation, he added, because they seem to have vitality and a moral stance. "That's why I welcome all the nonsensical movements among hippies and college students," he said. "At least they show that they aren't dead yet."

In reacting against the rigidity of Victorian child-rearing, he declared, parents today are notably reluctant to discipline their children or to teach them self-restraint.

"We must return to the goal of freedom for the child's mind, and not freedom for his impulses," Dr. Wolman asserted.

"If the new generation accepts stupid values, it just shows how hungry they are," he added.

According to Dr. Wolman, the hippie movement is one of the optimistic signs of revolt against moral aimlessness. "The hippies are searching for something. If we don't give our children the right values, they'll pick up their own."

He said, however, that on the whole he was pessimistic. "The abdication of parents seems general," he declared. "Society must have a complete revision of its values or we'll all wind up in nothingness."

October 19, 1967

Sex and the College Girl

By JANE E. BRODY

Many coeds of decades past avowed that if there were a perfect contraceptive they would not hesitate to indulge in premarital sexual intercourse.

Today's coeds have that foolproof contraceptive — The Pill — which has led many parents to worry that with the deterring fear of pregnancy gone their daughters would have a sexual free-for-all.

Authorities on the subject asserted recently that this has not occurred, that the coed of today is no more likely to express herself sexually than was the coed of 10 or 20 years ago. Their studies indicate that the pattern of premarital intercourse has changed relatively little in the past 30 years.

What has changed, the authorities said, is the emotional context of these sexual relationships.

The authorities participated in a symposium on changing sex behavior held at the annual meeting of the American Association for the Advancement of Science.

Dr. Paul Gebhard, director of the Institute for Sex Research at Indiana University, said that, for the coed of this decade, the premarital sexual relationship is surrounded by more pleasure and less guilt.

As in the past, he said, college girls almost invariable limit their sexual encounters to men they love. But, he added, girls seem more willing today to enter love relationships that they do not expect will lead to marriage.

College males, on the other hand, are more likely than in the past to be emotionally involved with their sexual partners, Dr. Gebhard said.

Dr. Gebhard based his statements on the early findings of a survey conducted last summer among 1,200 college students throughout the country. The results of this survey were compared with a similar one made 20 years ago by the late Dr. Alfred C. Kinsey.

Dr. Gebhard's data on the extent of premarital sex among today's college students is still to be processed, but other symposium participants said that the arrival of the Pill has not contributed significantly to its rise.

"Contraceptives are not changing sexual behavior. They are simply making safer sexual behavior that would have occurred anyway," said Dr. Mary Calderone, executive director of the Sex Information and Education Council of the United States. "People are going to behave sexually regardless of the availability and type of contraception."

Dr. Ira L. Reiss, sociologist at the University of Iowa, agreed that the effect of contraception on rates of premarital intercourse was small indeed. But, he observed, there is today "a new social context of premarital sexual permissiveness" evolving in America.

"In the old days," he said, "the highest degree of sexual permissiveness was found among the lower classes. Now it is highly rooted in the college-educated community. There is a more intellectualized attitude toward sex as acceptable, particularly when a love relationship is involved."

Dr. Reiss said that no change has occurred in the percentages of people performing sexually, but a change has occurred in male behavior — "from the prostitute to the girl next door."

He concluded that "males today are much tamer than their fathers or grandfathers."

January 7, 1968

235

Noise of Loud Bands Found To Harm Ears of Teen-Agers

GAINESVILLE, Fla., Jan. 12 (AP)—Teen-agers dancing to the pounding beat of rock'n' roll bands are blasting their eardrums into old age, a University of Florida researcher said today.

In front of the bandstand at The Place, a Gainesville club for teen-agers, his team found the noise measured 120 decibels—as loud as the Saturn 5 moon rocket measured from the press site at Cape Kennedy.

Dr. Kenneth C. Pollock said his associates at the audiology laboratory were 40 feet outside the club before the sound dropped below 90 decibels, which the American Medical Association says is the threshold above which damage is caused.

January 13, 1968

3,600 HEAR GURU URGE MEDITATION

He Tells Young Audience It Is Way to World Peace

By PAUL HOFMANN

An Indian guru who counts the Beatles among his world famous disciples drew a capacity audience, including many young people clutching flowers, to the 3,600-seat Felt Forum of the new Madison Square Garden yesterday.

Those in the audience paid $3 to $10 to hear Maharishi Mahesh Yogi, who fondled a yellow hyacinth while calling on Americans to practice "transcendental meditation" every day to bring about world peace.

Youth and an air of guilelessness were the main characteristics of the audience in the forum, at Eighth Avenue and 33d Street.

Listeners of the mystic's 105-minute address were quiet and attentive. Some kept their eyes closed as they took in the exhortations that the Indian addressed at them in a singsong voice that occasionally broke into a giggle or a birdlike interjection of "Hmm?"

Many in Miniskirts

Some of the many teen-age girls in the audience wore long granny dresses or flowing shirtlike garments. But most of them were in miniskirts. The young people also affected oversized,

The New York Times
Transcendental meditation is his message.
(The Maharishi yesterday)

round, metal-rimmed eyeglasses, bead necklaces, tinkling bells and long hair.

One girl who said she was Leila Schiff and lived on West 86th Street came with a large flower stenciled on the plaster cast on her left leg. "I broke my ankle on the sidewalk," she explained, "but wouldn't miss the Maharishi."

The Beatles had sent a large arrangement of pink tulips and carnations to the guru's suite

at the Plaza Hotel on the eve of his only public appearance here during his current visit to the United States.

The Indian, who is about 56 years old, paid an hour-long call on Secretary General Thant of the United Nations on Saturday and is scheduled to lecture at Harvard University today before returning home.

Floral Tribute

Many members of yesterday's audience at the Felt Forum placed floral offerings on the dais before the guru's appearance. Yellow was the dominant color. Yellow and brown chrysanthemums and gladioli provided backdrop decoration.

The diminutive, benign-looking guru was holding a nosegay of seven tea roses when he arrived at 3:35 P.M., more than half an hour late. He was wearing white vestments. A towering American aide, Charles F. Lutes, introduced him as His Holiness.

The lights were dimmed, and the Indian told his listeners: "My heart is bouncing with bliss." The reason for his happiness, he explained, was his conviction that permanent world peace could be achieved if global, national and regional problems could be reduced to the quest of individual peace.

Softly, gesturing with his right hand while the left gently defoliated a hyacinth, the guru talked about a happy world "where frowning will be missing, tensions will be absent." He spoke in English without notes.

"Wars, epidemics, famines, earthquakes are all symptoms of tensions," the guru declared. "Tension is as contagious as any other disease."

If only 1 per cent of the world's population followed his easy-to-learn method of half an hour's meditation every morning and night, the Indian said, "it will be enough to dispel the clouds of war for thousands of years."

Meditating also staves off heart attacks, a danger confronting the "aspiring individuals of the affluent society," while shaking underdeveloped countries out of their lethargy, the guru declared.

The first short applause came long after the guru had started, when he said that "people don't sleep because they don't know how to be awake."

Another one of the Indian's aphorisms brought a ripple of laughter: "It is natural to be material—the whole body is material." Far from preaching asceticism, he said man should live a life "100 per cent spiritual and 100 per cent material—when every man lives 200 per cent of life, then peace will be shared."

The guru professed to be "a firm believer in God," but said that "religion has failed . . . modern mind wants proof, experimentation, experience; the days of faith are over." He said he had come to the United States because it was the world's most advanced country "where people are used to trying something new."

"Maybe it works," the Indian concluded, drawing his feet up and sitting cross-legged on a deerskin for a three-minute meditation with closed eyes, while postulants of his Spiritual Regeneration Movement snatched souvenir flowers from the dais.

January 22, 1968

30,000 in Miami Join A Rally for Decency

By The Associated Press

MIAMI, March 23—Some 30,-000 hand-clapping persons, some waving signs saying "Down With Obscenity," rallied in the Orange Bowl today to support a teen-age crusade for decency in entertainment.

Teen-agers organized the rally after Jim Morrison, 24 years old, the lead singer of The Doors, a rock group, was charged with indecent exposure during a concert in Miami on March 1. Six warrants have been issued for Mr. Morrison's arrest.

Mike Levesque, 17, the originator of the rally, a senior at Miami Springs High School, said the idea had grown out of a Roman Catholic youth group discussion two days after the concert by The Doors.

"This is not a protest rally," said Julie James, 18, a member of the teen-age Rally for Decency. "We're not against something. We're for something."

Talks on God and Sex

Teen-age speakers gave three-minute talks on God, parents, patriotism, sexuality and brotherhood. There were appearances by professional entertainers, who donated their time.

"Five virtues," selected as the keynote of the rally, were "belief in God and that He loves us; love of our planet and country; love of our family; reverence of one's sexuality, and equality of all men."

"Sex is definitely being exploited and it is because society has been losing its reverence for one's sexuality," Miss James said.

The shirt - sleeved crowd basking in a warm sun cheered for Jackie Gleason, Anita Bryant and The Lettermen, popular music singers, who appeared in order to applaud the teen-age rally.

"I believe this kind of movement will snowball across the United States and perhaps around the world," Mr. Gleason said.

"I think it's great, there should be more things like that," said Tony Butala of The Lettermen.

Young Levesque said he was thrilled by the rapid growth, of the decency movement and the support it had gained from adults.

The crowd was about evenly split between teen-agers and adults.

March 24, 1969

Fathers and Sons—1969

In an effort to define the issues that currently divide young and old, CBS News has scheduled a three-part series under the over-all title "Generations Apart." The first of the series, "A Question of Values," will be broadcast Tuesday night from 10 to 11. The following excerpts from Tuesday's program were recorded on both sides of the generation gap in Boulder, Colorado.

ON HAIR AND CLOTHING

ADULT: To me, it's nauseating, it's disgusting. I think grooming and cleanliness, taking care of oneself, I mean this is important in everyday life.

YOUTH: I'm absolutely amazed at how upset people are about long hair. To see the things that are built into people's minds. It would be funny except for the fact that it perpetuates a lot of cruel, obnoxious attitudes. It's unfortunate.

ADULT: I dislike long hair and I dislike seeing boys and girls go out on dates without being dressed up. We used to put on the very best things we had each day when we went to school. We wouldn't be seen on a university campus without a tie and shirt on and a sport coat or jacket. But we were poor and all the kids on the campus were poor, so we tried to impress everyone to make them think that we weren't among the poor.

YOUTH: My father grew up during the Depression, and looking good—you know, shaving and stuff like that—was a big deal. You know, he had to pump the water, then heat it, and wash. A pair of shoes during the Depression was quite a thing. And so, looking straight a generation ago was a virtue because it took an effort to do it and people were trying to get into the middle class and get out of the Depression. That is a value to them. To us, because we've already had it—who cares?

ON SEX

ADULT: If we let down all the morals, we have nothing. I think children should know about sex, and if they have any questions about sex I think their parents should talk this out with them. But I don't believe in sex before marriage.

YOUTH: I think it's really a necessary part of growing up. I mean it's one of life's most beautiful experiences. And I do not see the reason why people say you should wait until you are really in love and this is the person you're going to spend the rest of your life with. See, because people are so afraid of being hurt, they think if you have a beautiful relationship for one year and then you decide that you're going to go your own ways, that's just terrible. You know? They want the security, not the love. They want the security of one person and therefore they say wait, don't give yourself to anybody. And I just—I don't know—I just can't go along with that.

ON MONEY

YOUTH: I could just get a haircut, stop using half of the vocabulary that I use, stop thinking three-quarters of the thoughts that I think, bathe more often, keep my teeth white, wear pretty clothes, and I could probably make a fortune. But then I wouldn't be a human being. Or the human being that I am right now.

ADULT: Success in my day, I think, was perhaps getting away from poverty and having enough bread and beans and potatoes and meat on the table—so your family could eat. Today the children have never gone through this.

YOUTH: Today, material success and all that goes with it are not necessarily the thing to be achieved in life. I mean we're not nearly as security conscious as our parents were, but I can't blame them because of the Depression and their times. But that contributes to our inability to communicate with them. I think now we've become affluent enough where we can find the deeper and more meaningful things in life.

May 18, 1969

300,000 at Folk-Rock Fair Camp Out in a Sea of Mud

By BARNARD L. COLLIER
Special to The New York Times

BETHEL, N. Y., Aug. 16 — Despite massive traffic jams, drenching rainstorms and shortages of food, water and medical facilities, about 300,000 young people swarmed over this rural area today for the Woodstock Music and Art Fair.

Drawn by such performers as Joan Baez, Ravi Shankar, Jimi Hendrix and the Jefferson Airplane, the prospect of drugs and the excitement of "making the scene," the young people came in droves, camping in the woods, romping in the mud, talking, smoking and listening to the wailing music.

Looking out over 20 acres of youths squeezed body to body, the festival's organizers, the state police and officials of the Sullivan County Sheriff's office agreed that the crowd was over 300,000.

Participants Well-Behaved

The crowd, which camped on the 600-acre farm of Max Yasgur near here for the three-day festival, was well-behaved, according to both the sponsors and the police, even though about 75 persons in the area were arrested, mostly on charges of possessing narcotics.

Most of the hip, swinging youngsters heard the music on stage only as a distant rumble. It was almost impossible for them to tell who was performing and probably only about half the crowd could hear a note. Yet they stayed by the thousands, often standing ankle-deep in mud, sometimes

237

GARBAGE piled up everywhere, causing a health hazard. The view here is to the stage; the towers support loudspeakers.

paying enterprising peddlers 25 cents for a glass of water.

Roadways leading from the site were lined tonight with thousands of weary-looking youths who had had enough, and were trying to reach places where they could get food or transportation.

During the first 24 hours of the fair, festival medical officers said that a thousand people had been treated at first-aid stations for various ailments, including exposure and a few accident cases. About 300 were ill because of adverse drug reactions.

Doctors Fly to Scene

A dozen doctors, responding to a plea from the fair's sponsors, flew from New York to the scene, about 70 miles northwest of the city, near the Catskill Mountain resorts of Liberty and Monticello.

Michael Lang, the 24-year-old producer of the event, said that the medical help was summoned not because of any widespread illnesses, but because of the potential threat of a virus cold or pneumonia epidemic among such a large gathering.

Parked cars jammed roadways in all directions for up to 20 miles, and thousands of festival-goers, weary after

Gary Azon

RAIN added another note of discomfort to the music festival. Performances were cut short because of bad weather.

long walks to get here, had to spend the night sleeping on the rain-soaked ground. They awoke to find food and water shortages.

But Mr. Lang said this afternoon: "It's about the quiet-est, most well-behaved 300,000 people in one place that can be imagined. There have been no fights or incidents of violence of any kind."

A state police official agreed. "I was dumfounded

The New York Times   Aug. 17, 1969

by the size of the crowd," he said. "I can hardly believe that there haven't been even small incidents of misbehavior by the young people."

Dr. Donald Goldecker, the fair's medical officer, said that most of those suffering from the ill effects of drugs had experienced "bad LSD trips." The symptoms are agitation, disorientation and fear, lasting three to four hours.

The fair's sponsors brought in 100 members of a group called the Hog Farm Commune of Santa Fe, N. M., who formerly used LSD, to act as security guards. They also attempted to treat "bad trips" with soothing, understanding talk and assurances that a sufferer is not dying or going insane.

Tonight, a festival announcer

238

Inc., which sponsored the festival, said today that the organizers expected to lose money on the enterprise.

The organizers had expected 150,000 to 200,000 persons to attend, and conceded today that they were unprepared for the numbers that actually arrived.

Six water wells were dug on the site and 600 portable toilets brought in.

The festival was originally scheduled to be held at Woodstock, 50 miles northeast of here, but a suitable location there was not available. The sponsors then turned to Wallkill, about 30 miles south of Woodstock, but were rebuffed and finally decided on Mr. Yasgur's farm here.

Many youths brought their own food, but there was a shortage at the concession warned from the stage that "badly manufactured acid" [a term for LSD] was being circulated. He said:

"You aren't taking poison acid. The acid's not poison. It's just badly manufactured acid. You are not going to die. We have treated 300 cases and it's all just badly manufactured acid. So if you think you've taken poison, you haven't. But if you're worried, just take half a tablet."

As the crowd swelled today, officials of the fair issued an urgent appeal for all those not already at the muddy site to stay away.

It was impossible, they said, to get to the site without walking for miles. Parked and stalled cars were bumper-to-bumper for 20 miles in all directions on Routes 17, 17B, 42, 55 and 97.

The Short Line Bus Company, which has provided the only bus service to the festival from New York, said yesterday it was canceling all buses to the festival and Bethel at the request of the police. "We're not driving into that disaster area," a company spokesman said.

Yesterday, 65 buses from New York City went to the festival. One took 12 hours to get there, with the average run-

LIVING QUARTERS were not always satisfactory. Most people stretched sleeping bags on the rain-soaked grass.

ning more than four hours. The customary travel time is two hours 20 minutes.

Despite the distance, columns of festival-goers were trudging on the highways toward the site. Their lines stretched back three to four miles in the afternoon.

Those reaching the site found tens of thousands of tents, campers and makeshift lean-to shacks—some of them rather elaborate—made of any materials at hand, including trees, wood, ropes, sheets and blankets.

Teepee for 20

One such was constructed as a teepee around a big elm tree. It had a fire inside and a hole at the top for the smoke to pour out. About 20 persons slept inside the tent last night with their heads toward the fire, like the spokes of a wheel.

The first day's music was to have ended at 4 A.M. today, but because of the weather the performances were concluded shortly after midnight.

Joan Baez ended it for the night by leading the crowd in singing "We Shall Overcome." Afterward, she told the audience, "I hope David can hear

it," referring to her husband, who is in jail for refusing to be drafted.

Today, thousands of fans, evidently discouraged by the weather and the press of the crowds, began leaving the festival site, which has turned into a giant mud puddle.

But they were quickly replaced by many more thousands seeking to get in.

Festival officials, unable to cope with the growing crowds, stopped selling tickets. "Now it's all a freebee," one said. The tickets had been sold for $7-day or $18 for the three-day weekend, which was scheduled to end tomorrow night.

Many of those leaving the festival today, encountering others just arriving on the roads outside the site, attempted to sell their weekend passes for money or food.

"Two tickets are worth a peach or half a sandwich," one departing youth said.

Festival officials today said they were sending representatives through the crowd seeking donations.

John Roberts, a 24-year-old officer of Woodstock Ventures,

stands set up around the festival site.

The members of one commune were passing out a free gruel of peanuts, oatmeal, raisins and sunflower seeds. Local farmers around the site complained to the police that corn and vegetables had been stripped in their fields by foragers.

Piles of garbage built up everywhere, and scores of men employed to collect it were hard pressed. Their work and other

200 in Security Force

Charged with keeping the peace was a 200-man "peace-security force," consisting of off-duty policemen from a number of communities as well as state troopers, off-duty state correction officers and Sullivan County Sheriff's deputies.

This afternoon, the festival promoters asked for more state policemen and aid from the Sullivan County Red Cross and Civil Defense organizations. The promoters said the reinforcements were being requested as a precautionary measure to help handle the large crowd and not because of any outbreaks of violence.

Additional sheriff's deputies also were brought from Dutchess, Saratoga and Rockland Counties.

In addition to a food shortage, festival officials said that a water shortage also was developing.

About 20 doctors and 50 nurses were on the site today before the arrival of the additional medical personnel. Some of the doctors said that the "bad LSD trips" had resulted from the circulation of some "flat blue acid tablets being passed around."

They also said tranquilizers were being peddled as LSD, which stands for lysergic acid diethylamide.

A state police sergeant said no one on the festival site was being arrested for the use of marijuana. "If we did [make such arrests], there isn't enough space in Sullivan or the next three counties to put them in," he said.

The music that brought the youngsters to the festival began last night with a folk orientation. Today's acts included the Who, the Jefferson Airplane and Janis Joplin. Tomorrow's billing included The Band, Jimi Hendrix, and Crosby, Stills and Nash.

The performers were at first ferried to the site by helicopter from an airport in nearby Liberty. But the promoters were forced to abandon this plan when most of the copters developed mechanical difficulties and the gasoline pumps at the airport ran dry. The theme of the festival was billed as "Peace and Music." There was plenty of music, and, according to the police, the peace was being kept.

FOOD SHORTAGE quickly became a problem. This girl's breakfast consists of an apple.

August 17, 1969

Why Do They Hate Long Hair?

To the Editor:

MOST of us leave a movie theater confident that what we have just seen is fantasy, not reality, fiction, not truth. Life is truth; the screen only a distorted reflection, or denial even, of the truth.

But a few weeks ago two movies and two ordinary events — all experienced in one day—left me wondering. The two movies were "Alice's Restaurant" and "Easy Rider."

In the first, Arlo Guthrie is thrown out of a restaurant through a plate-glass window by three young thugs who object to his long hair. Sitting alongside the curb, bleeding, he is arrested for disturbing the peace. When Arlo protests his innocence, the police simply look at his hair and throw him in jail.

In the second, Dennis Hopper's "Easy Rider," two long-haired motorcyclists set out cross-country from California to "discover" America. On their way, they pick up a hitchhiker, and just outside New Orleans the three of them stop for coffee at a roadside cafe. Several people in the cafe make caustic remarks about their appearance. The waitress does not serve them. Two local policemen joke about how they should book the "animals" and throw them in jail. Leaving the cafe without being waited on, the three men camp for the night on a roadside nearby. They are at-

tacked and one of them is killed. A few days later, the other two are blown from their cycles, off the face of America, by two passing motorists with shotguns.

After viewing the first movie, I sat in a cab that had stopped for a red light at 59th Street and Lexington Avenue. The driver and I watched a long-haired teenage boy cross 59th Street. He wore bell-bottomed jeans, a pullover sweater over an open-necked shirt, and his long, blond hair fell below his shoulders. Except for his hair, he was all masculine in appearance.

The driver turned to me just before the light changed, and, with deliberate hatred in his voice, said, "You see that? Boy, if I could get outa this cab right now, I'd go up and whip that kid and shave his skull naked." Judging from the cabbie's tone and physique, I didn't doubt for a moment his ability to carry out his threat. Acknowledging his attitude with a weak smile, I got out of the cab and walked to the Beekman Theater, where "Easy Rider" was playing.

On the way home to Kent, Conn., I picked up two young hitchhikers near Bedford, N. Y. They wore long hair, unkempt beards, sloppy blue jeans and well-worn hiking shoes. They carried knapsacks. When we reached Brewster, we had coffee together before parting. Over coffee, I learned that they were sophomores from the

Santa Barbara campus of the University of California. They had left California several weeks before, hitchhiking around the country, in their words, "to find the guts of America."

While our treatment in the cafe didn't resemble that of the three travelers in the cafe in "Easy Rider," I quietly observed that the waitress was hardly civil to us. And my two companions told me their experience:

While traveling with a young salesman, just outside New Orleans, a few days before I met them, the three had stopped at a roadside cafe for coffee. Inside, they were completely ignored by the waitress. Two parties of teen-age boys began a barrage of caustic remarks. Two local policemen entered the cafe, approached the travelers, yanked them out of their chairs, threw them against the counter and searched them. Finding a pocketknife on one of them, the police put the two hitchhikers in jail overnight for illegal possession of a dangerous weapon.

"Either of you see 'Easy Rider'?" I asked.

"Nope." They had been too busy the past few weeks searching for the guts of America.

Some weeks have passed now, and I'm still wondering: Has anyone beaten up and shaved the kid I saw crossing 59th Street? Have the two Californians returned to their classes, successful in having found the guts of their

country? Or have theirs been spilled on some highway because someone objected to their looks?

But this, of course, is fantasy. Things like this occur only on the screen.

Tom Andrews
Kent. Conn.

INSIDIOUS?

To the Editor:

After viewing such a kaleidoscopic diatribe of unmitigated cinematic junk as "Alice's Restaurant," I am amazed that this type of movie is even allowed to be shown to the public. The movie is nothing more than an instrument of rebellion and apparently the producer sought that the picture should be just that. It is a sneering, infantile portrayal of the lunacy fringe of the modern hippie generation of today. But more than that, it is a serious mockery of law and order, of religion, of military service, and even of patriotism.

Apparently anybody with a little money can hire a group of ham actors and put together a movie using the medium to propound whatever antisocial, antiestablishment ideas one may have. The movies have unquestionably reached a new low in taste, in theme, and in art. There should be some kind of protection against the insidious propaganda of individual ideas that, under the cloak of comedy and hilarity, seek to make a mockery of sacred and respected precepts of society.

Ernest R. Barra
Yonkers, N. Y.

November 2, 1969

'Just Too Much'

To the Editor:

RECENT letters in the Movie Mailbag concerning "Alice's Restaurant" and "Easy Rider" bring up a subject that deserves more than the simplistic treatment it has been given. They write about young people being "victimized" for the way they look, or the way they dress, and decry the "prejudice" that causes ordinary people to be angered by the presence of the long-haired young.

The question involved, however, is not individual dress but symbolic speech. If one young person blew into town with, say, a shaved head, I doubt that he would evoke more than curiosity and perhaps good-natured (or not so

good-natured) ribbing. It would be assumed that he was, in the current parlance, doing his own thing. But the long-haired unkempt young things who so arouse the public are a different phenomenon entirely. They are not individualists. They are wearing a uniform (albeit a sloppy one). Their reason for wearing it appears, to the man in the street, to be to express contempt for their parents, their elders, their homes, their country. Their dirtiness and contrived ugliness seem to bespeak a lack of respect for themselves, as well as for others.

To people whose lives have been struggles to maintain the thin veneer of civilization and civility that covers man's ir-

rationality, the sight of the children of affluence, the hope of the future, sinking to the depths of what appears to be animal degradation is Just Too Much! Aren't we demanding too much of human beings to expect them to respond with benevolent tolerance to what appears to be a gesture of utter contempt for all that is meaningful to them?

It sometimes seems that the ordinary people have more feeling for art than today's artists. Is not art the bringing of order out of chaos, beauty out of ugliness? I don't think we should blame the young people for their symbolic speech: I doubt that most of them realize the implications of their anarchic ways. But the artists who should be leading them to a higher civilization seem to be

pied pipers of barbarism.

What a man looks like should not enter into our evaluation of him. It is a trivial matter, at best. But if he chooses to use his appearance as a form of expression, he cannot complain if someone disagrees with his presence.

The symbolic speech of dress is a "cop out." Let these young people articulate their ideas, as they certainly have a right to do. They will then be open to refutation and counterargument. A dialogue may ensue and people on both sides might learn something. As long as the discourse is carried on by means of gestures, we cannot expect it to rise above the level of pre-verbal man, i.e., infants.

Joyce P. Davis
Teaneck, N. J.

November 30, 1969

240

Rock Concert's Statistics: Four Dead and Two Births

LIVERMORE, Calif., Dec. 7 (UPI) — The last of 300,000 young rock fans straggled out of debris-covered hills today, after a free concert by the Rolling Stones had left four persons dead.

Two births also occurred during the day-long concert yesterday.

Tons of empty wine bottles and other garbage were strewn on the hills around Altamont Speedway, a motorcycle and jalopy track that became the scene of the one-day music festival.

Hundreds of abandoned cars —many of which ran out of gas or broke down during the six-hour traffic jam after the concert—dotted the area.

December 8, 1969

Adolescents Today: Are They More Disturbed?

By ENID NEMY

THE subjec is discussed as casually today as a visit to the dentist. Everyone either knows or has heard of an adolescent who is undergoing psychiatric treatment.

Are today's adolescents sicker, or more disturbed, than those of past generations? No, say many of the psychiatrists who specialize in the field.

Are more adolescents more alienated from their parents and from society than they were a generation ago? The answer here is very likely to be yes.

"There's no reason whatsoever to believe that young people today are sicker," said Dr. Everett Dulit, director of the Adolescent Psychiatry Clinic and training program at Jacobi Hospital of the Albert Einstein College of Medicine.

Dr. Dulit, a wiry, articulate 40-year-old who commutes between the bustling Bronx hospital and a private practice in Westchester, sees the change that has taken place—one that has disturbed many adults—more as a matter of outer form. Many of his colleagues agree.

"There are equally as many disturbed adolescents in every generation," said Dr. Edward J. Hornick, who has been practicing 25 years and was at one time psychiatric consultant to Sarah Lawrence College. "They are just more visible today."

More Optimistic Than Parents

Psychiatrists, perhaps by the nature of their profession and perhaps because they are given the opportunity to probe beneath symptoms, are generally more positive and optimistic about the young than are many parents. The doctors are concerned about alienation, as they are about the broad aspect of drugs, but they explain the growing number of adolescents (an age group that theoretically ends at 18 to 20) undergoing treatment with ancillary factors.

Increasing visibility and relaxation of social restraints, which "allow the marginally disturbed kids we get in every generation" to express themselves more openly, are two of the most frequently given reasons.

There has also been:

¶A steady climb in the 13-through-19-year-old population from 22 million in 1960 to 24 million in 1965 and a probable 26.5 million this year.

¶More specialization by psychiatrists in the field of adolescence. The Society for Adolescent Psychiatry, organized in New York in 1958, now has about 350 members; nationally there are more than 800. "A decade ago, we were flying by the seat of our pants in this field," said one member.

¶Increasing availability of psychiatric services. An affluent society has made private treatment (anywhere from $30 to $50 for a 50-minute hour) more feasible, and there are a growing, if still insufficient, number of adolescent clinics.

There is no one pattern that leads adolescents to a psychiatrist's office. Sometimes the visit is initiated by a school, other times by parents or the young person involved.

Attitudes Have Changed

"There's no question that the attitude has changed in the last decade," said Dr. Aaron Esman, a graduate of the Cornell Medical School who has been practicing psychiatry 18 years and is director of training for the Jewish Board of Guardians.

"There's much greater acceptance now by young people. Parents are not as acceptive, but they tend to go along," he said.

To Dr. Malvina Kremer, the word "shrink" was itself symbolic.

"That meant someone was going to cut you down, take away from you," she said, sitting in the tranquil West Side apartment she uses as an office. Dr. Kremer is also chief of the Adolescent Clinic at Metropolitan Hospital and on the staff of the Bellevue medical school.

"Today, they essentially know we try to do the opposite—fulfill their needs."

The changes in adolescent problems are often linked to a changing pattern of family life, where the young find it difficult to emulate parents who are often unhappy and dissatisfied with their own lives. Some of the disillusionment stems from parents embracing, perhaps too wholeheartedly, a youth-oriented culture that plays down the values of maturity.

Good to Be Adult

"Secure parents would not feel a need to deviate from their own manners— they feel it a good thing to be an adult." Dr. Dulit said.

"At one time, parents said, 'You may

To many psychiatrists, the reiteration of issues such as Vietnam and civil rights on the part of their young patients is "party-line patter" and not the basic reason for problems.

241

have your own ideas, but we are sure we are doing things the right way,'" he said. "Adolescents have always rebelled, but there was a character growth out of pushing against a well-defined other way of life in which adults were sure of their values. There is no character growth pushing against a cream puff."

Dr. Esman, who spends his mornings at the Madeleine Borg Child Guidance Institute in a large office building in midtown Manhattan, has seen an increase in "the depressive type of kid—alienated and disoriented.

"They don't feel right, they feel depressed, unsure, uncertain about goals. They are looking for somebody to help them find clarity and meaning," he said.

Dr. James Masterson, a private practitioner and head of the adolescent psychiatry program of the Payne-Whitney division of New York Hospital-Cornell Medical Center, has his own definition of one root cause of trouble. He calls it the PIP syndrome—Permissive, Inconsistent and Punitive.

"Any one of them is harmful," he said. "All three together are a guaranteed prescription for a great deal of trouble. Parents have never taught children control, and when the kid does something they don't like—wham!"

The affluence that has made possible such things as private psychiatric care for adolescents, has also contributed to the necessity for such treatment. Psychiatrists who divide their time between private patients and clinics have found

---

"Parents want to put their children on an escalator. Adolescents want to walk up each step of the ladder themselves."

---

that children of middle- and upper-income families can be equally as emotionally deprived as those in slum areas.

"It's more subtle and masked in the middle-class home, but tension and lack of love may be there," said Dr. Robert E. Gould, who is in charge of adolescent services at Bellevue Hospital's psychiatric division.

"They see spiritual emptiness, the loneliness in the home, the lack of communication, the plain unhappiness, covered up by material possessions and frantic running around. They reject it totally."

To many experts, the reiteration of issues such as Vietnam and civil rights on the part of their young patients is

"party-line patter" and not the basic reason for problems. However, none deny that there is a genuine concern about these social and moral matters and that, if the concern is sometimes more emotional than knowledgeable, it does not lessen the degree.

"Thinking adolescents are as concerned as thinking adults," Dr. Dulit said. "Many of them may be minimally knowledgeable, but most people are. To hold the adolescent to a standard we don't have for adults is unfair."

The violence that has flared as a result of these and other issues, does not, according to many psychiatrists, reflect the majority of even the alienated adolescents. It has been described as stemming from a smaller group "who would rather have turmoil than change." There is a flat denial on the part of some, and doubts on the part of others, as to whether this group has increased over the decade.

Degrees of Rebelliousness

Most kids are middle-of-the-road rebellious," Dr. Dulit said. "There are rebellious adolescents recognized even by other rebellious adolescents as 'crazies.' They revel in the turmoil; they don't really want change. They are destructive. They used to do things in a more old-fashioned way. Now there are new ways."

The retreat to narcotics, perhaps the most oft-quoted common denominator as a reason for adolescents' undergoing treatment, is almost always cited as a symptom rather than the basic problem.

"First and most basic is that this is a drug society," Dr. Gould said. "Adolescents are emulating parents. There is not a home I know of where parents don't either drink or smoke cigarettes, have barbituates to go to sleep, tranquilizers to get through the day—not aspirin, but mood-changing drugs."

Dr. Gould noted that marijuana followed in the tradition of alcohol and had the added fillip of being different.

"It's important to the young to separate their actions from their parents'. Again, it's illegal, so it's the embodiment of the symbol of rebellion. Eighty per cent of my private patients are taking or have tried marijuana."

Marijuana Is an Experiment

"It depends on why marijuana is used," Dr. Masterson said. "Statistics show the majority use it for recreation purposes—in episodic ways. It's an experiment—they are seekers."

He defined heroin as "a kind of divider. The great majority of even sick adolescents who use many drugs (speed, LSD) are still wise enough not to take heroin. They know it is a one-way street. The focus of treatment is to substitute therapy for narcotics as a

means of dealing with problems.

"Some of the efforts of kids to make their parents aware [of their taking narcotics] are astonishing," he said. "They leave drugs around; they talk about them on the telephone. They want their parents to tell them to stop. And healthy parents will do something about it."

The sexual revolution among the young has been defined as part of the rebellion against hypocrisy—"so many adults they know practice adultery but indulge in sanctimonious preaching." But some psychiatrists are aware of an underlying guilt and conflict about sex.

"They know they are flouting conventional morality," Dr. Esman said. "One of the problems is to come to terms with this conflict of conventional morality against the expressed values of their generation."

To some psychiatrists, there has been a change in the degree of alienation experienced today.

"The ones I used to see fought with their parents, but it was a superficial struggle," Dr. Masterson said. "They sensed they would ultimately accept. The feeling now is that they are lost because they cannot accept their parents' values, and they feel they have nothing to replace them with."

No Answers About Future

There is no clear-cut opinion as to whether this generation of adolescents will come around to eventual acceptance or whether this time the split is permanent.

"Some are already moving back and some aren't. It will be another 10 years before we know," Dr. Dulit said.

No one has the prescription for an untroubled adolescent, but many psychiatrists would agree with some of the theories held by Dr. Kremer and Dr. Gould.

"Parents want to put their children on an escalator," Dr. Kremer said. "Adolescents want to walk up each step of the ladder themselves. They are trying to work things out. If parents understood this—that they don't want to just lean and duplicate, but want their own identities as they fit in with others of their own contemporary group—adolescents wouldn't have to retreat to drugs and hippie culture."

Dr. Gould considers guidance, structure, support and a relevant humanitarianism as among the basic needs.

"Adolescents need to be told a lot of things about what to do and what not to do because they simply don't know," he said. "This and a chance to stretch out and gain their own identity. It's a delicate balance."

February 20, 1970

Agnew Assails Songs and Films That Promote a 'Drug Culture'

By JAMES M. NAUGHTON
Special to The New York Times

LAS VEGAS, Nev., Sept. 14—Vice President Agnew said tonight that American youths were being "brainwashed" into a "drug culture" by rock music, movies, books and underground newspapers. He called these part of "a depressing life style of conformity that has neither life nor style."

After describing himself as a "bumpkin" earlier today in San Diego, the Vice President came to the capital of American gambling to lecture against "creeping permissiveness" and urge the election of "square" Republicans.

Mr. Agnew said in a speech to 1,000 Republicans at the

Space Center Auditorium of the Sahara Hotel that popular songs such as the Beatles' "With a Little Help From My Friends" or the Jefferson Airplane's "White Rabbit" were a message of drug use.

'Pill-Popping' Parents

He placed part of the blame on "pill-popping" parents and "growing adult alcoholism" that were setting examples for younger citizens "to do some experimenting on their own."

The Vice President urged Nevadans to "open your eyes and your ears" to the drug culture, "establish authority with com-

passion" in their families and elect William Raggio, the Reno District Attorney, who is the Republican senatorial candidate against Senator Howard W. Cannon, a Democrat.

He told the Republicans who paid $100-a-couple to attend the rally and those who saw it on a statewide telecast that he "may be accused of advocating 'song censorship' for pointing this out, but have you really heard the words of some of these songs?"

The Beatles' tune, he said, included these lines:

"I get by with a little help from my friends, I get high

242

with a little help from my friends. . . . "

A Catchy Tune

Mr. Agnew said that it was, like many of the rock songs, "a catchy tune, but until it was pointed out to me, I never realized that the 'friends' were assorted drugs."

He charged that a recent movie, which he did not name, but which apparently was "Easy Rider," promoted as heroes "two men who are able to live a carefree life off the proceeds of illegal sales of drugs."

Although the Nixon Administration is taking steps to curtail the spread of drugs and to advise against their use, and some news media are also warning against drug abuse, the Vice President said, "far too many producers and editors are still succumbing to the

temptation of the sensational and playing right into the hands of the drug culture."

Mr. Agnew said that "those who close their eyes to the pernicious influence of any form of drug—for fear of being out of step with the times— are dismally failing their own sons and daughters." If such an attitude brings down on him and others the label "squares," he added, "then we will just have to live with it."

Wave of the Future

His message here was part of the general Republican campaign theme. As Mr. Agnew rephrased it in a short speech to 1,000 persons, mostly school-children, at the Las Vegas Airport, "You need a Congress that will see to it that the wave of permissiveness, the wave of pornography and the wave of moral pollution never become

the wave of the future in our country."

The Vice President, his wife, Judy, and their 14-year-old daughter, Kim, who wore a gray minidress, traveled to the Frontier Hotel from the airport past signs that read "All You Can Drink, $2.25."

One hotel marquee advertised: "Welcome Vice President Spiro Agnew. Keno. Poker." Another declared: "The NOW Year. Folies Bergère. Welcome Vice President Agnew." A gas station sign said: "Free aspirin. Ask us anything."

Nevada Democrats were asking the Republicans to explain why schoolchildren had been bused to the airport to greet the Agnews. Republican state employes were given time off to take part in the reception and, according to the Democratic State Chairman, Philip

Carlino, pressure was put on casinos to sell tickets to the rally.

Before flying here, the Vice President told interviewers in San Diego:

"Speeches are of limited effect on the American people. Speeches and rallies and demonstrations, I think, have been grossly overrated as a way of appealing to the people to designate the kind of leadership they want to represent them."

He said that citizens were sophisticated, "even those of us who are described as the ordinary bumpkins throughout the countryside and may not be card-carrying members of the so-called intellectual community."

September 15, 1970

Dr. Spock Tells Youth: 'Civilizations Are Built on Restraints'

By JUDY KLEMESRUD

Not long ago, Dr. Benjamin Spock overheard a college psychiatrist say at a symposium that many students who don't consider themselves ready to enter into a premarital affair are made to feel "abnormal, frigid or perverse."

This incident and the fact that his antiwar activities have practically elevated him to sainthood among many segments of youth are two reasons why he decided to turn out another advice manual—this one for teen-agers.

According to the 67-year-old pediatrician, the book, "A Teen-Ager's Guide to Life and Love" ($4.95, Simon & Schuster), is "very conservative." He said that some of his more sophisticated young followers might even find it "pathetic," but he doesn't mind. The book, he says, is for "the shy kid who needs reassurance"— the kind of kid Dr. Spock says he was himself.

Friend or Foe?

"I'd thought for years that I had something to say to kids," he said yesterday in his apartment on East 83d Street. "But I didn't know whether youth would consider me a friend. I thought they might think of me as their enemy because I was a counselor of their parents in my book, 'Baby and Child Care.'"

He indicated that he

found out he was no enemy after he marched shoulder-to-shoulder with young people in peace demonstrations. He still talks about the time in 1965 when 8,000 jammed into an auditorium to hear him at a teach-in at Berkeley.

He also endeared himself to many youths in 1968, when he was convicted, along with four other men, including William Sloane Coffin Jr., the Yale chaplain, on charges of aiding and abetting violation of the Selective Service Act. (Their convictions were later overturned.)

"The main point I wanted to make to young people in the book is that inhibition is not unnatural," Dr. Spock said. "Many young people today feel that restraints are ipso facto immoral. Well, they aren't, because civilizations are built on restraints. Most unusually creative and productive people have almost always come from an inhibited group."

Wife's Concern

At that point, Dr. Spock's attractive wife, Jane, interrupted to remind him that since his back was bothering him, he should lie down on the couch while he talked. "Spocks aren't supposed to get sick," he muttered good naturedly, then did what he was told.

Although some women's liberationists have called him a male chauvinist ("Unconsciously what male isn't?"

he says), Dr. Spock repeated in his book his contention that child-raising was a woman's most important and satisfying job. But he added that he believed it was also a man's most important and satisfying job.

He said he saw some good in the current unisex movement among the young, especially when "sexual differences are exaggerated, and a woman is exploited just as a body." But he also said that when women become aggressive and dominating, they often produce submissive sons—"an unwholesome development."

"It goes against the whole biological plan," he asserted, his 6 feet 4 inches stretched out on the couch. "It leads to ineffectuality on the part of the male. In male children, it shows up in things like bed-wetting, phobias, tics and stuttering."

Among those things that Dr. Spock advises teen-agers against are smoking, drinking ("at least until the age of 18, and preferably until 20") and early dating.

"I deplore the social custom of early dating," he said, "especially when it's exploited by ambitious mothers who want daughters to be popular by arranging parties with dim lights."

Dr. Spock said that in at least one section of his book, "The Arrangement," he tried to show that he was "not just a rigid conservative." That section deals with

young people, especially college students, who live together without being married.

"It may be a wholesome thing for people who are mature enough," he said. "It's very natural for people who are 20 years of age and serious about each other to want to live together. Of course, they must use effective contraception."

Not a Recommendation

He quickly added that he wasn't urging undergraduates to try "The Arrangement." "It depends upon the individuals," he said.

When asked for his views on marijuana, Dr. Spock seemed on less firm footing than he was on other topics.

"I'm no expert," he said. "All I know is what I read as an interested citizen. I think it should be considered separately from all the rest of the drugs, which scare the hell out of me. Marijuana is certainly less harmful than alcohol. I don't know if it should be legalized, but I think the laws against its possession should surely be changed."

Dr. Spock retired three years ago, at the required age of 65, as a professor of child development at Western Reserve University in Cleveland. Since then, he said, he has been busy going "to every peace demonstration I hear about" and writing letters to Senators and Congressmen. He estimates he spends about 50 per cent of his time on the road, speak-

243

ing about peace, and, for the Civil Liberties Legal Defense Fund, on the right to dissent.

He also writes a monthly column for Redbook magazine, revises "Baby and Child Care" (more than 23 million copies have been sold since it was first published in 1946) now and then, and gives several guest lectures a year at Western Reserve.

"Every university is proud to show it has radicals on its faculty," he said.

He laughs when the subject of permissive child-raising is brought up, and how he is often blamed for the recent youth rebellions in this country.

On Spanking

"In the first place, as anybody who has read my books

knows, I was never permissive," he said. "I never said that parents shouldn't spank their children. To some parents, spanking is a natural way of making children behave.

"I would never tell them not to spank," he added, "just as I would never tell parents who abhorred the idea of spanking to spank their children."

Does Dr. Spock, who in fact spanked his own two sons "a couple of times," think he is responsible for today's rebellious youth?

He smiled. "I would be proud," he said, "if I were responsible in a small way for the idealism and courage of youths who are opposed to war and other injustices."

November 3, 1970

Rock Music Turns To Spiritual Ideas

By GEORGE GENT

It is perhaps too much to say that rock music is getting religion, but a large number of current records are dealing sympathetically with religious and spiritual ideals.

At the same time, rock music's once fashionably intense flirtation with drug lyrics appears to be abating in the face of industry disapproval. Some observers of the rock scene view both trends as interrelated. Here are some of today's bellwethers:

¶Decca Records has just released "Jesus Christ, Superstar," a rock opera based on Christ's Passion and Death by two young Englishmen, Andrew Lloyd Webber and Tim Rice. The work is recorded on two long-playing disks and runs more than 86 minutes.

¶Mylon LeFevre, formerly a member of the LeFevre gospel singers, is turning to gospel rock on Cotillon Records.

¶SSS International and Plantation Records is investing heavily in what it calls Jesus Rock, with a full slate of disks on the religious theme being readied, and including one recent release called "Remember Bethlehem," with lyrics about the birth of Jesus. Singleton recently issued an album of Jesus Rock by the U. S. Apple Corps. A single by the Sweet Revival is titled, "Will the Real Jesus Please Stand Up?"

¶Among current records on Billboard's chart of best-selling disks are Westbound's "God, Love and Rock & Roll," by Teagarden & Van Winkle; Dorothy Morrison's rendition of "Spirit in the Sky," on the Buddha label, and Neil Diamond's recording of "He Ain't Heavy . . . He's My

Brother," on Uni.

These are only a few of the records already issued or being readied that deal with the subject. There are various reasons for this apparent trend, but many observers see it as simply one more manifestation of American youth's search for values.

Trend to Spiritual Themes

There are skeptics who view the swing to religious themes as little more than a timely tapping of another commercial spring, but these are in a minority. Most agree that the search is sincere, but how deep the impulse runs is a matter of conjecture.

Rocco Laginestra, president of RCA Records, agreed that there was a trend toward lyrics with religious or spiritual themes, but he cautioned that the impulse might not be of a kind that would be acceptable to many churches.

"If these young people find an acceptable vision of God they will embrace it," he said. "I don't think this necessarily means they will embrace the structured religious organizations of the Establishment. More probably, they will believe on their own terms."

Jack Loetz, president of Decca, also discerned a trend toward religious subjects on the part of rock lyricists.

"I think it's because young people are looking for meaningful subject matter," he declared. "While there is a movement away from the church by young people, creative people may be able to stimulate a new interest in religion through music that questions and stirs controversy."

Some persons expressed a belief that the religious lyrics

might be a rebuttal to the drug lyrics of the recent past.

"They could be a reaction to the recent deaths by drug overdose of Janis Joplin and Jimi Hendrix," one observer maintained, "or it could be the rock stars' antidrug campaign. Antidrug lyrics are beginning to appear on the scene, but many rock stars don't like to be put in the position of lecturing their listeners. This could be their way of meeting the situation."

Censorship Is Denied

Record manufacturers were reluctant to admit that drug lyrics ever played a significant part on the rock scene —despite such entries as "Heroin" and "Take a Whiff" —but were unanimous in pronouncing the decline of such works in the last year.

And, while most denied that industry censorship existed, there was general agreement that decisions on lyric suitability usually was left to producers, who are not unaware of industry and Government disapproval. Others said it was no longer fashionable to insert drug references surreptitiously into song lyrics.

"It's all been done, anyway," one young record company executive explained. "Very few performers ever pushed hard drugs and it's no longer considered chic to push marijuana, because everyone's using it."

Although industry persons support this view, many manufacturers expressed strong disapproval of the recent action by Mike Curb, president of MGM Records, in dropping 18 rock groups for allegedly having exploited hard-drugs through music.

Many felt Mr. Curb's action was based more on economics—few of the acts were money-makers—than on altruism.

But it is the religious theme in rock lyrics that appears to have caught on. It began, as is so often the case, with a Beatles record,

"Let It Be," which contained some lines that many construed as religious.

About the same time, many young people got excited over the Who's rendition of "Tommy," a rock opera about a young man who goes through a drug experience and finds himself a figure of religious devotion.

Even Simon and Garfunkel's "Bridge Over Troubled Water," a song about an unnamed friend who helps the subject of the song during a dark night of the soul, is thought by some to have religious significance.

But these early attempts are considered ambiguous religiously, as much so, in their way, as some of the early drug lyrics.

Since then, the religious note has been hit more insistently. In addition to those already mentioned, there are two songs from Bob Dylan's new Columbia record, "New Morning," which contain specifically religious notes. They are "Three Angels," a lament on man's disregard for the spiritual, and "Father of Night," a hymn of praise to the Creator.

The Band's Capitol release titled "Stage Fright" has a cut called "Daniel and the Sacred Harp," and the Byrds' Columbia album, "Ballad of Easy Rider," has a song titled "Jesus Is Just Alright."

There can be little doubt that the most ambitious of the new religious records is "Jesus Christ, Superstar," which presents Christ's Passion and Death from a contemporary skeptical view of Jesus's claim to divinity, but with reverence for the person of Jesus and for the Biblical text from which it was adapted.

The work has been well received by clerics of all faiths, according to Decca, "although there have been a few charges of blasphemy from some sections of the country."

November 24, 1970

Communes Spread as the Young Reject Old Values

By BILL KOVACH
Special to The New York Times

BOSTON, Dec. 16—In remote valleys and canyons or cluttered city apartment houses, thousands of young adults, seeking economic advantages, social revolution, love, pot, God or themselves, are creating a new life style in America.

Whether the arrangement is called a commune, a colony, a cooperative, an affinity group or a family, these young adults have some form of sharing in common, and they reject the traditional style of living that groups people together largely because of blood or legal relationships.

It now is becoming clear that the commune phenomenon, which began most recently in the late nineteen-sixties with the hippie movement, is growing to such proportions that it may become a major social factor in the nineteen-seventies.

Nearly 2,000 communes in 34 states have been turned up by a New York Times inquiry seeking to determine how many permanent communal living arrangements of significant size could be found in the country, why they existed and who lived in them.

That number is believed to be conservative because it no doubt missed some smaller communes and does not include hundreds of small, urban cooperatives and collectives.

Several generalizations about the new life style were found, including the following:

¶No accurate count exists, largely because official agencies—except the police, who watch urban collectives and communes for narcotics—generally ignore the development. In addition, most are quiet and sometimes secretive, and thus go unnoticed by neighbors.

¶The average size of a communal group ranges from 5 to 15 persons, usually in their late teens or early 20's, but increasing numbers of groups whose members are over 30 are being reported.

¶All involve sharing space and finance and most go beyond this to share common work, goals or ideas. Others share themselves.

¶Despite general fears or assumptions, few successful group living arrangements are built around narcotics or promiscuous sexual relations, although both exist in some degree or other. But these attractions are too readily available outside the group to provide the basic cement.

¶Although communal living experiments are common throughout American history (such as Brook Farm, an intellectual experiment in 19th-century New England), few of the modern experiments have studied those historical roots. They regard themselves less as an experiment than, as a member of a West Virginia group expressed it, "a path from things as they are to things as they should be."

In such states as California, where communal living has become commonplace and is beginning to involve upper-middle-class elements, there is a rising official response to the phenomenon.

Albert Solnit, chief of advance planning for Marin County, which has several dozen hippie-style communes and will soon have a city of 20,000 for those who wish to live communally, recently called the movement to the attention of the American Institute of Planners.

'New Life Style'

"Here," Mr. Solnit says, "is a new life style that has dropped the idea of mother and father, dropped the single family living unit, dropped the idea of commuting to work, dropped the 40-hour work week."

"And yet," he continued, "we're still going to conferences to learn how to mediate with the land-rapers and developers. We're still thinking in terms of 1954 subdivision patterns."

Regardless of the specific drives that bring a group of unrelated people together in a family-style living arrangement, there seems to be an underlying motivation that suggests the new styles of living are more than a passing phase.

Dr. Louis West, chairman of the department of psychology at the University of California at Los Angeles, regards the commune phenomenon as one of three overlapping rebellions that the young have mounted against established society. The three rebellions, which he labels red, black and green, are, respectively, against the economic and governmental system, racism, and living style and conditions.

Suburbs Rejected

Dr. West says the green rebellion, is, among other things, a rebellion against the "sterile family and community life style of the suburbs, which produced most of these young people."

Current efforts to escape the mold cast by social arrangements break down into two basic trends—urban and rural group living experiments.

The urban experiments are by far the largest. San Francisco, Chicago, Boston, New York, St. Louis and other large cities report "literally hundreds" of such communes or collectives. Most of these are, to one degree or another, responses to the crowding and acute housing shortages in urban areas.

Probably the largest single group of communal living groups, and the type accounting for the rapid growth of the experiments, are those built near colleges and universities. Surrounding nearly every major college and university are houses in which the walls have been knocked down to make community rooms where students can live as one family.

"We're trying to share our lives and ideas in a way never possible in a dormitory or in separate apartments," a Harvard graduate student living in one of the Cambridge communes said. "It's an attempt to be truly human beings in the way we've always been taught to believe human beings are supposed to live with one another—with love and understanding."

There are more practical reasons, too. A group of three, six or 10 people sharing the rent can considerably reduce the cost of living for a student. It also eliminates the need for so many cars, telephones, television sets and radios, thus reducing pollution and striking a blow at an economic system based on duplicate consumption.

Overlapping these college-based communes is a group of revolution-oriented communes. These are usually composed of students or former students living together in collectives formed around the desire to change specific aspects of society. They include the women's liberation communes, political communes and those devoted to a specific but limited change.

Others work in draft counseling, day care centers and birth control and abortion clinics.

A third urban arrangement is built around common work situations and includes the following groups:

¶Cincinnati Health Department employes campaigning for a more efficient administration.

¶Former nuns of the Glenmary order working with Appalachian whites in the mountains of Kentucky and Tennessee.

¶Young men trying to develop counter-culture programs for the state of Maine in an attempt to prevent destruction of the state's open lands and shores.

¶The staffs of underground newspapers, which have sprung up in nearly every large city in the country.

In most of these urban-oriented communes, access to supplemental incomes keeps their members in the cities.

Many are on welfare rolls or receive Federal food stamps that contribute to the commune larders. Others work at odd jobs or at temporary jobs, which are much easier to find in the city.

Religious Principles

A fourth urban group is made up of collectives or communes built on philosophical or religious beliefs. In Iowa City, 10 adults—including a policeman—and four children share a house in which they "live simply by Christian principles." In New Orleans, a woman called Kumi Mantreya heads a Buddist commune. In Cambridge, a "lewd" commune has a nudist orientation.

Despite occasional disturbances, most urban communes seem to operate with little public reaction. The police occasionally raid them, searching for narcotics or runaway children, but generally the police report little real trouble from communal living.

The rural counterparts of these urban communal groups are less numerous, but they indicate a deeper commitment to the concept and are generally based on spiritual values or searches for utopian lives.

New Mexico became so overcrowded with rural communes that members of the first groups there have pleaded through underground media for others to "do your thing where you are; there's no more room here."

Although there are hundreds of rural communes in the Southwest and California, where the weather is usually mild, few people took the movement seriously until communes begain to crop up in the North — and the inhabitants stuck it out through bitter winters. Several communes in Vermont and at least one in northern Maine are going into their second winter with no indication of giving up.

Probably because these young people are deep into the "work ethic" — they build homes, manage farms, sell handicrafts and some even operate general stores — they are generally accepted, or at least tolerated, by their rural neighbors.

Many of the communes represent major investments. The following groups are some examples:

¶Near Nashville, Ind., Raintree Investments involves 500 acres that are farmed organically — without chemicals. Pests are controlled by birds, ladybugs and praying mantises.

¶Three Black Muslim communal farms are operating in Alabama despite harassment by whites who, at one point, apparently poisoned a dozen of their cattle.

¶"The Children of God,"

based on conservative Christian principles, has organized three communal farms, one each in California, Texas and Kentucky.

¶In Florida's Orange County, a school for children with behavorial problems operates communally and is moving toward self-sufficiency through farming and handicraft sales.

Both urban and rural, the idea of communal living has grown in the last two years at such a rate that many involved in these experiments suggest the energy devoted to the movement is largely responsible for the relative quiet that has settled over the under-30's protesters of recent years.

One student put it this way: "People are trying to get it together in their own communes this year. The movement has to reform itself to make way for things like women's liberation, and commune members have to learn how to relate to each other in a new situation."

Mr. Solnit, the California planner, compares communal living to a movement toward a new and permanent life style:

"A kind of new social frontier for the disaffected of the last third of the 20th century. Instead of claiming new lands, as the pioneers of the eighteen-hundreds did, they are claiming new human relationships. Just as the pioneers left established settlements behind, so these communicants have left established ties of family by blood line, marriage, class, race, occupation or anything else that boxes one in."

December 17, 1970

Analyst Says Mystics Flee Violence

By JOHN DARNTON

The mystical movements that are sprouting in this country represent an attempt by individuals to escape a world of aggression in order to renounce their own potential for violence, a psychoanalyst told the fall meeting of the American Psychoanalytical Association here yesterday.

"In practicing love and peace, they [mystics] try to cancel the aggression of the world and to do away with their own," said Dr. Peter Hartocollis, research director at the Menninger Hospital in Topeka, Kan.

"Such people are protesting the violence of their environment because they are burdened by their own potential for violence and the guilt of it," he said.

The resurgence of mysticism in America can be seen in the use of mind-expanding drugs, the proliferation of religious cults such as the "Jesus freaks" and a growing fascination with astrology, Oriental philosophies, rustication, monasticism and asceticism, and matters of the occult.

It is mainly extant among the young, who were characterized by Dr. Hartocollis as finding material progress valueless, science immoral and the corporate organization of modern society oppressive.

Historical Examples Cited

Mysticism asserts itself in certain historical moments, such as the Hellenistic period following the Roman conquest, which are marked by a superficial quest for universal peace, combined with undercurrents of violence expressed in long-lasting, "limited" wars of ideological origin, Dr. Hartocollis said.

The mystical experience, be it psychedelic or religious, extroversive or introversive, is characterized by an overwhelming belief in unity and a sense of oneness, he said.

Applying the psychoanalytic theory called "object relations"—which holds that psychological reality for an infant is his relationship with his mother — Dr. Hartocollis maintained that the mystic, in effect, has externalized and renounced an intense hatred against the Oedipean father.

At the same time, he re-experiences the early infantile sense of blissful omnipotence that stems from a fusion of his mother and his own undifferentiated self.

Dr. Hartocollis's paper, "Mysticism and Aggression," was one of 14 reports delivered during the opening of the four-day session at the Waldorf-Astoria Hotel.

The meeting, attracting more than 1,600 psychoanalysts from throughout the country, has temporarily transformed the ornate hotel into a many-chambered testing ground for new theories on dreams, creativity, drug use, self-pity and various other wrinkles in the human personality.

"In the fifties you used to hear a lot of German accents, but now that's all changed—we're American-trained," observed Dr. Irwin H. Marill of Washington.

However, the influence of Sigmund Freud was apparent at the proceedings.

The main speaker of the day —in a new spirit of ecumenism —was not a psychoanalyst, but Dr. Carl E. Schorske, the Princeton historian.

Dr. Schorske addressed the plenary session in the Starlight Roof ballroom. He offered a new interpretation of how Freud arrived at his psychoanalytical constructs, advanced in his "Interpretation of Dreams."

Dr. Freud, according to Dr. Schorske, was writing at a time of intense personal crisis that was mirrored by the civic crisis in Austria, where the radical right was on the rise. In turning to personal history, Dr. Freud was turning away from anti-Semitism and other contemporary developments — he was "neutralizing the pressure of politics."

In his "Interpretation of Dreams," he was working through three levels of crisis: professional, political and personal—each one forcing him to a deeper and more drastic break with the external world and pushing him further back on a journey into his own past.

The session included numerous discussion workshops, in which the psychoanalysts discussed new areas for inquiry.

A California psychoanalyst, Dr. Miriam Williams, told of the need for psychoanalytic treatment of the children of survivors of Nazi persecution who, she said, are influenced by their parents' "perennial mourning" and share in nightmares of persecution.

December 18, 1971

Sexual Activity Stable Among Youths in Study

BATON ROUGE, Aug. 28 (UPI)—The sexual revolution has not yet affected the behavior of middle America's teen-agers, two researchers reported today.

Profs. Arthur Vener and Cyrus S. Stewart, both Michigan State University social scientists, said that a study they conducted of the sex attitudes and conduct of junior and senior high school students indicated a "remarkable stability of incidence rates of sexual intercourse since World War II."

In a report prepared for a meeting of the American Sociological Association, the researchers concluded that the foment concerning sexuality in the nineteen-forties, fifties and sixties had apparently been one of attitude rather than conduct.

Their study was conducted in late 1969 in three Michigan communities, they said. It involved boys and girls who were white, did not plan to attend college, lived in rural areas and came from upper-working-class to upper-middle-class families.

August 29, 1972

They changed rock, which changed the culture, which changed us

By Jeff Greenfield

They have not performed together on stage for more than eight years. They have not made a record together in five years. The formal dissolution of their partnership in a London courtroom last month was an echo of an ending that came long ago. Now each of them is seeking to overcome the shadow of a past in which they were bound together by wealth, fame and adulation of an intensity unequaled in our culture. George Harrison scorns talk of reunion, telling us to stop living in the past. John Lennon told us years ago that "the dream is over."

He was right: When the Beatles broke up in 1970 in a welter of lawsuits and recriminations, the sixties were ending as well—in spirit as well as by the calendar. Bloodshed and bombings on campus, the harsh realities beneath the facile hopes for a "Woodstock nation," the shabby refuse of counterculture communities, all helped kill the dream.

What remains remarkable now, almost 20 years after John Lennon started playing rock 'n' roll music, more than a decade after their first worldwide conquest, is how appealing this dream was; how its vision of the world gripped so much of a generation; how that dream reshaped our recent past and affects us still. What remains remarkable is how strongly this dream was triggered, nurtured and broadened by one rock 'n' roll band of four Englishmen whose entire history as a group occurred before any of them reached the age of 30.

Their very power guarantees that an excursion into analysis cannot fully succeed. Their songs, their films, their lives formed so great a part of what we listened to and watched and talked about that everyone affected by them still sees the Beatles and hears their songs through a personal prism. And the Beatles themselves never abandoned a sense of self-parody and put-on. They were, in Richard Goldstein's phrase, "the clown-gurus of the sixties." Lennon said more than once that the Beatles sometimes put elusive references into their songs just to confuse their more solemn interpreters. "I am the egg man," they sang, not "egghead."

Still, the impact of the Beatles cannot be waved away. If the Marx they emulated was Groucho, not Karl, if their world was a playground instead of a battleground, they still changed what we listened to and how we listened to it; they helped make rock music a battering ram for the youth culture's assault on the mainstream, and that assault in turn changed our culture permanently. And if the "dream" the Beatles helped create could not sustain itself in the real world, that speaks more to our false hopes than to their promises. They wrote and sang songs. We turned it into politics and philosophy and a road map to another way of life. *(Continued)*

---

*Jeff Greenfield is a writer whose most recent book, "No Peace, No Place,"
deals with the rise of rock 'n' roll.*

The Beatles grew up as children of the first generation of rock 'n' roll, listening to and imitating the music of Little Richard, Larry Williams, Chuck Berry, Elvis Presley, and the later, more sophisticated sounds of the Shirelles and the Miracles. It was the special genius of their first mentor, Brian Epstein, to package four Liverpool working-class "rockers" as "mods," replacing their greasy hair, leather jackets, and on-stage vulgarity with jackets, ties, smiles and carefully groomed, distinctive haircuts. Just as white artists filtered and softened the raw energy of black artists in the nineteen-fifties, the Beatles at first were softer, safer versions of energetic rock 'n' roll musicians. The words promised they only wanted to hold hands; the rhythm was more insistent.

By coming into prominence early in 1964, the Beatles probably saved rock 'n' roll from extinction. Rock in the early nineteen-sixties existed in name only; apart from the soul artists, it was a time of "shlock rock," with talentless media hypes like Fabian and Frankie Avalon riding the crest of the American Bandstand wave. By contrast, the Beatles provided a sense of musical energy that made successful a brilliant public-relations effort. Of course, the $50,000 used to promote the Beatles' first American appearance in February, 1964, fueled some of the early hysteria; so did the timing of their arrival.

Coming as it did less than a hundred days after the murder of John Kennedy, the advent of the Beatles caught America aching for any diversion to replace the images of a flag-draped casket and a riderless horse in the streets of Washington.

I remember a Sunday evening in early February, standing with hundreds of curious collegians in a University of Wisconsin dormitory, watching these four longhaired (!) Englishmen trying to be heard over the screams of Ed Sullivan's audience. Their music seemed to me then derivative, pleasant and bland, a mixture of hard rock and the sounds of the black groups then popular. I was convinced it would last six months, no more.

The Beatles, however, had more than hype; they had talent. Even their first hits, "I Want to Hold Your Hand," "She Loves You," "Please Please Me," "I Saw Her Standing There," had a hint of harmonies and melodies more inventive than standard rock tunes. More important, it became immediately clear that the Beatles were hipper, more complicated, than the bovine rock stars who could not seem to put four coherent words together.

In the spring of 1964, John Lennon published a book, "In His Own Write," which, instead of a ghost-written string of "groovy guides for keen teens," offered word plays, puns and black-humor satirical sketches. A few months later came the film "A Hard Day's Night," and in place of the classic let's-put-on-a-prom-and-invite-the-TeenChords plot of rock movies, the Beatles and director Richard Lester created a funny movie parodying the Beatles's own image.

I vividly recall going to that film in the midst of a National Student Association congress; at that time, rock 'n' roll was regarded as high-school nonsense by this solemn band of student-body presidents and future C.I.A. operatives. But after the film, I sensed a feeling of goodwill and camaraderie among that handful of rock fans who had watched this movie: The Beatles were media heroes without illusion, young men glorying in their sense of play and fun, laughing at the conventions of the world. They were worth listening to and admiring.

The real surprise came at the end of 1965, with the release of the "Rubber Soul" album. Starting with that album, and continuing through

"Revolver" and "Sgt. Pepper's Lonely Hearts Club Band," the Beatles began to throw away the rigid conventions of rock 'n' roll music and lyrics. The banal abstract, second-hand emotions were replaced with sharp, sometimes mordant portraits of first-hand people and experiences, linked to music that was more complicated and more compelling than rock had ever dared attempt. The Beatles were drawing on their memories and feelings, not those cut from Tin Pan Alley cloth.

"Norwegian Wood" was about an unhappy, inconclusive affair ("I once had a girl/or should I say/she once had me"). "Michelle" and "Yesterday" were haunting, sentimental ballads, and Paul McCartney dared sing part of "Michelle" in French—most rock singers regarded English as a foreign language. "Penny Lane" used cornets to evoke the suggestion of a faintly heard band concert on a long-ago summer day. Staccato strings lent urgency to the story of "Eleanor Rigby."

These songs were different from the rock music that our elders had scorned with impunity. Traditionally, rock 'n' roll was rigidly structured: 4/4 tempo, 32 bars, with a limited range of instruments. Before the Beatles, rock producer Phil Spector had revolutionized records by adding strings to the drums, bass, sax and guitar, but the chord structure was usually limited to a basic blues or ballad pattern. Now the Beatles, with the kind of visibility that made them impossible to ignore, were expanding the range of rock, musically and lyrically A sitar—a harpsichord effect—a ragtime piano —everything was possible.

With the release of "Sgt. Pepper" in the spring of 1967, the era of rock as a strictly adolescent phenomenon was gone. One song, "A Day in the Life," with its recital of an ordinary day combined with a dreamlike sense of dread and anxiety, made it impossible to ignore the skills of Lennon and McCartney. A decade earlier, Steve Allen mocked the inanity of rock by reading "Hound Dog" or "Tutti-Frutti" as if they were serious attempts at poetry. Once "Sgt. Pepper" was re-

corded, Partisan Review was lauding the Beatles, Ned Rorem proclaimed that "She's Leaving Home" was "equal to any song Schubert ever wrote," and a Newsweek critic meant it when he wrote: "'Strawberry Fields Forever' [is] a superb Beatleizing of hope and despair in which the four minstrels regretfully recommend a Keatsian lotusland of withdrawal from the centrifugal stresses of the age."

"We're so well established," McCartney had said in 1966, "that we can bring fans along with us and stretch the limits of pop." By using their fame to help break through the boundaries of rock, the Beatles proved that they were not the puppets of backstage manipulation or payola or hysterical 14-year-olds. Instead, they helped make rock music the music of an entire international generation. Perhaps for the first time in history, it was possible to say that tens of millions of people, defined simply by age, were all doing the same thing: they were listening to rock 'n' roll. That fact changed the popular culture of the world.

■

Rock 'n' roll's popularity had never been accompanied by respectability, even among the young. For those of us with intellectual pretenses, rock 'n' roll was like masturbation: exciting, but shameful. The culturally alienated went in for cool jazz, and folk music was the vehicle for the politically active minority. (The growth of political interest at the start of the sixties sparked something of a folk revival).

Along with the leap of Bob Dylan into rock music, the Beatles destroyed this division. Rock 'n' roll was now broad enough, free enough, to encompass every kind of feeling. Its strength had always been rooted in the sexual energy of its rhythms; in that sense, the outraged parents who had seen rock as a threat to their children's virtue were right. Rock 'n' roll made you want to move and shake and get physically excited. The Beatles proved that this energy could be fused with a sensibility more subtle than the "let's-go-down-to-the-gym-and-beat-up-the-Coke-machine" quality of rock music.

In 1965, Barry McGuire recorded the first "rock protest" song (excluding the teen complaints of the Coasters and Chuck Berry). In his "Eve of Destruction," we heard references to Red China, Selma, Alabama, nuclear war and middle-class hypocrisy pounded out to heavy rock rhythms. That same year came a flood of "good time" rock music, with sweet, haunting melodies by groups like the Lovin' Spoonful and the Mamas and the Papas. There were no limits to what could be done; and the market was continually expanding.

The teen-agers of the nineteen-fifties had become the young adults of the nineteen-sixties, entering the professions, bringing with them a cultural frame of reference shaped in good measure by rock 'n' roll. The "youth" market was enormous—the flood of babies born during and just after World War II made the under-25 population group abnormally large; their tastes were more influential than ever before. And because the music had won acceptability, rock 'n' roll was not judged indulgently as a "boys will be boys" fad. Rock music was expressing a sensibility about the tangible world — about sensuality, about colors and sensations, about the need to change consciousness. And this sensibility soon spilled over into other arenas.

Looking back on the last half of the last decade, it is hard to think of a cultural innovation that did not carry with it the influence of rock music, and of the Beatles in particular: the miniskirt, discothèques, the graphics of Peter Max, the birth of publications like Rolling Stone, the "mind-bending" effects of TV commercials, the success of "Laugh-In" on television and "Easy Rider" in the movies—all of these cultural milestones owe something to the emergence of rock music as the most compelling and pervasive force in our culture.

This is especially true of the incredible spread of drugs —marijuana and the hallucinogens most particularly—among the youth culture. From "Rubber Soul" through "Sgt. Pepper," Beatle music

Helpmates: Former Beatle Paul McCartney with his wife, Linda Eastman.

was suffused with a sense of mystery and mysticism: odd choral progressions, mysterious instruments, dreamlike effects, and images that did not seem to yield to "straight" interpretation. Whether specific songs ("Lucy in the Sky with Diamonds," "A Little Help From My Friends") were deliberately referring to drugs is beside the point. The Beatles were publicly recounting their LSD experiences, and their music was replete with antirational sensibility. Indeed, it was a commonplace among my contemporaries that Beatle albums could not be understood fully without the use of drugs. For "Rubber Soul," marijuana; for "Sgt. Pepper," acid. When the Beatles told us to turn off our minds and float downstream, uncounted youngsters assumed that the key to this kind of mind-expansion could be found in a plant or a pill. Together with "head" groups like Jefferson Airplane and the Grateful Dead, the Beatles were, consciously or not, a major influence behind the spread of drugs.

In this sense, the Beatles are part of a chain: (1) the Beatles opened up rock; (2) rock changed the culture; (3) the culture changed us. Even limited to their impact as musicians, however, the Beatles were as powerful an influence

as any group or individual; only Bob Dylan stands as their equal. They never stayed with a successful formula; they were always moving. By virtue of their fame, the Beatles were a giant amplifier, spreading "the word" on virtually every trend and mood of the last decade.

They were never pure forerunners. The Yardbirds used the sitar before the Beatles; the Beach Boys were experimenting with studio enhancement first; the Four Seasons were using elaborate harmonies before the Beatles. They were never as contemptuously antimiddle-class or decadent as the Kinks or the Rolling Stones; never as lyrically compelling as Dylan; never as musically brilliant as the Band; never as hallucinogenic as the San Francisco groups. John Gabree, one of the most perceptive of the early rock writers, said that "their job, and they have done it well, has been to travel a few miles behind the avantgarde, consolidating gains and popularizing new ideas."

Yet this very willingness meant that new ideas did not struggle and die in obscurity; instead, they touched a hundred million minds. Their songs reflected the widest range of mood of any group of their time. Their openness created a kind of salon for

a whole generation of people, an idea exchange into which the youth of the world was wired. It was almost inevitable that, even against their will, their listeners shaped a dream of politics and lifestyle from the substance of popular music. It is testament both to the power of rock music, and to the illusions which can be spun out of impulses.

∎

The Beatles were not political animals. Whatever they have done since going their separate ways, their behavior as a group reflected cheerful anarchy more than political rebellion. Indeed, as editorialists, they were closer to The Wall Street Journal than to Ramparts. "Taxman" assaults the heavy progressive income tax ("one for you, 19 for me"), and "Revolution" warned that "if you go carrying pictures of Chairman Mao/you ain't gonna make it with anyone anyhow."

The real political impact of the Beatles was not in any four-point program or in an attack on injustice or the war in Vietnam. It was instead in the counterculture they had helped to create. Somewhere in the nineteen-sixties, millions of people began to regard themselves as a class separate from mainstream society *by virtue of their youth and the sensibility that youth produced.*

The nineteen-fifties had produced the faintest hint of such an attitude in the defensive love of rock 'n' roll; if our parents hated it, it had to be good. The sixties had expanded this vague idea into a battle cry. "Don't trust anyone over 30!"—shouted from a police car in the first massive student protest of the decade at Berkeley—suggested an outlook in which the mere aging process was an act of betrayal, in which youth itself was a moral value. Time magazine made the "under-25 generation" its Man of the Year in 1967, and politicians saw in the steadily escalating rebellion among the middle-class young a constituency and a scapegoat.

The core value of this "class" was not peace or social justice; it was instead a more elusive value, reflected by much of the music and by the Beatles own portrait of themselves. It is expressed best by a scene from their movie "Help!" in which John, Paul, George and Ringo enter four adjoining row houses. The doors open—and suddenly the scene shifts inside, and we see that these "houses" are in fact one huge house; the four Beatles instantly reunite.

It is this sense of communality that was at the heart of the youth culture. It is what we wished to believe about the Beatles, and about the possibilities in our own lives. If there is one sweeping statement that makes sense about the children of the last decade, it is that the generation born of World War II was saying "no" to the atomized lives their parents had so feverishly sought. The most cherished value of the counterculture—preached if not always practiced—was its insistence on sharing, communality, a rejection of the retreat into private satisfaction. Rock 'n' roll was the magnet, the driving force, of a shared celebration, from Alan Freed's first mammoth dance parties in Cleveland in 1951, to the Avalon Ballroom in San Francisco, to the be-ins in our big cities, to Woodstock itself. Spontaneous gathering was the ethic: Don't plan it, don't think about it, *do* it—you'll get by with a little help from your friends.

In their music, their films, their sense of play, the Beatles reflected this dream of a ceaseless celebration. If there *was* any real "message" in their songs, it was the message of Charles Reich: that the world would be changed by changing the consciousness of the new generation. "All you need is love," they sang. "Say the word [love] and you'll be free." "Let it be." "Everything's gonna be all right."

As a state of mind, it was a pleasant fantasy. As a way of life, it was doomed to disaster. The thousands of young people who flocked to California or to New York's Lower East Side to join the love generation found the world filled with people who did not share the ethic of mutual trust. The politicization of youth as a class helped to divide natural political allies and make politics more vulnerable to demagogues. As the Beatles found in their own personal and professional lives, the practical outside world has a merciless habit of intruding into fantasies; somebody has to pay the bills and somebody has to do the dishes in the commune and somebody has to protect us from the worst instincts of other human beings. John Lennon was expressing some very painful lessons when he told Rolling Stone shortly after the group's breakup that "nothing happened except we all dressed up . . . the same bastards are in control, the same people are runnin' everything."

He was also being unfair. If the counterculture was too shallow to understand how the world does get changed, the forces that were set loose in the nineteen-sixties have had a permanent effect. The sensuality that rock 'n' roll tapped will never again be bottled up. The vestiges of the communal dream have changed the nature of friendships and life-styles and marriages, in large measure for the better. And with the coming of harder economic times, the idea of abandoning private retreat for shared pleasures and burdens has a direct contemporary practicality.

For me, the final irony is that the Beatles themselves have unconsciously proven the value of communality. As a group, they seemed to hold each other back from excess: McCartney was lyrical, but not saccharine; Lennon was rebellious but not offensive; Harrison's mysticism was disciplined (Ringo was always Ringo, drummer and friend). Now, the sense of control seems to have loosened. Paul and Linda McCartney seem tempted by the chance to become the Steve and Eydie of rock; Lennon is still struggling to free himself from a Fad of the Month mentality; George Harrison's Gospel According to Krishna succeeded in boring much of his audience on his recent concert tour. Perhaps the idea they did so much to spread several years ago is not as dead as all that; perhaps we all need a little help from our friends. The enduring power of that idea is as permanent as any impact their music had on us, even if they no longer believe it.

February 16, 1975

"THE TIMES THEY ARE A-CHANGIN'"

The New Young Are Now Heard

A generation is emerging which asks of its elders, 'What do you know? What can you do?'

By HAROLD TAYLOR

EACH generation has its own style and its own truth, having lived through a particular expanse of time which belongs to it and to no other. Each member of a generation reflects some part of the character of his time and starts almost imperceptibly to transform it into something else.

In America at the beginning of the Nineteen Sixties, a new generation has appeared—even though we have not noticed it—and has already begun to transform that part of our society which belongs to youth. There is a new feeling of comradeship among the young, a growing sense of identity with their own generation, a sense of alienation from the older generation which dominated the Nineteen Fifties.

The feeling has now been deepened by the arrival of a new President who has put the past behind him and announced a new beginning. Mr. Kennedy has spoken for his generation—"born in this century, tempered by war, disciplined by a hard and bitter peace, product of our ancient heritage"—and has invited the younger generation to join with him in creating a new age.

Most of the talk about youth in the Nineteen Fifties made use of a public vocabulary created by the mass media, a vocabulary that blocked understanding of its true character. The words were "silent," "conformist," "beat," "security-minded," "delinquent," "soft," "apathetic." Most of the talk about education had to do with the faults of American youth and of their education in comparison with the European and Soviet systems.

WHAT we did not notice was that the young were not listening. They had quietly disappeared into their own world and left the older generation talking to itself. They had given up looking to their elders for leadership, having discovered for themselves that there has been little said which could either interest them or move them to action.

We have been talking about educating the young for a world they have already outgrown while they have been talking privately about a world they wished to bring about. In matters of principle and desire for positive action, the young have been ahead of their Government and their country.

Nor have we noticed the effects on ourselves of our absorption in the cold war. Through the whole of the Nineteen Fifties we impressed upon our young people the dangers to America of Soviet ideology and world policy, the necessity of competing with the Russians in science, technology and military power, giving to the young nothing but fear and negative strictures on which to subsist.

We have treated our students as adolescent members of their generation unready for the responsibilities of citizenship and political involvement. This we called "preparation for life." We have thought of education, not as the means of developing mature, independent-minded citizens, but as a system of taking academic courses in a congenial and bland environment. The public has then felt free to criticize the students for not working harder, for not believing more, for not showing the Russians that our system is better.

ON the other hand, whenever the students on our campuses have become involved in political and social issues, we have been anxious that they might be subverted by unseen hands, or that a visiting speaker might corrupt them with a single radical talk. We have then criticized these students for not being more outspoken, more willing to take risks, and we have been concerned that they have seemed to prefer the security of political silence and the safety of acquiescence to the excitement of social dissent and humanitarian action. An entire literature of alarm has been devoted to youth and its values. We seem surprised to have reaped a harvest of our own planting.

Yet there now exists among the new young an image of America which has survived the negative attitudes and inhibitions with which they have grown up. The silence of the generation of the Nineteen Fifties was in many ways deceptive; it did not mean either consent or lack of critical and creative thought.

HAROLD TAYLOR, former president of Sarah Lawrence and author of "On Education and Freedom," lectured and talked with students at more than a score of colleges last fall.

"They talk privately about a world they wish to bring about." Above, on the Columbia campus.

FOR many of that generation, the Eisenhower era with its public-relations culture, its policy of drift, its cultivation of affluence, and its political rhetoric was to them a total disaster of which they did not wish to speak. For others, the attitude has been one of neutralism, of standing outside the pressures on them to conform or to assume a patriotic posture.

The satirists were their spokesmen, the freedom of jazz and folk music their refuge; the philosophers, the composers, the authors, the poets wrote their texts. The rest, the majority, conformed, thus fulfilling the intention of the older generation.

A new generation has now emerged from the Nineteen Fifties with a style of its own. It has sophistication, skepticism, hard-headedness and idealism. Its critical faculties are highly developed. It asserts a new kind of equality for itself which cuts across the age groups and asks its elders: What do you know? What can you do?

The moral leadership of the new generation was established by the Negro students in the South who quietly and courageously began to assert their rights with the sit-in strikes at lunch counters. These were not organized from outside. They came from the Negro youth themselves, and everywhere in the country their example touched the moral imagination of white fellow students who formed groups to support their effort.

Other groups have been formed since then to protest the loyalty oath in the National Defense Education Act, to advocate the abolition of the House Un-American Activities Committee, to protest against our nuclear-arms policy, against compulsory R. O. T. C., to support Adlai Stevenson's nomination for President, to debate the issues of the Presidential election, to enlarge the dimensions of political discussion into the world of Asia, Africa, Russia.

THE National Student Association, representing more than a million students in nearly 400 colleges and universities, stated in a resolution passed at its Congress last August that the student "must be willing to confront crucial issues of public policy that affect him beyond the classroom and that determine the course of his society."

The most dramatic demonstration of the impulse behind the new generation came when the idea of a Peace Corps was launched a year ago by Representative Henry S. Reuss of Wisconsin and the late Senator Richard L. Neuberger of Oregon. Immediately students across the country responded to the idea that their contribution to world affairs and to the national purpose could be made through serving the

RETURN—President Kennedy, class of '40, is swamped by students on his recent visit to Harvard.

needs of the under-developed countries.

When President Kennedy on his campaign trip appeared at 2 A. M. one day last October at the University of Michigan, 10,000 students were there to hear him speak of the need for public service by American youth. Following his address, the Michigan students swung into action immediately with plans for a Youth Peace Corps.

HARVARD and M. I. T. students acted with equal directness, with two Harvard projects formed, one for teaching service in Nigeria, the other in Tanganyika. The sponsors were deluged with more than 350 applications for the twenty places in Nigeria. Eight M. I. T. graduate students in business and public administration gave up first-rate job opportunities in the United States, and went to Africa to work at the local wages offered.

Are we, then, in a new era in which the political and social enthusiasms of the Nineteen Thirties are again expressing themselves in the actions of youth?

As far as the college students are concerned, there is a new movement. But it is not the movement of the Nineteen Thirties. In those years, the common bonds of poverty, economic insecurity and unemployment drew together a liberal and radical movement of which the students were part, a movement which shared a common ideology and a partisan political program.

THE members of the new generation are not ideological. For the most part they are suspicious of orthodoxies, the liberal orthodoxy as well as the conservative. Some of them are radicals. Craig Comstock, a senior at Harvard and editor of The Harvard Crimson, says of them:

"Though often of the Left, they are done with ideology, and decline to content themselves with writing a manifesto, waving signs or circulating petitions. They are not old-style agitators but self-educators. Often they are starved by their formal academic courses. Like C. P. Snow's young scientists, they are radicals, who have seen the pace of technology, have heard the cry of the hungry and know that politics must respond."

On the other hand, there have been student demonstrations — at Harvard by the members of Tocsin, a disarmament group which staged a walk joined by close to 1,000 students on the campus in favor of unilateral initiative for disarmament; there was the demonstration by students in San Francisco against the hearings of the House Un-American Activities Committee; there has been national student picketing in sympathy with the sit-in strikers.

BUT this is not the main effort. Tocsin has a research-and-analysis project designed to prepare reports for students on the problems of disarmament and arms control; carefully documented reports on the Un-American Activities Committee in support of its abolition have been sent to Washington; students have conferred with or petitioned their Congressmen on issues of national importance.

"So many lies have been told," writes one student, "so many millions of lives have been casually yet brutally snuffed out, that no student will readily take anyone's word for anything."

Nor is there a cohesive student movement which can be identified by labels. There are, instead, groups of students who band together to develop the interests they have in common. These interests extend from writing and producing plays, organizing poetry readings, jazz groups and seminars in African studies to forming Russian-speaking choral groups to travel and sing in the Soviet Union.

WHEN Challenge, a student group, was formed last year at Yale, it came from the efforts of three students who worked outside the existing student organizations and political parties, elected no officers, and concentrated on seminars, study groups and week-end colloquia addressed by national and international figures with audiences of 1,000 to 1,500 students from Eastern colleges.

The issues of contemporary society, said the students, have become so complex that they begin to seem remote, and the university environ-ment tends to narrow the range of thought about the world outside it. The students therefore tackled world problems on their own, with such help as they could get, looking for new alternatives to existing policies. They respected the contribution of informed opinion and research in finding those alternatives.

In some cases, the interest in world issues and in politics has shown itself in more direct action. There are students now in college who are preparing to enter politics in their home states when they graduate and who have already had political experience in working for candidates in the recent election.

These are manifestations of a new spirit in a new generation. They occur against a background of conservatism in the American student body as a whole. This is a conservatism which mixes unconcern for social issues with acceptance of the status quo and considers a college education as the means of access to higher pay and wider range of employment opportunity.

Yet even here there are stirrings of new interest in political dialogue. Senator Barry Goldwater, who recently defended the fraternity system as a bulwark against communism in the colleges, has his own student following, and there are campus groups who have found in Senator Goldwater's principles of conservatism the first statement of conservative political belief around which they could rally.

The Intercollegiate Society of Individualists has some adherents on the campuses, with a program based on the fear that the influence of liberal professors is causing young Americans to lose faith in "the free enterprise system, the concept of limited government, the right of private property, and the moral and spiritual values which underlie this philosophy."

THERE is also a student conservatism which has nothing to do with politics, but which opposes any inclination by students to take part in political or social controversy. The attitude is shared by many faculty members and educators, who hold that the student in high school and college should be concerned primarily with passing his courses and that student government and student organizations and even student newspapers should confine themselves to local matters on the campus.

The student councils of several universities, including Columbia and the University of Colorado, voted to disaffiliate from the National Student Association after the association had declared its policies on the role of the student as a citizen. Other students have been critical of student government for taking action in matters of civil rights, the loyalty oath or other issues.

The argument is usually made that no student group can speak for all students, and that students are too imma-ture to understand and to act on the issues.

IT is this kind of argument which dampened the enthusiasm of students in the Nineteen Fifties, but which is no longer effective in muting the new voices of the Nineteen Sixties. The students have discovered a world of their own in which real issues in foreign countries are fought by students in the context of revolution and civil war, and can be fought at home, not only in Congress and in American communities, but in the schools and colleges where ideas for the future are generated.

It is time to pay attention to these young men and women. It is time to give them the support and encouragement they have failed to receive in the ten years just past. They need not only the opportunity for education, the financial support for their studies, the teachers who can give them the knowledge they desire, they need the faith of an older generation that they have a contribution to make, in their own terms, as free citizens whose ideas and energies can give us the shape and content of a new era.

President Kennedy knows the universities and what they have done and can do for his country. He knows the quality of this generation of Americans. If he and the Congress give them the chance they deserve, they will show the world what they can do.

January 29, 1961

KENNEDY SETS UP U. S. PEACE CORPS TO WORK ABROAD

Creates Pilot Plan and Asks Congress to Establish a Permanent Operation

RECRUITS TO GET NO PAY

By PETER BRAESTRUP
Special to The New York Times.

WASHINGTON, March 1 — President Kennedy issued an executive order today creating a Peace Corps. It will enlist American men and women for voluntary, unpaid service in the developing countries of the world.

The order set up the Peace Corps on a "temporary pilot basis." President Kennedy also sent Congress a message requesting legislation to make the corps permanent.

Announcing the move at his news conference, the President described the Peace Corps as a "pool of trained American men and women sent overseas by the United States Government or through private organizations and institutions to help foreign governments meet their urgent needs for skilled manpower."

The President's expressed hope was to have 500 to 1,000 Peace Corps workers "in the field by the end of this year."

Shriver Heads Planners

The Administration's planning effort on the Peace Corps has been headed since late January by R. Sargent Shriver, a Chicago business man and civic leader who is the President's brother-in-law. The President said today that a decision on who would head the agency would be made "in several days."

Life in the Peace Corps, the President stressed, "will not be easy." Members will work without pay but they will be given living allowances. They will live at the same level as the inhabitants of the countries to which they are sent.

The President emphasized that "we will send Americans abroad who are qualified to do a job," particularly those with technical skills in teaching, agriculture and health.

"There is little doubt," the President said in his subsequent message to Congress, "that the number of those who wish to serve will be far greater than our capacity to absorb them."

March 2, 1961

Rights Campaigners Off for Mississippi

By CLAUDE SITTON
Special to The New York Times

OXFORD, Ohio, June 19—The first phase of one of the most ambitious civil rights projects yet conceived has ended here in an atmosphere of mixed hope and doubt, fear and determination.

Some 200 college students, the vanguard of a volunteer force of 1,000, are drifting out of this quiet little college town to engage in a Negro voter registration drive in Mississippi.

There they will face white hostility in the smallest cities, dusty county seats, farms and plantations of the countryside. They, will attempt in two months to bring a lasting change in the pattern of segregation and discrimination under which Negroes have lived for a century.

No one can predict the outcome. But there is abundant evidence that the Mississippi project has already sharpened the controversy over the state's racial codes and customs. The consensus among observers is that, whether it leads to a serious crisis or not, the relationship between whites and Negroes there will be markedly different by the summer's end.

The national implications are symbolized by the red-lettered bulletin in the lobby of the Edith Clawson Hall at the Western College for Women, site of the first of two week-long orientation courses for the volunteers. It says:

"Before you leave Oxford, write your Congressmen asking them to act to insure your safety. Contact should be established with them before you reach Mississippi. The memo on Federal authority may help give background for your letters."

Many of the volunteers, most of whom are white, come from prominent and influential families in New York, California, Illinois and New Jersey. Civil rights leaders have complained that the Federal authorities have in the past shown little concern for the plight of Mississippi Negroes. They believe the presence of the students will involve the entire nation.

This objective was underscored by Robert P. Moses, a former New York City schoolteacher who has been working in Mississippi since 1961. He is a field secretary of the Student Nonviolent Coordinating Committee, the key civil rights group in the undertaking, and is director of the project.

"No administration in this country is going to commit political suicide over the right to vote of Negroes," he told an orientation session here.

"This is part of what we are doing, and getting the country involved through yourselves," he told the students, "that is, to open this up to the country and get the backing of the country and get pressure—public pressure, continual, mounting, steady public pressure—on all of the agencies of the Federal Government and on all of the informal processes of this country. That's the only way we'll get any kind of creative solution to what's going on down there."

Hope to Increase Interest

Not all the students in the 100 student committee workers, the National Council of Churches representatives, the lawyers and civil rights experts who have worked with them are certain that the project will bring greater Federal activity.

Neither are they convinced that the program of voter registration and other political action, education and vocational training and cultural activities will lead to sweeping change.

But they do believe the project will quicken the interest that whites outside the South have in the civil rights struggle. Philip Hocker of Corning, N. Y., said, "It will be something more than just a picture on a TV screen after this."

Mr. Hocker, the 20-year-old son of an engineering physicist, is typical of the volunteers. Like others in the group, Mr. Hocker, who was a freshman at Princeton last year, has some fear over the white hostility they may encounter. But he said his chief concern lay in another field — "whether I can get through to the Negroes."

Robert Berger, 25, a graduate student in government at Wesleyan, who is the son of a Hartford, Conn., insurance executive, said, "I think that a few of the people I meet will gain some feeling that there are some whites who understand their problems partially and who will work toward a solution of their problems."

Mr. Berger showed an awareness of the reaction of Mississippi whites to the project.

"They might really feel that they're being invaded," he said.

To avoid this impression, leaders of the project are trying to get the workers from Oxford to Mississippi with as little fanfare as possible. They said they wanted the first group, which will concentrate on voter registration, to start at once and thus demonstrate to Mississippians that the goal was not one of demonstrations or other tactics that might evoke violence.

Mr. Moses emphasized this point in a meeting with some 30 whites and Negroes assigned to southwestern Mississippi, where civil rights advocates contend a reign of anti-Negro terrorism exists.

"I think, it extremely important that you identify yourself as what you are, that you are working on voter registration, that you did not come down to organize any sit-ins, that you did not come down to organize any marches or demonstrations," he said.

However, there is a general belief that the volunteers may encounter trouble in some communities. The Rev. James M. Lawson, a Memphis pastor who is a consultant on nonviolence for the Southern Christian Leadership Conference, told the group, "Just your walking into Canton, Miss., or Ruleville or Shaw, just your being there, could be the catalytic agent that evokes violence."

Much of the orientation course has been devoted to preparing the volunteers for this eventuality. They have watched and taken part in "role-playing" — acting out scenes of violence and nonviolent confrontation with whites, as well as such less dramatic activities, as persuading Negroes to apply for registration and then accompanying them to the courthouse.

A handbook for political programs distributed to the students suggests the following safety precautions for voter registration workers:

¶Know all the roads in and out of town.
¶Know the location of sanctuaries and safe homes in the county.
¶Make arrangements for regular checks with the Jackson office and/or the county office of the campaign.
¶Decide whether night or day work is preferable

Suggests 'Track Practice'

Speakers have repeatedly warned the students that the students may be subjected to police brutality.

"They take you to jail, strip you, lay you on the floor and beat you until you're almost dead," said Cordell Reagon, a student committee field secretary from Nashville, Tenn.

"They'll beat you because you're white," said Mr. Reagon, a Negro. "They wouldn't do that to me."

Charles Morgan Jr., a civil rights lawyer and former resident of Birmingham, Ala., told the group, "Most of the people that you meet there are going to be just about as afraid of you as you are of them."

But he added, "I would suggest a little track practice between now and then, because I really believe it's going to be bad."

Miss Betty Garman, a white field secretary for the student committee, described the effect these lectures have had on the students. "There's fear, but the fear is not going to immobilize these people," she said.

Girl's Task Difficult

Mrs. Sandra Hayden, a field secretary who joined the student committee last year, said that most volunteers had a realistic attitude toward the project. She conceded that white girls would find their task more difficult than would boys.

Only a few girls will take part in registration activities. Most have been assigned to "freedom schools," community centers or to office work in the larger cities.

The major problem encountered by white women, Mrs. Hayden said, "is the psychological strain of knowing that you endanger the people you are around."

Not all the volunteers are students. Teachers, nurses, ministers and others are expected to participate. Some will have little contact with Negroes. They will work with persons in the white community, encouraging them to take part in the civil rights movement and studying white reaction to the project.

June 21, 1964

EXPERTS IDENTIFY MISSISSIPPI BODIES AS RIGHTS AIDES'

By CLAUDE SITTON
Special to The New York Times

JACKSON, Miss., Aug. 5—Experts working from dental charts and other evidence identified today the three bodies found buried deep inside a cattle-pond dam as those of three missing civil rights workers.

Federal Bureau of Investigation agents declined to say how the two white men and one Negro were killed six weeks ago after their release from the Neshoba County jail at Philadelphia, Miss.

There were persistent reports that an informer who received $25,000 to $30,000 had led F.B.I. agents to the crude graves five miles southwest of Philadelphia in the rolling hills of east-central Mississippi.

These reports and other circumstances surrounding the finding of the bodies early last night indicated that investigators knew some details of the slaying and had some idea of who was involved. However, it was learned that no arrests were imminent.

[In Honolulu, Dick Gregory, the Negro entertainer, said tonight that three weeks ago he had turned over a letter to the F.B.I. naming five persons as responsible for the deaths and pinpointing the location of the bodies, according to United Press International.]

Said to Have Been Shot

County Coroner Fulton Jackson, Sheriff L.A. Rainey, Deputy Sheriff Cecil Price and a six-man coroner's jury visited the site last night and again this morning. No finding was announced immediately.

"We are not certain what was the cause of death," Mr. Jackson said.

He drove an ambulance bearing the bodies to Jackson last night. The bodies were encased in three black plastic bags, tagged X-1, X-2 and X-3.

A waiting team of pathologists and F.B.I. identification experts at the University of Mississippi Medical Center began examination of the bodies after the ambulance arrived at 12:30 A.M.

Mr. Jackson was asked today if it were true the autopsies had shown that the three men had been shot to death and that bullets had been removed from all the bodies. Such a report was published by The Jackson Daily News.

"I'm just not going to make any statement at this time," the coroner answered. "The matter is still pending."

J. Edgar Hoover, director of the F.B.I., announced this morning in Washington that the two white men had been definitely identified as Michael H. Schwerner, a 24-year-old field worker for the Congress of Racial Equality from New York, and Andrew Goodman, 20, a Queens College student from New York, who was a volunteer in the summer civil rights campaign in Mississippi.

Further tests were being made to confirm the tentative identification of the body of James E. Chaney, 21, a Negro plasterer from Meridian, Miss., who also was a CORE field worker.

It was indicated that F.B.I. agents were certain the body was that of Mr. Chaney but that the identification could not be announced as positive until further tests were completed, to satisfy the legal requirements for establishing identification.

The three men disappeared late Sunday night, June 21. The last person known to have seen them is Deputy Sheriff Price.

He was among the law-enforcement officers who escorted the ambulance to Jackson and helped carry the bodies into the medical center.

Mr. Price has said he arrested Mr. Chaey for speeding on the afternoon of June 21 on Philadelphia's outskirts and held the others for investigation. The three men were returning to Meridian, Miss., from a visit to the site of a burned Negro church on the county's eastern edge.

Mr. Chaney posted a $20 bond, and he and the two white men were released at about 10:30 that night, according to the deputy. Mr. Price said he had told them to get out of the county and had seen them leave town in the direction of Meridian.

The station wagon in which they were riding was found burned in a swamp 10 miles north of Philadelphia two days later.

Despite a wide search across 10 counties by 400 sailors, 100 F.B.I. agents and 100 state highway patrolmen, there was no apparent progress toward a solution of the case until last Monday.

On that day the F.B.I. rented in Jackson a bulldozer and a dragline—a piece of heavy excavating equipment that uses a bucket shovel suspended by cable from a crane boom. The machinery left for Philadelphia that night.

The bulldozer cut a road through the pine woods and underbrush yesterday morning to the dam site, in a pasture between two hills, several hundred yards west of State Highway 21.

Joseph Sullivan, an F.B.I. inspector from Washington and chief of the search, obviously knew where the bodies lay. The dragline rolled out to the center of the 250-foot-long dam shortly after noon. The huge bucket shovel began tearing into the 25-foot-high earthen levee.

The question of how Mr. Sullivan knew the three bodies lay some 20 feet down, near the dam's base, remains to be answered. But a clue was provided last week in an interview with Roy K. Moore, special agent in charge of the new field office of the F.B.I. in Jackson.

Mr. Moore was asked if it were true that agents had passed the word around Philadelphia that $25,000 would be paid for information leading to recovery of the bodies.

He replied that it was well known that the F.B.I. offered rewards in cases of this kind.

According to one report, not immediately confirmed, an unidentified informant forced the bureau to raise the reward to $30,000 before disclosing the grave site.

Discovery of the bodies only intensified the F.B.I. search. While state troopers turned back the curious at roadblocks, agents streamed into the area of the dam at dawn today to examine the ground for hundreds of yards around it in a hunt for evidence.

Olen Burrage, 42, a truck-line operator, owns the farm, known locally as "the Old John Townsend Place." He said in an interview that he had employed Herman Tucker of Philadelphia to build the dam.

The pond was to serve as a catch basin for water for 20 cows pastured there. The work began in late May and was nearly finished.

Mr. Burrage said he had had no inkling that his property had been involved in the disappearance of the three men until yesterday, when agents came to his home, two miles northeast of the pond.

He said that the agents had told him they wanted to dig on his property and would reimburse him for any damages.

Agents returned last night to question him, he said.

"They were right nice to me," he added.

"I just don't know why anybody would kill them," he said in reference to the slayings. "I want people to know I am sorry it happened."

August 6, 1964

796 Students Arrested as Police Break Up Sit-In at U. of California

By WALLACE TURNER

Special to The New York Times

BERKELEY, Calif., Dec. 3 —The police arrested 796 University of California students in 12 hours today, dragging many on their backs down flights of stairs to end a sit-in demonstration. The mass arrests were made in removing demonstrators who took possession of the administration building on the campus last night. The Free Speech Movement, the protesting student group, retaliated by calling a student strike. Faculty members, at a special meeting, gave evidence of some support for the students. The dispute over students' political and protest activities has shaken the university for almost three months. The strike was called after Gov. Edmund G. Brown ordered early this morning that sit-in demonstrators be removed by force from the corridors of Sproul Hall, the administration building. Mr. Brown said that the students' action constituted "anarchy." Charges of police brutality were made as a result of the removals and arrests today. In this 27,500-student university, the effectiveness of the strike was difficult to measure. In the morning pickets wheeled in front of the doors of all the classroom buildings and, although students continued to pass through the lines, there were reports that many classrooms were empty.

Clark Kerr, president of the university, issued a statement tonight declaring that the Free Speech Movement represented an "understandable concern" last September but that it "has now become an instrument of anarchy and of personal aggrandizement."

Representatives of about 75 of the 82 academic departments at the university, in a meeting this afternoon, found that about 20 departments were functioning normally in the face of the strike. Prof. Charles Hulten, chairman of the Journalism Department, said that individual faculty members would decide tomorrow whether to hold classes.

A meeting of 500 of the 1,200 members of the faculty voted a resolution this afternoon stating that the university faced a "desperate situation."

The faculty members favor new and liberalized campus rules for political activity and setting up a committee to which students could appeal administration decisions on penalties for violating university rules on political action.

Plan Telegram to Brown

The resolution also asked "that all pending campus action against students for acts occurring before the present date be dropped."

At the meeting, faculty members drafted a telegram to be sent to Governor Brown. It condemned the use of the California Highway Patrol on the campus and the exclusion of faculty members from Sproul Hall.

Last night about 1,000 sit-in demonstrators filled the corridors of Sproul Hall before the doors were locked at 7:00 P. M. They sat there, sleeping, singing, studying and talking until about 3:10 A. M., when Edward W. Strong, the chancellor for this campus of the multi-campus university, went to Sproul Hall.

Mr. Strong read a statement asking the students to leave. A few did, but most stayed.

They had put up barricades at the stairways and were concentrated on the second, third and fourth floors.

The police took an elevator to the fourth floor and began removing students there.

Capt. Larry Waldt of the Alameda County sheriff's office made the estimate of the number of students arrested.

By midday, the routine was standard, as illustrated by the arrest of Jean Golson.

When she found herself at the head of the line of demonstrators, Sgt. Don Smithson of the Berkeley police force told her, "You are under arrest for trespass and unlawful assembly."

Another Berkeley policeman held a microphone to record her answers and the sergeant's statements. A third made notes on a booking form.

"If you talk out, you will not be charged with resisting arrest, but if we are forced to carry you out, you will be charged with resisting arrest," the sergeant said.

'Female on the Way'

Miss Golson said she would not walk out. A number was held to her chest and her photograph was taken. The Berkeley police pulled her by the arms for a few feet and then turned her over to two sheriff's deputies from Alameda County. They dragged her quickly down the corridor on her back, shouting, "Female on the way."

At a booking desk, she was pulled erect and was fingerprinted. Then she was pulled into an office for searching by two matrons from the sheriff's office.

Then she was dragged back into the elevator, where other girls were being held. When the elevator was full, the girls were taken to the basement and were loaded into a van for transportation to the county jail.

The bail schedule was $75 each on the trespass and unlawful assembly charges and $100 for resisting arrest.

Total Bail Is $150,000

Booking officers at the Alameda County sheriff's office said that about 25 of the demonstrators posted bail soon after being booked. Meantime, lawyers, parents and others were meeting with a municipal judge attempting to obtain an order freeing the demonstrators on their own recognizance. The total bail involved will be more than $150,000.

For men, the handling was significantly different once they were turned over to the sheriff's deputies after arrest. Those men who would walk were jogged down four flights of steps to the basement. Those who remained limp were dragged by the arms down the steps, departing to the cries of "Good luck" from their friends.

There were about a score of

sheriff's deputies whose job was to drag the men down the steps. As the day passed, their humor became more acid. Some bumped the buttocks of their male prisoners as they dragged them down the stairs.

"There'll be some sore rumps in jail tonight," one deputy said.

After the corridors of Sproul Hall were closed, a floor at a time, the litter of the sit-ins remained. There were empty fruit cartons, crushed soft-drink cans, a guitar, stacks of textbooks, sleeping bags and blankets and scores of notebooks with lecture notes in them.

Shouts 'This Is Wonderful'

When Mario Savio, a protest leader, was taken away by the police, he shouted, "This is wonderful—wonderful. We'll bring the university to our terms."

Another leader, Arthur Goldberg, said as he was led away. "Good! The kids have learned more about democracy here than they could in 40 years of classes. This is a perfect example of how the State of California plays the game."

Mr. Savio is a New Yorker who is the president of the Berkeley Chapter of Friends of S.N.C.C., the Student Non-violent Coordinating Committee. He was involved last spring in recruiting demonstrators who slept in at the Sheraton Palace Hotel. He was arrested on a charge of disturbing the peace. He also worked in the S.N.C.C. program in Mississippi last summer.

Another leader of the Free Speech Movement is Bettina

Aptheker. She is a member of the W. E. B. DuBois Club, which has been described by Department of Justice sources as a front among college students for the Communist party.

The dispute that led to the arrests began last September when the university administration announced that it would no longer permit the use of a strip of campus property for soliciting political funds and recruiting protests demonstrators.

The students objected, and a series of demonstrations resulted. Eight students were suspended and the demonstrations were stepped up.

Last month, the university regents ordered that the students be permitted to recruit demonstrators and collect political contributions on campus. But the regents said the students must be held accountable for off-campus violations of the law in projects begun on campus.

They also said that discipline must be tightened.

Earlier this week, four students received letters from the administration indicating that they were to be disciplined, and perhaps expelled. Yesterday the newest demonstration began in protest.

Conservatives Quit Group

The Free Speech Movement was organized with an executive committee of about 60 members, each representing some campus organization. Initially, conservative groups belonged, including the Young Republicans, but these recently disassociated themselves.

The leadership is concentrated in an 11-member steering committee that appears to be dominated by representatives of campus chapters of the Congress of Racial Equality, the Young Socialist League, the Young Socialist Alliance, Slate (a student political organization) and the W. E. B. DuBois Club.

At a noon rally of about 5,000 students, Steve Wiesman, leader of the Free Speech Movement, called for an investigation of what he termed police brutality. He also demanded the removal of the police "from this campus now and forever" and the removal of Mr. Kerr as president of the university.

In his statement tonight, Mr. Kerr denied that freedom of speech had ever been an issue and said, "The protest has been over organizing political action on campus."

Mr. Kerr accused the Free Speech Movement of violating the law, of intolerance, distortion of the truth, irrationality, indecency and ill will.

In Sacramento, Governor Brown said, "We're not going to have anarchy in the state of California while I'm Governor, and that's anarchy. I did plan to go to Berkeley, but I have other things to do."

Opposition to the Free Speech Movement was in evidence here today. Some students standing at the noon rally held signs reading "Throw the Bums Out" and "Law Not Anarchy—The Majority of Students Do Not Support This Demonstration."

December 4, 1964

Concern Over Adolescent Suicides Stirs Educators

Importance of Recognizing Symptoms Stressed by College Health Services

By JOAN COOK

A STUDENT at Yale University committed suicide on campus last month. A Princeton senior shot and killed himself last January. At Harvard there have been two suicides since July, 1963. There is even on record the incredible case of a child who tried to destroy himself more than 50 times between the ages of 3 and 7.

The number of adolescent suicides and suicide attempts is a source of alarm to an increasing number of educators, doctors and parents. Princeton added a second full-time psychiatrist to its health services this fall; other schools are expanding existing services; at Columbia University the number of students seeking professional help has tripled in the last 10 years.

And for every suicide there are five or six attempts, according to Dr. Dana L. Farnsworth, director of Harvard University's health services.

Latest available figures show that 550 teen-agers between the ages of 15 and 19 took their own lives in 1962. But statistics fail to tell the whole story.

Fewer than 50 per cent of juvenile suicides are reported as

such. The rest are covered up as accidents or illnesses by relatives, friends and sympathetic physicians, according to the Journal of the National Education Association.

Whether or not student suicide is on the rise remains for the present a moot question. Spokesmen for college health services vary in their opinions. Many are more inclined to believe that the recognition of mental illness and the rise in services open to troubled students has brought the formerly boo subject out into the open.

As to the causes of adolescent suicides or suicide attempts, they cite a number of reasons. These include:

¶Heightened academic competition

¶Increased tensions of modern life

¶Difficult personal adjustments

¶Unrealistic aspirations of parents

¶A combination of pressures beyond the youthful individual's capacity to cope.

Suicide is more frequent in boys than in girls, in whites than in nonwhites, in students than in workers, according to Dr. Henry Bakwin, professor of clinical pediatrics, New York University School of Medicine.

'Watch for Danger Signals'

Dr. Bakwin notes that the suicide rate is higher during spring months than in winter, more frequent during periods of economic crisis, less common during wars.

"Parents, teachers and doctors must learn to watch for danger signals and catch them in time, so that we may avert some of these tragedies," Dr. Leif J. Braaten has said.

The former Cornell University psychologist conducted an extensive study in cooperation with Dr. C. Douglas Darling, psychiatrist at the mental health division of Cornell's department of clinical and preventive medicine, in order to shed some light on youthful suicides.

"Evidence shows that at least one person often has been given

a clue to the young suicide's intentions," Dr. Braaten says. "This is a hopeful factor about this tragic situation, but it has been given scant attention."

The Cornell University study of student suicides uncovered information that might well apply to high-school and even grade-school students.

Surprisingly, Cornell doctors found that the student-patient who achieved the highest marks was the one most likely to do away with himself. Nonsuicidal students, on the other hand, were often doing poorly in their academic work. The bright students too often demanded far more of themselves than either their professors or the university.

The motives for student suicides, according to the study, included a desire to destroy themselves because of the gulf between what they wished to be and what they appeared to be to themselves; a need to punish others who had brought so much hurt upon them; an urge to repent from some sin, and a cry for help.

On the younger level, a child psychiatrist, Dr. Leo Kanner of Johns Hopkins University, has this to say:

"It is unnatural for a child to

be disgusted with life. An unhappy child is not a well child, and requires judicious psychiatric handling. In an atmosphere of fear and gloom, the soil is prepared for thoughts of self-destruction."

Unhappy Child Needs Help

Unhappiness can stem from a variety of things—the dread of failure in school with its ensuing punishment by strict, unrelenting parents; the fear of brutalities inflicted by an alcoholic or tyrannical father, and the mistaken idea that masturbation will have dire results, Dr. Kanner says.

On the college level, men such as Dr. Braaten, Dr. Willard Dalrymple, head of Princeton's

health services, Dr. Robert L. Arnstein, director of Yale's mental-health service, and Dr. Farnsworth feel the future is far from dark.

The increasing number of studies in this area, the broader dissemination of material about mental health and increased treatment facilities are big steps in the right direction. Teachers, parents and students themselves must be increasingly alert to the fact that when a young person mentions thoughts of suicide, trouble is brewing.

"The notion which many people have relied upon for years —that no one who talks about suicide is in danger of trying it—is often false," Dr. Braaten points out. "In fact, suicide

threats are probably the most important danger signal of all."

Parents' Responsibility

Parents, too, have a responsibility to curtail unreasonable demands and false expectations where their children are concerned. To force an adolescent to go to a particular school against his will for reasons of status; to map out career plans without regard to the individual's interest; to prevent withdrawal from one school in favor of another, where the student and a guidance counselor agree he might function better, are unfair.

At best, maturing is a slow and difficult business, educators note. It is sometimes advisable

for a student to drop out of college for a year or more and return to school when he is more sure of himself.

"We encourage young men of this sort [immature] to delay entering college or, if they have done so and run into trouble, to go on leave and put in their two years of military service," Dr. Arnstein says. "We once did a follow-up study of dropouts and found that the majority of those with personality disorders either came back and graduated or finished elsewhere or were successfully at work."

December 29, 1964

COLLEGIANS ADOPT A 'BILL OF RIGHTS'

Say Administrators Should Be Campus Housekeepers

By FRED POWLEDGE
Special to The New York Times

PHILADELPHIA, March 28 — A group of Eastern college students declared here this weekend that college administrators should be no more than housekeepers in the educational community.

The modern college or university, they said, should be run by the students and the professors; administrators would be "maintenance, clerical and safety personnel whose purpose is to enforce the will of faculty and students."

A manifesto, which is not likely to be adopted by any

college administrator, was adopted in draft form at an all-day meeting yesterday at the University of Pennsylvania. About 200 students attended the meeting, 45 remaining until the end when the "Student Bill of Rights" was adopted.

The 200 youths were from 39 colleges in the Philadelphia and New York areas, Harvard, Yale, the University of California at Berkeley, and from schools in the Midwest.

Their political beliefs represented a spectrum of campus activism. Some are members of campus chapters of the W.E.B. DuBois Clubs of America; one represented the National Student Association.

Many said they were independent of any student-left group. All appeared to believe that the wave of campus rebellion that started in Berkeley last fall should be brought to all American campuses.

National Panel Discussed

There was not complete agreement on the methods that should be employed to bring it there. A key portion of the

manifesto, proposed after hours of discussion, had been the pledge that, in order to achieve their demands, the students would not hesitate to start a general academic strike. The provision was voted down, 27 to 11.

The students then went on to discuss the possibility of forming a national coordinating committee to channel campus protest movements. They failed to reach agreement on this by 9 P.M. Saturday, which was the time the Christian Association Auditorium, where they met, closed. The question was to be settled at some later point.

A recurring theme in the meeting was that colleges and universities had become servants of the "financial, industrial, and military establishment," and that students and faculty were being "sold down the river" by administrators.

Among the provisions of the manifesto were declarations of freedom to join, organize or hold meetings of any organization and to extend the freedoms of speech and assembly to

the campus; abolition of tuition fees; control of law enforcement by the students and faculty; an end to the Reserve Officer Training Corps; abolition of loyalty oaths; student-faculty control over curriculum, and a number of safeguards against what the students considered wrongful search and seizure.

The conference, titled "Democracy on the Campus," was held under the auspices of the Emergency Civil Liberties Committee, which was formed in 1951 "to help meet the growing menace to the Bill of Rights."

One of the participants at the conference was the folk-singer and pacifist Joan Baez, who announced that she was about to start an "Institute for the Study of Nonviolence" in the Carmel, Calif., area.

Miss Baez said the institute would admit 10 or 15 students for six-week sessions, and that they would study nonviolence while remaining "politically active."

March 29, 1965

Youths March at School Barring Bearded Student

Special to The New York Times

STORRS, Conn., March 31 —Fifty chanting students marched outside the Edwin O. Smith High School today carrying signs defending beards.

The youths were demonstrating against an order barring James Steinman, an 18-year-old senior at the school, from attending classes until he shaved his three-month beard.

Young Steinman began picketing the school by himself yesterday after he had been given the order by the school principal, Arthur Goldberg. He was joined today by classmates and students from nearby schools and colleges, many of them wearing beards.

The signs bore such slogans as, "Beards Cannot Preclude Brains." The youths chanted, "Rhyme and reason, beards are in season."

April 1, 1965

PENTAGON FINDS DRAFT MUST STAY; URGES REVISIONS

Study Seeks Conscription at an Earlier Age and Wider Range of Deferments

By JACK RAYMOND
Special to The New York Times

WASHINGTON, May 8 — A year-long Defense Department study of military conscription concludes that the draft must be continued when the current law expires in 1967.

The results of the study indicate that the draft will have to be maintained for the foreseeable future if the size of the armed forces, now totaling 2.6 million, is kept at this strength.

However, the analysts who contributed to the study of the military draft made certain recommendations for changes in existing practices. These included:

¶The draft of younger persons. At present, the average draft age is 22 to 23 years, as draft boards consistently call up the oldest eligibles.

¶A widening of deferment possibilities. Deferments are based on occupations, educational activity and family status for reasons of national interest or personal hardship.

¶Increases in military pay and fringe benefits as an incentive to enlistment and re-enlistment.

Draft Inequities Scored

The study was ordered by President Johnson last year after a flurry of published criticism of inequities in the draft.

Subsequently, during the election campaign, Senator Barry Goldwater, the Republican candidate, advocated abolition of the draft.

At the time the President announced the study of the draft, he told a news conference that he would consider "alternatives to the present draft selection system, including the possibility of meeting our requirements on an entirely voluntary basis in the next decade."

He pointed out that the present draft law was more than 15 years old. The original principle of equal sharing "may have drifted in practice," he said.

Several Studies in One

The study ordered by the President was to have been completed within a year, that is by last month. Delays forced an extension of the deadline to July. The investigative part of the task has been completed, however.

Secretary of Defense Robert S. McNamara was scheduled to have the first complete written version of the report on his desk early next week.

The study is actually a series of studies, some of them prepared by private experts, under the direction of William Gorham, the Deputy Assistant Secretary of Defense Manpower.

The cost of the program of studies has been estimated at $1 million. It was described, when undertaken, as the most comprehensive analysis ever undertaken of the problems of military conscription in the United States.

The studies covered population growth, estimates of future military manpower needs, the effects of various economic and social conditions on enlistments, the attractions and vexations of military service, and various proposals for dealing with them that have been offered in the past.

The study's conclusion that the draft cannot be abandoned in the near future is not considered surprising, in the light of various recent comments by Pentagon officials.

Secretary of the Army Stephen Ailes, in testifying before the Senate Armed Services Committee, was asked what he thought about the possibility of ending the draft. He replied, "I know of no substitute for it at this time."

The Army is the only military service that consistently resorts to the draft to meet its manpower needs. There is general agreement, however, that volunteers for the other services are motivated in part by a desire to avoid being drafted into the Army.

Under the law, most young men between the ages of 19 and 26 may be drafted if they are not deferred because of occupation or studies whose continuance is believed in the national interest, or because of marital status or hardship.

Wealth Called Advantage

The draft has prompted criticism, however. It has been said that young men with enough money to get married or enter college have an advantage over those who must go to work immediately upon leaving high school.

In addition, the sometimes erratic way in which the draft has been carried out by various local draft boards has brought complaints. A youth drafted in one town might be spared in another.

The Army's rejection as a draftee of Cassius Clay, the heavyweight boxing champion, has never been explained to the satisfaction of many observers.

The armed services need about 600,000 new recruits a year. About 100,000 are drafted. But 200,000 of the remaining half-million are said to be motivated by the threat of the draft.

When talk of the possible elimination of the draft began to spread, enlistments fell. Each of the military services has complained about this recently during Congressional hearings.

The Navy, to avoid resorting to the draft, began accepting volunteers with lower physical and mental qualifications. The Army began raising its monthly draft requests. Yesterday, it announced a call for 17,000 in June — the biggest monthly draft quota since November, 1963.

Despite its comprehensive nature, the findings of the Pentagon draft study are expected to meet criticism. Many critics are expected to argue that a Presidential commission rather than the Pentagon should have conducted the study.

Former Senator Kenneth B. Keating argued for a Presidential commission when he raised the subject of the draft last spring. Similarly, James G. Patton, president of the National Farmers Union, has lately called for a Presidential commission and condemned the expected result of the Pentagon commission in advance.

Mr. Patton, an early critic of the draft whose correspondence with President Kennedy on the subject in August, 1963, disclosed Mr. Kennedy's concern, wrote recently in the National Union Farmer:

"It is probably true that the armed forces cannot be maintained at their present numbers without the draft, all other things remaining equal. The proper question is not, 'can we end the draft?' The proper question is 'what do we have to do to maintain the armed forces without the draft?'"

Most professional military men appear convinced that military conscription can not be abandoned. But counter to the prevailing opinion of their attitude, military men in this country generally oppose an all-professional military force.

Most military leaders believe that an all-professional military force would be regarded by the rest of the country as a class apart, whereas it is the intent of most military men to find acceptance and involvement between the uniformed forces and civilian society.

Some of these attitudes have been put forward in the Pentagon study, although it is believed probable that they will not be incorporated in the final report. The report itself is expected to stress the importance of easing the recruiting and retention problems through higher pay, better housing and educational and job-training opportunities.

May 9, 1965

STUDENTS URGED TO USE RESTRAINT

Graduation Speakers Across Nation Deplore Abuses of Right to Protest

By ERIC PACE

Speakers at commencements across the nation cautioned students yesterday not to abuse the right to protest.

The traditional college graduation ceremonies were bringing to a close an academic year that has been punctuated by student demonstrations.

In a commencement address at the University of Notre Dame, McGeorge Bundy said, "I observe that, as is true in other academic exercises of this spring, those who are the least learned make the most noise."

Mr. Bundy, Special Assistant to the President for National Security Affairs, was apparently alluding to teach-ins and other recent steps by teachers and students to protest Administration policies in Vietnam and the Dominican Republic.

Another high Administration official, Attorney General Nicholas deB. Katzenbach, said that student militancy in fields like civil rights was "healthy and commendable."

Sign of Health Discerned

In a commencement speech at Tufts University, in Medford, Mass., he encouraged students to take part in civil rights and other demonstrations but warned against using such protests "as a catharsis for a dull weekend."

Meanwhile, in a speech at Miami University, Oxford, Ohio, Under Secretary of State George W. Ball said that placards and protest marches against Administration policies were a sign of health and vigor among students. But he warned, "It behooves all of us—whether in government, in the academic world or in the press—to avoid that most dangerous disease, infectious omniscience."

"What is essential is that you apply the critical discipline you have learned in your student years to the intricate, and often intractable, problems faced by your country at the height of world power," he said.

Vice President Humphrey took humorous note of the Administration officials' speech-making activities yesterday, the day most commonly chosen for commencement exercises.

At a luncheon given by Syracuse University's chancellor, William P. Tolley, the Vice President joked, "We're not responsible in the executive branch for anything at home or abroad from now to June 15."

He observed with enthusiasm, "Now is the time we all go to commencements."

In formal remarks at the University's graduation ceremonies, Mr. Humphrey spoke in praise of political moderation.

"My willingness to compromise — and I have done so more times than I can count — is the respect I pay to the disagree," he said.

dignity of those with whom I

Other speakers echoed Mr. Humphrey's praise of moderation. Other large themes that speakers dealt with included problems of morality, world

peace and racial tension.

President Johnson, addressing graduates at Catholic Universit in Washington, called for world peace but did not indicate any new Administration policies to achieve that goal.

He said, "We of America—we of the free world—are ready, as we are always ready, to open that door and invite peace to enter, to dwell in the house of all nations forever."

Senator Robert F. Kennedy, Democrat of New York, made a more specific appeal in an address to graduates of State University College in Plattsburgh, N. Y.

U.S. Contribution Urged

He said that the developed nations must make a "greater contribution, of money and mind, of time and toil," to help underdeveloped countries.

"The United States must make the greatest share of these contributions," he declared.

Senator Margaret Chase Smith of Maine, a Republican, echoed the Democratic officials' pleas for student restraint. In Oneonta, N. Y., she told the 202 graduates of Hartwick College:

"Never be mental mutes, but resist the temptation to be irresponsible critics. Never shrink from protesting or criticizing."

"Leadership is not necessarily proved by carrying placards of protest, or by unruly demonstrations," she said. "It is more often proved by orderly, responsible and dignified expression in which opponents sit and reason with each other instead of indulging in name calling and character assassination."

Warns Aganst Vanity

Kingman Brewster Jr., president of Yale University, combined several of the day's most prevalent themes in an address to about 300 graduating seniors

at St. Lawrence University, Canton, N. Y. He warned against threats to freedom stemming from both "the radical right and the radical left," and against intellectual vanity.

"You have tasted the fruits of freedom here," he said. "You have seen that no person, no group, no generation is so allwise that it deserves to dictate final goodness, final truth, final beauty."

"Preserve that inheritance," he exhorted the St. Lawrence seniors, "against the highhandedness of others and against your own impatience."

Where most commencement speakers spoke against the perils of too passionate involvement in the causes of the day, Mr. Brewster also warned students not to seal themselves off from the world about them, not to "seek recourse in the selfpity now popularly dubbed alienation."

June 7, 1965

STUDENT SOCIETY WORKS ON AIMS

Finds Meeting Can Be More Trouble Than Campaign

By NATALIE JAFFE
Special to The New York Times

KEWADIN, Mich., June 12.— The executive secretary of Students for a Democratic Society climbed on a picnic table today and addressed more than 300 delegates to the organization's annual convention on its third day.

"How many think the food is lousy?" he asked.

A loud chorus of yeas.

"How many think there's not enough?"

More loud yeas.

"How many would put up a couple of extra bucks to improve things?"

Vehement boos.

"In that case, when you complain, please think of this in the context of the problem," concluded the speaker, Clark Kissinger.

A University of Texas student in blue jeans and boots muttered, "And they wonder why we spent all morning discussing how to create and op-

erate the participatory democracy?"

This exchange, which took place on a grassy, maplestrewn hillside here in northern Michigan, illustrates a major problem of Students for a Democratic Society, an organization that has taken a leading role in the movement known as the new student left.

In contrast to other student organizations such as the Student Nonviolent Coordinating Committee and the Free Speech Movement, the society does not have a specific mission in civil rights or university reform. It has served primarily as a forum where a rationale for the action groups can be developed.

Most of its 2,000 members belong to at least one student action group. They acknowledge that life is much simpler for them on a picket line or in a voter registration drive than at a society meeting.

A University of Michigan senior, who is also a member of the Nonviolent Committee, said, "Sure, it's much easier to make pronouncements or launch campaigns—and sometimes I get tired of all this talk."

He pulled at the chopped-off sleeve of his sweatshirt, gazed at a row of parked cars from nearly every state and added, "But here we can express ourselves and communicate with each other in ways that society today doesn't encourage—you

know, mull over what's wrong."

Standing on the lawn outside the big main house here at Camp Maplehurst and shouting over the clamor for more breakfast from the dining room, Mr. Kissinger said, "Maybe when all the forces finally get together, the country will remember this as the beginning of a real left opposition."

He looked down the row of bunkhouses, where many of the delegates were still rolled up in their sleeping bags.

"Right now, there's no correspondence for these kids between this organization and anything in the adult world," he said. "What we want to do is to collect all the sources of opposition so we'll have a constituency and a financial base that can really change the structure."

Unlike the civil rights and the university reform groups, the society has chosen its causes less to get results than to dramatize what it considers basic errors of national principle. From its national office comes an endless flow of documents analyzing these errors.

A march on Washington last April 17 to protest the war in Vietnam was sponsored by the group, its leaders explain, to underline the conviction that the war was being prosecuted without the consent of the nation.

The picketing last March 20 of the Chase Manhattan Bank in New York, Detroit and Boston was staged, they say, to point to the irresponsibility of financial power in dictating American foreign policy. The bank, they charged, is extending loans to the Government of South Africa, which practices racial separatism.

The sponsorship of community organizing projects—there are now 10 across the country —concentrates more on illustrating how much poor people can do for themselves rather than on changing a particular neighborhood.

In Newark, for example, the society-sponsored project recently captured control for neighborhood residents of the committee in the south ward that will direct the local antipoverty campaign. Five of the residents of the poor Negro neighborhood where the Newark Community Union Project has its base came to the convention.

Though many discussions have bogged down in arguments over method, the society's position appears to have emerged between the liberal and the radical left.

Said a student from Newark, "The liberals are too attached to working within the establishment, and the Trotskyists don't work at all, they just pronounce."

June 13, 1965

The Rioters

Roman candles and skyrockets were not the only fireworks set off over the long Fourth of July weekend. At resorts in Iowa, Missouri, New York and Ohio, thousands of teenagers and college students went on an orgy of rioting. Before the weekend was over, more than 600 had been arrested, 100 injured, and property damage ran into many thousands of dollars.

In recent years, vacation time for many youths has been a time for rampage. Florida resorts brace each spring for the invasion of Northern college students on vacation, many of whom spend time in jail before going back to school. On the West Coast, small towns have been terrorized by youthful motorcycle gangs. Music festivals at Newport, R. I., and elsewhere around the country have been scenes of wild outbreaks with

youths battling police and each other. These vacation-time riots, unlike the campus demonstrations over civil rights, Vietnam, free speech and other causes, seem to arise spontaneously and for no apparent reason.

"They don't need a reason," one psychiatrist said last week. "Remember, these are kids who are suddenly freed from school, from all responsibilities; they've been bottled up all year and it doesn't

take much to set them off. When you throw a thousand kids like this together, the explosion is going to be pretty loud." Another psychiatrist noted that "many of these young people are resentful at the uncertainty in society and in their lives, and when they explode in an adult world they are taking out that resentment in one of the few overt ways they can at the adults who have made the world the way it is." He added,

259

"Moderation has never been one of the strong points of youth."

Moderation was certainly not on display last weekend. At Arnolds Point, Iowa, it took tear gas and firehoses to put down 500 rioting youths who began by protesting the closing of the bars at 1 A.M. At two resorts in Ohio, the National Guard was called out and residents later said the area "looks as if there had been a war here."

In Missouri, it took 125 state troopers and police dogs to quell the youths who rampaged through the streets and stood on the dance hall roof and pelted police with beer bottles.

At Lake George, N. Y., however, police were ready when the youths appeared and they arrested anyone who stepped out of line. "What can you do?" asked the Mayor. "You've got to keep them under control." But one college student complained, "It's gotten so you can't sneeze in public around here without getting arrested." Of the 350 arrested at the resort, only one was charged with a felony - he bit the thumb of the village police chief

July 11, 1965

Vietnam Protesters Plan Drive to Avoid the Draft

With this weekend's protests against the war in Vietnam ended, organizations opposing the war are turning their attention to a nationwide movement against the military draft.

They hope to capitalize on a spirit that has already led thousands of youths to try to avoid the draft by burning their draft cards, by neglecting to register, by feigning homosexuality, madness or "football knee," by deliberately flunking a mental test, or simply by staying on in school or hastening marriage plans.

For some, the hero of this movement is 22-year-old David Mitchell, who a month ago was fined $5,000 and sentenced to up to five years in Federal prison for "willfully and knowingly failing to report for induction.

A spokesman for the Pentagon said the Defense Department was "not worried" by the plans. He noted that under the pressure of the increased draft calls voluntary enlistments were increasing for all services.

U.S. To Investigate

However, in Chicago, Attorney General Nicholas DeB Katzenbach announced that the Justice Department would begin an investigation into the "beat the draft" movement.

Asked about Communist influence in the movement, Mr. Katzenbach said that in such groups "you are likely to find some Communists involved."

It is a Federal crime, punishable by a fine of up to $10,000 and up to five years in jail, to evade the draft or counsel or abet another to "refuse or evade registration or service." Congress recently enacted a law making it a crime, punishable by the same penalties, to destroy a draft card.

Increase In Dodgers

"The tendency to avoid military service has considerably increased both in number and in the kind of ruses in the past year," according to Dr. Hugo Engel, a civilian psychiatrist employed as a consultant at the Army induction center at 39 Whitehall Street.

"There are artificial attempts to avoid service by pretending certain disorders — drug addiction, homosexuality, or some physical disorder," he said.

"Homosexuality is one of the predominate attempts," he continued. "Very often we find the appearance and mannerisms without any medical evidence.

"Quite often a person comes in, sometimes with other people, and gives the appearance of being mentally deranged, whereas the educational and professional history doesn't give any such evidence," he said.

Three Categories Noted

The movement against the draft can be roughly divided into three catagories:

¶Members of the new student radical organizations who are bitterly opposed to the war in Vietnam and who hope to build a mass antidraft movement as another form of protest.

¶Members of traditional religious and pacifist organizations who have long been conscientious objectors and who hope to replace wars with nonviolence as a means of settling disputes.

¶A sort of de facto underground, united by no other ideology than an antipathy for military service, who have quietly, undramatically, but successfully avoided the drill field, and hope to continue doing so.

The groups of what some call the "new left" range from the rapidly growing, campus-based Students for a Democratic Society to the splinter Spartacists, who are passing out leaflets charging the war is being run by "Imperialists and Stalinists." In recent months they have formed a special alliance to mount joint protests against the war.

This week the society, which also operates community organization projects in a dozen Northern cities will open a drive to encourage registration as conscientious objectors.

"From what we've seen, the level of dissatisfaction is very great," said Paul Booth, the organization's president. "We really might be able to get thousands of people."

The plan is in accord with a unanimous agreement drawn up Sept. 6 by the student group, in a national meeting near Bloomington, Ind. The group said there "that there should be a visible national antidraft program whose purpose would not necessarily be to abolish the draft, but build an antiwar movement around the draft issue and possibly make the draft system function less smoothly."

The group has already opened project workshops in New York, Los Angeles, Berkeley, Calif., Ann Arbor, Mich. and Chicago, and is working on a handbook for conscientous objectors.

An earlier plan to publish a 1book called "How to Cool the Military," which was to have contained all the lore on defeating the draft — such as founding one's own church so that one could be pastor of it —was abandoned two months ago, Mr. Booth said.

The May 2d Movement, named for the date of its sponsorship of the first public protest against the war in Vietnam, has also been counseling avoidance of the draft at forums at the Free University in New York, among other places. But it is not restricting itself to the conscientious objector approach.

The movement has, since its inception, been actively sympathetic to the National Liberation Front, which seeks to overthrow the South Vietnam Government, and has sent first aid supplies to the Vietcong. It holds that the struggle in Vietnam is between American "imperialists" and a "freedom movement of the oppressed people."

The group is discussing the formation of "antidraft unions," primarily on campuses, to provide mutual resources to resist the draft. It also is in the process of writing a book.

"We will discuss the experiences of people who came on expressing certain political views, other people who were rejected for psychiatric reasons, and other ways of dealing with this," Steve Newman explained in the movement's cluttered office in a shabby loft building at 640 Broadway.

One story being reprinted in radical student publications is the odyssey of Pieter Romayn Clark. On the day of his induction, he distributed 200 anti-Vietnam leaflets (the authorities thought he was performing an authorized task until an officer read one); drew up an anti-Vietnam petition on a brown envelope and obtained 21 signatures from his mates; shouted down a startled sergeant; gave a "loud talk" on the unjustness of the war, urging the draftees to join racial demonstrations instead, and refused to sign a loyalty oath.

"I was told that they would call me and for me not to call them," he wrote. "And that I should go home — which I did."

In contrast to the groups who are opposing the draft because of their position on Vietnam are the older pacifist organizations.

Their headquarters is at the top of narrow, twisting stairs that lead to the 10th floor of 5 Beekman Street. Hand-lettered signs on the walls of the stairway read: The War Resisters League; The Student Peace Union; The Catholic Peace Fellowship; The Teachers' Protest; Committee for Nonviolent Action; The Workshop in Nonviolence, and The Liberator.

It is the home of many of the traditional pacifist groups — some have existed since 1914. The posters of napalm-burned Vietnamese children are the same, but the voices are less strident.

The organizations deal primarily with counseling on the obligations of conscientious objectors.

"A year ago we'd have one or two people a month come to our group for advice," Ralph DiGia of the War Resisters League said. "Now we're getting three or four a day, including some people from the reserves."

The pressure has become so great that instructors from the Central Committee for Conscientious Objectors in Philadelphia will begin a three-week set of classes this week to train new counselors here.

"The trouble is," Maris Cakars of the New York Workshop in Nonviolence said, "it's almost impossible to find a draft card in the peace movement anymore. Last time, we had to use an honorable discharge, a disqualifying notice and some miscellaneous pieces of paper."

"It's the nature of this war," Mr. DiGia said. "We have people coming in who aren't objectors in the usual sense, not pacifists. But they're opposed to this war and they're thinking along these lines now.

"There are other ways out. For the poor, it's to get married and have kids; for the well-to-do, to stay in school."

October 18, 1965

Students Facing the Draft Seek an Out

Third-year students at Harvard Law School, resigned to the prospect of military duty but intent on serving as officers if serve they must, are thronging to hear about the Army's Judge Advocate General program.

At New York University, part-time students who have been working to pay for their studies are looking for full-time graduate programs and besieging officials with applications for financial aid.

And at Massachusetts Institute of Technology, job-hunting seniors are showing more interest than ever in the large defense companies that are considered vital to national security and thus offer special exemptions from the draft.

These students, and thousands like them, are responding to the pressure of this fall's rising draft calls. A recent tour of several Eastern campuses, whose students are registered with draft boards in all parts of the country, indicates that the Army has become nearly as much a topic of conversation as girls.

College administrators questioned about student anxiety over the draft invariably reacted with a weary laugh.

"I've seen a student every 20 minutes every day for the last month," said Robert A. Campbell, military adviser at Yale.

Students and officials said that concern intensified among young men of draft age last month when exemptions for childless married men were removed.

There were also reports from many colleges that full-time students had been denied deferments. School officials, however, said most such 1-A classifications were issued because draft boards had not received notice of enrollment or a complete description of the student's course of studies. In these cases deferments will be reinstated.

Most full-time students appear to be safe from the draft for the time being, although any general statement is subject to exceptions because each Selective Service board operates with considerable autonomy.

Draft boards in some well-to-do suburban areas, for instance, have a relatively small pool of nonstudents available since large numbers of the young men there go to college. Some boards have issued deferments without termination

dates, leaving them subject to review at any time. Others have warned that students will not be deferred for more than one graduate degree.

But part-time students, prospective graduates and men whose jobs are not clearly crucial to national defense are all being scrutinized by their draft boards.

In the Ivy League most undergraduates still seem to believe they can avoid military service. John D. Gerhart, a senior at Harvard, said:

"The majority think they won't have to go. They just have to make sure they take each step correctly so they won't get caught. Very few feel no obligation; they just don't want to be in the Army. You are abused and your talents are misused."

Many talk about, although few try, bizarre ways of getting deferred, such as feigning homosexuality or mental instability. But the best insurance for most top students is graduate school.

Officials estimate that 80 to 90 per cent of last year's graduates from Harvard and Yale continued their studies. But students who want to postpone further work, or study abroad, will have fewer opportunities.

Deans at several Ivy League schools' said June graduates might not be able to accept grants to travel or study abroad in a nondegree program. They agreed that students who joined no formal program who wanted to travel or work for a year — probably would be drafted immediately.

Qualify for Deferments

Graduate students at Ivy League schools almost all study full time and thus qualify for student deferments. And since only 10 per cent of the graduate students at a school like Yale finish their doctoral dissertations before turning 26, few normally would have problems. But this year some do.

Law students, however, usually graduate at 24 or 25 and become vulnerable for the draft immediately.

"My husband doesn't talk about anything else," said the wife of a third-year student at N.Y.U.

At Harvard Law last year 20 students attended a meeting to discuss the Army's Judge Advocate General program. This year 180 appeared. In Washington a spokesman said applications for the program, which requires a minimum three-year hitch, as an officer, would double this year.

Students report that many law firms and recruiters for clerkships in non-Federal courts are refusing to consider draftable men, no matter what their class standing.

Seek Government Jobs

Richard L. Levine, a third-year Harvard student, said his classmates were seeking jobs with Government agencies, such

as the Atomic Energy Commission and National Aeronautics and Space Administration, which they think could obtain occupational deferments for them. Companies such as International Business Machines and Bell Telephone are attractive employers for the same reason, Mr. Levine said.

Problems multiply at a big urban university, such as N.Y.U., where many students work during the day and study at night. Unlike the Ivy League and technical schools, these universities have many students who are worried not about the future, but the present.

John L. Landgraf, associate dean of the graduate school of arts and sciences, said:

"Our most serious problem is the student who has finished his course work and is writing a thesis. Courses would be a terrible burden, but if he's not taking them he's not full-time and thus draftable."

Dean Landgraf said draft boards had already classified some part-time graduate students 1-A. Several parents of part-time students secretly asked him to arrange full-time status for their sons, he said.

Finances Are Problem

Finances is another problem. Students cannot take a semester off to work or study part-time and maintain a job without risking induction.

"With the rising draft calls we've had a flood of applications for fellowships and loans so people can afford to study fulltime," Dean Landgraf said.

Married men with children are still exempt from the draft and for some couples parenthood is one way out. "The draft is knocking hell out of the birth control market," one N.Y.U. law student said.

The choice between military service and children, however, is not easy for poor couples or couples in which the wife wants to return to school.

"I suppose I have a duty to my husband," said the wife of a draftable third-year law student. "But a child would ruin my chance for a degree. The Army is really bothering us and all our friends."

At M.I.T. students seemed to take little time from their work in the laboratories to worry about the draft, but some showed concern when considering the future.

"The possibility for deferment is a frequent question asked of prospective employers," said Thomas W. Harrington Jr., head of the career counseling office. "Those companies which can get deferments for employees are getting a good play."

Time and Talent Cited

M.I.T. students are not unpatriotic, but afraid their time and talent would be wasted, Mr. Harrington said.

"Once you complete your education at M.I.T., there are a hell of a lot better ways to use your talent than carrying a rifle," he said. "I can understand a philosophy or history student being drafted, but to take a student in a technical school is idiotic."

Almost every student questioned—undergraduate, graduate or law student — said he wanted to avoid the Army "'because my talents would be wasted'" and "I would come back from the service rusty and have to compete with fresh graduates."

Many seemed to agree with Howard M. Moffett, a senior at Yale, who said he would rather fulfill his national obligation in the Peace Corps or similar service projects.

Mr. Moffett, chairman of The Yale Daily News, explained the students' attitude this way:

"More and more students are coming to look at war as it really is. The glory and parades are past history. The coverage from Vietnam and Korea heightens one's awareness of the effect of war on civilians. We stop to think what napalm bombing really means."

Many college officials, however, expressed sentiments similar to those of the dean who said:

"I don't like the attitudes growing up among students. They feel only suckers get drafted and if you're smart enough to go to college you shouldn't have to fight."

November 15, 1965

PROSPERITY BLAMED FOR CAMPUS UNREST

Special to The New York Times

CHICAGO, Nov. 27—Student unrest on college campuses is attributed by a prominent Eastern psychiatrist to the long prosperity in this country. According to Dr. Francis J. Braceland, a clinical professor of psychiatry at Yale University and senior consultant at the Institute of Living in Hartford, the prosperity is challenging students to search for an identity. Dr. Braceland, editor of the American Journal of Psychiatry, was in Chicago this week to accept the 1965 Stritch Medal from Loyola University, where he once served as dean of the Stritch School of Medicine.

Students used to be occupied with such problems as supporting themselves while going to college. Dr. Braceland said in an interview. With the decline of this outlet for their energies, however, they have turned to concern about prosperity in this country and the lack of it in other countries, he said.

"Most of these people are bright students who are in a period of turmoil," he said. "Many are undergoing a change from adolescence and feel a challenge toward responsibility. The conflict produces protest."

The Stritch Medal is presented annually to an alumnus or a present or former faculty member of the medical school.

November 28, 1965

Percentage of Negroes Drafted Is Higher Than That for Whites

Few Reach Officer Rank, but Many Become Sergeants— Re-enlistment Rate High

By ERIC PACE

Special to The New York Times

WASHINGTON, Dec. 31 — Negroes are more likely than whites to be drafted into the Army, Defense Department statistics showed this week. The statistics further revealed that once in the Army, Negroes were more likely to rise to the rank of sergeant and to re-enlist.

Pentagon figures showed the following:

¶In the 12-month period that ended last June, 16.3 per cent of the men drafted into the Army were nonwhite. The percentage of the nation that is nonwhite is about 11, mostly Negro.

¶In the lowest category of sergeants in the Army (and the equivalent, specialist 5), 17.4 per cent are Negroes.

¶The Negro re-enlistment rate in the Army after one hitch is 49.3 per cent, compared with 18.5 per cent for whites.

¶There are relatively few Negro officers in the Army, Navy and Air Force.

These and other figures were disclosed in an interview with Jack Moscowitz, Assistant Secretary of Defense for Civil Rights and Industrial Relations.

Pentagon officials explained that the main reason Negroes were being hit harder than whites by the draft was that whites were more likely to qualify for deferment because of their jobs or studies.

Officials said there had been no great change in the percentage of Negroes drafted during the last six months.

Mr. Moscowitz said his latest figures for the number of Negro enlisted men and officers were as of Dec. 31, 1964. They showed that the Negro presence in the armed services varied widely by branch and rank.

Negroes were proportionately most numerous in the Army, with 13.4 per cent of all enlisted men. The Air Force had 10 per cent and the Navy 5.8 per cent. Negroes tended to be most heavily represented in the middle enlisted men's ranks.

Mr. Moscowitz, a Michigan-born lawyer, pointed proudly to the Negro re-enlistment rate.

"That uniform," he said, "gives prestige and status to a guy who's been 100 years on the back burner."

In the Air Force, the Negro re-enlistment figure — again, as of one year ago — is slightly higher than in the Army — 50.3 per cent, compared with 27.4 per cent for whites.

In the Navy, which has been criticized for not providing high opportunities for Negroes, the first-time re-enlistment rate is only a little lower — 41.3 per cent of the Negroes, compared with 21.6 per cent of the whites.

The statistics showed that only 3.5 per cent of the Negroes in the Army were officers, 1.5 per cent were officers in the Air Force and 0.3 per cent were officers in the Navy.

There are no Negro admirals and only one Negro general, Lieut. General Benjamin O. Davis Jr. of the Air Force.

Mr. Moscowitz's figures showed 22 Negro colonels in the Army and the Air Force but no Navy captains, the naval equivalent of colonel.

However, a Navy Department spokesman said that a 54-year-old Negro chaplain, Comdr. Thomas D. Parham Jr. of the Naval Air Station at Quonset Point. R. I., would be promoted to captain around March. He said the chaplain, a Presbyterian, would thus become the highest-ranking Negro in the Navy's history.

"This is welcome news but certainly long overdue," a spokesman for the National Association for the Advancement of Colored People said.

James Farmer, national director of the Congress of Racial Equality, called the contemplated promotion "a splendid example of American racial tokenism."

Only one of the Navy's 1,000 vessels. from minesweepers to aircraft carriers, is commanded by a Negro. He is Lieut. Comdr. George Thompson of the U.S.S. Finch, a radar picket destroyer based in San Francisco.

January 3, 1966

DRAFT DEFERMENT SCORED AT RUTGERS

NEW BRUNSWICK, Sept. 11 (AP)—About 1,000 Rutgers University freshmen were urged today by Paul Goodman, author, to go out and campaign for the abolition of the student draft deferment.

Mr. Goodman, who gained national recognition for his books "Growing Up Absurd" and "Compulsory Miseducation," was the final speaker in the freshman orientation program at the state university.

"Why should Negro and Puerto Rican boys be fighting in the rice paddies of Vietnam while you're sitting safely here?" Mr. Goodman asked.

He told the freshman that society had "dragooned" them into college and that this gave them the right to demand that colleges teach them what they wanted to learn.

The author depicted colleges and universities as great gatherings of the young that are going to revolt against their elders.

Mr. Goodman, who has been a constant critic of American higher education, argued that freshman go to college for three main reasons: because society has set up rules requiring a diploma; because they don't know what else to do with themselves, and because they want to avoid the draft.

September 12, 1966

Most Students Are Conventional, Professor Says

Sociologist at Harvard Calls Them Politically Passive

By JOHN COGLEY
Special to The New York Times

WALTHAM, Mass., Oct. 9—Collegiate radicalism and free-wheeling morality are distinctly minority positions on the American campus, according to Prof. Seymour M. Lipset, a Harvard sociologist.

Most college students, he said, are politically passive, socially conservative and conventionally moral and are preoccupied with their private goals.

Professor Lipset voiced his views at an interfaith weekend institute here sponsored by Brandeis University. The institute was organized to commem-

orate the dedication of three chapels — Protestant, Roman Catholic and Jewish—that had been erected 10 years ago on the Brandeis campus.

The professor said students' greatest problem was getting into a first-rate college and later into a high-ranking graduate school.

Pressures on students have mounted drastically, he observed. While suicide rates have declined among older groups, he said, between 1952 and 1962 they jumped 48 per cent among youths 15 to 19 years old and 26 per cent among those 19 to 24.

"Some reactions to this pressure include getting off the treadmill, becoming beatniks and radicals, particularly among graduate students," he said, but added that the vast majority merely studied harder.

Dr. Lipset said national surveys reported that between

They're Social Conservatives, He Asserts at Institute

two-thirds and three-fourths of all students support the Vietnam war and are notably "more bellicose" than their elders.

Researchers associated with the Kinsey studies of sexual behavior, he added, find that while students today seem more permissive about norms, actual sexual behavior has not changed significantly in 30 years.

In a dinner speech, the Right Rev. John M. Burgess, Suffragan Bishop of the Protestant Episcopal Diocese of Massachusetts, said what while individual religious leaders have risen in every age to proclaim the faith delivered to the prophets

and saints, their followers have usually been "complacent and fat, stiff-necked and satisfied."

Bishop Burgess, who is a Negro, said that white backlashes would not frighten or discourage adherents of the civil rights movement. For 50 years, he said, white men have taught black men how to die for the high ideals of democracy.

Negro Americans learned this lesson well, he added, and have put it to use in Alabama, Mississippi, California and Illinois.

At the close of the dinner, Richard Cardinal Cushing, Roman Catholic Archbishop of Boston, was presented with a special citation by Dr. Abram L. Sachar, president of Brandeis.

"He wears the red hat of the College of Cardinals in a fashion all his own," Dr. Sachar said of the Cardinal.

October 10, 1966

At the risk of being 'old-hat, fuddy-duddy or a Colonel Blimp,' a member of the older generation lets some of today's young know what he thinks of them.

We Can't Appease The Younger Generation

By SPENCER BROWN

THE war of the generations has been going on a long time, and it is unlikely that anything really new can be contributed to it. But I should like to say a word on behalf of the elderly, remembering, of course, that whatever I say is suspect as reactionary, fuddy-duddy or dead.

We have spent a good deal of time in the last few decades trying to understand young people. It is no surprise when a conservative educator, someone perhaps like Jacques Barzun of Columbia or Douglas Bush of Harvard, tells us to pay no attention to what young people say; or to give them a standard curriculum —back to the three R's.

But it is high time for someone not committed to a rigid curriculum, for an admirer of Freud and Dewey, for one who has voted against conservative candidates in every election since 1932, for someone who rejoices in the march of modern science and is not the least interested in turning back the clock—for such a one to ask for understanding of the adult world and to argue against victory by the young in their warfare with the old.

SPENCER BROWN, headmaster of the Fieldston School, admits to being an elderly 57. He is the father of a married son, 30, and a daughter, 25, with whom he gets along much better now than when they were younger.

Thus, I wish to examine the fairly common claim that today's younger generation—the young people in the last years of high school and in college — are uniquely miserable, uniquely persecuted and uniquely virtuous. In examining that claim and determining what we elderly people should answer to it, I ask that we examine our own vocabulary, our thinking and our moral nerve. I ask that in addition to patience, which we have already shown in overwhelming abundance, we learn balance, common sense and humor.

At the outset we may well remember Logan Pearsall Smith's remark: "The denunciation of the young is a necessary part of the hygiene of elderly people, and greatly assists the circulation of their blood." But let us permit the elderly another word from the same essayist: "Uncultivated minds are not full of wild flowers, like uncultivated fields. Villainous weeds grow in them, and they are the haunt of toads." Having thus demonstrated our balance, we may proceed.

MUCH of our difficulty stems from our habits of talk. At one extreme we rejoice in being apocalyptic: we say that history is a race between education and catastrophe. But this race is no 100-yard or 100-year dash; if it were, catastrophe would have won long ago since education has not yet come up with a complete solution

to any major problem. The race must be at least a marathon. Or we say, as did a group of reporters interviewing Robert Frost on television, that this is the worst or most dangerous or most difficult time man has ever lived through. They kept trying to badger the octogenarian poet into saying what they wanted him to say; but at last he succeeded in outshouting them and making himself heard: "Yes, yes, yes, it's a terribly difficult time for a man to try to save his soul—about as difficult as it always has been."

Or at the other extreme, we speak gobbledygook sociologese - psychologese. We say that our young people are undergoing an identity crisis and think of them as alienated and suffering from anonymity. We remark that they are "acting out" their problems. We sympathize with their rebellion, for they have much to rebel against. We admire their courage when they "speak out" against their exploitation. And even when we are uneasy over what they are doing, we are glad that at least they are actively pro-

testing, and not behaving passively. We do not question their motives.

Phrases like these, I am convinced, corrupt our thinking. They suggest that these troubles are new, whereas they are as old as the human race. They change their form with each generation, sometimes oftener, since the best thing about youthful fads

263

is the rapidity with which they age and disappear. But our cant phrases, suggesting unprecedented gravity, deprive us of our sense of humor and perspective. "Growing pains" is an older phrase — half-mocking, half-tolerant—quite as useful as "identity crisis," since it suggests the recurring nature of the phenomenon. Youth has been lonely for centuries. What has "alienation" got that differentiates it from old-fashioned loneliness? And youth generally "acts out" its problems by raising hell, which is hardly a modern monopoly.

That youth has very real grievances, no sane man can doubt. Yet, just as surely, no sane man should subscribe to the statements of those grievances that we read in the press. As one example, there is the frequent assertion by Paul Goodman that college students are the most exploited class in our society; recently, he told a group of Rutgers freshmen that society had "dragooned" them into college. It is hard to take such things seriously: Mr. Goodman is merely working the old Shavian trick of taking an obvious truth and stating the opposite, to promote an uproar. College students are one of the most favored groups in our society, perhaps the most favored.

It may be that college students are miserable. At the same time, though, they are the largest leisure class in America. In comparison with the tiny numbers of immensely wealthy adults, they are more numerous and fairly wealthy. They are our mass consumers of culture, the advance guard of the great owning and managerial orders into which they will move at graduation, when they lose their leisure. Far from being exploited, they ride on the backs of all of us, and they sometimes use spurs.

True, the college student is usually not allowed free access to liquor; his sex life is often uncertain. His future, though rosy and assured in general, is unknown in detail and perhaps therefore frightening. He may debate whether it is more miserable to be young and unrealistically ambitious and therefore anxious about success or to be young and realistically unambitious and reconciled to anonymity.

Many have described these troubles, but few have done it better than Robinson Jeffers:

Age has infirmities
Not few, but youth is all one fever.

In short, the exploitation of youth is by its own ambitions, its own contradictions, its own hopeless passions, its own destructive violence—and certainly not, in middle-class America, by society's intervention and destruction. To equate the "exploitation of youth" with the exploitation of the Negro in Mississippi, as the Berkeley mutineers did, is a type of insanity. It reminds me of what E. B. White said about a certain kind of mad poet: he takes leave of his reason

66To equate the 'exploitation of youth' with the exploitation of the Negro in Mississippi, as the Berkeley mutineers did, is a type of insanity.99

deliberately, as a commuter might of his wife.

Doubtless one concern is with the draft, which does cramp youth and freedom. But whatever the inequities of the draft, most campus objections come from those who disapprove of the Vietnam war. And the reasonably well-to-do and reasonably astute collegians have so far found ways to beat the system, though often at the cost of becoming perpetual graduate students. There is some resentment at not being allowed to drop out freely—but no matter how horrible Harvard is, it is still preferable to Vietnam.

It is true, also, that the student is under pressure. Prof. Seymour M. Lipset, in a speech at Brandeis recently, reported on a survey he made of the ambitions and problems of students and noted that pressures on students have increased drastically. Their greatest problem, he said, is getting into a first-rate college and later into a high-ranking graduate school. "Some reactions to this pressure include getting off the treadmill, becoming beatniks and radicals, particularly among graduate students," Professor Lipset declared. But he added that the vast majority of students merely studied harder.

Is the pressure intolerable? Ob-

viously not. If it were, the activists on the campus (such of them as are not non-students) would all flunk out. College students have always had time to lead double and triple lives; they still do. They are certainly better off than the 9-to-5 jobholder.

As for worries, students today are considerably better off than their parents were, though they work harder than their parents ever did in college. The parents of today's students, plagued all through school by money worries, looked forward to a world of unemployment or, later, to a war of considerably larger size than the current phase of the cold war. Today's students, and younger faculty members, have never known a time when the country was not affluent. Indeed, in a romantic or nostalgic effort to regain the raptures of unemployment, the modern activist will drop out of his prosperity—like the activist students' idol, Bob Dylan, who "created his own Depression" by bumming about the countryside.

NEVERTHELESS, for most such dropouts-as-a-social-class the poverty is play-poverty. They can always write home for money. They make their own Depression, yet they insist also on an expensive hi-fi or electric guitar or wig or sports car or motorcycle or airplane tickets or drugs. These, they suggest, are what society owes them because society is hypocritical.

Society's hypocrisy is the great weapon in the hands of youth in the war with age. The older generation is bad, youth says, and only youth can be relied on to act with pure motives. From that notion stems the moral arrogance so noticeable in the pronouncements of youth leaders. For example, a high school editorial writer, protesting a school regulation, says that opposition to the rule is "a peaceful method of rebellion by a generation that has watched its parents solve problems by atomic bombs, napalm, civil rights murders, and genocide."

Though such a statement ought to be astonishing in the venom of its phrasing, it did not seem astonishing to any elderly person with whom I discussed it. I generally got a reply such as, "Well, it's true that the older generation has made a mess of things." Apparently the arrogance of moral superiority has become impudence too vast to be visible.

I imagine that the younger generation would become indignant—and properly so—if an elderly editorial writer said that youth solves problems by pouring kerosene over pathetic Bowery derelicts and igniting them, desecrating Jewish graves, breaking up peaceful meetings, filling the jails and hospitals with addicts, and murdering a President. Yet such a description would be no more venomous and misleading than their description of us.

The reaction of the elderly liberal (the elderly conservative merely gobbles like an angry turkey) is generally to turn away in silent shame when youth makes one of its monstrous general accusations. We must have lost our moral nerve if we cannot say, at least to ourselves, that such accusation comes with poor grace from a generation saved by its parents from Dachau and Belsen; a generation saved from physical destruction in World War II and political destruction in the cold war; a generation in which the diseases that slowly killed Schubert and Keats (those flowers of youthful genius) can be cured in a couple of weeks.

Instead, the young say, with Omar Khayyam, the poet of all poets of youth,

Ah Love! Could you and I with Him
conspire,
To grasp this Sorry Scheme of Things
entire,
Would we not shatter it to bits—and
then
Re-mould it nearer to the Heart's
Desire!

We oldsters have seen some master shatterers and remolders in our time —Mussolini, Stalin, Hitler, Castro, Mao. Hence, we have a right to be at least skeptical when some youngster advocates shattering as the essence of morality and the good life. But we are tempted to grin and put our hands over our ears rather than argue at the top of our lungs.

WHAT I am really concerned about is the addled pates of the older generation. We don't believe the incredible generalizations that youth makes about age, and we should have the grace not to pretend we believe them. We also don't have to believe the generalizations youth makes about youth. Professor Lipset found that the great majority of college students support the Vietnam war and are notably "more bellicose" than their elders. He added that though students are more permissive about sexual norms, Kinsey researchers find sexual behavior has not changed significantly in 30 years. In short, the Vietnik-beatnik image that some youth would have us accept about all youth is simply not so.

I recently asked a highly intelligent young man about alienation and loneliness. He said that young people felt alienated from society. I pressed him about loneliness, adducing for comparison the loneliness of a number of fictional heroes that we both knew. He said, "Oh, it's not that any more; it's mass alienation. When you're all alienated together, you're not really lonely."

I asked another young man if he

felt alienated. He said, "Nope." Was he undergoing a crisis of identity? Nope. This lad already has a direction: he is headed for medicine. And, by and large, the youngsters who are going to be our scientists and mathematicians do not seem rootless and alienated. Perhaps because they feel the future belongs to them, they have built-in sanity valves.

But it is not only they; the vast majority of young people are Men At Work. They have their enormous sorrows and world-weariness and hopeless love affairs. But in general they expect to be successful, and they see that the world has plenty of room for them to be successful in. As if these virtues were not enough, there are the virtues that belong peculiarly to the last 10 or 15 years — the altruism that shows itself, above all, in the Peace Corps.

SHOULD we then conclude that we clearly have no cause to concern ourselves with the troubles of this younger generation? Not altogether, for there is a small but significant portion of that generation at open war with society—or with the older generation.

The aim of militant youth in this war is to force us into either of two untenable positions: conservatism — the old-hat, the fuddy-duddy, Colonel Blimp; or radicalism — grooving with the youngsters, trying to outdo them in the art of appearing youthful and up-to-date, longing for the joys of playing left-wing in the good old Depression college days.

A political analogy is not far-fetched. The task of combating Communism is too often relegated to the reactionary and the lunatic right. The liberal, who should know the most and fight the most intelligently, pussyfoots. When he does what he calls Speaking Out, he deals a blow to the right and a lovetap to the left. Similarly, the young are denounced from conservative pulpits and platforms. But when the liberal educator Speaks Out, he usually delivers a blow to the old and a lovetap to the young. Even when the young have done something

everyone is ashamed of, he tells us their motives are good.

About a year ago I was asked by the father of a former student if I would attest to the good character of his son, who was about to be fined for his part in one of the Berkeley uproars. I am afraid I rather shocked the good man by saying: "Sure, he's a good boy, none better, but it was a damn fool thing to do." The father expected me to admire him for getting tossed into the paddy wagon in a foolish demonstration. We seem to have forgotten that not everything a good boy does is good. The father, wishing me to attest to his son's good character, did not wish me to object to his son's bad — or stupid — action. But if I did not object to the action, what was the point of my character endorsement?

In the old days, we might forgive the boy but not the action. If he raised hell, we might laugh, or secretly envy him, but we did not stultify ourselves by condoning his act. Today, if he breaks a window, for example, under the notion of the total

nobility of human motives we search for some principle of which window-breaking is an understandable manifestation.

When we tell youngsters that whatever they do is forgiven (in fact, approved in advance), we are telling them that their motives don't matter either. This is to make all youngsters as anonymous as a company of angels. Many young people resent their anonymity; nevertheless, by our abdication of moral judgment we are making them more anonymous. The crisis of identity, if it does exist in any form different from the personal crises of the past, must therefore reside in this absence of moral judgment. If anything goes, then I am no better than the worst, a youth tells himself. Since, like everybody else, I am perfectly virtuous, I am nobody.

This assumption of noble motivation is simply the argument of the natural depravity of man turned upside down. If we assume the depravity of man, we don't have to observe or understand the young — just beat the old Adam out of them. And if we believe in man's total virtue, we don't observe or understand him either; we forgive him without looking at him. Thus, youth has come to expect institutions such as our courts and our universities to have built-in forgiveness. Thus they have arrogated to themselves that sense of moral superiority which no human being has a right to. Thus, they raise hell.

In short, we have been had.

We have been had by a number of adults who have gained cheap approbation from young people by turning traitor, not to their class, since this is not a class struggle, but to their own wisdom. They have persuaded us, or loudly assumed, that left-wing activism is altruistic, but that right-wing extremism is the product of "the authoritarian personality" and neurosis. They have used academic freedom as a sort of Yalu River, behind which they are immune to attack but from which they are free to sally forth and attack anything else, including their own school or college.

In so doing they have done evil twice. They have hurt the adult world by their feckless policies and reckless tactics. And they have hurt the young by teaching them, not that good ends excuse bad means, but that bad means are a good end in themselves; that mere action is somehow mysteriously virtuous; that anger is wisdom.

They have hurt the young also by depriving them of their youth — of the opportunity to be different, private and naughty, rather than anonymously and monotonously violent; of the opportunity to make mistakes and suffer consequences; that is, of the opportunity to learn.

All of us, I think, and not only the professional camp followers of youth's army, have spent too much time flattering our children. As teachers, we abdicate the role of teacher. As parents, we abdicate the role of parent. We wish to be colleagues and brothers and sisters, forgetting that the difference in age makes us look awkward. In the meantime we are tolerated, at best, by the young and, at worst, used.

Youth is more likely to condemn us than to love us for such disrespect of ourselves, this refusal to take them seriously enough to tell them what we really think — or rather, what we ought to think as a result of our experience. If youth, looking at parents and teachers, sees no wisdom beyond what youth has learned, we should not blame youth for disregarding us.

In the war between the generations the elderly can often outmaneuver the young, but this is a poor way of doing business since the young can spend all their time thinking up tricks and the old have work to do. If we play for time, hoping they will grow up, they *will* grow up—but not as quickly as if we refuse to play their games. If we try only to outwit and wait, a new generation will take their place, trained by them and not by us.

The aim of the elderly should not be to try to win the war. Our aim should be to win our opponents to our side and make use of their energy. Our aim is to uphold society from attacks on it by young or old. Our aim is to improve society, not to destroy it in the transparently unlikely hope of making it better by making it worse. Our aim is to deny the validity of the war.

We cannot win, and society can only lose, if we alternate old-fashioned repression with new-fashioned appeasement. There are probably just as many wicked young people as wicked old people, and just as many virtuous people in both camps. Our young people have a right to look to us for balance, common sense and a sense of humor. With these unspectacular but indispensable qualities we can call off the war and proceed with the job of education. ∎

November 27, 1966

STUDENT LEADERS WARN PRESIDENT OF DOUBTS ON WAR

100, at 100 Schools, Assert Some Loyal Youths May Prefer Jail to Fighting

U.S. GOALS QUESTIONED

Collegians Write of Seeming 'Contradictions' Between Statements and Actions

By TERENCE SMITH

Student leaders from 100 colleges and universities have signed an open letter to President Johnson expressing their anxiety and doubts about United States involvement in the war in Vietnam. All of the signers are either student body presidents or campus editors.

Noting "apparent contradictions" between American statements and actions in the war, the students wrote:

"Unless this conflict can be eased, the United States will find some of her most loyal and courageous young people choosing to go to jail rather than to bear their country's arms."

The letter, which the student leaders signed as individuals, was mailed to the White House yesterday.

The 100 signers are from Harvard, Columbia, Manhattanville, Duke, North Carolina, Indiana and Stanford, as well as 93 other schools, both church and nonsectarian, in every region of the country.

'Mainstream' Students

As elected campus leaders, the students represent a far more moderate university group than the members of the student New Left, whose objections to the war are frequently and stridently demonstrated.

Several of the signers of the letter have described themselves as reflecting the "mainstream" of student thought in the country.

In the letter they refer to their contemporaries as "people as devoted to the Constitution, to the democratic process, and to law and order as were their fathers and brothers who served willingly in two world wars and in Korea."

The tone of the letter is restrained and respectful. The letter is presented to the President as a report on the sentiments of "significant and growing numbers of our contemporaries [who] are deeply troubled about the posture of their Government in Vietnam."

"There are many," the letter adds, "who are deeply troubled for every one who has been outspoken in dissent."

The goal of the letter is to "encourage a frank discussion" of some of the problems raised by the American role in the war.

"If such a discussion clarified American objectives in Vietnam," the students wrote, "it might help to reverse the drift, which is now from confusion toward disaffection.

"There is increasing confusion about both our basic purpose and our tactics, and there is increasing fear that the course now being pursued may lead us irrevocably into a major land war in Asia—a war which many feel could not be won without recourse to nuclear weapons, if then."

Urge Truce Extension

The students urged that the New Year's truce be extended by "de facto restraint on both sides, even if no formal agreement is reached."

The students reported "a growing sense—reinforced by Mr. Harrison Salisbury's recent reports from Hanoi—that too often there is a wide disparity between American statements about Vietnam and American actions there."

This was a reference to the dispatches filed in recent days by Mr. Salisbury, an assistant managing editor of The New York Times, reporting damage inflicted on North Vietnamese civilian areas by United States bombs.

The students' idea to write the letter to Mr. Johnson grew

out of a debate at the annual congress of the National Student Association last summer on the campus of the University of Illinois.

A Lawyer's Idea

The notion was put forward during the debate by Allard K. Lowenstein, a former president of the association who is now a lawyer and active Reform Democrat in Manhattan.

The idea caught the imagination of most of the audience, and at 2 A.M., after the debate concluded, a group of 200 students held a rump meeting on the campus and agreed to draft such a letter.

To cover the expense of mailing the letter to student leaders around the country, they passed a hat and raised $83.

"Some of the kids didn't have any money with them," ex-plained Abby Erdmann, a sophomore at Smith College who helped assemble the signatures.

Mailing Postponed

The letter was drafted and redrafted during September at meetings in Miss Erdmann's home at 119 East 79th Street, but the students postponed mailing it, first because of the President's Asian trip, and then because of the elections.

"We didn't want it to look like an election gimmick," Miss Erdmann explained yesterday, "and all the while we were hoping that something would happen that would make the letter unnecessary. Something like a cessation in the bombings or a major shift in the Administration's policy."

During the drafting, the campus leaders argued vehemently and at length over the wording of the letter. Some wanted the language to be stronger, others felt it should be less critical. In the end, several leaders refused to sign the letter because, one way or the other, they felt it did not reflect their sentiments.

Most of the students contacted, however, were anxious to lend their names.

"The response in my area of the country was much greater than I thought it would be," Robert Powell, the student body president at the University of North Carolina at Chapel Hill, said yesterday.

"I was astonished by the reaction," he said, "since the students in the South are not nearly so liberal. This letter is an expression of a new mood that should shock the President."

December 30, 1966

Turned-On Generation Rejects Adults' Inhibitions

By SHERMAN CHICKERING

"Don't trust anybody over thirty."

The nation heard the slogan for the first time two years ago during the student revolt on the University of California's Berkeley campus. Since the Berkeley uprising, students across the country have shown what that slogan means.

It reflects student culture and its confrontation with prevailing adult values. Not all students are members of the "student culture" by any means. But the common threads are there.

Student culture is characterized by intense involvement, the "participation syndrome." Students in the Sixties prefer to live, learn and love through intense interpersonal involvement. When these values run up against the values of adult society, crises occur.

American society is seen as one big system that inhibits interpersonal involvement.

Student culture—an opposition culture—takes many forms.

First, it seems to be a religion that finds its spiritual rewards in existential experience. Social causes and personal relationships supply the "religious" framework. Campus church groups and university chaplains concentrate not on church dogma but on helping students find themselves through social involvment.

Belmondo, Not Bogart

Culture with a capital "C," like Society, is rejected by those caught up in the participation syndrome. Some take instead to motorcycles, long hair, happenings and discothèques. Others produce their own version of culture: jazz, folk music and avante garde films are the main art forms adopted by student artists. All are "participatory" art forms in which the artist improvises and interacts with his audience.

Jean Paul Belmondo has replaced Humphrey Bogart as the student folk-culture hero. While Bogey was a cool hero for the Silent Generation, Belmondo is a carefree hero for the Turned-On Generation.

Students get equally excited by TV heroics, but for different reasons: The Man From Uncle and Batman, along with Mad and Marvel comic books, provide students with a chance to laugh at what they see as the absurdities of society.

Much has been made of the sexual revolution, too much: the revolution has passed. The participant generation is interested in "genuine relationships" as well as sex.

The Why of LSD

The presence of marijuana and LSD on campus has also received much comment in the national press, but little understanding.

Journalists seldom comment on the distinction students make between the drugs they take and those used by the rest of society. Students see the barbiturates used by adults as deadening to the senses; students consider LSD and marijuana ways of exploring the senses. Consequently, students consider legal restrictions on the availability of marijuana and LSD a psychotic measure taken by a society afraid of its senses. Students see the drugs they use as a means not of escape but of involvement.

The student culture of involvement often collides with the prevailing culture.

Perhaps the most dramatic crisis is suicide. Student suicides are, according to recent studies, above the national norm. A student committed suicide recently after his driver's license was revoked. Last year, a student leapt to his death through the window of a Selective Service System office building.

Less irrevocable confrontations take place on what has been called the New Left, whose organizations carry out the political implications of student culture.

Secretary of Defense Robert S. McNamara and Gen. Earle G Wheeler, chairman of the Joint Chiefs of Staff, recently were rudely treated at Harvard and Brown Universities. The ring leaders in each case were members of the Students for a Democratic Society. Their politics center on confrontation: to demand recognition of the wishes of various minority groups, including students, through civil disobedience.

Bringing teachers and students together is the main objective of student educational reform movements. Looking for participatory democracy in education, students are trying to set up an educational non-system in which there are no grades or classrooms, only students and teachers learning together.

This objective has actually been realized at San Francisco State College, where students were the main force in establishing a college within the college called the experimental college. There, students find sympathetic teachers to join them in preparing "courses" on subjects like "Neighborhood Renewal" and "the Educational Imagination."

This educational ideal is related to student community development work in slum areas, especially tutorials. There are now 200,000 college students spending at least an hour a week tutoring underprivileged children.

The most serious confrontation comes on the question of national defense and the questions of the Vietnam war and the draft.

On the one hand, students are remarkably quiescent on both counts. Polls indicate that 80 per cent of college students basically support the Administration's position on the war. Likewise, some 80 per cent prefer to retain their student deferments, thus endorsing the present draft law.

But statistics may be misleading. Senator Robert F. Kennedy points out the inconsistency in students who favor the war but also favor their own non-participation. Evidently, students are somewhat aware of this inconsistency: polls indicate substantial doubt about the war among many who endorse the administration position,

Though 80 per cent want to keep their deferments, an equal number would like to see sweeping changes in the draft law. Prominent among those changes would be alternative service. Students think national service should include the Peace Corps, Vista and similar voluntary work as well as military service.

Many students would like to see all service be voluntary. Behind this opinion may well be the feeling that the draft assumes unwillingness of the student to serve his country. Moreover, the Selective Service System is indeed a system, and students are increasingly confronting systems with hostility.

Students do not seem to understand the premises of a highly complex, highly organized society. When students say, "Do not trust anybody over 30," they are saying, "We understand people, but not systems."

Sherman B. Chickering is publisher of Moderator, a magazine by young adults for college student leaders.

January 11, 1967

Clark Kerr Calls It
The Exaggerated Generation

By CLARK KERR

THE current generation of college and university students is the most-berated, the most-praised—certainly the most talked-about—in America's history. The names are varied, even contradictory. They tend to reveal more of the biases of the observers than of the nature of the students.

To conservatives, this is a "discontented" generation — even though youth never had it so good; or a "distrustful" generation — distrustful of its elders, the schools, the Government, the Establishment, distrustful of all the elements that have brought the good life to Americans, and to young Americans in particular. University students of today are seen as "difficult" at best and "radical" at worst, disrupting society.

To liberals, students of today constitute a "generation of conscience" in a nation that badly needs a conscience; or a "prophetic minority" pointing the way for an evil society to evolve. Or they are said to be "committed" to reform and good works; or to constitute a "New Left," presumably carrying on the torch for the tired Old Left which sees in this new generation proof that it really was not defeated permanently and completely. Paul Goodman has called the students of today the "New Aristocrats" — "America's emergent power elite."

From a more neutral point of observation, today's youth has been called "cool" or "activist" or "alienated" or "permissive." The current generation is many of these things to some extent some of the time. It is, for example, certainly occasionally difficult; often committed to some cause or another; to a degree alienated. There are many facets to this generation, perhaps more than to any earlier generation. It is going in more directions and at a faster pace. Thus, any simple designation may hold an element of truth but not the whole truth.

Exaggeration is one word that fits this new generation. It has exaggerated itself. It has been exaggerated by the news media. It has been exaggerated and also used, for their own purposes, by the left and the right. And, as a result, seldom in his-

tory have so many people feared so much for so little reason from so few.

THE exaggeration is the work of many people. The students themselves are responsible in the first instance; some of them have wanted it that way. A few highly visible minorities, on a relatively small number of campuses, have become symbolic to the public at large of a whole generation. The dress has, at times, been outlandish. The speech, on a few occasions, has been without taste. The behavior of some, with sex and drugs, has been outside established norms. These characteristics have created an impression of widespread Bohemianism distasteful to large elements of the public. To distaste has been added actual fear and anger over actions of the political activists.

The student activists might be called the "McLuhan Generation." Their style is geared to the TV cameras and the flashbulbs, the bullhorn, the microphone and the walkie-talkie. Electricity powers this new student guerrilla warfare. It pulls in information, sends out instructions and carries the message of dissident views to a huge audience.

The media have also played their role in the exaggeration. Berkeley in the fall of 1964 and again in December, 1966, offered an example. The crowds were uniformly reported as being far larger than they were. Herbert Jacobs, a lecturer in journalism at Berkeley, has compared TV and press reports with analyses of photographs of the crowds. Thus, when reports said that 8,000 or 10,000 students voted to strike in Sproul Hall Plaza in December, 1966, the actual number of people there was 2,000 — and this number included wives, curious onlookers and nonstudents. Another count, on another occasion, showed a count of 2,400 actually present, when 6,000 to 7,000 had been reported.

"Crowdsmanship," as Jacobs calls it, is a game played by the sponsor, the

police and the media alike. They all have an interest in raising the score. Thus a demonstration becomes bigger and more violent than it really was. A sit-in becomes a riot, then a rebellion and finally the "revolution" at Berkeley.

I once said to some TV executives that, in the course of reporting history, they were changing it. They agreed, but said this was what their competition did—and what the public wanted.

EXAGGERATED accounts have, on occasion, produced exaggerated reactions. The Old Left has picked up each episode of campus protest around the nation and made it another omen of the second coming of the American Revolution. Its spokesmen saw these protests as involving more students, the students as more radical, the tactics as more effective and the "movement" as more permanent than the facts would seem to warrant. Some liberals went along, for they liked the goals, if not the methods; they wore their hearts on other people's picket signs.

The New Right, rising to the right of the Old Establishment, saw the long arm of Marx and trumpeted its discovery. The Old Establishment was the power structure and it did not like being pushed around; it liked law and order, and it did little to correct the exaggerations.

The middle class tended to be shocked. What it thought it saw of students disturbed it greatly—the biggest scare since the Korean war and Senator McCarthy. Politicians entered the game in more than one state to add their own misrepresentations. In California, "treason, drugs and sex" were said to be a part of the curriculum offered to the students on one campus, and student behavior was highlighted as involving an "orgy."

AMID these exaggerations, efforts to identify "cultures" and "typologies" of students are precarious at best.

CLARK KERR, removed as University of California president last winter by the Regents headed by Gov. Ronald Reagan, is now directing a study of higher education for the Carnegie Foundation and in the fall will also return to a teaching post at the university.

"Exaggeration is one word that fits. This new generation has exaggerated itself. It has been exaggerated by the news media. It has been exaggerated, and used, by the left and the right."

My own observation is that there are three main student types now vying to set the tone of campus life—Political Activists, Bohemians and the New Collegiates. These types, singly and together, constitute a minority of all students but contribute a majority of the off-campus impressions and impact of the modern generation.

The Political Activists: The protest element of issue-by-issue demonstrations first arose out of opposition to the House Un-American Activities Committee, atomic testing, capital punishment and other similar issues in the late nineteen-fifties and early nineteen-sixties, but particularly reflects in its style and content the civil-rights movement and then the opposition to the war in Vietnam. It rises and falls as issues rise and fall, and it attracts more or fewer or different people as the issues change. The radical element on campus finds its origins particularly in the Depression of the nineteen-thirties and the more recent developments in Cuba and China, and its fractionalization relates to the historical point of origin of each of its components. It has been undergoing a current revival

---

66 'Crowdsmanship' is a game in which all have an interest in raising the score—a sit-in becomes a riot, then a rebellion, finally the 'revolution.' 99

---

particularly as a corollary to the rise in protest sentiment. The protest element and the radical element together constitute the political activists.

The activist students have wanted to influence the Establishment but have often ended up, partly because of exaggeration on all sides, by energizing the right, giving ammunition to their worst enemies. They have been, on some occasions, self-defeating prophets, better in the long run at building resistance than getting results, more adept at bringing the counterrevolution than at getting basic reforms, fated to achieve minor successes and major failures. A few of the activists, on the far left, wanted it this way, since they believed that destruction must precede reconstruction. But the great majority of activists wanted to do good things with and for the existing society.

The Bohemians: The Bohemian element in American universities is largely a product of the post-World War II period. It is basically incompatible, in its temperament and use of time, with hard academic work, and superficial evidence is a poor test of the real hold that this culture has on students. Yet this element is certainly growing and, given the conditions out of which it

arises in modern society, it is almost bound to keep on growing. More fragmentation of life and less sense of purpose in the mass industrial society leads to more such behavior.

(Here we must note a subgroup, outside the campus itself but related to it. This comprises the nonstudents. It is a deviant group—deviant on politics, deviant on attitudes toward sex, morality, religion. Its members are children of affluence who often can make a life without having to make a living. They reflect the attraction of a large campus with its cultural programs, its political activism, its sense of freedom. They reflect the desire for the excitement without the hard work of intellectual pursuits. They reflect both Bohemianism and political activism—both of which reject the middle class. The period between emancipation from adult control and assumption of full adult responsibility can be prolonged almost indefinitely through nonstudent status. Left Banks are now found around a few of the great American universities. They will be found around more, and they will grow in size.)

The New Collegiates: Traditional collegiate culture took on its modern form before and after World War I with the development of intercollegiate athletics, formal student governments, debating clubs and the like. But, in terms of adherents, it has been losing ground rapidly since the G.I.'s came back to the campuses after World War II. What distinguishes the new collegiate culture is a sense of community service. It was hardly known in the nineteen-thirties and is particularly a product of the current decade, during which it has grown enormously.

In my student days at Swarthmore during the depths of the Depression, there were only two of us in my senior class who went to a Negro school in Philadelphia one morning a week to work on a Quaker project. Last fall, at the University of California, 8,000 students, or nearly 10 per cent of the total student body, engaged in projects such as these: tutoring Negro children in West Oakland; volunteer teaching in Watts; running a camp in the San Bernardino Mountains for disadvantaged children; serving as "Amigos Anonymous" in villages in Mexico; cleaning up freeways and parks as a beautification project around Berkeley; teaching in San Quentin prison; running summer schools for the children of migratory workers in the San Joaquin and Sacramento Valleys; helping to construct an orphanage in Baja California; working with delinquents in Riverside; providing free dental care to disadvantaged families in Northern California; "adopting" two orphanages in South Vietnam.

The report we issued on these and other projects was called "The Untold Story." The overtold story was about the "filthy nine" (only four of them students) who constituted the totality of the much-publicized Filthy Speech Movement on the Berkeley campus.

THIS generation, as a whole, has

some characteristics that mark the influences that have shaped it. No one today would describe students, as Philip Jacobs did in 1957, as "gloriously contented" and "self-centered" and satisfied with the "American assembly line." They might better be described as "aggressive"—at home, on the campus, off the campus; "concerned"—about the meaning of life and the quality of society; "serious"—about their studies and their actions; "experimental"—in their way of life and their attack on problems; "impatient"—with an education that sometimes lacks relevance and a society that often practices hypocrisy.

This is a generation that was born under the sign of the bomb and suckled at the breast of TV. The bomb created a feeling that there was a time limit on getting a better world. Some students have another sense of urgency—to get something done before they disappear forever into the flatland of the suburb and the wasteland of the corporation.

TV brought to this generation at an early age, as the newspapers never did to children and young people in the past, a view of the whole world and all aspects of it. It became interested in all the world, including Mississippi and Vietnam, and saw vividly that participation was not something to be postponed until adult life. The means were there, through the electronic revolution, for students to be citizens, to be informed and to participate.

This generation was raised at home according to new manuals that stressed permissiveness, and at school under new views that stressed participation. Too often, its members arrived at colleges and universities which still reflected the old manuals and the old views, and both the students and the colleges were unprepared for the meeting.

The quality of education has been improved all along the line, particularly in the high schools, and particularly since Sputnik I. There is a new emphasis on grades and on going into graduate work. The meritocracy is taking hold and school is the way to move up and to avoid being moved down. The pressure is greater at all levels and students are better educated. Among other things, they are better educated in basic American principles like equality, freedom and the pursuit of happiness. And they see around them discrimination, restrictions on their freedoms, and poverty. They are troubled by the gap between aspiration and attainment. They were told all through high school about the sins of omission of the apathetic generation and the conformity of the "organization man" and exhorted to do otherwise. They are doing otherwise.

American society is now, by and large, affluent — students stay in school longer and fewer of them support themselves while going to school. One result is to reduce their dependence on the world of work and the sense of reality that goes with it. As Eric Hoffer said, "They haven't raised a blade of grass, they haven't laid a brick." They are also, frequently, less oriented toward getting a job after graduation, since that is taken for granted. Thus, materialistic considerations and pressures are less evident now that materialistic welfare is taken more or less for granted and also given a lower value.

The American society of the future troubles them. They have read "1984," "Brave New World," "Animal Farm," and they know about I.B.M. cards and automation. The sense of a world in which the individual counts for less and less weighs heavily. Conformity to Big Brother and to science seems not so very far off. There is a countermove toward individuality as against the requirements of "the system." This move toward individuality is speeded as the new religion and the new anthropology remove some of the restraints on personal behavior.

The Rebel, to use the terminology of Camus, accepts society but wants to improve it. He accepts restraint but not the status quo. He rejects the absolutism of much of the left but not the need for reform. He rejects violence and seeks the possible. Part of his motivation is religious; part relates to a desire for a better future. The Rebel approach is at the heart of the community-service element as well as of the protest tendency among college students.

Confrontation politics, which has often been the special form of student protest, seems to be becoming a less significant weapon. Civil-rights victories are farther in the background. The radicals have taken over much of the guidance of confrontations, and conservative, religious and moderate support has dropped away. Vietnam, of course, remains an issue over which protest can easily be organized, but the great wave of student confrontations now seems to be passing. The sense of protest will continue, and may even rise in intensity, but it will find expression less through confrontation and more through other means.

New leaders are arising from what I have characterized as the New Collegiate group. The New Collegiate type has as one of its characteristics devotion to the campus and willingness to work with and through the campus power structure. The New Collegiate leaders, including those active in fraternities and sororities, are pushing academic reform instead of athletics, political discussion instead of activities, community projects instead of dances — and they appeal to the new interests of the students. They do not wish to bring a campus to a grinding halt, but to halt neglect of students and give voice to community and national concerns. The New Collegiate leaders reflect the student interest in service and protest and give organized expression to it. And then a number of them go overseas and become Peace Corps participants.

Nobody pays much attention to them, but in my opinion they are setting the tone of this generation. The campus revolutionaries are never going to win; this is not a revolutionary country. And the alienated Bohemians are parasites. What is most significant about this generation is the very high proportion of the Peace Corps type.

SOCIETY faces the campus just as the campus faces society. A reappraisal by society of the new generation is in order — a reappraisal which recognizes the diversity and the essential goodwill of the students of today. The communications media have a special responsibility to present the facts for this reappraisal. The public should read and hear and see the news about university students with sophistication and some tolerance. The excesses of youth are nothing new in history.

Aristotle once wrote: "They [young people] have exalted notions, because they have not yet been humbled by life or learned its necessary limitations; moreover, their hopeful disposition makes them think themselves equal to great things—and that means having exalted notions. They would always rather do noble deeds than useful ones: Their lives are regulated more by moral feeling than by reasoning—all their mistakes are in the direction of doing things excessively and vehemently. They overdo everything—they love too much, hate too much, and the same with everything else."

June 4, 1967

GUARDS REPULSE WAR PROTESTERS AT THE PENTAGON

6 Break Through Line Into Building — Mailer and Dellinger Are Arrested

THOUSANDS HEAR TALK

Spock Tells Demonstrators at Lincoln Memorial That Johnson Is Real 'Enemy'

By JOSEPH A. LOFTUS
Special to The New York Times

WASHINGTON, Oct. 21—Thousands of demonstrators stormed the Pentagon today after a calm rally and march by some 50,000 persons opposed to the war in Vietnam.

The protesters twice breached the lines of deputy Federal marshals backed by soldiers armed with bayonet-tipped rifles. But they were quickly driven back by the rifle butts of the soldiers and the marshals' nightsticks.

Six demonstrators succeeded in entering a side door at the main Mall entrance of the building but were pushed out immediately by marshals.

There were no reports of serious injuries but the Pentagon steps were spattered with blood.

128 Held at Pentagon

Soldiers and marshals arrested at least 128 persons at the Pentagon, including David Dellinger, Chairman of the National Mobilization Committee to End the War in Vietnam, which organized the rally and march.

Also arrested were Norman Mailer, the novelist, who was seized for technical violation of a police line, and the Rev. John Boyles, the Episcopal chaplain at Yale University.

The surging disorderly crowd that milled about the vast Pentagon shouted obscenities and taunted the forces on guard there. Some threw eggs and bottles as darkness fell, built bonfires and waved what they said were burning draft cards.

They clashed with the guards several times.

Use of Tear Gas Denied

Several tear gas canisters exploded outside the building at various times. The Defense Department announced that the Army had not used tear gas at any time and charged that the demonstrators had.

Two soldiers were reported to have been injured, one by tear gas and one by a missile that struck him in the eye.

As darkness fell, the demonstrators settled down to what some said would be an all-night vigil.

However, at midnight, United States marshals began systematically picked up demonstrators encamped at the east entrance of the Mall entrance steps and carried them to waiting vans. At that point it was estimated that the troops outnumbered the demonstrators on the Mall who had dwindled to about 1,000.

At the Lincoln Memorial and elsewhere, the police reported ten persons arrested, most of them for demonstrations against the demonstrators.

A police and military consensus put the size of the crowd at the Lincoln Memorial, where the demonstrators first gathered, at 50,000 to 55,000. A warm autumn sun lighted the crowds that filled the corridor stretching from the Lincoln statue to the east end of the reflecting pool nearly halfway to the Washington Monument.

John B. Layton, chief of the Metropolitan police, returned to his office at 5:30 P.M. and pronounced the demonstration "well controlled and orderly." His force was responsible only for the territory on the District of Columbia side of the Potomac.

At 2:15 the march leaders stepped off for the Pentagon, across the Potomac River. For three hours the trek continued across Memorial Bridge. The test of strength at the Pentagon began well before the stragglers arrived.

About 4 P.M., some 2,000 demonstrators pushed up the steps in front of the Mall entrance, which faces a spacious lawn and a big parking lot that the demonstrators had permission to use.

A rope at the top of the steps at the mall side separated the demonstrators from United States marshals, who were backed up by military policemen.

Blue and red flags with a yellow flag in the middle, identified by some as Vietcong emblems, were carried on poles by some of these demon-

Associated Press Wirephotos

U.S. marshals clubbing antiwar demonstrators who tried to storm the Pentagon

Demonstrators shouting at a military policeman at barrier

strators. One marshal was struck on the head by one of the poles. Eight or ten others in the crowd pushed over the rope and the marshals hit them with night sticks.

About 20 young persons started to crawl under a flat-bed press truck near the top of the steps. Marshals dived after them, whacking at hands and bodies. Helmeted military policemen carrying M-14 rifles, with bayonets fixed but sheathed, rushed out at that point to assist the marshals.

A few minutes later a second wave of military policemen carrying tear gas grenades emerged from the building and set up a third defense line. The confrontation lasted nearly a half-hour.

About 5:40 P.M., another crowd of 3,000 who had been outside the outer police lines around the highway got through a hole unopposed and dashed to an entrance used by the press. It was unguarded outside.

About a half-dozen got inside the door. Marshals used clubs to push them back. About 20 minutes before that about 300 military policemen had been brought up from the lower levels of the building and lined up in the corridor.

The M.P.'s, using rifle butts, pushed the intruders back and outside. Some of the demonstrators fell down the steps and left patches of blood behind. Some threw electric lamps, soft-drink cans, and sticks. It took the troops two to four minutes to expel the group.

Negroes Undecided

As darkness fell, the demonstrators settled down to what some said would be an all-night vigil. They made little bonfires with their posters on the Pentagon Mall and steps. The temperature, which had been 55 degrees in the afternoon, was expected to fall to 40 overnight.

Some began drifting away, but shortly before 8 P.M., the official Pentagon estimate of the throng was still 15,000 persons in the parking lot and grassy spaces. The atmosphere away from the building was

"like a picnic," one observer said.

The military, which had refused to identify the units brought to Washington for the demonstration, reported tonight that 2,500 soldiers had been used on the Pentagon grounds and that an undisclosed number had remained in reserve.

The units that saw service were:

503d M.P. battalion, Fort Bragg; 91st Engineer Battalion, Fort Belvoir, Va.; First Squadron of Sixth Cavalry Regiment, Fort Meade, Md.; 714th Transportation Battalion, Fort Eustis, Va.; four military police companies (one from Fort Dix, N.J.; one from the Presidio, San Francisco, and two from Fort Hood, Tex.).

The Pentagon troops were under the command of Maj. Gen. Charles S. O'Malley, commanding general of the Washington Military District. He said:

"No tear gas has been used by our troops. There is no evidence that any tear gas has

been used by our side."

Lieut. Gen. John Throckmorton, commanding general of the Third Army, who commanded troops in the Detroit riot a few months ago, was at the Pentagon as a special assistant to the Army Chief of Staff. Officials did not say what his duties were.

Robert S. McNamara, Secretary of Defense, was at his office in the Pentagon all day except for a helicopter trip to the White House to help brief Souvanna Phouma, the Laotian Premier. A heavily protected heliport is close to the Pentagon.

The vast majority of the demonstrators at the Lincoln Memorial were white.

The sprinkling of Negroes at the rally gathered in a special section and debated whether to join the march. About a hundred decided to go to a Negro rally in Banneker Park, across the street from Howard University, a few miles north of the Capitol.

A lesser number joined the

271

The New York Times   Oct. 22, 1967

SCENE OF PROTEST: Demonstrators at Lincoln Memorial (1) marched to Pentagon (2)

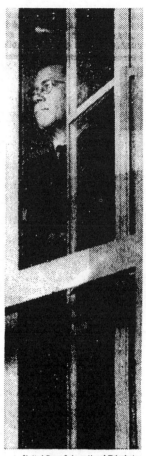

United Press International Telephoto

WATCHFUL: Secretary of Defense McNamara observing peace demonstration from window in **Pentagon.**

march to the Pentagon.

John Wilson of New York, director of the Students Nonviolent Coordinating Committee, who had spoken at the first rally, joined the Banneker Park crowd.

At the memorial, Mr. Wilson led the crowd in a chant of "Hell, no, we won't go." He later asked for a moment of silence to mark the death of Ernesto Che Cuevera, the Cuban revolutionary.

The trees around the basin, still untouched by frost, were in full leaf, though much of the green had turned to golden yellows and browns.

The mobilization committee, a loose confederation of perhaps 150 groups, established its platform at the top of the steps that rise from the basin to the circular drive around the Lincoln Memorial. The drive was closed to all motor traffic except police vehicles.

Mr. Dellinger, the chairman, said in his opening speech that "this is a beginning of a new stage in the American peace movement in which the cutting edge becomes active resistance."

Dr. Benjamin Spock, the pediatrician, said "we are convinced that this war which Lyndon Johnson is waging is disastrous to our country in every way, and that we, the protesters, are the ones who may help to save our country if we can persuade enough of our fellow citizens to think and vote as we do."

The enemy, "we believe in all sincerity," Dr. Spock went on, "is Lyndon Johnson, whom we elected as a peace candidate in 1964, and who betrayed us within three months, who has stubbornly led us deeper and deeper into a bloody quagmire in which uncounted hundreds of thousands of Vietnamese men, women and children have died, and 13,000 young Americans, too."

President Johnson worked in the White House, a few blocks east of the peace rally, and Mr. McNamara arrived at his Pentagon office at his usual hour of 8 A.M. Attorney General Ramsey Clark joined Mr. McNamara and other officials later at a command post inside the Pentagon's main entrance.

Hundreds of newsmen were admitted to the building but their movement was more restricted than on normal work days.

The mobilization committee, while agreed on the objective, peace in Vietnam, did not attempt to agree on methods and approaches to the objective. The participating groups reflected many shades of political and social philosophies.

The nominal leadership included, by their own acknowledgment, Communists and Communist sympathizers, but an authorized Government official said there was no evidence that the Communists were in charge or that there were more than "a very, very few" of them in influential roles.

Many youths carried United States flags; one carried a North Vietnam flag.

A small plane trailed a banner: "The Fallen Angels Love You."

At the Lincoln memorial rally, the crowd was orderly and the leaders seemed determined to maintain that order. The only disorderly occurrence there was an attack by three members of the American Nazi party who overturned the lectern and microphones.

Banners identified students from schools ranging from the Harvard Divinity School to colleges in California and Texas. High School of Music and Art A group of 37 came from the in New York City.

Three youths who said they were members of the American Nazi party tried to break up the program at the memorial at noon. Coming from behind, they rushed the lectern while Clive Jenkins of the British Labor party was speaking. The podium and a dozen microphones spilled down the stone steps leading to the reflection pool.

Young men from the mobilization group rushed the interrupters. Punches were exchanged and the three youths were hauled away to a patrol wagon shouting—"Heil Hitler."

The demonstrators had assigned marshals, coordinators, and controllers from their own group around the speakers' platform. As soon as the lectern tumbled, they linked arms and shouted "stay back," as newsmen tried to get closer. There were no uniformed policemen or soldiers in the platform area or on the steps.

The lectern and microphones were replaced within a few minutes, and Mr. Jenkins continued his speech.

The three youths who were taken away were arrested on disorderly conduct charges. They identified themselves as William G. Kirstein, 19 years old; Frank A. Drager, 27, and Christopher Vidnjevich, 24. All gave the address of the American Nazi party in Arlington, Va. The police called the three "storm troopers."

Mr. Dellinger made light of it all.

"I was just signing the last check for the sound **system,**" he said. "I thought he was after the check."

October 22, 1967

PRESIDENT ADVISES
YOUTH TO 'BUTT IN'

WASHINGTON, Jan. 26 (AP) —President Johnson said today that teen-agers who wanted to change the world should not "turn off" or "drop out" but should "butt in" to politics and change the world from within.

"Make no mistake," Mr. Johnson said. "When you young people speak up — people around here sit up. You won't see anyone wearing a hearing aid in the White House. You won't find anyone in this Administration who wants to tune you out. We hear you. We need you — maybe more than you know."

The President addressed the annual United States Senate Youth Program, which brings to Washington every year for a week two young people from each state who have been elected officers of their high school student bodies. This is done under a Senate resolution and through grants by the William Randolph Hearst foundation.

Mr. Johnson told the group:
"The test and art of leadership in a democracy is not the hand that rules, but the heart that hears. I want to leave you with a promise. So long as I lead, you will be heard."

January 27, 1968

If respect for authority, for the school, for the family has broken down,

Is It All Dr. Spock's Fault?

By CHRISTOPHER JENCKS

RESPECT for authority has never been an official American virtue. Our folk heroes include Puritan religious refugees who defied the Church of England, political revolutionaries who defied the British Government, and men we would now call psychological misfits who fled civilized America to make their own rule as frontiersmen. Our constitutional form of government placed unprecedented restraints on the authority of the state. Competition between denominations had the same effect on the traditional authority of the church, since potentially rebellious

CHRISTOPHER JENCKS, a resident fellow of the Institute for Policy Studies in Washington, is on leave, teaching at the Harvard Graduate School of Education. With David Riesman he wrote "The Academic Revolution," to be published soon.

parishioners could always leave a congregation whose demands they found burdensome. Even the informal authority that communities had traditionally exercised over their members was undermined by geographic mobility—today the typical American family stays in the same place only five years.

But every society must curb individualism in certain ways and induce men to submit to certain kinds of discipline. The family and the school have been America's principal institutions for doing this. Until fairly recently the American family was avowedly hierarchic: Men exercised power over women, and adults exercised power over the young. Those who had less power were expected to show respect for those who had more, to obey orders, to inhibit their feelings of resentment and to work hard to meet the demands placed upon them. It is true that even in the eighteen-thirties a European visitor like Alexis de Tocqueville was struck by the fact that American parents seemed more permissive and American children less obedient and less docile than their European counterparts. Nonetheless, earlier generations of children were generally kept in their place ("seen and not heard"), at least compared with children today.

American schools traditionally played a role rather similar to that of the family. One of their avowed purposes in the 19th and early 20th centuries was to teach children "to behave"—in particular to make them accept the impersonal discipline imposed first by a teacher and then by a textbook. While these efforts were not uniformly successful, especially when contrasted with Europe, neither were they totally without effect. The adults who emerged from these schools were by no means all pliant, subordinate bank clerks and secretaries, but neither were they all rebellious would-be cowboys. The genius of American institutions has been to find a place and a use for both these conflicting attitudes toward authority, making room

273

for both innovators and consolidators, entrepreneurs and "sound men," rebellious dreamers and stern adjudicators.

MODERN capitalism (like modern Socialism and Communism) relies on highly complex organizations. These can function only if most workers do what they are told most of the time. They must do it even when they feel the task is difficult, disagreeable or pointless, and they must do it with only minimal supervision. They must, in short, act precisely as parents used to urge their children to act and as teachers tried to make their pupils act. Yet capitalism also requires dissidents who will cut loose and go into business for themselves when their boss will not do something that obviously needs to be done. Without such men every organization would, sooner or later cease to serve the public and simply perpetuate itself—as, indeed, some have.

The American political system requires similar rebels who will continually argue the case against the status quo, formulate alternatives and try to create a constituency committed to those alternatives. When this kind of skepticism and resistance to established authority ceases, democracy becomes a mere facade for preserving the status quo—as, again, some radicals think it has. Yet at the same time every political system also needs dutiful civil servants who will carry out whatever program their political superiors inaugurate. If every civil servant had strong convictions of his own and then blocked anything which did not conform to these convictions, politics would become meaningless.

America has been built on a mixture of discipline and rebellion, but the balance between them has constantly shifted over the years. During the nineteen-forties and fifties the antiauthoritarian side of the American tradition lay politically dormant. Politicians and voters were mainly concerned with national security and prosperity. Conservatives expressed some alarm when pursuit of these objectives led to the growth and centralization of government power, and liberals expressed similar alarm when it led to the growth and centralization of corporate power, but almost

nobody opposed either trend in any serious way.

The nineteen-sixties, on the other hand, have seen a spectacular revival of the antiauthoritarian tradition. The most visible spokesmen for this revival are black militants and student radicals, but it has also affected many less outspoken liberals and conservatives—especially those under 30. It is important to ask why this questioning is taking place, for only if we know its roots have we much chance of predicting its consequences. This article offers some tentative speculations, but that is all anyone has to offer at the moment.

THE sources of the current unrest are many, but changes in the traditional structure of the American family strike me as playing a crucial role. The traditional, relatively hierarchical pattern of family relationships is being replaced by a new and far more egalitarian one, especially among the middle classes. This revolution began in the late 19th and early 20th centuries with the feminists' attack on masculine dominance. That battle was never entirely won, but relations between the sexes are certainly more equal today than they were in the 19th century. World War I and the Model A Ford encouraged a parallel change in the relation between parents and their adolescent children. This too is a continuing guerrilla war, but since the nineteen-twenties there has been little doubt that adolescents have been gradually gaining ground. During the nineteen-thirties this emancipation process began to have a dramatic effect on parents' relations with younger children as well.

Like most revolutions this one had its origins in a failure of nerve and loss of self-confidence among those who held power (in this case, adults). The origin of the crisis was probably the accelerating rate of social change. During the 19th century most parents had been able to assume that there were certain fixed standards of "civilized," "respectable" behavior to which every child should conform. These were the rules on which they themselves had been raised and (they assumed) their parents before them. In reality, of course, child-rearing practices have never been entirely stable. But until the past generation changes were fairly slow and hard to pinpoint.

A mother who upheld these standards was therefore not asserting her personal authority over her children; she was enforcing rules which, if not inscribed on golden tablets, were at least widely supported by her friends, her neighbors, her ancestors, her clergyman, and so forth.

By the nineteen-thirties the rate of social change and the amount of communication between dissimilar subcultures had increased to the point where no cosmopolitan parent could any longer cling to particular standards of behavior simply because "everyone" accepted them or because things had "always" been that way. Developments which would once have taken two or three generations now took one. Self-conscious choices were inescapable. Most urbane, educated parents knew they had been raised for a world very different from the one they lived in, and they at least suspected that their children would grow old in a world they could barely imagine. In such a context it was hard to be sure about anything, least of all whether children were better off on scheduled or demand feeding.

The anxiety accompanying these choices was heightened by the popularization in this same era of psychoanalysis. Millions of parents came to believe that they were responsible for whatever went wrong with their children's lives, that almost any parental act could have permanent traumatic consequences for a child, and that if they insisted on what had once been regarded as minimal standards they could easily turn their children into repressed neurotics. Many parents responded by trying to make as few choices as possible for their children, forcing the children to make more choices and (they hoped) take more responsibility for the consequences.

THE task of channeling parental anxiety into a new system of child-rearing fell to Dr. Benjamin Spock and his colleagues. Spock never urged complete permissiveness, but he did insist that a child's immediate needs had the same legitimacy and intensity as those of adults, that it was important for children to control their environment, and that authority should be rational and flexible rather than arbitrary and absolute. While this view is still by no means universally accepted, it has domi-

nated upper-middle-class child rearing since the nineteen-forties. Two features of this new style deserve particular attention in trying to understand contemporary America: the role of children in formulating the rules which govern their behavior, and the use of disapproval rather than actual punishment to keep children in line.

The idea that children can be implicated in the formulation of rules governing their behavior is certainly not entirely new. Parents have always tried to explain why certain rules existed, and by getting the child to acknowledge a rule's rationality they have in effect made him a partner in its preservation, if not its enforcement. But it is still fair to say that progressive-minded parents were more concerned with persuading their children that rules were legitimate and for their own good in the nineteen-forties and fifties than in earlier times. Such parents were also more willing to listen to their children's counterarguments. Children were encouraged to see themselves as equals who could use rationality to curb their parents' power, just as the parents used it to curb the children.

This ideal was, it is true, frequently violated. The child who asked his frazzled mother "Why?" 15 times in the same day sooner or later exhausted her patience and evoked the expected answer: "Because I say so." But forcing a "modern" mother to admit that her authority rested on superior power rather than reason made her feel guilty, and her children were quick to take advantage of this. By refusing to join the consensus which gave legitimacy to a particular request or rule, children could wear their parents down and eventually force them to retreat and reformulate their demands in a way that the children would accept. Child rearing in such families often became a process of overt negotiation. The fact of negotiation did not, of course, mean that the two parties were completely equal, but it was a long step in that direction. In a sense, Dr. Spock did for the young what the Wagner Act had done a few years earlier for the labor movement.

THE upper - middle - class family's emphasis on consensus, rationality and relative

DRAFT PROTEST — *"The Vietnam war has reinforced the feeling that hierarchical systems of government are destructive." A 1966 sit-in at City College, New York.*

equality was accompanied by new forms of discipline. If Johnny misbehaved he was made to feel that he was rejecting his parents and undermining the bonds of love which held the family together. For small children, this kind of fear and guilt seems to have been terrifying. As children grew older, however, they learned that their parents were vulnerable to the same tactics. A mother could keep a child in line by making him feel guilty and unlovable, but the child could do precisely the same thing to his mother. The result was a system of mutual deterrence.

When the products of these permissive, upper-middle-class homes entered school, they usually encountered teachers with more traditional standards of behavior and methods of control. A handful of progressive schools tried to recreate the atmosphere of a well-run permissive family, but these schools were almost all private. In the public schools rules were still rules, and teachers seem to have felt

less self-doubt when enforcing rules made by the administration than parents felt when trying to carry out the mandates of either their neighbors or Dr. Spock. The child who asked "Why?" all day in school was almost always silenced or at least subdued. Few schools even pretended to offer any answer but "Because we say so" (or "Because the book says so").

Yet even in the schools there was some change. More and more young teachers were anxious to win their pupils' love, reluctant to impose their will through physical punishment or intimidation, interested in dialogue rather than monologue, and hence more subject to both individual and collective pressure from their students. This was particularly true of the better suburban schools. So, while most schools continued to give children a foretaste of the "real" — i.e., nonfamilial — world, the flavor became more muted than in earlier times.

The first product of these semipermissive homes and

schools reached maturity in the nineteen-fifties. They—perhaps I should say "we," for this is my own generation—found that adult society was organized along very different lines from the families in which we had been raised, and that most employers were more like the teachers we had learned to hate than the teachers we had come to love.

Our reactions to this discovery were mixed. We were not sufficiently numerous to reinforce one another's prejudices, so we mostly assumed that our discontents were the result of personal maladjustments rather than societal ones. Even when we suspected that established institutions were unnecessarily hierarchic, authoritarian and repressive, it seldom occurred to us that they could be changed. The older generation which dominated America during the Eisenhower years had been so scarred by the nineteen-thirties and forties that it assumed fundamental change could only make America more totalitarian, not less, and its fatalism affected us too. Most of us therefore accepted the general principle that adult society could not be as egalitarian as our families had tried to be, and that we would have to subject ourselves to various kinds of remote, arbitrary authority.

Fatalistic as we were about reconstructing the adult world, we seldom threw ourselves into that world with much enthusiasm. Some of us took corporate or Government jobs, but few of us expected to get much satisfaction from them. They were simply a device for making a living. Those of us who wrote off the 9-to-5 portion of our lives pinned most of our hopes on creating a comfortable and comforting family life which embodied the ideals we had picked up in our own childhoods.

Others among us were slightly less pessimistic, and decided that while a corporate job would be intolerable we might find a habitable niche in one of the professions. Yet even this portion of my generation seldom saw its profession as an instrument for remaking the world.

Our professions were "just a job," preferable to a managerial career only because they gave us more day-to-day freedom and subjected us to less direct supervision and pressure from above. While many of us had an abstract sympathy with liberal causes,

we seldom let this affect our work in conspicuous ways. Most of us were even willing to let our professional knowledge and skills be used to strengthen the very hierarchic structures we disliked. Those of us who did scientific work, for example, had little compunction about working for the military as long as our personal independence was unaffected.

I DO not want to exaggerate the extent of these attitudes among people reaching adulthood in the nineteen-fifties. Indeed, World War II may have played a larger role than permissive ideology in shaping my generation. The war took millions of fathers away from their wives and children for long periods of time. This meant that the children in question did not encounter an impersonal, remote "law-giver," such as the American father had traditionally been, until they reached school. Even more important, mothers in these circumstances became more dependent on their children for emotional support, security and company.

Normally, a mother whose child rejects her can turn to her husband for reassurance; if the father is gone, she must make her peace with the child as best she can. This gives the child far more power than he usually has when dealing with two parents at once. (Where the two parents are in conflict, of course, a child may have more power when both are around and can be played off against each other than when one is away and the child has no potential ally.)

NONETHELESS, neither permissive ideology nor the war affected my generation during its earliest and presumably most formative years, and we must be viewed as a transitional group. Children born in the nineteen-forties were more clearly the products of the new ethos. Especially on leading college campuses in the sixties, the upper-middle-class children who set the tone are mostly products of permissive homes. Even those students whose parents had sought to preserve their traditional authority over their children had been affected by the national mood. All but the most self-confident of their parents had been troubled and ambivalent about imposing their will on the young, and had been vulnerable to pressures of the "Mrs. Smith lets

Johnny stay up as late as he likes" variety. Thus they learned that rules were, in fact, malleable under pressure, and that even apparently conservative authority figures could be made to yield.

Once the children of permissiveness arrived on campus in large numbers, they established their own cliques and way of life. Like all student subcultures, these were almost immune to adult control. Once established, such a milieu not only reinforced the prejudices of children from permissive homes but attracted—and to some extent resocialized — rebels from other backgrounds. Instead of one Greenwich Village in New York, populated by a handful of rebels from traditional homes, America developed scores of campus Villages, populated by young people whose values were shaped by the ideals espoused by their liberal parents. As the proportion of young people entering college grew, and the proportion going to work at 16 or 18 shrank, the new values flourished as never before.

Like young people in all eras, the present generation discovered what Kenneth Keniston calls the institutionalization of hypocrisy. No group of adults (or adolescents, for that matter) applies its ideals equally to all people and all areas of activity. Permissive parents, for example, often refuse to extend their generally libertarian values to sex. Many parents with strong ethical views are reluctant to apply the same standards to business relationships as to personal ones. Many who believe every American citizen has a right to elect the legislators and officials who exercise power over him are untroubled by the fact that America unilaterally determines the fate of hundreds of millions of foreigners who have no voice whatever in choosing American policymakers. The young have responded to such contradictions by growing cynical about America's professed ideals, even though these ideals are in most cases also their own.

Another difference between the old and the young is that many of the young have extended their parents' ideals about family life to society as a whole. This is not just a matter of rejecting traditional status distinctions or insisting that those who have power must respect the needs and feelings of those who lack it.

For this generation, private problems became public issues

That has been a recurrent theme in America for many generations, only marginally reinforced by recent changes in family structure. The really startling thing about the young is that so many of them have turned against the whole idea of industrial society and have tried to revive a complex of older ideals associated with the word "community."

COMMUNITY can mean as many things as there are men using the term. Nonetheless, certain common themes recur over and over in talking about it with today's students.

First, community means that nobody is expendable. Everyone has some kind of function, makes some kind of contribution to the group, and is accepted as a full member of the group for that reason. This means that every member of the community has a commitment to every other, regardless of whether he likes or dislikes him, just as every member of a family has a commitment to every other member, no matter how much bad blood there may be between them.

The liberal idea of voluntary association, especially voluntary association of like with like, has little place in this vision, for it allows too many "misfits" to fall through the cracks. The meritocratic idea that jobs should be ranked in terms of difficulty, and rewards given on the basis of where a man stands in the hierarchy, is also alien to this vision of community.

A second aspect of community as envisaged by the young is that everyone knows everyone else fairly well, so that even nonfamilial relationships involve "the whole man" rather than being confined to narrowly stylized roles. An employer sees his employes not just as subordinates but as neighbors. A seller sees a buyer not just as a source of cash but as a friend. A policeman who picks up a drunk deals with him not just as a violator of the law but, perhaps, as a fishing partner or a fellow P.-T.A. member. Because all relations are multifaceted—indeed, the ideal is that they should be total—there are very few impersonal, legalistic or "businesslike" encounters between people.

This has its dangers. A man who is, let us say, a "good" lawyer but a "bad" friend gets little business in such a society and makes little contribution. A student who does brilliant work in physics but is a poor neighbor does not get admitted to a selective graduate department, which makes the department pleasanter but may leave humanity more ignorant. And a policeman who finds a man he dislikes drunk in the street presumably gives him a kick and walks on rather than feeling obliged to act out his legally defined role and treat this particular drunk like every other.

If this vision of community sounds like an extended family, that is no accident. If it sounds unworkable for a society of 200 million people, that is no accident either. The young men and women who hold these ideas are not much taken with societies of 200 million people, which is one reason they talk continually about decentralization. Indeed, the young radical who suggested that Students for a Democratic Society should change its name to Students for a Small Society was speaking only half in jest.

GIVEN their dreams of an egalitarian, familistic world, the young men and women who came of age in the early nineteen-sixties were naturally quite appalled by the reality of American life. These young people were increasingly allergic to the idea of becoming organization men or organization wives, for example. Yet the hard fact was that new jobs for college graduates were almost all being created by large hierarchical organizations, either public or private. (The major exceptions to this were universities, which were creating openings for Ph.D.'s at a great rate, were subjecting these Ph.D.'s to relatively little supervision, and were, in most cases, allowing them a collective veto over those aspects of university policy which affected their own lives. Many rebellious young people therefore concluded that the only possible career for them would be an academic one.)

Yet, unlike my generation,

the undergraduates of the nineteen-sixties did not all retreat into quiescence. For them, private problems did become public issues. One key reason for this was the election of John F. Kennedy in 1960.

Kennedy was by no means similar to these young people in either style or temperament. He was an élitist whose greatest triumph (the Cuban missile crisis) involved a dozen men deciding whether 300 million others should live or die. One can hardly imagine a better symbol of the kind of hierarchical, authoritarian system the young were in revolt against—though most of them certainly applauded this particular coup.

Yet Kennedy shared the youthful conviction that some change was necessary, and he managed to persuade a great many people, young and old, that it was also possible. The Kennedy years were not a time of significant political achievement, but they were a time of hope, and that hope was communicated to the young. The future did not look bright to everyone, but at least it looked open. The missile crisis provided one kind of symbol, but the Peace Corps provided another and, a few years later, so did the atomic-test-ban treaty. Equipped with 20-20 hindsight, many now laugh at the naiveté of those who took these gestures seriously, but at the time they were widely seen as tokens of more and better things to come.

Another factor in breaking through the fatalism of the nineteen-fifties was the civil-rights movement. This was mainly a response to changes in the mood of the black lower classes on the one hand and the Federal courts on the other. It had almost nothing to do with the child-rearing revolution I have been describing. Nonetheless, the movement captured the imagination of many white undergraduates. It gave them something to do, and when they did it they often achieved tangible results. It was an extraordinarily decentralized movement, in which local action played an enormous role. (There was a Woolworth's within picketing distance of nearly every campus.)

Students' discovery that they could affect the seemingly remote and unshakable political system by both persuasion and civil disobedience transformed many of them, reinforcing their childhood dis-

PARADOX — *President Kennedy with Peace Corps trainees. "He was an elitist, a symbol of the system the young were in revolt against, yet he shared their conviction that some change was necessary."*

covery that their seemingly powerful parents could be pushed around by these same means. It is true that the achievements of this era were modest in comparison with the total problem. The movement produced only reforms, not a revolution. Nonetheless, the sense of movement was real and enormously important, as was the sense that individual citizens could affect the course of this movement by personal effort. History does not vouchsafe many people such potency, but when it does it usually takes a generation to restore order and re-create the general passivity which is normal in all political systems.

The net result of all this was that while large numbers of young people thought America a dreadful mess, many also thought it could be reconstructed along lines consonant with the values they had grown up believing in. Some of these young people became full-time political activists, but most entered the professions or went to work for the more glamorous agencies of the Federal Government. Most of them described themselves as liberals or radicals, but some of the young conservatives who rallied to the banner of Barry Goldwater were equally antiauthoritarian and dissatisfied with the status quo.

The difference between the two groups was that those or the left were usually concerned with the problems of the least competent and least privileged, while those on the right paid more attention to the problems of the most competent and most privileged. The right therefore tended, almost despite itself, to create centralized, authoritarian political organizations in which those who had advantages could maximize them. The left, on the other hand, created anarchic organizations in which the least competent members often neutralized the most competent.

THE Vietnam war has certainly not given the liberal-minded, open-hearted children of permissiveness any further grounds for supposing that they can affect the political events which most concern them. But it has reinforced their feeling that hierarchical systems of government which rely on *expertise* and technology to solve problems are fundamentally destructive. Some who draw this conclusion have become revolutionaries, demanding a complete reorganization of American life along nonhierarchical lines. (How this might be accomplished is unclear.) Many others, of whom the hippies are the visible fringe, have no interest in revolution or any other "political" solution. They think salvation is indi-

vidual, and, like their predecessors in the nineteen-fifties, they have "gone limp" politically. But, unlike their predecessors in the nineteen-fifties, many of them refuse even to go through the motions of conformity to rules they think absurd. Whereas members of my generation followed careers that bored them and sought solace in family life or alcohol, some of our successors have no careers at all. They simply drop in and out of the labor force in order to support themselves. Their solace, if any, is found in sex and drugs rather than drink.

Neither the political nor the psychological dropouts are yet anything like a majority. Most children, even from egalitarian and permissive homes, still climb through school and college into the established institutions of adult society, rather than trying to create alternatives. Yet their acquiescence should not be mistaken for support. The majority may have only a passing interest in LSD and may not respond to the New Left's demands for participatory democracy, but that does not mean they have any enthusiasm for the institutions their parents have created. They are a kind of fifth column within these institutions, unwilling to struggle very hard to preserve them and perhaps even available to support alternatives, should these come into existence.

WHAT does this imply for the future? First, it suggests that the current unrest of the young is not just a response to external events like the war in Vietnam or racial injustice. These events are real enough, but they evoke very different responses in people of more traditional temperament: rallying round the flag, support for established authority (rather than insurgency), repression (rather than acquiescence or compromise). Vietnam and Watts are symbols for the young and the alienated, but their elimination, even if it proved possible, would probably not make dissenters into passionate advocates of American institutions and social arrangements. As long as children are raised in increasingly permissive ways, and as long as the values developed in permissive families are reinforced by ever-longer immersion in adolescent subcultures, while adult life remains regimented and hierarchical for all but the most fortunate few, disenchantment will persist and probably grow even more intense.

This estrangement is unlikely to have much political effect in the near future. Recent events make an American victory in Vietnam seem unlikely even in the long run. If victory is impossible, the alternatives seem to be a larger land war in Asia, perhaps involving the use of nuclear weapons, or else a "compromise," probably involving an eventual take-over by the National Liberation Front. A settlement along the latter lines, while certainly preferable to the former, seems certain to produce a bitter reaction among American conservatives, just as Versailles and Panmunjom did in earlier times. Such a reaction would, most likely, be reinforced by continuing summer riots and "crime in the streets."

These appalling probabilities are not certainties; they could be averted with luck and leadership. But, if they materialize, America's "postwar"—i.e., post-Vietnam — politics are likely to be dominated by a combination "Red scare" and "black scare." The results would probably be irresistible pressure for a "return to normalcy," repression of past and potential radicals, and attempts to strengthen established authority against both external and internal enemies.

While many of the young people I have been talking about would greet such a development with sorrow, they are not likely to be either sufficiently numerous or sufficiently well-organized to prevent it. My guess is that it will take at least a decade, and possibly two, before they are in a position to dominate American politics — and by then they may well have internalized the very standards and assumptions they now question or reject.

THE fundamental challenge to the status quo posed by the recent revolution in child rearing may turn out not to be political but economic. I suggested at the beginning of this article that the viability of any social system depends on its ability to establish political and economic institutions which

SIGN — An antidraft march in Pittsburgh. The poster bears the ban-the-bomb symbol.

both serve the public and fit the character and temperament of those who staff them. A bureaucratic system which is tolerably efficient when staffed by conscientious Scandinavians or Prussians, for example, can be a complete disaster when staffed by self-indulgent Italians or cynical Latin Americans. Similarly, a capitalist system which

worked tolerably well when it attracted America's ablest and most public-spirited citizens could deteriorate into an unmanageable system of self-serving feudal baronies if its staff was less competent or entirely self-serving.

The rising distaste for managerial careers among the ablest and most altruistic students at leading colleges is

therefore an ominous portent. If the trend continues, the established machinery of business and government may be handed over by default to individuals who have neither the skill nor the wisdom to make the machinery serve the public interest. Those who could and should take a leading role in reshaping American life along more humane and civilized lines may simply slip quietly into the professions, where their influence will usually be marginal, even if their lives are comfortable. Some, indeed, may drop out of the economic system entirely.

It is too early to say whether this gloomy possibility will become a reality. One crucial variable in determining the outcome will be politics. If the nineteen-seventies turn out to be a conservative rerun of the nineteen-twenties or fifties, as seems possible, the egalitarian, familistic, antiauthoritarian youngsters I have been describing are likely to grow bitter, cynical and privatistic.

This has happened before, of course, both with the young people who nourished great hopes for progressivism before World War I and lost hope after Wilson's defeat, and with those who hitched their wagon to the star of radicalism during the nineteen-thirties and were defeated after World War II. The difference, I think, is that a far larger proportion of today's younger generation seems estranged from the American system than was the case in those earlier times. Unless that system does much more than it so far has to accommodate these young people's values and co-opt their talents, it could easily go into a decline similar to that which has undermined every previous civilization in history.

March 3, 1968

MORE YOUTHS JOIN M'CARTHY FORCES

Pour Into New Hampshire for the Final Push

By EDITH EVANS ASBURY
Special to The New York Times

CONCORD, N. H., March 9— A new wave of students from colleges and universities all over the nation poured into New Hampshire today to help

Senator Eugene J. McCarthy's campaign for the Democratic Presidential nomination.

Students began a McCarthy drive in the state six weeks ago, and their enthusiasm was so contagious that word had to be spread along the Eastern Seaboard yesterday canceling plans by 18 busloads of other students who wanted to join them in the final push this weekend.

But 1,000 more students who could not be reached in time arrived today.

Earlier two carloads of students who came from the University of Michigan to work for Gov. George Romney only to learn that the Michigan Governor had withdrawn from the race for the Republican Presidential nomination stayed on to work for Mr. McCarthy, Democrat of Minnesota.

Families Won Over

Some Republican families who agreed to let the students live in their homes are so won over to the students' idealism, shrewdness and painstaking at-

tention to detail that they says they plan to write in Senator McCarthy's name on their Republican ballots Tuesday.

"I never saw anything like it," declared Cort B. Antonson, a Republican, who took two students from New Jersey into his home.

"They are positively captivating," his wife, also a Republican, said.

"They get out at 8 o'clock in the morning and don't get home from their headquarters until 2 or 3 in the morning. I don't know where they get the strength."

The Antonsons are going to vote for Senator McCarthy. Mr.

Antonson, a sales representative, is trying to persuade his customers to do likewise, and Mrs. Antonson has persuaded their son to do so.

The students' campaign headquarters is in a one-story, store-front building, where electrical equipment used to be sold, a couple of blocks off Main Street.

Local students built tables and benches and partitions of rough lumber and plywood.

Here doctoral candidates in everything from English literature to nuclear physics study election district maps, plot routes for door-to-door canvassers, arrange for housing either in private homes or in churches and Y.M.C.A. gymnasiums for those who bring sleeping bags, obtain transportation to towns and villages all over the state, and supervise mass mailings of campaign literature.

There was a scream of anguish as word came that a busload with 50 more students was on the way.

"When I think how few we had six weeks ago and how we could have used them," said Dianne Dumonoski, 23-year-old Vassar graduate from Gardner, Mass. "Now I don't know where we are going to put them."

Miss Dumonoski, candidate for a Ph.D. in English at Yale, is among the estimated 50 per cent who are graduate students and of voting age. She is a slender, blue-eyed blonde with long straight hair and a fierce hatred of the war in Vietnam.

She and others interviewed consider the war immoral, a threat to students, a consumer of billions of dollars that should be used to rescue the cities and the poor.

March 10, 1968

McCarthy's Appeal to Youth

Eugene McCarthy has performed a service of value to his country quite apart from his astonishing showing in New Hampshire or his fate in future primary elections. He has rekindled the faith of thousands of intelligent young Americans in democratic machinery and the efficacy of the ballot.

In a climate of doubt and fear, Senator McCarthy has managed in particular to persuade great numbers of concerned youth that it is possible to make effective protest against existing American policies and practices by traditional democratic means. His chief basis for effecting this transformation was a willingness to act on his belief that honorable peace could be won in Vietnam through a more imaginative and energetic diplomatic effort coupled with military restraint.

College students, long ago convinced that the Johnson Administration is unable or unwilling to make this kind of fresh approach, flocked into New Hampshire to work the clock around for a man willing to challenge the President. Some frankly said they would have turned to violent protest if Senator McCarthy had not entered the lists to raise their sights with some of the most intelligent talk heard on the hustings of America since Adlai Stevenson burst on the national scene in 1952.

As it turned out, they delivered the most effective response possible to the nihilism and defeatism of their contemporaries of the New Left.

How many are thus committed and what possible impact can they have on the course of politics in this election year? In New Hampshire alone there were enough, and they were effective enough, to help Senator McCarthy win an unexpected 42 per cent of all Democratic votes, and now to encourage Senator Robert Kennedy to reconsider trying for the nomination, with incalculable results for the Democratic party.

Eugene McCarthy has done vastly more than mobilize an army of young Americans for doorbell-ringing and envelope-stuffing. He has demonstrated to the men who wield political power in America and to some who would like to wield it that it is still possible to close the generation gap and to counter the alienation of America's young people from the American system.

March 14, 1968

Mental Ills Linked to Disrespect

By JOHN LEO
Special to The New York Times

CHICAGO, March 21—A prominent psychologist warned here today that civil disobedience, contemptuous attitudes toward the police, and emotional attacks on President Johnson were damaging the mental health of the young.

Dr. Bruno Bettelheim, director of the Orthogenic School at the University of Chicago and author of "The Empty Fortress," a highly acclaimed study of infantile autism, said that the spreading disrespect for authority figures was "cheating the young" and leading to the breakdown of their inhibitions against violence.

Autism is absorption in fantasy to the exclusion of interest in external reality.

"What we've got to develop is trust in the institutions of society," he said, "the respect for the superego representations selected by society, from police and teachers all the way up to the President, whatever you may think of him personally."

Dr. Bettelheim spoke at the annual convention of the American Orthopsychiatric Association, a nationwide group of medical and academic professionals who collaborate on problems of mental health. About 7,000 are attending the four-day meeting at the Conrad Hilton Hotel.

Dr. Bettelheim said that liberals, the press and teachers who failed to assert their authority all shared some blame for denying superego models to the young, particularly the poor and disadvantaged.

"It's devastating to children," he said. "We send our children off to school to make their way into the system, and then tell them the system is lousy. We vilify the President as a man who is killing babies and then ask our children to respect authority."

"If we want to change the system," he continued, "we should change it in the voting booth, but we should keep adult concerns away from our children."

He said the mass media "make some of these riots" and further contribute to the breakdown of order by lavishing attention on Stokely Carmichael and H. Rap Brown, the militant black power advocates.

"There's no doubt about the underlying violence with which we are born," Dr. Bettelheim said. "Whether we're going to have violence depends to a very large degree on how we develop the superego and the controls of the coming generation."

Like Freud, he said, his own expectations about violence "are not optimistic, but realistic."

"I don't know whether we have to go back to the circus games and fights as satisfactions," he said, "but I don't know what the alternatives are. Maybe our riots are some of these extravaganzas. Maybe they are the price we have to pay."

March 22, 1968

'Respect' for Authority

To the Editor:

In The Times on March 22 appeared a summary of a paper by Dr. Bruno Bettelheim, from which it would seem that he has made a fundamental error in logic by confusing the institution with the individual. We cannot "trust" or "respect" an institution, since institutions cannot act.

We can only trust or respect the individual who fills the role in the institution. Therefore we must not confuse the Presidency with the President; a criticism of Mr. Johnson is a criticism of the man, not the institution. No one can demand respect for the President or for anyone else; respect and trust must be earned.

We were shocked by Dr. Bettelheim's remarks on civil disobedience and general criticism of the system. This man watched Hitler rise to power, and was himself a victim of the concentration camps.

While it is true that children learn control by internalizing relationships with authority figures, we must also teach our children to question rather than to accept submissively, and when necessary to act on their convictions.

Many individuals, young and old, deserve praise for their courage to stand up against an authority figure when they believe that individual is not acting for the good of the people. It seems to us that if this ability had not been lacking in the German people in the 1930's World War II could have been avoided.

Let us not teach our children automatic respect for "authority"; let us teach them to question and to examine the actions of all individuals, no matter what their rank or status—no human being is perfect. They should know that too.

DAVID GRAVES
JERILYN GRAVES
MAURICE YOUNG
JO LANG
New York, March 23, 1968

April 1, 1968

Observer: Round Holes, Square Pegs and Sore Kids

By RUSSELL BAKER

WASHINGTON, April 27—It is easy to laugh at the square, old-fashioned befuddlement and Blimpish choler with which the aging and institutionalized "older generation" responds to the present epidemic of youth rebellion. The old folks are in the classic comic plight of the fool at the party who has "Kick Me" written on his back but doesn't know it.

Something is going on, and he does not know what it is. His confusion, irritation and embarrassed sense of exclusion make him ridiculous, at least to the cruel. Among the initiates in the rites of the social lodge, there is a temptation to dismiss the uninitiated as fools.

Youth nowadays must surely be the biggest mystic lodge on earth, and the fact that the uninitiated—which is to say, the unyoung—do not know the secret handclasp or the secret of the mystic rites makes them seem slightly absurd, or in the current argot, "not with it."

It is plain enough that the old folks are "not with it." The interesting question is, are the young rebels "with it"? Something is going on, all right, but do they really have any clearer idea than the Blimps of what it is?

One curious aspect of the rebellion epidemic is that the rebels have no definable goals. Like mercenary soldiers, they seem perpetually available to swell the ranks of whatever cause may be on the wind.

Fashions in Issues

In 1963, it was civil rights, and when this went out of fashion, it became Vietnam. Now, with Vietnam temporarily fading as a cause, some are re-enlisting in civil rights. Dozens of lesser causes nurture them from time to time. The legalization of marijuana, the social stultification of German life, university administration, companionate marriage, unlim-

ited chapel cuts, and so on.

What becomes obvious, looking over the full range of causes—and it is as broad as the Rockies—is that the rebels don't know what's going on either. One suspects that if they were to be completely satisfied on one score, they would find two fresh grievances to fight against, and if victorious on those, would promptly find four or eight or sixteen more to fill their need for—what?

Their general inability to answer that question is best illustrated in the case of the bright precollege high-school dropouts who so baffle educators and psychologists. It is fashionable to say that the routine drudgery and discipline of formal education "bore" them. Perhaps so, but it appears to run deeper than that.

Often, they seem to have simply unplugged themselves from the entire society, not out of any particular hostility toward it, but rather out of a sense that it is irrelevant to the world of their intuitive perception. School is the principal mechanism by which the society reproduces itself, and the bright kids who cut out may be saying that they have no interest in being fitted, round peg in square hole, into a structure that has nothing to do with their personal vision of human existence.

The college-age rebels, having gone along with the system into adulthood, develop overt hostilities as well as the academic man's power to rationalize and articulate them in noble phrases. Even the natural lust of the puerile for violence is now justified by learned reference to Fanon's assertions that it is ultimately therapeutic.

It seems equally possible that the appetite for violent solution —"confrontation" is the popular learned word—is a natural retaliatory response against a system which blindly forces in-

telligent men to occupy lives that don't fit them. The bright hot young radicals of the New Left seem to be conceding the point when they argue for anarchy and reject the possibility of change without destruction.

Rebellion and revolution in this case are their own justifications. The goal of rebellion, is, very simply, rebellion. And the reason that the middle-aged and the institutionalized cannot cope with it by offering to satisfy its demands is that it does not know what its demands are. Neither do the rebels. In fact, they have no demands and no goals, but only an animal force focused against the outrage of authority.

Their motivating passion is, in Norman Mailer's phrase, "lust for apocalypse." What is the outrage that authority has committed against its children? Marshall McLuhan may have the best answer.

The New Environment

It has placed them in a revolutionary new environment which was bound inevitably to condition them to think and to see their world and their places in it in ways that persons bred by the old environment could not begin to comprehend. But the old breed, jealous of the old vision that worked so well for them, still man the institutions, which in turn demand square pegs to support them.

When the pegs are human, shaping a round one to fit a square hole is an act of torture. It should not be surprising if, after awhile, those who are tormented to fit in become more receptive to the notion that relief can be gained more rapidly from tearing the whole frame apart than by slowly reshaping the holes.

April 28, 1968

1,000 POLICE ACT TO OUST STUDENTS FROM FIVE BUILDINGS AT COLUMBIA; MOVE IN AT UNIVERSITY'S REQUEST

MEDIATION FAILS

Proposal by Kirk to End Dispute Spurned by Faculty Group

By SYLVAN FOX

A handpicked force of 1,000 policemen moved onto the Columbia University campus early today and began ordering student demonstrators out of five buildings the students have occupied in a tense, week-long protest.

The police moved with stunning suddenness at 2:30 A.M. while most of the city and much of the campus and its surrounding neighborhood slept.

As the hour for the police assault - approached, tension mounted sharply on the campus as groups of students held informal meetings. At 1:45 A.M., when word reached the Mathematics Building that "a bust," or police raid, was imminent, student demonstrators began strengthening their barricades and girding themselves for the assault.

WKCR, the campus radio station, at 1:30 A.M. reported that a police move appeared close, and it urged students to remain in their dormitories.

Move Delayed

The raid originally had been scheduled for 1:30 A.M. It was postponed several times because of what police officials described as "tactical delays."

A high police official said later that the raid had been delayed to wait until Harlem was asleep.

Wearing helmets and carrying flashlights, they fanned through the darkened campus, which they had divided for purposes of the assault into seven sectors that were designated "target areas."

These were Hamilton, Avery and Fayerweather Halls, the Low Memorial Library and the Mathematics Building—all occupied structures — and the areas of 115th Street and Morningside Drive and 116th Street and Amsterdam Avenue.

Target Gets Priority

Hamilton Hall, which Negro students and a scattering of off-campus black activists had occupied since the student uprising began last Tuesday afternoon, was the first police target.

As the police moved on Hamilton Hall, other policemen issued an ultimatum to the students occupying Low Library, demanding they leave peacefully or be ejected.

Speaking over a bullhorn, a white-helmeted policeman called to "the occupants" of Hamilton Hall, saying: "We want you to come out and come out now. We are authorized by the trustees of the university. This is it. Come out now. You made your point. Come out now."

It was understood to be the hope of the police commanders that they could remove the Negro students with a minimum of force, thus making it easier for them to evict the white students from the four other occupied campus buildings.

The police commanders, who led a force that included 200 men from each of five precincts, were said to be carrying written instructions from Police Commissioner Howard R. Leary to use necessary force but to show restraint in their handling of the students.

As the first move in their coordinated attack, the police at 2 A.M. severed all telephone service and water supplies to the five occupied buildings. The student protesters had depended heavily during the demonstration on telephone communication to keep in touch with the situation in each of the buildings they held.

Meanwhile, pockets of students, many huddled under blankets against the chill night air, moved from building to building trying to see what was going on. And outside the Low Library, where about 200 students gathered in a milling crowd, a "town crier" with a bullhorn issued minute-by-minute bulletins about events leading up to the raid.

Mr. Leary, accompanied by two representatives of the university administration, was directing the opation on the campus. Chief Inspector Sanford D. Garelik supervised the force, which included members of the Emergency Service Division, policewomen and detectives, as well as uniformed patrolmen.

University Made Request

The police acted in response to a request from the administration of the university it was understood. Under normal procedure, the police would take no action on the campus, which is private property, unless formally authorized to do so by university officials.

The police intervention came after a day of futile efforts to resolve the Columbia dispute by peaceful negotiations and mediation. The Columbia administration proposed a peace plan, but it was rejected by a key faculty grouy as inadequate.

The decision to request the police to move into control of the troubled campus was made about 5 P.M., according to high police officers.

During the next few hours, the operation, which had been planned long before on a contingency basis, was carefully reviewed by police commanders.

At midnight, the selected task force members assembled at each of five nearby station houses. An hour and 40 minutes later, the 1,000-man force grouped at the West 100th Street police station and prepared to move onto the campus.

Throughout the operation, the campus was tightly sealed. The police blocked all entrances in an attempt to prevent any off-campus groups sympathetic to the demonstrators from going to their support.

Faculty Intervenes

Police intervention had loomed as an almost constant prospect since the student uprising began. Last Friday morning, some 25 plainclothes policemen armed with clubs moved on Low Library at the request of university officials. There was a fracas as members of an Ad Hoc Faculty Group stood at the southeast entrance to the building and refused to permit the police to pass.

During the clash, one member of the faculty was struck on the head by a club and injured, although not seriously.

A faculty delegation immediately went to Dr. Grayson Kirk, the president of Columbia, and urged him to defer any police action until attempts to mediate the dispute had been exhausted. Dr. Kirk agreed to give the Ad Hoc Faculty Group, which has led mediation efforts, more time to seek a peaceful solution.

But ever since the confrontation, tension ran high on the Morningside Heights campus, which has about 17,500 students.

Over the weekend, rumors flew around the campus that some police action would be taken against the demonstrators on Sunday night to permit the university to reopen yesterday morning.

No action came, however, as mediators continued to seek a way out of the deadlocked dispute.

Police Remain

In the meantime, the police remained on the campus as a visible but inactive presence. About 20 policemen stood guard around Low Library. Several policemen were posted at 116th Street and Broadway and at 116th Street and Amsterdam Avenue—the only two campus gates that remained open when the university was officially closed Friday—to permit students and employes to enter.

The police had been requested to enter the campus by the university authorities on Thursday. It was the first time since May, 1965, when a campus demonstration disrupted graduation ceremonies of the Naval Reserve Officers Training Corps, that a police force had been asked to enter the university grounds.

The move by the police early this morning reflected the university administration's evident decision that negotiations and mediation had failed.

Earlier in the day, Dr. Kirk had offered a four-point peace plan that he said carried out "the essential spirit" of a faculty group's proposals to end the demonstration.

Leaders of the Ad Hoc Faculty Group, however, promptly declared that Dr. Kirk's plan fell far short of their proposals for drastic revision of Columbia's disciplinary machinery and abandonment of plans for the construction of a controversial gymnasium in Morningside Park. These were additional developments during the day:

¶A brief but angry clash erupted when supporters of students occupying President Kirk's office in Low Memorial Library and four other buildings attempted to smash their way through a human wall erected around Low by students opposed to the campus protest.

¶Theodore W. Kheel, the labor mediator, stepped into the Columbia dispute in an attempt to find a third-party solution.

Governor's Help Sought

At a meeting of the Ad Hoc Faculty Group last night, a proposal to ask Gov. Rockefeller to establish arbitration procedures to end the dispute was rejected.

But the faculty members who had been meeting in the Philosophy Building most of the day, approved a resolution asking Mayor Lindsay to intervene personally, according to one member of the group.

The group member said that two of the Mayor's aides had informed him that if the Ad Hoc Faculty Group requested the Mayor's help, the aides would recommend that Mr. Lindsay offer his services.

For the second day, there were no classes at Columbia yesterday. The university — except for Barnard, Teachers College and units removed from the Morningside Heights campus — was officially closed, as it had been on Friday.

Early this moring, about 450 students collected around the sundial in the center of the Columbia campus to listen to speakers urging support for the demonstrators.

One student speaker said he had been informed at 11:45 P.M. that "in the event of a bust" — a police raid on the demonstrators — members of

the Ad Hoc Faculty Group planned to circle the occupied buildings and interpose themselves between the police and the demonstrators.

The student urged those sitting around the sundial to remain there until they saw the faculty members taking up positions, then to join them.

Shortly after midnight, the campus was a strange and eerie place. Japanese music drifted from a window of Fayerweather Hall, one of the occupied buildings, and a show of red, blue and white lights payed on a window of the building. Everywhere else on the campus, there was almost deathly silence.

Dr. Kirk said last night that "in the present circumstances there will be an announcement on the radio each morning at 6 A.M. as to when classes will be resumed."

Dr. Kirk's announcement of his four-point plan, issued by the Columbia information office in midafternoon, brought a glimmer of hope to a campus that has been gripped for days by fear that it was heading for a potentially bloody confrontation between the police and demonstrating students.

In his plan, Dr. Kirk said he was prepared to accept a faculty committee recommendation for establishment of a tripartite disciplinary commission composed of students, faculty members and members of the administration and to appoint members recommended to him by the three-member faculty committee.

Dr. Kirk also said he would "recommend to the trustees that the statutes of the university dealing with disciplinary matters be re-examined in the light of the recommendations to be submitted by the tripartite commission."

Furthr, the Columbia president said "matters such as the question of uniform penalties" for students involved in the protest would be referred to the tripartite commission, which he proposed should consist of seven students, eight faculty members and three representatives of t' administration.

The idea of uniform penalties for the demonstrators had been proposed by faculty leaders as an alternative to the total amnesty that the student demonstrators have been demanding as a precondition to any formal negotiations to end the protest. Uniform penalties would mean that student demonstrators would receive token punish1 ient, probably nothing more than letters of warning from the administration.

Amnesty Is Rejected

The Columbia trustees and large numbers of faculty members have supported Dr. Kirk's rejection of amnesty. Aside from the letter of warning, the punishment for the demonstrators could range through probation, suspension or outright expulsion.

However, six leaders of the protesting group, including Mark Rudd, the Columbia chairman of the Students for a Democratic Society, are on probation because of earlier protests and even a letter of warning on top of probation would bring mandatory expulsion.

In his statement, Dr. Kirk said that he would "recommend to the trustees that they authorize me to proceed with discussions" on the problem of the gym in Morningside Park. Excavation work at the gymnasium site was halted at the request of Mayor Lindsay on Friday, and it is widely felt on the campus that work will never be resumed.

"I commend and fully share the objectives of the resolution adopted by the Ad Hoc Faculty Group on April 28," Dr. Kirk said in his statement. He went on to say that he was confident that his proposals "carry out the essential spirit of those proposals."

But a leader of the Ad Hoc Faculty Group, who asked not to be identified, said of Dr. Kirk's statement: "There's no give here."

Views of the Faculty

The faculty member said that Dr. Kirk had said only that he would recommend that disciplinary affairs be "re-examined," while the Ad Hoc Group had called in its resolution for establishment of a tripartite commission that would have "ultimate judicial review on all matters affecting university discipline."

The faculty member said also that Dr. Kirk's statement indicated only that he would undertake further discussion of the Morningside Park gymnaslum plan. The Ad Hoc Group, it was noted, had called for the creation by Mayor Lindsay of a panel to review the gymnaz:ium plan, adopt an alternative to the present plan and, if the alternative involved keeping the gym on its present site, submitting the matter to representatives of Harlem, where there has been strenuous opposition to construction of the gymnasium.

"He's taking the posture of a neutral party," the ad hoc leader said of Dr. Kirk.

As Dr. Kirk's statement was circulating around the campus, where thousands of students milled around and held informal meetings, Mr. Kheel arrived outside Hamilton Hall, which is occupied by Negro students and a scattering of off-campus black activists.

Mr. Kheel was with Dr. Kenneth Clark, a City College psychology professor and the president of the Metropolitan Applied Research Center.

The two men waited outside heavily barricaded Hamilton Hall, normally the focus of Columbia College undergraduate classroom activity, for

about 45 minutes. Then, at 1:45, Dr. Clark was invited inside.

Kheel on Crutches

Fifteen minutes later, Mr. Kheel, carrying two metal crutches to ease the strain resulting from a recent leg operation, was summoned inside.

The mediator, who has participated in settlements of transit strikes, newspaper strikes and a host of other labor disputes, climbed the tables and filing cabinets blocking Hamilton Hall's door. When som students reached out to aid him, he said: "No help, please I can make it."

Mr. Kheel remained in Hamilton Hall, meeting for about three hours with leaders of the `cc` cty of Afro-American Students, which, with the Students for a Democratic Society, has been leading the protest.

Afterward Mr. Kheel said that he and Dr. Clark had "made several suggestions for a possible resolution and the leaders have agreed to study the suggestions." He declined to divulge the nature of the proposals.

Mr. Kheel, who was joined in the Hamilton Hall talks by Dr. Clark and William H. Booth, the city's Human Rights Commissioner, then left for conferences with representatives of the Columbia administration.

He met for two hours with Dr. Kirk and David B. Truman, the vice president of the university.

"We had informal discussions with President Kirk and Dean Truman," Mr. Kheel said of his talks with the administrators. "We made some suggestions."

Before he entered Hamilton Hall, Mr. Kheel, who is chairman of the board of the Metropolitan Applied Research Center, said he had gone to Columbia at the invitation of Dr. Clark, who met with students in Hamilton Hall on Saturday.

While Mr. Kheel met with Negro students in Hamilton Hall, opponents of the protest, who have organized a group called the Coalition of the Majority, maintained a solid blockade around Low Library, where student demonstrators have occupied President Kirk's office since the uprising began on Tuesday afternoon.

About 250 antiprotest students stood shoulder to shoulder along the west side of the domed and pillared building vowing to prevent any food or medical supplies from reaching the demonstrators inside. The blockade, which was totally effective, was erected at 5:15 P.M. Sunday and maintained day and night.

At 3:35 P.M., as reports circulated on the campus that several of the students in Low Library were suffering from diarrhea and were running low on food, an attempt was made to breach the blockade.

About 60 supporters of the demonstration, which is aimed principally at halting construction of the Morningside Park gym and ending Columbia's association with the 12-university consortium known as the Institute of Defense Analyses, began marching around Low Library chanting "Food, food, food."

The foes of the demonstration locked arms and formed a solid wall along a hedgerow that skirts the building. Behind the wall of students, several faculty members wearing white arm bands braced themselves for trouble.

On their third circuit of the library building, the chanting supporters of the demonstration turned from the red brick walkway and threw themselves against the line of opposition forces.

Fists swung wildly as about 40 supporters and an equal number of opponents of the demonstration broke into open conflict for the first time.

"Hold that line, hold that line," the opposition forces shouted. "We're trying to get food up there," a student screamed.

"They're welcome to come out any time they want to," a majority coalition student replied.

While the battle raged, supporters of the demonstration hurled sandwiches, oranges,

grapefruits and cigarettes to the demonstrators poised on the second floor ledge outside Dr. Kirk's office. Much of the food fell short of its target, but some was caught by the demonstrators amid cheers from their supporters below.

Another Fight Flares

The violence subsided after few minutes as faculty members moved between the fighting students and separated them. But moments lafter, another fistfight erupted a short distance away. This, too, was halted by the faculty members. who walked up and down the line urging the students on both sides to "cool it."

Although about 30 policemen were within 100 feet of the scene of the violence, they did not move to interfere. One police official, explaining that "we don't go in unless there is a cross-complaint," said: "This is an administrative thing. It's a scholastic thing."

The failure of the police to take any action was a disappointment to at least one demonstrator on the ledge outside Dr. Kirk's office.

"We want the real cops," he cried as fist-fighting broke out. His remark was understood to reflect the feeling of some of the most militant demonstrators that a violent confrontation with the police would prove to the world the "brutality" of American society and the need

for revolutionary change.

No attempt was made by opponents of the demonstration to blockade any building except Low Library. In the other buildings, food moved freely to the demonstrators and they entered and left the buildings at will.

A leader of the Coalition of the Majority said no effort was being made to cut off supplies to the other buildings because "Low Library is a symbol of the administrative center of our university" and because "we don't have enough people."

At 6 P.M., as the potential danger of another confrontation between the opponents and supporters of the demonstration increased, about 40 policemen were moved into position along the west side of Low Library between the two student groups.

During the evening, several outside groups brought food for the beleaguered students occupying Hamilton Hall and the Low Library.

At about 9 P.M. 200 persons, mostly Negroes, gathered at the entrance to Columbia at 116th Street and Amsterdam Avenue —one of the two gates along with the one at 116th Street and Broadway that remained open—and sent a delegation of six persons into the campus carrying food for the students in Hamilton Hall.

The police checked each box

of food before permitting the bearers to enter the tightly sealed campus.

An hour later, about 35 persons, white and Negro, were allowed to pass through the Amsterdam Avenue gate with food. They went to Hamilton Hall first, but when they were informed there that food was plentiful, they moved to the blockaded Low Library.

The police there, however, would not permit the food to be passed in to the students occupying President Kirk's office.

500 Reported Involved

Estimates of the number of demonstrators who occupied the five buildings at Columbia varied. Student leaders claim about 1,000. Most faculty ces put the figure closer to about 500.

In addition to holding Dr. Kirk's offices in Low Library, the students are occupying Fayerweather Hall, Avery Hall, the Mathematics Building, where they have flown a red flag and declared the building a commune, and Hamilton Hall, which is held entirely by Negro students.

Two other buildings are occupied by students seeking to avoid their take-over by the demonstrators. One is held by a group of general studies students, and the other, Uris Hall, is held by a group of business students.

April 30, 1968

Student Survey Shows 38,911 Staged
221 Protests

By ANTHONY RIPLEY
Special to The New York Times

MANHATTAN, Kan., Aug. 26 — The National Student Association reported today that there were at least 221 major demonstrations at 101 colleges and universities from Jan. 1 to June 15 this year.

The demonstrations involved 38,911 participants or 2.6 per cent of the students enrolled in the colleges studied.

The study, done by the N.S.A., which ended its 10-day congress at Kansas State University today, was made by combing through 2,000 newspaper clippings. It included only those first-time occurrences on four-year college campuses led by students and including 35 or more participants. In some cases, smaller demonstrations that brought sharp administrative response were also included.

Such things as panty raids and football rallies were excluded.

Black power was given as the main reason for demonstrations, with 97 incidents. Includ-

ed in this group were protests against segregation, against poor facilities at Negro colleges, demands for more Negro students at white schools, and more Negro-related courses.

The second-largest category was student power, with 50 incidents. This included those strikes in which students demanded more control over university affairs.

Other topics included Vietnam, 26; the Dow Chemical Company, 14; supporting a professor or administrator, 14; against armed campus police, 6; poor people, 2; military recruitment 2; military officer training 2; bad food 2; the Central Intelligence agency 1, and unknown causes 4.

In 59 cases the demonstrations involved taking over a school building. There were 42 sleep-ins or sit-ins, 34 rallies, 24 picketing incidents, 13 fasts, 11 boycotts, 8 incidents of blocking or resisting arrest, 5 with the main aim of destroying life or property, 4 speech disruptions, and 2 teach-ins.

There were 417 arrests, with 228 for failure to leave a

building after closing hours, 117 for unknown charges and the rest of a miscellaneous nature.

There were 60 students suspended, 124 expelled, 50 expelled and reinstated pending hearings, 59 suspended until apologies were made, 34 placed on disciplinary probation and 50 expelled then reinstated pending hearings.

Professors participated in only 18 of the demonstrations.

There was "considerable violence" in 10 demonstrations.

The study did not include demonstrations at Columbia University, which was judged too difficult to categorize.

Sponsors of the demonstrations were identified as Negro student groups in 34 cases, the Students for a Democratic Society in 14 cases, campus committees in 5 cases, student government in 3 cases, draft resistance groups in 2 cases and the Southern Students Organizing Committee in 2 cases.

August 27, 1968

283

POLICE BATTLE DEMONSTRATORS IN STREETS

HUNDRED INJURED

178 Are Arrested as Guardsmen Join in Using Tear Gas

By J. ANTHONY LUKAS
Special to The New York Times

CHICAGO, Thursday, Aug. 29—The police and National Guardsmen battled young protesters in downtown Chicago last night as the week-long demonstrations against the Democratic National Convention reached a violent and tumultuous climax.

About 100 persons, including 25 policemen, were injured and at least 178 were arrested as the security forces chased down the demonstrators. The protesting young people had broken out of Grant Park on the shore of Lake Michigan in an attempt to reach the International Amphitheatre where the Democrats were meeting, four miles away.

The police and Guardsmen used clubs, rifle butts, tear gas and Chemical Mace on virtually anything moving along Michigan Avenue and the narrow streets of the Loop area.

Uneasy Calm

Shortly after midnight, an uneasy calm ruled the city. However, 1,000 National Guardsmen were moved back in front of the Conrad Hilton Hotel to guard it against more than 5,000 demonstrators who had drifted back into Grant Park.

The crowd in front of the hotel was growing, booing vociferously every time new votes for Vice President Humphrey were broadcast from the convention hall.

The events in the streets stirred anger among some delegates at the convention. In a nominating speech Senator Abraham A. Ribicoff of Connecticut told the delegates that if Senator George S. McGovern were President, "we would not have these Gestapo tactics in the streets of Chicago."

When Mayor Richard J. Daley of Chicago and other Illinois delegates rose shouting angrily, Mr. Ribicoff said, "How hard it is to accept the truth."

Crushed Against Windows

Even elderly bystanders were caught in the police onslaught. At one point, the police turned on several dozen persons standing quietly behind police barriers in front of the Conrad Hilton Hotel watching the demonstrators across the street.

For no reason that could be immediately determined, the blue-helmeted policemen charged the barriers, crushing the spectators against the windows of the Haymarket Inn, a restaurant in the hotel. Finally the window gave way, sending screaming middle-aged women and children backward through the broken shards of glass.

The police then ran into the restaurant and beat some of the victims who had fallen through the windows and arrested them.

At the same time, other policemen outside on the broad, tree-lined avenue were clubbing the young demonstrators repeatedly under television lights and in full view of delegates' wives looking out the hotel's windows.

Afterward, newsmen saw 30 shoes, women's purses and torn pieces of clothing lying with shattered glass on the sidewalk and street outside the hotel and for two blocks in each direction.

It was difficult for newsmen to estimate how many demonstrators were in the streets of midtown Chicago last night. Although 10,000 to 15,000 young people gathered in Grant Park for a rally in the afternoon, same of them had apparently drifted home before the violence broke out in the evening.

Estimates of those involved in the action in the night ranged between 2,000 and 5,000.

Although some youths threw bottles, rocks, stones and even loaves of bread at the police, most of them simply marched and countermarched, trying to avoid the flying police squads.

Some of them carried flags

The New York Times   Aug. 29, 1968
CENTER OF CONFLICT: Clash was on Michigan Ave. near Hilton Hotel (cross).

—the black anarchist flag, the red flag, the Vietcong flag and the red and blue flags with a yellow peace symbol.

Stayed Defiant

Although clearly outnumbered and outclassed by the well armed security forces, the thousands of antiwar demonstrators, supporters of Senator Eugene J. McCarthy and Yippies maintained an air of defiance throughout the evening.

They shouted "The streets belong to the people," "This land is our land" and "Hell no, we won't go," as they skirmished along the avenue and among the side streets.

When arrested youths raised their hands in the V for victory sign that has become a symbol of the peace movement, other demonstrators shouted "Sieg heil" or "Pigs" at the policemen making the arrests.

Frank Sullivan, the Police Department's public information director, said the police had reacted only after "50 hard-core leaders" had staged a charge into a police line across Michigan Avenue.

Mr. Sullivan said that among those in the charge were Prof. Sidney Peck, cochairman of the Mobilization Committee to End the War in Vietnam, the group that is spearheading the demonstration. He said Professor Peck had struck James M. Rochford, Deputy Superintendent of Police, with his fist. Mr. Peck was arrested and charged with aggravated assault.

As the night wore on, the police dragnet spread from Michigan Avenue and the area around the Hilton throughout

downtown Chicago.

On the corner of Monroe Street and Michigan Avenue, policemen chased demonstrators up the steps of the Chicago Art Institute, a neoclassical Greek temple, and arrested one of them.

As in previous nights of unrest here, newsmen found themselves special targets of the police action. At Michigan Avenue and Van Buren Street, a young photographer ran into the street, terrified, his hands clasped over his head and shrieking "Press, press."

As the police arrested him, he shouted, "What did I do? What did I do?"

The policeman said, "If you don't know you shouldn't be a photographer."

Barton Silverman, a photographer for the New York Times, was briefly arrested near the Hilton Hotel.

Bob Kieckhefer, a reporter for United Press International, was hit in the head by a policeman during the melee in front of the Hilton. He staggered into the UPI office on Michigan Avenue and was taken for treatment to Wesley Memorial Hospital.

Reporters Hampered

Reporters and photographers were repeatedly hampered by the police last night while trying to cover the violence. They were herded into small areas where they could not see the action. On Jackson Street, police forced a mobile television truck to turn off its lights.

Among those arrested was the Rev. John Boyles, Presbyterian chaplain at Yale and a McCarthy staff worker, who was charged with breach of the peace.

"It's an unfounded charge," Mr. Boyles said. "I was protesting the clubbing of a girl I knew from the McCarthy staff. They were beating her on her head with clubs and I yelled at them 'Don't hit a woman,' At that point I was slugged in the stomach and grabbed by a cop who arrested me."

Last night's violence broke out when hundreds of demonstrators tried to leave Grant Park after a rally and enter the Loop area.

At the Congress Street bridge leading from the park onto Michigan Avenue, National Guardsmen fired and sprayed tear gas at the demonstrators five or six times around 7 P.M. to hold them inside the park.

However, one group moved north inside the park and managed to find a way out over another bridge. There they met a contingent of the Poor People's Campaign march led by their symbol, three mule wagons.

Chase Youths

The march was headed south along Michigan Avenue and the police did not disrupt it, apparently because it had a permit. But they began chasing the youths along Michigan Avenue and into side streets.

The demonstrators were then joined by several thousand others who had originally set out from the park in a "nonviolent" march to the amphitheatre led by David Dellinger, national chairman of the Mobilization Committee to End the War in Vietnam, and Allen Ginsberg, the poet.

The climactic day of protests began with a mass rally sponsored by the mobilization committee in the band shell in Grant Park.

The rally was intended both as a mass expression of anger at the proceedings across town in the convention and as a "staging ground" for the smaller, more militant march on the amphitheatre.

However, before the rally was an hour old, it, too, was interrupted by violence. Fighting broke out when three demonstrators started hauling down an American flag from a pole by the park's band shell where speakers were denouncing the Chicago authorities, the Johnson Administration and the war in Vietnam.

Four blue-helmeted policemen moved in to stop them and were met by a group of angry demonstrators who pushed them back against a cluster of trees by the side of the band shell. Then the demonstrators, shouting "Pig, pig,"

pelted the isolated group of 14 policemen with stones, bricks and sticks.

Grenade Hurled Back

Snapping their Plexiglass shields down over their faces, the police moved toward the crowd. One policeman threw or fired a tear-gas grenade into the throng. But a demonstrator picked up the smoking grenade and heaved it back among the police. The crowd cheered with surprise and delight.

But then, from the Inner Drive west of the park, a phalanx of policemen moved into the crowd, using their billy clubs as prods and then swinging them. The demonstrators, who replied with more stones and sticks were pushed back against rows of flaking green benches and trapped there.

Among those injured was Rennie Davis, one of the coordinators for the Mobilization Committee to End the War in Vietnam, which has been spearheading the demonstrations in Chicago.

As the police and demonstrators skirmished on the huge grassy field, mobilization committee leaders on the stage of the baby-blue band shell urged the crowd to sit down and remain calm.

The worst of the fighting was over in 10 minutes, but the two sides were still jostling each other all over the field when Mr. Ginsberg approached

the microphone.

Speaking in a cracked and choking voice, Mr. Ginsberg said: "I lost my voice chanting in the park the last few nights. The best strategy for you in cases of hysteria, overexcitement or fear is still to chant 'Om' together. It helps to quell flutterings of butterflies in the belly. Join me now as I try to lead you."

So, as the policemen looked out in astonishment through their Plexiglass face shields, the huge throng chanted the Hindu "Om, om," sending deep mystic reverberations off the glass office towers along Michigan Avenue.

Following Mr. Ginsberg to the microphone was Jean Genet, the French author. His bald head glistening in the glare of television lights, Mr. Genet said through a translator:

"It took an awful lot of deaths in Hanoi for a happening such as is taking place here to occur."

Next on the platform was William Burroughs, author of "The Naked Lunch." A gray fedora on his head, Mr. Burroughs said in a dry, almost distant voice:

"I've just returned from London, England, where there is no effective resistance at all. It's really amazing to see people willing to do something about an unworkable system. It's not evil or immoral, just unwork-

able. And they're trying to make it work by force. But they can't do it."

Mailer Apologizes

Mr. Burroughs was followed by Norman Mailer, the author who is here to write an article on the convention. Mr. Mailer, who was arrested during the march on the Pentagon last October, apologized to the crowd for not marching in Chicago.

Thrusting his jaw into the microphone, he said: "I'm a little sick about all this and also a little mad, but I've got a deadline on a long piece and I'm not going to go out and march and get arrested. I just came here to salute all of you."

Then Dick Gregory, the comedian and Negro militant leader, took the platform. Dressed in a tan sport shirt and matching trousers with a khaki rain hat on his head, Mr Gregory said: "You just have to look around you at all the police and soldiers to know you must be doing something right."

Many of the demonstrators in Grant Park had drifted down in small groups from Lincoln Park, where 300 policemen had moved in at 12:15 A.M. yesterday and laid down a barrage of tear gas to clear the area. About 2,000 young protesters had attempted to stay in the park despite an 11 P.M. curfew.

August 29, 1968

AGNEW DEVELOPS HIS FATHER IMAGE

Puts a Stern Face Forward to Youths at Assemblies

By BEN A. FRANKLIN
Special to The New York Times

WASHINGTON, Oct. 12 — Gov. Spiro T. Agnew of Maryland, the Republican nominee for Vice President, is developing a stern father image in campaign appearances before youthful audiences and surprisingly, even to the Governor himself, the youths — at least middle-class youths — seem to love it.

Friends of Mr. Agnew, a gray-haired, 49-year-old father of four, whose only son is with the Navy in Vietnam, say the candidate is reflecting on the stump the same no-nonsense attitude toward child-rearing and the younger generation that has characterized him in his role as a strong paternal leader in his own home. One close observer of the Agnews has called him "authoritative, but not authoritarian" as a father and husband.

In his speeches in the last 10 days—a period in which he has

found new confidence in his prowess as a spontaneous orator who can establish rapport with an audience, sincere if not spell-binding—both his emphasis and his rhetorical successes have been on the theme of youth and before gatherings of youth.

It apparently was only an accident of scheduling that the Governor's decision to return to off-the-cuff speaking—occasionally glancing at notes— coincided with a series of encounters with youngsters. But the experience restored to him a semicharismatic knack he lost earlier in the campaign when his Republican speechwriters made him read prepared texts to avoid remarks that Mr. Agnew complained were "blown up in the press to make me look like a political stumblebum." And he was pleased with results. The rhetorical success seemed to reinforce the fatherly wisdom of his views.

The candidate has addressed his young hecklers for the most part in words more of sorrow than of anger. Except for one slip into open annoyance—he called after a group of students staging a walkout at his speech in Portland, Ore., "there goes the delegation from Hanoi"— Mr. Agnew has appeared to express more dismay for what he regarded as the pitiful appearance of his taunters than for

his own discomfort.

To the nonhecklers who remain, he has then spoken to in stern language about the superiority of middle class, educated adult judgments of the boundaries of "permissible dissent."

Mr. Agnew's boundaries of speech often seem restrictive, but his attack on "permissiveness" — coupled with the declaration that "the best crop of young people in our history" has been "grievously" misjudged by "a handful of rabble-rousing dissenters"—has been getting him some of his warmest applause of his campaign.

The Governor's instinctive belief in the idea that vocal dissent and the calculated disruption of youthful protest are social sicknesses — unpleasant fads made popular by the spread of "permissiveness"— was disclosed a week ago when an excited youth suddenly screamed "Warmonger!" at him in the middle of a speech in Spokane, Wash. The interruption came as the Governor was recalling the magnanimity of the United States for having failed to exploit its monopoly in nuclear weapons immediately after World War II by some easy military conquest.

As the police grappled with the young heckler and took him away, Mr. Agnew shook his head and remarked, "It is really tragic that somewhere somebody in that young man's life has failed him."

Later, in separate speeches to students at Belmont College in Nashville, and at Roanoke College in Salem, Va., last Tuesday, Mr. Agnew specified the "failure."

"I have always believed," he said, "that punishment is two things—first of all, the deprivation of personal liberty that comes with incarceration and, secondly, the social stigma that comes of conviction of a wrong doing."

Those who say that "no social stigma should be attached to wrong-doing where the person is morally convinced that what he is doing is within the boundaries of his own conscience," Mr. Agnew said, "remove the most effective deterrent to breaking the law, because it's the difference between being a martyr and being a disgraced law breaker that's involved."

Addressing the students at Roanoke College, where campus officials said the only student demonstration in the institution's 120 years had been a "20 minute sit-in for milk at all three meals each day," Mr. Agnew drew sustained applause by saying "I believe you young people know as well as I do that there are some people that just don't have the mentality, capacity or ability to make a judgment that's in the mainstream of opinion today. And

this country, fortunately for us, is still a democracy and is still governed by the majority."

Governor Agnew thus seemed to say that in the nation the majority should make the judgments and establish the "mainstream" limits of dissent. His fatherly formula for doing this is a reinforcement of the social pressure or "stigma" assigned to unacceptable behavior.

October 13, 1968

Antiwar Leaders Tell Hearing Youth Protests Will Get Worse

United Press International

Thomas E. Hayden, an organizer of the Chicago protests, talks to newsmen after testifying before the committee.

WASHINGTON, Dec. 3 (UPI) —The organizers of antiwar street protests during the Democratic National Convention told a Congressional committee today that youthful protests would get worse as today's "7 and 8-year-olds" grew up into rebels.

"There will continue to be

rebellions as long as we elect people like Mayor Daley and Richard Nixon," Rennard Davis told the House Committee on Un-American Activities.

Thomas E. Hayden, Mr. Davis's partner in planning the Chicago demonstrations, told the committee that today's American children were being

raised on a diet of hypocrisy that would turn them into dedicated firebrands.

"If you think you saw militant people at these hearings, you've seen nothing until you see the 7 and 8-year-olds in the next few years," Mr. Hayden said.

Leaders of Protests

Mr. Hayden, 28, of Oakland, Calif., a founder of Students for a Democratic Society, and Mr. Davis, also 28, of New York, a leader of the National Mobilization Committee to End the War in Vietnam, were called before the committee as the acknowledged leaders of the convention street demonstrations.

The committee is seeking evidence that Communists helped to lead the protests.

For the second straight day there were no pickets or protests at the hearing, and the witnesses answered questions readily. The atmosphere contrasted sharply with hearings in October on the same subject when throngs of hippies and yippies tried to disrupt the committee sessions.

Mr. Hayden told the committee that it, President Johnson and President-elect Nixon had lost the respect of American youth and "are finished."

"That's why I've been quiet," he said. "That's why no one comes to picket H.U.A.C. anymore. The job has been done already."

"No witness in the history of your silly committee has given you a fuller statement of his philosophy and views."

Mr. Davis, like Mr. Hayden, said that the Chicago protesters had tried to avoid violence, had no intention of disrupting the convention and only wanted to

demonstrate massive opposition to the Vietnam war and the policies of the Democratic party.

"The Democratic party is controlled by reactionary trade union fat men, big city machine men, tied to the military, to bankers and to Southern racists like yourself," Mr. Davis told Representative Albert Watson of South Carolina. Mr. Watson is a Republican.

Statement Acknowledged

Mr. Hayden acknowledged a statement, read to him by the committee, that he had made to demonstrators in Chicago's Grant Park during the convention.

"We must move out of the park and into the streets," the statement said. "We have to turn this overheated military machine against itself. If blood flows, we must make sure it flows all over the city."

Mr. Hayden said that demonstrators, including women and children, were being tear gassed at the time. He said that he wanted beatings by policemen to be seen throughout the city, not confined to the park.

"I hoped if I was going to pass out from gas, the gas would waft its way up to the 15th floor of the Conrad Hilton so that Hubert Humphrey would get the sweet smell of democracy in Chicago," he said.

Mr. Hayden answered one question, from Frank Conley, the committee counsel, with a muttered obscenity. The chairman, Representative Richard H. Ichord, Democrat of Missouri, admonished him, and Mr. Watson told him, "We have ladies in this room, and I shall not tolerate it."

December 4, 1968

Disorders Increase in High Schools

By JAMES P. STERBA

The nation's high schools are experiencing growing student protest and rebellion.

While the vast majority of high school students remain indifferent, and their schools

peaceful, more and more students are taking issue with school rules and policies, confronting nervous administrators with demands and participating in sometimes violent disruptions.

Scores of school racial dis-

orders were sparked by the slaying of the Rev. Dr. Martin Luther King Jr. last April. According to the Riot Data Clearinghouse or the Lemberg Center for the Study of Violence at Brandeis University, 91 such incidents were reported in

April, compared with 42 incidents for all of 1967.

This fall, racial disorders and general student protests continued to rise, according to School Management, a journal for school administrators.

Dispute Over Clothing

In Boston last September, disorders broke out in at least nine high schools after a dispute over whether black stu-

286

dents could wear African-style clothing in school.

High school underground newspapers, outlawed in most schools, have proliferated throughout the country. So-called student strikes, over such issues as cafeteria food, dress codes and newspaper censorship have occurred in some suburban and small-town schools, as well as in schools in urban areas.

A few educators, often unheeded, have sounded the warning for several years. Now the subject consumes discussions at state and national education conferences and pages in education journals.

For while high school student rebellion is generally welcomed with as much enthusiasm as greets a boy with shoulder-length hair and a pocketful of marijuana, it is hard to find anyone who doubts that it is present and growing.

'Increased Rebellion' Seen

"The evidence is mounting that we must be prepared for increased rebellion by high school students," according to Lawrence M. Brammer, chairman of educational psychology in the College of Education at the University of Washington.

Writing in the September issue of The Bulletin, a journal of the National Association of Secondary School Principals, he said: "Massive nonviolent protests and more active demonstrations sparked by increasingly sophisticated, yet disillusioned and frustrated teen-agers take place now.

"Targets are school regulations and routines, and larger issues such as civil rights and war." While irrational "hell-raising" continues, he added, there "are indications that this traditional explosive behavior will be redirected into educational, political and social controversies."

Where does the high school principal stand in this?

"He's up against the wall and that's where we're going to keep him," a 16-year-old New York City student joyously remarked during a recent demonstration against a school plan to make up class time lost in the teachers' strikes.

"It's a little of his own medicine," he added.

While student cure-alls range from reasonable discussion to burning down the building, principals and other school officials continue to debate the nature of the new trend.

A surprising number sniff a conspiracy. Paul A. Miller, a Cincinnati superintendent, is quoted in the November issue of School Management:

"Few of these demonstrations are spontaneous. They are planned by outside agitators. These demonstrations may be part of a national conspiracy and may be nationally directed."

Critics of this view say active students, black and white, tend to some degree to imitate their heroes, like Eldridge Cleaver, a Black Panther, or Tom Hayden, a founder of the Students for a Democratic Society.

Principal Backs Rebels

"I say it's about time," said Allan A. Glatthorn, principal of the Abington High School near Philadelphia.

Dr. Glatthorn pounced on his peers with such criticism at a conference in New York last week that some looked as if they had just bitten into a big lemon.

The typical high school deserves the student rebellion it is or will be confronted with, he said, adding:

"It is too big, overcrowded and impersonal...often with a principal who thinks he has all the answers to everybody's problems—students as well as teachers."

To which one New York city principal responded: "He can say all those things sitting comfortably in his little suburban ivory ower of a school. I'd like to see him come into town for some real life."

December 16, 1968

Chicago Tribune Omits Protest News as Protest

CHICAGO, Feb. 19 (UPI)— The Chicago Tribune in a front-page editorial tonight explained that it was refraining from publishing stories about student protests in tomorrow's editions as its own protest against "the attention, concern and indulgence" given such demonstrations.

"It is the fashion now to protest," the paper said. "Everybody seems to be doing it. For this day we choose to follow the fashion. We protest the attention, concern and indulgence that have been accorded to student protesters on the university campuses all over the world. We think that they have generated news out of all proportion to their numbers and importance.

"As a demonstration of our protest we are refraining from printing any news about protesting students today. Tomorrow we shall go back to reporting this story. It is our responsibility to print the news whether we find it pleasing or repugnant."

February 20, 1969

'Children must learn to fear'

By BRUNO BETTELHEIM

I CONSIDER it not at all startling that we encounter violence today on our campuses and on our streets. We are engaged in a process of removing both inner and outer controls, and as long as this process is not reversed, ours will become a time of more violence still.

Violence is the most primitive path to an objective. The temper tantrum, so typical of the young child, shows how the destructive outburst comes long before the ability to master inner drives and the external world.

Dr. Bruno Bettelheim, whose latest book is "The Children of the Dream" (Macmillan), is Rowley Professor of Education and Director of the Sonia Shankman Orthogenic School at the University of Chicago.

Almost any birthday party shows how normal this is. The birthday child will tear off the wrappings to get at his presents. And if the box he is ripping away at should have been part of the game, so much the worse for the game. Desire begets violence and violence may destroy the object desired.

Still, today's riots do not originate with small children, but with adolescents for the most part. It is a problem that calls for the most sensitive planning in earliest childhood, long before police action becomes necessary. To understand why pressures erupt in adolescence on a growing scale nowadays, and why controls seem to grow weaker, we must recognize that adolescent revolt is not a stage of development that follows automatically from our natural

makeup. What makes for adolescent revolt is the fact that our society keeps the next generation dependent too long.

Years ago, when schooling ended for the vast majority at 14 or 15, and thereafter one became self-supporting, got married and had children, there was no need for adolescent revolt. Because while puberty is a biological word, adolescence as we know it with its identity crises is not. All children grow up and become pubertal, but by no means do all become adolescents. To be adolescent means that one has reached and even passed the age of puberty, is at the very height of one's physical development—healthier, stronger, even handsomer than one has been, or will be, for the rest of one's life—but must nevertheless postpone full adulthood till long

ROAD TO VIOLENCE—When every wish has been granted in infancy and childhood, the adolescent tends to react to frustration with violence, which, Dr. Bettelheim says, is "the most primitive path to an objective."

beyond what any other period in history has considered reasonable. What preparation do we give youngsters for such a prolonged waiting, or for controlling their anger or violent impatience with the waiting?

Let me start with the obvious which is often neglected when we think about violence. Even Seneca knew in the first century that the best cure for anger begins with delay. Thus, to avoid violence, one must have learned first how to delay.

OUR modern infatuation with speed is a very real handicap. Our new yardstick of time, even in human affairs, tends to be the machine, not the living cell. Our image of time no longer rests on the slow growth of trees, nor on the nine months it still takes before a baby is ready to be born. In today's affluent society, satisfactions are so immediate that children are less likely to have learned about delay as a natural dimension.

Before bottle feeding, the infant had to learn to accept delay once he had drained his mother of milk. Now, almost from birth, things are instantly *here*. Baby's bottle is ready in the refrigerator; food comes precooked. Little wonder that youth expects instant solutions—even to problems that have plagued man for generations.

Photographs can be developed in an instant, the human fetus cannot. The same goes for inner controls. There are timetables in human development that can only

be hurried (or delayed) at a painful and deadening cost. We can now do many things at our own time, but we have not learned yet what is the right time to do them.

Until recently this slow inner growth was supported by early parental teachings, later by the schools, and then by society at large. Call it the teaching of a middle-class morality, if you will; in psychoanalysis we call it the "reality principle," which holds that if we want to direct our own fate, we must learn to let go of present pleasures at times for greater ones in the future. And frankly, unless we have learned how to wait, then the business of learning (most of which is hard work) cannot go on because there is always some learning that gives no immediate pleasure. If this is true for school learning, it is doubly so for the learning of self-control.

SO in the final analysis, whether or not violence occurs will depend on whether the individual has learned to brook delay, and whether better solutions are available and known. Violence is the behavior of the person who cannot wait and cannot visualize alternative solutions to his problem. For the mature adult, this search for alternatives is a rational process. But I am here less concerned with violence in adults than in how (and if) children learn delay and then control. My contention is that for self-control to develop, children must have learned to fear

something before they enter society, which for children means school. If it is not the once crippling fear of damnation, then in our more enlightened days it is at least the fear of losing parental love (or later, by proxy, the teacher's) and eventually the fear of losing self-respect.

To fear the loss of self-respect, however, one must first have acquired it. Self-respect (and what it demands of us) is merely what has taken the place of an earlier respect for the parent who protects us from physical and emotional pain. If there has been no such protection, there is no fear of losing this reliable source of satisfaction, and hence no respect for him and his commands. And without having established this early respect, no self-respect can replace it, nor any fear of the loss of self-respect.

I dwell on fear because of a common misunderstanding of Freud: the vague feeling among parents and educators that children should never be made to feel frightened at breaking a moral command. Not only are our children ill-prepared to brook delay, they have also been confronted with a morality from which we have done our best to remove the basic motivation. We want to remove fear from the life of the child and at the same time we want him to restrain his tendencies toward violence as if we had not removed fear. Children's earliest controls of violence rest on fear and are largely irrational; they come from the moral commands of adults. On the basis of fear, not of rational judgment, they tell the child what he "must do" and "must not do." Only later does the mature ego apply reason to these commands and slowly subject them to a critical judgment. Only as maturity grows can we slowly free ourselves of fear.

WHAT was wrong with old-fashioned, authoritarian education was not that it was based on fear. That is what was right with it. What was wrong was that it disregarded the need to modify the fear in a continuous process so that irrational anxiety would steadily give way to more rational motivation. Today, many parents are unwilling to face their children's displeasure when they impose controls. And they are also unwilling to invite the child to embark on the troublesome search for alternatives whenever frustration occurs. To such parents, modern psychology seems a way out. Certainly psychoanalysis suggests that we should not suppress our inner rages but should face them. But we were expected to face them only in thought, only when we had reached the age of reason, and only in the safely structured treatment situation. This has been understood by large numbers of the educated middle classes to mean that rage should always be expressed—and not just in thought. Thus, many children have no fear of lashing out and do not learn how to acquire control of their rages in childhood. Later, when adolescent pressures flood them with rage, they are helpless to control the rage or to restrict it to thought only. What Freud taught about the crippling effects of an over-repression of emotions due to excessive fear (that was where the shoe pinched in his day) has been wrongly extended to mean it is all right to discharge emotions in action without control of the discharge by thought.

EDUCATION also shows a parallel influence of psychoanalysis. We see it most typically in the tendency to applaud almost any disorganized thing the child does, because it reveals something. Or by viewing what he does as "creative," even when it is just an instinctual expression—such as smearing with paint or an outpouring in words of some formless inner pressures.

Now there is nothing wrong with the child's being able to mess and smear with paint or to voice aloud his chaotic feelings. At the right time and in the right place, it may be very good for him to enjoy the chance to let go, to be uncontrolled. It becomes damaging if the educator, who should know better, fools himself and the child into believing that if something has meaning as id expression, it is therefore ego correct (contains a meaningful message to others), which is not true.

It is very much the task of education to see that the sphere of the ego should grow. But to do that, the teacher must know clearly what is ego correct and what is not. We stunt the child's growth if we call id expressions creative, instead of being satisfied to recognize their possible value (that they may offer temporary relief to the child and deeper insight to the teacher into what is going on in the child). A dream may reveal what goes on in the unconscious. But dreaming is hardly an act of creation, nor will it advance intellectual growth.

EVEN when later scribbling or drawing becomes more expressive, it remains solipistic. It becomes meaningful to the child and possibly valuable to others only if through a slow process of education; through observing and appreciating the efforts of others; through criticism, self-criticism, and the use of appropriate standards his mere self-expression is transformed into a meaningful message.

Life would still be simple, though different, if middle class parents consistently encouraged their children to act on their instinctual tendencies. But where the old way of expression was at least all of a piece, the modern way is one of contradictions. Some instinctual tendencies are still repressed as before, while others are directed toward discharge without intervening thought and rational control. This makes no sense at all and is the source of the youngsters' insistence that our society does not make any sense. Even worse, the decisions on what to repress and what to discharge are based not on the interests of the child, but on the convenience of adults. And this is where the fatal error lies and what most enrages youth.

Let me use a minor example of what grates on many middle-class children every day.

WE'RE ONLY THINKING OF HER—
Parents who give in to a child's every whim are indulging themselves, not the child.

They are told they have a room of their own. But then they have to keep what has been called their possession just the way their parents see fit. And the same goes for toys: "It's your toy, but you must share it with others." Now it is possible to live without ownership, but it is more pleasant to have it. What is devastating is to be given to and then deprived in endless repetition. Some parents tell their children: "Since this is your room, you must take care of it," an utter perversion of the meaning of ownership leading to total rage and distrust. The same open lie and inner contradiction taints the unconscious of instinctual experience.

On the surface, it looks as if parents were indulging their children when they pick them up each time they cried. Actually they indulged the children only where it suited themselves, as if to say, "I indulge you now, but for that I'll expect you to be the brightest kid in school. Didn't I let you hang onto your bottle? Now go and be a whiz at school."

The same holds for toilet training. Yesterday's parents made up their minds when it was time for their child to be toilet trained and saw that it happened in a couple of weeks. There was nothing tentative about it, no if's or but's. Things were not easy for the child, but in two weeks the whole thing was over.

Modern parents let the child decide if he wants to toilet train or not. They say, "Do what you want, but by golly, it's time you did it." They say, "Oh, it's all right to make in your pants," but then they are disgusted. So the child must now live with the parents' disgust for six months or a year. And the message he gets is the following: "My parents are nice parents, but I'm a disgusting person." And this we call "permissive" training.

EVEN in families where I found a genuine desire to provide instinctual pleasure for children, it was expected that the children would therefore achieve intellectually even faster and at a much higher level. That is, instinctual pleasure was not given so the child could enjoy his own body and with it the world, but as a bribe held out to make the child a better feeder of parental narcissism.

I have known mothers of extreme campus activists who,

when the children were infants, fed them goodies against inner resistance because that is what good mothers were supposed to do. And soon even the child's pleasure evaporated as he realized he was being indulged to make the mother feel good about herself. I think of them as being "permissive if it kills me." Good reason then, for such youngsters to make a farce of permissiveness by asking for everything, with no sense of obligation to give in return.

When I see some of these wayout students, unwashed and unkempt — though, of course, nothing I say here is true of all of them—I cannot help thinking: "There goes another youngster who, as an infant, was practically scrubbed out of existence by his parents in the name of loving care."

Their dress or hairdo demonstrates how they rebel against parents who told them they could dress as they liked, provided their appearance pleased the parents' narciss-

ism and not the child's convenience. Yet in a strange contradiction—and I talk of the inner contradictions that tear the extremist apart and mark all his outer behavior, his hatred of self and society, of all adults over 30—he only seems to go contrary to his parents wishes or teachings. On the surface he seems to do the opposite; and he firmly believes that in his manner of dress he defies his parents, but, deep down, he merely copies their behavior. He mistreats and neglects the legitimate needs of his body just as much as his parents did, only this time not by total scrubbing, but by total neglect. It is the having been pushed out of infancy and childhood toward higher maturity in one area, while indulged or overstimulated in others, that tears them to pieces later on.

How natural it is that, as they strive for independence from their parents, some youngsters drop out while others resent the faculty, those

parental figures once removed. And that the faculty is resented for some of the reasons I mention, may be inferred from the angry charges made by students that professors care more for their research than for their teaching.

MY thesis, then, is that more than anything else it is the emotional contradictions, if not the outright emotional lies, in which both extremists and dropouts are raised by their educated, upper middle-class parents, that convinces them that ours is a society that deserves to be destroyed.

We know that each society can raise the new generation in its own way. If a society does not taboo sex, children will grow up in relative sex freedom. But so far, history has shown that such a society cannot create culture or civilization; it remains primitive. Without sex repression, there is no prolonged span of intellectual learning. And the same goes for fear. Without fear,

there is no inner control over instinctual tendencies.

Because Freud has shown the evil effects of too much fear, too much Victorian repression, because he concentrates on what most plagued the middle classes then, our own middle classes (to paraphrase Goethe) learned carefully how their master coughed and spat in order to totally disregard what he taught. Freud certainly knew that without strong inner controls, preferably conscious ones, man would sink back into barbarism. If he stressed it less, it was because the dominant pathology in his day came of too much, not too little, control. But with both teachings available, many middle-class families chose to follow Freud where it suited their convenience, and were as demanding of conformity as the worst Victorian parent where it did not. In either case, they evaded their adult responsibility.

April 13, 1969

You Have to Grow Up In Scarsdale to Know How Bad Things Really Are

By KENNETH KENISTON

THE recent events at Harvard are the culmination of a long year of unprecedented student unrest in the advanced nations of the world. We have learned to expect students in underdeveloped countries to lead unruly demonstrations against the status quo, but what is new, unexpected and upsetting to many is that an apparently similar mood is sweeping across America, France, Germany, Italy and even Eastern European nations like Czechoslovakia and Poland. Furthermore, the revolts occur, not at the most backward universities, but at the most distinguished, liberal and enlightened—Berkeley, the Sorbonne, Tokyo, Columbia, the Free University of Berlin, Rome and now Harvard.

This development has taken almost everyone by surprise. The American public is clearly puzzled, frightened and often outraged by the behavior of its most privileged youth. The

scholarly world, including many who have devoted their lives to the study of student protest, has been caught off guard as well. For many years, American analysts of student movements have been busy demonstrating that "it can't happen here." Student political activity abroad has been seen as a reaction to modernization, industrialization and the demise of traditional or tribal societies. In an already modern, industrialized, detribalized and "stable" nation like America, it was argued, student protests are naturally absent.

Another explanation has tied student protests abroad to bad living conditions in some universities and to the unemployability of their graduates. Student revolts, it was argued, spring partly from the misery of student life in countries like India and Indonesia. Students who must live in penury and squalor naturally turn against their universities and societies. And if, as in many developing nations, hundreds of thousands of university graduates can find no work commensurate with their skills, the chances for student militancy are further increased.

KENNETH KENISTON, associate professor of psychology at the Yale Medical School, is the author of "Young Radicals." This essay grew out of an article in The New Journal, an undergraduate publication.

290

These arguments helped explain the "silent generation" of the nineteen-fifties and the absence of protest, during that period, in American universities, where students are often "indulged" with good living conditions, close student-faculty contact and considerable freedom of speech. And they helped explain why "super-employable" American college graduates, especially the much-sought-after ones from colleges like Columbia and Harvard, seemed so contented with their lot.

But such arguments do not help us understand today's noisy, angry and militant students in the advanced countries. Nor do they explain why students who enjoy the greatest advantages —those at the leading universities—are often found in the revolts. As a result, several new interpretations of student protest are currently being put forward, interpretations that ultimately form part of what Richard Poirier has termed "the war against the young."

Many reactions to student unrest, of course, spring primarily from fear, anger, confusion or envy, rather than from theoretical analysis. Governor Wallace's attacks on student "anarchists" and other "pin-headed intellectuals," for example, were hardly coherent explanations of protest. Many of the bills aimed at punishing student protesters being proposed in Congress and state legislatures reflect similar feelings of anger and outrage. Similarly, the presumption that student unrest *must* be part of an international conspiracy is based on emotion rather than fact. Even George F. Kennan's recent discussion of the American student left is essentially a moral condemnation of "revolting students," rather than an effort to explain their behavior.

If we turn to more thoughtful analyses of the current student mood we find two general theories gaining widespread acceptance. The first, articulately expressed by Lewis S. Feuer in his recent book on student movements, "The Conflict of Generations," might be termed the "Oedipal Rebellion" interpretation. The second, cogently stated by Zbigniew Brzezinski and Daniel Bell, can be called the theory of "Historical Irrelevance."

THE explanation of Oedipal Rebellion sees the underlying force in all student revolts as blind, unconscious Oedipal hatred of fathers and the older generation. Feuer, for example, finds in all student movements an inevitable tendency toward violence and a combination of "regicide, parricide and suicide." A decline in respect for the authority of the older generation is needed to trigger a student movement, but the force behind it comes from "obscure" and "unconscious" forces in the child's early life, including both intense death wishes against his father and the enormous guilt and self-hatred that such wishes inspire in the child.

The idealism of student movements is thus, in many respects, only a "front" for the latent unconscious destructiveness and self-destructiveness of underlying motivations. Even the expressed desire of these movements to help the poor and exploited is explained psychoanalytically by Feuer: Empathy for the disadvantaged is traced to "traumatic" encounters with parental bigotry in the students' childhoods, when their parents forbade them to play with children of other races or lower social classes. The identification of today's new left with blacks is thus interpreted as an unconscious effort to "abreact and undo this original trauma."

There are two basic problems with the Oedipal Rebellion theory, however. First, although it uses psychoanalytic terms, it is bad psychoanalysis. The real psychoanalytic account insists that the Oedipus complex is universal in all normally developing children. To point to this complex in explaining student rebellion is, therefore, like pointing to the fact that all children learn to walk. Since both characteristics are said to be universal, neither helps us understand why, at some historical moments, students are restive and rebellious, while at others they are not. Second, the theory does not help us explain why some students (especially those from middle-class, affluent and idealistic families) are most inclined to rebel, while others (especially those from working-class and deprived families) are less so.

In order really to explain anything, the Oedipal Rebellion hypothesis would have to be modified to point to an unusually *severe* Oedipus complex, involving especially *intense* and unresolved unconscious feelings of father-hatred in student rebels. But much is now known about the lives and backgrounds of these rebels—at least those in the United States —and this evidence does not support even the modified theory. On the contrary, it indicates that most student protesters are relatively *close* to their parents, that the values they profess are usually the ones they learned at the family dinner table, and that their parents tend to be highly educated, liberal or left-wing and politically active.

Furthermore, psychological studies of student radicals indicate that they are no more neurotic, suicidal, enraged or disturbed than are non-radicals. Indeed, most studies find them to be rather more integrated, self-accepting and "advanced," in a psychological sense, than their politically inactive contemporaries. In general, research on American student rebels supports a "Generational Solidarity" (or chip-off-the-old-block) theory, rather than one of Oedipal Rebellion.

THE second theory of student revolts now being advanced asserts that they are a reaction against "historical irrelevance." Rebellion springs from the unconscious awareness of some students that society has left them and their values behind. According to this view, the ultimate causes of student dissent are sociological rather than psychological. They lie in fundamental changes in the nature of the advanced societies—especially, in the change from industrial to post-industrial society. The student revolution is seen not as a true revolution, but as a counterrevolution—what Daniel Bell has called "the guttering last gasp of a romanticism soured by rancor and impotence."

This theory assumes that we are moving rapidly into a new age in which technology will dominate, an age whose real rulers will be men like computer experts, systems analysts and technobureaucrats. Students who are attached to outmoded and obsolescent values like humanism and romanticism unconsciously feel they have no place in this post-industrial world. When they rebel they are like the Luddites of the past—workers who smashed machines to protest the inevitable industrial revolution. Today's student revolt reflects what Brzezinski terms "an unconscious realization that they [the rebels] are themselves becoming historically obsolete"; it is nothing but the "death rattle of the historical irrelevants."

This theory is also inadequate. It assumes that the shape of the future is already technologically determined, and that protesting students unconsciously "know" that it will offer them no real reward, honor or power. But the idea that the future can be accurately predicted is open to fundamental objection. Every past attempt at prophecy has turned out to be grievously incorrect. Extrapolations from the past, while sometimes useful in the short run, are usually fundamentally wrong in the long run, especially when they attempt to predict the quality of human life, the nature of political and social organization, international relations or the shape of future culture.

The future is, of course, made by men. Technology is not an inevitable master of man and history, but merely provides the possibility of applying scientific knowledge to specific problems. Men may identify with it or refuse to, use it or be used by it for good or evil, apply it humanely or destructively. Thus, there is no real evidence that student protest will emerge as the "death rattle of the historical irrelevants." It could equally well be the "first spark of a new historical era." No one today can be sure of the outcome, and people who feel certain that the future will bring the obsolescence and death of those whom they dislike are often merely expressing their fond hope.

THE fact that today's students invoke "old" humanistic and romantic ideas in no way proves that student protests are a "last gasp" of a dying order. Quite the contrary: All revolutions draw upon older values and visions. Many of the ideals of the French Revolution, for example, originated in Periclean Athens. Revolu-

tions do not occur because new ideas suddenly develop, but because a new generation begins to take old ideas seriously—not merely as interesting theoretical views, but as the basis for political action and social change. Until recently, the humanistic vision of human fulfillment and the romantic vision of an expressive, imaginative and passionate life were taken seriously only by small aristocratic or Bohemian groups. The fact that they are today taken as real goals by millions of students in many nations does not mean that these students are "counterrevolutionaries," but merely that their ideas follow the pattern of every major revolution.

Indeed, today's student rebels are rarely opposed to technology per se. On the contrary, they take the high technology of their societies completely for granted, and concern themselves with it very little. What they are opposed to is, in essence, the worship of Technology, the tendency to treat people as "inputs" or "outputs" of a technological system, the subordination of human needs to technological programs. The essential conflict between the minority of students who make up the student revolt and the existing order is a conflict over the future direction of technological society, not a counterrevolutionary protest against technology.

In short, both the Oedipal Rebellion and the Historical Irrelevance theories are what students would call "put-downs." If we accept either, we are encouraged not to listen to protests, or to explain them away or reject them as either the "acting out" of destructive Oedipal feelings or the blind reaction of an obsolescent group to the awareness of its obsolescence. But if, as I have argued, neither of these theories is adequate to explain the current "wave" of student protest here and abroad, how can we understand it?

*   *   *

ONE factor often cited to explain student unrest is the large number of people in the world under 30—today the critical dividing line between generations. But this explanation alone, like the theories just discussed, is not adequate, for in all historical eras the vast portion of the population has always been under 30. Indeed, in primitive societies most people die before they reach that age. If chronological youth alone was enough to insure rebellion, the advanced societies — where a greater proportion of the population reaches old age than ever before in history—should be the least revolutionary, and primitive societies the most. This is not the case.

More relevant factors are the relationship of those under 30 to the

established institutions of society (that is, whether they are engaged in them or not); and the opportunities that society provides for their continuing intellectual, ethical and emotional development. In both cases the present situation in the advanced nations is without precedent.

Philippe Aries, in his remarkable book, "Centuries of Childhood," points out that, until the end of the Middle Ages, no separate stage of childhood was recognized in Western societies. Infancy ended at approximately 6 or 7, whereupon most children were integrated into adult life, treated as small men and women and expected to work as junior partners of the adult world. Only later was childhood recognized as a separate stage of life, and our own century is the first to "guarantee" it by requiring universal primary education.

The recognition of adolescence as a stage of life is of even more recent origin, the product of the 19th and 20th centuries. Only as industrial societies became prosperous enough to defer adult work until after puberty could they create institutions—like widespread secondary-school education—that would extend adolescence to virtually all young people. Recognition of adolescence also arose from the vocational and psychological requirements of these societies, which needed much higher levels of training and psychological development than could be guaranteed through primary education alone. There is, in general, an intimate relationship between the way a society defines the stages of life and its economic, political and social characteristics.

Today, in more developed nations, we are beginning to witness the recognition of still another stage of life. Like childhood and adolescence, it was initially granted only to a small minority, but is now being rapidly extended to an ever-larger group. I will call this the stage of "youth," and by that I mean both a further phase of disengagement from society and the period of psychological development that intervenes between adolescence and adulthood. This stage, which continues into the 20's and sometimes into the 30's, provides opportunities for intellectual, emotional and moral development that were never afforded to any other large group in history. In the student revolts we are seeing one result of this advance.

I call the extension of youth an advance advisedly. Attendance at a college or university is a major part of this extension, and there is growing evidence that this is, other things being equal, a good thing for the student. Put in an oversimplified phrase, it tends to free him—to free him from swallowing unexamined the assumptions of the past, to free him from the superstitions of his childhood, to free him to express his feelings more openly and to free him from irrational bondage to authority.

I do not mean to suggest, of course, that all college graduates are free and liberated spirits, unencumbered by irrationality, superstition, authoritarianism or blind adherence to tradition. But these findings do indicate that our colleges, far from cranking out only machinelike robots who will provide skilled manpower for the economy, are also producing an increasing number of highly critical citizens—young men and women who have the opportunity, the leisure, the affluence and the educational resources to continue their development beyond the point where most people in the past were required to stop it.

So, one part of what we are seeing on campuses throughout the world is not a reflection of how bad higher education is, but rather of its extraordinary accomplishments. Even the moral righteousness of the student rebels, a quality both endearing and infuriating to their elders, must be judged at least partially a consequence of the privilege of an extended youth; for a prolonged development, we know, encourages the individual to elaborate a more personal, less purely conventional sense of ethics.

What the advanced nations have done is to create their own critics on a mass basis—that is, to create an ever-larger group of young people who take the highest values of their societies as their own, who internalize these values and identify them with their own best selves, and who are willing to struggle to implement them. At the same time, the extension of youth has lessened the personal risks of dissent: These young people have been freed from the requirements of work, gainful employment and even marriage, which permits them to criticize their society from a protected position of disengagement.

But the mere prolongation of development need not automatically lead to unrest. To be sure, we have granted to millions the opportunity to examine their societies, to compare them with their values and to come to a reasoned judgment of the existing order. But why should their judgment today be so unenthusiastic?

*   *   *

WHAT protesting students throughout the world share is a mood more than an ideology or a program, a mood that says the existing system—the power structure — is hypocritical, unworthy of respect, outmoded and in urgent need

Signs of the times

of reform. In addition, students everywhere speak of repression, manipulation and authoritarianism. (This is paradoxical, considering the apparently great freedoms given them in many nations. In America, for example, those who complain most loudly about being suffocated by the subtle tyranny of the Establishment usually attend the institutions where student freedom is greatest.) Around this general mood, specific complaints arrange themselves as symptoms of what students often call the "exhaustion of the existing society."

To understand this phenomenon we must recognize that, since the Second World War, some societies have indeed begun to move past the industrial era into a new world that is post-industrial, technological, post-modern, post-historic or, in Brzezinski's term, "technectronic." In Western Europe, the United States, Canada and Japan, the first contours of

this new society are already apparent. And, in many other less-developed countries, middle-class professionals (whose children become activists) often live in post-industrial enclaves within pre-industrial societies. Whatever we call the post-industrial world, it has demonstrated that, for the first time, man can produce more than enough to meet his material needs.

This accomplishment is admittedly blemished by enormous problems of economic distribution in the advanced nations, and it is in terrifying contrast to the overwhelming poverty of the Third World. Nevertheless, it is clear that what might be called "the problem of production" *can*, in principle, be solved. If all members of American society, for example, do not have enough material goods, it is because the system of distribution is flawed. The same is true, or will soon be true, in many other nations that are approaching advanced states of industrialization. Characteristically, these nations, along with the most technological, are those where student unrest has recently been most prominent.

THE transition from industrial to post-industrial society brings with it a major shift in social emphases and values. Industrializing and industrial societies tend to be oriented toward solving the problem of production. An industrial ethic—sometimes Protestant, sometimes Socialist, sometimes Communist—tends to emphasize psychological qualities like self-discipline, delay of gratification, achievement-orientation and a strong emphasis on economic success and productivity. The social, political and economic institutions of these societies tend to be organized in a way that is consistent with the goal of increasing production. And industrial societies tend to apply relatively uniform standards, to reward achievement rather than status acquired by birth, to emphasize emotional neutrality ("coolness") and rationality in work and public life.

The emergence of post-industrial societies, however, means that growing numbers of the young are brought up in family environments where abundance, relative economic security, political freedom and affluence are simply facts of life, not goals. to be striven for. To such people the psychological imperatives, social institutions and cultural values of the industrial ethic seem largely outdated and irrelevant to their own lives.

ONCE it has been demonstrated that a society can produce enough for all of its members, at least some of the young turn to other goals: for example, trying to make sure that society does produce enough and distributes it fairly, or searching for ways to live meaningfully with the goods and the leisure they already have. The problem is that our society has, in some realms, exceeded its earlier targets. Lacking new ones, it has become exhausted by its success.

When the values of industrial society become devitalized, the élite sectors of youth—the most affluent, intelligent, privileged and so on—come to feel that they live in institutions whose demands lack moral authority or, in the current jargon, "credibility." Today, the moral imperative and urgency behind production, acquisition, materialism and abundance has been lost.

Furthermore, with the lack of moral legitimacy felt in "the System," the least request for loyalty, restraint or conformity by its representatives—for example, by college presidents and deans—can easily be seen as a

moral outrage, an authoritarian repression, a manipulative effort to "co-opt" students into joining the Establishment and an exercise in "illegitimate authority" that must be resisted. From this conception springs at least part of the students' vague sense of oppression. And, indeed, perhaps their peculiar feeling of suffocation arises ultimately from living in societies without vital ethical claims.

Given such a situation, it does not take a clear-cut issue to trigger a major protest. I doubt, for example, that college and university administrators are in fact more hypocritical and dishonest than they were in the past. American intervention in Vietnam, while many of us find it unjust and cruel, is not inherently more outrageous than other similar imperialistic interventions by America and other nations within the last century. And the position of blacks in this country, although disastrously and unjustifiably disadvantaged, is, in some economic and legal respects, better than ever before. Similarly, the conditions for students in America have never been as good, especially, as I have noted, at those élite colleges where student protests are most common.

But this is precisely the point: It is because so many of the other problems of American society seem to have been resolved, or to be resolvable in principle, that students now react with new indignation to old problems, turn to new goals and propose radical reforms.

*   ○   ○

SO far I have emphasized the moral exhaustion of the old order and the fact that, for the children of post-industrial affluence, the once-revolutionary claims of the industrial society have lost much of their validity. I now want to argue that we are witnessing on the campuses of the world a fusion of two revolutions with distinct historical origins. One is a continuation of the old and familiar revolution of the industrial society, the liberal-democratic-egalitarian revolution that started in America and France at the turn of the 18th century and spread to virtually every nation in the world. (Not completed in any of them, its contemporary American form is, above all, to be found in the increased militancy of blacks.) The other is the new revolution, the post-industrial one, which seeks to define new goals relevant to the 20th and 21st centuries.

In its social and political aspects, the first revolution has been one of universalization, to use the sociologist's awkward term. It has involved the progressive extension to more and more people of economic, political and social rights, privileges and opportunities originally available only

to the aristocracy, then to the middle class, and now in America to the relatively affluent white working class. It is, in many respects, a quantitative revolution. That is, it concerns itself less with the quality of life than with the amount of political freedom, the quantity and distribution of goods or the amount and level of injustice.

As the United States approaches the targets of the first revolution, on which this society was built, to be poor shifts from being an unfortunate fact of life to being an outrage. And, for the many who have never experienced poverty, discrimination, exploitation or oppression, even to witness the existence of these evils in the lives of others suddenly becomes intolerable. In our own time the impatience to complete the first revolution has grown apace, and we find less willingness to compromise, wait and forgive among the young, especially among those who now take the values of the old revolution for granted—seeing them not as goals, but as rights.

A subtle change has thus occurred. What used to be utopian ideals—like equality, abundance and freedom from discrimination—have now become demands, inalienable rights upon which one can insist without brooking any compromise. It is noteworthy that, in today's student confrontations, no one requests anything. Students present their "demands."

So, on the one hand, we see a growing impatience to complete the first revolution. But, on the other, there is a newer revolution concerned with newer issues, a revolution that is less social, economic or political than psychological, historical and cultural. It is less concerned with the quantities of things than with their qualities, and it judges the virtually complete liberal revolution and finds it still wanting.

"You have to have grown up in Scarsdale to know how bad things really are," said one radical student. This comment would probably sound arrogant, heartless and insensitive to a poor black, much less to a citizen of the Third World. But he meant something important by it. He meant that even in the Scarsdales of America, with their affluence, their upper-middle-class security and abundance, their well-fed, well-heeled children and their excellent schools, something is wrong. Economic affluence does not guarantee a feeling of personal fulfillment; political freedom does not always yield an inner sense of liberation and cultural freedom; social justice and equality may leave one with a feeling that something else is missing in life. "No to the consumer society!" shouted the bourgeois students of the Sorbonne during May and June of 1968—a cry that understandably alienated French workers, for whom affluence and the consumer society are still central goals.

WHAT, then, are the targets of the new revolution? As is often noted, students themselves don't know. They speak vaguely of "a society that has never existed," of "new values," of a "more humane world," of "liberation" in some psychological, cultural and historical sense. Their rhetoric is largely negative; they are stronger in opposition than in proposals for reform; their diagnoses often seem accurate, but their prescriptions are vague; and they are far more articulate in urging the immediate completion of the first revolution than in defining the goals of the second. Thus, we can only indirectly discern trends that point to the still-undefined targets of the new revolution.

What are these trends and targets?

First, there is a revulsion against the notion of quantity, particularly economic quantity and materialism, and a turn toward concepts of quality. One of the most delightful slogans of the French student revolt was, "Long live the passionate revolution of creative intelligence!" In a sense, the achievement of abundance may allow millions of contemporary men and women to examine, as only a few artists and madmen have examined in the past, the quality, joyfulness and zestfulness of experience. The "expansion of consciousness"; the stress on the expressive, the aesthetic and the creative; the emphasis on imagination, direct perception and fantasy—all are part of the effort to enhance the quality of this experience.

Another goal of the new revolution involves a revolt against uniformity, equalization, standardization and homogenization—not against technology itself, but against the "technologization of man." At times, this revolt approaches anarchic quaintness, but it has a positive core as well—the demand that individuals be appreciated, not because of their similarities or despite their differences, but because they *are* different, diverse, unique and noninterchangeable. This attitude is evident in many areas: for example, the insistence upon a cultivation of personal idiosyncrasy, mannerism and unique aptitude. Intellectually, it is expressed in the rejection of the melting-pot and consensus-politics view of American life in favor of a post-homogeneous America in which cultural diversity and conflict are underlined rather than denied.

THE new revolution also involves a continuing struggle against psycho-

logical or institutional closure or rigidity in any form, even the rigidity of a definite adult role. Positively, it extols the virtues of openness, motion and continuing human development. What Robert J. Lifton has termed the protean style is clearly in evidence. There is emerging a concept of a lifetime of personal change, of an adulthood of continuing self-transformation, of an adaptability and an openness to the revolutionary modern world that will enable the individual to remain "with it"—psychologically youthful and on top of the present.

Another characteristic is the revolt against centralized power and the complementary demand for participation. What is demanded is not merely the consent of the governed, but the involvement of the governed. "Participatory democracy" summarizes this aspiration, but it extends far beyond the phrase and the rudimentary social forms that have sprung up around it. It extends to the demand for relevance in education—that is, for a chance for the student to participate in his own educational experience in a way that involves all of his faculties, emotional and moral as well as intellectual. The demand for "student power" (or, in Europe, "co-determination) is an aspect of the same theme: At Nanterre, Columbia, Frankfurt and Harvard, students increasingly seek to participate in making the policies of their universities.

This demand for participation is also embodied in the new ethic of

"meaningful human relationships," in which individuals confront each other without masks, pretenses and games. They "relate" to each other as unique and irreplacable human beings, and develop new forms of relationships from which all participants will grow.

IN distinguishing between the old and the new revolutions, and in attempting to define the targets of the new, I am, of course, making distinctions that students themselves rarely make. In any one situation the two revolutions are joined and fused, if not confused. For example, the Harvard students' demand for "restructuring the university" is essentially the second revolution's demand for participation; but their demand for an end to university "exploitation" of the surrounding community is tied to the more traditional goals of the first revolution. In most radical groups there is a range of opinion that starts with the issues of the first (racism, imperialism, exploitation, war) and runs to the concerns of the second (experiential education, new life styles, meaningful participation, consciousness-expansion, relatedness, encounter and community). The first revolution is personified by Maoist-oriented Progressive Labor party factions within the student left, while the second is represented by hippies, the "acid left," and the Yippies. In any individual, and in all student movements, these revolutions co-exist in uneasy and often abrasive tension.

Furthermore, one of the central problems for student movements today is the absence of any theory of society that does justice to the new world in which we of the most industrialized nations live. In their search for rational critiques of present societies, students turn to theories like Marxism that are intricately bound up with the old revolution.

Such theories make the ending of economic exploitation, the achievement of social justice, the abolition of racial discrimination and the development of political participation and freedom central, but they rarely deal adequately with the issues of the second revolution. Students inevitably try to adapt the rhetoric of the first to the problems of the second, using concepts that are often blatantly inadequate to today's world.

Even the concept of "revolution" itself is so heavily laden with images of political, economic and social upheaval that it hardly seems to characterize the equally radical but more social - psychological and cultural transformations involved in the new revolution. One student, recognizing this, called the changes occurring in his California student group, "too radical to be called a revolution." Students are thus often misled by their borrowed vocabulary, but most adults are even more confused, and many are quickly led to the mistaken conclusion that today's student revolt is nothing more than a repetition of Communism's in the past.

FAILURE to distinguish between the old and new revolutions also makes it impossible to consider the critical question of how compatible they are with each other. Does it make sense —or is it morally right—for today's affluent American students to seek imagination, self-actualization, individuality, openness and relevance when most of the world and many in America live in deprivation, oppression and misery?

The fact that the first revolution is "completed" in Scarsdale does not mean that it is (or soon will be) in Harlem or Appalachia—to say nothing of Bogotá or Calcutta. For many children of the second revolution, the meaning of life may be found in completing the first—that is, in extending to others the "rights" they have always taken for granted.

For others the second revolution will not wait; the question. "What lies beyond affluence?" demands an answer now. Thus, although we may deem it self-indulgent to pursue the goals of the new revolution in a world where so much misery exists, the fact is that in the advanced nations it is upon us, and we must at least learn to recognize it.

FINALLY, beneath my analysis lies an assumption I had best make explicit. Many student critics argue that their societies have failed miserably. My argument, a more historical one perhaps, suggests that our problem is not only that industrial societies have failed to keep all their promises, but that they have succeeded in some ways beyond all expectations. Abundance was once a distant dream, to be postponed to a hereafter of milk and honey; today, most Americans are affluent. Universal mass education was once a Utopian goal; today in America almost the entire population completes high school, and almost half enters colleges and universities.

The notion that individuals might be free, en masse, to continue their psychological, intellectual, moral and cognitive development through their teens and into their 20's would have been laughed out of court in any century other than our own; today, that opportunity is open to millions of young Americans. Student unrest is a reflection not only of the failures. but of the extraordinary successes of the liberal-industrial revolution. It therefore occurs in the nations and in the colleges where, according to traditional standards, conditions are best.

But for many of today's students who have never experienced anything but affluence, political freedom and social equality, the old vision is dead or dying. It may inspire bitterness and outrage when it is not achieved, but it no longer animates or guides. In place of it, students (and many who are not students) are searching for a new vision, a new set of values, a new set of targets appropriate to the post-industrial era —a myth, an ideology or a set of goals that will concern itself with the quality of life and answer the question, "Beyond freedom and affluence, what?"

What characterizes student unrest in the developed nations is this peculiar mixture of the old and the new, the urgent need to fulfill the promises of the past and, at the same time, to define the possibilities of the future.

April 27, 1969

High School Unrest Rises, Alarming U.S. Educators

By JOHN HERBERS
Special to The New York Times

WASHINGTON, May 8—Government officials and educators have become deeply concerned about the sharp increases this year in student protests and disruptions in high schools and junior high schools. The unrest has emerged in every region of the country, disrupting schools in suburbs and rural areas as well as in cities.

And officials and professional education groups are expecting, with growing anxiety, an even greater wave of protests in the future.

The extent of the unrest below the college level was disclosed in recent national studies by private and Government sources, in a New York Times check and in interviews with educators and officials.

"Three out of five principals report some form of active protest in their schools," according to a survey conducted this spring by the National Association of Secondary School Prin-cipals. "Many who note no protest as yet add that they expect it in the near future.

"One of the surprises of the survey was the fact that protest is almost as likely to occur in junior high schools as in senior high schools. Among junior high schools, 56 per cent report protest activities."

Robert H. Finch, Secretary of Health, Education and Welfare told a Chamber of Commerce audience here last month that "we must be prepared for much greater disorders in the secondary field" than have been seen in the colleges.

"The high school principal," said an official of the National Education Association, "is replacing the college president as the most embattled American."

Newspapers Studied

Alan F. Westin, director of the Center for Research and Education in American Liberties at Columbia University, has been monitoring 1,800 daily newspapers to determine the extent of disruptions. Dr. Westin is working under contract with the United States Office of Education.

In a four-month period, November through February, he counted 239 "serious episodes" of disorder—strikes, sit-ins, demonstrations, riots or other violence—in high schools. During the same period, 348 high schools in 38 states underwent some form of disruption that was reported in the newspapers studied.

Dr. Westin said in a telephone interview that the disruptions increased threefold from November through February. No detailed count has been made since then, he said, but the disorders have continued to increase. A conservative estimate, he said, is that 2,000 high schools have undergone disruptions from November through today.

A check by correspondents of The New York Times in 15 major cities across the country showed that the majority of high schools in some cities— San Francisco and Chicago, for example—experienced disruptions during the current school year. There has been a high incidence of violence, and police patrols at urban schools have become common.

Racial Conflict

In the large cities, racial conflict and protests are reported to have been the major cause of disruptions and of violence. Englewood High School on the South Side of Chicago, which is predominantly Negro, provides a current example.

Two weeks ago, the white principal, Norman E. Silber, notified a Negro teacher, George Spencer, that he would be dismissed for unsatisfactory performance. This sparked a campaign among blacks to have Mr. Silber dismissed.

On Monday, there was an outbreak of window-breaking and false fire alarms. A group of militants forced their way into Mr. Silber's office, and the police were called. The school was closed.

When Mr. Spencer refused Mr. Silber's order to report to the central personnel office for the public schools, he was arrested and charged with resisting arrest and criminal trespass.

The school was reopened yesterday under police guard, but about 500 students walked out in protest. Mr. Silber was removed by his superiors, and an assistant principal, a Negro, was named to replace him.

Freedom Central Issue

However, most protests outside the major cities, both disruptive and peaceful, appear to have been nonracial. The central issue is the growing effort toward more student freedom and involvement in school policy, according to the surveys.

Dr. Westin classified 361 disruptive cases as follows:

Type of Protest	Number of Incidents	States Involved
Racial	132	27
Political (including Vietnam)	81	21
Against dress regulations	71	25
Against discipline	60	28
For Educational reforms	17	14

The Secondary School Principals survey, compiled by J. Lloyd Trump and Jane Hunt, included all forms of protests and concluded:

"While dress and hair account for more protests than any other single topic, the principals enumerate many other regulations which students oppose. In fact, 82 per cent of the schools have protests against school regulations."

In suburban schools across the country, students have organized protests against everything from the food in the cafeterias to lack of toilet paper in the rest rooms.

A favorite target is the student councils, which in the nineteen-twenties were considered a daring innovation, but are now labeled by the students as meaningless or instruments of the administrators.

Underground newspapers, which have spread from the colleges to the high schools

and junior high schools, are considered an important part of the protest movement. Three months ago, Government officials estimated there were 500 such papers being published in the secondary schools.

Underground Newspapers

Douglas W. Hunt, director of administrative services for the National Association of Secondary School Principals, said the number was now "probably closer to 1,000."

B. Frank Brown, director of informational services for I/D/E/A, an educational research organization affiliated with the Charles F. Kettering Foundation, said in a speech to the Education Writers Association last February:

"The current wave of organized high school revolt has its origin in a position paper prepared by a Los Angeles high school student for the Students for a Democratic Society in 1965. This paper, entitled 'High School Reform,' was circulated in mimeographed form for a couple of years and published for wider distribution by the S.D.S. in 1967."

"The purpose of the position paper was to inform high school students on the best techniques for taking over a high school," he said. Part of the strategy was the establishment of an underground paper.

"If the underground paper is indeed a prelude to more militant activity as inferred by the

S.D.S. pamphlet," Mr. Brown said, "then the high schools of our country had best prepare for an excruciating era."

Most educators, however, attribute the protests mostly to changes in the society and the fact that teen-agers no longer automatically respect conventional values.

"In my view," said Dr. Westin, "it is a more decentralized and localized kind of thing. I haven't found any indication of a conspiracy, no blueprint. There is a common pattern, but this is more a cultural phenomenon."

School disruptions have occurred in such unlikely places as Edcouch, Tex., population 2,800, and Billings, Mont., 55,000, according to Dr. Westin's findings. Part of the trouble, he said, is that the public school system has been one of the last basic institutions to adapt to changes in the society.

Efforts to prepare school administrators for continued protests are encountering some difficulty. The National Association of Secondary School Principals prepared a 22-minute filmstrip on the subject for showing to parents and administrators.

It showed, among other things, teen-agers explaining the protest point of view, and it carried the voice of Thomas E. Hayden, the S.D.S. leader, presenting the view "of an increasing number of students."

The filmstrip was shown at a recent convention of the association. Principals from the large cities, a spokesman said, found it to be rather mild, but it created a furor among some of the principals from suburban and rural areas.

One reason for Mr. Finch's concern about the high school disorders is a belief among Federal officials that there is little the Government can do about the situation or even to collect meaningful intelligence about the scope of the trouble. There are 20,000 public school districts in the nation with 45 million students enrolled.

The Times check showed that much of the racial trouble in the city schools was occurring in those that had been fully integrated—a reflection of the increased tension between black and white adults.

In Pittsburgh, a spokesman for the Board of Education said the most difficulty had been in the schools with "the kind of racial balance we are striving for throughout the city."

"Appalling racial tensions have set black students against whites and whites against blacks," said Bernard McCormick, the Pittsburgh school superintendent. "I blame racial tensions that exist in our neighborhoods and are poisoning our city. Students bring into schools attitudes and hostilities that are bred in their homes and neighborhoods."

May 9, 1969

PRESIDENT SAYS CAMPUS RADICALS IMPERIL LIBERTIES

Sees Old Values Challenged by 'Moral Arrogance' and 'Permissive' Faculties

ASSAILS USE OF FORCE

By ROBERT B. SEMPLE Jr.
Special to The New York Times

MADISON, S. D., June 3— President Nixon said today that student revolutionaries — propelled by a "self-righteous moral arrogance" and abetted

by "permissive" faculties—were subjecting fundamental democratic values to perhaps their sharpest challenge in the life of the nation.

Only democratic restraint — the "reluctance of a free people" to apply force — has prevented a display of Government power against those who seek by force to disrupt the democratic process, he said.

Mr. Nixon chose a small college in the flat Dakota plains, General Beadle State College— to deliver a reflection on what he called this "deeply troubled and profoundly unsettled time," when racial discord, campus revolt and draft resistance threaten "old standards," "old values" and "old precepts."

Praise and Criticism

The President's language oscillated between lyrical defense of American democracy and sharp criticism of those who

cause and those who condone the present disturbances.

He said that the militants refused to acknowledge the "rights" of others and that as a result they risked the destruction of the political and constitutional liberties sheltered by the democratic process.

Of the radicals Mr. Nixon said:

"Scorning persuasion, they prefer coercion. Awarding themselves what they call a higher morality, they try to bully authorities into yielding to their 'demands.' On college campuses, they draw support from faculty members who should know better; in the larger community, they find the usual apologists ready to excuse any tactic in the name of 'progress.'"

"It should be self-evident," Mr. Nixon went on, "that this sort of self-righteous arrogance

has no place in a free community. It denies the most fundamental of all the values we hold: respect for the rights of others. This principle of mutual respect is the keystone of the entire structure of ordered liberty that makes freedom possible.

"The student who invades an administration building, roughs up the dean, rifles the files and issues 'nonnegotiable demands' may have some of his demands met by a permissive university administration.

"But the greater his 'victory,' the more he will have undermined the security of his own rights. In a free society, the rights of none are secure unless the rights of all are respected.

"It is precisely the structure of law and custom that he has chosen to violate—the process of freedom — by which the rights of all are protected."

June 4, 1969

297

Democratic Reform Commission Asks Full Party Participation for Youths From 18 to 20

By WARREN WEAVER Jr.
Special to The New York Times

WASHINGTON, Sept. 24—The Democratic party's reform commission voted today to give membership and full political status to a huge new block of young people that could remake the face of the party.

The commission, which is headed by Senator George S. McGovern of South Dakota, called on all state Democratic organizations to admit men and women 18 through 20 years old, whether or not they are eligible to enroll in a party or vote in the states where they live.

Under the McGovern commission plan, these young people could attend all party meetings, vote on such matters as delegates to county and state conventions and run for delegate posts themselves, up to and including the National Convention.

According to Census Bureau estimates, there were 10.3 million people in the 18-through-20 age bracket as of last July. Under previous party policy, they were restricted to joining young Democratic clubs on campuses or elsewhere.

The McGovern commission action was not just an idle recommendation. It carries a threat of strict enforcement.

After such final action any state organization that does not open its ranks to young people as prescribed will run the risk of having its delegates refused seats at the 1972 Democratic National Convention, about as serious a penalty as a political organization could face.

The same penalty may be applied by the Credentials Committee of the next National Convention to a delegation from any state that refuses to comply with any of the "guidelines" adopted by the McGovern Commission. The group gave initial approval to a dozen guidelines today.

The youth resolution raises the possibility that college students and other young people could take over some Democartic organizations by enlisting in large numbers, as supporters of Senator Eugene J. McCarthy did in some instances in the Presidential primary campaign last year.

The commission also voted to give insurgent groups further protection by prohibiting the casting of proxy votes on behalf of absentees at party meetings.

There were numerous reports in 1968 of Democratic leaders who frustrated the moves of a live majority at a party caucus by producing several hundred proxies signed by absent organization stalwarts and outvoting the opposition.

The commission was created at the request of the Democratic Convention of 1968 to make both delegate selection and party structure generally more democratic. The convention action was a response to protests from a number of party elements, among them young people.

The McGovern commission adjourned a two-day meeting today after postponing any decision on two of the most controversial issues before it: introducing proportional representation into the selection of National Convention delegates and insuring that those delegates represent roughly equal numbers of party members.

Senator McGovern said that a summary of the arguments on both sides of these issues would be mailed to party leaders with the guidelines adopted by the commission, so that comments by the leaders would be available at the next meeting, in five or six weeks.

Included in the unresolved proportional representation issue is the question of whether minority groups such as Negroes or Mexican-Americans should be guaranteed a number of convention delegates roughly reflecting their strength in the party.

Other guidelines approved by the reform commission today would:

¶Prohibit discrimination in party activity and advancement on the basis of sex.

¶Require state parties to make all possible efforts to eliminate laws and practices that restrict registration.

¶Call for the elimination of all excessive and burdensome fees charged convention delegates in some states.

¶Prohibit delegates from choosing their alternates and limit the power to fill delegation vacancies to the delegates themselves.

¶Require a quorum of 40 per cent to conduct business at all party meetings.

In addition to approving guidelines for the party, the commission approved resolutions calling for direct popular election of the President, extension of the vote to all those 18 and older and extension of the Voting Rights Act of 1965 for another five years.

September 25, 1969

A NEW ETHIC SEEN AMONG STUDENTS

Sociologist Cites Emphasis On Private Existence

A sociologist from Tulane University who conducted a national poll of 2,000 college seniors last year has reported that the results showed the emergence of a new ideology, which he calls "privatism," among the student generation.

In an article entitled "The Private Generation" that appears in the October issue of Psychology Today, Dr. Jeffrey K. Hadden says this ideology is "the most distinctive and obvious trait" to emerge from the replies to the survey's 246 questions. He adds that this new emphasis on the personal is both altruistic and selfish, because it "acknowledges the privileges of private existence — as rights — to all men" but tends to become self-indulgent at its "logical extreme."

Dr. Hadden defines personalism as the "whole ideology" that includes "student withdrawal from institutions into the self" and the rejection of "meaning or authority outside of the self."

Questions Commitment

Dr. Haddon says today's generation displays a high degree of idealism and social awareness, but he adds: "For all their abstract altruism, students lack a realistic sense of what their ideals imply in terms of social and public action. It is not clear, in fact, that they are fully committed to the ideals they talk about, especially when action may conflict with privatism."

He also says, however, that the students' idealism is often expressed in a rejection of the older generation's "hypocrisy . . . and failure . . . to act upon its stated ideals."

Dr. Hadden reports that 76 per cent of those responding "say that they feel morally obliged to do what they can to end racial injustice." But almost half — 42 per cent — accept as true "the most blatant stereotype . . . of the irresponsible and carefree Negro."

As another example, Dr. Hadden compares the 73 per cent who indicated a belief that the white exodus from the central city is a factor in "the ghetto crisis" with the 70 per cent who gave "every indication that they will join the exodus" to the suburbs.

September 29, 1969

300 in S.D.S. Clash With Chicago Police

By JOHN KIFNER
Special to The New York Times

CHICAGO, Oct. 8—Hundreds of young radicals charged through the Near North Side tonight, shouting, breaking windows and battling the police.

At least 40 demonstrators were arrested. Seven policemen and seven demonstrators in the rally called by the Students for a Democratic Society were treated at hospitals. Two of the demonstrators were shot but were not seriously wounded. The police used tear gas at least once.

The radicals, nearly all of them wearing helmets and carrying clubs and National Liberation Front flags, swarmed out of a rally in Lincoln Park at 10:20 chanting "Long live the victory of the people's war."

The crowd of 300 ran south down Clark Street. Rocks smashed through the high plate-glass windows of the North Federal Savings Bank at the corner of North Avenue. As the crowd moved on, the crashing of window panes and shops all along Clark Street blended with the chanting.

Plainclothes policemen ran ahead of them, urging motorists out of the way, apparently to avert further damage.

When the demonstrators saw a skirmish line of policemen forming ahead of them, they suddenly swung east, running along Goethe Street and then south on State Street.

As they reached the corner of Division Street, a line of police vehicles and dozens of policemen stretched across their path. Whooping, the youths charged into the police line. Many of them raced through the startled officers. Others were grabbed and pulled down.

At the corner of State and Division Streets the police threw two canisters of a mild tear gas at the demonstrators.

Several times the police and young demonstrators fenced with one another, using their clubs like medieval staves.

The radicals then broke up into small groups to roam through the streets of Old Town and the Near North Side. Sirens wailing, police cars hurtled through the night after them.

70 Hard-Core Weathermen

The action tonight began with a bonfire rally in Lincoln Park — the starting point for last year's Democratic convention disorders.

The rally was called by the dominant Weathermen faction of the Students for a Democratic Society in honor of the second anniversary of the slaying of the Cuban revolutionary Ernesto Che Guevara. It began a series of demonstrations here that members of the group say will be "very heavy."

At about 8 o'clock, 70 hardcore Weathermen marched into the park in a tight phalanx, wearing stiff new denim jackets with National Liberation Front flags stitched to the back and white motorcycle helmets with visors. They carried Vietcong flags and clubs.

A large part of this group were women, and a number of men seemed very young.

The Weathermen are proponents of militant street-fighting actions, and the rally could produce clashes between the police and roving "affinity groups" of from five to fifteen youthful dissidents.

Meanwhile, the rival Revolutionary Youth Movement II faction of S.D.S. has also announced plans for a series of marches and demonstrations running through Saturday.

Both sets of demonstrations are timed to coincide with the conspiracy trial here of eight radical leaders charged with fomenting disorders during the Democratic convention last August.

The Weathermen—who take their name from the line "You don't need a weatherman to see which way the wind blows" from Bob Dylan's "Subterranean Homesick Blues"—gained control of S. D. S. at last spring's convention of the organization.

Headed by Mark Rudd, a leader in the disorders at Columbia University last year, they believe that a worldwide revolution is in progress, spearheaded by black, brown and yellow "third world peoples." They hold that the potential revolutionary class in America is disaffected youths of high school age, and have written off the working class as hopelessly steeped in racism and college students as inherently bourgeois.

Over the summer, some Weathermen have developed a tactic of charging into high schools shouting "jailbreak"— and occasionally beating or tying up teachers—in hopes of radicalizing students by their action.

The Revolutionary Youth Movement II group has split off from the Weathermen, contending that their tactics are "adventuristic" and self-defeating because they will alienate potential supporters and lead to increased police crackdowns.

The Weathermen have announced plans for a "women's militia" to "destroy the armed services induction center" tomorrow morning and for "jailbreaks" at high schools tomorrow afternoon.

On Friday the Weathermen plan to "try and shut down the conspiracy trial" and on Saturday they have called for a march from Haymarket Square into the Loop.

All days off have been canceled for the Police Department's 10,000-man force, and hundreds of detectives have been ordered to report for duty in uniform. All but one door of the police headquarters building was barricaded with wooden horses today, and the police checked visitors' identification and packages.

October 9, 1969

The New Stage Of American Man— Almost Endless Adolescence

By BENNETT M. BERGER

WHEN I was an undergraduate 20 years ago, I was chairman of one of the radical student groups at my college and an active official in the regional intercollegiate association of that group. I marched in my share of picket lines, published an article attacking my college president for anti-Semitism, was sung to by the sirens of the local Communist party and even, in a burst of creativity, wrote what in this age of instant classics I suppose qualifies as a classic militant's love song. I called it, "You and I and the Mimeograph Machine" and dedicated it to all the youthful romances born amidst the technology of moral protest.

Later, when I got older and became a sociologist, I resisted becoming a "political sociologist," by which in this context I mean what a lot of the militants

BENNETT M. BERGER is a professor of sociology at the University of California, Davis. A collection of his essays, "Looking for America," will be published in the spring.

S-t-r-e-t-c-h! Campus unrest is a product, it is contended, of the artificial postponement of maturity. Colleges feel the strain.

mean: a former activist who traded his credentials as a conscious moral and political agent in exchange for the rewards of expertise about political behavior. Though the remarks about student militance which follow may be analytic, I yield nothing to the young in the way of moral credentials.

In trying to throw some sociological light on the nature and character of student unrest, I am not going to comfort the militants by saying that students protest because this is a racist, plastic society or because the curriculum is irrelevant or because the university has sold its soul to the military-industrial complex or because the university is a machine in which students are treated as raw material—when, indeed, their uptight teachers take time from their research to treat them as anything at all. On the other hand, I am not going to comfort their critics by saying that students rebel for kicks or because their upbringing was too permissive or because they are filled with a seething self-hatred or because they are symbolically murdering their fathers in a recurrent ritual melodrama of generational conflict.

What I will try to do is show how certain conditions generic to the direction of our present societal development have helped to bring about the present situation among youth and in the universities. I will also hazard a prediction as to the effects of these conditions during the next decade. An understanding of the problem will not make the solution any easier, for knowledge is not power, but it can at least arm us against panaceas.

* * *

THE problem of student unrest is rooted in the prolongation of adolescence in industrialized countries. But it should be understood that "adolescence" is only minimally a biological category; there are only a very few years between the onset of puberty and the achievement of the growth and strength it takes to do a man's or woman's work. As we know, however, culture has a habit of violating nature. Proto-adolescent behavior now begins even before puberty (which itself is occurring earlier) with the action — and the orientation — we call "preadolescent," while at the other end, technological, economic and social developments conspire to prolong the dependence of the young, to exclude them from many of the privileges and responsibilities of adult life, and therefore to *juvenilize** them.

The casual evidence in support of this deep institutionalization of adolescence is diffuse and quite remarkable. It includes such spectacles as 6-foot, 200-pound "boys" who in another time and place might be founders of dynasties and world-conquerors (like Alexander of Macedon) cavorting on the fraternity house lawn hurling orange peels and bags of water at each other, while tolerant local police, who chucklingly *approve*, direct traffic around the battlefield. It includes the preservation of childlike cadence and intonation in voices otherwise physically mature. It includes the common—and growing—practice (even in official university documents) of opposing the word "student" to the word "adult"—as if students were by definition not adults, even as the median age of university students rises with the increase of the graduate student population.

Adolescence, then, is not the relatively fleeting "transitional stage" of textbook and popular lore but a substantial segment of life which may last 15 or 20 years, and if the meaning of adolescence is extended only slightly, it can last longer than that. I have in mind the age-graded norms and restrictions in those professions which require long years of advanced training, and in which the system of sponsorship makes the advancement of one's career dependent upon being somebody's "boy" perhaps well on toward one's middle-age—a fact not uncharacteristic of university faculties.

Much of the discussion of "youth culture" in recent years reflects the prolongation of adolescence, since it is not surprising that a period of life which may last from age 12 to age 35 might develop its own cultural style, its own traditions and its own sources of motivation, satisfaction—and dissatisfaction. There is thus an enormous stratum of persons caught in the tension between their experience of peak physical strength and sexual energy on the one hand, and their public definition as culturally "immature" on the other.

This tension is exacerbated by a contradictory tendency: while modern industrial conditions promote juvenilization and the prolongation of dependence, they also create an "older," more experienced youthful cohort. They have more and earlier experience with sex and drugs; they are far better educated than their parents were; urban life sophisticates them more quickly; television brings into their homes worlds of experience that would otherwise remain alien to them. Young people, then, are faced not only with the ambiguity of the adolescent role itself and its prolongation but with forces and conditions that, at least in some ways, make for *earlier* maturity. The youthful population is a potentially explosive stratum because this society is ill-equipped to accommodate it within the status system.

ERIK ERIKSON'S well-known theory of the "psycho-social moratorium" of adolescence takes the facts of adolescent prolongation and transforms them into a triumph of civilization. By emphasizing the increased time provided for young persons to postpone commitments, to try on social roles and to play the game called "the search for identity," Erikson suggests that the moratorium on lasting adult responsibilities contributes to the development and elaboration of personal individuality. I have no wish to quarrel with Erikson's general thesis here; I have done so elsewhere. Instead, I want to emphasize a fact that is seemingly contradictory to Erikson's observations about the moratorium on adult commitments. Namely, there have actually been increasing and clearly documented pressures on young people for earlier and earlier occupational planning and choice. "Benjamin," ask that famous Graduate's parents repeatedly, "what are you going to *do?*" And the question is echoed by millions of prosperous American parents who, despite their affluence, cannot assure the future economic position of their heirs.

Logically, of course, prolonged identity play and early occupational choice cannot be encouraged at the same time; the fact is, they are. And like other ambiguous values (and most moral values are ambiguous, or can be made so), this pair permit different groups of youngsters to rationalize or justify the kinds of adaptations that differing circumstances in fact constrain them to make. The public attention generated by protesting youth in recent years (hippies, the New Left, black militants) obscures the fact that the majority of young people are still apparently able to tolerate the tensions of prolonged adolescence, to adjust to the adolescent role (primarily, student), to take some satisfaction from the gains it provides in irresponsibility (i.e., "freedom") and to sail smoothly through high school into college where they choose the majors, get the grades and eventually the certifications for the occupations which they want, which want them and which higher education is equipped to provide them—degrees in education, business, engineering, dentistry and so on.

For others, however, the search for identity (quote, unquote) functions as a substitute for an occupational orientation; it gives them something "serious" to do while coping with their problems of sex, education,

---

*"Juvenilize": a verb I have devised to describe a process through which "childish" behavior is induced or prolonged in persons who, in terms of their organic development, are capable of participating in adult affairs. If the process exists, there ought to be a verb to describe it.

family and career. In college most of these people tend to major in the humanities or social sciences (particularly sociology) where they may take 10 years or more between the time they enter as freshmen, drop out, return, graduate and go on to pursue graduate degrees or give up on them entirely. I will return to this matter, but for the moment I want to make two general points: (1) that the contradictions create understandable tensions in the young and feed their appetite to discover "hypocrisy" in their elders; (2) that this condition is largely beyond the control of the universities; it is generated by the exigencies of a "post-industrial" society which uses institutions of higher education as warehouses for the temporary storage of a population it knows not what else to do with.

The situation has become critical over the past 10 years because the enormous numbers of the young (even small percentages of which yield formidable numbers of troops for worthy causes) and their concentration (in schools and cities) have promoted easy communication and a sense of group solidarity among them. Numbers, concentration and communication regarding common grievances have made increasingly viable, in almost precisely the way in which Karl Marx described the development of class consciousness among workers, the creation and maintenance of "deviant subcultures" of youth.

THIS youthful population is "available" for recruitment to moral causes because their marginal, ambiguous position in the social structure renders them sensitive to moral inconsistencies (note their talent for perceiving "hypocrisy"), because the major framework of their experience ("education") emphasizes "ideal" aspects of the culture and because their exclusion from adult responsibilities means that they are generally unrestrained by the institutional ties and commitments which normally function as a brake upon purely moral feeling; they also have the time for it.

The two great public issues of the decade (the Vietnam war and the rights of despised minorities) have been especially suited to enlist the mili-

"For students who are 'around' a university for a long time, it tends to become a kind of 'home territory'—the place where they really live."

tant predispositions of the young precisely because these issues are clearly moral issues. To take a strong "position" on these issues requires no great *expertise* or familiarity with arcane facts. And the moral fervor involved in taking such a position nicely reflects our traditional age-graded culture to the extent that it identifies virtue with "idealism," unspoiledness and innocence, precisely the qualities adults like to associate with the young.

It is almost as if the young, in the unconscious division of labor which occurs in all societies, were delegated the role of "moral organ" of society—what with all the grown-ups being too busy running the bureaucracies of the world (with their inevitable compromises, deals, gives and takes) to concern themselves with "ideals." This even makes a sort of good structural sense because the unanchored character of the young (that is, their relative unfetteredness to family, community and career) fits them to perform their "ideal" functions—in the same sense and for the same reason that Plato denied normal family life to his philosopher-kings and the Roman Catholic Church denies it to their priests.

It is the combination of moral sensitivity and alienation that accounts both for the extreme juvenophile postures of moral critics like Edgar Friedenberg, Paul Goodman and John Seeley (which sometimes reach the belief that the young are simply better

people than the old or middle-aged, and hence even a belief in juvenocracy) and the fear of and hostility toward militant youth by writers epitomized by Lewis Feuer in his new book on student movements. In the latter view, the idealism of the young becomes corrupt, violent, terroristic and destructive precisely because, alienated, detached from institutions, youth are not "responsible"—that is, not accountable for the consequences of their moral zealotry upon the groups and organizations affected by it.

SO one is tempted to say that society may just have to accept youth's irresponsibility if it values their moral contributions. But evidence suggests that adult society is in general sympathetic neither to their moral proddings nor toward granting the young any greater responsibility in public affairs. Research by English sociologist Frank Musgrove clearly documents that adults are unwilling to grant real responsibilities any earlier to the young, and there is good reason to believe the same is true in the United States, as is suggested by the repeated failures of the movement to lower the voting age to 18. And as for the "idealism" of youth, when it goes beyond the innocent virtues of praising honesty, being loyal, true and brave and helping old ladies across the street, to serious moral involvements promoting their own group interests ("student power") or those of the do-

mestic or "third world" dispossessed, the shine of their "idealism" is likely to tarnish rather quickly.

Moreover, the moral activism of youth *is* sometimes vulnerable to attack on several counts. The "morality" of a political action, for example, is weakened when it has a self-congratulatory character (and the tendency to produce a holier-than-thou vanity in the actor). It also loses something when it does not involve substantial risk of personal interests or freedom (as it unambiguously *does* with the young only in the case of draft resisters). In the end, along with the society's prolongation of adolescence and encouragement of "the search for identity," continuing praise of the young for their "idealism" (except when it becomes serious) and continuing appeals to them to behave "responsibly"—in the face of repeated refusal to grant them real responsibilities (except in war)—are understandable as parts of the cultural armory supporting the process of juvenilization.

COLLEGES, universities and their environs are the places apparently designated by society as the primary locations where this armory is to be expended. It is clear that the schools, particularly institutions of higher learning, are increasingly being asked by society to perform a kind of holding operation for it. The major propaganda campaign to encourage students not to drop out of high school is significant less for the jobs which staying that last year or two in high school will qualify one for than it is for the reduced pressure it creates on labor markets unable to absorb unskilled 16- and 17-year-olds. The military institutions, through the draft, help store (and train) much of the working-class young, and the colleges and universities prepare many of the heirs of the middle classes for careers in business, the professions and the semiprofessions. But higher education also gets the lion's share of the identity seekers: those sensitive children of the affluent, less interested in preparing themselves for occupations which the universities are competent to prepare them for than in transcending or trading in the stigmata of their bourgeois backgrounds (work ethic, money-grubbing, status-seeking) for a more "meaningful" life.

It is these students who are heavily represented among the student activists and among whom the cry for "relevance" is heard most insistently. Does it seem odd that this cry should be coming from those students who are *least* interested in the curricula whose relevance is palpable, at least with respect to occupations? Not if one observes that many of these students are, in a sense, classically "intellectuals"—that is, oriented toward statuses or positions for which the universities (as well as other major institutions) have seldom been able or competent to provide certification.

The statuses such students want are those to which one appoints oneself or which one drifts into: artist, critic, writer, intellectual, journalist, revolutionist, philosopher. And these statuses have been undermined for two generations or more by technical and bureaucratic élites whose training has become increasingly specialized and "scientific." In this context the cry for relevance is a protest against technical, value-neutral education whose product (salable skills or the posture of uncommitment) contributes nothing to the search by these students for "identity" and "meaningful experience."

Adding final insult to the injury of the threatened replacement of traditional humanistic intellectuals by technical élites is the ironic transformation of some of their traditional curricula (social sciences particularly) into instruments useful to the "power structure" or "the establishment" in pursuing its own ends. It makes no sense to call a curriculum "irrelevant" and then to turn right around and accuse its chief practitioners of "selling out"; the powerful do not squander their money so easily. The ironic point, then, is not that these curricula are "irrelevant" but that they are far *too* relevant to the support of interests to which the left is opposed.

THE villains here are the methodological orthodoxies of the social sciences: their commitment to objectivity, detachment and the "separation" between facts and values. In the view of radical students, these orthodoxies rationalize the official diffidence of social scientists regarding the social

"Short of outright revolution, what one can expect to see over the next decade: for the radicals, academic credit for extension-type activities such as tutoring ghetto children; for the identity-seekers, classes emphasizing 'honesty.'"

consequences of their research, a diffidence which (conveniently—and profitably —for social scientists, goes the argument) promotes the interests of the established and the powerful. This is far from the whole truth, of course. There is plenty of research, supported by establishments, whose results offer the establishment little comfort. But like other "nonpartisan" or value-neutral practices and procedures, the methodological orthodoxies of the social sciences do tend in general to support established interests, simply because the powerful, in command of greater resources and facilities, are better able to make use of "facts" than the weak, and because avoidance of ideological controversy tends to perpetuate the inequities of the status quo.

But the demands for a more activist and "committed" social science and for social scientists to function as advocates for oppressed and subordinated groups may not be the best way of correcting the inequities. A thorough *doctrinal* politicization of social science in the university is likely to mean the total loss of whatever little insulation remains against the ideological controversies rending the larger society; and the probable result would be that the university, instead of being more liberal than the society as a whole, would more accurately reflect the still-burgeoning reactionary mood of the country.

For students who tend to be "around" a university for

a long time—the 10-year period mentioned earlier is not uncommon — the university tends to become a kind of "home territory," the place where they really live. They experience the university less as an élite training institution than as a political community in which "members" have a kind of quasi-"citizenship" which, if one believes in democratic process, means a right to a legitimate political voice in its government.*

This conception of the university is quite discrepant with the conception held by most faculty members and administrators. To most faculty members the university is the élite training institution to which students who are both willing and able come to absorb intellectual disciplines— "ologies"—taught by skilled and certified professionals whose competences are defined by and limited to those certifications. But which way one sees the university—as a political community or as an élite training institution — is not purely a matter of ideological preference.

The fact seems to be that where training and certification and performance in politically neutral skills are clearest, the more conservative view is virtually unchallenged.

---

*Much remains to be clarified about the nature of "membership" in academic communities. So much cant has gone down in the name of "community" that I often feel about this word much like that Nazi who has gone down in history as having said, "When I hear the word 'culture,' I reach for my revolver."

This is true not only for dentistry and mathematics but for athletics too. Presumably many militant blacks are not for any kind of a quota system with respect to varsity teams, and presumably football players in the huddle do not demand a voice in the decisions that shape their lives. But where what one's education confers upon one is a smattering of "high culture" or "civilized manners" or the detached sensibility and ethics of a science whose benefits, like other wealth, are not equitably distributed — in short, where the main result of liberal education is *Weltanschauung*—it indeed has "political" consequences.

These consequences were not controversial so long as the culture of the university was fairly homogeneous and so long as the "aliens" it admitted were eager to absorb that culture. They have become controversial in recent years because the democratization of higher education has revealed the "class" character of academic culture and because of the appearance on the campus of students who do not share and/or do not aspire to that culture. These newcomers have arrived in sufficiently large numbers to mount a serious challenge to the hegemony of traditional academic culture.

DESPITE their many differences, the new militant "ethnic" students and their supporters among "white radicals," "street people," hippies and other young people on the left have in common their anti-academicism, which is the campus version of the anti - establishment outlook. This is true notwithstanding the fact that the academy has been the most liberal sector of establishment thought and the most sympathetic to at least some of the aspirations of dissident students. Partly, of course, their hostility to the academy is rooted in the fact that the university is where they're at, the institutional location in which they have to work through their prolonged adolescence and the problems associated with it. But beyond this, there is real conflict between the traditional criteria of academic performance and what dissident students demand from academic life.

Research suggests that most of the white radical students have grown up in a milieu where "intellectual" matters were discussed, where books were probably present in their homes, where middle-class manners and style were their birthright, and where, therefore, they learned how to "talk"—that is, where they developed the sort of verbal facility enabling them to do well enough in high school and to seem like promising "college material" if only because they look and sound much like college students have always looked and sounded. With the ascendence of the view that everybody has a right to a higher education (along with the fact that there's no place else to send well-born adolescents), most of them wind up in colleges and universities.

Some of them, despite their verbal facility, are not really bright; many others, despite their ability to get good college grades, strongly resist "conforming" to many of the requirements for professional certification which they demean as mere "socialization." Confronted by academic demands for rigor in their thinking, for sufficient discipline to master a systematic body of knowledge, for evidence that they can maintain a line of logical thinking beyond one or two propositions, and bring evidence systematically to bear upon a problem, many of them are found seriously wanting—some because they are not bright enough, others because they think it a point of honor to resist the intellectual demands made on them. When their numbers are large enough to enable them to turn to each other for mu-

tual support, it is not surprising that they should collectively turn against the system of criteria which derogates them and, in a manner not unanalogous to the "reaction formation" of slum delinquents who develop a subculture in opposition to middle-class school norms which judge them inadequate, develop an anti-academic viewpoint which defines abstraction, logical order, detachment, objectivity and systematic thinking as the cognitive armory of a repressive society, productive of alienation, personal rigidity and truncated capacity for feeling.

Preoccupied as most of these students are with "identity problems" and moral protest, it is again not surprising that many of them should be less interested in the mastery of academic disciplines, even if they have the ability, than in pursuing what they are likely to call "gut-issues" or nitty-gritty. The kinds of problems they apparently are interested in studying can be inferred from the examination of almost any "Free University" brochure, and what these add up to is a sort of extension division for the underground: practical, topical "rap sessions" on Vietnam, civil rights, encounter groups, pottery, psychedelics, macrobiotics, Eastern religion, rock music and so on.

IN the conflict with the established interests of science and scholarship in the university, radical students do win significant victories. New courses do get approved; experimental curricula do get tried out; students do get appointed to important committees; greater weight is attached to teaching in the appointment and promotion of faculty members. But large numbers of these radical students, exhausted by conflict and depressed by negative criticism, drop out of school. In dropping out, however, they do not immediately disappear into the labor market. They tend to remain in the university community, employed occasionally or part time in dead-end jobs, living in furnished rooms or communal houses near the university, and most important for my purposes here, still participating in the marginal student culture which they know so well.

Their participation in this culture is made possible to some extent by the fact that their youth protects them from the degrading consequences of being poor and having no regular or "approved" status in the community. Part of the age-grading system which postpones adulthood is the temporary protection of the young against the stigmata which, for older people, are normally attached to poverty. But over time, this group of "nonstudents" can be regarded as downward mobile, and thereby hangs an inter-

esting prospect.

The United States has no major tradition of large-scale downward mobility. The only major image of intergenerational decline is associated with decadent aristocratic families in ruined Southern mansions. Given the general tendency for downwardly mobile groups to resent the system which derogates them, and given the fact that the channels of upward mobility today are largely through higher education, the hostility to the university of these radical, middle-class "nonstudents" is probably maintained even after they leave it. The irony is that in dropping out, the hippie and New Left children of the middle classes provide opportunity for the upward mobility of the new black and other ambitious "disadvantaged" students.

The blacks and other ethnic militants are presently using higher education in a manner different from that in which their predecessors from the lower class used it. For earlier ethnics, the university served as a channel of mobility for *individuals* from the talented poor; today, it is sought as a means of collective mobility. There are two aspects to this movement. There is the emphasis on ethnic studies programs designed to provide the members of the respective ethnic groups with a sense of pride in their history and culture, and there are the demands that the university play a more active role in ameliorating suffering in the ghettos, not merely through programs of research which exploit the cooperation of ghetto residents without helping them measurably, but by taking the university off the campus, bringing it to them, in their terms, on their turf, for their own purposes.

IN the struggle to achieve the ends of the militants, black and white, the traditional university is very vulnerable because the militants have great leverage. Just as the blacks can conceivably turn the urban core into a guerrilla battleground, militant students can bring the universities to the proverbial grinding halt. Continual rallies, classroom disruptions, picket lines, building seizures, student intimidation and general paranoia (to say nothing of the almost continual meetings by faculty and administration committees to cope with the crises and the continual corridor and coffee room gossip

"The young dissenters are unrestrained by the institutional ties and commitments which normally put a brake upon purely moral feeling; they also have the time."

by knots of faculty members) can bring the teaching and other academic functions of the university to a virtual standstill.

This prospect raises seriously for the first time the question of whether the traditional university, as we know it, is an expendable institution. And another question, as well: Is it possible that a decision has been made somewhere that it is better to risk the destruction of the university by confining the unrest to the campus than to allow it to spill over into more critical institutions? Pickets, sit-ins, building seizures and non-negotiable demands are one thing on the campuses. Imagine them at C.B.S. on Madison Avenue: no TV until S.D.S. gets equal time; at the Stock Exchange: the ticker tape does not roll until corporation X gets rid of its South African holdings; at the headquarters of the Bank of America: no depositors get through the doors until interest-free loans are made to renovate the ghettos. There would be machine guns in the streets in no time at all!

In 1969, despite the tear gas and the National Guard, it is still hard to imagine tanks and machine guns used against student radicals so long as their militance is confined to the campus. Because if they do close the universities down, exactly who would miss them? The most practical functions the university performs and its activities which are most directly relevant to the national economy (engineering, science, law, medicine, etc.) could be transferred to the private sector. The beginnings of such a transfer are apparent already in the educational functions carried on by private foundations, institutes and industrial corporations.

And if the departments of English and history and po-

litical science and sociology and art and so on closed tight shut tomorrow, who would miss them? Aside from the implication of some social science departments in the military-industrial complex, the studies in humanities and social science departments are civilized luxuries with very few sources of government or business support. The student radicals have little sympathy for them and there is probably even less sympathy for them among the students' severest critics. These days, even conservative legislators, in the same breath that they denounce student militance, will quickly add, "Of course, this doesn't mean that there isn't plenty wrong with the university; there is." And if the student revolution can be bought off by substituting Bob Dylan for Dylan Thomas, McLuhan for Freud, Marcuse for Plato, rock for Bach, black culture for Greek culture, rap sessions for formal examinations, how many will care? Who needs high culture anyway? For the radicals it's an instrument of class oppression, and their oppressors, at least in America, have never been too keen on it anyway, except as a tax dodge.

SHORT of machine guns in the streets and outright revolution, what one can expect to see over the next decade in academic life is greater adaptation by the university to the new kinds of students it must serve and to the new publics whose anticipated support or hostility it must take into account in its planning. By the new students I mean ghetto youth, middle-class white radicals and the identity seekers. By the new publics I mean those millions of citizens whose taxes support the great state universities but who never thought of the university as "theirs" until its politicization encouraged ambitious politicians to call this fact to

their attention. Having once been reminded (by Governor Reagan and others), the voters are not likely to forget it soon.

If it comes about, this adaptation is likely to occur in a manner not dissimilar to that in which the major political parties have adapted to third-party movements in the larger political community: by isolating the *most* radical through the adoption of some of their programs and demands, while at the same time adopting severe and punitive policies toward the more intransigent and violence-prone who are still unsatisfied.

FOR ghetto youth, then, there will be more ethnic studies programs and compensatory admissions and grading policies and practices and more energetic recruiting of ethnic students and faculty. But there will be less indecision or tolerance in the handling of sit-ins, seizures and other disruptions. For the radicals (ethnic as well as middle-class white), there will be greater emphasis on programs granting academic credit for extension-type activities such as tutoring of ghetto children, neighborhood seminars on consumer savvy and community organization. For the identity seekers there will be more encounter groups, more classes emphasizing 'openness and honesty" in dialogue, more experiments with less structured curricula and residential communities, more "retreats," more student-initiated courses on subjects which engage their sense of "relevance" to their interests, from sex to drugs to rock. For all, there will be further loosening of the *in loco parentis* restrictions which hardly anybody in the university believes in anymore, and a little more student power (at least influence) on faculty and administrative committees. All this, combined with a more effective public-relations campaign explaining the mission of the

university and its problems in coping with the consequences of prolonged adolescence, may just bring about a semblance of peace on the campus. But without peace in Vietnam, it will be an uneasy peace at best.

There will be opposition. Academic conservatives will see in these new programs the prospect of the dilution or outright abandonment of traditional standards of scholarship. The legitimation of ethnicity, the amelioration of suffering by the poor and the search for identity by the young may all be noble endeavors, they will say, but the major functions of the university are the creation and transmission of systematic bodies of abstract knowledge. Political conservatives will see in these programs harbingers of social changes which they oppose. Militant students imply more leaders and troops for restive ghettos; "the search for identity" and the self-exploratory activities the phrase suggests are redolent of the "liberalism," "permissiveness" and self-indulgence offensive to the traditional Protestant ethic which "made this country great."

Yet academic conservatives might well be reminded that the university is facing radically transformed constituencies, that academic disciplines which are well institutionalized and "traditional" today were themselves academically born in the blood of earlier periods of such transformations and that they were initially opposed by still more "traditional" fields. Political conservatives might well be reminded that student unrest was not invented by outside agitators, that its source is in social conditions conservatives affirm and that it is not repressible short of military measures. The alternatives to the adaptable university involve blood on the quad and an expendable university. ∎

November 2, 1969

THEY REALLY START EARLIER

To THE EDITOR:

Dr. Bennett Berger in "The New Stage of American Man — Almost Endless Adolescence," Nov. 2, overlooks the earlier causes of lengthening adolescence: the steady decrease of childhood. This is not a sociopsychological concept; it is a physical and anthropological fact. Two examples come to mind:

(1) In the Scientific American (218:21, 1968) it was pointed out that the stature of children in the United States and Europe averaged almost four inches taller at age 11 in 1965 than their counterparts 50 years before.

(2) Dr. Paul K. Ito's studies reveal that Japanese girls born and raised in California began normal menstruation 20 months earlier than Japanese girls born and raised in Japan or born in Japan and raised in

California.

Another reason why adolescence begins "prematurely" can be a result of civilization. For many years man has been amending natural laws with statutes of his own. Thus, children at puberty are physiologically mature and perfectly capable of mating and producing offspring, a common feature of primitive cultures. Western civilization has repressed nature for many reasons and yet is constantly

amazed that young persons in their earliest teens are interested in sex and other allied pursuits and endeavors. These and many more sociological, psychological and anatomic factors are some of the causes of protracted adolescence that Dr. Berger has omitted.

JAMES A. BRUSSEL, M.D.
New York.

November 23, 1969

Analysis of Student Protests Finds Most Nonviolent, With New Left a Minor Factor

By JOHN HERBERS
Special to The New York Times

WASHINGTON, Jan. 13—The first complete study of student protests last year at colleges and universities shows that most were nonviolent and did not interrupt routine, that new left groups were a minor factor, and that the protesters were less concerned with the Vietnam war and related issues than with conditions on the campuses.

The study, covering 232 campuses from January to June, 1969, was conducted by the Urban Research Corporation of Chicago, a private commercial organization that monitors trends on the domestic scene and prepares reports for a range of groups and institutions.

John Naisbitt, president of the corporation, a former assistant to John W. Gardner when Mr. Gardner was Secretary of Health, Education and Welfare, said that many of the findings "seemed to contradict the general wisdom" about campus protests and disorders.

He said that the formal study and analysis was undertaken when information arriving at the corporation in Chicago "seemed to conflict with many widespread impressions."

The study showed that 215,-000 students actively participated in 292 major protests on the 232 campuses, which have a total enrollment of 2,200,000 or one-third of the national college student population.

Although the study covers only the first six months of 1969, Mr. Naisbitt said that student protests in the current academic year were also monitored and added, "There have been no noticeable trends that contradict the findings."

The corporation compiled a profile of each protest, using a number of sources of information. Each profile was sent to students and administrators involved for corrections and comments. The information was coded for computer analysis. Some of the findings are listed in an advertisement on page 51 of the Wednesday issue of The New York Times, and the omplete study will be published later in a book.

Demands by Blacks

Forty-nine per cent of the 292 protests concerned demands by black students for such concessions as black studies, more black faculty and students, and better facilities.

Forty-four per cent were for more student power—by blacks and whites—and 22 per cent cocerned such war-related issues as military recruiting, the Reserve Officers Training Corps, military research and the war itself.

"The incidence of war as a major factor in protests was far less than the incidence of race or 'student power' issues," Mr. Naisbitt said. "This would tend to contradict major assumptions by national policymakers that an end to the Vietnam war and the draft will end campus problems. The draft, for example, was a major factor in only 1 per cent of all protests."

When students asked for more power, they usually sought a larger voice in policy, not control or veto, the study found. Students sought control in 4 per cent of the protests.

The protests occurred on campuses of all sizes and in every region of the country, but most occurred in large universities with more than 1,000 students. And schools with high admission standards had more protests than the average.

J. Edgar Hoover, director of the Federal Bureau of Investigation, and others have said that New Left political groups were to blame for much of the campus unrest. The study found that the New Left was involved more in white protests than in mixed or black protests, "but the striking finding about white student protests is that they were not dominated by the New Left."

"Students for a Democratic Society and other organizations with identifiably radical views, commitments and rhetoric were active in less than half of the white protests and in only 28 per cent of all protests," the study said.

The study found that 26 per cent of the protests involved blocking entry to classes or occupying a building so that its normal use was restricted. There were injuries in 22 per cent of the protests and property damage in 19 per cent.

Altogether, 3,652 students were arrested, 156 were expelled and 708 were placed on probation. The police were called to the campuses in 19 per cent of the protests.

Blacks were more successful than whites in gaining at least one demand from the authorities.

"Demands made by white students alone and mixed groups were rejected more than twice as often as those made by black students," Mr. Naisbitt said. In 49 per cent of the protests, at least one black demand was met.

The study also found that the longer the protest the more success the students had. Seventy per cent of the protests lasted more than two weeks.

January 14, 1970

What Generation Gap?

By JOSEPH ADELSON

CAN the truth prevail against a false idea whose time has come?

The idea that there is a generation gap is not totally false, perhaps. But it is false enough, false in the sense of being overblown, oversimplified, sentimentalized. This may be too strong a way of putting it. Let us say, then, that the idea of a generation gap is at the least unexamined, one of those notions that seems so self-evident that we yield to it without taking thought, and without qualms about not taking thought.

Once we examine the idea, we find it is almost too slippery to hold. What *do* we mean by a generation gap? Do we mean widespread alienation between adolescents and their parents? Do we mean that the young have a different and distinctive political outlook? Are we speaking of differences in styles of pleasure-seeking: greater sexual freedom, or the marijuana culture? Or do we simply mean that the young and the old share the belief that there is a significant difference between them, whether or not there is?

These questions—and many others one might reasonably ask—are by no means easy to answer. Few of them can in fact be answered decisively. Nevertheless, enough information has been accumulated during the last few years to offer us some new understanding of the young. As we will see, this evidence contains some

Construction by Robert Negrin, a student at the New York School of Visual Arts: ". . . the idea of a generation gap is a form of pop sociology, one of those appealing and facile ideas that sweep through a self-conscious culture from time to time. The quickness with which it has taken hold in the popular culture—in advertising, television game shows and semi-serious potboilers — should be sufficient to warn us that its appeal lies in its superficiality. . . ."

surprises; and persuades us to cast a very cold eye on the more simple-minded views about this young generation and its place in our society.

Parents and Children

ONE definition of generational conflict locates it in rebellion against parental authority, or in the failure of parents and their adolescent youngsters to understand and communicate with each other. (In short, "The Graduate.") On this particular issue, there is, as it happens, abundant evidence, and all of it suggests strongly that there is no extensive degree of alienation between parents and their children. Vern Bengtson, one of the most careful scholars in this area, has collected data from more than 500 students enrolled in three Southern California colleges. About 80 per cent of them report generally close and friendly relationships with their parents; specifically, 79 per cent feel somewhat close or very close, 81 per cent regard communication as good, and 78 per cent feel that their parents un-

JOSEPH ADELSON, professor of psychology at the University of Michigan, is co-author of "The Adolescent Experience."

derstand them all or most of the time.

Essentially similar findings have emerged from Samuel Lubell's perceptive studies of college youth. He reports that only about 10 per cent of the students he interviewed were in serious discord with their parents, and there was in most of these cases a long history of family tension. Any clinician working with college-age students would agree; among the rebellious or alienated, we find that their troubles with their families go back a long way and surfaced well before the college years.

In some respects the findings of Bengtson and Lubell are not really surprising. What they do is bring us up to date, and tell us that a long-established line of findings on adolescence continues to be true. A few years ago my colleague Elizabeth Douvan and I studied 3,000 youngsters of 12 to 18, from all regions of the country and all socio-economic levels. We concluded that there were few signs of serious conflict between American adolescents and their parents; on the contrary, we found that it was more usual for their relationships to be amiable.

The recently published study by psychiatrist Daniel Offer—of a smaller group, but using more inten-

sive methods of scrutiny—arrives at much the same conclusion. Incidentally, there is no support for the common belief that the adolescent is hostage to the influence of his friends and turns away from parental guidance. A number of studies, here and abroad, tell us that while peer opinion may carry some weight on trivial issues—taste, clothing and the like—on more central matters, such as career and college choice, it is parental opinion that counts.

Whatever the supposed generation gap may involve, it does not seem to include deep strains between the young and their parents. The idea of the adolescent's family milieu as a kind of *Götterdämmerung*, as the scene of a cataclysmic struggle between the forces of authority and rebellion, is exaggerated. As Lubell put it: "we found both much less authority and much less rebellion than popularly imagined."

Politics

THOSE who are convinced that there is a generation gap also tend to identify youth in general with radical or militantly liberal beliefs. Thus, the young are sometimes seen as a New Breed, impatient with the political pieties of the past, less subject to that fatigue and corruption of spirit characteristic of the older generation of voters.

There is indeed a generational element in politics; there always has been. But to identify the young with liberal or left militancy makes sense only from the perspective of the élite university campus. Once we look at the total population of the young a decidedly different picture emerges. We have, for example, a brilliant and revealing analysis of the 1968 election by the University of Michigan's Survey Research Center, based upon 1,600 interviews with a representative national sample of voters. Perhaps the most interesting finding was that the under-30 voter was distinctly over-represented in the Wallace constituency, and that the Wallace movement outside the South drew proportionately more of its strength from younger than from older voters.

Some of the center's commentary on generational influences is worth quoting at length. "One of the most important yet hidden lines of cleavage split the younger generation itself. Although privileged young college students angry at Vietnam and shabby treatment of the Negro saw themselves as sallying forth to do battle against a corrupted and cynical older generation, a more head-on confrontation at the polls, if a less apparent one, was with their own age mates who had gone from high school off to the factory instead of college, and who were appalled by the collapse of patriotism and respect for the law that they saw about them. Outside of the election period, when verbal articulateness and leisure for political activism count most heavily, it was the college share of the younger generation—or at least its politicized vanguard — that was most prominent as a political force. At the polls, however, the game shifts to 'one man, one vote,' and this vanguard is numerically swamped even within its own generation."

To overemphasize the role of generational conflict in politics is to ignore or dismiss what we have learned over the years about the transmission of political sentiments in the great majority of cases—it seems to average about 75 per cent in most studies—children vote the same party their parents do; it has often been noted that party preference is transmitted to about the same degree as religious affiliation. Political attitudes are also acquired within the family, though generally less strongly than party affiliation; among studies on this matter there is hardly one which reports a negative relationship between parental attitudes and those of their children.

My own research during the last few years has dealt with the acquisition of political values during ado-

lescence, and it is patently clear that the political outlook of the parents, particularly when it is strongly felt, tends to impress itself firmly on the politics of the child. Thus, the most conservative youngster we interviewed was the daughter of a leader of the John Birch Society; the most radical was the daughter of a man who had—in 1965—ceased paying income taxes to the Federal Government in protest against our involvement in Vietnam.

The strongest recent evidence on this subject seems to come from studies of the student radical. These studies make it evident that the "rebellious" student is, for the most part, not rebelling against the politics he learned at home. Radical activists are for the most part children of radical or liberal-left parents; in many instances, their parents are—overtly or tacitly—sympathetic to what their children are doing. (This is shown in the letters written to the press by parents of the students expelled by Columbia and Chicago; the rhetoric of these letters reveals how strong the bond of political sympathy is between the parents and their children. For instance, a letter from a group of Columbia parents states: "We are, of course, concerned about the individual fates of our sons and daughters, but more so with resisting such pressures against a student movement which has done so much to arouse the nation to the gross horrors and injustices prevalent in our country.")

Values

ARE the young abandoning traditional convictions and moving toward new moral and ideological frameworks? We hear it said that the old emphasis on personal achievement is giving way to a greater concern with self-realization or with leisure and consumption; that a selfish materialism is being succeeded by a more humanistic outlook; that authority and hierarchy are no longer automatically accepted, and are replaced by more democratic forms of participation; that rationalism is under attack by proponents of sensual or mystical perspectives, and so on.

The most ambitious recent survey on this topic was sponsored by Fortune magazine. Fortune seems to believe that its findings demonstate a generation gap and a departure from "traditional moral values" on the part of many of the educated young. A careful look at the survey suggests that it proves neither of these propositions, but only how badly statistics can deceive in a murky area.

The Fortune pollsters interviewed a representative sample of 18-to-24-year-olds, dividing them into a non-college group (largely upward-mobile youngsters interested in edu-

cation for its vocational advantages), and a so-called "forerunner" group (largely students interested in education as self-discovery and majoring in the humanities and social sciences). Some substantial, though not surprising, differences are found among these groups—the "forerunners" are more liberal politically, less traditional in values, less enchanted about business careers (naturally) than the two other groups. But the findings tell us nothing about a generation gap, since the opinions of older people were not surveyed. Nor do they tell us anything about changes in values, since we do not have equivalent findings on earlier generations of the young.

What the findings do tell us (and this is concealed in the way the data are presented, so much so that I have had to recompute the statistics) is, first, that an overwhelming majority of the young—as many as 80 per cent—tend to be traditionalist in values; and, second, that there is a sharp division within the younger generation between, on the one hand, that distinct minority that chooses a liberal education and, on the other, both those who do not go to college and the majority of college students who are vocationally oriented. In brief, the prevailing pattern (of intra-generational cleavage) is quite similar to that which we find in politics.

The Fortune poll brings out one interesting thing: many of those interviewed—well over 80 per cent—report that they do not believe that there are great differences in values between themselves and their parents. This is supported by other investigations. Bengtson's direct comparison of college students demonstrates that they "shared the same general value orientations and personal life goals." He concludes that "both students and parents in this sample are overwhelmingly oriented toward the traditional middle-class values of family and career." From his careful study of normal middle-class high-school boys, Daniel Offer states flatly, "Our evidence indicates that both generations *share the same basic values*" (his italics).

Despite the impressive unanimity of these appraisals, the question of value change should remain an open one. It is hard to imagine that some changes are not taking place, in view of the vast social, economic and technological changes occurring in industrialized countries: the growth of large organizations, shifts in the occupational structure, the rapid diffusion of information, etc., etc. Yet the nature of these changes in values, if any, is by no means evident, and our understanding remains extremely limited.

We simply do not know which areas

of values are changing, how rapidly the changes are taking place, which segments of the population they involve, how deeply they run, how stable any of the new values will turn out to be. Many apparent changes in "values" seem to be no more than changes in manners, or in rhetoric.

All in all, the most prudent assessment we can make, on the basis of the evidence we now have, is that no "value revolution" or anything remotely like it is taking place or is in prospect; and that if changes are occurring, they will do so through the gradual erosion, building and shifting of values.

Pleasure

LET us limit ourselves to the two areas of pleasure where generational differences are often held to be present: sex and drugs. Is there a sexual revolution among the young? And has a drug culture established itself as a significant part of youth culture?

Announced about 10 or 15 years ago, the sexual revolution has yet to take place. Like the generation gap itself, it may be more apparent than real. Support for this statement is provided by the Institute for Sex Research at Indiana University, which has just completed a new study, begun in 1967, in the course of which 1,200 randomly selected college students were interviewed. Comparing the findings with those obtained in its study of 20 years ago, the institute reports increasing liberalism in sexual practices but stresses that these changes have been gradual. One of the study's authors states, "There remains a substantial commitment to what can only be called traditional values." Most close students of the sexual scene seem to agree that the trend toward greater permissiveness in the United States probably began back in the nineteen-twenties, and has been continuing since. Sexual attitudes and habits are becoming more liberal— slowly. We are becoming Scandinavians—gradually.

The sexual changes one notes on the advanced campuses are of two kinds. First, there is a greater readiness to establish quasi-marital pair-ings, many of which end in marriage; these are without question far more common than in the past, and are more often taken for granted. Second, there is a trend, among a very small but conspicuous number of students, toward extremely casual sexuality, sometimes undertaken in the name of sexual liberation. To the clinician, these casual relationships seem to be more miserable than not— compulsive, driven, shallow, often entered into in order to ward off depression or emotional isolation. The middle-class inhibitions persist, and the attempt at sexual freedom seems a desperate maneuver to overcome them. We have a long way to go before the sexually free are sexually free.

As to drugs, specifically marijuana: Here we have, without much question, a sharp difference between the generations. It is a rare citizen over 30 who has had any experience with marijuana, and it is not nearly so rare among the young, particularly those in college. Still, the great majority of youngsters —almost 90 per cent—have had no experience with marijuana, not even to the degree of having tried it once, and, of course, far fewer use it regularly. Furthermore, a strong majority of the young do not believe marijuana should be legalized. What we have here, then, is both a generation gap and (as we have had before) a gap in attitude and experience within the younger generation.

It would be nice if we could keep our wits about us when we contemplate the implications of marijuana for our society. That is hard to do in the presence of hysteria on one side, among those who hold it to be an instrument of the devil, and transcendent rapture on the other, among those who see it as the vehicle and expression of a revolution in values and consciousness. In any case, the drug scene is too new and too fluid a phenomenon for us to foretell its ultimate place in the lives of the young. Drug use has grown rapidly. Will it continue to grow? Has it reached a plateau? Will it subside?

A more interesting question concerns the sociological and ideological factors involved in marijuana use. As marijuana has become more familiar, it has become less of a symbol of defiance and alienation. Lubell points out that just a few years ago the use of marijuana among college students was associated with a liberal or left political outlook; now it has become acceptable and even popular among the politically conservative. From what I have been able to learn, on some campuses and in some suburban high schools drug use is now most conspicuous among the *jeunesse dorée*— fraternity members and the like — where it succeeds or complements booze, and co-exists quite easily with political indifference or reaction and Philistine values. To put it another way, marijuana has not so much generated a new life style—as Timothy Leary and others had hoped—as it has accommodated itself to existing life styles.

*   *   *

IS there a generation gap? Yes, no, maybe. Quite clearly, the answer depends upon the specific issue we are talking about. But if we are talking about a fundamental lack of articulation between the generations, then the answer is — decisively — no. From one perspective, the notion of a generation gap is a form of pop sociology, one of those appealing and facile ideas which sweep through a self-conscious culture from time to time. The quickness with which the idea has taken hold in the popular culture— in advertising, television game shows and semi-serious pot-boilers—should be sufficient to warn us that its appeal lies in its superficiality. From another perspective, we might say that the generation gap is an illusion, somewhat like flying saucers. Note: not a

Carmen Cavazos

Drawing by Carmen Cavazos, a student at City College: ". . . whatever the supposed generation gap may involve, it does not seem to include deep strains between the young and their parents . . ."

delusion, an illusion. There *is* something there, but we err in our interpretation of what it is. There *is* something going on among the young, but we have misunderstood it. Let us turn now to the errors of interpretation which bedevil us when we ponder youth.

Parts and Wholes

THE most obvious conceptual error, and yet the most common, is to generalize from a narrow segment of the young to the entire younger generation. With some remarkable consistency, those who hold that there is a generation gap simply ignore the statements, beliefs and activities of the noncollege young, and indeed of the ordinary, straight, unturned-on, nonactivist collegian. And the error goes even beyond this: on the university scene, the élite campus is taken to stand for all campuses; within the élite university, the politically engaged are taken to reflect student sentiment in general; and among the politically active, the radical fraction is thought to speak for activists as a whole.

It is not surprising to come across these confusions in the mass media, given their understandable passion for simplification of the complex, and their search for vivid spokesmen of strong positions. Thus, the typical TV special on the theme, "What Is Happening to Our Youth?", is likely to feature a panel consisting of (1) a ferocious black militant, (2) a feverish member of S.D.S., (3) a supercilious leader of the Young Americans for Freedom (busily imitating William Buckley), and (4), presumably to represent the remaining 90 per cent, a hopelessly muddled moderate. But we have much the same state of affairs in the quality magazines, where the essays on youth are given to sober yet essentially apocalyptic ruminations on the spirit of the young and the consequent imminent decline (or rebirth) of Western civilization.

Not too surprisingly, perhaps, the most likely writer of these essays is an academic intellectual, teaching humanities or the social sciences at an élite university. Hence he is exposed, in his office, in his classes, to far more than the usual number of radical or hippyesque students. (And he will live in a neighborhood where many of the young adolescents are preparing themselves for such roles.)

On top of this, he is, like the rest of us, subject to the common errors of social perception, one of which is to overestimate the size of crowds, another to be attracted by and linger upon the colorful and deviant. So he looks out of his office window and sees what seems to be a crowd of thousands engaging in a demonstration; or he walks along the campus, noting that every second male face is bearded. If he were to count—and he is not likely to count, since his mind is teeming with insights—he might find that the demonstration is in hundreds rather than thousands, or that the proportion of beards is nearer one in 10 than one in two. It is through these and similar processes that some of our most alert and penetrating minds have been led astray on the actualities of the young; that is why we have a leading intellectual writing, in a recent issue of a good magazine, that there are "millions" of activist students.

It is not surprising, then, that both the mass media and the intellectual essayists have been misled (and misleading) on the infinite variety of the young: the first are focused upon the glittering surface of social reality, the second upon the darker meanings behind that surface (an art brought to its highest state, and its highest pitch, by Norman Mailer). What *is* surprising, and most discouraging, is that a similar incompleteness of perception dominates the professional literature — that is, technical psychological and sociological accounts of adolescence and youth.

Having attended, to my sorrow, many convocations of experts on the young, I can attest that most of us are experts on atypical fractions of the young: on heavy drug users, or delinquents, or hippies, or the alienated, or dropouts, or the dissident—and, above all, on the more sprightly and articulate youngsters of the upper middle class. By and large, our discourse at these meetings, when it is not clinical, is a kind of gossip: the upper middle class talking to itself about itself. The examples run: my son, my colleague's daughter, my psychoanalytic patient, my neighbor's drug-using son, my Ivy League students. Most of us have never had a serious and extended conversation with a youngster from the working or lower-middle classes. In our knowledge of the young we are, to use Isaiah Berlin's phrase, hedgehogs, in that we

know one thing, and know it well, know it deeply, when we also need to be foxes, who know many things less deeply.

What we know deeply are the visibly disturbed, and the more volatile, more conspicuous segments of the upper middle class. These are the youngsters with problems, or with *panache* — makers and shakers, shakers of the present, makers of the future. Their discontents and their creativity, we hear it said, produce the new forms and the new dynamics of our social system. Thus, they allow us to imagine the contours of a hopeful new order of things or, contrariwise, permit us visions of Armageddon.

Perhaps so, but before judging this matter, we would do well to recognize that our narrowness of vision has led us to a distorted view of adolescence and youth. We have become habituated to a conflict model of adolescence—the youngster at odds with the milieu and divided within himself. Now, adolescence is far from being a serene period of life. It is dominated by significant transitions, and like all transitional periods—from early childhood to middle age—it produces more than its share of inner and outer discord. Yet, we have become so committed to a view of the young based upon conflict, pathology and volatility—a view appropriate for some adolescents most of the time and for most some of the time—that we have no language or framework for handling conceptually either the sluggish conformity or the effectiveness of adaptation or the generational continuity which characterizes most youngsters most of the time.

Young and Old, New and Old

ANOTHER common error is to exaggerate the differences between younger and older generations. Differences there are, and always have been. But the current tendency is to assume that anything new, any change in beliefs or habits, belongs to or derives from the country of the young.

This tendency is particularly evident in the realm of politics, especially on the left, where "young" and "new" are often taken to be synonymous. Is this really so? To be sure, the young serve as the shock troops of New Left action. But consider how much of the leadership is of an

older generation; as one example, most of the leaders of the New Mobilization—Lens, Dellinger, Dowd and others—are in their forties and fifties. It is even more significant that the key ideologues of radical politics—such men as Marcuse, Chomsky, Paul Goodman — are of secure middle age and beyond. The young have, in fact, contributed little to radical thought, except perhaps to vulgarize it to a degree painful for those of us who can remember a time when that body of thought was intellectually subtle, rich and demanding.

For that matter, is New Left thought really new—that is, a product of the nineteen-sixties? I was dumfounded several weeks ago when I stumbled across a book review I had written in the nineteen-fifties, a commentary on books by Erich Fromm, Lionel Trilling and the then unknown Herbert Marcuse. My review suggested that these otherwise disparate authors were united in that they sensed and were responding to a crisis of liberalism. The optimistic, melioristic assumptions of liberalism seemed to be failing, unable to cope with the alienation and the atavistic revivals produced by technological civilization.

Thus, even in the sunny, sleepy nineteen-fifties a now-familiar critique of American society was already well-established. The seminal ideas, political and cultural, of current radical thought had been set down, in the writings of C. Wright Mills, Marcuse, Goodman and others, and from another flank, in the work of Norman O. Brown, Mailer and Allen Ginsberg. That sense of life out of control, of bureaucratic and technological things in the saddle, of malaise and restlessness were, in the nineteen-fifties, felt only dimly, as a kind of low-grade infection. In the middle and late nineteen-sixties, with the racial explosion in the cities and our involvement in Vietnam, our political and cultural crisis became, or seemed to become, acute.

What I am getting at is that there is no party of the young, no politics indigenous to or specific to the young, even on the radical left. The febrile politics of the day do not align the young against the old, not in any significant way. Rather, they reflect the ideological differences in a polarized nation.

What we have done is to misplace the emphasis, translating ideological conflict into generational conflict. We have done so, I believe, because it suits our various psychological purposes. On the left, one's weakness in numbers and political potency is masked by imagining hordes of radicalized youth, a wave of the future that will transform society. On the right, one can minimize the intense strains in the American polity by viewing it, and thus dismissing it, as merely a youth phenomenon—kid stuff. And for the troubled middle, it may be easier to contemplate a rift between the generations than to confront the depth and degree of our current social discord.

Present and Future

A THIRD error we make is to see the mood of the young—as we imagine that to be—as a forecast of long-term national tendencies. In our anxious scrutiny of youth, we attempt to divine the fu-

ture, much as the ancients did in their perusal of the entrails of birds. Yet consider how radically the image of the American young has changed within as brief a period as a decade.

Ten years ago, we were distressed by the apparent apathy and conformism of the young, their seeming willingness, even eagerness, to be absorbed into suburban complacency. We were dismayed by the loss of that idealism, that amplitude of impulse we felt to be the proper mood of the young. By the early nineteen-sixties we were ready to believe that that lost idealism had been regained; the prevailing image then was of the Peace Corps volunteer, whose spirit of generous activism seemed so much in the American grain. And for the last few years we have been held by a view of youth fixed in despair and anger.

It should be evident that these rapid shifts in our idea

of the young run parallel to changes in the American mood. As we moved from the quietude of the Eisenhower years, to the brief period of quickened hope in the Kennedy years, to our current era of bitter internal conflict dominated by a hateful war and a fateful racial crisis, so have our images of youth moved and changed. Yet, we were in each of these earlier periods as willing as we are today to view the then current mood of youth, as we saw it, as a precursor of the social future.

The young have always haunted the American imagination, and never more so than in the past two decades. The young have emerged as the dominant projective figures of our culture. Holden Caulfield, Franny Glass, the delinquents of the Blackboard Jungle, the beats and now the hippies and the young radicals—these are figures, essentially, of our interior land-

scape. They reflect and stand for some otherwise silent currents in American fantasy. They are the passive and gentle — Holden, Franny and now the flower children — who react to the hard circumstances of modern life by withdrawal and quiescence; or else they are the active and angry — the delinquents and now the radicals — who respond by an assault upon the system.

In these images, and in our tendency to identify ourselves with them, we can discover the alienation within all of us, old and young. We use the young to represent our despair, our violence, our often forlorn hopes for a better world. Thus, these images of adolescence tell us something, something true and something false, about the young; they may tell us even more about ourselves.

January 18, 1970

Problems of Youth

To the Editor:

Most of us share a concern for the youth of this country and recognize that we owe them more than just food and shelter. Most of us are disturbed by the extreme measures many young people are taking to effect change.

On the one hand the continuing difficulty young black people have in finding a place in our society, and on the other hand, the rejection of the society by the white youth, is causing a growing rift between the youth and the adults who represent this society.

Black fathers are blamed be-

cause they allow the "establishment" to deprive their sons and daughters of their human rights. White fathers are blamed because they are the "establishment" which causes these deprivations.

We are all in trouble because we are letting our youth lead us. We are, by default, watching young people burn, destroy, and flaunt our laws or drop out, shoot heroin and lose all interest in us or life, while we stand by waiting for somebody to do something. We look to the school, the police, the government or anywhere except to ourselves for the answer.

There are values in our cul-

ture which should be defended, not by paying lip service to them but by showing that they work. Some of our ideas are unworkable today and should be discarded. Only by working with, playing with, and living with our young people can we and they solve our mutual problems. The Black Fathers Association is exploring this possibility. We hope you will join us.

ROBERT MITCHELL
President
Black Fathers Association
New Brunswick, N. J.
April 2, 1970

April 21, 1970

Nixon Puts 'Bums' Label On Some College Radicals

By JUAN de ONIS
Special to The New York Times

WASHINGTON, May 1 — President Nixon referred today to some campus radicals who violently oppose his Vietnam policies as "bums" and, in contrast, he said American soldiers were "the greatest."

The President's remarks on violence at universities and the war were made to a group of civilian employes who greeted him at the Pentagon, where he went for a briefing on the new

United States military operations in Cambodia.

Mr. Nixon was cheered by public response to his television speech on Cambodia last night. Ronald L. Ziegler, White House press secretary, said telephone calls and telegrams received since Mr. Nixon spoke were "positive" in a ratio of six to one.

One such favorable comment came from a young woman in

a group of Pentagon employes who told the President: "I loved your speech. It made me proud to be an American."

Smiling and obviously pleased, Mr. Nixon stopped and told how he had been thinking, as he wrote his speech, about "those kids out there."

"I have seen them. They are the greatest," he said. Then he contrasted them with antiwar activists on university campuses. According to a White House text of his remarks, he said:

"You see these bums, you know, blowing up the campuses. Listen, the boys that are on the college campuses today are the luckiest people in the

world, going to the greatest universities, and here they are burning up the books, storming around about this issue. You name it. Get rid of the war there will be another one.

"Then out there we have kids who are just doing their duty. They stand tall and they are proud. I am sure they are scared. I was when I was there. But when it really comes down to it, they stand up and, boy, you have to talk up to those men. They are going to do fine and we have to stand in back of them."

The President's use of the term "bums" to refer to student radicals was the strongest language he has used publicly on the subject of campus violence, although he has been known to employ such terms in private.

Mr. Nixon's visit to the Pentagon this morning began a day that ended with his flying by helicopter to his Camp David retreat for a weekend of relaxation with his family and close friends.

Before departing from the capital, Mr. Nixon proclaimed Sunday a national day of prayer for all American prisoners and servicemen missing in action in Southeast Asia.

He was accompanied to the Pentagon by Henry A. Kissinger, his special assistant, and was briefed for one hour and 40 minutes by Secretary of Defense Melvin R. Laird and high miiltary officials in the presence of the Joint Chiefs of Staff.

On leaving, Mr. Nixon commented:

"I did what I believed to be right. What really matters is whether it comes out right."

According to Mr. Ziegler, the information given the President indicated that the operations in Cambodia across the South Vietnam border "appear to be going well."

Mr. Ziegler said the President stayed up after his speech last night until about 1:30 A.M., receiving visitors and talking by telephone with "friends and officials around the country."

May 2, 1970

4 Kent State Students Killed by Troops

8 Hurt as Shooting Follows Reported Sniping at Rally

By JOHN KIFNER
Special to The New York Times

KENT, Ohio, May 4—Four students at Kent State University, two of them women, were shot to death this afternoon by a volley of National Guard gunfire. At least 8 other students were wounded.

The burst of gunfire came about 20 minutes after the guardsmen broke up a noon rally on the Commons, a grassy campus gathering spot, by lobbing tear gas at a crowd of about 1,000 young people.

In Washington, President Nixon deplored the deaths of the four students in the following statement:

"This should remind us all once again that when dissent turns to violence it invites tragedy. It is my hope that this tragic and unfortunate incident will strengthen the determination of all the nation's campuses, administrators, faculty and students alike to stand firmly for the right which exists in this country of peaceful dissent and just as strongly against the resort to violence as a means of such expression."

In Columbus, Sylvester Del Corso, Adjutant General of the Ohio National Guard, said in a statement that the guardsmen had been forced to shoot after a sniper opened fire against the troops from a nearby rooftop and the crowd began to move to encircle the guardsmen.

Frederick P. Wenger, the Assistant Adjutant General, said the troops had opened fire after they were shot at by a sniper.

"They were under standing orders to take cover and return any fire," he said.

This reporter, who was with the group of students, did not see any indication of sniper fire, nor was the sound of any gunfire audible before the Guard volley. Students, conceding that rocks had been thrown, heatedly denied that there was any sniper.

Gov. James A. Rhodes called on J. Edgar Hoover, director of the Federal Bureau of Investigation, to aid in looking into the campus violence. A Justice Department spokesman said no decision had been made to investigate.

At 2:10 this afternoon, after the shootings, the university president, Robert I. White, ordered the university closed for an indefinite time, and officials were making plans to evacuate the dormitories and bus out-of-state students to nearby cities.

Robinson Memorial Hospital identified the dead students as Allison Krause, 19 years old, of Pittsburgh; Sandra Lee Scheuer, 20, of Youngstown, Ohio, both coeds; Jeffrey Glenn Miller, 20, of 22 Diamond Drive, Plainview, L. I., and William K. Schroeder, 19, of Lorain, Ohio.

At 10:30 P.M. the hospital said that six students had been treated for gunshot wounds. Three were reported in critical condition and three in fair condition. Two others with superficial wounds were treated and released.

Students here, angered by the expansion of the war into Cambodia, have held demonstrations for the last three nights. On Saturday night, the Army Reserve OOfficers Training Corps building was burned to the ground and the Guard was called in and martial law was declared.

Today's rally, called after a night in which the police and guardsmen drove students into their dormitories and made 69 arrests, began as students rang the iron Victory Bell on the commons, normally used to herald football victories.

A National Guard jeep drove onto the Commons and an officer ordered the crowd to disperse. Then several canisters of tear gas were fired, and the students straggled up a hill that borders the area and retreated into buildings.

A platoon of guardsmen, armed—as they have been since they arrived here with loaded M-1 rifles and gas equipment—moved across the green and over the crest of the hill, chasing the main body of protesters.

The youths split into two groups, one heading farther downhill toward a dormitory complex, the other eddying around a parking lot and girls' dormitory just below Taylor Hall, the architecture building.

The guardsmen moved into a grassy area just below the parking lot and fired several canisters of tear gas from their short, stubby launchers.

Three or four youths ran to the smoking canisters and hurled them back. Most fell far short, but one landed near the troops and a cheer went up from the crowd, which was chanting "Pigs off campus" and cursing the war.

A few youths in the front of the crowd ran into the parking lot and hurled stones or

United Press International

GUNS ON CAMPUS: Policeman, backed by National Guardsman, taking gun from youth at Kent State campus yesterday.

small chunks of pavement in the direction of the guardsmen. Then the troops began moving back up the hill in the direction of the college.

Students Cheer

The students in the parking lot area, numbering about 500, began to move toward the rear of the troops, cheering. Again, a few in front picked up stones from the edge of the parking lot and threw them at the guardsmen. Another group of several hundred students had gathered around the sides of Taylor Hall watching.

As the guardsmen, moving up the hill in single file, reached the crest, they suddenly turned, forming a skirmish line and opening fire.

The crackle of the rifle volley cut the suddenly still air. It appeared to go on, as a solid volley, for perhaps a full minute or a little longer.

Some of the students dived to the ground, crawling on the grass in terror. Others stood shocked or half crouched, apparently believing the troops were firing into the air. Some of the rifle barrels were pointed upward.

Near the top of the hill at the corner of Taylor Hall, a student crumpled over, spun sideways and fell to the ground, shot in the head.

When the firing stopped, a slim girl, wearing a cowboy shirt and faded jeans, was lying face down on the road at the edge of the parking lot, blood pouring out onto the macadam, about 10 feet from this reporter.

The youths stood stunned, many of them clustered in small groups staring at the bodies. A young man cradled one of the bleeding forms in his arms. Several girls began to cry. But many of the students who rushed to the scene seemed almost too shocked to react. Several gathered around an abstract steel sculpture in front of the building and looked at a .30-caliber bullet hole drilled through one of the plates.

The hospital said that six young people were being treated for gunshot wounds, some in the intensive care unit. Three of the students who were killed were dead on arrival at the hospital.

One guardsman was treated and released at the hospital and another was admitted with heat prostration.

In early afternoon, students attempted to gather at various area of the Commons but were ordered away by guardsman and the Ohio Highway Patrol, which moved in as reinforcements.

There were no further clashes, as faculty members,

graduate assistants and students leaders urged the crowd to go back to the dormitories.

But a bizarre atmosphere hung over the campus as a Guard helicopter hovered overhead, grim-faced officers maneuvered their men to safeguard the normally pastoral campus and students, dazed, fearful and angry, struggled to comprehend what had happened and to find something to do about it.

Students carrying suitcases and duffel bags began leaving the campus this afternoon. Early tonight the entire campus was sealed off and a court injunction was issued ordering all students to leave.

A 5 P.M. curfew was declared in Kent, and road blocks were set up around the town to prevent anyone from entering. A state of emergency was also declared in the nearby towns of Stow and Ravenna.

Statement by General

KENT, Ohio, May 4 (UPI)— Brig. Gen. Robert Canterbury, the commander of Guard troops on the Kent State campus, said today that no warning had been given to the students that the troops would shoot.

General Canterbury, at a campus news conference, said in reply to questioning that no official order had been given to open fire.

"The situation did not allow it," he said. "The emotional atmosphere was such that anything could have happened. It was over in two to three seconds."

He said a guardsman "always has the option to fire if his life is in danger."

"A crowd of about 600 students had surrounded a unit of about 100 guardsmen on three sides and were throwing rocks at the troops," he said. "Some of the rocks were the size of baseballs. The troops had run out of tear gas."

Governor Rhodes, who had ordered the National Guardsmen onto the campus Saturday after students began looting stores and breaking windows in the downtown area, said "a complete investigation" would be made into the shootings.

Dr. White, the university president, said:

"Everyone without exception is horror-struck by the tragedy of the last few hours. Unfortunately, no one is able yet to say with certainty what the facts of the situation are.

"There are many unconfirmed reports of gunfire from various sources," he went on. "We are asking for every possible appropriate investigation, which we shall undertake to pursue to the limit."

May 5, 1970

Two State Systems Shut

Illinois Deploys Guard

By FRANK J. PRIAL

More than 80 colleges across the country closed their doors yesterday for periods ranging from a day to the remainder of the academic year as thousands of students joined the growing nationwide campus protest against the war in Southeast Asia.

In California, Gov. Ronald Reagan, citing "emotional turmoil," closed down the entire state university and college system from midnight last night until next Monday. More than 280,000 students at 19 colleges and nine university campuses are involved.

Pennsylvania State University, with 18 campuses, was closed for an indeterminate period.

In the New York metropolitan area about 15 colleges closed, some for a day, some for the week, and some for the rest of the term.

A spokesman for the National Student Association said that students had been staying away

from classes at almost 300 campuses in the country.

Most, but not all, of the protesters eschewed violence. In Illinois, Gov. Richard Ogilvy ordered 5,000 National Guardsmen to duty at locations all over the state, with about 2,000 of them assigned to the Champaign-Urbana area, site of the downstate campus of the University of Illinois.

About 1,500 students clashed with the police there during the afternoon. One student and three policemen were reported injured. A similar clash was reported at Northwestern University, in Evanston, near Chicago.

Leaders on most campuses plan to organize participation Saturday in a national antiwar demonstration in Washington. At American University in Washington, the police fired tear gas at 1,000 demonstrators last night. Four policemen were hurt by rocks, and 17 protesters were arrested.

Other student groups, notably at Columbia University, Harvard University and the University of Rochester, organized support for a recently proposed Congressional amendment that would cut off funds for the war in Southeast Asia.

A spokesman for Senator

George S. McGovern, Democrat of South Dakota, one of five sponsors of the amendment, said the Senator's office had been in touch with "scores" of student leaders who voiced an interest in working for the amendment as an alternate to what they deemed less constructive forms of protest.

The amendment to the Defense Procurement Authorization bill is expected to reach the Senate floor in about 30 days.

At Brandeis University, in Waltham, Mass., a group called the National Student Strike Information Headquarters said it had counted 240 schools, mostly in the Northeast, where the students had voted to strike.

In Oberlin, Ohio, representatives of 15 northern Ohio colleges met and formed a coalition to combine student reaction to the Administration's Southeast Asian policies. The coalition called for a march Friday on Columbus and participation in the Saturday demonstration in Washington.

Similarly, representatives of 12 Eastern law schools met at New York University Law School to prepare for their participation in Saturday's demonstration in the Capital.

At least one government leader, New Jersey's Republican Governor, William T. Cahill, has responded to the student protests by criticizing the Administration's Southeast

Asian policies.

Governor Cahill, a supporter of Mr. Nixon, said he was personally disappointed by the President's decision to send troops into Cambodia, but added that he did not approve of student demonstrations as an effective way to protest that decision.

His statement came as 1,500 students from Rider and Trenton State Colleges, two New Jersey schools, marched on the New Jersey State House in Trenton to protest the war and the shooting to death of four students at Kent State University in Ohio.

Governor Cahill left the building as the students arrived, and an aide read his statement.

At the University of Kentucky, the state police and National Guardsmen "with mounted bayonets and live ammunition" were on hand in Lexington to enforce a dusk-to-dawn curfew.

Gov. Louie B. Nunn ordered the police and troops onto the campus when some 750 students ignored a 5 P.M. curfew.

At the University of Wisconsin in Madison, 3,500 students battled police all afternoon yesterday following a 1 P.M. rally. The university is officially open, but classroom attendance was light and some classes had to be ended because tear gas from the fighting drifted through campus buildings.

In Austin, Tex., former Ambassador John Kenneth Galbraith pleaded with 5,000 University of Texas students and sympathizers at a campus rally to avoid violence. There, had been threats yesterday to burn the Capitol in Austin.

"You are no longer an embattled minority," Mr. Galbraith said, as hundreds of policemen stood by, "but a majority and I ask you to maintain the discipline of a majority."

President Nixon was burned in effigy at least two campuses, the University of Cincinnati and Syracuse University. His impeachment was demanded by faculty members of five western Massachusetts colleges, including the ones attended by

his daughter, Julie, and his son-in-law, David Eisenhower.

The schools were the University of Massachusetts, Amherst, Smith, Mount Holyoke and Hampshire Colleges. Julie Nixon Eisenhower attends Smith; her husband attends Amherst.

The same group also called for the impeachment of Vice President Agnew for "crossing state lines with the intent of inciting riots."

One of the most singular protests was planned by Haverford College, a Quaker school in Haverford, Pa. There, the entire faculty, administration and student body voted to go to Washington tomorrow for discussions with Congressional leaders and to join Saturday's protest rally.

The following is a partial list

of colleges and universities that have announced they are closing:

All 19 state colleges and nine university campuses in California (through Sunday); Kent State University (indefinitely); all 18 campuses of Penn State University (indefinite); Boston University (end of term); Brown University (end of term); Tufts University (end of term); University of Notre Dame (end of week); Northwestern University (end of week); Bennington College (indefinite); Massachusetts Institute of Technology (end of week).

Also, the University of Connecticut (indefinitely); Seton Hall University (end of term); Princeton University (end of term); Rutgers University (indefinite); Sarah Lawrence (indefinite); Finch College (through Sunday).

Also Ohio State University (indefinitely); Fairleigh Dickinson University (indefinitely); C. W. Post College (indefinitely); Hofstra University (indefinitely); Syracuse

University (indefinitely); Brooklyn Polytechnic Institute (end of term).

Also University of New Mexico (through Sunday); Southampton College of Long Island University (until June 4); Manhattanville College (indefinite); Marymount College (indefinite).

Also Bronx Community College (indefinite); Hunter College (through Friday); City College of New York (through Friday).

Also, Adelphi University (end of week); Nassau Community College (end of week); Potsdam State University (undetermined); Queens College (through today); New School for Social Research (end of week); Manhattan Community College (through today); Siena College (undetermined); Wells College (undetermined); Paterson State College (end of week); Montclair College (end of term); University of Akron (through Saturday).

May 7, 1970

HICKEL, IN NOTE TO NIXON, CHARGES ADMINISTRATION IS FAILING YOUTH

AGNEW CRITICIZED

Discontent Is Believed Spreading in Ranks of Government

By MAX FRANKEL
Special to The New York Times

WASHINGTON, May 6 — In an extraordinary letter of protest, Secretary of the Interior Walter J. Hickel complained to President Nixon today that the Administration was turning its back on the great mass of American youth and thereby contributing to anarchy and revolt.

Mr. Hickel warned that further attacks by Vice President Agnew on the motives of young Americans would solidify their hostility beyond the reach of reason. Communication with them is still possible, he said, and alienation of them is wrong both politically and philosophically.

'Youth Must Be Heard'

Though carefully avoiding any frontal criticism of the President, Mr. Hickel complained that Mr. Nixon was ignoring his Cabinet officers, failing to make contact with

experienced community leaders and overlooking the lessons of history.

The lesson of the American Revolution by such "youth" as Patrick Henry, Thomas Jefferson, James Madison and James Monroe, he wrote, was that "youth in its protest must be heard."

The Hickel letter, which became available to newspapers within hours of its transmission to the White House, betrayed a deep-seated sense of frustration that is known to be shared by several members of Mr. Nixon's Cabinet. It was symbolic also of an even deeper discontent that is evident in the lower ranks of the Government and is inspiring widespread talk of resignation and protest.

Impact of Cambodia

Many different events, policies and examples of Presidential style have fed this discontent. It has been fueled by feelings of dismay over the handling of racial issues, the President's heated confrontations with Congress, the tone even more than the content of Mr. Agnew's speeches and the feeling that Mr. Nixon was slipping even further into isolation and under the influence of a parochial group of advisers.

It came to the fore here after

The New York Times
Secretary Walter J. Hickel

the sudden decision to move troops into Cambodia, the President's denunciation of some campus radicals as "bums" and the wave of student protest culminating in the death of four students at Kent State University. The head of the Administration's Office of Students and Youth, Anthony J. Moffett Jr., plan to resign tomorrow with a statement condemning the Administration, and several members of his staff are talking about resigning. Morale at the State Department has been described as particularly

low and several young Foreign Service officers report a widespread interest in resignation.

There is discontent in the White House, too, though it is usually expressed as unhappiness with Mr. Agnew's rhetoric. Aides say Mr. Nixon was disturbed by the Vice President's recent call for the ouster of Kingman Brewster Jr., president of Yale. But they think Mr. Nixon has also been impressed by the signs that Mr. Agnew's oratory is politically popular and advantageous.

Over the last 48 hours, however, there have been indications of a White House response to the discontent. The Justice Department was instructed to take an unusually conciliatory attitude toward the students massing here for protest marches this weekend. And Mr. Nixon today scheduled his first televised news conference since Jan. 31 for Friday.

Mr. Hickel is the father of six sons — aged 8 to 28 — including two in college and two at home. Like other Cabinet members with children of college age, he has been gaining insights into young people's thoughts that he has found lacking at the White House. He is known to have discussed his concern with Secretary of State William P. Rogers and other Cabinet officials, though he wrote to Mr. Nixon on his own behalf.

May 7, 1970

JACKSON POLICE FIRE ON STUDENTS

2 Killed and 12 Injured at Women's Dormitory

Special to The New York Times

JACKSON, Miss., Friday, May 15—Two persons were killed and 12 wounded early today after the police opened fire on a women's dormitory at Jackson State College here.

Fifteen students were carried out of the dormitory after the shooting. It was not determined immediately whether they had been wounded or cut by flying glass.

A heavy, concentrated barrage of gunfire, lasting seven to 10 seconds, was directed at the building. Students in front of the building dropped to the ground to take cover. The police said they returned fire after someone had shot at them.

[On five other campuses the police battled protesters Thursday, but elsewhere, the nationwide student antiwar protest appeared to have abated.]

National Guard troops moved onto the Jackson State campus after rock and bottle-throwing erupted for the second straight night.

There were conflicting reports as to how Wednesday night's disorder began. Several students said it was triggered by a white youth passing out antiwar leaflets, and others said it started when a handful of nonstudents started pelting passing cars. Sixteen persons were arrested.

There was no immediate explanation of why the disorder resumed.

Police Battle Protesters

By FRANK J. PRIAL

The police used gas yesterday on students at the Ohio University at Athens and at the University of Maryland campus in College Park, broke up a rock and paint-throwing session at Indiana University and battled with demonstrators at Eastern Michigan University in Ypsilanti and at Illinois State University.

Despite these incidents, however, the nationwide antiwar protest seemed to have abated.

Representatives of 250 colleges and universities met at Yale to plan constructive antiwar activities to replace that part of the student demonstrations in the last two weeks that has been violent.

As for those who support President Nixon on the war, New York City construction workers called off a parade and rally in lower Manhattan today. Instead, they will stage a giant rally in front of City Hall next Wednesday which they promised would be peaceful.

At a dinner at the Americana hotel, Mayor Lindsay asked the American Jewish Committee to try to ease tensions among ethnic groups to defuse the present explosive conflicts growing out of disagreements over the war.

At Ohio University, police wearing dungaree cover-alls hurled tear-gas cannisters into a crowd of more than 1,000 students who formed on the campus and marched toward the downtown area, throwing some rocks at a bookstore and smashing windows in a police cruiser. More than 1,000 National Guardsmen troops, alerted when disturbances broke out Wednesday night, remained on standby duty.

The Ohio University incident was apparently prompted by the suspension of seven students on Wednesday and the refusal by the university's president, Claude W. Sowle, to close the university in sympathy with the death of the four Kent State University students and opposition to the Vietnam war.

At the University of Maryland, one guardsman was reported injured by a missile thrown by students retreating down U.S. Route 1 near the campus. Guardsmen and state troopers marching shoulder to shoulder cleared the highway of 5,000 students.

Earlier, a group of students seized the administration building. A student strike has closed the university since May 1.

Eight Indiana University students were arrested in Bloomington when 300 demonstrated because classes were not suspended as they were at other colleges.

In Ypsilanti, streets were littered with broken glass, furniture and burned barricades after Eastern Michigan University students protested an 8 P.M.-to-5 A.M. curfew. The police used tear gas for the third night to confine the students to dormitories.

At Illinois State, an assistant dean was hospitalized with head injuries after a melee between 40 students and an equal number of policemen. There, too, students were challenging a night-long curfew.

In New York, a group of construction workers withdrew a request for a Police Department permit to stage a parade and rally at noon today. At the same time, the president of the Building and Construction Trades Council, Peter Brennan, said his group was planning a rally for Wednesday in City Hall Park.

Mr. Brennan said in a statement that the building trades unions hoped to have Wednesday declared "a special flag day," and urged supporters of the Nixon Administration's war policy to fly the flag on that day.

Alma Mater Bombed

Also in New York, a bomb partially damaged the statue of Alma Mater at Columbia University. The explosion, which occurred before dawn, tore a hole in the side of the statue. No one was injured, but the blast was heard for several blocks in the Morningside Heights area.

Later in the day, the police arrested three City College students on charges of breaking into R.O.T.C. offices in Townsend Harris Hall last week and destroying $5,000 worth of Government property.

They were Margot Goodman, 21 years old, of 245 East 180th Street, the Bronx; Ben Zion Ptashnik, 20, of 154-51 20th Road, Whitestone, Queens, and Robert Stirbl, 21, of 382 Wadsworth Avenue.

The incident followed a protest march of 2,000 students on May 5, the day after the fatal shootings of four students at Kent State University.

At Manhattan Community College, 134 West 51st Street, 58 students were arrested on charges of criminal trespass when, according to the police, they attempted to interfere with classes. Some teachers and administrators said antiwar protesters had terrorized other students, pulling them out of class and threatening them, even though the police were in the building at the time.

At New York University, the University Senate voted to "terminate as soon as legally possible" the school's relations with R.O.T.C. A spokesman said that the university's contract with the Air Force required a year's notice, but it was believed that the contract could be ended before then. A contract with the Army calls for termination "by mutual agreement."

At Rutgers University in New Brunswick, N.J., however, the board of governors overruled a faculty decision and voted to continue R.O.T.C. at the state school. Under the faculty plan, no incoming freshman in the class of 1974 would have been able to enroll in the military training program.

May 15, 1970

Voices of Fisk '70—

By C. ERIC LINCOLN and CECIL ERIC LINCOLN

NASHVILLE, Tenn.

THE Revolution has visited Fisk University in Nashville, as it has most other American colleges. But with a difference. Perhaps Fisk itself is different, as it perceives itself to be. Founded in 1866, the school is alma mater to generations of influential blacks, among them the late W. E. B. Du Bois, probably the most celebrated scholar Black America has produced; Congressman William Dawson of Chicago; A. Maceo Walker, millionaire Memphis banker and insurance company president; John Hope Franklin, chairman of the department of history at the University of Chicago, and Frank Yerby, best-selling novelist. While Fisk has a scattering of white students, the school has always considered itself to represent the aristocracy of "Negro" education, and the "Fisk tradition," though contested by other good schools like Morehouse in Atlanta, still suggests to many black households the best education available at a black college.

The Fisk graduate, class of '70, sees his situation as unique in a society torn between change and the *status quo ante*. He has learned the ambivalence and the anxieties of the black intellectual long before becoming one. It is as though his whole college career were a cleverly masked preparation for somehow surviving in a society so fraught with contradictions as to require some special psychological armor, or some chameleon versatility, "to make it." The Fisk student accepts and rejects the Fisk pattern for success and adjustment. He wants to make it in the world, but he does not like the kind of

"The law can be made to work. The system is the best we know about"

"We want a black university"

"You get power by being associated with power"

"The Fisk student is cool"

"The problem with this country is not race, it's war"

"Black people have always been motivated to get into the system"

world that is offered to him His ambivalence and frustration produce attitudes and behavior which are clearly inconsistent, and which are symptomatic of his longing for a respectable place in the society and his fear that he may succumb to values he cannot wholly accept.

For example, political science and government are popular courses, and a good proportion of Fisk graduates go to law school. Yet the Fisk student is contemptuous of both major political parties; and President Nixon's sustained but abortive support of Judge Carswell's nomination to the Supreme Court was interpreted as an official, cynical example of the quality of justice white America wants dispensed from the bench. Who can be for "law and order" if that is what it means?

The war in Southeast Asia has produced no protest at Fisk, and when the news media erroneously reported that Fisk students were involved in a demonstration over the expansion of the Vietnam conflict into Cambodia, the misrepresentation was highly resented. "It was a deliberate attempt on the part of the white press to make us look like fools," one student said. "We couldn't care less about Nixon and Cambodia. We've got problems here in Nashville."

Although Fisk maintains student exchange programs with several white colleges (such as Carleton, Colby, Whittier, Dartmouth), when the four students at Kent State University were killed by the National Guard, the reaction at Fisk was subdued. A student leader explained: "We were sorry the students were killed,

C. ERIC LINCOLN, M.A., Fisk '54, is a professor of sociology and religion at Union Theological Seminary. His son, **CECIL ERIC LINCOLN**, Fisk '69, is now a student at the University of Tennessee Law School.

but we saw no reason to get uptight about it. State troopers killed four black students at South Carolina State and another at Texas Southern, and nobody remembered to even call 'the law,' much less march on Washington." He paused for a moment in mock reflection. "But then, you see, we are used to being killed by 'the law,' and used to having it forgotten the next day."

A few days after this conversation, when six black youths were shot and killed by police in Augusta, Ga., and two students were gunned down by police at Jackson State College in Mississippi, several hundred Fisk students marched on the Fisk faculty complex demanding that representations be made to President Nixon to "stop the official slaughter of black people." Later the same night Livingstone Hall, a historic old dormitory being used as a classroom building, was burned. One Fisk freshman was arrested, but investigating authorities were inclined to believe the burning was prompted by some kind of national conspiracy.

The ambivalence toward institutionalized values even extends to such organizations as the Peace Corps, which is as taboo on the Fisk campus as it is on most other black campuses, though possibly for different reasons. Most black students simply cannot afford two years of financially unproductive engagement, but the Fisk student sees the corps as diversionary. "It takes your eye off The Man and your mind off The Problem," says a student, "and it takes you out of the country and out of The Action." The draft is viewed similarly; according to one student, it is "a diversionary tactic to get you iced for awhile—or if they're lucky, for good!" Most Fisk students try to avoid the draft as long as they can, within the limits of the law. However, there is no tradition there for draft-dodging or for leaving the

country to escape military duty.

THE one issue which has shaken the Fisk community more than any other has been the demand by some students that Fisk become a "black" university, beginning with its key faculty appointments. This is a very sensitive issue, and one which by implication challenges the basic scheme of education at Fisk. Fisk has always had a racially mixed faculty, and one could say that a substantial white presence is a salient aspect of the "Fisk tradition."

In the old days, many of the white teachers went to Fisk in the missionary spirit—when no black teachers were available. Others spent their retirement years at Fisk after a career of teaching at Northern or foreign universities. A few accepted no pay or refunded their paychecks to the school. Some, like the distinguished sociologist Robert Park, were accomplished scholars of international fame. Some others, like historian Theodore Currier, came "young" and spent their entire careers at Fisk. Still others, like historian August Meier (now at Kent State), stayed only a few years and moved on to other schools.

The proponents of the black university idea think it is time for *all* white instructors to move on—the sooner, the better. It is not just the white professors, however. In the words of William Owens, a Fisk senior, "It is the whole white-minded establishment at Fisk; it is all the symbols and trappings of the white man's stranglehold on the black mind that has to go. We want a *black* university."

WHAT is Fisk? Harvard University professors Christopher Jencks and David Riesman in their 1968 study, "The Academic Revolution," placed Fisk "at the head of the Negro academic procession." As far as most Fisk people are concerned, the Jencks-Riesman evaluation is gratuitous. The book caused a furor in black academic circles, which criticized it as being patronizing, insensitive and replete with errors of fact and judgment. But whatever the merits of the Harvard study, Fisk has always seen itself as first-rate, period; not just first among Negro colleges.

Fisk is a small school, as colleges go these days. Scarcely 10 minutes from downtown Nashville, it manages a student body of fewer than 1,300 on a campus of 40 acres. Its original campus was an expanse of blackberry bushes and honeysuckle surrounding the abandoned gun factory in which it was founded a year after the Civil War. A Union

315

officer, General Clinton B. Fisk, provided the impetus that founded the school—and gave it his name — and the American Missionary Association nurtured and applauded its growth for the next hundred years.

The Missionary Association was made up primarily of white New England Congregationalists who founded a number of schools and colleges in the South to educate emancipated blacks after the Civil War. But a more romantic legend which persists with the force of history is that Fisk was founded for the emerging Negro middle class, made up of the mulatto sons and daughters of the vanquished Southern gentry. The fact is that there was no "emergent Negro middle class" in 1866, but there did indeed emerge a *color* aristocracy which had its roots in the social structure of the plantation system. Color consciousness became at least a peripheral aspect of the "Fisk tradition," and remained so until the contemporary Black Revolution made color differences between black Americans everywhere taboo as a social value—or at least drove them underground.

BY most conventional standards, Fisk is a good school. The teacher-student ratio is about 1 to 12. Fifty members of the full-time faculty and 12 part-time instructors have earned doctorates from some of the world's most prestigious universities — Chicago, Yale, Stanford, Bombay, Munich, Havana, Columbia, Purdue and M.I.T., to name some of them. The president —hulking, affable, James (Big Jim) Lawson—is a physicist with a bachelor's degree from Fisk and a doctorate from the University of Michigan. Out of 226 members of the Fisk graduating class (two-thirds of them women), 75 per cent will go on to graduate or professional school.

To be admitted to Fisk, a student must rank in the upper third of his graduating class and take the College Entrance Examination Board tests. An early admissions program accepts exceptional students who have completed the 11th grade. Room, board, tuition and other fees run in the neighborhood of $2,500 a year. Once he has been admitted, the student has a variety of educational and extracurricular options open to him. He may work toward the usual undergraduate bachelor of arts or bachelor of science degree,

Michelle Moore. *Campus moderate and a second-generation Fisk woman, she has a scholarship to Harvard Law School. After getting her law degree, she plans to give some of her time to blacks in the ghetto. "But I don't want to make a crusade of it," she adds. "I want security for myself and my family."*

or on the graduate level, he may pursue study in seven departments, including religion and sociology. A recently effected agreement provides for limited cross-registration of students at Fisk, Vanderbilt, Scarritt and Peabody Colleges. Undergraduates may play football with the Fisk "Bulldogs," join a fraternity or a modern dance group or sing with the Fisk University Choir or the Fisk Jubilee Singers.

The famous Jubilee Singers are among the firsts at Fisk. When the college was founded, the students who enrolled did not have any money—being fresh from the stifling embrace of slavery. But they did have talent. They could sing. And they were fired with a determination to improve themselves, their college, and their race. As it turned out, the Fisk Jubilee Singers became a world-renowned company of black men and women singing their own songs—the Negro spirituals—before the world's most distinguished and discriminating audiences. They sang in Boston, New York, Philadelphia and Washington before the great names of American society and philanthropy, and they sang before European royalty. When they came home again, they brought enough money to insure the survival of their college and to build Jubilee Hall, four

stories of proud red brick in the antebellum style, which crowns a modest hill on the campus. This was the first permanent structure ever built for Negro education; if the Fisk tradition can be said to have a beginning, it began with the Jubilee Singers who took the black man's art and scholarship to the critical corners of the world, and returned in triumph to build a monument to their success.

The Fisk Jubilee Singers claimed international attention for three quarters of a century, but times change. Negro spirituals are no longer in vogue. Least of all is there much interest in performing them before white audiences, here or abroad. Today's Fisk student is turned off by the notion of performing for "whitey." He wants to find some other basis for evaluating his talent and his worth, and in his groping he has occasionally stumbled over the feet of the establishment, and not infrequently, his own.

WILLIAM OWENS is a symbol of the frustration and rage experienced by this generation of black youth, who feel that their revolution is perpetually derailed by the white man's presence and power in the "Negro" institutions they want to make black. But Owens is also

frustrated by the apathy and the obstruction of other blacks (or "Negroes," he would call them) of his own generation who may or may not engage in the rhetoric of black militance, but who are not anxious to be "locked in a black bag" if it means the renunciation of traditional values for which they have been taught to compete.

In what the students called a "Week of Reckoning" that began on Dec. 8, 1969, Owens, who was president of the student government, led a demonstration to have Fisk converted into a "black university"—which was defined as "an institution structured, controlled, and administered by black people ... devoting itself to the cultural needs of the black community ... identifying all black people as Africans ... and that addresses itself completely to black liberation." The demands made on the Fisk administration included "the removal of all white departmental a. administrative heads," and the severance of ties with "white institutions and foundations" not in sympathy with the notion of a black university.

The "Week of Reckoning" was aborted largely for lack of support from Fisk students, and 14 of the organizers, including Owens, were sus-

316

pended. He subsequently became president of "the student government in exile," carrying on his efforts from an off-campus apartment. The dissidents relieved their frustration (and revealed their ambivalence) by breaking windows in the school's new Main Library.

Owens does not fit the stereotype of the frothing-at-the-mouth black militant so beloved of the news media. The son of a Henderson, N. C., tobacco worker, he is quiet, controlled, persuasive. His task would be formidable at any erstwhile Negro college; at Fisk it is, for the time being, clearly improbable. "I came here," he confesses, "because all my life I had heard that this was a great college. The best. I figured that if it was the best, it would be doing something for black people. It isn't. It's still trying to teach them to be white. All of its emphasis is on job security, with none on the black man's need for power."

He is only half right. The need for power is recognized, but not necessarily the need for *black* power. The structure and the history of Fisk have committed it to finding power for its graduates where the power is—in existing institutions; and the Fisk students themselves are not convinced that this is not the place to look. "You can't create power out of no power," one student who is impatient with Owens' arguments insists. "You get power by being associated with power."

George Sampson, a transfer student from Morehouse, described Owens (with whom he is in basic agreement) as "too far ahead of his time. Like Che in Bolivia—too far ahead of the people." Sampson sees the Fisk student as being supersophisticated. "The Fisk student is cool. He's so cool, he's uncool. He listens to what Bill Owens is talking about, and then puts him down. It sounds great—but there ain't no bread in it. The issues Bill Owens is talking about are not issues we want to confront." The Fisk women "don't even give the Black thing the courtesy of listening," he complains. "They are all caught in an 'Edge of Night' [a TV soap opera] syndrome. You know—eating chocolates and thinking about how they can marry some cat who can make it for them in the suburbs. The brothers are no better. We're not together."

Owens agrees with Sampson about Fisk women. "They come in here *black* as fresh-

man," he says. "But then they pledge to the sororities and graduate into the 'Edge of Night.' The Afro is *in* at Fisk. Fisk women change their hair, but they don't change their minds."

MICHELLE MOORE is a Fisk woman, second generation. She is 21 years old, prim and pretty, and comes from San Francisco. If Bill Owens is the symbol of the alienated, frustrated black minority, Michelle poses an interesting contrast. As they sat in a booth rapping on the merits of revolution, Michelle, articulate and self-confident, ate a full Southern breakfast of sausage, eggs and grits; Owens jabbed gently with his finger and made short gestures with his cup of coffee ("No, thank you; I don't want any breakfast. Black people spend too much time eating!"). Michelle identifies with the need for a black revolution. "But it should occur," she says, "within the system. The law can be made to work. The system is the best we know about. The system doesn't corrupt the people. It's the people who corrupt the system. To tear down the system when you've got nothing to put in its place doesn't look much like progress to me."

At this point she is interrupted by an unidentified student playing cards in the next booth. "Yeah, baby, you're right. There's nothing wrong with this country that a little depopulation at the top won't cure!" Michelle does not think the men at Fisk are highly motivated, at least not during their campus years. "They spend their time goofing off, and expect the Fisk women to take care of them."

What does Michelle want? "I want to be a lawyer," she confides. "My grandfather has a good law practice in Washington. I want security for myself and my family—for my children. I can't see myself married to a man who is married to a revolution — black or otherwise. I'm interested in urban law, and when I have a practice, I expect to give some of my time to the problems of black people in the ghetto. But I don't expect to make a crusade of it. I want to help, but I want my own life, too." Michelle has a full scholarship to Harvard Law School.

Cheryl Armstrong is a sociology major who expects to go to graduate school. She likes to talk, and she has some original opinions on the state of things at Fisk and in the

larger world. She explains with a sober kind of tolerance that "the Fisk administration is not structured in a way that makes the introduction of new ideas possible. Patience and rejection is the Fisk defense against noncomprehension," she explains, "so we go around and round in circles of inanity." As for a black university, Cheryl says, "it isn't necessary that a black university be restricted to black people, but it should definitely have a black mentality. Money is more valuable than life in the United States, and the lives of black people are the least valued of all. A black university could ultimately offer some protection —economic, political, intellectual—to the black community."

At this point Cheryl was seconded by a senior who insisted that his name was not important, but who wanted to "make a couple of points we need to be clear on." The points: (1) A black university should accept all the white money it can get—"Who else has any money, and how did The Man get it?" (2) The courses at Fisk and elsewhere are irrelevant to the needs of black people in this kind of a world—"We need to know how to live as people whose existence makes a difference in the whole world. We aren't just a handful of niggers in a white man's country. That's *his* jive!"

Paula Livingston, who comes from Kansas City, Mo., is impatient with the black university idea. She is magnificently groomed, reminiscent of the "Fisk woman" of a decade ago. She is very attractive, but she is also pragmatic. "Let's face it," she says, "the kind of black university they're talking about is impossible. I feel that when I better myself I'm bettering my race *and* my country. We can't have Black Power without green power. We don't need a fantasy. We need money!"

BOBBY GUNN, the son-in-law of Fisk's president, Dr. Lawson, blames the racial situation on "the military-industrial-complex build-up." As he sees it, "The problem with this country is not race, it's war. Eliminate the war and you'll eliminate most racial tensions." Gunn, who is majoring in history, believes that every man has an obligation to his race *and* to his country, but "the way this country is geared makes conflict inevitable." He is sympathetic to the notion of a black university,

but when a group of students sought to occupy the president's office during the "Week of Reckoning" he assisted in their physical removal. "A lot of good ideas get lost in bad methods," Gunn declares.

William Bowens, who comes from a Nashville family of very modest means, wants to succeed within the system. He got into Fisk on a football scholarship, as did three brothers who preceded him. "Class structures will always exist," Bowens believes, "but racial discrimination of *any* kind is outmoded and childish." William Bowens, who studied history, aspires "to make it to the top without forgetting where I came from." The top? "The top is being at a point where you can be content with yourself, whether you are a professor, or whether you are a pimp."

Most Fisk students are more definite about where they want to go, and what being a success means. Herman Kelso, who comes from a poor family in a small town in southern Alabama, is a case in point. Kelso, who is the president of his fraternity, came to Fisk on a scholarship and studied economics: "Only the man with the dollar can have any influence on change in this society. It is one dollar, one vote." Kelso is going to medical school.

One of the most respected students at Fisk is Walter Searcy of Chicago, who spent three years preparing to become an architect. He sees Fisk as "a microcosm of the black community." "Black people have always been motivated to get into the system," he says, "so we have Fisk." Searcy plans "to take whatever expertise I have acquired at Fisk and elsewhere, and use it in the community to benefit black people."

Another student who rates high in popular acclaim is Lloyd Arrington, president of the senior class, who headed a caucus which tried to impeach William Owens as president of the student government. "The system must be changed from within," is the way Arrington sees it. "No handful of radicals can dictate what is best for everyone."

MEMBERS of the class of 1970 are self-conscious about their blackness and its implications in the kind of a world into which they are graduating, for they do not know yet how to resolve the dilemma of being black *and* middle-class. Nor do any of the rest of us. There are

Predictably, the "Real Fisk People" do not understand the class of '70

inherent contradictions there. These students are all black, but they are not all *black*. Nor are they all of one mind, obviously. The heroes they are willing to be publicly identified with run the gamut from Che Guevara to novelist John O. Killens (who was a resident writer at Fisk for a year) to Malcolm X. Martin Luther King is not usually mentioned, and James Baldwin, in one student's view, is "a cat we had to read in Black Lit." One can only guess who their private heroes are.

Predictably, they are not understood by the "Real Fisk People," older alumni for whom merely being at Fisk was in itself an accomplishment.* Take Bill Collier, who came to Fisk from Athens, Ala., in 1932, traveled with the Jubilee Singers, and stayed on after graduation to run a couple of small businesses he had founded while in college. "They don't ask the

---

*Fisk credentials still confer a kind of automatic status upon its graduates, although a distinction is made between the Real Fisk People—the true believers — and those who merely *went* to Fisk or happened to work there. As one R.F.P. put it, "Some of those 'other' people wandered in here and tumbled out after four years, and never knew where they were. Or why."

right questions, so they don't get the right answers," he says of the contemporary Fisk students. "They just don't know the ramifications of the situation." Collier, the president of the Nashville Alumni, stands in the doorway of his haberdashery and dry cleaning shop and looks across Jefferson Avenue at the back of Jubilee Hall. "We must have been doing something right over there," he muses half to himself. "Look at all the famous people we've turned out."

The probability is that the current crop of graduates are, for all the rhetoric of some, similarly motivated, and will produce their share of John Hope Franklins, Frank Yerbys, and perhaps a few A. Maceo Walkers as well. Certainly, that is an opinion supported by what their professors say of them. Dr. David Driscoll, professor of art, says: "True, our students are more aware, more community-minded, and this detracts from traditional academics. But our students are security-minded. There is lots of rhetoric, but few of them will ever use art as a revolutionary instrument."

Dr. Driscoll is echoed by Prof. Theodore Currier who has been at Fisk since 1929. Dr. Currier, who is white, sees the contemporary students as being in a "psychological straddle," characterized by "a

marked reluctance to take responsible positions on this black nonsense. Brighter students these days avoid controversy," he laments, "and the noise emanates from the least qualified." In 1964, a hundred Fisk alumni honored Professor Currier with a book of essays, 300 testimonial letters, a scroll and a purse of money. "That made me feel pretty good," he declares. "So how can you expect me to pay any attention to some shallow brain screaming, 'Go home, honky?' Go home? It's the silly-willies who need to go home! *This is Fisk!*"

To Dr. Lawson, who is in his second year as president, "change is inevitable, but Fisk will have orderly change." Dr. Lawson is very proud of the fact that "Fisk is a Phi Beta Kappa college —the first black one. We have demonstrated our quality and need not rely on the imitation of other colleges to know what is academically wholesome and viable." He adds: "We do not have to worry about living up to standardized yardsticks held up to … by the educational establishment."

This is not all presidential rhetoric. Fisk has made changes in its curriculum and some lesser capitulations of academic style to indicate its awareness of the new black

sensitivity. There is an African-Caribbean Studies Center, for example, offering a fair selection of interdisciplinary courses on the Black Experience; the center is headed by Prof. Chike Onwuachi, a Nigerian scholar well-known in the movement for black ethnicity. There is also an independent Center for Afro-American Studies, and the famous Institute of Race Relations, jointly sponsored by the university and the American Missionary Association. The Ford Foundation has given Fisk a grant of $300,000 for research on the Negro community.

Altogether, this would seem to constitute a respectable interest in the Black Experience at Fisk. It does not, however, signal a commitment to the notion of a black university. For President Lawson, it represents an attempt to "create at Fisk an environment of cultural diversity attractive to black and white students and faculty." To Bill Owens, the "exiled" student leader, "centers dependent on foundation money, and a few courses here and there with 'Negro' or 'black' in their titles, tell you that Fisk is still deep in a dream." To the class of 1970, now turned out to confront first-hand the raw contradictions of America's expectations for them, the Fisk experience, with its own contradictions, may after all be more consonant with present reality than any other. But for how long?

June 7, 1970

Agnew vs. Spock

Vice President Spiro T. Agnew speaking in Milwaukee, Wis., on Sept. 25, 1970:

Let me give you some everyday examples of the kind of permissiveness that has insinuated its way into our behavior.

A permissive parent sees his child come to the dinner table wearing dirty clothes, his hands unwashed and his hair unkempt. The parent finds this offensive and turns to Dr. Spock's book—which has sold over 25 million copies in the past generation—for guidance. He reads this on that subject: "As usual, you have to compromise. Overlook some of his less irritating bad habits, realizing that they are probably not permanent." The thing to be carefully avoided, says our foremost authority on children, is "bossiness."

Who do you suppose is to blame when, ten years later, that child comes home from college and sits down at the table with dirty, bare feet and a disorderly faceful of hair?

Dr. Benjamin Spock in "Baby and Child Care":

Good-hearted parents who aren't afraid to be firm when it is necessary can get good results with either moderate strictness or moderate permissiveness. On the other hand, a strictness that comes from harsh feelings or a permissiveness that is timid or vacillating can each lead to poor results. The real issue is what spirit the parent puts into managing the child and what attitude is engendered in the child as a result.

I think that good parents who naturally lean toward strictness should stick to their guns and raise their children that way. Moderate strictness—in the sense of requiring good manners, prompt obedience, orderliness—is not harmful to children so long as the parents are basically kind and so long as the children are growing up happy and friendly. But strictness is harmful when the parents are overbearing, harsh, chronically disapproving, and make no allowance for a child's age and individuality.

October 3, 1970

PRESIDENT'S PANEL WARNS SPLIT ON YOUTH PERILS U.S.; ASKS HIM TO FOSTER UNITY

VIOLENCE SCORED

Near-Civil War Feared Unless Division of Society Is Ended

By JACK ROSENTHAL

Special to The New York Times

WASHINGTON, Sept. 26 — The President's Commission on Campus Unrest appealed to President Nixon today to lead Americans back from the brink of what it described as a chasm in society so dangerous that it threatened the survival of the nation.

The division between established society and the new youth culture generates intensifying violence by both sides, the commission said. Unless it is stopped, the nation could disintegrate into near-civil war— "a brutal war of each against all," the unanimous commission warned in its final report.

All Sides Criticized

In strong, often passionate terms, the commission condemned with impartial fervor fanatical student terrorists, complacent campus officials, brutal law enforcement officers and vindictive acts and inflammatory words of politicians.

The commission, though it had only 90 days to prepare its report, offered dozens of detailed recommendations to universities, law enforcement agencies and government for avoiding or allaying campus disorder.

But what it called its most important recommendation for future action was directed to Mr. Nixon.

Pointedly recalling a theme of Mr. Nixon's inaugural address, the commission said, "It is imperative that the President bring us together before more lives are lost and more property destroyed and more universities disrupted."

Nixon Accepts Report

This was regarded as bold language for a Presidential commission. Nevertheless, Mr. Nixon personally accepted the report today from William W. Scranton, the chairman, in a meeting with the nine commissioners.

Mr. Nixon, who will not be able to study the report until he returns from Europe Oct. 6, made no direct comment on it. But sharp differences soon appeared, at least between his staff and the commission.

Under questioning today, Robert H. Finch, counselor to the President, said that on visits to campuses this fall, "I've been pleasantly surprised by the different climate."

Mr. Scranton, however, later told reporters he did not think the President or the Administration shared the commission's deep sense of urgency.

"Since last spring, up to this minute, there has not been the kind of leadership [needed] to bring about the kind of reconciliation that we're talking about," he said.

"The divisions are far deeper, far more compelling, and growing far faster than most Americans realize," he added.

Mr. Finch said the President had ordered the report sent out immediately to Governors, educators, and others in categories addressed by the commission. He alluded to the contrast between this reaction and the chilly silence from President Johnson when the controversial Commission on Civil Disorders published its report in 1968.

The Scranton commission was appointed by Mr. Nixon last June, following the killing of students by law enforcement officers at Kent State University in Ohio and Jackson State College in Mississippi. Its mission was to investigate the cause of and propose possible solutions to the disorders that have afflicted hundreds of campuses and to repot by Oct. 1

Separate investigative reports on Kent and Jackson will be issued next week.

To officials at various levels of government, the commission urged an end to the war in Southeast Asia; an end to harsh, divisive rhetoric; better planning for disorder; new off-campus alernatives to reserve officer training, and extensive assistance to black universities.

In the law enforcement sector, the commission sharply assailed the use of rifles and bayonets on campus. 'Sending civil authorities onto a college campus armed as if for war— armed only to kill—has brought tragedy in the past. If this practice is not changed, tragedy will come again," it said.

The report called for providing nonlethal weapons like tear gas to national guardsmen and for rules to insure that deadly force was used "only as the absolute last resort."

In a long list of recommendations to universities, the commission urged that they refocus on teaching and learning, as opposed to outside research and private consultancies for "entrepreneurial professors."

Larger universities, more susceptible to disorder, should decentralize to a more human scale, the report said. It further contended that all universities should remain politically neutral, while upholding personal and academic freedom, and all curriculums should be adapted to the new youth culture, with more flexible teaching methods and scheduling.

The commission urged students to recognize that "giving moral support to those who are planning violent action is morally despicable," to seek wider agreement by using less offensive language and to recognize that their own moral intensity could not automatically determine national policy.

The commission said that peaceful dissent must be defended, even encouraged, but asserted, "We utterly condemn violence. We especially condemn bombing and political terrorism." It continued:

"Students who bomb and burn are criminals. Police and national guardsmen who needlessly shoot or assault students are criminals. All who applaud these criminal acts share in their evil."

Violence, however, is only one part of a dual crisis on the campus, the report declared. The second, a crisis of understanding, was identified as the underlying cause of campus unrest.

This crisis of understanding, the commission said, flows from the development of the new youth culture. There is a growing lack of tolerance, a growing arrogance among members of this culture—and a growing rn to terror among a small minority of its members, the commission said. It continued:

"At the same time, many Americans have reacted to this emerging culture with an intolerance of their own. Distinctive dress alone is enough to draw insult and abuse. Some even say that when dissenters are killed, they have brought death upon themselves."

Addressing those on both sides of this division, the commission said:

"If this crisis of understanding endures, the very survival of this nation will be threatened. A nation driven to use the weapons of war upon its youth is a nation on the edge of chaos."

"A nation that has lost the allegiance of part of its youth is a nation that has lost part of its future.

"A nation whose young have become intolerant of diversity, intolerant of the rest of its citizenry and intolerant of all traditional values simply because they are traditional, has no generation worthy or capable of assuming leadership in the years to come."

The commission addressed a series of issues commonly regarded as causes of student unrest—the war in Southeast Asia, racial injustice, unresponsive universities and student perceptions of governmental repression.

The war must end, the report said, social justice must be realized, universities must be reformed and Government must take care to avoid appearing repressive.

Role of Affluence

But these actions, however necessary, would only allay, not remedy the fundamental cause of crisis, according to the commission. That cause, the great and growing gulf between the new culture and the old, is intensified but not created by issues like Vietnam, the commission said.

The members of the new youth culture are "part of the first generation of middle-class Americans to grow up in the post-depression American welfare state under the tutelage of a parental generation which embodied the distinctive moral vision of modern liberalism," the report said. It continued:

"The children, brought up in conditions of affluence and freedom from worldly struggle, began to live what their parents mostly preached. And as they brought their parents' high-minded ideals to bear upon American society in a thorough-going way, their vision of that society changed radically."

These young people, the commission said, are not only idealistic but also contemptuous of history and past experience and distrustful of liberal democracy. Such characteristics turn the puzzlement of older citizens into anger, the commission

319

said, continuing:

"Hostilities then intensify, the likelihood of violence and death increases, and civil society can disintegrate into a brutal war of each against all.

"We emphasize that the nation is not now in any such condition, but we must also warn that it could come to that if the escalation of hostility and fear does not stop."

The only way to bring about that halt is through a period of reconciliation—for which Presidential leadership is a critical necessity, the commission said. It explained:

"Only the President can offer the compassionate, reconciling moral leadership that can bring the country together again.

"Only the President, by example and by instruction, can effectively calm the rhetoric of both public officials and protesters whose words in the past have too often helped further divide the country, rather than unite it."

After receiving the report today, an aide said, the President told the commission members: "I can assure you that your report will be controversial. But don't worry about that. Worry if it isn't controversial. We don't want a bunch of intellectual eunuchs around here."

September 27, 1970

NIXON CONTESTS SCRANTON REPORT ON HEALING RIFTS

In Letter to Head of Panel on Unrest, He Cites Dispute on 'What Problems Are'

UNDERSTANDING URGED

Responsibility for Disruption of Campuses Is Attributed to Academic Community

By JACK ROSENTHAL
Special to The New York Times

WASHINGTON, Dec. 12 — President Nixon strongly contested today the principal recommendation of his Commission on Campus Unrest that he must lead the nation back from the brink of ominous divisions over social problems.

"There are widely divergent views within our society as to just what our problems are," he said, and no minority "has veto power over a President's decision to do what he believes is right in the nation's interest."

College students, he noted pointedly, make up 4 per cent of the population.

Cool to Some Themes

The commission made its report to the President 11 weeks ago. His response came in a letter to William W. Scranton, the chairman.

The letter endorsed some of the commission's recommendations, particularly those denouncing violence, and said the report was receiving close attention. But Mr. Nixon appeared cool to some of the report's major themes.

The commission identified multiple reasons for student unrest, including the war, social injustice, divisive official rhetoric, crude law enforcement methods, complacent campus administrators, a handful of fanatical young terrorists and a larger body of students who tolerate violence.

Panel Fears Chaos

But the President, using almost identical language twice in his letter, asserted that the responsibility for disruption "rests squarely on the shoulders" of some members of the academic community.

The commission pleaded for enlarged public understanding of the new "youth culture," declaring that "a nation driven to use the weapons of war upon its youth is a nation on the edge of chaos."

Mr. Nixon called for enlarged understanding by youth of their parents' generation. Overcoming depression, war and want, he said, "are not the achievements of a generation of men and women lacking either in idealism or courage or greatness."

Neither Mr. Scranton nor other members of the commission were willing to comment immediately on the President's letter, although several said they might make statements after reading it.

Mr. Nixon disclosed at his news conference Thursday that he had written the seven-and-one-half-page letter. He deferred comment until Mr. Scranton had received it.

The President praised several aspects of the commission report. He welcomed its emphatic condemnation of violence as a way to force social change and its view that Government cannot and should not assume responsibility for maintaining campus order.

History Endorsed

He also endorsed the report's history of student protest and its call for responsiveness by universities, and he noted that he had referred a number of specific recommendations to appropriate Cabinet officers for review.

The President not only stressed his belief that responsibility for unrest belongs on campuses, but he also contested additional causes described by the commission.

As to the war and social injustice, he said his Administration had "diminished America's involvement in the Asian war" and had made "new advances against America's ancient injustice — discrimination."

He did not respond directly to the commission's charges of divisive official rhetoric, but he praised national leaders who have denounced violence and said that "high in that category I would place the Vice President of the United States."

Agnew Not Named

The commission's criticism did not name the Vice President, but commission members have said their conclusions applied to speeches he made during the fall campaign.

The President also took exception to the commission's analysis of the youth culture. Just as that culture may have many adherents in the older generation, he said, "so also the traditional culture of American life has millions of adherents within the younger generation."

Mr. Nixon's most detailed rebuttal involved the commission's appeal for moral leadership.

"We will not pretend that it is easy for a President to inspire a diverse people or to set the tone for a nation: it is not," the commission report said.

"Yet he must strive to do just that. Especially in this time of division, every American must find in the President's leadership some reflection of what he believes and respects," the report said.

The President described this task as far more complex than it might appear. Even the views advanced by the commission, he said, range from those with widespread appeal to those "that may be shared by only a small minority."

Such differences reflect the vigorous opposition often confronted by a President, he said, "to his person, his policies, and his programs."

"But final determination in these maters must rightly rest with the elected representatives of all the American people," the President said.

In any event, the President said, moral leadership is not limited to the Presidency. The public looks also to thousands of others—clergy, teachers, public officials, scholars and writers, he said.

Mr. Nixon made few comments about either the law enforcement section of the commission's general report or about the panel's subsequent analyses of the killing of students last May at Kent State University in Ohio and Jackson State College in Mississippi.

These events, coupled with scores of campus disorders after the United States incursion into Cambodia, prompted the appointment of the commission.

The President did say, however, that "law enforcement officers should use only the minimum force necessary in dealing with disorders when they arise."

"A human life—the life of a student, soldier, or police officer—is a precious thing, and the taking of a life can be justified only as a necessary and last resort," Mr. Nixon said.

December 13, 1970

'The Horatio Alger Thing Is Dead'

By MICHAEL T. KAUFMAN

WITH its strewn volumes of Kurt Vonnegut Jr., Tom Wolfe and Hermann Hesse, and with the constant blare of George Harrison's new record coming from the stereo system, the cellar apartment on West 108th Street radiated the freedom of action of today that Charles A. Reich has called Consciousness III.

But amid all these complementing appurtenances of the youthful ethos, the conversation in the living room—furnished in Salvation Army eclectic — struck a jarring dissonance: Leonard Rose, a 22-year-old college senior and one of the tenants of the apartment, was discussing an offer he had received to join his uncle in a family printing business in California.

The offer involves a good salary, security, a chance for promotion and there is even the possibility that he could someday take over the business. It was right out of Professor Reich's Consciousness II, which he described in his book, "The Greening of America," as representing the values of an "organizational society."

For Leonard Rose and the flock in his living room, it was a cause of anxiety.

●

Mr. Rose is to graduate from City College this month with a degree in political science. For the last four years he has supported himself through intermittent periods of work as a cab driver, a merchant seaman, a bookstore clerk and a waiter. His average income in that time, he says, has been about $2,000 a year.

"Now I'm being offered about $10,000, and with the job situation being what it is, I doubt if I could get more anywhere else," he said, talking out one side of the argument he was having with himself. "I like my uncle and I've really nothing against business as such.

"But I don't know if I could take the hassles. I mean my uncle said I wouldn't have to shave my beard, but I don't know. And then you've got to put in all that time, and I guess you've really got to care more about making money than I do to like that sort of thing."

"What's wrong with making money?" asked Sam Millstein, a premedical student who is Mr. Rose's roommate.

"Not a damn thing, but it's all the time it takes," answered Mr. Rose. "Now, what I'd really like is to pull a miracle, make a lot of it and make it quickly. You know, do something that answers a need, that no one's done before."

The interloper in their midst, a man firmly rooted in Consciousness II½, asked them to name the heroes who had made miracles.

Kenneth Kessler, a senior political science major, replied, "The guy who made the first Humphrey Bogart poster, Bill Graham, the rock concert promoter, Dylan, people like that."

The conversation returned to Leonard Rose's dilemma. What, someone asked, did he think of the whole idea of business? "Wow," he said laughing. "Look, everybody I know is in business."

Then, with what seemed like a bit of bravado, the youths described the business enterprises of their acquaintances, all dealing with the marijuana trade, and all parodying conventional business enterprises.

"Some guys I know formed a partnership and they are looking to invest in a field," said one of the youths with the same tone that some of their elders use when discussing possible killings in soybean futures."

●

Mr. Kessler noted, humorously, that the illegal drug traffic aped the conventions of business. "Sometimes you listen to guys talking about Acapulco or Panama Red, about packaging and marketing techniques, of seasonal price fluctuations, and you have to laugh.

"I mean, these are the same guys who come down on their fathers for checking the stock tables every morning. I guess it's just a case of history repeating itself, the first time as tragedy, the second time as farce."

One of those present, a young law school student who asked that his name not be used, said that he was being drawn to "the kind of thing that Ralph Nader is doing, or legal and for the poor."

His father, a Wall Street lawyer, has different plans for him. "He thinks I'll be going to the Street and I haven't told him different, since he's paying my tuition."

The tall, clean-shaven youth continued, "I guess that social consciousness has a lot to do with it. I mean, how much are corporations putting into the struggle to clean up the environment? Not even 1 per cent of the advertising budgets, I'll bet. But I'd be lying if I said that was my main opposition. Basically, it's that everything is so dull in big business."

●

The group in Mr. Rose's living room all agreed that "the Horatio Alger thing is dead," at least as far as joining a big corporation was concerned. The youths all agreed that they could conceive of joining small business enterprises, as one said, "with no great separation between executive responsibility and actual production work."

And through the meandering discussion, Mr. Rose continued to waver in his choice. He could, he said at one point, go to sea again, and he has over the last year thought of starting a carpentry shop with his friends. Then, too, there is Vista, the domestic peace corps, but that doesn't pay enough.

Perhaps, he said, he'll write his uncle to say he'll join him on a provisional basis, say for six months, just to see how it is.

It is impossible to say whether the youths in the room were typical of their generation. Some of the things they said have been supported by a recent report showing that Harvard Business School graduates are becoming increasingly interested in jobs with smaller companies rather than the traditional prestigious and remunerative positions with major corporations.

And the increased rate of change in regard to consciousness makes almost anything possible. Perhaps Leonard Rose will buy a Brooks Brothers suit and shave his beard in two months. Perhaps he will be taking clients to lunch. Perhaps he will ship out to Marseilles.

January 10, 1971

Census Study Finds An 'Education Gap'

By JACK ROSENTHAL
Special to The New York Times

WASHINGTON, Feb. 3 — A Census Bureau study released today shows an explosive growth in the amount of education obtained by young Americans in the last 30 years.

The growth is so dramatic, scholars said, that what has been regarded as a generation gap is shown largely to be an education gap.

The study reports that the proportion of young adults with college degrees has almost tripled since 1940, going from 6 to 16 per cent.

The proportion of those with one or more years of college has more than doubled, going from 13 to 31 per cent.

And the proportion of those with at least a high school diploma has risen from 38 to 75 per cent.

These changes, to a greater degree than age differences, explain present social and political conflicts, authorities said today.

Theordore Newcomb, a professor of psychology and sociology at the University of Michigan said it was clear form extensive research that those who had attended college were generally more liberal in their attitudes toward politics, sex, child-rearing and religion than those who had not.

Education a Factor

"And there is much more in common between the educated young and the educated old," he said, "than between the educated young and the less-educated young."

The census report, based on a survey taken every 10 years, also offered the following aspects of a statistical profile of American youth:

¶The median age of the population dropped in 1970 to 27.6 years, the lowest since 1930. But the 1970 figure will be the lowest for the foreseeable future. As post-World War II babies age, the median age will rise, reaching an estimated 30 years by 1985.

¶The total number of young people—those aged 14 to 24—jumped 47 per cent since 1960 to 40 million. They now make up 20 per cent of the population, a 5 per cent increase over 1960. The 20 per cent figure is the highest since 1940. In

1910, young people constituted 22 per cent of the population.

¶The number of college students mushroomed from 4.6 million in the 1964-65 school year to 7.4 million in 1969-70. The number of black college students increased from 234,-000 to 492,000. In the decade, blacks went from 5 to 7 per cent of the college population. They compose 11 per cent of the population.

¶Young people are getting far more education than their parents. The fathers of nearly two-thirds of present college students did not go beyond high school.

¶Of all young people aged 16 to 24, 43 per cent are in school, 33 per cent are working, 7 per cent are in the service, 3 per cent are unemployed, and 14 per cent are not in the labor force. Young male college graduates average about $6,500 annual income. Their female counterparts average about $5,900.

In states where those under so far less frequently than their elders. In November, 1968, only 33 per cent voted, compared with 70 per cent of those over 25.

To population and education authorities, the most striking findings of the survey were those dealing with educational achievement.

"It is absolutely unprecedented in world history to have 75 per cent of an age group with at least a high school education," said Kenneth Kenniston of Yale University, a leading student of the youth culture.

"We're very much into a kind of society that has never existed before. No one can guess the full impact of these wide educational gains. But they certainly mean that a large segment of society will be more literate, more capable of dealing with complexity, less attached to the traditional pieties," he said.

"And social conflicts do flow from increased education. A person attached to traditional concepts accepts the idea of law and order, for instance. The college-educated person is more likely to ask, 'Is the law a just law?'"

In the view of James Q. Wilson, a Harvard political scientist, increases in college enrollment cannot come fast enough to offset the potential for such social conflicts.

"For a long time to come, we'll be a society divided between an élite of college graduates and a majority who have virtually no real exposure to a four-year college, with all the social and attitudinal differences that implies," he said.

Paul Weaver, who directed the preparation of the report of the President's Commission on Campus Unrest, said the new findings might help allay social tension.

"It's easier for society to deal with generational differences," he said, "if it recognizes that they flow from an educational reason. It is less threatening, less mystical than all the current generation gap talk."

The educational gains of the last generation pose two issues, cause and effect, according to Herman P. Miller, director of Census Bureau population studies.

More-affluent parents, he said, can afford to pay for increased education for their children, and an increasingly technical society requires it for employment.

"With a high school diploma, you can drive a bus for a transcontinental bus company. Without it, you're lucky to get a job with the podunk transit company."

But wahtever the causes, the effects are pronounced, he said, "We know from many different studies that college graduates hold different values. They tend to be more liberal politically, more concerned with the society around them than with their own particular needs. It's entirely possible that some, if not much, of what we call the generation gap is related to education," he said.

February 4, 1971

Census Reports a Drop In Median Age to 27.9

WASHINGTON, Jan. 16 (AP)—The median age of the United States population is 27.9 years, the Census Bureau reported today—higher than many people had thought.

The report, an updated one on characteristics of American youth, said that although the present median age was lower than it was in 1960, it was still high in relation to what it had been historically.

The bureau said that Americans widely believed that more than half of the population was under 25.

The new report shows a drop of 1.6 years in the median age between the 1960 census and 1971. During that time, the youth segment of the population—persons between the ages of 14 and 24—increased by 53 per cent, from 27.1 million to 41.6 million.

Youths made up 20 per cent of the 1971 population and only 15 per cent of the 1960 population, the Census Bureau said.

January 17, 1972

Working Youth: The 17 Million 'Invisible' New Voters

By STEVEN V. ROBERTS
Special to The New York Times

MIAMI, March 10—They are waitresses and gas station attendants, machinists and sales clerks and housewives. Some of them go to school part time. Many of them are unemployed. They probably know more about Elizabeth Taylor than Henry Kissinger, and might identify Che Guevara as an outfielder for the Chicago Cubs.

They have been called the "invisible youths."

Most of the interest about the "youth vote" — the 25 million young people who are eligible to vote in their first Presidential election this year — has focused on college students, particularly students at the prestige schools.

But in fact only 26 per cent of the new voters are in college, and only 4 per cent are in high school. The remaining 70 per cent—about 17.5 million youths — are mostly out in the world, working or looking for work. Almost half the women, and almost one-third of the men, are married.

Last night in Washington, Vice President Agnew urged a group of young Republicans to focus more attention on working youth. The party should not, he said, allow itself "to be trapped into pursuing a nonexistent phantom—somebody else's idea of the typical American."

What are these invisible youths like? What's bothering them, and what role are they likely to play in the politics of 1972?

The nonstudent group is highly diverse, subject to many pressures and changes, and very difficult to characterize. William Colson, campaign chairman for Paul Simon, a contender for the Democratic gubernatorial nomination in Illinois, put it this way:

"I don't see them considering themselves a separate and distinct group as their college counterparts do. I don't see the nonstudent youth as a bloc. I see it as a substratum of the society with pulls from both directions. They probably land somewhere between their parents and their college counterparts."

Scores of interviews in more than a dozen cities — with politicians, union leaders, the youngsters themselves — tend to validate Mr. Colson's view. Nonstudents are "pulled from both directions" by the conservation of responsibility and the iconoclasm of youth, and as a result seldom fit into neat categories.

Some generalizations are possible. Non-college youths are clearly less liberal than college students. George Gallup did a poll for Newsweek which showed that 49 per cent of the young workers identified themselves as "middle-of-the-road," as opposed to 38 per cent of the students.

Only 22 per cent called themselves "liberal or radical," while 43 per cent of the students did. Twenty-one per cent labeled themselves conservative, 6 points higher than the student group.

But labels do not mean much to youngsters like Teresa Reed, 19, who works part-time as a baby sitter, and Dale Couds, also 19, who has a job at a Ford assembly plant. They tend to be pragmatic, not ideological. What they know of the world comes mainly from experience, not books or speeches.

The other night they were sipping drinks in The Pub, a favorite hangout in their home town of Adrian, Mich., about 80 miles from Detroit. The clack of billiard balls, and the raspy voice of a rock singer, provided a background for their conversation.

"Most people don't like Nixon, but I do," said Teresa. "My dad complains about what he's done, but he put that price freeze on, and that helped."

"That freeze kept me out of work," retorted Dale, who had just been rehired after a long layoff.

"I think he's trying hard," answered Teresa, but Dale was not convinced.

'Main Concern Is the War'

"My main concern is the war," he explained. "My draft number is 43. He said he'd get us right out of Vietnam, but he's been in it three years, going on four. A neighbor of mine was killed a year ago, and all my other neighbors have been in the war. As far as I can see, no one likes Nixon."

Teresa and Dale seem rather typical. President Nixon enjoys sizable support from youngsters who think he is "trying hard" and "doing the best job he can."

But he is also vulnerable on two key issues, the economy and the war. Since they are often out looking for jobs and paying their own bills, most experts feel, this group is more sensitive to the unemployment issue than collegians.

And since they and their friends have not enjoyed college deferments over the last few years, they are more likely to have been personally affected by Vietnam. The troop levels might be down, but Dale Couds remembers

what the war has meant to his neighborhood, and can still mean to him.

But nonstudents will probably not take full advantage of their power, since the more educated a person is the more likely he is to vote. Gallup reports that while 79 per cent of the students are expected to register this year, only 59 per cent of the others will enroll.

The main reason is that nonstudents are so hard to find. They are not lumped together on a campus, and many of them are not in unions. One group that is trying to find them is Frontlash, an organization financed mainly by organized labor, which operates in about 50 communities across the country.

Frontlash organizers visit bars and bowling alleys, unemployment centers and office buildings, registering youngsters to vote. But the job is still tough, according to Cindy Amiotte, a 20-year junior college dropout who runs Frontlash in Contra Costa County, near San Francisco.

Apathy a Major Problem

"Look at all the organizations to which students belong," she said. "But it's very difficult to contact housewives, servicemen, working people. They constitute the largest bloc of new voters, and they should be reached if the youth vote is going to have any impact."

One major problem is apathy. At a bowling alley in Richmond, Calif., a Frontlash volunteer recently urged a pregnant young woman to register. "My husband does the voting in our family," she said, turning away.

Moreover, Miss Amiotte contended, nonstudents are often confused by the political process and embarrassed by their own ignorance. Many do not even know the names of the political parties, and feel powerless to influence public events anyway.

'I'm Just One Person'

An unemployed Vietnam veteran, playing the pinball machine in that Richmond

bowling alley, also declined to register. "My vote really doesn't make that much difference," he said. "I'm just one person; if I had a million votes, that would be a different story.

'Oh, I'll vote all right, but I sometimes wonder why," added John Schultz, assistant manager of a hamburger stand in Louisville. "It doesn't seem to matter too much who we put in Washington. We'll still have war somewhere; people will be without jobs and go hungry, and we'll still have corruption and crime. They all make big promises and don't keep them."

Most political observers believe that nonstudents will follow their parents' views more often than students. Nancy J. Shorter, a 24-year-old mother of two, recently registered at an unemployment office in San Pablo, Calif. When her mother saw her certificate, the older woman shouted:

"You're a Democrat, not a Republican. I'll disown you as a daughter."

Mrs. Shorter apologized. "I got confused," she said. "It's the Democrats who are for the poor people aren't they? And the Republicans for the rich?"

At the same time, nonstudent youth are showing some signs of independence. When asked to describe herself politically, one airline stewardess said, "Gemini." Brenda Huff, a 20-year-old black girl in Detroit, added:

"My parents are quite conservative, but I would tend to be more of a leftist. I was brought up in a different time than they were, things were more liberal. They're Democrats, but I registered independent. An independent is more willing to say what he feels, than what the party thinks is right."

Nonstudents Attitudes

Of nonstudents who do pick a party, according to Gallup, 40 per cent choose the Democrats, compared to 32 per cent of the collegians. The Republicans get only 18 per cent from either group. Frontlash reports that its reg-

istrations are running 3 to 1 Democratic, and in Contra Costa County it is closer to 5 to 1.

Like their collegiate counterparts, working youth seem less devoted to the concept of national honor than their parents. Paula Ralko, a 20-year-old medical assistant from Detroit, said:

"My parents dig the war, they feel we're doing the right thing. They're for this country no matter what the country does. But I think countries can make mistakes, just like people do."

There seems to be less disagreement on the subject of the economy. Few working youths know the details of Phase Two, but they know when they cannot find a job, or when prices go up.

Economic Crunch

Budd Cagle, the assistant manager of a variety store in Hamtramck, Mich., said:

"The economy is terrible, it's lousy. A guy I know got out of the service three months ago. He was a computer programer in the service for four years, and he can't find a job—nothing. I've often thought about switching jobs myself, but I wouldn't dare do it now.

"That price freeze wasn't worth 10 cents. As soon as it was over our prices went way up—but not wages. The only people it helped were the manufacturers. Big business is making out like a bandit."

The potential impact of the nonstudent youth vote, then, is still highly uncertain. But this is clearly a distinct group, fitting the stereotypes of neither youth nor age, battered by the forces of tradition and change, more pragmatic than ideological, cynical about politicians and not very confident of their ability to influence them.

Most experts agree that this group will probably not vote often enough or differently enough to topple empires. But it cannot be taken for granted by any candidate or party.

March 11, 1972

Nation Ends Draft, Turns to Volunteers

By DAVID E. ROSENBAUM
Special to The New York Times

WASHINGTON, Jan. 27—Defense Secretary Melvin R. Laird announced today that the military draft had ended.

As a result of the announcement, men born in 1953 and afterward will not be subject to conscription, and men born

before 1953 but not yet drafted will have no further liability to the draft.

These men will be the first in two generations to have no prospect of being drafted. Except for a brief hiatus in 1947 and 1948, men have been conscripted regularly since 1940.

President Nixon's authority to conscript troops into the military expires June 30. Since no one has been drafted since De-

cember, the President achieved his goal of turning the military into an all-volunteer force six months ahead of the deadline.

The President and Mr. Laird had promised repeatedly that the June 30 deadline would be met. But Mr. Laird had held out the possibility that as many as 5,000 men would be drafted this year from March through June.

But, in a message to senior defense officials that was

made public today, Mr. Laird said:

"With the signing of the peace agreement in Paris today, and, after receiving a report from the Secretary of the Army that he foresees no need for further inductions, I wish to inform you that the armed forces henceforth will depend exclusively on volunteer soldiers, sailors, airmen and marines.

"The use of the draft has ended."

Although no one will be drafted, the Selective Service machinery will most likely remain on the books for standby use in an emergency. Men will continue to have to register for the draft when they turn 18, and young men will still be assigned lottery numbers based on their birthdays.

Congress has mandated, however, that the Government call up Reserves and National Guardsmen before it turns to a reinstatement of the draft to meet future emergencies.

A spokesman for the Selective Service System said that men who had refused to report for induction would still be subject to criminal prosecution. But, he said, men with induction postponements that were due to expire before June 30 will not be drafted.

"We will draft nobody," the spokesman said.

January 28, 1973

WHAT DID IT ALL MEAN?

The Making Of a Counter Culture

Reflections on the Technocratic Society and Its Youthful Opposition.
By Theodore Roszak.
303 pp. New York:
Doubleday & Co.
Cloth, $7.95. Paper, $1.95.

By ROBERT PAUL WOLFF

The fool who misplaces his trust becomes a misanthrope and hates mankind for betraying him instead of berating himself for his unwisdom. So too, Socrates tells us in the "Phaedo," the novice philosopher who is taken in by a bad argument will often turn against logic, as though reason itself were to blame for his mistake. Misology, or the hatred of reason, is the greatest temptation of the fledgling intellect, and the only unforgiveable sin.

In recent years, many of our brightest and most gifted young men and women have been turning against reason. Horrified and revolted by the cruelties perpetrated by an established order which proclaims itself "reasonable," "pragmatic," "realistic" and "scientific," they conclude that a humane existence can be achieved only by a thoroughgoing rejection of the rational ideal which has dominated western civilization since the time of the ancient Greeks. So they turn to drugs, to mystical experience, to Zen, and to such other

Mr. Wolff teaches philosophy at Columbia University. His new book, "The Ideal of the University," will be published in November.

bits and snatches of Eastern religious practices as have made their way to our shores. So too, more than half in earnest, they consult horoscopes and conduct bowdlerized versions of the Black Mass, hoping to liberate themselves from the evils of modern society by rejecting that "reason" in whose name the evils are committed.

Theodore Roszak, a history professor at California State College, applauds the "great negation" of the rebel young. In his new book, "The Making of a Counter Culture," he argues that they are creating a new culture based upon a rejection of reason and the "objective consciousness" of science, and aiming at a liberation of the non-rational forces of the human personality. This new culture, as he sees it, is subjective rather than objective, tribal or communitarian rather than individualistic, transcendental rather than worldly. In a concluding chapter which we are apparently meant to take literally, Roszak calls for a renewal of the shamanistic worldview of our neolithic prehistory. Only through a release of the transcendent powers of the human spirit, he believes, can we break the all-encompassing, deadening, destructive domination of technocratic reason.

Roszak devotes almost half of his book to a discussion of the authors and practices to which dissident young people are drawn: Herbert Marcuse and Norman O. Brown, Allen Ginsburg and Alan Watts, Paul Goodman, LSD, marijuana, yoga, astrology, Zen, and so on. But these chapters, though well-written and insightful on a number of topics of contemporary dispute, are only ancillary to the main line of Roszak's argument, which can be summarized in four propositions: *First,* modern industrial society in general, and American society in particular, is ugly, repressive, destructive and subversive of much that is truly human;

Second, the youthful outbursts of rebellion and dissent are amalgamating into a coherent, though as yet uncompleted, "counter culture"; *Third,* the root of our troubles is western society's unquestioning acceptance of the "ideology of objective consciousness," the ideal and method of science; and *Fourth,* the anti-rationalist counter culture "that our alienated young are giving shape to . . . looks like the saving vision our endangered civilization requires."

The first of these propositions, I take it, is now acknowledged to be true by virtually every sensible man and woman. Anyone who still imagines that the United States is the land of opportunity and the bastion of democracy is a candidate either for a mental hospital or for Richard Nixon's Cabinet.

The second proposition is debatable, as Roszak himself says; but there is not much to be gained from disputing it. The crucial question is not whether a genuine counter culture is being born, but whether we wish to act as midwives or abortionists to it.

The fourth proposition depends for its plausibility on the third, and *that* is where the hard questions must be raised. Can we really trace the manifest evils of modern society to the methodology of science and a myth of objective consciousness? Roszak says yes. I say no.

First of all, Roszak is extremely ambiguous about the precise content of the "scientific world-view." His examples of repressive and inhuman social practices make it clear that his primary targets (and mine) are economic exploitation, political domination, and the depersonalization, which results from institutional bureaucratization. Hence his real villain is the social scientist, not the natural scientist.

Now, in a limited sense much explored by Max Weber, the bureaucratization of exploitation and domination can be traced to the functional principle of instrumental "reason." And it is certainly true that modern American political scientists, economists and sociologists are fatally prone to confuse functional rationality with reason itself. But one needn't take pot or study Zen to escape the grip of this fallacy. Countless rationalists, from Plato and Aristotle to Marx, Freud, Mannheim, and Weber himself have exposed the limitations of mere functional rationality and have recalled us to that substantive rationality on which a truly human existence is based.

The life of reason does not consist in planting symmetrical formal gardens, or in accumulating wealth out of all relation to one's desires, or in repressing spontaneous feelings, or in building weapons which no sane man could ever use. When twisted men offer for approval their efficient gas chambers and their utility-maximizing schemes of mutual annihilation, it is *they* who must be denied, not the ideal of reason which they falsely invoke.

Roszak reveals his confusion over the identity of his target in his quite insensitive discussion of the character of pure scientific investigation. He labors hard to persuade us that theoretical physicists and pure mathematicians are philistines whose work "depreciates our capacity for wonder" by reducing our majestic experience of the power of the uni-

verse "to manageable and repeatable terms, packaged up, mastered, brought under control." The beauties of creation, he says, can thus be "salted away in textbooks and passed onto posterity in summary form as established conclusions."

So it must seem to the humanistically inclined undergraduate laboring through a year of required science which he neither likes nor understands. But exactly the same soul-dampening tedium may be induced by reading half a dozen scholarly articles on the literary sources of William Blake's imagery. (Blake is one of Roszak's counter-cultural heroes.) If Newton and Einstein are to be believed, there is as much poetic wonder in the contemplation of the laws of the universe as in the worship of lightning or in reflection upon the sound of one hand clapping.

Despite the very great sophistication of his analysis, Roszak succumbs in the end to exactly the same sin of misology as the anti-rational students. When a farcical imposter like

> Herman Kahn hides his apologetics for Air Force policies behind a facade of "science" and "logic," Roszak is completely taken in. Instead of exposing the irrationalities in Kahn's sophistical arguments (not a very difficult task), Roszak retreats into oriental mysticism. One might as well for-

swear medicine because a quack once sold you snakeoil!

For a variety of historical reasons the promising young radical intellectuals of the thirties betrayed their faith in the forties and retreated in the fifties to the ranks of establishment liberal ideologues. The men who should have leading voices on the left became instead apologetic for capitalism at home and anti-Communism abroad. This generational failure has imposed a heavy burden on America's postwar young, for they have had to search the past or other lands for the heroes and mentors who can give them guidance.

But time passes and a new generation of radical scholars is coming upon the scene. The convenient celebrations of American life are giving way to critical new appraisals of the injustices of our society. Roszak may be right that our young people are fleeing from the ideal of reason, but to encourage them in their flight is to play into the hands of reaction. The only hope for a just and humane America is a renascence of true reason, which can hold their allegiance and guide their energies in fruitful directions.

September 7, 1969

Letters

Counter Culture

To the Editor:

Robert Paul Wolff's review of Theodore Roszak's "The Making of a Counter Culture: Reflections on the Technocratic Society and Its Youthful Opposition" (Sept. 7), hinges on Mr. Wolff's definition of "true reason." . . . His review scores Mr. Roszak for "misology" ("the hatred of reason . . . the greatest temptation of the fledgling intellect . . . the only unforgiveable sin"), without ever giving us a definition of "true reason" with which to

judge Roszak's "unforgiveable sin."

It seems to me that there are as many definitions of "true reason" as there are men willing to proclaim their definitions as definitive. . . . Therefore, to say that the "hope for a just and humane America is a renascence of true reason" is as fatuous an exercise as what your reviewer calls Herman Kahn's "apologetics for Air Force policies."

If the great majority of Americans miraculously accepted one definition of "true reason" (Mr. Wolff's, naturally) and lived strictly by its principles, I seriously doubt that the mess in that country would be ameliorated. Part of the trouble rests in the great intolerance of American society for differing opinions of such ideas as "reason," "democracy," "Communism." . . . Societies love to have their members believe in the one true faith. American society is hardly different in this respect—though it is somewhat more tolerant than, say,

Nazi Germany, which delighted in gassing its opponents.

It is little wonder, then, that the youthful "counter culture" Mr. Roszak's book describes seeks drugs and Zen to escape the hands of such absolutists as Mr. Wolff . . . who energetically defend their "Faith" (science, capitalism, true reason or whatever), and clobber the protestors.   Edward A. Kaufman
Quebec.

To the Editor:

I'm fully in accord with Mr. Wolff's opinion of Herman Kahn, that too-readily-endorsed "Big Brain." . . . I agree that hatred of reason is a woefully popular vice—and not only among the young. . . .

Where I'm inclined to question your reviewer is in the area of leftish leanings. When he notes that Mr. Roszak's book "applauds the 'great negation' of the rebel young," I don't think he comes down hard enough on those whose "philosophy" . . . is as mindless, basically, as the "thinking" of

emotional rightists.
Joseph Gancher
Albany.

To the Editor:

As a consultant to the Hudson Institute, any defense I might make of Herman Kahn (the subject of a vicious, gratuitous personal attack in Robert Wolff's review) might be discounted as an attempt by an employe to gain favor in the eyes of his superior. (And in any case, Herman is quite able to defend himself, if he so desires.)

I must protest, however, an editorial policy that allows a reviewer to describe an individual as a "farcical imposter" and to compare him to a quack.

As a minimum . . . reviewers should be obliged, if they are going to attack personalities, to give evidence of just what they are basing their opinions on— if only to give the readers of the review the opportunity to judge just who is a quack, and who is a responsible member of society.   Edward S. Boylan
Croton-on-Hudson, N. Y.

To the Editor:

It may come as a surprise to Mr. Wolff, but there are a great many sensible people who believe in this country's ideals of democracy and opportunity.

Because they take a common sense view of the imperfection of all human institutions, they recognize that a society is not only to be judged by its failure to attain all [essential] objectives . . . but by the process through which it permits improvement and reform.

Despite his evident disappointment with the outcome of the last national election, even Mr. Wolff should be able to detect a connection between the concept of "democracy," and the fact he is able to publish his opinions with impunity. . . . The people who, unlike Mr. Wolff, are able to perceive that connection may be referred to as intelligent adults.

Any person having the simple-minded arrogance to describe these people as candidates for a mental hospital is either a case of protracted infantilism . . . or a contributor to The New York Times.

Edward Greenbaum
Tarrytown, N.Y.

To the Editor:

Mr. Wolff, who teaches philosophy at Columbia University, illustrates the fallacy of Plato's ideas of rulers and philosophers (unintentionally). His logic is flawless, but his premises are nonsensical. . . .

Mr. Roszak argues, he says, that "modern industrial society in general, and American society in particular, is ugly, repressive, destructive and subversive of much that is truly human." . . . And he adds that this proposition, "I take it, is now acknowledged to be true by virtually every sensible man and woman. . . . Anyone who still imagines that the United States is the land of opportunity and the bastion of democracy is a candidate either for a mental hospital or for Richard Nixon's Cabinet."

If Mr. Wolff is correct, most of us will head for the hospitals, as the Cabinet is filled. Perhaps he should reread the first paragraph of his review . . . and then let us know who is the sensible man.

Jerome M. Harte
Bridgeport, Conn.

October 5, 1969

"The situation is very like 1510, when Luther went to Rome. There is everywhere protest, revaluation, attack on the Establishment."

The New Reformation

By PAUL GOODMAN

FOR a long time modern societies have been operating as if religion were a minor and moribund part of the scheme of things. But this is unlikely. Men do not do without a system of "meanings" that everybody believes and puts his hope in even if, or especially if, he doesn't know anything about it; what Freud called a "shared psychosis," meaningful because shared, and with the power that resides in deep fantasy and longing. In advanced countries, indeed, it is science and technology themselves that have gradually, and finally triumphantly, become the system of mass faith, not disputed by various political ideologies and nationalisms that have also had religious uses.

Now this basic faith is threatened. Dissident young people are saying that science is antilife, it is a Calvinist obsession, it has been a weapon of white Europe to subjugate colored races, and scientific technology has manifestly become diabolical. Along with science, the young discredit the professions in general, and the whole notion of "disciplines" and academic learning. If these views take hold, it adds up to a crisis of belief, and the effects are incalculable. Every status and institution would be affected.

PAUL GOODMAN is an educator, social critic and novelist. His works include "Growing Up Absurd," "People or Personnel" and "Adam and His Works."

Present political troubles could become endless religious wars. Here again, as in politics and morals, the worldwide youth disturbance may indicate a turning point in history and we must listen to it carefully.

In 1967 I gave a course on "Professionalism" at the New School for Social Research in New York, attended by about 25 graduate students from all departments. My bias was the traditional one: professionals are autonomous individuals beholden to the nature of things and the judgment of their peers, and bound by an explicit or implicit oath to benefit their clients and the community. To teach this, I invited seasoned professionals whom I esteemed—a physician, engineer, journalist, architect, etc. These explained to the students the obstacles that increasingly stood in the way of honest practice, and their own life experience in circumventing them.

To my surprise, the class unanimously rejected them. Heatedly and rudely they called my guests liars, finks, mystifiers, or deluded. They showed that every professional was co-opted and corrupted by the System, all decisions were made top-down by the power structure and bureaucracy, professional peer-groups were conspiracies to make more money. All this was importantly true and had, of course, been said by the visitors. Why had the students not heard? As we explored further, we

came to the deeper truth, that they did not believe in the existence of real professions at all; professions were concepts of repressive society and "linear thinking." I asked them to envisage any social order they pleased—Mao's, Castro's, some anarchist utopia—and wouldn't there be engineers who knew about materials and stresses and strains? Wouldn't people get sick and need to be treated? Wouldn't there be problems of communication? No, they insisted; it was important only to be human, and all else would follow.

Suddenly I realized that they did not really believe that there was a nature of things. Somehow all functions could be reduced to interpersonal relations and power. There was no knowledge, but only the sociology of knowledge. They had so well learned that physical and sociological research is subsidized and conducted for the benefit of the ruling class that they did not believe there was such a thing as simple truth. To be required to learn something was a trap by which the young were put down and co-opted. Then I knew that I could not get through to them. I had imagined that the worldwide student protest had to do with changing political and moral institutions, to which I was sympathetic, but I now saw that we had to do with a religious crisis of the magnitude of the Reformation in the fifteen-hundreds, when not only all institutions but all learning had been corrupted by the Whore of Babylon.

The irony was that I myself had said 10 years ago, in "Growing Up Absurd," that these young were growing up without a world for them, and therefore they were "alienated," estranged from nature and other people. But I had then been thinking of juvenile delinquents and a few Beats; and a few years later I had been heartened by the Movement in Mississippi, the Free Speech protest in Berkeley, the Port Huron statement of S.D.S., the resistance to the Vietnam war, all of which made human sense and were not absurd at all. But the alienating circumstances had proved too strong after all; here were absurd graduate students, most of them political "activists."

ALIENATION is a Lutheran concept: "God has turned His face away, things have no meaning, I am estranged in the world." By the time of Hegel the term was applied to the general condition of rational man, with his "objective" sciences and institutions divorced from his "subjectivity," which was therefore irrational and impulsive. In his revision of Hegel, Marx explained this as the effect of man's losing his essential nature as a cooperative producer, because centuries of exploitation, culminating in capitalism, had fragmented the community and robbed the workman of the means of production. Comte and Durkheim pointed to the weakening of social solidarity and the contradiction between law and morality, so that people lost their bearings — this was anomie, an acute form of alienation that could lead to suicide or aimless riot. By the end of the 19th century, alienation came to be used as the term for insanity, derangement of perceived reality, and psychiatrists were called alienists.

Contemporary conditions of life have certainly deprived people, and especially young people, of a meaningful world in which they can act and find themselves. Many writers and the dissenting students themselves have spelled it out. For instance, in both schools and corporations, people cannot pursue their own interests or exercise initiative. Administrators are hypocrites who sell people out for the smooth operation of the system. The budget for war has grotesquely distorted reasonable social priorities. Worst of all, the authorities who make the decisions are incompetent to cope with modern times: we are in danger of extinction, the biosphere is being destroyed, two-thirds of mankind are starving. Let me here go on to some other factors that demand a religious response.

There is a lapse of faith in science. Science has not produced the general happiness that people expected, and now it has fallen under the sway of greed and power; whatever its beneficent past, people fear that its further progress will do more harm than good. And rationality itself is discredited. Probably it is more significant than we like to think that intelligent young people dabble in astrology, witchcraft, psychedelic dreams, and whatever else is despised by science; in some sense they are not kidding. They need to control their fate, but they hate scientific explanations.

Every one of these young grew up since Hiroshima. They do not talk about atom bombs—not nearly so much as we who campaigned against the shelters and fall-out—but the bombs explode in their dreams, as Otto Butz found in his study of collegians at San Francisco State, and now George Dennison, in "The Lives of Children," shows that it was the same with small slum children whom he taught at the First Street School in New York. Again and again students have told me that they take it for granted they will not survive the next 10 years. This is not an attitude with which to prepare for a career or to bring up a family.

Whether or not the bombs go off, human beings are becoming useless. Old people are shunted out of sight at an increasingly earlier age, young people are kept on ice till an increasingly later age. Small farmers and other technologically unemployed are dispossessed or left to rot. Large numbers are put away as incompetent or deviant. Racial minorities that cannot shape up are treated as a nuisance. Together, these groups are a large majority of the population. Since labor will not be needed much longer, there is vague talk of a future society of "leisure," but there is no thought of a kind of community in which all human beings would be necessary and valued.

The institutions, technology and communications have infected even the "biological core," so that people's sexual desires are no longer genuine. This was powerfully argued by Wilhelm Reich a generation ago and it is now repeated by Herbert Marcuse. When I spoke for it in the nineteen-forties, I was condemned by the radicals, for example, C. Wright Mills, as a "bedroom revisionist."

A special aspect of biological corruption is the spreading ugliness, filth, and tension of the environment in which the young grow up. If Wordsworth was right—I think he was—that children must grow up in an environment of beauty and simple affections in order to become trusting, open, and magnanimous citizens, then the offspring of our ghettos, suburbs, and complicated homes have been disadvantaged, no matter how much money there is. This lack cannot be remedied by art in the curriculum, nor by vest-pocket playgrounds, nor by banning billboards from bigger highways. Cleaning the river might help, but that will be the day.

IF we start from the premise that the young are in a religious crisis, that they doubt there is really a nature of things, and they are sure there is not a world for themselves, many details of their present behavior become clearer. Alienation is a powerful motivation, of unrest, fantasy and reckless action. It leads, as we shall see, to religious innovation, new sacraments to give life meaning. But it is a poor basis for politics, including revolutionary politics.

It is said that the young dissidents never offer a constructive program. And apart from the special cases of Czechoslovakia and Poland, where they confront an unusually outdated system, this is largely true. In France, China, Germany, Egypt, England, the United States, etc., most of the issues of protest have been immediate gut issues, and the tactics have been mainly disruptive, without coherent proposals for a better society. But this makes for bad politics. Unless one has a program, there is no way to persuade the other citizens, who do not have one's gut complaints, to come along. Instead one confronts them hostilely and they are turned off, even when they might be sympathetic. But the confrontation is inept too, for the alienated young cannot take other people seriously as having needs of their own; a spectacular instance was the inability of the French youth to communicate with the French working class, in May 1968. In Gandhian theory, the confronter aims at future community with the confronted; he will not let him continue a course that is bad for him, and so he appeals to his deeper reason. But instead of this Satyagraha, soul force, we have seen plenty of hate. The confronted are not taken as human beings, but as pigs, etc. But how can the young people think of a future community when they themselves have no present world, no profession or other job in it, and no trust in other human beings? Instead, some young radicals seem to entertain the disastrous illusion that other people can be compelled by fear. This can lead only to crushing reaction.

All the "political" activity makes sense, however, if it is understood that it is not aimed at social reconstruction at all, but is a way of desperately affirming that they are alive and want a place in the sun. "I am a revolutionary," said Cohn-Bendit, leader of the French students in 1968, "because it is the best way of living." And young Americans pathetically and truly say that there is no other way to be taken seriously. Then it is not necessary to have a program; the right method is to act, against any vulnerable point and wherever one can rally support. The purpose is not politics but to have a movement and form a community. This is exactly what Saul Alinsky prescribed to rally outcast blacks.

And such conflictful action has indeed caused social changes. In France it was conceded by the Gaullists that "nothing would ever be the same." In the United States, the changes in social attitude during the last 10 years are unthinkable without the youth action, with regard to war, the military-industrial, corporate organization and administration, the police, the blacks. When the actors have been in touch with the underlying causes of things, issues have deepened and the Movement has grown. But for the alienated, again, action easily slips into activism, and conflict is often spite and stubbornness. There is excitement and notoriety, much human suffering, and the world no better off. (New Left Notes runs a column wryly called, "We Made the News Today, O Boy!") Instead of deepening awareness and a sharpening political conflict, there occurs the polarization of mere exasperation. It often seems that the aim is just to have a shambles. Impatiently the ante of tactics is raised beyond what the "issue" warrants, and support melts away. Out on a limb, the leaders become desperate and fanatical, intolerant of criticism, dictatorial. The Movement falls to pieces.

Yet it is noteworthy that when older people like myself are critical of the wrongheaded activism, we nevertheless almost invariably concede that the young are *morally* justified. For what is the use of patience and reason when meantime millions are being killed and starved, and when bombs and nerve gas are being stockpiled? Against the entrenched power responsible for these things, it might be better to do something idiotic now than something perhaps more practical in the long run. I don't know which is less demoralizing.

Maybe the truth is revea'ed in the following conversation I had with a young hippie at a college in Massachusetts. He was dressed like an (American) Indian—buckskin fringes and a headband, red paint on his face. All his life, he said, he had tried to escape the encompassing evil of our society that was trying to destroy his soul. "But if you're always escaping," I said, "and never attentively study it, how can you make a wise judgment about society or act effectively to change it?" "You see, you don't dig!" he cried. "It's just ideas like 'wise' and 'acting effectively' that we can't stand." He was right. He was in the religious dilemma of Faith vs. Works. Where I sat, Works had some reality; but in the reign of the Devil, as he felt it, all Works are corrupted, they are part of the System; only Faith can avail. But he didn't have Faith either.

INEVITABLY, the alienated seem to be inconsistent in how they take the present world. Hippies attack technology and are scornful of rationality, but they buy up electronic equipment and motorcycles, and with them the whole infrastructure. Activists say that civil liberties are bourgeois and they shout down their opponents; but they clamor in court for their civil liberties. Those who say that the university is an agent of the powers that be, do not mean thereby

to reassert the ideal role of the university, but to use the university for their own propaganda. Yet if I point out these apparent inconsistencies, it does not arouse shame or guilt. How is this? It is simply that they do not really understand that technology, civil law, and the university are *human* institutions, for which they too are responsible; they take them as brute given, just what's there, to be manipulated as convenient. But convenient for whom? The trouble with this attitude is that these institutions, works of spirit in history, are how Man has made himself and is. If they treat them as mere things, rather than being vigilant for them, they themselves become nothing. And nothing comes from nothing.

In general, their lack of a sense of history is bewildering. It is impossible to convey to them that the deeds were done by human beings, that John Hampden confronted the King and wouldn't pay the war tax just like us, or that Beethoven too, just like a rock 'n' roll band, made up his music as he went along, from odds and ends, with energy, spontaneity and passion—how else do they think he made music? And they no longer remember their own history. A few years ago there was a commonly accepted story of mankind, beginning with the Beats, going on to the Chessman case, the HUAC bust, the Freedom Rides, and climaxing in the Berkeley Victory—"The first human event in 40,000 years," Mike Rossman, one of the innumerable spokesmen, told me. But this year I find that nothing antedates Chicago '68. Elder statesmen, like Sidney Lens and especially Staughton Lynd, have been trying with heroic effort to recall the American antecedents of present radical and libertarian slogans and tactics, but it doesn't rub off. I am often hectored to my face with formulations that I myself put in their mouths, that have become part of the oral tradition two years old, author prehistoric. Most significant of all, it has been whispered to me—but I can't check up, because I don't speak the language—that among the junior high school students, aged 12 and 13, that's really where it's at! Quite different from what goes on in the colleges that I visit.

What I do notice, however, is that dozens of Underground newspapers have a noisy style. Though each one is doing his thing, there is not much idiosyncracy in the spontaneous variety. The political radicals are, as if mesmerized, repeating the power plays, factionalism, random abuse, and tactical lies that aborted the movement in the thirties. And I have learned, to my disgust, that a major reason why the young don't trust people over 30 is that they don't understand them and are too conceited to try. Having grown up in a world too meaningless to learn

anything, they know very little and are quick to resent it.

THIS is an unpleasant picture. Even so, the alienated young have no vital alternative except to confront the Evil, and to try to make a new way of life out of their own innards and suffering. As they are doing. It is irrelevant to point out that the System is not the monolith that they think and that the majority of people are not corrupt, just browbeaten and confused. What is relevant is that they cannot see this, because they do not have an operable world for themselves. In such a case, the only advice I would dare to give them is that which Krishna gave Arjuna: to confront with nonattachment, to be brave and firm without hatred. (I don't here want to discuss the question of "violence," the hatred and disdain are far more important.) Also, when they are seeking a new way of life, for example when they are making a "journey inward," as Ronald Laing calls it, I find that I urge them occasionally to write a letter home.

As a citizen and father I have a right to try to prevent a shambles and to diminish the number of wrecked lives. But it is improper for us elders to keep saying, as we do, that their activity is "counterproductive." It's our business to do something more productive.

Religiously, the young have been inventive, much more than the God-is-dead theologians. They have hit on new sacraments, physical actions to get them out of their estrangement and (momentarily) break through into meaning. The terribly loud music is used sacramentally. The claim for the hallucinogenic drugs is almost never the paradisal pleasure of opium culture nor the escape from distress of heroin, but tuning in to the cosmos and communing with one another. They seem to have had flashes of success in bringing ritual participation back into theater, which for a hundred years playwrights and directors have tried to do in vain. And whatever the political purposes and results of activism, there is no doubt that shared danger for the sake of righteousness is used sacramentally as baptism of fire. Fearful moments of provocation and the poignant release of the bust bring unconscious contents to the surface, create a bond of solidarity, are "commitment."

But the most powerful magic, working in all these sacraments, is the close presence of other human beings, without competition or one-upping. The original sin is to be on an ego trip that isolates; and angry political factionalism has now also become a bad thing. What a drastic comment on the dehumanization and fragmentation of modern times that salvation can be attained simply by the "warmth of assembled animal bodies," as Kafka called it, describing his mice. At the 1967 Easter Be-In in New York's Central Park, when about 10,000 were crowded on the Sheep Meadow, a young man with a quite radiant face said to me, "Gee, human beings are legal!"—it was sufficient, to be saved, to be exempted from continual harassment by officious rules and Law and Order.

The extraordinary rock festivals at Bethel and on the Isle of Wight are evidently pilgrimages. Joan Baez, one of the hierophants, ecstatically described Bethel to me, and the gist of it was that people were nice to one another. A small group passing a joint of marijuana often behaves like a Quaker meeting waiting for the spirit, and the cigarette may be a placebo. Group therapy and sensitivity training, with Mecca at Esalen, have the same purpose. And I think this is the sense of the sexuality, which is certainly not hedonistic, nor mystical in the genre of D. H. Lawrence; nor does it have much to do with personal love, that is too threatening for these anxious youths. But it is human touch, without conquest or domination, and it obviates self-consciousness and embarrassed speech.

Around the rather pure faith there has inevitably collected a mess of eclectic liturgy and paraphernalia. Mandalas, beggars in saffron, (American) Indian beads, lectures in Zen. Obviously the exotic is desirable because it is not what they have grown up with. And it is true that fundamental facts of life are more acceptable if they come in fancy dress, e.g. it is good to breathe from the diaphragm and one can learn this by humming "OM," as Allen Ginsberg did for seven hours at Grant Park in Chicago. But college chaplains are also pretty busy, and they are now more likely to see the adventurous and off-beat than, as used to be the case, the staid and square. Flowers and strobe lights are indigenous talismans.

IT is hard to describe this (or any) religiosity without lapsing into condescending humor. Yet it is genuine and it will, I am convinced, survive and develop — I don't know into what. In the end it is religion that constitutes the strength of this generation, and not, as I used to think, their morality, political will, and common sense. Except for a few, like the young people of the Re-

sistance, I am not impressed by their moral courage or even honesty. For all their eccentricity they are singularly lacking in personality. They do not have enough world to have much character. And they are not especially attractive as animals. But they keep pouring out a kind of metaphysical vitality.

Let me try to account for it. On the one hand, these young have an unusual amount of available psychic energy. They were brought up on antibiotics that minimized depressing chronic childhood diseases, and with post-Freudian freedom to act out early drives. Up to age 6 or 7, television nourished them with masses of strange images and sometimes true information— McLuhan makes a lot of sense for the kindergarten years. Long schooling would tend to make them stupid, but it has been compensated by providing the vast isolated cities of youth that the high schools and colleges essentially are, where they can incubate their own thoughts. They are sexually precocious and not inhibited by taboos. They are superficially knowledgeable. On the other hand, all this psychic energy has had little practical use. The social environment is dehumanized. It discourages romantic love and lasting friendship. They are desperately bored because the world does not promise any fulfillment. Their knowledge gives no intellectual or poetic satisfaction. In this impasse, we can expect a ferment of new religion. As in Greek plays, impasse produces gods from the machine. For a long time we did not hear of the symptoms of adolescent religious conversion, once as common in the United States as in all other places and ages. Now it seems to be recurring as a mass phenomenon.

WITHOUT doubt the religious young are in touch with something historical, but I don't think they understand what it is. Let me quote from an editorial in New Seminary News, the newsletter of dissident seminarians of the Pacific School of Religion in Berkeley: "What we confront (willingly or not we are thrust into it) is a time of disintegration of a dying civilization and the emergence of a new one." This seems to envisage something like the instant decline of the Roman Empire and they, presumably, are like the Christians about to build, rapidly, another era. But there are no signs that this is the actual situation. It would mean, for instance, that our scientific technology, civil law, professions, universities, etc., are about to

vanish from the earth and be replaced by something entirely different. This is a fantasy of alienated minds. Nobody behaves as if civilization would vanish, and nobody acts as if there were a new dispensation. Nobody is waiting patiently in the catacombs and the faithful have not withdrawn into the desert. Neither the Yippies nor the New Seminarians nor any other exalted group have produced anything that is the least bit miraculous. Our civilization may well destroy itself with its atom bombs or something else, but then we do not care what will emerge, if anything.

But the actual situation is very like 1510, when Luther went to Rome, the eve of the Reformation. There is everywhere protest, revaluation, attack on the Establishment. The protest is international. There is a generation gap. (Luther himself was all of 34 when he posted his 95 theses in 1517, but Melanchthon was 20, Bucer 26, Münzer 28, Jonas 24; the Movement consisted of undergraduates and junior faculty.) And the thrust of protest is not to give up science, technology, and civil institutions, but to purge them, humanize them, decentralize them, change the priorities, and stop the drain of wealth.

These were, of course, exactly the demands of the March 4 nationwide teach-in on science, initiated by the dissenting professors of the Massachusetts Institute of Technology. This and the waves of other teach-ins, ads and demonstrations have been the voices not of the alienated, of people who have no world, but of protestants, people deep in the world who will soon refuse to continue under the present auspices because they are not viable. It is populism permeated by moral and professional unease. What the young have done is to make it finally religious, to force the grown-ups to recognize that they too are threatened with meaninglessness.

The analogy to the Reformation is even closer if we notice that the bloated universities, and the expanded school systems under them, constitute the biggest collection of monks since the time of Henry VIII. And most of this mandarinism is hocus pocus, a mass superstition. In my opinion, much of the student dissent in the colleges and especially the high schools has little to do with the excellent political and social demands that are made, but is boredom and resentment because of the phoniness of the whole academic enterprise.

Viewed as incidents of a Reformation, as attempts to purge themselves and recover a lost integrity, the various movements of the alienated young are easily recognizable as characteristic protestant sects, intensely self-conscious. The dissenting

329

seminarians of the Pacific School of Religion do not intend to go off to primitive love feasts in a new heaven and new earth, but to form their own Free University; that is, they are Congregationalists. The shaggy hippies are not nature children as they claim, but self-conscious Adamites trying to naturalize Sausalito and the East Village. Heads are Pentecostals or Children of Light. Those who spindle IBM cards and throw the dean down the stairs are Iconoclasts. Those who want Student Power, a say in the rules and curriculum, mean to deny infant baptism; they want to make up their own minds, like Henry Dunster, the first president of Harvard. Radicals who live among the poor and try to organize them are certainly intent on social change, but they are also trying to find themselves again. The support of the black revolt by white middle-class students is desperately like Anabaptism, but

God grant that we can do better than the Peasants' War. These analogies are not fanciful; when authority is discredited, there is a pattern in the return of the repressed. A better scholar could make a longer list; but the reason I here spell it out is that, perhaps, some young person will suddenly remember that history was about something.

Naturally, traditional churches are themselves in transition. On college campuses and in bohemian neighborhoods, existentialist Protestants and Jews and updating Catholics have gone along with the political and social activism and, what is probably more important, they have changed their own moral, esthetic and personal tone. On many campuses, the chaplains provide the only official forum for discussions of sex, drugs and burning draft cards. Yet it seems to me that, in their zeal for relevance, they are badly failing in their chief

duty to the religious young: to be professors of theology. They cannot really perform pastoral services, like giving consolation or advice, since the young believe they have the sacraments to do this for themselves. Chaplains say that the young are uninterested in dogma and untractable on this level, but I think this is simply a projection of their own distaste for the conventional theology that has gone dead for them. The young are hotly metaphysical—but alas, boringly so, because they don't know much, have no language to express their intuitions, and repeat every old fallacy. If the chaplains would stop looking in the conventional places where God is dead, and would explore the actualities where perhaps He is alive, they might learn something and have something to teach.

September 14, 1969

The Rebirth of a Future: I

By CHARLES A. REICH

Day-to-day events leave us with a feeling of chaos; it seems as if we must be mere powerless spectators at the decline and fall of our country. But these same events are capable of being understood as part of a larger process of social change — a process that is fearsome and yet fundamentally hopeful. And we may be participants—we may regain the power to make our own future—if only we understand what is taking place.

In Spain, the American President rides in an open car with a military dictator who by using lawless force has repressed all meaningful social progress. In Vietnam, halfway around the world, young Americans are compelled to fight in support of another corrupt dictatorship. These are not separate events, they are symptoms of a larger pattern. Women's liberation, black militancy, the campaign against the S.S.T., Gay Liberation, the long hair of youth are not separate events either; they too are related. The many wars, the many revolutions, are one.

The agonies of the great industrial nations, and especially our own, are no mystery. They have been fully predicted and explained by many social thinkers. There is much room for argument among schools of thought, but the main outline is clear. Neither machines nor material progress is inherently bad. But we have achieved our progress by a system which shortsightedly wastes man and nature by failing to protect them in the haste for gain. A rising crime rate, extremes of inequality, neglect of social needs, personal alienation and loss of meaning, disorder and war are all manifestations of the underlying process of corrosive exploitation.

This process has now reached a point where remedial action is desperately urgent. Knowing this, why are we unable to guide our progress along more rational lines? Why is our system so rigid that it ignores even the mild remedies proposed by its own Presidential Commissions? This brings us to a second element of our crisis, an element which also can be explained. American society has been amalgamated into a single monolith of power—the corporate state—which includes both the private and public structures. This monolith is not responsible to democratic or even executive control. The Corporate State is mindless and irrational. It roils along with a momentum of its own, producing a society that is ever more at war with its own inhabitants. Again, there is plenty of room for different theories of the state, but the major pattern of unthinking and uncontrolled power must by now be accepted.

If our nation's immobility can be explained and understood, we must ask once more: why are we unable to refashion our system? All social systems are merely the creations of men; men make them and men can change them. But the power to act is limited by our consciousness. Today most Americans are not conscious of the realities of their society.

One segment of the American people remains at a level of consciousness that was formed when we were a land of small villages and individual opportunity; Consciousness I is unable to accept the reality of an interdependent society that requires collective responsibility. A second segment of the American people understands the realities of organization life but does not see that organizations and their poli-

cies are, by themselves, inhuman. Consciousness II supports the Corporate State and seeks happiness in its artificial rewards, mistakenly believing that such a state is necessary and rational in this industrial age.

These two forms of unreality, Consciousness I and II, render us powerless. We cannot act constructively so long as we are the prisoners of myth. Consciousness I exhausts its energy blaming scapegoats such as Communists, hippies, and liberals. Consciousness II offers solutions that would but strengthen existing structure. But the moment that our eyes are opened to the true causes of our self-destruction, there is hope.

What the times urgently demand, what our survival demands, is a new consciousness that will reassert rational control over the industrial system and the Corporate State, and transform them into a way of life that protects and advances human values. It is not necessary to destroy our machines or our material well-being; it is only necessary to guide them. Such a new consciousness must reject the old myths, must reject the mindless operation of the State, must reassert the reality of nature and of man's nature. Today, in this moment of most desperate need, that new consciousness is at last emerging—the spontaneous outgrowth of the fears and hopes of the new generation.

Charles Reich is Professor of Law at Yale University. This article and one which follows tomorrow synthesize his views of the American condition as presented in "The Greening of America," to be published Friday.

October 21, 1970

The Rebirth of a Future: II

By CHARLES A. REICH

All around us today we see new ways of thinking and living: long hair, student protest, rock music, rejection of old careers. Many people find all of this shocking, frightening, senseless. But against the background of what has gone wrong with America, it all makes sense. There is a logic to it that explains each large and small experiment. Taken as a whole, it represents the only large-scale search for common sense and self-preservation that can be found in America today, the only major effort to come to grips with reality and reassert man's control of his own fate. This is the beginning of a new consciousness, Consciousness III.

If the American Corporate State is, despite the wishes of a majority of its people, mindlessly destroying the land, culture, and people of a country in Southeast Asia, it is rational to refuse to become an instrument of that war, and to refuse obedience to laws that seek to compel a human being, despite his deepest convictions, to kill other human beings. If the State wants its citizens identically boxed and packaged, all the better to serve its rigid organizational structure, it makes sense to wear long hair and beards and clothes that constitute a refusal to be regimented. If the State wants all decisions made by remote central managers or by even more remote computers, it makes sense to insist that real people be allowed to participate in the making of decisions that affect their lives. If official language has been so debased that making war is called "making peace," and human needs are described in terms of manufactured appliances, there is a genuine need for the new language of rock music to aid in the effort to regain truth.

A revolution usually means the seizure of power by one group from another. But the revolution of the new generation is very different. It is not directed against other people, but against an impersonal system. And its objective is to place that system under the guidance of a mind—to reassert values where none are now recognized. The first stage of this revolution must be personal and cultural—the reassertion of values in each individual's life. The revolution will change the political structure of the State only as its final act. This is revolution by consciousness.

Revolution by consciousness is possible—and an orthodox revolution is not—because the Corporate State, while almost impregnable from outside, is astonishingly vulnerable from within. It is operated not by force but by willing workers and willing consumers. They have been persuaded to pursue goals set for them by the State. But if young lawyers will work only in firms that do some public service, if consumers refuse to buy the furs of endangered animal species, the State will be forced to obey, and it will begin to be turned to human ends. Opinion is not enough. People must change their working and consumer lives. And they can do this only by a rediscovery of self. It is only by a renewed self-knowledge that we can learn what work gives our lives meaning, and what material things will not impoverish us but affirm us.

Recovery of self is possible for people of all ages and conditions. The coming revolution has started with youth, but all others can join. They need not adopt the specifics of the youth culture; a sixty-year-old person does not have to wear bellbottoms. All that he needs is to make as honest a search for his own happiness and meaning as youth are making for theirs. There need be no unnatural warfare between generations, incited by promoters of hate. Parents do not want to hate their children. And children—our children of the new generation—desperately want the support and the wisdom of older people, who have too long left it to the young to carry alone the burden of resisting the inhuman Corporate State.

The generation of Consciousness III does not seek anything alien and strange. It is the Corporate State that has turned our country into a foreign and unrecognizable land. The new consciousness dreams the old American dream—of individual fulfillment and brotherly love. It is the old dream restated in terms of the realities and the promise of a technological society, where man must understand and master his machines.

To write about the coming revolution in terms of abstract concepts like "consciousness" is to risk missing its essence. This revolution does not find expression in theories. It is expressed all around us by the bloom of renewed life. Faces are gentler and more beautiful. People are better with each other. There are more smiles, more love. There is new hope, for young people have rediscovered a future, where until recently no future could even be imagined. This is the Revolution: the rebirth of people in a sterile land.

October 22, 1970

Where Is Youth's Individualism?

By MARYA MANNES

Those with open minds and hearts would want to share Professor Reich's faith that the "new consciousness" of the young is our best hope for bringing America back to its senses and its roots. This is the core of their revolution against the inhumanity of the Corporate State we have become; a revolution of which the first stage, he writes, "must be personal and cultural—the reassertion of values in each individual's life."

Nowhere, of course, is this reassertion more evident than in their new life-style: "a refusal," Reich says "to be regimented."

The reasoning ear begins to prick at the words "individual" and "regimented." Where is the individual in the generation that prefers to move in swarms, suspended in a single beam of sensation and the contagion of crowds? Where is the individual in the armies of the young who, catered to by the

*A Skeptical Look at
The 'New Consciousness'
Of Professor Reich*

mass-media and profit-makers, adopt the same styles and growth of hair as their peers? Have they not produced their own form of regimentation?

What is the meaning of this uniform of revolution, the core of a life-style that has made them the most decorative generation in over a hundred years?

Has their new consciousness a new esthetic? If it has, it has nothing to do with what was called refinement of taste. When the young say "beautiful!", it is not so much a hymn to externals as a salute to experience: the shared experience of their fiercely exclusive community. It has much more

to do with subject than with object; far more an appreciation of meaning —the mystical core—than of form, the visible shell.

It has a great deal to do with two states of being: the natural, as against the artificial; the fluid, as against the static. Long hair is natural; it flows and moves. Cropped hair doesn't. Fringe moves. So do beads, scarves, ponchos, and the body free under fluid fabrics.

Television taught this generation a craving for movement. Film now feeds it. Blacks taught them the visceral frenzy of African dance and sound.

What doesn't move is dead. The repose and serenity which invest so many of the great creative works of man is sought by the young largely in states of trance. They accept tranquillity through drugs.

But this life-style is shot through with paradox. There is nothing "natural" about highly amplified sound. There is nothing "natural" about anything which blunts rather than refines any sense.

The loudest explosion of rock is an assault against consciousness itself. The relentless speed of shifting images in so much of the new film culture splits the retina and splinters the mind. These manifestations are as against nature as the whine of an SST.

So is dirt—another symbol of the new "esthetic" of the natural. Healthy animals keep themselves clean. The assumption that matted hair and soiled clothes are signals of freedom and honesty is as silly as the assumption that short hair and a white shirt are marks of morality.

The scruffiest of the young are only depriving themselves in denying the esthetic of pleasure given as well as received. Embroiled in their own mystique of self, they ignore or deliberately offend the sensibilities of others.

One manifestation of beauty, however, that the young seem to share with others is nature itself. A generation reared in hideous cities, sterile homes, and stenciled suburbs finds in untampered earth a very real joy. Yet the thousands who travel hundreds of miles to experience this joy in communion with their kind, in music and drugs, leave behind them a sea of garbage.

The new consciousness has produced beauty in ballads and the best of rock, in the theatre of exuberance, protest, and flesh, and in fragments of film. Fragmentation is, in fact, the signature of their esthetics. And although they talk about "getting it all together," they seem constitutionally unable or unwilling to do so.

In an interview, Professor Reich conceded that "The new generation doesn't know how to work or how to create a structure of society that will work or that will reflect its values."

When they do, it might indeed be "beautiful!"

———

Marya Mannes, essayist and social critic, is the author of "They."

October 23, 1970

Charles Reich—A Negative View

By HERBERT MARCUSE

If you read a critical essay in The New Yorker, you can be reasonably sure of at least three things: (1) It is beautifully written; (2) it comes very close to the truth; (3) you are satisfied: no reason to get frightened, everything will be all right—or beyond your (and anybody else's) power.

Take as example the by now classical piece on "Hiroshima": there is to my knowledge no better, no more moving description on what happened, and all this appears like a natural catastrophe, an earthquake, the last day of Pompeii—there is no evidence, no possibility of crime, of guilt, of resistance and refusal.

The most recent example is Charles A. Reich's long piece, "The Greening of America," a condensation of the book with the same title. We should admire the sensitivity and good instincts of the editors: they must have realized immediately the vital importance of the piece. The opening sentences read as follows:

"There is a revolution under way. It is not like the revolutions of the past. It has originated with the individual and with culture, and if it succeeds, it will change the political structure only as its final act. It will not require violence to succeed, and it cannot be successfully resisted by violence."

So we are advised that we are in the middle of a revolution which is "spreading with amazing rapidity," and at the same time assured that there will be no violence.

If true, this revolution would indeed be very much unlike the revolutions of the past. All that has to happen (and it is already happening, according to Reich) is that more and more people develop a new consciousness (Consciousness III as contrasted with Consciousness I, corresponding to the early American tradition, and Consciousness II, corresponding to the "Corporate State"), with new values, new goals, a new sensitivity which reject the values and goals of the Corporate State—and the latter will collapse. There will be, there can be no resistance, for the people will just stop working, buying, selling, and they will have won. For the State is nothing but a machine, controlled by nobody, and if the machine is no longer tended to, it will stop.

Consciousness III is of course that of the young generation in rebellion against the Establishment. What are the new revolutionary values of the rebels? The author formulates them in three "commandments"; the first: "thou shall not do violence to thyself"; the second: "no one judges anyone else"; the third: "be wholly honest with others, use no other person as a means." The astonished reader might ask: What is revolutionary about these commandments which from the *Bible* to Kant and beyond have graced the sermons of the moralists?

In a sense, they are indeed present in "Consciousness III" but in a sense essentially different from the tradition which has professed and "sublimated" them so that they get along well with repression, misery, frustration. For the militant young, they are desublimated so that they are no longer compatible with repression, misery and frustration. They are a little less nonviolent: they presuppose the abolition of the established system of institutions, a new society, a new way of life.

For Reich, this is not really a serious problem. One day in the foreseeable future, men and women, boys and girls from all walks of life will have enough of the old, will quit. And since there is "nobody in control," this will be it.

Nobody in control of the armed forces, the police, the National Guard? Nobody in control of the outer space program, of the budget, the Congressional committees? There is only the machine being tended to? But the machine not only must be tended to, it must be designed, constructed, programed, directed. And there are very definite, identifiable persons, groups, classes, interests which do this controlling job, which direct the technical, economic, political machine for the society as a whole. They, not their machine, decided on life and death, war and peace—they set the priorities. They have all the power to defend it—and it is not the power of the machine but *over* the machine: human power, political power.

Even granted that the dream comes true—is it conceivable that this will come about, all over the nation, spontaneously and at the same time? Without any form of preparation, organization, mobilization?

Violence is ingrained in this society: in its institutions, its language, its experience, its fun—violence of defense and violence of aggression. Nobody in his right mind would "advocate" violence: it is there. The task is to reduce it as much as is humanly and socially possible. But this goal cannot be attained by an ostrich policy.

Reich recognizes that the revolutionary changes to come will have a pattern very different from the preceding historical revolutions, that their scope and depth will be greater, that the traditional concepts do not suffice to understand the emerging radical forces. His analysis of the hippie subculture is sensitive—although again much too sensitive—sentimental sublimation.

The best part is perhaps his picture of the Corporate State—not its evaluation. But all this is distorted by the false perspective, which transfigures social and political radicalism into moral rearmament. Notwithstanding its insights and critiques, "The Greening of America" is the Establishment version of the great rebellion.

Herbert Marcuse, until June 1970 Professor of Philosophy, University of California, San Diego, is author of "Reason and Revolution" and "One Dimensional Man."

November 6, 1970

Campus Activism Fades, Style of 1950's Prevails

By ROBERT D. McFADDEN

Political activism is moribund at colleges and universities in New York, New Jersey and Connecticut, and students have taken on the superficial appearance of their self-centered, socially indifferent, All-American campus counterparts of the nineteen-fifties.

They are cutting their hair, studying harder, shunning esoteric life-styles and their behavior is generally so docile that a few formerly embattled school administrators call it eerie. A few other school officials say this has been going on so long it is just boring.

After three years of campus calm that followed the uprisings over the Cambodia invasion and the Kent State killings, this postwar spring has settled in with a politica sleepy - headedness unequaled since the Eisenhower years. Many students cannot recall when they last heard fiery rhetoric, let alone saw a demonstration.

National issues — as well as most state and local ones—are all but ignored. Even the Watergate scandal hardly raised an eyebrow. And while some questions involving women's rights, local housing and campus safety occasionally cause a stir, the remaining radicals are Pirandello - like characters in search of a cause.

This seems all the more dramatic today, the fifth anniversary of the student uprising at Columbia University, where hundreds were injured and arrested in clashes with the police.

Though reasons vary considerably, the vast majority of students now appear to be devoted to themselves—to achieving success, acquiring money and having a good time—all in the most cherished, middle-class Establishment style.

These are the major conclusions drawn from interviews in recent weeks with hundreds of students, faculty members and school administrators by campus correspondents of The New York Times at tristate colleges and universities.

The survey of student interests, activities, concerns and life-styles, supplemented by the correspondents' own observations, also pointed up the following:

¶Most students believe that demonstrations and other forms of protest by students over the Vietnam war and other issues in the nineteen-sixties achieved little or nothing. The idealism of the effort is admired, but the effort itself is thought to have been unrealistic and the issues too abstract.

¶Students are most concerned about their own pursuits and futures—about their grades, chances of getting into graduate schools and lucrative careers, marriage prospects, personal ambitions, personal friendships and, occasionally, what they consider a realistically solvable problem, such as a rash of thefts in a dormitory.

¶They also chase the bluebirds of happiness of the nineteen-fifties. Liquor, wine and beer are increasingly popular, as are on-campus pubs and schmaltzy juke - box dancing. There have even been a few mock-nostalgic formal dances. Marijuana, pill-popping and sex are big party favorites, but opiates have virtually no takers.

¶Alienation as a general attitude and the generation gap in particular are not in vogue. Many faculty members and school administrators talk of student courtesy, civility and attentiveness; many students praise their teachers, discount the radicals' perception of administrators as reactionary and talk effusively about their parents as understanding and generous.

¶Long hair, scruffy blue jeans and faded shirts—once symbols of defiance—have lost their radical connotations, and barbers and stylish clothiers are making a comeback. Students say there is more freedom and less pressure to conform in matters of personal appearance.

¶Besides ignoring nearly all political and social issues of public concern, students at many schools have lost interest in what was once a major push to gain a voice in the policies and operations of their schools. Student-government organizations also lack support generally, though they are important at a few schools.

¶Race relations appear to be generally good, but many blacks and Latin students maintain "Third World" corridors in classrooms and dormitories and a voluntary separatism in social life that may hide tensions to some extent. Much of the white-liberal guilt in campus race relations of the last decade seems to be gone.

Interviews suggesting these general trends were conducted at Fordham, Columbia and New York Universities and the City College of New York here; the State University centers at Stony Brook and Binghamton; Vassar College at Poughkeepsie, N.Y., Rutgers and Princeton Universities in New Jersey and Yale University and Connnecticut College in Connecticut.

The end of direct American involvement in Vietnam and the end of the military draft are the most obvious and frequently cited reasons for the vanishing stock of political activism. But others cited a disillusionment with radicals and many said they thought the era of demonstrations had accomplished nothing and left the student body-politic benumbed.

"I thought the persons who organized us were out for peace, love and happiness," said Dorinda Deodata, a Fordham senior. "Then we got to Washington and they started throwing rocks through windows and chanting 'Ho-Ho-Ho-Chi-Minh.' They used us."

"The killing of millions and discrimination just does not arouse the feeling that it did five years ago," said Mark Dawson, a student-government leader at Stony Brook. "Things like the Watergate caper don't shock anybody. Nothing shocks anybody anymore."

"Lobbying is the style for the seventies," said Mitch Medine, the student-government president at Binghamton. "Ten well-informed people making their cases in Congress or in the State Legislature can ' be more effective than a half-million people in the streets."

Not all issues of public concern are dead. Housing and tenants' rights have drawn attention recently at Rutgers, Binghamton and Columbia. Crime—mainly thefts and assaults—are cited as concerns at Stony Brook and Columbia. Homosexual movements received considerable attention this year at Fordham, and just last week—contrary to the general apolitical trend—the Student Peace Union at Fordham said its 30 members had raised $700 on campus for Quaker relief efforts in Vietnam.

Apathy Called a Problem

At Yale, about 70 people turned up at a recent demonstration against a Marine recruiter on campus. But the Yale Political Union, which brings notables to speak on campus, made its big splash of the year in February with the appearance of Ann Landers, the syndicated-advice columnist, who was applauded for favoring abortion on demand.

In general, the women's liberation movement is the most prevalent political force on college campuses, but its leaders say apathy rather than opposition is their biggest problem.

Outwardly, the broad retreat in the last three years from political activism to personal and parochial concerns appears to be a resurgence of the middle-class values and apathetic innocence of the nineteen-fifties.

But there are numerous indications that the similarities are only superficial, that the upheavals of the nineteen-sixties have left permanent imprints on the student psyche.

"Less Hypocritical"

Today's college student appears to be more aware but more cynical about the nation's problems, less inhibited but less inclined to act in situations without concrete aims and the prospect of success. Many object to being called apathetic, and refer to themselves as "practical" or "realistic."

"People who got involved in politics found out they were ineffective," said Elisa Curialle, a 20-year-old N.Y.U. senior, voicing a popular view.

"They're facing personal problems now," she went on. "I think those problems are really harder to solve. Anyone can sit down and discuss what to do about poverty. People realize now that you can't live without money. They're less hypocritical. It's no longer unfashionable to say you're looking for a job to get money."

A C.C.N.Y. student, Larry Peobles, said students had a "monumental ambivalence toward all issues that have nothing to do with their own ambitions or goals." As for idealism, he added: "Once you give up wanting to be a fireman or a cowboy, you're only in it for the money."

Lucrative Goals Cited

Citing inflation, rising unemployment and increasing competition in graduate schools and the professional job markets— plus their own desires to make lots of money—students are spending more time studying and directing their efforts toward the lucrative goals.

"We're caught in a professional sandwich," said Carolyn Grillo, a Yale Junior. "One slice is law school, the other is medical school."

At Princeton, Jay Lucker, a

librarian, said: "If you come to the main library at 9 P.M., it looks like Grand Central Station." This was echoed in reports from most schools surveyed. Though academic performance is difficult to measure, school officials generally said they thought it was improving.

The rapidly increasing costs of education also have added to the mood of student seriousness, with many working to pay part of their expenses. At Princeton, where next year's minimum costs will be $5,400, nearly half of the 4,000 undergraduates hold part-time jobs.

Students are, nonetheless, relaxing. At Columbia this year, there have been beer-drinking contests, tugs-of-war, an ice-skating party and a performance by a stripper hired by 150 freshmen. The latter prompted a protest by women editors of The Columbia Daily Spectator.

Drinking and dancing, somewhat tarnished relics of yesteryear, have been revived with gusto. Students regularly drink beer and dance to records in the Lion's Den in the basement of Ferris Booth Hall at Columbia—once a radical command post. "It's straight out of American Bandstand," said 21-year-old Marcy Glanz of Barnard.

The Yale prom, which died in 1971, was resurrected last winter. Many considered it a joke, but other groups are now considering formal dances.

At Princeton, a new pub is the most popular spot on campus. Plans are under way to set up a bar in the student recreation building at Connecticut College in New London, and the pub in the student center at Binghamton had to be doubled in size recently to accommodate overflowing crowds.

Drinking tastes are also being upgraded. Sangria and jug wines used to be most popular among N.Y.U. students who patronize the Astor Place Liquor Store, according to the manager, Dominique Manzone. "Now they buy the better Italian and French wines," he said. "They have graduated."

Marijuana and various types of pills, including depressants called Quaaludes, are widely popular.

Jim Borzilleri, a Vassar freshman, said that student energies formerly devoted to protests now "are in Quaaludes, alcohol, bad grass and good women." Another Vassar student said: "The energies have paired off and gone to bed, locking the door behind them."

The sexual revolution is perhaps the clearest illustration that any similarity between students of today and those of the nineteen-fifties is superficial. Co-ed dormitories are now commonplace, as are apartment-living arrangements between unwed men and women students. Many say an emotional commitment is no longer a prerequisite for sexual relations.

Personal appearance is increasingly amoral as well as apolitical. "There's no longer a romanticism about poverty," said one N.Y.U. student. "For awhile it was very fashionable to look poor, especially if you weren't."

Barbers in and around campuses report brisk business, as do clothing stores with mod styles. But despite the appearance of dark fingernail polish and lipstick, unisex clothes and platform shoes—all seemingly faddish — most students say they feel little or no pressure to conform sartorially.

"Last year, I'd walk into a class with a skirt on and people would look at me like I had bad breath," said a Princeton co-ed. "Now, you can even wear stockings and not get the crazy stares."

The quest for student power in school operations and policies, which achieved some successes in the sixties, has left few traces at most schools. At C.C.N.Y., for example, student senate elections in the last three years have failed to draw more than 15 per cent of the voters. Some senate seats are unfilled because of dropouts, and the deadline for senate-president nominations had to be extended recently because there were no contenders.

Princeton's undergraduate assembly is an exception, influencing academic, financial and social functions considerably. "The perceptions of students have been very helpful in guiding the university committees to make balanced judgments,"

said Princeton's provost, Sheldon Hackney.

In a similar tone of amity, Fordham's president, the Rev. James Finlay, said his campus had experienced "a return to a spirit of warmth," adding: "I don't run into hostility much anymore. There is a growth of civility among students."

Some students said the so-called "generation gap" no longer existed. "My mother and father are the best people I know," said Herbert Michaels, a member of the Students for a Democratic Society at C.C.N.Y. "I also know a lot of teachers who are good people."

Another C.C.N.Y. student, Tom McDonald, put it another way: "There are an awful lot of 20-year-olds here with 50-year-old values. I've met people here whose only justification for taking education is [that] it pays $18,000 after seven years."

At most schools surveyed, little or no apparent racial tension was reported, though it was noted at several that blacks and Latin students maintain a "Third World" voluntary separatism in living accommodations and social situations.

Dr. Lamar Miller, professor of education and the director of the Institute of Afro-American Affairs at N.Y.U., said: "Black students have sort of been beaten back. They still complain about racism and discrimination and bias on the campus, but the effort to change things is not as it was."

April 23, 1973

Streaking: A Mad Dash To Where?

By ROBERT D. McFADDEN

Is it an art form? Is it an uncontrollable urge? Is it political? Perhaps perverse? Healthy? Naughty?

Streaking—the new spring rite of sprinting in the nude, preferably before a big gawking audience — was praised, put down and generally laid bare yesterday in a series of interviews with psychiatrists, sociologists and other educated guessers, including some streakers.

And even as these experts expounded their theories, the phenomenon spread from the nation's collegiate campuses to shopping centers, factories, spring-training baseball diamonds, the hallowed halls of the Michigan State Capitol and on Wall Street.

'A Form of Assault'

Clad in the latest accessories — sneakers, neckties, masks and body paint— streakers pranced at West Point, rode bicycles in Rhode Island, took to motorcycles in Iowa and hopped a firetruck in Florida. It was, in fact, a big day for streakers.

A coterie of devotees at the State University Center at New Paltz, N. Y. organized the New Paltz Intramural Streaking Club. And at Fordham University, where jaybirds swung in the trees outside a coed dormitory, officials pronounced streaking— and inciting to streaking — an offense punishable by suspension.

Last night at Colombia, 50 streakers appeared around 11 o'clock, followed by a band and a crowd of 500 that blocked traffic on Broadway. There were some unverified reports of streakers being struck by bystanders.

Amid the frolicking, there emerged some more or less considered analyses.

"Streaking is a put-on, a form of assault," said Marshall McLuhan, the author and communications theorist who is director of the Center

for Culture and Technology at the University of Toronto. In a telephone interview, he added:

"It's an art form, of course. All entertainment has elements of malice and power in it. Streaking has a political point, too. It's a form of activism."

Professor McLuhan also had a linguistic point to make, noting that streakers are nude but never naked. "It's only when you don't want to be seen that you're naked," he said. "A stripper backstage is naked, but when she is in front of an audience she is wearing her public."

Dr. Robert Michels of the New York Psychiatric Institute at the Columbia Presbyterian Medical Center, described streaking as "the defiance of accepted cultural norms—more naughty than sexual."

"I see it as a continuation of fads of provocative and socially amazing behavior," Dr. Michels continued, "much more in line with panty raids, swallowing goldfish and doing consecutive whatevers . . .

startling and astounding. Disturbing. The inherent meaning is just silly."

If there is a political point, he said, it is that young people are telling an older and more powerful generation that "social customs and norms are based on arbitrary rules."

Energy Crisis Cited

Dr. David Abrahamsen, a Manhattan psychoanalyst and the author of 10 books, said he thought streakers were "trying to liberate themselves" after a "long winter without sexual outlets." Dr. Abrahamsen also drew a relationship of sorts between streaking and the energy crisis.

The gasoline shortage, he said, has made it more difficult for youngsters to use cars parked in shady lanes. The resulting sexual frustration, he said, has contributed to the streaking phenomenon. Dr. Abrahamsen, a Norwegian, also suggested that streaking might "give a lift to nudism."

Dr. Robert J. Lifton, a professor of psychiatry at Yale

University, called streaking a prank in the long collegiate tradition—"a challenge to authority and a mockery of authority." But more is involved, he said, "like sex, the sexual revolution and social mores."

But, Dr. Lifton added, "there are three things I'm sure it's not: It's not a return to the fifties; it's not a sign of the corruption of American morality and it's not a threat to national security."

A Yale streaker, one of four placed on probation for a midnight dash with a flaming torch, said it was simply a prank. "We had no message to get across," he said. "It's very important for everyone to keep a perspective on the fact that we're college students and college students are supposed to

have fun."

A cadet at the United States Military Academy at West Point, said that he was one of dozens of streakers who dashed around the post in the buff "with the officers chasing us."

"We did it to relieve the monotony," he said. "Everybody was hanging out the windows cheering."

In other streaking action yesterday, Mark W. Nunes, a 21-year-old self-styled drifter from Crow's Landing, Calif., dashed down the center aisle of the Michigan House of Representatives at Lansing, while stunned lawmakers bolted from their chairs agape at the figure in boots and ski mask. He was seized by a sergeant-at-arms but was released without charges after a friend brought his clothes from the legislative bathroom.

Wall Street had its first streaker yesterday, an un-

named 28-year-old bond broker without portfolio. He was said to be an employe of the First National City Bank, but he dashed through Chase Manhattan Plaza.

Baseball games in Miami, Atlanta and Statesboro, Ga., were invaded by seventh-inning streakers, and a pitcher at Jacksonville State in Alabama said a streaker ruined his no-hitter by forcing him to serve up a double.

In Deland, Fla., 28 men wearing only towel masks hopped aboard a fraternity fire truck and toured the town. A young man wearing boots, a bow-tie and a frozen smile introduced streaking to Calgary, in Alberta, Canada, dashing down the main thoroughfare when the temperature was 2 degrees below zero. Witnesses called it a numbing performance.

Fifteen students at Michigan State University in East Lansing staged what they

contended was the first classroom streak.

A "Streak for Impeachment" had about a dozen participants on the Fairleigh-Dickinson campus in Rutherford, N.J.

A few arrests were made around the country, but the police in most instances were looking the other way. That was the case at Syracuse University, where 18-year-old Rob Sedwin raced about in sneakers and a wristwatch as 3,000 of his classmates chanted: "Streak! Streak! Streak!"

"Today was a good day to let yourself go," he said as he buttoned up his blue jeans after the romp. "You feel like a flower taking off its winter clothes. Deep down, everybody has the urge to streak in them."

March 8, 1974

Youth's New Values

By Fred M. Hechinger

The nation's college students have learned to enjoy life in a sick society, and noncollege youths would like to share the fun. A cynical view? Yet, this is the general picture that emerges from the latest study by Daniel Yankelovich, "Changing Youth Values in the Seventies: A Study of American Youth."

The dramatic change on campuses from war to peace was, as the survey stressed, an extraordinarily quick transition. A superficial view of the new scene might suggest much to cheer about.

Traditionalists may well applaud the students' "new central theme" of trying to "find self-fulfillment within a conventional career." The rejection of violence, even to attain desirable objectives, is a definite gain. Education—only so recently denounced as "irrelevant"—now is strongly endorsed.

It need not be a mystery or surprise that most of the discontent that was the mark of collegians during the nineteen-sixties is now registered by noncollege youths.

This could, in part, be explained simply as the normal time lag—the masses catching up with the mores of the trend-setting élite. It would then be safe to predict that the present blue-collar discontent will in turn eventually catch up with the collegians' current quiescent accommodation.

Far more disturbing is the composite of what the survey calls the "new values" that the total youth group—collegians and working-class—apparently subscribe to and that are in-

creasingly shared by the older generation as well.

It is easy to welcome the scuttling of the old-fashioned "my country right or wrong" kind of patriotism. It is a mark of progress that the war in Vietnam was denied the jingoistic support of, say, the Spanish-American War.

Nor can there be any serious quarrel with youth's alienation from religious Establishments that have often identified themselves with the conservative political Establishment, in disregard of the demands of social justice and reform.

Certainly, no legitimate objections should be raised to young people's rejection of the authority of institutions — governmental or corporate — that have grown unresponsive, oppressive or corrupt.

The nagging questions concern the nature of the new values that were found to have replaced the old. Using a polite sociological term, the survey suggests that "self-fulfillment" has become the central new value, and it offers this summary:

"Stress on the theme of gratification is the individual's way of saying that there must be something more to life than making a living, struggling to make ends meet, and caring for others. The self-fulfillment concept also implies a greater preoccupation with self at the expense of sacrificing one's self for family, employer and community."

No amount of rationalizing can pretty up a picture of a new cult of the self. The old rugged individualism had its seamy side; a new turn toward hedonistic individualism is no more appealing.

If it is true that collegians and working youths are discarding the belief that "living a clean moral life is a very important value," then it is difficult to take seriously these same young people's demand for the reform of big business and of the political parties.

It is even harder to square an easy-going private morality with the almost universal view among the young that business is too much concerned with profits and not enough with public responsibility. If individuals show little concern over their private morality, is it realistic to expect business and politics to be clean and public-spirited? Those who eventually move into executives suites—or into the White House —will, after all, bring with them the values of their own previous morality, of campus or Main Street.

One might be encouraged by the reported new noninterest in making money, were it not that these attitudes appear to have been shaped by the existing high level of economic security rather than by a measurable decline in materialism. The two most neglected groups, the racial minorities and the Vietnam veterans, who lack such security, clearly do not share the majority's cavalier attitude toward money. One cannot help but worry about the impact of a self-centered and self-satisfied majority on the fate of those disadvantaged groups.

Yet, it is the continued sense of despair among those groups—55 per cent of black youths consider the society sick and 76 per cent see it as undemocratic — that needs public-spirited attention. Will such attention

335

be forthcoming if a majority is primarily interested in self-fulfillment? Is there much hope for a spirit of *noblesse oblige* from an upper middle-class that, according to Mr. Yankelovich, is "the most satisfied group . . . most at ease with the society as it exists . . ."?

That, of course, is a classic description of an élite whose values are shaped by enjoyment of the good life. If the majority of the nation's youth aspire to membership in that "large and growing social class" and if a college education is seen primarily as the admission ticket to a society of happy Bourbons, then the outlook is bleak indeed for those outside the charmed circle—and for the nation governed by the "new values."

Fred M. Hechinger is a member of the Editorial Board of The Times.

May 28, 1974

Students Flock to Job-Related Courses

By GENE I. MAEROFF
Special to The New York Times

STATE COLLEGE, Pa., Nov. 1—The nation's troubled economy and the accompanying complications of the energy shortage are causing an unprecedented boom in business and energy-related courses at colleges and universities across the country.

In a quest for better job credentials and an improved understanding of the forces that they think will shape their lives in years to come, students are deserting the humanities and many of the social sciences for academic programs that they consider more practical.

Here at Pennsylvania State University, which has an on-campus enrollment of 31,583 and 21,393 others at its branches, the nationwide trend is reflected in record enrollments in business administration, economics, engineering, agriculture, mining and mineral sciences.

Officials of the rapidly growing College of Earth and Mineral Sciences say they have received more liberal arts transfers in the last six months than in the previous 20 years. One of the new graduate students in metallurgy got her bachelor's degree in French.

Accounting and economics are bearing the brunt of the stampede into business-related programs at Penn State and elsewhere. Many of the students are seeking vocationally oriented minors to go with their less marketable majors, and others want one or two basic courses so they will at least be conversant on the economy.

Economics has become the largest undergraduate department at Harvard. Class sections in economics filled up so quickly at Brooklyn College that registration had to be closed early. More than 2,660 students signed up for lower-division economics courses at Ohio State, an increase of 24 percent, and 120 students had to be turned away.

"It is testing our ingenuity to find enough classrooms and instructors for all these students," said Dr. Grant N. Farr, chairman of Penn State's economics department.

An academic offshoot of the energy shortage has been the whetting of students' curiosity in programs dealing with the Middle East and the Arab people, whom they see as holding a pivotal spot in determining the course of the future. New and enlarged programs are appearing regularly.

The Middle Eastern Studies Center at the University of Texas gets more than 30 letters of inquiry a week from people considering a master's program tying in with business and petroleum engineering.

In the business area, students everywhere have developed a special fascination for courses in accounting. Jobs in that field are plentiful: the average starting salary for an accountant with a bachelor's degree is now $11,760.

Enrollment at Bentley College in Waltham, Mass., which produces more accountants than any school in the country, increased almost 20 percent in one year, from 4,065 to 4,860, at a time when many other private institutions are withering from a lack of applicants.

Five Bentley faculty positions are vacant because Ph.D's in accounting are not being graduated fast enough to keep up with the hiring demands of college and university faculties.

What bothers Dr. Edward Sommers, chairman of the accounting department at the University of Texas, is that "there has been a tremendous influx of marginal students" into accounting because of the employment opportunities.

Not only has this led to a massive quality control problem, Dr. Sommers said, but it also has made crowding so severe that fire marshals have expressed concern.

Recruiting Campaign

This enrollment pressure in a few select areas is coming at a time of fiscal exigency for many universities, when the number of students entering other departments is leveling off.

Thus, faculty expansion in the newly popular disciplines frequently does not occur, even though it seems warranted.

Not only are payrolls weighted down by tenured professors in fields no longer attractive to students, but there also is institutional anxiety over the possibility that the enrollment shifts may be a fad.

Brandeis University in Waltham, Mass., which had three sections of about 35 students each last year in introductory economics, is saving money this year by putting them all in one class, even though the number of students taking the course has risen to 200.

An impetus for the dramatic enrollment increases is the new-found interest of women in some fields they have traditionally shunned. By and large, their motives appear to parallel those of their male counterparts.

"What do I expect out of majoring in accounting?" Susan Phillips, a junior at the University of Texas, asked rhetorically. "A good job with lots of money," she said.

Carol Leisenring, who joined the economics faculty at Penn State in September as the only woman in a 46-member department, has about 10 women among the 60 students in her "Introductory Microeconomics Analysis and Policy."

"Just a few years ago, I wouldn't have expected more than two or three women in a class like that," remarked Miss Leisenring.

A radio and television recruiting campaign by Penn State has raised the number of women in engineering from less than 1 percent five years ago to 8 percent today, helping the College of Engineering to show a 40 per cent enrollment growth in the last three years.

The prospect of readily available jobs for men and women who can help the world satisfy its hunger for energy and minerals is raising enrollments on a wide front.

A mining engineering program that was allowed to die 10 years ago at the University of Pittsburgh has been reinstituted. Lamar University in Beaumont, Tex., is offering a new degree in energy resources management.

Disdain and Jealousy

Meanwhile, liberal arts professors at many institutions, their enrollments tumbling, view the flurry of activity in such fields as business, mining and engineering with a mixture of disdain and jealousy. One response has been to try to draw back students by infusing the liberal arts with a vocational element.

Penn State's French department is considering a program with the College of Business Administration. Eastern Michigan University will train managers for cultural institutions. Baruch College in New York has a similar program to give history majors the business expertise to run historical societies.

Some academicians are wondering where the accent on vocationalism will lead, and whether a steady erosion of the liberal arts is inevitable. But, whatever the effects on the rest of the curriculum, the trend is clearly toward more career orientation, and the troubled economy and the energy shortage are promoting that trend.

November 3, 1975

Many Rebels of the 1960's Depressed as They Near 30

By ROBERT LINDSEY
Special to The New York Times

LOS ANGELES, Feb. 28—The rebellious, idealistic generation of adolescents who reached maturity in the 1960's is now approaching 30, and for many, according to psychiatrists and mental health counselors, the trip into adult life is being dogged by disillusionment and depression.

Many young Americans who matured during the 60's—when many traditional standards of behavior and morality came under challenge—have glided easily into adulthood, they say. Many never joined the rebellion. Others have assimilated easily into the system they once rebelled against, while still others are continuing happily to pursue alternative life styles.

But, according to dozens of specialists who counsel

336

young people, interviewed in 14 cities across the country, large numbers of the men and women who grew up in the 60's are now experiencing a generational malaise of haunting frustrations, anxiety and depression.

The malaise, they say, is reflected in an increase in the number of people in their late 20's and early 30's receiving psychiatric help; by a rise in suicides and alcoholism in this age group, and a boom in the popularity of certain charismatic religious movements, astrology, and pop psychology cults that reflect part of this generation's search for contentment.

The reasons cited for its problems range from disillusionment following the Watergate scandals, to disorientation caused by new sexual freedom, to the failure of life to fulfill the expectations established for themselves and society during the idealistic 60's.

Many who "dropped out" are said to be depressed about the difficulties they are now having in trying to enter a competitive job market at a time of economic retrenchment, while others, with little work experience and accustomed to having parents pay their bills, are having difficulty coping with responsibilities of a job, especially ones they regard as unglamorous or not socially "meaningful."

"They are threatened by the future," Dr. Edward Stanbrook, chairman of the department of human behavior at the University of California School of Medicine, observed about the adolescents of the 60's. "They see the possibility of not having jobs, not having a lot of things their parents and grandparents took for granted. They see the possibility of not having an adequate role in society."

"The values that worked for their parents are not holding today, so they don't have the same values to hold them on their journey; they feel alone," said Dr. William Ackerly, a staff psychiatrist at Metropolitan State Hospital in Waltham, Mass.

Pattern of 'Alienation'

Dr. Leonard Bachelis, director of the Behavior Therapy Center in New York, sees a pattern of "alienation" among many in this generation, a force that he says brings young people into his office to tell him: "I've got a good job, I'm successful, and I want to kill myself. Life doesn't mean anything."

"People spent the 60's trying to get closer to each other, getting to learn intimacy, shedding their hang-ups, finding that it's okay to be authentic, to let it all hang out, as the jargon goes," he said. "But now they find that somehow, something is missing—that it

didn't do the trick."

Meanwhile, just behind the generation that matured in the 60's is a newer crop of young people, and some are said to be experiencing a different kind of disillusionment.

Many, said the counseling specialists, have enthusiastically enrolled in the "system" that many of their predecessors spurned. They are hitting the books and striving for success, but suspect the system is betraying them by failing to deliver what they expected—a good job.

Counseling specialists emphasize that it is impossible to generalize about the millions of young people who lived through the social changes that began a decade ago. A soldier who turned 21 under fire in Vietnam, changed differently than one who went through the campus revolt at Columbia University, they said.

Distortion Conceded

The psychiatrists and other counselors also stressed that their vision of this generation was distorted because they tended to see only its middle-class members who seek help. They say that many factors—such as the environment in their homes—are responsible for emotional difficulties, and they say that young people in general are more inclined to seek psychiatric help now than they did in the past.

Nevertheless, the interviews, conducted in all regions of the country, disclosed a pattern of problems that suggest they are being experienced by many members of this generation. (There were regional variations to the pattern. Psychiatrists in Kansas City, Mo., and Lincoln, Neb., for example, reported fewer such problems than those in areas such as New York, Los Angeles and Chicago, where the social turmoil of the 60's was more intense.)

The young people of the 60's were probably the most widely studied and publicized generation ever in this country and, one, according to many psychiatrists, that developed high levels of self-awareness, self-esteem, confidence and high expectations.

Much of the current malaise, the experts say, stems from the failure of many of this group to fulfill the visions of success they were led to believe would be theirs.

"To put it in simplistic, laymen's terms," a Los Angeles psychiatrist said, "a lot of these kids were led to believe the world would be handed to them on a silver platter. They got spoiled by permissive parents, and aren't prepared for a cruel world."

"However," he added, "you still have to point out that a lot of kids went through this period and became good doctors, good lawyers, good politicians, and weathered the storm."

'Already Done Everything'

Several psychiatrists reported that some young persons appeared emotionally to be, in effect, "burned out." While still young, they sampled fruits forbidden to other generations—drugs, many sexual partners, a freedom to experiment in many ways—and now have a sense of emptiness that they've "already done everything," it was said.

The counselors said depression was common among young women who have not succeeded in the business or professional worlds, despite being well educated and having their hopes raised by the women's movement.

"The women's movement has caused a lot of anxiety among both males and females," said Dr. Felix Ocko, a Berkeley, Calif., psychiatrist. "Many men don't know how to handle the more aggressive women. And although women are more aggressive, many don't know what they want, what their role should be, how they should fit in, how much femininity they'll lose by pursuing a professional career."

Although many people in their 20's are said to have no problems coping with modern sexual permissiveness, several psychiatrists said pressure to perform has caused higher rates of impotence among men, and depression among some women who feel they are "being used."

Sex and Wisdom

"There's a tremendous amount of sexual freedom," said Dr. Fred E. Davis, director of Tulane University's counseling center, "but there has not been a parallel increase in wisdom on how to handle the new freedom."

Dr. George Mallory, chief of adult psychiatry at a hospital in the predominantly black community of Watts here, said many young blacks in this age group were also suffering from problems of depression.

He attributes their problems to a number of factors—aftereffects on many of serving in Vietnam; failure of society to fulfill many of the dreams that seemed attainable at the peak of the civil rights movement; a shortage of attractive jobs, and for some, a sense of guilt for having succeeded.

"I think depression among successful blacks in their late 20's and early 30's," he said, "is sometimes caused by their great fear of success. I had one patient, a girl in her late 20's from a wonderful family; she had a college education and seemed to be doing well, but she had a fear of success. She kept thinking it was wrong for her to succeed.

"With the civil rights movement," he went on, "blacks could find positive ways of expressing anger at not having jobs, not having a place to live, not having good schools; now these opportunities are gone, and there's no way people can express this anger except by directing it back upon themselves and becoming depressed."

Most of the specialists stressed that it was impossible to determine exactly the percentage of this generation having trouble. Most said that it could be a small minority and that it was clear many young people had adapted to adulthood. But they emphasized that problems were clearly a pattern among many of the young adults, and said a clearer picture would have to await studies that could measure the extent of the problems.

Dr. Robert S. Brown, a psychiatrist in Collegeville, Pa., estimated that, based on a study he made using standardized tests, about one-third of the people in their 20's and 30's are "very depressed and anxious" much of the time.

Dr. Perry Ottenberg, senior attending psychiatrist at the Institute of the Pennsylvania Hospital, estimated that adolescents and young adults probably account for 50 to 75 percent of the patients in many psychiatric hospitals and clinics, a trend that partly reflects the greater awareness of this generation of emotional stresses, as well as in church programs that now finance much of this kind of care.

According to the National Center for Health Statistics, the suicide rate for Americans aged 20 to 24 jumped from 8.9 per 100,000 persons in 1965 to 15.1 in 1974. In the 25-to-29 age group, the increase was from 11.3 per 100,000 to 15.9.

Commenting on the increase, Dr. Seymour Perlin, a professor of psychiatry at George Washington University who is an editor of "The Handbook for the Study of Suicides," said:

"Kids now don't see any way to change things. There are no rallying points in their lives, so they look to existential questions. It seems to many that one of the few things they have control over is the taking of their own lives."

"In my opinion, the 1960's raised the hopes of young people a little too high and now they have met with disillusionment and depression in the 70's," said Dr. Kenneth Silvers, a psychiatrist who teaches at the University of California, Los Angeles. Many young people, he said, have set unrealistic goals—of achieving glamorous jobs that they are unlikely to attain.

The nation's depressed job market — especially the gap that has developed between the number of college graduates and the number of available jobs that usually go to college graduates—appears to be a major cause of the depression experienced by many young people.

"You'd be amazed at the number of young people who

put themselves through college working as barmaids, bunnies, selling marijuana, working at anything to achieve their goal —which is to graduate; and when they reach the date and can't find a job, that's really a big wipe-out," said Betty Spencer, a clinical social worker at the Pontchartrain Mental Health Clinic in New Orleans.

Many of the young people that visit Seattle's East Side Mental Health Center, said Karol Marshall, a psychologist,

have a sense of "despair." She continued:

"It's puzzling, as if no one taught them how to shape their future, how to make the future responsive to their wishes. They seem to have been taught: 'You can expect to get what you want out of life and it will come your way.'

"Now they're finding that this philosophy doesn't necessarily work. They can't get the job they want. They have a sense of helplessness, direc-

tionlessness, and purposeless-ness, and this deteriorates into depression."

Dr. Graham Blaine, a former head of psychiatric services at Harvard, said:

"The most fascinating aspect of youth today is the narrowing of the generation gap. Somehow, the end result of the recent revolutionary period, including the Vietnam War, worked as a lever with which the young moved older people.

"Today, youth is in a unique

position of being allowed—not necessarily officially—to smoke marijuana and to bring their sweetheart home and share a bedroom."

Meanwhile, he said, younger people are slowly becoming more conventional than they were a decade ago, and beginning to see their own goals as compatible with those of their parents.

February 29, 1976

'76 Politics Fail to Disturb Campus Calm and Cynicism

BY JON NORDHEIMER

KENT, Ohio — Harriet Begala was pleased. The Democratic Party's rally at Kent State University the other night was the best political showing on campus since 1972.

On a campus with more than 20,000 full-time students, most from working-class backgrounds, fewer than 30 students had turned out in a show of support for Jimmy Carter. And even those who came seemed nervous and wary, hesitant to volunteer their time.

"It's not like '72, when we had more than 400 student volunteers manning the phones for George McGovern," Mrs. Begala, a local Democratic worker, said later, "but it's far better than 1974 when we had to pay 10 women to make phone calls in the campaign for governor when we couldn't get student volunteers."

The fact that anyone could be pleased by such an anemic turnout was indicative of how low political activism has fallen on Kent State's campus, where National Guard troops killed four students after opening fire on an anti-Vietnam War protest demonstration in 1972.

But all across the nation this fall, not just Kent State, both rebellion and activism seem far from students' minds. Protest, to this generation of college students, is not only dead—it is "uncool."

Beer busts and R.O.T.C. are back in vogue.

The current Presidential campaign, for the most part, has a remote, detached presence on campuses where four years ago thousands of students plunged into the volunteer work of the Nixon-McGovern race. On nearly every campus, with the possible exception of schools in Georgia, campaign organizers report finding little student enthusiasm for either Mr. Carter or President Ford, the Republican incumbent.

Apathy vs. Anomie

Some observers have compared today's campus mood to the buttoned-down apathy of students in the 1950's. But the causes of the current inaction are different.

In the 50's there was apathy: Students complacently sought individual goals within the context of an ordered society that had their general approval and confidence. Today there is anomie: a general mistrust of and lack of involvement with the nation's leadership and institutions; a bewilderment and confusion over what to do, how to do it, and little faith in the effectiveness of any kind of action.

"What we are seeing today is a move toward privatism," said Prof. Sandford M. Dornbusch, a sociologist at Stanford University in California since 1959.

"Instead of joining others for change, this generation of students is giving up and saying, 'How am I going to survive?'. There's a great stress on individual fulfillment rather than societal improvement."

"Politicians don't understand human feelings," remarked Jean Stone, a sophomore at Miami-Dade Junior College, the largest two-year community college in the East, "and the country is being run by big businesses that have no concern for the average guy. I don't think I can trust either Carter or Ford."

From Palo Alto to Miami, from Boston to Los Angeles, a check with students and faculty members on a dozen campuses turned up the same theme of political alienation coupled with strivings by individuals to impose some form of structure on their personal lives.

Almost everywhere, students were engrossed by the pursuit of grades and jobs. There was universal concern that a tight job market created by an economic turndown, and the sheer numbers of the post-World War II baby boom generation now competing for work, would dominate their lives for years to come.

This pragmatism has created a rush in applications to business schools, and everywhere students appear to be turning away from interest in education and the humanities, areas of study that were highly popular among activist students of the 60's.

"Money is the most important value to students today," said Dr. James H. Lewis, professor of agriculture business at Colorado State University. "They are aware of the fact that the free lunch is over."

'No Atmosphere for Radicalism'

"It is not an atmosphere for bold departures in radicalism," commented Dr. Richard Smoke, a political scientist at the Wright Institute of the University of California at Berkeley, where the student rebellion took its first massive step during the Free Speech Movement in 1964.

Berkeley today has a quiet, almost benign climate compared with the foment of the 60's. In Sproul Plaza, the issues nerve center of the campus, spokesmen of the radical Left are still present, but their rhetoric seems less impassioned— and their audience is almost nonexistent. Much more attention at Sproul seems

focused on the advocates of religious cults.

The seniors who now face decisions about their future entered college in the fall of 1973. For the most part, they had no involvement in the years of campus rebellion and political activism. Most played no role in the McGovern campaign of 1972, and only a small minority possess emotional links to the "Keep It Clean For Gene" slogan of the 1968 Presidential campaign of Eugene McCarthy, the former Democratic Senator of Minnesota who is an independent Presidential candidate this year.

Instead, their political instincts have been shaped by the Watergate and intelligence agency scandals and by scary unemployment figures. Their common outlook is cynical and pragmatic, in the view of many who study the evolving nature of the American campus.

The Now Generation has become the Me Generation.

There are no heroes on the campus today. In scores of interviews, when the question was put to them, no student proposed the name of an individual who combined those traits worthy of universal respect and emulation: No politicians, no politicians, no rock stars or football heroes.

There are, however, trends on campuses that demand comparisons with the untroubled 50's. Social fraternities have rebounded from the low period of 1971-72, when they were widely seen as "not relative" to society's needs, and membership dipped to about 150,000. There are now more than 202,000 members in about 4,600 chapters across the country.

Similarly, Reserve Officer Training Corps units are flourishing nearly everywhere, with the impetus derived from three sources: Peace has eliminated much of the risk factor involved in participation, compensation (upper classmen receive $100 a month in pay and full scholarships cover all tuition and other campus fees) helps thousands of students who otherwise could not afford a higher education and careers in the military are a part of the general craving for economic security.

Socially, the sexual and drug revolutions of the past decade have created a behavior pattern beyond anything that existed a generation ago. Open dormitories on most campuses mean that men and women students can have affairs without fear of administration or peer disapproval.

Use of alcohol—mainly beer, vodka and tequila—has returned to the campus, but the trend still keeps company with widespread use of marijuana and an assortment of other, nonaddictive drugs.

Trend Toward Frivolity

There is also a trend toward silliness: nonserious, frivolous activities with no other objective but fun. At Cornell University, for example, dances, parties, trivia contests and even campus beauty contests are in vogue.

A pronounced "preppy" look is returning to campus dress, with clothes in better repair than during the shopworn look of the radical era. There is less reluctance to wear expensive casual clothes; women on mid-American campuses are appearing more often than before in dresses, wearing bras and using more cosmetics.

There also appears to be a return to dormitory life by underclassmen, now that the sexual barriers have been eliminated. Some of the motivation is financial —it is perhaps cheaper in terms of room and board, and life there is not as dependent on transportation to classes and study halls. But observers also see in the trend the same search for structure and control, freedom from too much freedom, that appears in other modes of the new behavior.

Racial lines at most campuses are sharply drawn, with very little interracial dating or social integration. Like their white counterparts, black students today thrive in the structure and form of clubs and fraternities; they are also less likely to rise in protest when programs or privileges won during the days of revolt are diluted or withdrawn by campus administrations today.

When the National Guard troops killed the four Kent State students in the demonstration against the United States incursion in Cambodia in 1970, the incident, and the days that followed, represented perhaps the high water mark of protest on college campuses in this country.

The Kent State tragedy had a special irony because the campus, situated in the rolling hills of Ohio about 50 miles southeast of Cleveland, was a typical state-supported institution that was as representative of mid-American values and attitudes as any that could be found in the nation.

There is no discernible cult surrounding the shedding of student blood on the grassy knoll outside Taylor Hall on May 4 seven years ago, but Kent State students appear sensitive to the memory of the event and keep it alive as a kind of oral history. However, student activism at Kent State is as moribund as on any campus in the nation.

When the administration recently imposed rules on dormitory behavior and designated "quiet hours" and "quiet floors," there was not a hint of protest, despite the fact that the new regulations infringed on "freedoms" won during the campus revolt.

"The students," said Gary Begala, a 25-year-old Kent State graduate who is running for the State Legislature, "are turned off by political media technicians selling their candidates like soapsuds. I'm personally offended by Carter's and Ford's staffs' telling reporters how they're going to merchandise their man and how they won't let them talk about issues. It turns everybody off."

Mr. Begala, a Democrat, had scheduled "rap sessions" at student dormitories to discuss the election. At the first session he was the only person to show up.

John Gargin, 42, a professor of political science at Kent State, said in a recent interview:

"Most of our students are from low-to middle-income families, many Catholics and ethnics, and they are here to get the credentials they believe are central to admission to the Dream. Everyone does the rhetoric bit—fascist pig this and that —but push them and they ask you to write recommendations for jobs with banks and insurance companies."

Dr. Gargin said that this generation of college students lacks commitment to either major political party and that that fact has implications for the future that no one has fully explored.

Over at the student psychological counseling center, Dr. Richard C. Rynearson, the director, told of a new melancholy among students on campus who come to his clinic to discuss their emotional problems.

'Symptoms of Depression'

"Their symptoms look like depression but they can still handle their studies," he said. "They're coming in more frequently and asking to see older advisers. 'I don't want to talk to someone my age,' they say as though they don't trust anyone their own age. 'I want someone who's been around longer and knows more.' That's quite different than a few years ago when they feared older advisers would criticize their new life styles."

So far, no individual or group has touched a significant nerve to distract the students from their present course, however undefined and uncharted it is.

Graffiti at times can be useful in measuring a community's concern. At Kent State this fall there is an astonishing lack of it outside of the standard bathroom wall jottings. In the turbulent 60's the campus walls were covered with political graffiti, not ivy, and the slogans, however romantic or fierce, indicated movement and direction: "Power to the People!" or "Right On!"—such phrases at least showed a sense of purpose.

Outside the beer hall at the student center at Kent State today there were only a couple of scrawled lines worthy of note.

"Will the real God please stand up?" said one.

"Death must be the ultimate trip because they save it for last," read the other.

Inherent in the smudgy penciled statements was a despair that seemed so discordant for the walls of an American university.

October 17, 1976

Increased Marijuana Use Is Found

WASHINGTON, Nov. 23 (AP)—More than half this year's class of high school seniors tried marijuana and three out of 10 were users at graduation, according to Government surveys.

The National Institute on Drug Abuse surveyed 17,000 high school seniors in 130 schools last spring and found that 53 percent had tried marijuana, as against 48 percent for the class of 1975.

The survey, released today, said that 32 per cent regarded themselves as current marijuana users.

Meanwhile, 53 per cent of those 18 to 25 years old had tried marijuana, according to another institute survey, and 25 per cent were current users. It showed that 22 per cent of 12-to-17-year-olds had experimented with marijuana and 15 per cent were regular or occasional users.

Cigarettes Feared by Most

Although cigarettes and alcohol were used more frequently than marijuana by young adults, 57 per cent of high school seniors thought there was a serious health risk for cigarettes while only 40 per cent felt the same way about marijuana.

The findings indicated that the use of LSD has remained virtually constant the last four years and that abuse of heroin and psychotherapeutic drugs has been unchanged the last two years. The rate of cocaine use was the same this year as in 1975.

Dr. Robert L. DuPont, the institute's director, said that comparison of the surveys showed "an apparent stabilization in drug use and the attitudes toward drugs in general."

"The public, including youth, clearly recognizes the addictive effects of tobacco and alcohol and has very negative attitudes toward the use of all illicit drugs except marijuana," he said. "Although drug abuse continues to be widespread in every region of the country, we are seeing some slight downward trends for amphetamines, LSD and barbituates. Marijuana is the only drug showing a definite upward trend."

Two other Government-sponsored surveys released at the same time showed that drug abuse cost the nation from $8.4 billion to $12.2 billion a year, more than alcoholism but less than tobacco smoking.

The school survey showed that only 39 per cent of the class of 1976 disapproved of experimenting with marijuana, down from 47 per cent in 1975. The number disapproving of regular marijuana use was 70 per cent, as against 72 per cent last year.

November 24, 1976

Campus Mood: The Focus Is on Grades

By EDWARD B. FISKE

Shortly before noon one day recently, 18 members of the Spartacus Youth League gathered near the sundial at Columbia University and, chanting slogans and carrying placards, began marching in a circle to protest a visit to the campus by recruiters from the National Security Agency.

About 100 yards away a larger group of students, apparently oblivious to the demonstration, gathered quietly in a line to await the noon opening of the new student-run cooperative grocery store.

The relative size of the two groups suggested much about the interests and priorities of the current generation of students of campuses throughout the metropolitan area.

In contrast to the 1960's—when student activists such as Mark Rudd at Columbia were drawing large numbers of students to antiwar demonstrations and leading takeovers of campus buildings—students now show little outward interest in social and political issues.

Libraries and study areas are populated into the early hours of the morning, and the main priority on most students' minds would seem to be what the Columbia College dean of students, Henry S. Coleman, termed "the almighty grade point average."

The 'Silent Generation'

The common wisdom is that the pendulum of campus life has swung back to where it was in the 1950's, when writers spoke of the pervasive apathy of the "silent generation." In fact, interviews by The New York Times at a dozen local colleges and universities suggest that the situation is not quite that simple. If there is a new "silent generation" today, it is one whose character has been profoundly shaped by the turbulence of the intervening decade.

Though outwardly inactive, students who grew up watching a war on their living-room television sets seem to be far better informed about current issues and injustices in the world than their predecessors of two decades ago.

"It's just that we're much more cynical about our ability to change things," said Gary Cohen, a senior at Columbia. "With all of the political protest of the 1960's, very little happened."

The economic situation means that even relatively affluent students must now help support themselves, and the intense competition for jobs and places in graduate schools has put pressures on present-day students that were unknown in the 1950's.

"Most of them are so weighted down by the academic challenges they face that they don't seem to enjoy college," said Howard Crosby, dean of students at Rutgers. "I don't think today's students have enough fun."

Generalizations about the mood of an entire campus—much less that of an entire college generation—are always dangerous, but the themes of declining political activism and increased academic seriousness run through interviews on all of the campuses surveyed.

The Kent State Issue

At Rutgers, for example, only 200 students showed up for a recent appearance, sponsored by the student government, of one of the students wounded by National Guardsmen at Kent State in 1970, and a group of students at Barnard College recently abandoned plans for a rally in favor of elective abortion. "We were afraid that no one would show up," said Joan Storey, one of those involved.

Polls indicate that students are informed about issues such as the racial situation in South Africa, but many did not know who Mark Rudd was when he recently surrendered to the police after years of hiding. And efforts to encourage divestiture by the colleges of stocks in companies doing business in South Africa will often draw considerable support.

By and large, though, the issues that inspire student action are local. Students at Queens College, for example, have organized lobbying efforts in behalf of low tuition and increased legislative support for the City University, and a one-day boycott of the food service at Columbia last spring to protest its quality was 95 percent effective. "People are more concerned with what affects them directly," said Howard Leib, a sophomore.

At Cornell a student recently started a campaign of "civil disobedience" urging people to violate parking regulations to protest inadequate parking space on the campus. The dome of Sibley Hall now bears the painted inscription "Protest Student Activism."

A search for security seems to dominate much of student life. "There's a trend toward nice safe curriculums," said David Alexander, a law student at the State University Center at Buffalo.

Placement offices have extended their hours, and last spring at New York University more than 500 juniors signed up for workshops on topics such as résumé-writing and interviewing skills. At Rutgers, lines begin forming the night before when such major companies as Bell Telephone announced job interviews.

'A Lesson in Frugality'

"There's a sense of scarcity around," said the Rev. William Starr, Episcopal chaplain at Columbia. "The idea of dropping out and dropping in—taking a year off to do tenant organizing or something—is really gone. At Columbia the children of the middle class are getting a lesson in frugality."

Such attitudes affect social activism. "We circulated a petition on [stock] divestiture, and some students told us they wouldn't sign because they didn't want trouble from the C.I.A.," said Mr. Starr. "Maybe they're right."

Students suggested other factors in the social attitudes of the mid-1970's, including the absence of leaders and the lack of a single overriding issue like the war in Vietnam. "There's so much ambiguity today," said Marianne Goldstein, a junior at Barnard. "Everyone was against the war, but on an issue like abortion you can find right and wrong on both sides."

Students on local campuses are clearly part of the turning inward that seems to be evident in society as a whole. The best-seller lists at campus stores invariably include the popular self-help works such as "Your Erroneous Zones."

"The key is finding a place for yourself—answering the question: Where do I go in a huge world?" said Sari Sweden, an 18-year-old student at the State University of New York at Buffalo.

Some see the developing pragmatism as unfortunate. "In turning inward there is a danger people may be becoming more selfish," said Richard Cheshire, vice president for public affairs at Colgate University. Others take a somewhat longer view and suggest that today's students are no different from those of the 1960's.

Kenneth Goodsell, a Columbia sophomore, argued that the antiwar youth of the last decade had a life and death stake in the war's being ended. "The sellout came not in the 70's but in the 60's, when the civil-rights movement gave way to antiwar protests and students began to overlook what was still happening on the domestic front."

Extracurricular activities such as glee clubs and campus radio stations seem to be doing relatively well, though here again some significant changes have taken place.

"College students are more interested in smaller, more specialized groups than in large national movements," said Brian Guillorn, president of the Student Union Polity, which coordinates student activities at Columbia. "I imagine it's because in a smaller group they have more control."

The gymnasium at Columbia, which was the focus of bitter controversy when it was built a decade ago, draws large numbers of students for jogging and intramural sports, and spectator sports are making a big comeback on some campuses.

Escape From Pressure

"People here go nuts over sports," said Rob Gleaner, a student-government official at Rutgers. "The reason is simple—escape from the growing pressures associated with high academic standards and the demands of tightening job market."

"Escapism" is a word that tends to pop up frequently in discussions with students and faculty members. Science-fiction clubs are thriving at several local colleges. Asked why his own group seems to be doing so well, Richard Lappin, a junior who heads the one at Columbia, replied: "It's entertainment. It fits in with the times."

The consumption of alcohol is clearly on the increase, and it now ranks alongside marijuana and cocaine at the top of student preference. "In private, students use dope, but at public events alcohol is taking over," said Miss Storey at Barnard. The use of hard drugs is said to be rare, and marijuana has taken on a different function than in the past.

"Ten years ago pot smoking was a radical political act," said Tim Weiner, a Columbia senior. "Now everyone does it, and it's become personalized and depoliticized. If it can be said that there is a cogent reason for smoking pot, it's inward-directedness."

Students at some colleges reported that it was customary now to serve wine at campus gatherings, and that its presence or absence would sometimes determine the attendance level. "Drinking is an occupational hazard of being a student activist," said Ellen Doherty, a student member of the Barnard board of trustees. "I could easily get drunk three or four times a week just going to meetings."

Some universities have become concerned about the level of student drinking. Colgate, for example, recently set up a committee of students, faculty

members and administrators to study the question of alcohol abuse on the campus.

College students have always been known for their penchant for beer, and many faculty members believe that, despite some problems, the trends of the last few years have essentially consisted of what some called a healthy "return to normalcy."

Others, though, are disturbed by what they see happening, especially in relation to academic work. For example, Charles R. Decarlo, president of Sarah Lawrence College, expressed fear that education had become a process for

earning credentials to the exclusion of any sense of a joy in learning for its own sake.

"There's a curious paradox," he said "Students work hard, but there is a decline in serious intense intellectual focusing. They don't know how to concentrate. They are full of anxiety about getting a job; but there is no motivation that proceeds from within, and when that happens there is a decline in quality. The only goal seems to be to get enough work together—to put some sort of mental act together to go out and get a job."

November 23, 1977

Most College Freshmen in Poll Shun Liberal Label

By GENE I. MAEROFF

The nation's first-year college students are less willing to identify themselves as liberals in their attitudes, according to a survey that also showed that the spectrum of political philosophy was slowly shifting to the left and that what is now considered "middle of the road" used to be left of center.

A poll of 1.79 million current freshmen found that 56.6 percent, the most in the 12-year history of the survey by the American Council on Education, considered themselves at the center of the political spectrum.

"These trends show that labels can be misleading," said Alexander W. Astin, the survey director, "since the decline in students who call themselves liberals has been accompanied by increasing liberalization of student attitudes about legalization of marijuana, student power and autonomy and equal rights for women."

"Apparently," he continued, "views that were once considered liberal are now a part of the mainstream of opinion among today's college freshmen."

More Favor Legal Marijuana

Support for legalization of marijuana, for instance, increased from 19.4 percent in 1968 to 48.4 percent in 1976 and to 52.9 percent last year, the first time that a majority of the nation's freshmen has taken this stand.

Similarly, the proportion of freshmen favoring busing to achieve school desegregation rose from 37 percent in 1976 to 40.6 percent.

Yet, only 25.1 percent of the freshmen called themselves "liberal" and 1.9 percent identified themselves as "far left."

On the other hand, there were 15.6 per-

cent who said that they were "conservative" and eight-tenths of 1 percent who called themselves "far right."

There were several issues on which attitudes moved markedly toward positions traditionally considered right of center. For example, the proportion of freshmen who felt "there is too much concern in the courts for the rights of criminals" grew from 48.1 percent in 1971 to 59.7 percent in 1976 and 64.3 percent in 1977.

For the last several years, some observers of the campus scene have maintained that many values have been swinging back to those prevalent in the 1950's. Some of the findings of the survey of the current freshmen tended to support that belief.

For instance, the proportion of young people who said that they wanted to be "very well off financially" increased from 40.1 percent in 1967 to 53.1 percent in 1976 to 58.2 percent in 1977.

Also, those who said that a key reason for going to college was "to be able to make more money" rose from 49.9 percent in 1971 to 53.8 percent in 1976 to 62.1 percent in 1977.

The proportion interested in a career in business—often cited as an indication of the shift back to earlier values grew from 11.6 percent in 1966 to 16.4 percent in 1976 to 18.1 percent in 1977.

"Evidence supports the notion that students are becoming increasingly more materialistic," said Mr. Astin, a professor at the University of California, Los Angeles, who is regarded as an authority on the attitudes of college students.

There were signs, too, that the students shared society's general concern about the adequacy of teaching of the basic skills. More students than ever, 42.6 percent, said that an important reason for

going to college was to "improve reading-study skills."

In 1971, only 22.2 percent said that this was an important reason for higher education. Furthermore, by their own admission, 25.6 percent of the students said that they needed remedial work in mathematics.

In rating their ability to perform specified tasks, 14.3 percent said that they could speak a second language, 5.2 percent said that they could program a computer and 7.4 percent said that they could name the divisions of the animal kingdom.

A comparison with past years found that the proportion of freshmen who said that they knew the freedoms guaranteed in the Bill of Rights fell from 48.8 percent in 1967 to 29.7 percent in 1977. The number who said that they knew the difference between stocks and bonds dropped from 40.6 percent to 22.2 percent in the same period.

The survey findings are based on questionnaires filled out by 198,641 first-year students at 374 two-year and four-year schools. The information was weighted to reflect the entire freshman class at all colleges and universities.

Three million students have been polled on similar questions since the project, the Cooperative Institutional Research Program, was launched in 1966 to provide information for a continuing study of student attitudes.

The project is administered for the American Council on Education by the Laboratory for Research on Higher Education at the University of California, Los Angeles. Copies of the survey report are available for $6 from the Graduate School of Education at the university.

January 22, 1978

Survey Finds Teen-Agers Ignorant of Government

WASHINGTON, Feb. 1 (AP)—Nearly all teen-agers know who the President is, but for many that is where their knowledge of government stops. Fewer than half can name even one of their senators or representatives in Congress, a nationwide survey has found.

In the first half of the 1970's, an era

that included the Vietnam War, campus disturbances and the Watergate scandal, understanding of the way democracy works declined among American youth 13 to 17 years old, the National Assessment of Education Progress reported. The federally sponsored survey tested 145,000 teen-agers in 1970, 1972 and 1976 to chart their political knowledge and attitudes.

It found that among 17-year-olds, the ability to explain the basic concept of

democracy—namely, that the people elect their leaders—declined from 86 percent to 74 percent. Among 13-year-olds, it fell from 53 to 42 percent.

More than 96 percent of both groups could name the President, but only 20 percent of the 13-year-olds and 48 percent of the 17-year-olds could name any of their representatives in Congress.

Experts who took part in the study attributed the results to a shift from civics courses to electives.

February 2, 1978

In Our Colleges, an 'Emersonian' Generation

By Martin Duberman

It's being widely labeled the "me" generation, derided as complacent and careerist, dismissed as a mere replica of the 50's generation. Before the portrait gets cast in textbook cement, I'd like to toss a few pebbles into the mix.

The students I teach at Lehman College and meet in travels to other campuses are not, contrary to reputation, oblivious to social ills. They're informed and angry about the vast disparities of income and opportunity in our country. They place primary blame on the interlocking alliance of hereditary wealth, political officialdom, Pentagon brass and multinational corporations. There's a marked resurgence of interest among them in Marxist analysis (though more typically confined to informal study groups than to membership in socialist organizations).

Feminist analysis has had still wider appeal (and has been far better reported in the news media). In the 16-25 age group, the transformation in sociosexual values has been "startling," to quote the respected pollster Daniel Yankelovich.

Suppositions about human nature that have long had the stature of axioms are increasingly viewed as culture-bound norms subject to scrutiny and redefinition. What does (should) it mean to be "male" or "female"? Do marriage and family life provide optimal conditions for human happiness? Does sexual pleasure require the justifying context of a love relationship? Is there any organic connection between sexual and emotional fidelity?

Marxists and feminists often view each other with deep suspicion. Male Marxists doubt that the challenge to sex-role stereotyping and normative definitions of sexual morality can prove the cutting edge for a broad social transformation; they think it more likely to prove yet another self-indulgent middle-class diversion. Feminists fear that Marxists are eager to destroy class privilege but tardy in challenging gender privilege; they view most male Marxists as cultural conservatives—committed to patriarchal values of hierarchy, authority, order and discipline, given to over-rationalizing experience, impatient with personal idiosyncrasy ("subjectivism"), distrustful of aspects of reality (intimacy, say) that cannot be closely measured and defined.

The vast majority of the young stand apart from these concerns but are not indifferent to them. Many seem attracted to socialist economic analysis and to feminist values. But the flirtation tends to be intermittent, the commitment sporadic. Not because of callow self-absorption (the standard view), but from profound wariness. They are neither obtuse nor heartless. They suffer, if anything, from a surfeit of knowledge, a deep revulsion against moralizing, a painful distrust of all

Drawings by Sué Coe

prescriptions for social change—even as they profoundly wish it otherwise, wish to end the stalemate between their ethical insights and their political pessimism.

I've come to think of this pervasive ambivalence as essentially "Emersonian" in spirit, though I may be over-elaborating (and overdignifying) what is in essence a banal set of generational characteristics.

Ralph Waldo Emerson, the historical figure, has always been most unmanageable. The problem (as with the generation of the 70's) is his plenitude, his multiplicity of personae. No sooner does his image seem fixed than it dissolves. He declares decisively on this or that question—then shifts ground (or the question). He asserts the absolute claims of the self, the need to reject the world's "conspiracy to importune you with emphatic trifles," the delusion of schemes for social reform. Yet turn a page in Emerson, pick up another essay, and the disdainful Olympian turns into an egalitarian democrat, the hermit scholar disdains books as "crutches," the radical individualist demands that attention be paid to the claims of the world.

Is this a spirit at war with itself, a temperament unable to choose? Or a multitudinous nature refusing to reduce itself to a single impulse, a fixed identity? In the 50's, my students couldn't have cared less. They simply found Emerson boring: too serious, too introspective, too abstract. In the 60's, they found him repellent: overcultivated, indifferent to suffering, smothered in self-importance. He was no

one's Representative Man. For a time, I gave up pleading his case, increasingly uncertain he had one.

But in the past year or two, students have begun to respond to him again—and to that very ambiguity, that divided consciousness that has long seemed foreign in a culture attuned to categorizing. Even this generation, newly sympathetic to aspects of Emerson's personal style and thought, still sees him in certain central ways as on the other side of an immense divide.

Emerson's serene affection for his own shifts in opinion puzzles those who have learned to live with equivocation, but not to cherish it. His conviction that the universe is at base benign—that an underlying "moral order" ultimately converts evil into good—produces astonished disbelief (New York not being a benign universe). To most Marxists and feminists, Emerson remains what he was to the 60's generation: a complacent patrician, a remote, fastidious figure unable to translate ideas into action.

But almost everyone else—the centrist majority—finds something to identify with in Emerson, something to admire. His themes once more have takers: the illusion of "reality," the need to cultivate indifference to circumstances, the importance of becoming a "system instead of a satellite," the sense that the demands of the community and the cultivation of a sovereign self must always be somewhat at odds. The single line, "Perhaps all that is not performance is preparation, or performance that shall be," produces a particularly deep response. Perhaps because the image is comforting: concentration on career will someday justify itself in performance.

But when I hear them talk of "performance," they put emphasis on a particular kind: one that combines personal advancement with some form of public service.

They are not comfortable—as students in the 50's were—with the former alone. Nor can they devote themselves—as could the activists of the 60's and the more dedicated of today's young socialists and feminists—with the latter alone.

Theirs is a divided consciousness, the Emersonian double vision that prevents single-minded commitment, whether to personal or public goals—which fears to participate and fears not to. A canny awareness that corruption is endemic and available solutions shopworn—but in tandem with a guilty recognition that the subtlest form of corruption may be resignation.

Martin Duberman is professor of history at Lehman College of the City University of New York. This article appears in longer form in the current issue of Liberation magazine.

Suicides Among Young Persons Said to Have Tripled in 20 Years

SAN DIEGO, Feb. 9 (UPI) — Suicides among teen-agers and young adults have tripled in the last 20 years, and children as young as 6 are now killing themselves, according to the director of a suicide prevention center.

"I think the major reason is the way our society has of alienating kids," Charlotte Ross, director of the San Mateo Suicide Prevention Center, said Wednesday.

Miss Ross, who was in San Diego for a conference on juvenile justice, said that the yearly suicide total for people between 15 and 24 years old was now almost 5,000. "We have validated attempts by kids as young as 6 or 7 years old," she said.

February 11, 1979

Fraternities' Antics Turn Violent on Some Campuses, at Cost of Money and Privileges

By MARYANN BIRD

Hijinks have given way to violence on a few American campuses, keeping law enforcement officials busy, prompting neighbors to consider moving away and costing some fraternities their campus welcome and hundreds of dollars in damages.

Merry- and mischief-making existed on most campuses in the United States long before Universal Studios gave them a starring role in the film "Animal House." The celluloid antics had little effect on pranks and partying, most officials said at more than a dozen colleges checked by The New York Times, including Harvard, Duke, Michigan, Ohio State, Antioch, Texas, Princeton, Stanford and the University of California at Berkeley.

But some schools had battles to report, paralleling or sometimes exceeding those of the movie.

One such school was the University of Texas, where Austin residents have banded together as Save University Neighborhoods and demanded relief from "drunken, lawless, ugly and retaliatory behavior." Much of the rowdyism has been traced to fraternity men.

"I just spoke to three people who said they were going to move because of the situation," said the group's president, Betty Phillips, who teaches educational psychology. "To me, that's when cumulative nuisances become a menace."

At the same university, a freshman's assertion that he was abducted, beaten, robbed and sexually molested last August has led to a $1.1 million civil suit, as well as criminal assault charges, against three members of Alpha Tau Omega, the fraternity itself and its president at the time of the alleged incident.

The defendants, who pleaded not guilty, are no longer connected with Alpha Tau Omega, and the fraternity's national office has placed the Austin chapter on probation.

At Duke University in Durham, N.C., a Halloween food fight developed into a barrage. The dining room was closed for a week, while food and broken tableware were scraped from the room's carpeting, furniture, paneling and windows at a cost of over $3,000. The dining hall manager called it "a preplanned thing inspired by

'Animal House,' " in which Bluto, portrayed by John Belushi, and his brother "Deltas" engage in food fights, among other disreputable activities.

Two campus groups were accused of initiating the incident. The Beta Phi Zeta fraternity is appealing the charge, while residents of the Wilson House dormitory have acknowledged their involvement and paid a fine.

"Animal House was a small pocket of resistance," said Joshua Agrons, a senior from New York City who lives in the dorm, "and Wilson House is the same thing, against the conformity of the apathetic 70's."

Small Minority Involved

Whether or not the new wave of campus rowdyism is inspired by the film, college and police officials generally acknowledge the problem, although they are careful to say that only a small minority of students are involved.

Incidents reported recently on college campuses include the following:

¶In 57 hours over one fall weekend, the University of Massachusetts police answered more than 180 emergency calls and arrested 29 people, most of them intoxicated. It was estimated that vandals cost the university $15,000 that weekend, a 10th of the school's vandalism tab for all of 1978.

¶Officials at the University of Florida banned the Omega Psi Phi fraternity from the campus after allegations that at least 18 pledges had been beaten.

¶At their annual banquet at Princeton University, Rugby Club members spilled a keg of beer on the floor and on one another, fed a chair to a fireplace, emptied fire extinguishers and left the university-owned Gun Club littered with food, cans and paper, according to a proctor's report. The club was assessed $115 for damages.

"'Animal House' hasn't affected us very much," said Henry Maguire, a senior and Rugby Club's president, "since we have a long tradition of wildness."

University administrators, along with fraternity and sorority advisers and members, emphasize the groups' constructive aspects — charity fund-raising, for example — and downplay the pranks and police reports. And most campuses

are fairly sedate, including the University of Oregon campus at Eugene, where "Animal House" scenes were filmed in the fall of 1977.

"Outsiders come expecting to see it reincarnated, going full bore on the edge of the campus," said the college's dean of students, Robert Bowlin. "There is much clearer recognition by the students that it was another era."

Report From Columbia

Crime is low, too, in the Columbia University fraternities, which are scattered on the side streets around the New York campus, according to Frank Evers, the college's security supervisor. "There is a little noise now and then from the parties, but no vandalism or anything like that," he said.

Some of the fraternities on 114th Street, near the campus's south gate occasionally yell insults at residents of German Hall, a nearby dormitory, who respond with water balloons or eggs, one student said.

"Fraternities are pretty innocuous until they start trying to outdrink each other," said one security officer at Southern Methodist University in Dallas. After a fraternity member fell two stories to his death last spring while trying to do handstands on a balcony, attempts have been made to curtail drinking at parties.

Hotels in the Dallas area have increasingly refused to rent rooms to students, however, especially since two partying fraternity men tried to remove bathroom stalls and another waltzed with a six-foot popcorn popper, costing their group more than $1,000 in damages.

Despite the rowdyism — or perhaps because of it — men are still being attracted to fraternities.

Justin Berta, president of Phi Gamma Delta at Ohio State University, said that "Animal House" has spurred such interest in fraternities that many men have been turned away.

"I know my brother who saw it — he's in the eighth grade — thought it was a riot," said John Labinsky, the Inter-Fraternity Council president at the University of Texas. "He can hardly wait to go to college, to join a fraternity."

April 16, 1979

Is Rock the Music of Violence?

By JOHN ROCKWELL

Eleven young men and women died at a Who concert in Cincinnati on Dec. 3. Most of the responsible commentary — and refreshingly enough, most of the commentary *has* been responsible — has dealt with questions of how rock concerts can be better organized and controlled. It would seem that so-called "festival" seating of the sort used in Cincinnati — unreserved tickets that lead to a buildup of impatient fans at the gates followed by a mad dash for the best positions when the hall finally opens its doors — will be curtailed. And legislation may be enacted to ensure a proper degree of concert security.

This is indeed a reasonable response, but there are two larger issues to be addressed in the wake of this tragedy: is there something inherently violent about rock music, and do rock concerts serve a constructive social function?

To begin with, one has to understand what rock music is and what it represents. Rock was born as an unprecedented free expression of adolescent sexual and aggressive energy. Before the advent of rock, the arts had never attempted to deal with such passions in quite so direct and democratic a way.

Pre-rock popular music had reflected the sturdier hierarchies of an earlier age, and the pieties of its dominant morality. If vaudeville and burlesque were allowed to get a little bawdy, that bawdiness was still sequestered from the mainstream. The mainstream — the Hit Parade of the early 1950's, for instance — was full of Moon-June songs and deliberately silly novelty numbers. The music was syrupy and bland, more an escape from social tension than an expression of it.

All that changed, dramatically, with the sudden — and, to older folk, shocking — advent of rock in the mid-50's. From the pelvic gyrations of Elvis Presley and the suggestiveness of early rock lyrics to the pounding beat of the music to the very name, "rock-and-roll," the new music and the very institution of the rock concert became part of our culture's way of dealing with teen-age rebellion.

This only reflected the new realities of mid-20th-century American life — the sudden coming of age of members of the post-war baby boom, the move of millions from tightly-structured rural America to a life of freedom and loneliness in the cities, the new self-assertiveness and social impact of black Americans, the loosening bonds of a previous century's social, moral and religious rigidities.

There are those who feel that the pre-rock attitude was as it should have been; that some things about human nature are best left alone, or repressed, or at the very least not encouraged. Some rock does indeed exploit sex and violence in a manner akin to pornography and exploitation films — and like them, is created for for simple commercial gain. But the finest rock bands have had a higher aim; they have taken the sexual yearning and violent propensities of a newly assertive yet often frustrated adolescent social group and transformed them into art.

The best rock stands in relation to human experience as does all art, revealing us to ourselves. Rock art speaks directly to teenagers. It may be unhealthy that our society has tolerated the evolution of an isolated youth culture. But that culture exists: rock lives.

That doesn't mean, however, that rock only becomes "art" if it simply serves to tame violent energies Art plumbs life more deeply than entertainment, and the Who and the Rolling Stones, the class of the hard-rock field, are better than lesser bands in part because they confront in the most unflinching manner the aggressive instincts of their audiences.

It is thus ironic, at least on the surface, that it was the Who, and not some lesser band, that was the catalyst of the events in Cincinnati. Because the Who, by the very nature of its music and career, might have seemed able to defuse the sort of violence that erupted in Ohio. And the nature of the Who still may be able to help us explore the ramifications of this tragedy.

Pete Townshend has always been the soul and the leader of this band — its guitarist, chief songwriter and principal spokesman. Nobody in rock has spoken more thoughtfully about what it means to be a teen-ager, and about the mystical relationship that exists between the true rock fan and his favorite band.

Mr. Townshend is an avowed mystic, a follower of the late Meher Baba, the Indian guru. In the days after Cincinnati, many thoughts swirled through Mr. Townshend's head, and among them was the notion that "the whole purpose of a rock concert is for people to forget themselves, to lose their egos in the crowd and to disappear — a temporary sort of flight."

It is an alluring idea, and one that helps explain not only the *positive* connection between rock and violence, but also the Who's own seemingly bifurcated image as the band that, on the one hand, introduced ritualized destruction to the rock stage — the smashing of guitars and drum kits — and, on the other hand, created an entire "rock opera" about transcendental experience in "Tommy." Mr. Townshend feels that young people will never accept preaching from the outside; he himself tried to make television commercials a decade ago warning against drug use, and felt them to be a ludicrous failure. Since then he has concentrated his energies on music — and, more recently, on films.

Right now a film called "Quadrophenia" is playing around the country. It was produced by the Who, and is based on Mr. Townshend's rock opera of the same name, about the riots between the Mods and the Rockers in England 15 years ago, when the Who was just beginning. What's interesting is that the film takes an empathetic but still bleak view of those riots, fueled as they were by amphetamines and ultimately expressive of little more than adolescent despair.

Mr. Townshend feels that what a rock band can do is evoke and sympathize with adolescent passions, and then try through the medium of music to transform them — to "help young people come out whole on the other side."

Sitting in a Cleveland hotel room the other day, Mr. Townshend looked haggard and spoke with a quiet intensity. "If this had to happen at all, I'm glad it happened to us and not some other group," he said. "I think we're strong enough to turn it into something good — not just in terms of improving concerts, but of improving rock itself."

To summarize: the answer to the first question posed here is yes, there is

something inherently violent about rock music. Moreover, there are groups that pander to such violence. But the best groups, while seeming to plunge most deeply into the heart of the violence, seek to transform it into an artistic or even a religious experience.

The second broader issue to be addressed in the wake of Cincinnati is whether rock concerts serve a socially constructive function. To begin with, there is no point in disguising the realities of the situation. Most rock concerts are reasonably well run, but at their worst, cost-cutting by promoters and hall managers turns concerts into

---

'Rock music is a way of dealing with teen-age rebellion.'

---

anarchic pigsties — that more people aren't hurt at them is a tribute to the inherent good sense of the vast majority of our young people. At the worst concerts, the restrooms are disgusting, there is litter everywhere, the aisles are impassable and reserved seating a farce.

The justification for such squalor is that "the kids like it that way." That attitude suggests a toleration for teenage rowdiness at rock concerts that doesn't exist elsewhere in society. Rock concerts are places where young people are allowed to yell and shout, push and shove, drink and use both hard and soft drugs.

When a facility attempts to crack down on such behavior, the management quickly realizes the folly of its ways. A few years ago the Nassau Coliseum on Long Island made a fairly serious effort to prevent drinking and drug use at rock concerts; sometimes hundreds of teen-agers were arrested on a single night.

The result was widespread protests from young people, their parents and from the rock music business. Bands refused to play there because their fans were being "hassled," booking agents didn't include Nassau on tours, and attendance dropped off seriously at concerts that *were* scheduled.

Things are back to normal at the Nassau Coliseum now, and the reasons are two. On the one hand, most people prefer to look the other way at teenage drug use; until Cincinnati, at least, it seemed a victimless crime. Furthermore, there is big money in the rock concert business, and large facilities such as the Nassau Coliseum derive a considerable portion of their income from them.

Esthetically, rock concerts in arenas and stadiums leave a lot to be desired. The actual music in these environments is seriously compromised. The acoustics are generally terrible. The volume is screwed up to a roar. The difficulties of buying tickets and getting to an arena can be daunting. And with an audience dominated by loudly enthusiastic teenagers, an adult is almost assured of feeling awkwardly out of place.

On the other hand, there is generally not much wrong with an innocent little teen-age Saturnalia — except when something terrible happens. Naturally, there are invariably a few drunken, punkish louts in every such crowd, and sometimes the T-shirted security personnel can be downright brutal. But real physical conflict is rare (a lot rarer than at sports events, one suspects, on or off the ice); the more prevalent mood is of good-natured rough-housing.

Even so, it is not surprising that these concerts have helped bring about a split between record-buyers and concert-goers. Some people simply give up rock music as they grow out of their teens. More commonly adults keep buying the occasional record and listening to the music on the radio, but would never dream of going to a concert.

Given the realities of rock concert life today, as a tacitly licensed preserve for teen-age libertinism, what should be done? Even if a majority in this country should come to the conclusion that such formalized outlets are unnecessary or undesirable, it seems unlikely that they will be "outlawed,"

barring a nationwide wave of repression.

Thus we are left with the prospect of improvements in the regulation of such concerts. Rock concerts can and should be run in such a way that young people are encouraged to behave responsibly, rather than like cattle.

Still, there is a danger of overreaction on the local level. To avoid that, we must understand that rock carries with it the potential for a transformation of anti-social behavior into something that serves the highest of human ideals. But it can do so only by accepting the reality of human nature. ■

December 16, 1979

Thousands Register in U.S. Despite Draft Protests

By DAVID BIRD

Despite demonstrations at New York City's main post office and in other major cities across the country yesterday, thousands of 19- and 20-year-old men quietly signed up on the first day of registration for a possible military draft.

The protests were generally peaceful. Fifteen demonstrators were arrested at a sit-in inside the main post office in Boston, and in Hartford eight demonstrators were carried out by the police after they sat down on the floor of the State Street post office and refused to move.

Selective Service officials said they were pleased with the turnout.

"It seems to be going very well," said

Brayton Harris, a spokesman at the service's headquarters in Washington, where protesters staged a sit-in in the lobby. Mr. Harris said it would take at least a week to determine how many had registered.

The law requires men born in 1960 and 1961 to register. Those born in 1960 are registering this week, and those born in 1961 have been asked to register next week. The Government estimates that four million men are affected and predicts that at least 98 percent of them will show up at the nation's post offices to fill out green and white cards with their names, addresses and telephone numbers. The 98 percent prediction is disputed by registration's opponents. The

registration law was declared unconstitutional last Friday by a Federal court in Philadelphia because it excluded women. But Saturday, Associate Justice William F. Brennan Jr. of the Supreme Court, without deciding on the constitutionality of the law, ruled that the registration could proceed pending a review later this year by the full Supreme Court. He argued that the potential harm to the Government if registration were delayed would be greater than the potential harm to those required to register if it were not.

In front of the main Manhattan post office on Eighth Avenue from 31st to 33d Streets, marchers paraded under banners that said: "Hell No. We Won't Go,"

United Press International and The New York Times/Vic DeLucia

Dean Poulios was the first to register for the draft yesterday morning at Manhattan's General Post Office at 33d Street and Eighth Avenue. Later in the day, another registrant had to hand his card over demonstrators protesting the draft.

and "No Draft for Women or Men."

Many protesters said that they would oppose the draft even if it were modified to include women but that they welcomed any way to attack the law.

"We celebrate anything that stops registration, anything that stops the war machine," said Glenn Tepper, a leader of the demonstration in New York.

As the heat inched up to 100 degrees, demonstrators used placards as fans and for shade.

At 12:25 P.M. the picket line, which had been scheduled to go until 1 P.M., was called off.

"We're going to be merciful." Mr. Tepper said as he mounted the steps. "You don't have to keep the picket line going. It's too hot."

Inside, demonstrators sat in front of Multi-Service Window No. 77, which had been designated to receive the filled-in registration forms. But those who came to register worked their way through the crowd or simply handed in their forms at other windows.

When they saw the protesters, some young men said they would come back later, but many stayed to go through the process.

"It's something you have to do," said Jacob Sayraf. "Besides, all you're doing is sending in your name."

"Nobody wants to die," said Floyd Thomas, a student at Long Island University, as he filled in his form. "But you can't fight the Government."

Protesters engaged in debates with registrants as they filled out their cards at the post office.

"Do you want to go?" Linda Owoie said to John P. Mele as he started writing out his name in block letters.

"It depends on what it's for," Mr. Mele answered, continuing to fill in his form.

"Any war is bad," Miss Owoie said.

"Not if it's against fascism and dictatorship," Mr. Mele said.

"This is fascism right now," Miss Owoie said, jabbing a finger at Mr. Mele's registration card.

After completing the card, Mr. Mele stepped over and around protesters and handed it to a clerk at window 77. The protesters were chanting loudly, "No draft, no war."

By 3 P.M., 76 men had registered at the main post office in Manhattan, according to Mildred Lee, a spokesman for the office.

Many registrants said they felt it was their duty to register.

"I thought a lot about it over the weekend," said 20-year-old Mark Putnam, a Nyack College senior after registering in Nyack in Rockland County. "It seems to me that for anything in life you have to pay a price. If I want to continue to enjoy freedom in this country I think my responsibility as a citizen is to make myself available for the draft."

In Pittsburgh, protest messages were sprayed on three post offices in 14-inch-high block letters. They read: "Don't register for World War III" and "No Draft, No World War III, No Fascist U.S.A." They were signed "CWP" for Communist Workers Party, according to Postmaster George T. Harkins.

But 70 miles north of Pittsburgh, Kevin Foust, who was first in line to register at the post office at Greenville, Pa., said: "I'm for it 100 percent. I think it's more or less my duty to sign up."

In Portland, Ore., Allen Nellis said after filling out his card: "It wasn't hard. The way I feel about it is that America may not be perfect, but it's better than any other country in the world. If it comes down to it, I'll fight for my country."

But at the Columbia University Post Office in Morningside Heights, Michael Lamble, a Columbia College student from Muncie, Ind., said: "I hate it. We're being used as pawns and I hate it. Registration is asinine, it's stupid. It's nonsensical. It's a damned crime. There is no compelling reason for registration now, and I resent Carter using us to bolster his popularity."

In Dallas, where he was campaigning last evening, President Carter again defended the registration as a precautionary move. "We do not anticipate departing from an all-volunteer force," he said. "We're registering today just in case we are challenged in the future."

In Hartford, where the eight protesters were arrested, Lance Wyse, a protester who was nearby, said: "They didn't block anything. They were not here to stir things up or anything, just to make an official statement by getting arrested."

The protesters were later released. They were scheduled to be arraigned on charges of criminal trespass today.

July 22, 1980

YOUTH UNEMPLOYMENT

LEGIONS OF TRANSIENT BOYS CREATE A NATIONAL PROBLEM

Children's Bureau Suggests Ways of Handling the Rapidly Increasing Numbers Forced to "Take to the Road"

By C. W. B. HURD.

WASHINGTON.

THE United States has a new social phenomenon—great numbers of transient boys. This is a development of the depression, especially noticeable during the past year, and has become a serious problem for social agencies. Conservative and reliable authorities estimate that between 200,000 and 300,-000 boys between the ages of 12 and 20 are "on the road," cut loose from their home surroundings and unable to adjust themselves into any normal picture. And the total is constantly increasing.

So grave is the problem, first called to its attention by the railroads, that the Federal Government has taken a hand. At the request of the President's Organization for Unemployment Relief, the Children's Bureau of the Department of Labor has completed a national survey; it has presented its findings informally to a "steering committee" of representatives of national welfare agencies organized by the National Association sandlots or with companions in the open country. The fear is that unless they are helped they will become, sooner or later, a charge on society, if not criminals at least seasoned vagrants schooled by their hardships and their contacts in the methods of "getting by."

The extreme possibility is that numbers of them may become similar to the "wild boys" of Russia, who some years ago by sheer force of necessity organized themselves into pillaging bands. Small communities in America already hold such fears; the railroads in many cases have found themselves unable to cope with the situation.

When faced with this new problem, the ordinary agencies for caring for transients find themselves under a severe handicap, for their activities must be directed toward caring for wandering families. More than that, the transient boy is usually a timid type who exists outside of the circle where ministering agencies might be able to reach him. When he is seen, he is found to be not a youthful smart aleck intent on seeking adventure, but a hungry, ill-clad youngster needing and welcoming attention.

"Boys accustomed to decent standards of living," says the bureau's report, "find themselves going for days at a time without taking off their clothes to sleep at night, becoming dirty, unkempt, a host to vermin. They may go for days with nothing to eat but coffee, bread and beans. In Winter they suffer from exposure. Last Winter, in one Western city, thirty-five young men and boys were removed from box cars, seriously ill, some in an advanced stage of pneumonia."

How the Survey Was Made.

In the bureau's survey, visits were paid to twenty-five communities in widely scattered parts of the United States, and much information was gathered through correspondence with responsible organizations.

Railroad men in Kansas City told investigators that in May no fewer than 1,500 men and boys a day rode freight trains through that city alone. In Yuma, Ariz., on the main line of the Southern Pacific, 30,000 men and boys were fed at public soup kitchens between Nov. 1, 1931, and March 15, 1932. The Salvation Army reported that during April and May it fed and lodged 9,551 men and boys at El Paso, Texas, alone, 2,059 of these being under 21 years of age.

The proportions of the problem grow even greater when it is realized that those boys who come in contact with agencies that keep statistics are only the barest minority of the whole —that the great mass of them shun the cities.

The transient boy is not the product of any individual locality. The Community Boys' Lodge in Los Angeles reported it had served boys from forty-five States and from the District of Columbia among the 623 to whom it gave shelter in the five months ended March 31.

As for the plight of communities faced with the problem of the transient boy, the following is taken from the bureau's report about to be sent to social welfare agencies:

"Most of the communities through which this hungry, tired and dirty horde passes are no longer able to meet the needs of their own unemployed adequately. They have no choice but to spend as little as possible on non-residents. Therefore, in city after city the transient boy finds that if he pauses to seek food or to rest he can remain but twenty-four hours. The local agency, charged with service to transients, will usually give him lodging for one night and two meals. Then he must move on.

"In the urban centres the time limit is sometimes a little longer. But in the whole mass of evidence assembled the universality of the policy of keeping these wanderers moving stands out conspicuously.

"Shelter facilities range all the way from a basement jail devoid of sanitary arrangements or from permission to sleep in the sandhouse on railroad property, where the warmed sand lends some degree of comfort on a frosty night, up to a well-regulated lodging house with beds,

equipped with fresh linen and with bathing arrangements and a place to launder soiled clothing.

"In cities where the conservation of resources is a primary consideration the food given the transients has sunk to a dead level of monotony. Coffee, bread, beans and an occasional vegetable stew constitute the menu at station after station. Occasionally, persons with imagination and initiative have found ways to vary this diet at little increase in cost.

Lack of Special Facilities.

"Riding freights and hitch-hiking are hard on shoes and clothes. Cities are now providing little help in this line to non-residents. Medical care for those sick as a result of hardship or exposure is practically not to be had until the sufferer is in an obviously serious condition. Except in a very few of the larger cities no case work, even of the most rudimentary character, is attempted. In most places a simple form of registration is all that is undertaken.

"Freight yards are policed. Hence trains must be boarded outside the yard limits while trains are in motion. One railroad alone reported more than fifty young men and boys killed and more than 100 crippled in this way last Winter.

"It is no longer possible to pick up odd jobs here and there. Communities jealously reserve even the occasional short-time job for local residents. Therefore the unwelcome non-resident boy must either depend on the bread line or the soup kitchen, or he must beg or steal.

"In the box cars, in the 'jungles,' as the camping sites adjacent to the

railroad yards are called, or even in the municipal shelters, he will meet men whose entire influence is destructive—criminals, fugitives from justice planning new 'jobs' and looking for clever new recruits—degenerates and perverts eager to initiate new boys into evil habits and to teach them how they can pick up a few odd dollars in any big city.

"Such men are in the great minority, but one or two can do an incalculable amount of damage. Worst of all, perhaps, because it is so contagious, is the workless philosophy, the 'getting-by' attitude everywhere encountered and very easily acquired on the open road. To this species of demoralization the 'keep them moving' policy universally in vogue not only offers no opposition but in fact contributes."

Publicity Campaign Planned.

With these conditions established, it is suggested that welfare agencies embark on a coordinated program for the dual purpose of arresting the movement of boys away from their homes and of rehabilitating those who have become waifs and strays. First of all, there is planned a national publicity campaign for the month of September, warning boys of the hardships that will be encountered by "taking to the road."

Beyond that, however, the work of necessity must extend to families, with the creation of more satisfactory environments. For instance, in the report no blame was attached to a 15-year-old boy found in a "jungle" in Utah, who had left his home in an Eastern industrial district because his family, containing nine persons, was reduced to living on county re-

lief which amounted to $3.20 a week "with a prospect of further reduction as county funds dwindled."

Even with proper family surroundings established, there will remain other problems, such as providing activities for idle hands so as to ward off the restlessness of youth. California is cited as an example of progressiveness in this regard; it has established camps where reforestation is carried on, providing boys with interesting work as a natural outlet for their energy.

"A community that seriously sets out to organize such a program," the bureau states, "would certainly find among its own unemployed many men and boys of imagination and enterprise with executive ability and qualities of leadership to whom much of the development of the projects might be entrusted. State leadership and probably State financial assistance doubtless will be needed, with all communities participating in intelligent planning on a State-wide cooperative basis."

However, it is recognized that despite such preventive measures "many boys will continue to take to the road." For these it is hoped that national and local agencies will provide a higher standard of food and shelter, together with attention to individual cases and some effort toward assimilating these transients into permanent surroundings. It is urged that those boys who have homes be returned to them and that the cities pay more attention to absorbing those who have none.

August 14, 1932

THE FORESTRY ARMY THAT LIVES BY WORK

In the Camps of the Conservation Corps 250,000 Youths Find a New Outlook

By DOROTHY D. BROMLEY.

PRESIDENT ROOSEVELT, on the radio last Monday night, talked to more than 250,000 young men in more than a thousand Civilian Conservation Corps camps throughout the country. They were evidence, he said, "that we are seeking to get away as fast as we possibly can from soup kitchens and free rations," and they were "the vanguard of the new spirit of the American future," namely, "that satisfying reward and safe reward come only through honest work."

It was in the belief that the average American prefers honest toil to a dole that the President conceived the idea of putting this army of unemployed young men at work in the forests. Congress approved the project on March 31 and the Department of Labor hastened to select a quarter of a million men of good character and physique, between the ages of 18 and 25, whose families were on the relief rolls. They were enrolled for a six months' period at $1 a day plus subsistence and clothing, and the greater part of their pay, from $20 to $25 a month was to be allotted to their families.

It was the task of the United States Army to examine, equip and

organize these men and establish them in work camps before July 1, so that they might complete their service before the dead of Winter. As many as 52,000 boys had to be moved from East to West, since all but 7,000,000 of our 161,000,000 acres of national forests lie west of the Great Plains.

Composition of the C. C. C.

Today the boys are settled in groups of 200 in 1,330 different camps, and the work is well under way. The 25,000 war veterans who were enrolled on June 26 will soon be established in camps of their own, bringing the grand total of C. C. C. camps up to 1,435.

The work is under the direction of the forestry experts and engineers of the Departments of Agriculture and the Interior, but it has been necessary to supplement their staffs with 22,000 foresters, landscape men and construction engineers who will act as superintendents and foremen at salaries ranging for the most part from $100 to $125 a month. In addition 35,000 local unemployed men at $1 a day

with no age limit specified have been taken on by the camps in order to insure the cooperation of the communities where the camps are situated. Finally 14,400 Indians have been enrolled at $1 a day to work on their own reservations. This makes, all told, 324,000 men who have been given employment with the C. C. C.

The disbursement of large sums of money for wages and supplies is already being felt throughout the country. On July 1 pay checks for $6,250,000 were mailed to the boys' families. While the expense to the government is great around $20,-000,000 a month in rough figures the wide distribution of the money and the investment being made in the public domain are held to justify this novel public works project.

The camps are scattered along the Pacific Coast, all through the Rockies, along the Appalachian chain in the East, down into the Great Smokies in Tennessee and up into the White and Green Mountains in New England. In the Middle West, the Ohio and Mississippi

Valleys are dotted with camps that will do work to prevent soil erosion and floods. Every State except Delaware has at least one camp. California, with her great stretches of national forests, has the largest number, 164. In the East, Pennsylvania leads with sixty-odd camps, while New York has thirty-three.

The Program Ahead.

The plan, breath-taking in its magnitude, is to rehabilitate, protect against fire and improve 161,-000,000 acres of national forests, the 4,353,000 acres of timbered lands in the national park system and also the State forests and parks wherever the States have agreed to share with the government any future profit that may accrue from planting that is done. It is the first great step in the offensive against the deterioration and wasting of forest lands, both public and private, which, if allowed to continue at the present rate, would, it is held, leave us without a domestic timber supply in thirty or forty years.

In the national and State forests trails are to be made for fire-fighters, wide fire-breaks are to be cut out of the forests and fire lines are to be built along motor roads. Insect pests and blights are to be eradicated, and fallen timber is to be cleared away. Undesirable growths are to be eliminated, the valuable trees nurtured and many millions of saplings planted.

In the national parks, in the national military parks and in the State parks the same kind of conservation work is to be done, with the aim not of cutting and selling in the future, but of preserving and improving the parks for the use and enjoyment of the public.

Hard Work to Start With.

When the boys arrived in camp they soon found that there was hard work to be done. The camp site had to be cleared, tents pitched, a road built into camp, a water system put in, and a mess hall built.

The sense of strangeness—there were a good many cases of homesickness among the younger boys—and the worst of the discomforts are over now. In whatever camp you may visit, the boys seem to belong to their camp and their camp to them. Here, in a cleared space on the side of the mountain, are brown khaki tents, some fifteen or twenty of them, standing high and dry on wooden floors. The company street which they face is outlined in white stones and landscaped with a few baby fir trees. At one end is the combined mess hall and recreation room.

Every day has its rhythm. At 6:30 in the morning the camp bugle blows. Morning "chow" is at 7 and the boys in blue denim shirts and jeans troop into the mess hall intent on ham and eggs, bread and potatoes. They eat, the officers say, as though they had been starved for a year; the food allowance is 30 cents a day.

At 8 o'clock they set out in groups of fifteen and twenty under the supervision of forestry foremen, piling into trucks, or trekking on foot, depending on the job location. Shirts are peeled, revealing some bronzed torsos and others painfully sunburned. Eager to get a tan, the boys cannot be persuaded to keep their shirts on. Some of them are narrow-chested, with the mark of meager lives still upon them; almost all of them look under 20, still very much boys.

The work that they are doing, no matter whether it is chopping trees, digging out rocks, or building trails, looks hard, almost backbreaking, for such youngsters. They toil away stoically, without much singing and joking; that comes later in the day.

At 12 o'clock the "chow" wagon if they are working far from camp is greeted with whoops of joy. These boys get a full hour for lunch. They are supposed to work eight hours a day five days a week, but the time spent going to and from camp and the lunch hour are taken out, so that they actually work only about six and one-half hours a day.

At 4 o'clock they are back in camp, starting out for the swimming hole with towels over their shoulders, loafing in their tents until supper time, or playing baseball. Interest in baseball is at white heat in all the C. C. C. camps and rivalry between neighboring outfits is keen.

Army Discipline Lacking.

The army Captain in charge of one camp happens to be a great baseball enthusiast and he complains loudly that he has been ruled off the team under the C. C. C. rules. He coaches the boys, mixing with them, contrary to army tradition, in a very democratic fashion. There is no military discipline in the C. C. C., no saluting, no standing at attention. There is not supposed to be any drilling, either, although the boys in this camp had asked for a little, so that they could make a showing in Fourth of July parades.

After supper there are classes in English, mathematics, geology, &c., for those who are interested. They are taught by college boys and one or two by the officers. Last week there were talks on personal and sex hygiene and the bulletin board announces a series on forestry. The camp string quartette is scheduled for an evening's entertainment and a minstrel show is rehearsing.

The musical members of the camp hope to follow the brilliant example of a near-by outfit, which recently put on a show for the townspeople and made some money.

They are 100 per cent American, these boys of the C. C. C.—cocky and boastful, alive with the competitive spirit, awed by no one. Every camp flatters itself that it is the best outfit—with the best baseball team, the best boxers, the best musical talent—in the C. C. C. A few of the camps have had their baptism of fire, and have told the world, through the C. C. C. newssheet, Happy Days, how gloriously they have acquitted themselves. A company in South Carolina claims "the fire-fighting derby" for having put out a 700-acre forest fire in five hours, while a company in Georgia boasts of having spent three days and nights on the fireline, with its meals brought up in a roller-kitchen.

Reaction of the Youths.

Most of the boys seem to like the life. The majesty of nature is somehow calming young nerves that had been made jumpy by enforced idleness and by knocking about city streets.

Just as the war aroused new emotions and sensations, the experience of life in the open and the feeling of oneness with a quarter of a million other human beings is having its effect on these youngsters. Some are writing poetry; crude, but from the heart. One of them thinks it's a "grand corps" and dedicates a poem to "President Roosevelt, Our Deliverer." Another calls his poem "A New View."

Word comes from Massachusetts that a number of the boys in one camp were offered jobs when they were home over the Fourth, but turned them down; they were so well satisfied with life in the C. C. C.

Discipline is a problem but so far not a serious one. Regulations provide that a boy who misbehaves or refuses to work may be confined to camp for a week, lose three days' pay, have certain privileges suspended, or, in extreme cases, be discharged. If a boy goes a. w. o. l. the only penalty that can be inflicted is discharge. Very often the officers have been just as glad to see the trouble-makers eliminated.

By July 1, 5 per cent of the original 250,000 had been separated from the service, some for refusal to work, some for misconduct, some for being a. w. o. l., some for medical reasons, a few for having been arrested by the civil authorities and a certain number to take proffered jobs. All are being replaced.

Morale Declared Good.

There have been rumors of drunkenness among the boys and of some stealing in the countryside. Yet the army reports show that such cases are rare and that in general the morale "is better than was to be expected." There have been a few disturbances in different camps, chiefly about food.

The fact that most of the camps are isolated in the most healthful kind of surroundings and are limited to 200 men insures them to a certain extent against bad moral and health conditions. So far nothing worse than measles has broken out. Many of the boys have gained an average of six or seven pounds.

July 23, 1933

YOUTH CRIES OUT FOR A SALVAGING HAND

It Asks for Guidance Toward Solid Goals And, Above All, a Chance to Work

By EUNICE FULLER BARNARD

AMERICA is traditionally a young man's country, a land of opportunity and boundless hope. Yet recently, at a national conference in Washington, a hundred experts—officially chosen for their intimate knowledge of the younger generation—petitioned the government to salvage our youth from futility and despair. Not as an emergency aid but as a continuing national prop, they asked for a Federal commission to help youth find a foothold and a faith.

Some six or seven million young people, it is estimated, in that ardent decade between the ages of 16 and 25, when new-found energies cry out to be tried, are paralyzed by enforced inertia. They have no jobs, and they are not preparing for any. They have left school. Most of them have not even facilities for constructive play. They are tramping the streets, "riding the rods," or just idling in the very years when normally youngsters make their first straight, spirited dash toward careers and homes of their own. Like so many sprinters poised for the race, a generation is being held back at the starting tape.

For five successive Junes, during the depression, high schools and colleges have poured their hundreds of thousands of eager-eyed, lean-limbed graduates into a society which apparently has little need of them. In a world for which they have spent from twelve to sixteen years in training, they find, by and large, less occupation, less hope and less concern for their welfare than do the inmates of an Old Men's Home.

* * *

CUMULATIVELY we are beginning to realize that the years just past have been peculiarly a depression of the young. In former business emergencies youth has been served, frequently at the expense of the older generation. With its readiness to accept bargain wages as a weapon, it has often wrested many of the available jobs from expert middle age. In the severer recent crisis, age, forced to fight on youth's terms, has not usually been under-cut. Today we are quite properly protecting the experienced worker, the older "family man," against youth's competition, both by the wage levels set by the NRA and by the minimum age provisions of 60 per cent of the codes.

Thus, however, on every count today's youngster loses. He lacks, as a rule, even that chance to begin at the bottom which has been America's traditional promise to youth. Industry and trade, in sad plight themselves, have felt neither obliged nor able to look after him. High schools and post-high school courses have not often been equipped to deal with his realistic vocational interests. The alternative of putting him to wholesale social use we have as yet tried only in such an experiment as the Civilian Conservation Corps. In large part that force and enthusiasm of youth which Russia and Germany are making their main motive power are here an unharnessed Niagara.

Even of the nine or ten million

youth estimated as employed, not all by any means are at satisfying or necessary work. Nearly three million young people who in normal times would have moved to towns or cities, are for instance, still on farms, where they are not needed, according to Dr. O. E. Baker of the Department of Agriculture.

How many of the unemployed or mal-employed youth have turned to anti-social lives is not known. Some fifty thousand are among the homeless, destitute wanderers recently registered at the government transient camps. As for crime, George F. Zook, United States Commissioner of Education, has pointed out that this age group, which already furnished the largest proportion of our criminals, increased in State and Federal prisons about 9 per cent in the single year 1929-30. Scattered reports also indicate that many young people have become discouraged to the point of mental derangement.

We are accustomed to think of the youth of the World War era as the lost generation. But before their disillusion, they had their moment of service and applause. These present youngsters, most of them, have never felt either socially needed or acclaimed.

Alike for Ph. D. and prospective porter, would-be stock-broker and stenographer, the "No Help Wanted" sign has stood across the path like a barrier to life itself. Education, brawn, technical training—none of these has been able to assure its possessor of a chance at necessary or remunerative work. Recently the National Student Federation estimated that at least 350,-000 young college graduates have not yet found jobs. Since then the class of 1934, some 150,000 strong, has stepped into the outer world.

Current crops of teachers, nurses, architects, lawyers, engineers have glutted the market like those of cotton and wheat. All too literally these young people are being plowed under by circumstances, or turned to uses foreign to their abilities. Beaux arts graduates are behind grocery store counters, and French teachers are working as floor-walkers. For the first time young white-collar workers are sharing the misfortune of wholesale unemployment and maladjustment with their contemporaries of factory and shop.

* * *

VAGUELY, perhaps, but none the less surely, youth is gaining a new solidarity, a kind of class consciousness in the working world. Like women of the pre-suffrage era, young people are beginning to feel the bond uniting victims of a common discrimination. It is a tie far stronger than that of the smart escapades, intended to defy and shock an elder morality, which distinguished the youngsters of a decade ago. Then they were referred to as "the younger generation," an appendage obviously of

the older society. Now, in significant contrast, they are "youth," a class apart with a cause of its own.

Already the more articulate are calling themselves the "frustrated generation." Blocked in their desire for self-support, they are withheld from marriage as well. Many are vocally dissatisfied with their education, which they feel has not adequately prepared them for the modern world. This August they are to air some of these views at a first American Youth Congress to be held at New York University. To this meeting have been invited heads of seventy-odd youth organizations in the United States and some 400 young "leaders in new thought." Called by a recently organized "Central Bureau for Young America," the congress will discuss three "basic needs" of present-day youth: employment; education for job and leisure; and "leadership toward goals which youth itself believes worth while."

* * *

MORE and more youth is demanding a finger in the pie of its own collective future. At the conference which recommended a continuing Federal commission to map out a national youth program, representatives of youth itself were prominent. At least a third of such a commission, they insisted, should be made up of persons less than 30 years old.

Again and again these young leaders intimated that youth is tired of having its course charted by age, well meaning but ignorant of its real desires. New plans for youth's education and leisure activities, they urged, should "grow out of the needs of youth as expressed by youth."

But no amount of recreation or higher schooling is, in their view, a substitute for a paying job. Both, they are apt to say, are mere narcotics to reconcile them to an abnormal existence. "Sitting in choral clubs and weaving baskets is not enough," one girl explained. "We want jobs, success and marriage." These "society, for its own preservation," should be obliged to provide for them, the youthful leaders made clear. Not just any jobs, but jobs in the line of their special talents and therefore of their best contribution to the general welfare. According to their theory, society should assure every individual "opportunities for exercising his abilities in an occupation which will provide adequate support."

Many of them admit that success in terms of individual fortunes may be a thing of the past. They envisage the probability that youth, as one of them put it, "must learn to find in social service the same satisfactions its elders once gained in industrial pioneering."

The youth leaders and those elders closely in touch with the situation seem to cherish little hope of a return for youth to the pre-depression status quo. Its present plight, they believe, is no mere emergency. Instead, the depression has served to reveal a new situation, caused, in the phrase of the national conference, by "the social, economic and industrial changes

that have taken place so rapidly during the past decade." In this altered society, youth, in the conference's opinion, "can no longer look forward to employment even in juvenile occupations."

The success story, dear to commencement orators, about the boy who won his way by honesty and hard work, was even before the depression increasingly becoming a myth, it is said. Analyses of jobs open to youth, made in a number of places in the pre-1929 era, uniformly revealed work of "routine or repetitive type, offering practically no educational advantages," according to Courtenay Dinwiddie, secretary of the National Child Labor Committee. "These work opportunities were, therefore, in the main, not stepping stones leading the youthful occupants to anything better, but were entrances to blind alleys," he said.

* * *

HERE, then, permanently on our hands may be millions of young people who, in Commissioner Zook's phrase, "are simply not wanted in industry or business in competition with wage-earners with families." Most of them doubtless would profit by using these years of youth in further training. But for many such opportunities are either not open, not desired or are not of the right sort.

It is a colossal riddle for Uncle Sam. Dr. Zook has put it this way: "We have therefore the problem of affording these young people a chance to work at something that is real, something which has further educational opportunities in it, and yet something which does not result in a product in competition with the great army of wage-earners. Truly, it would seem as if we were faced with a paradox."

Already dozens of solutions have been proposed, and many tried. The Federal Government has poked at the problem through several of its new alphabetical departments. So have counties and cities and private agencies. But much of what has been done has been only palliative.

For instance, the most extensive attack on the dilemma thus far has been through direct aid. Something less than 2,000,000 of these youths at the last check-up were counted as being in the families on direct relief. It is the contention of most students of the question that less money would go further, and would stimulate a heightened morale, if it could be paid to these boys and girls for some form of useful work.

That of course is what is being done for the 300,000 boys enrolled in the CCC camps. Five-sixths of the $30-a-month wage earned by these sons of relief families is automatically sent home. Tenement lads, bronzed and hardened by forest life and the first balanced rations many of them have ever had, have gained in a single month pounds in weight and quarter inches in height.

What is more significant, they have added cubits to their morale, as letters and statements amply testify. That is because their work, better than many other projects, meets most of the conditions of the riddle, as Commissioner Zook has

pointed out. These boys are on a real job, not a "set-up," and a job of whose social benefits they can be proud. Yet they are not competing with existing industry, agriculture or business.

The main objection which has been raised to the camps as a solution of youth's dilemma is that they are not in themselves a permanent answer. When after some months the boy goes back home, he is vocationally often as much at a loss as ever. The new educational program which is now functioning in most of the camps may, however, partly still this criticism. Most of the men are taking advantage of it to study for some occupation, or, in a few cases, by teaching others, to keep a skill already gained.

Another government answer to the riddle is a new type of apprenticeship now being evolved as a permissive plan by the NRA. This would allow private employers to hire boys and girls over 16 at wages averaging half the basic rates, provided they give them approved training, with at least 100 hours of class instruction.

A similar plan of having the young graduate "sing for his supper," so to speak, is being discussed both within and without the relief administration. Under this scheme, for a year or two after leaving school or college, the boy or girl would enter the public service as a sort of interne at subsistence wages, doing socially necessary work and gaining a job technique. Thus young surveyors, draftsmen, engineers and physicians might be employed by the scores in the Tennessee Valley project and other construction centres, as the National Student Federation has recently proposed.

* * *

FROM preparing museum exhibits to running playgrounds or controlling insect pests, there is apparently no end to the tasks in which youth might help and learn, and even lead to its own and the country's benefit. Take one accomplished case in Schuylkill County in the Pennsylvania coal-mining region, where youth with a slight start has taken its own problem in hand. There last Spring, in an area with a high juvenile crime record, the FERA organized some twenty so-called Youth Community Centres, with classes in music, dramatics, art and home-making. Unemployed young people managed the project and became the teachers, janitors, hostesses, laborers and students. It was a pure democracy—"college graduates and thugs working side by side," as an organizer put it.

Soon, particularly in the rural districts, the need of libraries was felt. The youngsters adopted it as a youth problem. Today they have organized traveling libraries of 1,200 to 2,500 volumes in almost a score of towns, serving themselves as librarians.

FERA funds, which at first had paid them subsistence wages, gave out. But the youngsters did not. Classes and libraries are still going, and small dues are remunerating the workers. Meanwhile the juvenile crime record has been lowered.

Collectively also these young people evolved salable commercial products. They discovered, for instance, that coal with long polishing would take a hard, brilliant finish that would not rub off. Out of coal therefore they designed thermometers and clocks and other novelties, which they sold to the coal companies as advertising souvenirs.

* * *

SPENDING of government money to help youth help itself, to assemble in youth centres of this sort and develop pioneer activities is a remedy more and more strongly advocated. The American Youth Council of Springfield, Mass., conducts a self-governing group of a type which it seeks to have the Relief Administration aid and promote in other places. For a year now, with no money but with an eighteen-room house loaned as headquarters, this mutual benefit society of 100 unemployed young

people has been carrying on. In various clubs and classes the members have tried to maintain morale and keep themselves employable. In a business practice room, for instance, stenographers have kept their skill alive, supervised by one more experienced than the rest. In the kitchen, girls with domestic interests have been making, for sale, candy, cake and salted nuts.

Such centres as this are necessary, many leaders believe, to compensate for the lack not only of employment but of suitable opportunities for either education or recreation for young people. The National Conference on Youth Problems asked for two special United States commissions, one to plan a proper educational program, and another to coordinate leisure-time activities for youths.

"In the end," Commissioner Zook

has said, "the responsibility of dealing with this situation rests squarely on the regular school system." Two years more added to the high school, he believes, should provide technical courses giving any young man or woman a chance to learn "one of the many new vocations which a changing economic life is constantly producing."

Part of such a course must be the opportunity to work at actual jobs in industry and elsewhere on a part-time basis. This would give students, he feels, "the satisfaction of beginning to earn and at the same time to learn something of the technical and human-relations requirements of a job."

A subsistence wage to be paid to young people for pursuing such an approved educational program was recommended by the national conference. Such a subsidy, at the

rate of $15 a month, has been given by the government to some 70,000 students during the past year to enable them to remain in college, but only in return for actual work in connection with the college plant or services. It has recently been proposed also to pay a small wage to the army of youngsters who have found refuge and work opportunities at the transient camps.

Whether any or all of these plans are adopted, they at least betoken a new attitude toward the problem. We are accustomed to think of our great and expanding national future. Youth, we are beginning to realize, is that future. And no training or development or hope that we can give it can be too much.

July 1, 1934

$50,000,000 Youth Project Is Established by the President

Sets Up National Administration, Which Expects to Aid 500,000 in Finding Jobs in Industry, Giving Special Training, Helping in School and College, and Providing Work Relief.

Special to THE NEW YORK TIMES.
WASHINGTON, June 26.—President Roosevelt set aside $50,000,000 from work relief funds today to give more than half a million young Americans the educational and vocational opportunities of which the extended depression has threatened to rob them.

To provide a unified program to school and find employment for those between the ages of 16 and 25, the President created a National Youth Administration under the direct supervision of Aubrey Williams, assistant FERA administrator.

Objectives of the drive were listed as follows:

1. To find employment in private industry for unemployed youth.

2. To train and retrain young people for industrial, technical and professional employment opportunities.

3. To provide for continuing attendance at high school and college.

4. To provide work relief upon projects designed to meet the needs of youth.

In a White House announcement of the program, Mr. Roosevelt asked for the cooperation of industry, commerce and agriculture, and of leaders in every walk of life, to save young morale by opening up fields of normal endeavor to those under 25.

"The yield on this investment should be high," he declared.

With still heavier taxation looming if work is not provided soon for the jobless, the Chief Executive made clear that the primary objective of this new program was to find jobs in private industry for youthful unemployed. The plans for industrial and civic training and

high school and college aid were outlined with this goal in view.

At least 150,000 youths should be taken care of under the job training program, 150,000 should receive work relief jobs, 100,000 be aided in attending high school, 120,000 in attending college, and several thousand in taking post-graduate work, it was declared.

"I have determined that we shall do something for the nation's unemployed youth because we can ill afford to lose the skill and energy of these young men and women," the President said. "They must have their chance in school, their turn as apprentices, and their opportunity for jobs."

With this end in view, Mr. Roosevelt tonight provided for a closely correlated nation-wide organization. He named Josephine Roche, Assistant Secretary of the Treasury, to head an executive committee for the National Youth Administration.

Advisory Council to Be Named.

He also prepared to select a National Advisory Council to work under the general supervision of Harry L. Hopkins, Works Progress Administrator, and the specific direction of Mr. Williams.

On the advisory council will serve representatives of labor, business, agriculture, education and youth itself. Under the central organization will be forty-eight State Youth Divisions, each with its own advisory committee. Similar committees will be formed in counties and communities.

Available school-shop facilities for basic trade training, as well as private factories and shops, will be used for training youth to hold specialized jobs under the plan. Special afternoon or evening classes will be established in the schools

and factory shops will be used after the regular day's work is done.

In both cases instruction will be given "by needy unemployed persons qualified to teach the special field."

In addition, an "apprentice" system will be established.

Job placement, under this plan, will be developed in cooperation with re-employment offices. A service will be developed "in each Youth Centre" for the purpose of guidance, adjustment and job placement.

PRESIDENT'S STATEMENT.

In his statement, issued as he signed the executive order creating the Youth Administration, the President said:

"Satisfactory progress in setting up the work program for the unemployed is being made. This program calls for the removal of unemployed from direct relief to jobs and should be well under way during July.

"I have determined that we shall do something for the nation's unemployed youth because we can ill afford to lose the skill and energy of these young men and women. They must have their chance in school, their turn as apprentices and their opportunity for jobs—a chance to work and earn for themselves.

"In recognition of this great national need I have established a National Youth Administration, to be under the Works Progress Administration.

"This undertaking will need the vigorous cooperation of the citizens of the several States, and to insure that they shall have an important part in this work a representative group will be appointed to act as a national advisory board with similar boards of citizens in the States and municipalities throughout the country.

Youth to Have Say.

"On these boards there shall be representatives of industry, labor, education and youth, because I want the youth of America to have something to say about what is being done for them.

"Organizations along State and municipal lines will be developed. The work of these organizations will be to mobilize industrial, commercial, agricultural and educational forces of the States so as to provide employment and to render other practical assistance to unemployed youth.

"It is recognized that the final solution of this whole problem of

unemployed youth will not be attained until there is a resumption of normal business activities and opportunities for private employment on a wide scale. I believe that the national youth program will serve the most pressing and immediate needs of that portion of unemployed youth most seriously affected at the present time.

"It is my sincere hope that all public and private agencies, groups and organizations, as well as educators, recreational leaders, employers and labor leaders, will cooperate whole-heartedly with the national and State youth administrations in the furtherance of this national youth program.

"The yield on this investment should be high."

Training for Federal Service.

Included in the "job" program is a plan of training selected youths for government service, foreshadowing a permanent civil service organization like that of England, and the President stresses that particular efforts must be made to find jobs for college graduates of 1935.

Boys and girls unable to attend high school for want of money for carfare, lunches and incidentals will, if over 16 years of age, receive an average of $6 a month to permit them to continue their secondary education.

An average of $15 a month will be given to unemployed high-school graduates under 25 to assist them in obtaining college education. No subsidies will be granted institutions under this plan, and students will be expected to pay part of the costs themselves, as in the past.

The present rule that those receiving work-relief aid in colleges shall not exceed 12 per cent of any institution's enrolment was held likely to be changed to permit more work-relief students to attend.

Aid for taking graduate courses, to be given to a selected group of those who are unable to find private employment on leaving college, will not be put on any fixed basis.

$15 a Month for Work Relief.

It is provided that only "unemployed youths in families that are certified for relief" shall receive outright work relief jobs, and an average wage of $15 a month will be paid to the young laborers. It is assumed that the heads of their families will hold better paid work relief jobs.

In this connection the announcement of the objectives of the plan said:

"Particular stress should be laid upon the building and the use of recreational and community centres which, depending upon local conditions and the energy, ability and enthusiasm of local youth groups, can be anything from an old-fashioned 'swimming hole' to a complete centre including all types of athletic facilities, community houses, library, class rooms, &c.

"In most communities these recreational and community centres can be made self-liquidating. Substantially all of the direct labor in the creation of these centres shall be performed by youths themselves,

working as apprentices under the direction of skilled mechanics."

It is further provided that " a national census of all youths in the United States between the ages of 16 and 25 is to be undertaken, using competent youths within that age group to carry on the work."

During the afternoon Mr. Roosevelt conferred briefly with leaders of the Youth Administration and went over details of the plan. The leaders promised that the program will be under way within ten days.

Among those present were Mr. Hopkins, Secretary Morgenthau, Miss Roche and Mr. Williams.

"It is certain that we will be well under way in ten days and, I hope,

in full swing by mid-July," Mr. Williams remarked.

Director for Each State.

A small central organization to be manned by men and women drawn from other governmental organizations would be set up separately from the FERA and the Works Progress Administration, he added, with an Assistant Youth Administration Director selected for each State.

It was noted here that two of the aims of the President's youth program are similar to phases of Senator Long's "share-the-wealth" plan. Training for industrial, technical and professional jobs and pro-

visions for continued attendance at high schools and colleges are urged by Mr. Long.

Enrolment of 30,189 recruits for the enlarged Civilian Conservation Corps during the first week of enlistment was announced today by Robert Fechner, CCC Director, as another program designed to aid the young gathered headway again.

By the week of July 4 there will be 400,000 workers in the organization receiving $30 a month, Mr. Fechner estimated. The limit of 600,000 youth would probably be reached by August, officials said.

June 27, 1935

JOBLESS YOUTH MAJOR PROBLEM

Decline of Work for the Unskilled Increases Teen Unemployment

By JOHN D. POMFRET
Special to The New York Times

WASHINGTON, June 8—The evidence is mounting that the United States is faced with a long-range unemployment situation of serious dimensions.

The underlying difficulty is that the economy is not growing fast enough to create the new jobs that would provide work for those who want it.

This strikes hardest at the young people who are looking for their first permanent jobs and the burden of unemployment is falling on them with ever greater severity.

The employment figures for May, issued last week by the Labor Department, gave striking evidence of this and prompted Labor Secretary W. Willard Wirtz to say that teenage unemployment could develop into "one of the most explosive social problems in the nation's history."

The figures showed that the unemployment rate among teen-agers was nearly 18 per cent—the highest since the department began keeping a separate figure for teen-agers in 1949.

Critical Situation

Mr. Wirtz thinks the situation is critical and called for broad action to improve the educational system, eliminate racial discrimination, train jobless youths and reduce the number of students who drop out of high school.

President Kennedy recently emphasized the gravity of the general manpower situation in

a message to Congress that was accompanied by a Labor Department analysis that is the most thorough to date.

Between 1947 and 1962 the number of jobs rose by 17 per cent, but the labor force went up by 21 per cent. The obvious result of this discrepancy was that unemployment rose from an average of below 4 per cent of the labor force in the immediate post-war period to more than 5 per cent in more recent years.

As unsatisfactory as this situation is, it may very well get worse.

Flood of Job Seekers

An unusual flood of new job seekers is about to hit the economy. The experts' estimates are that the country's labor force will grow by 13,000,000 during the sixties and by another 7,-000,000 between 1970 and 1975, reaching 93,000,000.

But these are net changes. Within the figures will be even larger shifts.

Thus, 26,000,000 young persons under the age of 25 are expected to enter the labor force in the sixties — a far greater number than the country ever has had to train and absorb before in a ten-year period.

Success would mean a new level of prosperity as the young people get jobs, marry and begin to rear families and contribute to the economy's output and demand.

But the experts do not be-

lieve that success will come easily or automatically.

Further, two statistics in the manpower report indicate that the economy will have to run faster and faster just to stay even.

Research and development expenditures rose from slightly over $5,000,000,000 in 1953-54 to $14,750,000,000 in 1961-62. The impact of this so far has not been reflected by a rise in the rate at which output per man-hour is increasing, but it is inconceivable to the experts that it will not be soon.

Secondly, even without any rise in the rate at which productivity is increasing, the real output of the private economy in this country grew 59 per cent between 1947 and 1961 with an increase in total man-hours of just 3 per cent. The fact that private employment increased by 10 per cent in this period was due to the very large rise in the number of part-time workers.

In the first place, the economy's performance at creating jobs has been lack-lustre in recent years. The slowdown has been centered in the private sector. This, between 1947 and 1957, grew at a rate of 700,-000 jobs a year. But between 1957 and 1962 the gain was 175,000 annually.

Growth in the public sector—mostly state and local government—has absorbed some of this slack. Total civilian government employment has been rising in the post-war period at a rate more than two and a half times that of total non-farm employment. State and local governments have been creating 285,000 jobs a year on the average since 1957, compared with 185,000 before then.

More Idleness Feared

But the experts estimate that if the economy does not begin to grow faster, unemployment which now is about 4,500,006 will grow by 1967 to beyond 5,500,000, or more than 7 per cent of the labor force.

If the challenge is large in the aggregate, it gets even bigger when looked at up close.

Technological change is demanding an ever-higher level of skill. An underlying shift in employment from goods-producing to service-producing industries is leaving many stranded. Drastic shifts in demand, depletion of natural resources or relocation of industries have left large groups of persons and sizeable areas in the backwash of the general prosperity.

Thus, unemployment last year among unskilled nonfarm laborers was 12 per cent—higher than any other occupational group. Semi-skilled workers had a jobless rate of 8 per cent; the skilled, 5 per cent, and professional people, 2 per cent.

The jobless rate among construction workers ran 12 per cent and among manufacturing employes, 5.8 per cent. In the service industries, it was 4.3 per cent and in public administration, just under 2 per cent.

Negroes, often deprived of training as well as job opportunities by discrimination, have an unemployment rate of twice the national average.

Skills Needed

Unemployment among teenage boys many of whom had not finished high school, was more than twice as high as the average rate last year. And although older workers are not as often out of work as their juniors, they have a much harder time finding a job when they are.

West Virginia, hard hit by the decline of coal-mining, had a jobless rate of 10.9 per cent last year. Pennsylvania, with the mining and steel industries both contributing to joblessness, had a rate of 7.9 per cent.

To meet the unemployment challenge, the Administration has proposed a $10,300,000 tax cut to stimulate the economy and create jobs.

June 9, 1963

351

BOYS LACK CHANCE TO STAY ON FARMS

Fewer Rural Jobs Are Available for Youths

By DONALD JANSON

Special to The New York Times

STILLWATER, Okla., Sept. 24—If it were possible, most farm boys would farm.

The technological revolution in agriculture, however, has ruled this out. Science and machines have replaced not only the horse but also millions of farmers.

Last decade there was a 41 per cent decline in farm workers, the biggest decrease yet. It is continuing.

Today fewer than 1 in 10 of the nation's population farms, and only one-tenth of today's farm boys will ever become farmers.

The youths, however, are coming out of rural schools ill-prepared for anything else. When forced to go to the city in search of work, they find that the number of unskilled jobs has shrunk because of automation, just as farm work has. Better trained city dwellers take the bulk of skilled work.

As a result, unemployment among farm youths is 50 per cent higher than among urban youths.

About 500 education, farm, labor and youth authorities are meeting here at Oklahoma State University this week to try to determine how the farm boy can cope with his plight.

The chairman of the National Conference on Problems of Rural Youth in a Changing Environment is Winthrop Rockefeller. The sponsor is the National Committee for Children and Youth.

"Foremost among the pressing needs," Assistant Secretary of Labor Esther Peterson said today, "is that of adequate education and training."

Mile J. Peterson, chairman of the department of agricultural education at the University of Minnesota, said the emphasis or college preparation at the expense of vocational training was "the most glaring maladjustment of our high schools."

Comparatively few farm youths go to college, many experts pointed out. They are interested in working with machines and tools, though, and if trained might outdo city youths in the competition for the increasing number of skilled and technical jobs.

However, many farm youths receive no competent vocational guidance and have little idea what the urban employment opportunities of the present and future are, the authorities continued.

September 29, 1963

WAR ON POVERTY WILL FOCUS ON YOUTH

By MARJORIE HUNTER

Special to The New York Times

WASHINGTON, March 14—In keying his chief domestic program of the year to the youth of the nation, President Johnson is seeking an answer to an age-old problem: How to prevent today's children of poverty from becoming tomorrow's parents of poverty.

The problems of youth are not new, nor have they been ignored. Untold thousands of agencies and organizations and groups — public and private — have programs geared to the needs of youth.

But certainly not in recent years has the nation's youth—— variously identified as 16 through 21 or 16 through 24 — been singled out as chief benefactor of a President's principal domestic program, in this case, President Johnson's "unconditional war on poverty."

The President's war — which some critics already are saying will involve more smoke than actual shooting—will seek to deal with the poverty of adults as well as youth. But, as the President himself has said, the emphasis will be on youth.

There are no estimates on the number of poor among those identified as youth—approximately 25,000,000 aged 16 through 24.

Many Findings

But the decision to concentrate the antipoverty campaign on this relatively small segment of the population was based on findings of a number of Government surveys.

"High and mounting unemployment of young people may well be the nation's most formidable manpower problem of this decade," the Department of Labor concluded in its manpower report sent to Congress.

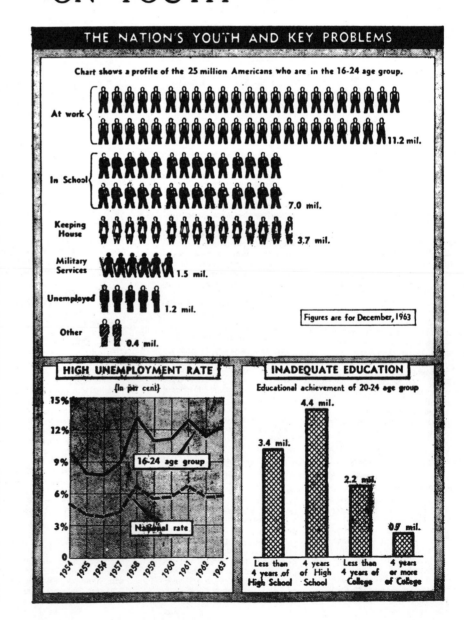

THE NATION'S YOUTH AND KEY PROBLEMS

Chart shows a profile of the 25 million Americans who are in the 16-24 age group.

At work — 11.2 mil.
In School — 7.0 mil.
Keeping House — 3.7 mil.
Military Services — 1.5 mil.
Unemployed — 1.2 mil.
Other — 0.4 mil.

Figures are for December, 1963

HIGH UNEMPLOYMENT RATE
(In per cent)
16-24 age group
National rate
1954 1955 1956 1957 1958 1959 1960 1961 1962 1963

INADEQUATE EDUCATION
Educational achievement of 20-24 age group
3.4 mil. — Less than 4 years of High School
4.4 mil. — 4 years of High School
2.2 mil. — Less than 4 years of College
0.9 mil. — 4 years or more of College

last week by the President.

The report cited these statistics:

(1) The unemployment rate for young people, aged 16 through 24, is twice the average for workers of all ages (12.2 per cent for youths, as compared with a national rate of 5.7 per cent).

(2) There are 1.2 million jobless young people in this age bracket, representing one of every three unemployed workers in the United States.

(3) More than 350,000 young people, 16 through 19 years old, are neither in school nor hold a job.

(4) More than a fourth of the non-white teen-age boys, not in school, cannot find work.

A Senate subcommittee on employment and manpower reported this month that unless steps were taken to reverse the trend 26,000,000 young people, aged 16 through 24, would enter the labor force (either by working or seeking work) during the present decade and that 7,500,000 of them would be school dropouts.

The dropouts, the Labor Department has predicted, will form the nucleus of the hardcore unemployed — the future parents of poverty as most of them had been children of poverty.

For this reason, the President and his economic advisers decided that the time had come to close in on the problem.

He will seek to do this in two ways: Help alleviate present poverty through job training

and remedial education. And help prevent it in the future through providing young children from poor families with better opportunities, including study centers at which to do home work, remedial education classes and a variety of other educational and health services.

Perhaps the cornerstone of his program will be something tentatively called the jobs corps, designed to aid unemployed, out-of-school male youths who need either job skills, basic education or both.

Tests Planned

Youths in need of such help will be identified through educational and physical examinations given under Selective Service. This does not mean that they face induction into the military service earlier than the present age minimum of 18, but will mean earlier identification of their particular problems.

The decision to use the draft examinations in this program to combat poverty stemmed largely from the fact that a task force named by President Kennedy reported last year that if Selective Service examinations were given to everyone at age 18—sometimes, such exams are not given for several years—a third of the young men would be found either educationally or mentally unqualified.

The task force report, "One Third of a Nation," showed an obvious pattern of inherited poverty. Most of the rejectees, it was found, were either unemployed or working at low-pay jobs that held little fu-

ture. Four out of every five were school dropouts.

The antipoverty program will set up youth camps—somewhat similar to the Civilian Conservation Camps of the 1930's—to teach these draft rejectees job skills and basic education and to attend to their health needs.

Other phases of the antipoverty program will include special youth counseling in employment offices, and work - study programs to encourage poor students to stay in school or even go on to college by providing them with needed part-time jobs.

Many of the guidelines for what the Administration hopes to do have already been laid down in many communities. There are a number of work-study programs — on both the high-school and college level—in many states, including New York.

There are remedial-education classes and job-training centers, many privately staffed and financed, throughout the nation.

Agriculture extension services in all states operate 4-H clubs to direct young people in self-improvement projects. Numerous programs to combat school dropouts have been instituted throughout the nation.

There are guidelines to be found, too, in various Federally assisted programs designed primarily to combat juvenile delinquency, such as the $12.6 million mobilization for youth on the Lower East Side of New York, a three-year program to

strike at the roots of delinquency.

The Federal Government, under an expanded vocational-education program enacted by Congress just last December, is preparing to put $150 million into an experimental four-year program of resident vocational-education schools and work-study programs for youths.

And there are numerous other Federal, state, local and private programs — largely keyed to education and training—designed to help youth.

But all too often, these programs have lacked several needed ingredients:

(1) Job training is available, but often not in the areas where it is needed. Too, many of those who need training are unable to absorb it because they lack basic education.

(2) Many programs are geared to middle - income youth, who need it far less than those from the families of poverty.

The Administration's war on poverty hopes to offer programs of its own, but, even more important, to mobilize and coordinate existing programs and agencies, particularly on the local level.

For, as President Johnson said in his economic message to Congress this year, a solution to the problem of poverty "will not be found in any single new program directed from Washington."

The entire nation, he said, must mobilize for "a frontal assault."

March 15, 1964

JOBLESSNESS RATE OF NEGRO YOUTHS INCREASES TO 25%

U.S. Statistics Show Figure Is Twice as High as That of White Teen-Agers

By EDWIN L. DALE Jr.
Special to The New York Times

WASHINGTON, Aug. 22 — Twenty-five per cent of the male Negro teen-agers who are in the labor force are out of work, according to normally unpublished Government statistics obtained today.

In addition, the jobless rate among Negro teen-age boys, which was only slightly higher than that among their white counterparts 10 years ago, is now nearly twice as high. The jobless rate for both groups has

grown, as was expected because of the teen-age population explosion, but the Negro rate has grown far faster.

The huge percentage of unemployment among Negro boys is not new. The jobless rate for this group, according to the Government figures, has ranged between 21 per cent and 25 per cent since 1958. The big growth in this group of jobless was in the years 1953 to 1958, and it has remained high ever since.

26 Per Cent Last Month

The rate was 25.4 per cent for all of last year and it was 26 per cent last month, though the latter figure is not adjusted for seasonal variations.

These facts, taken together, are regarded by many officials here as a major explanation for what has been taking place in Harlem, Rochester, Elizabeth, N. J., and elsewhere, where rioting has been led by youths.

The jobless figures refer to male Negroes between the ages of 14 to 19, inclusive, who count themselves as in the labor force and looking for work. It is

highly probable that a significant additional percentage of Negro youths are out of school but are not even looking for work and thus are not counted in the labor force.

No Problem in 1953

In 1953, a boom year in the economy until the last three months, the percentage of unemployment among the Negro teen-agers was only 7.1 and that among white boys 6.3. There was, in effect, no problem. By 1957, a comparable year for economic conditions, the jobless rate among white boys had risen to 10.6 per cent. But among Negroes it had soared to 17.7 per cent.

In 1958, a recession year, the jobless rate for white teen-age boys rose to 14 per cent and for Negroes it rose to 24.3 per cent. For the Negroes it has not dropped below 20.7 per cent since. In 1959 the Negro rate was 22.8 per cent, in 1960 it was 22 per cent, in 1961 it was 24.7 per cent, in 1962 it was 20.7 per cent and last year it was 25.4 per cent.

For white boys last year's

jobless rate was 14.2 per cent—a rate that was also broadly stabilized since 1958.

The sharp divergence since 10 years ago in the rate of unemployment as between white and Negro boys is not accounted for by different rates of population growth. Both groups grew in numbers by just under 50 per cent in the period.

There is no ready explanation here for the continuation of a huge army of Negro teen-age unemployed in a generally prosperous economy.

One explanation, covering both whites and Negroes, is simply the teen-age explosion, coming at a time when the labor force in general is not fully employed. But this does not account for the sharp relative jump in unemployed Negroes.

A familiar explanation, but one not accepted by all students of the problem, is that the skill requirements for jobs in recent years have grown rapidly and that Negroes tend to have fewer skills because they tend to leave school earlier.

Another related theory is that a sizable portion of today's Negro teen-agers—larger than in the past—comes from the Negro "problem families." These include the ones with little education who have migrated to cities from rural areas, and those headed only by a mother who has been deserted or never married.

Many War Babies

These families tend to produce culturally deprived children, and large numbers of those children were born in the years during and shortly after World War II.

The Government has begun several efforts to get at the problem, though not explicitly or overtly designed to aid Negroes as such. The antipoverty program will provide jobs and training for scores of thousands of youths, of whom Negroes will probably be in far larger proportion than their share of the population.

The Defense Department has begun an experimental program to accept youths for the service who do not qualify under normal medical and mental standards. And here again there will be large numbers of young Negroes.

In addition, there is a strong belief in the Government that further expansion of the economy at the rapid pace achieved this year will open up jobs for more and more of the presently unemployed youth, even those without skills.

But all of this is a relatively slow process. Meanwhile, possibly more than a third of the Negro youths on city streets—counting those in the labor force and those technically not in it—are without useful work.

August 23, 1964

Job Corps Opens First Center For Training Underprivileged

Special to The New York Times

THURMONT, Md., Jan. 15—The Federal Job Corps became a reality here today. The beginning was modestly low-key.

It became a reality when 30 young men from the slums of Baltimore and from the mountain poverty of the coal counties of Kentucky and Virginia arrived at Catoctin Center.

The Center is the first of 87 training camps scheduled to be opened by July 1 under President Johnson's antipoverty program, which offers basic education and job skills to underprivileged youths.

The opening of this Frederick County center, a former Civilian Conservation Corps camp in the Catoctin National Forest adjoining Camp David, the President's retreat, was the final step in preparations for receiving the first 500 to enroll at three training centers during the weekend of Feb. 7.

The 36 men who arrived here today are members of an advance group that will be split into three cadres to provide staff assistance at the camps, which open Feb. 7.

Reassigned in three squads of 10 men each, they will serve as reception committees here, at Winslow Center, Ariz., and at Ouachita Center, Ark., when these three camps receive their full complements of 100 to 200 youths three weeks from now.

President to Participate

President Johnson is expected to participate in ceremonies marking the formal opening of one of the three camps.

In addition to filling their cadre assignments, the youths beginning their Job Corps training here today also will serve as guinea pigs for the next three weeks, giving adult Job Corps instructors their first experience with live young men.

The program calls for parallel courses of training in basic education for youths who are school dropouts, and work training. At the 87 rural centers to be opened by midsummer, the job training will be largely in conservation work but training will be provided in skills such as carpentry, masonry work and the operation of heavy machinery, such as bulldozers.

The corps has announced plans to open 10 additional and much larger urban centers. They will provide the same basic education program, but the vocational training will be industrial. One such center, near New York, will be at Camp Kilmer, N. J.

Observing the three-week breaking-in process here were the professional staffs of two other Job Corps centers that are scheduled to open later. They are Tillamook Center, Ore., and Arrowood Center, N. C.

Each of the conservation camps, which will accommodate from 100 to 200 men, will have a staff of about 21, including 14 to 15 adult instructors in forestry and other skills, and six to seven members of Volunteers in Service to America, who conduct the domestic Peace Corps program."

Those who enroll in the Job Corps will receive a $30 a month allowance plus $50 a month, which will be held for them until they complete the one-year term. Those who choose to do so may allocate up to $25 a month of the withheld funds in month-by-month payments to their families and the Job Corps will match this sum, yielding $50 a month in family support funds.

January 16, 1965

SUMMER EVENTS FOR YOUTH URGED

U.S. Asks Help of Cities to Head Off Racial Unrest

WASHINGTON, June 10 (AP) — The Federal Government is trying to get local communities to turn on fire hydrants this summer, hold block parties and sponsor basketball tournaments for youngsters.

The Government also wants to find summer jobs for some 12.5 million boys and girls between the ages of 16 and 21, send youngsters from poor neighborhoods to camp and otherwise keep the nation's youth occupied.

Much of the Government's interest is designed to head off racial unrest in the nation's cities.

Vice President Humphrey, in seeking the support of the Advertising Council, told its annual Washington conference last month:

"Let me put it clearly and simply: If we want this summer to be a cool summer and not a hot one, if we want our young people to grow up as decent, constructive citizens and not as embittered, disappointed dwellers of the ghetto, if we want our America to be an America that is strong and free, it will depend on us."

Humphrey Heads Drive

Mr. Humphrey, chairman of the President's Council on Youth Opportunity, has led an information project aimed at getting local communities to develop work, recreational and social summer programs for the nation's youth.

The council, with covering letters by Mr. Humphrey, has written to mayors and city managers, newspapers and national and local volunteer agencies in an effort to get local communities moving as quickly as possible.

"We've been asking them what they're doing for their youngsters and telling them what other communities are doing," a council spokesman said. "We don't expect every community to do everything—many of them can't—but we hope to give them plenty of ideas so they can do something."

Mr. Humphrey and the council have told the communities that though the Federal Government is spending some $678-million this summer — more than ever before—it will take a local effort to succeed.

The council has urged the nation's 2,700 mayors and city managers to establish local youth opportunity councils and to tell the Federal Government about programs they plan or have done in the past.

Projects Held

Among the projects held or in effect:

¶Chicago—Sears Roebuck on the West Side made available four of its lighted parking lots which were used for basketball and football clinics, costume parties, an art fair, movies and dances.

¶Washington—Neighborhood street dances were held last year, with the music provided by each youngster bringing a transister radio. The dances were so successful that one was held on Halloween and some 1,000 youngsters attended.

¶Dayton, Ohio—The school system taught swimming last summer to 5,760 6-to-11-year-olds from poverty areas. Eight portable and two permanent pools were used.

¶Philadelphia — In cooperation with the water, fire, police and streets departments, the recreation department issues permits to attach approved shower equipment to a fire hydrant for periods not to exceed one hour. The permit is issued to responsible adults in each block.

¶New York—Movies and plays were shown on flat-body trucks in slum neighborhoods.

¶Omaha — In addition to dancing and swimming programs, the city is making vacant lots available where older youths may bring their cars for waxing and polishing and do-it-yourself repair work.

¶Los Angeles — Track and field meets were held at five locations Monday through Friday for an eight-week period. Competition was restricted to those 15 or older. More than 9,000 youngsters learned to swim in the portable pool program conducted throughout the summer months.

¶Cincinnati — Kroger grocer stores served as local sponsors of a combined physical fitness pentathlon and junior Olympics track and field competition for more than 900 boys and girls 6 to 18.

New York is also sponsoring a 12-city United States Youth Games with the finals to be held Aug. 18 and 19.

Youngsters will compete in track and field, basketball and bowling. Preliminaries will be held in Atlanta, Baltimore, Boston, Cleveland, Detroit, New Orleans, New York, Pittsburgh, St. Louis, San Juan, San Francisco and Washington.

Teams representing those cities will compete in New York.

June 11, 1967

JOB CORPS STUDY DEPICTS BENEFITS

Training Increases Wages, Harris Report Says

WASHINGTON, April 17 (AP)—a widespread new study of the Job Corps shows that it has substantially increased wages and reduced unemployment among youths who complete their training, Congress was told today.

Louis A. Harris, who conducted the study for the Office of Economic Opportunity, said it was the most extensive ever made of disadvantaged young people.

He presented his findings to the House Education and Labor Committee only a day after turning the study over to the Government.

Although Mr. Harris said he was not taking sides in the dispute over the Administration's decision to close 59 Job Corps centers and merge the program into other manpower training programs, critics of his decision praised his testimony.

Representative Carl D. Perkins, Democrat of Kentucky who is the committee chairman, said he hoped the Administration would study the Harris report carefully before carrying out its plan.

Mr. Harris said the study was based on interviews with 9,463 former Job Corpsmen and 1,850 persons associated with them. Those interviewed included people of various age groups, including high school and non-high school graduates.

All States in Poll

A wide variety of questions was asked, including why the person liked or disliked the Job Corps. Every state was represented in the poll. The poll was begun last November and completed two weeks ago.

Mr. Harris said the study led to two conclusions that he termed inescapable:

1. The Job Corps has had a positive impact on its enrollees in terms of decreasing unemployment and increasing earnings.
2. The achievements of Negro enrollees showed that Negro youths "can make it" in society if given an equal opportunity with whites.

April 18, 1969

YOUTH CORPS AID TO DROPOUTS CUT; HIRING IS LIMITED

Labor Department Officials Depict Moves as Effort to Spur Return to School

Special to The New York Times
WASHINGTON, June 6—The Labor Department has ordered an immediate one-third reduction in enrollment of the Neighborhood Youth Corps's year-round out-of-school program and a complete halt in hiring those 18 or older for the program.

The $129-million authorization for the fiscal year 1969 provided training opportunities for 46,100 persons. Under the cutback, this will be slashed by approximately 15,000 this summer.

Department officials say that the moves are part of an effort to get young dropouts to return to school. The purpose of the corps, they say, is to keep youngsters in school or persuade them to return when they drop out.

Those over 18, who will no longer be accepted, will be encouraged to enter other Labor Department training programs, particularly the Job Opportunities in the Business Sector program sponsored by the National Alliance of Businessmen. They will be trained for jobs in industry.

Find Placement Hampered

Some local Neighborhood Youth Corps administrators feel that the age cutoff cripples job placement under the program and reduces the corps to supporting 16-and-17-years olds for whom they cannot find work.

The corps is a "work experience" program that provides funds for summer employment, year-round in-school employment, and year-round out-of-school employment for youths 16 through 21.

Its most visible effect is in the summer employment program, which pays minimum wages to vacationing youngsters and keeps them busy with special work projects.

The people most affected by the Labor Department directives will be older dropouts, who looked on the Neighborhood Youth Corps as a training and placement operation.

Loss for New York City

The age limitation eliminates this group and leaves local administrators with teen-agers too young to be placed in most union, civil service, heavy industrial or bondable jobs.

June 7, 1969

BLACK YOUTH CRISIS OF JOBS HELD WORSE

A Twentieth Century Fund study group on unemployment among black youth reported yesterday that "despite the sixties, despite all the corrective action," the employment situation for young black men and women is still "social dynamite."

"Since 1969, the softening economy has led to a serious deterioration in the over-all employment situation. But its effect on black youth has been a disaster," the study group wrote. "During the second quarter of 1971, the over-all black teen-age unemployment rate was 34.9 per cent . . . in poverty areas it was 39.1 per cent."

These data, and the group's recommendations, have been published in a book entitled: "The Job Crisis for Black Youth."

The book consists of the report of the fund's Task Force on Employment Problems of Black Youth and a background paper by Sar A. Levitan, an economist at George Washington University who is a member of the study group, and Robert Taggart 3d, executive director of the National Manpower Policy Task Force who is also a graduate student at George Washington University.

December 1, 1971

Slump Killing Black Teen-Agers' Hopes

By CHARLAYNE HUNTER

Tens of thousands of black and Puerto Rican teen-agers in New York City are "piling up at the bottom" of the recession. With no jobs and no prospects of jobs, they are abandoning their dreams of education, and their belief in the other institutions of a civilized society, and are slipping back toward the drugs and hustling of "the street."

"I'm up at 5, going places, getting rejected," said one South Bronx teen-ager who has a small daughter. "I'm not a moron, but it feels degrading."

"Once they know I never worked and have no skills—no work skills—no job," said Migdalia Colon, 20 years old, also of the South Bronx. "That's not right. We need a chance."

"Best that you can do is hang out, get high," said a young black woman. "All that's out there is reefer. Either smoke it or sell it, or both."

Anger. Frustration. Hopelessness. Such is the picture that emerged over the last two weeks in interviews with scores of black teen-agers in the city's most deprived neighborhoods, where unemployment levels for the youths are as high—many say—as 60 per cent.

No one is exactly sure just how many that represents, or if, indeed, the percentage is accurate, since, for one thing, the United States Department of Labor, which counts teen-agers, contends that the sample among black teen-agers is "too small" to separate from over-all figures.

The New York State Employment Service estimates that there are about 150,000 people between the ages of 16 and 21 who are out of school and looking for work, with approximately 45 to 50 per cent of that number—or 82,500—black and Hispanic.

There are about 400,000 more, officials say, who are out of work, out of school and not looking, with some 45 to 50 per cent of that number black and Hispanic, officials say.

Black and Hispanic teen-agers find that looking for work is itself a full-time occupation, costly, but unrewarding.

They say that they are exploited by both legitimate and "fly by night" employment agencies, and by prospective employers who seek sexual favors—from young men as well as young women.

Many who counted at least on summer employment are complaining that "you have to know somebody" to get the limited number of jobs available—about 50,000 so far for all teen-agers through combined Federal and city programs.

Further, many of the teen-agers are living on their own, frequently with families of their own to support. In numerous cases, young women with babies have rejected marriage to the fathers because, as one young woman put it, "they don't have jobs either."

Little Recreation

Community workers and others stress that while jobs are paramount, it is going to be even rougher for the thousands of unlucky teen-agers "walking the beat," as they say of idleness in the Bronx, without expanded plans for recreational programs.

Two students at Harlem Prep, waiting their turn to play on a Harlem basketball court, said recreation was no substitute for jobs.

"I don't want to be out here in the street with no job, you can get in trouble," said Eric Griffin, 17, of the Bronx.

"I had no idea it was going to be this rough," said Sylvester MacKay, 18, from Jamaica, Queens.

For many of the youngsters who are still at home, relationships with parents are often strained—on one hand, because parents—many of whom have only marginal jobs themselves —tend to blame the young people for not finding work; on the other hand, because the teen-agers feel betrayed by their parents who advise them that staying in school would insure their getting ahead.

Eliud Alicea turned 18 this year, which means, among other things that the Housing Authority raises the rent in his parent's public-housing apartment. But he cannot find a

job, so that while he is the cause of the rent increase, he can neither move out or help with meeting it.

A dilemma for these young people—many of whom are high-school dropouts—is that they have few, if any, skills. But as they look around, they see college graduates out of work and competing for the same jobs. Others, applying for training programs, are being told they have to have experience to get in.

For some, who have held on to the hope that college may mean something to them in the long run, their optimism is fading as programs designed to give them needed financial aid, such as Search for Education, Elevation and Knowledge (SEEK) and Model Cities, are being cut back and terminated.

"They're piling up at the bottom," said Royston Nero, director of a Harlem Manpower Center, as he explained that he had more than 1,500 applications for 265 summer jobs.

New federally financed public-service jobs are not benefiting them because their criteria is just "out of work for 30 days," he continued. And there is only a very small," number of even the most-menial jobs.

The responses of the youth tend to be angry, generalized denunciations of systems: Education, they say, has failed them. Politics, they say, has used them, and welfare, they say, has abused them.

The people who deal with young people's problems feel that such a response is likely to lead to explosive, spontaneous acts that may also lack direction.

Societal Conditions Stressed

Probation officers and others who deal with youthful offenders generally agree that many of the crimes committed by them—robbery, muggings, burglary—are tied in some way to both societal conditions generally and joblessness specifically.

"It's leading to apathy and depression, which is more harmful than physical abuse," said Dr. James P. Comer, associate professor of psychiatry at the Yale University Child Study Center.

"That's what happened in slavery and that's what we've created again in young blacks and Puerto Ricans."

Some youngsters still come to the city from the South, under the illusive hope that brought the masses of blacks here in the first place—"more businesses here than down there," as Willie Thompson, 19, put it, as he waited in the State Employment office in Harlem.

What Mr. Thompson left behind in Orangeburg, S.C., early this year was a situation in which his two oldest brothers were among many blacks being laid off because of industrial cutbacks, or one in which work-

ers were making a three-day week, or one week on and one week off at the local cotton mill.

Mr. Thompson wants to be a physical-education teacher, but he has to make some money to go to school.

Two weeks ago, he heard of a situation in which a young man who was working as a shipping clerk was discharged because he had had no experience and wasn't doing the job.

"The employment agency sent me because I had some experience. But all of them tell you they'll call you in a day's time. I'm still waiting."

Marie Smith, a slightly built 17-year-old who supports herself, spoke of the special problems of being female as well as young and black.

Last month, she paid $30 to one employment agency on 14th Street. They sent her to Brooklyn, for a job as a seamstress in a factory, but the employer told her that the Bronx was too far for her to commute.

"That was three hours and two car fares I wasted because the lady didn't tell me where I lived."

The next place they sent her was an office building where they had an opening for a coffee server she said. "But," "as soon as he saw me, he said, 'I wouldn't hire you anyway.' And I was looking presentable."

Too Good a Friend

After wasting $10 on a defunct employment agency, Miss Smith decided to give up on them. Then, she said:

"The elevator man once told me about a man who needed a receptionist in a garage. I went down and this big old garage was all but empty, with one telephone on the wall.

"He told me to come in, closed the door and locked it and began asking me if I knew how to cook, take things to the laundry. Stuff like that. Then he told me he'd be a good friend. I got out of there, but that man made me cry."

George Grant, who is 19 and a student at John Jay College, had a similar experience at a major department store, where he said, "the dude in charge wasn't correct."

"He told me I could get the job if I would be his playmate," he said. "I told him—politely, because I wanted the job—that I had a wife and son. And he told me that was all right. He just wanted to share me for a while."

Scheryl Underwood, who lives in the South Bronx, said that the only way she could go to college was through Model Cities and Basic Education Opportunity Grants. But, she, too, has been trying to find a job because she feels insecure relying on government funding.

"Once all the funds stop," she was saying the other day, "that's the end for me." She

paused for a moment, then added:

"You know, a diploma had value until all the blacks and Puerto Ricans started getting them."

Despite the frequent cynicism of young people toward college as a "social control," a way to keep people out of the job market, the attitude of Eleanor Peterson, who had to drop out of school four years ago because she was pregnant, is typical.

"I've been running back and forth to my mother's house and that's a rut. I've been running back and forth to welfare and that's a bigger rut. I'm just running around and running around.

"Now, I'm planning to go into the Army because I know that's income every month. And then after I serve my time, I can come out and the Army can take care of me for a while after I get out. They can help me go to college."

Many of the young people interviewed expressed the feeling that they were coming to the end of their patience as their options narrowed.

There is a widely held belief that young people are going to start "acting out," as the sociologist and psychiatrist describe antisocial behavior. One young woman in the Bronx, indicating a readiness for violent protest in the streets, said, "I'm ready to get down."

For in spite of all of the hardship that they know and see, they nevertheless, see around them success stories and role models—but not of the traditional sort.

Choosing a Career

One young woman said that "even my little brother is saying, I want to grow up to be a big-time dope dealer. Then he tells you about some dope dealer's bathroom. 'He had a bad house, and he had himself a bathroom,' my brother told me."

One young man said that he had been in the streets, had a Cadillac when he was 17, but lost it when he almost lost his life in a street altercation.

"In hustling, there's this thing called an unauthorized zone and if you cross it, they will kill you. I wanted to get out before somebody killed me or I had to kill somebody. So when the dude fired at me and hit my friend and said, 'Oh, I hit the wrong person,' I said, 'Oh no, you didn't I left town, went and stayed with my grandmother until things blew over. Now I don't want to get back out there, but I may have to."

"Even the people that's scared are getting out there now," said another young man. "It's not about being scared, it's about surviving."

Probation officers, policemen and the young people themselves say that street hustlers, particularly those dealing in

356

narcotics, are getting younger.

"The adult dealers are now using the young blacks because they figure they won't slap those heavy sentences on them," said a probation officer in the Bronx.

But if black teen-agers in general are having a hard time finding jobs, those with records are having it worse.

"Their records are not supposed to be held against them or even known about," said a probation officer. "But many of the personnel people are former cops who have connec-

tions down at the Bureau of Criminal Identification. They may not be able to do a fingerprint check, but they'll run a name check every time."

Some probation officers argue that there is little correlation between joblessness and crime among young offenders, including one who attributed much of the antisocial behavior among black teen-agers to "a general sense of rage" over their conditions.

But even those who argue that there is a correlation, agree that it is the conditions

out of which many of the youngsters come that contributes to their attitudes.

"It's true," said one probation officer. "A lot of these kids who have committed offenses don't really want to work. They come from backgrounds where the value system is so different that their whole life-style is not consistent with work.

"They are poorly educated, so they drop out of school out of boredom. They are poorly trained and don't even know how to look for a job, or what to wear, or how to talk to

an interviewer once he gets there."

Nevertheless, they argue, that blaming the victim for the failure of the systems, and institutions is the wrong approach.

"The Army will not even take anyone actively on probation," one probation officer said. "We have resorted to telling them that if the job does not involve bonding, and nobody is going to do a background check, then cheat a little bit. Don't tell them. Otherwise, where's he going to go?"

May 19, 1975

A New Approach To Job Problem Of City Youths

By ROGER WILKINS

Urban affairs experts agree that one of the most important problems facing American cities is the unemployment, and perhaps the unemployability, of large numbers of poor youngsters, many of them members of minority groups.

Affairs Urban

The dimensions of the problem are defined by the official unemployment figures—17 percent for white youths, nearly 40 percent for black youths, with unofficial estimates that the black rate may actually be around 65 percent. The experts agree that much of the social pathology that big cities experience, particularly violent street crime, flows directly from the idleness and the hopelessness that those figures suggest.

The problem is almost put in the "too hard" category by critics of the social programs that were enacted in the 60's. They argue that job-training programs were far too expensive and that they rarely matched newly trained people with real jobs at the end of the line.

Even people who disagree with that view acknowledge that the problem is extremely difficult. Dr. Sar A. Levitan, director of the Center for Social Policy Studies at George Washington University, argues that the Great Society training programs were much more effective than the critics contend, but he underscores how fundamental the youth unemployment problem is by saying:

"The real trouble, is that the economy really doesn't need these kids as far as production is concerned."

The Carter Administration has just announced a program that, according to some experts, will pose an imaginative test of both the critics' gloom about the feasibility of government intervention

and Dr. Levitan's optimism at last about the possibilities of job training. It is a $115 million pilot project designed to "entitle" poor youngsters who agree to remain in or return to school, to jobs that will provide "employability" training.

16 Cities Receive Grants

Six cities—Baltimore, Boston, Detroit, Cincinnati, Denver and Seattle—have been given more than $15 million each and 10 other cities have been awarded about $1 million. The idea is not so much to attack the unemployment problem itself, although Government officials expect lower youth unemployment rates to result, but to attack the unemployability problem. Many of the youngsters the Labor Department hopes to reach are not only children who are willfully undereducated and who have never had any experience in the world of work, but also children whose parents have never had that experience either.

"Many of the kids in this program are the kinds of students the schools have absolutely given upon." said Harriet Michel, director of the Labor Department's Office of Community Youth Employment Programs. "The question we're posing now is whether they can accommodate them.

"This program has forced the local manpower offices and school systems to work together, often for the first time. We hope there will be long-lasting benefits from these marriages."

Though manpower experts agree that the Labor Department's design for the program and its execution have been excellent, they say they think that the proof of this will be in the local delivery systems. Dr. Levitan had some thoughts on the problems the cities would encounter.

Reservations of Employers

"The private employers," he said, "and sometimes others too, but particularly the private employers have real reservations about taking these youngsters. Sometimes it's race: sometimes they think the kids will just play around: or perhaps it is hard to arrange a work schedule for them."

If these problems are to be put to an effective test anywhere, Dr. Levitan and others say they think that it would be

in Baltimore, which, by all accounts, received the largest of the six major grants. One of the key figures in the Baltimore program is Marion Pines, director of the Mayor's Office of Manpower Resources.

"This program is a significant addition to our manpower resources," Mrs. Pines said recently. "It adds about 25 percent to the funds we already had. That's a lot."

But Baltimore seems ready for it. The city has already identified 9,000 jobs. Some of them are public jobs, some are with private, nonprofit agencies and 1,000 of them are in 100 private-sector companies.

The program will test, according to the Baltimore official, whether the certainty of having a job will motivate poor youngsters to stay in school. It will also test a variety of academic models designed to enrich and prolong their academic experience.

"We're concerned about the quality of the labor force," Mrs. Pines said, "so we have academic programs to motivate and to train. For example, some of these youngsters will learn in 'occupational clusters.' If they're in a health-related job, their math and their English will be related to health programs. That way they'll know why they're in the classrooms, because their work will be relevant.

"We'll also have a lot of one-on-one work with youngsters who are illiterate and special courses at the community colleges for participants who need more sophisticated training."

"The program is sharply targeted," she continued. "Sixty percent of the participants are from welfare families and 72 percent live in public housing. We're ready and eager to get started."

If Mrs. Pine's optimism proves justified and the drop-out and truancy rates drop dramatically and the training is effective, the mesh of local and Federal government will have proved a lot, say the experts. But the biggest problem of all still remain for the nation to face. Dr. Levitan put it sharply:

"The question then is, how do you create jobs for these people so they can function effectively?"

January 16, 1978

Changes in Society Holding Black Youth in Jobless Web

By JOHN HERBERS

The extraordinary growth in unemployment among black youths, a trend that has persisted through both recession and prosperity and through more than a decade of civil rights enforcement and minority job programs, is largely a result of major changes in the nation's economy, in the structure of its society and in its political climate.

That is the consensus of many people who have been searching for the causes of one of the most perplexing troubles of the times — the inability of hundreds of thousands of young black adults and teenagers to move into productive work.

The problem should be of concern to more than blacks, they say, because the whole nation bears its burden in social costs, the expenses of dealing with increased criminal activity and the loss of potential economic infusions.

But there is also the psychological cost: the fear felt by city dwellers and by business people in poorer, crime-ridden areas and the despair felt by those who want to work and cannot find jobs.

The unemployment picture for minority youths, particularly blacks, is now roughly what it was for the entire nation in the depths of the Great Depression, the experts say — a fourth or more of those who want to work are unable to find jobs.

And the experts' search for the causes and cures has been given new urgency with President Carter's announced intention of cutting the Federal budget and curbing inflation. Many black leaders fear that the Administration's economic policy, with its almost certain side effect of higher unemployment, will hurt young blacks disproportionately.

Congressional testimony, interviews with public and private experts and the statements of job seekers suggest complex reasons for the persistence of the high rate of unemployment for black youths. The best documented, most frequently cited causes include the following:

¶A large influx of aliens, legal and illegal, who are taking jobs once held by blacks.

¶The entry of white women into the labor market in great numbers. According to the Bureau of Labor Statistics, the work force grew by three million last year, and 1.9 million were women. Only 400,000 of them were black women.

¶The rise of an underground economy of illegal activities at which youths find they can make more money with less effort.

¶The continued movement of jobs out of the central cities where many blacks live.

¶A fractured society in which various groups militantly defend their own interests, creating a new political climate that makes assimilation of blacks and other poor minorities more difficult.

Discrimination Persists

Those reasons, added to the original causes of the problem — lingering discrimination in the marketplace, the failure of Federal programs to reach those

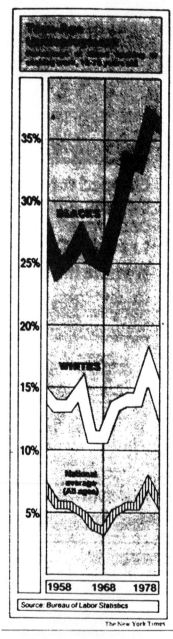

1958   1968   1978

Source: Bureau of Labor Statistics

The New York Times

most in need, and the inability or unwillingness of many youths to perform the kind of jobs that are available — have created massive unemployment for young blacks.

Although racial discrimination in employment was made illegal by the Civil Rights Act of 1964, and although successive court decisions have upheld the right of equal access to jobs, authorities say that job discrimination, while more subtle than before, nonetheless remains.

And the situation may seem all the more hopeless to young blacks because they are caught in what President Johnson described more than a decade ago as a "seamless web" of social pathology perpetuated by poor home training, poor

schools, poverty and crime.

Parents who have been unable to find work themselves cannot offer guidance to their teen-age children, and the schools frequently fall short, graduating students who cannot even fill out a job application, labor experts say. It is more than an unemployment problem, they say; it is a community problem, a home problem.

Some Fear the Worst

Some speak of the situation in cataclysmic terms.

"Black America today verges on the brink of disaster," Vernon E. Jordan Jr., president of the National Urban League, said in a recent report that highlighted chronic youth unemployment.

And Herbert Hill, former labor director of the National Association for the Advancement of Colored People, said: "It is evident that a permanent black underclass has developed, that virtually an entire second generation of ghetto youth will never enter into the labor force. This means that a large part of the young black urban population will remain in a condition of hopelessness and despair and that the social and psychological costs in wasted lives continues a major tragedy in American life."

Secretary of Labor Ray Marshall is more sanguine about the future. He says the Federal job and vocational education programs on which billions of dollars have been spent are beginning to help young blacks.

There is general agreement, however, that the reasons for the continuing problem are exceedingly complex and difficult to sort out.

As Robert Shranck, projects director for the Ford Foundation and a former manpower commissioner for New York City, explained, no one yet understands the relative impact of even those causes that are known.

The Background

The unemployment problem can be traced to the rural South and the time when the number of farms shrank and the remainder became mechanized. Blacks who had been engaged in agriculture moved by the millions to the cities just as factory and laboring jobs were drying up or going to the suburbs with the middle class.

Through the 1960's, they were systematically barred from construction and other jobs by union or company discrimination, and they were seldom where the jobs were. Industrialization in the South usually took place in areas where whites predominated or where discrimination was still strong enough to give whites job preference, despite civil rights laws and judicial rulings.

Those old patterns and practices have combined with changes in the economy and in social practices to keep the overall black unemployment rate where it has been for many years, at about twice that for whites.

For black youth, however, both men and women, the gap has widened. In 1954, the unemployment rate for blacks 16 to 19 years old was 16.5 percent, as against a 12.1 percent rate for whites of the same age; in 1978, the rate for blacks of that age was 36.3 percent, as against 13.9 percent for whites. The rate for teen-age blacks then dropped, hitting 32.7 percent in January 1979. But figures released Friday show that the rate climbed again last month, to 35.5 percent, while the rate for whites has held almost steady, fluctuating between last year's 13.9 percent and 13.6 percent.

The picture has been better for blacks 20 to 24 years old than for teen-agers. In

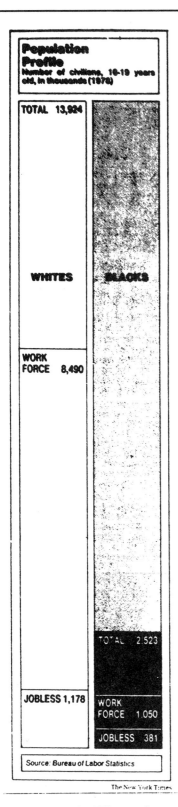

Population Profile
Number of civilians, 16-19 years old, in thousands (1978)

TOTAL 13,924

WHITES | BLACKS

WORK FORCE 8,490

TOTAL 2,523

JOBLESS 1,178 | WORK FORCE 1,050

JOBLESS 381

Source: Bureau of Labor Statistics

The New York Times

613,000 to 669,000, mostly because of new jobs created by Government programs. The rate of unemployment declined slightly, from 38.3 to 36.3 percent, about where it stood in the recession year of 1975.

Based on the 1978 figures for those seeking work, it would require 445,000 jobs for blacks from 16 to 24 to equalize the unemployment rates for whites in the same category. This is a comparatively small number of jobs; the national work force now stands at about 100 million.

But even if the 445,000 jobs were added, labor officials believe, other blacks, currently not counted as jobless because they are not actively seeking work, would be encouraged to do so, thus raising the unemployment rate again.

Without the Government programs, the situation would have worsened considerably for blacks, Mr. Taggart said. And the unemployment rate would have been lower, he said, had not many young blacks, encouraged by the opening of new government jobs, entered the labor market and got themselves counted in the ranks of those actively seeking work.

Yet that only underscores the depth of the difficulty and gives credence to the belief of some black leaders that unemployment rates do not begin to reflect the number of idle young people in communities across the country.

Inaccuracies Conceded

Even the census interviewers who collect data for the Bureau of Labor Statistics say there are inaccuracies in the figures. Occasionally the one person interviewed per household is not honest or is mistaken in thinking a teen-ager is looking for work, they say, and sometimes, because the interviewer may be required to work in areas that can be dangerous, answers are faked, interviews never conducted.

But John Bregger, of the Bureau of Labor Statistics, says unemployment for black youths has been so widespread for so long that any statistical errors in the employment rate are not of a magnitude that is meaningful.

The unemployment statistics show about 677,000 blacks 16 to 24 years old looking for work. About half are younger than 20, and Mr. Taggart estimated that to put that group alone in jobs would cost the Government roughly $9 billion a year, almost as much as it spends on its overall manpower program, the Comprehensive Employment and Training Act.

But black leaders say the statistics do not reflect many more youths — in the central cities but also in suburbs, small towns and rural areas — who are out of school and have quit trying or have never tried to find a job.

The Underground Economy

No one knows how many are on the streets, hustling in dope, prostitution and gambling or staging robberies and burglaries, but the number is not inconsequential.

Several studies have shown a direct correlation between unemployment and youth crime. More youths 18 to 24 years old are in local jails than in the Job Corps and other Federal service programs put together, according to census figures. Others crowd the penitentiaries, and the number of idle on the streets increases.

Joseph Cooper, a black student at Harvard Law School who is a research economist at the National Bureau of Economic Research, recently told of the underground economy at a hearing in Washington conducted by Youth Work, Inc., a privately financed group created to monitor the new Federal youth job programs.

In preparation for a bureau study on jobless youth, Mr. Cooper talked with about 60 unemployed youngsters in Boston. Although it was too small a sample from which to draw conclusions, he said, he nevertheless came away with some impressions.

The Desire for Work

"More than half of the youngsters interviewed said that they had engaged in illegal activity during the course of the survey week," he said. "These youths sold marijuana frequently, and some reported that robbery, pickpocketing, burglary and breaking and entering took up most of their time the week prior to the survey week. All of the teen-agers wanted a full-time permanent job."

There is a widely held belief that a system has evolved in the United States in which poor members of minorities in many areas find little stigma attached to crime and prefer to make a living that way.

Black leaders say this is obviously true for some, but they cite evidence of a desire for legal work in legal pursuits on the part of many others. Whenever new Federal jobs are opened in a city or rural area, officials are besieged with applications. In Atlanta, the crush was so great for one offering that the crowd broke through a plate glass window to get in line. Almost every day, young people crowd the Urban League's public employment offices waiting for openings. When substantial numbers of jobs were filled in the experimental youth programs last year in Syracuse and other cities, the authorities noted a decline in crime.

Who Gets the Jobs?

Eli Ginzberg, the Columbia University economist who heads the National Commission on Employment Policy, noted in an article in "Scientific American" in November 1977 that 28 million jobs had been added to the economy in the past quarter of a century, an increase of almost 50 percent in the civilian work force. But in that period the number of Americans seeking jobs increased even more rapidly. Young people reaching working age and married women accounted for most of the rise.

With more competition for the jobs available, minority teen-agers began to lose out even more than in the past. Orley Ashenfelter of Princeton University described this development in a paper for the Labor Department that said:

"Apart from a small drift upward, adult employment has remained at around 60 percent of adult population throughout most of the last two decades. Though more erratic and at a lower level, the employment-population ratio of white male teen-agers 14 to 19 has followed a similar pattern.

"Employment-population ratios for white females 14 to 19, on the other hand, have drifted continually upward in a qualitative pattern much the same as that for white female adults.

"For black youngsters, however, the employment-population ratio for males and females have been tending steeply downward for the past two decades. It is this latter, largely unexplained phenomenon that has suggested a cause for alarm."

Mr. Ashenfelter said the decline in employment was particularly sharp for black males, not only for teen-agers but also for those 20 to 24.

'Education Is Critical'

"Cities like New York, where many blacks live, have become white-collar factories," said Mr. Schranck. "Educa-

that category, the 1978 unemployment rate was 20.7 percent, as against 9.5 percent for whites. Nevertheless, the rate for blacks is twice what it was in 1968, the year the urban riots reached a peak, when it stood at 10 percent.

A Less Negative View

Labor Secretary Marshall and Robert Taggart, administrator of the Office of Youth Programs, say a better way to view the picture is through employment. In 1978 the number of employed black youths 16 to 19 years old grew from

tion is critical. If you are illiterate you are in a lot of trouble, the school system is turning out a lot of kids who can't read or do arithmetic."

While the public schools have been widely condemned in Congressional and other testimony for not educating pupils, the problem goes deeper.

Representative Parren J. Mitchell, Democrat of Baltimore, said in the Youth Work hearings:

"The most difficult thing that we have to deal with in our youth problem of unemployment is a constellation of attitudes which come together and create what is essentially apathy. I don't blame young people for being apathetic. I don't blame them for saying, 'There is no way I can win in this system,' because they look at their fathers, who have been unemployed for the past five years if they are black or Hispanic, and they say, 'If Dad can't win, I can't win.' "

The Overqualified Applicant

Some blacks who continue to knock on doors for jobs encounter yet another change in the society that works to their disadvantage — lower-level jobs are being taken by persons trained as professionals who cannot find jobs at the higher level.

And a number of economists say the minimum wage, now $2.90 an hour, is partly responsible, although they do not think it a major factor. Businessmen forced to pay the minimum wage either reduce the number of jobs or hire the more productive adult or both, they say.

"I have young applicants who are qualified for jobs that used to go to high school graduates," said Ross Knight, employment director for the Richmond Urban League. "But now people who are college graduates will come in and take those jobs because that is the best they can find. Naturally, the employer is going to take the higher-qualified person."

And the more qualified person is likely to be older and white.

A variation on that theme has occurred in the jobs created by government. When the Carter Administration made a commitment of $10 billion to public service jobs two years ago as part of its package to stimulate the economy, one of the purposes was to reach those groups most in need, a category that includes young blacks because of their high unemployment rate and their relative poverty.

Best Qualified Were Hired

The bulk of the jobs, however, were provided through the state and local governments. And many of those governments, especially the cities, were so hardpressed for revenue that they had reduced their payrolls and personnel for basic services. Therefore, they hired the best-qualified people they could find under the Federal guidelines, and those people usually were not black youths.

The Carter job initiatives helped lower the overall unemployment rate but had only a marginal impact on that for young blacks. A renewed effort is under way to direct the jobs more to those in need, but few outside the Government believe that in a time of declining domestic appropriations the effort will have much effect.

In communities around the country, there is visual evidence of what has happened. Iranians are driving taxis. Asians and South Americans are doing restaurant work. Hispanics are picking vegetables and citrus fruits in fields and orchards where blacks once labored. The statistics show it, too. Unemployment is high for all poor minorities, but is highest for blacks.

The Illegal Immigrant Factor

Some members of those other minorities are in this country illegally. Secretary of Labor Marshall says nobody knows the number of illegal aliens, that the estimates vary from four million to 12 million. Nevertheless, he says, their presence is a significant factor in black unemployment.

There are those who say black leaders, trying to instill pride in black youths, also instilled an unwillingness to labor at menial jobs. The accepted view has become that aliens take the undesirable jobs that blacks, who may be on welfare, do not want to perform.

But Mr. Marshall said in an interview that it was not that simple. Employers from apple-growers to housewives prefer to hire foreigners because, whether they are here illegally or hold visas, they are in no position to complain about pay or working conditions. Most blacks are American citizens with the full protection of the law.

The Fractured Society

Vernon Jordan says there is a "creeping malignant growth of a new negativism that calls for a weak passive Government and indifference to the poor." However defined, the experts agree that the nation has developed a political climate that makes it more difficult to address minority needs than a few years ago.

The movement on behalf of some whites to halt "reverse discrimination" in the great middle-class uprising for lower taxes in college tax credits are cited as symptoms.

Further, various special interest groups — the aged, the handicapped, women, farmers, even salesmen — have become increasingly active in competing for public attention and funds.

M. Carl Holman, president of the National Urban Coalition, said that causes have so proliferated since the civil rights movement of the 1960's that the nation has difficulty sorting out the most important needs. Some interest groups that once worked in consort for the disadvantaged have become defensive and splintered.

In an interview, Harold Fleming, president of the Potomac Institute, who has spent his career in race relations, said in response to a question about new divisions in America, "How can I help but believe that part of our problem is that we are losing the ability to create a common culture? We are a more fractured society than at the time when we were carrying out such atrocities as segregation. It was easier then to move back and forth between groups because there were more commonly held values."

A Lack of Awareness

A number of persons interviewed about black youth unemployment said there was a greater tendency than before for each different group to look after its own and to find jobs for its own. Blacks, as a group, control fewer jobs than any other group, so their teen-agers cannot avail themselves of the time-honored practice of finding work through adults or friends.

A New York Times/CBS News Poll conducted last year showed that one-fifth of those questioned in a national sample believed that unemployment was higher for whites than for blacks. The experts agree that a middle class revolting against taxes and inflation has not noticed, or does not care, about continued discrimination.

"There are companies in this town that belong to the Urban League," said Mr. Knight of Richmond. "They carry the sign that they are an equal opportunity employer, but they do not have blacks. I placed black salesman for the first time with one company but he was harassed by the other employees until he left. It still goes on."

March 11, 1979

Economists Studying Minimum Pay And Effects on Jobless Teen-Agers

By STEVEN RATTNER
Special to The New York Times

WASHINGTON, May 4 — The minimum wage, long considered a protector of the poor, may do more harm than good, at least for teen-agers, a growing number of economists believe.

The economists are hotly divided on many aspects of the question, but there is general agreement on one central point: The minimum wage means fewer jobs for the young, many of whom are black.

"The evidence is in that direction, although I don't suggest that the effect is enormous," said Arthur M. Okun, who was chairman of the Council of Economic Advisers under President Johnson and who is now a senior fellow at the Brookings Institution. "The minimum wage won't explain why black youth unemployment is 35 percent but only why it is 35 percent instead of 32 percent."

When businessmen are forced to pay a minimum wage, now $2.90 an hour, they would rather hire a more productive adult. Were there no minimum wage, businessmen would replace some adult employees with lower-paid, albeit less-skilled and less-trained, youths. In essence, the economists say, the minimum wage distorts the workings of the labor market in favor of adults.

That distortion has led a number of economists and politicians to propose a "youth differential," a lower minimum wage for young adults, perhaps those between 16 and 24.

In a way, that would mirror a free market situation, where businessmen are able to choose between high wages with high productivity and low wages with low productivity. The youth differential exists in many European countries.

"The youth differential is an idea worth testing," said Edward M. Gramlich, a professor of economics at the University of Michigan, who has done a basic study on minimum wage effects. "But I have to admit we have no way of knowing precisely how much it would do."

The idea of a lower minimum wage for the young has more than its share of opposition, principally from those who believe that the effect would be to take jobs away from heads of households and give them to teen-agers.

"You do have to worry about the substitution effects," confirms Lyle Gramley, a member of the Council of Economic Advisers.

The Possible Job Shift

And statistics developed by Mr. Gramlich in his 1976 study show that about 70 percent of those earning the minimum wage now are adults.

However, only 20 percent of the total are men, which tends to contradict the fear that household heads would lose their jobs. And total incomes of the adults were substantially higher than those of the youths, meaning that a shift of jobs from adults to young people would in essence be a shift of jobs from a higher income group to a lower income group.

The fears of substitution ultimately turn on the related question of whether the level of the minimum wage affects the total number of jobs in the economy.

Some economists believe that the minimum wage encourages business to cut the number of employees, by installing more machinery, for instance. That implies that, just as raising the minimum wage costs jobs, lowering it would increase the total number of jobs.

"As far as I can tell, increasing the minimum wage reduces jobs and labor

force participation," said Finis Welch, a professor of economics at the University of California at Los Angeles. A variety of estimates of the effects of a minimum wage for teen-agers indicate that a 10 percent reduction would increase total employment by 1 to 2.5 percent.

But other economists believe that the minimum wage has little impact on overall employment, leading them to the conclusion that a lower wage for teen-agers would mean few new jobs and a lot of jobs taken away from adults.

Easy Resolution Is Unlikely

The question obviously is nowhere near resolution.

Congress, however, almost included a youth differential in 1977, while considering increases in the minimum wage, and the subject seems sure to be raised again.

The push for a youth minimum wage may coincide with efforts in some quarters to postpone the next increase in the minimum wage — a 20 cent rise is scheduled for 1981 — on the ground that it would be inflationary.

A possible middle course could be deferring the increases for youths only. That might be satisfactory to the Carter Administration, which has been opposed to a youth differential, although not

strongly, and which has been split over the effect of the minimum wage increases on inflation.

Private economists are generally in favor of trying the differential, but they fear that Congress would institute the gap by raising adult minimums rather than by reducing the youth standard.

And raising the minimum wage does not find favor with those who believe, as Mr. Okun stated, that "the minimum wage is a lousy antipoverty program."

To the extent that minimum wage programs reduce the total number of jobs, black youths are likely to bear a disproportionate burden, since outlets for working-class high school graduates or summer jobs for middle-class whites are not likely to be the jobs eliminated.

However, most economists believe that the minimum wage is but a small part of the black youth unemployment problem. The real trouble, they believe, lies in the noneconomic problems most often mentioned by sociologists: poor role models, disenchantment, even such problems as illegal immigration, the baby boom and the underground economy.

May 5, 1979

Count of Jobless Among Youths Called Very Low

By PHILIP SHABECOFF

Special to The New York Times

WASHINGTON, Feb. 28 — An unpublished Government report concludes that unemployment among American youth is much higher than the official figures show and that the unemployment gap between white and black young people is even wider than had been believed.

The report, based on a long-term Labor Department survey of youths, also tends to refute the widely held opinion that unemployment among young people, particularly those from minority groups, is high because they will not accept low-paying jobs or work considered menial. A summary of the report was obtained by The New York Times.

The official data published by the Labor Department's Bureau of Labor Statistics, based on a monthly survey of a sample of households, showed a 14.1 percent jobless rate among all 16- to 21-year-old youths and a 28 percent rate among black youths of the same age in the spring of 1979.

Magnitude of Problem

But the unpublished long-term survey of young people concluded that overall youth unemployment in the same period was 19.3 percent, while black youth unemployment was 38.8 percent. For young black people in school but seeking work, the official Labor Department jobless figure was 36.9 percent, while the long-term survey showed a rate of 55.4 percent.

However, the survey suggests that the problem is of even greater magnitude than these rates indicate because it shows a higher participation rate in the labor market than the monthly Labor De-

partment report and, therefore, a much higher absolute number of young people seeking work. According to the survey, there were 775,000 16- to 21-year-olds seeking jobs last spring, while the regular monthly report showed 478,000 young job-seekers.

The results of the survey suggest that unemployment among youths in general and among youths from minority groups in particular, already recognized as a major social and economic problem, is even more severe than generally believed.

According to a summary of the report, "Its major findings are of critical importance in the formulation of youth policies for the 1980's."

The findings represent the first results of the Labor Department's National Longitudinal Survey, which is following a representative sample of 12,693 youths over an extended period, with particular attention paid to their training and employment experiences.

The results directly challenge the contention made by a number of manpower economists that the Labor Department's monthly reports overstate unemployment among black teen-agers.

The unpublished report says that the disparity between the long-term survey results and the monthly household survey used for the Bureau of Labor Statistics's regular reports on employment and unemployment stems from the fact that the youths involved in the long-term survey were interviewed, rather than the head of a household.

The report states that "it has been documented" that responses differ significantly when the youth is asked directly and that the evidence suggests that the direct youth interviews are more accurate.

The survey indicates that the labor force participation rate — those who either have jobs or are looking for them — for 16- to 21-year-olds is 11 percent higher than that reported by the monthly survey and that the participation rate for blacks is 27.5 percent higher.

It also said that while the racial differentials in rates in employment and unemployment were "massive," they were "only the most visible dimensions of relative deprivation."

"In almost every aspect of their labor

market experience, black and Hispanic youths are significantly worse off than white youths," it added.

Other Impacts Cited

In addition to having higher unemployment rates, the survey indicated, black and Hispanic youths are consigned to lower-wage, lower-skilled jobs than whites. Young minority group workers must travel longer to reach their jobs and derive less satisfaction from their work. They also tend to be laid off more often than their white counterparts.

Young female workers, regardless of color, tend to be laid off more often than their white counterparts, young women, regardless of color, tend to lag well behind white males in most employment categories.

The report states that contentions that youths will not take available jobs because they demand higher wages, find the nature of the work unacceptable or simply do not like to work are often used "to gainsay the seriousness of youth labor market problems."

But such arguments are now "deflated" by the survey results, the report asserted.

The survey found that a majority of the young people would be willing to take low-paying jobs in such areas as fast-food restaurants, cleaning establishments, supermarkets as well as dishwashing. A substantial number of the young people surveyed said they would work at below the minimum wage.

The survey suggests that the younger the worker the lower the wage and level job he is willing to accept. It also indicates that young minority group workers will take lower level work than young white people.

"The evidence suggests that the majority of these young people are not unsuccessful because of inflated expectations," the report states.

Finally, the survey found that "employment and training programs are an important factor in mitigating the problems of disadvantaged and minority youths."

The full report is 400 pages long. It was prepared for the Labor Department by the Center for Human Research of Ohio State University.

February 29, 1980

LEGAL RIGHTS OF MINORS

Provisions of the Laws of Various States Relating to Parents and Children.

THEIR AUTHORITY AND DUTIES

Phases of the Common Law and Special Statutes—Facts Collected by the Federal Department of Labor —F. J. Stimson Points Out Interesting Features.

All minors, male or female, attain their majority by marriage in Iowa, Texas, and Louisiana. In Nebraska, when a woman over sixteen years old is married her minority ends. In most of the States, however, children male or female, become of age at twenty-one, as provided by the common law of England. There are special laws in several States providing that a married woman of any age may exercise all the powers of majority, and in Vermont, Ohio, Illinois, Iowa, Minnesota, Kansas, Nebraska, Maryland, Missouri, Arkansas, California, Oregon, Nevada, Washington, Dakota, Montana, and Idaho a woman comes of age at 18. These facts are set forth in The Bulletin of the Department of Labor, by F. J. Stimson, who discusses the "Mutual rights and duties of parents and children, guardianship, &c., under the law."

It is an established principle that minors cannot make any contract. But in Connecticut, California, Nevada, Dakota, Idaho, Montana, and Utah every person, male or female, may make a will of real or personal estate. In Georgia every person aged fourteen, male or female, may make a will of real or personal estate, and in New Mexico every male of fourteen and female of twelve; while in Kentucky a person under twenty-one may make a will only in pursuance of a power specially given to that effect. As a general rule, contracts of a minor are void, except for necessaries, and in Georgia they are not valid even for necessaries unless the party furnishing them proves that the parent or guardian fails to supply sufficient necessaries for the minor. By the California code, and in some other States, if a parent neglects to provide for his child, who is under his charge, articles necessary according to his circumstances a third person may, in good faith, supply such necessaries and recover the reasonable value thereof from the parent.

Under the Georgia laws, if an infant, by permission of his parent or guardian, or that of the law, practices any trade or engages in business, he is bound for all contracts connected with such trade or business. It is frequently provided that debts for liquor sold to minors shall not be collected, or it is made a penal offense to sell liquor or cigarettes to minors, and debts contracted by students for such articles are often, by the statutes of the older State, declared void. As liquor can hardly be considered a necessary article, Mr. Stimson thinks it probable that debts for liquor sold to minors are not valid by the common law.

The earnings of an infant in most States belong to the parents if claimed by them. By the common law, however, wages paid to a minor not living with the parents cannot be recovered by the latter, so that in a few States there are special statutes. There is an old New York statute that requires a parent to give notice within thirty days after the beginning of work, or a payment of wages to his child will be valid. In the States where the California code prevails, when a wife is living separate from her husband, the earnings of minor children with her are declared by statute to be her separate property.

There is a new and comprehensive statute in Ohio which provides that no person shall employ a minor without a written statement from parents or guardians that such minor is of legal age to be so employed; nor without agreeing with said minor what compensation he shall receive. This same statute provides that employers shall not withhold wages from minors by reason of their negligence, failure to comply with rules, incompetence, breakage of machinery, &c. In a majority of the States minors may make and withdraw deposits in savings banks or loan institutions and give valid receipts therefor.

With regard to the rights and duties of parents in the matter of the custody of children there are a diversity of statutes in the several States. By the common law the father or, in case of his death, the mother, is entitled to the custody of the children. The California code provides that the parent entitled to the custody of the child must give him support and education suitable to his circumstances. If the father is unable to give adequate support the mother must assist him to the best of her ability. By the Georgia code it is the duty of the father to provide for the maintenance, protection, and education of his child until majority, and the child remains under the control of the father, who is entitled to his services and the proceeds of his labor.

Parental control may be relinquished by the parent under certain conditions, and the State takes it away on proof of cruel treatment of the child. In Ohio, when there are children ten years of age or more, they are allowed to choose which parent they prefer to live with in cases of dispute between the father and mother. If the child selects a parent unfitted to take charge of it by reason of moral depravity, habitual drunkenness, or incapacity, then the Court shall determine the custodian. There is a clause in the California code that provides that a husband is not bound to maintain his wife's children by a former marriage.

In New York, whenever a parent abandons an infant child, such parent is deemed to have forfeited all claim to the custody of the said child as against any other person who may have adopted it. When husband and wife live in a state of separation without being divorced, the Supreme Court, upon habeas corpus, may award the custody of the child to the mother for such time and under such regulations and restrictions as the case may require. The statutes of all the States provide for awarding the custody of the children to either wife or husband upon divorce or during pendency of divorce proceedings.

Several of the States have enacted laws providing that nothing contained in the statutes concerning apprentices shall affect the father's right at common law to assign or contract for the services of his children during their minority. In Vermont a married woman whose husband deserts her, or from intemperance or other causes becomes incapacitated, or neglects to provide for his family, may make contracts for the labor of her minor children, shall be entitled to their wages, and may in her own name sue for and recover them. In many States it is made a penal offense for a father to fail to support his minor children. As a rule, a parent may not disinherit his children except for certain specified causes. In New York there is a statute forbidding a person having children, or issue, to will more than half his estate to charities. At the common law a parent is answerable for the acts of his minor children.

In treating of the relations between guardian and wards, Mr. Stimson says that in New York, Colorado, and Nebraska, every married woman is declared the joint guardian of her children with her husband, with equal powers, rights, and duties in regard to them with him.

In some States no guardians can be appointed over children while the parents are living; but in most of the States guardians, at least of the property, or general guardians having powers over the property, may be appointed by the courts for any minor under legal age, and so generally, where the parent is incompetent, or unfit, a habitual drunkard, or neglects the child. Guardians ad litem must usually be appointed in all States when an infant is represented in any litigation pending before any court. It is customary in nearly all the States to permit minors over fourteen years of age to nominate their guardians, subject to the approval of the court.

September 26, 1897

HIGH COURT RULES ADULT CODE HOLDS IN JUVENILE TRIALS

Finds Children Are Entitled to the Basic Protections Given in Bill of Rights

ONLY STEWART DISSENTS

By FRED P. GRAHAM
Special to The New York Times

WASHINGTON, May 15—The Supreme Court ruled today that juvenile courts must grant children many of the procedural protections required in adult trials by the Bill of Rights.

The landmark decision is expected to require that radical changes be made immediately in most of the nation's 3,000 juvenile courts.

In New York, judges said that the Supreme Court ruling would not affect juvenile cases, since "it already is the law" that minors have the same rights as adults. The change became effective in September, 1962, with the adoption of a new Family Court Act by the State Legislature.

In a detailed opinion by Justice Abe Fortas, the Supreme Court held that, in delinquency hearings before juvenile court judges, children must be accorded the following safeguards of the Bill of Rights:

¶Timely notice of the charges against them.

¶The right to have a lawyer, appointed by the court if necessary, in any case that might result in the incarceration of a child.

¶The right to confront and cross-examine complainants and other witnesses.

¶Adequate warning of the privilege against self-incrimination and the right to remain silent.

Rights Applied to All

"Neither the 14th Amendment nor the Bill of Rights is for adults only," Justice Fortas declared. He went on:

"Under our Constitution, the condition of being a boy does not justify a kangaroo court."

The decision was supported at least in part by eight of the justices, with only Justice Potter Stewart dissenting outright. He said the decision was "a long step backwards into the nineteenth century," because, he contended, it would abolish the flexibility and informality of juvenile courts, and would cause children once more to be treated as adults in courts.

Chief Justice Earl Warren and Justices William J. Brennan Jr., Tom C. Clark and William O. Douglas joined Mr. Fortas's opinion.

Justice Byron R. White and John M. Harlan both joined it in part and disagreed in part.

Justice Hugo L. Black wrote a separate concurring opinion, in which he disclosed that he had opposed reviewing the matter in the first instance because the case "strikes a well-nigh fatal blow to much that is unique about the juvenile courts in the nation."

But Justice Black agreed with the outcome because of his belief that all of the guarantees of the Bill of Rights are applicable to all state criminal trials, including juvenile ones, by the 14th Amendment.

Justice Fortas took pains to state that the decision applied only to juvenile trials, and did not affect the handling of juvenile cases before or after trial. This means that the decision does not automatically apply the Supreme Court's limitations on police interrogation to the investigation of juvenile suspects.

However, the Court's opinion mentioned several instances of improper questioning of young suspects, and Justice Fortas noted that "it would indeed be surprising if the privilege against self-incrimination were available to hardened criminals but not to children."

He found it unnecessary to deal with this issue, or with the rights of indigent children to free appellate transcripts and legal assistance, because the case before the Supreme Court could be decided solely on Constitutional deficiencies at the trial level.

The case before the Supreme Court was brought by Paul L. and Marjorie Gault, parents of Gerald Gault of Globe, Ariz., with the assistance of attorneys furnished by the American Civil Liberties Union. Gerald was adjudged to be a juvenile delinquent in June, 1964, when he was 15 years old, after a juvenile court judge found he had made lewd telephone calls to a female neighbor.

Young Gault served 6 months in the state industrial school. His parents challenged the constitutionality of the Arizona juvenile court law in a habeas corpus petition for his release.

They asserted, among other things, that they had been given inadequate notice of the charges, that the woman had not testified, that they had not been offered the assistance of counsel, that Gerald had not been warned that his testimony could be used

against him, that no transcript had been made of the trial and that Arizona law does not permit an appeal of juvenile court decisions.

Old Doctrine Rejected

Justice Forta's opinion rejected a basic premise on which juvenile courts have operated since the first one was established in Chicago in 1899—that juvenile court trials are essentially civil in nature and that the children's rights are adequately protected by the judges, acting as parens patriae, or substitute parents.

He cited studies to show that about half of the nation's juvenile court judges have no undergraduate degree, a fifth have no college education and a fifth are not members of the bar.

He also cited data from the national crime commission showing that persons under 18 accounted for about one-fifth of all arrests for serious crimes and over one-half of all the arrests for serious property offenses, in 1965. About one out of nine children will eventually face charges of juvenile delinquency, the Justice further said.

While remarking that juvenile courts are failing to cope with this criminality, Mr. Fortas referred to a report by the District of Columbia Crime Commission showing that 66 per cent of the 16 and 17-year-old persons before the juvenile court there had been in court before. Fifty-six per cent of those in the juvenile receiving home were repeaters, the report said.

Justice Fortas noted that this was the first Supreme Court case involving the constitutional rights of children in juvenile court. He concluded that the parens patriae concept had not protected them, and held that they must be accorded the protection of the Bill of Rights. The most far-reaching aspect of today's decision is expected to be the new requirement that counsel be provided in juvenile court.

According to the opinion, only New York, California, Minnesota and the District of Columbia now provide free counsel, and some of them do so only when the charge would be a felony in adult court. Today's decision requires counsel whenever the child might be incarcerated.

Initially, this could cause some paralysis in juvenile courts across the country, which could be followed by a scramble to make lawyers available. Few lawyers are familiar with the procedures of juvenile courts. With the annual number of juvenile cases in the country at 600,000 and rising, the burden on the legal profession could be considerable.

In declaring that the Fifth Amendment's privilege against compulsory self-incrimination applied in juvenile cases, Justice Fortas acknowledged that in practice it might not operate as rigidly as in adult cases, since children are encouraged to talk things out informally with the judge.

But he said that the privilege had been violated in this case because young Gault had not first been told of his right to remain silent.

Justice White disagreed. He said the failure to give warnings did not prove that self-incriminating testimony had been compelled. He declared that the Court was repeating the same mistake in reasoning that led it last year to declare, in Miranda v. Arizona, that confessions are always coerced unless the suspects are first warned of their rights.

Justice Harlan agreed that the Gault decision should have been reversed, because the boy had been denied the "fundamental fairness" required of all criminal proceedings by the due process clause of the 14th Amendment.

In juvenile cases, this would require only timely notice, the right to be represented by retained counsel and an adequate

transcript for appeal, Justice Harlan said.

Justice Black's concurring opinion was aimed primarily at this "fundamental fairness" approach.

"Due process of law," he said, means merely that persons must be tried under the law that existed when the offense was committed.

It should not be stretched by judges to "give courts power to fashion laws in order to meet new conditions, to fit the decencies of changed conditions, or to keep their consciences from being shocked by legislation, state or federal."

The dissent by Justice Stewart conceded that the record of juvenile courts did not measure up to their ideals, but he said that the solution "does not lie in the Court's opinion in this case, which serves to convert a juvenile proceeding into a criminal prosecution."

To illustrate the possible abuses of this, he related the case of a 12-year-old New Jersey boy named James Guild, who was hanged for murder in the nineteenth century.

"It was all very constitutional," he said.

In a footnote, he repeated Blackstone's report of a 10-year-old boy who was sentenced to death for murder to squelch any "notion that children might commit such atrocious crimes with impunity."

In the Gault case, he found that despite the lack of formal procedures, Gerald's parents had known of the charges and their rights. He said he would dismiss the appeal.

Norman Dorsen of New York argued for the Gaults. Frank A. Parks, assistant Attorney General of Arizona argued for the state, and Merrit W. Green of Toledo, Ohio, argued as friend-of-the-court in support of the state, for the Ohio Association of Juvenile Court Judges.

May 16, 1967

High Court Upholds A Student Protest

By FRED P. GRAHAM
Special to The New York Times

WASHINGTON, Feb. 24—The Supreme Court ruled today that public school officials may not interfere with students' rights to express political opinions in a nondisruptive way during school hours.

In a 7-to-2 decision, the Court held that school officials in Des Moines, Iowa, had violated the First Amendment rights of three children, 13 to 16 years of age, when they suspended them for wearing black armbands to protest the Vietnam war.

The ruling provoked a heated

dissent from Justice Hugo L. Black, who insisted that it would encourage students to demonstrate and would embroil the Supreme Court in public school affairs.

Justice Abe Fortas emphasized in the Court's opinion that school children's free speech rights are limited to conduct that does not disrupt discipline or interfere with the rights of others.

He also said that their rights included only political expression, and that the Federal courts would not become involved in disputes over the permissible length of students' hair or skirts.

But he noted that some students in Des Moines had been permitted to wear political campaign buttons, and some had worn the Iron Cross. The school principals ruled out only the armbands protesting the Viet-

nam war. Justice Fortas saw this as an attempt to suppress expressions of opposition to the war.

"In our system, students may not be regarded as closed-circuit recipients of only that which the state chooses to communicate," he said. "In the absence of specific showing of constitutionally valid reasons to regulate their speech, students are entitled to freedom of expression of their views."

The Supreme Court declared as early as 1943 that schoolchildren have First Amendment rights, when it struck down a West Virginia law that required students to salute the flag, even if they had religious scruples against it. Lower Federal courts have extended this to safeguard the rights of students to wear political or civil rights insignia.

However, today's ruling marked the Supreme Court's first ruling on the question of

free speech rights, and Justice Fortas emphasized that the decision related only to "symbolic speech" or speech itself, and not to protest demonstrations.

He said that the courts should consider if curbs school officials imposed on students' political expression were reasonable in the light of the probability of disruption, and should enjoin unreasonable restrictions.

Despite efforts by Justice Fortas to confine the ruling to narrow limits, it may make it more difficult for public schools to censor student publications or to purge school libraries or curriculums of "objectionable" material. Principals and deans may also encounter legal difficulty when they attempt to discipline student protesters.

Justice Black insisted that after today's ruling many students "will be ready, able, and willing to defy their teachers on practically all orders."

"This is the more unfortunate for the schools," he said. "since groups of students all over the land are already running loose, conducting break-ins, sit-ins, lie-ins and smash-ins."

He objected that young persons are currently too prone to try to teach their elders rather than to learn from them, and that today's ruling would make the situation worse. Moreover, he said, the Court's "reasonableness" standard would put the Federal judiciary in the position of second-guessing actions of school officials without clear standards

to guide either.

Justice John M. Harlan also dissented in a short opinion.

Justice Black, whose dissents have tended to become longer and more acid in recent years, spoke extemporaneously for about 20 minutes this morning.

At one point he used mocking tones to quote from an old opinion with which he disagreed, and he finished by stating that "I want it thoroughly known that I disclaim any sentence, any word, any part of what the Court does today."

Justice Black will observe his 83d birthday next Thursday.

The events leading to today's decision go back to December,

1965, when antiwar groups in Des Moines began to plan the armband protest. The Board of Education voted to prohibit the wearing of armbands.

Seven children defied the rule and wore armbands. Those who refused to remove them were suspended and were permitted to return later without the armbands.

The suit, sponsored by the American Civil Liberties Union, was brought in the names of three of the suspended students: John F. Tinker, then 15; his sister Mary Beth, then 13, and Christopher Eckhardt, 16.

The father of the Tinker children is a Methodist minister

employed by the American Friends Service Committee. Young Eckhardt's mother is an officer in the Women's International League for Peace and Freedom.

The United States District Court in Des Moines refused to enjoin the school officials from forbidding the armband protests, and the United States Court of Appeals for the Eighth Circuit affirmed.

Dan Johnsston of Des Moines argued for the children. Allan A. Herrick, also of Des Moines, argued for the school board.

February 25, 1969

NIXON SIGNS VOTE-AT-18 BILL BUT ASKS FOR COURT TEST

By JACK ROSENTHAL

Special to The New York Times

WASHINGTON, June 22—President Nixon resolved a political dilemma today by signing into law a historic measure lowering the voting age from 21 to 18—and then immediately calling for a court challenge to decide if it is constitutional.

The measure was a rider on a bill that extends for five more years the protection of the Voting Rights Act of 1965 against racial discrimination. Since its passage, nearly a million Negro residents of Southern states have registered to vote.

The measure lowering the voting age, if it survives a challenge, would make 11 million more young people eligible to vote in the next Presidential election. It goes into effect on Jan. 1 and applies to all elections, Federal, state, and local.

Approves Despite Doubts

President Nixon emphasized, in a statement, that the voting rights extension was of such great importance that he was giving his approval to the entire measure, despite his serious constitutional doubts about the 18-year-old vote provisions.

Mr. Nixon's action was promptly hailed by Roy Wilkins, executive director of the National Association for the Advancement of Colored People. Mr. Wilkins said the association noted "with satisfaction that President Nixon regards the safeguarding of the Negro's

right to vote as a prime consideration in his signing of the measure."

'Act of Statesmanship'

Clarence Mitchell, director of the N.A.A.C.P.'s Washington bureau, said the signing was "an act of statesmanship undergirded by faith in the rule of just law."

Mr. Nixon took pains in his statement to reiterate his support of the 18-year-old vote and his belief that it was the method of achieving it, not the result, that he questioned.

The Constitution leaves the establishment of voting qualifications to the states. Mr. Nixon said he believed, "along with most of the nation's leading constitutional scholars," that lowering the voting age thus required a constitutional amendment, not simply an act of Congress. The dilemma for the President, White House sources said, lay between the constitutional argument and the feelings of youth and Negroes, neither of whom are likely to be attentive to constitutional subtleties.

His answer to the dilemma, in the view of a White House aide, was for the executive branch to seek the aid of the judicial branch in correcting what it regarded as a mistake of the legislative branch.

Mr. Nixon directed Attorney General John N. Mitchell "to cooperate in expediting a swift court test of the constitutionality of the 18-year-old provision."

Speed is essential, he said, because the results of any election under the new law could be clouded by legal doubt unless its constitutionality was upheld by the courts.

Mr. Nixon made it clear that he felt such approval was unlikely, referring to "the likelihood that the 18-year-old vote provision of this law will not survive its court test."

As if to underscore his feelings about this provision, Mr. Nixon signed the bill in his hideaway office this afternoon with only an aide for an audience and with his own silver fountain pen, forswearing the ceremonial signing and distribution of souvenir pens often associated with historic bill signings.

Mr. Mitchell has not yet decided what form the court challenge to the new law will take, but some unusual types of action are being discussed.

"After all, it's a rare situation," a Justice Department spokesman said.

An important consideration, the spokesman said, is which kind of action would produce the most rapid final determination by the courts.

One strong possibility is an original action—a case initiated in the Supreme Court — thus saving the time required for consideration by lower courts. In such an original action, a state could seek to bar the Federal Government from enforcing the new law.

Since the Department of Justice resists challenges to Federal laws, such an action would have an ironic result. The Administration would be in the position of defending, legally, a provision with which it disagrees against a challenge

that, philosophically, it supports.

In his statement, the President urged Congress to act promptly on establishing the 18-year-old vote in what he regards as the correct way—"by amending the Constitution."

He asked Congress "to act now upon the new constitutional amendment" already pending and speed it along to the states for ratification. Approval by 37 state legislatures is required for adoption of an amendment.

Even if upheld by the courts, the new law is not generally expected to result in many of the 11 million potential new voters actually voting.

One study of states that now permit those under 21 to vote showed that only about 30 per cent did so. This compares with 51.1 per cent participation among those 21 to 24 and 75.1 per cent for those 45 to 54, according to census figures.

Controversy over the constitutional issue has obscured several other important — and uncontroversial — provisions of the new law. One is the elimination of long residency requirements for voting in Presidential elections.

Such requirements, sometimes of a year or more, have excluded large numbers in the past. The new law establishes a 30-day residency requirement.

Another new provision extends the present prohibition against the use of literacy tests as a condition to voting registration to all states until 1975.

A further amendment to the Voting Rights Act changes a basic definition. Originally, the act was applicable to any county in which 50 per cent of the eligible residents were not registered or did not vote in 1964.

The year has now been changed to 1968, leaving Southern states covered, but also extending its potential applicability to Manhattan Brooklyn and seven counties in four Western states.

June 23, 1970

SUPREME COURT BACKS VOTE AT 18 IN FEDERAL ELECTIONS, NOT STATE

A 5-TO-4 DECISION

Residency Rule Eased and Literacy Tests Are Abolished

By FRED P. GRAHAM
Special to The New York Times

WASHINGTON, Dec. 21 — The Supreme Court upheld today the 18-year-old vote in Federal elections but ruled that Congress acted unconstitutionally when it lowered the voting age to 18 for state and local elections.

At the same time, the Court upheld other provisions of the voting rights amendments of 1970 that abolished residency requirements of longer than 30 days and outlawed literacy tests for voting.

Five separate opinions, totaling 184 pages, were issued by the Justices in the 5-to-4 decision that cleared the way for 11.5 million young Americans to vote for President and members of Congress. It also cleared the way for 11 million others to vote — 10 million penalized by residency requirements in 38 states and the District of Columbia of up to one year—and a million now barred by literacy tests.

The ruling on the 18-year-old vote also raised the possibility of widespread confusion in voting. Only three states—Alaska, Georgia and Kentucky—now permit 18-year-olds to vote, and most of the other states would have to amend their constitutions before they could let 18-year-olds vote for Governors, state legislators, mayors and other state and local officials.

Thus today's ruling may require these states to provide separate registration books and perhaps separate ballots or voting booths for young voters.

Senator Edward M. Kennedy, Massachusetts Democrat who was the author of the 18-year-old provision, quickly issued a statement predicting that the decision would encourage states to enact 18-year-old vote laws in the interest of uniformity.

He introduced, as a speedier settlement, an amendment to the Federal Constitution to lower the voting age to 18 in state and local elections. Senator Kennedy called upon Congress to approve it and send it to the states for ratification before the present session ends.

The surprise ruling came from a Court that was so splintered that only one Justice, Hugo L. Black, agreed with the entire outcome. This happened because four Justices—William J. Brennan Jr., William O. Douglas, Thurgood Marshall and Byron R. White—considered the 18-year-old vote provision fully constitutional for Federal and state elections. Four others—Warren E. Burger, Harry A. Blackmun, John M. Harlan and Potter Stewart—believed it was unconstitutional as to both state and Federal elections.

Justice Black wrote an opinion stating that "Congress has ultimate supervisory power" over Congressional and Presidential elections, and thus the 18-year-old vote law could stand as to Federal elections.

"The Constitution allotted to the states the power to make laws regarding national elections but provided that if Congress became dissatisfied with the state laws, Congress could alter them."

Justice Black said, however, that the authority of Congress under the 14th Amendment to overrule the voting standards of the states applies only when the rules of the states discriminate on the basis of race and not age. Thus, he found that Congress lacked the authority to change the voting standards of states on the theory that they discriminate against persons between 18 and 21 years of age.

Although no other Justice joined in the 84-year-old Justice's opinion, he became the "swing" man between the two blocs and declared the judgment of the Court in his opinion. He joined with the Brennan - Douglas - Marshall - White group to uphold the law as to Federal elections and with the Burger-Blackmun-Harlan-Stewart bloc to strike the law down as to the states.

Unanimity on Literacy

All of the Justices agreed that the ban on literacy tests was constitutional as an expression of Congress's authority under the 15th Amendment to counteract voting discrimination on grounds of race or color. Congress had declared in the statute that it passed the law because literacy tests tended to weed out members of minority groups who had been denied equal educational opportunities.

The court's vote supporting Congress in abolishing the residency rules was 8 to 1. The majority declared that the Federal Constitution safeguards the right of individuals to travel freely from state to state and that Congress has the power to blot out any state laws that impede this right.

Justice Harlan dissented. He called the right to travel a "nebulous judicial construct" that has been recognized in some Supreme Court decisions but that does not appear in express terms in the Constitution. Because he reads the Constitution as clearly leaving the question of voting standards in the states' hands, he concluded that Congress lacked the power to pass a law regulating state voting residency laws.

The Court had been expected to decide the case today, the last session before the 18-year-old-vote provision goes into effect on Jan. 1. The Court will be in recess until Jan. 11.

Shortly after President Nixon signed the law on June 22, the stage was set for a rapid Supreme Court review when original suits were filed in the high court under a constitutional provision that permits states and the United States to skip the lower courts and sue directly in the Supreme Court. In these suits, the United States asked the Court to uphold the law, while Arizona, Idaho, Oregon and Texas urged the Court to strike it down.

The states asserted that the Constitution gives the states the sole power to set voting standards. As proof that Congress cannot change these standards short of a constitutional amendment, they pointed out that constitutional amendments were used to extend the vote to women and to eliminate the poll tax in Federal elections.

When the case was decided today, Congress's theory in passing the 18-year-old vote provision was accepted by three Justices — Brennan, Marshall and White — in an opinion written by Justice Brennan. He reasoned that the 14th Amendment's equal-protection clause outlaws state voting standards that discriminate invidiously against any class of voters. He then noted that 18-year-olds were subjected to the same laws as older persons on criminal responsibility, marriage, education and military service but were denied the right to vote.

Justice Brennan concluded that when Congress found that this constituted discrimination against the 18-to-21-year group in violation of the 14th Amendment, the Supreme Court should not disturb the law as long as there was "a rational basis" for Congress's findings. He said there was such a basis for this act of Congress.

14th Called Sufficient

Justice Douglas argued in a separate opinion that the 14th Amendment's prohibition against discrimination in voting was enough to sustain Congress's power to pass all three of the disputed provisions.

Justice Stewart, joined by Chief Justice Burger and Justice Blackmun, argued that state laws that deny the vote to voters under 21 "do not invidiously discriminate against any discrete and insular minority." They concluded that the laws do not violate the 14th Amendment's antidiscrimination ban and thus Congress was in error when it passed the law to combat the "discrimination" against youths.

In his opinion, Justice Harlan rekindled a long-standing controversy on the Court as to whether the 14th Amendment was ever intended to apply to denials of political rights, as it clearly was intended to cover denials of civil rights. He noted that the Supreme Court decided in its 1962 reapportionment ruling, Baker v. Carr, that equal rights in voting were guaranteed by the amendment.

But Justice Harlan, who dissented in that case and in one-man, one-vote rulings that have followed it, declared today that he was still convinced that the framers of the 14th Amendment never intended it to modify the sole power of states to regulate voting. Although he is a strong believer in the doctrine of "stare decisis" — that judges should follow established precedents — he said that he would not follow it in voting equality cases because he remained "deeply convinced" that they misstated the Constitution.

This declaration by Justice Harlan appeared to raise a possibility that, with the recent changes in the high court's membership, it could begin to take a new line in one-man, one-vote cases.

Justice Brennan, who wrote the court's Baker V. Carr decision, insisted in his opinion today that the Court has been right in holding that the 14th Amendmen bars discrimination in elections. Otherwise, he said, states would be free to deny Negroes the right to run for public office, because the 15th Amendment protects only their right to vote.

December 22, 1970

Court, 6-3, Says Jury Trial Is Not Required for Youths

Opinion by Blackmun Warns of an End to the 'Intimate, Protective Proceeding' Sought Under the Juvenile System

By JOHN HERBERS
Special to The New York Times

WASHINGTON, June 21—The Supreme Court ruled 6 to 3 today that juveniles do not have a constitutional right to a trial by jury.

Justice Harry A. Blackmun said in the majority opinion that although the juvenile system of justice may have fallen far short of perfection the requirement of a jury trial could "put an end to what has been the idealistic prospect of an intimate, informal protective proceeding."

The decision nevertheless went against a 23-year trend in which the Court in a succession of cases had extended Bill of Rights protections to juvenile proceedings.

Opinion by Douglas

Justice William O. Douglas said in the dissenting opinion that because many law enforcement officials had treated juveniles as criminals, and not as delinquents, they were entitled to the same procedural protections as adults.

Joining Justice Blackmun in the majority were Chief Justice Warren E. Burger and Justices John M. Harlan, Potter Stewart and Byron R. White and, to a partial extent William J. Brennen Jr. Voting with Mr. Douglas in dissent were Justices Hugo L. Black and Thurgood Marshall.

The ruling upholds laws existing in most states. Twenty-nine states and the District of Columbia have laws barring jury trials in youth courts, which provide for proceedings before a judge in closed hearings. In five other states there are no jury trials by virtue of court rulings. In the remaining states trials for youths are allowed under certain circumstances.

The judgment was based on cases from Pennsylvania and North Carolina in which teenagers adjudged to be delinquent petitioned for jury trial.

In 1968, Joseph McKeiver of Philadelphia, then 15 years old, was charged with robbery, larceny and receiving stolen goods after he participated with 20 or 30 other boys in pursuing a teen-ager and taking 25 cents from him. He was adjudged a juvenile and placed on probation.

In 1969, Edward Terry, then 15, also of Philadelphia, was accused of assaulting a policeman with his fists. He was committed to a youth center after it was learned he also had assaulted a teacher.

In the North Carolina case, Barbara Burnrus and 45 other black minors, ranging from 11 to 15 years old, were charged with impeding traffic and found to be delinquent after a demonstration against a school consolidation in Hyde County.

In the majority decision, Justice Blackmun summarized the long list of rulings that had extended more and more constitutional guarantees to accused youths. He said that the "fond and idealistic hopes" of juvenile court proponents of three generations ago had not been realized.

"Too often the juvenile court judge falls far short of that stalwart protective and communicating figure the system envisaged," he wrote. "The community's unwillingness to provide people and facilities and to be concerned, the inefficiency of time devoted, the scarcity of professional help, the inadequacy of dispositional alternatives and our general lack of knowledge all contribute to dissatisfaction with the experiment."

But he said that despite these disappointments and failures "there is a possibility, at least, that the jury trial, if required as a matter of constitutional precept, will remake the juvenile proceeding into a fully adversary process and will put an effective end to what has been the idealistic prospect of an intimate, informal protective proceeding."

He said it would bring "the traditional delay, the formality and clamor of the adversary system and, possibly, the public trial."

"If the formalities of the criminal adjudicative process are to be superimposed upon the juvenile court system, there is little need for its separate existence," he said. "Perhaps that ultimate disillusionment will come one day, but for the moment we are disinclined to give impetus to it."

Justice Douglas wrote on the other hand that, "Where a state uses its juvenile court proceedings to prosecute a juvenile for a criminal act and to order 'confinement' until the child reaches 21 years of age or where the child at the threshold of the proceedings faces that prospect, then he is entitled to the same procedural protection as an adult."

Justice Brennan concurred in the Pennsylvania cases in the conclusions of the majority but joined the dissent in the North Carolina cases because the prosecutions in that case were carried out in secret.

June 22, 1971

THE STATES RATIFY FULL VOTE AT 18

Ohio Becomes 38th to Back the 26th Amendment

By R. W. APPLE Jr.
Special to The New York Times

WASHINGTON, June 30—The 26th Amendment to the Constitution, lowering to 18 years the minimum voting age in local and state as well as Federal elections, was ratified tonight.

Ohio became the 38th state to approve the Amendment when the state's House of Representatives, meeting in extraordinary evening session, gave its assent, 81 to 9. The Ohio Senate had approved the measure yesterday, 30 to 2.

The ratification of at least 38 states, or three-quarters of the total, is required for constitutional amendments.

An atmosphere of near-panic attended Ohio's climactic vote. The Republican Speaker of the House, Charles F. Kurfess, had planned to let a number of members, both Republicans and Democrats, speak on the issue before calling for a vote.

But after only three short speeches, the Republican floor leader, Robert E. Leavitt, interrupted to warn:

"I've just been informed that the Legislature of Oklahoma has gone into special session tonight. The time for debate and discussion is over. The time for action is here."

Over the shouted protests of several back-benchers, Mr. Kurfess then gaveled through a motion cutting off debate. To the accompaniment of more cat-calls, he ordered an immediate roll-call, which ended at 8:05 P.M.

In fact, Ohio had no reason to worry that it would lose its place of distinction. The Oklahoma Legislature was not scheduled to go into session until tomorrow.

Ratification means that millions of young voters will be able to participate in elections this year, including contests for Governor in Mississippi and Kentucky, mayoral elections in Boston, San Francisco and other large cities and scores of races in towns and counties.

In addition, it removes the legal cloud that had hung over the right of young voters to cast their ballots in Presidential primaries next year.

Political commentators have gradually arrived at the conclusion, which runs counter to their earlier thesis, that the Democrats will be aided by the enfranchising of the young. The most recent analysts to state that view is Samuel Lubell, in an article in this week's issue of Look magazine.

But one issue, still unresolved, could blunt the effect of the change: the question of where students can register—where they live or where they attend school. Most states have forbidden students to register at school, and experience indicates that they will not vote heavily if forced to resort to the absentee ballot.

Challenge Under Way

Local politicians have expressed the fear that they could be voted out of office, particularly in college towns, by students with no proprietary interest in the towns. Their views already under challenge in state courts and will soon be challenged in Federal courts in several states as well.

The Voting Rights Act of 1970 gave the franchise to young people in all elections. But the Supreme Court earlier this year struck down the measure to the degree that it would have affected state and local elections, while upholding its applicability to Federal voting.

On March 23, in order to avoid widespread confusion, Congress gave final approval to the proposed amendment.

Ratification has come with a rush as opposition to youth voting collapsed. It has been only two months and seven days since the process of getting the requisite 38 assents began—by far the shortest time in which the process has ever been accomplished. The old record was six months and six days in 1804 for the 12th Amedment, which provided for separate balloting for President and Vice President.

North Carolina 37th

Illinois became the 35th state to ratify yesterday.

Then, this morning, Alabama became the 36th. The House of Representatives had acted last Thursday, and the Senate concurred, 31 to 4, after a filibuster

failed. Its leader, Senator James A. Branyon, a 64-year-old conservative from Fayette in central Alabama, said, "I'm physically unable to stand here any longer," sat down, and the vote followed.

At 4:21 P.M., the North Carolina Senate made that state the 37th to ratify. After House approval in March, the measure had been held up in the Senate by rural Democrats, but Lieut. Gov. Pat Taylor, hoping to make North Carolina's the decisive vote, managed to push aside the opposition. The final vote was 38 to 7.

Conceivably, a mild squabble over who was 38th could break out. North Carolina officials, apparently still hoping to play the decisive role, delayed in signing an "enrolled bill"—the official copy—until tomorrow morning.

According to Common Cause, the citizens' lobbying organization that played a prominent role in the ratification effort, the Amendment does not actually take effect until the General Services Administration in Washington has received an official record of each state's action. But that is considered

a mere formality.

When notified of the ratification, President Nixon said at the White House, "Some 11 million young men and women who have participated in the life of our nation through their work, their studies and their sacrifices for its defense now are to be fully included in the electoral process of our country.

"I urge them to honor this right by exercising it—by registering and voting in each election."

July 1, 1971

Youths See Little Effect From Newly Won Rights

By AGIS SALPUKAS
Special to The New York Times

DETROIT, Dec. 31—Maureen Doyle, an 18-year-old student in Vermont, got not only the right to vote last July but also the right to enter contracts, serve on juries, sue in court and marry without her parents' consent.

But she is not ready to marry, has no wish to sue anyone, has not yet sat on a jury or cast a vote, and has been turned down by a bank in an attempt to get a loan for a car without her mother's signature.

In other words, not much has changed in Miss Doyle's life as a result of her newly acquired rights.

And her experience has been the rule for hundreds of thousands of other young people around the country who are finding that what they have won on paper is often slow to be granted in practice.

In the nine states that have lowered the age of majority from 21 to 18—and in Maine, where it was lowered to 20—many of the young people have begun to express disappointment.

"The law about entering into contracts is a farce," said Steward Fallings, a 20-year-old service station attendant in Oregon. "If you try to buy a car on time, they won't talk to you unless you have a co-signer. It has nothing to do with age; it's economic."

When the legislatures were deliberating whether to lower the age, the main fear was that young people would be taken advantage of by shady businessmen who would try to saddle them with homes, cars and goods that they could not afford.

Walter L. Kennedy, the Republican Speaker of the House in Vermont, said in an interview that he had opposed the change because "there are many outfits that would try to pull a fast one and get young people into contracts they couldn't afford."

But in the 10 states where the age of majority has been lowered—Vermont, Maine, Tennessee, North Carolina, Michigan, New Mexico, Oregon, Washington, North Dakota and Alaska—there have been few reports of young people being victimized by dishonest businessmen.

Lenders Reluctant

Instead, the main complaint has been that banks, stores and other institutions are still reluctant to give loans to 18-to 20-year-olds without the guarantee of an older person, even though it is no longer required by law.

"We're not concerned about age, but rather about job history and income," a credit manager of a department store in Portland, Ore., explained. "Let's face reality; it is not very often that someone that young has established a financial capability to pay back a loan. The 18 to 20-year-olds, frankly, are simply not good credit risks."

In Tennessee, James Lewis, president of the First Federal Savings and Loan Association in Johnson City, said that his lawyers had advised him not to make mortgage loans to those under 21 until their right to make a contract had been tested in the courts.

Not only has the change left some young people disappointed, but they are also bewildered by the actions of some of the legislatures.

Washington, Oregon, Tennessee, North Carolina, North Dakota and New Mexico, for example, gave most majority rights except the right to drink

beer and liquor.

Oregon and North Dakota also withheld the right of 18-to 20-year-old males to marry without permission from their parents.

Roger Johnson, a 19-year-old student at Portland State University, said: "I can't understand the logic of the legislature. They'll let us sell beer and wine, but they won't let us drink it. That's sort of a double standard of morality, don't you think?"

In Tennessee, some liquor and beer dealers refused to sell to 18 to 20-year-olds even after the law permitted it, until the state's Attorney General ruled it legal. Several cities such as Franklin and Nashville tried to prevent it through local ordinance, but they were overturned by the state.

Also legislators in Tennessee had second thoughts after lowering the age. When voters in their districts began to complain, they urged repeal; but nothing came of it because the legislature was in a hurry to adjourn.

Attempts to lower the age failed in numerous other states —such as Florida, Arkansas, Connecticut, Wyoming, Nevada and Hawaii — but they will be renewed when the legislatures convene for their next sessions.

Legislators Spur Drive

Up to now there has been little support from young people for the change. The initiative has come from legislators who felt that since 18 to 20-year-olds had gotten the right to vote under the 26th Amendment to the Constitution, they should also be made adults before the law.

David Desjardin, an 18-year-old student in Augusta, Me., is an exception to the general lack of interest in the issue by young people. He has organized a drive by 100 high school volunteers throughout the state to get signatures on a petition asking that the Legislature lower the age of majority from 20 to 18.

"A lot of us feel that we're more mature today in handling responsibilities," he said. "By the time you're out of high school you're 18 and ready to

go—you're ready to get some good job and start preparing for later on."

Major gains in income, education and employment during the last decade among 18- and 20-year-olds, who now number about 11.1 million, have been a major argument used by those who favor lowering the age.

During the last decade, the number of 18- and 19-year-olds who stay in school has gone from 38 per cent to 50 per cent. The number of men employed has remained about the same, but the number of working women has jumped dramatically in the last 10 years, according to the United States Census Bureau.

Gov. William G. Milliken of Michigan, who helped push a measure lowering the age of majority through the Legislature, said recently that "when we permit and often require young people to enter the labor market and earn their own way, it is illogical and inconsistent to bind our young adults to archaic guardianship."

Legal historians have traced the origins of 21 as the adult age to English common law. It was set at the time of William the Conquerer as the age when a young man could hold a sword and a lance while dressed in full armor.

"The weight of armor in the 11th century," Mr. Milliken said, "should not govern the age at which a 20th-century couple can get a mortgage in Michigan."

Legal Inconsistencies

States have also been spurred to lower the age after they examined their laws and found it hard to justify numerous legal inconsistencies.

A special commission appointed by the Governor of Michigan, for example, found that a 17-year-old does not need a guardian if he is a defendant in a legal case; but he must get an adult guardian if he wants to bring a suit, unless he wants a divorce. Also a married man who has not reached the age of majority cannot make a will to leave property to his wife, but a state law requires that he provide for her support.

367

It also found that 18 to 21-year-olds could not commit themselves to a mental hospital and unwed mothers under the age of majority could not get prenatal care without the consent of their parents.

Even though many of the sponsors of bills to lower the age of majority have not lost interest, the process of making the new rights effective is expected to be slow and difficult.

Mr. Kennedy, the House Speaker in Vermont, who owns two car agencies, has been able to get about 15 cars financed for young people without the guarantee of their parents. But in each case he has had to write a long personal letter to the bank explaining the change

in the law and that he would vouch for the young people's standing.

'Going to Take Time'

"Even then I get some reluctance," he said. "The rights will come, but it's going to take some time for people to accept it."

The courts could also become an important ally to the young in exercising their new rights.

In North Carolina, last summer, a Superior Court judge granted a motion to dismiss an indictment against three Black Panthers because the grand jury did not reflect the racial composition of the county and did not have any

18- to 20-year olds serving on it.

The case is being appealed in the state's Supreme Court, but meanwhile every county has made extra efforts to get 18- and 20-year-olds on its juries.

The prospect of having young people on juries has not aroused much concern on the part of judges or lawyers in other states that have lowered the age.

William N. Gale, Presiding Judge for Multnomah County Circuit Court, the largest court in Oregon, summed it up by saying: "Age, I feel, is not a factor in determining a good jurist. Some teen-agers might be better equipped and more

mature to handle these responsibilities than their parents may be."

He also predicted that not too many 18-year-olds would serve on juries since they could be excused if they were students.

Miss Karolyn Brown of Gresham, Ore., a 19-year-old student, was the first young jury member to be called under the new law.

"It's so new and sort of scary," she said in an interview. "I think I can remember enough about the American jury system from civics class to do a good job."

January 1, 1972

Supreme Court, 5-4, Backs Rights of Suspended Pupils

By WARREN WEAVER Jr.
Special to The New York Times

WASHINGTON, Jan. 22 — Public school pupils cannot be suspended without notice of the charges against them, an explanation of any adverse evidence and a chance to give their side of the story, the Supreme Court ruled today.

Dividing 5 to 4, the high court held for the first time that young people are entitled by the Constitution to the same sort of protection against unfair interference with their education that adults enjoy when the Government tries to deprive them of their rights.

The ruling, sharply disputed by the minority Justices, was certain to have broad impact on public school disciplinary procedures. Surveys have indicated that more than 10 per cent of urban pupils are suspended at least once a year, as many as 20,000 a year in New York City alone.

Leading the dissenters, Associate Justice Lewis F. Powell Jr. called the decision an "unprecedented intrusion into the process of elementary and secondary education" and argued that injury caused by short suspensions was "too speculative, transitory and insubstantial" to justify the courts in invoking the Constitution.

With today's ruling, the high court ventured into what the minority called a "new thicket," the question of whether minors have the same constitutional rights, enforceable by the Federal courts, as adults do.

Still awaiting decision by the Justices are another case involving disciplinary expulsion from high school without an adequate hearing and an appeal by the school authorities from a ruling that they violated the First Amendment by barring distribution of an underground student paper they regarded as obscene.

Maintaining that "young people do not shed their rights at the schoolhouse door," Associate Justice Byron R. White concluded for the majority that a state that has guaranteed its residents free primary and secondary education "may not withdraw that right on grounds of misconduct, absent fundamentally fair procedures to determine whether the misconduct has occurred."

The Court divided along ideological lines. Joining Justice White were another moderate, Associate Justice Potter Stewart, and three liberals, Associate Justices William O. Douglas, William J. Brennan Jr. and Thurgood Marshall.

Voting in the minority were all four of former President Richard M. Nixon's appointees to the bench: Justice Powell, Chief Justice Warren E. Burger and Associate Justices Harry A. Blackmun and William H. Rehnquist.

The decision had apparently been reached before Justice Douglas suffered a stroke on New Year's Eve and was formally ratified by the eight other Justices at their closed conference last Friday. Justice Doug-

las, who is still hospitalized, has not participated in any of the conference decisions in January on accepting cases for review or rejecting them.

The case (No. 73-898, Goss v. Lopez) involved nine students who were suspended from Columbus, Ohio, high schools in 1971 during student unrest and racial demonstrations. They then challenged in Federal District Court the state law that permitted such suspensions for up to 10 days without any hearing.

The students argued that this procedure deprived them of both property (their statutory right to an education) and liberty (by damaging their school record without proof) without due process of law, in violation of the 14th Amendment to the Constitution.

A three-judge District Court panel agreed with the Columbus students, and the school authorities appealed directly to the Supreme Court, as is permitted in constitutional cases.

1969 Ruling Recalled

Only once before, in 1969, has the high court enforced high school students' constitutional rights, ruling that they could not be suspended for wearing black armbands in an otherwise nonviolent Vietnam protest.

With that exception, the minority said, "until today . . . the educational rights of children and teen-agers in the elementary and secondary schools have not been analogized to the rights of adults or to those accorded college students."

Justice Powell maintained that the Federal courts would now be called upon to review for fairness decisions by teachers or the school authorities to fail a pupil in a course, deny him promotion, exclude him from extracurricular activities or assign him to a vocational rather than a college program.

The minority predicted that there would be no way to limit today's holding that "Government infringement of any inter-

est to which a person is entitled, no matter what the interest or how inconsequential the infringement, requires constitutional protection."

Steps Are Listed

Speaking through Justice White, the majority ruled that public school officials must take these steps when they suspend pupils for 10 or fewer days.

¶Give the pupil oral or written notice of the charges against him.

¶If he denies the charges, furnish "an explanation of the evidence" against him.

¶Give the pupil "an opportunity to present his side of the story."

Mr. White called these "rudimentary precautions against unfair or mistaken findings of misconduct and arbitrary exclusions from school." But the majority stopped short of ruling that pupils suspended for short periods had the right to hire a lawyer, cross-examine witnesses for the school authorities or call witnesses in their own defense.

"Longer suspensions or expulsions for the rest of the school term, or permanently, may require more formal procedures," Justice White said.

If unchallenged charges of misbehavior are allowed to remain on pupils' records, the majority said, they could damage their standing in the school and impair their chances of getting into college or finding a job after graduation.

Underlying the Columbus lawsuit were charges by civil rights organizations that white school officials across the nation had been increasingly relying on unjustified suspensions as a discriminatory weapon against black pupils in the city districts where their relative numbers had been on the increase.

January 23, 1975

Teen-Agers Leave Home — Legally

By MARK BLACKBURN

Special to The New York Times

Terrence McCarthy

**Noriko Blue hopes
to go on to college.**

SAN FRANCISCO

UNDER a law in California designed to help teen-agers who have fled intolerable family situations, children who are at least 14 years old can be declared independent of their parents and receive the right to be treated as adults for most legal purposes.

The new law applies to children up to the age of 18 who are living away from home and supporting themselves. Their parents must either consent to or acquiesce in the process — acquiescence meaning that they are not making an active effort to get the child back.

The law, known as the Emancipation of Minors Act, took effect 13 months ago, but, with amendments, has been on the books in its present form only since September. New as it is, the law has already attracted wide interest in California. The National Center for Youth Law, which helped draft the legislation, says it is receiving an inquiry a week about emancipation. Noriko Blue, for example, now 18 years old and an orphan, was able to sever her relationship with a stepfather who attempted to abuse her sexually. And Maria Leon, 16, when independent of her mother and a hated stepfather, will be able to apply for admission to the University of California at Davis and seek financial aid in her own right.

For Charlie Eagle, 17, whose Legal Services lawyer calls him "one of our failures," there have been no advantages, however. (The names of the children have been changed.)

Among other things, the law permits emancipated teen-agers (the word "emancipation" in this context dates to Roman times) to get driver's licenses, to sign contracts such as leases, and to buy cars and other goods on credit. It also facilitates legal abortions and permits the youngsters to take responsibility for their schooling.

Similar laws exist in other states: minors under 18 can be emancipated in Mississippi, Louisiana, Oklahoma, Kansas and Arkansas. Also, a law like California's was enacted in Oregon in 1977, and a similar one took effect in Connecticut last year. Moreover, the courts in most states will, under some circumstances, free a child from its parents. Still, California, the most populous state and one that has often been a legal trend-setter, now has the youngest age for emancipation — 14 — and its experience with the law is being closely watched by other states.

How do children so young survive outside the shelter of the family? For Noriko, at least, the prospects seem good. She was born in Japan of a Japanese mother and an Australian father who were not married. Her mother died of a cerebral hemorrhage while she was living with an American sailor stationed in Japan.

He brought Noriko back to the United States when she was 12 and three years later married a woman six years older than Noriko. A year later the couple had a baby girl of their own, and subsequently another child. Problems began then for Noriko. "I was going through a really hectic time," she said. "My grades started slipping. I had been getting A's and B's."

Noriko was in a class for gifted children, took part in student government and cheerleading and went out on dates. Meanwhile, the stepmother sat at home. The two women competed for the stepfather's attention. Their differences were so strong that each had her own iron and sewing machine.

"It came to the point where my father said, 'Noriko, you can't wear the same perfume your mother wears,'" she said. She also said that her father "came close to the point where he abused me sexually."

When the family moved to San Francisco a year ago, Noriko moved out, living with an aunt, then with friends and finally on her own. At first she went to high school from 11:30 A.M. to 2 P.M. and worked in a movie theater from 6 P.M. until midnight. But, unable to keep up her studies, she quit school and took a job at a McDonald's restaurant from 5 to 10 P.M.

Emancipation had been suggested to her stepfather by the police a year earlier when he had asked them if there was a home he could put her in. Now Noriko began to consider emancipation. She was helped by a public service group here called Legal Services for Children. Noriko's plan now, since she has dropped out of school, is to take a proficiency examination next month to get a diploma. This will enable her to go to junior college.

Noriko appears to be a mature young woman who knows where she is going and how to get there. Her main problem at the moment is getting a job that provides her more than the minimum wage offered by McDonald's.

Charlie, who is black, also had a difficult childhood. In his case, it seems to have traumatized him. He describes life in a family with frequent changes of stepfather and frequent fights with mother and younger sisters. Charlie hinted that his real father, who lives in Oakland, is a numbers runner.

Charlie seems agreeable, but much of what he says is hard to believe. He says he ran away from home at 11 and has wandered all over the country, living with friends and going to school here and there ever since. In an interview, he boasted of love affairs and of badly beating someone in a fight. The person he beat turned out to be one of his sisters.

The lawyer who obtained Charlie's emancipation was deceived into thinking Charlie was stable and independent enough to benefit from it. But seven months after his emancipation last April, Charlie lost what seemed to be a promising job in the offices of the Hotel, Restaurant and Bartenders Union here.

Neither he nor the lawyer was able to cite any benefit emancipation had brought him, and all Charlie can say now is, "I want to get unemancipated." The law as amended does include a provision for reversing emancipation that would require Charlie's family to support him.

Maria, too, had a hard childhood. Both her mother and father are from Nicaragua, though her mother has been in this country for 18 years and is an American citizen. Her father divorced her mother and disappeared when Maria was 3 or 4. Her mother then married a San Francisco deputy sheriff, and they had children together.

"He used to beat up the little babies," Maria said. "He locked my mother in handcuffs. I used to get re-

The New York Times   Terrence McCarthy

Charley Eagle is uncertain about his future.

stricted for leaving rusty bobby pins in the bathtub. I moved out after four or five years of living with that crazy man." She left when she was 13 and went to stay with relatives, moving from one set to another. She is now living with cousins who are college students here, barely older than she.

They live in Oakland, and she gets up at 6 A.M. each day to cross the San Francisco Bay Bridge to her high school. She goes to high school from 8 A.M. to 1 P.M., works as a keypunch operator from 1 to 6 and then returns home to study. It is not an easy life, but she is cheerful.

Besides enabling her to ask the university for financial aid when she applies for admission, emancipation

will permit her to get her own apartment if her cousins return to Nicaragua.

"And third there is the fact that my mother is funny," Maria said. "She causes problems sometimes. Sometimes she wants me home. She'll call the police and say I'm a runaway." Emancipation will make it impossible for the police to arrest her if her mother, who now consents to Maria's decision, calls. Under current law, a suspected runaway can be taken to Juvenile Hall but not held.

A more pressing problem for Maria is money. She works 25 hours a week for $4.25 an hour and, like Noriko, needs more.

Both are exceptional women, and it

may be that only exceptional young people can benefit from the emancipation law. As the case of Charlie shows, emancipation offers no benefits to those who are at odds not only with their families but also with themselves.

There are no records on how many children have become emancipated. Probably only a handful have. The Los Angeles County school system, which has half the schoolchildren in the state and supported the measure, says it knows of none in its jurisdiction, though it does know of one student who is planning to seek emancipation. Maria, who intends to file in Oakland, will be the second child emancipated there.

February 20, 1980

Rise in Drinking Age Becoming Issue Over Nation

GAINESVILLE, Fla., May 17 (AP) — Georgia will raise its minimum legal age for drinking in four months. New Hampshire and Massachusetts did it last spring. Florida and at least eight other states are thinking about doing it, too.

In statehouses as well as high schools and colleges the question of how old people should be before they may legally consume alcoholic beverages is being debated around the country.

A new Georgia law will go into effect Sept. 1 raising the age from 18 to 19 but exempting young people in the armed forces. Illinois, Massachusetts, Michigan, Montana, New Hampshire, New Jersey and Tennessee all raised the minimum age in the last year.

But Dr. Gerardo Gonzalez, a University of Florida researcher who operates a college alcohol awareness program called Bacchus, contends that such laws are backfiring.

More Problems Than Solutions

"My feeling is that raising the drinking age causes more problems than it solves," Dr. Gonzalez said after a recent visit to the University of New Hampshire to talk to college officials about the effects of the new law in that state.

"What they have found are problems like their residence assistants' being assaulted by students when they try to enforce the new law and increasing fatal-

ities among the 18-to-20 age group," said Dr. Gonzalez. In mentioning fatalities he meant traffic deaths.

When the issue came up in the Florida Senate earlier this month, it was sent back to committee after Senator Jack Gordon, Democrat of Miami, jokingly suggested an amendment to prohibit people 34 to 36 years old from drinking, noting statistics that showed this age group had the highest incidence of alcoholism.

He also used the main argument against raising the legal drinking age, saying it was hypocritical to permit 18-year-olds to vote and serve in the military but bar them from buying a drink.

Proponents have argued all along that the higher drinking age would reduce the number of alcohol-related highway deaths.

"The No. 1 killer of young people in this state is not cancer; it is not heart disease; it is alcohol-related accidents," said Representative Fran Carlton, a Democrat. "Raising the drinking age will help to save the lives of young people who are dying by the hundreds in alcohol-related accidents."

Dr. Gonzalez and others contend that there is no such proof. "While the efforts are well-intentioned, the evidence does not support such a move," he said. In Massachusetts, he said, an increase in arrests for driving while intoxicated has followed the raising of the drinking age.

"We get the opposite effect of what it intended," he said.

Alcoholism Group's View

The same thoughts were voiced in Washington at the National Institute of Alcohol Abuse and Alcoholism, which picked the Bacchus program as a national model.

"There's no conclusive evidence that the drinking age makes any difference because young people are drinking at a younger age, prior to any age limit," an institute spokesman, Paul Garner, said. "Let's face it, most of the kids get the liquor out of their homes anyway."

Mr. Garner and Dr. Gonzalez say that what was needed were programs like Bacchus to inform young people about what will happen when they drink to excess. Death in an automobile should be high on the list, they say.

"I think it's pretty well established that laws in and of themselves do not change social customs," Dr. Gonzalez said. "What we need is to support a comprehensive and sustained commitment toward alcohol education."

Dr. Gonzalez's program is used on at least 14 college campuses around the nation.

May 18, 1980

Suggested Reading

Aiken, William and La Follette, Hugh, eds. *Whose Children?: Children's Rights, Parental Authority and State Power*. Totowa, N.J.: Littlefield, Adams, 1980.

Bremner, Robert H. et al. *Children and Youth in America: A Documentary History*. 3 vols. Cambridge, Mass.: Harvard University Press, 1971-1974.

Chase, Naomi F. *A Child is Being Beaten: Violence Against Children, an American Tragedy*. New York: McGraw-Hill, 1976.

Coles, Robert. *Children of Crisis: Eskimos, Chicanos, Indians*. Boston: Atlantic-Little Brown, 1980.

_____. *Children of Crisis: Privileged Ones*. Boston Houghton Mifflin, 1974.

Cottle, Thomas J. *Black Children, White Dreams*. Boston: Houghton Mifflin, 1974.

_____. *Children in Jail*. Boston: Beacon Press, 1977.

Fyvel, T.R. *Troublemakers: Rebellious Youth in an Affluent Society*. New York: Schocken, 1964.

Gould, Shirley. *Teenagers: The Continuing Challenge. New York: Hawthorn, 1979.*

Greenleaf, Barbara K. Children Through the Ages: A History of Childhood. New York: Barnes and Noble, 1979.

Hechinger, Grace and Hechinger, Fred M. *Teenage Tyranny*. New York: Morrow, 1963.

Kett, Joseph F. *Rites of Passage: Adolescence in America 1790 to the Present*. New York: Basic Books, 1979.

Melody, William. *Children's Television: Economics of Exploitation*. New Haven, Conn.: Yale University Press, 1973.

Platt, Anthony. *The Child Savers: The Invention of Delinquency* 2nd, enl. ed. Chicago: University of Chicago Press, 1977.

Rosenberg, Morris. *Society and the Adolescent Self-Image*. Princeton University Press, 1965.

Rush, Florence. *The Best Kept Secret: Sexual Abuse of Children*. Englewood Cliffs, N.J.: Prentice-Hall, 1980.

Sanders, William. *Juvenile Delinquency: An Introduction*. New York: Holt, Rinehart & Winston, 1980.

Sparge, John. *Bitter Cry of the Children*. New York: Times Books, 1972.

Taylor, Ronald B. *Sweatshops in the Sun: Child Labor on the Farm*. Boston: Beacon Press, 1972.

Yankelovich, Daniel. *The New Morality: A Profile of American Youth in the Seventies*. New York: McGraw-Hill, 1974.

Index